A Review of the Events of 1975

The 1976 World Book Year Book

The Annual Supplement to The World Book Encyclopedia

Field Enterprises Educational Corporation
Chicago Frankfurt London Paris Rome Sydney Tokyo Toronto

A subsidiary of
Field Enterprises, Inc.

Staff

Editorial Director
William H. Nault

Editorial Staff
Executive Editor
Wayne Wille

Managing Editor
Paul C. Tullier

Chief Copy Editor
Joseph P. Spohn

Senior Editors
Robert K. Johnson,
Edward G. Nash,
Kathryn Sederberg,
Darlene R. Stille,
Foster P. Stockwell

Assistant Copy Editor
Irene B. Keller

Index Editor
Marilyn Boerding

Editorial Assistant
Madelyn Krzak

**Executive Editor,
The World Book Encyclopedia**
A. Richard Harmet

Art Staff
Executive Art Director
William Dobias

Art Director
Alfred de Simone

Senior Artists
Roberta Dimmer,
Gumé Nuñez

Photography Director
Fred C. Eckhardt, Jr.

Photo Editing Director
Ann Eriksen

Senior Photographs Editors
Blanche Cohen, Marilyn Gartman,
John S. Marshall

Assistant Photographs Editor
Paul Quirico

Research and Services
Director of Educational Services
John Sternig

Director of Editorial Services
Carl A. Tamminen

Head, Editorial Research
Jo Ann McDonald

Senior Researcher
Robert Hamm

Head, Cartographic Services
J. J. Stack

Pre-Press Services
Director
Richard A. Atwood

Manager, Pre-Press
John Babrick

Assistant Manager, Pre-Press
Marguerite DuMais

Manager, Art Production
Alfred J. Mozdzen

Assistant Manager, Art Production
Barbara J. McDonald

Manufacturing Staff
Executive Director
Philip B. Hall

Production Manager
Jerry R. Higdon

**Manager, Research
and Development**
Henry Koval

Year Book Board of Editors
Harrison Brown, Alistair Cooke, Lawrence A. Cremin, John Holmes, James Murray, Sylvia Porter, James Reston

World Book Advisory Board
Phillip Bacon, Professor and Chairman, Department of Geography, University of Houston; Jean Sutherland Boggs, Director, The National Gallery of Canada; George B. Brain, Dean, College of Education, Washington State University; Alonzo A. Crim, Superintendent, Atlanta Public Schools; William E. McManus, Director of Catholic Education, Archdiocese of Chicago; Robert K. Merton, University Professor, Columbia University; A. Harry Passow, Jacob H. Schiff Professor of Education and Director, Division of Educational Institutions and Programs, and Chairman, Department of Curriculum and Teaching, Teachers College, Columbia University; John Rowell, Director, School Libraries Programs, School of Library Science, Case Western Reserve University; William M. Smith, Professor of Psychology and Director, Office of Instructional Services and Educational Research, Dartmouth College.

Preface

Voltaire's naïve young wanderer of the 1700s, Candide, obviously was never a member of the YEAR BOOK Board of Editors. And nobody mentioned him at either of the board's two meetings in 1975. If somebody had, an exception might have been made to Candide's cynical assertion that optimism is "a mania for maintaining that all is well when things are going badly."

The board first gathered in a special session in midyear for an all-day discussion about the United States after 200 years as a nation in the making. The result of that discussion–tape-recorded, transcribed, and

The YEAR BOOK Board of Editors discuss "America: Then, Now, and Tomorrow."

edited–is the Special Report on page 76. It is YEAR BOOK's contribution to the American Revolution Bicentennial celebration. The board noted that not all was well, but that while some things had been going badly, a number of things nonetheless had been going very well. They did not deny the serious problems that the United States and the world face today, but they generally expressed optimism about the future.

Six months later, the board assembled again, this time for their regular three-day meeting, at which plans for the Focus section were made. Again the things going badly were acknowledged: a crisis of democracy in several countries, a leadership vacuum, threats to economic recovery, man's effect on the environment, and so on. But again, just as in May, the consensus was one of cautious optimism. It was a judicious judgment. Contrary to the assertion of Voltaire's youthful Candide, an optimist is one who sees the whole cloth; the pessimist sees only the ravelings. WAYNE WILLE

Contents

A chronology of some of the most important events of 1975 appears on
pages 8 through 16. A preview of 1976 is given on pages 607 and 608.

Contributors

Abrams, Edward, Ph.D.; Director of Technical Development, Chemetron Corporation. [CHEMICAL INDUSTRY]

Alexiou, Arthur G., M.S., E.E.; Associate Director, Office of Sea Grant Programs, National Science Foundation. [OCEAN]

Anderson, Joseph P., M.S., LL.D.; Director, Social Legislation Information Service, Inc. [POVERTY; Social Organizations]

Anderson, Leo S., B. A.; Editor, *Telephony Magazine*. [COMMUNICATIONS]

Antonini, Gustavo A., B.S., M.A., Ph.D.; Associate Professor of Latin American Studies and Geography; Director of Research Center for Latin American Studies, University of Florida. [WORLD BOOK SUPPLEMENT: GRENADA]

Araujo, Paul E., Ph.D.; Assistant Professor, Human Nutrition, University of Florida. [NUTRITION]

Banovetz, James M., Ph.D.; Chairman, Department of Political Science, Northern Illinois University. [CITY; City Articles; HOUSING]

Barabba, Vincent P., B.S., M.B.A.; Director, United States Bureau of the Census. [CENSUS, UNITED STATES]

Barber, Peggy, B.A., M.L.S.; Director, Public Information Office, American Library Association. [AMERICAN LIBRARY ASSOCIATION]

Bare, Frank L., B.S., M.S.; Executive Director, U.S. Gymnastics Federation. [WORLD BOOK SUPPLEMENT: GYMNASTICS]

Bautz, Laura P., Ph.D.; Associate Professor of Astronomy, Northwestern University. [ASTRONOMY]

Beaumont, Lynn; Travel and Public Relations Consultant. [BICENTENNIAL, UNITED STATES; FAIRS AND EXPOSITIONS; TRAVEL]

Beckwith, David C., J.D.; Correspondent, *Time* Magazine. [COURTS AND LAWS; CRIME; PRISON; SUPREME COURT]

Benson, Barbara N., A.B., M.S.; Instructor, Biology, Cedar Crest College. [BOTANY; ZOOLOGY]

Berkwitt, George J., B.S.J.; Chief Editor, *Industrial Distribution Magazine*. [MANUFACTURING]

Bornstein, Leon, B.A., M.A.; Labor Economist, U.S. Dept. of Labor. [LABOR]

Boyum, Joy Gould, Ph.D.; Professor of English, New York University. [MOTION PICTURES]

Bradsher, Henry S., A.B., B.J.; Correspondent, *Washington Star*. [Asian Country Articles]

Brown, Kenneth, Editor, *United Kingdom Press Gazette*. [EUROPE; Western Europe Country Articles]

Brown, Madison B., M.D.; Senior Vice-President, American Hospital Association. [HOSPITAL]

Cain, Charles C., III, B.A.; Automotive Writer, Associated Press. [AUTOMOBILE]

Carroll, Paul, M.A.; Professor of English, University of Illinois at Chicago Circle. [POETRY]

Clark, Phil, B.A.; Free-Lance Garden and Botanical Writer. [GARDENING]

Cook, Leon F., B.S., M.S.W.; Director, Minnesota Indian Resource Development. [WORLD BOOK SUPPLEMENT: INDIAN RESERVATION]

Cook, Robert C., former President, Population Reference Bureau. [POPULATION, WORLD]

Cromie, William J., B.S.; Executive Director, Council for the Advancement of Science Writing. [Special Report: UPDATING OUR PERSPECTIVE ON THE PLANETS; SPACE EXPLORATION; SPACE EXPLORATION (Close-Up)]

Csida, June Bundy, former Radio-TV Editor, *Billboard* Magazine. [RADIO; TELEVISION; TELEVISION (Close-Up)]

Cuscaden, Rob, Editor, *Building Design & Construction* Magazine. [ARCHITECTURE]

Cviic, Chris, B.A., B.Sc.; Editorial Staff, *The Economist*. [Eastern Europe Country Articles]

Dale, Edwin L., Jr., B.A.; Reporter, *The New York Times*, Washington Bureau. [INTERNATIONAL TRADE AND FINANCE]

DeFrank, Thomas M., B.A., M.A.; Correspondent, *Newsweek*. [NATIONAL DEFENSE]

Delaune, Lynn de Grummond, M.A.; Assistant Professor, College of William and Mary; Author. [LITERATURE FOR CHILDREN]

Derickson, Ralph Wayne, Public Information Associate, Council of State Governments. [STATE GOVERNMENT]

De Simone, Daniel V., LL.B., J.D.; Deputy Director, Office of Technology Assessment, U.S. Congress. [METRIC SYSTEM]

Dewald, William G., Ph.D.; Professor of Economics, Ohio State University. [Finance Articles]

Dixon, Gloria Ricks, B.A.; Director of Public Relations, Magazine Publishers Association. [MAGAZINE]

Eaton, William J., B.S.J., M.S.J.; Washington Correspondent, *Chicago Daily News*. [U.S. Political Articles; WATERGATE]

Esseks, John D., Ph.D.; Associate Professor of Political Science, Northern Illinois University. [AFRICA and African country articles]

Evans, Earl A., Jr., Ph.D.; Professor of Biochemistry, University of Chicago. [BIOCHEMISTRY; BIOLOGY]

Farr, David M. L., D. Phil.; Professor of History, Carleton University, Ottawa. [CANADA; LEGER, JULES; TRUDEAU, PIERRE ELLIOTT]

Feather, Leonard, Professor of Jazz History, University of California, Riverside; Author, *The Encyclopedia of Jazz in the Sixties*. [MUSIC, POPULAR; RECORDINGS]

French, Charles E., Ph.D.; Head, Agricultural Economics Department, Purdue University. [AGRICULTURE]

Gayn, Mark, B.S.; Foreign Affairs Columnist, *The Toronto Star*; Author. [Special Report: RUSSIA TODAY: REALITY AND THE FADING DREAM; ASIA and Asian Country Articles]

Goldner, Nancy, B.A.; Critic, *Dance News*, *The Nation*, and *Christian Science Monitor*. [DANCING]

Goldstein, Jane, B.A.; U.S. Representative, International Racing Bureau. [HORSE RACING]

Goy, Robert W., Ph.D.; Director, Wisconsin Regional Primate Research Center; Professor of Psychology, University of Wisconsin. [PSYCHOLOGY]

Grasso, Thomas X., M.A.; Chairman, Department of Geosciences, Monroe Community College. [GEOLOGY]

Graubart, Judah L., B.A.; former Columnist, *Jewish Post and Opinion* (Chicago). [JEWS]

Griffin, Alice, Ph.D.; Professor of English, Lehman College, City University of New York. [THEATER]

Gross, Beatrice, B.A., M.A.; Associate Professor, State University of New York, Old Westbury. [WORLD BOOK SUPPLEMENT: ALTERNATIVE SCHOOL]

Gross, Ronald; Vice-President, Academy for Educational Development. [WORLD BOOK SUPPLEMENT: ALTERNATIVE SCHOOL]

Handlin, Oscar, B.A., M.A., Ph.D.; Carl H. Pforzheimer University Professor of American History, Harvard University. [WORLD BOOK SUPPLEMENT: UNITED STATES, HISTORY OF THE]

Havighurst, Robert J., Ph.D.; Professor of Education and Human Development, University of Chicago. [OLD AGE]

Healey, Gerald B., Midwest Editor, *Editor & Publisher* Magazine. [NEWSPAPERS; PUBLISHING]

Hechinger, Fred M., B.A.; member, Editorial Board, *The New York Times.* [EDUCATION]

Hudson, Michael C., M.A., Ph.D.; Associate Professor of Political Science, Johns Hopkins University. [WORLD BOOK SUPPLEMENT: PALESTINE LIBERATION ORGANIZATION]

Jacobi, Peter P., B.S.J., M.S.J.; Professor, Medill School of Journalism, Northwestern University. [MUSIC, CLASSICAL]

Jessup, Mary E., B.A.; former News Editor, *Civil Engineering* Magazine. [DRUGS; Engineering Articles; PETROLEUM AND GAS]

Joseph, Lou, B.A.; Manager, Media Relations, Bureau of Public Information, American Dental Association. [DENTISTRY]

Karr, Albert R., M.S.; Reporter, *The Wall Street Journal.* [TRANSPORTATION and Transportation Articles]

Kind, Joshua B., Ph.D.; Associate Professor of Art History, Northern Illinois University; Author, *Rouault;* Midwest Correspondent, *Art News.* [VISUAL ARTS]

Kingman, Merle, B.A.; Senior Editor, *Advertising Age.* [ADVERTISING]

Kisor, Henry, B.A., M.S.J.; Book Editor, *Chicago Daily News.* [LITERATURE]

Klis, John B., M.S.; Director of Publications, Institute of Food Technologists. [FOOD]

Koenig, Louis W., Ph.D., L.H.D.; Professor of Government, New York University; Author; *Bryan; A Political Biography of William Jennings Bryan.* [CIVIL RIGHTS; CIVIL RIGHTS (Close-Up)]

Levy, Emanuel, B.A.; Editor, *Insurance Advocate.* [INSURANCE; INSURANCE (Close-Up)]

Lewis, Ralph H., M.A.; Collaborator, Division of Museum Services, Museum Operations, National Park Service. [MUSEUMS]

Litsky, Frank, B.S.; Assistant Sports Editor, *The New York Times.* [Sports Articles]

Livingston, Kathryn Zahony, B.A.; Senior Editor, Special Projects, *Town and Country.* [FASHION]

Maki, John M., Ph.D.; Professor of Political Science, University of Massachusetts. [JAPAN]

Marcum, John A., B.A., M.A., Ph.D.; Provost, Merrill College, University of California, Santa Cruz. [WORLD BOOK SUPPLEMENT: GUINEA-BISSAU]

Marty, Martin E., Ph.D.; Professor, University of Chicago. [PROTESTANT; RELIGION]

Mattson, Howard W., B.S.; Director of Public Information, Institute of Food Technologists. [FOOD]

Maxon, John, Ph.D.; Vice-President, Art Institute of Chicago. [VISUAL ARTS (Close-Up)]

Mikdashi, Zuhayr, B.A., M.A., B.Litt., Ph.D.; Professor of Business Administration, American University, Beirut, Lebanon. [WORLD BOOK SUPPLEMENT: ORGANIZATION OF PETROLEUM EXPORTING COUNTRIES]

Miller, J. D. B., M.Ec.; Professor of International Relations, Research School of Pacific Studies, Australian National University. [AUSTRALIA; NEW ZEALAND; PACIFIC ISLANDS]

Morton, Elizabeth H., LL.D.; former Editor in Chief, Canadian Library Association. [CANADIAN LIBRARY ASSOCIATION; CANADIAN LITERATURE]

Moss, Robert, M.A.; Special Correspondent, *The Economist.* [Latin American Country Articles]

Mullen, Frances A., Ph.D.; President, International Council of Psychologists, Inc. [CHILD WELFARE]

Neil, Andrew F., M.A.; Political Correspondent, *The Economist.* [GREAT BRITAIN; IRELAND; NORTHERN IRELAND]

Nelson, Larry L., Ph.D.; Executive Vice-President, Snyder Associates, Inc. [AGRICULTURE]

Newman, Andrew L., M.A.; Information Officer, U.S. Department of the Interior. [CONSERVATION; ENVIRONMENT; FISHING; FOREST AND FOREST PRODUCTS; HUNTING; INDIAN, AMERICAN]

Oatis, William N.; United Nations Correspondent, The Associated Press. [UNITED NATIONS]

O'Connor, James J., E.E.; Editor in Chief, *Power* Magazine. [ENERGY]

Offenheiser, Marilyn J., B.S.; Free-Lance Writer. [ELECTRONICS]

O'Leary, Theodore M., B.A.; Special Correspondent, *Sports Illustrated* Magazine. [BRIDGE, CONTRACT; CHESS; COIN COLLECTING; GAMES, MODELS, AND TOYS; HOBBIES; PET; STAMP COLLECTING]

Pearl, Edward W., Supervisory Meteorologist, University of Chicago. [WEATHER]

Plog, Fred, Ph.D.; Associate Professor of Anthropology, State University of New York, Binghamton. [ANTHROPOLOGY; ARCHAEOLOGY]

Poli, Kenneth, Editor, *Popular Photography.* [PHOTOGRAPHY]

Rabb, George B., Ph.D.; Deputy Director, Chicago Zoological Park. [ZOOS AND AQUARIUMS]

Rafalik, Dianne, B.S., M.S.; Editor, *The New Physician.* [HEALTH AND DISEASE; MEDICINE; MENTAL HEALTH]

Remsberg, Bonnie, B.S.; Free-Lance Writer. [Special Report: THE UPROOTED]

Remsberg, Charles, M.S.J.; Free-Lance Writer. [Special Report: THE UPROOTED]

Rowen, Joseph R., A.B.; Vice-President, National Retail Merchants Association. [RETAILING]

Rowse, Arthur E., I.A., M.B.A.; President, Consumer News, Inc. [CONSUMER AFFAIRS]

Schmemann, The Reverend Alexander, S.T.D., D.D., LL.D., Th.D.; Dean, St. Vladimir's Orthodox Theological Seminary, New York. [EASTERN ORTHODOX CHURCHES]

Schubert, Helen C., B.S.; Home Furnishings Writer. [INTERIOR DESIGN]

Shaw, Robert J., B.S.B.A.; former Editor, *Library Technology Reports,* American Library Association. [LIBRARY]

Shearer, Warren W., Ph.D.; former Chairman, Department of Economics, Wabash College. [ECONOMICS]

Sheerin, John B., C.S.P., A.B., M.A., L.L.D., J.D.; General Consultor, American Bishops' Secretariat for Catholic-Jewish Relations. [ROMAN CATHOLIC CHURCH]

Simmons, Henry T., B.A., LL.B.; Correspondent and Science Writer, *Interavia.* [SCIENCE AND RESEARCH]

Spencer, William, Ph.D.; Professor of Middle East History, Florida State University; Author, *Land and People of Algeria.* [MIDDLE EAST and Middle Eastern Country Articles; North Africa Country Articles]

Thompson, Carol L., M.A.; Editor, *Current History* Magazine. [U.S. Government Articles]

Tofany, Vincent L., B.L.; President, National Safety Council. [SAFETY]

von Smolinski, Alfred W., Ph.D.; Associate Professor of Chemistry, University of Illinois at the Medical Center. [CHEMISTRY]

Westin, Alan F., Ph.D.; Professor of Public Law and Government, Columbia University. [Special Report: PROTECTING PRIVACY IN THE COMPUTER AGE]

White, Thomas O., Ph.D.; Research Officer, Nuclear Physics Laboratory, Oxford University, Oxford, England. [PHYSICS]

Contributors not listed on these pages are members of the WORLD BOOK YEAR BOOK editorial staff.

Chronology 1975

January

Sun	Mon	Tue	Wed	Thu	Fri	Sat
			1	2	3	4
5	6	7	8	9	10	11
12	13	14	15	16	17	18
19	20	21	22	23	24	25
26	27	28	29	30	31	

1   **Jury convicts Nixon aides** H. R. Haldeman, John N. Mitchell, John D. Ehrlichman, and Robert C. Mardian of Watergate cover-up charges stemming from the June, 1972, break-in at Democratic National Committee Headquarters.

3   **Argentine President** María Estela Martínez (Isabel) de Perón names José López Rega as secretary to the president, her closest adviser.

5   **Vice-President Nelson A. Rockefeller** heads an eight-member commission to investigate charges of illegal domestic spying by the Central Intelligence Agency (CIA).

7   **North Vietnamese and Viet Cong forces** capture Phuoc Binh, the first provincial capital to fall to the Communists since 1972.

9   **Danish elections** give Social Democrats 54 seats and Prime Minister Poul Hartling's Liberal Party 42 in the *Folketing* (parliament). Hartling refuses to resign.

10   **Russia cancels 1972 trade agreement** with the United States, blaming the Trade Reform Act signed by President Gerald R. Ford on January 3. The act linked most-favored-nation trade status to freer Russian emigration policies.

13-17   **China's National People's Congress,** meeting for the first time in 10 years, re-elects Premier Chou En-lai and revises the 1954 Constitution.

14   **President Ford nominates** Edward H. Levi to be U.S. attorney general and William T. Coleman, Jr., to be U.S. secretary of transportation.
The 94th U.S. Congress convenes with 291 Democrats and 144 Republicans in the House of Representatives and 60 Democrats, 37 Republicans, 1 Conservative, and 1 Independent in the Senate.

15   **President Ford presents** an economic recovery plan to Congress that includes a $16-billion tax cut and a $3-per-barrel increase in the tax on crude oil.

21   **Prime Minister Gough Whitlam** returns to Australia from a 5½-week tour of Europe and Asia, reports "meaningful relations" with all power blocs.

28   **President Ford asks Congress** for $522 million in added military aid for South Vietnam and Khmer.

29   **Danish Prime Minister Hartling** resigns after defeats in parliament.
British Prime Minister Harold Wilson meets Canadian Prime Minister Pierre Elliott Trudeau in Ottawa. He offers to help Canada establish special relations with the European Community.

Jan. 15

Feb. 3-4

Feb. 11

February

Sun	Mon	Tue	Wed	Thu	Fri	Sat
						1
2	3	4	5	6	7	8
9	10	11	12	13	14	15
16	17	18	19	20	21	22
23	24	25	26	27	28	

1   **Common Market pledges** $4 billion in aid and trade over five years to 46 developing nations in Africa, the Caribbean, and the Pacific.

1-5   **Russian Foreign Minister** Andrei A. Gromyko visits Syria and Egypt to discuss defense.

1-6   **Civil war in Ethiopia** pits government troops against rebels in the province of Eritrea. As many as 1,200 persons die in Asmara.

3-4   **French President** Valéry Giscard d'Estaing and West German Chancellor Helmut Schmidt agree in Paris to propose a joint meeting of oil-consuming and oil-producing nations to work out differences.

3-8   **Representatives** of 110 developing nations meet in Dakar, Senegal, and resolve to unite for higher prices and better trade terms.

4   **"The economy is in a severe recession,"** President Ford tells Congress.

4-7   **Common Market** and Council for Mutual Economic Assistance (COMECON) delegates meet officially for the first time in Moscow but fail to reach agreement.

5   **Congress ends U.S. military aid** to Turkey because of lack of "substantial progress" in Cyprus peace negotiations.

5-7   **International Energy Agency,** a group of 18 oil-consuming nations, sets a temporary goal of reducing 1975 oil imports 10 per cent.

7   **Unemployment hits a 33-year high** at 8.2 per cent in January, the U.S. Department of Labor reports.
Canada's Minister of Energy Donald S. Macdonald announces an energy-conservation

program that includes a 55-mile (88.5-kilometer)-per-hour speed limit.

11 **Margaret Thatcher becomes** leader of the British Conservative Party, defeating former Prime Minister Edward Heath.

13 **Turkish Cypriots proclaim a separate state** in the northern 40 per cent of Cyprus.
Carla Anderson Hills is named secretary of housing and urban development by President Ford.
Anker Henrik Jorgensen, head of the Social Democratic Party, is sworn in as prime minister of Denmark.

13-21 **Organization of African Unity** meets in Addis Ababa, Ethiopia.

21 **Judge sentences Nixon aides** John D. Ehrlichman, H. R. Haldeman, and John N. Mitchell to from 2½ to 8 years in prison for their parts in the Watergate cover-up. Robert C. Mardian gets 10 months to 3 years.

March

Sun	Mon	Tue	Wed	Thu	Fri	Sat
						1
2	3	4	5	6	7	8
9	10	11	12	13	14	15
16	17	18	19	20	21	22
23	24	25	26	27	28	29
30	31					

1 **The American Revolution Bicentennial** observance of the 200th anniversary of United States independence officially begins.

2-22 **Argentine political killings** claim 59 lives.

5 **Eighteen die in Tel Aviv, Israel,** in attack by eight Palestinian guerrillas.

8-13 **U.S. Secretary of State** Henry A. Kissinger resumes shuttle diplomacy, meets with Egyptian President Anwar al-Sadat and Israeli Prime Minister Yitzhak Rabin.

10-11 **Common Market renegotiates** Great Britain's membership terms.

11 **Portuguese revolt** by forces loyal to the former provisional president, General António de Spínola, fails. He flees to Spain.

18 **Russian General Secretary** Leonid I. Brezhnev addresses the 11th Hungarian Socialist Workers' Party Congress in Budapest, calls for renewed East-West détente.

18-20 **South Vietnamese forces abandon** seven provinces, about 40 per cent of the country's land area, to Communist forces.
International Energy Agency agrees to a minimum price for imported oil to encourage investment in other sources of energy.

21 **Malcolm Fraser** succeeds Billy M. Snedden as head of Australia's Liberal Party.

22 **Fire threatens nuclear power plant** near Athens, Ala. Damage is estimated at $50 million, but reportedly no radiation escapes.

23 **Israeli-Egyptian peace talks break down,** and Secretary of State Kissinger returns to the United States.

25 **King Faisal of Saudi Arabia is shot** to death by his nephew Prince Faisal ibn Musad Abdel Aziz.

26 **A new left wing Portuguese Cabinet** is sworn in, the fourth since May, 1974.

29 **President Ford signs** a $22.8-billion tax cut bill aimed at spurring United States recovery from recession.

31 **Turkey's Prime Minister** Suleyman Demirel forms a four-party coalition government, ending a six-month crisis.
U.S. clemency program for military deserters and draft evaders ends. About 22,500 of the 124,400 eligible signed up for a chance to "earn return" to the United States.

Feb. 13

March 11

March 25

April 1

April 18

April 30

April

Sun	Mon	Tue	Wed	Thu	Fri	Sat
		1	2	3	4	5
6	7	8	9	10	11	12
13	14	15	16	17	18	19
20	21	22	23	24	25	26
27	28	29	30			

1   **Chicago's Mayor** Richard J. Daley is re-elected to his sixth consecutive four-year term by a margin of almost 5 to 1.

1-3   **North Vietnam** seizes major coastal cities in South Vietnam as defending forces flee.

4   **March unemployment hit 8.7 per cent,** the highest rate since 1940, the U.S. Department of Labor announces.

7-15   **Talks between oil-exporting** and oil-importing nations end without agreement in Paris.

8   **Canadian unemployment** hit 7.2 per cent in March, a 14-year high, reports Statistics Canada.

9-10   **Canada's provincial premiers** meet in Ottawa with Prime Minister Trudeau but fail to agree on future prices for oil and natural gas.

15-16   **Greek Prime Minister** Constantine Caramanlis visits Paris. France agrees to sponsor Greece as full Common Market member.

16   **Khmer Rouge rebel troops** capture Phnom Penh, ending the five-year civil war in Khmer (Cambodia).

17   **John B. Connally, Jr.,** former U.S. treasury secretary, is acquitted of bribery charges.

18   **International conference** to update the 1949 Geneva Conventions ends in Geneva, Switzerland, after delegates approve 77 articles aimed at protecting civilians in time of war.
     President Ford speaks from the pulpit of Boston's Old North Church during a Bicentennial celebration.

19-26   **North Korean President** Kim Il-song visits China.

21   **South Vietnamese President** Nguyen Van Thieu resigns after 10 years in office.

22   **Honduras President** Oswaldo López Arellano is ousted by the military because he allegedly accepted a $1.25-million bribe from the U.S.-based United Brands Company.

25   **Prince Norodom Sihanouk** is named president for life by the new Khmer government.
     Portuguese moderates win in first free elections in 50 years.

28   **Greek and Turkish Cypriot** leaders agree to form a group to study proposals for a new government.

30   **South Vietnam surrenders** to Viet Cong and Communist forces. U.S. airlift ends hours before the fall.

May

Sun	Mon	Tue	Wed	Thu	Fri	Sat
				1	2	3
4	5	6	7	8	9	10
11	12	13	14	15	16	17
18	19	20	21	22	23	24
25	26	27	28	29	30	31

1   **Northern Ireland Protestants,** who oppose sharing power with Roman Catholics, win 46 of 78 seats for a constitutional convention.
     Rising malpractice insurance costs cause about 2,000 physicians to strike in northern California.

| 5 | **President Ford asks Congress** for $507 million to aid the estimated 125,000 refugees who fled South Vietnam. |

May 5-8

5	**President Ford asks Congress** for $507 million to aid the estimated 125,000 refugees who fled South Vietnam.
5-8	**Senator George McGovern** (D., S. Dak.) visits Cuba. Prime Minister Fidel Castro calls for improved U.S.-Cuban relations.
8-19	**The Organization of American States** holds its fifth General Assembly in Washington, D.C., and agrees to review Cuban relations.
9	**United States and Canada** renew the North American Air Defense (NORAD) agreement for five years.
	United Nations Law of the Sea Conference ends in Geneva with a draft treaty providing a 200-nautical-mile economic zone within which coastal states have fishing and mining rights.
	Canadian Finance Minister John N. Turner says 11.1 per cent annual inflation rate and 8.1 per cent unemployment in April can no longer be blamed on international events.
	France decides to rejoin the Common Market's joint currency float, which it left in January, 1974.
11	**Israel signs trade agreements** with the Common Market, the first Mediterranean nation to do so.
12	**U.S. freighter *Mayaguez* is seized** in the Gulf of Thailand by Khmer forces. On May 14, 15 U.S. servicemen die in rescue operation to free the ship and its 39 crewmen.
12-17	**China's Deputy Premier** Teng Hsiao-ping visits France, agrees to promote more high-level meetings and increase trade.
14	**President Ford refuses** federal aid to New York City Mayor Abraham Beame to pay $1.5 billion in debts by June 30.
15	**Gyorgy Lazar** replaces Jenö Fock as Hungary's prime minister.
16	**Congress appropriates $405 million** for the resettlement of Vietnamese refugees.
19	**U.S. Senate votes to end embargo** on military aid to Turkey.
19-27	**Fighting in Lebanon** between Palestinian guerrillas and Christian Phalangist militia leaves more than 130 dead in Beirut and causes government crisis.
21	**Daniel P. Moynihan** is named chief U.S. representative to the United Nations.
22-23	**North Atlantic Treaty Organization** (NATO) defense ministers discuss Spain's role in European defense and agree to standardize equipment to cut costs.
23	**The U.S. Environmental Protection Agency** proposes sharp reductions in the maximum radiation from nuclear power plants to protect the public.
	Former Prime Minister John Gorton quits the Liberal Party in Australia to become an Independent.
27	**President Ford announces a second hike** of $1 per barrel in the tariff on imported crude oil, effective June 1. U.S. reverses policy, agrees to discuss raw material prices at future meetings of oil producers and industrial nations.

May 19-27

May 22-23

June

Sun	Mon	Tue	Wed	Thu	Fri	Sat
1	2	3	4	5	6	7
8	9	10	11	12	13	14
15	16	17	18	19	20	21
22	23	24	25	26	27	28
29	30					

| 3 | **President Ford returns** from his first European visit as President. He met other heads of state at the NATO meeting in Brussels, Belgium; visited Spain and Italy; and met Egypt's President Anwar al-Sadat in Salzburg, Austria. |

June 5

June 10-11

June 10

June 12

June 25

4   **Finland's government resigns.** The four-party coalition Cabinet of Prime Minister Kalevi Sorsa fell to economic ills.

5   **Egypt reopens the Suez Canal** after eight years. It was closed during the 1967 Arab-Israeli war.
British voters approve Common Market membership by a 2-to-1 margin.
Australian Prime Minister Gough Whitlam shuffles Cabinet members following a parliamentary crisis.

6   **Arms embargo against South Africa** is vetoed by France, Great Britain, and the United States in the UN Security Council.

7   **Greek Parliament** adopts a new Constitution.

8   **May unemployment rate** reached 9.2 per cent, the U.S. Labor Department announces.

9   **China and the Philippines** establish diplomatic relations.

9-11   **Organization of Petroleum Exporting Countries** (OPEC) agrees not to raise prices until September.

10   **Rockefeller Commission** accuses CIA of activities that were "plainly unlawful and constituted improper invasions upon the rights of Americans" in a 299-page report to President Ford.
House fails to override veto of the strip-mining bill by President Ford.

10-11   **The International Monetary Fund** fails to reform the world monetary system because of differences between the United States and France over gold and exchange rates.

12   **Two million Khmer refugees** have been forced to flee from the cities to the countryside, reports *The New York Times*.
Ban aerosol sprays that are propelled by fluorocarbons, the President's Council on Environmental Quality says. They might destroy the earth's protective ozone shield.
Court in India convicts Prime Minister Indira Gandhi of illegal campaigning practices before the 1971 election.

15-16   **Communists gain** in Italian regional elections with 33.4 per cent of the vote compared to 35.3 per cent for the Christian Democrats.

16   **The U.S. Supreme Court** rules that lawyers who set uniform minimum fees violate antitrust laws.

17   **Mariana Islands residents vote 4 to 1** in favor of becoming a commonwealth of the United States.

18   **Howard H. Callaway** resigns as secretary of the army to head President Ford's re-election campaign.

19   **Constantine Tsatsos** is elected president of Greece by the new Parliament.

25   **People's Republic of Mozambique,** formerly Portuguese East Africa, becomes an independent state with Samora M. Machel as president.

26   **Prime Minister Indira Gandhi** declares a state of emergency in India. She arrests opposition party leaders and begins press censorship.

27   **West Germany agrees to supply Brazil** with a complete nuclear power industry by 1990.

July

Sun	Mon	Tue	Wed	Thu	Fri	Sat
		1	2	3	4	5
6	7	8	9	10	11	12
13	14	15	16	17	18	19
20	21	22	23	24	25	26
27	28	29	30	31		

1   **Swiss government fights recession** by passing three emergency decrees.
Australia's new National Health Scheme—Medibank—begins.

2   **Prime Minister Whitlam** dismisses Deputy Prime Minister James F. Cairns in Australia for alleged overseas loan irregularities.

U.S. senators meet Leonid I. Brezhnev, Communist Party general secretary, during four-day visit to Russia.
A world conference for women in Mexico City, Mexico, ends after two weeks. Delegates from 113 nations adopt a 10-year plan to promote equal rights and greater participation in national development.

3 **John N. Mitchell is barred** from practicing law in New York state.

4 **The Indian government bans** more than 25 opposition political organizations.
The National Association for the Advancement of Colored People's annual convention calls for the protection of minority jobs.

5 **Cape Verde Islands gain independence.** Portuguese rule ends after 515 years.

7-9 **Mayors want federal aid** to fight recession. Theme dominates the 43rd annual U.S. Conference of Mayors in Boston.

10-11 **United States-Russian talks** in Geneva between Secretary of State Kissinger and Foreign Minister Andrei A. Gromyko center on nuclear arms limitations and the Middle East.

11-17 **Portuguese moderates quit** the provisional government in protest over alleged dictatorial acts by the ruling Armed Forces Movement.

14 **North Korea rejects proposal** by South Korea to resume reunification talks.

16-17 **Russia agrees to buy wheat** from U.S. and Canadian grain exporters.

17 **U.S., Russian spacecraft** link up in space.

28 **The Organization of African Unity** begins its 12th annual summit meeting in Kampala, Uganda.

29 **The Organization of American States** lifts its diplomatic and commercial sanctions against Cuba.
Congress overrides a Ford veto and enacts a $2-billion health bill.
Turkish troops take over U.S. bases after the U.S. House of Representatives refuses to lift an arms embargo.

30 **European summit conference** in Helsinki, Finland, attracts leaders from 33 European nations, the United States, and Canada, and produces a nonbinding treaty.
Italy's government announces a $5.25-billion plan to stimulate the sluggish economy.

31 **Portuguese military junta** led by General Francisco da Costa Gomes, the provisional president, assumes power.
U.S. Congress votes to extend price controls on domestic oil for six months.
New York Mayor Beame presents an economy program aimed at restoring confidence in the city's fiscal integrity.
James R. Hoffa, former international president of the Teamsters Union is reported missing by his family.

August

Sun	Mon	Tue	Wed	Thu	Fri	Sat
					1	2
3	4	5	6	7	8	9
10	11	12	13	14	15	16
17	18	19	20	21	22	23
24	25	26	27	28	29	30
31						

1 **Brazilian President** Ernesto Geisel rejects a return to democracy in a nationwide speech.

2 **Poland agrees** to let ethnic Germans in Poland emigrate to West Germany.

3 **Romania gets most-favored-nation** trade status as President Ford meets President Nicolae Ceausescu in Bucharest.

5-6 **Japanese Premier Takeo Miki** and President Ford meet in Washington, D.C., and reaffirm mutual cooperation and security.

July 17

July 31

July 30

Aug. 9-10

Aug. 23

Sept. 3-10

Sept. 5

6	**More than 2,300 U.S. scientists petition** the White House for a "drastic reduction" in the pace of building nuclear power plants.
9-10	**Violence in Belfast,** Northern Ireland, is the worst in two years.
	U.S. congressmen visit Russian Communist Party leader Brezhnev in Yalta.
15	**Prime Minister Sheik Mujibur Rahman** is assassinated in Dacca, Bangladesh, in an army coup d'état.
18	**British government starts subsidizing** companies that retain rather than lay off employees. The highest unemployment rate in 35 years prompted the plan.
18-21	**San Francisco's police** and fire fighters strike.
19	**Australian Treasurer Bill Hayden** introduces an inflation-fighting budget.
21	**U.S. eases Cuban embargo** in keeping with an earlier decision by the Organization of American States.
	Venezuela nationalizes oil industry, effective Jan. 1, 1976.
	Two policemen die in violence as separatists demand self-government for the French-controlled island of Corsica.
21-22	**Premiers of Canada's 10 provinces,** at their annual meeting in Saint John's, Nfld., urge more federal help in paying for such programs as hospital insurance.
23	**Death sentences** are given to former Greek President George Papadopoulos and two others who led the 1967 military coup. The Greek Cabinet later commuted the sentences to life imprisonment.
27	**France and West Germany** announce joint economic plans to stimulate their sagging economies and provide more jobs.
29	**Peru's President** Juan Velasco Alvarado is replaced by General Francisco Morales Bermudez Cerruti. Peru's military commanders want less government repression.

September

Sun	Mon	Tue	Wed	Thu	Fri	Sat
	1	2	3	4	5	6
7	8	9	10	11	12	13
14	15	16	17	18	19	20
21	22	23	24	25	26	27
28	29	30				

1-5	**International Monetary Fund** and World Bank officials reach gold agreement in annual Washington, D.C., meeting but postpone the question of establishing a new currency-exchange rate until 1976.
3-10	**Teachers strike** in 12 states over wages, class size, and fringe benefits. Nearly 2 million students are affected at peak of strikes.
4	**Israel and Egypt sign an interim peace pact** in Geneva, Switzerland.
5	**President Ford escapes assassination** in Sacramento, Calif., when a Secret Service agent deflects a gun pointed at him by Lynette Alice Fromme, 26, a follower of convicted murderer Charles M. Manson.
5-6	**Portugal's Prime Minister** Vasco dos Santo Gonçalves steps down.
9	**President Ford** selects Thomas S. Kleppe to be secretary of the interior.
	Prince Norodom Sihanouk returns to Khmer (Cambodia) after five years of exile in China.
10	**Congress overrides veto** of a $7.9-billion education aid bill, but fails to override Ford's veto of a bill to continue price controls on domestic oil production for six months.

Cyprus peace talks in New York City between Greek and Turkish Cypriots adjourn after two days of no progress.

11 **Canada's Finance Minister** John N. Turner quits as prices continue to climb and unemployment reaches 14-year high.

13 **Argentine President Isabel Perón** begins a month-long leave of absence for health reasons. The 1975 death toll from political killings tops 400.

14-18 **Christians and Moslems battle** in Beirut, Lebanon, killing nearly 100 and leaving the city a shambles.

15 **China and the Common Market** set formal ties.

16 **New Hampshire special election** for a U.S. Senate seat goes to Democrat John A. Durkin.
The 30th UN General Assembly session convenes in New York City.

18 **Patricia C. Hearst is arrested** by FBI agents in San Francisco 19 months after being kidnaped. William and Emily Harris of the Symbionese Liberation Army are also captured.

19 **New Portuguese Cabinet** headed by José Pinheiro de Azevedo is sworn in.

22 **Mexico's Finance Minister** José Lopez Portillo gains the presidential nomination of the ruling Institutional Revolutionary Party, virtually assuring his election in July, 1976.
President Ford escapes bullet fired from a crowd in San Francisco. Sara Jane Moore is accused of firing the shot.

26 **Canadian Prime Minister Trudeau** reshuffles his Cabinet, names Donald S. Macdonald finance minister.

27 **Organization** of Petroleum Exporting Countries raises oil prices 10 per cent. The price hikes will cost the rest of the world about $10 billion annually.
Spanish authorities execute five members of the Basque separatist movement convicted of killing police. Widespread street and diplomatic protests throughout Europe follow their deaths.

29 **New York State Court of Appeals** strikes down a part of the plan to save New York City from default.

October

Sun	Mon	Tue	Wed	Thu	Fri	Sat
			1	2	3	4
5	6	7	8	9	10	11
12	13	14	15	16	17	18
19	20	21	22	23	24	25
26	27	28	29	30	31	

1 **Italy and Yugoslavia** formally end their Trieste dispute; Italy cedes territory south of Trieste to Yugoslavia.

4 **Canada formally opens** the $500-million Mirabel International Airport near Montreal, Que.

5-8 **Nine persons die in Spain** in protest violence after the execution of five political terrorists.

6 **President Ford calls** for a $28-billion cut in the current permanent tax rates. He also asks for reduced federal spending to match.

9 **U.S. Senate confirms** Thomas S. Kleppe as secretary of the interior.

10 **Russia criticizes** human-rights advocate Andrei D. Sakharov, winner of the Nobel Prize for Peace.

13 **Canada adopts wage and price controls** in an attempt to "knock the wind out of inflation."
Japanese Emperor Hirohito ends a two-week goodwill tour of the United States, the first by a reigning Japanese monarch.

President Ford signs congressional authorization for 200 U.S. civilian technicians to monitor Egyptian-Israeli disengagement in the Sinai Desert.

14 **Australia's Minister of Minerals** and Energy Rex Connor resigns over a controversial foreign-loan case.
The UN Commission on Human Rights charges Chile with continued abuse of civil liberties, including arrest without trial and torture of political prisoners.

14-18 **President Giscard d'Estaing** visits Russia for the first joint top-level consultations between the two countries since 1971.

15-16 **Arab League** foreign ministers meet in Cairo, Egypt, to try to stop the Christian-Moslem fighting in Lebanon. Death toll in Beirut alone is more than 400.

16 **Moroccan King Hassan II** calls for a peaceful mass march of 350,000 persons into the disputed Spanish Sahara.

20 **Russia agrees to buy** up to 8.8 million short tons (8 million metric tons) of U.S. corn and wheat each year for five years.

21 **Canadian postal workers strike.**
Unemployment in Britain tops 1 million; the jobless rate is the highest since World War II.

22 **A Russian unmanned spacecraft** lands on Venus and transmits the first pictures sent to earth from the surface of another planet.

26 **President Anwar al-Sadat** of Egypt begins a 10-day U.S. visit to seek economic and military assistance.

29 **President Ford says he would veto** any federal "bailout" of New York City.

Sept. 13

Sept. 27

Sept. 18

November

Sun	Mon	Tue	Wed	Thu	Fri	Sat
						1
2	3	4	5	6	7	8
9	10	11	12	13	14	15
16	17	18	19	20	21	22
23	24	25	26	27	28	29
30						

3   **President Ford fires** Secretary of Defense James R. Schlesinger and Central Intelligence Agency Director William E. Colby.
Vice-President Rockefeller announces he will not run with Ford in 1976.

6   **UN Security Council** calls on Morocco to withdraw its marchers as tens of thousands pour across the border into the Spanish Sahara.

9   **King Hassan II** ends the peaceful march of thousands of Moroccans into the Spanish Sahara.

10   **UN General Assembly votes** 72 to 35 that Zionism is "a form of racism."

11   **Portugal grants independence** to Angola as rival groups, backed by Russian, Chinese, and U.S. aid, battle for control.
Australian Governor General Sir John Kerr removes Prime Minister Gough Whitlam following a month-long political crisis. Malcolm Fraser is sworn in to serve until December 13 general election.

12   **William O. Douglas retires** from the Supreme Court of the United States for health reasons after 36 years of service.

15-17   **Heads of state** of Britain, France, Italy, Japan, West Germany, and the United States hold an economic summit conference in France.

17   **Judge orders Patricia Hearst** to stand trial on charges of bank robbery and use of a firearm to commit a felony.

18   **The U.S. Senate confirms** Donald Rumsfeld as secretary of defense.
Senate committee reveals that the FBI used electronic bugs in an extensive illegal campaign to discredit Martin Luther King, Jr., in the 1960s.
Spain's parliament votes to withdraw forces from the Spanish Sahara and end Spanish rule of the disputed territory by Feb. 28, 1976.

20   **General Francisco Franco dies** in Madrid, Spain. He ruled as dictator since 1936.

22   **Juan Carlos I** becomes king of Spain.

24   **Maryland Governor Marvin Mandel** and five others are indicted on charges of mail fraud and bribery.
President Ford expresses "complete confidence" in outspoken UN Ambassador Daniel P. Moynihan following rumors that he was about to resign.

26   **President Ford approves federal aid** for debt-ridden New York City.
Nearly 900,000 Japanese workers strike, crippling transportation and communications systems.

29   **Robert D. Muldoon** is elected prime minister of New Zealand.

30   **Martti Miettunen** heads a new government in Finland.

Nov. 15-17

Nov. 20

Dec. 13

December

Sun	Mon	Tue	Wed	Thu	Fri	Sat
	1	2	3	4	5	6
7	8	9	10	11	12	13
14	15	16	17	18	19	20
21	22	23	24	25	26	27
28	29	30	31			

3   **Japanese public employees end strike.**
Russian report shows most disastrous grain harvest in 10 years, one-third below target.
Laos government coalition falls ; 600-year-old monarchy abolished as all of former French Indochina is formally under Communist rule.
The FBI illegally compiled dossiers, wiretapped phones, and spied on citizens under six U.S. Presidents—Roosevelt through Nixon—a Senate panel charges.

5   **President Ford concludes** a state visit to China.

7   **Cuban forces using Russian equipment** allegedly spearhead a drive by pro-Communist forces in Angola.

8   **Indonesian troops seize Dili,** the capital of Portuguese Timor, after months of civil war.
The United States vetoes a UN Security Council resolution to condemn Israel for air attacks against Palestinian refugee camps in Lebanon.

9   **President Ford signs** a $2.3-billion loan to help New York City avoid default.

11   **Spain's Prime Minister** Carlos Arias Navarro forms a new, more moderate Cabinet.
U.S. Senate votes banking reform.

13   **Australians elect** Malcolm Fraser's Liberal-National Country Party to office in landslide victory over Gough Whitlam's Labor Party.

19   **John Paul Stevens** is sworn in as associate justice of the Supreme Court of the United States.

31   **U.S. postal rates go up.** First-class letter rises from 10 cents to 13 cents.

Section One

The Year
In Focus

THE YEAR BOOK Board of Editors analyzes some significant
developments of 1975 and considers their impact on contemporary
affairs. The Related Articles list following each report directs the
reader to THE YEAR BOOK's additional coverage of related subjects.

Focus on The World

John Holmes

SYRIA DENOUNCES
SINAI AGREEMENT

U.N. Delegates Says It Will
Cause Arab Discord

Special to The New York Times

UNITED NATIONS, N. Y.,
10—Syria attacked the
disengagement agreement

It was a year in which economics dominated the world scene, and the Communist and third world states seemed to need a buoyant United States

Economics dominated the world scene in 1975. Inflation, unemployment, and the shortage of food were uppermost in the relations between states. The system of international economic institutions so laboriously created after the end of World War II was severely tested. It was still holding, however. Desperate practical considerations for each nation finally induced a mood of moderation in a year of otherwise intense ideological confrontation. The Russians needed American wheat and technology. The third world of developing nations cooled its political passions for Western aid and markets. And the West had to keep a cautious eye on energy supplies and shipping lanes. On the whole, it was the power with the soundest and most versatile economy that best survived a rough year – the United States, on the eve of what had looked like a gloomy 200th birthday.

Security considerations had not vanished, but the force of circumstances relegated them to a secondary priority. The world was still an armed and arming camp. The Communist and Western countries were holding to détente, but they were largely stalled for the year. Neither the Strategic Arms Limitation Talks between Russia and the United States, nor the two-year-old effort in Vienna, Austria, by the North Atlantic Treaty Organization and Warsaw Pact countries to reach agreement on a mutual reduction of forces made much headway.

An agreement on security and cooperation in Europe was finally reached at Helsinki, Finland, however, after a two-year effort by 33 European and two North American countries. Whether it actually promoted security or cooperation was much debated. In exchange for what was, in fact, a guaranteed acceptance at last of the division of Germany and of Europe, the Western countries, in an unusual display of solidarity, both obtained and gave pledges on the exchange of peoples, ideas, and trade. If honored, the pledges could greatly reduce human tensions. Few expected scrupulous fulfillment, but, it was argued, some leverage had been gained to press the Communist states for more liberal practices. Such interference in their national policies was painful to the Communist states, but the bait for them – apart from removing uncertainties about their borders – was the widened opportunity for trade and advanced technology. The East Europeans may not need Western markets and Western technology to survive, but their leaders considered them necessary to preserve the rising standards of consumption that have become essential to maintain domestic tranquillity. That was one side of the inescapable paradox of détente. Strategic and ideological competition between the East and West continued as usual in Europe – most notably in Portugal – and also in Africa (especially Angola) and the Middle East. Détente, however, was increasingly encouraged not only by the old fear of nuclear

John Holmes

escalation, but also by the compulsions of consumer societies. For economic reasons, most industrialized countries were trimming their defense spending, and the pressure of consumers in the Communist states was challenging their defense priorities.

What should have been the most destabilizing event of the year, the swift capitulation in the spring of all the Indochinese states to Communist forces (whoever they might be), seemed to have upset the equilibrium very little. Americans quickly put it in the back of their minds. The impact may, of course, have been falsified by the silence that descended upon Vietnam and Khmer (formerly Cambodia) and permitted few headlines. The dominoes had fallen, but they weren't picked up, as once feared, by "international Communism." In victory, Communism's disunity was starkly revealed. Thailand and the Philippines quickly established relations with China and planned the withdrawal of United States bases and the liquidation of the Southeast Asia Treaty Organization. However, the Chinese told the visiting prime minister of Thailand and the president of the Philippines that they hoped the reduction of American influence would not lead to an increase of Russian influence. With Peking and Moscow at cross-purposes, Hanoi looked more than ever like its own master and another center of Communism in South Asia. The "vacuum" in that area was likely to be filled by a new balance of powers.

The United States had lost face, of course, but it had also lost an appalling drain on its health and strength. It was rather like the European powers that had realized—after shedding their colonies in the 1950s and 1960s—that they were better off, rid of a military and financial burden and better able to concentrate their forces. Defeat or victory is sometimes a way of looking at things. By accepting the inevitable without loud lamentation, Americans minimized their setback. There was no vigorous protest when Thailand and the Philippines quite understandably shifted to a more neutral posture. As U.S. Secretary of State Henry A. Kissinger said in a speech in August, the United States was accepting nonalignment at a time when the nonaligned were aligning. The United States reduced its forces on Taiwan, Chiang Kai-shek died, and little attention was paid.

Nor did the United States resist later when a majority in the Organization of American States decided to resume relations with Cuba. The nonaligned powers met in Lima, Peru, and launched salvos against American imperialism, but Washington did not get excited. By looking less like a loser than a confident power that takes the inevitable in its stride and adjusts, the United States reassured those who had worried about the Vietnam aftermath. Congress and the public were leery of commitments, but the Ford Administration showed little disposition to retreat from Europe and the Middle East. In the Middle East, the United States retained the diplomatic initiative through Kissinger's further successful negotiations, which led in September to an Israeli-Egyptian agreement for partial withdrawal from the Sinai Peninsula. It was a precarious agreement, of course,

The vacuum in South Asia was likely to be filled by a new power balance

Kissinger on the move

but Russia and the other Arab states, while growling, still seemed cautious about defying it. It was significant that the United States agreed to man early-warning stations in the Sinai to detect violations of the agreement. This is a job that should be done by the United Nations (UN), but it was presumably undertaken, on request, by the only power whose behavior Egypt and Israel would trust.

The old bipolar concept, the struggle of the Free World against Communism in which the Vietnam War had been conceived, seemed less and less applicable in a world of new confrontations. Communism remained a serious challenge for power in many countries, especially as democratic regimes faced economic and governmental crises grave enough to raise doubts as to whether their system was workable in an overcrowded world. But the Communist parties were increasingly schismatic. China and Russia, snarling and arming against each other, seemed to want continued détente bilaterally with the United States, but not as a trio. The Chinese played a modest role in world diplomacy, uncertain, according to speculation, of their direction because of the uncertainties about their ailing leaders and the succession to power.

Divisions within the Communist system were notable also in Europe. Maoists and Moscow-oriented Communists opposed each other in Portugal. The Italian and French parties drew further away from Moscow to adapt themselves to their national political scenes and get closer to power. However, international Communist disunity did not necessarily mean weakness. The Communist parties made gains in France and Italy, hovered close to power in Portugal, and looked like a factor to be reckoned with in Spain if there were eruptions after General Francisco Franco's death in November. Greater flexibility in doctrine and detachment from a superpower–Russia–that has been less and less respected in radical circles strengthened their national appeal as an alternative to democracy in trouble.

The most serious threat to the industrialized countries was not a shift of the strategic balance, but a crisis of confidence. It was stimulated by worldwide inflation and the apparent inability of governments and international institutions to cope with the increasing complexity of man's interdependence. Democracy had flourished in the context of economic growth. Could it accomplish the redistribution of wealth? It was encouraging to watch the Greeks re-establishing democratic practices and the Portuguese Socialists defying traditional Communist tactics. Even the South Africans and Rhodesians were showing some tentative signs of bending under world pressure and the collapse of Portuguese imperialism. But the odds against democracy in countries unused to it and facing desperate economic and social problems seemed overwhelming. Most disheartening was the sharp swerve from liberal practices by the world's largest democracy, India, where Prime Minister Indira Gandhi arrested members of the opposition and imposed censorship. Further coups in Bangladesh and Nigeria, the extension of military rule in Africa, corruption in Kenya,

The nonaligned meet

civil war in Lebanon, repression in Chile, and anarchy in Argentina raised grave doubts whether liberal democratic practices would work in the postimperial age. The fear was no longer that countries that slipped from grace joined "the other side," but rather that their defection contributed to the breakdown of international good government.

The UN was going through a perilous stage. A majority of developing countries–unnaturally swollen by the addition of ministate remnants of the Portuguese and other empires–was displaying, in the eyes of Western peoples, a reckless disposition. This took the form of demands for the instant creation of a new world economic order. Although justifiable in principle, this seemed impossible of realization. Even more inflammatory on public opinion in the West, especially in the United States, was the developing countries' even bolder espousal of the Palestinian case against Israel. A resolution of the General Assembly majority equating Zionism with racism provoked a wave of protest in Western countries against the UN itself.

The UN was reflecting the third world's increasing militancy

The UN, however, was merely reflecting, not creating, the increasing militancy of the third world. As a widely diversified framework within which to negotiate vital issues, it was more important and indispensable than ever. The Western powers, particularly the United States, set out to warn the third world of the threat to their own hopes if they alienated the electorates of countries that had the funds to contribute. Moderates in the third world got this message. There was a notable improvement in the tone of the debate when the United States presented to the special session of the Assembly in September a set of proposals that at least made clear that the West recognized the basic justice of the demand for a new economic order. This "détente" between North and South lasted through the regular session of the General Assembly. If it could hold, it would mean that the UN was performing its basic function–to force opposing sides to recognize the futility of confrontation and the need to look for accommodation.

The crisis seemed to have frightened most of those concerned into a new sobriety, a mood that could do much to counteract the growing cynicism about efforts in the UN to maintain orderly international progress. Economic distress had begotten the rough challenge of the third world, but it also encouraged pragmatism. In spite of all the strategic calculations of East and West, North and South, the poor knew that they needed help from the industrialized nations. The Russians needed dollars and trade and technology and–most of all–the food from North America that they were still unable to produce in sufficient quantities for their own expanding needs. And the West wanted raw materials, secure supplies, and more trade to pull them out of recession, and that required business relations with the Communists and the less developed. It was a situation that tended to fortify the world power that, for all its internal problems and strategic rebuffs, was the soundest and richest of them all–the United States. When the Russians had bad harvests again and requested more wheat than the U.S. could spare, it made dramatically clear the extent to

Wheat in the United States

which expanding world populations depended on the unique capacity of North America to produce a surplus of food. Russia was by no means without economic power, of course. During the year, it surpassed the United States as the world's leading oil producer, and the possibility of trading wheat for oil was pondered.

Economic relations across the Atlantic were considerably improved in spirit in November when leaders of four European powers met near Paris with leaders of Japan and the United States and produced a set of guidelines that would counter the trend toward protectionism. It even resulted in a compromise between France and the United States on an issue that had been sharply divisive–exchange-rate stability. It was a notable gesture of Western solidarity, but the intention was to prepare for fair bargaining with representatives of the third world. This got off to a businesslike start at a December conference in Paris of 27 industrialized and developing nations, which set up four commissions to look for some feasible solutions. The hard issues of coexistence remained to be tackled, but the international machinery, after a disastrous spring, seemed pointed again in the direction of dialogue.

If the United States was likely to continue as the principal object of third world resentment, this was because the U.S. could best provide the answers. Russia or China or a European Community without much cohesion did not have the diversified power and influence to be decisive. The United States also was more likely than other Western powers to move out of recession, and the rest of the world was counting on American prosperity to pull them out, too.

There was no question of the United States retrieving, even if it wanted to, the authority it had exercised in the 1950s and 1960s. For one thing, there were too many other centers of power now. It was extraordinary, nevertheless, that the United States could emerge resilient in the year in which all it had fought for in Indochina had been lost. There was no doubt that the disastrous involvement in Indochina and the nasty revelations of Watergate and the Central Intelligence Agency had contributed to the universal uneasiness of democracy. It was, nevertheless, counteracted by the capacity of a democracy to purge itself and change course. Perhaps also a chastened and humbled United States had more human appeal than the self-confident giant of yesterday. Whatever the long-range plans of the Communist and third world states, they seemed to need for the time being a buoyant United States as part of their equilibrium. Not that any of them would say this out loud, of course.

The rest of the world was depending on United States prosperity

Discussing world economics

Related Articles

For further information on international relations in 1975, see the articles on the various nations in Section Four, and also the following:

Africa	International Trade	Middle East
Asia	and Finance	Pacific Islands
Europe	Latin America	United Nations

Focus on The Nation

James Reston

There was in 1975 a pause for reflection in American life, a summing-up of the past, and an examination of the country's institutions

At the beginning of 1976, the 200th anniversary of the Declaration of Independence, the American people had many reasons to rejoice. No other people on earth were so prosperous, or had lived for so long under the liberties and constraints of such an enduring written political constitution. Also, for the first time in a decade, they were not at war anywhere in the world, and they were in the forefront of a strenuous effort, as they had been from the beginning, to bring about a new and just order among the nations and peoples of the world.

And yet, at the beginning of their third century, the American people were not rejoicing. They were measuring their progress against their ideals, and their present leaders against the founders of the republic. They were concentrating, not on their successes but on their failures and disappointments. They were still engaged in "the pursuit of happiness," but they were still troubled about what happiness meant.

In short, the long and remarkable history of the United States—its triumphs over adversity, its conquest of the continent, and its rise to world leadership—oddly did not dominate the mind of the nation at the beginning of its Bicentennial year. Somehow, the problems of the present temporarily overwhelmed the achievements of the past, and clouded the hopes for the future.

"If we could first know where we are, and whither we are tending," President Abraham Lincoln said, in the darker days of the Civil War, "we could better judge what to do, and do it better." But paradoxically, at the start of 1976, with all the triumphs over slavery, disunion, depression, and world war before us, it was clear in the Bicentennial year that the nation was divided about where it was, and where it was heading.

Part of the reason for this division was that the nation early in 1976 was in the midst of the worst economic slump in over 30 years. It was also heading into a presidential election with an unelected President and an unelected Vice-President in office. Both these facts added a quarrelsome spirit to the discussion of public affairs and perhaps made things seem worse than they actually were.

Beyond this, the nation was troubled by the psychological depression of the Vietnam War and the Watergate political scandals. And also by the disclosures in 1975 that succeeding presidents from Franklin D. Roosevelt and Harry S. Truman to John F. Kennedy, Lyndon B. Johnson, Richard M. Nixon, and—to a lesser extent—Dwight D. Eisenhower had used the Federal Bureau of Investigation and the Central Intelligence Agency against the personal liberties of the American people and against the ideals of the nation abroad.

The year 1975, then, was a time of self-examination and criticism in the United States. Its most spectacular city, New York, symbol of

James Reston

the most successful economic system in the history of the world, had come to the verge of bankruptcy. Its political system, based on the balance of power among Congress, the President, and the courts, had got wildly and even scandalously out of balance in the Watergate controversy. The military assumptions that money, machines, and scientific knowledge would prevail over any potential enemy were destroyed in Vietnam. And even the American experiments with the welfare state, from Roosevelt to Gerald R. Ford, were under serious attack at the beginning of 1976.

Accordingly, it was not the specific events of 1975—the prices, the inflation, the interest rates, and the unemployment at home, and the controversies over trade, money, and military arms abroad—that dominated the American mind at the beginning of its Bicentennial year. Rather, it was the larger philosophical questions of whether something had gone wrong with the American political and economic systems and with the American spirit of confidence and optimism.

For example, the American historian Richard Hofstadter thought of the period from the Civil War to the 1890s as a period of industrial and continental expansion, and the ensuing period from 1890 to the Roosevelt New Deal as the Age of Reform. But by 1975, even the liberal reformers seemed· to be questioning many of their own economic and political reforms and to be turning to more conservative policies.

Also, in 1975, with the retirement of Justice William O. Douglas from the Supreme Court of the United States after 36 years of service, the court had a conservative majority for the first time in over 30 years. In reaction to the abuses of presidential power under Richard Nixon, the authority of the executive branch was reduced without a similar rise in the power of Congress.

There was, naturally, in respect for the nation's birthday, a tendency to look back at the historical assumptions of the past to see whether they were still valid. On the whole, contemporary historians were in a doubting mood.

In 1902, when Brooks Adams wrote *The New Empire*, he emphasized a theme that had been popular in previous generations with the French political scientist Alexis De Tocqueville and the British historian and statesman James Bryce. This was that America was not only "unique," but also had established a system of liberty that would be the model of the coming age.

"The seat of energy has migrated from Europe to America," Brooks Adams wrote. "Supposing the movement of the next 50 years only equal to the last ... the United States will outweigh any single empire, if not all empires combined. The whole world will pay her tribute. Commerce will flow to her from both East and West, and the order which has existed from the dawn of time will be reversed."

The 19th-century German philosopher Georg Hegel, in his *Philosophy of History*, had been more specific. "America," he said, "is therefore the land of the future, where, in ages that lie before us, the

James Bryce

burden of the World's history shall reveal itself. . . . It is the land of desire for all those who are weary of the historical lumber room of old Europe."

Similarly, Bryce had said in *The American Commonwealth* (1888) that America "sailed a summer sea," that American institutions would inherit the future because they were the institutions "towards which, as by a law of fate, the rest of mankind are forced to move."

The tone of most comment about the United States in 1975 was strikingly different—one ventures to think excessively pessimistic because the prophecies of the past had been excessively optimistic. The quarterly magazine *The Public Interest,* for example, invited a group of distinguished historians and scholars to compare the American commonwealth of Bryce's vision with the American commonwealth of 1976.

Daniel P. Moynihan of Harvard University, United States ambassador to India and later to the United Nations, introducing these studies in the magazine, remarked: "Neither liberty nor democracy would seem to be prospering—or in any event, neither would seem to have a future nearly as auspicious as their past. . . . Seemingly nothing at present brings forth more gloom than the contemplation of the future. . . ."

The American Dream has not ended—there simply are more dreamers

Harvard's Daniel Bell was more hopeful, but even he commented: "The belief in American exceptionalism has vanished with the end of empire, the weakening of power, the loss of faith in the nation's future. . . . Internal tensions have multiplied and there are deep structural crises, political and cultural, that may prove more intractable to solution than the domestic economic problems. "What happened," he asked, "to the American Dream?"

One answer might be merely that in the 1960s and the first half of the 1970s, the nation woke up to the daylight realities of a rapidly changing world. The days of its military dominance as the sole possessor of atomic weapons were over, and with them, the security of its oceans.

Likewise, its long leads in science and technology, in mass production and distribution, were under challenge by other nations. The other industrial countries may not have followed the example of American politics, as Bryce and Hegel thought they would, but they mastered the techniques of mass production, mass education, mass communications, and computers.

Some of them—West Germany and Japan, for example—developed partnerships of management and labor that made them even more competitive with the United States in the growing markets of the world. Other nations, those in possession of most of the oil resources of the planet, also learned from the United States how to extract their wealth from the earth and charge as much for it as the free market could possibly pay.

The American Dream didn't end, at least in economic terms—there are simply more dreamers. The dream began 200 years ago in the American Declaration of Independence and a revolution against

Daniel P. Moynihan

foreign domination. That is what almost a hundred new nations have done in changing the map of the world in the past 30 years.

The American ideal was not only for independence, but also for equality. It was still going on in the United States at the beginning of 1976 in the struggles over jobs, taxes, housing, busing, women's rights, interest rates, and many other things. And this ideal of equality is still envied, if not being copied, all over the world, even in the totalitarian states of Russia and China.

The old tug and haul, push and shove of American life were going on

What the American people were debating at the beginning of 1976 was not whether democracy was still a valid system of government, but whether individual liberty–the first principle of the Declaration and the Constitution–had gone too far and created what the American historian Samuel P. Huntington of Harvard University called "the democratic distemper."

In a report to the Trilateral Commission–itself a symbol of the American dream of bringing the industrial nations of the United States, Europe, Japan, and the rest of the world into a study of their common problems–Huntington noted that the 1960s had witnessed a dramatic upsurge of democratic fervor in America.

The predominant trends of that decade, he suggested, "involved challenges to the authority of established political, social, and economic institutions. Also, a reaction against the concentration of power in the executive branch of the federal government; the emergence of 'public interest' lobbying groups; increased concern for the rights of minorities and women; and a pervasive criticism of those who possessed or were even thought to possess excessive power or wealth.

"The spirit of protest, the spirit of equality and the impulse to expose and correct inequalities were abroad in the land. The themes of the 1960s were those of Jacksonian democracy and the muckraking Progressives; they embodied ideas and beliefs which were deep in the American tradition but which did not usually command the passionate intensity of commitment [in the 1970s] that they did in the 1960s."

In other words, the old tug and haul, push and shove of American life were still going on at the beginning of the nation's third century as they had 200 years before. Even on the question of the Declaration and the revolution against the British, the American people of 1776 were divided–about one-third warriors for war, one-third loyalists for the British, and one-third for peace and quiet. Thomas Jefferson and James Madison differed, too, about whether too little or too much democracy was the greater danger. So the ancient debate goes on.

At the beginning of 1976, the American people were complaining about the quality of the men seeking the presidency, but Bryce, who thought America was a model for the world, was complaining about precisely the same sort of thing back in 1888.

Samuel P. Huntington

No form of government needed great leaders more than democracy, Bryce wrote, so why were they so scarce? In a chapter on "the true faults of American democracy," he protested that in America there was "a certain commonness of mind and tone, and want of dignity and elevation, in and about the conduct of public affairs, an insensibility to the nobler aspects and finer responsibilities of national life."

In explaining "why great men are not chosen" for the presidency, Bryce concluded that "the ordinary American voter does not object to mediocrity," but in the end, he thought, we would come out all right. "The problem of conducting a stable executive in a democratic country," he said, "is indeed so difficult that anything short of failure deserves to be called a success. . . ."

The main difference between Bryce's analysis of the American problem almost a hundred years ago and now, is that the old boy defined it so much better and in such nobler language than his successors in 1976.

In short, there was in 1975 a pause for reflection in American life, a summing-up of the past, and a practical examination of all political, economic, and social institutions. The same sort of thing happened between the Declaration of Independence in 1776 and the writing of the Constitution in 1787, and that earlier period of self-examination proved to be one of the great chapters in American history.

In the end, the historian Bryce thought, we would come out all right

Related Articles

For further information on United States affairs in 1975, see also Section One, FOCUS ON THE ECONOMY and FOCUS ON EDUCATION; Section Two, AMERICA: THEN, NOW, AND TOMORROW; and the following articles in Section Four:

Focus on The Economy

Sylvia Porter

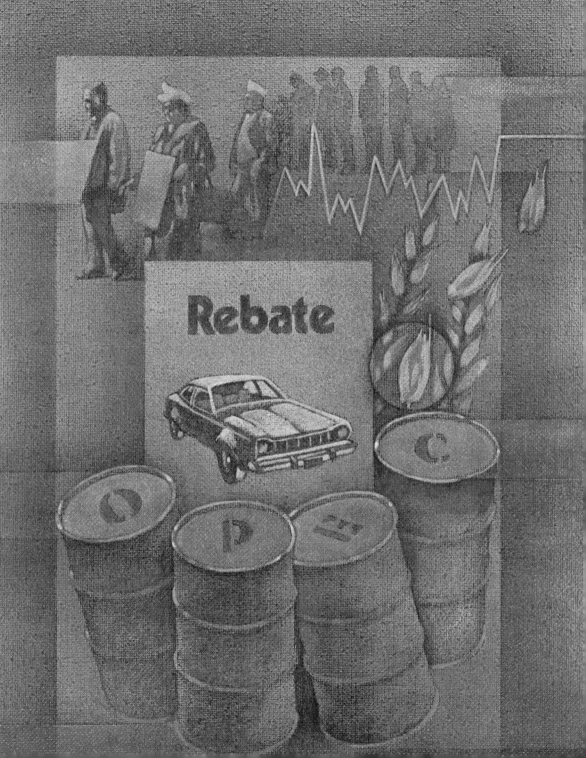

The United States was recuperating from its most prolonged slump since the depression 1930s, but the recovery was blotched by several threats

As 1975 ended, the United States was well into its initial recuperation from the deepest, broadest, most prolonged slump since the depression 1930s. But despite surface evidence suggesting it was a sturdy, even strong, recovery, it was blotched by threats that, if permitted to become realities, could abort the upturn in a matter of months. Some nationally respected economists, in fact, openly predicted that we would again be sliding downward as early as mid-1976 – with all that would imply for jobs, paychecks, and profits, as well as for the November, 1976, elections.

The anxieties were indisputable. Until the very year-end, skepticism was widespread among consumers and businessmen that the slump had even ended (not so surprising if the skeptic was in one of the still-weak industries, such as housing, or lived in a neighborhood where joblessness was alarmingly high, or was among the nearly 8 million unemployed). And the challenges were enormous. Among them: an unacceptably high rate of inflation, a steep level of interest rates, a huge total of unemployed, tremendous budget deficits, and the unforeseeable "domino" impact on the economy of the nation, should there be a series of debt defaults and forced retrenchment in spending by cities and states.

Thus, 1975's was a fragile and uncertain recuperation – just as the feverish boom that bred the 1974-1975 slumpflation was joyless and unsustainable. But, even admitting all the ifs, ands, and buts, an expansion it was. To document:

■ "Real" gross national product (GNP) – meaning total U.S. output of goods and services with the impact of price increases on the dollar totals eliminated – started to rise in the second quarter of the year, after five consecutive quarters of decline. And real GNP was continuing to increase at a 6 to 8 per cent rate as 1976 began. This is the broadest measure of our nation's economic health.

■ Production of U.S. factories, mines, and utilities climbed back from the trough to the highest level since late 1974.

■ The total number of employed in the United States jumped by an impressive 1.6 million to 85.4 million, the highest since November, 1974. Layoffs bottomed out; rehiring rose. Although the unemployment rate remained intolerably high at 8.3 per cent of the nation's labor force – and the rate was much higher among blacks and teenagers and women – the rate was down from the summer's peak of 9.2 per cent, and joblessness among married men heading households fell to 5.2 per cent.

■ Personal incomes surged upward to an adjusted annual rate of $1.3-trillion, propelled primarily by expanding factory payrolls and other wage-salary payments.

Sylvia Porter

- "Real" spendable earnings of workers turned upward for the first time since February, 1973, mostly reflecting the reduction in federal income taxes that went into effect in May, 1975. These are weekly earnings, minus federal income and social security taxes, adjusted to reflect the erosion of buying power caused by price increases.
- Consumer confidence perked up, and retail sales rebounded in response to increased spending and buying on the installment plan. While still depressed, the auto and housing industries came back a bit.
- Business slashed its inventories at a spectacularly brutal pace during the slump, and goods in warehouses plunged to levels where businesses were forced to renew buying and restocking merely to meet current consumer demands.
- The stock market as measured by the New York Stock Exchange index soared 56 per cent between the fall of 1974 and July, 1975. Stock price ups and downs are considered a key leading indicator—telegraphing in advance the ups and downs in the economy as a whole.

Nevertheless, the threats to the life of this economic recovery were very real and frightening. They could halt what almost surely would otherwise be a long, healthy uptrend. The threats:
- An extraordinarily rapid rate of inflation in the 6 to 8 per cent range piled on top of an all-time-high price level. There are few precedents for a galloping inflation throughout a deep business decline, but that's what happened in 1974 and early 1975. And the deceleration in the inflation rate after that was only moderate. If inflation returns to and stays in the double-digit ranges of the recent past, this fragile upturn is doomed.
- A suffocatingly steep level of interest rates, also starting from astoundingly high rates for so early in a recovery. The cost of raising funds was inhibiting borrowers across the board—businesses that wanted to modernize and expand; consumers who wanted to buy and build houses; cities and states; and so on. Without this support, the expansion cannot thrive.
- An unacceptably high rate of joblessness—which translated into the most human of terms and meant that our economy was not expanding fast enough to create jobs both for our unemployed and for new workers entering the labor force. Although White House policymakers argue that a high rate of unemployment is essential to curb inflation, this, in effect, makes the unemployed American a first line of defense against price increases. To me, a jobless worker is a criminally cruel, callous, barbaric "weapon" to put into an anti-inflation arsenal.
- A dangerously depressing setback in economic activity across the board while troubled cities and states fight bankruptcy, just as New York City and New York state fought it throughout the year. The retrenchment was sharply underlined in November's elections, when voters throughout the nation turned down proposals for spending, seemingly without reference to value or need. And long before December, when there appeared to be at least a temporary relief from the default crisis in New York City, other cities and states already had

Filing unemployment claims

been compelled to add billions of dollars to their costs for borrowing money merely because of New York City's plight and the fact that they, too, were cities and states issuing tax-exempt securities. There is no way to forecast accurately at this time what could be the ultimate economic effect of major cutbacks in state and local spending.

■ A specter of *disintermediation*, the huge outflow of savings from institutions as savers seek to reinvest their funds in securities carrying higher rates than the institutions are permitted to pay under federal ceilings. A persistent, major drain of savings from these institutions would slash the total available for mortgages and throw the feebly recovering housing industry into a tail spin.

■ A continuing lag in business spending for new factories and modern equipment because of the big percentage of idle plant capacity at year-end as well as the high cost of borrowing. Unless auto sales, housing starts, and business spending perk up markedly, this recovery cannot gain much speed.

■ The approach of a period of unprecedented labor contract negotiations in five major industries. The outcome of any one of the five–trucking, rubber, electrical, autos, construction–could slow the pace of the upturn.

■ The prospect of horrendously swollen deficits in the U.S. budget. While deficits were welcomed by most liberal economists in mid-1975 as an effective antirecession cushion, both liberals and conservatives were deeply worried about the coincidence of an expanding economy with annual U.S. deficits of the magnitude of $70 billion-plus. In this case, the U.S. Treasury Department could "crowd out" lesser borrowers from the financial markets, with unforeseeably adverse results. And the deficits themselves could lead to an overheating of the economy and from there to another phase of runaway inflation.

Are we running out of answers to inflation, the evil behind other evils?

And this, mind you, is only a sampling of the threats. Others range from deep doubts about oil supplies and oil prices over the long term, to the untested impact of "tax reform" legislation, to the ability of the international monetary system to withstand constant pressures.

Yet, the fundamental question of all the fundamental questions facing us as 1975 ended was beyond any of these. In blunt summary, it was: Are we running out of answers to inflation, the basic evil that is behind all other evils?

If prices were to continue soaring at the 12.2 per cent rate of 1974, the value of the $1 that bought you 100 cents of goods and services at the start of 1975 would be worth only 51 cents in 1980, only 36 cents in 1983, only 26 cents a mere 10 years from now, and only 5 cents by the year 2000. Today's price level would double as early as 1980, triple by 1983, quadruple within the decade, and be 19 times as high in 2000 as now. You couldn't make stable plans for the future. Your very expectations of the disaster of relentless inflation would help make the disaster a self-fulfilling prophecy.

If the pace of rise in prices were to fall into the "good news" range of 6 to 8 per cent–which many experts say is the best we can expect in

Setting oil prices

the months ahead—the future still would be too bleak to be accepted without protest. Assume the rate fell to and stayed at 7 per cent a year compounded (meaning each year's 7 per cent rise would be built on top of the previous year's 7 per cent and on and on).

At a 7 per cent annual rate of rise, today's dollar would be worth only 51 cents in 1984, only 34 cents in 1990, only 26 cents in 1994, only 17 cents less than 25 years from now. Today's price level would double by 1984 and be almost six times as high by 2000.

Certainly, even a sharp business slump isn't the answer to curbing inflation in this era, as first the Nixon Administration and later the Ford Administration have tried to convince us. In depth, the 1973-1975 slump was the most severe business decline since the 1930s, much worse than any other post-World War II drop. Real gross national product fell almost 8 per cent, in contrast to declines in recessions 1969-1970 and 1960-1961 of under 2 per cent. No decline since 1929-1932—except 1973-1975—has exceeded 4 per cent. The 1973-1975 slump lasted 16 months, by far the longest of any retreat since the 43-month depression of 1929-1932. In breadth—impact on number of industries, services, occupations of all types—it was the worst in a generation. Industrial output dropped almost 14 per cent, again the worst drop since 1929-1932. In unemployment, too, the 9 per cent-plus ranked as the most severe since the catastrophic 1930s.

And in one very real sense, this was the worst slump of all. For in 1929-1932, prices at least fell along with incomes. This time, though, prices were galloping at the start of the decline and even after 16 months of contraction were still climbing at an intolerable rate. Clearly, in addition to being cruel and primitive, the traditional "slump" weapon of unemployment has been inadequate to deal with the inflation spirals cursing not only our society, but also those of other countries around the globe.

What might be the answers, then? Each of the following has as many vocal opponents as defenders. But each should at least be examined in the open by an aware public—not shrugged off by policymakers determined to rely on the economics of anxiety, to err on the side of too little rather than too much economic stimulation. To illustrate:

■ A workable "incomes" policy, involving "jawboning with teeth in the jaws," so that inflationary price hikes do not occur when the law of supply and demand actually is dictating price cuts. This does not mean formal price-wage controls. It does mean a policy of nonmandatory restraints, under which the giant corporations and unions would have to give prenotification of price increases and wage demands, and the price increases as well as wage hikes could be reduced or even suspended by a responsible incomes board.

■ Courageous, innovative moves to speed productivity (output per worker), which is a fundamental offset to spiraling prices. (A worker who wins a 7 per cent hourly wage hike but turns out 10 per cent more units per hour has cut the cost of his work by 3 per cent per unit; his

Announcing deficit budget

The possible answers must be examined in the open by an aware public

pay raise can easily be absorbed while his employer prospers.) Productivity climbed sharply in 1975, but the challenge is to maintain the pace of rise.

- A public commitment by business and labor to help curb inflation, with the commitment under the policing of a federal council. A public commitment by consumers, too, to favor businesses that try to hold the price line.
- A balanced drive to enforce our antitrust laws more strictly–which could save consumers tens of billions of dollars a year.
- Tax policies and incentives designed to spur business expansion and modernization in order to increase efficiency.
- Stretching out of timetables for achieving environmental goals where it can be demonstrated this would reduce inflationary pressures.
- Elimination of regulations that are harmful, but not deregulation for deregulation's sake. Among the candidates: requirements that trucks make return trips empty when cargoes are available, or that wholesome farm produce be destroyed so that it cannot be sold at cut-rate prices.
- More escalator clauses for more types of compensation (or indexing in some form) to keep incomes rising with rises in living costs.

This is a short, random listing; many other ideas are being seriously debated (though not, apparently, at the White House). There *are* answers among these or other proposals. And to close on a further note of optimism: Just as the most-publicized threats of 1974 did not become reality in 1975, so the threats of 1975 can be averted. Moreover, if the recuperation that began in the spring of 1975 were only to match the average life of the previous upturns of the post-World War II period, our economy would continue expanding until at least mid-1979. Even if the spectacularly long expansion that began under President John F. Kennedy in 1961 and ended under President Richard M. Nixon in 1969 is omitted from the figures, the average span of the other post-World War II recoveries would keep us on an upturn until the spring of 1978. This more modest upturn would boost employment by 19 per cent and send production up 40 per cent.

We are not doomed to be victims of our own economic creations. We can become the masters, not settle for being helpless slaves, of our man-made systems. We can so manage our economy that inflation rates and interest rates fall to within tolerable ranges. While the decade of the 1970s is far more turbulent than we anticipated, we can still turn it into a span of above-average economic health and well-being. One point is sure: The economic policies the current Administration in Washington, D.C., adopts to achieve this will be at the heart of the 1976 presidential and congressional elections.

We are not doomed to be victims of our own economic creations

Stock-exchange action

Related Articles

For further information on economics in 1975, see Section Four, Agriculture; Banks and Banking; Economics; International Trade and Finance; Labor; Manufacturing; Stocks and Bonds.

Focus on Science

Harrison Brown

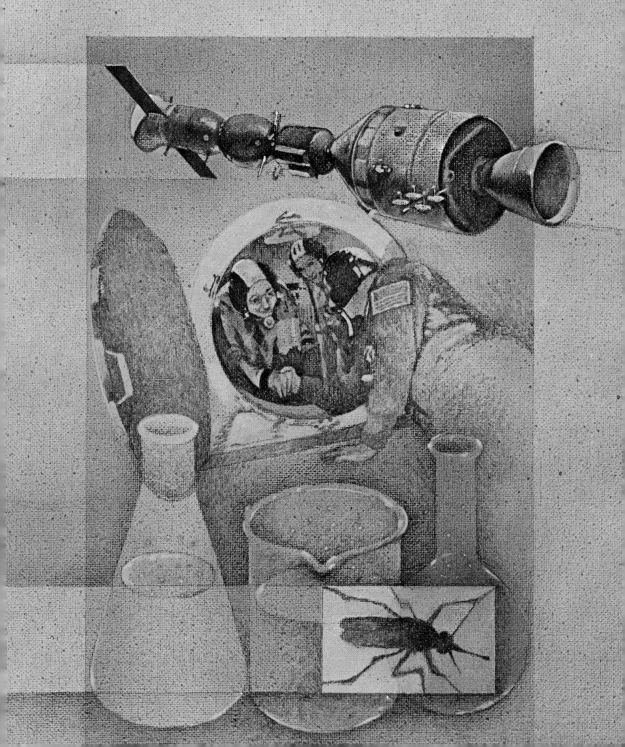

Aerosol spray cans became the subject of a lively scientific-political controversy, and mankind may be faced with some of its most difficult decisions

As recently as one year ago, it would not have seemed likely that aerosol spray cans such as those used for hair sprays, deodorants, or insect repellents would ever be the subject of a lively scientific-political controversy, but in 1975 that is exactly what happened. In 1974, F. Sherwood Rowland and Mario J. Molina of the Department of Chemistry at the University of California, Irvine, reported that the propellent gases used in spray cans might result in the destruction of ozone in the so-called ozone layer that exists in the stratosphere about 15 miles (24 kilometers) above the earth. The ozone layer protects terrestrial life from the damaging effects of the sun's ultraviolet rays, and the alarming implications of Rowland and Molina's calculations triggered considerable additional investigation, as well as a great deal of heated debate.

Ozone, which is made up of three combined oxygen atoms instead of the two that combine to make up a molecule of ordinary oxygen, is continuously being formed at high altitude by the action of sunlight. The sun's rays of short wave length decompose oxygen molecules into free oxygen atoms, and those atoms in turn combine with oxygen molecules to form ozone. But the action of sunlight also destroys ozone, primarily indirectly, by creating intermediate substances with which the ozone reacts. The ratio of the rate at which ozone is produced to the rate at which it is destroyed depends upon the presence of *catalysts* – atoms or molecules that react with the ozone but that are regenerated in a "catalytic cycle." Thus, even small concentrations of certain substances in the stratosphere can give rise to considerable ozone decomposition.

Most propellants used in aerosol sprays are compounds of chlorine, fluorine, and carbon known as chlorofluorocarbons and are usually referred to by a widely used trade name, Freon. These gases are also widely used as refrigerants as well as for other industrial purposes. They are remarkably *inert* (chemically inactive), which makes them particularly suitable for these purposes. They are harmless to living organisms. Human tissue is not hurt in any way by direct exposure to those chlorofluorocarbons in widespread use.

But the very inertness of chlorofluorocarbons enables them to travel freely from the home to the stratosphere. They do not dissolve in water, so rainfall does not wash them away. They do not react rapidly with gases in the lower atmosphere, so, once released, they slowly diffuse upward into the stratosphere.

Harrison Brown

Rowland and Molina suggested that ultraviolet light in the stratosphere could *dissociate*, or separate, the chlorofluorocarbons, causing them to release free chlorine atoms. These atoms appear to be extremely effective catalysts for the decomposition of ozone. Subsequent calculations indicated that if the manufacture of chlorofluorocarbons continues increasing at its current rate, the ozone layer might be depleted by 15 per cent by the year 2000.

The argument over aerosol sprays is really a continuation of an earlier argument over the supersonic transport (SST). In 1971, Paul J. Crutzen, an atmospheric physicist, now at the National Center for Atmospheric Research near Boulder, Colo., and Harold S. Johnston, a chemist at the University of California, Berkeley, pointed out that nitric oxide is an effective catalyst for ozone decomposition. They warned that the amount of this substance in the stratosphere might be increased significantly if supersonic aircraft became an important part of air transport. Nitric oxide is produced when air is heated to the very high temperatures characteristic of jet engines. A supersonic plane flying at an altitude of about 12½ miles (20 kilometers) would deposit the nitric oxide near the layers of maximum ozone concentration. Crutzen has estimated that a fleet of 500 Boeing SST's, each flying at such an altitude for seven hours every day, would result in an average ozone reduction of 16 per cent in the Northern Hemisphere. Similar fleets of the British-French Concorde and the Soviet Union's Tupolev 144 would cause smaller reductions of ozone because they are smaller planes and fly at lower altitudes.

The recognition that supersonic transport on a substantial scale could lead to a significant reduction of ozone was an important factor in the 1971 decision by the Congress of the United States to cancel financial support for development of the Boeing SST. Regrettably, though that decision was probably a wise one, the debate that preceded it was far more political and emotional than scientific in both nature and content.

In 1975, some of the predictions made earlier concerning chlorofluorocarbons in the atmosphere were confirmed. Chemists at the National Bureau of Standards in Washington, D.C., firmly established in the laboratory that mechanisms for the decomposition of chlorofluorocarbons do exist in the upper atmosphere and that free chlorine atoms result from the process. Balloon measurements conducted by the National Oceanic and Atmospheric Administration (NOAA) confirmed the presence of chlorofluorocarbons in the stratosphere at heights of about 11 to 14 miles (18 to 22 kilometers). The concentrations and vertical distributions of the chlorofluorocarbons agreed with those predicted by scientists using theoretical computer models.

Thus, it is now clear that chlorofluorocarbons are indeed transported efficiently into the stratosphere with very little loss in the lower atmosphere. Further, the NOAA group found no evidence of a chemical reaction that would remove the active chlorine from the stratosphere once it was formed. In other words, once the active chlorine is in the stratosphere, it remains there and continues its work of decomposing ozone for a very long time. Its concentration seems destined to increase as long as we use substantial amounts of chlorofluorocarbons.

Supersonic transport on a large scale could reduce the ozone layer

Rowland and Molina

In order to have an effect on the ozone layer, chlorofluorocarbons must diffuse upward into the stratosphere, and this takes time. The delay between the release of the gases in the home and their maximum effect in the stratosphere seems to be about 10 to 20 years. So, even if we stopped using aerosol sprays tomorrow, the effects of those we have already used would continue to increase for at least a decade. And the effects would persist for several decades beyond that.

Nuclear explosions in the atmosphere provide another mechanism for the destruction of ozone. Such explosions heat the air and create large quantities of nitric oxide. In the case of thermonuclear explosions, the hot air with its high concentration of nitric oxide rises into the stratosphere, where it can accelerate the destruction of ozone. A committee of the National Academy of Sciences in Washington, D.C., has estimated that a 10,000-megaton nuclear exchange between the great powers would result in a fivefold-to-fiftyfold increase in the nitric oxide concentration in the stratosphere. (A megaton equals 1 million short tons [907,000 metric tons] of TNT.) The committee estimates that ozone in the Northern Hemisphere might be reduced by 30 to 70 per cent. Natural atmospheric processes would restore almost 60 per cent of the loss in two to four years. Such figures are awesome, but it is clear that—because of their long-term effects upon the ozone layer—aerosol spray cans seem mightier than the thermonuclear bomb.

Man's use of agricultural fertilizers may become a very critical matter

Lastly, the ozone layer is subjected to an assault that in the long run may be more ominous than any of the others. Nitric oxide is also produced in the stratosphere by oxidation of the nitrous oxide made biologically by bacteria from nitrites and nitrates in soil and ocean waters. The quantitative aspects of the production and flow of nitrous oxide in the atmosphere are not fully known. If most of it is made in the oceans, it is unlikely that man will be able to have much effect on that aspect of nitrous oxide production. On the other hand, if biological production of nitrous oxide in the soil turns out to be of paramount importance, man's use of agricultural fertilizers may turn out to be a critical matter.

Most *nitrogen fixation* (the process by which nitrogen in the air is converted into a form useful to plants) takes place biologically. A lesser amount is fixed as a result of such processes as lightning and combustion. Today, fertilizer manufacture accounts for about 15 per cent of all terrestrial nitrogen fixation. But the extremely serious shortage of food in the world has caused the industrial production of nitrogen fertilizers to increase rapidly. It is not unreasonable to expect a fivefold increase in fertilizer use in the next 25 years. Under those circumstances, nitrogen fixation by man would about equal fixation by nature, and the injection of nitrous oxide into the atmosphere would also be greatly increased.

Chemical reactions in the atmosphere, it is hoped, would prevent all but a small part of the nitrous oxide from reaching the stratosphere, where it would be converted to the effective catalyst, nitric oxide. Should this not happen (which is quite possible), we would find our-

The culprit?

selves in an unenviable position. We need to use more fertilizer if we are to grow more food. But the increased fertilizer use might decrease the concentration of ozone in the protective ozone layer.

What would be the effects upon human beings, were the ozone layer to be depleted? Unfortunately, because of our inadequate knowledge, the estimates embrace a wide range of possibilities.

One clear effect would be an increase in skin cancer, particularly if human beings did not take actions to compensate for the increase in ultraviolet radiation. A 5 per cent depletion of ozone, which would result in a 10 per cent increase in radiation, might cause an additional 20,000 to 60,000 cases of skin cancer in the United States each year. Fortunately, most such cancers are curable. Indeed, by applying chemical creams to the skin to screen the ultraviolet, most such cancers could be prevented.

The problem of how ultraviolet radiation affects natural *ecosystems* – systems of ecological relationships upon which lives of living organisms are based – is far more complex. It is known that such radiation can have significant genetic effects. It is also known that intense ultraviolet radiation is harmful to plants and can even destroy them. But the overall effects of an increase of ultraviolet intensity of, say, 20 per cent upon an ecosystem are extremely difficult to estimate. The effects might be very small; on the other hand, they might be substantial. In any event, the effects would be global.

The problem of the vulnerability of the ozone layer may well turn out to be relatively easy to handle. Then again, it could be a disaster. Our major difficulty is that our knowledge is too limited. But even if the problem turns out to be less serious than it now appears, there are lessons to be learned from this experience. First of all, our natural environment is extremely complex. Second, our knowledge of that environment is inadequate – so much so that we can easily paint ourselves into a corner. Third, we are confronted by a global problem that requires a global political solution embracing *all* nations. Fourth, although we are now aware of the problem of ozone vulnerability, there are undoubtedly many other problems that will result from man's actions and inactions and that will eventually become apparent.

The fact is that from the time man first appeared upon the scene he has had profound effect on the patterns of life around him and on his physical environment. The use of fire enabled him to burn vegetation over extremely large areas of land. As he improved the effectiveness of his hunting, he drove numerous species of animals to extinction.

With the invention of agriculture, man's effect upon the environment increased dramatically. Deforestation, slash-and-burn agriculture, and erosion changed the nature of many landscapes and living systems. Irrigation schemes made deserts bloom, but they also led to catastrophe because of faulty practices stemming from too little knowledge.

Over the centuries, the changes wrought by man's actions were enormous, but they took place extremely slowly. People would die in

A Concorde takes off

We are facing a global problem that requires a global solution

a world that appeared virtually identical to the one into which they had been born and in which their parents and grandparents had lived before them. But when small annual increments of change are multiplied by centuries and millenniums of time, the cumulative change can be very large.

Society today is characterized by extremely rapid rate of change brought about largely by numerous scientific and technological developments. As a result, man has become a global geological and ecological force on a time scale of years instead of centuries. The earth's surface, oceans, and atmosphere are being transformed more rapidly than they have ever been changed by nature on such a large scale. The changing ozone layer is but one potential manifestation of these developments.

By burning petroleum, coal, and natural gas to satisfy our needs for heat and power, we pour vast quantities of carbon dioxide into the atmosphere. Some of this passes into the oceans, but much of it stays in the atmosphere. We know that the carbon dioxide content of the atmosphere has increased appreciably during the 1900s and that it is destined to increase even more. We also know that these changes will affect our climate. Unfortunately, beyond saying that the earth will "warm up," we cannot specify the details of the climatic changes ahead.

Under the circumstances, what should we do? Certainly we need not panic; nor should we take precipitous action. Certainly we should carefully monitor the changes that are taking place. We should also prepare ourselves to change our ways of doing business if such changes seem to be dictated by the facts.

With respect to the ozone layer, this obviously gives us yet one more reason to avoid thermonuclear war. We should approach the supersonic transport gradually, monitoring its effects at all stages. It may well turn out that we must abolish aerosol sprays, but more facts are needed before such an action can be clearly justified. With respect to the problem of nitrogen fixation, there may well be no clear-cut answer. It might turn out not to be a problem. But if that hope is unwarranted, mankind will be confronted by some of the most difficult decisions it has yet been called upon to make.

We must neither panic nor take actions that are precipitate

Related Articles

For further information on science and technology in 1975, see Section Two, UPDATING OUR PERSPECTIVE ON THE PLANETS; and the articles on the various sciences in Section Four.

Spreading fertilizer

Focus on Education

Lawrence A. Cremin

**The big news of the year concerned the family,
where profound changes were working a revolution
in the education children receive in their homes**

Census statistics rarely make headlines, but in 1975 it was census statistics that marked the most significant educational news of the year. Some of that news concerned the schools and colleges, where the effects of declining birth rates during the late 1960s were beginning to be felt in empty elementary school classrooms across the country and in debt-ridden colleges that had formerly devoted their principal energies to the preparation of schoolteachers. But the more important news concerned the family, where profound changes in structure and composition were working a revolution in some of the most fundamental aspects of American education, namely, the education children receive in their homes.

Consider three sets of related data. First, 1 out of every 6 children under the age of 18 in 1975 was living in a single-parent household, a proportion almost double what it had been in 1950. Moreover, the single-parent household was especially prevalent among young parents of young children, with almost 1 out of every 4 parents under the age of 25 listed as heads of households actually living without a spouse (most of these were women). Second, at the same time as the percentage of single-parent households was rising, the number of adults in the average household was falling, to the point where in 1975 it hovered at around two adults per household. What this meant was that there were fewer aunts and uncles and especially grandparents living in American households with children; or, put another way, there were fewer extended or three-generation households. Moreover, the number of children per family was also declining, with more than 60 per cent of those families listed as having any children at all having either one or two. Thus, not only were there fewer adults per household, but also fewer children, and therefore fewer siblings for any given child. Third, more than half of all married women who were living with their husbands in 1975 and who had children between the ages of 6 and 17 were either working or looking for work, as were one-third of all such women who had children under the age of 6. What is more, the great majority of the working women were working full time.

How did all of this bear on education? To answer the question, one must call to mind the fundamental educational role of the family. Americans have become so accustomed to identifying education with schooling that they have sometimes forgotten that the family is the first—and some would say the foremost—educator, and further that the family continues to educate throughout an individual's lifetime. It is, after all, in the context of association with parents, siblings, and other kin that children first learn to give and receive affection, to use language, to play games, to follow rules, to perceive and enjoy beauty, to know and explore the world. Sociologists refer to such learning as

Lawrence A. Cremin

socialization (the learning of social roles), and anthropologists refer to it as *enculturation* (the learning of cultural beliefs and behaviors). Much of this learning seems to take place through the processes of imitation and trial and error. But much of it is also the result of deliberate teaching, as when parents help a child learn to walk or say "thank you," or when brothers and sisters explain to a sibling how to use a toy, or when grandparents tell grandchildren stories about the past, thereby conveying a sense of history and the passage of the generations.

Much learning is the result of deliberate teaching at home by kin

It is in the context of the family, too, that youngsters have their first experiences with other educators and educative agencies—with churches and synagogues, playmates and friends, radio and television, books and magazines. And even after schooling begins, and with it visits to libraries, museums, zoos, summer camps, and county fairs, the family remains a powerful interpreter of these experiences, assigning them particular meanings and significances depending on the values and understanding of family members. Finally, when children become adults, they in turn marry and form new families and in the process establish additional contexts in which they themselves continue their education as spouses, parents, and grandparents, and as kin to an entirely new set of relatives called "in-laws." At the same time, they also maintain their changing relationships with their own parents, grandparents, brothers, sisters, and kin.

Behavioral scientists have given a good deal of attention to these phenomena in recent years, though they differ among themselves in how they interpret and explain them. Those within the psycho-analytical tradition tend to view the earliest emotional relationships with parents as decisively important in all later education. Others, within the tradition of stimulus-response psychology, prefer to look instead at the continuing modification of habits and beliefs over a lifetime, depending on which ones happen to bring rewards of one kind or another. Others within the several developmental traditions tend to conceive of successive stages of development, each marked by its own characteristic problems, outlooks, and behaviors, through which individuals pass during the course of their lives. And still others within the various sociological traditions tend to see the social structures and institutions within which individuals maintain their relationships with others as exercising the most significant influence. Needless to say, there are also eclectic interpretations that draw from several of these (and other) theories, depending on how well they seem to explain particular phenomena.

It is also important to bear in mind that the family itself has assumed very different forms at different times in history and in different parts of the world. It has ranged in structure from the nuclear family prevalent in present-day North America (father, mother, and offspring) to various kinds of composite family based on polygyny (one husband, several wives, and their offspring), or polyandry (one wife, several husbands, and their offspring), or the co-residence of a nuclear family with additional kin (uncles, aunts, cousins, grandparents) or of more

A family then

than one nuclear family. Moreover, different family structures combine in very different ways such diverse functions as reproduction, economic maintenance, religious observance, recreation, and education. And even within a particular structure—say, the nuclear family—it is possible to organize such functions variously. Thus, a nuclear family may or may not live near kin; it may or may not worship in common; and it may or may not maintain arrangements whereby husband and wife share in wage earning, housekeeping, or child rearing.

Given the centrality of the family in the life of any society, family arrangements are commonly codified and sanctioned in law, religion, and custom. Some arrangements are judged legal, moral, and proper; others are judged illegal, immoral, and improper. For that reason alone, significant changes in family life—or even perceived changes—are likely to become matters of intense public concern. And in an education-conscious society such as the United States, that concern is likely to be all the more profound. Hence, given the changes indicated by the census data, it should be no surprise that the situation of the American family in general and of familial education in particular had become matters of heated public discussion in 1975. As *Newsweek* magazine put the question in extrabold letters on the cover of a September issue, "Who's Raising the Kids?"

As might be expected, public interest did not arise all at once. It had been developing since the late 1960s in connection with four widely discussed social concerns. First, as the number of working mothers steadily increased, there was the demand that decent child-care facilities be made available for preschool children. Second, as educators began to trace some of the roots of educational inequality back to early experience in the family, there was the demand for compensatory projects that would afford poor children the same educational opportunities as their more fortunate age-mates received at home. Third, as the number of unskilled and unemployed mothers receiving public welfare funds increased and as concern mounted to "break the continuing cycle of poverty," there was the demand that child-care assistance be provided so that welfare mothers could obtain the kind of training that would enable them to find employment. And fourth, there was the whole complex of demands associated with the highly charged issue of changing sex roles—of what rights, responsibilities, and options ought to go with being male or female.

All of these concerns flowed into the discussions of the White House conferences on children and youth held, respectively, in December, 1970, and April, 1971. The reports of the two conferences dealt with a wide range of problems, from infant health and nutrition to compulsory military service, and there was considerable controversy on many of the issues. But the conference participants were virtually unanimous about the need for national policies that would provide supplementary child-care services to children of all ages and families of all social backgrounds, through a variety of alternative programs and with ample

The situation of familial education was a matter of hot discussion

A family now

45

opportunity for parent participation in planning, policymaking, and management.

Now, there are numerous ways in which supplementary child-care services can be provided. The government can provide money directly to individual families, which can then purchase the services they need and desire. Or the government can provide money to small groups of families, and the groups can purchase the services cooperatively. Or the government can provide money to private and public organizations, which can then furnish the services to those who desire them, at little or no cost. Or the government can simply make its own arrangements to provide the services through public agencies. Similarly, the government can offer services solely to those who cannot otherwise obtain them; or it can offer services to everyone at nominal cost and then waive the cost for those who cannot afford it; or it can offer services to everyone free of charge. The possibilities are legion, and there are many examples available in other countries, from the mixture of private and public facilities characteristic of Switzerland and Great Britain to the communal arrangements of the Israeli kibbutz or the People's Republic of China.

In any case, the political pressures generated by the White House conferences were brought to bear on Congress, which in late 1971 enacted legislation establishing a Comprehensive Child Development Program that would (1) authorize $100 million in 1972 and $2 billion in 1973 to support health, nutritional, and educational services for all children whose parents or guardians desired the services, regardless of economic or social background; and (2) make federal funds available to state and local government agencies as well as to private nonprofit agencies for the planning, development, and operation of child development programs, provided that parents were involved in policymaking and that certain guidelines were followed with respect to program. President Richard M. Nixon, however, vetoed the bill, claiming that the need for such a program had not been demonstrated, that the cost could not be justified, and that the ultimate effect would be to undermine the American family.

President Nixon's action effectively stymied efforts to enact a comprehensive child development program during the remainder of his time in office. Yet public and congressional interest persisted. Bills of various sorts continued to appear in both houses of Congress, and in September, 1973, the Subcommittee on Children and Youth of the Senate Committee on Labor and Public Welfare, headed by Senator Walter F. Mondale (D., Minn.), held hearings on "trends and pressures affecting American families." An impressive array of scholars, clergymen, and organizational representatives appeared before the subcommittee. All sketched in dramatic terms the devastating social costs of family breakdown–in infant mortality, child illness, adolescent alienation, and adult crime–and all pointed to the need for a broad range of public programs that serve in effect as a family "support system." Anthropologist Margaret Mead, speaking out of a lifetime of

Many examples of child-care services are available in other nations

Day-care center

46

research on children and youth in different societies, called for "some new recognition of how we can strengthen and support our families, rebuild our communities, bring the old people back into the community to be useful and warm to the young, provide many kinds of education instead of only one, stop giving priority to miles and miles of cement [highways] above the well-being and safety of our children." Psychologist Edward Zigler, who had formerly headed the federal government's Office of Child Development, called for a monitoring of the impact of government policies on family life, so that the unintended consequences of some laws (welfare laws, for example, that literally drive fathers out of impoverished homes) could be remedied and beneficent use made of "the regulating, taxation, research, and moral powers of the federal government." And psychologist Urie Bronfenbrenner proposed a comprehensive "American Family Act" that would recast welfare legislation so as to keep poor families together, provide homemaker services for single-parent families, establish day-care facilities for all who wanted them, expand training programs for day-care workers, and change fair employment practices laws to take account of the special needs of women with young children.

Some sort of policy for strengthening family life seems needed

Senator Mondale, acting in collaboration with Congressman John Brademas (D., Ind.), introduced a bill based on this testimony into Congress, but it remained in committee through 1975. It authorized a wide range of services from prenatal care for mothers to day-care arrangements for young children, at an initial cost of $1.85 billion over three years. The bill had the support of many social, religious, and women's organizations; but it drew sharp opposition from conservatives, who saw any comprehensive public day-care program as subversive of family life; from radicals, who saw institutionalized day-care as a middle-class program for "other people's" (meaning "poor") children; and from representatives of teacher organizations, who wanted control of all public day-care programs explicitly placed in the hands of public school authorities. Given such controversy, and given, too, the opposition of President Gerald R. Ford to all new federal spending programs, it seemed unlikely that the Mondale-Brademas program or any resembling it would become law. Yet, given the trends indicated by the census data, it seemed equally unlikely that the American people could afford much longer to go without some sort of rational policy for the strengthening of family life, and with it the improvement of familial education.

Related Articles

For further information on education in 1975, see Section Four, EDUCATION; Section Five, ALTERNATIVE SCHOOL.

The big question

Focus on The Arts

Alistair Cooke

The Bicentennial exploitation was underway, a theater strike underlined some of Broadway's problems, and Hollywood enjoyed a boom year

Long before the dawn of the Bicentennial year of American independence, patriotism–stimulated by the itch for 10 per cent–began to stir in the breasts of countless museum directors, historical societies, city councils, and manufacturers of medals, spoons, Toby jugs, pistols, furniture, belt buckles, toys, jewelry, coffee-table picture books, calendars, and T-shirts. Through television, magazine, and mail-order advertising, the United States citizenry was bombarded with invitations to celebrate the proclamation of the republic with everything from $750 sets of reproduced "colonial" silver to a miniature branding iron that would stamp "U.S.A." on the family hamburgers.

It was difficult in this haystack of commercial exploitation to find a few needles of any true value. But there were some. The National Trust for Historic Preservation published a comprehensive list of buildings–from statehouses to crumbling railroad stations and post offices–that are in imminent danger of rot or destruction. And in a heartening precedent, the trust persuaded an old Massachusetts construction firm to sponsor a statewide competition, run by a committee of architects, craftsmen, and historians, to supervise the restoration of 115 chosen projects. A good many towns that claim some colonial heritage started subscription funds to rid the old village green, or the courthouse square, of mediocre modern buildings, gasoline stations, and the like that blurred the pristine appearance of the original. A conservation society in Virginia prescribed a limit, by way of size and construction, to advertising signs within the precincts of an old colonial town. And another county had the wit to raise enough money to send a delegation to Britain to learn from its experience in curbing industrial sprawl by way of acquiring public lands for parks and recreation, and requiring screens of trees to hide proposed factory sites. It is a hard question whether this expertise can be of much use in a country whose laws affecting the right of public seizure of land are diffused among competing jurisdictions. Still, the effort was made toward introducing a view of conservation policy that does not set industrialists against environmentalists as natural enemies but seeks to bring them together with a common aim of making the use of the land both productive and aesthetic.

But since the bogging down of the Highway Beautification Act of 1965 in a mire of special interests, there is not in sight any federal law that begins to approach, in imagination and civic sense, Britain's great Town and Country Planning Act of 1951. Passed by an overwhelming majority of both the Conservative and Labour parties, the British act restricts billboard advertising to an area within 2 miles (3.2 kilometers) of all city centers. The billboard lobby in the United States, however, is one that is far too strong to be resisted, and Ver-

Alistair Cooke

49

mont provides the noble, and lonely, example of a legislature that has banished billboards throughout the state.

A Broadway theater strike in the late summer of 1975 underlined some of the more painful problems of staging theatrical productions for profit. We have mentioned before the show-business axiom that Broadway is not organized to tolerate modest successes. The high mortality rate among new productions, in any Broadway season, is due not so much to the mediocrity of the playwrights and their offerings as to the bounding costs of staging anything at all. Production costs have quadrupled in the past 20 years. Although many of New York City's theaters are physically decaying—shocking outlanders from Florida, Illinois, Minnesota, and California by their grubbiness and discomfort—their rents go soaring along with those of the rat-traps of Harlem. Production materials are four or five times as expensive as they were in 1950. And labor regularly increases its demands for higher wages and more relaxed working conditions.

The producers and theater managers tend to see labor as the villain of the piece. But faced by the nightly competition of the motion pictures and television, the production crews that mount and maintain a theater production see themselves as vanishing craftsmen, on a par with butlers and caddies. The Broadway strike, on the face of it a straightforward demand for higher salaries for less work, was a variation on the old Luddite protest against the tyranny of the machine. It had to do with the minimum size of an orchestra for a musical show. The producers have long complained of an excess of "walkers"—that is, nonplaying musicians—who must be hired and paid to meet the union requirement that an orchestra be of a certain size. This requirement is based, in hard fact, on the large orchestra that was called for by the musical comedies of the 1920s or, say, by musical comedies as they were known before the advent of small rock groups, choral casts, and electronic music. In the past decade, small musical productions have managed to flourish off-Broadway because the gross box-office revenue—which conditions a union's quota for stagehands, orchestras, and so on—was small enough to allow the musical accompaniment to be provided by a handful of musicians, sometimes by no more than an electric guitar, a drummer, and a flute. The rising popularity of such groups, and their frequent appearance as part of the onstage cast, encouraged young composers no longer attracted to the full-blown orchestras, and orchestrations, of the Gershwin-Rodgers-Porter years. Naturally, the best of them invaded Broadway, to the alarm of old fiddlers, cellists, oboe players, and triangle artists who saw their occupation gone or going. The union dug their heels in. They demanded, and got, a minimum orchestra of 13 musicians for all new Broadway musicals. If only six of them were called for by the composer and orchestrator, then there would remain seven walkers, who must be paid as performers, whether or not their performance included anything more than a backstage game of pinochle. In line

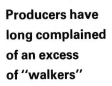

Producers have long complained of an excess of "walkers"

Bicentennial belt buckles

50

with the implacable advance of inflation, they were to receive a base weekly pay of $290, rising in two years to something between $350 and $380.

And there it stands. Unless there is a revival of gaudy shows with large orchestras, the producers will simply have to pay the walkers for treading water until they die off and their specialties become antiquarian whimsies in the oncoming era of electronic synthesizers played by one man. In the waiting interval between one era and another, negotiations are already underway to set permissible conditions for the staging of shows that require nothing but taped music.

The Met loses $44,000 every time it raises the curtain

If economics is one anxiety of Broadway producers, it threatens to be the bane of opera in the United States. As each summer wanes, the rumor starts that either New York City's Metropolitan Opera season may have to be postponed until Christmas, or that there will be no season at all. The wolf cry is now as predictable as the Canada geese flying south in the fall. But the fact that it is obscures from the public the grimmer fact that the wolf is annually kept from the door only by emergency rations donated by the remaining rich patrons. They, too, like the triangle players, are dying off, and—sooner than later—the opera houses of this country will have to find some more dependable saviors. The United States is alone among the self-governing nations of the West (not to mention the Soviet Union) in denying all but a pittance to its opera companies by way of government subsidy. The average annual budget of the Metropolitan Opera is $27.7 million, toward which the National Endowment for the Arts contributes $600,000 and the state of New York $1 million. The annual operating loss is more than $9 million, which is made up, more or less, by those moneyed individuals whose automatic largess the opera lover has come to take for granted. The Metropolitan calculates that it loses $44,000 every time the curtain goes up.

By odious comparison, Hamburg's opera house is sustained by a joint subsidy from the West German government, the state, and the city. Only 25 per cent of its revenue comes from the box office—compared with 49 per cent at the Metropolitan. Austria, Italy, and Great Britain all provide heavy government subsidies, enough to guarantee the permanence of their opera houses as state institutions. In Britain, the main subsidy is provided by the national Arts Council, and a supplementary one by the City of London through its governing authority, the Greater London Council. In Italy, operatic salaries are tax-free.

Even, however, in these Western countries, where subsidizing the opera is not thought of as the unmistakable clip-clop of galloping Socialism, inflation is shrinking the value of the government's subsidy. An international meeting of opera administrators and directors in 1975 concluded that the chronic drain on all of them was the unconscionable salaries demanded by opera stars. The meeting agreed to freeze stars' salaries for three years, a decision that provoked a resounding howl of pain from coloratura sopranos and basso profundos alike. The pain of this decision was aggravated in London by the lowly

Striking musicians

status of the British pound, which has stiffened the preference of many opera stars to receive their salaries in practically any other currency than sterling.

In New York City, the telling argument has been made that the city might at least recognize that since the construction of Lincoln Center, the surrounding properties have risen enormously in value, and the city could surely reward this recognition by granting fractional financial relief to the opera. However, New York's new and unenviable reputation as the most financially profligate of U.S. cities is not likely to encourage any such reward.

Hollywood, which has for a decade or more been thought of as the former film capital that relapsed into a television company town, had in 1975 its most profitable film production year since the 1940s. And this during the worst recession since 1937.

There are glib persons ready to say that this surprising boom was due to nothing *but* the recession, on the analogous argument that Hollywood's golden age coincided with the Great Depression of the 1930s and that nothing drives people out of their own careworn lives into the escape hatch of the movies like hard times. It is true, and it is paradoxical, that when one American family in four had nothing coming in, millions swarmed, without audible protest, to the fantasy life of Ginger Rogers and Fred Astaire, to Ernst Lubitsch's upper-crust romances, to the preposterously conspicuous waste of the Busby Berkeley musicals, and in general to the comforting spectacle of rich people having fun.

But this was not the sort of daydream sought by Americans during the 1975 recession. While Hollywood reported no noticeable gain in the size of the average motion-picture audience, no general flight from the television tube, it attributed its 1975 box-office boom to the crashing success of a few big films. Most people who are not inveterate moviegoers see two or three films a year. They are the people who turned *Gone with the Wind* and *The Sound of Music* into the biggest money-makers of all time. Of all time, that is, until our time. Suddenly, there are three or four films that, on their box-office take in a single year, have already broken the records of the record breakers. The very occasional moviegoers went in their millions to see *The Godfather* and *Jaws*.

The huge profits of these, and one or two other totally unexpected world-beaters, was partially offset by the crashing failures of some heavily promoted high-budget films, such as *Nashville* and *The Day of the Locust*. But there was evidently nothing freakish or accidental about Hollywood's 25 per cent increase in profits. It discovered a new and profitable trend, a new anodyne for the downcast, in films of callow or overwhelming violence. There is a new breed of producer, recruited mostly from the old race of actor's agents. According to one veteran observer of Hollywood manners and mores, they are shrewder than the old-timers at guessing the box-office prospects of the new

Ginger and Fred

high-budget films. They can also identify more shamelessly with the need to produce what one of them calls "films with gut grab." And if that prescription sounds annoyingly abstract, its relevance to the box-office is made terrifyingly concrete in the huge revenues taken in by such films of brutality or catastrophe as *The Godfather, The Exorcist, Earthquake,* and *The Towering Inferno.*

It is not, on the whole, a financial instinct to envy or admire. It is, to this critic, yet another symptom of the unexplained sickness of a land overrun by rising crime and violence, both in fact and in fantasy.

It has become almost standard procedure for these annual reports to add a tailpiece on the current status of pornography. There is nothing innately fascinating in the topic, but it continues to provide us with the most teasing legal test of freedom of speech. In a previous Focus article, I traced the steps we have taken, over the past century, toward our present state of extreme permissiveness, from our adoption of the British Obscene Publications Act of 1857 down to a ruling of the Supreme Court of the United States in December, 1969, that the First Amendment to the Constitution does not bar states from suppressing what their own statutes deem to be obscene, unless it is proved that their definition of obscenity "is wholly out of step with current American standards." This judgment made some liberals fear that we were in for a wave of reactionary local legislation that would swamp all erotic art or literature by reviving the repressive prudery of the early 1900s. It has not happened. The phrase "current American standards" is wide enough to permit pornographers to drive whole trainloads of hard-core films through it.

My own guess, a year ago, was that the audience for hard-core films was declining, and that the theaters showing them would be abandoned, as local communities began to apply liquor and zoning ordinances to put topless bars and sleazy massage parlors out of business. This, too, has not happened. Hard-core pornography, both in films and in publications, has graduated into more respectable theaters and more pretentious production. And the reason is a menacing one: The Mafia has discovered a gold mine in pornography and now controls its distribution and much of its production. It is a sobering thought—it would certainly have sobered the Founding Fathers—that almost 200 years after the First Amendment was written, the Mafia has become its most affluent beneficiary.

The repressive prudery of the early 1900s has not been brought back

Crowd at *Jaws*

Related Articles

For further information on the arts in 1975, see the following articles in Section Four:

Focus on Sports

Jim Murray

Baseball was becoming too slow for the jet age; time
had passed it by, and it would be gone in a decade,
they said — and then, along came the 1975 World Series

You may remember Baseball, a well-beloved friend and companion of all of us, died some years ago. Its obit was in all the newspapers.

Its coming demise was heralded on all the talk shows. It was noted that it had become too slow to keep up with today's pace. Its color was gray. Its step was faltering. Rigor mortis was detected.

Time had passed it by. Football was the new undisputed monarch of sport. Basketball was making grave inroads. Even Tennis had a boom. Who needed this set-piece sport right out of the Gay Nineties with its cobwebbed characters standing around waiting for something to happen? It was the Dinosaur of Sports, the Sick Man of Athletics. It would be gone in a decade. Bring on the 7-foot (210-centimeter) centers, the 300-pound (135-kilogram) linebackers. Put Baseball in the Smithsonian Institution along with the Lincoln letters and the *Spirit of St. Louis*.

Well, a funny thing happened to the corpse of the Grand Old Game on its way to the cemetery. It sat up, sold tickets, and soon had the whole country in a community sing of "Take Me Out to the Ball Game."

The 1975 World Series was seen by more people than had ever seen a sporting event before. It cut across age lines, sex lines, class lines. It was a prime-time show that ran movies, talk shows, sitcoms, cartoons, and soap operas right out of the living rooms. And it was institutional advertising at its best. Seventy-one million persons watched game number six—which may go down in history as The-Game-That-Saved-Baseball—and saw one of the finest athletics contests it is possible to see.

The Cincinnati Reds won the World Series. But, in a larger sense, Baseball won it.

In the first place, it had a cast of highly recognizable characters. Any showman will tell you that's an essential—marquee value. Audiences are comfortable with the familiar. And the Cincinnati Reds had four of the most visible celebrity-athletes in the game today: Johnny Bench, whom they may name a candy bar or a car after; Joe Morgan, everybody's favorite 5-foot 7-inch (170-centimeter) giant killer; Pete Rose, everybody's kid brother, who always looks as if someone just bought him a balloon; and Tony Perez, always riding to the rescue in the nick of time and saving the fort with prodigious Ruthian home runs.

On the Red Sox, you had Luis Tiant. It would be impossible to fabricate a more sympathetic character than this noble, balding, *appealing*, old-young man with the solemn goatee, the barber-pole pitching style—surely this was such a man as Cervantes imagined, a Don Quixote tilting at the hated Reds, dreaming the Impossible Dream.

Could you *invent* a Fred Lynn, Frank Merriwell in center field, quiet, modest, self-effacing—but marvelously gifted? Rookies don't win Most Valuable Player awards. MVP's are not collar-ad college graduates but wire-bearded, tobacco-chewing, 15-year veterans who have

Jim Murray

learned to outguess the crafty old types on big-league mounds. But who could not be captivated by that smooth, flowing swing, that graceful antelopelike pursuit of a fly ball into the deeper reaches of Boston's Fenway Park? Not since the great Joe DiMaggio or the ever-young Willie Mays has the game seen such effortless perfection. Fred Lynn is that well-worn cliché of the game—too good to be true.

Add the Red Sox catcher, Carlton Fisk, the Yankee from the rock-bound crags of Vermont. Catchers like Bench and Fisk come along in baseball only every other total eclipse, and here were two of them in the same series.

Carl Yastrzemski—was there ever a more charismatic outfielder in Boston save for the storied Ted Williams? Yaz, with the angriest bat in the big leagues for so many years, a picture outfielder, an older, more experienced Fred Lynn who played the left-field wall the way Willie Mosconi played cushions.

A great series can be four, five, or six games. There have been some memorable ones over quickly. But a truly vintage series must go seven games. It must get down to a situation where an inch or centimeter one way or the other can mean the difference between winning or losing—a team must never be more than one long hit away from being toppled over the precipice. This series went seven games. And it was decided by one run.

A great series must have controversy boiling out of it. And the 1975 series had the quintessential controversy—an umpire's call. Come back with us now to the ninth inning of game three. The score is 5-5, and it's the bottom of the 10th. Cincinnati is at bat. A runner is on first, and no one is out. The batter, Ed Armbrister, is at the plate. He bunts. A bad bunt. It stops 3 feet (90 centimeters) in front of home plate. So does Ed Armbrister. So does the catcher trying to field the ball, which is a double-play ball. They start up again, collide briefly. And the "double-play ball" is thrown into center field. Is it interference? An error? The luck of the draw? The rub of the green? The umpire takes the high road. That's the way the ball bounces, he says, in effect, to the outraged Red Sox.

The rulebook is ambiguous. The Supreme Court of the United States couldn't unravel this. In Tennis, they could play a let. In Football, the official would probably wisely apply offsetting penalties. In Baseball you have to say whether it's fair or foul. You can't equivocate. There are no cop-outs. Umpire Larry Barnett decides the World Series. Cincinnati wins the argument. And the game. And the series.

Across the United States, fans happily take sides. A vintage series is not seven games long. It is all winter long. It is the stuff and substance of Baseball competition and controversy. You couldn't script a better hot-stove-league debate.

A great series needs extra-inning games. There's nothing like a man on third in the bottom of the 12th of a tie game to keep even the casual fans from swinging over to Johnny Carson. This series had two extra-inning games, both won by the home team.

Center fielder Lynn, center

The series had *five* games decided by one run and three games decided in the last inning. A great series must have home runs. This one had 13.

But what this series especially had was a special quality of *caring* because of the towns involved. New York City can yawn over a series champion. Chicago or Los Angeles could take it in stride.

Cincinnati and Boston are two towns that may belong culturally or sociologically to a more leisurely time in this country. A championship team is very important to them. They are largely made up of people who have lived there all their lives, perhaps all their fathers' or grandfathers' lives. They are unabashed loyalists. They take pride in their teams, their towns. This Mudvillian, turn-of-the-century kind of civic identification and loyalty was impressively present to the visiting journalists—electronic and print—in the home games. The World Series was an *event* to them. The towns *cared*—therefore, the country cared.

What the series especially had was a special quality of caring

One of the things missing from World Series of late has been exactly that kind of community identification with the goings on at the ballpark. Oakland, Calif., greeted its three-time champions with the kind of apathy you'd expect for a second-division team in Peoria, Ill.

It turned out there was nothing wrong with Baseball that a good, old-fashioned, bare-knuckle World Series couldn't fix.

Great World Series are not as common as you might think. There were heady ones in the early years when John McGraw v. Connie Mack matched brawling teams and whirring brains. But, by and large, when fans think of great World Series, they think of 1926 and Grover Cleveland Alexander striking out Yankee sluggers with the bases loaded.

Or, they think of 1931 and Pepper Martin, a little-known outfielder at the time, become the "Wild Horse of the Osage" and stealing everything but the clubhouse clock on the Philadelphia Athletics.

The 1934 World Series was the Dean Brothers, a comedy-drama in seven acts, Joe Medwick being thrown out of the game in a shower of garbage. A series that had a cast of characters like Dizzy Dean, brother Paul, Frankie Frisch, Leo Durocher, Schoolboy Rowe, and Mickey Cochrane had all the socko appeal of a college musical.

Tiant's victory yell

The 1947 World Series had the sociological impact of the first black player in major-league history, Jackie Robinson, in it. The Bad Guys (the Yankees were always the guys in the black hats at World Series time, the team you loved to hate) won it, as usual. But civil rights had come to Baseball and, as a matter of fact, batted .259 with three runs batted in, not a bad debut for a man or a movement. That series had other great moments—a no-hitter not only spoiled in the bottom of the ninth, but also a victory, the only series game in history where the winners made only one hit.

The 1955 World Series makes the pantheon because it was the one where the haughty, hated Yankees finally lost their dignity and got their top hats knocked off with the snowball. Brooklyn had never won a World Series—or much of anything else—before, and the borough blasted off and its joy was the nation's.

World Series 1975 was one for the ages, a return to the verities

A whole series of lackluster World Series followed that one. The Yankees faded from view, taking with them the villain of the piece, thus leaving the autumn olios without a third act, usually. They were cooky-cutter World Series, one the same as another, except for brief incandescent performances by a Sandy Koufax or an occasional Charlie Finley flare-up, firing a second baseman in midgame. They were listless affairs, often, mere Saturday afternoon games, and the nation usually gratefully cut to football—sometimes by the late innings. Sometimes earlier.

The Cassandras of the press box served up their gravest doomsaying for Baseball. It would never play in a jet age. Nothing ever happened. And kept on not happening. It was losing its heroes, its grip on the imagination. Get the hearse. Here lies Baseball, R.I.P. It died in its sleep. Cause of death: acute boredom.

Well, the funeral has been indefinitely postponed. The corpse is doing a buck and wing. The deceased is out on the banquet circuit.

World Series 1975 was one for the ages. It was a return to the verities. The players on both sides were clean-cut, clean-shaven—one (the Reds) by managerial fiat, the other because they, and Boston, liked it that way.

The show they put on was as wholesome as Andy Hardy, as melodramatic as Bulldog Drummond, as charming as Disney. Rated "G." And it was box-office. Bigger than *Sound of Music* for its split week. Not even rain delays, usually fatal to a World Series, could blight or blunt the interest.

Two fine, young, enthusiastic teams with plenty of star appeal, as crowd-pleasing as a fighter-who-gets-up (four wins were come-from-behind) showed on the tube. Game number six goes directly to Cooperstown, joins Great Moments In Sport. This series even had that show business staple, A Star Is Born. By series end, Dwight Evans had gone to join Pepper Martin, Roberto Clemente, and others who first displayed their virtuosity in a World Series.

But the 50 young men in the red stockings did more than titillate an audience. They resurrected an industry. They provided The Happy Hour, made the nation redolent of peanuts, popcorn, and Crackerjack and hot dogs again. The sport became a freckle-faced kid again. It was a great day for bubble gum and razor blades and breweries and Baseball. It was 1910 again for nostalgia buffs. And it was that happiest, hoariest, and heartiest of all war cries for the home nine in Boston— "Wait Till Next Year!" But as far as Baseball was concerned, *this* was Next Year. *This* was The Good Old Days.

Related Articles

For further information on sports in 1975, see SPORTS and the articles on individual sports in Section Four.

Reds' fans celebrate

Section Two

Special Reports

Five articles give special treatment to subjects
of current importance and lasting interest.

The Uprooted

By Charles and Bonnie Remsberg

There are 14 million refugees adrift in the world today; with help, many of them rebuild their lives, but millions will always be strangers in strange lands

*T*hirty-two-year-old Vladimir Elperin, his wife, Rachel, 28, and their 9-year-old daughter, Miriam, were gambling their lives on what would happen inside the dimly lighted customs room in the lonely railroad station on the Russian-Czechoslovak border. As Jews trying to leave Russia, they knew the risks—contraband planted among their belongings, rejection of their exit visas on an unforeseen technicality, or some deliberate provocation to violence to cause their arrest. "Expect anything," Vladimir had cautioned. For most of the afternoon and evening, they had traveled by train from their native city in the Ukraine, over the Carpathian Mountains and down to the border town of Chop. The tension mounted with every click of the rails. At the customs office door, they had tearfully kissed and hugged the handful of relatives who came to see them off. A guard now barred further communication.

"Empty your pockets," a customs officer commanded. He began to search the boxes and luggage that held all the worldly goods they had any hope of taking with them—clothing, a few personal effects, and 300 rubles (about $330). No

After months of worry and government delays, a tense train ride takes the Elperin family from their native Ukraine to a new and uncertain life in the Free World.

original documents could leave the country. Still, Vladimir had brought one he considered indispensable, his university diploma. He kept it hidden inside his shirt. When the guard was not looking he slipped it furtively into a suitcase that had already been examined.

The search dragged on. Vladimir was swept with doubts. Then the officer challenged a package of phonograph records. He declared that he had no record player, so he could not verify that they were merely music. He stared expressionless at the Elperins. At last, trying not to tremble, Vladimir took a chance and offered him two bottles of cognac "as a present to yourself."

With a grunt, the officer grabbed the bottles, stamped their visas, and waved them aboard a waiting train. It was nearly midnight when their car suddenly lurched forward. As their compartment window glided past the station, Vladimir, for a split second—"just like that"—glimpsed his brother and his parents for the last time. Moments later, the train rumbled in darkness across the border.

In that instant, Vladimir, Rachel, and Miriam joined the ranks of a special and growing subculture: the ever-changing, never-ending tide of the stateless and dispossessed, the world's refugees....

Since Adam and Eve were expelled from the Garden of Eden, refugees have been an enduring phenomenon. The persecution of the followers of Moses 1,200 years before Christ in Egypt; the ravaging advances of Genghis Khan across Asia 2,400 years later; the oppressive religious intolerance of the Middle Ages; the great Zulu expansion in southern Africa in the 1700s—all forced threatened men, women, and children, "the tempest-tossed," to flee their native lands.

In the 20th century, World Wars I and II uprooted tens of millions. Human displacement has reached such unprecedented proportions that this could be called the Century of the Refugee. Since 1915, when hundreds of thousands of Armenians fled the Ottoman Empire to escape Turkish persecution, more than 30 major refugee migrations and scores of lesser ones have crisscrossed the globe. In 1975, the 132,000 Vietnamese and Cambodians airlifted to the United States dominated headlines, but waves of forced emigrants also rolled out of Angola, Ethiopia, Iraq, and Timor.

Exactly how many are adrift in the world is clouded by a controversy over who they are. Nearly 70 countries, including the United States and Canada, have signed treaties defining a refugee as anyone outside his homeland because of "well-founded fear of being persecuted for reasons of race, religion, nationality, membership of a particular social group, or political opinion" and unable or unwilling to return. But interpretations of this definition vary markedly.

The authors:
Charles and Bonnie Remsberg, husband and wife, are a writing team specializing in today's social issues.

The Office of the United Nations High Commissioner for Refugees (UNHCR) excludes from UN refugee aid and protection Jews fleeing the Soviet Union, for example, on grounds that they are leaving "voluntarily," with proper visas. Officials in the U.S. Department of State, citing clear documentation of mistreatment of Jews in Russia, argue privately that the UNHCR is splitting hairs under political pressure from Russia. "When you speak of a refugee fleeing from his

The future is uncertain for refugees leaving a ship by cargo sling at Da Nang just before South Vietnam's fall.

country," says Laurence A. Dawson, a State Department senior adviser, "it doesn't mean literally that he has to go across barbed wire or an electrified border." The State Department includes in its statistics even people who have never crossed international frontiers but are displaced *within* their own countries by persecution or strife. Some private monitoring agencies, such as the U.S. Committee for Refugees (USCR) in New York City, count victims of natural disasters.

Depending on definition, the latest estimates of "active" refugees range from 2.3 million (UNHCR) to 14.2 million (USCR), located in more than 80 countries on every continent. In all, upwards of 40-million persons have become refugees since the end of World War II.

For many, this upheaval comes suddenly, amid the frenzy and panic inflicted by advancing armies, guerrilla harassment, political collapse, or edicts of expulsion. But others, victims of religious, ethnic, or political persecution during peacetime, must often struggle against tremendous odds to win freedom.

When the Kurdish revolt against Iraq collapsed in 1975, thousands of Kurds fled to Iran, *top.* Unrest in Africa has displaced thousands.

Vladimir Elperin (he asked that we use a fictitious name because of the relatives he left behind) had looked to the world outside Russia with yearning since the day, at 17, despite triumphant entrance exams, he was denied admission to college because he was a Jew. He eventually bribed his way into another school with "presents under the table," and gained a mechanical engineering degree. His internal passport declared his "nationality" as "Jew," and in Russia's officially nurtured atmosphere of anti-Semitism he had only feeble chances of professional advancement.

Of the estimated 240,000 Jews who have sought to leave Russia since 1968, fewer than half have succeeded. For trying, many are fired from their jobs, then arrested for parasitism *(being without work) or "slandering the Soviet system." Approval or denial is arbitrary and sometimes takes years. "If you are lucky, you get permission," says a former refugee. "If you don't, your life is broken." One night in 1971, Vladimir told Rachel he was going to apply for exit visas to Israel. "I was scared," she remembers. "When you decide to go, you have to be not a chicken. Nobody knows what's going to be."*

As the Elperins slogged through the morass of procedural documentation required by the OVIR (visa office) in their city, growing tension shadowed every move. Delay was piled upon delay over technicalities—the pictures they submitted were 1 inch (2.5 centimeters) too wide; long forms were rejected because of a misspelling. Day after nerve-racking day, they feared they would be arrested.

More than eight interminable months passed after every trifle had been met before the OVIR rendered its decision—visas denied, no explanation. Then in

April, 1972, more than a year after their initial application, they were unexpect-edly given permission to leave. In less than a month, President Richard M. Nixon would be making the first visit by a U.S. President to Moscow, and Russia was temporarily easing Jewish emigration for propaganda purposes. (That year, 31,082 Jews were granted exit visas, a number that plunged to about 3,500 in the first half of 1975.) The Elperins had 30 days to get out.

In May, after the last, long train ride through the Ukrainian countryside they had never left before, they said good-by to their families at Chop. "We had been such a big family, lots of relatives," Rachel remembers. "All of a sudden, it was just three of us."

Weeping, wondering, they sat awake as the train clattered through the Czechoslovak night toward Austria. In Vienna, the conductor said, they would be met and helped, like others before them....

In 1921, after the Russian Revolution and civil war had sent 1.5-million Russians fleeing to other countries, the League of Nations took history's first formal international action on behalf of refugees. A spe-cial identification certificate known as a "Nansen passport" was issued to refugees, in the hope that it might shield them from arbitrary ac-tions by authorities of the countries they entered. Today, that primi-tive beginning has developed into a sophisticated worldwide network of governmental and voluntary agencies that can shepherd refugees at least to safety and often to a better life.

Dominant among government-sponsored groups is the UNHCR. Headquartered in Geneva, Switzerland, and financed by more than 60 member nations, the UN agency works with governments to ensure the legal and political protection of refugees it recognizes–to prevent, for example, their being returned home against their will. In addition, it helps needy countries suddenly swamped with large numbers of refugees to provide emergency relief, such as food, clothing, shelter, and medical care, and also helps bankroll special economic develop-ment projects designed to make the newcomers self-sufficient. For instance, in Africa the UNHCR has helped organize job-counseling services for refugees in major cities beset with acute unemployment, and in some rural areas has helped build entirely new villages. Work-ing in close cooperation to provide emergency relief, transportation, immigration aid, and other supportive services are more than 100 voluntary social service agencies.

"Once a refugee is outside his country of origin," says Dale de Haan, staff director for the U.S. Senate Subcommittee on Refugees and Migration, "an aid group can help him act on any of his three options: He can be repatriated if circumstances change and he feels safe to go home, he can stay in the country where he first seeks asylum, or he can resettle elsewhere." Peasants or uneducated tribesmen tend to favor eventual repatriation. But among students, skilled laborers, and professionals, resettlement is most popular.

Often when masses of refugees arise suddenly–as with the Indo-china evacuation or the exodus to India of 10 million Bengalis fleeing

Pakistani troops in Bangladesh in 1971 – they make their decisions in crude cities of tents, shacks, or barracks hastily prepared for them under national or international auspices. From bitter experience, government and voluntary workers have learned to disperse refugees as swiftly as possible from these "temporary" shantytowns lest, like the 30-year-old Palestine Arab encampments, they turn into bases for troublesome political agitation.

In Europe, once dotted with vast camps for the displaced persons of World War II, refugees now assemble in certain cities that have become "staging areas" for their scattering. One is Vienna, capital of Austria; a country that, in the words of Alton Kastner, deputy director of the International Rescue Committee, a voluntary refugee agency, "has an unsurpassed record for granting asylum to refugees." Another is Rome, the scene many times each year of the final break with the Old World.

A representative of the Jewish Agency, an aid group for refugees bound for Israel, met the Elperins in Vienna and drove them to "a beautiful, marvelous place," an old castle called Schonau on the outskirts of the city that served as a processing center for refugees in transit. For three days, they rested and mapped their future there.

The Jewish Agency bought them plane tickets to Israel, which they paid for later, and less than a week after leaving the temperate climate of the Ukraine, they found themselves in a remote "absorption center" on the sparsely settled, sun-blistered Negev Desert. "I saw on my wife's face that she was shocked," says Vladimir.

They were to have stayed there five months, gradually learning about Israeli life. But as the weeks passed, Vladimir realized that while he and his family might adapt to desert rigors, his elderly parents, whom he hoped eventually could join them, would never adjust.

After four months, Vladimir repaid the Jewish Agency with money he saved working part time in a factory and booked steamer passage to Italy for himself, Rachel, and Miriam. There were many refugee resettlement organizations in Rome, and the Elperins were still technically refugees because they had been in Israel less than a year.

In Rome, the Elperins decided to seek admission to Canada. They were told that a national voluntary agency in Canada called the Jewish Immigrant Aid Service (JIAS) would act as their official sponsor and help them settle into a new life. With a counselor's guidance, they filled out a required evaluation form for the Canadian Embassy to match their skills, education, and background against Canada's labor demands.

Aside from English classes they attended with other refugees, the Elperins had few obligations for the seven months they waited. United HIAS Service, a refugee aid group, paid their rent on a new one-bedroom apartment and gave them a modest monthly maintenance allowance. "It was a sweet time," Rachel recalls. She loved to walk the city's streets because the pattern of bricks was "the same as like home." "We swam, we traveled a little, we visited places of history," Vladimir remembers. "Now when I see Rome on TV, I feel in my heart something warm."

Then in April, 1973, word came that they were accepted by Canada. They took the long jet ride to North America—and to a period of adjustment that would prove a jarring contrast to their Roman holiday....

In her 1972 book *Canada and Immigration*, Canadian political scientist Freda Hawkins estimates that 75 per cent of the refugees resettled since World War II have gone to the United States, Canada, or Aus-

Months of wandering, from Vienna to Israel and then to Rome, end as the Elperins arrive in their new home, Canada.

Where Do They Come From?
Where Do They Go?

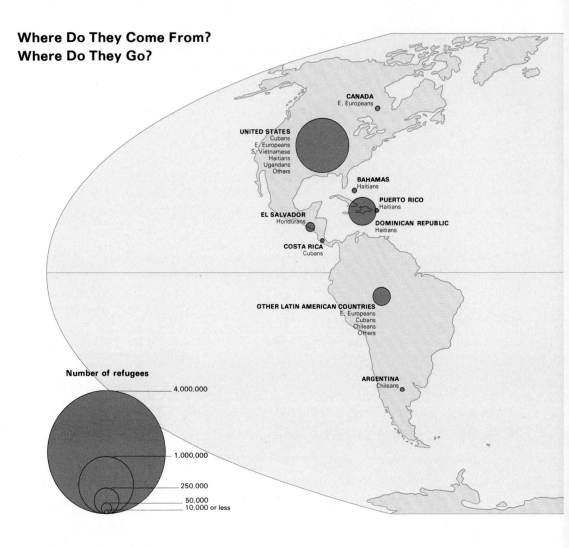

Long after headlines are forgotten, the refugees remain. The map includes "internal refugees," those who are displaced in their native land. Refugee groups are shown under host nations.

tralia, in that order. These governments have consistently stretched their immigration restrictions to help the homeless.

Refugees can enter the United States through two channels. Under present immigration laws, 10,200 are allowed to enter each year as "conditional entrants." After two years, their status can be changed to "permanent resident alien," making them eligible for citizenship after five years. Since 1956, when this quota proved inadequate to handle the mass of refugees who fled the Hungarian revolution, the U.S. attorney general has often invoked a provision allowing him to "parole" into the United States any alien seeking admission. Sizable groups of refugees have been admitted as parolees, the largest being some 675,000 Cubans who fled Fidel Castro's Cuba and settled, to a great extent, in Miami, Fla.

The Vietnamese refugees of 1975 were admitted to the United States under the parole system. Evacuated from Indochina to the Philippines or Guam and then dispersed among four military bases in

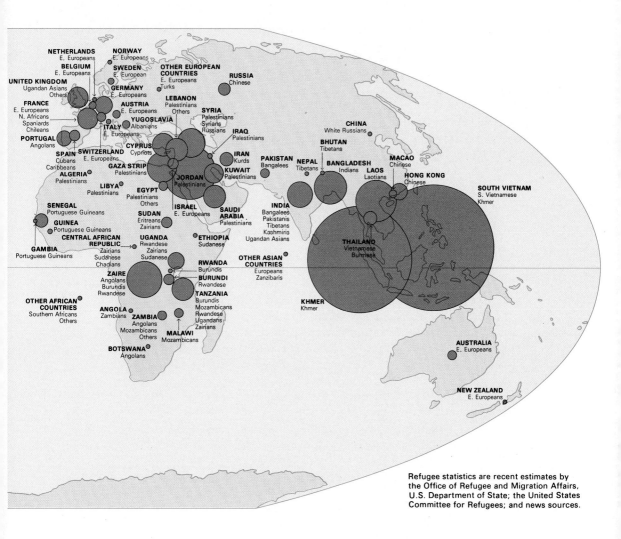

NETHERLANDS
E. Europeans

NORWAY
E. Europeans

BELGIUM
E. Europeans

SWEDEN
E. European

OTHER EUROPEAN
COUNTRIES
E. Europeans
Turks

RUSSIA
Chinese

UNITED KINGDOM
Ugandan Asians
Others

GERMANY
E. Europeans

FRANCE
E. Europeans
N. Africans
Spaniards
Chileans

AUSTRIA
E. Europeans

YUGOSLAVIA
E. Europeans

LEBANON
Palestinians
Others

SYRIA
Palestinians
Syrians
Russians

CHINA
White Russians

PORTUGAL
Angolans

ITALY
Albanians

CYPRUS
Cypriots

IRAQ
Palestinians

BHUTAN
Tibetans

SPAIN
Cubans
Caribbeans

SWITZERLAND
E. Europeans

IRAN
Kurds

PAKISTAN
Bangalees

NEPAL
Tibetans

BANGLADESH
Indians

MACAO
Chinese

ALGERIA
Palestinians

GAZA STRIP
Palestinians

JORDAN
Palestinians

KUWAIT
Palestinians

LAOS
Laotians

HONG KONG
Chinese

LIBYA
Palestinians

EGYPT
Palestinians
Others

SOUTH VIETNAM
S. Vietnamese
Khmer

SENEGAL
Portuguese Guineans

ISRAEL
E. Europeans

SAUDI
ARABIA
Palestinians

INDIA
Bangalees
Pakistanis
Tibetans
Kashmiris
Ugandan Asians

SUDAN
Eritreans
Zairians

GUINEA
Portuguese Guineans

CENTRAL AFRICAN
REPUBLIC
Zairians
Sudanese
Chadians

UGANDA
Rwandese
Zairians
Sudanese

ETHIOPIA
Sudanese

THAILAND
Vietnamese
Burmese

GAMBIA
Portuguese Guineans

OTHER ASIAN
COUNTRIES
Europeans
Zanzibaris

ZAIRE
Angolans
Burundis
Rwandese

RWANDA
Burundis

BURUNDI
Rwandese

TANZANIA
Burundis
Mozambicans
Rwandese
Ugandans
Zairians

KHMER
Khmer

OTHER AFRICAN
COUNTRIES
Southern Africans
Others

ANGOLA
Zambians

ZAMBIA
Angolans
Mozambicans
Others

MALAWI
Mozambicans

AUSTRALIA
E. Europeans

BOTSWANA
Angolans

NEW ZEALAND
E. Europeans

Refugee statistics are recent estimates by
the Office of Refugee and Migration Affairs,
U.S. Department of State; the United States
Committee for Refugees; and news sources.

the United States, some spent months in tent cities or barracks awaiting final relocation. During this period, they underwent intensive public health screenings and security checks, completed orientation programs about American life, and were interviewed by representatives of
voluntary resettlement agencies who worked to reunite families and to
match them with private sponsors willing to help them get established
in new homes. Transportation arrangements were also made for those
wishing to resettle in Europe or return to Vietnam. The program was
one of the smoothest mass movements of refugees in history.

Refugees are not specifically mentioned in Canada's immigration
laws, so they are subject to the same selection standards as other
would-be immigrants. In practice, though, the evaluation test that
measures an applicant's skills and training against labor demand is
simply relaxed enough to ensure a refugee's entry. On arrival, a refugee has the status of "landed immigrant," and can seek citizenship
after five years.

69

Australia generally has followed a "flexible" policy toward refugees. But in recent years, with a soft economy and less need for new immigrants, it has granted permanent residency rights to fewer and fewer refugees. "Large-scale immigration, which can be considered importing unemployment, is no longer considered a socially desirable thing," explains Duncan S. Waddell, Australia's immigration attaché in Washington, D.C. For example, refugees from strife-torn Portuguese Timor were admitted in August, 1975, on temporary visas and will have to qualify by more rigorous regular immigration standards in order to remain in Australia.

Australia and Canada offer more direct services to refugees once they are admitted than does the United States, which dispenses most of its refugee aid funds—about $323 million in 1974—through contributions to the intergovernmental organizations and in subsidies to voluntary resettlement agencies. In Canada, however, a refugee can get government aid for food, clothing, rent, and the tools of his trade until he is employed. Under the Canadian Manpower Training Program, he can also draw a living allowance for six months while receiving daily English lessons or other instruction.

But no matter how great the assistance, adjustment is rarely painless. As Maurice Benzacar, caseworker for JIAS in Toronto, Ont., points out, "The refugee is coping with massive cultural shock."

*D*espite the classes in Rome, the Elperins landed in Toronto with only a rudimentary grasp of English. "When you don't speak the language," says Vladimir, "everything is like a dog barking around you." That was to prove their greatest, but not their only, problem.

From the Toronto airport, a JIAS representative took them to a small hotel where they were quartered at government expense until JIAS rented an apartment for them and furnished it with a sparse assortment of donated furniture. Then— seven hours a day, five days a week for nearly six months—Vladimir and Rachel attended English classes, together drawing about $145 a week in allowances from the Canadian government.

Like most Soviet refugees, an unusually high percentage of whom are professionals, they expected to find jobs comparable to those they had in Russia, where personal status is virtually synonymous with the assigned occupation. But even with an English certificate and his carefully smuggled university diploma, Vladimir could find work only in a sweaty assembly line in a furniture factory. Rachel, who had been a textile technologist, worked as a clerk in a sewing factory. "For morale," says Vladimir, "it was rough." Moreover, they discovered, Canadian workers can be fired for reasons that go largely unnoticed in bureaucratic Russia, such as taking sick leave without phoning in or arriving on the job after starting time.

In public school, Miriam struggled to adapt to an educational system that encourages such foreign concepts as free expression, self-discipline, and independent thought. Meanwhile, her parents grappled with Canada's freewheeling economic system fraught with potential pitfalls (such as easy credit) and new confusions (such as managing a checking account) for the unwary newcomer.

Oddly, their religion, which had been a leaden weight in Russia, now produced strain of a different sort. The local Jewish community had accorded almost celebrity status to the 1,200 Soviet refugees settling in Toronto in recent years, but the enchantment has increasingly turned to disillusionment because the new arrivals have evidenced little knowledge of Jewish traditions and scant interest in practicing Judaism. "The community wants to make Jews of these people," explains Don Schwartz, a professor of Soviet politics at the University of Toronto, but the refugees are "primarily concerned with the assimilationist gut issues of jobs, schooling, and housing." Also, the refugees usually have at best ambivalent feelings toward an identity that has brought them stigma and discrimination. The other Jews they were most comfortable with, the Elperins found, were fellow refugees from the Soviet Union, a number of whom lived in their apartment building.

"One of the hardest things," says Rachel, "is to live without family and old friends. In your old town, every store even is close to you. I didn't write probably all my life so many letters as here."

JIAS caseworkers provide free counseling on adjustment problems, but some of the refugees with whom the Elperins became friendly seemed shattered beyond help by the new environment. One Russian doctor who cannot practice because of licensing restrictions "cried like a kid" and talked of suicide. A neighbor who had been a college teacher in Russia could find only a loading-dock job and said he wanted to go home, regardless of the consequences.

Thoughts of returning teased the Elperins, too. But Vladimir told himself, "You have to be a man, you are not a child anymore. Only people who are not strong enough try to run away."

Traumatic stress is inevitable among refugees because, as Canadian Minister of Manpower and Immigration Robert K. Andras points out, "All are experiencing more change at one time than many natives experience in a lifetime." In trying to adapt, writes researcher Kazys C. Cirtautas, who lived among World War II refugees in Europe, "The expatriate is like a caged eagle. Feebly and clumsily he turns around in his strange, bewildering surroundings."

Age is often the critical factor in the ability to adjust. Children assimilate most easily as a rule; indeed, their quick adoption of new manners and mores frequently becomes a source of conflict with their slower parents. The older generation, particularly those over 40, "in many ways will never fully adapt," says Don Schwartz. Their capacity for adjustment becomes severely impaired, observes Cirtautas in his book *The Refugee: A Psychological Study,* because "the course of their whole life has been disorganized."

In many cases, failure to adapt leads to deep depression. The refugee, Cirtautas says, becomes "uneasy, restless. He may have sudden outbursts of violent anger. He does not seem to fit in anywhere, can no longer accomplish anything. He lives too largely in his imagination. In fantasy, the familiar world of the old country becomes a paradise, the unfamiliar new country a hell....The most dangerous thing for the expatriate is falling into a pattern of compulsively thinking, 'If I were

After 25 years, Palestinians still live in camps, *top,*
and pose grave world problems. But Cubans in Florida
and Tibetans in Switzerland have successfully integrated.

Refugees, the orphans of the world, seek freedom and safety, food and shelter, and the chance to build new lives.

at home....' Loneliness and nostalgia create a state of mind which frequently ends in complete apathy."

The refugee will never feel wholly at home in a foreign country, Cirtautas asserts, but the degree of comfort he achieves is linked closely to his skill at mastering the new language. "Halting use of language can cause intelligent, educated persons especially to feel stupid. To the person who cannot speak or understand the language of the country in which he lives, that country remains unintelligible."

In his struggle to establish a new life, Cirtautas notes, "The refugee is likely to discover within himself tendencies and characteristics whose presence he never suspected in his normal, settled mode of life. How successful a given individual will be in his adjustment depends entirely on his emotional capacity."

Vladimir Elperin never heard of Horatio Alger, but he has bought the Alger story (strive and succeed) and so far has made it work. After less than three years in Toronto, he has become a partner in a small company that installs electrical equipment, and he is earning about $15,000 a year. Rachel works as a factory supervisor for $185 a week. With Miriam, they live in a two-bedroom apartment in a sleek suburban high-rise, complete with balconies, a swimming pool, and an obligatory North American status symbol—a meaningless piece of sculpture in the driveway. They have made a down payment on a condominium.

After the dishes are cleared from the dining room table and a new bottle of wine is uncorked, Vladimir, a warm, engaging, intense man, talks to us of the need to undercut his competition. "Everything here must be cheap, cheap, cheap," he declares. Then he frets about the power of labor unions, and rails against the naïveté of Western politicians in dealing with Russia. Rachel talks about the most exciting purchase they have made, a car. "It is like a dream to have one."

Miriam now attends Hebrew school. "I want my daughter to be more Jewish than I am," explains Rachel. "Not necessarily religious, but to know everything about Jewish history." Teen-aged Miriam, almost electric with vivacity and speaking English with no trace of accent, bounds into the room with a girl friend to babble something about boys, and then is gone again. Vladimir sighs. "We argue sometimes about her using her mind more," Rachel says. "She watches too much TV. It's TV and outside."

Vladimir is worried about his brother, who filed an application a few months ago to leave Russia with his family. Now in a coded letter, he has told Vladimir of being fired from his job, and the visa has not come through.

"I want he should be here with us, same city, same street," Vladimir says. "And my parents, yes, I want them, too. And Rachel's parents also. And then.... Well, there is always someone...."

There is always someone. And for every success like the Elperins, there are many refugees still languishing in camps and slums around the world. The embittered Palestinians are a potent and disruptive force in the unsettled Middle East. The proud Kurds have fled their ancient homeland in Iraq for camps in Iran. Greek Cypriots are exiles on their native island. Millions of Cambodians have been uprooted and moved to other parts of their own land. Thirty years of war have broken and scattered other millions in Vietnam. Africans, both black and white, have been forced from their homes by the thousands. Even the United States has its refugees–living in Canada, Sweden, and other countries–who would not fight in what they felt was an unjust war, or would not live in the country that fought that war.

For all these victims of politics and war, racial and religious hatreds, and the whims of nature, there will be months and perhaps years of hardship, alienation, and readjustment. For many, there will be help from national and international organizations. But this traditional refugee aid may be more difficult to obtain in the future, for both economic and political reasons. "The very ready acceptance of refugees won't be so ready any more," says Waddell in explaining Australia's position, which seems typical. "They'll be looked at harder: Where are they going to go when they get here? Are they going to pose major sorts of problems? Are they going to take jobs? Once those questions would have been heresy. That position no longer applies." He proposes "a unified dispersal package, some sort of international allocation" of refugees under the United Nations.

Some observers fear that a new flood of refugees, such as flowed into India from Bangladesh in 1971, might outstrip available resources and touch off an even greater crisis. It is not certain where the next waves of refugees will come from, nor where they will go. But, in this uncertain world, they are sure to come.

Harrison Brown, professor of geochemistry and professor
of science and government, California Institute of Technology

Wayne Wille, Executive Editor,
THE WORLD BOOK YEAR BOOK

Sylvia Porter, financial writer
and syndicated columnist

Alistair Cooke, author, journalist,
and broadcaster

Lawrence A. Cremin, President,
Teachers College, Columbia University

America:
Then, Now,
And Tomorrow

**Observing the U.S. Bicentennial, members of the
YEAR BOOK Board of Editors discuss the heritage
of America's past and the challenge of its future**

Jim Murray, sports columnist
for *The Los Angeles Times*

William H. Nault, Editorial Director,
Field Enterprises Educational Corporation

John Holmes, Research Director,
Canadian Institute of International Affairs

James Reston, columnist for
The New York Times

As a contribution to the American Revolution Bicentennial celebration, the YEAR BOOK Board of Editors met at Teachers College, Columbia University, in New York City in mid-1975 for an informal discussion about the nation, its successes, shortcomings, and progress over the past 200 years.

The board of editors meets with YEAR BOOK staff members each fall to discuss the year just ending and to plan the Focus section for the forthcoming edition. But the New York City meeting was special, in that the editors looked back not one year, but 200. And they also looked ahead to the challenges facing the nation and the world and the role that the United States must play in bettering the human condition. The following pages present, in conversation form, some of the board's views on the state of the nation, how it performed in the past, and how it may perform in the future.

William H. Nault: I think we all recognize that the Founding Fathers, wise as they were, could not possibly have anticipated the kind of world we live in today. And we can't predict what America will be like 200 years, or even 20 years, from now. But just as the Founding Fathers had their dreams for the country's future, we also have our dreams. So we want to talk about two broad and related subjects: the United States as it is now and how it may be tomorrow, given the realities of today.

As just a bit of background to our conversation, it's interesting to recall what some of the Founding Fathers thought about human nature. John Adams warned that anyone who would found a nation had to presume that "all men are bad by nature." James Madison was more encouraging. He said that he was aware of "the infirmities and depravities of the human character," but Madison said he also saw "other qualities which justify a certain portion of esteem and self-confidence." Thomas Jefferson held a more balanced view. Jefferson be-

How well do you feel our constitutional system has withstood the onslaught of what Adams and Madison saw as failings in the human character? And how well will it be able to cope with the future? [Nault]

lieved that man had an "innate sense of justice," that he could be "restrained from wrong and protected in right." It was this diversity of viewpoints that came together in the American Colonies in the late 1700s, went through a process of discussion and compromise, and finally resulted in the Declaration of Independence and the United States Constitution, two truly world-shaking documents that arose from the American Revolution.

How well do you feel our constitutional system, over the past 200 years, has withstood the onslaught of what Adams and Madison saw as failings in the human character? And how well, in your opinion, will it be able to cope with the future? Let's begin with Scotty Reston.

James Reston: Well, I think that I'm probably the last of the optimists around here about those two questions. When you realize that the documents we're talking about were produced in the 1700s by a group of men from 13 small colonies on the Eastern Seaboard, and that these documents have gone through 200 years and adjusted to a series of revolutions the like of which the world has never seen, I think you have to wonder at the genius of these men and the documents they produced. Look at the last of our revolutions, in the 1930s during the time of President Franklin D. Roosevelt. The economy adjusted at that time to a tremendous crisis—the Great Depression. Look at the political challenge of the 1970s—the Watergate scandal of Richard M. Nixon's Administration. Presidential power was out of hand in a way the Founding Fathers never imagined, even when they were thinking of the power of the British Crown. Still, the system of balanced power set up under the Constitution operated very well. The judiciary played its role. Congress did also. Outside government, the press, under the First Amendment, acted, I think, precisely as the nation's founders thought it would act. Therefore, I am enormously encouraged by the way the system has operated under tremendous pressure, and I'm very hopeful that it will go on into the 21st century, with modifications as it goes along.

Another thing that I believe has contributed enormously to the United States success as a nation—as a revolutionary society—has been the growth of our free institutions. In addition to the press, the churches and the universities and the labor union movements have all acted as a bulwark to the Constitution.

Alistair Cooke: I would like to say something about the Constitution and why I think the republic has survived until today. What it's going to do tomorrow is something else, of course. But, to me, the great hero of the Constitution—and the man we should be celebrating during 1976—was the most undramatic person there. He was physically unattractive, tedious, and scholarly, and yet he was the man whose main principles forged the system we have today—James Madison.

Madison saw what hardly anybody else saw—that the Thirteen Colonies were only the beginning. He saw that this was a continent, that it would open up, that it would be explored and settled. There would be regions developed, with regional interests and regional economies. A man in the Far West would be different from a man in Maine. And that's why Madison went on pounding away at Alexander Hamilton and other idealists, really laying the groundwork for what seems to me the anchor of American survival—sectionalism. A lot of the idealists wanted to have a life-appointed President, life-appointed senators, no House of Representatives at all, and no strong state governments. Madison said that inevitably you are going to get factions. When the country opens up, you are going to get different kinds of regional interests and ambitions. And Madison said that what this new national federation needs is a system of checks and balances whereby "ambition counteracts ambition."

Madison was afraid that if you had a strong, centrally ruled federation, you would get dictators. And he thought that, with many strong factions, it would be impossible for any one to override the others. His idea was that a House of Representatives should represent totally separate sectional constituencies and be in conflict with the Senate, which would represent national interests for each section.

Madison saw that the Thirteen Colonies were only the beginning, that when the country opens up, you are going to get different kinds of regional interests and ambitions. [Cooke]

We The People

Reston: But wasn't it that very sectionalism and the power of the state government that after a hundred years almost destroyed the republic in the Civil War?

Cooke: Sure. Madison took that risk. He knew that if you set up the national government against any local government or region, you will have a civil war. Well, of course, the South began to form a separate economic culture, and it happened. We had a civil war. But the nation's founders had to take that risk.

Jim Murray: Alistair, tell me, how do you square that idea with the massive dependence of sections, states, and municipalities on the federal government today?

Cooke: Well, of course, we *may* have come to the end of the workability of this theory, of the whole idea of sectionalism. I think one of the most telling examples of what you say is the fact that more people now, mayors and so on, go to Washington–to their congressmen and senators–for help, rather than to the state governor. Since the states are pretty well strapped, there is no point in going to the governor, because he is bankrupt, too. And it may be that we are moving into something totally new because of the mammoth corporations and the mammoth unions, and that we will have to be much more national. Maybe the whole sectional system is breaking down.

Harrison Brown: I agree that the group of individuals who put our Constitution together was a most remarkable group. But to what extent is the fact that the Constitution has lived this long, and survived a number of revolutions or crises, due to the wisdom of these men and to what extent is it due to a number of other circumstances that have helped us enormously? I am thinking, for example, of the country's fantastic natural resources, which enabled us to quickly pile up tremendous wealth, agriculturally and industrially. The young nation also had tremendous physical space and a degree of isolation from outside dangers provided by two oceans. It seems to me that these good circumstances must have had some effect.

As to the Constitution itself, I would like to raise the question of how good a document it is for our society today. With all due respect to our Founding Fathers, the fact is that the United States as it was at the time the Constitution was drafted was dramatically different from the United States today: There were 4 million people then; we have more than 200 million people now. It took months to cross the continent then; it takes a matter of a few hours now. There were very poor communications links then; we have fantastic communications links now. Most people were farmers then; very few people are farmers now. Most people lived in the countryside then; most people live in the cities now. Yet somehow, this document known as the Constitution seems to work now, maybe not as well as it did then, but nevertheless it works. Is this because the document is so remarkable that it would apply in any culture in any civilization at any time? Or is it that we've just learned how to work with it? Here's what I am getting at: If a new Constitution were to be drafted today, would it be about the same as the Constitution that was drafted by our forefathers?

Sylvia Porter: One thing is for sure. A document that would be drafted today would not need an amendment, which is still trying to get through the states, guaranteeing equal rights for women. It would certainly take into consideration the equality of women under all circumstances. That is one fundamental way that it would be changed. I think that in many other ways it would not be. The amendments that have already been added tell you where the changes would come. And these changes have come slowly, tortuously slowly.

Cooke: I must say it seems to me the Constitution works better in many respects today than it did in the beginning. Consider that in the early days Jefferson thought there would be a revolution every 10 years. Many people, including Hamilton, thought the country would be absolutely gone by the early 1800s. Andrew Jackson alone could say, forget what the Supreme Court says on the right of the Indians to keep their tribal lands to the east of the Mississippi. He said bring on the Army and kick them out, which they did. Imagine what kind of a hullabaloo there would be about that today. We tend to see the system as a continuous tapestry when, in point of fact, you could give 30 or 40 examples of total breakdowns.

As to the fact that there were 4 million people then and more than 200 million now, that they lived in the country then and in cities now, there is no mention of countryside or cities in the Constitution, and it has gotten along very well without it. And that's because, it seems to

I would like to raise the question of how good a document it is for our society today. If a new Constitution were to be drafted today, would it be about the same as the Constitution that was drafted by our forefathers? [Brown]

me, the role of the Supreme Court is the supreme achievement of what happened to the Constitution. The Constitution is only what the court says it is. But if the justices are in touch with public opinion, it seems to me that there is no limit to their hold on the Constitution as it is, though there have been and will be amendments.

Murray: I like what you said, that the viability and strength of the Constitution is in its interpretation.

Cooke: Yes. Perhaps Europeans think it's a weakness that the Supreme Court can and has reversed itself. For instance, the Supreme Court said that it is in the Constitution that you cannot deny an 11-year-old child the right to work 18 hours a day. Thirty years later they said an employer has no right to employ a child under 14 years of age. Look at the races. The most striking case was the "right" of blacks and whites to be kept separate and equal; and then the "right" *not* to be kept separate and equal. But it's up to the justices. It's up to the quality of the people who constitute the Supreme Court.

Lawrence A. Cremin: You know, Alistair, there's a very important point about education to be made here. The Founding Fathers believed that of all the institutions that educate, the law was the most fundamental. One reason why the Constitution works better today than it did in the early decades of our nation is that the Constitution itself has been educating generations of Americans. Think of the shift in Presidents from Richard M. Nixon to Gerald R. Ford. The President, with his great power, resigned and moved out, and this was all done peacefully. This is testimony to the extent to which the laws have educated the American people.

Nault: Well, is it an acceptable summary to Harrison's question that we feel that the Constitution has withstood well the test of time? That if it were rewritten today, it would not be significantly different—except for some specific points—and that the genius of it certainly is the interpretation of it?

John Holmes: I have an objection—foreign policy. I think the early critics of the Constitution wondered how the system would work when, eventually, the United States had to have an effective foreign policy. There was an awful lot of fumbling in the beginning, and this is a question that has been raised often up to the present day. At the time the United States entered fully into World War II, the Allies wondered: Will the U.S. foreign policy system be sufficient and swift enough for the United States to play a leading role? Well, the U.S. record certainly hasn't been a failure. On the other hand, I'm just wondering if it isn't somewhat self-indulgent. It makes it very difficult for other countries to deal with you. From the point of view of your ideal state, this division of powers—executive branch, legislative branch, and so on—is fine. But try to deal with a country in which you don't know who can make a promise. You can talk to the State Department, but the State Department cannot commit the Senate.

Reston: I don't question for a minute that this makes it terribly awkward for the leaders of Canada, Western Europe, all the leaders. Yet I wonder if there is not a certain wisdom in this separation. I think

The Founding Fathers believed that of all the institutions that educate, the law was the most fundamental. One reason why the Constitution works better today is that the Constitution itself has been educating generations of Americans. [Cremin]

we have to remember that we got into trouble about who makes promises because promises were made to South Vietnam that the President had no power to make. And it was then the division of powers that pulled them back. I admit this made South Vietnam's President Thieu rather unhappy, but I'm not sure it's a valid criticism of our way of doing things.

Wayne Wille: While we are talking about the Constitution, I wonder if we could define the qualities of the American character that have enabled us to operate it successfully for so long.

Reston: One thing is that, as a people, we have no memory. There is, for instance, no anti-Japanese or anti-German feeling in this country despite World War II. Another thing–which, paradoxically, may seem to be a weakness–is a kind of indifference to politics and to ideology. For example, we would never have been an independent country if it had been put to a vote or referendum on whether to fight the British. I think the historical record there is fairly clear. I don't know where politics rates on the scale of the most popular subjects in this country. You could make a long list beginning with the family and the job, with recreation, with sports, with business, and so on, before you would ever come to the point where you would say, "Now politics fits in there in the attention of the American people."

I would argue that this has been a good thing. There is very little ideology in this country, because we as a people have a very practical nature. We want to know how things work. If they work, you do them, but you don't tie them to an ideology. This, I think, has enabled us to roll with historical forces and has given a certain stability to the country as things change. It's given us a capacity for change.

Holmes: There's an extent to which America itself is your ideology, isn't there? Your Founding Fathers saw the United States as democracy and republicanism made flesh, a challenge to monarchs and tyrants–with a mission to change the world. But I think they wanted the United States to change the world by its example, rather than by imposing its beliefs on others. It was a noble vision, and it did change the world–mostly for the better. But because you did not recognize your convictions as an ideology, you were often intolerant of other ideologies. Increasingly, since World War II, you have been tempted to impose your ideology on others. I believe you did this because you believed it was good for them, not just for you. But the military means defeated the ends.

Murray: I think that, rather than ideology, we have a sort of *anti-*ideology in this country. People know communism is bad, but they really don't know what communism is. They just know it's like the bogeyman. It's evil. So I think people are a little bit uneasy about ideology–communism, fascism, whatever.

Cooke: Well, I must say, for a practical people we get off more ideological prose than any nation I know. We just pour it out. Of course, all this ideological rhetoric may be just a big cloak. You know, we wear a sword and a cloak in public, and then we throw them out as soon as we get home.

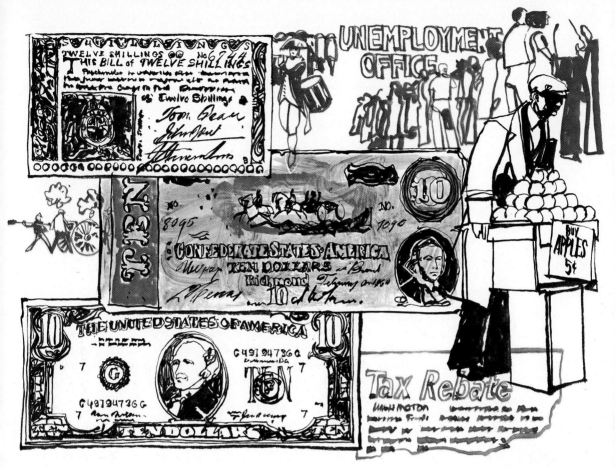

Reston: Well, you might say it's hypocrisy.

Cremin: Or you could say it's piety rather than ideology. Some scholars have said that we Americans have secularized the Protestant religious values–the dominant values at the time of the founding of the republic–into a civic religion. We celebrate those religious values that bind us together in statements like Abraham Lincoln's Gettysburg Address and presidential inaugural speeches that are somewhere between ideology, which is a driving force, and piety, which has no force. These statements, in a sense, celebrate communal values in a country that has no memory.

Nault: Perhaps we should turn in our discussion now to what progress we've made as a nation in the past and what hopes and aspirations we have for the future in some specific areas. Let's first look at economics. Sylvia, the economic climate today, I think, has caused a great many people to wonder just how far the United States has come in the past 200 years. The Revolution in part resulted because of British blunders in the economic area: taxes on newspapers and tea, "taxation without representation," and so forth. And right after the Revolution there was a severe economic recession. Paper money became worthless, trade fell into confusion. Would you say that it almost sounds like a description of today?

We have learned since the catastrophic depression of the 1930s how to control recessions. In terms of money, we haven't learned too much since 1776. The history of paper money has been to become progressively worth less and less. [Porter]

Porter: Not quite—not by any means. Let's put the optimistic point first, with a deep bow to economist John Maynard Keynes, and to those economists who helped translate his theories into American facts. Because of these people, we have learned since the catastrophic depression of the 1930s how to control recessions. We are now recuperating from the most severe, the most prolonged, the most pervasive slump since those depression 1930s. I think this slump ended because we took the classic measures to end it. A massive tax cut, tax rebates, one-stop tax bonuses, easier credit, and the building of massive federal budget deficits. This may very well lay the basis for another inflation blowoff in 1976 or 1977. But right now, it's sending our economy upward again. So we have learned how to control recession. In that sense, we have come a long way since 1776. That deep recession, which the young country felt because it didn't know what to do, was governed by the *laissez faire* economic theories of the time.

In terms of money, we haven't learned too much since 1776. You've all heard the expression "not worth a continental"? Well, the continental was the money issued by the Continental Congress to fight the Revolutionary War. It was backed by nothing except "we'll pay you." By 1780, it was absolutely worthless. The history of paper money has been to become progressively worth less and less. You issue it, eventually you take its backing away in order to finance expanding trade, and eventually its value goes down, down, down. I fear that the only weapons we have relied on to fight inflation are unacceptable morally and socially—economic slumps with high unemployment rates and price and wage controls, which the country would accept for only a short period of time.

As far as the international scene is concerned, we have learned to trade and to live with other nations through such international groups as the North Atlantic Treaty Organization, the International Monetary Fund, and the World Bank. And, among the states that make up this nation, we've crossed borders freely. From the very beginning, we were a heartening example of a customs union that worked. As the United States became more complicated, we really broke down all barriers completely. We pay no tariffs or taxes to cross state borders. We used to have individual state currencies; we now have one federal currency. We are a real United States. So, to sum up, we've made great progress in most economic areas. One, inflation, remains the great challenge of the rest of the 1900s.

Brown: At the present time, the rate of economic growth in the United States is around zero. Even if we averaged the past several years, our rate of growth has been less than that of some other countries of the world, including Japan and the Soviet Union. A part of the reason for this might well be that we already are the most affluent nation in the world. But do you view this with any alarm, Sylvia? Do you look upon this as a relative weakening of the United States compared to other countries?

Porter: It has important implications in terms of unemployment. We have to grow at a much higher rate than that of recent years in order to employ the new members of the labor force and to keep the ones who *are* working in jobs. I don't view the current slow growth rate with alarm, though, because there are ways for this country to expand. I think that the slowdown is part of our becoming a little less first among equals, and I don't particularly find that trend frightening. I would much rather have the gap narrowed between our contribution to the world and other nations' contributions to the world, and the responsibilities, as well as the pleasures, shared more equally. It doesn't scare me; it concerns me. And we'll have to reach a solution.

Reston: In my lifetime alone, the population of this country has increased by 100 million persons. Now, it seems to me absolutely astonishing that we've managed to adjust and absorb this torrent of people in the last 65 years. But I wonder whether the promises we're making to our people now, which are quite different from those made by the Founding Fathers, are valid. Can we really do it?

Porter: Talking about employment?

Reston: Well yes, employment, and all the other things we're promising. The whole welfare state gamut plus virtually full employment and all the rest of it.

Porter: I think young people reading this book will be interested in whether they are going to have a job when they get out of school, whether there is going to be anybody to employ them, whether there are going to be any professions to go into, and—if they are going to earn anything—what it's going to be worth. The Employment Act of 1946 states as a national objective of U.S. policy high employment, maximum production, and maximum income. The only thing we left out was stable prices. More's the pity, because that's where the weakness of our policies has been since World War II. But that is quite an ideal to set in a national law, to work toward employing people.

Brown: Well, I think, Sylvia, it's going to be very interesting to see how this employment act holds up during the course of the next 30 years, because we've only, in my opinion, seen the beginning of some dramatic social changes, which have at their roots massive technological changes. We have already passed through the time when most people were farmers to the point where there are very few farmers. I can easily conceive of our reaching a time when virtually all industries are operated essentially without people. Oh, you'll need a few people. But modern oil refineries, for example, now are so completely automated that they have one person on each shift who looks after the dials to make sure that everything is all right. And they have another person to sit with him just in case the first one drops dead.

We have already passed from an industrial economy into a service economy. This is going to become accelerated in the future, I suspect, and what are people going to do? Are we all going to be in the service industries? Are we all going to sit around and watch our machines?

Reston: Sylvia knows much more about this than I. But I can remember the horrendous prophecies produced on the subject of automation about 15 years ago. The idea that the machine was going to put everybody out of work just hasn't proved to be true.

Porter: Precisely the answer. New occupations or variations of old ones always will arise to absorb people.

Brown: But the point I was trying to make, I suppose, is that the avenues of employment that are considered conventional now—manufacturing industries and so forth—are going to decrease with time, just as the avenues of employment on farms have decreased to practically zero. This means that full employment in the future will involve most people in working in the services. Most people are going to be teachers, doctors, travel agents, hotel managers, what have you. And this, of course, has tremendous implications in regard to the educational levels that will have to be reached.

Nault: I agree, Harrison, that this has profound implications for education in the United States. Jefferson said that education was one of the tools society had for ameliorating the human condition and advancing the happiness of men. Larry, *is* our educational system preparing us for tomorrow?

Cremin: I want to emphasize, Bill, that by *education* Jefferson meant the family, the press, the churches, the laws, and immersion in politics, as well as the schools. He thought the schools would do a limited part of the job. Nevertheless, the Founding Fathers knew that the system they had built into the Constitution wouldn't work without a new arrangement for education. Jefferson deeply believed that citizens had to be educated as to their responsibilities. He enunciated the principle that unless your entire electorate is educated, and unless you train

If you ask me, the most revolutionary aspect of this society is what it's done in education. [Cremin]

leaders to perform the leadership responsibilities of society, the system is not going to work.

If you ask me, the most revolutionary aspect of this society is what it's done in education. I think our American contribution in free, universal education is the most radical departure from the past and probably our most innovative contribution to Western civilization.

But let me go back to the point about Jefferson to set the groundwork for some of our dissatisfactions today. Jefferson's generation knew full well that families educated, that the press educated, that education went on in lots of places. But in the mid- to late-1800s, when we began to build our public school systems and state universities, we got so excited about the notion of universal schooling that we began to assume that universal *schooling* would do all the things that Jefferson's generation had hoped universal *education* would do. The astounding thing is how well the schools did do. I think they have made an enormous contribution to political education, to the democratizing of culture, to making music and the other arts widely available. I think our American schools have done a better job of providing vocational education and equal opportunity and access to positions of influence than have any other schools in history.

But for every success the schools have had, the public has wanted more success. The result is that, along with the acknowledgment of tremendous accomplishment, there's a great sense that not enough has been done. I think our schools have done a better job of making education available to the population as a whole than any school system in the past, but the schools haven't worked nearly well enough with many *segments* of the population—blacks, Spanish-speaking Americans, American Indians, Asian Americans, migrant workers, and others. I think the schools have done an admirable job of popularizing the curriculum and making new subjects available to improve the life of the citizenry. But one of the problems is that they've popularized so much that a lot of nonsense has crept into the curriculum. By introducing many innovations, the schools have created both their own success and their own problem. And after 200 years, I think that's where we find ourselves, with tremendously significant innovations and accomplishments as well as some glaring inequities and some immensely high public expectations, and, therefore, with very ambivalent feelings, partly of success and partly of failure.

Porter: In view of the question of jobs and what's going to happen to the youngsters if we have a period of slow economic growth, what about the vocational school system? What about the training for blue-collar jobs, jobs that we certainly have learned are more vital to the sustenance of our form of life than many a philosophical Ph.D?

Cremin: Well, I would make three points, Sylvia. First, the vocational schools were very much out of style 10 or 20 years ago, but they are coming back into style again today. As a matter of fact, they are very much sought after. Secondly, in 1974, there were three major reports on secondary education in the United States. The common thrust of all three reports is that some educational tasks are better performed outside the school. One of the very interesting developments we're having in vocational education today is a return to cooperative education, where part of the training is done in the school and part out in factories and businesses or on farms.

The third point is that the American system has resisted undertaking a great sorting process at 14 or 15, the age when some youngsters in other countries are channeled into vocational education and are forever cut off from college and culture. What's more, the youngsters who make it into the academic secondary schools in those systems rarely do anything by way of vocational learning. *We've* tried to bring the vocational and the cultural together, not only in comprehensive high schools, but also in our vocational schools, where a good deal of cultural education is available. And we've tried to delay any final decisions, so that even if a student chooses a vocational high school, it is easier than it is in most societies to go on to a more academic course at the age of 18 or 20 or even 50.

There's a lot to find wrong with us, because there's a great deal still to be accomplished in the direction of fulfilling our ideals. But I think often we need to compare what we've achieved with what's going on in other countries and what's gone on in the past. When you look at it that way, we don't come off so badly.

Nault: How real is the ideal of every child having the opportunity of going as far as he or she might up the educational ladder?

Cremin: I think it's more real than in any other society in history—and to say so is in no way to deny that millions of American children have not yet been afforded decent educational opportunities, and that the inequity needs to be remedied. Yet the fact remains that a black child in the United States has a better chance of going to college than children of any color in most other countries of the world.

Porter: Yes, but wait a minute, Larry. In view of the enormity of our federal, state, and local budget deficits, and the very real danger of another burst of inflation later in this decade, how really free is the disadvantaged child? Who is going to pay if, for instance, the city university is no longer free?

Cremin: I predict that by the year 2000, whatever the inflation rate, the college-age population will have universal access to higher education and that 60 to 70 per cent will make use of this access. It will be financed by a mixture of federal, state, local, and private funds.

Porter: A major, and to me a most fundamental advance, has been made in the education of women. For the first time in modern history, a woman is born into a society which has acknowledged her right to an education and her right to the freedom to choose the role that she wants. Now, the education of the women of this country is very ambivalent at this stage, because they are being taught, in many cases, by men who were caught unprepared for the suddenness of their demands. But despite the current ambivalence, which may last for a few more years, the picture is pretty clear. Being born a girl in the United States in the last quarter of the 20th century is being born a person. The girls, the women, feel that they have the right to use the educa-

I think the television revolution of the last 25 years is as significant an educational revolution as the original invention of the school. Now, what does this mean in reference to Jefferson's idea of educated public opinion? [Cremin]

tional system just as the boys and the men do, and that they may take advantage of it to their own limits.

Reston: You pointed out an interesting distinction between schooling and education, Larry. How hard do you think American society is working to absorb the education offered?

Cremin: This is a very interesting problem that I wish more educators were working on today. I think the television revolution of the last 25 years is as significant an educational revolution as the original invention of the school. I would contend that this television revolution has fundamentally changed education in the family; it's fundamentally changed the education of the public. For example, the brief television news reports leave much less room for divergent thinking than do the more detailed newspaper reports.

Now, what does this mean in reference to Jefferson's idea of educated public opinion? What does this mean about the formation of public opinion? Where are the basic values being formed about the use of education, the use of opportunity? Where is moral education going on? If you ask an American parent, the parent will reply that moral education takes place in the family, the church, and the school. The parent doesn't think of television as providing moral education. Yet much that comes over television undermines what the schools are daily trying to do. The school may be the last dike, the last bulwark. The youngsters are being educated, but it's the television education that's washing over them and over their teachers. Schools get blamed because they are there, but it may be that if it were not for the schools, the situation would be much worse.

Reston: I don't think you answered my question. That is, whether the children, with the educational opportunities they have, are even coming close to using the opportunities they're given.

Cremin: No, they're not, Scotty, because they're glued in front of the television set five or six hours a day. And I believe that society and the government have been remiss in their responsibility for ensuring that television is a social good as well as an entertainment delight.

Porter: In the 1920s, when Herbert Hoover was secretary of commerce, he remarked about radio that it would be unthinkable that the society would allow such a powerful medium of public education to be used solely to sell soap, and I think we've used radio and television mostly to sell soap.

Nault: This discussion about television leads us now into another specific area we want to explore. It seems to me that if there is one aspect of life today that could never have been imagined by the Founding Fathers, it must be the fruits of science and technology. Try to explain to George Washington in the year 1789, for example, the role of television in a presidential election today. Yet the leaders back then had great faith in science. Jefferson wrote that each succeeding generation is a bit wiser than the one before because of what he called "the progressive march of science." But I wonder if we are still justified in having that Jeffersonian faith in science. There must be limits to what science can do and the problems it can solve, if only because of such conditions as population growth and limited supplies of natural resources, energy, and so on. Harrison, what do you think?

Brown: Well, first of all, we have to remember that society back then was primarily an agricultural society. And although the basic sciences were praised by Jefferson and by Franklin, the actual level of science and technology in the United States was very low 200 years ago. It was to remain lower than that of Europe for a very long time. The change eventually came about in part because of our wealth but, in large measure, also because of the remarkable law passed in 1862 that created the land-grant colleges. This had a great impetus not only on university education, but also on scientific research. Superimposed on that was what one might call a massive technical assistance program on the part of Europe generally and Germany in particular. They provided space for our professors to study there, and large numbers of professors from Europe came over here. And it has been a terribly interesting transformation, because until World War II, we were basically second-rate in the sciences.

Nevertheless, when the land-grant colleges were created, there was almost an explosion in scientific research in this country, most of it of an applied nature. And that research eventually led to a high level of agricultural productivity in the United States that is still unparalleled anywhere, with the exception of Canada. This really had a profound effect on our entire economy, and that effect is destined to last for a

The actual level of science and technology in the United States was very low 200 years ago. When the land-grant colleges were created, there was almost an explosion in scientific research. [Brown]

very long time. We now are the largest exporter of agricultural products in the world. We are destined to be the largest agricultural exporter for a long time.

Nault: A former member of this editorial board, the scientist and science writer Isaac Asimov, has projected that by the year 2000 the earth will have a population of between 7 and 8 billion, and that about three-fourths of the people will be in some stage of hunger. What's your reaction to that, Harrison, in terms of the ability of the United States to help solve this problem?

Brown: First of all, I think that perhaps the most important single development since World War II has been the very rapid evolution of a process I like to call the fissioning of human society into two cultures — the rich and the poor. Before World War II, there were lots of poor people, lots of rich people, yet lots of people in-between.

The poor countries are now the majority, characterized by rapid rates of population growth. The rich countries have totally different characteristics. Our population growth is low, but our growth rate of affluence is very high. And when we talk about hunger, we always point the finger of shame at the poor countries because of their rapid rates of population growth. But I think we have got to recognize that because of our growth of affluence, we end up consuming far more food than do the poor countries. This is largely because we consume large quantities of meat, which takes a lot of cereal to produce. We probably feed far more cereals to chickens and pigs and cows than all of India feeds to its own people. And I don't know how one gets out of this. But the fact that the rich countries are eating so much, coupled with the fact that the population in the poor countries is increasing so rapidly, leads to a situation which borders on the insolvable. It's a situation that is fraught with enormous dangers. Hungry people often do irrational things, as do well-fed people. The combination of these factors, I think, is one of the paramount problems of our time, and I don't know how we're going to get out of it.

Nault: I think this raises a very critical question, one that we have to turn to at the end of this discussion; namely, what will be America's role in world leadership as we look ahead. But I'd like first to go on to another area and take a look at America and the arts. Historian Russel Nye in his book *The Cultural Life of the New Nation* wrote that immediately after the Revolution, American critics, editors, and authors clamored for the immediate creation of a native, indigenous, and original art. Jamie Wyeth, the American artist, recently commented that we've always had an inferiority complex in terms of European art, and that it's time we shook off that stepchild attitude. Alistair, what do you think? Have our painters, writers, composers, and architects created an original American style?

Cooke: I don't think there's any question about that. But I would challenge the statement that immediately after the Revolution, or for a very long time, there was any great clamor for a popular art. The most striking thing right after the Revolution — and for the next 60 years — was that the Americans, especially the writers, ached to show that they were just as genteel and literary as the English. Washington Irving, James Russell Lowell, Oliver Wendell Holmes, Sr., even Henry Wadsworth Longfellow, were all branches of English literature. The material was new, but the diction was as proper as could be.

American literature did achieve its genius in Mark Twain. The interesting thing is that it was the English critics who decided that Mark Twain was the American Chaucer. Twain was despised in Boston and Philadelphia and the Southern towns as a comic-strip buffoon. There was outrage when *Tom Sawyer* and *Huckleberry Finn* came along. But the Europeans decided they were probably the first two great works of American literature. And, of course, what Twain did was take the spoken language and write it as it was spoken. And that, I think, is an indigenous movement that has been characteristically American, going from Mark Twain through many people like Ernest Hemingway, through the writing of movies.

Back to the protest, which is repeated about every 40 or 50 years, that we are not English, that we have our own style, our own character. It comes, I think, from sort of an inferiority feeling that we're not being appreciated. This happened in the 1930s in painting. Suddenly you got people like Thomas Hart Benton and Grant Wood and Reginald Marsh saying, "Let's stop imitating the French impressionists. Let's do our own." So you get *American Gothic* and you have Benton showing a mule team. Of course, the fact that you have an American

I would say that the major American contribution has been to produce art, not just for a few people in the village, but for the masses. [Cooke]

subject doesn't make it a great work of art. And I think we have made that mistake all along.

Actually, without any protest or much notice we developed an indigenous school of painting. We started out with the perfectly straightforward portrait painters of the 1700s, and then we went into genteel landscape painting—the Hudson River school and so on—sometimes very good and sometimes not. But the Western artists, such as George Catlin and Alfred J. Miller, who followed the pioneers, were the first, I think, genuine American artists with American themes. In abstract painting, I think there's no question that Americans were the pioneers and that they were the best.

But I would say that what I think is indigenous more than anything else is the 12-bar blues, a distillation out of work song combined with the religious music that the blacks picked up from missionaries. As you know, the harmonic base is absolutely still there. That, of course, was the great black contribution to American music. The white contribution was country music, mountain music, originally derived from Scottish and Irish ballads.

In architecture, there was the skyscraper. I think the feature film, made under the star system, was a native American product. Then there's the popular song that will sell 2 million copies. Actually, I would say that the major American contribution has been to produce art, not just for a few people in the village, but for the masses.

Nault: Yes, and it seems to me that another area in which America has captured the attention of the masses is sports. It's interesting to note that away back in 1794, *New York Magazine* warned that too much of sports could lead to dangerous excesses in other areas of life: "The path of amusement can become the broadway to destruction." The world of sports certainly has changed tremendously in 200 years, and many a television viewer thinks it has long since passed the point of excess. What do you think, Jim?

Murray: Well, we have to recognize that sports were not a big factor in this country at all for a long, long time. The colonials followed the Protestant-Puritan work ethic, and sports were frowned upon. Once in a while, there would be a sporting competition, but it always had a practical application. You had a contest in railsplitting, or you matched your horses, or you had a boat race, or something like that, but there really wasn't any kind of organized sport.

As near as I can tell, journalism—first the newspaper, then radio, then television—made sports what they are today. In the 1890s, James Gordon Bennett and William Randolph Hearst discovered that reporting sports events was a very good way to sell newspapers. People would buy a paper to see whether the Cincinnati Red Stockings had beat the whomever. The newspapers were in such frantic competition for circulation that they almost tangentially promoted sports. They gave so much attention to them, that they became more and more economically worthwhile.

Sylvia mentioned earlier that Hoover said it was a pity to use radio to sell soap. Well, David Sarnoff of the Radio Corporation of America

Journalism—first the newspaper, then radio, then television—made sports what they are today. [Murray]

had exactly the opposite point of view. He felt that radio should move goods, and that that was the great contribution it could make to American society. When he began to broadcast baseball games, advertisers with products to sell bought the rights.

And sports gave a tremendous impetus to television. So sports have really had a tremendous influence in the growth of the media in this country and have tied themselves to the advertising industry. Advertisers pay tremendous amounts of money to telecast sports these days.

But today, paradoxically, the major danger facing sports, it seems to me, is television. Television helped to kill boxing, I think, and affluence helped kill it, too. A man who is going to go out and risk a subdural hemorrhage for a $200 pay night has got to need money very badly, and most people don't need to do that now. They can make $200 far more easily.

Brown: There are boxers getting more money than that. Just take, for example, Muhammad Ali. He gets millions of dollars a match.

Murray: Sure, but that's a one-shot thing. When Muhammad Ali goes, he'll probably take boxing with him, because nobody else will be able to command $5 million for one match. Television killed boxing, because it killed small-club fighting where young boxers developed their skills. Television very nearly killed baseball, too. It ruined the minor leagues totally in baseball.

As for sports today, we may have reached the saturation point. But it's curious that politicians from the days of the ancient Roman Empire have felt that people have to have sports. For instance, President Roosevelt, during World War II, closed down the race tracks. But he decided that he had better not close baseball parks, because the swing-shift workers had to have someplace to go, someplace to spend money that they couldn't use to buy tires or automobiles or other things. Despite the fact that we may have too much sports on television now, we have to admit that sports have been part of our burgeoning economy, an integral part of our society.

Wille: It seems to me that the American public accepts a certain level of dirty tricks or cheating, whatever you want to call it, in politics or in business. But we won't accept the same kind of thing in sports. We think this is a violation of some ethic, I guess, where it might not be a violation in other areas. We hope that sports are a lot purer, in other words, than just about any other activity.

Murray: I think we Americans do want our heroes to be people of tremendous probity and character and integrity. There is a high level of integrity in sports. No baseball umpire has ever been found guilty of anything but blindness. On the golf course, very few people have been caught cheating. You'd think with the amount of money put out for the golf tours nowadays that the temptation to cheat would be monumental. And yet, there are people who come in and call penalties on themselves. Now this isn't always true in every sport. In baseball, you trap the ball, and pretend you caught it. And in football, you'll hold the man. But that's just considered good old American gamesmanship, not really cheating.

Nault: Well, so far in our discussion today, we all seem to agree that, despite certain shortcomings, America has made revolutionary contributions to virtually every area of living during the past 200 years. But many critics take the view that America's role in the world today is not consistent at all with our revolutionary past and the roots of this country. They say that we seek the status quo and oppose revolution as a matter of national policy. John, how do you feel about that?

Holmes: Well, I think the United States is still the most revolutionary country in the world, and perhaps also the most counterrevolutionary. One of your revisionist historians said that imperialism is as American as apple pie, and he is probably quite right. But so is anti-imperialism just as American as apple pie. And you have the struggle between these two different instincts. It's largely American historians who make the point that the United States always was an imperialist power and that this can be seen from the beginning. It is true that certainly in the beginning, as far as your own continent was concerned, you were very imperialistic – territorially aggressive and ideologically aggressive, as well.

But as to the suggestion that the United States has arrogated unto itself the role of maintainer of world stability, one has to remember that it was, after all, the chosen leader. The rest of us wanted this very badly. After World War I, we tried to get the United States into the League of Nations. We felt that the League didn't work because the United States didn't join. At the end of World War II, the most important thing was to get the United States involved in a role of world leadership. We thought of it as a sort of senior partnership. The United States did take that role, and on the whole, really played it magnificently, even though it did get into the habit of running things itself. The record, nevertheless, is very good, and everyone in the world is praying that the United States will still participate in the international system, but as a leading partner rather than as director.

Wille: John, I'd like you to expand a little bit on the point that some critics say our present posture in regard to maintaining the status quo seems to be inconsistent with our revolutionary past.

Holmes: I think there's inconsistency there. But it seems to me that the criticism is essentially a Marxist one. In Marxism, the United States is a supporter of the status quo; it is counterrevolutionary; it's not supporting the right people. But I can't accept that perspective. I do think that the United States has had some awfully curious allies. And you have chosen what I would think – and a great many people would think – were the wrong people as friends. But I think you did this from the beginning, and I also think you have had to. After all, if it hadn't been for your alliance with the corrupt French monarchy, you wouldn't have won the Battle of Yorktown. These are practical politics. I think that the significance of the United States in the world has been and is as sort of a social laboratory. It's the most avant-garde country in the world. It's where things happen.

Brown: You're right, John. As I travel around the world, I have become more and more convinced that in the United States today, we

*I would like to
question whether this
society—after 200 years—
is producing leaders
who can define the
problems of the age
and the coming age,
the way the Founding
Fathers did.* [Reston]

have the closest approximation to a truly revolutionary society that
exists anywhere, without question, in any area of substantial size.
Only in the United States do you find tremendously rapid social
changes taking place, a willingness to accept a new idea. And there is a
surprisingly minimal amount of blockage by what you might call the
more conservative forces. By contrast, change comes very slowly in the
Soviet Union. There has been a lessening of this inertia in Europe in
recent years. Still, it is terribly interesting to see how slowly they are
able to change relative to the United States. Certainly, revolutionary
change is a characteristic of the United States, and it is probably
destined to be for some time in the future.

Reston: Yes, but I would like to question whether this society—after
200 years—is producing leaders who can define the problems of the age
and the coming age, the way the Founding Fathers did. I'm not talking only about political leaders; I'm talking about leaders in the universities, in the press, and so on. I'm talking about leaders who can
reduce the enormous diversity and confusion of our time so that people
can say, "Yes, that is my problem," or "That helps me." We have
come out of both Watergate and Vietnam, and I can't remember a
single speech that I would regard as memorable, a speech that really
defined the essential issue. John Gardner of Common Cause says we

are producing managers, not leaders. As things have become more and more complicated, the specialist has taken over, and he handles a little bit of the problem. But the overall view of what an institution is doing, where it is going, is absent.

Cremin: Gardner has another point, Scotty, that I think is extremely important. He calls it the problem of the antileadership vaccine. He said we inoculate our youngsters with the fear of leadership. If you look at the young revolutionary generation of the late 1700s, they had a sense of standing on the threshold of history. But we have inoculated our own generation into a fright of that idea. So one of the problems of America today is the fear of leadership–the fear of the hot seat, of the buck stopping here. Some very talented people feel, "I don't need that. I'd rather take home less and have my freedom."

Reston: That's not the way I hear it at all. In some ways, I wish it were that way. There is, I find, an enormous longing, almost a scary longing, for leadership. And with the kinds of problems we've got in this country, I can imagine ourselves going not to the revolution of the left, but to the revolution of the right. The leader of the right could say, "Look, let me deal with this problem, we'll get you order."

Cremin: But they go together, saying "I don't want to do it, you do it. And if you lead, you have my vote. Just leave me alone."

Brown: I think that Scotty raised a very important issue. When we look at the horrendous spectrum of problems facing our country and the world today–nuclear war, energy shortages, depletion of natural resources, unemployment–we find that these problems cannot be isolated in terms of any one discipline. They cut across virtually all areas of our knowledge and our experience.

The university traditionally was the area where these problems were grappled with. But this can't happen within the framework of our modern university, simply because the universities are patterned along traditional lines. We have a department of physics, of chemistry, of economics, of this, of that. But they do not cross. I think what is happening within our universities today is typical of our society as a whole. We have plenty of specialists, as Scotty said, but too few people who are able to look at the problems across the board, the political and economic aspects along with the technological. I really don't know how one comes to grips with this. The problem of changing our universities, I think, is not the most important problem confronting us, but it certainly is numbered among them.

Reston: Doesn't this discussion now raise a fundamental question about America at the end of 200 years–whether we are not now challenged to apply to the world the ideals and techniques that have made us a successful society within our own borders? We have gone through mass education, we have gone through and are going through a massive redistribution of wealth, we have raised the question of equity between rich and poor, and black and white. And now, if I understood Harrison correctly a while back, we are in the midst of a new class war between the rich nations and the poor nations. If America is a great leader in the world, what will America say to that?

There was a time when the United States offered refuge to the poor and wretched of the earth. I presume this is out on any large scale from now on. [Holmes]

Holmes: There's one difference between the role of the United States in post-revolutionary times and in the present that might be noted in this connection. There was a time when the United States offered refuge to the poor and wretched of the earth. If they were in trouble, they could come to the United States, become Americans, and share in this civilization. I presume this is out on any large scale from now on because of employment problems and other things. But I think this is likely to be a very serious cause of tensions in the world. Many other countries will be establishing stricter rules of immigration. So you'll have more and more refugee crises. Things like that will have something to do with a changing image of the United States in the world, because you're not taking these people anymore.

Nault: The late Belgian statesman, Paul-Henri Spaak, a former YEAR BOOK editorial board member, once mentioned a feeling of self-doubt that he had started to see in America. He said, "There used to be a feeling of 'Where's the job? We'll do it. We can do it, and we will do it.'" I wonder how that idea fits in with what we've just mentioned about America's role of leadership in the world as we look ahead to the next 20 or 200 years.

Reston: I think any self-doubt regarding our role—America's role—given the new conditions and attitudes within and without, is temporary. If there is one theme that runs through the whole of American history, surely it is to rebuke the idea that we will not adapt. Even if

I think any self-doubt regarding our role is temporary. If there is one theme that runs through the whole of American history, surely it is to rebuke the idea that we will not adapt. [Reston]

Mankind today is going through the most difficult period of our history. We are in several crunches—the energy problem, the food problem, the division of the world into rich and poor countries, the problem of armaments. [Brown]

you begin at the very beginning, before we were a country, we have always made progress in the face of intolerable conditions. At least a third of the people in the American Colonies felt the impositions of the British government were intolerable. When they finally got to that point, they produced a revolution. We knew for a hundred years that slavery was an abomination to everything we believed in, and we had to go through a terrible civil war before we corrected it. But we corrected it. The same thing is true of the era of American isolation from world affairs; we corrected that after two world wars. The same is true of our economy. After the depression of the early 1930s, we acted. And after Watergate and the Vietnam War, we got control of campaign financing and excessive use of presidential power. So that record, I think, justifies us in believing that the people are smart enough and their institutions malleable enough so that they can change.

Cooke: But after a catastrophe.

Reston: I must say that I am more hopeful about our capacity to deal with adversity than I am with our capacity to deal with prosperity. I think our great periods, really, have been the periods when things were tough. The challenge now is to deal with affluence and with peace rather than the opposite.

Holmes: I've just been meeting with some Europeans together with some Americans. And I realized that the Europeans were trying to say to the Americans, "Cheer up. You know, you're really all right. You're better than you think you are, and don't get into the dumps." I do think the United States has an extraordinary ability to absorb experience, and I think it will absorb its recent experiences of Watergate and Vietnam and be wiser. That old self-confidence, the feeling that you have the capacity to do anything, was one of the causes of your trouble. To me, it was your great technological ability that led you astray in Vietnam, into a war that defeated its own purpose. But I am fairly confident that you'll learn from that experience.

Reston: Perhaps our assumptions have been too grandiose. The concept of "We're number one" was true for years, and it was very much part of our psychology and our goals. But there has been a change in the world. We can't just assume that our advanced technology is better than everybody else's advanced technology—that we can charge any price for our products because our technology is good enough to overcome any competitive disadvantage with the rest of the world. I think we've been forced by the rise of other centers of power to put aside the concept that as soon as we take the field, everybody else is going to run away. To realize that, in my view, is a good thing.

Murray: We found out we weren't completely the guys in the white hats anymore. Vietnam really shook us.

Reston: Yes, but that's a little too bad. If we have begun to realize that machines and money can't do everything, that is good. But our real power was that we *were* the guys in the white hats. We *did* conduct ourselves in the world in ways that were more generous than most other powerful nations. In our relations with other nations, the United States believed that power wasn't really anything if it was not morally

based. Now I do think that we Americans have rather lost that. However, I hope that we can get back to it.

Nault: Larry, are we still exporting educational know-how to the extent that we were 20 years ago? Are we still leaders in that field?

Cremin: A colleague of mine used to say that every major country in the world, in one way or another, was moving toward American ideals in education, with one notable exception—the United States. The idea of free, equal, universal public schooling coupled with widespread access to public universities continues to engage educational reformers around the world. Of course, there are a few countries determined to create their own new educational ideals—the Chinese, for example, with the educational program they have in their communes and their "red-and-expert" universities. But American ideals in education still exercise a very powerful hold on the imagination of many other countries, even though we ourselves have lost faith in some of those ideals.

Porter: I think the self-doubt that came over us in the wake of Vietnam and Watergate has been a cathartic we've needed. And I think we'll be much more willing to work with our allies in various international organizations, because we've had this rather essential reminder that we, too, are mortal.

Brown: May I sort of neutralize some of the optimism? As a result of the convergence of a number of effects, of historical trends, mankind today is going through what I personally consider to be the most difficult period of our history. I'm speaking of mankind's history, not just America's history. We are in not just one crunch, but several crunches. And these are bound to become more severe as time goes on.

The Bicentennial has provided us with a unique opportunity to look back on our nation's history. However, it is also necessary that we, as a people, look ahead, and I hope that the discussion today will contribute to that by spurring others to do the same. [Nault]

One can mention the energy problem, the food problem, the division of the world into rich and poor countries, the problem of economic development, the problem of armaments, and the dangers presented by the flow of arms from the richer countries to the poorer. When a country like India has fantastic malnutrition, and tremendous frustrations, and also possesses nuclear weapons, what is the prognosis for the future? I would submit to you—without any feelings of demagoguery or any feelings that we in the United States are any better than anyone else—that our sheer power, productivity, wealth, and tremendous technological expertise put a tremendous responsibility upon us. Although we have shown in the past that we can cope with that responsibility, I hope that our recent experiences will not cause us to withdraw to the point where we do not make use of our influence and our power to help solve these problems. And if these problems are not solved, we go down with the rest of the world. Isolationism from that point of view doesn't make any difference anymore.

I hope that we are going to really play a major role. I'm not speaking of a military role. I'm talking about an intellectual role, an economic role, a human role in solving these problems. Because if America doesn't play that role, I suspect it's curtains for all of civilization.

Cooke: I really think that the country is bewildered by the complexity of its problems and doesn't know what job it *is* that has to be done. So there's no point in rolling up your sleeves. I see in this two dangers. One is, if the complexity produces 40 million unemployed or a hopeless future for blacks, they will literally blow up the complexity. I think that's a very real possibility. The other danger is the appearance on the scene of a first-rate demagogue who could say to people, "Things are not complex at all. We're in this mess because of the blacks or the Jews or the mammoth corporations" or whoever the scapegoat may be. "I will take hold and I will give you some simple disciplinary laws." I agree with Scotty that if a dictatorship or a totalitarian government came about, it would be of the right.

Reston: It's very interesting, though, that nobody has taken that line during this whole recent period of frustration. I've often wondered what would happen if you had an attractive demagogue who would take that line. But I would not really be worried about the common sense of the American people confronted even with a demagogue. We'd go through a rough time, but I don't think the demagogue would win. I think the country still believes in believing in many of the ideals on which the republic was founded. And I think if push came to shove on that, the good side of America would prevail.

Nault: I want to thank all of you for taking time out from your busy schedules to participate in what has been a stimulating and thought-provoking discussion. The occasion of the Bicentennial has provided us with a unique opportunity to look back on our nation's history and assess both our revolutionary contributions and the areas in which we still need to make a great deal of progress. However, it is also necessary that we, as a people, look ahead, and I hope that the discussion today will contribute to that by spurring others to do the same.

Updating Our Perspective On the Planets

By William J. Cromie

An unexpected and still-changing picture of the solar system emerges from the space exploration and astronomical studies of the past 10 years

Spinning through the darkness beyond the Earth, two spacecraft hurtle toward a rendezvous with Mars. They are *Vikings* and, like the Norsemen of old, they seek to explore unknown lands. By January, 1976, they were halfway to their destination. If all goes well, they will go into orbit around the red planet in July. As scientists on Earth anxiously await results, a lander will separate from each orbiting vehicle and descend by parachute. On the Martian surface, a long, mechanical arm will stretch out and scoop up a metallic fistful of soil and rock. Inside the lander, instruments will subject the sample to a battery of chemical and biological tests in the hope of answering one question: Is there life on Mars?

At the same time, other equipment will analyze the soil's mineral content, study the Martian atmosphere, measure the winds, and radio the data back to Earth. Television cameras will provide color and black-and-white pictures of the landscape. If successful, the *Viking*

Jupiter's north pole, first photographed by *Pioneer 11,* looks like a boiling pot of porridge, with bubbles that may be similar to thunderstorms on Earth.

Mapping the Moon

Worn-down craters

Moderately sharp craters

Crater chains and clusters

Furrowed and hilly areas

Ce₁

Young, sharp craters

Im

Smooth, dark *maria* (plains)

A geologic map of the Moon, *facing page,* aids scientists in decoding its complex history. Colors, *above,* identify various lunar features.

The author:
William J. Cromie is a free-lance science writer and executive director of the Council for the Advancement of Science Writing.

landers will be the first man-made vehicles to operate on the surface of Mars. The results should profoundly influence our picture of Earth's ruddy neighbor, just as *Viking's* predecessors have drastically altered our view of the solar system during the past decade.

As recently as 1965, some scientists saw the Moon as a cold, dead world, basically unchanged since the birth of the solar system, some 4.6 billion years ago. Others pointed to its large craters as evidence that the Moon was hot and young. People argued about what kind of plant life caused the seasonal changes of color on Mars and wondered if the mysterious Martian canals were cut by nature or by living creatures. Some scientists declared that the dry, frozen surface of Mars foreshadowed what the Earth would be like in the distant future. They pictured Venus as a steamy, primitive swamp like that which covered most of the Earth's land 310 million years ago. Mercury was only a fuzzy disk, even through the most powerful telescopes. Equally mysterious were the colored bands and Great Red Spot of Jupiter. Science-fiction writers peopled these planets with strange creatures.

But as new information came in, from both spacecraft and Earth-based instruments, the picture changed. Some data supported previous theories, but more often, the theories were overturned. Faced by unchallengeable facts, many science-fiction writers packed up and moved to other planetary systems. But the scientists, fascinated by the constantly changing picture, moved in for a closer look.

One of the most unexpected and fundamental discoveries during the past golden decade of astronomy involved the extent of the physical and chemical changes on the inner planets. Before the first Moon landing by *Apollo 11* in 1969, most scientists considered the Earth unique because geophysical and geochemical forces clearly had remolded its surface features at regular intervals. They believed that the other planets had not experienced such geologic resculpturing.

The return of the first Moon rocks enabled scientists to date events on another world for the first time. To their surprise, they found that the Moon was not always cold and dead, but had gone through violent periods of melting and bombardment. From studying these rocks, they concluded that the entire surface of the Moon had once been covered by an ocean of molten rock. Heavy elements sank toward the Moon's center, while lighter elements floated to the top and formed a crust of lightweight rock. Astronauts searched for a rock that had been part of that original crust, thinking it might hold the key to the origin of the Earth and other planets. They finally found one in 1972 on the last lunar landing mission, *Apollo 17.* Geochemists dated the rock at about 4.55 billion years.

The difficulty in finding a piece of the original crust stems from a tremendous early bombardment suffered by the Moon, which virtually eliminated the geologic record of its birth and early life. For some 500 million years after the crust hardened, gigantic meteorites hammered the surface into a pocked chaos, punching out basins up to 700

miles (1,100 kilometers) in diameter. Many of the rocks picked up by the astronauts were part of the debris spread by this cosmic assault. Other rocks came from a later period of volcanic eruptions that began about 4 billion years ago. Dark, molten lava welled up and filled the largest craters, forming smooth plains that are easily visible from the Earth—the eyes, nose, and mouth of the "man in the Moon." The Moon's volcanic fires went out about 3.1 billion years ago and the Moon has been quiet ever since.

Far from solving the mystery of the Moon's origin, the *Apollo* samples only raised more questions. Despite the 840 pounds (380 kilograms) of rock samples and a large amount of other data gathered in six manned landings, the Moon's birthplace remains obscure. Because its composition is so different from the Earth's, few planetary scientists still cling to the theory that the Moon was torn out of the Earth when the latter was partly molten. More fashionable theories suggest that the Moon formed in orbit around the Earth, or that it originated somewhere else and was captured later by the Earth's gravity. One thing seems certain—the Moon does not belong where it is today.

Several years before the first lunar landing, scientists got their first close-up look at Mars when *Mariner 4* flew by in 1965. Photographs showed a crater-pocked surface much like that of the Moon, but there was no sign of geologic activity—no mountains, no elevated land masses, no deep valleys, no hint of serious disturbance. It was a disappointing finding for those who expected to see traces of ancient oceans and other evidence that Mars resembled the Earth.

Four years later, *Mariners 6* and *7* passed within 1,990 miles (3,200 kilometers) of the Martian surface, sending back hundreds of photographs. These showed that not all of the surface was cratered—some areas had jumbled ridges and valleys; others seemed smooth and featureless. However, the picture remained that of a barren world.

Then, in November, 1971, *Mariner 9* went into orbit above Mars. To the dismay of the scientists working on the project, the spacecraft arrived as Mars was enveloped in a dust storm. All that could be seen through the haze were the polar caps and four dark spots. But, as the dust gradually settled, the spots were revealed as huge *calderas* (circular basins at the tops of volcanic mountains). One gaping caldera, about 40 miles (65 kilometers) in diameter, crowns the top of the largest known mountain in the solar system—*Olympus Mons* (Mount Olympus). It is 310 miles (500 kilometers) across at its base, and it rises more than 15 miles (25 kilometers) above the surrounding plain, almost three times as high as Mount Everest, the Earth's tallest peak.

Mariner 9 sent back photos and other data for nearly a year, until it was finally shut off in October, 1972. Its photographs show volcanic plains and uplands, blocks of crust uplifted into mountains, and long *faults* (breaks) in the Martian crust. These include a great series of canyons that stretches one-sixth of the way around the Martian equator, dwarfing Earth's Grand Canyon.

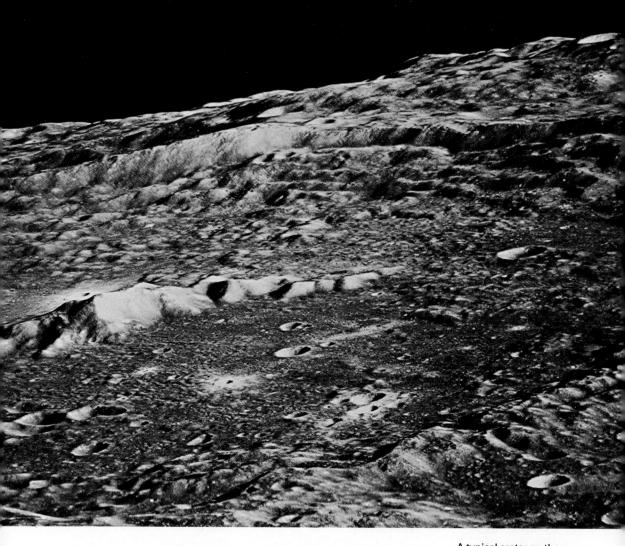

A typical crater on the far side of the Moon shows terraces and central peaks like those seen in large craters on the Moon's near side.

The mysterious canals could not be found. As it turned out, man had been studying and mapping creations of his own imagination ever since Italian astronomer Giovanni V. Schiaparelli announced his discovery of geometric lines he called *canali* (channels) in 1877. The idea of seasonal changes in vegetation literally turned to dust as scientists decided that dust storms, following seasonal winds, caused the shifting patterns of light and dark colors.

But there is a new puzzle. Strange, winding valleys snake across the surface for hundreds of miles or kilometers, with braided patterns and branching tributaries that seem very similar to watercourses on the Earth. Yet liquid water cannot exist in the thin atmosphere of Mars— it evaporates instantly. How, then, were the channels carved? Some scientists believe the channels point to a past era when atmospheric pressure was high enough to allow water to flow freely. Some suggest that the climate may run in long-term cycles, alternating between cold, dusty ice ages like the present and more clement times when higher temperatures and a denser atmosphere might allow some forms

A huge rift canyon cuts across the center of Mars, *above.* A closer look, *opposite,* shows branching channels that resemble streams on Earth. This suggests that water may once have flowed on Mars.

of life to flourish. Such long-term variations in the climate are expected because of irregularities in the Martian orbit.

Mars retains its mystery. Far from being an old and dying Earth, it turned out to be geologically active, meteorologically active, and, perhaps, biologically active, with its own unique history.

Nor is Venus a primitive, swampy Earth. Seven Russian *Venera* spacecraft penetrated its thick clouds between 1968 and 1975. Four reached the surface and radioed back information for up to an hour. They found the surface hot enough to melt lead, with an average temperature of about 900°F. (485°C). The visible clouds are thought to be composed of sulfuric acid droplets, while the atmosphere below—95 per cent carbon dioxide—has a surface pressure at least 90 times that of the Earth. Because of the thick atmosphere, the surface is probably suffused in a deep red gloom, though the most recent Russian landing craft were able to radio back pictures that showed a surface covered with jumbled rocks and a formation that looks like it might be an old mountain.

Radar signals bounced off the surface from Earth indicate there are craters, mountain ranges as large as the Rocky Mountains, and deep canyons that may surpass those of Mars in their grandeur. Radar

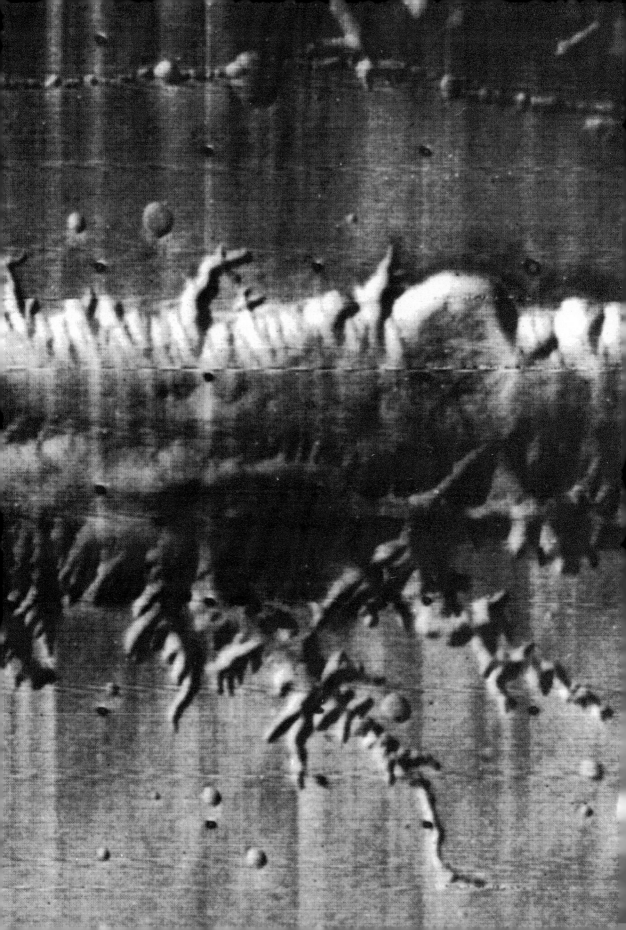

studies underway at Arecibo Observatory in Puerto Rico are expected to give a detailed picture of the structures and elevations of the surface. *Venera 8* sent back evidence of surface rocks resembling granite, a lightweight rock that makes up most of the Earth's crust. This suggests that Venus, like the Earth, is differentiated, or separated into layers of rocks that become progressively heavier toward the center.

Mercury is the most recent planet to yield its secrets to scientists. It is so far from the Earth and so close to the Sun that even the strongest telescopes cannot resolve any detail through the glare. But when *Mariner 10* sped past Mercury three times in 1974 and 1975, it took pictures of surface features as small as 0.6 mile (1 kilometer) in diameter. On the surface, Mercury looks much like the Moon—with craters, ridges, basins, and smooth plains. But there are some differences. Long *scarps* (cliffs), so far found only on Mercury, cut across the surface, slashing through craters and plains. Geologists believe the scarps formed when the core of the cooling planet shrank, causing the crust to buckle. The gigantic Caloris Basin, 800 miles (1,300 kilometers) across, dominates one side of the planet. But the biggest surprise lay under the surface.

The surface crust is lightweight rock, much like the surface of the Moon, but scientific measurements indicate that the planet must have a heavy iron core, like that of the Earth. Moreover, Mercury, like the Earth, acts as if it contains a giant magnet. The magnetic field is weak —only 1 per cent as strong as the Earth's—but that is still far stronger than most scientists predicted.

The discovery of Mercury's magnetism has cast doubt on the previously accepted theory about how the Earth's magnetic field is generated. Most scientists thought the Earth's magnetism is caused as the planet's rotation sets up movements in its liquid iron center. The swirling of the molten metal generates electric currents, which in turn produce a magnetic field. The discovery of Mercury's magnetic field poses a problem, however. Even though its core may be liquid, as demanded by the theory, Mercury rotates too slowly to set up the motion needed to produce the measured magnetism. "The only conclusion you can reach," says astronomer Carl Sagan of Cornell University, Ithaca, N.Y., "is that we don't understand as much as we thought we did about our own planet."

Bruce C. Murray of the California Institute of Technology (Caltech) looks to Mercury for a solution to the problem. "As we study Mercury's field and begin to understand it, we may reach an understanding of Earth's field," Murray says. "We don't get natural experiments like this often. You can't drill to the Earth's core. Therefore, having a captive planet that has the same kind of field, scaled down, provides an extraordinary laboratory to test our theories. Since magnetic fields are intimately associated with the origin and history of a planet, and on Earth with the evolution of life, I think that information about magnetic fields will prove to be one of the most important contributions of planetary exploration."

Jupiter, some 483 million miles (778 million kilometers) from the Sun, is different from the rocky terrestrial planets such as Mars, Venus, and Mercury. It is 318 times as massive as the Earth, and contains three-fourths of all the mass in the solar system beyond the Sun. Jupiter is a whirling gaseous globe with a stormy atmosphere, and no one is quite sure where the atmosphere ends and the solid surface begins, or indeed whether the planet has a solid surface or core. There may be no real surface, only a gradual transition from thin gas to dense hydrogen fluid. At a depth of 12,000 miles (19,300 kilometers) from the top of the atmosphere, the fluid hydrogen becomes so dense that it behaves like metal and conducts electricity.

In 1972 and 1973, two spacecraft—*Pioneers 10* and *11*—set off to explore the region around Jupiter. Radiation was the greatest danger facing the mission. To study the radiation trapped in Jupiter's magnetic field, scientists sent *Pioneer 10* through the heart of the radiation zone. Even while it was on its 21-month journey toward the giant planet, estimates of the radiation intensity were revised upward. Project scientists crossed their fingers, fearing that the instruments might not be able to withstand the bombardment. Fortunately, though the spacecraft received a radiation dose 1,000 times greater than that needed to kill a human, none of the instruments were badly damaged. *Pioneer 11*, coming in at a different angle over the planet's poles, suffered less from radiation.

The *Pioneers* discovered that Jupiter's magnetic field is substantially different from any other encountered so far. Compared to the Earth's, the field is upside down, and the magnetic axis is tilted about 15 degrees to the rotational axis. The center of the field is offset from the center of the planet by about 10,000 miles (16,000 kilometers), which means that the strength of the field on the planet's surface varies widely, being as much as five times greater in some places than in others. The field also is far more complicated than the Earth's and about 10 times as strong at the surface. The Earth behaves as though it contained a simple large magnet, but Jupiter's field acts as if it comes from several magnets inside the planet.

Jupiter's intense, rapidly rotating magnetic field shields it from the *solar wind* (energetic radiation streaming from the Sun) and traps high-energy charged particles that produce radio signals detected on Earth. *Pioneer 10* found that this region of charged particles—the *magnetosphere* —was much larger than expected and that it changes both in shape and size in response to pressure from the solar wind. Early observations suggested that the outer magnetosphere was stretched out in a thin disk, which wobbles as the planet spins. But *Pioneer 11* found that the disk model is only an approximation of the actual situation. Many questions still remain.

As massive as it is, Jupiter is far from being a star, but it still pours out up to 2.5 times as much heat as it receives from the Sun. So much excess heat indicates that the interior of the planet must be extremely

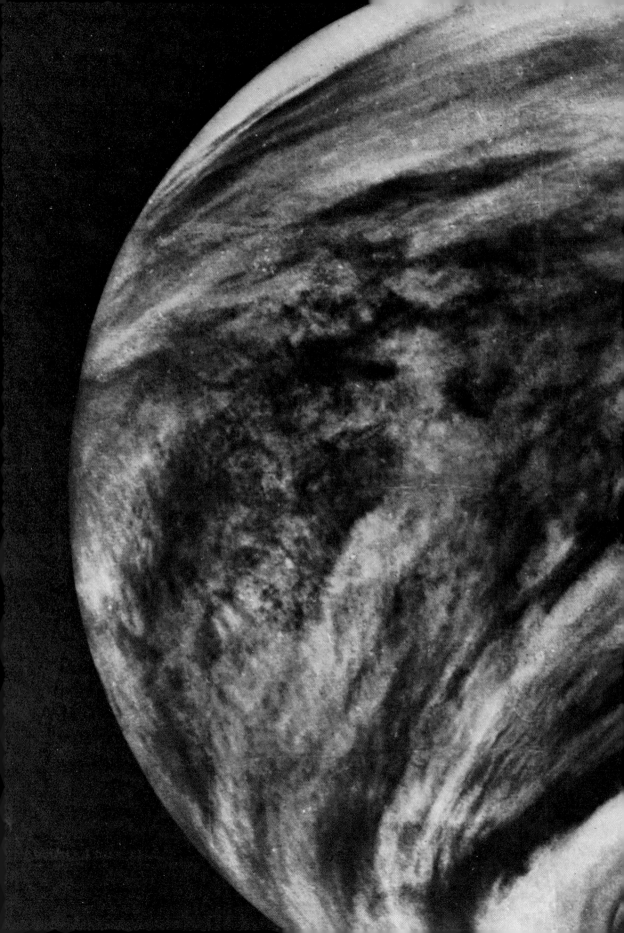

hot—hotter than the surface of the Sun. Some astronomers have suggested that the heat is produced because Jupiter is still contracting, or shrinking in size.

Like everything else about the planet, Jovian weather processes are more complicated than expected. Jupiter is a planet of storms, with the Great Red Spot the largest of them. It appears to be a gigantic hurricane, several centuries old, that towers above the surrounding clouds. It varies in size, ranging up to 25,000 miles (40,000 kilometers) long and 8,500 miles (13,700 kilometers) wide, large enough to swallow up three Earths. Most of the planet is ringed by light and dark clouds that are stretched out in bands by the planet's rapid rotation. The atmosphere at the poles looks like a pot of bubbling porridge, which some observers interpret as huge thunderstorms.

Planetary exploration has brought practical dividends, including breakthroughs in communication, meteorology, geology, and other areas. Some of the most immediate benefits are expected in the area of weather and climate, thanks to a better understanding of planetary atmospheres. Atmospheric conditions on Earth fall between the extremes of its neighbors in space. Mars has a thin carbon dioxide atmosphere, with a surface pressure less than 1 per cent of Earth's, few clouds, and galelike winds. Venus has a continuous blanket of thick clouds, a surface pressure at least 90 times greater than Earth's, a fast-moving upper atmosphere, and relatively calm winds at the surface. Earth's atmosphere is much more complicated, with a variable cloud cover and shifting winds. But by studying the bracketing conditions on Mars and Venus, scientists can obtain clues to general processes that will help them understand how the Earth's atmosphere works.

"**M**ost of our ideas about Earth's weather should work on Mars," says Richard M. Goody, atmospheric physicist at Harvard University, Cambridge, Mass. "If Earth possessed a thin atmosphere like Mars, lower gravity, and vast accumulations of dust, we also would experience months-long dust storms that covered the whole planet. The difference is a matter of scale, not of process. Weather patterns in the winter hemisphere of Mars involve unstable westerly winds like those in temperate latitudes on Earth. The Martian summer hemisphere probably has easterly winds similar to those that blow in our tropics. We see what look like cirrus clouds and cold fronts on Mars. Over a two- or three-day period, they behave the way we would expect them to on Earth."

John S. Lewis, geochemist at the Massachusetts Institute of Technology (M.I.T.) in Cambridge, expands this point: "Circulation patterns found on Venus resemble those in the tropics. A better understanding of these patterns should provide clues to the mechanism of climate change on Earth. Understanding tropical circulation is the key to understanding what causes deserts and severe droughts, such as the recent one on the south edge of the Sahara. If we can learn the basic principles of atmospheric circulation, we may be able to avoid

Streaks and swirls in the thick cloud layers blanketing Venus show up in an ultraviolet photograph. Circulation patterns parallel those found in Earth's tropics.

119

Bright rays, created by
debris thrown out when
a crater was dug, stream
across the pock-marked
landscape of Mercury.
The Moon-like surface
may hide a heavy core
like that of the Earth.

disastrous droughts and break up deserts by making a small change in weather patterns."

Caltech's Murray agrees that information gained from the study of climate on other planets can have a significant impact on man's future. "Climatic change is a critical question because of the growing food problems on Earth," he points out. "Looking back 30, 50, or 100 years from now, the results of planetary exploration, now considered esoteric, may come to be regarded as the most practical knowledge ever obtained for managing the destiny of man on his own world."

Observations of Venus' atmosphere already have alerted scientists to a possible danger in the Earth's atmosphere. In the upper atmosphere of Venus, *Mariner 10* discovered hydrogen chloride, a compound that is broken down into hydrogen and chlorine by the Sun's ultraviolet radiation. Chlorine, a powerful catalyst, causes oxygen to combine with carbon monoxide to form carbon dioxide on Venus.

After studying this reaction, scientists realized that a similar process could destroy the Earth's ozone shield. Ozone is an oxygen molecule that contains three oxygen atoms, rather than the normal two. High in the atmosphere, the ozone molecules absorb much of the Sun's ultraviolet radiation, completely blocking out the most dangerous rays. But ozone is highly unstable. Even small amounts of chlorine in our upper atmosphere could break it down into ordinary oxygen molecules that offer no protection against the radiation.

At first, no one worried, because no source of chlorine was known at those high altitudes. Then, researchers at the University of California at Irvine discovered in 1974 that chlorine can be released when sunlight breaks down the fluorocarbons used as propellants in spray cans. If the fluorocarbons work their way into the upper atmosphere, as some scientists believe they do, they could be a serious threat. Some scientists argue that thinning the ozone layer by as little as 10 per cent could result in thousands of additional cases of skin cancer each year, as well as cause detrimental environmental changes. Several studies now are underway to determine the true extent of the problem. If a danger does exist, we will have been warned of it by what scientists found in the atmosphere on Venus.

Planetary exploration, then, has produced surprises, delights, disappointments, and astonishments. The activity of the past decade has resulted in what one planetary scientist calls "the beginning of a new coherent perspective of the solar system."

In general, astronomers believe that the solar system formed some 4.6 billion years ago out of a large, slowly turning, nearly spherical cloud of dust and gas—the solar nebula. Something caused the cloud to collapse and, as it contracted, it began spinning faster. The rapid spinning caused it to flatten, eventually forming a thick disk at least 11.8 billion miles (19 billion kilometers) across. As the disk became dense enough to absorb its own radiation, temperatures at the center rose to at least 3450°F. (1900°C), hot enough to *vaporize* (turn to gas)

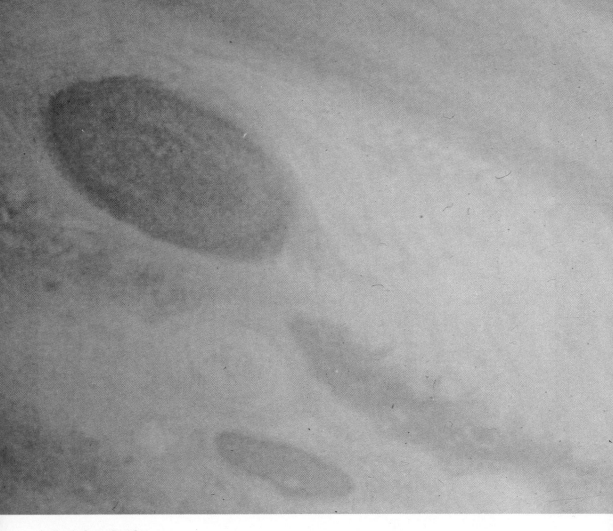

Jupiter's Great Red Spot towers above nearby clouds. It is probably a gigantic hurricane, several centuries old. Computer enhancement of a *Pioneer 11* photo gives the most detail scientists have seen.

any material in the vicinity. When the center became hot enough for nuclear reactions to occur, the Sun turned on.

Although astronomers generally agree on how stars like our Sun are born, the details of how planets form are more disputed. One prominent theory suggests that, as the spinning cloud cooled, various compounds condensed out of the hot gas, forming tiny pebbles that rained down and settled in a thin sheet in the mid-plane of the disk. At this point, the disk began to break up and the pebbles collided to form clusters perhaps 0.6 mile (1 kilometer) in diameter. As the clusters grew, they formed protoplanets, somewhat smaller than the Moon. Protoplanets collided and formed the inner planets—Mercury, Venus, Earth, and Mars—and perhaps rocky inner cores for such outer planets as Jupiter and Saturn. Heat in the center of the disk boiled away the lighter elements, such as hydrogen and ammonia, eliminating them from the rocks and atmospheres of the inner planets. These light elements collected farther out, around Jupiter, Saturn, and the other large planets and their satellites.

The greatest mystery for scientists concerns the origin and evolution of life in the solar system. If the 1976 *Viking* landers find living organisms on Mars, it will be one of the most important discoveries in history. It would indicate that the conditions scientists believe necessary for life to arise can exist somewhere besides the Earth, and that living creatures may inhabit many planets in the universe.

But if the *Viking* project fails to find signs of life, scientists will not despair. Sagan, for example, talks of molecules that are the building blocks of life "falling from the skies of Jupiter like manna from heaven." Suggesting that the color red may signal the potential for life on other worlds, Sagan points to laboratory experiments with chemical mixtures resembling the hydrogen-ammonia atmosphere of Jupiter –and, incidentally, similar to the original atmosphere on Earth. Bombarding these mixtures with charges of electricity or ultraviolet radiation produces a reddish goo that contains the complex hydrocarbon molecules that are the precursors of life. The rusty color matches that of the dark cloud bands that circle Jupiter.

As the two *Vikings* spin toward their rendezvous with Mars, scientists back on Earth busily rewrite textbooks on the solar system. The revisions are just beginning. Each new discovery brings in its wake new questions, and new ideas to be tested.

What do we do next to keep the revolution in planetary knowledge going? Gerald Wasserburg, a Caltech geophysicist, advocates a balanced series of explorations "to get the facts clearly missing in our knowledge about the inner planets, and to determine the composition and other basic information about the outer planets."

Virtually every planetary scientist wants a closer look at Saturn, Uranus, Neptune, and their satellites. These gaseous outer planets, with their strange frozen satellites, are quite different from the rocky inner planets. "We need to make a preliminary reconnaissance of all the large objects in our solar system," Sagan insists. "Some of the answers we seek must come from beyond Jupiter."

Only by getting to know all of its members will we be able to complete a coherent picture of the solar system. Toward this end, two *Mariner* spacecraft are due to leave for Jupiter and Saturn in 1977. *Pioneer 11* is already on its way to Saturn, and should arrive in 1979. In 1978, a *Pioneer* spacecraft will attempt to discover more about the atmosphere and surface of Venus. The National Aeronautics and Space Administration hopes to send a spacecraft to Uranus in 1979. Scientists also are studying information from two Russian spacecraft that reached Venus in October, 1975.

"It is no longer possible or desirable to consider Earth entirely apart from the other planets," says Goody. "We may never have a totally acceptable theory of the origin and early history of Earth, or the other planets. But it is our nature to keep learning more and more. Someday we may arrive at a point where we are content."

Then there will be other solar systems to explore.

Protecting Privacy in the Computer Age

By Alan F. Westin

Western nations have started to safeguard what may well be our most fundamental right against abuse by new technological tools

Scarcely a week went by during 1975 without a major news story about invasion of the citizen's right to privacy – the claim by individuals to decide what personal information to share with others. Even for Americans painfully educated by Watergate about the use of wiretaps, break-ins, dirty tricks, and "enemies lists," the 1975 disclosures were most disturbing.

There were revelations that government agencies had repeatedly invaded the privacy of millions of citizens. The U.S. Central Intelligence Agency illegally opened thousands of letters to and from Russia in a mail-interception operation in New York City between 1953 and 1973. A woman charged

that the Internal Revenue Service hired her in 1972 to spy on about 30 prominent Miami, Fla., public officials and uncover information about their sex lives and drinking habits. The attorney general disclosed that the Federal Bureau of Investigation (FBI) had planted spies, forged papers, leaked damaging material to reporters, and used other dirty tricks to disrupt the activities of certain political organizations between 1956 and 1971. The target groups included the American Communist Party, the Ku Klux Klan, the Southern Christian Leadership Conference, and the Students for a Democratic Society. The U.S. Senate Select Committee on Intelligence disclosed in November that the FBI had undertaken a campaign in the 1960s to discredit the late civil rights leader Martin Luther King, Jr. The FBI bugged King's hotel rooms many times and mailed tape recordings along with threatening unsigned notes to him. FBI officials acknowledged before the committee that such activities were illegal.

There were also disclosures during 1975 that private organizations invaded the privacy of individuals and groups. An automobile insurance company investigated a woman's private life and denied her a policy because she was living with a man without being married to him. A computer manufacturer sued a competitor who allegedly hired private detectives to wiretap the company's phones and gather trade secrets. A national loan company improperly used confidential personal data obtained from its income tax preparation service to solicit new loan business. Many employers refused to hire job applicants unless they took lie-detector tests.

Finally, the year was filled with stories about future threats to privacy. The head of the U.S. Passport Office set off alarms in February by suggesting that every American citizen should be required to carry a government identity card with photo, fingerprints, and identification number. A Department of Justice agency criticized FBI plans to manage, through a central telecommunications facility, the computerized criminal-history records of local and state police. Congressmen considering national health insurance plans voiced concern that future centralized health records be securely protected so that medical records remain confidential.

Public opinion polls documented how widely concern over privacy had spread by 1975. A Roper poll showed that 4 out of 5 Americans believed new laws were needed to require organizations to notify individuals that personal information is kept on file, to regulate the sharing of the information, and to let citizens see and challenge these records. A Louis Harris poll found that 1 out of every 2 Americans felt that their privacy was threatened.

Reflecting these public attitudes, President Gerald R. Ford warned in a speech in September, 1975, that a combination of well-intentioned new laws and new technology "threaten to strip the individual of his privacy or her privacy," reducing the individual "to a faceless set of digits in a monstrous network of computers." While "we cannot

Privacy reflects each person's need to be alone. But it must be balanced against the needs at other times for disclosure and for companionship.

The author:
Alan F. Westin is professor of public law at Columbia University and author of *Databanks in a Free Society* and *Privacy and Freedom.*

126

scuttle worth-while programs which provide essential help for the helpless and assist the deserving citizen," the President said, "we must protect every individual from excessive and unnecessary intrusions by a Big Brother bureaucracy." The extent of government's personal-record keeping had just been made public under the Federal Privacy Act of 1974, the federal government's first attempt to regulate data-banks containing personal information held by its agencies. In com-plying with the act, about 90 federal agencies disclosed that they held individual files on Americans in some 6,000 separate record systems.

More congressional committees and national commissions were in-vestigating privacy issues in 1975 than ever before. Committees in the United States studied government intelligence activities, national-security wiretapping, the privacy of bank records, police information systems, private health records, and arrest records. Similar committees in Australia, Canada, Great Britain, and other Western nations were also hard at work. Given such high concentration on privacy in 1975, we should come to grips with what we mean by the "right to privacy," and what we are doing to redefine and protect privacy in Western urbanized nations in the 1970s.

A t its most fundamental level, psychologists tell us, privacy reflects a person's need to be alone, away from other persons. At other times, we desperately need to communicate and we feel greatly deprived if we cannot share in the intimacy of family and friends. Sometimes we need to be with others even though we do not disclose our inner thoughts. We may seek out strangers in a bar or at a football game. Each person's need and desire for personal privacy changes from time to time, even from hour to hour, as he balances this need against his needs for disclosure and companionship.

Democratic societies allow each individual to strike his or her own balance, within limits, in deciding what personal information should be disclosed to others, when, and under what conditions. Such socie-ties recognize the individual's need to protect his privacy in order to develop his personality and talents effectively, to enjoy the intimacy of trusted relationships and obtain confidential advice, and to decide when he is ready to "go public" with his ideas. Democracies extend a similar right of privacy to voluntary associations so they can develop new ideas and places for fellowship, and provide for political expres-sion. Government itself has a claim to privacy for the temporary confi-dentiality of advisory communications and impending decisions. However, the importance of the public knowing what its representa-tives are doing, and how, generally requires rapid disclosure of gov-ernment action.

Throughout the past 2,000 years, this democratic tradition has com-peted with the authoritarian tradition in defining the relationship of authority to the individual, and thereby setting the basic framework for social balances regarding privacy. Such modern totalitarian states as Russia regard close surveillance of individual and group activity

and compulsory disclosure of thoughts as the legitimate function of a moral state. An editorial in *Pravda*, the Russian Communist Party newspaper, said only those who are "morally untidy" worry about privacy. Such societies collect extensive personal data on citizens and do not allow them to see and contest the state's records.

By contrast, democratic societies limit the power of such authorities as churches, governments, and employers to spy on individuals and groups. Yet, free societies have never treated privacy as an absolute right. They have had to balance three competing social values – the individual's need to be let alone, the government's need for personal information in order to act intelligently and fairly, and government's duty to monitor antisocial activity to protect lives, property, and public order. Balancing privacy, disclosure, and surveillance has been a major concern of law and politics in democratic societies for centuries.

This concept of balance is reflected directly in the way American law has dealt with privacy. A specified "right to privacy" appears neither in the Bill of Rights to the U.S. Constitution nor in the state constitutions during the nation's first century. Basically, courts protected privacy during the 1800s and early 1900s through the Fourth Amendment's guarantee against unreasonable search and seizure and the Fifth Amendment's guarantee of the right to remain silent and not incriminate oneself in any criminal case.

Technological advances – especially the revolution in microminiaturized electronic circuitry – undercut the physical limits and legal rules on which democracies depended to protect individual privacy.

In the 1950s and 1960s, the Supreme Court of the United States also began to defend privacy under the First Amendment's guarantee of freedom of expression – free speech, press, religion, assembly, and association. The court argued that an individual must be free to decide if and when he or she discloses personal expressions or beliefs for the First Amendment to have meaning. For government to force disclosure without a person's consent – sometimes even without his knowledge – would make a mockery of the First Amendment. Accordingly, the courts have let organizations keep membership lists private and allowed parents to decide about such matters as birth control and education for their children.

Simultaneously, legal decisions have extended the "due process of law" clause in the federal and state constitutions to cover an individual's access to information being kept about him or her. This principle of access to data gives any person judged in a criminal or civil proceeding, or whose employment, licensing, welfare, or other rights and opportunities are judged by government, the right to know the evidence used in those proceedings, and to inspect and challenge it.

While the courts continued to refine a legal definition of the citizen's right to privacy in the 1960s, a microelectronics revolution made available low-cost, easily hidden tools for dissolving the walls and windows that once helped ensure privacy. Complete radio transmitters were developed that are smaller than a matchbox but can operate continuously for a year, broadcasting room conversation over a distance of 50 yards (150 meters). Closed-circuit television cameras no larger than a cigarette package can send pictures to a nearby receiver. Nowhere is the threat clearer than in the enormous capacity of electronic computers to collect, store, manipulate, and distribute information, including personal data about individuals. Suddenly, the old physical limits and legal rules on which democracies relied to protect privacy have been outrun by technological advances.

If the issue were simply to regulate new technology and punish those who use these new tools for illegal personal or political gain, revising privacy laws would be a relatively easy matter. But there are usually difficult questions of social value to resolve. For example, when should government be entitled to tap telephone conversations to solve major crimes or avert threats to human life? What strict safeguards and controls should prevent abuses? What personal information—credit record, educational background, prior employment, and personal habits—is a government agency, an employer, or a licensing agency legitimately entitled to know, and how should such personal data be collected and stored?

Because records are kept on all of us, we can best trace the move to new definitions of privacy and protections by taking one example—control over personal-record keeping and computer databanks. The magnitude of the technological threat is best illustrated by the fact that a single computer system can now store a 20-page typewritten *dossier* (information file) on every man, woman, and child in the United States and retrieve any record in 10 seconds or less.

Such an increase in the power of data collection seemed to threaten many of the traditional protections that had evolved throughout American history. From the beginning, the United States rejected population registers and internal passports, which were common in Europe. It kept few police dossiers and almost no government dossiers in peacetime, and it cloaked the statistical census in strict confidentiality. It was an article of faith that much information about the American citizen was simply none of the government's business. A decision by the Supreme Court in 1881 prohibited congressional investigations from probing into "the private affairs of individuals."

But by the 1960s, the American way of life had changed fundamentally. Mass education programs created kindergarten-to-college "permanent records." The increased mobility of workers led employers to compile detailed personnel records. Such social welfare programs as the Social Security Act of 1935 led administrators to create huge record systems to identify, qualify, and monitor each participant. Detailed information began to flow freely among schools, employers, creditors, and government agencies.

Some observers saw the threat and began sounding alarms in the 1960s. They warned that computers made it easier to collect more detailed and sensitive personal data than had been feasible or affordable before and to create secret files and make secret decisions. Organizations with computer databanks could easily exchange information with one another. Many said these possibilities were, in fact, inevitable consequences of using computers in government, industry, and private organizations to improve efficiency and standardize records. Books on these themes were published not only in the United States, but also in Australia, Britain, Japan, and the Netherlands. Such international organizations as the United Nations joined the chorus.

The governments of most Western nations and some private organizations began studying the databank problem between 1969 and 1973. They came up with remarkably similar findings that experts considered still valid in 1975. They concluded that computerization of personal records and files had not yet created the revolutionary effects that the critics assumed were already taking place in the 1960s. They carefully noted that a combination of factors have limited the uses made of the computer's capacity. For example, because automation is a costly process, organizations computerize only the most objectively worded and frequently used data. Bureaus and departments within large organizations generally oppose putting the data they collect into someone else's central databank.

The study groups did agree, however, that Western industrial nations need to develop both private policies and public regulations to safeguard rights of privacy and confidentiality for personal information stored in large data systems, especially computerized systems. But they stressed that the key privacy or civil liberties issues involved in record keeping are not basically matters of technology, of computer files instead of paper folders. The computers only underscore the fact that the basic issues involve social values and public policy. The key issue is not whether to computerize data, but rather what personal information organizations such as police, universities, and banks should collect. Should they share that information with others inside the organization or with other organizations? When should individuals have the right to know that an organization has records on them? Should individuals have the right to inspect such records and challenge their accuracy, completeness, or relevance?

Although most Western nations share a common democratic tradition, they have begun to regulate computer databanks in ways that reflect important differences in their constitutional and legal systems, political cultures, and administrative traditions. For example, the Swedish and German people have confidence in powerful administrative agencies, state registration, and detailed codes of procedure. The British expect their government officials and private managers to observe codes of proper behavior. They stand ready to intervene with legal enactments and criminal penalties only if self-regulation proves inadequate. In the United States, a concept of fair information practices for federal agencies has developed out of long-standing American legal concepts that forbid unfair labor or trade practices, and rely on public notices, citizen complaints, and supervision by the courts through privately initiated lawsuits.

To restore the balance between the individual's right to privacy and government's need to know in order to protect the public, the 1970s have become a period of new regulation.

At one extreme is Britain. The Younger Committee on Privacy, a parliamentary group, has strongly endorsed public support for the right to privacy. But there has been no legislation and no major new court decisions. Lacking a common-law right of privacy, and pressed by economic problems, Britain's government is not likely to act soon. Privacy is being protected through the enunciation of codes of good practice for organizations using computers, rather than by establishing stiff civil and criminal penalties.

Britain's fellow Commonwealth members Australia and Canada similarly had no national privacy laws at the end of 1975. However, Canada had legislation pending to cover federal department data files, and Australia built privacy safeguards into Medibank, the computerized National Health Scheme that began operating in July.

Sweden took the opposite regulatory approach. Sweden's National Data Act of 1973 created a Data Inspection Board (DIB), whose nine members are appointed by the king. All private automated personal-data systems must be registered and licensed. The law also covers all

government databanks except those operated by the *Riksdag* (parliament). No databank is licensed if the board concludes that there might be "undue intrusion" into the privacy of the people covered. The DIB also sets security standards for automated systems, regulates transfers between automated and manual systems, and serves as what the Swedes call a "wailing wall" to receive complaints from anyone who believes that the data law is being violated. Sweden's law makes it a crime to commit "data trespass"–enter a data system without authorization to obtain, alter, or destroy data. The punishment is up to two years in jail.

Already the DIB has denied licenses to computerized dating bureaus that collect information about the sexual preference of their clients, even with their compliance. The DIB ruled in 1975 that personal information on some 80,000 Swedes could not be sent to Britain for the preparation of encoded health identity cards because Britain's privacy laws are so weak. The DIB also stopped a multinational firm from putting Swedish personnel records into a central computer system in West Germany. In several West German states, data-protection commissioners oversee government data systems and protect citizens' rights, but West Germany does not have national privacy laws like Sweden's.

In the United States, the extent of databank regulation falls between that in Britain and Sweden. The Federal Privacy Act of 1974, which went into effect on Sept. 27, 1975, requires virtually all federal agencies to disclose their information activities, justify their collection and use of data in public proceedings, and allow individuals to see almost all of their records. Telling the citizen what the federal agencies are doing is at the heart of U.S. fair information practices.

When it asks an individual to supply personal information, each agency must tell that person what legal authority authorizes the solicitation, whether supplying the information is compulsory or voluntary, and how the information is to be used. At least once each year, each agency must publish a notice about each system of records it maintains, indicating the system's name and location, the categories of persons covered, who uses the information and how, and how the data is stored, retrieved, protected, and eliminated. The public notice must also spell out procedures by which a citizen can find out if he or she has a record and, if so, how it can be inspected and contested. The law provides tough penalties for federal officials who knowingly violate its provisions. Violators may be fined up to $5,000, and individuals may sue in federal court and collect damages and legal fees if their privacy is willfully violated.

In addition to implementing general codes of fair information practices for federal agencies, the United States has also moved to protect privacy and due-process rights in specified areas of social activity. For example, the Family Educational Rights and Privacy Act passed in 1974 checked the widespread practice by which teachers and other school personnel put highly subjective evaluations and personal observations about students into the students' files, then made that information available—without the knowledge or consent of the students or their parents—to potential employers, licensing authorities, government security investigators, and many others. The law gives students over 18 and parents of school-age children the right to see their school and college records and requires their permission for such information to be released to others.

Major controversies arose over application of the law. Many university administrators backed faculty members who told students that they would not write frank recommendations unless the student signed a waiver giving up the right to see what had been written. Consequently, college placement offices issued recommendation forms that stated the student's right under the law and also provided a place to sign and waive the right to see the letter. The student must thus decide which is more important to him—his right to see his records or a recommendation that may vitally affect his career. Supporters of the right-of-access principle denounced these practices as a violation of the spirit of the law and possibly of its letter as well. Test cases have been filed to get court rulings on their legality.

The U.S. Congress has also moved to give people some control over personal information gathered by consumer credit agencies. The Fair Credit Reporting Act of 1970 provides that if a person is denied credit, employment, or insurance on the basis of a report prepared by a commercial reporting agency, he or she must be notified of the report and the agency that made it. The individual can inspect a copy of the report and require the agency to reinvestigate. Should he still dispute the facts, he can enter his own statement in the agency's file, and it must be included when the agency sends out a report. If still aggrieved by the agency's version of events, he can sue in federal court challenging the truth of the report.

Many legislators consider the 1970 act too weak and are proposing amendments that would allow greater access to credit records and broader legal grounds for contesting a credit refusal. Further legislation has been proposed to extend the fair information concept of the federal privacy act to protect privacy in arrest, bank, health, and personnel records. For example, liberal Congressman Edward I. Koch (D., N.Y.) and conservative Barry M. Goldwater, Jr., (R., Calif.) are jointly sponsoring a bill that would extend the provisions of the act to state and local governments and private organizations. State governments, such as in Minnesota, have enacted laws governing state databanks containing information on individuals.

Court cases will decide just what each of these acts means. And with a growing awareness of the issues, administrators in unregulated sectors are critically examining their record-keeping procedures with an eye to adopting rules and practices that might convince legislators to exempt them from future legal controls.

Alarms have sounded throughout the Western world and study groups have identified the issues. The late 1970s are unfolding as a period of regulation by legislation, by court decision, and by administrative self-regulation. New rules must be devised to control intrusion by government and private parties, the use of wiretapping and other physical surveillance techniques, the use of lie detectors and personality tests by employers, and the collection and use of personal data in dossiers and databanks. We must protect privacy as we move toward an increasingly checkless and cashless society, in which the electronic records of our daily business transactions will contain full profiles of our lives.

We may not be quite the single "electronic village" that Marshall McLuhan, the Canadian expert on mass communications, said we have become as a result of computer and communications technologies. But most of the people in the Free World recognize that it will take creative and sustained action to keep alive the tradition of personal and group privacy in the computer age.

Russia Today: Reality and the Fading Dream

By Mark Gayn

Russian citizens live in a split-level society as they learn to exist in two different worlds—official and private

I was having dinner at the home of a Russian family during a recent tour of that country, and their 17-year-old son was describing his morning at the movies. With other senior students from half a dozen Moscow high schools, he had been taken to see the supercolossal film, *The Difficult Road to Peace*, featuring the Communist Party general secretary, Leonid I. Brezhnev. Each pupil had to buy his own 30-kopeck (43-cent) ticket to see this celluloid hymn of praise to the Russian leader. It showed his journey to the United States, France, and West Germany in determined pursuit of peace and détente. He was seldom off the screen–cheered by adoring multitudes, showered with flowers, greeted by the officials of Western governments, and shaking the hands of innumerable foreign admirers.

Such films are nothing new for the Russian moviegoer. They were produced after each of Nikita S. Khrushchev's major trips abroad. But this time, the audience reaction was unexpected. As Brezhnev was shown delivering one speech after another in foreign capitals, the students began to shout *"Oohrah!"* ("Hurrah!") at the wrong places. Still later, things got out of hand. There was loud laughter, hooting, and mimicry at climactic points in the oratory.

Brezhnev has an odd speech defect. He swallows some vowels in long words. He says "S-tsializm" and "K-mmunizm," and soon the words echoed in the hall, "S-tsializm, S-tsializm, oohrah!" One youth shouted to a friend seated three rows ahead, "Hey, Sasha, you think the jaw operation helped him?" (Moscow rumor has it that Brezhnev has had operations on his jaw.) Sasha yelled back, "Not sure. But the teeth are definitely false."

The teachers were frantic. They ran up and down the aisles asking the pupils to quiet down. But the youngsters were now beyond control, and the hooting and jeering continued. When *The Difficult Road* at last ended, and the lights went on, the teachers sighed with relief.

Why this extraordinary scene? Was it a display of contempt for Brezhnev? Had these Russian youths tapped a public vein of resentment unsuspected by their elders? I was assured it was not so. The answers are far more complex.

The 17-year-old explained to me at dinner that "when it comes to propaganda, most youths are cynics." As for Brezhnev, he said, the young actually hold him in some esteem; he is a *dyelovoi muzhik* (businesslike peasant), which is a compliment in Russia.

The adults in the room offered other explanations. The teen-agers, they said, resented having to pay 30 kopecks to see a film they would not have gone to see on their own. The young people are restless, and they find such official movies a stupefying bore. "Our youth has changed," someone finally said, "while our propaganda remains where it was decades ago."

This is one of the keys to what is happening in this vast and dynamic nation. Russian society is changing as a result of the technological revolution, a growing affluence, and a new mobility. But the political framework remains unaltered.

Most of the Russian sociologists I talked with insisted there has been no radical change. "Although living conditions may improve, a Socialist society will remain unchanged," they told me. Yet I have traveled in Russia many times, and I have seen various changes taking place that no Russian official will recognize publicly. In fact, an entire generation has come into life since Joseph Stalin's death in 1953, a generation that does not remember the dictator, the terrifying sound of a midnight knock on the door, or, indeed, World War II.

The unruly scene at the Brezhnev film was just one symptom of these changes. While Stalin was alive, nobody dared jest about him. Now, a teen-ager reels off half a dozen current jokes at Brezhnev's

The author:
Mark Gayn, who has visited Russia many times, is the foreign affairs columnist of *The Toronto Star.*

expense. At night, the young turn on short-wave radios and listen to broadcasts from the British Broadcasting Corporation, the Voice of America, Radio Free Europe, or Deutsche Welle. If a boy turns his set on too loud and is reminded that the neighbors might hear, he may retort, "They're listening to the same broadcasts."

Like sons, like fathers. A doctor told me about a rainy night in a tourist camp when he went to his car to listen to a West German broadcast of excerpts from Alexander I. Solzhenitsyn's book, *The Gulag Archipelago,* an indictment of Stalin's slave-labor camps. The antenna of the doctor's short-wave set protruded through the half-open window. In a few minutes, a bit uneasily, he saw the approaching figure of a man in a shiny leather coat (favored by members of the secret police). The man reached the car, and said formally, "Comrade, do you mind if I listen, too?" Soon, a small circle of people ringed the car, listening to Solzhenitsyn's harrowing recital.

Tuning in on Western broadcasts is known in Russia as "listening to the voices." Anyone who knows the basic principles of electronics can adapt a Russian-made radio to pick up Western broadcasts. If not, a university instructor told me, "You can always find an ex-serviceman who studied electronics in the army. For a bottle of vodka, he'll fix the set for you."

The youth of Russia—open to new ideas, fashions, and values, and not tied to memories of the past—are playing a major role in effecting change, just as youth have effected changes in many other countries. They have rising expectations and want comforts not yet available to most of the Russian people. They are thus one of the keys to the continuing social change occurring in Russia.

Political parades are a frequent event in Russia, and political posters are found on every street and factory wall, but few people stop to read them or to look at them anymore.

The official view of Russian youth conflicts with reality. For example, the official position was put to me by Alexander B. Chakovsky, the vigorous editor of the *Literaturnaya Gazeta* (*Literary Gazette*) and a man of few doubts. He compared the Vanya (Johnnie) of today with the Vanya of 25 years ago:

"The Vanyas of our day are more intellectual, better educated, more curious, and better dressed. They own more things. They are eager to move—and they tend to move east. In the United States, the young once went west, but they were driven by the gold fever, by the desire to get rich. Perhaps some of our young people, too, go east to build the Baykal-Amur Railway because of the high pay, but that's not the main reason. Ask them, and they will tell you that they're working for Communism."

Party imagemakers such as Chakovsky like to describe the youth as *romantiki* (dreamers), young men and women driven by a sense of adventure to explore new frontiers in Siberia or the Arctic. It is a word used to tempt them from the comfortable cities of European Russia into the wilderness of Asian Russia. And many young people are drawn by the lure of the wild, by danger and adventure, as many young Americans were tempted to go west a century ago. But the romantiki of today demand fashionable high boots, blue jeans, and a good choice of American jazz recorded from Voice of America broadcasts. And the restless ones quickly drift back to the comfortable cities once they have had a look at Asian Russia, sailed its immense rivers, climbed its peaks, and searched for its oil and iron.

The realists insist that the young are apolitical, tired of party clichés, and eager for privacy. The ambitious among the young do join

The pursuit of well-being, combined with increased availability of money but shortage of automobiles, leads to the popularity of sidecar motorcycles on the streets of Russia.

The increasing number of modern, well-built homes and factories whet the interest of the average Russian in acquiring the comforts of modern life. A lunchroom at the Kama River truck plant and the new scientific research city, Akademgorodo, are among the many examples of such modern facilities.

the Komsomol (Young Communist League), which offers the path to a career in the party machine. But most youths attend only the required minimum of political seminars and meetings, and they read few editorials in the party press. Most of them are far less preoccupied with the triumph of Communism than with jazz, the purchase of a good motorcycle for a trip to the Baltic or the Black Sea, or—especially—with living space of their own.

There was a time when asceticism and self-denial were hallmarks of this lean, revolutionary society. Every resource was needed to industrialize and arm, and there was little to spare for the individual. Necessity became a virtue. Three and four families were crowded into an apartment, and stores displayed half-empty shelves. The people were told that sacrifices had to be made for the sake of survival. But now, half a century later, Russians insist that their needs, and even comforts, be met. And the leadership of the country can no longer ignore these expectations.

This poses two problems, one material and the other ideological, for Kremlin officials. The material problem is that Russia still does not produce enough goods to satisfy the demand. The puzzle for ideologists is: How can this perfect Socialist society reconcile its ideals with barefaced consumerism?

A visitor quickly discovers the universal hunger for *vyeshchi* (things) in Russia. Almost every dinner conversation inevitably drifts to a discussion of items–nylon shirts, fur hats, or good shoes–that have suddenly appeared at this or that store. More frequently, the talk centers on shortages of such things as chinaware and razor blades, tomatoes in October, or skis in November.

While we in the West suffer from a glut of tape recorders, transistor radios, and automobiles, gleeful Russians are just discovering them. I heard exclamations of envy when a man boasted that he used influence to buy a car out of turn. Others in the group still had to wait from 6 to 12 months before they could get new automobiles, for which they had each paid the full price–about 7,200 rubles ($9,400)–in advance. It is such consumers who create a problem for the ideologists. As Chakovsky puts it bluntly:

"*Vyeshchism,* or the pursuit of well-being as a goal, is an especially acute problem for us, for it runs counter to our efforts to create a new Soviet man and his goal of Communism. In the West, there are men who yearn to accumulate things. We find that such ideas conflict with our own social objectives."

Yuri Zamoshkin, a leading sociologist, told me about a public opinion poll he conducted among 1,700 workers in an industrial city in the Ural Mountains and among 500 students and their families in Moscow. Their responses proved a conclusion that was predictable, that pleased the party, and that startled at least this listener.

"We found people who bought because others did," Zamoshkin reported. "We found fetishism–purchase of shiny novelties. The total of all these was 4 to 5 per cent. Some others, on the contrary, were ascetic–they felt we already have too many things. But the vast majority felt that to buy things was to help develop Socialism, to improve one's ability to mix with others in society, to help develop one's abilities. Unlike the people in the West, we have no cult of things. If we buy a car, it is so that we can visit our friends, and thus bind our society together."

I told Zamoshkin that I bought my car because I, too, wanted to go places and visit friends, so there was no difference between my brand of consumerism and that of Ivan Ivanov. My argument was dismissed out of hand. But two facts impressed me: While the young people in Western nations have been in open rebellion against consumerism during the past 10 years, the Russian people are only now becoming familiar with consumerism–and enjoying it hugely. And the Communist Party sees consumerism as such a threat to its faith that it has to recruit sociologists to justify Soviet vyeshchism while denouncing it in the West. Of course, putting a red jacket on it doesn't really change the reality of consumerism.

Just as vigorously as they deny the existence of consumerism in Russia, the party leaders argue that theirs is a classless society. In fact, it is more stratified than American society. Perhaps one-third of the people—the bulk of the collective farmers, construction workers, unskilled laborers, and pensioners—live on incomes that would be well below the poverty level in Western countries. At the other end of society, the élite own comfortable suburban *dachas* (summer homes), go to special hospitals when they are ill, and shop in special stores that offer everything from sturgeon to imported shoes.

These class distinctions were graphically illustrated for me in an incident at Tyumen airport in Siberia, where all planes were grounded because the airport runways were turned into sheets of ice by a blizzard. There I met a famous member of the élite. He was an

The hunger for *vyeshchi,* or things, is universal in Russia today. Even in small stores such as this one in Gorodnya, near Moscow, customers keep the clerks busy.

urbane, handsome man who had supervised the construction of dams, refineries, and mills in South America and the Middle East, as well as in Russia. He was in Siberia for the purpose of erecting an immense synthetic rubber plant.

We spent the stormy night in the VIP room, trading stories and drinking champagne and vodka. Every now and then, the man's chauffeur came in to bring the gloomy latest word on the state of the runways, and to receive the injunction, "But don't you go away, Kolya, until I take off. If we remain iced in, I may still want to return to the hotel."

Kolya sat in the car throughout the night because the airport building was packed with people squatting or sleeping on the floor and on the steps leading to our waiting room. Not once did the man suggest that Kolya take a nap on one of the vacant couches in our suite.

Prefabricated high-rise apartment buildings have replaced the shacks and hovels of old Czarist Russia. But the modern country still has a housing shortage, and apartments are small by American standards.

We finally took off for Moscow long after daybreak. And when we arrived, the Very Important Person gave me a lift to my hotel in another official car that was waiting for him. Its driver had arrived the previous night and, like Kolya, waited 8 or 10 hours for our plane. I tried to visualize the same scene in North America, but could not.

Just as the growing class distinctions no longer reflect Communist ideals, neither do relations between the sexes. World War II tended to loosen earlier sexual constraints. So did such huge postwar youth projects as the development of virgin lands, which brought millions of young men and women together in unforgivably bad living conditions, with little diversion other than sex and vodka. The automobile, too, has helped to break old moral restraints, as have tourist camps and the growing number of private rooms and apartments.

However, the Communist Party, and those who preach its ideals, continue to pursue a line the Puritans might have envied, acting as if Russia were a mid-Victorian rather than a revolutionary state. A "Kinsey" report on the new Russian sex habits? Perish the thought. One such study was made in 1926, another some 40 years later. But both were circumspect. One can find published records of, say, pregnancy in U.S. and Canadian high schools. Clinics in Russia also keep these statistics, but they are released only to scholars—and, says one sociologist, "If I wanted to publish them, I could have trouble."

Russian high schools offer virtually no sex education, except in the more broad-minded Baltic republics—Estonia, Latvia, and Lithuania —which provide a modest program. Leningrad runs the only counseling center for those about to be married. It offers two lectures—one on the economics of married life, the other on sex methods. But it is not widely advertised, and few young couples attend.

"We may be on the threshold of a sexual revolution," one Russian sociologist told me, "but how much sexual attitudes have changed no one in this country knows precisely." Some scholars blame the Academy of Pedagogical Sciences for this because it has published no textbooks on sex. But the responsibility really lies with the Communist Party. To admit that sex morals have been loosened is to chip away at its idealized image of Soviet youth, and this might be socially destructive. As a result of census studies published in 1975, the party has had to lift a corner of the veil on the sexual byways of Soviet youth. Although they seek divorce less frequently than do the middle-aged, many young people are said to have a "frivolous" attitude toward marriage ("if it doesn't work, we'll just get divorced"). In general, millions of Russians are said to be living together out of wedlock. Thus, in the latest census, 1.3 million more women than men said they were married. The divorce rate, though not yet as high as that in the United States, has already reached 28 in 100 marriages.

The sexual revolution is but one of a number of social phenomena that are kept hidden in Russian society. There is an undercurrent of anti-Semitism that no one admits, nourished by the official anti-Israel campaign. And no one talks about the way youth are now making a cautious reacquaintance with religion. I saw churches filled with young people, not worshiping, but at least being attentive. I was told by one observer that they are turning to the church in their "search for inner tranquility." Whether this is a true explanation or not, the fact remains that the young now flock to the churches on major holidays.

But contrary to a popular belief in the West, the Russian people are not rebellious, or even bitterly discontented. They demand that their material expectations be met—and they are being satisfied, if only slowly and inadequately. Reports of Russian dissenters, secret trials, underground literature, and packed exhibits of anti-Establishment art are true, but they distort reality by magnifying the scale of the dissent.

Samizdat, the body of underground literature passed from hand to hand, is a fascinating example of how dissent operates in Russia's cultural and political life. In Moscow, a mimeographed transcript of Solzhenitsyn's account of Stalinist terror may cost 50 rubles ($72). The work is taperecorded from Western broadcasts, typed out, and then secretly mimeographed by young secretaries in government offices. The risks are great, but the rewards are tempting.

Yet, only a limited number of people buy such transcripts. And a group of well-placed intellectuals, all of whom admire Solzhenitsyn's genius, agree that only a small fraction of 1 per cent of Russia's 259-million people were at all troubled when Solzhenitsyn was driven into exile in the West.

But, though Russian society is not rebellious, it has long learned to accommodate itself to bureaucratic abuses by adopting a double standard. To illustrate this, a senior official described for me a *vstrechny*

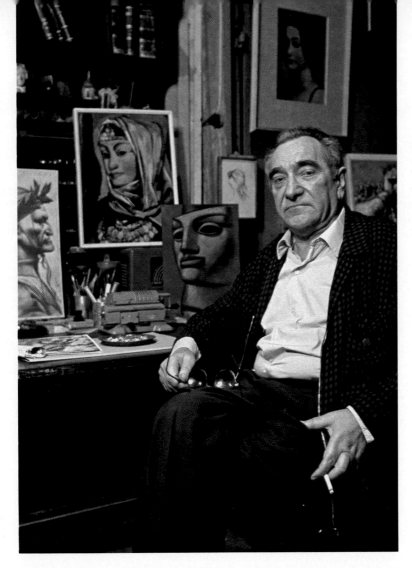

Sergei Kobuladze, painter and professor of art in Tbilisi, is a member of the upper class in this officially classless state. His income brings him comparative affluence.

plan (counterplan). Each year, the government planners in Moscow set production targets for every factory and farm in the country. And, in this curious Soviet ritual, workers and peasants then hold mass meetings and "unanimously" vote resolutions for counterplans that are much higher than the ones dictated from Moscow.

"The planners," the official said, "tell a shoe factory, 'Your daily production is to be 10,000 pairs a day.' The workers then protest, 'Oh, no, that's not enough. We will undertake to make 15,000 pairs a day for our Socialist motherland.' But, in fact, both the planners in Moscow and the workers know well that, in the end, the factory will produce only 7,500 pairs a day."

This ritual, or double standard, is reflected in private lives. Even members of the Communist Party élite, who during the day speak only in lofty clichés and try to devise ways to strengthen the loyalty and dedication of the people, make cruel jests about the clichés and the system at night among their trusted friends.

Despite official denials, Russian life is changing, and young Russians long to imitate Western ways. State-owned stores in Moscow display clothing like that in the West, and elaborate weddings, once censured in Russia, are very much in style.

As part of this accommodation to Soviet life, Russian society has become cellular, particularly in the big cities. This is especially true among intellectuals, many of whom are now grouped into informal bands, or cells, of 10 or 20 people bound only by friendship and total trust. In these groups, a person can criticize the latest bit of bureaucratic stupidity, tell the latest antisystem jokes, recount the latest instance of official injustice, pass on a *Samizdat* item, or criticize a new policy. There, too, they hear the latest reports from "the voices"—the broadcasts that come from the West.

Such circles were unimaginable under Stalin. A man could trust neither his close friends nor his family. This fear has vastly diminished today, no matter what some commentators in the West might say, and the cells have become safety valves that enable the new urban intelligentsia, in and out of the Communist Party, to air its complaints and resentments against the government.

Yet the social changes taking place in Russia have not been accompanied by any comparable political change. The nation still is ruled much as it has been for more than 50 years. The party machine retains its monopoly of power, and Communist ideologists resist change. But one finds a gap between society and the party, between the governed and the governors. It is almost as if the people and the party live on different planets. They are in close contact during office hours. Even after work, the party tries to involve the people by summoning them to seminars and meetings.

But the people avoid involvement. They may attend a meeting at 5 P.M. at which speakers denounce Solzhenitsyn. But at 9 P.M., they will listen to "the voices" reading excerpts from Solzhenitsyn's works indicting the Soviet system. The people may join in official denunciations of the "decay and immorality" of American "imperialism," but they continue to admire the *Amerikantsi,* and listen to the Voice of America "to get the real story." This does not detract from their passionate nationalism, but it does reflect their admiration of Western culture and the things it produces, and their distrust of propaganda.

Along with this goes every Russian's insatiable curiosity about Soviet society. But if the party regards a problem as "sensitive," this curiosity goes unsatisfied. I asked half a dozen young women at an Intourist Russian travel agency office to recommend a play. They all told me that *Last July in Chulimsk* was the best show in town. I found it to be a third-rate *Peyton Place* revolving around life in a small provincial town. The play opened with extramarital sex and closed with unpunished rape. The amazing thing about the play, however, was the impact it had on the young women who commended it to me. Obviously, it touched them deeply.

A few days later, I met Fyodor Konstantinov, an old-time hardliner, party philosopher, and ex-editor of the party magazine, *Kommunist.* Konstantinov denied there had been any breach in the puri-

Although few Russians use drugs, drinking is a problem. The walls of this cafe in Tbilisi are decorated with primitive art rather than the officially sanctioned "socialist realism."

tanical ways of his society. "Oh, sure enough, you might see couples walking hand in hand on Gorki Street," he said. "Or perhaps a young man might even steal a kiss on a girl's cheek. But that is all. Our young people remain good." When I told him about the play, he dismissed it brusquely. Unfortunately, it is men like Konstantinov who set the ideological line.

It is also men like him who have made sociology an abused orphan among the Russian sciences. Typical of what happens in this field is the case of a young woman sociologist who became interested in a textile town that had scores of women to each man. The scholar took a job there, and soon began to unravel a story of deep psychological maladjustment and nervous breakdowns. When she returned from the town to work on her report, she was forced out of the institute at which she worked and her findings were locked up in "closed" files.

The party's position is logical. Its authority rests on a rigid dogma and general acceptance of the images it has created. It cannot allow any of these to be challenged. This is why the party stalwarts will not accept the free exchange of men and ideas that the West expects to see as a result of détente. And this is why it will not allow sociological studies that might show its people the tremendous changes taking place in Russia. Not surprisingly, then, Russian sociologists turn to studies of such "safe" subjects as American society or that of under-developed countries.

In summary, Russian society today has three notable features. While society continues to change, the nature and scope of this change is largely concealed from the public. The people, moreover, have learned to live on two different levels, official and private, which do not touch. Finally, social change has not been accompanied by any comparable political change. Détente with the West is having little, if any, effect on Russian political life, and I doubt that it will have any.

Party ideologists hate *convergence*—narrowing of the gap between Soviet and Western society. They denounce Western scholars who suggest that convergence is underway. They try to persuade their people that, while great powers with differing social systems can live side by side in peace, the ideological battle must go on with undiminished fury. Any other course would compel them to concede that Soviet society is drifting closer to our capitalist ways—and agree that there is some merit in the capitalist system.

But government leaders must eventually make some political concessions to account for the social changes that are taking place. These changes are a natural outgrowth of modernization and industrialization, and they reflect a natural desire for more goods, privacy, and individual freedom. In fact, Russian society is now going through many of the same torments, discoveries, and revolutions that the West went through decades ago. Even if the ideologists refuse to acknowledge it, Russian society is steadily becoming more and more like our own in the West.

A Year
In Perspective

THE YEAR BOOK casts a backward glance at
the furors, fancies, and follies of yesteryear. The
coincidences of history so revealed offer substantial
proof that, though the physical world continually
changes, human nature—in all its inventiveness,
amiability, and even perversity—remains fairly
constant, for better or worse, throughout the years.

1875

Rough Seas, Safe Harbor

By Paul C. Tullier

Neither domestic storms nor worldwide tempests could disrupt the birthday voyage of America's ship of state

Anniversaries, to those who cherish them, serve a threefold purpose. They are the pinnacles from which one compares the present with the past and by so doing places the past in its proper perspective. They are the way stations at which one pauses to take stock of the present and evaluate the role one plays in it. They are the milestones from which one can seek the potentials of an all-too-elusive future.

In 1975, the United States stood at just such a three-way point as it approached the 200th anniversary of its nationhood. That such a point had been reached was unanimously conceded. There was less unanimity over the ways in which the occasion should be celebrated. Some favored pageantry, re-enactments of great events that would turn the American Revolution Bicentennial celebration into a self-congratulatory worship of the past. Others, not convinced that the past was flawless, proposed that the occasion be used to define contemporary problems and resolve them with contemporary techniques. A third group found neither approach satisfactory. They thought the occasion should be ignored or given only a sidewise glance. "With money tight, Social Security benefits eroding, the cost of food rising," wrote one such disenchanted citizen to *The New York Times*, "why continue federal funds for America's Bicentennial celebration? Besides, what is there really to celebrate in America today?"

What indeed? It was a rhetorical question that brought indignant reactions from readers who deplored the writer's "un-Americanism" and "unheard of insolence not previously recorded in American history." The question—and the reactions—were truly contemporary. But they were not unprecedented—as a glance into the past would have

National concerns in 1875 included (clockwise) health, government scandals, vanishing wildlife, and the search for spiritual truths.

revealed. The same element of cynicism and disenchantment toward the Centennial celebration had made itself heard in 1875 in *Leslie's Illustrated Weekly Newspaper*, a respected journal of its day. "What," demanded an anonymous complainant 100 years ago, "are we to boast of, when our Centennial celebration comes, if all we have to show the nations of the world as a result of 100 years of freedom is...political corruption, financial skulduggery, and the drifting of a constantly inflated currency toward the bottomless gulf in which the French *assignats* [promissory notes] sank?"

In many respects, it was a justifiable complaint. In 1875, the United States was still reeling from the aftereffects of the Credit Mobilier scandal and the ensuing financial panic that had plummeted the purchasing power of the dollar to a new low. Of political corruption there was plenty; no better example could be offered than that of the Whiskey Ring scandal, which exploded in the public eye on May 1. High officials in the Treasury Department and others had collaborated with the nation's major whiskey distillers over a three-year period to defraud the U.S. government of millions of dollars in tax revenue. The scandalous collusion–and payoffs–had even reached into the White House via General Orville E. Babcock, President Ulysses S. Grant's private secretary. It was yet another blemish on the record of the Grant Administration, for all of which the President, in an apologetic end-of-term farewell letter to Congress, accepted responsibility but insisted (as President Richard M. Nixon would do almost verbatim about a hundred years later) that he was guilty only "of errors of judgment, not of intent."

This cheerless news at home was depressing enough to the average reader. News from abroad–of wars, pestilence, and famine–did little to reassure even those who had hoped that world conditions might offer something to celebrate. In Italy, a threatened eruption of Mount Vesuvius overshadowed news that Italian troops were being armed with modern repeater rifles. Russia was also experimenting with armaments, including a circular ironclad vessel for harbor defense that measured 99.2 feet (30 meters) in diameter with a spar deck rising 2.6 feet (79 centimeters) above the water line. Turkey had troops in Bosnia, where an insurrection was raging. Great Britain, which then had 46 colonial governments scattered over four continents, was having difficulties with rebellious Ashanti tribesmen in West Africa. Spain was in the throes of a government upheaval involving succession to the throne; the Carlists were determined that their man (Don Carlos) would wear the crown. In perennially drought-stricken India, 500,000 persons perished from starvation. An outbreak of cholera in Poland resulted in 26,000 deaths.

Switzerland's livestock was being ravaged by a cattle plague so virulent that all cattle fairs were suspended. In Australia, on the other hand, wild horses were reproducing so rapidly that farmers had to kill them in order to protect the crops. The reverse was true in Germany.

The author:
Paul C. Tullier is Managing Editor of THE WORLD BOOK YEAR BOOK.

Great Britain's Queen Victoria busied herself with dynastic marriages in 1875, and Germany's Otto von Bismarck charted Europe's fate. Meanwhile, civil war raged in Spain, and Russia tested new naval armaments.

A decree published on March 4, 1875, prohibited the export of horses because of a growing shortage. The decree was heartily approved by Germany's Iron Chancellor, Otto von Bismarck, who was recovering from a gunshot wound inflicted by an insane barrel maker who had attacked him near the town of Bad Kissingen.

And yet, despite such dismal developments, the year offered diversions, either vicariously or through direct participation. The vicarious pleasures included royalty watching. The emperor of Japan was especially fond of a donkey, imported from Georgia, that was guaranteed not to buck. The khedive (ruler) of Egypt was in such financial straits that he was forced to sell all of his remaining shares in the Suez Canal –44 per cent–to the British. King Kalakaua of Hawaii, whose recent visit to the United States had made him the first royal potentate to visit American shores, had just signed a protocol with the United States permitting it to establish a coaling and naval station at a small inlet called Pearl Harbor. England's Queen Victoria, who spent much time arranging dynastic weddings, had just presided over the marriage of the Duke of Edinburgh, her second son, to Maria, the only daughter of Russia's Czar Alexander II. Soprano Adelina Patti sang at the wedding.

If royalty watching was one form of escape from the trials and tribulations of the times, the arts offered an even more rewarding one. The Paris Opéra, an opulent citadel of music designed by Charles Garnier, opened its doors in 1875. Hans von Bülow, the celebrated German piano virtuoso and conductor, was concertizing in piano recitals in the United States where, among other things, he introduced Peter Ilich Tchaikovsky's *Concerto No. 1 in B flat minor* for piano and orchestra to Americans at the Music Hall in Boston on October 25. Richard Wagner had just been commissioned by conductor Theodore Thomas to compose an American Centennial March for the opening of the Centennial Exposition in Philadelphia in 1876.

A memorable failure in 1875 was the première of Georges Bizet's *Carmen* at the Opéra-Comique in Paris. The critics tore it to shreds as "devoid of color, undistinguished in melody, and undramatic." Johannes Brahms had better luck with his *Ein deutsches Requiem*, which was sung complete for the first time in America on January 24. The audience greeted with sustained applause the Liederkranz Singing Society, which performed the work at their hall in New York City. Also warmly welcomed was Gilbert and Sullivan's *Trial by Jury*, which was given in New York City on November 15. Its first performance was at the Savoy Theatre in London on March 25, 1875.

Jacques Offenbach's operas *La Grande Duchesse de Gérolstein* and *Robinson Crusoe* served as vehicles for the New York season's musical novelty: a children's group from south of the Rio Grande called the Mexican Juvenile Opera Company. The company's demure *prima donna*, one Señorita Nina y Morón, was 8 years old. Another children's group— this one all boys—was making news on what would 100 years later be called off-Broadway. The youngsters, most of them messengers or newspaper hawkers, had joined forces to form The Grand Duke's Opera House Company, which was housed on Barter Street near Park. The hall, a low subterranean room entered by a rickety staircase, was owned and managed by the boys, who also served as stage carpenters, money takers, ushers, and actors. On the strictly dramatic side, Edwin Booth was appearing in *Hamlet* and *Julius Caesar*. He had ushered in the new year by burning, piece by piece, the contents of his brother John Wilkes Booth's wardrobe trunk. (An embalmed body, allegedly that of John Wilkes Booth, President Abraham Lincoln's assassin, was being toured around the country as a profitable sideshow attraction.)

Bowling, one of America's oldest sports, was a nationwide diversion pursued in dingy alleys as well as on the flawlessly manicured lawns of the upper classes. The game's rules, however, were chaotic and often conflicting until they were standardized on Nov. 13, 1875. Horse racing gained status when a new race track, known as Churchill Downs, began operating near Louisville, Ky., on May 17. Its first race, which forever after would be known as the Kentucky Derby, was won by a horse named Aristides. The purse was $2,850.

Baseball, by 1875, had assumed the dimensions of a national sport. About 2,000 baseball clubs were in existence. Yale boasted the best college team, with Harvard, Princeton, Columbia, and Rutgers in hot pursuit of that distinction. Professional baseball, however, ended the year under a cloud. Because of a public scandal involving dishonesty, gambling, and contract jumping among the players, the National Association of Professional Baseball Clubs was forced to disband. Almost overshadowed by this event was the intriguing news that the first glove especially designed for baseball was worn by Charles C. Waite, first baseman for a Boston team. The glove was unpadded. The first football uniform made its appearance at a game between Harvard and Tufts that same year.

Croquet, which had been introduced in the United States by the early settlers, was still widely popular in 1875. Roller skating was also attracting enthusiasts, thanks to James Leonard Plimpton, who had invented a skate that had two sets of parallel wheels. Plimpton, cashing in on the craze, had built a $100,000 roller-skating rink in New York City; its cost—like that of the Louisiana Superdome that opened in New Orleans in 1975—was widely criticized as being exorbitant.

The money, detractors said, could have been spent to better advantage; for example, on the new educational facilities that were springing up everywhere. In Cincinnati, Ohio, the Hebrew Union College—the first Jewish seminary in the United States to train men for the rabbinate—was established on October 3. The college opened with an enrollment of nine men. Earlier, in January, New York City had inaugurated the nation's first municipal nautical school. The Connecticut Agricultural Experiment Station—the first in America, and one to be operated "for the general...improvement of agriculture and kindred interests of the State"—was set up by law on July 20.

A cause badly in need of both financial and moral support was that of the conservationists, who were becoming concerned about the wholesale slaughter of America's wildlife. In 1875, they were generally considered to be crackpots, and their warnings that the vast herds of buffalo were in danger of extinction met not just indifference but deliberately provocative defiance. Buffalo hides were big business, especially in the East. In 1875 alone, Western railroads hauled 1,379,-000 of them to market, where they were enormously popular as bedcovers that could also serve as wraps in case of emergency. Many citizens aroused during the night by a nearby fire would rush forth to watch with buffalo coverlets hastily thrown over their nightgowns. The covers were soon referred to jokingly as "fire buffalos," a phrase that eventually was shortened to fire buffs and subsequently broadened to include the wearers.

Another conservationist cause was given focus in a book that had just been published, called *The Earth as Modified by Human Action*. Its author, George P. Marsh, warned that there were limits to America's natural resources and that unregulated exploitation could lead to exhaustion. A prophet before his time, he argued that wildlife, including snakes, should be protected. Above all, he insisted that the ground-water level depended on a forest cover, thus making it imperative that forests be preserved. One immediate result of his plea, which otherwise fell mostly on deaf ears, was the founding of the American Forestry Association on September 10 in Chicago.

The health of the nation's resources may not have aroused much national concern, but personal health was a major preoccupation in 1875. On July 19, the *Emma Abbott*—America's first floating hospital—was launched in Boston. The launching almost coincided with the opening in Asheville, N.C., of the first private sanatorium for the treatment of tuberculosis.

Patent medicines—elixirs, potions, and tonics—were available in abundance and for a variety of ailments. Sufferers from intestinal disorders were invited to use Tarrant's Seltzer Aperient. Its superb "regulatory properties," asserted the advertisements, were "unparalleled." The Tarrant formula, however, was considered inappropriate to the needs of small children insofar as cathartics were concerned. For them, there was a new formula, one whose birch-beer odor and sweetly pungent taste were well calculated to conceal the not-so-pleasant senna content. Its formula was devised by Dr. Charles E. Fletcher; its slogan, eventually, was "Children Cry For It." Its name was Fletcher's Castoria. Those born the year it was patented included violinist Fritz Kreisler, humanitarian Albert Schweitzer, conductor Pierre Monteux, poet Rainer Maria Rilke, statesman and novelist John (*The 39 Steps*) Buchan, motion-picture pioneer D. W. Griffith, novelist Edgar Rice (*Tarzan of the Apes*) Burroughs, composer Maurice Ravel, and novelist Thomas (*Buddenbrooks*) Mann.

One way to forestall intestinal distresses while simultaneously improving the constitution was to follow a proper diet. A leading crusader for such a diet was a Presbyterian minister named Sylvester Graham, who had developed a special flour consisting solely of coarsely ground whole-wheat kernels. Graham's flour, when lightly sweetened and baked in cookie-sized squares, proved tasty to the palates of 1875. Graham Crackers, as they eventually became known, remain a staple on supermarket shelves today. Another of today's staples owes its origins to a 22-year-old medical student who, in 1875, was enthralled by Graham's idea. His experiments during the year with a daily diet of seven Graham Crackers and one apple led him to branch off on his own research. Neither he nor the world could have foreseen the enormous impact his experiments with corn would have on humanity's eating habits—particularly at breakfast. His name was John Harvey Kellogg.

America's search for panaceas was but an echo of its search for those reassuring eternal truths that make life's burdens more bearable. One dedicated seeker was Mary Baker Eddy, who published her principal book, *Science and Health with Key to the Scriptures*, in 1875. Eddy, whose

As Americans put down the shovel, symbol of the nation's enterprise, to celebrate the Centennial, suffragette Louisa May Alcott appeared at the opening ceremonies in Concord, Mass., deploring the limited role society had imposed on women.

Christian Science movement stressed spiritual healing, had thus provided the foundation on which the movement would build its church. On November 17 of that same year, the American Theosophical Society was founded in New York City with Madame Elena Petrovna Blavatsky as its founder, leader, and chief inspiration. Madame Blavatsky, a short, heavily built woman with extraordinarily piercing blue eyes, had reached her particular convictions–including a belief in reincarnation–during a long sojourn in India.

Two extremes characterized, for the most part, the discussions of religion in 1875. At one end was Robert G. Ingersoll, an orator as well as a lawyer, who was known among his followers as the "Great Agnostic." He inveighed against the four Gospels, he denounced divine forgiveness, and he called immortality a fraud. At the opposite extreme was Dwight L. Moody, a shoe-salesman-turned-evangelist. On March 9, 1875, Moody and his partner–a gospel singer and hymn writer named Ira D. Sankey–launched their biggest campaign to date in London. Moody's call for "out-and-out" Christians with "heart and brain on fire for Christ" struck a responsive chord in the 15,000 persons who assembled to hear him. Many who had come to literally hurl brickbats left showering the evangelist with verbal bouquets.

Appeals to the average American's literary tastes in 1875 were as varied as those appealing to his or her spiritual pursuits. Gustave Flaubert's latest book was a fantasy entitled *The Temptation of St. Anthony*. One of Flaubert's admirers, Émile Zola, had begun work on a projected series of novels, one of which was tentatively titled *Nana*. A frequent visitor to Paris, and an acquaintance of both Flaubert and Zola, was the Russian novelist Ivan Turgenev.

In the United States, Herman Melville, a $4-a-day employee of the New York Custom House, was putting the finishing touches to his 600-page, 10,000-line, narrative-philosophical poem entitled *Clarel*. Poet Walt Whitman, still limping perceptibly from a paralytic stroke, whiled away some of his happiest hours in 1875 riding on Philadelphia's horsecars—with kind assists from the drivers. General William Tecumseh Sherman, who had led the Union Army "marching through Georgia," published his personal memoirs.

The grande dame of American letters was 43-year-old Louisa May Alcott, whose books *Little Women* (1868) and *Little Men* (1871) had helped make her one of the wealthiest of American authors. In 1875, Alcott was furious, and the object of her wrath was nothing less than the planning for the nation's Centennial celebrations. Nothing, she said, was being done to include American women in the celebrations; no recognition was being given to the role women played in the American Revolution. True enough, she said, it was the minutemen who fired the shots heard round the world at Concord, Mass., in 1775. But the colonial women had helped cast the bullets for those muskets, and she thought that service, among others, should be recognized in the commemorative ceremony scheduled at Concord on April 19, 1875. Undaunted by the rebuffs she received from officialdom, Alcott—who was an ardent suffragette—issued a call to arms. On the day of the Centennial kickoff ceremonies, with President Grant on the speakers' platform, the protestors were ready.

A phalanx of women, with Alcott front and center, marched into the vast speakers' tent that had been erected on the site of the revolutionary skirmish. Moving directly to the speakers' platform, Alcott handed a declaration of women's rights to the program chairman. The women then retreated to the back of the hall, where they paused, regrouped, and began a song that described a time when women would have equality with men, and government would no longer be all male. The title of the song was "A Hundred Years Hence."

The song title was provocative, but no one, least of all Louisa May Alcott, really knew where the country was going—though there were some who said it was going to the dogs. Yet almost everyone, by the end of 1875, was suddenly, exuberantly aware that the country was 100 years old and that, doubts and dissensions notwithstanding, the country had something to sing about. A previously niggardly Congress had finally appropriated $2 million to help defray the costs of the exposition, which was to be held in Philadelphia. A site covering 236 acres (95 hectares) had been set aside for the exposition grounds. A flood of support was pouring in to the Centennial Commission Headquarters. By year's end, some 60,000 exhibitors from throughout the world had agreed to take space in the 50 available buildings. There would be Krupp guns from Germany and woodcarvings from Belgium; crockery, stoves, and a narrow-gauge locomotive were promised by Sweden; France would send paintings, porcelains, and crystal. Great Britain's Queen Victoria, whose grandfather George III had once ruled—and lost—the American Colonies, promised needlework done by herself and her daughters.

American donors were not to be outdone. Their promised contributions ranged in scope from models of sugar mills to mountains of machinery, from miniature railroads to multipurpose gadgets, from stuffed birds and mammals to silkworms, fishing craft, and spice grinders. From the colonial past came such heirlooms as pewter candleholders, butter churns, spinning wheels, weather vanes, and *Psalters* (hymnbooks) used by the Puritans of Plymouth. A place of honor was reserved for a venerable handpress that had belonged to Benjamin Franklin. W. A. Washington of Denison, Tex., sent a box of George Washington's relics that included camp equipment the "Father of His Country" had used on his campaigns.

Unnoticed and unsung amid this outpouring of the Titanesque and the trivial was a simple, everyday tool that was to be displayed by the O. Ames Company, whose founding in Bridgewater, Mass., predated the Boston Tea Party. The tool would be all but lost in the welter of displays, yet it epitomized what was quintessentially a history of the republic in capsule form. An Ames tool had been used by the early colonists to beat back the hostile wilderness and plant their crops. It had been useful at the Battle of Bunker Hill, at Valley Forge, and in the recently ended Civil War. Here, in one simple object, was summarized America's past. It was equally a symbol of the present for, in 1875, the Ames tool was being used to build the Brooklyn Bridge; Luther Burbank, the great botanist, was using one in his scientific garden in Santa Rosa, Calif.; Irish gandy dancers were utilizing them as they built the railroads that had begun to lace the country.

As for the future, the Ames tool would be there; strong hands would be wielding it in constructing the Panama Canal, New York City's subway system, and the Empire State Building. Its services would be equally valued at the site of the United Nations Headquarters and in the war in Vietnam. A shovel (for that was what it was) even performed a service for the *Apollo 15* crew who used one—albeit from another manufacturer—specially designed to gather specimens from the surface of the moon.

Over a 200-year period, the shovel had changed in shape, size, and composition. But its purpose—to build for a better world—had remained unchanged. It was the kind of message the true observer of anniversaries would receive loud and clear.

Section Four

The Year
On File, 1975

Contributors to THE WORLD BOOK YEAR BOOK report on
the major developments of 1975 in their respective fields. The
names of these contributors appear at the end of the articles
they have written. A complete roster of contributors,
giving their professional affiliations and listing the articles
they have prepared, appears on pages 6 and 7.

Articles in this section are alphabetically arranged by subject
matter. In most cases, titles refer directly to articles in
THE WORLD BOOK ENCYCLOPEDIA. Numerous cross references
(in bold type) are a part of this alphabetical listing. Their
function is to guide the reader to a subject or to information that
may be a part of some other article, or that may appear under
an alternative title. *See* and *See also* cross references appear
within and at the end of articles and similarly direct the reader
to related information contained elsewhere in THE YEAR BOOK.

ADVERTISING. One of the painful aspects of U.S. advertising in 1975 was its sharply rising cost. The average media schedule cost 13.7 per cent more in 1975 than it did in 1974. Some price tags rose by an even higher percentage. A 30-second spot on prime-time TV cost $40,900, up 18 per cent. N. W. Ayer ABH International, New York City, which computed the figures, offered advertisers some comfort by predicting the average cost increase in 1976 would drop to 7.2 per cent.

This meant that rising media rates accounted for most of the increased advertising expenditures in 1975. Varying factors, pulling in different directions, affected the final picture. The recession brought an abrupt drop in advertising for some big-ticket consumer products. At the same time, sluggish sales led other advertisers to step up their advertising during the year in an effort to clear out heavy inventories.

Advertising Volume in 1975 increased an estimated 6 per cent to about $28.4 billion. The media department of McCann-Erickson estimated that the biggest revenue increase went to television, with network TV up 8 per cent to $2.3 billion and spot TV up 8 per cent to $1.6 billion. McCann-Erickson estimated that newspaper ad volume rose 4 per cent to more than $1.2 billion, while magazine volume dipped 1 per cent to $1.5 billion.

Adding to magazine woes was a 42 per cent hike in postage rates for second-class mailers, including magazines. The Postal Rate Commission approved the increase in late summer. It could have been worse – publishers had feared a proposed 121 per cent boost. Although rates varied by category, a weekly news magazine such as *Time* had been paying slightly more than 4 cents per copy in postage. The increase added about 1 cent to this amount.

Top Advertisers. The 100 largest national advertisers accounted for a big part of the money spent on advertising in the United States. *Advertising Age's* annual compilation showed the 100 leading advertisers entered 1975 with a record $6-billion total expenditure for the preceding year. The number-one national advertiser was Procter & Gamble of Cincinnati, Ohio, whose $325-million total was bolstered by heavy advertising for its new Era liquid laundry detergent and increased expenditures for such established products as Pampers disposable diapers, Crest toothpaste, and Tide laundry detergent. The second biggest advertiser was General Motors of Detroit, which spent $247-million – an 8 per cent boost – to help shore up sagging car sales.

Despite the recession, the stocks of leading advertisers were well represented among the gainers on the stock market in 1975. The *Advertising Age*

Hungry pussycat cha-cha-chas on the way to dinner in scenes from a pet-food commercial, one of many television commercials using animal performers.

Starvation stalks millions.

Who cares?

"To save starving families abroad, I pledge to have one 'Empty Plate' meal a week and send the money saved to CARE"

I care

CARE World Hunger Fund   660 First Ave., New York, N.Y. 10016

Ad for CARE's Empty Plate campaign asks people to skip one meal each week and give the money saved to feed starving people in famine areas.

interested in looking at advertisements that do not involve significant economic or physical harm to consumers.

Time v. Simmons. Advertisers viewed with concern a wrangle between Time, Incorporated, and W. R. Simmons Research over readership findings. Time sued Simmons in January, alleging that inaccurate Simmons data indicated a dramatic loss of readers. The results left *Time* magazine's audience roughly equal to *Newsweek's*, despite *Time's* greater circulation. Simmons denied the charges in court. A settlement was reached in June. Simmons lawyers promptly drew up new contract terms aimed at avoiding future lawsuits based on claims of negligence.

A Newsworthy Campaign was that of Bristol-Myers for Datril nonaspirin pain reliever. Hotly competitive TV and print ads bucked Johnson & Johnson's (J & J) Tylenol "for people who can't take aspirin." Datril ads pushed the item as identical to Tylenol and $1 cheaper per 100 tablets. Johnson & Johnson protested to TV networks that both initial Datril spots and later ones that were toned down were incorrect because J & J slashed prices as soon as it learned of the Datril ads. As Bristol-Myers and J & J spent to expand the market, American Home Products was quietly testing Trillium, and Sterling Drug tested a nonaspirin Bayer pain reliever.   Merle Kingman

National Advertisers Index showed that stocks of 30 leading advertisers rose 26.3 per cent in the six months ending June 30. Norton Simon, Incorporated, scored the biggest gain among these top advertisers as its stock soared 102.2 per cent. Other big gainers were RCA Corporation, up 90.7 per cent; Coca-Cola Company, up 71 per cent; and Chrysler Corporation, up 70.6 per cent.

Washington Influence. Disagreements about advertising developed among various national bureaus during the year. The Advertising Council, demonstrating independence from federal officialdom, thwarted the wishes of the Federal Energy Administration (FEA) by refusing to approve FEA fuel-conservation ads that blamed the nation's energy problems on the oil cartel. The Advertising Council's volunteer agency, Cunningham & Walsh, joined in the refusal to turn out "ads we didn't believe in."

In a decision likely to be the most important in several years for advertising, the Federal Trade Commission (FTC) dropped its case against television commercials for Bristol-Myers' Dry Ban deodorant. The commercials demonstrated that the product showed up clear when sprayed on a surface, while a competitive product appeared white and gritty. The FTC, whose administrative law judge earlier had proposed prohibiting "rigged" product demonstrations, served notice that it is not

AFGHANISTAN. President Mohammad Daoud's government entered its third year in power in 1975 with sufficient public confidence and internal stability to begin restoring civil liberties and civilian control. Daoud overhauled the Cabinet in September, dismissing a number of ministers with military backgrounds in favor of civilian technicians. Another significant step was the release of 284 political prisoners on the October 5 celebration of the end of Ramadan, the Moslem fasting month.

The nation started a program of basic economic and social reforms. A banking law issued in July placed all private banks under state control. An Afghan Agricultural Bank was established to make loans to farmers from a $13-million World Bank fund. Tax and tariff reforms enacted in July will produce a 47 per cent increase in income from local sources. Investment in education increased by 50 per cent during the year. In a July speech, Daoud promised land reforms within a year and a final draft of the new republican constitution and announced a seven-year development plan including more than 200 separate projects.

New copper deposits discovered at Ainak in Logar province and an increase in natural gas production to 102 billion cubic feet (2.9 billion cubic meters) marked the growth of Afghan mineral production.   William Spencer

See also ASIA (Facts in Brief Table).

AFRICA

The liquidation of Portugal's colonial empire was the single most important development in Africa in 1975. Other developments had potential long-term effects on the financial well-being of African nations. Severe drought ended in West Africa but persisted in the east, and high prices for imported oil continued to damage African economies.

Portugal granted independence to the last four of its five African colonies in 1975. Guinea-Bissau had gained independence in 1974. Mozambique became independent on June 25, 1975; Cape Verde Islands, on July 5; São Tomé and Príncipe, on July 12; and Angola, on November 11.

In all of these new countries, except Angola, the transfer of power went smoothly. But in Angola, civil war raged on the day of formal independence. Two rival governments claimed to rule the country. Portugal refused to recognize either one. The Angolan situation assumed international importance, with Russia supplying arms to one side. China, along with the United States and several other Western countries, aided the other side. See ANGOLA; CAPE VERDE ISLANDS; MOZAMBIQUE; SÃO TOMÉ AND PRÍNCIPE.

The Comoro Islands, a French holding, unilaterally declared independence on July 6. The islands lie between the east coast of Africa and the island of Madagascar.

The people of one island, Mayotte, decided to retain ties with France. On July 21, the Organization of African Unity (OAU) accused France of invading Mayotte. France denied the charge. However, a coup in August by a group favoring close ties with France overthrew the first Comoran government.

Remaining White-Ruled Countries. The white-minority government of Rhodesia faced strong pressure from neighboring African-ruled countries to negotiate a constitutional settlement granting majority rule to Rhodesian blacks. Botswana, Zambia, and Mozambique surround Rhodesia on all sides, except a portion of its southern border. And it was clear that their territories could be used to launch guerrilla operations against the Rhodesian regime in the event that negotiations failed. South Africa's white-minority government, trying to avoid such a conflict, also applied pressure on Rhodesia to begin talks and avoid civil war. Negotiations between black and white Rhodesians took place in August, but broke off after one session. See RHODESIA.

South Africa's white government was pressured by both internal dissidents and neighboring black-ruled nations to eliminate its policy of racial segregation and to grant independence to the territory of Namibia (South West Africa). South Africa continued to administer Namibia under a disputed mandate, even though the United Nations (UN) had repeatedly called for Namibian independence. See SOUTH AFRICA.

The Drought. Normal rains fell on the Sahel in West Africa, the area just south of the Sahara, in 1975. Near-normal rainfall in 1974 had broken a drought that began in 1968. As a result, the region's governments and foreign relief donors switched their attention to rehabilitating the people, land, and livestock victimized by the long drought. The United States and other nations in 1975 worked with Sahelian countries on plans to protect the region against famine in the event of future droughts. The plans included irrigating land and building up grain reserves.

Drought persisted, however, in East Africa. During 1975, drought conditions grew worse in the southeastern part of Ethiopia and in the province of Eritrea. A civil war between secessionists and Ethiopian government forces hampered relief aid to Eritrea. Between 1973 and September, 1975, an estimated 230,000 Ethiopians died as a result of the drought. See ETHIOPIA.

The Russian Presence. United States Secretary of Defense James R. Schlesinger charged on June 10 that Russia was developing naval, air, and missile facilities at the Somali port of Berbera. The Somali government denied the charge and invited U.S. congressmen to visit Somalia and investigate. One delegation arrived in Somalia on July 4, a second visited the following week. Both groups concluded that Russia had indeed built missile-storage facilities there. The major purpose of the base was apparently to support Russian operations in the Indian Ocean. The U.S. Department of Defense used this information to justify developing a U.S. naval and air base on Diego Garcia, a British-occupied island about 1,000 miles (1,600 kilometers) south of the tip of India.

Apparently trying to gain a stronger foothold in Africa, Russia sent massive military aid to one faction struggling for control of Angola. United States diplomats and officials repeatedly warned Russia that its intervention in Angola was threatening the future of détente. The aid also brought Russia into conflict with the OAU. See RUSSIA.

U.S. Relations. President Gerald R. Ford's appointment of Nathaniel Davis as assistant secretary of state for African affairs strained U.S.-African relations. On February 21, the OAU's Council of Ministers criticized Davis' nomination because he

Thousands of citizens watch intently on June 25 as Mozambique is declared independent, ending centuries of Portuguese colonial rule.

A family of nomads enjoy their first meal at a refugee camp in southern Somalia after being airlifted from the drought-stricken north.

had been U.S. ambassador to Chile when the U.S. Central Intelligence Agency was operating to weaken the Socialist government of the late President Salvador Allende Gossens. Nevertheless, Davis was sworn in as assistant secretary on April 2. But the Department of State reported on September 1 that he had submitted his resignation, apparently because of continued hostility toward him on the part of African governments.

The U.S. ambassador to the UN, Daniel P. Moynihan, also became a focus of U.S.-African controversy during the year. On October 3, he accused Uganda's President Idi Amin Dada of being a "racist murderer" and implied that the OAU, which had elected Amin chairman in July, condoned the alleged murders of Amin's opponents in Uganda. African governments strongly resented these remarks. See UGANDA; UNITED NATIONS.

European Relations. Africa's relationship to the European Community (Common Market) changed substantially when the market and developing nations signed the Lomé Convention on February 28. This five-year agreement covers trade and aid relations between the Common Market and 36 African nations, plus developing countries in the Caribbean Sea and the Pacific Ocean.

Previous Common Market agreements in Africa had been restricted almost entirely to former French and Belgian colonies. The 1975 agreement expanded coverage to all former British territories.

Under the Lomé Convention, all exports from these developing nations may enter Common Market countries tax-free or with lowered tariffs. For some of their exports, the developing countries will receive special compensation from the Common Market if prices drop sharply. The pact also committed the Common Market to provide $4.1 billion in development aid over the five-year period.

OAU Summit Meeting. The OAU's 12th summit conference was held in Kampala, Uganda, from July 28 to August 1. However, Botswana, Tanzania, and Zambia boycotted the meeting, because they opposed Ugandan President Amin, who hosted the conference.

The conference turned down a resolution calling for economic sanctions against Israel and for its expulsion from the UN. The meeting approved a declaration on southern Africa endorsing efforts for a negotiated settlement in Rhodesia. But it committed the OAU to intensified financial, material, and diplomatic support for African nationalist guerrillas if majority rule cannot be achieved peacefully. The declaration also called for independence for Namibia, either through negotiations or armed struggle, and for the end of racial separation in South Africa.

Oil Prices. Many African governments were angered by a 10 per cent increase in oil prices that was announced in September by the Organization of Petroleum Exporting Countries (OPEC). A Tanzanian official accused the exporting states of "appearing to turn their backs on the developing countries...."

On February 27, Nigeria proposed to sell its oil to other African nations at reduced rates, provided the countries had their own refineries and did not export products made from Nigerian oil. However, Nigeria withdrew its offer in early March, explaining that pricing was the responsibility of OPEC.

As of late February, a special fund established by Arab members of OPEC in 1974 to aid African countries hurt by high oil prices had reportedly disbursed $125.6 million to 31 countries.

Regional Economic Groups. One of the most important regional organizations for economic cooperation among several African nations is the East African Community (EAC). It links Kenya, Tanzania, and Uganda in a common market. They also share several services, such as railroads, airlines, and telecommunications. However, the EAC had such a difficult year that its future was in doubt. All three member governments withheld payments of funds for the regional corporations that operate the shared services.

The payments problem was reportedly resolved on August 12, but on August 14, the three governments announced they would review the treaty on which the EAC is based. Observers speculated that

Facts in Brief on African Political Units

Country	Population	Government	Monetary Unit*	Foreign Trade (million U.S. $) Exports	Imports
Algeria	17,523,000	President Houari Boumediene	dinar (4.1 = $1)	4,587	4,048
Angola	6,240,000	Contested	escudo (27 = $1)	727	529
Botswana	701,000	President Sir Seretse M. Khama	rand (1 = $1.15)	84	148
Burundi	3,760,000	President & Prime Minister Michel Micombero	franc (78.8 = $1)	30	43
Cameroon	6,540,000	President Ahmadou Ahidjo; Prime Minister Paul Biya	CFA franc (217.63 = $1)	478	437
Cape Verde	322,000	President Aristides Pereira; Prime Minister Pedro Pires	escudo (27 = $1)	2	34
Central African Republic	1,825,000	President Jean-Bedel Bokassa; Prime Minister Elizabeth Domitien	CFA franc (217.63 = $1)	37	52
Chad	4,103,000	Supreme Military Council President F. Malloum Ngakoutou Bey-Ndi	CFA franc (217.63 = $1)	38	82
Comoro Islands	310,000	National Executive Council President Ali Soilih	CFA franc (217.63 = $1)	5	15
Congo	1,070,000	President Marien N'Gouabi; Prime Minister Henri Lopez	CFA franc (217.63 = $1)	62	84
Dahomey (Benin)	3,192,000	President & Premier Mathieu Kerekou	CFA franc (217.63 = $1)	44	112
Egypt	38,456,000	President Anwar al-Sadat; Prime Minister Mamduh Muhammad Salim	pound (1 = $2.56)	1,516	2,349
Equatorial Guinea	310,000	President Francisco Macias Nguema Biyogo	ekpwele (58.3 = $1)	32	36
Ethiopia	27,961,000	Provisional Military Administrative Government Chairman Teferi Bante	dollar (2.1 = $1)	267	273
Gabon	1,008,000	President Albert Bernard Bongo; Prime Minister Leon Mebiame	CFA franc (217.63 = $1)	932	360
Gambia	416,000	President Sir Dawda Kairaba Jawara	dalasi (1.86 = $1)	43	47
Ghana	10,188,000	Supreme Military Council Chairman Ignatius Kutu Acheampong	new cedi (1.15 = $1)	752	819
Guinea	4,500,000	President Ahmed Sekou Toure; Prime Minister Lansana Beavogui	syli (20.7 = $1)	70	100
Guinea-Bissau	533,000	President Luis de Almeida Cabral	escudo (27 = $1)	3	44
Ivory Coast	4,976,000	President Felix Houphouet-Boigny	CFA franc (217.63 = $1)	1,214	969
Kenya	13,900,000	President Jomo Kenyatta	shilling (8.16 = $1)	603	1,026
Lesotho	1,065,000	King Motlotlehi Moshoeshoe II; Prime Minister Leabua Jonathan	rand (1 = $1.15)	13	88
Liberia	1,850,000	President William R. Tolbert, Jr.	dollar (1 = $1)	400	288
Libya	2,410,000	Revolutionary Command Council President Muammar Muhammad al-Qadhaafi; Prime Minister Abd as-Salam Jallud	dinar (1 = $3.38)	7,596	3,138
Malagasy	7,737,000	Supreme Revolutionary Council President Didier Ratsiraka	franc (217.63 = $1)	203	203
Malawi	5,170,000	President H. Kamuzu Banda	kwacha (1 = $1.12)	119	186
Mali	5,690,000	President & Prime Minister Moussa Traore	franc (435.3 = $1)	35	100
Mauritania	1,339,000	President Moktar Ould Daddah	ouguiya (44.2 = $1)	177	170
Mauritius	897,000	Governor General Sir Abdul Raman Osman; Prime Minister Sir Seewoosagur Ramgoolam	rupee (6.4 = $1)	310	309
Morocco	18,450,000	King Hassan II; Prime Minister Ahmed Osman	dirham (4.1 = $1)	1,706	1,913
Mozambique	9,140,000	President Samora Moises Machel	escudo (27 = $1)	226	465
Namibia (South West Africa)	928,000	Administrator B. J. van der Walt	rand (1 = $1.15)	no statistics available	
Niger	4,669,000	Supreme Military Council President Seyni Kountche	CFA franc (217.63 = $1)	62	86
Nigeria	64,043,000	Head of State Murtala Ramat Muhammed	naira (1 = $1.60)	9,567	2,737
Rhodesia	6,479,000	President Clifford Dupont; Prime Minister Ian D. Smith	dollar (1 = $1.68)	652	541
Rwanda	4,419,000	President Juvenal Habyarimana	franc (92.8 = $1)	36	35
São Tomé and Príncipe	84,000	President Manuel Pinto da Costa; Prime Minister Miguel Trovoada	escudo (27 = $1)	13	10
Senegal	4,532,000	President Leopold Sedar Senghor; Prime Minister Abdou Diouf	CFA franc (217.63 = $1)	361	450
Sierra Leone	2,788,000	President Siaka Stevens; Prime Minister Christian A. Kamara-Taylor	leone (1 = $1.04)	144	223
Somalia	3,221,000	Supreme Revolutionary Council President Mohamed Siad Barre	shilling (6.3 = $1)	54	110
South Africa	25,572,000	President Nicolaas J. Diederichs; Prime Minister Balthazar Johannes Vorster	rand (1 = $1.15)	4,979	7,179
Sudan	18,343,000	President Sayed Gaafar Mohamed Nimeiri	pound (1 = $2.87)	350	642
Swaziland	481,000	King Sobhuza II; Prime Minister Makhosini Dlamini	lilangeni (1 = $1.15)	109	99
Tanzania	15,499,000	President Julius K. Nyerere; Prime Minister Rashidi Kawawa	shilling (8.16 = $1)	427	811
Togo	2,318,000	President Gnassingbe Eyadema	CFA franc (217.63 = $1)	189	120
Tunisia	5,870,000	President Habib Bourguiba; Prime Minister Hedi Nouira	dinar (1 = $2.42)	921	1,128
Uganda	11,684,000	President Idi Amin Dada	shilling (8.16 = $1)	315	213
Upper Volta	6,097,000	President & Prime Minister Sangoule Lamizana	CFA franc (217.63 = $1)	25	99
Zaire	26,640,000	President Mobutu Sese Seko	zaire (1 = $2.00)	1,004	754
Zambia	4,898,000	President Kenneth D. Kaunda; Prime Minister Elijah Mudenda	kwacha (1 = $1.55)	1,406	904

*Exchange rates as of Dec. 1, 1975

A train parked on the Victoria Falls Bridge provides neutral territory
for Rhodesian white regime's negotiations with black nationalists.

Tanzania might limit its ties with Kenya and Uganda and establish closer relations with Zambia and newly independent Mozambique. Those governments were ideologically closer to Tanzania's. Moreover, Zambia and Tanzania were linked by the new 1,200-mile (1,900-kilometer) railroad that opened on October 23.

On October 25, the three EAC nations devalued their currencies about 14 per cent to increase exports and curb imports. See KENYA; TANZANIA; UGANDA.

Fifteen states signed a treaty on May 28, creating the Economic Community of West African States (ECOWAS). ECOWAS was composed of Dahomey, Gambia, Ghana, Guinea, Guinea-Bissau, Ivory Coast, Liberia, Mali, Mauritania, Niger, Nigeria, Senegal, Sierra Leone, Togo, and Upper Volta. The treaty called for an economic community in which goods and people would circulate freely. There would be a common system of tariffs, a coordinated transportation system, and regional economic planning.

Border Dispute. Both Mali and Upper Volta claimed an area along their common border, which is about 90 miles (150 kilometers) long and 9 to 13 miles (15 to 20 kilometers) wide. In July, presidents Sangoule Lamizana of Upper Volta and Moussa Traore of Mali reportedly agreed to establish a joint technical committee to define the border in the disputed territory. The territory is valuable for its good water supply and possible mineral deposits. In December, 1974, units of the two countries' armies clashed three times in the area.

Military Regimes. The number of military regimes ruling black African countries increased to 16 on April 13 when the army overthrew Chad's civilian government. In Nigeria, a group of junior officers overthrew the military regime of General Yakubu Gowon. The new Nigerian government was also controlled by the military. However, the new government pledged to return Nigeria to civilian rule by October, 1979. See CHAD; NIGERIA.

On February 11, Gabriel Ramanantsoa, president of the Malagasy Republic, was ambushed and assassinated. A rebel police unit was blamed for the attack. However, apparently in the interest of restoring calm, the assassination suspects were acquitted in June, just before a civilian government, headed by Didier Ratsiraka, assumed power.

Genuinely competitive elections continued to be a rarity in Africa. However, in Tanzania's parliamentary elections on October 26, voters had the opportunity to choose between two candidates of the same party for each seat. See TANZANIA.

In November, President Mathieu Kerekou of Dahomey announced that the country's name had been officially changed to the People's Republic of Benin.

John D. Esseks

AGRICULTURE. A very good harvest in the United States and a spectacularly bad one in Russia dominated the news of agricultural production in 1975. The bountiful crop picture in the United States was in sharp contrast to the more difficult food situation reported in many other parts of the world. "The world food problem is so widespread, deep-rooted, and potentially explosive as to constitute perhaps the most serious challenge of our times . . . ," said Director-General Addeke H. Boerma of the United Nations Food and Agricultural Organization. "Never before has the world had such need of its farmers nor indeed such an obligation to them."

Hot, dry weather in the Soviet Union reduced Russia's grain output to as low as an estimated 152-million short tons (138 million metric tons). That was about 60.6 million short tons (55 million metric tons) below Russia's production goal. The poor harvest affected Russian economic plans in other areas, and seemed certain to have an impact on world food trade, because Russia returned to the market place to make up its staggering losses. See FOOD; RUSSIA.

World Production. In spite of the reduced Russian output, world crop production was generally up in 1975. Total world grain production was estimated at 1.29 billion short tons (1.17 billion metric tons), up from 1.26 billion short tons (1.14 billion metric tons) in 1974.

Corn and soybeans, boosted by huge U.S. harvests, led the increase in crop production. Soybean production was also aided by a 28 per cent increase in Brazil's crop.

Large crops in Argentina, Australia, Canada, and the United States resulted in wheat production of 392 million short tons (355.5 million metric tons), second only to the record 1973 crop of 405 million short tons (367.4 million metric tons). A one-third reduction in Russia's crop, usually the world's largest, resulted in the smallest rye crop since World War II. Cotton production dropped slightly, primarily because of a reduced U.S. crop.

Coffee production dropped, but the sharp reductions expected after killing frosts in Brazil did not materialize because the frosts came too late to significantly affect the 1975 output. The frosts are expected to cut the 1976 crop in half, however. They will probably cut production for several years because trees damaged by the freeze must be pruned or replaced.

Data on 1974 world red-meat production showed an increase of 6 per cent to 77 million short tons (70-million metric tons). Led by expanded production in the United States and France, beef and veal production was up 6.4 per cent to 41.1 million short tons (37.3 million metric tons). Pork output (excluding China) was 31.1 million short tons (28.2-million metric tons), up 6.5 per cent, but lamb and

mutton production was down 1 per cent to 4.7 million short tons (4.3 million metric tons).

The U.S. Crop Harvest set a new record, 11 per cent above the 1974 harvest. Livestock production began to recover; the number of cattle on feed increased in October for the first time in two years. Undersecretary of Agriculture J. Phil Campbell said at the National Agricultural Outlook Conference in November, "This harvest means many things to many people. To farmers . . . a good income . . . to marketers . . . big volume [and] efficient use of their facilities. To foreign purchasers . . . a godsend because crops have been poor in many countries . . . and to consumers . . . less of a rise in food prices."

For U.S. agriculture, it was a year to catch its breath. No period in recent history had put the agriculture and food industry under such economic stress as the period from 1972 through 1974. The industry had been caught in the cross-currents of erratic domestic and foreign production, pressing consumer demands, materials shortages, worldwide inflation, explosively high food prices, and soaring costs for marketing and transportation.

The importance of agriculture to the total economy was re-emphasized. One study showed 1.2 million full-time civilian jobs that are related directly to agricultural exports. The continued increase in agricultural exports in 1975 was a major factor in offsetting a deficit trade balance. The record agricultural production was a significant impetus to general economic recovery, and larger food supplies worked against inflation.

U.S. production rebounded from a sharp decline in 1974 to establish a record in 1975. The all-crops production index stood at 122 (1967 = 100), up from 110 in 1974 and two points above the previous record, 1973's 120. Cotton was the only major crop showing a production decline.

Adverse weather was a major factor in 1974, but 1975's weather assisted production. Warm, dry days in the Great Plains and Corn Belt states during the fall harvest season helped farmers bring the bumper crop to market. By November, 82 per cent of the nation's corn crop was harvested, compared with 62 per cent in 1974 and 58 per cent in an average year.

The major feed and food grains led increased crop production. Corn production jumped 25 per cent and was 3 per cent above the previous record set in 1973. Sorghums and soybeans also registered major gains, but both were below the record 1973 output. Rice output also rose to a new high, 9 per cent above the record 1974 crop and 24 per cent above 1973 production.

Livestock production, responding to reduced feed-grain production in 1974 and consequent higher feed prices, was curtailed during 1975. Of the major livestock categories, only beef and milk production showed gains. By November, 1975,

Empty freighter waits at Houston dock after longshoremen protesting
the effect on U.S. prices stopped loading grain sold to Russia.

however, livestock production was again expanding as higher livestock prices and the bumper 1975 grain crop combined to paint a better profit picture for livestock producers.

Farm Prices, on the average, were near 1974 levels. The index of all prices received by farmers was 185 (1967 = 100) on November 15, compared to 182 on the same date in 1974. There was a sharp contrast between livestock and crop prices.

Cutbacks in the production of many classes of livestock boosted livestock prices throughout much of the year. During one week in October, the average hog price at seven major markets reached a record $63 per hundredweight (45 kilograms). Prices for cattle, chickens, turkeys, eggs, milk, and most other livestock and livestock products were also up substantially.

But record or near-record outputs in most major crops depressed crop prices. On November 15, the all-crops price index was 188 (1967 = 100), down 16 per cent from 1974.

Farm Income, boosted by higher livestock prices and increased crop output, improved substantially in the second half of the year. Net farm income was estimated at $25 billion, down from $27.7 billion in 1974, but still the third highest on record and substantially above pre-1973 levels.

A summary published in 1975 showed that during 1974, for the first time in 50 years, total receipts from sale of crops exceeded receipts from sale of livestock. This situation continued in 1975, though livestock receipts regained some of their lost ground.

U.S. Agricultural Trade surpassed all prior records in dollar value during the fiscal year that ended June 30. Agricultural exports totaled $21.6-billion, up $289 million from 1974's record trade performance.

All of the increase in value resulted from higher prices, however; the actual volume of goods shipped dropped 15 per cent. Factors contributing to the decrease in volume of exports were the reduced 1974 U.S. grain crop and expanded crop production in some other countries.

Prices for exported commodities were up an average of 14 per cent. The export price for wheat climbed as high as $4.80 per bushel and to $3.55 per bushel for corn, both new records.

Japan remained the single largest buyer of U.S. farm products with purchases totaling $3.2 billion. Japanese purchases were down 5 per cent in dollar value and 18 per cent in volume, however.

Major new markets for U.S. agricultural products were developing in the Middle East. Egypt became the 15th largest buyer of U.S. farm goods with purchases totaling $388 million, 47 per cent above 1974 and up from only $83 million in 1973. Exports to the Arabian Peninsula tripled from 1973 levels and are expected to show further dramatic increases during 1976.

The five-year U.S.-Russian grain agreement signed on October 20 committed Russia to buy up to 8.8 million short tons (8 million metric tons) of wheat and corn annually through 1980.

Farmers' Financial status as of Jan. 1, 1976, showed total assets of $594 billion, up 14 per cent. Land prices were also up 14 per cent and had more than doubled in the 1970s. Total debt in the farm sector increased only 11 per cent, so farmers had a 14.9 per cent increase in their net worth and their debt-to-asset ratio hit a 10-year low.

The farm labor force continued to decline. The total work force, including family labor, totaled 4.5-million in October, 1975. However, the number of hired farmworkers increased from 1.395 million in 1974 to 1.396 million in 1975. This was the third consecutive year the number of hired workers increased, perhaps reflecting the rise of corporate farming. Hired workers were paid an average of $2.63 per hour in October, up from $2.43 a year earlier.

Federal Policies. The so-called "market-oriented" policy of Secretary of Agriculture Earl L. Butz was dramatized when the last government-owned commodity-storage bin, used to store farm surpluses, was sold to a private owner on August 22. "Three years ago, American taxpayers were paying up to $4 billion a year for farm programs," Butz was quick to remind his critics. Now, farm-program costs are under $1 billion, "and most of that goes for disaster payments . . . ." the secretary said.

The Agriculture and Consumer Protection Act of 1973 remained in effect as President Gerald R..Ford vetoed on May 1 a new program proposed by Congress. Congress showed little enthusiasm for stronger price-support legislation in light of earlier farm bill vetoes. Yet, the federal suspension of foreign grain trade during late harvest periods made some observers wonder how committed the government really was to its "market orientation," and some expressed concern that the nation-to-nation trading implied by the U.S.-Russian grain agreement was inconsistent with an open-market policy.

The record harvests highlighted a number of potential transportation problems. The most serious was the probable loss of rural railroad outlets under proposed railroad legislation, which could slow crop shipments. The strength shown by the maritime unions in boycotting grain shipments to Russia also aroused concern. There was a major controversy in August between the agricultural establishment and George Meany, president of the American Federation of Labor and Congress of Industrial Organizations (AFL-CIO), over the boycotts.

Grain Scandals. More than 50 persons involved in international grain trading had been indicted on federal charges in the United States by November.

Agricultural Statistics, 1975

World Crop Production
(million units)

Crop	Units	1974	1975*	%U.S.
Corn	Metric tons	281.7	315.4	46.2
Wheat	Metric tons	350.3	355.3	16.4
Rice	Metric tons	325.1	NA	1.6[1]
Barley	Metric tons	159.9	148.6	5.6
Oats	Metric tons	50.7	51.3	19.2
Rye	Metric tons	32.7	26.1	1.8
Soybeans	Metric tons	52.0	61.2	65.5
Cotton	Bales[2]	63.2	57.8	15.7
Coffee	Bags[3]	79.7	72.5	0.3
Sugar	Metric tons	78.6	83.4	7.5

*preliminary
[1]Based on 1974 production
[2]480 lbs. (217.7 kilograms) net
[3]132.276 lbs. (60 kilograms)
NA Not Available

Output of Major U.S. Crops
(millions of bushels)

	1962-66†	1974	1975*
Corn	3,876	4,651	5,804
Sorghums	595	628	770
Oats	912	621	678
Wheat	1,229	1,793	2,138
Soybeans	769	1,233	1,520
Rice (a)	742	1,141	1,241
Potatoes (b)	275	341	310
Cotton (c)	140	115	90
Tobacco (d)	2,126	1,990	2,191

†Average; *Preliminary
(a) 100,000 cwt. (4.54 million kilograms)
(b) 1 million cwt. (45.4 million kilograms)
(c) 100,000 bales (50 million lbs.) (22.7 million kilograms)
(d) 1 million lbs. (454,000 kilograms)

U.S. Production of Animal Products
(millions of pounds)

	1957-59†	1974	1975*
Beef	13,704	23,138	23,825
Veal	1,240	486	875
Lamb & Mutton	711	465	410
Pork	10,957	13,805	11,425
Eggs (a)	5,475	5,489	5,270
Chicken	5,292	11,322	11,200
Turkey	1,382	2,426	2,240
Total Milk (b)	123	115.4	116.0

†Average; *preliminary
(a) 1 million dozens
(b) billions of lbs. (454 million kilograms)

Federal investigators, concentrating on grain trading in New Orleans, found evidence of mislabeling, short-weighting, theft, and adulteration of millions of dollars worth of grain bound for foreign ports from that important grain-shipping center. Other investigations were begun in such grain ports as Baltimore; Norfolk, Va.; and Seattle, Wash.

Forty-seven defendants had either pleaded guilty or had been convicted of such charges as bribery and fraud. The Bunge Corporation, third largest grain exporter in the United States, pleaded no contest on October 8 to conspiracy charges in the theft of grain and cover-up of the thefts. Usually secretive major grain traders, still reeling from charges of windfall profits in the 1972 Russian

Demonstrating for higher prices for their product, angry Japanese dairy farmers dump gallons of milk in front of a Tokyo processing plant in July.

grain deal, were buffeted anew by the Gulf Coast scandals.

On December 5, Butz announced an increase in 1976 foreign food aid to $1.5 billion. At the same time he announced an $85-million, 1976 Agricultural Conservation Program designed to encourage soil and water conservation. The Department of Agriculture's (USDA) Food Stamp Program cost an estimated $4.8 billion and touched 20 million persons. There were reports of losses due to negligence in states' administration of the program, and, late in 1975, USDA sent bills of more than $1 million each to three states for such violations.

New Technology and Research continued to strengthen American agriculture in 1975. One important field of research was on nitrogen fixation, the process of making nitrogen from the air useful to plants. Scientists are now trying to get the nitrogen-fixing bacteria that live in nodules on the roots of such legumes as soybeans and peas to associate with other important crops, especially such grains as wheat and corn. Johanna Dobereiner, a microbiologist at the Agricultural Institute in Rio de Janeiro, Brazil, has found a strain of bacteria that lives with several tropical grasses. She reported in July that she had grown corn with these bacteria on the root surfaces and the bacteria appeared to be fixing nitrogen for the plants. Other researchers were developing strains of bacteria that would fix nitrogen independently in the soil, so that fields may someday be inoculated with bacteria rather than sprayed with nitrogen fertilizer. The petroleum price increases in recent years have spurred research on nitrogen fixation, because much chemical fertilizer is made from petroleum. Research in both public and private laboratories also promised to improve the very low efficiency of photosynthesis, the process by which plants convert solar energy into food carbohydrates.

Animal Researchers hope to increase the number of high-quality offspring by transplanting eggs from high-quality sows to lower-quality sows. They also believe research will increase cattle twinning.

Waste disposal problems and high feed costs have stimulated a variety of new feeding techniques. Manure is being recycled through cattle at an Iowa Agricultural Experiment Station with promising results; USDA researchers pelletized straw with good feeding results; University of Nebraska researchers treated corncobs for use as feed; and University of Hawaii researchers tested the use of treated sugar-cane waste and pineapple field trash for livestock feeding.　Charles E. French and Larry L. Nelson

AIR FORCE. See ARMED FORCES.

AIR POLLUTION. See ENVIRONMENT.

AIRPORT. See AVIATION.

ALABAMA. See STATE GOVERNMENT.

ALASKA. See STATE GOVERNMENT.

ALBANIA continued its anti-Russian, pro-Chinese political stance in 1975. It was the only European nation to boycott the Conference on Security and Cooperation, which opened in Helsinki, Finland, on July 30. In tune with Chinese denunciations, the Albanian Communist Party newspaper *Zeri i Popullit* denounced the meeting as a "dangerous Russian-American undertaking" that would produce only "pretentious statements and deceptive illusions."

The Chinese alliance also remained the cornerstone of Albania's economic development. China agreed in June to a large loan for economic development. Reports in August suggested that Albania turned down a similar loan from Russia. Albania tried to improve relations with its neighbors, especially Yugoslavia. In June, it began negotiations to link Albania's rail network with that of Yugoslavia at Bar, an Adriatic port about 30 miles (50 kilometers) from the Albanian border.

Industrial production exceeded planned targets during the first six months of 1975 in copper, ferronickel (iron-nickel alloy) and pyrite mining, and in road and sea transportation.

Albania's Communist Party Central Committee met on October 10 and decided that Albania should have a new constitution. Chris Cviic

See also EUROPE (Facts in Brief Table).
ALBERTA. See CANADA.

ALGERIA played host to several international conferences in 1975 as President Houari Boumediene continued to assert his country's leadership among nonaligned third world countries. During the Organization of Petroleum Exporting Countries (OPEC) conference in March, Boumediene mediated talks between Iran and Iraq on their longstanding border dispute. The two nations reached an accord on March 5. See IRAN; IRAQ.

Tension Grew between Algeria and neighboring Morocco over the fate of Spanish Sahara. Algeria rejected Morocco's claim to the phosphate-rich area and backed an independence group. Thousands of Algerian troops were reported massed around the Tindouf Oasis near the Algeria-Spanish Sahara border. Tensions mounted in November when Algeria refused to accept a Spanish proposal to turn over the Spanish Sahara to Morocco and Mauritania. See MOROCCO.

On April 10, President Valéry Giscard d'Estaing became the first French head of state to visit Algeria since that nation gained its independence in 1962. Boumediene and Giscard d'Estaing agreed to work for better housing and wages for Algerians working in France.

Several political developments marked the 10th anniversary of the coup that brought Boumediene to power. Elections were held for labor councils in state-owned industries on February 7, and for the popular assemblies of the 15 *wilayas* (provinces), Algeria's basic political units, on March 30. About 79 per cent of the voters turned out. Boumediene also announced on June 19 that elections would be held within a year for the National Assembly and the presidency, the first since the 1965 coup.

The July dismissal of Minister of State Cherif Belkacem, former National Liberation Front head, and the death of Interior Minister Medeghri left Boumediene and Foreign Minister Ahmed Abdelaziz Bouteflika as the only 1965 coup leaders in power.

Economic Affairs. A $5.9-billion budget, 55 per cent larger than in 1974, was approved on January 15. It included $820 million in price subsidies for basic foodstuffs to combat an 8 to 10 per cent annual inflation rate.

Boumediene officially began Algeria's massive "green belt" program on February 9. The 20-year forestation scheme is designed to halt the northward advance of the Sahara by planting 6 billion trees, mostly pine and eucalyptus, in a barrier 10 miles (16 kilometers) wide and 950 miles (1,500 kilometers) long, south of the Atlas and Aurès mountains. Planners hope to reclaim almost 70,000 square miles (181,000 square kilometers) of agricultural land. William Spencer

See also AFRICA (Facts in Brief Table).
AMERICAN LEGION. See VETERANS.

President Valéry Giscard d'Estaing of France, left, is welcomed to Algiers in April by President Houari Boumediene of Algeria.

AMERICAN LIBRARY ASSOCIATION (ALA).

More than 11,000 librarians, authors, publishers, trustees, and information scientists attended the annual ALA conference in San Francisco in July 1975. Allie Beth Martin, director of the Tulsa (Okla.) City/County Library, took office as president of the association.

Association Activities in 1975 involved a review of progress in library service during the past 100 years and development of plans to meet new needs. Recognizing that millions of Americans are functionally illiterate, the ALA designed a program to help librarians provide literacy training. The first phase of the program, funded by a grant of $49,951 from the United States Office of Education, involves preparation of a manual to help librarians coordinate and initiate literacy training activities.

The ALA took over the National Library Week program from the disbanded National Book Committee. The 1975 program, from April 13 to 19, focused national attention on library and information services.

The ALA also joined in plans for the American Revolution Bicentennial celebration by producing an extensive reading, viewing, and listening resource list. A nine-month national discussion program, called "The American Issues Forum," is designed to involve the public in a thoughtful examination of American society. Grants from the National Endowment for the Humanities and the ALA Carnegie Endowment financed the distribution of millions of copies of the ALA American Issues Forum resource lists.

The Year's Awards. The J. Morris Jones-World Book Encyclopedia-ALA Goals Award went to the ALA Intellectual Freedom Committee and the Intellectual Freedom Round Table to promote the First Amendment freedom of access to information. The first Bailey K. Howard-World Book Encyclopedia-ALA Goals Award was presented to the ALA Centennial Conference Program Committee for the achievement of excellence in the centennial conference program.

Virginia Hamilton won the Newbery Medal for her novel *M. C. Higgins the Great,* the year's most distinguished children's book. Gerald McDermott received the Caldecott Medal for *Arrow to the Sun,* the most distinguished picture book. The Laura Ingalls Wilder Medal, awarded every five years, was given to Beverly Cleary for her contribution to children's literature. The Mildred L. Batchelder Award for the most outstanding children's book originally published in a foreign language went to *An Old Tale Carved Out of Stone,* translated from Russian by Maria Palushkin and published by Crown Publishers, Incorporated.   Peggy Barber

See also CANADIAN LIBRARY ASSOCIATION (CLA); LIBRARY; LITERATURE FOR CHILDREN.

ANDORRA. See EUROPE.

Portuguese refugees in Angola wait to be evacuated from Nova Lisboa to escape fighting between nationalist factions.

ANGOLA became independent of Portugal on Nov. 11, 1975. However, the new nation, with a population of 6 million persons and an area about twice the size of Texas, was in the midst of a civil war. Two rival governments claimed to rule.

Rival Factions. The Popular Movement for the Liberation of Angola (MPLA) established a government headed by Agostinho Neto in Luanda, the former colonial capital. Its rival, a coalition of two other nationalist groups – the National Front for the Liberation of Angola (FNLA) and the National Union for the Total Independence of Angola (UNITA) – set up their capital in Nova Lisboa, changing its name to Huambo. Holden Roberto (FNLA) and Jonas Savimbi (UNITA) were its two main leaders.

From late January until early August, the three nationalist movements joined with the Portuguese in a shaky coalition government. However, each movement had its own army, and they clashed frequently, particularly in Luanda. In early July, the MPLA launched an offensive against both the FNLA and UNITA, capturing Luanda on July 15. This move led to the fall of the coalition government on August 14.

Portugal and the Organization of African Unity tried in vain to bring the three groups back together before independence. But there was strong personal enmity between Neto and Roberto and ethnic rivalries among the rank-and-file members.

Foreign Powers fueled the conflict by supplying arms to the two sides. From January to November, Russia provided the MPLA with about $100 million worth of weapons and ammunition. Cuba, Russia's ally, sent about 3,000 men to operate complex Russian arms.

The FNLA-UNITA coalition received some military aid from Zaire, the United States, China, France, and South Africa. These diverse aid sources apparently had a common goal, that of trying to prevent Russia from gaining a strong influence in Angola.

From August until late October, the tide of war seemed to favor the MPLA. But beginning in the last week of October, a FNLA-UNITA armored column, apparently led by white South Africans or Portuguese, or perhaps both, pushed north and captured major inland and coastal towns. However, in early December, the tide reversed again. The MPLA gained ground north of Luanda and in the central region.

The FNLA-UNITA coalition hoped for increased U.S. aid to offset Russian aid to their opponents. But considerable opposition developed in Congress against deeper U.S. involvement. See CONGRESS OF THE UNITED STATES.   John D. Esseks

See AFRICA (Facts in Brief Table); PORTUGAL.

ANTHROPOLOGY. Mary Leakey reported in October, 1975, that she has found fossil evidence in Tanzania that man lived and perhaps evolved in East Africa about 3.75 million years ago. She found the jaws and teeth of at least 11 individuals who appear to belong to the genus *Homo* in a region called Laetolil, about 25 miles (40 kilometers) south of the Olduvai Gorge, where she and her late husband, Louis Leakey, made many spectacular fossil discoveries over the last two decades. The fossils were found in sediments that have been dated by radioactive methods at the University of California, Berkeley.

Awash River Discoveries. C. Donald Johanson of Case Western Reserve University in Cleveland and Maurice Taieb of the French Scientific Research Center in Paris discovered about 75 fossil bones from a single australopithecine, a close relative of man, in the Awash River Valley in central Ethiopia in October, 1974, but they did not report the find until 1975. The remains were estimated to date from more than 3 million years ago.

The two anthropologists had found the remains of another individual of about the same age earlier in 1974, including teeth and jaws. But the australopithecine remains included many parts of the body. The remains, named "Lucy," were those of an 18- to 20-year-old female about 3½ feet (106 centime-

Medical researchers at Wayne State University in Detroit unwrap an Egyptian mummy for an autopsy as part of an anthropological study.

ters) tall. Preliminary studies indicate that she almost certainly walked with an erect posture.

The two finds appear to support the argument some anthropologists have made in recent years that the australopithecines were contemporaries, not ancestors, of early humans. They also suggest that the two evolved from a common ancestor more than 4 million years ago.

Support for this theory came from a study carried out by anthropologists David Pilbeam of Yale University and Stephen J. Gould of Harvard University. They examined the relationship between body and tooth size, brain capacity, and skull shape of three species of early hominids – *Australopithecus africanus, Australopithecus robustus,* and *Australopithecus boisei* – as well as in the remains of a hominid that some anthropologists have called *Homo habilis* and others consider an australopithecine. Their study indicates that all of the australopithecine species are "variants of a single animal," and that differences in skull shape and tooth size are explained by differences in body size. They reject the notion some anthropologists propose that *Australopithecus africanus* was a meat-eater while *Australopithecus robustus* was a vegetarian. Pilbeam and Gould argue that the diets of the two hominids were similar. *Homo habilis,* on the other hand, shows some differences in characteristics that cannot be explained solely on the basis of changes in body size. Pilbeam and Gould say these reflect new adaptive patterns.

Genetic Patterns. In a related study, Mary-Claire King of the University of California, San Francisco, and Allan C. Wilson of the University of California, Berkeley, reported on a comparison of the molecular biology of modern humans and chimpanzees in which they focused on the proteins and nucleic acids found in the cells of men and apes. They discovered that, while the genetic distance between humans and chimps measured in this fashion is 25 to 60 times greater than the distance between various human groups, it is actually extraordinarily small. It is smaller than the distance between, say, related species of squirrels.

Hunting and Male Dominance. Many scholars have attributed the dominance of males in most existing societies to the pivotal role men played when hunting was a primary source of subsistence. Richard B. Lee of the University of Toronto in Canada has challenged this argument on the basis of his studies of the !Kung Bushmen, hunter-gatherers who live in the Kalahari Desert of southern Africa. The !Kung women, Lee points out, are neither economically nor politically dependent on the men. They obtain food by gathering while the men hunt, and the gathered food is as important to the group as that obtained by hunting.   Fred Plog

ARAB EMIRATES, UNITED. See UNITED ARAB EMIRATES (UAE).

ARCHAEOLOGY. Construction workers in July, 1975, uncovered a pottery army of life-sized figures of warriors and horses that had been buried for more than 2,000 years near the city of Sian in northwestern China. The figures were in a huge tomb that was built for the remains of Ch'in Shih-huang, an emperor of the Ch'in dynasty (221-206 B.C.). About 530 figures have been excavated, and Chinese archaeologists estimate that there may be up to 6,000 such life-sized statues in the tomb.

The warriors, laid out in rows and phalanxes, were armed with such weapons as swords, spears, crossbows, and bows and arrows. The weapons were in excellent condition, and some of the swords were still shiny. The excavators also unearthed almost 10,000 artifacts from the site, including wooden chariots, iron farm implements, and objects of gold, jade, bone, linen, silk, and leather.

Workmen building a dam near Senta, Yugoslavia, unearthed the remains of a 1,900-year-old city in June that may yield important discoveries about the Sarmatians, Huns, and other predatory neighbors of the Roman Empire. Archaeologists took charge of the digging in early September.

Cultural Resource Management. New federal and state environmental protection laws are having a great impact on archaeology in the United States. Many of these laws include guidelines for the preservation of historic and prehistoric cultural resources. Implementing such laws requires that archaeologists survey the site of any proposed construction project, identify prehistoric or historic sites found there, and propose ways to save important resources from destruction.

This is important to archaeologists because most existing archaeological sites in the United States will be destroyed within 25 to 50 years at the current rate of construction. The new laws have created a demand for archaeologists, and new university programs are being developed.

The Mammal Mystery. Several members of the mammal class, such as mastodons and saber-toothed tigers, became extinct at about the time that man colonized the New World. Archaeologists have long debated whether their disappearance resulted from climatic changes at the end of the last Ice Age or from hunting by primitive people. After making a computer study of the problem, anthropologist Paul S. Martin of the University of Arizona and statistician James Mosemann of the National Institutes of Health in Bethesda, Md., pointed a finger of suspicion at primitive man.

Martin and Mosemann assumed that about 100 persons entered the New World about 12,000 years ago, and that there were more than 75 million large animals on the continent at that time. Given the abundant food supply of this previously unexploited area, they postulated a population growth rate of 2.4 per cent per year, which would result in

Archaeologists uncovered some 530 life-sized pottery warriors and horses, buried for more than 2,000 years near an emperor's grave in north China.

an overall population of around 300,000 people in 293 years. Martin and Mosemann found that this many people could easily have killed off the game in this time.

In another study, Martin and Austin Long, also of the University of Arizona, demonstrated that the giant ground sloth disappeared from western North America and South America at about the same time that people appeared there. Radiocarbon dates for dung balls left by the sloths correspond closely with the arrival of the first people.

Mayan Collapse? Archaeologists have developed a number of theories to account for the collapse of Mayan civilization in Mesoamerica in about A.D. 900. Disease, warfare, and ecological disasters have all been listed as possible causes of the collapse. However, Jeremy A. Saboloff of Harvard University and William L. Rathje of the University of Arizona suggested in October that there may have been no collapse at all. They cited evidence from recent archaeological excavations on Cozumel Island off the coast of Mexico's Yucatán Peninsula. These excavations showed that, though various Mayan monuments disappeared about A.D. 900, the well-being of the average Mayan was unchanged. The so-called collapse may represent no more than the replacement of a religious government with a far more secular organization based on trade and economics.   Fred Plog

ARCHITECTURE in the United States struggled through a very poor year in 1975. A gloomy financial picture resulted in sharp cutbacks in both public and private funding of new buildings. Many projects that were already on the drafting boards were stopped, leaving great numbers of buildings and complexes abandoned or postponed.

The larger architectural firms managed to stay in business by severely cutting back on personnel and by diligently searching out work in such related areas as interior design. But for the smaller firms, the year was disastrous. Many simply closed their doors, and their skilled designers and engineers sought work with larger firms or drifted into other careers.

The AIA Convention. "Spaces for the Species" was the official theme of the American Institute of Architects (AIA) national convention held in Atlanta, Ga., in May. But "survival for the species known as architect" more adequately described the overriding concern of the 4,000 who attended.

Because of the crisis in the profession, the convention program dispensed with much of the usual philosophical discussion on the nature of design. Instead, more practical sessions concentrated on marketing design services, remodeling existing structures, and the architect as developer.

These signs of the times were accurately reflected in the 1975 design award competitions staged

The Herbert F. Johnson Museum of Art at Cornell University, designed by I. M. Pei & Partners, won a 1975 AIA honor award.

by the AIA's two most influential chapters – New York City and Chicago. In New York City, five of the 10 citations were for building renovations, and four of the five were modest-budget projects. The renovations "are projects that architects should be doing rather than selling monuments," one of the jurors said.

In the Chicago competition, architect Stanley Tigerman won two awards – one for a barn in Michigan that he remodeled into a residence and one for an old store that he remade into a clothing boutique on Chicago's Near North Side.

Preservation Affected. The money crunch also directly affected architectural and historical preservation efforts. For example, St. Louis had high hopes of restoring and preserving the Wainwright Building of 1891, designed by Dankmar Adler and Louis Sullivan. The state of Missouri had purchased the building to save it from demolition and had also sponsored a national competition for a design incorporating the landmark within a proposed one-block state-office complex. Winners were Mitchell-Giurgola of New York City and Philadelphia, in association with Hastings & Chivetta of St. Louis. Unfortunately, restoration was barely underway in 1975 when the Missouri legislature cut the project's funds.

Another significant shift in the profession's direction was away from the one-man, form-giver

concept and toward the team approach. Symbolic of this, The Office of Mies van der Rohe announced in July that it was changing its name to Fujikawa, Conterato, Lohan & Associates, representing the three architects who have guided the Chicago firm as equal partners since the death of Ludwig Mies van der Rohe in 1969.

A spokesman said the firm was "proud to acknowledge its debt to Mies and to a tradition of architectural professionalism and excellence of design." But he added: "The practice of architecture has changed drastically during the past decade. Social, economic, and technological changes have increasingly directed the firm toward a team approach to architectural practice."

Notable New Prisons. New structures completed in 1975 revealed further signs of changing architectural times. Three metropolitan correctional centers were constructed for the U.S. Bureau of Prisons. Each is a bold departure from the traditionally stark prisons of the past. In fact, the three $10-million to $15-million facilities could easily be mistaken for modern college dormitories.

San Diego architects Tucker, Sadler & Bennett designed a 21-story correctional center for that city that broke up each 48-person floor into individual living units oriented around a bilevel multipurpose area. In Chicago, architects Harry Weese & Associates opted for a 28-story, triangular structure. Each floor is bisected into two living modules – each having individual accommodation for 11 persons – facing a small lounge area. And in New York City, Gruzen & Partners designed an 11-story facility, with living units, classrooms, recreation areas, and multipurpose rooms interspersed throughout each floor.

Two Tall Buildings in the Southwest will provide focal points for their respective cities, Dallas and Tulsa, Okla. They will also result in urban revitalization in those cities. In Dallas, Woodbine Development undertook a $75-million endeavor, called the Reunion Project, on a 70-acre (28-hectare) downtown site. A Los Angeles architectural and engineering firm, Welton Becket & Associates, designed the 50-story Reunion Tower, a cylindrical office building topped by a revolving observation deck, restaurant, and cocktail lounge. The tower will be very much like Seattle's Space Needle. Becket also designed a 27-story, 1,000-room Hyatt Regency Hotel and a shopping area.

In Tulsa, the Williams Realty Corporation began developing its 22-acre (8.9-hectare) Williams Center. The $200-million project includes a 51-story Bank of Oklahoma Tower and a Performing Arts Center, both designed by Minoru Yamasaki. There will also be two auto parking facilities – one aboveground and one underground – and a 2.5-acre (1-hectare) park designed by C. F. Murphy Associates of Chicago.   Rob Cuscaden

ARGENTINA. All the conditions for a military coup d'état seemed to be present in Argentina in 1975; the remarkable thing was that one did not occur. The army chiefs were reluctant to assume responsibility for a situation in which the rate of inflation climbed over 260 per cent in a year, terrorist attacks claimed more than 600 lives, and the trade unions – using threats of a general strike as a weapon – dictated economic policy. Avoiding a coup was not due to any political skills displayed by President María Estela (Isabel) Martínez de Perón, the widow of General Juan D. Perón. Her sole claim to power was her married name.

Isabel Perón's Regime. President Perón's personal weakness became obvious through her prolonged absences because of physical and nervous breakdown. It made her depend heavily on intimate, but controversial, counselors such as José López Rega, a former policeman and amateur astrologer who was later accused by army intelligence of organizing the right wing terrorist group, the Argentine Anticommunist Alliance. It took the combined pressure of the trade union federation (CGT) and the generals to oust López Rega as social welfare minister on July 11.

Perón's second choice as strongman brought Argentina to the very brink of a coup. She named a young colonel, Vicente Damasco, as interior minister of Argentina. The army chiefs were outraged and issued a statement insisting on their "total independence" from the government. In quick succession, conservative generals forced the retirement on August 27 of the army chief, General Alberto Numa Laplane, who had backed Damasco, and encouraged Perón to take an extended holiday at an air force base. The president of the Senate, Italo Luder, was promptly named interim president on September 19; he fired Damasco.

Although it was widely believed that Perón's vacation would be permanent, she resumed her duties on October 17. But she found herself with an even narrower power base than before.

Political Violence went almost unchecked throughout most of the year. The Montoneros, rooted among radical Peronist youth, overtook the Trotskyist People's Revolutionary Army (ERP) as the most formidable urban guerrilla group. After collecting a ransom reputedly between $26 million and $60 million for the release of financiers Jorge and Juan Born, who were kidnaped in September, 1974, the Montoneros staged a new series of kidnapings. The victims included the U.S. honorary consul in Cordoba, John P. Egan, who was murdered after his capture on February 26; British businessman Charles A. Lockwood, who was kidnaped by the ERP in 1973, and again seized on July 31; and the chief justice of Buenos Aires.

The scale of terrorist operations became far more ambitious as the year progressed. The most spectacular was the Montoneros' October 5 attack on a military barracks at Formosa, near the Paraguayan border, in which 30 persons were killed; the guerrillas made their escape in a hijacked plane. They also set a precedent for international terrorists by blowing up a frigate, the *Santísima Trinidad,* in August. Shortly after the Formosa attack in October, the army was given powers to tackle the problem. Mass arrests followed.

The Economy spun out of control in 1975. Devaluations of the peso never caught up with the plunging black-market rate. Ministers of economy following each other in quick succession contributed further to the instability. During his brief period in office, Minister of Economy Celestino Rodrigo experimented with a relatively conservative program – a realistic exchange rate, a wage ceiling, and free-floating prices. This, however, was destroyed by the CGT, which organized a 48-hour general strike on July 5 after the government imposed a 50 per cent limit on wage increases. Ten hours before the strike was due to finish, the government gave way and wage increases of up to 150 per cent were approved. Rodrigo was dismissed soon after. Robert Moss

See also LATIN AMERICA (Facts in Brief Table).

ARIZONA. See STATE GOVERNMENT.

ARKANSAS. See STATE GOVERNMENT.

Argentina's ailing President María Estela Martínez de Perón, wearied by political and economic problems, leaves on a needed vacation.

ARMED FORCES. The United States and Russia continued efforts in 1975 to build on the Strategic Arms Limitation Talks (SALT) agreements reached in Vladivostok, Russia, in November of 1974, but they reported little progress. Both sides continued to develop a variety of strategic new programs. United States officials reported the Soviet Union had successfully deployed multiple independent re-entry vehicle (MIRV) nuclear warheads on their intercontinental ballistic missiles (ICBM's) in January. And in his annual report on February 5, Secretary of Defense James R. Schlesinger reported, "We are now beginning to witness in the Soviet Union the largest initial deployment of improved strategic capabilities in the history of the nuclear competition."

The United States continued development of the *Trident* ballistic missile submarine, the B-1 strategic bomber, and more accurate and potent Minuteman III ICBM's. President Gerald R. Ford warned on August 19 that he would be forced to recommend a $2- to $3-billion annual increase in defense spending for the foreseeable future unless a SALT agreement is reached with the Russians.

The Cruise Missile, a new U.S. weapon, may further complicate disarmament negotiations. Powered by a small jet engine and guided by a miniature computer, the cruise missile can deliver its nuclear payload over a range of up to 1,500 miles (2,400 kilometers) with an accuracy of about 30 yards (27 meters). It can be launched by bombers or submarines, and it can elude many air-defense systems by flying at low altitudes.

Two major technological advances lie at the heart of the cruise missile's ability. The development of small, efficient jet engines allowed the missiles to be designed to fit submarine torpedo tubes, which are only 21 inches (53 centimeters) in diameter. Advances in microelectronics made possible the sophisticated guidance system, which matches the terrain of the target area against terrain information stored in the missile's computer. Accurate, hard-to-detect, and relatively economical (from $500,000 to $1 million each), the cruise missile could "drastically alter the conduct of both tactical and strategic warfare," nuclear physicist Kosta Tsipis of the Massachusetts Institute of Technology warned in the 1975 *Yearbook on World Armaments and Disarmament.*

The cruise missile's first test flight was scheduled for early 1976, but it was already creating disarmament problems. Russia, far behind the United States in cruise-missile technology, insists that the missiles should be included in the overall SALT limitation of 2,400 "strategic delivery vehicles" that the 1974 Vladivostok agreement sets for both

The F-16 jet fighter proved a bonanza for General Dynamics Corporation when the U.S. and other NATO countries ordered nearly 1,000 planes.

nations. While the United States may agree to include 3,000-mile (4,800-kilometer) missiles in this category, it said that shorter-range missiles should not be included, though they could reach most targets in Russia from bombers or submarines.

New Sea Power. Almost unnoticed, China has developed into the world's third-largest naval power in recent years, with more officers and men than the French and British navies combined. China reportedly has more than 1,000 vessels, including 60 submarines.

Big Arms Deal. The F-16 lightweight fighter plane, built by the General Dynamics Corporation of St. Louis, won out over the Northrop Corporation's F-17 and the French-built Mirage F-1 in early June. In what many observers called "the arms deal of the century," Belgium agreed to buy 102 of the F-16 jets. Denmark, Holland, and Norway had previously agreed to buy more than 200 of the planes, but their order was contingent on the Belgian agreement. The deal will cost the four North Atlantic Treaty Organization countries more than $2 billion.

Experts generally agreed that the F-16 was the best of the three planes. But the agreement to buy the plane was preceded by intense political and commercial pressures. Charges of bribery and political arm-twisting were widespread.

The United States remained the world's largest arms dealer. The nation sold $9 billion worth of weapons to other countries in fiscal 1975, a record increase of $2 billion. The Pentagon reported arms sales to 72 countries, nearly half of them to three Persian Gulf nations – Iran, $2.5 billion; Saudi Arabia, $1.4 billion; and Kuwait, $366 million.

U.S. Military Strength. The United States continued to trim its military forces. On October 31, troop strength stood at 2,096,620, the lowest level in 25 years and 60,000 less than in 1974. Nearly 500,000 troops were stationed overseas, including 220,000 in West Germany, 46,000 in Japan, and 42,000 in South Korea. At the insistence of the Thai government, the United States began reducing its 20,000-man force in Thailand.

In his annual report, General George S. Brown, chairman of the Joint Chiefs of Staff, warned that American military power was declining with respect to that of Russia. "The strategic balance today remains in dynamic equilibrium," Brown said, "with the Soviet numerical edge by some indicators offset by the United States qualitative advantage. The U.S.S.R., however, has embarked upon a mass program of major strategic-force improvements and deployments which, if not constrained by the negotiating process or balanced by major U.S. arms initiatives, will result in serious superiority over the United States in the years ahead...."

Defense Budget. The U.S. Department of Defense submitted a budget request for fiscal 1976

(July 1, 1975, to June 30, 1976) of $92.8 billion, an $8-billion increase. Officials attributed the increase almost entirely to inflation. The budget would support 14 Army and 3 Marine divisions, 22 Air Force tactical wings, 17 Navy and Marine air wings, and a Navy fleet of 502 vessels. An estimated $7.7 billion was recommended for strategic forces, $35.9-billion for conventional forces, and $9.4 billion for research and development. The Navy was scheduled to receive the largest share of the budget, $34.1 billion; the Air Force, $30.6 billion; and the Army, $25.1 billion.

The Navy asked for $2.1 billion for the *Trident* ballistic missile submarine, $1.1 billion for guided missile frigates, $819 million for nuclear attack submarines, $516 million for the S-3A antisubmarine-warfare plane, $102 million for a cruise missile, and $620 million for F-14 Tomcat jet fighters.

The Air Force requested $1.7 billion for the F-15 Eagle jet fighter, $780 million for Minuteman III ICBM's, $749 million for the B-1 bomber, $690-million for the Airborne Warning and Control System (AWACS) radar plane, $460 million for the A-10 close-air-support fighter, and $273 million for the F-16 lightweight fighter.

The Army asked for $498 million for M-60 tanks, $312 million for Tow and Dragon antitank missiles, $130 million for the SAM-D missile, $65-million for an advanced attack helicopter, and $65-million for a short-range air-defense missile system. The Army made plans to create two new divisions by the end of fiscal 1976.

Congress passed a $25.5-billion military procurement bill for fiscal 1976 on September 28. The bill authorized $3.1 billion less than the Pentagon had sought, but virtually every major weapons system survived attempts to reduce spending.

Command Changes. In a surprise move on November 1, President Ford dismissed Secretary of Defense Schlesinger and appointed White House chief of staff Donald H. Rumsfeld to the post. Schlesinger had been a hard-liner on defense issues, and his removal was viewed by many as a political victory for Secretary of State Henry A. Kissinger and his policy of détente with Russia.

Howard H. Callaway resigned as secretary of the Army on July 3 to become director of President Ford's 1976 election campaign and was succeeded by Martin R. Hoffmann. General Robert E. Cushman, Jr., retired as commandant of the Marine Corps and was succeeded by General Louis H. Wilson, Jr., on July 1. Daniel James became the first black four-star general on August 29, when he was promoted from Air Force lieutenant general and named commander of the North American Air Defense Command.   Thomas M. DeFrank

ARMY. See ARMED FORCES.

ART. See ARCHITECTURE; DANCING; LITERATURE; MUSIC, CLASSICAL; POETRY; VISUAL ARTS.

ASIA

War ended in Indochina in the spring of 1975, and the United States abandoned its footholds there. Non-Communist Asian countries spent the rest of the year adjusting to the reality of several new Communist regimes in their midst.

For the U.S.-backed regimes in Indochina, the end came with dramatic suddenness. In Khmer (formerly Cambodia), President Lon Nol's government simply disintegrated, and, on April 16, the Communist Khmer Rouge marched into Phnom Penh. With South Vietnamese forces in panicky flight, Saigon fell to North Vietnamese and Viet Cong troops on April 30. Ambassador Graham A. Martin was one of the last Americans to board an evacuation helicopter on the roof of the United States Embassy. The Communist Pathet Lao gained the upper hand in Laos in the spring, but it was not until December 3 that they deposed King Savang Vatthana and proclaimed a People's Democratic Republic.

Asia Adapts. Observing the scene, Indonesia's Foreign Minister Adam Malik spoke soberly of "a new political configuration in Southeast Asia to which all nations have to adapt themselves." Adaptation to the new realities and fears was hasty. Barely three weeks after Saigon's fall, President Ferdinand E. Marcos of the Philippines announced new foreign policy guidelines. He said his government would try more vigorously to establish diplomatic relations with Socialist states, particularly the People's Republic of China and Russia, and try to "find a new basis compatible with the emerging realities in Asia for a continuing healthy relationship with the United States...." Philippine leaders, like those of Burma, Malaysia, and Thailand, made pilgrimages to China and announced recognition of the new governments in Indochina.

Only a few Asian leaders were far-sighted enough to realize the need for long-delayed domestic reforms. One of the most perceptive was Singapore's Prime Minister Lee Kuan Yew. After a melancholy survey of inequities in non-Communist countries, Lee predicted "more and more of the third world going Communist" in the near future.

At least for the moment, the fears seemed justified. Communist influence was spreading, and the elaborate network of old alliances was falling apart. Much as it had during the birth of the People's Republic of China in 1949, the Communist triumph in Southeast Asia presaged a long, uncertain, and—to many—frightening season of continuing readjustment.

Red Feuds. Into the power vacuum left by the U.S. departure moved Russia and China, obsessed

North Vietnamese soldiers atop a Russian tank celebrate victory on April 30 after crashing through gates of Saigon's Presidential Palace.

with their relentless feud. They picked their favorites in Indochina. The Russians backed Laos, and the Chinese supported Khmer—which let it be known it might establish diplomatic relations with Moscow in about two years. They also picked their allies on the subcontinent of India, with Russia providing heavy military and industrial aid to India and China helping to arm Pakistan. The two countries engaged in competitive wooing of North Korea's strongman, Kim Il-song.

Japan, which once hoped to play one Communist giant against another, was distressed to find itself suddenly under massive pressure from both. China refused to conclude a peace and friendship treaty with Japan unless the document included a phrase denouncing *hegemony* (political domination) by another power, meaning Russia. Moscow, in turn, warned Tokyo it would regard any such phrase in the treaty as a hostile act.

A New Rival. But the two great Communist powers had their own problems, at least in Southeast Asia. On November 21, much sooner than expected, the two halves of Vietnam agreed to hold joint elections in 1976, as a step toward unification. Once rejoined, this will be a nation proud of its triumphs over the French in 1954 and the Americans in 1975 — heavily armed, disciplined, and determined to have its own zone of influence. Russia and China could contend against each other in most of Asia, and they could competitively romance Hanoi. But they would have to be constantly aware of Hanoi's interests and sensitivities.

Some of the non-Communist Asian states saw a hope for survival in this Communist triangle. If once they pinned their dreams to U.S. generosity and protection, now they would try to play Moscow against Peking, and Hanoi against both.

Obsolete Treaties. For the United States, defeat in Indochina did not mean a total break with the region; it only meant the withdrawal of armed forces and a search for a new political and military strategy. The United States was still the richest nation in the world, and for most of the non-Communist countries of Asia, the American market meant the difference between economic well-being and stagnation. This gave Washington considerable leverage in the area. But, in 1975, U.S. leaders also began to consider forging a new anti-Communist barrier in the Pacific, notably in Indonesia and the Philippines.

U.S. Armed Forces Deaths from Enemy Action During the War in Vietnam

Killed	38,433
Died of wounds	5,168
Died while missing	2,782
Died while captured or interned	80
Total deaths	46,463

*Jan. 1, 1961, through Sept. 30, 1975

The fiasco in Indochina had exacted its price. One of the earliest casualties was the anti-Communist Southeast Asia Treaty Organization (SEATO). Thailand and the Philippines, the two remaining Asian members since Pakistan quit in 1973, proposed in July that SEATO be dissolved. On September 23, the non-Asian members – Australia, Great Britain, New Zealand, and the United States – agreed that this should be done "in view of the changing circumstances." SEATO was never a significant force in Asia, but its passing was symptomatic of the new reality there.

Other agreements were also being dissolved. Although Manila agreed to let the United States continue to use the bases it had on Philippine soil, Manila demanded in July that control over the bases be surrendered to the Philippines. Significantly, China had hinted to both Manila and Washington, D.C., that it preferred to see the United States maintain its naval presence in the region as a counterweight to Russia.

A Time of Missiles. Not the least disturbing feature on the Asian scene in 1975 was the growing proliferation of sophisticated weapons. India, which tested a "peaceful" nuclear device in the sands of Rajasthan state in 1974, vigorously pressed its nuclear program. China carried out yet another nuclear test in 1975, launched two earth satellites, and added to its 75 or so medium-range missiles that were in place for action against Russia.

Reasonably sophisticated earth satellites were being produced by China, India, and Japan. And Indonesia expected to join the United States, Canada, and Russia in 1976 as the possessor of a communications satellite. The *Palapa,* to be orbited in July by the United States for that country, became the subject of sharp controversy. Critics in Indonesia argued that the $5-billion price tag on *Palapa* and the rest of the communications program was extravagant for a nation that has had trouble paying its debts.

The immense quantities of modern arms captured by the Communists in Indochina presented another problem. The danger was that these weapons would soon find their way into the hands of Communist guerrillas in Indonesia, Malaysia, and Thailand. Some of the arms were already appearing in local black markets, and gunrunners in Thailand were offering U.S. M16 rifles for $100 each in 1975, half the price they had demanded a year earlier.

Economic Woes. All Asian countries would remember 1975 as a year of deep economic crisis. With the notable exception of Japan, these nations are mainly hewers of wood and diggers of minerals for the industrial West. The recession in the West meant less demand for Asia's products and a sharp drop in prices. This was true in Malaysia, which found its markets for rubber, palm oil, tin, and lumber shrinking. It was true in Bangladesh, India, Indonesia, the Philippines, and Sri Lanka. And, for all their claims of immunity from capitalist crises, it also proved true in some of the Communist states. Even with its growing oil exports, China saw its 1975 trade deficit growing beyond $1 billion. North Korea, too, found itself temporarily unable to meet its foreign payments. While Asia's raw materials brought in less money, the products these countries wanted to buy – oil, fertilizer, manufactured goods, and industrial machinery – cost much more.

This, inevitably, led to a sharp drop in the rate of growth. The poorer countries, in which the annual per capita income is under $200, saw the growth rate drop from about 5.3 per cent in 1973, to 2.4 per cent in 1974, to less than 2 per cent in 1975. In fact, a World Bank study showed that India's gross domestic product (gross national product minus net payments on foreign investments) averaged only 1.3 per cent growth annually between 1970 and 1974. This was worse than stagnation. With the birth rate in most Asian countries ranging upwards of 2.5 per cent, this meant a decline in the already low living standards. It was hardly comforting to learn of a United Nations estimate that by the year 2000 Asia's population would soar to 3.8 billion people. This would be a larger population than the entire world had in 1970.

Rice and Oil were two bright spots in the bleak Asian picture. After a series of crop failures, the rice harvest in key countries, notably China, India, and Thailand, was bountiful.

But it was oil that formed the stuff of dreams in many of the Asian countries. Oil was found in 1975, usually offshore, in Bangladesh, India, South Korea, Malaysia, Pakistan, and Taiwan. China and Indonesia were already self-sufficient in petroleum production.

Facts in Brief on the Asian Countries

Country	Population	Government	Monetary Unit*	Foreign Trade (million U.S. $) Exports	Imports
Afghanistan	19,660,000	President & Prime Minister Mohammad Daoud	afghani (45 = $1)	122	145
Australia	13,972,000	Governor General Sir John R. Kerr; Prime Minister Malcolm Fraser	dollar (1 = $1.26)	11,046	12,411
Bangladesh	82,785,000	President Abu Sadat Mohammed Sayem	taka (13.7 = $1)	347	1,096
Bhutan	953,000	King Jigme Singye Wangchuck	Indian rupee	no statistics available	
Burma	31,496,000	President U Ne Win; Prime Minister U Sein Win	kyat (6.7 = $1)	196	127
China	845,441,000	Communist Party Chairman Mao Tse-tung; Premier Chou En-lai†	yuan (1.9 = $1)	4,900	5,000
India	614,744,000	President Fakhruddin Ali Ahmed; Prime Minister Indira Gandhi	rupee (8.8 = $1)	3,925	5,043
Indonesia	133,180,000	President Suharto	rupiah (415 = $1)	7,094	3,842
Iran	34,384,000	Shah Mohammad Reza Pahlavi; Prime Minister Amir Abbas Hoveyda	rial (65.3 = $1)	24,000	5,672
Japan	111,742,000	Emperor Hirohito; Prime Minister Takeo Miki	yen (305 = $1)	55,596	62,075
Khmer (Cambodia)	7,860,000	President Norodom Sihanouk; Prime Minister Penn Nouth	riel (1,650 = $1)	15	98
Korea, North	16,394,000	President Kim Il-song; Premier Kim Il	won (1.3 = $1)	133	267
Korea, South	35,180,000	President Chung Hee Park; Prime Minister Choi Kyu Ha	won (484 = $1)	4,461	6,844
Laos	3,415,000	President Prince Souphanouvong; Prime Minister Kayson Phomvihan	kip (750 = $1)	4	57
Malaysia	12,057,000	Paramount Ruler Yahya Petra ibni Al-Marhum Sultan Ibrahim; Prime Minister Abdul Razak bin Dato Hussein	dollar (2.5 = $1)	4,232	4,155
Maldives	120,000	President Ibrahim Nasir	rupee (6.9 = $1)	2	3
Mongolia	1,463,000	People's Revolutionary Party First Secretary & Presidium Chairman Yumjaagiin Tsedenbal; Council of Ministers Chairman Jambyn Batmonh	tugrik (3.3 = $1)	130	157
Nepal	12,315,000	King Birendra Bir Bikram Shah Dev; Prime Minister Tulsi Giri	rupee (12.5 = $1)	65	70
New Zealand	3,083,000	Governor General Sir Denis Blundell; Prime Minister Robert D. Muldoon	dollar (1 = $1.05)	2,434	3,651
Pakistan	73,321,000	President Fazal Elahi Chaudry; Prime Minister Zulfikar Ali Bhutto	rupee (9.9 = $1)	1,113	1,732
Papua New Guinea	2,849,000	Governor General Sir John Guise; Prime Minister Michael Somare	kina (1 = $1.26)	516	343
Philippines	43,940,000	President Ferdinand E. Marcos	peso (7.4 = $1)	2,671	3,436
Russia	258,542,000	Communist Party General Secretary Leonid I. Brezhnev; Premier Aleksey N. Kosygin; Supreme Soviet Presidium Chairman Nikolay V. Podgorny	ruble (1 = $1.43)	27,405	24,890
Singapore	2,324,000	President Benjamin H. Sheares; Prime Minister Lee Kuan Yew	dollar (2.5 = $1)	5,810	8,379
Sri Lanka (Ceylon)	14,274,000	President William Gopallawa; Prime Minister Sirimavo Bandaranaike	rupee (7.5=$1)	521	691
Taiwan	16,372,000	President C. K. Yen; Premier Chiang Ching-kuo	new Taiwan dollar (37 = $1)	5,519	6,983
Thailand	40,999,000	King Bhumibol Adulyadej; Prime Minister Khukrit Pramot	baht (19.6 = $1)	2,470	3,090
Vietnam, North	24,136,000	President Ton Duc Thang; Prime Minister Pham Van Dong	dong (2.4 = $1)	150	250
Vietnam, South	21,080,000	Head of Government Pham Hung	piaster (2.4 = $1)	58	656

*Exchange rates as of Dec. 1, 1975; †died Jan. 8, 1976

A bowing representative of Sikkim presents a
ceremonial scarf to India's foreign minister
as the Himalayan state is merged with India.

China, in fact, provided the year's most exciting
oil success story. In 1963, it produced 6.3 million
short tons (6 million metric tons) of crude oil. By
1975, production had grown more than tenfold,
and China's oil brought in more than $700 million
in foreign sales.

But oil also produced serious international fric-
tions. Japan wrangled with South Korea and Taiwan over potential offshore fields. China, which
landed a garrison on the potentially oil-rich Para-
cel Islands off South Vietnam in February, 1974,
also appeared to be interested in Spratly Island,
already claimed by the Philippines, Taiwan, and
Vietnam.

Repression. Communist triumphs in Vietnam,
Khmer, and Laos were followed by purges, with
penalties ranging from periods of "re-education"
to the firing squad. The people in the "liberated"
countries soon became accustomed to mass meetings at which cringing enemies of the new government were required to repent their sins. And students found themselves recruited for compulsory
farm work or for service in vigilante squads to fer-
ret out enemies.

But repression was not confined to the Communist countries. Generals continued to rule in
Burma, Indonesia, and South Korea, and their
only remedy for social unrest was to put dissidents
in prison. In Indonesia, some 55,000 persons arrested 10 years earlier on suspicion of involvement
in a Communist uprising still sat in the jails awaiting trial in mid-1975.

But civilian rulers were scarcely more gentle
with their people. President Marcos continued to
rule the Philippines under martial law, with his
opponents in jail, the press muzzled, and numerous
relatives — including his wife — holding top offices.

The year's most stunning reverse for democracy
came in June in India, where Prime Minister Indira
Gandhi, faced with an adverse court ruling and vast
public discontent, suspended many constitutional
provisions, put tens of thousands of people behind
bars, and placed the press under tight control.
While Gandhi insisted she was merely protecting
democracy, her critics argued she had destroyed
what democracy there was in India.

Racial minorities also fared badly in 1975, none
so much as the Chinese in Indonesia, Malaysia,
and the Philippines, and the Moslems in the last of
these countries. Students continued to provide
some of the social ferment, but they were rigor-
ously suppressed. Still, they sought civil rights in
South Korea and justice for the landless peasants
in Malaysia and Thailand.

Other Changes. Fighting raged through much
of Portuguese Timor, a colony that occupies half of
an island 360 miles (580 kilometers) north of Dar-
win, Australia. The western half of the island is
ruled by Indonesia. Nearly 600,000 persons live in
Portuguese Timor, in an area of about 5,800
square miles (15,000 square kilometers).

A conference to decide the status of the colony
ended on March 28 with Portuguese officials and
representatives of two political parties there fore-
casting a smooth transition to independence. However, fighting erupted between rival factions in August after an attempted coup d'état. It continued
off and on through the rest of the year. Indonesian
troops invaded the colony on December 7, and Portugal broke diplomatic relations with Indonesia.
China and several other countries protested Indonesia's action. On December 8, Indonesia's Foreign Minister Adam Malik announced that pro-
Indonesian parties in Portuguese Timor had set up
a provisional government in the wake of the take-
over by Indonesia. However, there were reports at
the end of the year that opposition forces had withdrawn to the jungle for the purpose of fighting a
guerrilla war.

In the Maldives, about 400 miles (650 kilometers)
southwest of Sri Lanka, President Ibrahim Nasir
ousted Premier Ahmed Zaki on March 10. Zaki was
exiled to a remote island.

More orderly change came in Sikkim, which
voted on April 15 to abolish the 300-year-old monarchy and merge with India.   Mark Gayn

See also the various Asian country articles; Section One, FOCUS ON THE WORLD.

ASTRONOMY. Two especially good examples of the added information that can be gained by making composite pictures from several individual exposures of celestial sources excited astronomers in 1975. The first shows how astronomers can artificially eliminate movements in the Earth's atmosphere in order to see the surface of a star other than the Sun. The second reveals the added size perceived for galaxies when atmospheric lights are suppressed.

Betelgeuse Resolved. Most stars are so far away that they look like mere points of light even through the largest telescopes. If the Earth's atmosphere were perfectly still, a few nearby giant stars could be seen as disk surfaces rather than as points. But winds and eddy currents in the atmosphere smear images so that marginal details are lost. Until now, the Sun was the only star close enough to reveal surface detail.

Working with the 158-inch (4-meter) telescope at Kitt Peak National Observatory near Tucson, Ariz., Roger Lynds and his co-workers used a new technique called *speckle interferometry* to see the surface of Betelgeuse, a cool supergiant star in the constellation Orion. They took large-scale, short-exposure photographs through filters that picked out either the hot or cool regions on the star's surface. Short exposures freeze the Earth's atmos-

pheric turbulence and yield a mottled, diffuse picture with many small speckles showing the star surface. A single speckle is not reliable as a clear picture, but thousands added together give astronomers confidence in the resulting picture.

Betelgeuse is hundreds of times larger than the Sun, and it shows faint hints of dark markings that indicate cool spots on the surface. This is the first time astronomers have been able to measure the size of another star directly from photographs and see hints of surface markings resembling sunspots.

Whirlpool Galaxy. M51 is a striking spiral galaxy with an irregular companion dangling at the end of one arm. Martin Burkhead of Indiana University at Bloomington combined five exposures of M51 to get the equivalent of 9½ hours exposure. This procedure greatly reduced the background light from the Earth's atmosphere. The composite picture shows faint outer extensions of the companion galaxy extending thousands of light-years farther than seen before.

Search for Planets. Planets orbiting stars other than the Sun are impossible to see because they are so faint compared to their parent stars. Most searchers use indirect methods to find them. The most recent attempt concentrated on 123 stars like the Sun, or slightly hotter, that are visible to the naked eye.

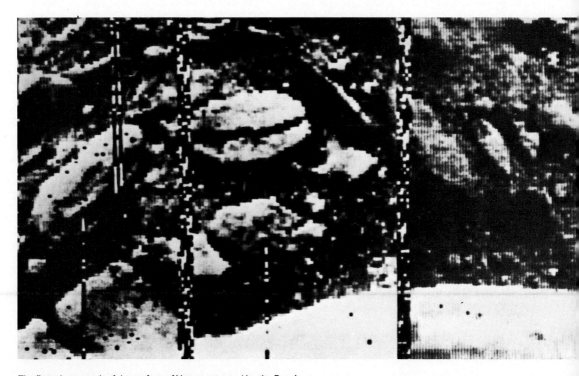

The first photograph of the surface of Venus, returned by the Russian *Venera 9* spacecraft in October, shows an area covered with rocks.

Helmut Abt and Saul Levy of the Kitt Peak observatory systematically looked for variations in the speed of approach or recession of these stars on the theory that an unseen companion could change the motion of the visible star through gravity, causing it to move in a small orbit around the common center of mass. This type of study will reveal the existence of faint stars and massive planets the size of Jupiter or larger.

Abt and Levy found that about 42 per cent of the stars they studied showed no evidence of a companion. But 46 per cent were double objects; 9 per cent, triple; and 2 per cent, quadruple. Thus, most stars seem to have at least one companion star.

Allowing that some companions were probably missed in this search, Abt and Levy concluded that roughly two-thirds of all stars have a companion massive enough to be a star. If the companion's mass is less than 7 per cent that of the Sun, it will not heat up enough during formation to produce the nuclear reactions that make it a star, and it will end up as a planet. We can expect that virtually all stars have some kind of celestial body – either another star or a planet – in orbit around them. Searches for extraterrestrial signals should concentrate on stars with undetected companions.

Farthest Galaxy. Objects moving away from the Earth look redder than if they were standing still because, figuratively speaking, their motion stretches out the light waves and changes their color as seen from the Earth. In general, more distant objects or galaxies are receding faster than nearby galaxies. The farther away a galaxy is, the more its light is shifted toward longer, redder wave lengths. By measuring the shift, astronomers can estimate the distance to a remote stellar system.

Hyron Spinrad of the University of California at Berkeley announced in July that he had identified the most distant galaxy yet found. The galaxy, 3C-123, is only a faint smudge on long-exposure photographs. Using a spectrum scanner on a telescope at Lick Observatory in Mount Hamilton, Calif., Spinrad determined that the galaxy's radiation is shifted toward the red side of the spectrum by almost 64 per cent. Thus, bright lines of oxygen and dark lines of calcium, usually found in the ultraviolet, showed up as orange-red. This shift means the galaxy is moving away from us at a speed equal to 45 per cent the speed of light and is about 8-billion light-years away. From the size of the smudged image, Spinrad predicts the galaxy is a supergiant, 5 or 10 times larger than our Galaxy, the Milky Way. The light we see now left the galaxy more than 3 billion years before our solar system was formed some 4.6 billion years ago. This is about halfway back to the birth of the universe.

The previous recordholder was a supergiant galaxy with a red shift of 46 per cent, discovered in 1960. Many quasars have larger red shifts, but there are so many unanswered questions about them that astronomers hesitate to draw conclusions about the early history of our universe from them.

Variable Quasars. Martha and William Liller of Harvard University in Cambridge, Mass., studied photographs going back to 1885 to investigate the recent history of two celestial objects, one known as a quasar and the other a similar object that lacks certain identifying features common to quasars. They announced their results in July.

The quasar, PKS 1510-089, showed a phenomenal outburst in 1948 when it flared to more than 100 times its usual brightness for 10 days. The short duration of the outburst indicates that the active part of the quasar must be less than about 10 *light-days* across. A light-day is the distance light travels in one day. During the flare-up, PKS 1510-089 was the brightest object ever measured in the universe – roughly 10,000 times brighter than the entire Milky Way.

The other object studied is similar to a quasar except that it has no bright lines that can be used to measure the red shift. The first object of this type singled out for study was BL Lacertae. A few others have also been identified. The one studied by the Lillers has become about 25 times brighter than normal at times.   Laura P. Bautz

See also Section Two, UPDATING OUR PERSPEC-TIVE ON THE PLANETS.

ATLANTA. Mayor Maynard H. Jackson, the first black mayor in Atlanta's history, encountered political difficulties in 1975 that threatened to provoke racial strife when he refused to fire the city's first black public safety commissioner. The commissioner, Reginald Eaves, had been a college friend of Jackson's. Eaves was charged with cronyism and influence peddling. City Council President Wyche Fowler, a leading white politician, called for Eaves's resignation on April 16. Fowler and Jackson then traded charges that each was trying to polarize the city's black and white communities.

Exploring Expansion. Atlanta's businessmen and state political leaders began discussing possible means of expanding the city's boundaries in order to expand its tax base. The alternatives under consideration included both annexation of additional land and the merger of city and suburban services. Some black leaders supported the movement, seeing it as a solution to city revenue problems and also as a means of desegregating Atlanta's schools. But other black leaders were concerned that such moves would dilute the growing political power of blacks within the city.

A special report by the U.S. Census Bureau issued in mid-1975 estimated that Atlanta's population as of July 31, 1973, was 451,123. This represented an 8.9 per cent loss of population since the 1970 census. In another report, however, the Na-

The 70-story Peachtree Center Plaza Hotel, topped out in October, dominates Atlanta's skyline and is the tallest hotel in the world.

tional Planning Association listed the Atlanta urban area as one that would continue to grow significantly.

Economic Situation. The number of persons receiving unemployment-insurance payments in the Atlanta area rose from 10,200 to 25,000 between August, 1974, and August, 1975. In mid-1975, the area's unemployment rate was 9.5 per cent. Competition for the few jobs available was fierce. About 3,000 unemployed persons started gathering at 3 A.M. on January 10 at Atlanta's Civic Center Auditorium to apply for 225 new public service jobs.

Living costs in the area rose 9.3 per cent between June, 1974, and June, 1975, with food prices up 10.4 per cent and housing costs up 11.7 per cent. Department store sales rose 1.4 per cent, while construction activity dropped 16.6 per cent. The average income of a factory worker rose 11 per cent. Regular gasoline prices rose 3.4 per cent between June, 1974, and June, 1975, to an average of 57.8 cents per gallon (3.8 liters).

A Tornado struck Atlanta on March 24, killing 3 persons, injuring at least 170 others, and causing an estimated $20-million to $30-million damage. The storm severely damaged the front of the Georgia governor's mansion, destroyed a U.S. mail truck terminal, and disrupted schools, businesses, and electric and telephone services. James M. Banovetz

ATOMIC ENERGY. See ENERGY.

AUSTRALIA. Voters gave a sweeping victory to Malcolm Fraser and his Liberal Party-National Country Party coalition in a national election on Dec. 13, 1975. The vote climaxed months of political bickering and propelled Fraser into office as prime minister by the largest majority ever recorded in an Australian election.

Fraser had been acting prime minister since November 11, when Governor General Sir John Kerr dismissed Prime Minister Gough Whitlam because Whitlam could not get Senate approval of the government budget. The precedent-shattering move touched off violent reaction throughout the country, but by election day, economic issues had become paramount.

Whitlam's Problems centered in the Senate. For the first time in history, an Opposition Senate majority rejected the government's financial plans, triggering a constitutional crisis in October. Fraser, who replaced Billy M. Snedden as Opposition leader on March 21, argued that the Senate had a constitutional right to reject money bills and that the government must resign and face the people in an election if it could not obtain funds.

Whitlam replied that his Labor government, with a continuing majority in the House of Representatives, could not be forced to resign by any action of the Senate. He termed the Senate a corrupted body, because two state governments had

failed to observe convention and fill two vacant Labor Senate seats with Labor nominees. Whitlam also said that the Senate is not as representative of the people as the House because each state has the same number of members regardless of population.

Kerr dismissed Whitlam because he would neither resign nor recommend a general election when the Senate refused to pass his budget. He installed Fraser as a caretaker prime minister on condition that Fraser obtain financing from the Senate and recommend a dissolution of Parliament.

The "Loans Affair" was the most serious of the government problems that precipitated the Senate's defiance in October. It arose from attempts by several ministers to borrow Arab "petrodollars"

Two cars hang on the edge of a damaged bridge in Tasmania after an ore carrier knocked out one of its sections on January 5, killing 12 persons.

in order to finance government projects and, in particular, to increase Australian ownership in the minerals and energy industries. Setting aside Australia's traditional loan sources, Treasurer James F. Cairns and Reginald F. X. (Rex) Connor, minister for minerals and energy, sought loans through unusual intermediaries. Both lost their ministerial posts, Cairns for giving an inaccurate reply to a parliamentary question and Connor for continuing negotiations after his authorization was withdrawn. On October 15, the day after Whitlam requested Connor's resignation, Fraser announced that the Senate Opposition would stop the government's supply of money.

The Whitlam government also found itself in conflict with the four non-Labor state governments, especially Queensland's. These governments resisted the federal government's Medibank health-care scheme, which will refund at least 85 per cent of a patient's doctor bill. They also refused a federal offer to take over their ailing railway systems, and, along with the national Opposition, boycotted the second session of the Australian Constitutional Convention, which met in Melbourne from September 24 to 26. However, some advances were made in federal-state cooperation on Aborigines and urban development.

The Economy had a mixed year. Inflation, which had been such a feature of Australian life in 1974, began to moderate. Replacing it as a major national preoccupation was unemployment, which reached 4 per cent of the work force. However, Australia continued to be highly prosperous by world standards.

Both price and wage increases began to ease. Wages were affected by the trial adoption of a policy of wage indexation by the Conciliation and Arbitration Commission on April 30. Indexation ties wage increases to rises in the cost of living.

Private investment was low, and the use of manufacturing capacity fell to 75 per cent. Consumer spending and capital investment by business were both affected by the political crisis at the end of the year. The federal government began to restrict increases in spending compared with 1973 and 1974.

Australia's trade position remained good, though a net outflow of private capital and heavy payments for services caused a balance-of-payments deficit in certain months. Mineral exports continued to grow, and future prospects appeared bright. Wheat also continued to find good markets. Beef exports remained a problem, though there were encouraging signs that Japan would buy more. In October, the government and Opposition produced similar policies limiting the degree of foreign ownership in resource industries. The government tried to encourage oil companies to increase exploration by authorizing a higher price for crude oil from new wells.

Foreign Policy was not especially troublesome, except for two issues in Southeast Asia – the collapse of anti-Communist resistance in Indochina in April, with its consequent refugee problem, and the upheaval in Portuguese Timor in October. The Whitlam government was cautious about accepting more than a small number of Vietnamese refugees, and was quick to recognize the new Communist regimes in South Vietnam and Khmer (Cambodia). The Opposition attacked the govern-

ment in both cases. In general, however, Australians accepted the collapse in Indochina as the end of an unsuccessful episode in Western policy.

Timor, a Portuguese colony near Indonesia, proved an awkward and persistent problem. The situation there had been disturbed since the 1974 changes in the Portuguese government. The new government's policy of freeing Portuguese colonies in Africa aroused both hopes and fears in Timor. The policy aroused mainly fears in Indonesia, where some leaders believed that Timor might come under Chinese or Russian influence. If Timor became independent, they feared it would encourage secessionist tendencies in the outer islands.

Whitlam discussed the Timor question with President Suharto of Indonesia at an informal meeting in Townsville, Queensland, in April. When fighting broke out in Timor in October, the Australian government provided relief supplies and accepted refugees. Eventually, the government offered to allow round-table talks to be held in Australia to resolve the conflict. Don R. Willesee, minister for foreign affairs, said on October 30 that the government was concerned about widespread reports that Indonesia was involved in military intervention in Timor. Previously, the government had been criticized for taking too indulgent a view of Indonesian intentions. See PORTUGAL.

When Papua New Guinea, Australia's largest dependency, became an independent state on September 16, Whitlam attended the independence ceremonies in Port Moresby. He gave "categorical and unequivocal" assurance that Papua New Guinea would have first call on an expanding Australian aid program. See PAPUA NEW GUINEA.

Australia also extended its control over the tiny Cocos Islands in the Indian Ocean to counter the century-old sway of the Clunies-Ross family, which was granted the islands in 1886 by Queen Victoria. Australia took over administration of the group in 1955, but John Clunies-Ross, known as the "king of the Cocos," continued to govern the 654 mostly Malay inhabitants. Australia tried to buy the islands in September. Clunies-Ross rejected the offer.

Social Change. Population growth was slow. The birth rate of 18 per 1,000 population was the lowest since 1938-1939. Immigration gains also declined because of the rise in unemployment. A report suggested that future population growth would continue to be slow, affecting government planning in such areas as education and urban development.

In two other areas, Australian laws were modified to reflect changing social attitudes. South Australia became the first state to legalize homosexual acts between consenting adults. On the federal level, the Family Law Act became effective in January, 1976. Its new system of courts and conciliation was to administer a single form of divorce, based upon the breakdown of marriage over a 12-month period, without either party judged at fault.

Other Developments. The arts, a field in which the Whitlam government had markedly increased spending, continued to grow in importance. Australian movies – including *Between Wars, Petersen, Picnic at Hanging Rock,* and *Scobie Malone* – gained audiences abroad, as well as at home. Cost problems in the publishing industry restricted book publication, but authors began to receive payments under a system designed to compensate them for the use of their books in public libraries.

The government also increased its aid to the Aborigines. The minister for Aboriginal affairs announced on August 22 that spending on Aboriginal housing, health, and education would increase to $273 million in fiscal 1976.

The Order of Australia was first awarded in June. The government created it to replace British honors that had previously been awarded on Australian recommendation. Among those who became Companions of the Order, its highest award, were opera singer Joan Sutherland, Nobel Prize-winning novelist Patrick White, historian Charles Manning Clark, economist Herbert C. Coombs, and heads of the armed services.　　J. D. B. Miller

See also ASIA (Facts in Brief Table); FRASER, MALCOLM.

AUSTRIA. The ruling Socialist Party won a resounding victory in general elections on Oct. 5, 1975. Chancellor Bruno Kreisky's party captured 94 of 183 seats in the *Nationalrat* (National Council), 1 more than in the outgoing council. The conservative People's Party won 78 seats, and the rightist Freedom Party won 11.

Increasingly, Austrian leaders acted in 1975 to fulfill a world role in building a bridge with Europe's Eastern bloc. On March 26, Austria signed a consular agreement with East Germany, becoming the first Western nation to recognize a separate German nationality. The accord followed months of dispute between Austria and West Germany, which insists it represents all German nationals.

The Economy. Despite continuing stability, a firm Austrian schilling against other currencies, high employment, and only 58,000 working hours lost through strikes, Austria did not escape the world recession. Industrial output during the first three months of 1975 fell 10 per cent below that during the first three months of 1974. The drop ended six years of industrial growth. The trade deficit reached $1.7 billion, but expansion of the state-owned energy industry helped offset the imbalance. Austria kept fuel-import costs down in 1975 by completing eight electric power stations, three of them hydroelectric, with an investment of $700 million. However, inflation slowed investments in more large-scale energy projects. Austria plans to produce 7,400 megawatts of electric power by 1984, and will have enough storage facilities to export power to other European nations. Exports fell 4 per cent in the first six months, and the Federal Chamber of Economy decided to launch a worldwide export-promotion campaign in 1976.

Austria and Russia signed a new 10-year trade agreement in Vienna on June 1. The two countries reported in September that they had signed their third contract by which Austrian steel pipes would be exchanged for Soviet natural gas from 1978 through the end of the century.

Faced with a 20 per cent drop in tourism in 1974, Austria tried in 1975 to win back the travelers. Hotel owners pressured the government to decrease the value-added tax on meals and drinks.

Mountain Farmers, who live in regions that cover about two-thirds of the country's 32,374 square miles (83,849 square kilometers), pressed the government for state subsidies tied to the amount of land cultivated rather than to production. The farmers believe the present system of subsidies is unfair because industrial incentives have drastically cut the farm labor force. The government appointed a state secretary for mountain farming to study the farmers' problems and protect Alpine farm settlements.　　Kenneth Brown

See also EUROPE (Facts in Brief Table).

AUTOMOBILE. For the world's automakers, 1975 began badly, then improved late in the year. Higher fuel prices, inflation, recession, and lack of consumer confidence combined to produce a weak, unstable automobile market. Layoffs were common throughout the industry. Volkswagen, faced with slumping sales and rising inventories, laid off some 79,000 of its 133,000 German workers in February. In April, it announced it would cut its work force by 25,000 by the end of 1976. Fiat of Italy laid off 70,000 early in the year, and Great Britain's automakers put 46,000 workers on a reduced workweek in February.

The United States market took some of its roughest knocks early in the year, despite rebate schemes by which all four U.S. carmakers refunded from $200 to $500 on most new cars purchased. Some 300,000 U.S. auto workers, 40 per cent of the work force, were on reduced work schedules or extended layoffs at various times during the first quarter. But the picture brightened noticeably in October, November, and December. December sales in the surging U.S. market ran 30.6 per cent over those in 1974. By December 1, only about 75,000 of the industry's 701,000 hourly employees were still idle.

U.S. Auto Production for 1975 was estimated at 6.7 million cars, off 8 per cent from the 7.3 million assembled in 1974 and 31 per cent below the all-

Sportscaster Joe Garagiola prepares to film a television commercial for
an advertising campaign used by auto dealers to hike sales in 1975.

time high of 9.7 million assembled in 1973. United
States auto sales for 1975 were 7.05 million cars,
down from 7.4 million in recession-plagued 1974
and the record high of 9.7 million sold in 1973.

Despite the sales drop, the profit picture was not
all bad. General Motors Corporation (GM) said a
strong third quarter helped its nine-month profits
to climb to $635 million, up from $442 million in
the same 1974 period. Ford Motor Company's
nine-month earnings were $162.8 million, which
was down from $228.8 million a year earlier, but the
troubled Chrysler Corporation had a nine-month
loss of $225 million against a $21.4-million profit in
1974.

Import Car sales through November were estimated at nearly 1.5 million, up 11 per cent from
last year, giving foreign cars a record 18.6 per cent
of the 1975 U.S. car market. But in November, the
imports suffered their biggest drop in 11 years,
falling 4 per cent below the preceding November.

Market Mix. United States carmakers in 1975
trimmed the number of models available to 295, a
reduction of 30. The trend had been down since the
high of 375 models in 1970. For the second consecutive year, the average car was smaller, both in
wheelbase and overall dimensions.

Chevrolet unveiled its Chevette in 1975, becoming the first American manufacturer to get a true
subcompact car into the sales race. Chevette, the

smallest U.S.-built car, had a $2,900 base price.
The Japanese Honda, smallest car sold in the
United States, had a $2,729 price tag.

Ford, which has a European subcompact, the
Bobcat, on the way, said in early December that it
could not get the car into the U.S. market place
until 1979 at the earliest. Chrysler introduced two
new compact cars, the Volaré and the Aspen.

Labor. The average auto worker earned $6.77
per hour in pay and cost-of-living allowances in
1975. Thomas A. Murphy, chairman of the board
of GM, said in advance of the 1976 auto-contract
talks that the total annual labor cost for the average full-time GM hourly employee is about
$20,000, with about $15,500 of this going to the
employee directly in wages, cost-of-living allowances, and vacation and holiday pay. The other
$4,500 represents the cost to GM of other benefits,
such as insurance, pensions, supplemental unemployment benefits, state unemployment payments,
and federal social security. The United Auto
Workers indicated a four-day workweek probably
would be one of its prime goals in 1976 talks.

Automobile Prices increased substantially on
1976 models, though prices were hard to figure
because automakers shuffled standard and optional
equipment on their cars. Chrysler announced a
$144 increase, while GM's figure was $206 and
Ford's was $216. After taking all the pricing fac-

tors into consideration, the trade publication *Automotive News* came up with an average 1976 price increase of $200. Ford led off what could have been another round of industry price increases in mid-December when it raised prices 2.2 per cent, effective on Jan. 5, 1976. But Ford rescinded most of the price increase on Jan. 15, 1976, probably because its main competitor, General Motors, had not increased prices.

Government Standards. General Motors president Elliott M. Estes voiced the views of most auto executives when he said in early December that the industry is convinced there should be a five-year freeze on current federal auto-emission levels. Estes said considerable progress had been made in making engines cleaner and that there was $215 worth of emission controls on the average 1976 car. Meeting standards that various congressional subcommittees have set will cost an additional $150 to $340 per car. Industry spokesmen said that proposed government controls, if not modified, could result in a fuel-economy loss ranging from 5 per cent to 30 per cent. Environmental Protection Agency officials disputed that opinion.

Experimental Engines. GM said federal efforts to lower nitrous oxide emissions would rule out, for the immediate future, the possible use of some alternatives to the conventional piston engine – the diesel and stratified-charge engines. GM also put on the back burner its program to develop the Wankel rotary engine for use in Chevrolets. "For some strange reason that nobody can explain," a high GM official said, "without any controls on it, the rotary will emit three to four times as many hydrocarbons as a comparable piston engine. We have a research program underway to determine why the engine acts like that."

Personnel Change. The biggest shakeup in top management came at Chrysler, where Lynn A. Townsend bowed out as chairman of the board on October 1. President John J. Riccardo was promoted to chairman, with Executive Vice-President Eugene A. Cafiero moving up to president.

Chrysler faced many problems, including negotiations with the British government for capital to keep Chrysler operating in Great Britain. Chrysler's plants in Great Britain employ 25,000 workers. "Even if the capital is guaranteed by the government," the British trade publication *Ward's Auto World* said, "Chrysler will also have to accept massive layoffs to keep above water."

On August 11, the British government nationalized another auto company, British Leyland Motors Corporation, Limited, which had been in serious financial difficulty.

Unwilling to take over still another auto company, the British government on December 19 came up with a $330-million agreement to bail Chrysler out of its difficulties.   Charles C. Cain III

AUTOMOBILE RACING. Niki Lauda, a 26-year-old Austrian, became the world driving champion in 1975 in a series of Grand Prix races on four continents. A. J. Foyt of Houston and Richard Petty of Randleman, N.C., won America's most important championships, and Bobby Unser of Albuquerque, N. Mex., won America's best-known (and the world's richest) race, the $1,001,321 Indianapolis 500.

The world championship series encompassed 14 races for Formula One cars. Lauda won three races in a row – the Grands Prix of Monaco, Belgium, and Sweden – lost the next race (in the Netherlands) by 1 second, and won the next (in France). He also won the year's last race, the $350,000 United States Grand Prix at Watkins Glen, N.Y. He drove a 3-liter Ferrari.

The Formula One cars are highly dangerous because they are so light – 1,200 pounds (544 kilograms) – and fragile. An accident on August 17 took the life of 38-year-old Mark Donohue of Media, Pa., who had retired from racing at 36 but returned to the track a year later.

Donohue, driving an American-built Penske-Ford in practice for the Austrian Grand Prix at Zeltweg, blew a tire at 160 miles (257 kilometers) per hour and crashed. He underwent emergency surgery to remove a blood clot on the brain, and died two days later. He had won 57 major races in almost every type of car, and ranked as one of America's greatest drivers.

Eight days before his fatal accident, Donohue set a world closed-course speed record of 221.16 mph (355.9 kph) over the 2.6-mile (4.2-kilometer) tri-oval at Talladega, Ala. He drove the 1,100-horsepower, 12-cylinder Porsche 917-30 in which he had won the 1973 Canadian-American Challenge Cup (Can-Am) title.

The Indianapolis 500, America's classic race, had two unexpected developments near the end. First, Wally Dallenbach of Basalt, Colo., seemed a sure winner until the 161st lap of the 200-lap race. But he suffered a slow tire leak, cut his speed too much, and burned out a piston. Then a violent rainstorm inundated the track after 174 laps, with Unser leading, and the race was terminated.

Foyt, 40, the fastest qualifier, was favored to win at Indy for a record fourth time. Instead, he finished third. However, Foyt won the Ontario 500 and Pocono 500, the other major races on the United States Auto Club's (USAC) championship-car circuit, and won the season title for a record sixth time. He raised his lifetime race earnings to more than $2.5 million.

Stock Cars. Petty, at 38, became the first stock-car driver to reach $2 million in career earnings. Driving his 1974 Dodge, he easily dominated the National Association for Stock Car Auto Racing's (NASCAR) Grand National series and won it for a

Clay Regazzoni wins the Swiss Grand Prix, revived in Dijon, France, in August after 21 years because auto racing is banned in Switzerland.

record sixth time. He won 13 races and earned $342,980.

There were 30 races for these late-model stock cars, and Petty failed to win the richest in this series, the $282,375 Daytona 500 on February 16 at Daytona Beach, Fla. Benny Parsons, of Ellerbe, N.C., won it in a Chevrolet.

Formula 5000. The USAC and NASCAR championship races were run on oval tracks. The major competition on American road courses was in the Formula 5000 series. The chassis were similar to those on Indianapolis and Formula One cars; power came from 5-liter stock-block engines.

The series attracted many European drivers and such Americans as Al Unser (Bobby's brother) of Albuquerque and Mario Andretti of Nazareth, Pa. The overall champion for the second straight year was Brian Redman of England in a Lola. Redman, 38, had quit Grand Prix and endurance racing because he disliked the pressure.

The big endurance cars again raced in Europe and the United States for the world manufacturers' championship. Alfa-Romeo of Italy became champion. The famous 24 Hours of Le Mans in France no longer was part of the series, but negotiations were underway to change that. Le Mans, which had limited fuel consumption to encourage smaller cars to enter, decided to return to unlimited fuel consumption.   Frank Litsky

AVIATION fell on hard times in 1975. Jet fuel and other costs continued to climb, and business was temporarily depressed by an economic slump. Airline finances reflected a partial recovery later in the year, however, as improving traffic and airline belt-tightening measures helped out.

United States scheduled airlines, after solidly profitable earnings of $322 million in 1974, plunged into deficits in 1975. George W. James, the industry's chief economist, estimated in December that the carriers would show a loss of $100-million to $125 million for the year on a slight drop in traffic. Industry losses were attributable mainly to a few major airlines – Trans World Airlines (TWA), American Airlines, Pan American World Airways (PanAm), and Eastern Airlines. Costs in 1975 outstripped revenue gains, and widespread business-stimulating discounts lowered the revenue yield for each passenger. Moreover, United Air Lines was struck in December. A strike against National Airlines that began in September ended in January, 1976. Only the grounding of some aircraft, employee layoffs and wage cuts, a fare increase on November 15, and a stronger autumn air-travel pickup than expected kept losses down.

Domestic airline-passenger traffic through December gained slightly after running behind 1974 in the early months. Total air freight fell 4.1 per cent through November. Domestic air freight was down 4.2 per cent, with international air freight hauled by U.S. carriers declining 3.9 per cent.

International Flights. International Air Transport Association figures showed 8.1 per cent fewer revenue passengers flown by scheduled airlines on major North Atlantic routes through September, and cargo declined 15 per cent. United States carriers' international passenger traffic was off 7.4 per cent for the year.

Air Canada announced in September it was trimming some flights from its schedule, including transatlantic flights and flights to the United States. It expected a $10-million deficit for 1975.

For the two major U.S. lines with world routes — PanAm and TWA — international flights bolstered 1975 finances. Mutual route swaps, service cuts, and cost trimming bore fruit in fuller planes and other economies. PanAm reported record third-quarter profits of $42 million, but said it would still wind up 1975 with a loss. TWA's overall prospects worsened as domestic problems wiped out international gains. TWA posted a record deficit of $86.3-million for the year.

New Regulation Policies. The U.S. Civil Aeronautics Board (CAB) became less accommodating to airlines as a debate over possible deregulation grew hotter. John E. Robson, a Chicago lawyer and former U.S. Department of Transportation undersecretary, became CAB chairman on April 21 in an effort by President Gerald R. Ford to loosen federal transportation regulation. Under pressure from various critics, the CAB rejected several 1975 proposals to raise domestic fares. It finally allowed a 3 per cent fare increase on November 15.

The CAB also relaxed its policy against promotional fare discounts and permitted widespread bargain fares for "no-frills" flights and excursion-fare travel, offered by carriers to revive slumping air travel. Following a federal court decision criticizing the CAB for permitting airlines to jointly reduce flight schedules to boost profits without thorough analysis, the CAB canceled the agreement on July 21. On August 8, it issued rules opening the way for liberalized low-cost charter packages involving combined cut-rate fares and ground charges such as hotel prices.

The Senate Administrative Practice and Procedure Subcommittee, chaired by Senator Edward M. Kennedy (D., Mass.), conducted lengthy hearings on the CAB. Its draft report recommended sharp deregulation, concluding that the agency had severely restricted airline competition to the consumer's detriment. On October 8, the Ford Administration announced legislation that would strip the CAB of much of its power to regulate airline service, fares, and mergers, over five years.

Canada's new $500-million Mirabel International Airport, northwest of Montreal, was formally opened on October 4.

Officials said the plan would lead to lower fares, better service, and more competition. Industry spokesmen opposed the measure, saying it would "tear apart" the nation's air-transport system, wipe out much scheduled air service to smaller cities, and lead "inevitably" to higher fares.

Supersonic Transport. In December, Russia began scheduled cargo service of its supersonic TU-144 between Moscow and Alma-Ata, Kazakstan. The first British-French Concorde international passenger flights began on Jan. 21, 1976. Pending U.S. approval, a total of six round-trip flights daily were scheduled to start in the spring of 1976 serving John F. Kennedy International Airport in New York City and Washington, D.C.'s Dulles International Airport.

The Federal Aviation Administration (FAA) issued a statement on March 4, saying the Concorde posed some noise and air-pollution problems. However, the FAA recommended that the limited number of flights be allowed. Environmental groups mounted opposition, and on November 13, Secretary of Transportation William T. Coleman, Jr., released another FAA environmental statement, which said the Concorde flights would produce "high noise levels" and have other "adverse" environmental effects.

Air Safety. Airline fatalities declined from 1974's disastrous level. The Flight Safety Foundation, a private U.S. group, counted 617 deaths in airline crashes through September, far below the full 1974 total of 1,816. In the United States, 124 airline-accident deaths occurred in 1975, according to figures from the National Transportation Safety Board.

The worst single-plane air disaster in United States history took place in 1975, however. An Eastern Airlines Boeing 727 crashed on approach to Kennedy airport on June 24, killing 113 persons. Safety experts blamed the crash on severe wind gusts. See DISASTERS.

The FAA moved to correct air-traffic control and other U.S. air-safety deficiencies that had been widely cited as responsible for some earlier accidents. On April 30, Coleman directed the FAA to carry out recommendations promoting flight safety made by an advisory task force. A series of midair near-collisions in November and December focused attention on this type of danger.

The FAA ruled that jetliners be equipped with a device to warn pilots when the plane is descending too fast, ordered air-traffic controllers to tell pilots when their planes are too low, and gave pilots and controllers limited immunity from disciplinary action, to encourage reports of unsafe flight practices. It also ruled that wide-bodied jets must be equipped to avoid crashes in case the fuselage is suddenly punctured.   Albert R. Karr

See also TRANSPORTATION.

AWARDS AND PRIZES presented in 1975 included the following:

Arts Awards

American Institute of Architects. *Allied Professions Medal,* Carl M. Sapers, Boston attorney, for legal counsel to more than 50 architectural firms. *Architectural Firm Award,* Davis, Brody and Associates, New York City, for continuing collaboration in producing consistently distinguished architecture. *Fine Arts Medal,* Josef Albers, artist, for distinguished achievement in the fine arts related to architecture. *Industrial Arts Medal,* Gemini GEL, a Los Angeles lithography firm.

Avery Fisher Prize, for excellence among young instrumentalists, Lynn Harrell, New York City, cellist, and Murray Perahia, New York City, pianist.

Brandeis University *Creative Arts Awards. Award for Notable Achievement,* Aaron Copland. *Medal for Fiction,* Christopher Isherwood. *Medal for Film,* King Vidor. *Medal for Music,* Vincent Persichetti. *Medal for Painting and Visual Arts,* Isabel Bishop.

Capezio Dance Award, Robert Irving, music director and principal conductor, New York City Ballet, "for bringing unequaled musical distinction to . . . the dance."

Dance Magazine Award, for contributions to the dance, Alvin Ailey, Cynthia Gregory, Arthur Mitchell.

National Academy of Design. *The Benjamin Altman Prize for Figure Painting,* Jack Levine, for *Perpetrator. Landscape Painting,* Giovanni Martino, for *Winter.*

National Academy of Recording Arts and Sciences. *Grammy Awards: Record of the Year,* "I Honestly Love You," Olivia Newton-John. *Song of the Year,* "The Way We Were," by Marvin Hamlisch and Marilyn and Alan Bergman. *Album of the Year, Pop,* "Fulfillingness' First Finale," by Stevie Wonder. *Classical,* Berlioz' *Symphonie Fantastique,* the Chicago Symphony conducted by Sir Georg Solti. *Best Classical Performance, Orchestra,* the Chicago Symphony's *Symphonie Fantastique. Best Solo Classical Performance with Orchestra,* violinist David Oistrakh in *Concerto No. 1* for violin by Shostakovich. *Best Solo Classical Performance Without Orchestra,* Alicia de Larrocha in *Iberia* by Albéniz. *Best Chamber Music Performance,* Brahms and Schumann Trios, by Arthur Rubinstein, Henry Szeryng, and Pierre Fournier. *Best Opera Recording, La Bohème,* the Chicago Symphony conducted by Sir Georg Solti. *Best Jazz Performance, Big Band,* "Thundering Herd," by Woody Herman; *Group,* "The Trio," by Oscar Peterson, Joe Pass, Niels Pedersen; *Solo,* "First Recordings," by Charlie Parker. *Best Country Vocal Performance, Female,* "Love Song," by Anne Murray; *Male,* "Please Don't Tell Me How the Story Ends," by Ronnie Milsap; *Combo,* "Fairytale," the Pointer Sisters. *Best Contemporary Vocal Performance, Female,* "I Honestly Love You," Olivia Newton-John; *Male,* "Fulfillingness' First Finale," Stevie Wonder; *Combo,* "Band on the Run," Paul McCartney and Wings.

National Academy of Television Arts and Sciences. *Emmy Awards: Best Actor and Actress in a Special,* Sir Laurence Olivier and Katharine Hepburn in the comedy "Love Among The Ruins." *Best Actor and Actress in a Drama Series,* Robert Blake in "Baretta" and Jean Marsh in "Upstairs, Downstairs." *Best Actor and Actress in a Comedy Series,* Tony Randall in "The Odd Couple" and Valerie Harper in "Rhoda." *Best Supporting Actor,* Will Geer in "The Waltons." *Best Supporting Actress,* Zohra Lampert in "Kojak" and Cloris Leachman in "The Mary Tyler Moore Show." *Best Actor and Actress in a Limited Series,* Peter Falk in "Columbo" and Jessica Walter in "Amy Prentiss." *Best Dramatic Series,* "Upstairs, Downstairs." *Best Comedy Series,* "The Mary Tyler Moore Show." *Best Limited Series,* "Benjamin Franklin." *Best Comedy, Variety, or*

Music Series, "The Carol Burnett Show." *Best Comedy, Variety, or Music Special,* "An Evening with John Denver." *Best Special,* "The Law."

National Institute of Arts and Letters and American Academy of Arts and Letters. *Gold Medal for Belles Lettres and Criticism,* Kenneth Burke. *Arnold W. Brunner Award,* Lewis Davis and Samuel M. Brody. *E. M. Forster Award,* Seamus Heaney. *Howells Medal,* Thomas Pynchon, for *Gravity's Rainbow. Charles E. Ives Scholarships,* Chester Biscardi, Stephen Chatman, David Koblitz. *Award of Merit,* Galway Kinnell. *Gold Medal for Painting,* Willem De Kooning. *Richard and Hinda Rosenthal Foundation Awards,* Richard Merkin, for painting, Ishmael Reed, for literature. *Marjorie Peabody Waite Award,* Leo Ornstein. *Morton Dauwen Zabel Award,* Charles Newman. *National Institute Awards. Art,* Barbara Falk, Claus Hoie, Leonid, Seymour Pearlstein, Calvin Albert, Harry Bertoia, William Talbo. *Literature,* William S. Burroughs, J. P. Donleavy, John Gardner, William Gass, Terence McNally, Tillie Olsen, John Peck, Mark Strand, Colin M. Turnbull, Helen Hennessy Vendler. *Music,* Marc Antonio Consoli, Charles Dodge, Daniel Perlongo, Christian Wolff.

Journalism Awards

American Institute of Physics and United States Steel Foundation. *Science Writing Award,* to Robert H. March, for "The Quandary over Quarks" in SCIENCE YEAR, *The World Book Science Annual.*

Long Island University. *George Polk Memorial Awards: Book,* Mary Adelaide Mendelson for *Tender Loving Greed,* an exposé of nursing homes in the United States. *Foreign Reporting,* Donald Kirk, the *Chicago Tribune,* for dispatches describing corruption in South Vietnam. *National Reporting,* Seymour M. Hersh, *The New York Times,* for revealing illegal domestic surveillance operations of the Central Intelligence Agency. *Metropolitan Reporting,* Richard Severo, *The New York Times,* for reports on watering down milk by Dairylea Cooperative, which started both state and federal investigations. *Community Service,* William E. Anderson, Harley R. Bierce, and Richard E. Cady, *The Indianapolis Star,* for investigative reporting of police corruption. *Magazine Reporting,* Edward M. Brecher and Robert H. Harris, *Consumer Reports,* for the series "Is the Water Safe to Drink?" *News Photography,* Werner Baum, Deutsche Presse-Agentur (German Press Agency) for his photo of a German policeman killing a Hamburg robber who was holding a knife to a hostage's throat. *Television Documentary,* NBC News for "And Who Shall Feed This World?" a report on malnutrition. *Special Award,* Sydney H. Schanberg, *The New York Times,* who remained in Khmer (Cambodia) to report on the fall of Phnom Penh to the Khmer Rouge.

National Cartoonists Society. *Reuben,* Dick Moores, for the comic strip "Gasoline Alley."

The Newspaper Guild. *Heywood Broun Award,* Selwyn Raab, *The New York Times,* for an article revealing new evidence that raised doubts about the murder convictions of boxer Rubin (Hurricane) Carter and John Artis.

The Scripps-Howard Foundation. *Roy W. Howard Public Service Award,* to seven reporters of *The Milwaukee Journal* for the series "Judging Justice: A Report on Our Criminal Courts," and to WABC-TV, New York, for "The Willowbrook Case: The People vs. the State of New York," a program on conditions in the Willowbrook, N.Y., mental institution. *Edward J. Meeman Conservation Award,* David Johnston, *The Detroit Free Press,* for exposing a Michigan state legislator as the secret boss of a foundry cited for pollution violations.

The Society of Professional Journalists, Sigma Delta Chi. *Newspaper Awards: General Reporting,* Frank Sutherland, *The Tennessean,* Nashville, Tenn., for a series on conditions in Tennessee's mental hospitals. Sutherland posed as a mental patient for a month while researching his articles. *Editorial Writing,* Michael Pakenham, *The Philadelphia Inquirer,* for 23 hard-hitting editorials on police corruption in the Philadelphia Police Department, which led to 18 indictments. *Washington Correspondence,* Seth Kantor, *Detroit News,* for reporting on secret government plans to set up a $100-million computer network to store data on citizens and institutions. The report led eventually to the cancellation of the project. *Foreign Correspondence,* Donald L. Barlett and James B. Steele, *The Philadelphia Inquirer,* for their series "Foreign Aid: A Flawed Dream," which detailed how U.S. foreign aid programs missed their goals. *News Photography,* Werner Baum, Deutsche Presse-Agentur, Frankfurt, West Germany, for a photograph of a German policeman firing point-blank at a bank robber holding a hostage. *Editorial Cartooning,* Mike Peters, *Dayton* (Ohio) *Daily News,* for penetrating and humorous cartoon on the Watergate trials. *Public Service in Newspaper Journalism,* the *Indianapolis Star,* Indianapolis, Ind., for exposing widespread police corruption in Indianapolis. *Magazine Awards: Reporting,* John Guinther, *Philadelphia* magazine, for two articles, "Sweet Are the Uses of Immunity" and "Probing the Grand Jury," which documented inequities in the grand jury system and pointed out the civil rights dangers from grand juries controlled by political officeholders. *Public Service, Philadelphia* magazine, "Nothing to Eat" by Loretta Schwartz, an article describing the thousands of elderly and infirm persons and children who go hungry in Philadelphia. *Radio Awards: Reporting,* Jim Mitchell, Gary Franklin, and Herb Humphries, KFWB, Los Angeles, for their coverage of the gun battle between police and members of the Symbionese Liberation Army in 1974. *Public Service,* WIND Radio, Chicago, for its documentary "EMH: Board of Education Dumping Ground for Spanish Students," which revealed that more than half of the Spanish-speaking students in special education classes for the mentally handicapped in Chicago were found to be normal when they were tested by bilingual psychologists. *Editorializing,* Jim Branch, WRFM, New York City, for his well-researched, clearly written, and consistently listenable editorials. *Television Awards: Reporting,* Lee Louis, KGTV, San Diego, Calif., for coverage of a police shootout with a suspect in Ocean Beach, Calif. *Public Service,* ABC News, New York City, for its documentary "ABC News Close-up – The Paper Prison: Your Government Records," which examined the threat to personal privacy by extensive government records on private citizens. *Editorializing,* Jay Lewis, WSFA-TV, Montgomery, Ala., for editorials calling for a new jail in Montgomery, which prompted county commissioners to investigate conditions in the jail and led to recommendations for a new jail. *Research in Journalism,* Loren Ghiglione, *The Evening News,* Southbridge, Mass., for his book *Evaluating the Press,* a survey of New England daily newspapers.

Literature Awards

Academy of American Poets. *Lamont Poetry Selection Award.* Lisel Mueller, for her second book of poems, *The Private Life.*

American Library Association. *Beta Phi Mu Award,* Kenneth R. Shaffer, former director of the School of Library Science, Simmons College, Boston. *Caldecott Medal,* Gerald McDermott, for illustrating *Arrow to the Sun. Clarence Day Award,* Margaret McNamara, founder and director of the "Reading Is FUNdamental" program. *Dartmouth Medal,* the New England Board of Higher Education. *Joseph W. Lippincott Award,* Leon Carnovsky, professor emeritus, Graduate Library School, University of Chicago. *Newbery Medal,* Virginia Hamilton, author of *M. C. Higgins the Great,* the most distinguished contribution to children's literature.

Columbia University. *Bancroft Prizes,* for "books of exceptional merit and distinction in American history . . . diplomacy and international relations. . . ." Stanley L. Engerman and Robert W. Fogel, for *Time on the Cross,* a two-volume study of American slavery; Eugene D. Genovese, for *Roll, Jordan, Roll;* Alexander L. George and Richard Smoke, for *Deterrence in American Foreign Policy: Theory and Practice.*

Copernicus Society of America. *Copernicus Award,* to Kenneth Rexroth, for lifetime achievement and his latest book, *New Poems. Edgar Allan Poe Award,* to Charles Simic, for *Return to a Place Lit by a Glass of Milk. Walt Whitman Award,* to Reginald Saner, first winner of a competition for poets who have not had a book published.

National Book Committee. *National Book Awards: Arts and Letters,* Roger Shattuck, for *Marcel Proust,* and Lewis Thomas, for *The Lives of a Cell. Biography,* Richard B. Sewall, for *The Life of Emily Dickinson. Children's Literature,* Virginia Hamilton, for *M. C. Higgins the Great. Contemporary Affairs,* Theodore Rosengarten, for *All God's Dangers: The Life of Nate Shaw. Fiction,* Robert Stone, for *Dog Soldiers,* and Thomas Williams, for *The Hair of Harold Roux. History,* Bernard Bailyn, for *The Ordeal of Thomas Hutchinson. Philosophy and Religion,* Robert Nozick, for *Anarchy, State, and Utopia. Poetry,* Marilyn Hacker, for *Presentation Piece. Science,* Silvano Arieti, for *Interpretation of Schizophrenia. Translation,* Anthony Kerrigan, for his translation of Miguel D. Unamuno's book *The Agony of Christianity and Essays on Faith.*

Yale University Library. *Bollingen Prize in Poetry,* A. R. Ammons, professor of English, Cornell University, Ithaca, N.Y., for *Sphere: The Form of a Motion.*

Nobel Prizes. See NOBEL PRIZES.

Public Service Awards

National Association for the Advancement of Colored People. *Spingarn Medal,* to Henry Aaron, baseball's home-run king, of the Milwaukee Brewers.

Ralph Bunche Institute of the United Nations. *Award,* Alva and Gunnar Myrdal.

Ramon Magsaysay Award Foundation. *Magsaysay Award for International Understanding,* Father Patrick A. McGlinchey, an Irish missionary working on the Island of Cheju, South Korea. *Journalism, Literature, and Creative Communications,* George Verghese, editor, *The Hindustan Times,* India. *Government Service,* Tan Sri Mohamed Suffrian bin Hashim, lord president of the courts of Malaysia and pro-chancellor, University of Malaysia. *Community Leadership,* Lee Tai-Young, South Korea's first woman lawyer. *Public Service,* Phra Charoon Parnchandara, abbot, Wat Tharn Krabok Monastery, Saraburi, Thailand.

Science and Technology Awards

American Chemical Society. *Priestley Medal,* George Hammond, professor of chemistry, University of California at Santa Cruz.

American Chemical Society, Chicago Section. *Willard Gibbs Medal,* Herman F. Mark, dean emeritus, Polytechnic Institute of New York.

American Section, Society of Chemical Industry. *Perkin Medal,* Carl Djerassi, professor of chemistry, Stanford University, and chief executive officer, Zoecon Corporation, Palo Alto, Calif.

American Institute of Aeronautics and Astronautics. *Goddard Awards,* Gordon E. Holbrook, General Motors Corporation, and George Rosen, United Aircraft Corporation. *Louis W. Hill Space Transportation Award,* Rocco A. Petrone, associate administrator, National Aeronautics and Space Administration.

American Institute of Physics. *Dannie Heineman Prize for Mathematical Physics,* Ludwig Faddeev, sen-

ior scientific worker, Leningrad Branch, Steclov Mathematical Institute, Leningrad, Russia.

American Museum of Natural History. *Gold Medal for Distinguished Service,* Willi Hennig, director of phylogenetic research, State Museum of Natural History, Stuttgart, West Germany.

American Physical Society. *Bonner Prize in Nuclear Physics,* Chien Shiung-wu, professor of physics, Columbia University. *Buckley Solid State Physics Prize,* Albert W. Overhauser, professor of physics, Purdue University, Lafayette, Ind. *High-Polymer Physics Prize,* Walter H. Stockmayer, Dartmouth College, Hanover, N.H. *Langmuir Prize,* Robert H. Cole, professor of chemistry, Brown University, Providence, R.I.

Columbia University. *Louisa Gross Horwitz Prize,* for outstanding research in biochemistry, Sune Bergstrom, professor of chemistry and rector, Karolinska Institutet, Stockholm, Sweden, and Bengt Samuelsson, professor of medical and physiological chemistry, Karolinska Institutet, for their research on prostaglandins, hormonelike regulators of many bodily functions.

The Gairdner Foundation. *Gairdner Awards,* for medical research, John Dow Keith and William T. Mustard, the Hospital for Sick Children, Toronto, Canada; Ernest Beutler, City of Hope National Medical Center, California; Baruch S. Blumberg, Institute for Cancer Research, Philadelphia; Henri G. Hers, University of Louvain, Belgium; Hugh E. Huxley, Medical Research Council, Cambridge, England.

Franklin Institute. *Franklin Medal,* John Bardeen, professor of physics and electrical engineering, University of Illinois, Champaign-Urbana, Ill., for his insights and work on electrical conductivity of solids, semiconductor devices, and superconductivity.

Geological Society of America. *Penrose Medal,* Francis J. Pettijohn, professor of geology, Department of Earth and Planetary Sciences, Johns Hopkins University, Baltimore. *Arthur L. Day Medal,* Allan V. Cox, professor of geophysics, Department of Geophysics, Stanford University, Stanford, Calif.

Kittay Scientific Foundation. *Kittay International Award,* Harry F. Harlow, director, Primate Research Center, University of Wisconsin, Madison, for his work with primates on the mother-infant attachment bond.

Albert and Mary Lasker Foundation Awards. *Albert Lasker Clinical Medical Research Award* to Godfrey N. Hounsfield, head, Medical Systems Section, EMI Central Research Laboratories, Hayes, Middlesex, England; and William Oldendorf, medical investigator, Brentwood Veterans Administration Hospital, and professor of neurology, School of Medicine, University of California, Los Angeles, for independent research that led to the development of computerized X-ray brain scanners, which have revolutionized neurological diagnosis. *Albert Lasker Basic Medical Research Awards,* to Roger C. L. Guillemin, research professor and resident fellow, The Salk Institute, LaJolla, Calif., and Andrew V. Schally, senior medical investigator, Veterans Administration System, New Orleans, La., for new discoveries about the role of the hypothalamus in both the neural and endocrine systems; to Frank Dixon, director, Scripps Clinic and Research Foundation, LaJolla, and Henry G. Kunkel, professor, The Rockefeller University, for their work on immunologic diseases. *Albert Lasker Special Award,* to Karl H. Beyer, Jr., pharmacologist and physician, James M. Sprague, organic chemist, John E. Baer, pharmacologist, and Frederick C. Novello, organic chemist, a research team for Merck Sharp and Dohme Research Laboratories, Rahway, N.J., and West Point, Pa., for developing new medications to control high blood pressure and edema associated with heart failure. *Albert Lasker Public Service Award,* to Jules Stein, chairman, Research to Prevent Blindness, New York City, for his efforts to prevent blindness, preserve vision, and restore sight.

National Academy of Engineering. *Founders Medal,* James B. Fisk, former chairman of the board, Bell Laboratories, for leadership in the advancement of communications technology for the benefit of society. *Zworykin Award,* Jack S. Kilby, consultant, Dallas, Tex., for "contributions to the development and application of monolithic integrated electronic circuits."

National Academy of Sciences (NAS). *National Medal of Science,* Nicholaas Bloembergen, Harvard University, applied physics; Britton Chance, University of Pennsylvania, biophysics; Erwin Chargaff, Columbia University, biochemistry; Paul J. Flory, Stanford University, chemistry; William A. Fowler, California Institute of Technology, physics; Kurt Gödel, Institute for Advanced Study, Princeton, N.J., mathematics; Rudolph Kompfner, Bell Laboratories, electronics; James Van Gundia Neel, University of Michigan, genetics; Linus C. Pauling, Stanford University, chemistry; Ralph B. Peck, private consultant, Albuquerque, N. Mex., civil engineering; Kenneth S. Pitzer, University of California, Berkeley, chemistry; James A. Shannon, Rockefeller University, biomedicine; Abel Wolman, Johns Hopkins University, sanitary engineering.

Pepperdine University. *John and Alice Tyler Ecology Award,* Ruth Patrick, chairman, Academy of Natural Sciences, Philadelphia, for ecological studies of polluted streams.

Theater and Motion Picture Awards

Academy of Motion Picture Arts and Sciences. *"Oscar" Awards: Best Picture, The Godfather, Part II. Best Actor,* Art Carney in *Harry and Tonto. Best Supporting Actor,* Robert De Niro in *The Godfather, Part II. Best Actress,* Ellen Burstyn in *Alice Doesn't Live Here Anymore. Best Supporting Actress,* Ingrid Bergman in *Murder on the Orient Express. Best Director,* Francis Ford Coppola for *The Godfather, Part II. Best Foreign Language Film, Amarcord,* directed by Federico Fellini. *Best Original Screenplay,* Robert Towne, for *Chinatown. Best Documentary Feature, Hearts and Minds,* produced by Peter Davis and Bert Schneider. *Best Song,* "We May Never Love Like This Again" from *The Towering Inferno,* music and lyrics by Al Kasha and Joel Hirshhorn. *Honorary Awards,* French director Jean Renoir and American director Howard Hawks for their film achievements over the years.

Antoinette Perry (Tony) Awards. *Drama: Best Play, Equus* by Peter Shaffer. *Best Actor,* John Kani and Winston Ntshona in *Sizwe Banzi Is Dead* and *The Island. Best Actress,* Ellen Burstyn in *Same Time, Next Year. Best Supporting Actress,* Rita Moreno in *The Ritz. Best Director,* John Dexter for *Equus. Musical: Best Musical, The Wiz. Best Actor,* John Cullum in *Shenandoah. Best Actress,* Angela Lansbury in *Gypsy. Best Choreographer,* George Faison for *The Wiz. Best Musical Score,* Charlie Smalls for *The Wiz. Best Director,* Geoffrey Holder for *The Wiz. Special Award,* Al Hirschfeld, for 50 years of theatrical cartoons.

Cannes International Film Festival. *Grand Prix International, A Chronicle of the Years of Heat,* Algeria. *Best Actor,* Vittorio Gassman, *A Woman's Perfume. Best Actress,* Valerie Perrine, *Lenny. Best Director,* Michel Brault, *Les Ordres,* and Constantin Costa-Gavras, *Special Section.*

New York Drama Critics Circle Awards, *Best Play of 1974-1975, Equus,* by Peter Shaffer. *Best American Play, The Taking of Miss Janie,* by Ed Bullins. *Best Musical, A Chorus Line,* by Michael Bennett.

New York Film Critics Circle Awards. *Best Film, Amarcord,* directed by Federico Fellini. *Best Actor,* Jack Nicholson, *Chinatown* and *The Last Detail. Best Actress,* Liv Ullmann, *Scenes from a Marriage. Best Director,* Federico Fellini, *Amarcord. Best Screenwriting,* Ingmar Bergman, *Scenes from a Marriage.* Edward G. Nash

AZEVEDO, JOSÉ PINHEIRO DE (1917-   ), became prime minister of Portugal on Aug. 29, 1975, replacing General Vasco dos Santos Gonçalves. Unlike Gonçalves, Azevedo was not controversial and was at first not opposed by either the Communists or the Socialists. See PORTUGAL.

Azevedo was a navy captain when the armed forces overthrew the civilian government of Prime Minister Marcello Caetano in April, 1974. Azevedo reportedly was chiefly responsible for organizing navy support for the coup. Within a week after the overthrow, the coup leaders made him a member of the ruling junta, promoted him to vice-admiral, and named him chief of staff of the navy. During his brief service on the junta, Azevedo avoided voicing his opinions publicly. This restraint was seen as one of the major factors in his becoming prime minister.

Azevedo was born on June 5, 1917, in Luanda, Angola, where his father was a Portuguese colonial official. He entered the naval academy at the age of 17. He received his first command, a destroyer, in 1946, and was an instructor at the naval training school from 1955 to 1963, then took charge of the naval defense of Angola. From 1968 to 1971, he served as naval attaché in London, and from 1971 to 1974, he was the commander of the Portuguese marines. Darlene R. Stille

BAHAMAS. See WEST INDIES.

BAHRAIN. Opposition to the rule of Amir Isa bin Salman Al Khalifa and the royal family delayed plans to develop more representative government in 1975. The Cabinet, headed by Amir Isa's brother, Prime Minister Khalifa bin Salman Al Khalifa, resigned on August 24, charging the 30-member National Assembly elected in 1973 with obstruction of government policies. Amir Isa then suspended the Assembly and reappointed the prime minister to head a caretaker government. About 60 persons, most of them students and Assembly members, were arrested on charges of endangering state security. Amir Isa also postponed Assembly elections.

Because of internal unrest and pressure from other Arab states, the government announced on September 26 it would terminate the U.S. naval base in Bahrain, effective in 1977. The annual rent was raised in March from $600,000 to $4 million.

Bahrain's economy continued to prosper. Oil production averaged 68,000 barrels a day. Aided by a September order from the People's Republic of China for 6,950 short tons (6,300 metric tons) of aluminum, the Bahrain Aluminum Company inaugurated a $38-million expansion program. Bahrain also reported a 100 per cent increase in crime and traffic congestion during the year. William Spencer

See also MIDDLE EAST (Facts in Brief Table).

BALLET. See DANCING.

BALTIMORE. Mayor William D. Schaefer easily won re-election on Nov. 5, 1975. He defeated his Republican opponent, Claudette M. Chandler, a black activist, by a vote margin of more than 5 to 1.

The city's school board fired Baltimore's first black school superintendent, Roland N. Patterson, on July 17. The board charged Patterson with short-changing the city's predominantly black schools by failing to curb violence and by deliberately lowering academic standards. Three of the school board's five black members joined with the four white members to vote for his ouster.

City Finance. Mayor Schaefer joined forces in February with the chief executives of Maryland's most populous counties – Anne Arundel, Baltimore, Montgomery, and Prince Georges – to urge adoption of an increase in the state sales tax from 4 per cent to 5 per cent. They estimated that the increase would generate an additional $70 million yearly for distribution to local governments.

In comparison with other large U.S. cities, Baltimore was in relatively strong financial condition in 1975. The city concluded its fiscal year on June 30 with a surplus of $52 million.

Urban Energy. The Regional Planning Council in Baltimore reported on June 10 that more area residents were using mass transit than before the 1974 gasoline shortage. The report noted that the number of riders in April, 1975, was 6 per cent higher than in April, 1973.

The pump price of regular gasoline averaged 58.7 cents per gallon (3.8 liters) in June, up 3.2 per cent from the previous year.

A new garbage-disposal system began operating on a limited basis in Baltimore during the year. The $16-million facility converts garbage into usable energy, iron, steel, and other products.

Area Economy. The number of persons in Baltimore receiving unemployment-insurance payments doubled between August, 1974, and August, 1975. The unemployment rate in the area was 8.4 per cent by mid-1975, up only 0.4 per cent from 1974. Living costs rose 8.8 per cent between June, 1974, and June, 1975. During the same period, food and housing costs rose 9.4 per cent, and health and recreation costs went up 9.7 per cent.

A U.S. Census Bureau report issued in mid-1975 indicated that Baltimore had lost 3.1 per cent of its population between 1970 and 1973. The Census Bureau estimated the city's population at 877,838 persons as of July 1, 1973.

On November 24, a federal grand jury in Baltimore indicted Maryland Governor Marvin Mandel and five associates on charges of mail fraud, bribery, and racketeering. The grand jury charged that Mandel used his official position to favor associates with insurance, real estate, and race track interests. Mandel then allegedly shared secretly in the profits.   James M. Banovetz

BANGLADESH. President Sheik Mujibur Rahman, the spellbinder who liked to be called "father of his nation," was assassinated on Aug. 15, 1975. The young officers who killed him also shot his wife, his three sons, his brother, and his nephew, Sheik Fazalul Huq Moni, one of the most hated figures in Mujibur's government. One of the principal plotters, Major Shariful Huq Dalim, dismissed by Mujibur when he became too zealous in pursuing official grafters, went on the radio a few hours later to announce the coup.

Radio Dacca provided the details. The regime of "corruption, injustice, and autocracy" had ended and Mujibur was dead. His minister of commerce, 56-year-old Khandakar Mushtaque Ahmed, conservative, pro-American, and a strong believer in a Moslem state, had been sworn in as president.

Pakistan recognized the new regime and promised a gift of 50,000 short tons (45,000 metric tons) of rice and 15 million yards (14 million meters) of cloth. China soon followed. India and Russia granted recognition reluctantly.

The August coup was followed by another one on November 3. In the next fortnight, Dacca went through a series of coups, arrests, and murders. Eventually, Lieutenant General Ziaur Rahman, chief of army staff, emerged as the new strong man. After 87 days in the presidency, Mushtaque

Tanks move into the heart of Dacca on August 15, following the first of two army-backed revolts that overturned the government of Bangladesh.

Ahmed yielded his post to Abu Sadat Mohammed Sayem, chief justice of the Supreme Court. One of his first acts was to deal with an army mutiny in which 34 officers and some 100 enlisted men were killed on November 7.

Mujibur's Errors. Just three years earlier, Mujibur was the idol of Bangladesh's millions. By mid-1974, his popularity had waned. The people were hungry and misgoverned, while Mujibur's favorites grew rich.

Public resentment mounted with the growth of distress. Mujibur sought the answer in personal authority. He suspended the Constitution on Dec. 28, 1974, after three members of his Awami (People's) League were murdered. On Jan. 25, 1975, Mujibur gave up the post of prime minister to become president with near-absolute powers. Meanwhile, the price of rice more than doubled.

In the Red. There were heavy infusions of foreign cash and grain, but it was never enough. Thousands of people died. For the second straight year, the country suffered from a major cholera epidemic. Western nations gave $900 million in credits, but the trade deficit ran to $1.1 billion. The country needed 2.3 million short tons (2 million metric tons) of imported grain, but the supply ran short by more than 350,000 short tons (318,000 metric tons). Mark Gayn

See also ASIA (Facts in Brief Table).

BANKS AND BANKING. The worst world-wide recession since the 1930s touched bottom in 1975, and interest rates throughout the world began to fall. In the United States, interest rates fell sharply after reaching a 100-year high in the third quarter of 1974. Rates on short-term securities dropped roughly 50 per cent to cyclical lows in the second quarter, but long-term rates came down only about 10 per cent. Interest rates for some borrowers actually increased as a result of New York City's threatened default.

Long-term rates remained high, even for the best credit risks. This was because of the need to finance an enormous federal government deficit – $43.6 billion in fiscal 1975 – and general public expectations of continued high inflation rates. Although price advances slowed during the year, dropping to about half the 12 per cent annual increase in 1974, recognition of this filtered through to consumer expectations only after the recovery was well underway in the last half of 1975.

Congress Acts. The U.S. Congress made a major effort to exert more effective controls over federal fiscal and monetary policies than it had in the past. Fiscal policy is the government's use of its spending and revenue-producing activities in order to achieve certain goals. Monetary policy is the management of the nation's money supply to gain desired objectives.

To gain greater control over fiscal policy, the Democratic-controlled Congress established a Congressional Budget Office, headed by economist Alice M. Rivlin. The office tried to force the legislative branch to scrutinize the budget as a whole, rather than leaving that responsibility to the President and his Office of Management and Budget.

A bipartisan coalition in Congress in March passed a joint resolution on the conduct of monetary policy over the objections of Arthur Burns, chairman of the Board of Governors of the Federal Reserve System. In addition to asking the Federal Reserve to ease its monetary policy, the resolution requires the Federal Reserve for the first time to reveal to Senate and House banking committees each quarter what its target is for the rate of monetary growth in the forthcoming year. Although the Federal Reserve has always been legally responsible to Congress since its founding under the Federal Reserve Act, previous Congresses had received only periodic reports on past monetary policies; they had not received a specific forecast for a planned policy stance.

Monetary Disputes. Passage of the resolution reflected general concern in Congress because the Federal Reserve had permitted the growth rate of the money supply – demand deposits and currency held by the public – to slow down during the recession of 1974 and early 1975.

Characteristically, the Federal Reserve lowered the proportion of required reserves for member banks on February 13 after watching the money supply drop by an annual rate of 11 per cent in January. This move brought the required ratio of reserves against deposits down from 7.5 per cent to 7 per cent. Consequently, each dollar of reserves could support more deposits than before.

For some years, a small band of so-called monetarist economists, most notably Milton Friedman of the University of Chicago, has criticized Federal Reserve authorities for crediting themselves for expansionary policies during recessions solely because interest rates decline. Monetarists argue that such interest rate decreases really reflect relative declines in the demand for money and credit, not an increase in supply. Hence, the Federal Reserve could be fooled into permitting a slower rate of monetary growth in a recession just when the opposite policy would be more appropriate.

Targets for Growth. Burns cooperated fully with Congress in the first hearings held under the congressional resolution on May 1. He revealed a monetary growth target of from 5 to 7.5 per cent for the coming 12 months, and he stuck to that target the rest of the year. There was some question whether the Federal Reserve could control the money supply even if it wanted to. Actual performance during the year did not show steady monetary growth. But through the end of November, the av-

"Don't panic. It's a note of introduction. I'd like to buy your bank."

erage monetary growth rate over the previous seven months remained within the designated target range.

After the recovery was underway, liberal economists increasingly criticized the target growth rate. Walter W. Heller and Arthur M. Okun, both former chairmen of the Council of Economic Advisers, argued that too slow a rate of monetary growth might cut short the recovery by permitting interest rates to rise sharply in the face of unusually heavy public demands for credit to finance a federal budget deficit projected at $60 billion or more in fiscal 1976.

New York City. There was considerable controversy about whether the federal government should help stave off default on the debt owed by New York City. Some 75 banks around the country held New York City debt amounting to 50 per cent or more of their assets, and half of them could be in serious trouble if New York defaulted. Some feared that a default might precipitate an old-fashioned financial panic, because commercial banks held about $100 billion, or about 15 per cent of their assets, in state and local government bonds. The Federal Reserve stood ready to lend to individual banks if they were adversely affected.

President Gerald R. Ford and Secretary of the Treasury William E. Simon initially opposed any special federal aid for the city until New York City came up with a program to keep its expenditures within the bounds of its revenues. When the state of New York finally approved such a plan for the city in late November, Congress passed a bill providing federal loans of up to $2.3 billion through June, 1978. Ford signed it on December 9. See NEW YORK CITY; STOCKS AND BONDS.

Credit and Saving. Consumer credit, which fell in early 1975, rose briskly in the third quarter, led by renewed demand for automobile financing. The housing market also recovered somewhat from the poor showing of the previous year. Mortgage loans increased 7 per cent in the year ended June 30. Interest rates on mortgages, which had peaked in October, 1974, were down at least 1.5 percentage points by midyear.

Consumers, whose confidence had been strained by the simultaneous inflation and recession in 1974, led the economic advance in late 1975. They saved an unusually high 10.6 per cent of their income in the second quarter, as incomes were temporarily swollen by federal tax rebates. But in the third quarter, savings dropped to 7.7 per cent of income as spending advanced at a rapid 16.7 per cent annual rate.

Currency and demand deposits totaled more than $300 billion, about 20 per cent of the gross national product, down from 25 per cent a decade earlier. Other financial assets held by the public included about $350 billion in commercial bank time and savings deposits, $110 billion in mutual savings banks deposits, and $280 billion in savings and loan associations.

Banking Services. The attempt of two Chicago banks to offer a form of automatic computer-linked banking to their customers was ruled illegal in December under an Illinois law that prohibits branch banking. However, the remote teller stations, which can handle deposits and withdrawals and make small loans, were allowed to continue to operate pending appeal. Check-verification devices were not affected by the ruling. Also unaffected were savings and loan associations.

The Federal Reserve Board adopted a rule in April that allows bank customers to withdraw funds from savings accounts by telephone. In a joint ruling with the Federal Deposit Insurance Corporation, the Federal Reserve also proposed that banks allow customers to pay bills from their savings accounts.

International Finance. The value of the dollar continued to float in relation to other currencies — that is, its value was determined on the basis of market demand for dollars and foreign currencies. The average exchange rate of the dollar against other currencies at year-end was about 10 per cent lower than it was in mid-1971, when the United States began allowing the dollar to float.

H. Johannes Witteveen, managing director of the International Monetary Fund (IMF), proposed in October that the fund evolve into a central world bank. The IMF now serves mainly as an international lending agency to help member countries stabilize the foreign exchange values of their currencies. Witteveen proposed that the IMF establish reserve requirements under which member countries would agree to hold a specified fraction of their international reserves in Special Drawing Rights (SDR's), the so-called "paper gold" set up by the IMF. By controlling the amount of SDR's or changing the required ratio of SDR's to other international reserves, the IMF could regulate the total amount of international reserves and prevent the uncontrolled pile-up of foreign currencies that can lead to heightened inflation. This happened in 1971 when an explosion in official dollar holdings outside the United States was a factor in triggering worldwide inflation. Witteveen also favored further reducing the international monetary role of gold by having countries exchange their gold for SDR's.

Anticipated increases in the price of gold after U.S. citizens became legally free to hold gold in 1975 failed to materialize. Although the U.S. Treasury auctioned off small amounts of its gold stock, U.S. citizens bought little of the gold. The price in early December was about $140 a troy ounce (31 grams). William G. Dewald

BARBADOS. See WEST INDIES.

BARYSHNIKOV, MIKHAIL (1948-   ), a ballet star, gained great acclaim in North America in 1975, following his 1974 defection from Russia. He joined New York City's American Ballet Theatre and made his U.S. debut in *Giselle* in July, 1974.

Baryshnikov was born in Riga, the capital of Latvia, a Russian republic. His childhood fascination with the stage led him to enroll in a ballet school there. At 12, he was older than most of the other students, but his obvious talent soon conquered that handicap. When he was 16, he went to Leningrad with a touring dance group and stayed to study under Alexander Ivanovich Pushkin, who also taught Rudolph Nureyev and Valery Panov. After three years, he joined the famed Kirov Ballet company as a soloist.

Baryshnikov enjoyed his first Western triumph when he danced in London in 1970, but his interest in things Western was noted with disapproval at home. By 1974, Baryshnikov had decided to defect. He felt hamstrung by the limited classical repertory and longed for new choreographic challenges that could be found only in the West. His chance came one evening in June, 1974, while he was dancing in Toronto, Canada, with a visiting Russian dance group. With characteristic flair, Baryshnikov broke away from the group after an evening performance, sprinted across the street, and leaped into a waiting car. Kathryn Sederberg

BASEBALL. The Cincinnati Reds, with one of the best records in modern baseball history, became 1975 champions in one of the greatest World Series in history. But a labor arbitrator's ruling soon pushed the series into the background.

Arbitrator Peter M. Seitz ruled on December 23 that pitchers Andy Messersmith of the Los Angeles Dodgers and Dave McNally, who quit the Montreal Expos in mid-season, were free agents and could sign with any club. A 1974 Seitz ruling made pitcher Jim (Catfish) Hunter a free agent on the grounds that Oakland A's owner Charles O. Finley had breached Hunter's contract. Hunter then signed with the New York Yankees. But Seitz said the Messersmith and McNally cases were not the same as Hunter's. He said Messersmith and McNally, by playing in 1975 without having signed contracts, had completed their contracts, and he ruled against the club owners' contention that player contracts can be renewed indefinitely. If upheld on appeal, the ruling strikes a blow at baseball's reserve clause, which binds a player to one team until he is released, sold, or traded, or retires.

On the Field. The Reds, champions of the National League, barely defeated the Boston Red Sox, champions of the American League, 4 games to 3, in the World Series.

The division races were all one-sided. The Reds won the National League's Western Division for

Carlton Fisk claims interference after he bumped
Reds bunter Ed Armbrister, then threw wildly.
Boston lost the argument and third series game.

the third time in four years. Their 20-game margin
was staggering, and their September 7 clinching
date was the earliest in league history.

The Pittsburgh Pirates won the National League
East for the fifth time in six years. Their margin
was 6½ games. The American League winners
were the Red Sox by 4½ games in the East and the
Oakland A's by 7 games in the West.

The pennant play-offs lasted only three games
each. The Red Sox surprisingly eliminated the A's,
who had won the three previous World Series, and
the Reds won quickly from the Pirates.

Reds and Red Sox. Except for pitching that
was sometimes erratic, the Reds had everything —
power, good fielding, and speed. They stole 168
bases in 204 attempts during the regular season
and 11 for 11 in the play-offs. Their most exciting
player was Joe Morgan, a 5-foot 7-inch (170-cen-
timeter) second baseman, who batted .327 during
the regular season, hit 17 home runs, scored 107
runs, coaxed 132 bases on balls, and stole 67 bases.
He was named the National League's Most Valuable Player in the most one-sided voting in history.

Morgan was not the only heavy hitter. Johnny
Bench drove in 110 runs; Tony Perez, 109. Pete
Rose batted .317, led the majors in runs scored (112)
and doubles (48), and was second in hits (210).

The Red Sox, managed by Darrell Johnson, received special help from Luis Tiant, Carl Yastrzemski, Fred Lynn, and Jim Rice. Tiant, a wily,
aging pitcher from Cuba, pitched shut-outs in two
of his last three regular-season games and stopped
the A's on three hits in the play-off opener.

Lynn and Rice were rookie outfielders. Lynn
batted .331, hit 21 home runs, batted in 105 runs,
led the American League in three categories (runs
scored with 103, doubles with 47, and slugging
percentage with .566), and starred in center field.
He became the first man in major-league history to
be voted his league's Most Valuable Player and
Rookie of the Year in the same season. Rice batted
.309, hit 22 home runs, and drove in 102 runs. His
left hand was broken by a pitch one week before the
season ended. He missed the play-offs and World
Series. Lynn was voted Rookie of the Year with
23½ votes. The remaining half vote went to Rice.

World Series. The first two games were played
in Boston. The Red Sox won the opener, 6-0, on
Tiant's five-hit pitching. The Reds won the second
game, 3-2, with two runs in the ninth inning.

Then the series moved to Cincinnati and an immediate controversy. In the 10th inning of the
third game, the Reds led off with a single. Ed Armbrister, attempting to sacrifice, bunted. The ball
rolled perhaps 3 feet (91 centimeters) in front of
home plate. Armbrister hesitated, and Carlton
Fisk, the Red Sox catcher, ran for the ball and
bumped into Armbrister. Fisk grabbed the ball and
threw wildly to second base, allowing the base run-

ner to reach third base and Armbrister to reach second. The Reds soon scored and won, 6-5.

The Red Sox protested vigorously that Armbrister had interfered with Fisk's attempt to get to the ball. Umpire Larry Barnett disagreed.

The Red Sox tied the series by winning the fourth game, 5-4, behind Tiant, and the Reds won the fifth game, 6-2, behind Don Gullett. That sent the series back to Boston, where rain and a soaked field caused three consecutive postponements.

When the sixth game was finally played, it was unbelievably exciting. The Red Sox fought off defeat in the eighth inning when a three-run pinch homer by Bernie Carbo tied the score. In the 11th inning, Dwight Evans' circus catch against the right-field stands saved a home run. In the 12th inning, at 12:33 A.M. and after four hours of play, Fisk hit a home run to win it for the Red Sox, 7-6.

The next day, almost as an anticlimax, the Reds won the decisive game, 4-3, on Morgan's ninth-inning single.

The Oakland A's, as usual, were a talented, flamboyant team in almost constant turmoil, a condition stemming from the freewheeling moves of Finley, who served as general manager.

After the season, Finley fired manager Alvin Dark, not for losing the pennant but for a personal remark Dark made about him to a church group.

Top Players. Jim Palmer of the Baltimore Orioles and Hunter led American League pitchers with 23 victories each, and Palmer's 2.09 and Hunter's 2.58 were the lowest earned-run averages among American League starters. Tom Seaver of the New York Mets won 22 games, the only National Leaguer over 20, and his 243 strikeouts led the league. He set a major-league record of 200 or more strikeouts a year for eight consecutive years.

Nolan Ryan of the California Angels defeated the Orioles, 1-0, on June 1 for his fourth no-hit, no-run game, tying Sandy Koufax' major-league record. On September 28, four A's pitchers—Vida Blue, Glenn Abbott, Paul Lindblad, and Rollie Fingers—combined to pitch a 5-0 no-hitter against the California Angels. It was the first by more than two pitchers. Rod Carew, Minnesota Twins second baseman, won the American League batting title for the fourth straight year with a .359 average.

Henry Aaron, who broke Babe Ruth's home-run record in 1974, was traded after that season, at his request, from the Atlanta Braves to the Milwaukee Brewers. Aaron, 41 and in his 22nd major-league season, hit 12 home runs as the Brewers' designated hitter. He finished the season with a lifetime total of 745 home runs, 2,261 runs batted in, and a host of other all-time records, and said he would be back in 1976.

Final Standings in Major League Baseball

American League	W.	L.	Pct.	GB.
Eastern Division				
Boston	95	65	.594	
Baltimore	90	69	.566	4½
New York	83	77	.519	12
Cleveland	79	80	.497	15½
Milwaukee	68	94	.420	28
Detroit	57	102	.358	37½
Western Division				
Oakland	98	64	.605	
Kansas City	91	71	.562	7
Texas	79	83	.488	19
Minnesota	76	83	.478	20½
Chicago	75	86	.466	22½
California	72	89	.447	25½

Leading Batters
Batting Average—Rod Carew, Minnesota — .359
Home Runs—George Scott, Milwaukee, and Reggie Jackson, Oakland — 36
Runs Batted In—George Scott, Milwaukee — 109
Hits—George Brett, Kansas City — 195

Leading Pitchers
Games Won—Jim Palmer, Baltimore; Jim Hunter, New York — 23
Win Average—Rogelio Moret, Boston (14-3) — .824
(162 or more innings)
Earned-Run Average—Jim Palmer, Baltimore — 2.09
Strikeouts—Frank Tanana, California — 269

Awards
Most Valuable Player—Fred Lynn, Boston
Cy Young—Jim Palmer, Baltimore
Rookie of the Year—Fred Lynn, Boston
Manager of the Year—Darrell Johnson, Boston

National League	W.	L.	Pct.	GB.
Eastern Division				
Pittsburgh	92	69	.571	
Philadelphia	86	76	.531	6½
New York	82	80	.506	10½
St. Louis	82	80	.506	10½
Chicago	75	87	.463	17½
Montreal	75	87	.463	17½
Western Division				
Cincinnati	108	54	.667	
Los Angeles	88	74	.543	20
San Francisco	80	81	.497	27½
San Diego	71	91	.438	37
Atlanta	67	94	.416	40½
Houston	64	97	.398	43½

Leading Batters
Batting Average—Bill Madlock, Chicago — .354
Home Runs—Mike Schmidt, Philadelphia — 38
Runs Batted In—Greg Luzinski, Philadelphia — 120
Hits—Dave Cash, Philadelphia — 213

Leading Pitchers
Games Won—Tom Seaver, New York — 22
Win Average—Alan Hrabosky, St. Louis (13-3) — .813
(162 or more innings)
Earned-Run Average—Randy Jones, San Diego — 2.24
(162 or more innings)
Strikeouts—Tom Seaver, New York — 243

Awards
Most Valuable Player—Joe Morgan, Cincinnati
Cy Young—Tom Seaver, New York
Rookie of the Year—John Montefusco, San Francisco
Manager of the Year—George (Sparky) Anderson, Cincinnati

Managers. Frank Robinson became the first black manager in major-league history, and his Cleveland Indians finished only half a game below .500. The Indians signed him to manage in 1976.

Robinson fared better than Dark and a small army of other managers. The Texas Rangers fired Billy Martin and replaced him with Frank Lucchesi. Martin soon became manager of the Yankees, who fired Bill Virdon. The Houston Astros then dropped Preston Gomez and hired Virdon. Kansas City released Jack McKeon in favor of Dorrel (Whitey) Herzog. The Mets fired Yogi Berra and named Joe Frazier, and the Braves dropped Clyde King for Dave Bristol. The Montreal Expos fired Gene Mauch and hired Karl Kuehl. Milwaukee fired Del Crandall and named Alex Grammas. The Twins replaced Frank Quilici with Mauch, and San Francisco released Wes Westrum. Bill Veeck, who bought the Chicago White Sox a second time, hired Paul Richards to replace Chuck Tanner, who went to Oakland.

Hall of Fame. Ralph Kiner, who hit 369 home runs in 10 years as a major-league outfielder, was voted into the Baseball Hall of Fame. Kiner was inducted with Earl Averill, Billy Herman, and Stanley (Bucky) Harris, who were chosen by a veterans' committee, and William Julius (Judy) Johnson, who was chosen by a Negro Leagues committee. Frank Litsky

BASKETBALL. The Golden State Warriors, the Kentucky Colonels, and the University of California, Los Angeles (UCLA), won the major U.S. basketball titles in 1975, all in upsets. But as has happened so often in recent years, the struggle among professionals to acquire players and player moves from team to team and league to league often overshadowed the games themselves.

The travels of George McGinnis, who led the Indiana Pacers to the American Basketball Association (ABA) championship finals, commanded the widest attention. McGinnis, a 24-year-old forward, is big and strong at 6 feet 8 inches (203 centimeters) and 240 pounds (109 kilograms). He led the ABA in scoring, averaging 29.78 points per game, and ranked second in steals, third in assists, and fifth in rebounds. He shared the Most Valuable Player award with Julius Erving of the New York Nets.

The Philadelphia 76ers held the National Basketball Association (NBA) rights to McGinnis. The New York Knickerbockers acquired those rights in October, 1974, only to forfeit them when they failed to induce McGinnis to switch to the NBA. In May, 1975, the Knickerbockers convinced McGinnis to join them. They were unable to conclude a new agreement with Philadelphia for his rights, but they signed him anyway for $400,000 a year for six years plus a $500,000 nonreturnable bonus.

The 76ers charged the Knicks with piracy, later amending that to treason. Larry O'Brien, who became the NBA's new commissioner in June, revoked the signing and, as punishment, ordered the Knickerbockers to forfeit their first-round draft choice in 1976. In July, the 76ers surprisingly signed McGinnis to a six-year, no-cut, no-trade, no-option contract worth $3.2 million. In addition, they refunded the $500,000 bonus to the Knicks.

Despite his salary of $500,000 a year, Kareem Abdul-Jabbar, the 7-foot 2-inch (218-centimeter) center of the Milwaukee Bucks of the NBA, was unhappy in Milwaukee. He said that he would play out his option year and thus be free to sign with anyone if he were not traded to the Knicks or the Los Angeles Lakers. The Bucks soon traded him to the Lakers for two veteran players and two rookies.

McGinnis and Abdul-Jabbar thrived in a players' market because the 18 NBA teams and the 10 ABA teams fought to acquire veterans and draftees. As a result, salaries remained high. The Denver Nuggets of the ABA contested the Atlanta Hawks of the NBA for the two most coveted college players and signed both—David Thompson of North Carolina State for $2.5 million and 7-foot (213-centimeter) Marvin Webster of Morgan State for $1.5 million.

NBA Season. The Washington Bullets and the Boston Celtics had the best records in the NBA during the regular season, which ran from October, 1974, to April, 1975. The Bullets reached the play-off finals against the Golden State Warriors, and many thought the Bullets would win easily. Instead, the Warriors, coached by Al Attles, won in four straight because of the inspirational play and shooting of Rick Barry and a near-anonymous supporting cast.

Barry was voted the Most Valuable Player in the play-offs, and Bob McAdoo of the Buffalo Braves won that honor during the regular season. During the season, Barry led the NBA in steals and free-throw accuracy and was second in scoring to McAdoo. Barry and McAdoo made the all-star team along with Elvin Hayes of Washington, Walt Frazier of New York, and Nate Archibald of the Kansas City-Omaha Kings.

ABA Season. Denver, the strongest team during the regular season, lost to Indiana in the Western Division play-offs. Then Kentucky defeated Indiana, 4 games to 1, in the play-off finals, and Artis Gilmore, Kentucky's 7-foot 2-inch (218-centimeter) center, was voted Most Valuable Player in the play-offs. After the season, the ABA attacked two franchise problems by moving the Memphis team to Baltimore and finding a buyer for the San Diego Conquistadors for $2 million. But the ABA was soon down to seven teams. Baltimore was dropped in October, San Diego folded in November, and Utah quit in December.

Final Standings in Major League Basketball

National Basketball Association

Eastern Conference

Atlantic Division

	W.	L.	Pct.
Boston	60	22	.732
Buffalo	49	33	.598
New York	40	42	.488
Philadelphia	34	48	.415

Central Division

	W.	L.	Pct.
Washington	60	22	.732
Houston	41	41	.500
Cleveland	40	42	.488
Atlanta	31	51	.378
New Orleans	23	59	.280

Western Conference

Midwest Division

	W.	L.	Pct.
Chicago	47	35	.573
Kansas City-Omaha	44	38	.537
Detroit	40	42	.488
Milwaukee	38	44	.463

Pacific Division

	W.	L.	Pct.
Golden State	48	34	.585
Seattle	43	39	.524
Portland	38	44	.463
Phoenix	32	50	.390
Los Angeles	30	52	.366

Leading Scorers	G.	FG.	FT.	Pts.	Avg.
McAdoo, Buffalo	82	1,095	641	2,831	34.5
Barry, Golden State	80	1,028	394	2,450	30.6
Jabbar, Milwaukee	65	812	325	1,949	30.0
Archibald, K.C.-Omaha	82	759	652	2,170	26.5
Scott, Phoenix	69	703	274	1,680	24.3

American Basketball Association

Eastern Division

	W.	L.	Pct.
*Kentucky	58	26	.690
New York	58	26	.690
St. Louis	32	52	.381
Memphis	27	57	.321
Virginia	15	69	.179

Western Division

	W.	L.	Pct.
Denver	65	19	.774
San Antonio	51	33	.607
Indiana	45	39	.536
Utah	38	46	.452
San Diego	31	53	.369

*Beat New York, 108-99, in play-off game to win division championship

Leading Scorers	G.	FG.	FT.	Pts.	Avg.
McGinnis, Indiana	79	811	545	2,353	29.7
Erving, New York	84	885	486	2,343	27.8
Boone, Utah	84	862	363	2,117	25.2
Grant, San Diego	53	575	182	1,335	25.1
Barnes, St. Louis	77	777	295	1,849	24.0

College Champions

Conference	School
Atlantic Coast	Maryland (regular season) North Carolina (ACC tourney)
Big Eight	Kansas
Big Ten	Indiana
Ivy League	Pennsylvania
Missouri Valley	Louisville
Ohio Valley	Middle Tennessee
Pacific-8	UCLA
Southern	Furman
Southeastern	Kentucky-Alabama (tie)
Southwest	Texas A&M
Western Athletic	Arizona State

College. This was not expected to be a memorable year for UCLA. For one thing, its all-America center, Bill Walton, had graduated to the Portland Trail Blazers of the NBA. But UCLA reached the National Collegiate Athletic Association (NCAA) championships in March in San Diego, and won the title by defeating a taller, more physical Kentucky team, 92-85, in the final. The championship was UCLA's 8th in 9 years and its 10th in 12 years. It was also the last for John Wooden, UCLA coach for 27 years. After the final, he retired at age 64.

Thompson, North Carolina State's 6-foot 4-inch (193-centimeter) forward, was named Player of the Year for the second straight year and all-American for the third straight year. The Coach of the Year was fiery Bobby Knight of Indiana University, whose team posted the only undefeated record during the regular season. Consensus all-Americans, in addition to Thompson, were Adrian Dantley of Notre Dame, David Meyers of UCLA, Scott May of Indiana, John Lucas of Maryland, and Luther (Ticky) Burden of Utah.

The Associated Press final poll, taken after the postseason tournaments, voted UCLA national champion, with Kentucky second, Indiana third, and Louisville fourth. The final United Press International ratings, made before the tournaments, ranked Indiana first, UCLA second, Louisville third, and Kentucky fourth.

Frank Litsky

BAYH, BIRCH EVANS, JR. (1928-   ), Democratic senator from Indiana, became the ninth candidate for the Democratic nomination for President on Oct. 21, 1975. He promised to provide "moral leadership" that would create more jobs, close tax loopholes, break up "monopolistic oil companies," reform the Federal Reserve System, and aid the old and needy.

Born near Terre Haute, Ind., Bayh graduated from Purdue University in 1951. He received his law degree from Indiana University in 1960 and was admitted to the bar the following year. He served in the Indiana House of Representatives from 1954 to 1962 and was speaker from 1959 to 1960. In 1962, when he was elected to the U.S. Senate, he used a catchy jingle to help voters identify him: "Hey, look him over, he's your kind of guy. His first name is Birch, his last name is Bayh."

Bayh is a member of the Senate Appropriations Committee and the Judiciary Committee, where he waged successful fights against the nominations of Clement F. Haynsworth, Jr., and G. Harrold Carswell to the Supreme Court of the United States. The pending constitutional amendment on equal rights is a product of his work as chairman of a judiciary subcommittee.

Bayh still operates the family farm near Terre Haute. He and his wife, Marvella, have one son, Evan.

Kathryn Sederberg

BAYI, FILBERT (1953?-   ), Tanzanian runner, set a world record of 3 minutes 51.0 seconds for the mile run on May 17, 1975, breaking Jim Ryun's 1967 record of 3:51.1. Bayi beat most of the world's leading milers in the International Freedom Games in Kingston, Jamaica. However, his record stood only until August 12, when John Walker of New Zealand ran a 3:49.4 in Götenborg, Sweden.

An air force lieutenant in Dar es Salaam, Bayi won the mile run in his American and indoor debut in Madison Square Garden, New York City, in January, 1975. He also won the mile in the Los Angeles Times Indoor Games, the Maple Leaf Games in Toronto, Canada, and the National Amateur Athletic Union Indoor Championships.

Bayi introduced a new racing style to the mile run. Instead of pacing himself, he runs as fast as he can from start to finish. The slender Tanzanian learned to run in the fields near his home village, Karatu, near Kilimanjaro. He ran after dogs hunting hares and gazelles to develop his endurance. "And since the altitude there is in excess of 5,000 feet (1,500 meters), this gave me the needed stamina for long-distance running, he explains. Bayi trains by running about 10 miles (16 kilometers) cross-country every morning. After work, he spends four hours running sprints of up to 1,000 yards (900 meters).   Joseph P. Spohn

See also TRACK AND FIELD; WALKER, JOHN.

BELGIUM. The coalition government of Prime Minister Leo Tindemans survived a parliamentary vote of confidence by 112 to 91 on June 12, 1975. The crisis arose when the small Walloon Union Party, which holds a 12-seat balance of power, opposed the parliamentary decision to buy U.S.-built F-16 jet fighter aircraft rather than the French Mirage. Tindemans cut Belgium's order from 116 planes to 102 and said he would use the money saved to set up a European aeronautics and development fund. Denmark, the Netherlands, and Norway, part of a four-nation group with Belgium, had already selected the F-16 in a North Atlantic Treaty Organization deal for 306 planes.

Severe Inflation, running at more than 15 per cent annually, was Belgium's biggest problem. The government imposed a 60-day price freeze on May 7 and placed a 14 per cent limit on annual growth of credit and reserve requirements for commercial banks. Tindemans said on April 30, "The terrifying problem facing us is how to make our prices competitive again." Because 53 per cent of Belgium's gross national product comes directly from exports, he emphasized slowing inflation.

Unemployment rose to 156,000, or 6 per cent of the working force, by June. Earlier, to combat it, the government had started a public works program to provide an additional 20,000 jobs. On October 1, it acted again to boost the economy and provide more jobs by reducing the social security contributions of businesses with large labor forces; lowering taxes on company stocks; and providing tax relief on some investments. The plan froze dividends and rents until mid-1976. The government also voted to loosen the tight link between prices and wages under which wages automatically rise with each cost-of-living increase.

By October 15, registered unemployment had reached 204,507 and the government decided to go along with union proposals to ban overtime to help ease the situation. The ban was to begin Jan. 1, 1976, and last for a year. Executives and their staffs would be excluded from the ban.

Labor Disputes. Thousands of oil and water workers went on strike on March 3, and oil refineries were closed for 24 hours. Teachers struck for a week over delayed payment of salaries. On June 11, a strike of self-employed business and professional men over high taxes and the government's price freeze deprived Belgians of medical and other services.

Tindemans visited China for 10 days in April, meeting Chairman Mao Tse-tung and Premier Chou En-lai. In June, King Baudouin I and Queen Fabiola made a visit to Russia.   Kenneth Brown

See also EUROPE (Facts in Brief Table).

BELIZE. See LATIN AMERICA.

A scoreboard in Belgium's parliament tallies a vote of confidence that Prime Minister Leo Tindemans won by 112 to 91 on June 12, 1975.

BENN, ANTHONY WEDGWOOD (1925-   ), became one of Great Britain's most controversial political figures in 1975. Despite his Cabinet post as secretary for industry, Benn went against the Labour Party position and led opposition to Britain's continued membership in the European Community (Common Market).

Despite Benn's efforts, an overwhelming 67 per cent of the voters approved membership in a June referendum. Prime Minister Harold Wilson immediately transferred Benn from his Cabinet post to a different one as secretary of energy.

Benn, the son of the first Viscount Stangate, was born in London on April 3, 1925. After graduating from Westminster School, he served as a pilot in the Royal Air Force from 1943 to 1945. He graduated from Oxford University in 1949 and spent a year as a producer for the British Broadcasting Corporation. Elected to the House of Commons in 1950, he was unseated in 1960 when he inherited the family title. He was re-elected to Commons in 1963, after renouncing the title.

Benn is a leader of the left wing in British politics. After becoming secretary for industry in 1974, he offered government proposals for more industrial nationalization, often pursuing goals that went beyond party policy.

He married Caroline de Camp in 1949. They have four children.　　　　　Kathryn Sederberg

BENTSEN, LLOYD MILLARD, JR. (1921-   ), United States senator from Texas, announced on Feb. 17, 1975, that he would seek the 1976 Democratic presidential nomination. The Texas senator made his move after a year of testing the political waters in public appearances across the country. Bentsen has generally taken a moderate to conservative stance on most issues.

Bentsen was born on Feb. 11, 1921, in Mission, Tex., where his father was a successful land speculator. He earned a law degree from the University of Texas in 1942 and served in the U.S. Army Air Corps during World War II, flying 50 missions. After the war, he practiced law in McAllen, Tex. In 1955, Bentsen began a successful career in insurance. By 1970, he was the millionaire president of Lincoln Consolidated, a holding company with large insurance interests.

Bentsen was elected to Congress in 1948 and served until 1955 in the House of Representatives. He maintained close ties with the conservative wing of the Texas Democratic Party, dominated by Lyndon B. Johnson and John B. Connally, Jr. In a bitterly fought 1970 primary, Bentsen defeated the liberal incumbent, Ralph W. Yarborough, and went on to be elected to the Senate.

Bentsen married Beryl Ann Longino in 1943. They have three children.　　　　　Edward G. Nash

BHUTAN. See ASIA.

BICENTENNIAL, UNITED STATES. Plans for the nation's 200th birthday celebration moved into high gear in 1975. Congress appropriated about $41 million to finance various Bicentennial projects on a national level. State, local, and corporate interests were planning to spend an additional $45-million. Under a congressional matching-grants program set up for fiscal 1976, the 50 states, Puerto Rico, and the District of Columbia would be eligible for $40,000 each to augment their Bicentennial budgets.

By year's end, the American Revolution Bicentennial Administration had recognized more than 7,000 U.S. communities as official participants in the celebration. About 20 federal agencies were engaged in more than 200 Bicentennial programs, including commemorative events in 298 national parks. About 450 colleges and universities, with activities ranging from commissioned musical compositions to scholarly dissertations, were formally recognized as "Bicentennial campuses." Private corporations were also involved in programs of their own, including Walt Disney Productions, which spent two years and $8 million preparing for a 15-month series of parades at Disney World in Florida and Disneyland in California.

A Major Event of the 1975 Bicentennial celebration took place on April 18 when the 200th anniversary of Paul Revere's ride was observed in a commemorative lantern service in Boston's Old North Church. The following day, about 160,000 Americans gathered in Concord and nearby Lexington, Mass., to witness re-enactments of the two skirmishes that launched the Revolutionary War in 1775. The only untoward incident occurred when an unruly crowd jeered President Gerald R. Ford during his commemorative address at Concord.

Numerous other re-enactments occurred during the year. On May 10, Ethan Allen's Green Mountain Boys "recaptured" Fort Ticonderoga in New York. An estimated 1.5 million people turned out on May 10 in Philadelphia to commemorate the convening of the historic Second Continental Congress. On September 20, a contingent from Cambridge, Mass., restaged the epic march made through Maine to Quebec, Canada, in 1775 under the command of Benedict Arnold. They were joined by a 600-man uniformed Maine unit and a New York unit that moved north from Manhattan, following General Richard Montgomery's route along the St. Lawrence River to Quebec. There, the two groups joined forces for a mock frontal assault on that Canadian city.

Cultural Exhibits were both popular and widespread. Particularly appropriate was "Paul Revere's Boston: 1735-1818," a display of the visual arts at the time of Revere's famous ride. It was on exhibition in the Boston Museum of Fine Arts from April through October. "The Die Is Now Cast:

A re-enactment of the historic skirmish at Concord, Mass., in April, 1775, was a major event of the U.S. Bicentennial celebration held in 1975.

The Road to American Independence," a sampling of portraits, documents, and artifacts produced between 1774 and 1776, opened a seven-month stay in Washington, D.C.'s National Portrait Gallery in mid-April. The Denver Art Museum sponsored "USA '76: The First 200 Years," which ran from September 1 through October 13. "The World of Franklin and Jefferson," a display of paintings, photographs, and texts reflecting the America both men knew between 1706 and 1826, opened in Paris on January 9. It was later mounted in Warsaw, Poland, and in London, with other stops scheduled in New York City, Chicago, and San Francisco.

"Industrial Heritage USA," a traveling exhibit developed by Greenfield Village and the Henry Ford Museum in Dearborn, Mich., completed a 10-month tour of 34 metropolitan areas in 23 states. The 25-car Freedom Train, carrying 700 historical items, began a two-year tour of 80 U.S. cities at Wilmington, Del., on April 1. The Wagon Train pilgrimage of covered wagons from each state, a "replay of history – in reverse," began its journey from the West to Valley Forge, Pa., on June 8.

Community Groups across the nation took an active role in focusing attention on the Bicentennial. Between April and June, Greater Miami conducted a series of public forums on "paradoxes of

the Bill of Rights." Residents of Potomac, Md., held a series of living-room panel discussions to promote community-style debates on current issues in terms of the country's basic documents. A series of town meetings began on August 3 in Milwaukee to discuss tax reform in the context of the Bicentennial year.

Foreign Participation. More than 40 foreign governments agreed to participate in the celebration. France installed a sound-and-light presentation at Mount Vernon, George Washington's home in Virginia. Great Britain presented a reproduction of the Liberty Bell from the Whitechapel Foundry in London, which cast the original in 1752. West Germany established the John J. McCloy Foundation for German-American student exchanges.

Iran gave $100,000 to establish a scholarship fund for American students wishing to pursue specialized fields of education in Iran during the Bicentennial period. Australia endowed a chair of Australian studies at Harvard University. In the largest single cultural enterprise of its kind ever undertaken by Canada, the government sent the Royal Winnipeg Ballet, the National Arts Centre Orchestra, the Mendelssohn Choir, the Shaw Festival, and two opera companies for a two-week festival beginning on October 13 at the John F. Kennedy Center for the Performing Arts in Washington, D.C.

Lynn Beaumont

Man-made microbes munch crude oil in the flask at right. They may be used to convert oil spilled on waterways into food for marine life.

BIOCHEMISTRY. Henry A. Lardy, a University of Wisconsin biochemist, offered a biochemical explanation of what causes crib death, or the sudden infant death syndrome, in August, 1975. Crib death is the leading cause of death among babies from 1 month to 1 year of age. As many as 10,000 infants die from it annually in the United States.

Autopsies have failed to yield any clues as to the cause of the deaths, other than small bleeding spots in the lungs. However, some medical researchers have suggested recently that periods of *apnea* (temporary suspension of breathing) during sleep deprive the infants of oxygen, causing crib death.

Lardy believes that apnea results from the infant's failure to maintain a normal blood sugar level because the child lacks an enzyme that can convert amino acids to sugar. Lardy examined the enzyme content in the livers of 100 crib death victims and found a significant decrease in the enzyme phosphoenolpyruvate-carboxykinase in all but four. This enzyme plays a central role in converting amino acids into sugars to maintain normal blood sugar levels between meals. Most crib deaths occur during the winter months and at night when infants first begin to sleep through the night without a feeding. Lacking the enzyme, an infant might die of an otherwise minor infection.

Emphysema and Liver Cirrhosis. The protein alpha$_1$ antitrypsin is a constituent of normal human blood serum that inhibits the action of trypsin, an enzyme that breaks down large, complex protein molecules into amino acids. In some people who have a defective genetic inheritance, the alpha$_1$ antitrypsin concentration may be only from 10 to 50 per cent of normal. These people tend to develop emphysema early in life.

In January, Sten Eriksson and Christer Larsson at the University of Lund in Sweden isolated and characterized the inclusion, or stainable, bodies in cells from the cirrhotic livers of patients with an alpha$_1$ antitrypsin deficiency. They discovered that a protein about the same size as serum alpha$_1$ antitrypsin is the main component of the inclusion body. Both the normal serum antitrypsin and the isolated protein possess similar immunological properties in forming antibodies and in reacting with immune serum. However, the protein from the deficient individuals does not inhibit trypsin and other protein-splitting enzymes. It does not contain sialic acid, a complex nitrogen-containing sugar molecule that is a part of the normal antitrypsin structure. The researchers believe that the genetic defect apparently blocks the manufacture of normal sialyated trypsin.

Gene Structure. A group of researchers in the Laboratories of Molecular Biology and of Histology and Genetics at the University of Ghent in Belgium reported in July that they had determined the sequence of nucleotides in an entire gene. They investigated the gene that codes for the A protein of the bacterial virus MS2. Using a variety of chemical techniques, the researchers found the nature and order of the gene's 1,355 constituent nucleotides. Their impressive technological feat permits biochemists to propose a model for the three-dimensional structure of the polynucleotide and also confirms the relationship between protein and gene structure expressed by the genetic code itself.

Cellular Morphine Addiction. Werner Klee, Dinesh Sharma, and Marshall W. Nirenberg of the National Institutes of Health in Bethesda, Md., reported in July on the process of morphine tolerance and dependence at a cellular level. They found that cultured cells adapt to continued exposure to morphine by increasing the amount of adenylate cyclase, the enzyme that makes cyclic AMP (3'-5' adenosine monophosphate). Cyclic AMP controls many metabolic processes in cells. The cultured cells showed tolerance in that their cyclic AMP levels were similar to those of normal cells despite the continued presence of morphine, and they showed dependence in that cyclic AMP levels became abnormally high when the morphine was removed from the culture. These findings support the view that opiates may act as enzyme inducers in the process of addiction.

New Amino Acid. Johan Stenflo of the University of Lund first reported in 1974 finding a new amino acid that is a building block of prothrombin, a sugar-containing protein that is involved in blood clotting and that requires vitamin K for its synthesis. Prior to this discovery, most biologists believed that they had found all the amino acids that make up proteins in humans. For example, 22 amino acids are known to be the primary building blocks that are linked together to form long, chain-like protein molecules.

The new amino acid, γ-carboxy glutamic acid, is a post-translational amino acid. That is, it is formed in a chemical reaction after the primary amino acid (glutamic acid) is already in place in the growing prothrombin protein molecule.

In animals treated with the anticoagulant drug dicoumarol, normal prothrombin is replaced by an abnormal protein that fails to bind calcium ions. Consequently, clotting does not occur. The abnormal protein molecule contains glutamic acid that has not been converted to γ-carboxy glutamic acid.

Steffan Magnusson and his co-workers at the University of Arhus in Denmark found that all 10 of the glutamic acid amino acids in normal prothrombin are in the form of γ-carboxy glutamic acid, which does bind calcium ions. The researchers continued their work through 1975 in hopes of pinpointing the molecular role of vitamin K in the clotting process and understanding the anticoagulant effect of dicoumarol. Earl A. Evans, Jr.

BIOLOGY. Scientists from 16 countries agreed in February, 1975, on voluntary guidelines to control experiments in which genes are transmitted from one organism to another. Their meeting at the Asilomar Conference Center in Pacific Grove, Calif., grew out of a call in 1974 by a group of American molecular biologists for a temporary ban on such genetic-engineering experiments. The conferees concluded that such experiments should continue, but with great care to deal with potential hazards to laboratory personnel or to the public.

Risky experiments should be performed in laboratories similar to those designed to contain highly infectious microbiological agents. They must be isolated from other areas by airlocks, have vacuum environments, and have treatment systems that inactivate or remove biological agents from air exhaust systems and liquid and solid wastes. There also must be requirements that personnel change clothes and shower before entering and leaving the area. The conferees listed those experiments that are too hazardous to perform now.

In August, the Advisory Committee on Medical Research of the World Health Organization (WHO) urged that WHO "strongly support" these genetic studies but "fully recognize possible risks involved."

"These new methods [for transferring genes] have already opened up many lines of experimental investigation of the chromosomes of nucleated cells," said microbiologist Joshua Lederberg of Stanford University, co-winner of the 1958 Nobel Prize for Medicine and Physiology and a member of the committee. "In the case of medicine, [they] may allow the reproduction of an unlimited variety of human proteins." Similar applications in fermentation processes, he said, could permit the cheap manufacture of essential nutrients, antibiotics, or special chemicals.

Genetic Screening. Since 1968, all babies born in the Boston Hospital for Women have been screened for chromosomal aberrations, particularly for XXY and XYY patterns. The normal pattern is XX for females and XY for males. Directed by psychiatrist Stanley Walzer and geneticist Park Gerald of Harvard Medical School, the project was dropped under pressure in June, 1975.

In the fall of 1974, members of Science for the People, led by Jonathan R. Beckwith of Harvard and Jonathan King of the Massachusetts Institute of Technology, protested the study. Males carrying the XYY gene are likely to be stigmatized, they said, because this chromosome is popularly, though incorrectly, called the "criminal chromosome." This unfortunate terminology resulted from a study claiming that prisons contained an abnormally high proportion of individuals carrying the XYY gene. However, there is no information concerning the proportion of XYY males in

Stanford University biologist Paul Berg,
foreground, makes a point at Asilomar
conference on genetic-engineering risks.

the general population and no evidence that the presence of the XYY chromosome indicates any particular type of behavior, antisocial or otherwise.

Nevertheless, opponents of the Walzer-Gerald screening process believed that labeling an infant, even incorrectly, as a potential criminal would be psychologically damaging. The screening program was approved by the Committee on Medical Research of the Harvard Medical School and an overwhelming majority of the medical faculty.

In July, a committee of the National Academy of Sciences reported the results of their 2½-year study of genetic screening. The committee decided that it was too soon to recommend mass screening programs for communities. However, it strongly endorsed the genetic screening of individuals under the proper circumstances – for example, when the medical history of a parent suggests the possibility of genetic abnormalities in a child.

Screening for sickle cell anemia has been carried out in some areas, and some states and localities actually require it. The committee emphatically opposed any laws or regulations that make screening mandatory because individuals, informed that they have an incurable disease trait that could become active when transmitted to their children, become alarmed.   Earl A. Evans, Jr.

BIRTHS. See CENSUS, U.S.; POPULATION, WORLD.
BLINDNESS. See HANDICAPPED.

BOATING. The U.S. pleasure-boating industry held its own financially during 1975, with sales about the same as the near-record level of the previous year. Boating-industry spokesmen said that sales of new boats and equipment exceeded $2 billion. There were increases in the sales of stern-drive boats (up $58 million to $444.7 million) and sailboats (up $12.6 million to $192.6 million).

Powerboats. The national championship series for unlimited hydroplanes consisted of 10 races with $350,000 in purses. *Pride of Pay 'N' Pak*, with a remodeled hull and sponsor, won the series for the third consecutive year after a season-long battle with *Weisfield's*. Both boats were based in Seattle and used Rolls-Royce engines. *Pride of Pay 'N' Pak*, driven by George Henley of Eatonville, Wash., won five of the year's last six races.

The American Power Boat Association staged a series of 11 races for the national offshore championship. Sandy Satullo of Cleveland won in a 36-foot (11-meter) Cigarette hull powered by twin 482-cubic-inch (7,900-cubic-centimeter) MerCruiser engines.

Carlo Bonomi of Italy, the world offshore champion in 1973 and 1974, went into semiretirement because of business demands. He had been racing 36-foot (11-meter) Cigarettes with twin 468-cubic-inch (7,700-cubic-centimeter) Kiekhaefer Aeromarine engines – one boat for American races and one for the European circuit.

Yachting. The year's most successful yachts included two owned and sailed by Californians. They were *Stinger*, a 36-foot (11-meter) sloop owned by Dennis Conner of San Diego, and *Kialoa II*, a 79-foot (24-meter) ketch owned· by James Kilroy of Los Angeles.

Stinger, sailing in the One Ton Class, was overall winner of the Southern Ocean Racing Conference's six-race series from January 31 to February 28 off Florida and the Bahamas. *Stinger* was designed by Doug Peterson of San Diego, who also designed *Pied Piper*, another new $100,000 sloop. Lowell North of San Diego sailed *Pied Piper* to the One Ton world championship in September off Newport, R.I.

Kialoa was the largest craft in most of the year's major races, and perhaps the fastest in the world. In race after race, it was the first to finish, but it seldom won the overall prize because it could not overcome the time handicaps it gave to the smaller yachts.

Kialoa overcame the handicaps once, in the 811-mile (1,305-kilometer) race from Miami, Fla., to Montego Bay, Jamaica, which it finished on March 18. It was also first finisher (but not first overall) on June 16 in the 485-mile (780-kilometer) race from Annapolis, Md., to Newport and the transatlantic race from Newport to the Isle of Wight off England. *Kialoa* crossed the ocean in 15 days.   Frank Litsky

BOLIVIA. President Hugo Banzer Suarez continued to insist in 1975 that there would be no return to civilian government before 1980. In September, however, he conceded that political parties and trade-union activity would eventually be legalized.

The government faced a series of challenges from militant tin miners. The temporary closing of four radio stations in the mining region on January 13 led to a two-week miners' strike.

The state-church conflict became more embittered during the year. On July 14, 32 organizers of the new *Central Obrera Boliviana* (Bolivian Labor Center) were arrested in Oruru. They were said to have been plotting a general strike on August 6 that would coincide with the 150th anniversary of Bolivian independence. They met in the home of three Spanish nuns – who were promptly expelled – and this gave the government an excuse to expel several clergymen.

The main political threat to President Banzer, as always, came from younger, radical military officers who looked to neighboring Peru as a model. They seized on the furor that followed admissions in May by Gulf Oil Corporation chairman Robert R. Dorsey that his company had made large payments to former President René Barrientos Ortuño for the removal of senior officers – notably the army and air force commanders – who had been associated with Barrientos. But there was no significant change in the high command, and no serious plot against the president.

Exit to the Sea. President Banzer made it his personal goal to realize landlocked Bolivia's century-old ambition for a corridor to the Pacific Ocean through negotiations with Chile's President Augusto Pinochet Ugarte. Banzer received support for his claims to a corridor from a series of visitors, including President Juan M. Bordaberry Arocena of Uruguay and President Carlos Andres Pérez of Venezuela. In his meeting with Pinochet in February – when formal diplomatic relations with Chile were restored – Banzer was widely believed to have secured a secret agreement giving Bolivia a port and a land corridor through northern Chile. But this part of Chile is also claimed by Peru. On December 20, following further negotiations, Chile announced it was prepared to cede the sea outlet to Bolivia in return for part of Bolivia's land.

The Economy. Bolivia ended 1974 with a comfortable balance-of-payments surplus and foreign reserves in excess of $200 million. Although the economy was buffeted in 1975 by slackened world demand for oil and tin, domestic inflation was held to manageable levels after a wage-and-price freeze in January.   Robert Moss

See also LATIN AMERICA (Facts in Brief Table).

BOOKS. See CANADIAN LITERATURE; LITERATURE; LITERATURE FOR CHILDREN; POETRY; PUBLISHING.

BOSTON. Mayor Kevin H. White was re-elected on Nov. 4, 1975. He narrowly defeated state Senator Joseph F. Timilty in a hotly contested race clouded by controversy over school busing. Although neither candidate approved of forced busing and both avoided the issue, observers believed that busing damaged White's political standing.

The Busing Controversy that began in 1974 flared anew after the final integration plan for Boston's schools was announced on May 10, 1975, by U.S. District Court Judge W. Arthur Garrity. Judge Garrity ordered the busing of about 21,000 students, 3,000 more than were being bused under the temporary plan he ordered in 1974. Mayor White, indicating his disappointment with the new plan, suggested that it guaranteed continued racial tension and hostility throughout the city. The Boston School Committee, which had voted unanimously on January 23 to approve a voluntary school desegregation proposal, also opposed the final busing plan.

The controversy erupted in occasional violence when the school year began in September. On September 7, Mayor White reinforced the city police with 600 National Guard men and U.S. marshals in an effort to keep order for the school opening. More than 250 policemen had called in sick because of a union contract dispute.

A crowd of more than 2,500 persons wave flags and banners in Boston at the end of the first National Anti-Busing Convention.

Fewer than 60 per cent of the students attended school on the first day. Protest demonstrations and attendance problems continued to plague school and law-enforcement officials long after the start of the fall term. On December 9, Judge Garrity placed South Boston High School, center of the controversy, in federal receivership.

The school integration plan was temporarily interrupted on September 22, when 90 per cent of Boston's 5,000 teachers defied a court injuction and went on strike to protest longer workdays and to demand higher pay and greater job security. Two union leaders were found in contempt of court the next day. The strike ended on September 29.

Living Costs in Boston rose 8.9 per cent between July, 1974, and July, 1975. Midyear figures showed that food costs had risen 9.1 per cent, department store sales were up 6.1 per cent, the unemployment rate was down 0.7 per cent to 12.8 per cent, and construction activity was down 6.9 per cent. Factory workers' average annual income was $10,020 in mid-1975, up only 4.9 per cent from mid-1974. Regular-grade gasoline sold for 56.1 cents per gallon (3.8 liters) in June, up from 54.6 cents in June, 1974.

Figures released by the U.S. Census Bureau in June showed that Boston's population fell an estimated 3.6 per cent between 1970 and 1973, or to 618,275 as of July 1, 1973.   James M. Banovetz

BOTANY. Three groups of scientists in Australia and Canada succeeded in 1975 in getting the nitrogen-fixing bacteria *Rhizobium* to *fix* (change the form of) nitrogen while living apart from legume plants. These bacteria ordinarily live in nodules on the roots of such legumes as alfalfa, beans, peas, and soybeans and change nitrogen from the air into ammonia and then nitrates that can be used by the plants. Prior to the 1975 work, scientists believed the bacteria could not perform their task if separated from legume plants. But this work proves that *Rhizobium* can fix nitrogen independently of legumes if supplied with two simple nutrients, a pentose sugar and a dicarboxylic acid.

Because these requirements for independent nitrogen fixation by *Rhizobium* seem so simple, it is strange that *Rhizobium* limits its association only to legume plants. If the bacteria can be effectively combined with other types of plants, the need for expensive, commercially produced nitrogen fertilizers might be reduced throughout the world. The teams that did this work were at CSIRO in Canberra, Australia; the University of Western Australia in Nedlands; and the National Research Council of Canada in Saskatoon, Sask.

Shrubs. The arid lands of the world are often shrub lands that are considered by many to be wastelands. However, botanist Cyrus M. McKell of Utah State University in Logan, believes that shrubs are a neglected resource. He pointed out in an article in *Science* magazine in March, 1975, that shrubs make various adaptations to their favored habitat that allow them to flourish in seemingly harsh conditions. Shrubs have drought tolerance and roots that spread widely or penetrate deeply. They can control water loss by regulating transpiration, and they have a remarkable ability to grow quickly when conditions are temporarily good. They can tolerate high salt loads, or they can excrete salt if they cannot tolerate it.

Misconceptions about shrubs are prevalent, according to McKell. Contrary to widely held beliefs, some shrubs are high in food value and excellent for livestock and wildlife food. Some are quite palatable and are even preferred as food by various animals. Some shrubs have fruits, flowers, fibers, and oils that could be of commercial value. Most types effectively stabilize soils and would be especially useful as highway plantings in arid regions. Some shrub lands provide good wildlife habitats. Great expanses of land are unsuited for any other form of development than as shrub lands. The smartest procedure, according to McKell, is to leave these lands as shrub lands. He contends that random burning and replanting in exotic grasses, as advocated for shrub lands by some range managers, is not ecologically sound.   Barbara N. Benson

BOTSWANA. See AFRICA.

BOWLING. Earl Anthony, who led the Professional Bowlers Association (PBA) 1974 tour in earnings (setting a record), scoring average (setting a record), and victories (tying the record), did even better in 1975.

Anthony, a 37-year-old left-hander from Tacoma, Wash., won a record seven tournaments in 1975. His earnings topped $107,500.

He won the Los Angeles Open in January; the Long Island Open in Garden City, N.Y., in February; the PBA national championship in Downey, Calif., in May; the Quad Cities Open in Davenport, Iowa, in July; the Jackson (N.J.) Open and the Waukegan (Ill.) Open in August; and the Buzz Fazio Open in Battle Creek, Mich., in October. In major tournaments, he won the PBA title, finished third in the Tournament of Champions and Brunswick World Open, and was fourth in the United States Open.

Anthony ended the year with 20 career victories, third in the all-time standing behind Dick Weber of St. Louis and Don Johnson of Las Vegas, Nev., who had won 24 each. Johnson's 24th triumph came in July in the Tucson (Ariz.) Open, and ran his record to at least one victory a year for the previous 10 years.

A Satisfactory Year. The quiet, conservative Anthony said it cost him $30,000 in expenses for one year on the tour, but his 1975 earnings, in addition to his record prize money, included $60,000 in contracts. He also posted the top average for the year – 219.060 pins.

He won the PBA national title for the third consecutive year. He led the qualifying rounds and defeated Jim Frazier of Seattle in the final.

Steve Neff of Sarasota, Fla., captured the U.S. Open in March in Grand Prairie, Tex. He beat Paul Colwell of Tucson in the final, 279 to 217.

Dave Davis of Atlanta, Ga., won the Tournament of Champions in April in Akron, Ohio. He defeated Anthony, 247 to 193, to qualify for the final, where he beat Barry Asher of Costa Mesa, Calif., 201 to 195. Two weeks earlier, Davis won the Miller Open in Milwaukee, his first triumph in five years; and in November, he won the Brunswick World Open.

Women Bowlers usually played for smaller purses. Paula Sperber of Miami, Fla., earned $6,000 for winning the United States Open, and Pam Rutherford of Oroville, Calif., $4,000 for winning the Professional Women's Bowlers Association championship. But in a special one-game match for television, Carolyn Anderton of Fort Worth, Tex., defeated Vesma Grinfelds of San Francisco, 182 to 157, on October 11 in Las Vegas, Nev., and earned $50,000, the richest prize ever awarded to a bowler, male or female.　　Frank Litsky

BOXING. No professional boxing champion defended his title more frequently or with more attention in 1975 than Muhammad Ali. And no athlete in any sport ever came close to earning as much money in one year as Muhammad Ali.

From March to October, the 33-year-old Ali successfully defended the world heavyweight title four times. His purses totaled at least $8.6 million, and that did not include the $5 million he earned in October, 1974, when he regained the title from George Foreman in Zaire.

Ali's Year started on March 24 at Richfield, Ohio, near Cleveland, when he stopped Chuck Wepner of Bayonne, N.J., in the 15th round. Next came a May 16 fight against Ron Lyle of Denver in Las Vegas, Nev. Lyle lasted until the 11th round in the only one of the fights seen on home television. The others were shown on closed-circuit television. Then came a July 1 fight in Kuala Lumpur, Malaysia, against Joe Bugner of England. Ali won a 15-round decision.

"Thrilla in Manila." The fourth fight, an October 1 defense in Manila, the Philippines, against former champion Joe Frazier of Philadelphia, was the best. Ali and Frazier split two previous fights. This one turned out to be the roughest and best, and probably the most lucrative fight in history. Ali was guaranteed $4 million.

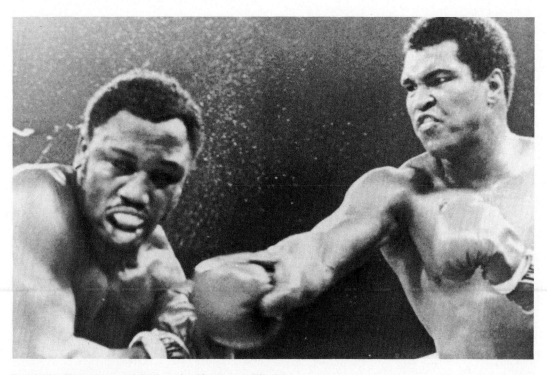

Perspiration flies as heavyweight champion Muhammad Ali's right bounces off challenger Joe Frazier's jaw. Ali won their October fight in Manila.

World Champion Boxers

Division	Champion	Country	Year Won
Heavyweight	Muhammad Ali	U.S.A.	1974
Light-heavyweight	*Victor Galindez	Argentina	1974
	†John Conteh	England	1974
Middleweight	*Carlos Monzon	Argentina	1970
	†Rodrigo Valdes	Colombia	1974
Junior-middleweight	*Yu Jae Do	South Korea	1975
	†Elisha Obed	Bahamas	1975
Welterweight	*Angel Espada	Puerto Rico	1975
	†John Stracey	England	1975
Junior-welterweight	*Antonio Cervantes	Colombia	1972
	†Shengsak Muangsurin	Thailand	1975
Lightweight	*Roberto Duran	Panama	1972
	†Gattu Ishimatsu	Japan	1974
Junior-lightweight	*Ben Villaflor	Philippines	1973
	†Alfredo Escalera	Puerto Rico	1975
Featherweight	*Alexis Arguello	Nicaragua	1974
	†David Kotey	Ghana	1975
Bantamweight	*Alfonso Zamora	Mexico	1975
	†Rodolfo Martinez	Mexico	1974
Flyweight	*Erbito Salavarria	Philippines	1975
	†Miguel Canto	Mexico	1975
Junior-flyweight	*Jaime Rios	Panama	1975
	†Luis Estaba	Venezuela	1975

*Recognized by World Boxing Association
†Recognized by World Boxing Council

Frazier, after a slow start, gave Ali such a beating that Ali wanted to quit in the 10th round. Instead, he kept fighting and gave Frazier such a beating that Frazier's manager stopped the fight after the 14th round. Columnist Red Smith wrote: "Say what one will about this noisy extrovert, this swaggering, preening, play-acting slice of theatrical ham, the man is a gladiator... a champion of genuine quality." Ali was also, as always, controversial. After the Wepner fight, he called referee Tony Perez "a dirty dog, a dirty referee," and Perez promptly sued him for $20 million. While training for the Frazier fight, Ali had a girl friend in Manila and a wife and four children in Chicago. Dave Anderson wrote in *The New York Times:* "Muhammad Ali always has plots. Boxing has never been a sufficient theme for him. Through the years, his plots have involved his brashness, his religion, his defiance. . . . his return from exile. . . ."

Other Divisions. Except for Ali, there were two champions in every division as the World Boxing Association and World Boxing Council listed different champions. The most durable were middleweight Carlos Monzon of Argentina, who won his title in 1970; lightweight Roberto Duran of Panama, 1972; and junior-welterweight Antonio Cervantes of Colombia, 1972.   Frank Litsky

BOY SCOUTS. See YOUTH ORGANIZATIONS.
BOYS' CLUBS. See YOUTH ORGANIZATIONS.

BRAZIL remained in the firm grip of President Ernesto Geisel's military regime in 1975. It appeared likely to remain so, following a nationwide address by President Geisel on August 1. Geisel had relaxed press censorship and had indicated that some political and social liberalization might be permitted. But in his address, he pointedly rejected all proposals that he expand Congress, reduce powers of the presidency, and grant political amnesties.

Geisel's chief critic was the Brazilian Democratic Movement (MDB), the only opposition party permitted to function. Government harassment included dozens of arrests of MDB members because of their alleged links to the outlawed Communist Party. Nevertheless, MDB Chairman Ulysses Guimaraes continued to denounce the regime's claims that job opportunities had increased, illiteracy had decreased, and social security benefits had risen since the 1964 military take-over.

Guimaraes particularly denounced government repression and its inhumane treatment of political prisoners. According to press reports, dozens of Communists, doctors, journalists, and trade-union leaders — including Essio Rossetti, president of the São Paulo textile workers' union — were arrested and tortured during February, March, and April. The MDB asked that Minister of Justice Armando Falcão be summoned to testify on the treatment of political prisoners, but the congressional motion was voted down by Geisel's ruling Arena Party.

Political Arrests increased throughout Brazil as the year progressed. In late September and October, large numbers of lawyers, labor-union leaders, students, and MDB members were jailed in the states of Goiás, Paraná, Ceará, Rio Grande do Sul, São Paulo, and Rio de Janeiro. All were accused of subversive activities.

The arrest and death on October 24, allegedly by suicide, of journalist Vladimir Herzog caused a nationwide furor. Roman Catholic and Jewish leaders were particularly vehement in their anti-government protests. Some 15,000 students at the University of São Paulo went on a two-day strike, and the school's professors joined them.

Despite mounting dissatisfaction, government intolerance of criticism increased and press censorship tightened. Police abuse also increased, despite the growing unrest and increasing pressures on the regime to restore some semblance of democracy.

Economic Scene. Inclement weather severely affected the nation's crops. The wheat harvest, hurt by heavy fall rains, was expected to be about 40 per cent less than the 3 million short tons (2.7-million metric tons) forecast. Frost that damaged or destroyed cattle feed throughout Paraná state also threatened an estimated 6 million head of cattle. To relieve the situation, Brazil bought 55 million bushels of wheat from the Canadian Wheat

A farmer in southern Brazil walks disconsolately amid the shriveled stalks of his coffee crop, which was severely damaged by a heavy frost.

Board on November 1, to be delivered over a three-year period.

Earlier, in July, a heavy frost ruined about half of the anticipated coffee crop of 28 million bags. The Coffee Institute promptly ordered a temporary ban on coffee exports. In other areas, bad weather damaged produce, and vegetable prices rose as much as 900 per cent in some of Brazil's larger cities. Milk production was down 10 per cent.

Energy Resource development programs continued to flourish. In May, work began on the 12.6-million-kilowatt Itaipu Dam project on the upper Paraná River. It was scheduled for completion in 1988 at a cost of about $5 billion.

Brazil signed a controversial nuclear pact with West Germany on June 27. Under its terms, West Germany agreed to supply Brazil with a complete nuclear industry by 1990. In addition to eight nuclear reactors, Germany is to provide a uranium-enrichment facility, a fuel-fabrication plant, and installations to turn fuel waste into plutonium.

The agreement was criticized abroad, and the United States and Russia said it would supply Brazil with the potential to produce nuclear weapons. Construction began late in the year on the first of the eight plants at Agra dos Reis, 60 miles (97 kilometers) southwest of Rio de Janeiro. Paul C. Tullier

See also LATIN AMERICA (Facts in Brief Table).
BRIDGE. See BUILDING AND CONSTRUCTION.

BRIDGE, CONTRACT. Aided by a dramatic grand slam on the 92nd deal of the final round, defending champion Italy won its 16th world contract bridge championship in 19 years on Feb. 1, 1975, at Southampton, Bermuda. The grand slam, made by Benito Garozzo and Giorgio Belladonna, veterans of the famed Italian Blue team, clinched victory over the United States team. Italy's winning margin in the Bermuda Bowl was 215 to 189.

The World Bridge Federation severely reprimanded two members of the Italian team – Gianfranco Facchini and Sergio Zucchelli – for allegedly using foot signals in a first-round Bermuda Bowl match. The U.S. players threatened to withdraw. However, Facchini and Zucchelli were allowed to continue playing.

In the American Contract Bridge League's spring tournament in Honolulu, Hawaii, the Harold A. Vanderbilt knockout team championship was won on March 24 by George Rosenkranz of Mexico City, Mexico, and Roger Bates, John Mohan, Larry Cohen, and Richard Katz, all of Los Angeles. Theodore M. O'Leary

BRITISH COLUMBIA. See CANADA.

BRITISH COMMONWEALTH OF NATIONS. See AUSTRALIA; CANADA; GREAT BRITAIN; NEW ZEALAND; and articles on other Commonwealth countries.

BRITISH HONDURAS. See LATIN AMERICA.

BUILDING AND CONSTRUCTION. Spending for 1975 construction in the United States was estimated at $124 billion, down 17 per cent from the $143 billion spent in 1974. The tentative forecast for spending in 1976, assuming a sustained improvement in the economy, was $144 billion, a rise of 16 per cent. Spending for housing in 1975 was down 8 per cent to $46.8 billion. On the optimistic side, the Department of Housing and Urban Development announced in August that it planned a huge increase in new approvals for federally subsidized multifamily housing units.

Wages in the building trades climbed 8.9 per cent in the year that ended on July 1, 1975, a substantial increase over the preceding year's rise of 7.4 per cent. The Bureau of Labor Statistics reported that the average construction worker earned $10.54 an hour. Plumbers topped the list, earning $12 an hour, followed by electricians at $11.21 an hour, and carpenters at $10.54 an hour.

Codes and Specifications. The New York state government announced in February that it would install an automatic sprinkler system on the 55 floors it occupies in one of the two 110-story towers of the World Trade Center in New York City. The towers have been plagued by fires since their completion. The most recent, in early February, 1975, caused damage estimated at $1 million. New York City now requires sprinkler systems in all buildings

Five of the most powerful tugboats in the world tow the Condeep Beryl A oil-drilling platform from Stavanger, Norway, to the North Sea oil fields.

over 100 feet (30 meters) high, or compartmentalization of buildings with fire-rated walls.

Two studies are looking into development of building codes for new structures in earthquake-prone areas. Under a contract from the National Bureau of Standards, the Applied Technology Council of the Structural Engineers Association of California is investigating architectural, mechanical, and electrical design standards for such areas. And at the University of Michigan in Ann Arbor, civil engineering professors Glen Berg and Robert Hanson are conducting a study that includes testing precast wall structures under earthquake conditions and developing advanced computer techniques to analyze structural response to dynamic forces.

New Building Techniques. A $70-million addition to the National Gallery of Art is under construction in Washington, D.C. It will consist of four parts connected by concrete slabs and supported by a combination of steel bridge trusses and concrete girders. The eight-story addition to the gallery will be divided into two adjacent triangular structures. The smaller will house a library and offices. The other will consist of three 8-story galleries called *pods*. The pods will flank two sides of a triangular courtyard.

Raman Kurkchubasche, of Frankfurt, West Germany, sliced 6 per cent off the cost of a Frank-furt office tower by stacking one-piece girder-and-slab floors on top of one another to a height of 43 stories. The floors, which measure 46 by 130 feet (14 by 40 meters), are similar in design to continuous-span bridges. The $25-million building consists of twin towers flanking a central core.

Work started in September will expand the world's busiest bus terminal, the mid-Manhattan facility of the Port of New York Authority. The extension, covering 75,000 square feet (7,000 square meters) is scheduled to be completed in about three years at a cost of $137.5 million.

IBM Plaza, the IBM office building in Chicago, received a Federal Energy Administration award for energy conservation. This conservation resulted even though the building's outer wall is largely made of glass, a notably poor insulating material. Energy is saved mainly by using a heat pump that circulates the large amounts of excess heat generated in the inner offices to the cooler outer rooms.

Bridge Building. The California Toll Bridge Authority announced in August that it planned to call for bids on a 1.2-mile (2-kilometer) bridge at the southern end of San Francisco Bay to replace the existing low-level Dumbarton Bridge. The new bridge will have a 340-foot (104-meter) main span with a 230-foot (70-meter) span on one end and five 200-foot (61-meter) spans on the other. The cost is estimated at $94 million.

The low bid for a bridge over the Columbia River from Pasco to Kennewick, Wash., was nearly $7.4 million above the $16.3 million estimated by the engineers. The structure, 2,503 feet (763 meters) long, will have a main span of 981 feet (299 meters) and will be the world's second-longest concrete stayed-girder bridge. The longest, with a main span of 1,050 feet (320 meters), is under construction in Rouen, France. The Washington bridge will be 80 feet (24 meters) wide and will have four traffic lanes.

North Carolina legislators criticized the state transportation department and its bridge-safety program following the March collapse of a one-lane bridge that killed 4 persons and injured 16. North Carolina is not the only state with bridge-replacement problems, according to the Federal Highway Administration (FHWA). The FHWA estimated there are 32,400 inadequate bridges in the United States, based on a national bridge inventory. The agency also estimated that it would cost about $1 billion to replace these bridges, even under the most optimistic conditions.

Wildlife-Protection Groups forced a halt in work on the world's largest system of sea dams, designed to prevent disastrous floods in the southwest Netherlands. Environmentalists want to preserve breeding grounds for fish in the Eastern Scheldt River estuary, even though this means that more than 100,000 persons would be threatened with flooding from the North Sea. All other sea arms and inlets have been dammed since a 1963 spring tide, driven by a gale, overwhelmed dikes in the delta region and drowned at least 1,850 persons. The solution to the problem may be to sink dozens of floating concrete caissons across the mouth of the river.

Environmentalists won a 14-year battle against the U.S. Army Corps of Engineers when the governors of New York, New Jersey, and Delaware voted in August to scrap plans for constructing the proposed $400-million Tocks Island Dam on the Delaware River.

New Tunnels. Austria started construction in midsummer of 1975 on a highway tunnel 7.7 miles (12.4 kilometers) long near the western tip of the country. It would be the world's second-longest road tunnel, except that the two-lane highway will emerge into the open partway along the route to cross the Rosanna River Valley.

Construction of a tunnel and reservoir system in Chicago started in September, 1975. The project, intended to solve the city's sewer overflow problem, involves construction of a deep-rock tunnel system 125 miles (200 kilometers) long and three underground reservoirs to store sewage.   Mary E. Jessup

The Lower Granite Dam at Lewiston, Ida., opened in 1975, is the last link in an inland waterway connecting landlocked Idaho with the Pacific Ocean.

BULGARIA remained Russia's closest ally in 1975 while building closer political and economic ties with other Communist and Western nations. In June, Russia and Bulgaria signed 12 major agreements for joint ventures in the chemical, food, motor, machine-building, and heavy and electrical engineering industries. Communist Party First Secretary Todor Zhivkov visited Romania in May and signed a number of trade pacts, including one to build a huge hydroelectric project on the Danube River. Also in May, France and Bulgaria signed long-term industrialization and trade agreements. In September, Bulgaria accepted a Greek invitation to a meeting of Balkan nations.

Zhivkov visited Pope Paul VI in Rome on June 27, and in August the pope appointed two bishops for the country's 70,000 Roman Catholics.

In April, Kiril Zarev replaced Ivan Iliev as chairman of the state planning committee. Zarev had been president of the national bank and minister of labor and social welfare. Zhivkov's daughter, Lyudmila Zhivkova, became chairman of the Committee for Art and Culture, and Pencho Kubadinski was elected to the State Council.

Industrial output rose 11.6 per cent during the first six months of 1975. Labor productivity reportedly rose 9.5 per cent, but efficiency and quality control remained serious problems.   Chris Cviic

See also EUROPE (Facts in Brief Table).

BURMA remained immersed in war, civil unrest, and economic crisis in 1975. Much of the turmoil was traceable to December, 1974, when 20,000 students and monks seized the body of U Thant, the former United Nations secretary-general, for burial on the campus of Rangoon University. In clashes that followed, 15 persons were killed, 2,887 were arrested, and there was widespread looting. Significantly, the students chanted, "Down with one-party dictatorship."

Riots broke out anew in early June, 1975, with the students demanding the release of those arrested in December, as well as measures to check unemployment and soaring prices. President U Ne Win's government responded by closing all universities and arresting 213 students. But this time, the students were joined by railroad, dock, and jute workers, who had gone on strike to protest low wages, shortages, and high rice prices.

Ne Win reacted with a heavy hand. On June 24, he told the leaders of his Burma Socialist Program Party that "resolute measures must be taken against any breakdown of discipline resulting from economic hardship." Taking the hint, the Burmese Supreme Court on July 13 ordered the courts to issue the harshest penalties for such crimes as strikes, defamation of the state or the governing party, illegal flight from the country, or smuggling buffaloes, elephants, and cows across the border.

Eight days later, a lower court sentenced 28 strikers to terms ranging from 10 to 16 years for "opposition to Socialist economic construction."

The Durable Enemy. The government announced in March that it had broken the back of the Communist rebellion. The Communist Party chairman, the party secretary, and 179 followers were reported killed in battle. The claim, however, was premature. The pro-Chinese Communist Party kept growing. Ne Win's army of 130,000, busy with rebellious hill tribes that demanded independence, could not cope with the 10,000 Communist guerrillas.

Trip to Peking. The military regime continued to mean scarcity and official corruption to the 30-million Burmese. It also meant self-imposed isolation from the world. However, Communist triumphs in Indochina made such isolation untenable. Thus, in mid-November, Ne Win joined other Asian pilgrims to Peking, where he obtained promises of expanded trade and political cooperation.

Another blow in this bleak year was an earthquake on July 8 that wrecked most of the great pagodas and temples around the ancient capital of Pagan. Art historians had ranked Pagan with the renowned Khmer temples of Angkor Wat — both were royal capitals — or such European centers as Venice and Florence, Italy.   Mark Gayn

See also ASIA (Facts in Brief Table).

BURSTYN, ELLEN (1932-   ), won the Academy of Motion Picture Arts and Sciences Award as best actress of 1974 for her performance in *Alice Doesn't Live Here Anymore.* She played a 35-year-old widow who journeys to California with her 12-year-old son in an attempt to build a new life after the death of her husband. The film was a critical and popular success in part because it viewed life essentially from a female point of view. Burstyn also won the 1975 Antoinette Perry (Tony) Award as best actress of the year for her work in the Broadway comedy *Same Time, Next Year.*

Burstyn was born Edna Rae Gillooly on Dec. 7, 1932, in Detroit. After leaving Cass Technical High School there, she worked in a variety of jobs, often changing her name. As Edna Rae, she was a model in Texas; as Keri Flynn, a nightclub dancer in Montreal, Canada. She played many small film and television parts, but her career did not begin to take shape until she began serious acting studies in the mid-1960s. She has appeared in such films as *The Last Picture Show* (1971), *The King of Marvin Gardens* (1972), and *The Exorcist* (1973).

Burstyn has been married three times and lives near New York City.   Edward G. Nash

BURUNDI. See AFRICA.

BUS. See TRANSIT; TRANSPORTATION.

BUSINESS. See ECONOMICS; LABOR; MANUFACTURING; Section One, FOCUS ON THE ECONOMY.

CABINET, UNITED STATES. President Gerald R. Ford appointed new members to all but three Cabinet posts in 1975. Only Secretary of State Henry A. Kissinger, Secretary of the Treasury William E. Simon, and Secretary of Agriculture Earl L. Butz remained in the same positions.

The commerce and interior posts changed hands twice during the year. Rogers C. B. Morton, former interior secretary, was confirmed by the Senate on April 25 as secretary of commerce, replacing Frederick B. Dent. Then, on November 3, Ford named U.S. Ambassador to Britain Elliot L. Richardson to replace Morton in the Commerce post.

After Ford named Morton commerce secretary, he appointed former Wyoming governor Stanley K. Hathaway secretary of the interior. The Senate confirmed Hathaway on June 11, but Hathaway resigned on July 25, claiming physical exhaustion and depression. Ford replaced him with Thomas S. Kleppe, who was sworn in on October 17. See KLEPPE, THOMAS S.

Minorities, Women, Academics. On March 3, the Senate confirmed William T. Coleman, Jr., a black Philadelphia lawyer, as secretary of transportation, replacing Claude S. Brinegar. See COLEMAN, WILLIAM T., JR.

On March 10, Carla A. Hills, assistant attorney general of the Department of Justice Civil Division, became secretary of housing and urban development. She replaced James T. Lynn, who became director of the Office of Budget and Management in February. See HILLS, CARLA A.

John T. Dunlop, a Harvard University economist, replaced Peter J. Brennan as secretary of labor on March 16, then resigned in January, 1976. University of Chicago President Edward H. Levi was confirmed as attorney general on February 5, replacing William B. Saxbe. On July 22, F. David Mathews, University of Alabama president, replaced Caspar W. Weinberger as secretary of health, education, and welfare. See DUNLOP, JOHN T.; LEVI, EDWARD H.; MATHEWS, F. DAVID.

National Security Shakeup. On November 3, Ford named White House Chief of Staff Donald H. Rumsfeld to replace Secretary of Defense James R. Schlesinger. Kissinger gave up his post as head of the National Security Council to Air Force Lieutenant General Brent Scowcroft. George H. W. Bush, head of the U.S. liaison office in China, replaced William E. Colby as head of the Central Intelligence Agency (CIA).   Darlene R. Stille

CALIFORNIA. See LOS ANGELES-LONG BEACH; SAN FRANCISCO-OAKLAND; STATE GOVERNMENT.

CAMBODIA. See KHMER.

CAMEROON. See AFRICA.

CAMP FIRE GIRLS. See YOUTH ORGANIZATIONS.

President Ford congratulates a joyous Carla Hills after she is sworn in as secretary of housing and urban development.

CANADA

In common with most other countries, Canada wrestled with worrying economic problems in 1975. The recession that began in 1974 worsened, producing higher unemployment and a continuing stiff rate of inflation. The exports so necessary to economic health suffered because of the worldwide

The Canadian National Communications Tower in Toronto, 1,805 feet (550 meters) high, is the tallest free-standing structure in the world.

recession, producing an unusually large trade deficit of $5 billion. The cost of such government services as welfare and health rose faster than revenues, leading to a substantial deficit.

Pierre Elliott Trudeau continued as prime minister and leader of the governing Liberal Party, but his style was cautious and managerial for much of the year. His Administration seemed unable to come to grips with the country's economic difficulties. Finally, in October, following the unexpected resignation of Finance Minister John N. Turner in September, Trudeau and his Cabinet came forward with a sweeping set of income and price restraints.

Only 15 months before, in the general election of July 8, 1974, the Trudeau government had campaigned strongly against the Conservative Opposition's demand for wage and price controls. The Liberals argued then that controls would be ineffective and would produce inequities throughout the economy. By returning Trudeau to office with a strong majority, the voters showed that they shared the misgivings about controls.

Production Down. The Canadian economy registered its poorest production performance in 20 years. The real gross national product (GNP) was expected to decline about 0.5 per cent. In current dollars, the GNP reached $150.3 billion on a seasonally adjusted basis, an increase of about 9.5 per cent. Exports were sluggish as the United States, Canada's principal market, climbed slowly out of the recession. For the first nine months of the year, exports totaled $23.8 billion, only slightly above the 1974 total. Imports were valued at $25.6 billion, a 12.5 per cent increase.

Finance Minister Turner presented his fifth budget on June 23. It allowed the domestic price of oil to rise to $8 a barrel and increased the federal excise tax on gasoline to provide more revenue for the subsidy required to hold down the price of imported oil in eastern Canada. Federal expenditures were expected to climb to more than $31 billion for fiscal 1975-1976, leaving a deficit conservatively estimated at $3.6 billion.

Economic Woes. The state of the economy during the first half of 1975 led increasing numbers of Canadians to demand strong measures from the central government. Prices continued to increase at a yearly rate of more than 10 per cent, while unemployment rose to 7 per cent of the labor force. Fear of the consequences of inflation led to industrial unrest across Canada. Strikes and demonstrations were widespread. Working days lost through labor disputes were almost double the total for 1974.

Since 1972, the Trudeau government had taken several steps to cushion the impact of inflation on disadvantaged Canadians. It adjusted payments to pensioners and the unemployed to reflect increases in the cost of living, and gave income tax relief to the lowest wage earners. Through the Bank of Canada, it sanctioned high interest rates in 1975. But the government did not restrict the growth of the money supply or check increases in its own expenditures. Most of the provinces also committed themselves to large deficits for the 1975 fiscal year.

During the spring, Ottawa became concerned that the level of Canadian wage settlements was running substantially above that in the United States, endangering Canada's competitive export position. Finance Minister Turner drew attention to the problem in his budget of June 23 and tried to persuade business and labor leaders to accept voluntary price and wage controls. Turner was

Olympic City in Montreal, a cluster of four 19-story buildings, will house 9,250 athletes and officials for the 1976 Olympic Summer Games.

eventually forced to admit that he could not get a consensus in favor of controls. After three years as finance minister, he dramatically resigned from the government on September 11.

Trudeau's Solution. On October 13, the Canadian Thanksgiving holiday, Trudeau announced on a nationwide broadcast that legislation to restrain incomes and prices would be introduced immediately. The new policy, passed by Parliament in December, was intended to jolt Canadians into realizing that incomes could not "continue growing at a faster rate than the economy." Canadian wage earners were trying to "overcompensate for the worst conceivable rate of future inflation." If this state of mind continued, Canada's employment and income prospects would be seriously damaged, Trudeau said.

The guidelines announced by Trudeau were mandatory for the following groups: companies employing more than 500 persons; construction companies with more than 20 workers; all federal, provincial, and municipal employees; and all professionals, such as physicians and lawyers, who charge fees for their services. Income increases for these groups would be limited to 10 per cent in the first year of the three-year program – 8 per cent to cover expected inflation and 2 per cent for greater productivity. Another 2 per cent was allowed for workers who were felt to have fallen behind other

The Ministry of Canada
In order of precedence

Pierre Elliott Trudeau, prime minister
Mitchell Sharp, president of the queen's privy council
Allan Joseph MacEachen, secretary of state for external affairs
Charles Mills Drury, minister of science and technology, and public works
Jean Marchand, minister without portfolio
Jean Chrétien, president of the treasury board
Bryce Mackasey, postmaster general
Donald Stovel Macdonald, minister of finance
John Carr Munro, minister of labor
Stanley Ronald Basford, minister of justice and attorney general of Canada
Donald Campbell Jamieson, minister of industry, trade, and commerce
Robert Knight Andras, minister of manpower and immigration
James Armstrong Richardson, minister of national defense
Otto Emil Lang, minister of transport
Jean-Pierre Goyer, minister of supply and services
Alastair William Gillespie, minister of energy, mines, and resources
Eugene Whelan, minister of agriculture
Warren Allmand, solicitor general of Canada
Hugh Faulkner, secretary of state of Canada
André Ouellet, minister of consumer and corporate affairs
Daniel J. MacDonald, minister of veterans affairs
Marc Lalonde, minister of national health and welfare
Jeanne Sauvé, minister of communications
Raymond Perrault, leader of the government in the Senate
Barnett Danson, minister of state for urban affairs
Judd Buchanan, minister of Indian affairs and northern development
Romeo Leblanc, minister of fisheries and acting minister of the environment
Marcel Lessard, minister of regional economic expansion
Jack Cullen, minister of national revenue

Premiers of Canadian Provinces

Province	Premier
Alberta	Peter Lougheed
British Columbia	William H. Bennett
Manitoba	Edward R. Schreyer
New Brunswick	Richard B. Hatfield
Newfoundland	Frank Moores
Nova Scotia	Gerald A. Regan
Ontario	William G. Davis
Prince Edward Island	Alexander B. Campbell
Quebec	J. Robert Bourassa
Saskatchewan	Allan Blakeney

Commissioners of Territories

Northwest Territories	Stuart M. Hodgson
Yukon Territory	James Smith

groups in wage settlements in recent years. For the rest of the labor force, the guidelines were to serve as a model for income settlements. Prices would be allowed to rise only to the extent necessary to cover higher costs.

Trudeau established an Anti-Inflation Review Board to monitor the program. Jean-Luc Pepin, a former minister of industry, trade, and commerce, was named to head the board, which also included Beryl Plumptre, the former head of the Food Prices Review Board. The board was to watch wage and price increases and report infractions of the guidelines to a special administrator, who could roll back increases if they exceeded the guidelines.

Trudeau also announced a freeze on federal public service appointments and said that government spending would be curtailed in many areas. However, he did not intend to reduce essential services such as the subsidy to reduce the cost of imported oil, allowances for the aged and disabled, or unemployment assistance. In December, the government announced plans to impose a 10 per cent surcharge in 1976 on incomes over $30,000.

National Reaction. The anti-inflation measures encountered a mixed reaction. The Conservatives welcomed them, while the New Democratic Party (NDP) criticized their vagueness in dealing with price rises. Organized labor strongly attacked the new policy.

The reaction of the provinces, critical to the success of the new policy, was generally supportive. A number of provinces agreed to allow the federal board to administer the program within their borders. British Columbia decided on October 24 to supplement the federal guidelines by freezing the prices of all essential goods and services until the end of the year.

Political Changes. Trudeau shuffled his Cabinet on September 26 in order to plug the hole created by the resignation of Turner. Six senior ministers changed office, and two new faces were brought in from the Liberal back-bench. Energy Minister Donald S. Macdonald moved into the crucial finance post and Alastair W. Gillespie became minister of energy, mines, and resources. Otto E. Lang, the minister of justice and the government's most prominent western member, went to the difficult transport ministry, replacing the ailing Jean Marchand.

The electorate rejected another minister after he had served two months. Pierre Juneau, appointed minister of communications on August 29, was defeated in a by-election in a Montreal district on October 14 and thus failed to win a seat in the House of Commons. According to Canadian practice, he then resigned from the Cabinet. In a second by-election on the same day, the Liberals retained a seat in northern New Brunswick. These changes left the Liberals with 140 seats in Com-

Prime Minister Pierre Trudeau holds the door for his wife, Margaret, as she leaves the hospital with their third son, Michel Charles-Emile.

mons; Progressive Conservatives, 95; NDP, 16; Social Credit, 11; and independent, 1. One seat was vacant.

All three of the Opposition parties changed, or made plans to change, their leaders. The socialistic NDP, founded in the depression of the 1930s, chose a leader from the second generation of its members for the first time. The veteran socialist David Lewis gave way to a former university lecturer, Edward Broadbent, 39, who has represented the automobile-manufacturing center of Oshawa, Ont., in Parliament since 1968. Broadbent won election at a party convention in Winnipeg, Man., on July 7. Joyce Nash of Nanaimo, B.C., was named the NDP president (see NASH, JOYCE). The national leader of the Conservatives, Robert L. Stanfield, announced his resignation, but continued as leader pending a party convention in February, 1976. Réal Caouette, the outspoken leader of the Social Credit group, was in ill health during 1975 and also announced his resignation.

Parliament was in session for most of the year, beginning on Sept. 30, 1974, and continuing until July 30, 1975, when it recessed for 10 weeks. The House of Commons spent a great deal of time debating energy policies before approving a petroleum administration bill that gave the federal government power to set oil prices across Canada. A second bill established Petro-Canada, a public pe-

troleum company designed to assist in the exploration and development of oil resources. A series of tax measures also required legislative approval.

Members of Parliament considered a measure to increase their salaries by 50 per cent, but the increase was lowered to 33 per cent following public criticism. The increase was the first since 1971. The government in December announced plans to freeze salaries for Parliament and high-level civil servants.

A number of measures stabilized agricultural incomes from such commodities as wheat, cereals, milk, soybeans, and livestock. Several federal statutes were amended to give women the same status as men. In a lighter vein, Parliament designated the beaver as an official symbol of Canada.

Oil Developments. Canada's declining oil reserves meant that exports to the United States averaged well below the levels laid down by the Canadian government. The average flow was just over 700,000 barrels a day during the second half of the year, even though the ceiling was 750,000 barrels. At the same time, eastern Canada was importing 825,000 barrels a day from members of the Organization of Petroleum Exporting Countries. The oil export tax, used to subsidize consumers in Quebec and the Maritime Provinces for the higher cost of this imported oil, was increased. A pipeline was begun to carry western Canadian oil to eastern

CANADA

Canada and thus reduce the dependence on off-shore supplies. It was expected to carry 250,000 barrels a day.

Ottawa made a major decision to participate in the long-term development of the Athabasca tar sands in northern Alberta when it agreed in February to contribute $300 million to the Syncrude Canada, Limited, project to extract oil from the tar sands. The federal government joined Alberta, Ontario, and three oil companies in financing the giant plant, which is expected to produce 125,000 barrels a day when it gets underway in 1978.

Foreign Affairs. Canada challenged Russia's overfishing along the Atlantic coast by closing Canadian ports to Russian fishing vessels on July 23. Quotas for catches in the area are laid down by the International Commission for the Northwest Atlantic Fisheries, but Canada had evidence that Russian captains were ignoring the limitations. Russian ships visited Canadian Atlantic Coast ports about 400 times in 1974, providing considerable business to merchants and suppliers. Prime Minister Trudeau discussed the issue with Leonid I. Brezhnev, Russian Communist Party general secretary, at the Conference on Security and Cooperation in Europe in Helsinki, Finland, on July 31. An agreement was reached when Russian Foreign Minister Andrei A. Gromyko visited Ottawa in

September, and Canadian ports were reopened to Russian vessels on September 29.

Trudeau devoted considerable attention to the possibility of putting Canada's trade with the European Community (Common Market) on a firmer basis. He sought what he called "a contractual link." This would not be a preferred trading arrangement that might discriminate against other countries, but rather a relationship in which the Common Market countries and Canada would consult closely on a range of economic subjects.

Trudeau visited Europe twice to discuss his ideas with European leaders. From February 27 to March 15, he visited the Netherlands, West Germany, Italy, England, and Ireland. From May 25 to 31, he was in Europe for the North Atlantic Treaty Organization (NATO) summit meeting in Brussels, Belgium, and continued the discussions with other leaders. The commission of the European Community recommended on May 22 that negotiations begin on a cooperative agreement with Canada.

Defense Efforts. Two members of the United States Administration visited Canada in the autumn to urge a greater Canadian defense effort in NATO. Secretary of Defense James R. Schlesinger was in Ottawa on September 15 and 16 to brief Canadian ministers on the Russian military threat in Europe. He urged Canada to rethink its military priorities, which place the protection of national sovereignty and North American defense ahead of strengthening Western Europe. A month later, U.S. Secretary of State Henry A. Kissinger raised the same subject on his first official visit to Canada. Nevertheless, Canada announced on November 27 that it planned to purchase 18 long-range patrol aircraft for North American defense from the Lockheed Aircraft Corporation at a cost of almost $1 billion. Defense Minister James Richardson also promised that Canada's forces in Europe would soon be provided with new or modernized tanks.

Canada set up a new air command, with headquarters at Winnipeg, Man., in May. This restored the air, land, and sea division of operational duties that was eliminated in the Canadian armed forces by the 1967 unification arrangements.

A second North American Air Defense Command (NORAD) district was created within Canada as part of a reorganization of continental air defenses. The new western Canadian region is headquartered at a base in Edmonton, Alta., while the eastern region uses the existing headquarters at North Bay, Ont.

The Provinces

Alberta. Premier Peter Lougheed's Conservative government, in power since 1971, won a landslide electoral victory on March 26. Lougheed called for endorsement of his position that Alberta should receive the world price for its oil, rather than the

Excessive heat and heavy rains in the prairie provinces caused Canada to revise grain harvest estimates downward and limit exports in autumn.

lower price set for domestic oil. The Conservatives won 69 of the 75 seats in the legislature. The Social Credit Party, which held 24 seats before the election, elected only 4 members. A lone NDP member and 1 independent were also elected.

British Columbia. The NDP government, under Premier David Barrett, took a tough line with labor on October 7. It passed emergency legislation to send back to their jobs almost 50,000 workers who were on strike or locked out by their employers. Pulp workers, retail clerks, provincial railway employees, and truckdrivers had been engaged in the costly strikes, which began when forest workers walked out in July. Although the British Columbia Federation of Labor denounced the move, the workers complied with the law.

On October 24, Barrett imposed a price freeze on all basic commodities, including food, until the end of the year. Both that move and the strike-breaking legislation were widely popular, which may have encouraged Barrett to call an unexpected election for December 11. A dramatic upset took place when the free enterprise forces combined to give 37 of the legislature's 55 seats to the Social Credit Party under William H. Bennett, son of former Premier W.A.C. Bennett. Barrett and seven of his cabinet ministers were defeated as the NDP took only 16 seats. One Liberal and one Conservative were also elected.

Manitoba. The NDP, under Premier Edward R. Schreyer, lost a midterm popularity test on June 25, when its candidates ran third in two Winnipeg by-elections. Conservatives won both elections, giving them 23 seats in the provincial legislature compared with the NDP's 31. Unhappiness with a huge increase in rates for the government's automobile-insurance plan and with what was seen as unwise spending in developing new industries hurt the six-year-old Schreyer government.

New Brunswick. The plan to build a quality two-seat sports car, the Bricklin, in New Brunswick collapsed when Bricklin Canada, Limited, went into receivership on September 26. The car's U.S. designer, Malcolm Bricklin, opened a plant near Saint John in 1973. The New Brunswick government advanced $21 million in loans to the project, receiving in turn a 67 per cent ownership in the company. The failure was attributed to problems in attracting capital and difficulties in preparing an operating plan acceptable to the province.

Newfoundland. A lackluster election campaign produced a surprising political comeback for Joseph Smallwood, 74, on September 16. Smallwood, who led the province into Confederation in 1949 and governed it for 23 years, led a splinter group of Liberals that he formed in 1974, and split the Liberal vote in the election. This allowed the Conservatives under Frank Moores to retain office, winning 46 per cent of the popular vote. The official Liberals received 37 per cent, and Smallwood's Liberal Reform Party, 12 per cent.

Nova Scotia was upset by a number of major labor disputes. Communications employees were on strike for several weeks in late summer, and 1,000 of the province's nurses walked out in June. The government introduced legislation on June 12 to force the nurses back to work, but it was withdrawn when a settlement was reached.

Ontario witnessed a startling political reverse in the September 18 election. After 32 years of majority government, the Conservative Party was reduced to a minority position. The Conservatives won 78 seats against a combined opposition of 39 in 1971. In 1975, they won only 51 seats in a legis-

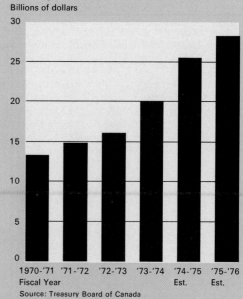

Federal Spending in Canada
Estimated Budget for Fiscal 1976*

	Millions of Dollars
Health and welfare	7,854
Economic development and support	4,657
Public debt	3,575
Defense	2,802
Fiscal transfer payments to provinces	2,625
Transportation and communications	2,080
General government services	1,437
Internal overhead expenses	1,149
Foreign affairs	701
Culture and recreation	690
Education assistance	672
Total	28,242

*April 1, 1975, to March 31, 1976

Spending Since 1970
Billions of dollars

Source: Treasury Board of Canada

lature that had been expanded to 125 members, leaving a combined opposition of 74. The NDP took over as the official Opposition party, winning 38 seats to the Liberals' 36.

Prince Edward Island. The Supreme Court of Canada on June 26 upheld a controversial land-ownership law, prohibiting nonresidents of the island province from holding more than 10 acres (4 hectares). Prince Edward Island, the only province completely dependent on oil for electric generation, was to be connected with the mainland power grid by an electric cable across Northumberland Strait. The federal government promised to pay up to half of the cost of the connection.

Quebec. The provincial labor scene was stormy as Premier J. Robert Bourassa's Liberal government tried to bring order and acceptable standards of conduct to the construction industry. A three-man commission under Judge Robert Cliche examined the industry and found evidence of "corruption and banditry" in the Quebec Federation of Labor, to which most of the construction unions belong. The commission recommended that four Montreal locals be placed under government trusteeship and that legislation be passed to bar persons with criminal records from union office.

The labor movement protested against the legislation by staging a series of walkouts and strikes at the Montreal site of the 1976 Olympic Summer Games, at several hotels under construction in Montreal, and at the new international airport, Mirabel, north of the city. The disturbances raised doubts as to whether Olympic facilities would be ready in time for the official opening of the games on July 17, 1976. The provincial government took control of Olympic construction on November 18 in an effort to restrain further growth in a deficit of $600 million.

Saskatchewan gave a reduced majority to Premier Allan Blakeney and his NDP administration in a June 11 election. The NDP, which took 45 of 60 seats in 1971, won 39 of 61 in this election. Three Cabinet ministers were defeated, and the party's share of the popular vote was sharply cut. The most surprising result was the resurgence of the Conservatives, who had no seats in the legislature. They won seven seats and increased their share of the popular vote from 2 per cent to 28 per cent. The Liberals were the chief losers, with a decline in their share of the popular vote from 43 to 31 per cent.

Facts in Brief: Population: 23,280,000. Government: Governor General Jules Léger; Prime Minister Pierre Elliott Trudeau. Monetary unit: Canadian dollar. Foreign Trade: exports, $34,-228,000,000; imports, $34,573,000,000. David M. L. Farr

See also CANADIAN LIBRARY ASSOCIATION (CLA); CANADIAN LITERATURE; LÉGER, JULES; TRUDEAU, PIERRE ELLIOTT.

CANADIAN LIBRARY ASSOCIATION (CLA) held its 30th annual conference in Toronto, Ont., from June 13 to 20, 1975. More than 1,800 persons attended. In keeping with the conference theme, the delegates discussed the opportunities and problems of women librarians and the need for and availability of continuing education. The participants passed 24 resolutions, setting an ambitious program for 1976. Young Canada's Book Week was discontinued, and Paul H. Kitchen of the National Library was appointed executive director.

Medals and Awards. The Book of the Year for Children Medal was awarded to Dennis Lee for *Alligator Pie.* The Amelia Frances Howard-Gibbon Medal for excellence in illustration in a children's book went to Carlo Italiano for *The Sleighs of my Childhood (Les Traîneaux de mon Enfance).* The Merit Award of the Canadian Library Trustees Association went to Donald Craw, Saint Boniface Public Library Board in Manitoba; the Canadian School Library Association Merit Award went to Agnes Florence, chief librarian, Library Service Centre, Winnipeg, Man., and Margaret I. Gayfer, former editor of *School Progress.* The Order of Canada awarded a Medal of Service to Claude Aubry for library leadership and for his legends and stories in French and English. The seventh Howard V. Phalin-World Book Graduate Scholarship in Library Science was awarded by a CLA standing committee to Lorne J. Amey, associate instructor, Faculty of Library Science, University of Toronto. The scholarship was sponsored by World Book – Childcraft of Canada, Limited.

The CLA published *Canadian Reference Sources, Supplement,* edited by Dorothy E. Ryder, and *Canadian Library Systems and Networks, Their Planning and Development,* CLA Winnipeg Conference papers.

Libraries. The first fully integrated library system under the new library program was established in the Thompson-Nicola District in British Columbia. Meanwhile, Aubry and G. Laurent Denis surveyed metropolitan Montreal, Que., for library service. The National Library established a division for the visually and physically handicapped and named a children's literature librarian.

Two research libraries opened for complete service. The Canada Institute for Scientific and Technical Information, formerly the National Science Library, opened in Ottawa, Ont. It has 360,000 square feet (33,400 square meters) of space and uses the latest mechanized techniques to store, retrieve, and disseminate information. The John P. Robarts Research Library for the Humanities and Social Sciences in Toronto stands 14 stories high and serves the universities of Ontario. Its rare books are housed in a specially constructed, windowless, adjoining building, the Thomas Fisher Rare Book Library. Elizabeth Homer Morton

CANADIAN LITERATURE was marked in 1975 by a geographic-historical strain that one critic dubbed "geohistory." Four of the most outstanding works are *Canada: The Heroic Beginnings* by Donald Creighton; *Rivers of Canada* by Hugh MacLennan; *The National Atlas of Canada*; and *The Mammals of Canada* by A. W. F. Banfield.

Regional Canada. Books on western Canada include *Salt of the Earth* by Heather Robertson and *The Mountains and the Sky* by Lorne E. Render. *Indian Petroglyphs of the Pacific Northwest* by Beth and Ray Hills and *A Guide to Vancouver* by Chuck Davis cover the Pacific. Books on the north include *Goggles, Helmets, and Air Mail Stamps* by Georgette Vachon; *Denison's Ice Road* by Edith Iglauer; and *The Snow Walker* by Farley Mowat. Writings of the Atlantic include *Sailing Ships of the Maritimes* by Charles A. Armour and Thomas Lackey; *Nova Scotia* by Harry Bruce and 14 photographers; and *Shaped by This Land* by painter Tom Forrestall and poet Alden Nowlan. Books on central Canada include *The Beautiful Old Houses of Quebec* by P. Roy Wilson.

Biography. *Dictionary of Canadian Biography Vol III (1741-1770)* was edited by Francess G. Halpenny. *Don't Have Your Baby in the Dory, a Biography of Myra Bennett* was written by H. Gordon Green. Political biographies include *The John A. Macdonald Album* by Lena Newman; *Edward Blake: the Man of the Other Way (1833-1881)* by Joseph Schull; *Amor de Cosmos, Journalist and Reformer* by George Woodcock; *Mike: The Memoirs of the Right Honourable Lester B. Pearson, Volume 3, 1957-1968* edited by John A. Munro and Alex I. Inglis; and *René Lévesque, Portrait of a Québécois* by Jean Provencher, translated by David Ellis.

Politics. *The Power and the Tories, Ontario Politics 1943 to the Present* was written by Jonathan Manthorpe. David E. Smith is author of *Prairie Liberalism, the Liberal Party in Saskatchewan 1905-1971. The Dynasty, the Rise and Fall of Social Credit in Alberta* is by John J. Barr.

The Arts. *A People's Art, Primitive, Naïve, Provincial and Folk Painting in Canada* was produced by J. Russell Harper. Ernst Roch edited *Arts of the Eskimo. Canadian Water-colours and Drawings in the Royal Ontario Museum* was catalogued by Mary Allodi. William Duff wrote *Images Stone B.C. Thirty Centuries of North-West Coast Indian Sculpture.*

Fiction. Outstanding titles include: *A Fine and Private Place* by Morley Callaghan; *Crackpot* by Adele Wiseman; and *Sawbones Memorial* by Sinclair Ross.

Poetry. New collections include *The Collected Poems of A. M. Klein* compiled by Miriam Wad-

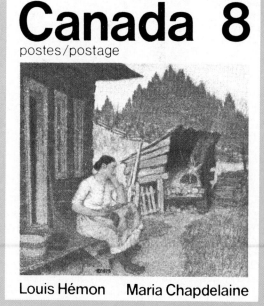

Canadian 8-cent stamps issued in May honor authors Lucy Maud Montgomery for *Anne of Green Gables, left,* and Louis Hémon for *Maria Chapdelaine.*

dington; *The Full Furnace* by Douglas Lochhead; and *Light Bird of Youth: Selected Poems* by Fred Cogswell. Volumes by individuals include *I'm a Stranger Here Myself* by Alden Nowlan; *In Search of Owen Roblin* by Al Purdy; *Atlantic Crossing* by David Helwig; and *Change-Up: New Poems* by Raymond Souster.

Governor-General's Literary Awards for books published in 1974 went to Ralph Gustafson for *Fire on Stone* (English poetry); Margaret Laurence for *The Diviners* (English fiction); Charles Ritchie for *The Siren Years* (English nonfiction); Nicole Brossard for *Mécanique jongleuse suivi de masculin grammaticale* (French poetry); Victor-Lévy Beaulieu for *Don Quichotte de la démanche* (French fiction); Louis Dechêne for *Habitants et marchands de Montréal au XVIIᵉ siecle* (French nonfiction).

Stephen Leacock Memorial Award for humor went to Morley Torgov for his book *A Good Place to Come From.*

The Canada Council Translation Prizes. Sheila Fischman won for her English translations of *Le deux-millième étage* (*They Won't Demolish Me*) by Roch Carrier and *Le Loup* (*The Wolf*) by Marie-Claire Blais. Michelle Tisseyre won for her French translation of *Such Is My Beloved* (*Telle est ma bien-aimée*) and *Winter* (*L'Hiver*), both by Morley Callaghan, and *Seasons of the Eskimo* (*Les Saisons de l'Eskimo*) by Fred Bruemmer.   Elizabeth Homer Morton

CAPE VERDE ISLANDS became independent on July 5, 1975, after 500 years of Portuguese colonial rule. Cape Verde consists of 10 islands and five islets off the west coast of Africa. Praia, on the island of São Tiago, is the capital.

In parliamentary elections just preceding independence, the African Party for the Independence of Guinea-Bissau and the Cape Verde Islands (PAIGC) won 96 per cent of the votes. Aristides Pereira, secretary-general of the PAIGC, became the first president of the Cape Verde Islands. As a result, observers expected Cape Verde to collaborate closely with the government of Guinea-Bissau, which won independence from Portugal in 1974.

Portugal and the United States promised economic aid to the 300,000 persons living in this very poor country. At the time of its independence, Cape Verde had little industry. Its chief exports were canned fish and salt. Adding to its economic woes, several successive years of drought drastically reduced agricultural output.

The Cape Verde Islands are strategically located, and the departing Portuguese left behind a military air base and a naval installation. These facilities might interest both Eastern and Western powers. However, the new government announced on July 7 that Cape Verde would be nonaligned and would ban foreign bases.   John D. Esseks

See also AFRICA (Facts in Brief Table).

CARNEY, ART (1918-   ), won the Academy of Motion Picture Arts and Sciences Award as best actor of 1974 for his portrayal of a 72-year-old widower who wanders with his orange cat, Tonto, in *Harry and Tonto.* The role was Carney's first lead in a feature-length motion picture. He won several Emmy Awards in the early 1950s for the best supporting role in "The Jackie Gleason Show" and "The Honeymooners," in which he played the part of sewer cleaner Ed Norton.

Arthur William Matthew Carney was born on Nov. 4, 1918, in Mount Vernon, N.Y. He was the youngest of six sons of a newspaperman. He began his career singing and doing impersonations with Horace Heidt's band from 1936 to 1939. His talent for mimicry won him a job on radio with the Columbia Broadcasting System (CBS) on "Report to the Nation."

He joined the U.S. Army infantry in World War II, and was wounded in France. He returned to CBS radio in 1947 and broke into television in 1949 as a comedian. In 1957, he made his Broadway debut in *The Rope Dancers.* Carney won critical acclaim for his portrayal of Felix in a Broadway production of Neil Simon's comedy *The Odd Couple* in 1965.

Carney married Jean Myers in 1940. They were divorced in 1965, and he married Barbara Isaac in 1966.   Robert K. Johnson

CARTER, JIMMY (1924-   ), former governor of Georgia, campaigned during 1975 for the Democratic presidential nomination. As governor from 1971 to 1975, Carter built a reputation as a moderate on racial issues, a new politician of the so-called New South.

As a presidential contender, he presented himself as a populist, calling for tax reforms, a cleanup of "the mess in Washington," and reorganization of the federal bureaucracy. Carter describes himself as a conservative on budgetary and financial matters and a liberal on social issues. He sees his skill and experience at reorganizing and managing as his major qualification for the presidency.

James Earl Carter, Jr., was born on Oct. 1, 1924, in Plains, Ga. He graduated from the U.S. Naval Academy at Annapolis, Md., in 1946 and served seven years in the Navy. Toward the end of his naval career, he helped develop nuclear submarines.

Carter resigned his commission as a lieutenant commander in 1953, returned to Georgia, and became a successful peanut farmer. In 1962, he was elected to the first of two terms in the Georgia Senate. He ran unsuccessfully for governor in 1966, but was elected in 1970. His four-year term ended in January, 1975, and he began his campaign for the Democratic presidential nomination.

Carter married Rosalynn Smith in 1946. They have four children.   Darlene R. Stille

A medieval joust climaxes an Elizabethan fair held at Stratford-on-Avon in 1975 to mark the centenary of the Royal Shakespeare Theatre.

CELEBRATIONS and anniversaries observed in 1975 included the following:

Amsterdam Septicentennial. The 700th anniversary of the founding of one of Europe's major cities was celebrated throughout the year in the Netherlands. Events included a series of parades, art exhibits, concerts, and ballets.

Hans Christian Andersen Centennial was celebrated worldwide, notably in Denmark, his birthplace. The author of numerous children's tales was honored with a festival in Copenhagen in April that included concerts and story-telling sessions.

Jane Austen Bicentennial. The Jane Austen Society marked the 200th anniversary of the British novelist's birthday with a yearlong series of events including a country festival in Steventon, England, her birthplace, from July 25 to July 27.

Edgar Rice Burroughs Centennial. A birthday celebration honoring the prolific author of 26 *Tarzan* novels and 11 science fiction books, was observed during the North American Science Fiction Club convention held from August 28 to September 1 in Los Angeles. A highlight was the appearance of many of those who had played Tarzan — and his mate, Jane — in motion-picture versions of the books.

Gilbert and Sullivan Centenary honored the first performance of *Trial by Jury,* a collaborative effort by Sir William Schwenck Gilbert and Sir Arthur Seymour Sullivan, in London. The Pierpont Morgan Library in New York City held an exhibition in April of memorabilia, including a full autograph score of *Trial by Jury.*

D. W. Griffith Centenary. The 100th birthday of perhaps the most innovative director in American cinema history was observed at New York City's Museum of Modern Art with a two-part retrospective in January and May.

Royal Greenwich Observatory Tercentenary celebrations marked the founding of the world-renowned facility by King Charles II of England in 1675. A year-long series of exhibits were held at the observatory's two installations — Herstmonceux Castle and Greenwich Hill.

Thomas Mann Centenary, honoring the author of *Buddenbrooks* (1901), *The Magic Mountain* (1924), and *Death in Venice* (1912), was observed at various times throughout the year. In Lübeck, West Germany, his home on the Baltic Sea, a Thomas Mann Week of nightly readings of his works was held, climaxed by a performance of Benjamin Britten's opera based on *Death in Venice.*

Michelangelo Cinquecentennial, honoring the 500th birthday of one of the world's great sculptors and painters, was widely observed. See VISUAL ARTS (Close-Up).

Norwegian Emigration Observance. The 150th anniversary of the year the first boatload of Norwe-

Movie stars who played lead roles in cinema
versions of Edgar Rice Burroughs' *Tarzan*
novels celebrate the author's 100th birthday.

gians emigrated to the United States was marked
with a two-day re-enactment of their voyage in
Stavanger Harbor, Norway. King Olav V later visited the United States.

Albert Schweitzer Centenary. An all-Bach concert by soloists and the American Symphony Orchestra was given in New York City's Carnegie
Hall in January in honor of the doctor, musician,
and humanitarian who won the 1952 Nobel Prize
for Peace. Schweitzer was also given philatelic tribute in new stamps issued in Gambia, Hungary, and
Pakistan.

Royal Shakespeare Theatre Centenary celebrations included a vast Elizabethan fair at Stratford-on-Avon, England, featuring medieval jousting
and a command performance of William Shakespeare's *Henry V* attended by Queen Elizabeth II.

Soviet Academy of Science Anniversary. The
academy, founded by Peter the Great in 1724, celebrated its 250th anniversary a year late with a gala,
weeklong rally in Moscow in October attended by
scientists from 28 countries.

Johann Strauss, Jr., Festival, marking the composer's 150th birthday, was held from May 24
through June 22 in Vienna, Austria. Strauss works,
including *Die Fledermaus* and *The Gypsy Baron,*
were performed.   Paul C. Tullier

See also BICENTENNIAL, U.S.; Section Three, A
YEAR IN PERSPECTIVE.

CENSUS, UNITED STATES. The Bureau of the
Census reported on May 25, 1975, that the United
States population grew only 0.75 per cent during
1974 as the declining birth rate reached a record
low of 14.9 per 1,000 persons. By comparison, the
population growth rate averaged 1.26 per cent a
year during the 1960s, while the average birth rate
stood at 20.2 per 1,000 persons.

In addition to the birth rate decline, there were
more persons living alone between 1969 and 1974.
This reduced the average size of American households from 3.19 to 2.97 persons.

More Housing. Between the 1970 census and
October, 1974, the nation added nearly 7.5 million
housing units for a total of 77,602,000 units. Census surveys showed that the proportion of large
apartment buildings increased and that of single-family dwellings and two- to four-unit apartment
buildings declined slightly.

Distribution of household heads by age also has
changed. Those under 35 years increased from
about 25 per cent in 1969 to about 29 per cent of all
household heads in 1974. The 35- to 64-year-old
group dropped from about 56 to 51 per cent of the
total. The proportion of household heads 65 years
of age and over remained at 19 per cent.

Census demographers say this age shift reflects
the movement of people born in the "baby boom"
after World War II into young-adult brackets.

Other Findings:

■ Population growth in metropolitan areas from
1970 to 1974 slowed to about the rate of nonmetropolitan growth. More whites moved to the South,
and fewer blacks left there. Southern and Western
states showed the greatest growth.

■ Compared with whites in 1974, blacks and Spanish Americans were less likely to have voted and
had less education; they also had a significantly
higher rate of unemployment and a larger proportion of blue-collar workers.

■ A new population estimate showed that 1 of every 20 Americans is of Spanish origin, a total of
11.2 million persons. About 60 per cent of these —
6.7 million — are Mexican Americans.

The U.S. population in the year 2000 is expected
to be from 245 million to 287 million, slightly below
past bureau projections. These projections assume a
small reduction in the death rate, and a net annual
immigration of 400,000.

The United States began 1975 with an estimated
population of 213,224,000, including the populations of the 50 states, the District of Columbia, and
servicemen and federal employees living overseas
with their dependents. The U.S. population, including all government personnel overseas, was estimated at 214,813,000, as of Dec 31, 1975, an
increase of 1,589,000.   Vincent P. Barabba

CENTRAL AFRICAN REPUBLIC. See AFRICA.
CEYLON. See SRI LANKA.

CHAD. President N'Garta Tombalbaye, Chad's president since 1960, was overthrown in a military coup on April 13, 1975. Tombalbaye reportedly died during heavy fighting against the insurgents. A nine-member Supreme Military Council, headed by F. Malloum Ngakoutou Bey-Ndi, a former army chief of staff, was set up to rule the country. See MALLOUM, F. NGAKOUTOU BEY-NDI.

The new government almost immediately announced a policy of national reconciliation designed to end an armed rebellion by Moslem tribesmen in the north.

In late 1974, the rebels had taken six hostages, several of whom died. French military bases in Chad faced a doubtful future because of a dispute over one of the hostages, a French woman. The rebels demanded a ransom of cash and military supplies for the release of archaeologist and anthropologist Françoise Claustre. Against the wishes of the Chad government, French officials negotiated directly with the rebels and reportedly agreed to pay a large sum in cash, but not to deliver arms. The government regarded France's action as a violation of Chad's sovereignty and, on September 27, insisted that France withdraw about 2,000 troops. At about the same time, a rebel leader demanded that France pay a $1.5-million ransom for Claustre.   John D. Esseks

See also AFRICA (Facts in Brief Table).

CHEMICAL INDUSTRY declined in 1975 because of the worldwide recession in such chemical-consuming industries as automobiles, housing, plastics, steel, and synthetic fibers. For example, West Germany's chemical industry profits fell 60 per cent for the first six months of 1975, compared with the same period of 1974. France's chemical production was down 16 per cent for the same period.

In the United States, the recession bottomed out in April and May, but recovery was slow. Nevertheless, the chemical industry did better than the economy as a whole. Value of output was $306.7-billion, but the 15 per cent increase over 1974 was mainly the result of inflation. Output rose about 2 to 3 per cent, and prices gained 10 per cent. The major factor contributing to high chemical prices was the unrelenting upward thrust of capital, feedstock, energy, and other costs.

On the bright side, labor productivity in the third quarter increased at a 17.6 per cent annual rate, more than double the average annual rate since 1967. But overall productivity was about the same as 1974 because of a bad first quarter. Chemical exports rose 36 per cent to $7.9 billion, but fell off during the last half of the year.

Capital spending, both domestic and by U.S. firms abroad, remained strong. Domestic spending rose 14 per cent to $6.1 billion. More than 9 per cent of this investment was in pollution-control equipment. Foreign capital investment by U.S. firms increased 36 per cent to $3.4 billion, indicating confidence in the economic recovery of the countries involved.

Chemicals and Health. The aerosol industry felt the effects of the ozone-depletion warning as the chlorinated fluorocarbon propellants used in many spray-can products continued to be implicated in destroying the protective ozone layer in the upper atmosphere. See ENVIRONMENT (Close-Up); Section One, FOCUS ON SCIENCE.

On April 29, the Occupational Safety and Health Administration (OSHA) proposed standards for worker exposure to inorganic arsenic. OSHA's permanent standards for worker exposure to vinyl chloride monomer (VCM) – a cancer-causing material – went into effect in April. VCM is the basic material for the plastic polyvinyl chloride (PVC). The Environmental Protection Agency (EPA) proposed standards limiting VCM emissions to the atmosphere, and the Food and Drug Administration (FDA) proposed on August 28 that "rigid or semirigid" polyvinyl chloride food packages be banned. The FDA adopted a limit of no detectable level for VCM on foodstuff-grade PVC packaging materials. The Health Research Group, which sought a total ban on PVC materials, protested the exclusion from the ban of the common film food wraps made of PVC.

Spurred by the VCM controversy and proposed legislation on toxic substances, 11 leaders of the chemical industry formed the Chemical Industry Institute of Toxicology. The institute will conduct toxicological studies on common chemicals.

On May 12, the National Cancer Institute issued a warning regarding the chlorinated solvent, trichloroethylene, because it produced tumors in mice that ate it. At about the same time, Dow Chemical Company reported studies indicating that chlorinated solvents trichloroethane and perchloroethylene, a dry-cleaning solvent, do not produce cancer. But General Foods Corporation discontinued use of trichloroethylene for decaffeination of coffee.

Sweeteners. After more than two years of study requested by the FDA, the National Academy of Sciences announced in January that the synthetic sweetener saccharin cannot be judged a carcinogen until further studies are completed. But, reversing its stand on cyclamates, the FDA requested the National Cancer Institute to review data regarding its *carcinogenicity*, or tendency to cause cancer. A report is expected in early 1976. In December, the FDA withdrew approval for G. D. Searle & Company's aspartame because of the possible development of harmful breakdown products.

Pesticides. The EPA suspended the use of the pesticides heptachlor and chlordane on July 30 because of evidence that they cause tumors in laboratory animals.   Edward Abrams

CHEMISTRY. A team of scientists from the University of Arizona's Lunar and Planetary Laboratory headed by Harold P. Larson announced in March, 1975, that they had detected oxygen, combined in water vapor, in the atmosphere of Jupiter. They used the National Aeronautics and Space Administration's C-141 flying infrared observatory plane, which is equipped with a 36-inch (91.5-centimeter) infrared telescope. The plane flew at more than 45,000 feet (13,700 meters) above the ground to eliminate the infrared obscuring effects of water vapor in the earth's lower atmosphere.

According to Larson, the water vapor was found "deep down in the atmosphere where it is warm, about room temperature, and where the pressure is about 20 times atmospheric pressure on earth." Larson believes that the presence of water vapor suggests that organic compounds are being formed in the Jovian atmosphere.

Insulin Synthesis. A team of researchers at Ciba-Geigy in Basel, Switzerland, led by Werner Rittel have used a new approach to a chemically directed total synthesis of human insulin. Insulin is a hormone that is essential for the metabolism of the sugar glucose. When the pancreas does not produce enough insulin, *diabetes mellitus* occurs. The body cannot use or store glucose normally.

The human insulin molecule comprises two polypeptide chains. One chain has 21 amino acid residues, and the other has 30. The two chains are linked by three disulfide bridges. Previous synthetic approaches consisted of building up the two chains independently, then coupling them at the proper positions – an extremely difficult task. The Swiss team built fragments of the amino acid chains and linked them together in a way to consistently form the three key disulfide bonds. More than 170 individual steps are involved in the complex synthesis, and Rittel believes that the stepwise approach might lead to the synthesis of similar molecules that are more active than the natural insulin hormone.

Isotope Enrichment. Several groups of scientists, working independently, separated isotopes of different elements using new methods based on irradiation with a laser beam. Isotopes of a specified element differ only in the number of neutrons in their nuclei. The laser method may someday provide less expensive isotopes for research, medical diagnosis, and nuclear power fuel.

A team of scientists from the University of California's Los Alamos Scientific Laboratory in New Mexico headed by C. Paul Robinson announced in April that they used carbon dioxide laser pulses to change the ratio of boron and chlorine isotopes from its natural value in a gaseous sample of boron trichloride. The method works because energy from the laser beam selectively excites only one of the isotopes in the mixture. The excited isotope can then react with a third substance to form a new compound that can be removed. Thus, the unexcited isotope accumulates in the mixture.

Irradiating sulfur hexafluoride in the presence of hydrogen, they obtained a 500 to 3,300 per cent increase, or enrichment, of the sulfur 34 isotope. Robinson points out that sulfur 34 is a nonradioactive isotope that would be a valuable tracer in biological research. The cost of energy needed to produce it by laser enrichment is about 40 cents per gram (0.035 ounce). The total cost for producing it by conventional methods is about $1,000 per gram.

Laser-enrichment research is conducted also at the University of California's Lawrence Livermore Laboratory under the direction of Benjamin B. Snavely. Focusing a beam from a tunable dye laser and a beam of ultraviolet light from a mercury vapor lamp on a stream of vaporized uranium, the Lawrence researchers selectively ionized uranium 235 (U-235) atoms. The positively charged U-235 ions were collected at a negatively charged electrode. By June, the researchers were able to produce milligram quantities of enriched uranium after several hours of operation.

Uranium 235 is the nuclear fuel used in most nuclear power reactors. If laser separation can be made to work on a large scale, U-235 could be produced using 100 to 1,000 times less energy than by the conventional methods.   Alfred W. von Smolinski

CHESS. Anatoly Karpov, a Russian economics student, became world chess champion on April 3, 1975, by default over reigning champion Bobby Fischer of the United States. Karpov is the first player to win the title without proving his right to it in a showdown match.

Fischer had been scheduled to play Karpov beginning June 1 in Manila, the Philippines, in a $5-million championship match with about $3.2 million going to the winner and the remainder to the loser. Fischer had demanded two changes in the International Chess Federation rules for the match. On March 19, the federation allowed one of the changes, removing the 36-game limit on the championship series. The title was to be won by the first player gaining 10 victories, with draws not counting. But the federation refused Fischer's demand for a rule that would permit him to retain his title in the event the number of games won reached a 9 to 9 tie.

Fischer was given a deadline of midnight, April 1, to accept the federation's terms. Federation president Max Euwe of the Netherlands even gave Fischer an extra 24 hours to agree to play, but Fischer did not reply and consequently lost his title. Later, Fischer and Karpov considered the possibility of arranging an unofficial match, but nothing came of it. After Fischer's default, Edmund E. Edmondson, president of the United States Chess

New world chess champion Anatoly Karpov
gets laurel wreath in Moscow ceremony in
April after Bobby Fischer of the U.S. defaulted.

CHIANG CHING-KUO (1910-   ), prime minister of Taiwan since 1972, assumed leadership of the Nationalist Chinese government on Taiwan following the death of his father, Chiang Kai-shek, on April 5, 1975. See DEATHS OF NOTABLE PERSONS (Close-Up).

Chiang was born in Chekiang Province of mainland China and attended several Chinese schools. He went to Russia in 1925. He broke with his father and joined the Communist Youth Corps there. Chiang graduated from Sun Yat-sen University in Moscow in 1927 and from a military academy there in 1930. He married an orphaned Russian girl, Faina, in 1933. In 1937, he returned to China and was reconciled with his father. He then joined the Kuomintang Party and held a series of positions of increasing importance in the Nationalist government during World War II.

Toward the end of the war, Chiang, who speaks Russian fluently, went to Moscow with a delegation that tried to reach agreement on decisions made concerning China at the Yalta Conference.

After the Chinese Communists conquered China in 1949, Chiang moved to Taiwan with his father and the Nationalist government. He took charge of the secret police and directed youth and veterans' organizations. He was minister of defense from 1965 to 1969. From 1969 to 1972, he was deputy prime minister.   Foster Stockwell

Federation, said, "Poor Fischer won't have his title, Karpov will have a paper title, and the world won't have its match. We're all losers."

Karpov assailed Fischer on April 22 for having "brought suspiciousness, mercantilism, and psychological pressure" to chess. However, as the international tournament in Milan, Italy, opened on August 20, Karpov again expressed his desire to play Fischer. Fischer ignored an invitation to play in the tournament, which ended on September 14. Karpov won the $12,000 first prize by defeating Lajos Portisch of Hungary, 3½ to 2½, in the six-game final round.

Other Matches. Walter Browne, an Australian living in Berkeley, Calif., won his second consecutive United States Chess Championship in Oberlin, Ohio, on June 29. His 8½ points gave him a half-point margin over runner-up Kenneth Rogoff of Rochester, N.Y. William Lombardy of Ridgefield, N.J., and Pal Benko of Jersey City, N.J., tied for first place with 10 points each in the United States Open Chess Championship, which ended on August 22 in Lincoln, Nebr. Diane Savereide, a 19-year-old player from Culver City, Calif., won the United States Women's Chess Championship with 10 points in Milwaukee on July 27. Runners-up, with 6½ points each, were Ruth Herstein of Los Angeles and Ruth Orton-Haring of Fayetteville, Ark.   Theodore M. O'Leary

CHICAGO. Mayor Richard J. Daley won re-election to an unprecedented sixth four-year term on April 1, 1975. He amassed a record-breaking 77.7 per cent of the votes in defeating his main opponent, Republican John J. Hoellen. See DALEY, RICHARD.

Corruption Charges. A grand jury was convened in March to investigate charges that Chicago police had illegally spied on politicians, businessmen, and citizens' groups. Although the grand jury did not return any indictments, it issued a report on November 10 condemning the activities.

On October 27, the City Council abolished the Civil Service Commission, which controls about 40,000 city jobs, and replaced it with a personnel board. Daley critics complained that the new system placed all city workers under political control.

The city's schools were severely criticized during the year by several sources, including the Chicago Urban League. The Urban League's report "flunked" the schools in the areas of integration, decentralization, and student progress. Joseph P. Hannon became superintendent of schools on July 23, replacing James F. Redmond.

Strikes. Chicago's 25,000 public-school teachers went on strike on September 3, seeking pay increases, smaller classes, and dental insurance. Already foreseeing a $24-million budget deficit, the Board of Education opposed the teachers' demands and threatened to cut 1,500 teaching positions. The

Mayor Richard J. Daley thanks his supporters after winning re-election to an unprecedented sixth term as mayor of Chicago on April 1.

strike ended on September 17 with a settlement including salary boosts averaging 7.1 per cent.

Chicago City College teachers went on strike on August 25 in a dispute about class size and cuts in extra-assignment pay. A circuit court judge issued a restraining order, which the teachers ignored, and the judge found the union in contempt of court. A settlement was reached on September 14.

About 250 interns and resident doctors at Cook County Hospital struck on October 27 in a dispute over salaries, patient care, and working hours. What became the longest doctors' strike in U.S. history finally ended on November 13. The doctors won a pay increase, a committee for patient-care issues, and a reduction in the workweek from 100 to 80 hours.

Local Economy. The number of persons in Chicago receiving unemployment insurance payments increased 203 per cent to 146,000 between August, 1974, and August, 1975. Living costs rose 7.6 per cent in the area between August, 1974, and August, 1975. Food prices rose 7.6 per cent; housing costs, 9.1 per cent; and health and recreation prices, 8.0 per cent. The price of regular gas averaged 57.7 cents a gallon (3.8 liters) as of June.

The U.S. Census Bureau announced in mid-1975 that Chicago's population had declined 5.8 per cent between 1970 and 1973 to 3,172,929 persons as of July 1, 1973.　　James M. Banovetz

CHILD WELFARE. Concern over child abuse continued to mount throughout the world in 1975, as evidence piled up of the great number of children affected and the proportion of deaths and serious injuries. The National Clearing House on Child Abuse and Neglect found 14,083 cases of child abuse in the United States during 1974.

Child abuse was a frequent topic in professional journals. The *Bulletin of the World Organization for the Safeguard of Youth* frequently published articles on child abuse in many countries. The entire spring, 1975, issue of the *Journal of Clinical Child Psychology* was devoted to the subject, as was the May/June issue of *Children Today,* published by the Children's Bureau of the Department of Health, Education, and Welfare (HEW).

HEW proposed new regulations in February to curb child abuse. The proposal would require states to investigate reports of suspected child abuse and neglect. Existing rules place the primary responsibility for safety on the child's parents or legal guardians. The new proposal extended this obligation to anyone responsible for the child's care in the child's own home, a relative's home, a foster home, or an institution.

The National Center on Child Abuse and Neglect awarded grants in 1975 for research projects. The center was established in 1974 within the Children's Bureau of the Department of Health, Education, and Welfare.

Social Legislation of any kind met high resistance in the United States Congress in 1975. Both the Senate and the House of Representatives held hearings on a comprehensive Child Development Act designed to improve and expand such services as day care, preschool education, family support, health, nutrition, and prenatal care.

Legislation providing increased financing for educational services for handicapped children passed both houses of Congress by an overwhelming margin. President Gerald R. Ford signed it on December 2. The bill provides incentive grants to states that do not now provide educational services to handicapped children under 5 years of age. In order to be eligible for funds, a state must demonstrate that it has a right-to-education policy ensuring that, by 1980, all handicapped children from 3 to 18 will have appropriate public education available. States are required to concentrate aid first on those children not receiving any education help, and then on those receiving inadequate special education.

Child Advocacy. Concerned citizens and professionals adopted child advocacy tactics to implement existing legislation and judicial decisions. They defended the rights of handicapped children to an appropriate education; of institutionalized children to effective treatment and return to family or community settings wherever possible; of delinquents and those before the courts to due process of law; of parents to access to all school records concerning their children; and of all children to protection from abuse and neglect.

A growing number of federal, state, and local organizations helped to demand and secure the rights of children. The Council for Exceptional Children in Reston, Va., published *A Primer on Due Process: Education Decisions for Handicapped Children.* The Children's Defense Fund in Boston conducted studies of the large number of children who are out of school because they were expelled, encouraged to drop out, or not admitted.

The American Psychological Association, along with other professional organizations in law, medicine, and social work, established a task force on children's rights. Los Angeles County, California, like many other local governments, has a team of public defenders, with specific personnel assigned to investigate complaints concerning mental health services for adults and children.

Controversy continued over the growing use of amphetamines to treat hyperactive children. Research literature indicated that there is no clear evidence that these drugs should be used as often as they are in treatment.   Frances A. Mullen

See also CIVIL RIGHTS (Close-Up).

CHILDREN'S BOOKS. See LITERATURE FOR CHILDREN.

CHILE suffered another year of international isolation and bitter economic recession in 1975. President Augusto Pinochet Ugarte and the military junta continued to govern under a state of siege. Press controls tightened, trade union leaders were jailed, and there were new charges that political prisoners were tortured. The newly established National Intelligence Directorate, headed by Colonel Manuel Contreras, was a target for criticism by church and Christian Democrat Party leaders.

Politically, it became clear that the armed forces were determined to hold power indefinitely. Pinochet was unchallenged within the regime, which seemed likely to evolve – under the guidance of a small group of presidential aides headed by Jaime Guzman – into an authoritarian system. Christian Democrat opposition grew, partly as a result of the arrest of party militants. Former President Eduardo Frei Montalva openly attacked the junta's economic policies.

Guerrilla Opposition was decisively crushed in a series of shoot-outs with the Movement of the Revolutionary Left (MIR). Andres Pascal Allende, leader of the MIR and nephew of the late President Salvador Allende Gossens, sought refuge in the Costa Rican Embassy in November, and the junta claimed it had uncovered a Marxist plot to infiltrate 1,200 revolutionaries into the country from bases in Argentina.

Foreign Relations with most Western governments continued to be strained, and Pinochet's decision to block a July visit by the United Nations Commission on Human Rights provoked criticism from Washington, D.C. But Pinochet scored a notable diplomatic success in his meeting with Bolivian President Hugo Banzer Suarez in February. The two leaders agreed to restore diplomatic relations, suspended in 1962; a secret part of the agreement reportedly allows Bolivia to supervise freight moving on the Antofagasta-La Paz railway.

The Economy. The top priority for Chile's economic planners continued to be controlling inflation. A ruthless cutback in public spending and monetary expansion began to produce results in July, when the monthly rate of inflation fell to 9.5 per cent, compared with 35 per cent in January. But unemployment rose to over 16 per cent, and in the 12 months ending in March, the index of industrial production fell 15 per cent.

Chile's payments deficit was increased by the low world price of copper, which provides 75 per cent of its foreign-exchange earnings. A campaign to attract foreign loans and investment by denationalizing state-run firms and guaranteeing repatriation of capital was disappointing.   Robert Moss

See also LATIN AMERICA (Facts in Brief Table).

CHINA, NATIONALIST. See TAIWAN.

President Augusto Pinochet Ugarte, head of the military junta that ousted the Marxist regime in Chile, reviews troops in Santiago.

華人民共和国第四届全国人民代表大会第一次会

Delegates to the Fourth National People's Congress of China
approved a new Constitution at their January meeting in Peking.

CHINA, PEOPLE'S REPUBLIC OF. Party slogans came to life in electric lights in Peking and fireworks brightened the sky on the evening of Jan. 18, 1975. Street loudspeakers announced that the Fourth National People's Congress had begun its work. In fact, China's People's Congress had ended its five-day secret session the previous day, and most of the 2,864 deputies who attended had already left for the provinces.

The People's Congress has no real power. It is a tool of the Communist Party's Central Committee, which put the final touches on the congress's agenda at its own meeting, held from January 8 to 10. But even if it was no more than a rubber stamp, the congress's session was newsworthy. It presented the nation's new Constitution, replacing that of 1954. It also revealed that China's Old Guard, led by Premier Chou En-lai (who died a year later, on Jan. 8, 1976, after a long illness), at last had won its struggle for power with the generals and Shanghai-based radicals. Chairman Mao Tsetung, 82, did not attend the congress. He remained somewhere in central China, receiving a few Western visitors.

The New Government Leadership, announced at the congress, gave proof of Chou's success. His close ally, 72-year-old Teng Hsiao-ping, who had been roundly criticized by the Red Guards during the Cultural Revolution that started in 1966, was

made first among the 12 deputy premiers, the men who direct the day-to-day governing of the nation. Before January was over, Teng had also become one of the five vice-chairmen of the Communist Party and chief of the armed forces general staff. Another close Chou ally, 76-year-old Yeh Chienying, became defense minister.

The army's influence was diminished. Its representative among the deputy premiers was Chen Hsi-lien, former commander in Manchuria and now commander of the Peking military district. He began his revolutionary career at the age of 15 as a member of a children's arson squad. Now, at 62, he was a wily politician attuned to the opportunities of the moment.

This gallery of old-time revolutionary leaders was not meant for permanence. Its task was to ensure orderly transition after the deaths of Chou and Mao, as younger men elbow their way to the top.

The New Constitution granted a number of rights the Chinese did not have under the previous charter — freedom of speech and assembly, freedom to demonstrate, and freedom to strike. This last one, according to Chang Chun-chiao, a Shanghai leader who presented the document to the congress, was inserted on the personal instructions of Mao. The new Constitution also promised freedom from arrest, "except by decision of a people's court or with the sanction of a public security organ."

The new Constitution abolished the post of head of state, which had been vacant since it was formally stripped from the disgraced Liu Shao-chi more than six years ago during the Cultural Revolution. The Constitution described the congress as "the highest organ of state power," but it emphasized that the congress is "under the leadership of the Communist Party."

The Economy. The leaders in Peking had been engaged for three years in a debate on where the economy was to go, and how fast. One of their decisions led to a cut in defense spending to free more funds for the economy. The crucial decision to embark on an all-out drive to industrialize China was finally reached in the fall of 1974.

Premier Chou gave only a hint of this in reminding the People's Congress of Mao's injunction 10 years earlier to lay the groundwork for industrialization by 1980 and to have "comprehensive modernization" of industry, agriculture, and defense by the year 2000. If this is done, Chou said, "our national economy will be advancing in the front ranks of the world."

By April, 1975, the people were told at thousands of mass meetings that industrial production would have to be more than doubled by 1980. This would clearly involve an extraordinary effort, because the target set in the Fifth Five-Year Plan, which ended in 1975, was 10 per cent a year. Although that goal was surpassed in some areas, in such key provinces as Liaoning it had not yet reached 7 per cent.

The peasants were also told in April that farms would have to be completely mechanized by 1980. In September, the theme was underlined at a national conference of 3,700 agricultural delegates in Shansi province. In one of the main speeches, Mao's wife, Chiang Ching, urged the country's estimated 650 million peasants to modernize, mechanize, and study her husband's teachings.

New Priorities. The plan to industrialize required a radical change in priorities. Late in 1974, Peking began to re-examine its purchases abroad. In January, 1975, it canceled two-thirds of its contracts for U.S. wheat to be delivered by mid-1976. Peking also deferred the delivery of some steel and fertilizer ordered from Japan. At the same time, Peking sent missions abroad to shop for items on its new list of priorities — from steel mills and oil rigs to sophisticated computers. The government also opened diplomatic relations with the European Community (Common Market) in September, in the hope of increasing trade.

For the first time since 1949, China went into debt. The foreign trade deficit for 1974 was $1.3 billion, and experts predicted it would reach $3 billion by 1978, before beginning to decline. China expected to meet its debts with the soaring production and exports of oil. Oil output, which reached 475 million barrels in 1974, was estimated

Member of a Chinese surveying team probes an ice cave from a precarious perch on a slope of Mount Everest, world's highest mountain.

at about 600 million barrels in 1975. Some specialists thought that China, with its offshore fields, might rival Saudi Arabia as a major oil producer by the end of the 1980s. Japan was expected to remain China's principal buyer.

Unrest Grows. Even as the workers were urged to work harder, Peking insisted that they toil for the revolution, not for money. Pay had long been frozen at low levels – an average factory salary was about $25 a month – and the bonuses, on which workers once relied to supplement their pay, had been declared "counterrevolutionary." This had resulted in ferment.

The most striking display of unrest came in July in Hangchow, in central China. The trouble in this city of more than a million people dated back to 1974, when workers began to complain about poor food in the canteens, lack of transport for the night shift, absence of barbers, inadequate nursery facilities, and the low piecework pay made even lower by the often inadequate supply of raw materials.

Violence finally broke out, and buildings, equipment, and electric installations were reported damaged. Peking acted firmly in mid-July, replacing the army commander and political commissar of the Hangchow area. A "stability and unity" directive bearing Mao's signature instructed the party and the army to restore order and resume production. A reported 10,500 troops were moved into the factories.

The soldiers' task was a complex one. Not only did they join the workers at the lathes, but they also held political seminars, helped the factory cooks, and did barbering and laundering for the workers. Other military teams visited homes to talk to the workers' families about the need to follow Mao's injunction.

Down with Détente. Rivalry with Russia continued to dominate China's view of the world. One of Peking's fears was that détente in the West would allow Russia to increase its pressure on China. Consequently, Peking concentrated its fire on détente.

When U.S. Secretary of State Henry A. Kissinger visited China in October, his hosts tried to convince him that the Russians were treacherous, and that the West, instead of being lulled by détente, should strengthen its armed forces. Lest Moscow misunderstand the happenings in Peking, Kissinger eventually found it necessary to defend the U.S. policy of avoiding "needless confrontations" with the Soviet Union in a speech before his hosts. The differences did not prevent a four-day state visit to Peking by President Gerald R. Ford in December.

Through the year, Peking's men had gone to European capitals to recommend Western unity, a stronger North Atlantic Treaty Organization, and firmness in dealing with Moscow. But the rivalry with Russia was not confined to such exchanges. Peking warmly welcomed two top-drawer missions from Romania and Yugoslavia, hoping to undermine the conference of European Communist parties that Moscow had been trying to convene.

Japan, with a two-way trade worth about $4 billion, remained China's main trading partner. The diplomatic dealings of the two countries ran into snags, however, when Peking insisted on inserting a sentence denouncing "great-power *hegemony*" (political domination) into a proposed coexistence treaty. Tokyo resisted this, for fear it would offend Russia.

In September, China released 144 Nationalist spies and raiders from Taiwan who were captured between October, 1962, and September, 1965. The Chinese said they did this "as an expression of leniency," and that they would be given jobs or allowed to go back to Taiwan, if the government there permitted them to do so. See TAIWAN.

The action was an obvious embarrassment to the Nationalist government on Taiwan. In 1974, the Chinese released a group of Nationalist officers captured before 1949, during the civil war. Some of these men wanted to rejoin relatives in Taiwan, but the Nationalists refused their request, fearing they had been brainwashed with Maoist ideas.   Mark Gayn

See also ASIA (Facts in Brief Table).

CHRONOLOGY. See pages 8 through 16.

CHURCH, FRANK FORRESTER (1924-   ), an Idaho Democrat, was appointed chairman of the Senate Select Committee on Intelligence Activities in January, 1975. Committee hearings on Central Intelligence Agency (CIA) and Federal Bureau of Investigation activities disclosed some new information about covert CIA activities abroad but primarily focused on possible misdeeds relating to the American people. "My overriding concern is the growth of Big Brother in this country, and the implicit threat that this represents to the freedom of people," Church said. Late in the year, his name was entered in Florida's 1976 presidential primary.

Church was born on July 25, 1924, in Boise, Ida. He attended Stanford University and the Harvard University Law School. During World War II, he served as an Army intelligence officer in China, Burma, and India. From 1950 to 1956 he practiced law in Boise. He became a Democratic senator from Idaho in 1957 and won re-election in 1968 and 1974. He has served as chairman of the Foreign Relations Subcommittee on Western Hemisphere Affairs, of the Interior Subcommittee on Public Lands, and the Special Committee on Aging. In 1966, he was a member of the U.S. Mission to the 21st General Assembly of the United Nations.   Foster Stockwell

CHURCHES. See EASTERN ORTHODOX CHURCHES; JEWS; PROTESTANT; RELIGION; ROMAN CATHOLIC.

CITY. A deepening financial crisis confronted cities all around the world in 1975, threatening their public service programs and even their very solvency. The crisis was most marked in the United States, where the world's third largest city, New York City, faced bankruptcy and was forced to turn over partial control of its financial affairs to a new Municipal Assistance Corporation (see NEW YORK CITY). But the crisis was real in other parts of the world, too. Both London and Rome staggered under massive municipal debts, for example, and the mayor of Ankara, Turkey's capital, staged a three-day hunger strike in late July to protest the national government's lack of financial support for his city.

Causes of the Crisis. A principal culprit in the crisis was the economic recession that afflicted much of the world in the wake of rising energy prices. In Rome, the recession's effects crippled the city's construction industry, leading to a shortage of some 100,000 housing units. The recession caused severe unemployment in Cleveland, Detroit, and Seattle. As a result, local tax revenues fell and cities had to curtail services and cut their municipal payrolls. The U.S. Congressional Joint Economic Committee reported on June 6 that local governments had enacted some $3.6 billion in new taxes and cut spending by an estimated $3.3 billion in an effort to balance their 1975 budgets. See CLEVELAND; DETROIT; SEATTLE.

Another cause of the fiscal plight of U.S. cities was the exodus of residents to new homes in the suburbs. A U.S. Census Bureau report released in June showed that nearly every major American city lost population between 1970 and 1973. Losses ran as high as 12 per cent in Minneapolis, Minn.; 10.3 per cent in St. Louis; and 9.6 per cent in Cleveland. Houston was a major exception to the trend. Because it has been able to annex developing suburban areas, Houston registered a 7 per cent gain since 1970. See HOUSTON; ST. LOUIS.

City Workers' Strikes. Many mayors attributed part of the blame for the crisis in New York City and other cities to increasing militancy among unionized municipal employees. The employees demanded pay increases and better pension programs, and some resisted labor-saving measures.

Policemen went on strike during the year in Albuquerque, N. Mex.; Kansas City, Mo.; and San Francisco. About half the members of Albuquerque's striking police force turned in their badges and resigned on July 16 rather than defy a court order to return to work.

Eighteen policemen in Skokie, Ill., a Chicago suburb, reported for work on July 6, but they were not in uniform. They were protesting the village's offer of a 5 per cent pay increase. Other Skokie policemen joined the action, which lasted 11 days, and 34 were fired for not wearing uniforms.

Firemen struck in Berkeley, Calif.; Kansas City; and San Francisco. Kansas City officials charged that firemen set fires during their four-day strike in October to pressure the city into meeting their demands. Transit workers walked off the job in Philadelphia and New Orleans. There were strikes by teachers and doctors in Chicago and by nonuniformed city employees in Cleveland. Pittsburgh was hit by a teachers' strike. Even New York City, while on the verge of bankruptcy, had to deal with strikes involving teachers, garbage collectors, and other municipal employees. See CHICAGO; LABOR; NEW ORLEANS; PHILADELPHIA; PITTSBURGH; SAN FRANCISCO-OAKLAND.

Federal Aid. The Administration of President Gerald R. Ford in April asked Congress to enact a five-year, nine-month extension of the general revenue-sharing program. Under the program, set to expire at the end of 1976, federal money is made available to support state and local governments. The Ford extension plan would allocate about $39.8 million over the life of the extended program. The Administration bill also proposed minor changes in the aid-distribution formula designed to benefit larger and poorer cities at the expense of wealthier suburban counties.

Congress enacted the $2-billion Health Revenue Sharing and Health Services Act on July 29, over-

FLOOD STAGE

Aquapolis, Japan's model floating city of the
future, leaves Hiroshima under tow in April
for display at an ocean exposition in Okinawa.

cessful attempt to get more federal aid for the cities
or federal guarantees of municipal bonds. Another
delegation of mayors and other municipal officials
on October 8 urged congressional leaders to renew
the revenue-sharing program.

The U.S. Conference of Mayors held its annual
meeting in Boston from July 7 to 9. New Orleans
Mayor Moon Landrieu became the new conference
president. The conference voted to support legislation that would provide $2 billion in grants for
cities and states having a 6 per cent unemployment
rate for three consecutive months. In addition to
the general revenue-sharing program, the group
also supported a proposed $2.5-billion federal aid
program for public works and an Administration
program to give cities greater flexibility in transferring highway money to mass transit systems.

Other Urban Problems. A Gallup Poll released
on July 26 reported that residents of U.S. cities
having 500,000 population or more listed crime as
the top urban problem. The poll showed that a
record 45 per cent of big-city residents were afraid
to walk in their neighborhoods at night. Other major concerns, listed in order, were unemployment,
transportation, education, poor housing, and the
cost of living.

Statistics released by the Federal Bureau of Investigation on March 31 showed that serious
crimes increased by 17 per cent in the United
States in 1974, and that every major city, except
San Francisco-Oakland, reported an increase in its
crime rate. Despite the rising crime rate, President
Ford recommended a cut of $100 million in the
fiscal 1976 budget (July 1, 1975, to June 30, 1976)
for federal aid to local law-enforcement agencies.

Limiting Urban Growth. The U.S. Court of Appeals for the Ninth Circuit ruled on August 13 that
ordinances enacted by Petaluma, Calif., to regulate
growth were valid. The appeals court overturned a
lower court's 1974 ruling in the case. The appeals
court ruled that local ordinances restricting the
number of houses that could be built each year did
not violate the constitutional right to travel. Plaintiffs in the case had argued that such ordinances
unconstitutionally restricted the mobility of persons in search of housing. They also argued that
the ordinances were detrimental to the general welfare of the surrounding area and that they were in-
sensitive to the needs of low-and moderate-income
persons.

In another important judicial action, the Supreme Court ruled on June 24 that Southern cities
with high black populations could annex predominantly white suburbs without violating constitutional law. But the court warned that such annexations must preserve proportional black representation on city councils. Also, the cities must prove
that such annexations are not undertaken with the
intent of diluting the black inner-city vote. The

riding a presidential veto. The bill authorized
$125 million for health revenue-sharing block
grants. It also extended funding for family planning programs, community health and mental
health centers, migrant health centers, and rape-
prevention programs.

President Ford signed into law on June 16 a bill
appropriating $473 million for summer employ-
ment and recreation programs for 840,000 disadvantaged youths.

On February 18, the Supreme Court of the
United States ordered the release of $6 billion for
construction of municipal waste-treatment plants.
The funds had been impounded in 1973 by President Richard M. Nixon. However, the Environmental Protection Agency said it might take several years to disburse the money.

Militant Mayors. A group of big-city mayors
representing the U.S. Conference of Mayors and
the National League of Cities met with congressional leaders on January 30, seeking assistance to
help balance city budgets. They criticized the Administration's urban budget as a mere holding action against the impending tide of financial disaster. Twenty-two mayors went to Washington,
D.C., in March to lobby for more federal aid.

A delegation of nine mayors met on September
24 with the Congressional Joint Economic Committee and later with President Ford in an unsuc-

case involved an attempt by Richmond, Va., to annex portions of neighboring Chesterfield County. Black leaders had opposed the move, claiming it would reduce black voting strength in the city from 52 per cent to 42 per cent.

City Government Survey. Fewer than 1 per cent of all U.S. elected officials are black, even though blacks make up an estimated 11 per cent of the nation's population, according to a study completed in mid-1975 by the Metropolitan Applied Research Center. The survey showed that there were 3,503 elected black officials as of May 1, 1975. This included 135 black mayors, 66 black vice-mayors, and 276 state legislators.

Foreign Cities. Socialist Mario Rigo became mayor of Venice, Italy, in August, ending 24 years of Christian Democratic control in the city. Communist mayors were elected in Naples and Florence. The Viet Cong said that Saigon, South Vietnam, would also be called Ho Chi Minh City.

With prayers and the release of birds symbolizing peace, Japan, on August 6, marked the 30th anniversary of the atomic bombing of Hiroshima.

Preparations for the 1976 Olympic Summer Games in Montreal, Canada, were slowed during 1975 by a series of financial and labor problems. However, Mayor Jean Drapeau expressed confidence that preparations would be completed in time. See OLYMPIC GAMES.   James M. Banovetz

CIVIL RIGHTS became a suspenseful concern in Portugal, India, and elsewhere in 1975. Portugal, after overthrowing a 40-year dictatorship in 1974, seemed about to slide into a hybrid Communist-military domination that had the support of only a minority among the people. But moderates – aided by city demonstrations, rural opposition, and dissenting military leaders – formed a new government in September. The new government's ability to retain power by developing popular support was yet to be tested. See PORTUGAL.

In India, a democracy since it gained independence from Great Britain in 1947, Prime Minister Indira Gandhi suspended civil rights in June after a local court found her guilty of illegal campaign practices in the 1971 elections. Gandhi proclaimed a state of emergency on June 26 because of "the threat of internal disturbances." Thousands of her political opponents were arrested, press censorship began, and her parliamentary majority passed a new election law that retroactively legalized the acts for which she had been convicted. See INDIA.

More favorable for civil rights was a court ruling on October 1 that rejected the British government's effort to halt publication of the diaries of the late Richard Crossman, a Labour Party Cabinet minister from 1964 to 1970. The decision broke the tradition of keeping all Cabinet discussions secret, even those that do not involve national secu-rity. Equally favorable for civil rights was a U.S. Supreme Court decision affecting the rights of public school pupils (see Close-Up).

School Desegregation in the United States, through court-imposed busing, experienced many moments of tension and conflict. In Boston, police were assailed with stones, darts, and slingshots. Fire bombs were also thrown at a school, and horn-honking protest caravans visited the homes of public officials. Most of the trouble occurred at night. The schools were quiet in the daytime, thanks to the efforts of police, federal marshals, and community leaders, though school attendance declined significantly. See BOSTON; EDUCATION.

A somewhat less troubled atmosphere prevailed in Louisville, Ky., and surrounding Jefferson County. The metropolitan area became the first in the nation to carry out court-ordered, cross-district busing of children to establish racial balance in the public schools. Although an organized boycott group helped keep attendance down early in September, other residents conducted an advertising and public relations campaign, featuring the slogan, "Nobody wins when you lose your cool."

The courts were a busy arena for school desegregation questions. On September 16, a federal district court rejected a desegregation plan for Dallas that, despite the projected busing of 18,000 pupils,

George Brown of Colorado, first black to be elected lieutenant governor of a state, takes the oath of office in Denver in January.

Rights
For
Pupils

Public school pupils have the same constitutional rights against unfair disciplinary action that adults have when the government violates their civil rights. The Supreme Court of the United States issued that ruling on Jan. 22, 1975, in a case, *Goss v. Lopez,* involving nine students who were suspended from a Columbus, Ohio, high school in 1971 during a period of unrest and racial disorder.

The discipline was authorized under a state law permitting suspensions of up to 10 days without a hearing. The Supreme Court, in a ruling of marked potential importance, concluded that this procedure violated the students' rights to due process of law under the 14th Amendment to the U.S. Constitution. That amendment bars the states from depriving "any person of life, liberty, or property, without due process of law."

The court accepted the contention of the pupils that the suspension procedure deprived them of "property" in barring the exercise of their statutory right to an education, and of "liberty" by damaging their school records without providing evidence that could be evaluated in a hearing. The blemished records, the court agreed, could injure the pupils' ability to get into college or to obtain a job after graduation.

Justice Byron R. White's majority opinion specified the steps school officials must take in order to comply with the 14th Amendment when they suspend pupils for 10 days or less. Officials must give the pupil oral or written notice of the charges against him. If the pupil denies the charges, the school officials must provide "an explanation of the evidence." Then the pupil must be given an opportunity "to present his side of the story."

Justice White termed these steps "rudimentary precautions against unfair or mistaken findings of misconduct and arbitrary exclusions from school." However, he did not hold that these "precautions" gave pupils the right to be represented by counsel, cross-examine witnesses appearing on behalf of the school authorities, or call witnesses in their own defense. In many other decisions, the court has ruled that some

Beneficiaries
of court decision

or all of these procedures are necessary to protect adult rights. White said only that, "Longer suspensions or expulsions for the rest of the school term, or permanently, may require more formal procedures."

Nonetheless, *Goss v. Lopez* is a landmark case in recognizing that the educational rights of children and teen-agers are protected under the Constitution, just as are the rights of adults or college students. Only once before has the Supreme Court recognized constitutional rights for high school students. It ruled in 1969 in *Tinker v. Des Moines Independent Community School District* that students could not be suspended from high school and junior high school in Des Moines, Iowa, for wearing black armbands during a protest against the Vietnam War.

Goss v. Lopez was especially welcome to civil rights organizations. Some have charged that white school officials in many parts of the nation were resorting increasingly to unjustified suspensions as a discriminatory device against black pupils.

Any assessment of *Goss v. Lopez* must acknowledge the closeness of the decision. The court was divided 5 to 4, with the liberal and moderate justices joined in a majority, while the four conservative appointees of President Richard M. Nixon composed the minority.

Justice Lewis F. Powell, Jr., speaking for the minority, termed the ruling a "new thicket," foreshadowing innumerable court reviews to determine the fairness of decisions by teachers or school authorities to fail a pupil in a course, withhold his promotion, or decide that he is better suited for vocational training than a college program.

One month later, on February 25, the Supreme Court ruled in another case involving pupil rights that school officials who discipline pupils unfairly cannot defend themselves against civil rights suits by claiming ignorance of the pupils' basic constitutional rights. Again, the court was divided 5 to 4 on the issue. Undoubtedly, the question of children's rights will come before the Supreme Court again soon.
                                        Louis W. Koenig

would still leave the city with 46 one-race schools. See DALLAS.

A new weapon against school segregation was introduced on May 22 when the Department of Justice filed suit against local and state officials, charging that Ferndale, Mich., a Detroit suburb, illegally operated segregated schools, and, consequently, the state was illegally channeling general revenue-sharing funds into a retirement fund for school employees, including those in Ferndale.

Voting Rights. The important Voting Rights Act of 1965, which outlawed literacy tests in many Southern states, was renewed by Congress on July 28 for seven years. At the same time, its protection was extended to Spanish-speaking Americans and other "language minorities."

Black civil rights organizations and other minority groups assailed a new procedure, proposed on June 7 by the U.S. Department of Health, Education, and Welfare (HEW), for handling complaints of discrimination. Instead of investigating each complaint of bias, HEW would use individual complaints as the basis for investigating broad patterns of discrimination and pursue individual grievances only when it chose to. The National Association for the Advancement of Colored People objected that the proposal left too much to the discretion of an agency that had to be sued in the past before it would use its powers.

Federal Spying. Federal agencies were repeatedly exposed in 1975 as violators of civil liberties. The Rockefeller Commission, during its study of the Central Intelligence Agency (CIA), disclosed that the Internal Revenue Service had secretly given information to the CIA from individual income tax returns. Both the Federal Bureau of Investigation (FBI) and the CIA were reported to have illegally opened and photographed mail, maintained files on thousands of citizens, and engaged in widespread electronic surveillance and break-ins. Congressional investigators contended that the CIA had informants on President Richard M. Nixon's White House staff and in government departments and agencies. See Section Two, PROTECTING PRIVACY IN THE COMPUTER AGE.

Several government employees were the unwitting subjects of a CIA program of drug experiments. Even plots to assassinate heads of foreign governments were attributed to the CIA. The FBI was disclosed to have sent a note and tape recording to civil rights leader Martin Luther King, Jr., who believed it was an effort to drive him to suicide. Domestic political groups, including the Socialist Workers Party, were harassed.

The courts issued important rulings in 1975, and moved to consider cases with significant implications for civil liberties. On January 1, the California Supreme Court ruled that law enforcement officers do not have automatic access to a bank's

records in order to develop a case against one of its customers. The court said the law officers must first obtain a warrant or court order. On May 27, the Supreme Court of the United States upheld a lower court order requiring a former CIA employee to submit his future writing about the agency for pre-publication censorship.

The news media in the United States struggled on several fronts for freedom of the press. One, a proposed federal criminal code that Congress considered in August, threatened to impose new restrictions on reporters. The code would make it illegal, for example, for the press to disclose information the government had classified as restricted.

Women's Rights. The U.S. Supreme Court on March 19 invalidated a provision of the Social Security law that authorized survivor's benefits for the widow of a deceased worker with children, while denying them to a widower in similar circumstances. The Constitution, said the court, "forbids the gender-based differentiation that results in the efforts of women workers required to pay Social Security taxes producing less protection for their families than is produced by the efforts of men." The Supreme Court also ruled that it was unconstitutional for states to deny women equal opportunity to serve on juries.   Louis W. Koenig

See also articles on individual countries; COURTS AND LAWS.

CLEVELAND. Ralph J. Perk, a Republican, won re-election to his third two-year term as mayor of Cleveland on Nov. 4, 1975, defeating Cleveland School Board President Arnold R. Pinkney, a Democrat. While the election was legally nonpartisan, both candidates ran with the backing of their respective political parties.

A Financial Crisis. Mayor Perk was faced with a $16-million budget deficit in 1975. In an effort to balance the budget, Perk dismissed 1,100 city workers, including some police and firemen. He reduced garbage-collection services and closed four fire stations, but voters rejected his proposal for an increase in the city's income tax. As an example of the city's financial plight, 17.9 per cent of the budget was committed to paying off debts, the highest percentage of any major U.S. city.

Mayor Perk offered municipal employees only a 10-cent-an-hour pay increase. As a result, 3,600 employees representing five different unions went on strike from July 21 to July 27 and accepted a contract that would allow them to work out compromises. Eight other unions accepted the city's offer without striking.

Local Economy. Massive automobile-industry layoffs in the Cleveland area adversely affected other businesses. State banking authorities closed the Northern Ohio Bank of Cleveland on February 14. Banking officials reported that the bank had assets in 1975 of more than $115 million. When it closed, it had more than $10 million outstanding in uncollectible loans and only $5 million in capital and $2 million in loan-loss reserves.

On January 9, the bankrupt Erie-Lackawanna Railroad, which serves the Cleveland area, asked to be included in the government's new Consolidated Rail Corporation system.

The number of persons receiving unemployment-insurance benefits in the Cleveland region rose to 27,000 by mid-August, a 180 per cent increase over the previous year. Living costs rose 8.3 per cent between August, 1974, and August, 1975. Food costs rose 10.2 per cent, and department store sales reportedly increased 3 per cent between mid-1974 and mid-1975. The average annual earnings of a factory worker rose only 2.6 per cent to $11,813. A midyear report by the U.S. Census Bureau, meanwhile, showed that the city of Cleveland lost 9.6 per cent of its population between 1970 and 1973. The report estimated Cleveland's population at 678,615 as of July 1, 1973.

Flood. Heavy thunderstorms dumped 2 to 4 inches (5 to 10 centimeters) of rain on the Cleveland area on August 24, causing severe flooding in some areas. United States Coast Guard and police harbor units were called out to rescue persons from flooded houses. James M. Banovetz

CLOTHING. See FASHION.

With their horns blaring, about 600 coal trucks form a convoy in Washington, D.C., on April 8 to protest Congress's tough strip-mining bill.

COAL. Great Britain, the United States, and West Germany agreed in November, 1975, to cooperate in building and operating a $20-million coal-test facility. To be built in Britain, the plant will enable engineers to test ways to burn coal more efficiently.

The United States consumed a record 624 million short tons (566 million metric tons) of bituminous coal in 1975, according to estimates by the National Coal Association (NCA). The 2 per cent increase over 1974 was met partly from stockpiles. The NCA also estimated bituminous coal production at 640 million short tons (580 million metric tons) in 1975 – an increase of 6 per cent over strike-ridden 1974. A month-long wildcat strike originated in West Virginia on August 11 and spread to other states before ending a month later. See LABOR.

New Sources Sought. President Gerald R. Ford outlined his goal for coal in February as part of an energy-conservation program. He called for the opening of 250 new mines. The NCA president, Carl E. Bagge, said President Ford's goal is "a minimum figure if we expect to double coal production by 1985." The NCA saw environmental obstacles to the goal. The group called for revisions in the Clean Air Act to allow utilities to burn high-sulfur coal and urged passage of a new strip-mining bill so that extensive new leases in the West can be opened up for mining. But the NCA and

utilities lobbied strongly for President Ford to veto a second tough strip-mining bill. He did, and the U.S. House of Representatives fell three votes short of overriding the veto on June 10.

Under pressure from the mining industry, the Department of the Interior moved in September to resume leasing federally owned Western coal reserves to private energy companies without obtaining the approval of environmentalists or Western governors. In a 400-page final statement on the impact its coal-leasing program would have upon the environment, the government began clearing the way to resume sale of coal leases.

Feasibility studies were underway for pipelines that would carry coal long distances in a water slurry. Energy Transportation Systems, Inc., of San Francisco, announced in February it was planning a 1,036-mile (1,667-kilometer) coal-slurry pipeline to carry coal from the mineral-rich fields of Wyoming to Arkansas. A skirmish developed as environmentalists tended to favor the enterprise while railroads and railroad unions opposed it. Middle South Utilities, Incorporated, the Arkansas utility that plans to use the pipeline, calculated that the line could deliver coal at about one-fourth the railroad transport rate over a 30-year period because it would not incur inflated costs for labor and new equipment. Mary E. Jessup

See also MINES AND MINING.

COIN COLLECTING. Ending the ban on private ownership of gold by United States citizens did not result in the expected rush to buy gold bullion in 1975. After the ban was ended on Dec. 31, 1974, gold bullion proved to be less popular than gold coins. Small buyers favored coins because coins are more marketable and less subject to forgery.

On January 7, less than seven days after order forms had gone out from the U.S. Mint, the 1,500 special gold medals commemorating President Gerald R. Ford's inauguration were sold. The medal sold for $395.

Bicentennial Issues. Collectors showed some resentment at the way the U.S. Mint handled sales of the double-dated (1776-1976) Bicentennial quarters, half dollars, and dollars. In January, the mint reduced the price of the 40 per cent silver proof sets from $15 to $12 and offered rebates to earlier purchasers. But the price of the less attractive uncirculated sets remained at $9. Their sales lagged, and, on September 1, the mint began offering them in bulk lots of 50 or more sets at $7 each. Collectors protested that the new policy discriminated in favor of dealers and other bulk buyers. Apparently to placate those who had paid $9 for the uncirculated sets, the mint in mid-September offered full refunds for sets returned by September 30.

The mint mailed 350,000 Bicentennial proof sets to buyers after July 4. Regular issues of the Bicentennial half dollars were released on July 7, and quarters were released on August 18. Dollars came out on October 13.

Dollars had originally been scheduled to come out first, but imperfectly prepared dies resulted in flaws in the relief of the dollars. Collectors were naturally interested in whether the flawed dollars would eventually be released. However, they suspected the mint might release these dollars in large quantity to reduce their value as rarities. No 1975-dated U.S. quarters, half dollars, or dollars were issued because the mint's resources were devoted to turning out the Bicentennial coins.

Sagging Prices. There was some evidence that poor economic conditions had affected rare-coin prices, which had continuously climbed in recent years. An uncirculated specimen of the first 1794 U.S. silver dollar, which sold in August, 1974, for $127,500, sold at auction for only $75,000 six months later. An auction at the annual convention of the American Numismatic Association, held in Los Angeles from August 19 to 24, grossed a record $3.7 million. But some sellers were disappointed, because many so-called hard-line coins, such as early American colonial issues and other rarities — which recently sold for record prices — did not even equal those prices.

Theodore M. O'Leary

The designers proudly display the dollar, half dollar, and quarter issued in 1975 to commemorate the United States Bicentennial.

COLEMAN, WILLIAM THADDEUS, JR. (1920-
), a noted legal expert in transportation and civil rights, became United States secretary of transportation on March 7, 1975. He succeeded Claude S. Brinegar, and is the second black to serve in a Cabinet post. At the time of his appointment, he was senior partner with the Philadelphia law firm that he joined in 1952.

Born in the Germantown section of Philadelphia, on July 7, 1920, Coleman graduated *summa cum laude* from the University of Pennsylvania in 1941 and *magna cum laude* from the Harvard Law School in 1946. After a year as a law secretary, he became a law clerk on the staff of Supreme Court Justice Felix Frankfurter in 1948.

Coleman coauthored the brief that helped persuade the Supreme Court of the United States to outlaw public school segregation in 1954. He has served as president of the Legal Defense and Educational Fund of the National Association for the Advancement of Colored People.

In public service, Coleman served as a senior consultant and assistant counsel to the Warren Commission in 1964; a member of the United States delegation to the United Nations in 1969; and as a consultant to the U.S. Arms Control and Disarmament Agency from 1963 to 1975.

Coleman married the former Lovida Hardin in 1945. They have three children. Robert K. Johnson

COLOMBIA. President Alfonso Lopez Michelsen in 1975 faced the familiar plight of every would-be reformer. He was under attack from those who thought he was moving too fast and those who thought he was not moving fast enough. Confronted with street violence, renewed guerrilla activity, and rumors of a right wing coup d'état attempt, Lopez gradually shifted his ground toward the conservative camp.

Despite severe stresses, Lopez managed to preserve a power-sharing arrangement with the Conservative Party that allowed that party to hold as many seats in the Cabinet as his own Liberal Party. Minister of the Interior Cornelio Reyes, a Conservative, continued to hold overall responsibility for internal security. This arrangement survived a crisis in October, when the Liberal majority in Congress voted to replace the Conservative comptroller general, who had been charged with embezzlement, with a Liberal.

Lopez Michelsen was less successful in holding his own party together. With the support of left wing groups, former President Carlos Lleras Restrepo thrust himself forward as the Liberal candidate for the 1978 elections. His maneuver was seen as an attempt to undermine Lopez.

State of Siege. Lopez also had to contend with army unrest. He sacked the army commander, General Alvaro Valencia Tovar, in May, amid rumors of a military conspiracy. In September, a group of right wing officers formed the National Liberation and Reconstruction Brigade, and claimed it included some of Tovar's followers.

The army was inevitably drawn deeper into politics as the government tried to grapple with labor and student unrest and a major guerrilla campaign waged by the Castroite National Liberation Army (ELN), led by Fabio Vasquez Castano, the pro-Russian Colombian Revolutionary Armed Forces, and the Maoist-inclined People's Liberation Army (EPL). One of the latter's leaders, Pedro Leon Arboleda, was killed by security forces in August. Traditionally rural-based movements, these dissident groups turned to urban operations. The murder of the army's inspector general, General Ramon Rincón Quinónes, on September 8, and the kidnaping of Donald Cooper, a Sears, Roebuck and Company executive, were both attributed to the EPL.

On June 26, because of labor upheaval, the illegal occupation of private lands by peasants, and student riots, Lopez was obliged to abandon an earlier promise and declare a state of siege. Martial law was declared, and the army staged massive house-to-house searches. Robert Moss

See also LATIN AMERICA (Facts in Brief Table).
COLORADO. See STATE GOVERNMENT.
COMMON MARKET. See EUROPE.

COMMUNICATIONS. The recession hindered growth in communications facilities throughout the world during 1975. Nevertheless, it was a year of net gain. Satellite systems and terrestrial and undersea cable systems expanded, while advances in electronics speeded call switching.

Oil-rich Middle Eastern nations surged forward in efforts to provide their lands with modern communications facilities. Iran, for example, ordered $500 million worth of equipment. More developed nations linked up with satellites, automated their telecommunications systems, and reorganized for greater efficiency. Mexico, Puerto Rico, Singapore, and Sweden reorganized their telephone administrations; and Austria, Finland, Norway, Sweden, and West Germany were among the countries moving toward automating international and local communications switching and transmission as quickly as possible.

In the United States, which has the world's most widespread and sophisticated telecommunications system, the emphasis was on changing central offices to electronic switching. During the year, the Bell System, which provides 80 per cent of the telephone service in the country, installed new electronic central offices at the rate of one every two days, bringing the total to nearly 900 by year-end. The computer-controlled electronic switches work many times faster than older electromechanical devices, they can diagnose their own internal malfunctions, and they provide such new services as abbreviated dialing, automatic call forwarding, and "camping" on a busy line until it is free.

The largest long-distance telephone switch in the world was put into service on May 3 in the General Telephone Company of California toll center in Long Beach. The all-electronic switch can switch 150,000 calls per hour at full capacity. The Bell System finished installing its first all-electronic long-distance switching machine in Chicago at the end of the year. It can process about 550,000 long-distance calls an hour.

Legal and Regulatory Actions. The massive task of gathering evidence for the antitrust suit filed against the American Telephone and Telegraph Company (A.T.&T.) began in November, 1974. The U.S. Department of Justice suit charges A.T.&T. with obstructing competition and restricting buying. It seeks to force the company to divest itself of its manufacturing company, Western Electric Company; its research arm, Bell Laboratories; and its long-distance transmission company, A.T.&T. Long Lines.

In another major antitrust case, General Telephone & Electronics Corporation, which owns the second largest U.S. telephone system, won reversal of a decision ordering the company to sell its man-

ufacturing companies and several telephone operations because of restrictive buying practices. A higher court sent the case back to be resolved without divestiture.

The U.S. telephone industry spent an estimated $12.5 billion in 1975 to expand and improve facilities. This was about a 1 per cent decrease from 1974. It was the first time in 16 years that the industry did not increase its construction spending.

Telephone companies filed a spate of rate-increase requests with state commissions. In addition to general increases, they sought to charge for directory assistance calls and to change the basis for local charges from a flat rate to one based on use.

Satellite Service. By midyear, there were 88 earth stations in 64 countries. One new *Intelsat IV* satellite was launched in May, and the first *Intelsat IV-A* satellite was launched at the end of the year. It provides 6,600 voice circuits, 2,600 more than the *Intelsat IV*.

Despite the advantages of satellites, undersea cables continue to be laid and planned for the future. A 7,500-mile (12,000-kilometer) cable between San Luis Obispo, Calif., and Okinawa was laid during the year. Leo S. Anderson

COMORO ISLANDS. See AFRICA.

CONGO (BRAZZAVILLE). See AFRICA.

CONGO (KINSHASA). See ZAIRE.

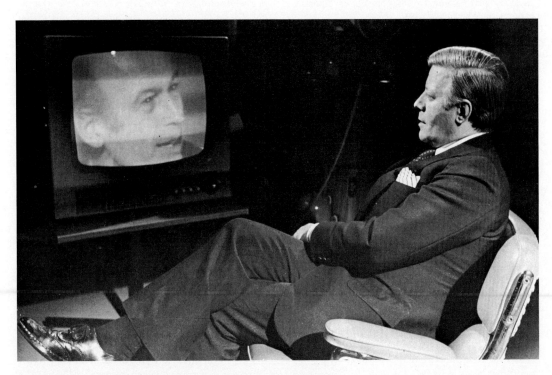

West German Chancellor Helmut Schmidt, right, talks with French President Valéry Giscard d'Estaing via a new French-German communications satellite.

CONGRESS OF THE UNITED STATES. Young liberal House Democrats challenged the congressional seniority system in 1975, sweeping three committee chairmen from their posts on January 22. Wright Patman (D., Tex.) was replaced as chairman of the Banking and Currency Committee by Henry S. Reuss (D., Wis.). Thomas S. Foley (D., Wash.) replaced W. R. Poage (D., Tex.) as head of the Agriculture Committee. Charles Melvin Price (D., Ill.) was elected chairman of the Armed Services Committee, ousting F. Edward Hébert (D., La.). Conservative Congressman John Jarman of Oklahoma switched his party affiliation from Democrat to Republican on January 23, after the full House approved the change.

Al Ullman (D., Ore.) became the new chairman of the House Ways and Means Committee. He replaced Wilbur D. Mills (D., Ark.), who resigned in the wake of scandal involving his personal life.

The first session of the 94th Congress convened on Jan. 14, 1975. In the Senate, there were 60 Democrats, 37 Republicans, 1 Independent, and 1 Conservative. One New Hampshire seat was vacant. In the House of Representatives, there were 291 Democrats and 144 Republicans.

The Senate tried unsuccessfully to resolve who won a New Hampshire Senate seat in the November, 1974, election – Republican Louis C. Wyman or Democrat John A. Durkin. On July 30, it declared the seat vacant. In a September 16 election, Durkin won. See ELECTIONS.

The Budget. On February 3, President Gerald R. Ford sent Congress a $349-billion budget for fiscal 1976 (July 1, 1975, to June 30, 1976). He estimated a federal budget deficit of $34.7 billion in fiscal 1975 and projected a deficit of $51.9 billion for fiscal 1976, the largest peacetime deficit in U.S. history. See UNITED STATES, GOVERNMENT OF.

On March 24, the Office of Management and Budget estimated that the fiscal 1976 budget deficit might reach $100 billion. As deficit estimates rose, the President repeatedly asked Congress to stop proposing further federal expenditures. On May 14, the House and the Senate approved a concurrent resolution to hold federal spending at $367-billion in fiscal 1976 and keep the deficit to no more than $68.8 billion. On July 28, the Administration reported the fiscal 1975 deficit at $44 billion.

Energy Policy Controversy. Disagreement between the President and Congress about a federal energy policy preoccupied the executive and legislative branches of government. On February 19, the Senate completed final action on a bill suspending for 90 days the President's power to increase import taxes on foreign oil. The President vetoed it on March 4. On July 17, Congress completed action to roll back the price of domestic oil from $13 a barrel to $11.28 a barrel. On July 21, Ford also vetoed this measure.

The disagreement continued. Twice in July, the House rejected presidential suggestions that oil price controls be lifted and prices allowed to rise gradually. On July 31, Congress voted to extend the President's power to control oil prices for six months after the Emergency Petroleum Allocation Act expired on August 31. The President allowed the act to expire, and he vetoed the extension on September 9.

The President and Congress reached a temporary compromise on September 26. Price controls were reinstated until November 15, retroactive to September 1. On November 12, Administration officials and Congress worked out an energy policy agreement, and on November 15, the President signed another extension to December 15.

Both houses passed the compromise energy bill on December 17, and the President signed it on December 22. The measure extended domestic oil price controls for three years and four months. It also called for an average rollback in oil prices of $1.09 a barrel. However, future oil prices could rise according to the rate of inflation. The bill also contained energy-conservation measures, such as requiring U.S. automobile makers to produce cars that would deliver an average of 18 miles per gallon (7.6 kilometers per liter) by 1978, and 27.5 miles per gallon (11.6 kilometers per liter) by 1985.

Foreign Policy. On October 9, Congress approved the plan to station U.S. civilians in the Sinai Peninsula to monitor the Sinai agreement that ended the conflict between Egypt and Israel. See MIDDLE EAST.

On April 10, the President asked Congress to provide nearly $1 billion in humanitarian and military aid for South Vietnam. He also asked for authority to send U.S. troops to evacuate Vietnamese who feared reprisals in the wake of the Communist victory in Southeast Asia. Congress refused.

Congress, displeased with the fact that Turkey used U.S. arms in its 1974 invasion of Cyprus, enacted a six-month arms embargo against Turkey on February 5. The House refused on July 24 to suspend the embargo. However, both the House and the Senate voted in October to partially lift the embargo. The bill was signed by President Ford on October 10. See TURKEY.

On December 19, the Senate passed a measure cutting off funds for a faction struggling for control of Angola. Congress adjourned before the House could vote, so the matter was carried over to the 1976 session. See ANGOLA.

Social Welfare Legislation. Faced with a mounting federal deficit, continuing inflation, and the nation's worst recession since the 1930s, the President and Congress differed sharply on social welfare legislation. The House voted on February 4 to freeze food-stamp prices through 1975, and the Senate approved the bill the next day. President

Members of the United States Senate

The Senate of the second session of the 94th Congress consists of 61 Democrats, 37 Republicans, 1 Independent, and 1 Conservative, compared with 60 Democrats, 37 Republicans, 1 Independent, and 1 Conservative, with 1 seat contested, for the first session of the 94th Congress. Senators shown starting their term in 1975 were elected for the first time in the Nov. 5, 1974, elections (with the exception of John A. Durkin, who was elected in a special New Hampshire senatorial election Sept. 16, 1975). Those shown ending their current terms in 1981 were re-elected to the Senate in the same balloting. The second date in each listing shows when the term of a previously elected senator expires. For organizational purposes, the one Independent will line up with Democrats, the one Conservative with Republicans.

State	Term	State	Term	State	Term
Alabama		**Louisiana**		**Ohio**	
John J. Sparkman, D.	1946—1979	Russell B. Long, D.	1948—1981	Robert Taft, Jr., R.	1971—1977
James B. Allen, D.	1969—1981	J. Bennett Johnston, Jr., D.	1972—1979	John H. Glenn, D.	1975—1981
Alaska		**Maine**		**Oklahoma**	
Theodore F. Stevens, R.	1968—1979	Edmund S. Muskie, D.	1959—1977	Henry L. Bellmon, R.	1969—1981
Mike Gravel, D.	1969—1981	William D. Hathaway, D.	1973—1979	Dewey F. Bartlett, R.	1973—1979
Arizona		**Maryland**		**Oregon**	
Paul J. Fannin, R.	1965—1977	Charles McC. Mathias, Jr., R.	1969—1981	Mark O. Hatfield, R.	1967—1979
Barry Goldwater, R.	1969—1981	J. Glenn Beall, Jr., R.	1971—1977	Robert W. Packwood, R.	1969—1981
Arkansas		**Massachusetts**		**Pennsylvania**	
John L. McClellan, D.	1943—1979	Edward M. Kennedy, D.	1962—1977	Hugh Scott, R.	1959—1977
Dale Bumpers, D.	1975—1981	Edward W. Brooke, R.	1967—1979	Richard S. Schweiker, R.	1969—1981
California		**Michigan**		**Rhode Island**	
Alan Cranston, D.	1969—1981	Philip A. Hart, D.	1959—1977	John O. Pastore, D.	1950—1977
John V. Tunney, D.	1971—1977	Robert P. Griffin, R.	1966—1979	Claiborne Pell, D.	1961—1979
Colorado		**Minnesota**		**South Carolina**	
Floyd K. Haskell, D.	1973—1979	Walter F. Mondale, D.	1964—1979	Strom Thurmond, R.	1956—1979
Gary Hart, D.	1975—1981	Hubert H. Humphrey, D.	1971—1977	Ernest F. Hollings, D.	1966—1981
Connecticut		**Mississippi**		**South Dakota**	
Abraham A. Ribicoff, D.	1963—1981	James O. Eastland, D.	1943—1979	George S. McGovern, D.	1963—1981
Lowell P. Weicker, Jr., R.	1971—1977	John C. Stennis, D.	1947—1977	James G. Abourezk, D.	1973—1979
Delaware		**Missouri**		**Tennessee**	
William V. Roth, Jr., R.	1971—1977	Stuart Symington, D.	1953—1977	Howard H. Baker, Jr., R.	1967—1979
Joseph R. Biden, Jr., D.	1973—1979	Thomas F. Eagleton, D.	1968—1981	William E. Brock III, R.	1971—1977
Florida		**Montana**		**Texas**	
Lawton Chiles, D.	1971—1977	Mike Mansfield, D.	1953—1977	John G. Tower, R.	1961—1979
Richard B. Stone, D.	1975—1981	Lee Metcalf, D.	1961—1979	Lloyd M. Bentsen, D.	1971—1977
Georgia		**Nebraska**		**Utah**	
Herman E. Talmadge, D.	1957—1981	Roman Lee Hruska, R.	1954—1977	Frank E. Moss, D.	1959—1977
Sam Nunn, D.	1972—1979	Carl T. Curtis, R.	1955—1979	Edwin Jacob Garn, R.	1975—1981
Hawaii		**Nevada**		**Vermont**	
Hiram L. Fong, R.	1959—1977	Howard W. Cannon, D.	1959—1977	Robert T. Stafford, R.	1971—1977
Daniel K. Inouye, D.	1963—1981	Paul Laxalt, R.	1975—1981	Patrick J. Leahy, D.	1975—1981
Idaho		**New Hampshire**		**Virginia**	
Frank Church, D.	1957—1981	Thomas J. McIntyre, D.	1962—1979	Harry F. Byrd, Jr., Ind.	1965—1977
James A. McClure, R.	1973—1979	John A. Durkin, D.	1975—1981	William L. Scott, R.	1973—1979
Illinois		**New Jersey**		**Washington**	
Charles H. Percy, R.	1967—1979	Clifford P. Case, R.	1955—1979	Warren G. Magnuson, D.	1944—1981
Adlai E. Stevenson III, D.	1970—1981	Harrison A. Williams, Jr., D.	1959—1977	Henry M. Jackson, D.	1953—1977
Indiana		**New Mexico**		**West Virginia**	
Vance Hartke, D.	1959—1977	Joseph M. Montoya, D.	1964—1977	Jennings Randolph, D.	1958—1979
Birch Bayh, D.	1963—1981	Pete V. Domenici, R.	1973—1979	Robert C. Byrd, D.	1959—1977
Iowa		**New York**		**Wisconsin**	
Richard C. Clark, D.	1973—1979	Jacob K. Javits, R.	1957—1981	William Proxmire, D.	1957—1977
John C. Culver, D.	1975—1981	James L. Buckley, Cons.	1971—1977	Gaylord Nelson, D.	1963—1981
Kansas		**North Carolina**		**Wyoming**	
James B. Pearson, R.	1962—1979	Jesse A. Helms, R.	1973—1979	Gale W. McGee, D.	1959—1977
Robert J. Dole, R.	1969—1981	Robert Morgan, D.	1975—1981	Clifford P. Hansen, R.	1967—1979
Kentucky		**North Dakota**			
Walter Huddleston, D.	1973—1979	Milton R. Young, R.	1945—1981		
Wendell, H. Ford, D.	1975—1981	Quentin N. Burdick, D.	1960—1977		

Members of the United States House

The House of Representatives of the second session of the 94th Congress consists of 290 Democrats and 145 Republicans (not including representatives from the District of Columbia, Puerto Rico, Guam, and the Virgin Islands), compared with 291 Democrats and 144 Republicans for the first session of the 94th Congress. This table shows congressional districts, legislator, and party affiliation. Asterisk (*) denotes those who served in the 93rd Congress; dagger (†) denotes "at large."

Alabama
1. Jack Edwards, R.*
2. William L. Dickinson, R.*
3. William Nichols, D.*
4. Tom Bevill, D.*
5. Robert E. Jones, D.*
6. John H. Buchanan, Jr., R.*
7. Walter Flowers, D.*

Alaska
† Don Young, R.*

Arizona
1. John J. Rhodes, R.*
2. Morris K. Udall, D.*
3. Sam Steiger, R.*
4. John B. Conlan, R.*

Arkansas
1. Bill Alexander, D.*
2. Wilbur D. Mills, D.*
3. J. P. Hammerschmidt, R.*
4. Ray Thornton, D.*

California
1. Harold T. Johnson, D.*
2. Don H. Clausen, R.*
3. John E. Moss, D.*
4. Robert L. Leggett, D.*
5. John L. Burton, D.
6. Phillip Burton, D.*
7. George Miller, D.
8. Ronald V. Dellums, D.*
9. Fortney H. Stark, D.*
10. Don Edwards, D.*
11. Leo J. Ryan, D.*
12. Paul N. McCloskey, Jr., R.*
13. Norman Y. Mineta, D.
14. John J. McFall, D.*
15. B. F. Sisk, D.*
16. Burt L. Talcott, R.*
17. John H. Krebs, D.
18. William M. Ketchum, R.*
19. Robert J. Lagomarsino, R.*
20. Barry M. Goldwater, Jr., R.*
21. James C. Corman, D.*
22. Carlos J. Moorhead, R.*
23. Thomas M. Rees, D.*
24. Henry A. Waxman, D.
25. Edward R. Roybal, D.*
26. John H. Rousselot, R.*
27. Alphonzo Bell, R.*
28. Yvonne B. Burke, D.*
29. Augustus F. Hawkins, D.*
30. George E. Danielson, D.*
31. Charles H. Wilson, D.*
32. Glenn M. Anderson, D.*
33. Del M. Clawson, R.*
34. Mark W. Hannaford, D.
35. Jim Lloyd, D.
36. George E. Brown, Jr., D.*
37. Shirley N. Pettis, R.

38. Jerry M. Patterson, D.
39. Charles E. Wiggins, R.*
40. Andrew J. Hinshaw, R.*
41. Bob Wilson, R.*
42. Lionel Van Deerlin, D.*
43. Clair W. Burgener, R.*

Colorado
1. Patricia Schroeder, D.*
2. Timothy E. Wirth, D.
3. Frank E. Evans, D.*
4. James P. Johnson, R.*
5. William L. Armstrong, R.*

Connecticut
1. William R. Cotter, D.*
2. Christopher J. Dodd, D.
3. Robert N. Giaimo, D.*
4. Stewart B. McKinney, R.*
5. Ronald A. Sarasin, R.*
6. Anthony J. Moffett, D.

Delaware
† Pierre S. du Pont IV, R.*

Florida
1. Robert L. F. Sikes, D.*
2. Don Fuqua, D.*
3. Charles E. Bennett, D.*
4. William V. Chappell, Jr., D.*
5. Richard Kelly, R.
6. C. W. Young, R.*
7. Sam M. Gibbons, D.*
8. James A. Haley, D.*
9. Louis Frey, Jr., R.*
10. L. A. Bafalis, R.*
11. Paul G. Rogers, D.*
12. J. Herbert Burke, R.*
13. William Lehman, D.*
14. Claude D. Pepper, D.*
15. Dante B. Fascell, D.*

Georgia
1. Ronald Ginn, D.*
2. Dawson Mathis, D.*
3. Jack T. Brinkley, D.*
4. Elliott H. Levitas, D.
5. Andrew Young, D.*
6. John J. Flynt, Jr., D.*
7. Lawrence P. McDonald, D.
8. Williamson S. Stuckey, Jr., D.*
9. Phillip M. Landrum, D.*
10. Robert G. Stephens, Jr., D.*

Hawaii
1. Spark M. Matsunaga, D.*
2. Patsy T. Mink, D.*

Idaho
1. Steven D. Symms, R.*
2. George Hansen, R.

Illinois
1. Ralph H. Metcalfe, D.*
2. Morgan F. Murphy, D.*
3. Martin A. Russo, D.
4. Edward J. Derwinski, R.*
5. John G. Fary, D.
6. Henry J. Hyde, R.
7. Cardiss Collins, D.*
8. Dan Rostenkowski, D.*
9. Sidney R. Yates, D.*
10. Abner J. Mikva, D.
11. Frank Annunzio, D.*
12. Philip M. Crane, R.*
13. Robert McClory, R.*
14. John N. Erlenborn, R.*
15. Tim L. Hall, D.
16. John B. Anderson, R.*
17. George M. O'Brien, R.*
18. Robert H. Michel, R.*
19. Thomas F. Railsback, R.*
20. Paul Findley, R.*
21. Edward R. Madigan, R.*
22. George E. Shipley, D.*
23. Charles Melvin Price, D.*
24. Paul Simon, D.

Indiana
1. Ray J. Madden, D.*
2. Floyd J. Fithian, D.
3. John Brademas, D.*
4. J. Edward Roush, D.*
5. Elwood H. Hillis, R.*
6. David W. Evans, D.
7. John T. Myers, R.*
8. Philip H. Hayes, D.
9. Lee H. Hamilton, D.*
10. Philip R. Sharp, D.
11. Andrew Jacobs, Jr., D.

Iowa
1. Edward Mezvinsky, D.*
2. Michael T. Blouin, D.
3. Charles E. Grassley, R.
4. Neal Smith, D.*
5. Tom Harkin, D.
6. Berkley Bedell, D.

Kansas
1. Keith G. Sebelius, R.*
2. Martha E. Keys, D.
3. Larry Winn, Jr., R.*
4. Garner E. Shriver, R.*
5. Joe Skubitz, R.*

Kentucky
1. Carroll Hubbard, Jr., D.
2. William H. Natcher, D.*
3. Romano L. Mazzoli, D.*
4. Marion Gene Snyder, R.*
5. Tim Lee Carter, R.*
6. John B. Breckinridge, D.*
7. Carl D. Perkins, D.*

Louisiana
1. F. Edward Hébert, D.*
2. Lindy Boggs, D.*
3. David C. Treen, R.*
4. Joe D. Waggoner, Jr., D.*
5. Otto E. Passman, D.*
6. W. Henson Moore, R.
7. John B. Breaux, D.*
8. Gillis W. Long, D.*

Maine
1. David F. Emery, R.
2. William S. Cohen, R.*

Maryland
1. Robert E. Bauman, R.*
2. Clarence D. Long, D.*
3. Paul S. Sarbanes, D.*
4. Marjorie S. Holt, R.*
5. Gladys N. Spellman, D.
6. Goodloe E. Byron, D.*
7. Parren J. Mitchell, D.*
8. Gilbert Gude, R.*

Massachusetts
1. Silvio O. Conte, R.*
2. Edward P. Boland, D.*
3. Joseph D. Early, D.
4. Robert F. Drinan, D.*
5. Paul E. Tsongas, D.
6. Michael J. Harrington, D.*
7. Torbert H. Macdonald, D.*
8. Thomas P. O'Neill, Jr., D.*
9. John J. Moakley, D.*
10. Margaret M. Heckler, R.*
11. James A. Burke, D.*
12. Gerry E. Studds, D.*

Michigan
1. John Conyers, Jr., D.*
2. Marvin L. Esch, R.*
3. Garry Brown, R.*
4. Edward Hutchinson, R.*
5. Richard F. Vander Veen, D.*
6. Bob Carr, D.
7. Donald W. Riegle, Jr., D.*
8. Bob Traxler, D.*
9. Guy Vander Jagt, R.*
10. Elford A. Cederberg, R.*
11. Philip E. Ruppe, R.*
12. James G. O'Hara, D.*
13. Charles C. Diggs, Jr., D.*
14. Lucien N. Nedzi, D.*
15. William D. Ford, D.*
16. John D. Dingell, D.*
17. William M. Brodhead, D.
18. James J. Blanchard, D.
19. William S. Broomfield, R.*

Minnesota
1. Albert H. Quie, R.*
2. Thomas M. Hagedorn, R.
3. Bill Frenzel, R.*
4. Joseph E. Karth, D.*
5. Donald M. Fraser, D.*
6. Richard Nolan, D.
7. Bob Bergland, D.*
8. James L. Oberstar, D.

Mississippi
1. Jamie L. Whitten, D.*
2. David R. Bowen, D.*
3. G. V. Montgomery, D.*
4. Thad Cochran, R.*
5. Trent Lott, R.*

Missouri
1. William L. Clay, D.*
2. James W. Symington, D.*
3. Leonor K. Sullivan, D.*
4. William J. Randall, D.*
5. Richard Bolling, D.*
6. Jerry Litton, D.*
7. Gene Taylor, R.*
8. Richard H. Ichord, D.*
9. William L. Hungate, D.*
10. Bill D. Burlison, D.*

Montana
1. Max S. Baucus, D.
2. John Melcher, D.*

Nebraska
1. Charles Thone, R.*
2. John Y. McCollister, R.*
3. Virginia Smith, R.

Nevada
† James Santini, D.

New Hampshire
1. Norman E. D'Amours, D.
2. James C. Cleveland, R.*

New Jersey
1. James J. Florio, D.
2. William J. Hughes, D.
3. James J. Howard, D.*
4. Frank Thompson, Jr., D.*
5. Millicent Fenwick, R.
6. Edwin B. Forsythe, R.*
7. Andrew Maguire, D.
8. Robert A. Roe, D.*
9. Henry Helstoski, D.*
10. Peter W. Rodino, Jr., D.*
11. Joseph G. Minish, D.*
12. Matthew J. Rinaldo, R.*
13. Helen Meyner, D.
14. Dominick V. Daniels, D.*
15. Edward J. Patten, D.*

New Mexico
1. Manuel Lujan, Jr., R.*
2. Harold Runnels, D.*

New York
1. Otis G. Pike, D.*
2. Thomas J. Downey, D.
3. Jerome A. Ambro, Jr., D.
4. Norman F. Lent, R.*
5. John W. Wydler, R.*
6. Lester L. Wolff, D.*
7. Joseph P. Addabbo, D.*
8. Benjamin S. Rosenthal, D.*
9. James J. Delaney, D.*
10. Mario Biaggi, D.*
11. James H. Scheuer, D.
12. Shirley Chisholm, D.*
13. Stephen J. Solarz, D.
14. Frederick W. Richmond, D.
15. Leo C. Zeferetti, D.
16. Elizabeth Holtzman, D.*
17. John M. Murphy, D.*
18. Edward I. Koch, D.*
19. Charles B. Rangel, D.*
20. Bella S. Abzug, D.*
21. Herman Badillo, D.*
22. Jonathan B. Bingham, D.*
23. Peter A. Peyser, R.*
24. Richard L. Ottinger, D.
25. Hamilton Fish, Jr., R.*
26. Benjamin A. Gilman, R.*
27. Matthew F. McHugh, D.
28. Samuel S. Stratton, D.*
29. Edward W. Pattison, D.
30. Robert C. McEwen, R.*
31. Donald J. Mitchell, R.*
32. James M. Hanley, D.*
33. William F. Walsh, R.*
34. Frank Horton, R.*
35. Barber B. Conable, Jr., R.*
36. John J. LaFalce, D.
37. Henry J. Nowak, D.
38. Jack F. Kemp, R.*
39. James F. Hastings, R.*

North Carolina
1. Walter B. Jones, D.*
2. L. H. Fountain, D.*
3. David N. Henderson, D.*
4. Ike F. Andrews, D.*
5. Stephen L. Neal, D.
6. L. Richardson Preyer, D.*
7. Charles Rose, D.*
8. W. G. Hefner, D.
9. James G. Martin, R.*
10. James T. Broyhill, R.*
11. Roy A. Taylor, D.*

North Dakota
† Mark Andrews, R.*

Ohio
1. Willis D. Gradison, Jr., R.
2. Donald D. Clancy, R.*
3. Charles W. Whalen, Jr., R.*
4. Tennyson Guyer, R.*
5. Delbert L. Latta, R.*
6. William H. Harsha, R.*
7. Clarence J. Brown, R.*
8. Thomas N. Kindness, R.
9. Thomas L. Ashley, D.*
10. Clarence E. Miller, R.*
11. J. William Stanton, R.*
12. Samuel L. Devine, R.*
13. Charles A. Mosher, R.*
14. John F. Seiberling, D.*
15. Chalmers P. Wylie, R.*
16. Ralph S. Regula, R.*
17. John M. Ashbrook, R.*
18. Wayne L. Hays, D.*
19. Charles J. Carney, D.*
20. James V. Stanton, D.*
21. Louis Stokes, D.*
22. Charles A. Vanik, D.*
23. Ronald M. Mottl, D.

Oklahoma
1. James R. Jones, D.*
2. Theodore M. Risenhoover, D.
3. Carl B. Albert, D.*
4. Tom Steed, D.*
5. John Jarman, R.*
6. Glenn English, D.

Oregon
1. Les AuCoin, D.
2. Al Ullman, D.*
3. Robert B. Duncan, D.
4. James Weaver, D.

Pennsylvania
1. William A. Barrett, D.*
2. Robert N. C. Nix, D.*
3. William J. Green, D.*
4. Joshua Eilberg, D.*
5. Richard T. Schulze, R.
6. Gus Yatron, D.*
7. Robert W. Edgar, D.
8. Edward G. Biester, Jr., R.*
9. E. G. Shuster, R.*
10. Joseph M. McDade, R.*
11. Daniel J. Flood, D.*
12. John P. Murtha, D.*
13. Lawrence Coughlin, R.*
14. William S. Moorhead, D.*
15. Fred B. Rooney, D.*
16. Edwin D. Eshleman, R.*
17. Herman T. Schneebeli, R.*
18. H. John Heinz III, R.*
19. William F. Goodling, R.
20. Joseph M. Gaydos, D.*
21. John H. Dent, D.*
22. Thomas E. Morgan, D.*
23. Albert W. Johnson, R.*
24. Joseph P. Vigorito, D.*
25. Gary A. Myers, R.

Rhode Island
1. Fernand J. St. Germain, D.*
2. Edward P. Beard, D.

South Carolina
1. Mendel J. Davis, D.*
2. Floyd D. Spence, R.*
3. Butler C. Derrick, Jr., D.
4. James R. Mann, D.*
5. Kenneth L. Holland, D.
6. John W. Jenrette, Jr., D.

South Dakota
1. Larry Pressler, R.
2. James Abdnor, R.*

Tennessee
1. James H. Quillen, R.*
2. John J. Duncan, R.*
3. Marilyn Lloyd, D.
4. Joe L. Evins, D.*
5. Clifford R. Allen, D.
6. Robin L. Beard, Jr., R.*
7. Ed Jones, D.*
8. Harold E. Ford, D.

Texas
1. Wright Patman, D.*
2. Charles Wilson, D.*
3. James M. Collins, R.*
4. Ray Roberts, D.*
5. Alan Steelman, R.*
6. Olin E. Teague, D.*
7. Bill Archer, R.*
8. Bob Eckhardt, D.*
9. Jack Brooks, D.*
10. J. J. Pickle, D.*
11. W. R. Poage, D.*
12. James C. Wright, Jr., D.*
13. Jack Hightower, D.
14. John Young, D.*
15. Eligio de la Garza, D.*
16. Richard C. White, D.*
17. Omar Burleson, D.*
18. Barbara C. Jordan, D.*
19. George H. Mahon, D.*
20. Henry B. Gonzalez, D.*
21. Robert Krueger, D.
22. Robert R. Casey, D.*
23. Abraham Kazen, Jr., D.*
24. Dale Milford, D.*

Utah
1. K. Gunn McKay, D.*
2. Allan T. Howe, D.

Vermont
† James M. Jeffords, R.

Virginia
1. Thomas N. Downing, D.*
2. G. William Whitehurst, R.*
3. David E. Satterfield III, D.*
4. Robert W. Daniel, Jr., R.*
5. W. C. Daniel, D.*
6. M. Caldwell Butler, R.*
7. J. Kenneth Robinson, R.*
8. Herbert E. Harris, D.
9. William C. Wampler, R.*
10. Joseph L. Fisher, D.

Washington
1. Joel Pritchard, R.*
2. Lloyd Meeds, D.*
3. Don Bonker, D.
4. Mike McCormack, D.*
5. Thomas S. Foley, D.*
6. Floyd V. Hicks, D.*
7. Brock Adams, D.*

West Virginia
1. Robert H. Mollohan, D.*
2. Harley O. Staggers, D.*
3. John M. Slack, D.*
4. Ken Hechler, D.*

Wisconsin
1. Les Aspin, D.*
2. Robert W. Kastenmeier, D.*
3. Alvin J. Baldus, D.
4. Clement J. Zablocki, D.*
5. Henry S. Reuss, D.*
6. William A. Steiger, R.*
7. David R. Obey, D.*
8. Robert J. Cornell, D.
9. Robert W. Kasten, Jr., R.

Wyoming
† Teno Roncalio, D.*

Nonvoting Representatives

District of Columbia
Walter E. Fauntroy, D.*

Guam
Antonio Won Pat, D.*

Puerto Rico
Jaime Benitez, D.*

Virgin Islands
Ron de Lugo, D.*

259

CONGRESS OF THE UNITED STATES

Congressman Al Ullman (D., Ore.), one of four new House committee chairmen, took over the House Ways and Means Committee in January.

Ford favored raising food-stamp prices, but he announced on February 13 that he would allow the bill to become law without his signature.

On May 29, the President vetoed a $5.3-billion bill to create 1 million jobs for the unemployed. But on June 26, both houses of Congress approved a 65-week extension of the emergency unemployment-compensation bill, which the President signed on June 30. The Senate completed congressional action on June 12 on a bill providing $373 million to create summer jobs for poor youths. Ford signed it on June 16.

The President also opposed emergency housing legislation. On June 11, the Senate completed congressional action on a $1.2-billion emergency housing bill, but the President vetoed it on June 24. Congress then passed a modified version of the act on June 27, and the President signed it on July 2. The law made $10 million available for the government purchase of housing mortgages at 7.5 per cent. See HOUSING.

On December 19, President Ford vetoed a $36-billion education bill that would also have limited forced school busing because he considered the bill inflationary. On Jan. 2, 1976, he vetoed a bill that would have allowed striking construction workers to shut down an entire building site, even if only one contractor was involved in the labor dispute.

Veto Overrides. The President vetoed a $2-billion health-care bill on July 26, but the Senate overrode the veto that same day and the House overrode it on July 29.

The bill provided $1.42 billion in 1976 and 1977 for grants to states for public health service programs, family-planning programs, and migrant health centers, and an additional $553 million for a two-year training program for nurses.

On July 25, the President vetoed a $7.9-billion education appropriations bill. The House overrode the veto on September 9; the Senate, the next day.

The House passed the National School Lunch and Child Nutrition Act of 1975 on September 18 and the Senate approved it the following day. Charging that the bill was inflationary and provided lunches for children who did not need them, the President vetoed the $2.7-billion measure on October 3. On October 7, both houses overrode.

Price Supports and Strip Mining. The President vetoed price-support bills in 1975 because he viewed them as inflationary. On April 22, the House completed congressional action on a bill to raise price supports for wheat, cotton, and feed grain and to provide price-support loans for milk products. The President vetoed it on May 1. On September 30, the President vetoed a bill providing higher price supports for tobacco.

He also vetoed a strip-mining-control bill. On May 5, the Senate passed a bill requiring stricter regulations for restoring strip-mined lands to productive use after mining operations ceased. The bill passed the House on May 7. But Ford vetoed the bill on May 20, and Congress was unable to override the veto.

Tax Legislation. On March 26, the House and Senate approved a federal tax cut to pump more consumer money into the economy. The bill provided for a $22.8-billion net federal income tax reduction in 1975 and rebates of between $100 and $200 per family on 1974 taxes. It also called for partial repeal of oil and gasoline depletion allowances. The President signed the bill on March 29 with reservations, noting that the tax cuts would mean a federal budget deficit of $60 billion.

In a televised speech on October 6, he suggested that Congress should make $17 billion of the 1975 tax cuts permanent and that another $11 billion in tax cuts should be added. However, he said that he would veto such a measure unless Congress simultaneously made a commitment to reduce federal spending by $28 billion in fiscal 1977.

On December 17, Congress completed final action on a bill calling for $18 billion in tax cuts, but the bill contained no provisions for limiting federal spending. President Ford vetoed the bill the same day. Congress failed to override the veto on December 18. However, to prevent taxes from rising on Jan. 1, 1976, Congress passed a compromise bill on December 19, extending the tax cuts for six months. Since the bill contained some language about holding down spending, the President signed it on December 23.

Transportation Bills. The United States Railway Association, on July 28, submitted a plan to Congress calling for a sweeping reorganization of seven bankrupt Northeastern railroads. Because Congress did not reject it within 60 working days, the plan went into effect at midnight November 8. Under the terms of the plan, the federally financed Consolidated Rail Corporation will take over freight-hauling operations in a 17-state area. It will also operate commuter railroads in the New York metropolitan area.

During the year, Congress also approved $347-million in emergency grants and loans for Northeastern and Midwestern railroads, including the Penn Central. On December 19, Congress passed a $6.5-billion railroad aid bill. However, the Senate did not send the bill to President Ford while Congress was in recess, reportedly because it wanted to prevent a pocket veto. See RAILROAD.

Aid to New York City. New York City came perilously close to bankruptcy and default on its municipal bonds four times during 1975. President Ford at first strongly opposed federal aid for New York City, but on November 26, he proposed legis-

lation that would provide $2.3 billion in short-term seasonal loans. The loans would be administered by the secretary of the treasury at an interest rate 1 percentage point above the federal borrowing rate. Congress passed the bill, and Ford signed it on December 9. See NEW YORK CITY.

Other Measures passed by the first session included:
- Repealing fair-trade laws that allowed price fixing on some consumer products.
- Granting state use of some of the $11.1 billion of impounded highway-construction funds by temporarily relaxing requirements for matching funds.
- Extending the Voting Rights Act of 1965.

Committee Investigations. House and Senate select committees investigated the activities of the Central Intelligence Agency (CIA) and the Federal Bureau of Investigation (FBI) in 1975. The Senate report, issued on November 20, revealed that the CIA was involved in assassination plots against foreign heads of state and in illegal domestic spying activities. The FBI, too, was allegedly involved in illegal burglaries, wiretapping, and other activities. See UNITED STATES, GOVERNMENT OF.   Carol L. Thompson

See also FORD, GERALD RUDOLPH; PRESIDENT OF THE UNITED STATES.

CONNECTICUT. See STATE GOVERNMENT.

"...7, 8, 9, 10...22, 23, 24, 25...32, 33, 34...."

CONSERVATION. Thomas S. Kleppe, former congressman and head of the Small Business Administration, was confirmed as U.S. secretary of the interior on Oct. 9, 1975. Kleppe, a millionaire businessman from North Dakota, succeeded Stanley K. Hathaway as head of the department, in which key environmental actions are centered. See KLEPPE, THOMAS S.

Hathaway, former governor of Wyoming, resigned on July 25 after only 43 days in office. His nomination was vigorously opposed by conservation organizations for what they considered his anti-environment record as governor. Friends said mental pressures resulting from his six-week confirmation battle led to his resignation and hospitalization for depression.

Kleppe struck a middle-of-the-road environmental stance when he told the Senate Interior Committee on September 23: "We must keep in mind that the economic penalty for an error in the direction of overprotection can always be corrected, while the damage from resource abuse may be irreparable. At the same time, we must not permit the proper development of our natural resources to be paralyzed by baseless fear of damage to the environment."

Parks and Recreation. The National Park Service (NPS) was beset by problems as it struggled to

An elephant is airlifted to safety in Rwanda's Kagera National Park. About 100 others were shot to death in the crowded African country.

cope with a record load of nearly 250 million visitors in 1975. It also prepared for even larger crowds, 270 million persons, in 1976, when the United States marks the American Revolution Bicentennial. Services were reduced in some parks because of budget cuts. Park officials campaigned for additional funds by pointing out that the ratio of visitors to employees was 27,000 to 1 in 1960, compared with 44,000 to 1 in 1975.

Some unusual challenges confronted the NPS during the summer. Crater Lake National Park in Oregon was closed between July 11 and August 1 because more than 500 persons became ill after drinking sewage-contaminated water. On May 19, the service banned nudity on the Cape Cod National Seashore. In a "free the beach" gathering on August 23, however, hundreds of nude sunbathers defied the ban at the Truro, Mass., beach, which has been a Mecca for nudists for 40 years.

Gary E. Everhardt, former superintendent of Grand Teton National Park in Wyoming, was named director of the NPS on January 9. Everhardt faced increasing pressure from conservationists stressing preservation of prime scenic and wilderness areas over the accommodation of large numbers of visitors. Congressional and conservationist views often conflict on this issue and on such specific park issues as the role of urban parks, the concession system, and whether roads and accommodations within the parks should be limited. With the park system and the visitor load both expanding rapidly, Everhardt said $3 billion would be required to maintain and restore parks properly. The Department of the Interior asked Congress on October 7 to halt new mining claims in the Death Valley National Monument in California and Nevada. In July, conservationists urged a ban on mining in all park areas when it was reported that strip mining for borates in Death Valley threatened one of the country's most scenic areas. The department's recommendation against banning the filing of claims in the Glacier Bay National Monument in Alaska, in which new mineral discoveries were predicted, also drew criticism.

Endangered Wildlife. Protests against the killing of whales by Japanese fishermen greeted Emperor Hirohito of Japan when he was received at the White House on October 2. The Animal Welfare Institute chartered an airplane that towed a 100-foot (30.5-meter) banner proclaiming "Hirohito, Please Save Our Whales" across the sky in the emperor's view. The action highlighted an unrelenting drive by conservation groups for a complete moratorium on the harvesting of whales. The campaign continued despite Japan's acceptance of the International Whaling Commission's action in London on June 27 that gave almost total protection to the finback whale and drastically reduced catch quotas for other whale species.

In April, conservation workers chased nine migrating whooping cranes from a Nebraska marsh boiling with infectious avian cholera. The U.S. Fish and Wildlife Service trial of a new foster-parent concept in which whooper eggs were snatched from nests in Canada and slipped under nesting sandhill cranes in Idaho also succeeded. Nine of 14 eggs hatched, and six young whoopers survived to begin their migratory flight south.

Three species of trout were eliminated from the endangered species list on July 16 in the first such action since passage of the Endangered Species Conservation Act in 1969. The Fish and Wildlife Service hailed the action as signaling a new era of progress in protecting wildlife. The alligator was removed from the list on September 19 in parts of Louisiana.

In a sweeping but belated action on September 26, the service added 216 species to the endangered list. Those added were listed as "critical" by an international wildlife conference in 1973. The Fund for Animals on May 28 threatened legal action against the Interior Department for "neglect" in not moving more speedily to list 175 animals that the 1973 conference had agreed were nearing extinction.

The National Marine Fisheries Service held hearings in October on proposals to provide greater protection for porpoises. About 100,000 porpoises drown each year when they are trapped in the nets of tuna fishermen. The Marine Mammal Protection Act of 1972 was designed to reduce porpoise kills to an "insignificant level," but progress has been limited in developing fishing methods that reduce the drownings. Conservationists urged Congress to require observers on tuna boats.

Pesticides. The U.S. Environmental Protection Agency (EPA) banned further production of chlordane and heptachlor on July 30 (see CHEMICAL INDUSTRY). On September 17, the EPA lifted its ban on use of cyanide poison guns to kill coyotes on Western rangelands. Charges by woolgrowers that coyotes were taking a heavy toll of sheep had steadily mounted since the ban was imposed in 1972. The National Wildlife Federation called the action a "significant setback." Congress defeated on October 3 a proposal to give the secretary of agriculture veto power over EPA's pesticide-control programs.

Water Resources. A national conference on water produced warnings on April 23 that the drive to develop new energy supplies in Western states may create a water crisis. The Water Resources Congress told the meeting in Washington, D.C., that better planning is needed to avert a water crisis by 1985.   Andrew L. Newman

See also COAL; ENVIRONMENT.

CONSTITUTION, UNITED STATES. See UNITED STATES CONSTITUTION.

CONSUMER AFFAIRS. The cost of living continued as the biggest problem for U.S. consumers in 1975, though the rate of increase slowed somewhat. The government's Consumer Price Index rose 9.1 per cent, substantially higher than officials in President Gerald R. Ford's Administration had predicted. However, it was below 1974's 12 per cent rise. A sudden jump of 1.8 per cent in the Wholesale Price Index for October, the largest increase in 12 months, foreshadowed significant increases at the retail level as the year ended.

Fuel prices again rose faster than the average of all other commodities. But gasoline prices dropped a few cents per gallon (3.8 liters) in October before resuming their upward march, mainly because of import prices.

American consumers could take credit for helping to restrain — and even reverse — some price advances. Ironically, President Ford's WIN (Whip Inflation Now) program sputtered to a halt just as the public appeared to take matters into its own hands. A silent but massive buyer boycott of sugar at the beginning of the year was generally credited with wiping out a 300 per cent price jump in this commodity registered late in 1974.

The Rebate Craze. Buyer resistance to huge price increases for 1975 automobiles — averaging $630 — cut deeply into sales. The sales losses were so large that manufacturers offered $100 to $500 in rebates to stimulate purchases. Despite these rebates, sales declined more than 15 per cent from 1974-model levels, which were also below normal. As a result, automakers limited price increases on 1976 models to an average of $248, only 57 per cent of actual cost increases, according to the government's Council on Wage and Price Stability.

Price rebates also spread to other commodities, notably small appliances. The word *rebate* became a popular sales ploy featured by retailers, even where there were no actual savings. Catching the spirit, the Civil Aeronautics Board approved, on an experimental basis, a discount air-fare plan for several airlines that lasted most of the year. The U.S. Congress and the President authorized a $12-billion income tax cut, including rebates of as much as $200 to taxpayers, to stimulate the economy.

Higher fuel prices, along with government pleas for energy conservation, noticeably reduced total fuel consumption. Figures released in 1975 showed that the annual growth rate in the use of electric power, which had averaged 7 per cent, slowed to less than 1 per cent in 1974. The growth rate increased in 1975 but went no higher than 3 per cent. As a result, many public utilities canceled plans for new power plants, and rate increases fell far below those of the previous year. Public resentment of large increases in fuel bills, particularly for electricity, spawned new citizen organizations and helped to slow the rising price of fuel.

Changes in Living Styles. Pressed by constantly rising prices, especially for such basic commodities as food and fuel, millions of Americans changed their way of living. Highway travel, as measured by fuel consumption, continued below the 1973 level, though slightly above that of 1974.

The trend toward buying smaller cars that use less fuel continued, as U.S. auto manufacturers fought off foreign-car competition by introducing their own small models. To meet the demand for greater fuel economy, Detroit managed to boost the miles-per-gallon ratio on their 1976 models 26.6 per cent above what it was two years earlier.

Public interest in energy efficiency also reached into the field of appliances. Many advertisements for appliances focused on fuel costs. And the U.S. Department of Commerce launched a campaign to get appliance manufacturers to reduce energy consumption by an average of 20 per cent by 1980.

One major bottleneck to consumer savings cropped up, however, for people who had planned to beat the high price of food by canning produce from home gardens. The supply of canning lids fell far short of demand, causing much home-grown food to be wasted. No explanation was found for the "Great Canning Lid Shortage," despite investigations by several government agencies and congressional committees.

Simplified Language

The old Master Charge agreement of the First National Bank of Boston:

Cardholder and any other person applying for, using or signing the card promise, jointly and severally, to pay to Bank the principal of all loans plus, as provided in paragraph 4. FINANCE CHARGES. Payments shall be made each month at Bank or as Bank may direct, on or before the Payment Due Date, in the amount of (a) the greater of $10 or an amount equal to 1/36th of the Total Debit Balance not in excess of the Maximum Credit on the related Statement Date plus (b) any amounts owing and delinquent plus (c) any excess of the Total Debit Balance over the Maximum Credit.

The new agreement, in simplified terms:

You must pay us a monthly minimum payment. This monthly minimum payment will be 1/36 of the balance plus, of course, any amounts which are past due, but at least $10. If the balance is less than $10, the minimum payment will be the entire balance. The balance will include the outstanding amount that you have borrowed plus a finance charge.

As a service to customers, several banks use simpler loan contracts that are written in language that is easy to understand.

Legislative Changes. Consumer leaders reaped a meager legislative harvest. A four-year battle in Congress to set up a new federal agency to monitor other government agencies on behalf of the consuming public once again faced defeat. President Ford threatened to veto a compromise measure that passed the House by only nine votes. The National Association of Manufacturers, the U.S. Chamber of Commerce, and the National Federation of Independent Business led opposition to the proposed plan.

However, several major pieces of legislation became effective during the year. The Magnuson-Moss Warranty Act, which became effective on July 5, requires any manufacturer offering a product warranty under the law's jurisdiction to declare the warranty either "full" or "limited." Under a full warranty, the product must be repaired or replaced free of charge "within a reasonable time" if found defective, or the purchase price must be refunded in full. The Federal Trade Commission (FTC), the agency in charge of administering the law, spent the rest of the year drawing up regulations and definitions that would make the law work effectively.

A law requiring home-mortgage lenders to issue statements before settlement disclosing closing costs also became effective, on June 20. Lenders also must provide borrowers with a booklet explaining their rights under the law and the various costs involved. But within a few weeks, complaints from both lenders and borrowers began flowing into congressional offices. In response, legislators began drafting revisions to the law to relax its most controversial requirement—that the disclosure statement be furnished 12 days before final settlement is made.

Also becoming effective in 1975 were two amendments to the Truth-in-Lending Law—the Fair Credit Billing Act and the Equal Credit Opportunity Act. The billing act gives credit purchasers new rights to get monthly bill errors corrected. In brief, a store must respond within 30 days when a billing error is alleged in writing. The store has 90 days to either correct the error or explain why there is no error. During that time, the customer does not have to pay the disputed amount or finance charges on the bill, and the store cannot report the account as delinquent to a credit bureau. The Equal Credit Opportunity Act makes it illegal for lenders to deny credit to any individual on the basis of sex.

Law Enforcement. An anticonsumer trend became discernible in key decisions by the Supreme Court of the United States, reversing an earlier trend. The court decided to restrict sporadic efforts of the government to enforce laws against merger and monopoly, curb the right of citizens to recover for injuries and damages, and reduce the rights of shareholders. A notable exception was the court's ruling that "minimum" lawyers' fees for real estate settlements violate antitrust laws.

The FTC created an unprecedented flurry of activity against deceptive advertising. In August, the agency announced complaints against diet pills, facial-hair removers, home-improvement companies, mail-order firms, retail chain stores, skin-care products, tax-preparation services, and truckdriver schools. The agency also proposed guidelines to reduce deceptive advertising claims for automobile fuel economy, funeral services, and protein food supplements.

Private Organizations. Voluntary groups organized to fight against consumer abuse continued to proliferate. They tended to focus on specialized rather than broad consumer interests. Typical were several new groups created to combat utility rates and policies.

Traditional consumer organizations fell on hard times, however, because of the recession and an apparently hostile Administration in Washington, D.C. Consumers Union of the United States (CU), the largest such group, reported a $3-million loss in fiscal 1974-1975 in contributions and subscriptions to its monthly magazine *Consumer Reports,* requiring it to slash its staff and curtail many of its operations.

Arthur E. Rowse

See also BANKS AND BANKING.

COPPOLA, FRANCIS FORD (1939-   ), in April, 1975, won the Academy of Motion Picture Arts and Sciences award as best director of the year for *The Godfather, Part II.* The tale of a family in the world of organized crime, it was a sequel to his 1972 award-winning movie, *The Godfather.*

Coppola was born on April 7, 1939, in Detroit, but grew up in New York City. His father was a flutist and composer; his mother, a film actress.

He earned his B.A. degree in theater from Hofstra University in Hempstead, N.Y., in 1959 and his M.A. from the University of California, Los Angeles, film school. While there, he worked with a producer of horror films and also began building his reputation as a screenwriter. His critically acclaimed *You're a Big Boy Now* was released in 1966.

He then directed two films for Warner Brothers, *Finian's Rainbow* and *The Rain People.* But he became unhappy with the "overcontrol" he felt the major studios exerted, and set up his own film company in 1969. However, he ran into financial trouble and had to accept a job with Paramount Pictures Corporation directing *The Godfather.*

Among his other screenwriting and directing credits are *Reflections in a Golden Eye, Patton, The Conversation,* and *The Great Gatsby.* He also owns interests in a film-distributing company and a magazine.

Darlene R. Stille

COSTA RICA. See LATIN AMERICA.

COURTS AND LAWS. Attempts to promote international law by strengthening the United Nations International Court of Justice in The Hague, the Netherlands, met with disappointing results in 1975. One proposal, endorsed by a group of South American jurists, would have encouraged appointment of distinguished jurists to the 15-member court and given it some authority. Most of the court's opinions are nonbinding. But little enthusiasm developed for increasing the importance of the court. When Australia's Prime Minister Gough Whitlam announced in February that his government would recognize International Court opinions as binding, for example, he was heavily criticized for yielding potential Australian sovereignty over matters such as use of the continental shelf.

The International Court's major opinion of the year, a nonbinding advisory on disposition of the Spanish Sahara, was all but ignored by the countries involved. After accepting on January 16 a petition to review the case, the court determined that neither Morocco, Mauritania, nor Algeria had legally binding claims to annex Spain's African desert colony. The court urged on October 16 that the decolonization process should honor the rights of the territorial people "to determine their future political status by their own freely expressed will." This call for a referendum went unheeded, however. King Hassan II of Morocco ordered thousands of unarmed Moroccans to march into the Sahara and then proceeded to work out a political solution with Spain that gave Morocco half of the territory. See MOROCCO.

Legal Fees. In the United States, a series of rulings by the Supreme Court of the United States that attacked traditional precepts jolted the legal profession. The most significant decision removed lawyers' immunity from antitrust laws. In a unanimous decision on June 16, the court, through Chief Justice Warren E. Burger, labeled bar association setting of minimum-fee schedules as "a classic illustration of price fixing," and ordered that free market price competition in fee setting be restored.

The decision and its implications occupied much of the annual American Bar Association (ABA) convention, in Montreal, Canada, in August. Amid threats of further Department of Justice antitrust action, an ABA study committee recommended on December 6 that the association consider allowing attorneys to place tasteful advertising for their services in mass media.

The Supreme Court's decision on June 30 that a criminal defendant has the constitutional right to reject his court-appointed attorney and defend himself, and a May 12 ruling prohibiting parties bringing environmental class-action lawsuits from collecting attorney's fees unless such awards are specifically authorized by statute, also bothered some lawyers.

Criminal Code. After five years of sporadic study and revision, the longest bill ever submitted to the U.S. Congress, the Criminal Justice Reform Act, a 750-page recodification of the federal criminal code, was submitted in December for formal congressional debate. Although critics charged that the bill endangered First Amendment freedoms, particularly those of free speech and free press, the ABA House of Delegates endorsed recodification.

The bill included controversial sections that would punish persons who disclose or receive national defense information, define and limit insanity defenses, reinstate the death penalty for specific crimes, legalize temporary government wiretapping without court order, and facilitate the conviction of persons goaded into illegal action by police trickery. Code defenders asserted the provisions were either found in existing laws or were necessary to meet the challenge of rising crime rates.

A long-awaited Supreme Court review of the new death-penalty laws, on the books in 34 states, was delayed because of Justice William O. Douglas' health. He retired in November. John Paul Stevens was sworn in as his replacement on December 19. See STEVENS, JOHN PAUL.   Davis C. Beckwith

See also CIVIL RIGHTS; CONSUMER AFFAIRS; SUPREME COURT OF THE UNITED STATES.

CRIME. Terrorism, particularly by urban guerrillas, continued to plague governments worldwide during 1975, prompting increased calls for international cooperation in combating the widespread violence. In the United States, the bloodiest single incident occurred on December 29 when a bomb exploded in a locker near a crowded baggage claim area at New York City's La Guardia Airport, killing 11 persons and injuring 75.

President Gerald R. Ford was the target of two assassination attempts in California during the year. On September 5, as Ford was walking through a Sacramento park, a .45-caliber semiautomatic pistol was pointed at him from 2 feet (61 centimeters) away. A Secret Service agent collared Lynette Alice (Squeaky) Fromme, 26, a follower of cult leader Charles Manson. Fromme was convicted on November 26 of attempted assassination of the President and was sentenced on December 17 to life imprisonment.

On September 22, a .38-caliber bullet was fired at Ford as he emerged from a hotel in San Francisco. Oliver Sipple, a retired marine, noticed a gun in the hand of Sara Jane Moore, 45, and deflected the shot. Moore, active in social causes and a onetime informer for the Federal Bureau of Investigation (FBI), pleaded guilty; she received a life sentence on Jan. 15, 1976.

Guarded by a policewoman, Emily Harris, left, and Patricia Hearst raise defiant fists after their court arraignment in San Francisco.

Low in Hijacking. Due to tightened security measures, airplane hijackings declined, with half a dozen serious incidents throughout the world during the year. But kidnaping, bombing, extortion, and murder by political activists were plentiful. The year's most spectacular terrorism was the December 2 hijacking of a Dutch train and the takeover of the Indonesian consulate in Amsterdam, the Netherlands, two days later by South Moluccan extremists. The Moluccans, seeking Dutch assistance in obtaining independence from Indonesia for their Pacific islands, grabbed 88 hostages at the two locations and murdered three hostages held on the train. On December 14, the six Moluccans on the train surrendered, and seven confederates in the consulate followed suit five days later.

In the United States, crime continued to rise significantly. FBI statistics showed that major crime rose 13 per cent during the first six months of 1975. Continuing a trend, crimes against property showed the most sizable gains. Burglary rose 14 per cent; larceny, 14 per cent; and auto theft, 4 per cent. The FBI index of violent crimes also reflected increases. Murder was up 4 per cent; aggravated assault, 9 per cent; robbery, 17 per cent; and rape, 4 per cent. As in recent years, the greatest increase was in rural and suburban crime, with gains of 15 and 14 per cent, respectively. Urban crime rose 12 per cent.

The FBI, stung by criticism in recent years over its failure to capture wanted radical leftists, recouped during 1975 by snaring half a dozen longtime fugitives – Susan Saxe, Patricia Swinton, Cameron Bishop, Patricia Hearst, and Emily and William Harris. Capture of the Harrises and Hearst on September 18, along with Wendy Yoshimura, ended one of the largest federal manhunts in history. On October 2, Hearst and the Harrises were indicted in Los Angeles on 11 counts each of robbery, kidnaping, and assault. On November 7, a federal judge ruled Hearst was fit to stand trial, after receiving psychiatric reports on her mental state. She entered a plea of not guilty.

Hoffa Missing. James R. Hoffa, 62, former international president of the Teamsters Union, disappeared on July 30 in a Detroit suburb. Months of intense work by federal and local investigators failed to find Hoffa. One theory was that Hoffa was killed because he had threatened to disclose syndicate infiltration of the Teamsters Union and misuse of Teamster pension funds.

The year's most celebrated criminal trial resulted in acquittal on August 15 for Joan Little, a black accused of murdering a white guard with an ice pick while trying to escape from the Washington, N.C., jail in 1974. Little claimed she was defending herself against rape, and her case attracted widespread interest from feminist and civil rights groups.   David C. Beckwith

CUBA moved closer to normal relations with other American nations in 1975. Sixteen of the 24 members of the Organization of American States (OAS) voted on July 29 to lift the diplomatic and economic sanctions adopted in 1964 and allow more normal relations on a bilateral basis.

There was a thaw in the frosty relations between Prime Minister Fidel Castro and the United States following a speech in Houston by U.S. Secretary of State Henry A. Kissinger on March 1. Kissinger held out the possibility of détente with Cuba. In July, Castro announced his readiness to return a ransom of nearly $2 million paid by the Southern Airways airline to three U.S. hijackers who landed in Havana in 1972; a check was sent to the airline in August.

A number of U.S. senators visited Havana during the year, including Senator George S. McGovern (D., S. Dak.) and Senator Edward M. Kennedy (D., Mass.). But there were no specific moves toward lifting the U.S. economic embargo imposed in 1962 or restoring diplomatic relations. Following the OAS vote, the United States relaxed trade curbs. In particular, foreign subsidiaries of U.S.-owned companies were no longer banned from exporting to Cuba.

Despite assurances by Vice-President Carlos Rafael Rodríguez that Cuba was no longer inter-

U.S. Senator George McGovern, center, takes a sightseeing tour of Cuba in a jeep chauffeured by the island's Prime Minister Fidel Castro.

ested in backing guerrilla groups, Castro's foreign policy still generated U.S. concern. Two examples were Cuban support of Puerto Rican independence groups at a conference held in Havana in September and the sending of Cuban troops to Angola to fight with the pro-Russian Popular Movement for the Liberation of Angola.

Political Reorganization. In April, it was announced that the first congress of the Cuban Communist Party would be held in December, at which approval would be asked for a new constitution that would establish a governing national assembly elected by all citizens over the age of 16. On December 22, a draft constitution was adopted, making Cuba's conversion into a Communist state complete. Castro's informal style of government would be replaced by a hierarchy of rigidly structured institutions, with the Communist Party as "the overall directing force." A referendum was scheduled for Feb. 15, 1976.

The Economy. Despite another low sugar harvest, partly because of a winter drought, Cuba managed to produce another modest trade surplus. This resulted mainly because of the high world sugar price and a new price agreement with Russia, which will pay about 30 cents a pound (0.45 kilogram) for Cuban sugar until 1980, compared with about 19.6 cents in 1974.   Robert Moss

See also LATIN AMERICA (Facts in Brief Table).

CYPRUS. Turkish Cypriot leaders, on February 13, 1975, proclaimed a federated Turkish state in the northern part of Cyprus. Rauf Denktash, leader of the Turkish Cypriot community, was declared head of the new state. He denied that the action amounted to partition or that it was a unilateral declaration of independence. He claimed it was purely in preparation for the birth of a federal state of Cyprus.

Thousands of Greek Cypriots demonstrated peacefully against the proclamation in Nicosia, and the Greek Cypriot leader, Archbishop Makarios III, pledged resistance. Prime Minister Constantine Caramanlis of Greece described the measures as "arbitrary, unlawful, and in contradiction of international treaties and resolutions." Russia backed Makarios and restated its call for a United Nations (UN)-sponsored conference on Cyprus.

The UN Security Council expressed "regrets" on March 12 over the unilateral decision. The Council unanimously approved a resolution calling for a resumption of talks under the "personal auspices" of UN Secretary-General Kurt Waldheim.

Waldheim met Denktash and Greek Cypriot leader Glafcos Clerides in Vienna, Austria, on April 28, and the two Cypriot leaders agreed to form a committee to consider proposals for a new central government for the island. They also discussed the disposition of refugees during four days of meetings. Negotiations continued through the summer, but a fourth round of UN-sponsored talks in New York City ended in deadlock in September.

Greek Cypriots staged mass rallies in Nicosia and other towns on November 10 demanding a settlement "through the United Nations." Denktash talked with Turkish Prime Minister Suleyman Demirel in Ankara on November 24 to push his demands for a unilateral declaration of independence. "Makarios," he said, "has no intention of reaching an agreement with the Turkish-Cypriot community to establish a two-zone federated independent state."

Women Walk Home. More than 20,000 Greek Cypriot women and about 200 foreign women staged a peaceful demonstration on April 20 to draw attention to the plight of an estimated 200,000 refugees made homeless by the 1974 civil war. Men were barred from taking part in the 2½-mile (4-kilometer) token walk to a UN checkpoint dividing Greek Cypriot and Turkish troops outside the Turkish-held port of Famagusta. Turkish authorities refused to accept a petition presented by the women. Sympathy walks in Athens, Greece; Berlin, West Germany; London; New York City; and Toronto, Canada, were supported by more than 700 women's organizations.   Kenneth Brown

See also GREECE; MIDDLE EAST (Facts in Brief Table); TURKEY; UNITED NATIONS.

CZECHOSLOVAKIA. The Federal Assembly elected Communist Party First Secretary Gustav Husak president of Czechoslovakia on May 29, 1975, signaling a more moderate policy line. He replaced the ailing 79-year-old Ludvik Svoboda. But in July, Viliam Salgovic, former chief of the secret police, became chairman of the Slovak National Assembly. He was also named to the party's Central Committee and to the Presidium.

Former liberal party leader Alexander Dubček was expelled from his trade union in April after a 1974 letter he had written criticizing the Presidium was published in the West. Husak branded Dubček a traitor, and on April 16, police reportedly searched the homes of some 100 prominent Czechoslovaks who were suspected of supporting Dubček. They confiscated a 250-page manuscript from Zdenek Mlynar, a former Central Committee secretary. The document, which analyzed the 1968 Russian invasion of Czechoslovakia, was to have served as a point of discussion at a European Communist Party conference.

Dissident writers Vaclav Havel and Ludvik Vaculik and philosopher Karel Kosik published attacks in the West on the Husak regime. However, two well-known authors, Jiri Sotola and Bohumil Hrabal, joined the Czechoslovak Writers' Union.

Daring Airlift. Czechoslovakia charged on August 21 that West Germany and Austria had aided an American helicopter pilot who flew several East Germans out of Czechoslovakia on August 15 and 17. The official Czechoslovak news agency called the flights "gross infringements of the Czechoslovak border." The pickups were made on a sand bar in the Vltava River in southern Czechoslovakia near the Austrian border. In the August 17 attempt, the pilot was wounded and the copilot, a Pole living in West Germany, was captured.

Martina Navratilova, a Czechoslovak tennis star who was playing in U.S. tournaments, announced on September 6 that she wanted to stay in the United States permanently.

Economic Moves. Czechoslovakia signed 10-year economic trade agreements with West Germany in January and with France in November. The government said in November that Western firms will be allowed to set up independent representation in Czechoslovakia. Imports from both East and West went up 14.5 per cent. Exports rose 11.7 per cent, and industrial output rose 7 per cent in the first six months, compared to the first six months of 1974. Coal output, however, was only 0.2 per cent higher, and the country's grain harvest dropped to 10.8 million short tons (9.8 metric tons) – below the 1974 record crop.   Chris Cviic

See also EUROPE (Facts in Brief Table).

DAHOMEY. See AFRICA.

DAIRYING. See AGRICULTURE.

DALEY, RICHARD JOSEPH (1902-   ), easily won election to an unprecedented sixth 4-year term as mayor of Chicago on April 1, 1975. He has been in office since 1955, longer than any other mayor in Chicago's history. He crushed token Republican opposition by more than 400,000 votes, despite only lukewarm support by much of Chicago's press, the indictment and conviction of several aides and associates for political corruption, and concern for his health. Daley suffered a stroke in May, 1974.

Daley controls the powerful Cook County Democratic organization, the strongest political machine in the nation. He is expected to be a powerful force at the 1976 Democratic National Convention, despite his humiliation at the 1972 convention, when his regular Democratic delegation was unseated by a group of independent Democrats.

In July, Daley received the Distinguished Service Award of the United States Conference of Mayors at the conference's annual meeting in Boston.

Daley was born in Chicago and has spent his life in politics. He received his undergraduate and law degrees from DePaul University there and served in both state legislative houses, as state revenue director, and as Cook County clerk before becoming mayor. He and his wife, Eleanor, live in a modest home in the neighborhood in which he was born. They have seven children.   Edward G. Nash

See also CHICAGO.

DALLAS-FORT WORTH. The population of both Dallas and Fort Worth declined between 1970 and 1973, according to a report issued in mid-1975 by the U.S. Census Bureau. Dallas lost 3.4 per cent of its population, while Fort Worth suffered an 8.6 per cent decline. The estimated population as of July 1, 1973, was 815,866 in Dallas and 359,542 in Fort Worth.

Dallas imposed its first property-tax increase in four years in 1975, increasing its levy by 4.5 cents per $100 of property valuation. City leaders saw the tax increase as necessary to help finance the city's $272-million budget. Dallas also cut back on the city budget, including eliminating 481 municipal jobs.

Wes Wise was re-elected on April 1 to serve a third term as mayor of Dallas.

School Desegregation Ordered. The U.S. Fifth Circuit Court of Appeals ordered the Dallas Independent School District on July 23 to devise a desegregation plan for Dallas schools. The appeals court ruled that a 1971 desegregation plan drawn up by U.S. District Court Judge William M. Taylor, Jr., was inadequate and directed that the new plan be implemented by January, 1976.

The school district presented a new plan, but Judge Taylor rejected it as inadequate on September 16. Then on October 16, the judge announced that a new desegregation plan might have to be delayed until August, 1976. He noted that implementing a busing plan in the middle of the school year would be very disruptive.

Transportation Developments. The National Railroad Passenger Corporation (Amtrak) began passenger service between Dallas and Chicago on July 1. The service is a branch of Amtrak's Chicago-Houston train, the *Lone Star*, which also serves Fort Worth.

A federal grand jury indicted Braniff International Airways and Texas International Airlines on February 14 on charges of conspiring to monopolize airline business in Dallas-Fort Worth as well as in the Houston and San Antonio areas. The airlines allegedly attempted to exclude Southwest Airlines from operating at the major airports in those cities.

The Economy. Living costs in the Dallas area rose 8.9 per cent between August, 1974, and August, 1975, while the average annual earnings of factory workers increased 10 per cent by midyear, to $9,013. During the same period, food costs in the area rose 10.2 per cent. Department store sales increased 10.3 per cent, while construction activity fell 22.3 per cent. The unemployment rate dropped 1.8 per cent to 5.8 per cent by midyear.

The *Fort Worth Press* published its last edition on May 30. The afternoon newspaper, financially ailing for some years, had a daily circulation of about 40,000 when it was shut down.   James M. Banovetz

DAM. See BUILDING AND CONSTRUCTION.

DANCING

Although dance has been booming for the last five years, it was never as glamorous as it was in 1975. Individual personality, rather than choreography or artistic achievement, was the keynote.

Valery and Galina Panov, who had been fired from Leningrad's Kirov Ballet and otherwise harassed for wanting to emigrate to Israel, finally made their United States debut on February 4 in a sports arena in Philadelphia. What and how they danced was not as important as the mere fact that they performed.

Mikhail Baryshnikov, a 1974 defector from the Kirov, drew sellout audiences wherever and whenever he performed with the American Ballet Theatre. He appeared on the cover of both *Time* and *Newsweek* magazines, and he was the reason CBS could broadcast a film of an obscure, nine-year-old dance competition staged in Varna, Bulgaria. He had been a participant. See BARYSHNIKOV, MIKHAIL.

Rudolf Nureyev was the only one who rivaled Baryshnikov's popularity. Only Nureyev could successfully organize a dance package known as *Nureyev and Friends.* The production was no more than a potpourri of dancers and dance styles, held together by Nureyev. *Nureyev and Friends* first held forth in New York City's Uris Theater from Dec. 26, 1974, to Jan. 25, 1975. It was a varied program, ranging from a 19th-century pas de deux by Bournonville to a modern dance by Paul Taylor, and the dancers' abilities were equally diverse. Nureyev danced in each of the four ballets every night.

A second version of *Nureyev and Friends,* including Margot Fonteyn, appeared at the Kennedy Center in Washington, D.C., for two weeks in July and for another two at the Uris Theater in November. Although different in programming and personnel, it again was viable because of Nureyev. The same might be said of the National Ballet of Canada's engagement at the Metropolitan Opera House in New York City from July 22 to August 10. Nureyev danced in every performance but one.

The biggest Nureyev wave, however, occurred when he joined ranks with the grand lady of modern dance, Martha Graham. The Graham company held a benefit for itself on June 19 in New York City that was highlighted by a new piece, *Lucifer,* created by Graham especially for Nureyev. Cross-fertilization between modern dance and ballet has been an important trend recently, but Nureyev's virtual transplant from ballet to Graham technique, the epitome of modern-dance style, was unprecedented. Graham's new production was interesting primarily because of Nureyev's participation in it. However, she also revived a number of her dance masterpieces from the 1930s and 1940s for her company's spring tour of the East and Midwest. Based on American themes, they constitute a formidable contribution to the American Revolution Bicentennial celebration.

American Ballet Theatre (ABT) had the most successful year of its 35-year history, partly because its principal dancers and repertory of full-length ballets dovetailed with the audience's attraction to glamour. In addition to its usual roster of Baryshnikov, Gelsey Kirkland, Fernando Bujones, Cynthia Gregory, and Natalia Makarova, it hosted several illustrious guest artists.

Erik Bruhn came out of retirement on January 11 to dance an excerpt from *Miss Julie* for a gala 35th birthday party. So electrifying was his performance that he decided to dance with ABT during its New York season, from July 1 to August 9, at the New York State Theater.

ABT's second gala, on July 28, featured Alicia Alonso, now head of the National Ballet of Cuba, but formerly the prima ballerina of ABT. This was her first appearance in the United States since the 1959 Cuban revolution and it pointed to a possible cultural exchange between the two nations.

Finally, there was the ever-present Nureyev, this time in the role of choreographer as well as dancer. The vehicle was a reconstruction of Petipa's full-length *Raymonda.* Nureyev's version of the Russian classic premièred in Houston on June 26 and opened ABT's New York season on July 1. Nureyev and Bruhn danced the male lead roles. Although critical reception was generally poor, *Raymonda* offered a fine opportunity for stargazing. It was the only item on the bill during ABT's miniseason at the Uris Theater from November 4 to 16, which preceded the company's major winter season at the City Center.

New Works. More significant, but less sensational, for ABT was a new ballet by Antony Tudor that premièred on July 17. *The Leaves Are Fading* is Tudor's first nonnarrative ballet and the first ballet he has created in a decade. Most critics appreciated Tudor's new-found lyricism, though some felt that *The Leaves Are Fading* lacks the trenchancy of his psychological works of the 1940s. Because Tudor ballets are rare, revivals of any of them are always noteworthy. In 1975, there were two: *Shadowplay,* danced by ABT for the first time on July 23, and *Offenbach in the Underworld,* unveiled by the City Center Joffrey Ballet at Chicago's Ravinia Festival in August.

The New York City Ballet's big event centered, typically, around choreography. It presented a

Vladimir Vasiliev and Natalya Bessmertnova starred in the Bolshoi Ballet's presentation of *Spartacus* during a United States tour.

Dancers of the Dutch National Ballet, appearing in Toronto, Canada, portray the agony of not belonging, in Rudi van Dantzig's *Ramifications*.

Ravel Festival of 16 new ballets by George Balanchine, Jerome Robbins, John Taras, and Jacques d'Amboise between May 15 and 31. Much fanfare surrounded the festival, but the artistic rewards were considered feeble. Still, there was one fine ballet from Balanchine – *Le Tombeau de Couperin*, possibly a masterpiece. Set for two quadrilles, it is a perfect example of Balanchine's genius for geometrically precise construction and for calling forth the most delightful aspects of courtly manner and style.

Other New Works were Eliot Feld's *Mazurka*, set to music of Chopin, premièred by the Eliot Feld Ballet on July 8 at Wolf Trap Farm in Virginia, and *Excursions*, first seen on October 15 during the company's six-week season at the Public Theater in New York City. Paul Taylor came up with a winner in *Esplanade*, which premièred March 1 in Washington, D.C. He formulated such activities as walking and falling into theatrical shape. Setting these activities to the music of Bach added great punch.

Visiting Troupes. The Bolshoi Ballet's visit to the Metropolitan Opera House from April 22 to May 24 and its subsequent eight-week tour of major U.S. cities was very controversial. The debate centered around Yuri Grigorovich's mammoth spectacles, *Spartacus* and *Ivan the Terrible*. Did Grigorovich really blend dance and drama, or was

each sacrificed to the other? Were they propaganda pieces, or epic dramas? Was the flamboyant style of choreography hopelessly backward compared to Western standards, or just different? However, there was nothing but acclaim for many of the dancers, such as Vladimir Vasiliev, Ludmilla Semenyaka, and Vyacheslav Gordeyev, as the standardbearers of the great Russian ballet tradition.

Other visitors to the United States included the Stuttgart Ballet, under the direction of Glen Tetley. It appeared at the Metropolitan Opera House from May 27 to June 21, and at Washington's Kennedy Center for the next two weeks. The program included new ballets by Tetley and old favorites by John Cranko, the Stuttgart's director until his death in 1973. Dancers and musicians of the Burmese National Theater visited the United States and Canada for the first time in October. But a transcontinental tour by the Performing Arts Troupe of the People's Republic of China was canceled when the U.S. Department of State objected to a song referring to the liberation of Taiwan.

Charles E. Weidman, who, with Doris Humphrey, was a pioneer of modern dance as a dancer, choreographer, and teacher, died on July 15. The Harkness Ballet disbanded at the end of March after a tour of the Eastern Seaboard. Rebekah Harkness, its director, attributed the demise to financial troubles.   Nancy Goldner

DEATHS OF NOTABLE PERSONS in 1975 included those listed below. An asterisk (*) indicates the person is the subject of a biography in THE WORLD BOOK ENCYCLOPEDIA. Those listed were Americans unless otherwise indicated.

Adderley, Julian E. (Cannonball) (1928-Aug. 8), jazz saxophonist whose hits included "African Waltz" and "Mercy, Mercy, Mercy."

*__Anderson, Clinton P.__ (1895-Nov. 10), a Democratic senator from New Mexico from 1949 to 1973 and secretary of agriculture from 1945 to 1948.

Anderson, Leroy (1908-May 18), composer of popular music whose works included "Sleigh Ride."

*__Andrić, Ivo__ (1892-March 13), Yugoslav writer who won the 1961 Nobel Prize in Literature for his novel *Bridge on the Drina* (1945) and other works.

Angle, Paul M. (1900-May 11), historian and director of the Chicago Historical Society who published many books on Abraham Lincoln.

Arendt, Hannah (1906-Dec. 4), German-born author who became one of America's foremost political philosophers. Her many books include *On Violence* (1970).

Bailey, John M. (1904-April 10), Democratic national chairman from 1961 to 1968.

Baker, Josephine (1906-April 12), American-born singer and dancer who became one of France's greatest music-hall stars.

Baring, Walter S. (1911-July 13), Democratic politician, Nevada's lone congressman for 20 years.

Beatty, Morgan (1902-July 4), news correspondent and radio broadcaster for more than 50 years.

*__Benton, Thomas Hart__ (1889-Jan. 19), the crusty old man of American painting whose bold, stylized murals reflect homespun Americana.

Black, Eli M. (1921-Feb. 3), chairman of the billion-dollar United Brands Company, a former rabbi, and a generous patron of the arts.

Blaise, Pierre (1951-Aug. 31), French film actor who starred in the acclaimed *Lacombe, Lucien* (1974).

Blue, Ben (Ben Bernstein) (1900-March 7), sad-faced comedian-pantomimist.

Borbón, Prince Jaime de (1908-March 20), oldest son of the late King Alfonso XIII of Spain, who renounced his claim to the Spanish throne in 1931 in favor of his brother Don Juan.

Botkin, Benjamin A. (1901-July 30), authority on American folklore whose many books include the trail-blazing *Lay My Burden Down: A Folk History of Slavery.*

Branigin, Roger D. (1902-Nov. 19), Democratic governor of Indiana from 1965 to 1969.

Bronk, Detlev W. (1897-Nov. 17), biophysicist, president emeritus of Rockefeller University and former president of the National Academy of Sciences.

Brown, Pamela (1917-Sept. 18), British actress who won an Emmy for her performance as the Duchess of Kent in *Victoria Regina* (1961).

Brundage, Avery (1887-May 8), president of the International Olympic Committee from 1952 to 1972.

Buckley, Tim (1947-June 29), composer and rock singer whose records included "Goodbye and Hello" and "Move with Me."

*__Bulganin, Nikolai A.__ (1895-Feb. 24), Russian premier from 1955 to 1958.

Bundy, May S. (1887-Oct. 4), whose forehand drive and fighting spirit made her the first American to win a tennis championship at Wimbledon, in 1905.

Burkhalter, Everett G. (1897-May 26), Democratic congressman from California from 1962 to 1964.

Burns, John A. (1909-April 5), Democratic governor of Hawaii from 1962 to 1974.

Carpentier, Georges (1894-Oct. 28), French boxer who lost on a fourth-round knockout to Jack Dempsey in boxing's first $1-million gate in Jersey City, N.J., in 1921.

Nikolai Bulganin was Russian premier from 1955 to 1958.

Cardinal Mindszenty, a religious leader.

Thomas Hart Benton was a renowned mural artist.

Susan Hayward, an Oscar-winning star.

Charles, Ezzard M. (1921-May 28), world heavyweight boxing champion from 1949 to 1951.

*__Chiang Kai-shek__ (1887-April 5), political and military leader of Nationalist China since 1928. He headed the Nationalist government in Taiwan after the 1949 Communist victory in China. See Close-Up.

Considine, Bob (Robert Bernard) (1906-Sept. 25), adventurous reporter and columnist whose "On the Line" column ran for more than 40 years.

Conte, Richard (1916-April 15), actor who often portrayed gangsters and world-weary heroes.

Coolidge, William D. (1873-Feb. 3), physical chemist and engineer who developed the "Coolidge tube," the basis of modern X-ray units, in 1913.

Cordier, Andrew W. (1901-July 11), president emeritus of Columbia University and executive assistant to the secretary-general of the United Nations, 1946 to 1962.

Craig, May (1889-July 15), Washington correspondent for the *Portland Press Herald,* noted at presidential press conferences for her dodge-proof questions and her stunning hats.

Crerar, Thomas A. (1876-April 11), minister of mines and resources in Canada from 1929 to 1936 and member of the Senate from 1945 to 1965.

Cross, Milton (1897-Jan. 3), radio announcer who narrated the Metropolitan Opera's Saturday afternoon broadcasts from their inception in 1931.

*__Dallapiccola, Luigi__ (1904-Feb. 19), Italian composer and musical theorist. His works include an opera, *The Prisoner* (1948), and *The Songs of Imprisonment* (1955).

Richard Tucker, a
famous opera tenor.

Haile Selassie I, ruler of
Ethiopia for 50 years.

Aristotle Onassis,
a Greek shipowner.

Josephine Baker, U.S.-born,
starred in Paris music halls.

DeSpirito, Tony (1935-May 26), jockey who set a record of 390 victories on U.S. thoroughbred tracks in 1952.

***De Valera, Eamon** (1882-Aug. 29), American-born founder and leader of Ireland's *Fianna Fáil* (Soldiers of Destiny) party. He became president of the Irish Free State in 1932, prime minister of Ireland three times after 1937, and president of Ireland from 1959 to 1974.

Donohue, Mark (1937-Aug. 19), champion race driver who won the Indianapolis 500-mile race in 1972.

Doxiadis, Constantinos A. (1913-June 28), Bulgarian-born Greek architect and visionary city planner.

Driscoll, Alfred E. (1902-March 9), Republican governor of New Jersey from 1947 to 1954.

***Dunning, John R.** (1907-Aug. 25), physicist who helped develop the method of isolating the uranium-235 used in nuclear weapons.

Dunninger, Joseph (1892-March 9), magician and "mind reader" who mystified millions.

Egtvedt, Claire L. (1892-Oct. 19), aeronautical engineer and former president of the Boeing Company.

Evans, Walker (1903-April 10), photographer known for his eloquent studies of poverty-stricken Appalachians in James Agee's *Let Us Now Praise Famous Men* (1941).

***Faisal ibn Abdul Aziz al Faisal al Saud** (1906-March 25), king of Saudi Arabia from 1964 until his murder.

Felsenstein, Walter (1901-Oct. 8), Austrian opera director who headed the East Berlin Komische Opera.

Feltin, Maurice Cardinal (1883-Sept. 27), former archbishop of Paris and president of the French Roman Catholic Bishops Conference.

Fine, Larry (1902-Jan. 24), frizzy-haired member of the Three Stooges comedy team that made 218 motion pictures in 24 years.

Flanders, Michael (1922-April 14), British actor and humorist who performed from a wheel chair.

Fox, Nellie (Jacob Nelson) (1927-Dec. 1), former second baseman for the Chicago White Sox, voted the American League's Most Valuable Player in 1959.

***Franco, Francisco** (1892-Nov. 20), dictator of Spain since 1936.

Gibbons, Euell (1911-Dec. 29), author and naturalist who achieved national fame because of his TV appearances promoting natural foods.

Gleason, Ralph J. (1917-June 3), jazz and pop music critic with the *San Francisco Chronicle* from 1950 to 1975 and a founder of *Rolling Stone* magazine.

Green, Martyn (1899-Feb. 8), British actor with London's D'Oyly Carte for over 30 years who set the standard for Gilbert and Sullivan operetta roles.

Grove, Robert M. (Lefty) (1900-May 22), star pitcher for the Philadelphia Athletics and Boston Red Sox who won 300 major-league games and is in the National Baseball Hall of Fame.

***Haile Selassie I** (1892-Aug. 27), emperor of Ethiopia, who ruled for more than 50 years until he was deposed in a military coup d'état in September, 1974.

Hanfstängl, Ernst (Putzi) (1887-Nov. 6), Hitler's piano-playing, Harvard-educated press chief, who aroused Hitler with Harvard football songs and soothed his nerves with the lilting strains of *The Merry Widow*.

***Hansen, Alvin H.** (1887-June 6), economist who helped create the Social Security System in 1935.

Hayward, Susan (1919-March 14), Brooklyn-born motion-picture actress who won a 1958 Academy Award for her role in *I Want to Live!*

Heald, Henry T. (1904-Nov. 23), president of the Ford Foundation from 1956 to 1965.

Hepworth, Dame Barbara (1903-May 20), British sculptor who put the hole in modern sculpture and made it her signature.

***Hertz, Gustav** (1887-Oct. 30), German nuclear physicist who shared the Nobel Prize for Physics in 1925 for proving the validity of Niels Bohr's theory of the atom.

Hibbs, Ben (1901-March 30), long-time editor of *The Saturday Evening Post*.

***Hill, Graham** (1929-Nov. 30), British racing driver who won the Indianapolis 500 in 1966. He was world racing champion in 1962 and 1968 and was awarded the Order of the British Empire in 1968.

Hogben, Lancelot (1895-Aug. 22), British physiologist and science writer whose *Mathematics for the Million* (1936) has been translated into 30 languages.

Howard, Moe (1897-May 4), leader of the slapstick Three Stooges comedy team. He wore a soup-bowl haircut and wildly bopped the others.

Huston, Luther A. (1888-Nov. 26), author and former reporter for *The New York Times* who won the Polk Prize in 1954 for coverage of the school desegregation struggle.

***Huxley, Sir Julian S.** (1887-Feb. 14), British biologist and author, grandson of biologist Thomas H. Huxley and brother of the late author Aldous L. Huxley.

Jenckes, Virginia (1877-Jan. 9), Democratic state representative from 1932 to 1937, first woman to represent Indiana in Congress.

Jodoin, Claude (1913-March 1), founding president of Canadian Labour Congress from 1956 to 1966.

Johnson, Crockett (1906-July 11), artist, writer, and illustrator of children's books who created the comic strip "Barnaby."

Jones, Laurence C. (1883-July 13), black educator who founded the Piney Woods School near Braxton, Miss., in 1909 with $1.65 and three students.

Jordan, Louis (1908-Feb. 4), saxophonist, blues singer, and popular bandleader of the 1940s.

Last of The Giants

Chiang Kai-shek, who died on April 5, 1975, had been in declining health for a long time and had not appeared in public for two years. The once austerely erect generalissimo could stand for only a few minutes during the 1973 ceremony inaugurating his fourth six-year term as president of Nationalist China. But to the end, Chiang, an exile on the island of Taiwan, still clung to the almost sacred illusion that he was the father of all modern China and the only legitimate ruler of the mainland's 845 million people.

Chiang fought hard and bravely to shape history to his personal specifications. To his admirers, he was a stanch anti-Communist and supporter of Chinese democracy. To his detractors, he was at best corrupt and ineffectual. But everyone agreed he was a patriot. Even Premier Chou En-lai of the mainland's Communist government described him as such, though Chiang's form of patriotism had long since lost touch with the course of Chinese history. Perhaps he outlived the other three World War II Allied leaders—Franklin D. Roosevelt, Winston Churchill, and Joseph Stalin—by too many years.

Chiang had an epic career as a revolutionary and ardent Nationalist. Most of his life was taken up with fierce struggles against opponents of his Nationalist cause. He fought against the crumbling Manchu dynasty and the warlords that flourished in its ruins in the 1920s, then against Japanese invaders in the 1930s and 1940s, and finally against the Communist peasant army that drove him and his supporters into exile on Taiwan in 1949.

Chiang was born in 1887, the son of a salt merchant in Chekiang Province on China's central coast. He was trained as a soldier in Japan, where he first met Sun Yat-sen, and returned to China to join Sun's revolutionary movement to depose the Manchus. Sun sent Chiang to Russia in 1923, and when he returned, Sun appointed him head of the Whampoa Military Academy. By the time Sun died in 1925, Chiang had become a powerful figure in the Kuomintang (Nationalist Party). He took

command of the Nationalist army in 1926, and the Nationalist government of China was formed in 1928.

At first, Chiang collaborated with the Communists, who were part of the coalition that composed the Kuomintang. But after he had solidified his power and started to reunify the country, he turned on them, executing thousands and driving the rest into hiding. For the next 20 years, there was sporadic civil war between the Nationalist and the Communist forces.

Chiang was named the first constitutional president of China in 1948. But the Communists were excluded from that government, so the civil war continued. But Chiang could not solve China's basic problems—poverty, illiteracy, unjust taxation, and excessive land rents. His idea of progress was the New Life Movement, a campaign he initiated to stress reverence for family elders and other Confucian virtues. His lack of any real political program increasingly isolated him from the masses of Chinese.

Meanwhile, the Communists were promising land reform and total government reorganization. With each passing year, Chiang became increasingly autocratic, ruling China with the aid of a small clique of personal friends, Shanghai bankers, and former warlords.

Later, Chiang's fleeing Nationalist government did effect some land reform on Taiwan, while thwarting Taiwanese aspirations for self-rule. It also attracted enough foreign capital investment to turn the island into Asia's second fastest-growing state, after Japan.

But Chiang lived long enough to see the United States, Japan, and other postwar friends turn from his government to the Communist government in Peking. Finally, the United Nations voted in 1971 to eject the Nationalists and to grant China's membership to the Communist government. Through these reverses, Chiang maintained an outward stoicism, holding that the recovery of the mainland was "the inalterable national purpose." But no one listened to him anymore.   Foster Stockwell

Chiang Kai-shek
(1887-1975)

King Faisal, ruler
of Saudi Arabia.

Dimitri Shostakovich was a
renowned Russian composer.

Casey Stengel, a
madcap manager.

P. G. Wodehouse was a
prolific writer of humor.

Journet, Charles Cardinal (1891-April 15), Swiss theologian and educator who became Switzerland's only cardinal in 1965.

Judson, Arthur (1881-Jan. 28), leading concert manager in the 1930s and a founder of what became the Columbia Broadcasting System in 1926.

*Julian, Percy L.** (1899-April 19), organic chemist who discovered a low-cost synthesis for cortisone and a way to mass-produce physostigmine, used to treat glaucoma.

Kay, Marshall (1904-Sept. 3), Canadian-born geologist who won the 1971 Penrose Medal for his early model of continental drift.

Keating, Kenneth B. (1900-May 5), Republican senator from New York from 1958 to 1965.

Kellems, Vivien (1896-Jan. 25), colorful businesswoman who battled the federal tax system.

Kenny, John V. (1893-June 2), Democratic mayor of Jersey City, N.J., from 1949 until he was convicted of income tax evasion in 1970.

Keres, Paul P. (1916-June 5), Estonian grandmaster who ranked among the world's leading chess players.

Laing, Arthur (1904-Feb. 13), Canadian Liberal Party leader in British Columbia from 1953 to 1962.

Laniel, Joseph (1889-April 9), premier of France from 1953 to 1954.

Leinster, Murray (Jenkins, Will E.) (1896-June 8), science fiction writer who wrote such books as *The Forgotten Planet* and *Time Tunnel*.

Levi, Carlo (1902-Jan. 4), Italian writer and painter, best known for his book *Christ Stopped in Eboli* (1947).

Lochner, Louis P. (1887-Jan. 8), chief of the Associated Press in Berlin from 1924 to 1942 and winner of a Pulitzer Prize in 1939 for general correspondence.

Londos, Chris Theophelus (Jim) (1895-Aug. 19), the "Golden Greek" of professional wrestling and former world heavyweight champion.

Lopez, Vincent (1894-Sept. 20), bandleader whose popularity on radio and TV lasted for more than 50 years.

Lowson, Sir Denys S. F. (1906-Sept. 10), English investment banker and former lord mayor of London whose business ethics were roundly condemned in a 1974 government report.

Mabley, Moms (Jackie) (1900-May 23), raucous-voiced comedienne and television personality.

MacPhail, Larry (Leland Stanford) (1890-Oct. 1), baseball impresario with a Midas touch at the box office who pioneered major-league night baseball in Cincinnati in 1935.

Main, Marjorie (1890-April 10), stage and screen actress known for her role as Ma Kettle.

March, Fredric (1897-April 14), stage and film actor who won the Academy Award for Best Actor in 1932 for *Dr. Jekyll and Mr. Hyde* and in 1946 for his role in *The Best Years of Our Lives*.

Marshall, George E. (1891-Feb. 18), Hollywood film director who made more than 400 films in 62 years, including *How the West Was Won*.

Maxwell, W. Donald (1900-May 22), editor of the *Chicago Tribune* from 1955 to 1966 and later head of the Tribune Company.

McAuliffe, General Anthony C. (1898-Aug. 11), commander of the 101st Airborne Division in World War II. He answered "Nuts!" to a German surrender demand when his paratroops were encircled in the Battle of the Bulge in 1944.

McCoy, Ella (1877-May 9), the Hatfield who married a McCoy in 1898 and sent shock waves through their feuding families in the mountains of Kentucky.

McGiver, John (1913-Sept. 9), character actor of stage, screen, and television.

McWhirter, Ross (1925-Nov. 27), co-editor with his twin, Norris, of the *Guinness Book of World Records*.

Medwick, Joe (Ducky) (1911-March 21), star major-league outfielder from 1932 to 1948.

Meouchi, Paul Pierre Cardinal (1894-Jan. 11), patriarch of the Maronite Church, largest Christian community in Lebanon, since 1955.

Mesta, Perle (1890-March 16), Washington, D.C., "hostess with the mostes'"for almost 30 years.

*Mindszenty, Joseph Cardinal** (1892-May 6), Roman Catholic religious leader of Hungary who left that country in 1971 under pressure from Pope Paul VI and President Richard M. Nixon after eight years imprisonment by the Hungarian Communist government and 16 years sanctuary in the U.S. Embassy in Budapest.

Moley, Raymond (1886-Feb. 18), journalist and political adviser who coined the term *New Deal* in 1933 during President Franklin D. Roosevelt's Administration.

Mollenkopf, Jack (1903-Dec. 4), football coach at Purdue University from 1946 to 1960.

Mollet, Guy (1905-Oct. 3), French Socialist Party leader, premier of France from 1956 to 1957.

Montana, Bob (1920-Jan. 4), cartoonist who created the "Archie" comic strip.

Mudd, Stuart (1893-May 6), microbiologist who helped develop a valuable technique for freeze-drying blood plasma during World War II.

*Muhammad, Elijah** (1897-Feb. 25), spiritual leader of the Black Muslims' Nation of Islam for 41 years.

Nelson, Oliver (1932-Oct. 27), composer and jazz saxophonist with Duke Ellington and Count Basie.

Nelson, Oswald G. (Ozzie) (1907-June 3), who produced, directed, and co-starred in "The Adventures of Ozzie and Harriet" radio and television show.

Niesen, Gertrude (1913-March 27), Broadway and Hollywood star of the 1930s.

Norfolk, 16th Duke of (Bernard Marmaduke Fitz-Alan-Howard) (1908-Jan. 30), Earl Marshal of England, who choreographed state processions with such clockwork precision that he complained when Winston Churchill's funeral was two minutes late.

Novotný, Antonín (1904-Jan. 28), Czechoslovak Communist Party leader and president of Czechoslovakia from 1957 to 1968.

O'Hara, Joseph P. (1895-March 4), ranking Republican member of the House Interstate and Foreign Commerce Committee who represented Minnesota's second district from 1941 to 1959.

Olivier, Charles P. (1884-Aug. 14), astronomer who cataloged 294,000 meteors between 1901 and 1959.

*Onassis, Aristotle S. (1906-March 15), Greek shipowner and one of the world's wealthiest men, who married Jacqueline Kennedy, widow of President John F. Kennedy, in 1968.

Park, Sir Keith R. (1892-Feb. 5), New Zealander who commanded the Royal Air Force group that bore the brunt of the German onslaught in 1940.

Parks, Larry (1914-April 13), Hollywood film actor best known for his title role in *The Jolson Story*.

Pasolini, Pier Paolo (1922-Nov. 2), Italian film director, columnist, and poet whose many films include the prizewinning *Acsattone* (1961).

Payson, Joan Whitney (1903-Oct. 4), owner of the New York Mets and the Greentree racing stables.

Perey, Marguerite (1909-May 13), French nuclear chemist and educator, co-worker of Marie Curie, who discovered the radioactive element 87, which she named francium.

*Perse, Saint-John (Alexis Léger) (1887-Sept. 20), French poet and diplomat who won the 1960 Nobel Prize for Literature. Perse led a double life until World War II as secretary-general of the Ministry of Foreign Affairs from 1932 to 1940 and as a poet under his pen name.

Pettis, Jerry L. (1916-Feb. 14), Republican state representative from California who was a self-made millionaire when he was elected to Congress in 1966.

Pinilla, Gustavo Rojas (1900-Jan. 17), strongman president of Colombia from 1953 to 1957.

Prefontaine, Steve (1951-May 30), top U.S. long-distance runner who died in an automobile accident four hours after winning a 5,000-meter race in Eugene, Ore.

Priest, Ivy B. (1905-June 23), treasurer of the United States from 1953 to 1961.

Pulliam, Eugene C. (1889-June 23), publisher of many newspapers including *The Arizona Republic* and *The Phoenix Gazette*.

Radhakrishnan, Sarvepalli (1888-April 16), philosopher who was president of India from 1962 to 1967.

Ray, John H. (1886-May 21), Republican congressman from Staten Island, N.Y., and part of Brooklyn from 1952 to 1962.

Revson, Charles H. (1906-Aug. 24), who built the multimillion-dollar Revlon, Incorporated, cosmetic firm from a formula for nail polish.

Rooney, John J. (1903-Oct. 26), Democratic congressman from Brooklyn, N.Y., for 30 years.

Salmaggi, Alfredo (1886-Sept. 5), Italian-born impresario of bargain price opera who once staged *Aïda* in Soldier Field in Chicago for an audience of 45,000.

Sapir, Pinhas (1909-Aug. 12), Polish-born Israeli Cabinet minister from 1955 to 1974 and a founder of the state of Israel.

*Sato, Eisaku (1901-June 3), premier of Japan from 1964 to 1972 who shared the 1974 Nobel Peace Prize.

Schiotz, Aksel (1906-April 19), the "Voice of Denmark," Danish tenor and educator whose voice became a symbol of Danish resistance to the German occupation during World War II.

Perle Mesta was Washington's "hostess with the mostes'."

Elijah Muhammad, Black Muslim leader.

Eamon de Valera was the prime minister of Ireland three times.

Sir Julian Huxley, renowned biologist.

*Seredy, Kate (1896-March 7), Hungarian-born author and illustrator of children's books who won the 1938 Newbery Medal for *The White Stag*.

*Serling, Rod (1924-June 28), playright and producer who won six Emmy awards for such TV scripts as *Patterns* (1955) and *Requiem for a Heavyweight* (1956).

Sheean, Vincent (James Vincent) (1899-March 15), author and journalist whose style influenced a whole generation of reporters in the 1930s and 1940s. His many books include *Mahatma Gandhi* (1955).

Shipstad, Roy (1910-Jan. 20), who helped found the Shipstads & Johnson Ice Follies in 1936.

Short, Luke (Frederick Glidden) (1908-Aug. 18), author of many Western novels whose hard-riding stories were often adapted into films.

*Shostakovich, Dimitri (1906-Aug. 9), Russian composer, best known for his 15 symphonies. He gained international recognition as a student in 1926 with his famous *Symphony No. 1*.

Singleton, Zutty (1898-July 14), jazz drummer who was a member of the Tuxedo Brass Band with Louis Armstrong in New Orleans in 1917.

*Slobodkin, Louis (1903-May 8), sculptor and author-illustrator of children's books. He won the 1944 Caldecott Medal for illustrating James Thurber's *Many Moons*.

Soglow, Otto (1900-April 3), cartoonist who created "The Little King" character.

Steen, Marguerite (1894-Aug. 4), prolific English novelist whose many books included *The Sun Is My Undoing* (1941).

Eisaku Sato was a
premier of Japan.

Moe Howard was the leader of
the slapstick Three Stooges.

Hannah Arendt, noted
political philosopher.

Thornton Wilder won Pulitzer
Prizes for plays and a novel.

*Stengel, Casey (Charles Dillon) (1890?-Sept. 29), baseball personality for over 60 years as player, coach, and manager of four major-league teams, including the New York Yankees. He was elected to the Baseball Hall of Fame in 1966.

Stevens, George (1905-March 8), Hollywood film director who won Academy Awards for *A Place in the Sun* (1951) and *Giant* (1956).

Stevenson, Coke R. (1888-June 28), Democratic governor of Texas from 1941 to 1947.

Stillman, Irwin M. (1895-Aug. 26), physician and author of best-selling diet books.

*Stout, Rex T. (1886-Oct. 27), whose Nero Wolfe detective stories were published in 22 languages.

Sullivan, Annette Kellerman (1888-Nov. 5), Australia's "million-dollar mermaid" who combined swimming with vaudeville and shocked Boston in 1907 with her daring one-piece bathing suit.

Svenson, Andrew E. (1910-Aug. 21), writer who co-authored such popular children's stories as the Bobbsey Twins and the Hardy Boys adventure series under a variety of pen names.

*Tatum, Edward L. (1909-Nov. 5), biochemist who shared the 1958 Nobel Prize for Medicine for proving that individual genes are coded messages specifying the makeup of individual proteins.

Thomson, Sir George Paget (1892-Sept. 10), British physicist, co-winner of the 1937 Nobel Prize for Physics with American Clinton J. H. Davisson for discovery of the diffraction of electrons by crystals.

Tolson, Clyde A. (1900-April 14), associate director of the Federal Bureau of Investigation from 1947 to 1972 and closest friend of the late director J. Edgar Hoover for more than 30 years.

*Toynbee, Arnold J. (1889-Oct. 23), British historian whose 12-volume *A Study of History* covers the rise and fall of 26 civilizations in dazzling detail.

Treacher, Arthur (1894-Dec. 14), the proper British butler of Hollywood films who also appeared on television talk shows.

*Trilling, Lionel (1905-Nov. 5), acclaimed literary critic whose paramount interest was the interaction between society and the work of art. His books include *The Liberal Imagination* (1950), a collection of essays.

*Tucker, Richard (1914-Jan. 8), Metropolitan Opera star for 30 years who was considered the greatest American tenor of his time.

Tung Pi-wu (1886-April 2), a founder of the Chinese Communist Party of the People's Republic of China and deputy chief of state from 1959 to 1975.

Tunis, John R. (1889-Feb. 4), author of popular sports books for young people, including *The Iron Duke*. His books deal with sportsmanship and downgrade the idea of winning at all costs.

Tunnell, Emlen (1925-July 23), who played 14 seasons in the National Football League as defensive back, including 11 with the New York Giants. In 1967, he became the first black named to the Pro Football Hall of Fame.

Ure, Mary (1933-April 3), Scottish actress whose films included *The Luck of Ginger Coffey* and *Sons and Lovers*.

Vreeland, Albert L. (1901-May 3), Republican congressman from New Jersey from 1939 to 1943.

Walls, William J. (1885-April 23), bishop and former leader of the African Methodist Episcopal Zion Church.

Walters, Basil L. (Stuffy) (1896-Aug. 29), editor of the *Chicago Daily News* from 1959 to 1961.

Weidman, Charles E. (1901-July 15), modern dance choreographer and teacher whose gift for comic pantomime brightened such works as *Fables for Our Time*.

Wellman, William A. (1896-Dec. 9), motion-picture director of such highly acclaimed films as the original *Beau Geste* and *A Star Is Born,* and the classic Western, *The Ox-Bow Incident*.

*Wheeler, Burton K. (1882-Jan. 6), Democratic senator from Montana from 1923 to 1947 and Progressive Party candidate for Vice-President in 1924.

*Wheeler, Earle G. (1908-Dec. 18), U.S. Army general and chairman of the Joint Chiefs of Staff from 1964 to 1970.

Whitton, Charlotte E. (1896-Jan. 25), Canadian politician, mayor of Ottawa from 1951 to 1954 and 1960 to 1964. She was the first woman to serve as mayor of a Canadian city.

*Wilder, Thornton N. (1897-Dec. 7), writer who won three Pulitzer Prizes — in 1928 for his novel *The Bridge of San Luis Rey* and in 1938 and 1943 for his plays *Our Town* and *The Skin of Our Teeth,* respectively. He said we "have to use the comic spirit. No statement of gravity can be adequate to the gravity of the age in which we live."

Wills, Bob (1905-May 13), country singer and composer who originated Western swing country music and wrote "San Antonio Rose."

*Wodehouse, P. G. (1881-Feb. 14), English-born author and humorist, noted for his outlandish parodies of life among the British aristocracy in over 100 novels, including several featuring Bertie Wooster and his butler, Jeeves.

Yakobson, Leonid (1904-Oct. 20), Russian ballet master whose works include the choreography for the Soviet-American film *The Bluebird*.

Yergan, Max (1892-April 11), black educator and civil rights leader. He won the 1933 Spingarn Medal for interracial achievements.   Irene B. Keller

DELAWARE. See STATE GOVERNMENT.

DEMOCRATIC PARTY. A large number of candidates entered the race in 1975 for the 1976 Democratic presidential nomination. Ten contenders had announced their candidacy by the end of November, and more were expected before the Democrats assemble for their national convention in July, 1976. The lagging U.S. economy and low public-opinion ratings scored for President Gerald R. Ford raised Democratic hopes that the party could recapture the White House after eight years of Republican rule.

The Field included three senators, one former senator, two governors, two former governors, one member of the U.S. House of Representatives, and the 1972 Democratic candidate for Vice-President. Senator Edward M. Kennedy of Massachusetts, one of the most popular men in the party, repeatedly stated that he would not be a candidate. Another liberal, Senator Walter F. Mondale of Minnesota, dropped out of the running.

On January 11, former Senator Fred R. Harris of Oklahoma announced his candidacy, joining Congressman Morris K. Udall of Arizona and former Georgia Governor Jimmy Carter, both of whom had announced in late 1974. In February, senators Henry M. Jackson of Washington and Lloyd M. Bentsen of Texas entered the race.

Former North Carolina Governor Terry Sanford announced his presidential bid on May 29. He was followed by Sargent Shriver, the 1972 Democratic vice-presidential candidate, on September 20; Pennsylvania Governor Milton J. Shapp on September 25; and Senator Birch Bayh of Indiana on October 21.

Alabama Governor George C. Wallace, crippled by a would-be assassin's bullet in 1972, toured Europe in October, partly to prove he had the stamina to be President despite being paralyzed below the waist. Wallace declared his presidential candidacy on November 12.

Senator Hubert H. Humphrey of Minnesota, who ran a close race against Richard M. Nixon in the 1968 presidential election, said he would not compete in the 30 presidential primary elections but would be available if the convention deadlocked. Humphrey rated above all other Democratic contenders in a public-opinion survey taken in December. Another Democrat, former Senator Eugene J. McCarthy, declared himself an independent presidential candidate on January 12.

Party Funds. Wallace, who raised more than $4-million in two years as an undeclared candidate, in April became the first Democrat to claim matching federal campaign funds under the new campaign-financing law. The law requires candidates to raise $5,000 in contributions of $250 or less in 20 states

in order to qualify. The federal campaign aid can go as high as $10 million for presidential candidates. In September, Jackson, Bentsen, Udall, Carter, and Shriver also said they met the financing requirement.

The Democratic Party itself, however, remained debt ridden. A telethon on July 26 and 27 fell $1-million short of its $6-million goal before deducting expenses. The funds were needed to pay off a $2.6-million debt and raise money for the 1976 presidential election. After deducting costs, the party netted less than $2.5 million from the lengthy telethon.

The American Federation of Labor and Congress of Industrial Organizations (AFL-CIO) leadership said it would stay out of the fight for the nomination. But observers expected several AFL-CIO affiliate unions, along with the United Automobile Workers, to take part in the Democratic presidential primaries. The president of the Service Employees' International Union, for example, endorsed Harris.

Convention Plans. The Democrats decided on August 27 to hold their national convention, beginning on July 11, 1976, in New York City's Madison Square Garden. In October, the Democratic National Committee approved rules changes making it more difficult for dissenters to force floor fights. Minority reports from delegations at the 1976 convention must have support from 25 per cent of the credentials, rules, or platform committees to be brought before the full convention, rather than the 10 per cent required in 1972. The Democrats also made it more difficult to challenge a delegate's credentials.

The national committee approved a new formula for allocating delegates among the states. The South will lose some convention voting strength, and big industrial states will gain slightly. The new formula gives equal weight to the size of a state's congressional delegation and the size of its Democratic vote in the last three presidential elections.

The party won backing for its rule-making authority from the Supreme Court of the United States. In an 8 to 1 decision on January 15, the court held that the party's rule prevailed over state election laws. The case was brought by the 1972 convention delegates loyal to Chicago Mayor Richard J. Daley, who were rejected. The convention seated a rival, pro-McGovern slate instead. An Illinois judge had ruled in favor of Daley and cited the pro-McGovern group for contempt when they refused to give up their seats.   William J. Eaton

See also BAYH, BIRCH; BENTSEN, LLOYD M.; CARTER, JIMMY; DALEY, RICHARD J.; HARRIS, FRED R.; HUMPHREY, HUBERT H.; JACKSON, HENRY M.; KENNEDY, EDWARD M.; SANFORD, TERRY; SHAPP, MILTON J.; SHRIVER, SARGENT; UDALL, MORRIS K.; WALLACE, GEORGE C.

DENMARK. Anker Henrik Jorgensen, leader of the Social Democratic Party, formed a minority government on Feb. 13, 1975, after the Liberal Party failed to gain support for a tough economic program. In parliamentary elections on January 9, former Prime Minister Poul Hartling's Liberal Party gained 20 seats but still held only 42 in the 79-seat *Folketing* (parliament). The Social Democrats, who built Denmark's extensive social-welfare system, picked up 7 seats for a total of 54.

Hartling continued his shaky hold on power until January 28, when a motion calling for his resignation passed 86 to 85. Queen Margrethe II then asked the 10 political parties to seek a compromise solution to the crisis. Hartling struggled to form a four-party minority coalition, but the right wing Progress Party withdrew its support on February 7. Jorgensen then formed a minority government.

Labor Package. On March 11, the Folketing approved an economic program to avert threatened strikes by labor unions. Collective wage contracts were extended for two years, giving an average annual wage increase of 2 per cent. The package also froze prices and profit levels of products and professional services.

Unemployment Surged by 216 per cent during the year ending July 31, 1975, the largest percentage increase for any European Community (Com-

Denmark's Queen Margrethe II and her husband, Prince Henrik, tour Leningrad in May on first visit to Russia by European royalty since 1917.

mon Market) country. More than 9 per cent of the work force was jobless. On September 8, the Folketing accepted Jorgensen's plan to pump $850 million into the economy to create new jobs. The value-added tax was reduced 5.75 percentage points to 9.25 per cent on all goods and services except new automobiles. The plan boosts government spending on construction and public works, provides financial aid for fisheries and export promotion, and releases revenue from a compulsory savings scheme introduced by the previous Liberal government.

Jorgensen explained that the economic stimuli were possible because the inflation rate had fallen and the balance of payments was favorable. Indeed, June's trade deficit was the smallest since 1973, and the Bureau of Statistics reported on August 12 that the trade deficit for the first six months of 1975 was about one-third that for the same period in 1974. "We want to give the economy a boost now, and then gear down as international conditions improve," Jorgensen said. He plans a second-phase program involving long-term policies to stabilize prices, incomes, and costs.

U.S. Planes. With Belgium, the Netherlands, and Norway, Denmark decided to buy U.S.-built F-16 jet fighter aircraft instead of French jets. See ARMED FORCES.   Kenneth Brown

See also EUROPE (Facts in Brief Table).

DENTISTRY. A London psychiatrist warned dentists in April, 1975, that their patients may mask the amount of anxiety or discomfort they are experiencing during dental treatment. F. G. Spear told the annual meeting of the International Association for Dental Research in London that dentists should get to know their patients better so they will not be misled by the patient's overt behavior.

Fluoride Paradox. A study released in April of children living in New Britain, the first city in Connecticut to fluoridate its water supply (in 1950) shows a continuing decline in tooth loss and decay but an increase in the number of unfilled cavities. Cosmo R. Castaldi, head of the Department of Pediatric Dentistry at the University of Connecticut, told the annual meeting of the American Association for Dental Research in New York City that this apparent paradox implies that New Britain youngsters are not going to the dentist as often as they once did.

Ironically, Castaldi believes one reason for this is that fluoridation is no longer a controversial subject in New Britain. He also noted a population change that has produced more children who may come from a lower economic group and do not receive adequate dental care.

Child Dental Care. A Children's Dental Health Act, introduced by Senator Warren G. Magnuson (D., Wash.) and developed in cooperation with the American Dental Association, was approved by the Senate in August, 1975, as an amendment to a disease prevention and control measure. The bill seeks federal grants for children from low-income families, who are eligible for Medicaid, to step up early and periodic screening, diagnosis, and dental treatment. It provides funds for demonstration projects for dental-health education programs in schools. The amendment also establishes a dental advisory committee to the secretary of health, education, and welfare. The measure calls for awarding one-time federal grants to states and communities that plan to initiate fluoridation programs.

Babies' Cavities. Infants given sugar water or highly sweetened formula at bedtime are in danger of developing massive tooth decay, James P. Carlos, associate director of the National Institute of Dental Research's national caries program, warned in April. Carlos said research findings and clinical reports strongly reaffirmed that sugar is a major factor in tooth decay, especially in children and young adults. "From the evidence, it is clear that how frequently sugar is eaten is even more important than how much is consumed." For children and teen-agers, he recommended substituting sugar-free beverages and gums for sugar-containing snacks. "Sugar-sweetened foods should be eaten only at regular meals and only as part of a well-balanced diet," he said.   Lou Joseph

DETROIT. The recession's impact on the automobile industry created economic havoc in Detroit in 1975. Growing unemployment rolls and falling tax receipts produced a series of crises for city leaders.

The U.S. Department of Labor reported on May 3 that unemployment in Detroit and surrounding suburban areas averaged 9 per cent throughout 1974, the highest in any U.S. metropolitan area. The city's rate was even higher – near 25 per cent by some estimates.

Living costs in the Detroit area registered a relatively modest increase of 6.9 per cent between August, 1974, and August, 1975. But the average annual income of factory workers rose by only 3.1 per cent during the same period. Food costs increased by 4.9 per cent between mid-1974 and mid-1975, while housing costs rose 9 per cent. Other economic indicators did poorly during the same period. Department store sales increased by only 1.2 per cent; construction activity fell 19.6 per cent.

Shrinking City Funds. The recession produced a sharp decline in city revenues. One report indicated that city income tax revenues had declined by from $12 million to $15 million. The fiscal year ended with a budget deficit of $17.6 million.

Seeking to reduce a projected $65-million to $75-million budget deficit in fiscal 1976 (July 1, 1975, to June 30, 1976), city officials announced on March 30 that 25 per cent of the city's 23,000

A new, 80,000-seat domed stadium opened in Pontiac, Mich., on August 23. Its prime tenant is the Detroit Lions football team.

workers would be laid off. Between February and June, 1,980 workers were laid off, but a planned layoff of 10 per cent of the police force was averted. On May 21, the policemen and the city agreed on a plan that included each officer's taking 14 consecutive working days off without pay between June, 1975, and Dec. 31, 1976.

Race Relations. Massive citywide busing to integrate Detroit's schools was ruled out by a federal court order on August 16. The court directed the Detroit Board of Education to draw up a desegregation plan for the city's more than 300 schools, using busing only as a last resort to mix the races in the remaining predominantly white schools. On November 4, the court accepted a busing plan involving only 56 schools and about 28,000 students. It was scheduled to begin in January, 1976.

Former Teamsters Union President James R. Hoffa was reported missing on July 31, a day after he allegedly had a luncheon date with union leaders and a reputed Detroit crime figure. Hoffa was still missing at year's end. See CRIME.

A census report issued in June, 1975, by the U.S. Census Bureau showed that Detroit lost an estimated 8.4 per cent of its population between 1970 and 1973. The city's population as of July 1, 1973, was estimated at 1,386,817.   James M. Banovetz

DICTIONARY. See Section Six, DICTIONARY SUPPLEMENT.

DISASTERS. Two massive earthquakes shook parts of China and Turkey during 1975. On February 4, a tremor struck a heavily populated industrial area in Manchuria. Communist officials did not release casualty figures, but the force of the quake caused tremors as far away as Vladivostok, Russia. The earthquake that hit Turkey on September 6, though weaker than the Chinese tremor, killed more than 2,000 persons.

Other disasters that resulted in 10 or more deaths in 1975 included the following:

Aircraft Crashes

Jan. 4 – Romania. Officials reported that an airliner crashed in a mountainous area, killing 33 persons.

Jan. 8 – Neiva, Colombia. An airliner crashed and burned soon after take-off, killing all 20 persons aboard.

Jan. 9 – Whittier, Calif. A commuter plane collided with a private plane, killing 14 persons.

Jan. 30 – Istanbul, Turkey. A Turkish airliner crashed in the Sea of Marmara when a power failure at the airport caused the runway lighting system to fail. The 37 persons aboard were killed.

Feb. 3 – Manila, the Philippines. Fire in an airliner engine forced the pilot to crash-land. Thirty-one persons were killed.

Feb. 9 – Island of Crete. All 42 persons aboard were killed when a West German military transport crashed into a mountain during a storm.

March 16 – Near San Carlos de Bariloche, Argentina. An airliner carrying 47 passengers and 5 crew members crashed into an Andes peak while attempting to land, killing all aboard.

March 20 – Olympic Mountains, Washington. A U.S. Air Force jet crashed, killing 16 men.

April 4 – Saigon, South Vietnam. A U.S. Air Force transport plane crashed during take-off, killing at least 155 persons. The plane was carrying at least 247 Vietnamese orphans to safety before the collapse of the South Vietnamese regime.

June 24 – New York City. In the worst U.S. air accident involving a single plane, 113 persons were killed when an Eastern Airlines jet crashed while trying to land at Kennedy International Airport during a rainstorm.

July 15 – Batumi, Russia. A Russian airliner crashed, killing at least 28 persons.

July 31 – Taipei, Taiwan. The landing gear of a Taiwan airliner apparently collapsed as the plane touched down on the runway, causing it to crash. Twenty-seven persons were killed, and one was listed as missing.

Aug. 3 – Near Agadir, Morocco. A chartered Boeing 707 carrying Moroccan workers home from France crashed into a mountain shrouded in fog, killing the 188 persons on board.

Aug. 20 – Damascus, Syria. A Czechoslovak plane crashed into a hill while attempting to land, killing 126 of the 128 persons aboard.

Sept. 1 – Leipzig, East Germany. An East German airliner carrying West German businessmen to a trade fair crashed while landing, killing 26 persons.

Sept. 24 – Palembang, Indonesia. An airliner crashed while attempting to land in foggy weather, killing 23 persons. Two others were missing.

Oct. 22 – Near Cairns, Australia. A turboprop airplane crashed during a thunderstorm, killing at least 11 persons.

Oct. 27 – Andes Mountains, Bolivia. A Bolivian Air Force transport plane crashed into a mountainside, killing at least 50 persons.

Oct. 30 – Prague, Czechoslovakia. A chartered Yugoslav jetliner crashed into a fog-shrouded hillside while trying to land, killing 68 of the 120 persons aboard.

Rescue workers attempt to reach injured passengers trapped in a Mexico City subway train after a crash on October 20 that killed 26 persons.

Bus and Truck Crashes

Jan. 1 – The Japanese Alps. A ski-tourist bus went off the highway and plunged into a mountain lake, killing 23 passengers.

Jan. 30 – Northern Ecuador. A bus plunged over an embankment, killing 30 persons.

Feb. 7 – Near Ahvaz, Iran. A small bus collided with a trailer truck, killing all 21 persons in the bus.

Feb. 8 – Near Mexico City, Mexico. A freight train struck an overcrowded bus at a railroad crossing, killing 29 persons and injuring 28 others.

March 25 – Rio de Janeiro, Brazil. Thirty-one persons drowned when a commuter bus skidded off a rain-slick highway and into a river.

May 19 – New Delhi, India. A train struck a truck carrying a large wedding party, killing 66 persons and injuring 18 others.

May 27 – Hebden, Yorkshire, England. Thirty-two persons died in Great Britain's worst highway accident when the brakes failed on a chartered bus and it crashed through a bridge retaining wall into a ravine.

July 2 – Izmir-Ankara Highway, Turkey. A head-on collision between two buses killed 25 persons and injured 54 others.

July 5 – Near Bandar Abbas, Iran. Officials reported that 21 persons were killed when a bus and a truck collided head-on.

July 21 – Near Culiacán, Mexico. A bus collided with a car and burst into flame, killing 30 persons.

Sept. 20 – Near Ciudad Obregón, Mexico. A passenger bus slid off a road and into a river, and 18 persons drowned.

Dec. 12 – Toronto, Canada. A city bus stalled on a railroad track and was struck by a fast-moving train. Eleven persons were killed and 15 others injured.

Earthquakes

Sept. 6 – Lice, Turkey. A devastating earthquake that leveled parts of Lice and surrounding towns and villages killed more than 2,000 persons.

Explosions and Fires

Jan. 22 – Manila, the Philippines. Fifty-one persons were burned, suffocated, or leaped to their death when a blaze swept through a suburban factory. At least 79 others were seriously injured.

March 28 – Rijeka, Yugoslavia. A fire caused by faulty wiring killed 25 newborn infants in a hospital nursery. The nurse on duty was asleep at the time.

June 10 – Southern India. An apparently stolen cache of explosives blew up in a small village, killing 12 persons and injuring 65 others.

Aug. 16 – Near Durban, South Africa. A raging brush fire killed at least 25 persons.

Dec. 12 – San Francisco. A blaze in an apartment hotel killed at least 12 persons. Police suspected arson.

Dec. 12 – Near Mecca, Saudi Arabia. Fire swept through a tent camp, killing 138 Moslem pilgrims.

Dec. 25 – Sydney, Australia. Fire swept through a small hotel, killing 18 persons and injuring 23 others.

Floods

Jan. 11 – Southern Thailand. Floods caused by heavy rains killed 131 persons and destroyed rubber plantations and mines. More than 10,000 persons were left homeless.

Feb. 22 – Between Cairo and Aswan, Egypt. Fifteen persons were killed and 20 villages devastated by flooding along the Nile River.

March 13 – Neuquén Province, Argentina. Floods caused by heavy rainstorms killed 20 persons and left more than 6,000 homeless. Eleven others were listed as missing.

DISASTERS

July 28 – Pakistan. Two weeks of heavy flooding killed 63 persons, with the worst damage occurring in the Punjab Province.

Aug. 26 – Yemen (Sana). Monsoon-caused floods killed at least 70 persons and left thousands homeless.

Sept. 6 – Patna, India. Officials reported that 17 persons were killed by floodwaters. At least 50 more deaths were caused by a cholera outbreak following the flood.

Hurricanes, Tornadoes, and Other Storms

Jan. 10 – Mississippi. Tornadoes ripped through the state, killing 12 persons and injuring 200 others.

Jan. 12-13 – Midwestern United States. A blizzard followed by bitter cold temperatures killed 50 persons. The states worst affected were: Illinois (1 dead), Iowa (9 dead), Michigan (2 dead), Minnesota (6 dead), Nebraska (5 dead), and North Dakota (2 dead).

Jan. 25-26 – The Philippines. At least 30 persons were killed during a tropical storm, including 11 who were buried by a landslide and 7 fishermen who died at sea.

April 2-3 – Chicago. An unusual spring blizzard paralyzed the city and killed about 25 persons in the metropolitan area.

May 11 – Burma. Officials reported that a cyclone with winds up to 90 mph (145 kph) killed 187 persons.

Aug. 17 – Japan. Typhoon Phyllis swept across Japan, causing floods and landslides that killed at least 68 persons. One week later, a second typhoon struck, killing 26 persons and leaving 3 missing. Both storms struck hardest on the island of Shikoku.

Sept. 16 – Puerto Rico. At least 35 persons in Puerto Rico were killed when Hurricane Eloise swept through the Caribbean, leaving thousands homeless and causing more than $40 million damage. The storm killed a total of 51 persons in the Caribbean and the eastern United States.

Mine Disasters

May 5 – Baluchistan Region, Pakistan. Nineteen miners were killed by a gas explosion in a coal mine.

Sept. 20 – Queensland State, Australia. An explosion and fire in a coal mine about 450 miles (725 kilometers) northwest of Brisbane killed 13 workers.

Nov. 19 – Near Johannesburg, South Africa. A methane-gas explosion in a gold mine killed 12 miners and injured 4 others.

Dec. 27 – Bihar State, India. Water from a reservoir flooded deep shafts after explosions ripped through a coal mine. At least 372 miners were trapped underground and were feared dead.

Shipwrecks

Jan. 25 – Near Dacca, Bangladesh. A ferryboat collided with a river steamer, killing about 100 persons.

June 29 – Near Patna, India. Eighty persons drowned when a ferryboat capsized in the Ganges River.

June 30 – Lake Victoria, Tanzania. A water taxi capsized, killing 40 persons.

July 23 – Off Southeastern France. Twelve persons were killed and eight others injured when fire broke out on a ferryboat carrying vacationers.

Aug. 3 – Near Canton, China. Two triple-deck passenger boats collided on a river west of Canton, killing about 500 persons.

Sept. 18 – Uttar Pradesh State, India. About 100 persons drowned when an overcrowded ferryboat capsized in a flood-swollen river.

Nov. 10 – Lake Superior. Twenty-nine crewmen were missing and presumed drowned after the ore carrier *Edmund Fitzgerald* sank during a violent storm.

Dec. 29 – Pacific Ocean. A Norwegian tanker carrying 32 crewmen sank. Two survivors were found.

English police search the wreckage of a chartered bus that plunged off a bridge in Hebden, Yorkshire, on May 27. The crash killed 32 persons.

A Turkish shopkeeper returns to his ruined shop to salvage what remains after a severe earthquake struck eastern Turkey in September.

Train Wrecks

Jan. 18 – Cairo, Egypt. A speeding passenger train derailed, killing 27 persons and injuring 52 others.

Feb. 17 – South Africa. An express train from Cape Town to Johannesburg collided with a freight train, killing 16 persons and injuring 30 others.

Feb. 22 – Near Oslo, Norway. Twenty-seven persons were killed when two express trains collided head-on.

Feb. 28 – London. A rush-hour subway train failed to stop at the last station and crashed into the wall at the end of the line. Forty-one persons were killed.

May 23 – Near Rabat, Morocco. Officials reported that a passenger train bound for Tangier derailed, killing 34 persons and injuring 200 others.

June 8 – Near Munich, West Germany. Two passenger trains collided head-on, killing 35 persons and injuring 60 others.

Oct. 20 – Mexico City, Mexico. A subway train crashed into the rear of a train stopped at a station, killing 26 persons.

Other Disasters

Jan. 5 – Hobart, Australia. An ore freighter crashed into a bridge over the River Derwent, killing seven crewmen and five passengers in cars on the bridge.

April 6 – The Swiss Alps. Swiss officials reported that 10 persons were killed by avalanches following a heavy snowfall. Ten others were missing after a snowslide buried part of a mountain village.

March 9 – Seoul, South Korea. A cement embankment supporting two houses gave way, crushing several dormitories where industrial workers lived. Seventeen women who worked in a wig factory were killed and 12 others were injured.   Darlene R. Stille

DOMINICAN REPUBLIC. See LATIN AMERICA.

DRUGS

DRUGS. A task force of the President's Domestic Council issued a report in October, 1975, that strongly urged a de-emphasis of U.S. law-enforcement measures against users and possessors of small quantities of marijuana. The main efforts, the report said, should be concentrated on stopping the use of the most harmful drugs, such as heroin. It also recommended that firm steps be taken to stop the rivalry that has developed between the U.S. Drug Enforcement Administration (DEA) and the U.S. Customs Service, the nation's two top narcotics law-enforcement agencies. The task force was headed by Vice-President Nelson Rockefeller.

The Customs Service has long objected to the 1973 reorganization plan, in which the DEA received primary responsibility for investigating narcotics smuggling in the United States and abroad. The reorganization limited the role of the Customs Service to seizures of contraband at the border.

Vernon D. Acree, commissioner of the Customs Service, criticized the Domestic Council report, saying he feared it would encourage massive and illegal marijuana smuggling. In the three months before the report appeared, customs agents seized nearly 100 short tons (91 metric tons) of marijuana that smugglers had tried to slip into the United States by boat, airplane, "and every other conceivable means."

Hard Drugs. The number of Turkish farmers allowed to grow the opium poppy increased during the year from 70,000 to 103,000, despite Turkey's 1974 agreement with the United States to limit production. Much of the 100 short tons (91 metric tons) of Turkish opium produced is processed into heroin in France, and part of it is then smuggled into New York City and other East Coast cities. The Midwest and other parts of the country are supplied mainly by Mexican traffickers.

Congressional hearings revealed in June that the Department of Health, Education, and Welfare (HEW) had administered potentially dangerous drugs, including the mind-altering LSD, to about 2,500 prisoners, mental patients, and paid volunteers from 1954 to 1968, to determine if the drugs had any medical value. It was also disclosed that both the Central Intelligence Agency and the Army had given LSD to scientists and servicemen without their knowledge to study the drug's effects.

Drugs Investigated. Two widely used tranquilizers, Librium and Valium, came under strict government control on July 2. The action was aimed at preventing abuse of the drugs. The DEA and HEW said evidence indicated the drugs could produce physical and psychological dependence. The agencies also placed under control two similar but lesser-known tranquilizers, Tranxene and Serax; the sedative Dalmane; and Clonopin, a new drug designed to control convulsions. Valium was described as the largest-selling drug on the commercial market. Nearly 3 billion Valium tablets and over 1 billion Librium tablets were sold in 1974. Doctors' prescriptions for these drugs may not be refilled more than five times.

The Federal Trade Commission acted on June 2 to invalidate state laws and private agreements that prohibit druggists from advertising the price of prescription drugs. Economists for the commission said this action may save consumers more than $300 million a year. A 694-page study said the action was necessary because a complex web of state and local laws meant that consumers in almost every state could not learn the price of prescription drugs before they bought them.

Alcohol Use remained the most serious problem among the young. A report issued by the New York City Department of Mental Health Services in February revealed that 12 per cent of the juniors and seniors in city high schools were drinking enough to make them potential alcoholics.

Cyclamate Ban Restudied. The scientist whose research helped the federal government to ban cyclamates in 1970 said in July that he believed the decision was not justified on the basis of his study. Bernard L. Oser, now an independent researcher, told a panel of scientists in Bethesda, Md., that he was shocked when the widely used artificial sweetener was ordered off the market by the Food and Drug Administration.   Mary E. Jessup

DUNLOP, JOHN THOMAS (1914-   ), an economist and labor mediator, became United States secretary of labor on March 6, 1975. But he resigned in January, 1976, after President Gerald R. Ford vetoed a labor-backed bill Dunlop favored.

Dunlop, a professor of economics at Harvard University, served under President Richard M. Nixon as chairman of the Construction Industry Stabilization Committee from 1971 to 1973. Nixon appointed him head of the Cost of Living Council in February, 1973, a post Dunlop held until the council was dissolved in July, 1974. He then returned to Harvard until he was nominated as secretary of labor.

Dunlop, the son of missionary parents, was born on July 5, 1914, in Placerville, Calif., and grew up on Cebu in the Philippines. He received his Ph.D. in economics from the University of California, Berkeley, in 1939.

In 1938, he joined the faculty at Harvard, becoming professor of economics in 1950. From 1970 to 1973, he was also dean of arts and sciences. In addition to his academic career, he has served as a government adviser on labor relations and as a labor mediator, specializing in construction industry disputes.

Dunlop married Dorothy Emily Webb in 1937. They have three children.   Darlene R. Stille

EARTHQUAKES. See DISASTERS.

EASTERN ORTHODOX CHURCHES. The recent cordiality between the Greek Orthodox and Roman Catholic churches was broken in July, 1975, when the Vatican decided to appoint a new bishop for the Uniate Church, a small sect in Greece that recognizes the pope but follows Eastern Orthodox liturgy.

According to Archbishop Seraphim of Athens, Greece, the Vatican made its decision despite the objections of leaders of the Greek Orthodox Church. The Greek Orthodox leaders had assumed that a delay in appointing a successor had been a deliberate move to continue improving relations between the Roman Catholic and Greek Orthodox churches. The Uniate Church has long been a source of friction. Greek Orthodox leaders regard the sect as existing primarily to convert unsuspecting members of the Orthodox faith.

In Russia. The historic Assumption Cathedral in Vladimir, Russia, was closed by the Russian government in 1975, and the harassment of religious dissidents was intensified. Vladimir Ossipov, editor of the underground magazine *Veche,* received an unusually harsh sentence of eight years in prison. Campaigns against Roman Catholics in the Baltic States, especially Lithuania, continued.

In the United States. A delegation of the Moscow Patriarchate, headed by Metropolitan Filaret of Kiev, was received in February by the National Council of Churches, whose delegation had visited Russia in August, 1974. Theological conversations were held in Princeton, N.J., and in Chicago. In these and other cities visited by the Russian clergymen, there were organized demonstrations to denounce persecution of Christians in Russia.

Bishop Stephen, head of the Albanian Diocese within the Orthodox Church in America, died on April 30 in Boston at the age of 74.

Author Alexander I. Solzhenitsyn visited Canada and the United States in May. He spent the Orthodox Holy Week at the Orthodox Church in America's Cathedral in Montreal, a guest of Archbishop Sylvester. Solzhenitsyn then went to Alaska to visit old Russian shrines and churches.

In August, the two American dioceses in the jurisdiction of the Patriarchate of Antioch, headed by Metropolitan Philip (Saliba) of New York City and Metropolitan Michael (Shaheen) of Toledo, Ohio, agreed to end 30 years of rivalry and animosity. The agreement, to be approved by the Synod of the Patriarchate of Antioch in Damascus, Syria, restores the unity of the Antiochian jurisdiction in North America.

The Fourth All-American Council of the Orthodox Church in America was held in November in Cleveland. The council made plans to make the "voice of Orthodoxy" heard in America through the mass media.   Alexander Schmemann

See also RELIGION.

ECONOMICS. All the industrialized countries of the world, including the United States, experienced similar maladies in 1975 – inflation, unemployment, and recession. As of September, only West Germany, with its traditional tight monetary controls, and Switzerland had inflation rates lower than the 9.1 per cent average in the United States – West Germany with about 6 per cent and Switzerland with 5.4 per cent. Japan, Canada, Norway, and Sweden all reported rates of more than 10 per cent. In Great Britain, the rate was more than 25 per cent and the hard-pressed Labour government of Prime Minister Harold Wilson, over the objections of other Western nations, imposed selective import curbs on December 17 in an effort to save several important segments of British industry from going into bankruptcy.

The situation in the less-developed areas of the world was even worse. The rise in prices in Latin America ranged from 20 per cent in Mexico to 500 per cent in Chile. Rates among the African nations generally ranged from 30 to 40 per cent, but the statistics are not very meaningful because so many people in these countries are not part of a market economy.

Economic problems were worldwide, as reflected in editorial cartoons from Sri Lanka, *below left;* the United States, *below right;* and Mexico, *bottom.*

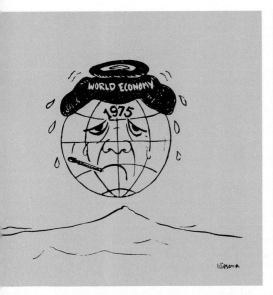

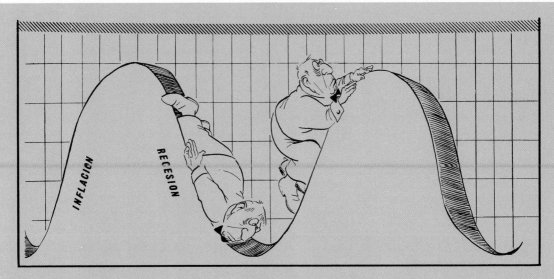

The U.S. Economy in mid-spring began to make a hesitant recovery from the longest and deepest recession since World War II. The recovery picked up speed during the third quarter, but the pace slackened in the fourth. The net result was that the year's output, after being corrected for inflation, declined for the second successive year. In current dollars, the gross national product (GNP) hit an estimated $1.47 trillion, up slightly from 1974's $1.4 trillion. But prices rose even faster. Department of Commerce measurements showed that the GNP in 1958 dollars would be slightly under $800 billion, compared with $821-billion in 1974.

Even more disturbing to economists, both unemployment and inflation remained unacceptably high. The most widely watched index, that of consumer prices, averaged about 161 for the year, an increase of more than 9.1 per cent (with the 1967 average equal to 100). This was a slower rate of increase than in 1974, and it showed signs of slowing even further at year-end. Yet it was still a disturbing phenomenon when accompanied by unemployment levels that ranged from 9.2 per cent in May down to 8.3 per cent in December.

The 11 per cent inflation rate in 1974 had been explained as resulting from the enormous increase in crude-oil prices imposed by the oil-exporting nations and a rapid increase in food prices caused by unusually heavy grain exports in 1973. These influences had relatively little impact in 1975. Oil prices crept up slightly at the start of the year, but then were stable for the last nine months. Prices received by farmers tended to drop slightly. Under these conditions, economists would normally expect a substantially lower rate of inflation – perhaps 4 or 5 per cent – or at least a lower unemployment rate.

The Labor Picture. No sector of the American economy was completely immune from the effects of the slump. Wage earners perhaps felt the least impact. Average hourly earnings in manufacturing industries rose from $4.41 in 1974 to about $4.80, and weekly earnings from $176.40 to slightly more than $188. But in terms of 1967 dollars, the estimated purchasing power of the average weekly wage dropped from $119.43 to about $117.

Average total employment dropped from 85.9-million in 1974 to 84.7 million for the first 10 months of 1975. Of this total, nearly 77 million were payroll employees. Somewhat over 18 million of these worked in manufacturing, about 17 million in wholesale and retail trade, and just under 15-million held federal, state, or local government jobs. The latter figure does not include those in the armed forces. A steady increase in government employment over the past few years has made government on all levels the third largest category of employer in the United States.

Despite the gloomy employment picture, a look at developments since 1967 reveals that wage earners who have been fully employed during this period actually improved their relative position. Prices rose slightly more than 60 per cent over the eight years, but average hourly earnings in manufacturing went up 71 per cent. Government employees and service workers did even better in recent years, while those engaged in wholesale and retail trade generally lagged behind the rise in the cost of living.

Other Measures of economic activity were no more cheering. The Federal Reserve Board index of industrial production was down from 124.8 in 1974 to an estimated 113, though it recovered somewhat in the last half of the year. As is almost always true in recessions, the production of durable goods suffered more heavily than nondurables. The durables index fell more than 10 per cent below 1974's 120.7. Nondurables dropped from 129.7 to about 120 for the year, but by year-end had achieved a level of operation only slightly below the average for 1974.

Surprisingly, estimated new plant and equipment expenditures rose from $112 billion to almost $114 billion, but much of this went for environmental purposes and did not add to productive capacity. When inflation is taken into account, the physical volume of new plants was down almost 10 per cent. Corporate profits after taxes were down about 15 per cent, from $85 billion to about $72-billion.

The drop in corporate profits from the record level of 1974 was not unexpected and, as often happens, the stock market anticipated the later economic recovery by running up prices about 40 per cent in the first three months of the year. But when the recovery seemed less strong than had been hoped for and the problems of inflation and unemployment continued, investors backed away and the stock market ended at about the same level it had reached in March.

Consumer Status. Despite the generally unsatisfactory economic conditions, consumers came off somewhat better than might have been expected. Thanks to a tax cut that took effect at the beginning of the year and increased unemployment compensation and social security payments, per capita disposable income after taxes rose from $4,623 in 1974 to about $5,000. Estimated net farm income, however, decreased from $27.7 billion to about $25 billion. At the same time, the farm parity ratio – the prices at which farmers sell relative to those at which they buy, compared to 1914 levels – dropped from 81 per cent to an estimated 76 per cent. However, this was still a high level compared with most of the 1960s.

Food prices the consumer paid were about 175 per cent of the 1967 level, and services other than

Selected Key U.S. Economic Indicators

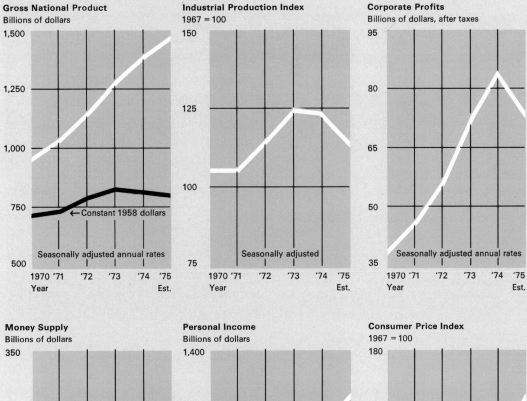

Gross National Product
Billions of dollars

1,500

1,250

1,000

750

500

← Constant 1958 dollars

Seasonally adjusted annual rates

1970 '71   '72   '73   '74   '75
Year   Est.

Industrial Production Index
1967 = 100

150

125

100

75

Seasonally adjusted

1970 '71   '72   '73   '74   '75
Year   Est.

Corporate Profits
Billions of dollars, after taxes

95

80

65

50

35

Seasonally adjusted annual rates

1970 '71   '72   '73   '74   '75
Year   Est.

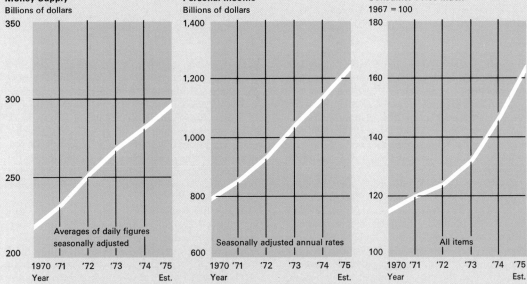

Money Supply
Billions of dollars

350

300

250

200

Averages of daily figures
seasonally adjusted

1970 '71   '72   '73   '74   '75
Year   Est.

Personal Income
Billions of dollars

1,400

1,200

1,000

800

600

Seasonally adjusted annual rates

1970 '71   '72   '73   '74   '75
Year   Est.

Consumer Price Index
1967 = 100

180

160

140

120

100

All items

1970 '71   '72   '73   '74   '75
Year   Est.

The most comprehensive measure of the nation's total output of goods and services is the *Gross National Product* (GNP). The GNP represents the dollar value in current prices of all goods and services plus the estimated value of certain imputed outputs, such as the rental value of owner-occupied dwellings. *Industrial Production Index* is a monthly measure of the physical output of manufacturing, mining, and utility industries. *Corporate Profits* are quarterly profit samplings from major industries.

Money Supply measures the total amount of money in the economy in coin, currency, and demand deposits. *Personal Income* is current income received by persons (including nonprofit institutions and private trust funds) before personal taxes. *Consumer Price Index* (CPI) is a monthly measure of changes in the prices of goods and services consumed by urban families and individuals. CPI includes 300 goods and services. All 1975 figures are *Year Book* estimates.

Volkswagen workers in Salzgitter, West Germany, carry a coffin to
dramatize protest against closing an auto plant that employed 3,000.

rent were roughly 170 per cent of 1967. Commodities other than food were the lowest item, at about 149 per cent.

Individuals continued to save at a relatively high rate—about 8 per cent of their disposable income. For the first time in several years, the volume of outstanding consumer credit declined, dropping to about $187 billion from slightly more than $190-billion in 1974.

New York City's Problems. Uncertainty surrounded the financial solvency of New York City. Early in the year, it became apparent that the largest U.S. city would be unable to meet its debt obligations without substantial outside assistance. Temporary help was provided by banks and investors who, though unwilling to purchase the direct obligations of the city, purchased enough bonds issued by an independent agency—the Municipal Assistance Corporation—to meet the city's cash needs until early fall. Then another crisis occurred, and only last-minute investment by the state of New York and municipal pension funds avoided default in early November.

Finally, after the city enacted new taxes and stringent budget limitations that virtually deprived Mayor Abraham D. Beame and the other elected city officials of any control over municipal expenditures, President Gerald R. Ford proposed on November 26 that the United States lend the city

enough funds to meet the temporary cash-flow problems that have been predicted for the next three years. Congress passed the bill in December.

The scheme will not cost the taxpayers in the rest of the country anything. However, New York City's already high taxes will go up, and the budgetary restraints that have been imposed will unquestionably have an unhappy effect on municipal services, especially on wage contracts, which had become increasingly generous in recent years. See NEW YORK CITY.

Municipal Bond interest rates reflected the uncertainty affecting New York City, plus the sudden realization that many large U.S. cities could face similar, if less severe, problems in the future. The rates rose from slightly more than 6 per cent in 1974 to about 7 per cent. Meanwhile, other interest rates were falling, so that municipal bonds, whose interest is free from federal income tax, were in effect yielding more than taxable United States Treasury bills by year-end.

Lower interest rates resulted more from the lack of demand for loans than any lack of monetary restraint. Fearful of stoking the fires of inflation again, the Federal Reserve Board limited the increase in the money supply—defined as currency and demand deposits—to an average of about 5 per cent over the year. Total cash in circulation and demand deposits rose from $292 billion in December, 1974, to more than $300 billion a year later. Time and savings deposits rose by a somewhat higher rate.

Early in the year, the tight-money policy of the Federal Reserve Board brought Chairman Arthur F. Burns into conflict with many liberal members of Congress, a conflict that continued throughout the year. The congressmen wanted a relatively easy monetary policy that would permit more rapid expansion of the money supply. They argued that, with unemployment running at more than 9 per cent in May and with idle resources, injecting funds into the market place could bring interest rates down and stimulate the economy without fueling more inflation.

Burns, on the other hand, argued that inflation was the number-one problem and that it had not yet been brought under control. With consumer prices still rising at a rate of 7 or 8 per cent at year-end, the control of inflation still appeared to lead the nation's priorities.

Balance of Payments. Normally, a country suffering a high rate of inflation becomes a good place for other countries to sell their goods and a poor place in which to buy. This produces a deficit in the balance of payments on merchandise accounts. Far from suffering this fate, the United States was expected to chalk up its biggest trade surplus in history, with exports exceeding imports by about $10 billion or more. The current account balance, which includes exchanges of services, was expected to show an even higher surplus. This contrasted with a trade deficit of more than $5 billion in 1974, when a sharp rise in crude-oil prices had a major influence on imports. Largely as a result of the trade surplus, the total balance of payments on current account plus long-term capital movements also showed a slight surplus, compared with a $10.7-billion deficit in 1974.

The total value of U.S. exports reached an estimated $107 billion, up about 10 per cent, while imports were expected to decline slightly to about $97 billion. Agricultural products led the exports, followed by transportation equipment and general manufactured goods. Petroleum products — largely crude oil — led the import list, followed by machinery, transportation equipment (primarily foreign cars), and general manufactured goods.

Trading Abroad. American grain seemed assured of a generally firm market abroad for the next few years. After President Ford placed a temporary embargo on further grain sales to Russia in August, the United States and Russia signed an agreement in October whereby Russia could annually buy from 6.6 million to 8.8 million short tons (6 million to 8 million metric tons) of wheat and corn. If the Russians want more than 8.8 million short tons of grain, they must consult with U.S. officials before closing the deals. The agreement

becomes effective in October, 1976. Although it is not likely to eliminate the ups and downs of export trade, it is expected to smooth the previously erratic and sudden Russian purchases in the U.S. market that caused sharp price fluctuations like those that occurred in 1973.

As usual, Canada was the United States largest trading partner, leading in both exports and imports. Following on the export side were Japan, West Germany, Mexico, and Great Britain. Japan, Saudi Arabia, West Germany, and Venezuela were the next most important sellers to the United States. The two oil-producing states, Saudi Arabia and Venezuela, are on the list as a result of the tremendous increases in oil prices that began in late 1973. In that year, United States petroleum imports totaled only $7.6 billion. They rose to $24.3 billion in 1974 and remained at about the same level in 1975. The last round of oil price increases occurred in September, when members of the Organization of Petroleum Exporting Countries agreed to raise prices 10 per cent and hold them at that level until June, 1976. Actual increases following this decision were somewhat less than 10 per cent because several members made price adjustments to preserve their market shares.

Energy Problems. President Ford and Congress disagreed sharply about how best to meet the energy crisis, especially the troublesome question of pricing crude oil and natural gas. Oil was under a two-price system that provided a low ceiling price on so-called "old oil," from wells in production at the time of the 1973 Arab oil embargo, while allowing "new oil" to be sold at a price roughly equal to the price of imported oil. The President and most of his energy advisers wanted to remove controls from domestic oil, while many members of Congress favored continuing the present controls.

Controls expired on August 31, but most oil companies delayed raising prices until they saw what Congress would do. The controls were temporarily extended in September and again in mid-November. Meanwhile, President Ford and the Congress attempted to work out a compromise long-term energy program.

Under consideration was a compromise bill that would roll back oil prices at the start, then allow prices to rise over the next 40 months. At first, it was predicted that the initial rollback would reduce the price of gasoline by 3.5 cents per gallon (3.8 liters) — not an unimportant consideration in an election year — but this estimated saving was later reduced to 1 cent. Congress passed the bill on December 17, and the President signed it on December 22.

It was a compromise that left nobody happy. Oilmen claimed that it would hold back the search for new wells because it would limit the funds needed for exploration and development drilling.

Others, who believe that the government should intervene in the market place to prevent prices from rising, were unhappy to have the controls phased out.

The International Scene. The United States economic problems were not unique. Those of other countries were, if anything, even greater. Industrial production fell in the four major European countries – West Germany, France, Italy, and Great Britain. Unemployment rose in all four countries to more than 4 per cent of the labor force. Only West Germany had lower inflation than the United States.

Economic policies in the four countries did not follow parallel lines. Great Britain, with inflation running at more than 25 per cent, gave primary emphasis to controlling inflation, while West Germany, with only 5 per cent inflation, concentrated on economic expansion. The West German government decided in August to boost the federal deficit in order to spur the lagging building industry, even though the country's economy was considered the strongest in Europe. The deficit was the country's first in a number of years. See GERMANY, WEST.

In August, France announced a plan to boost its lagging economy with heavy public-works spending – including investments in roads, canals, and railroad tracks – along with additional funds to industry and low-cost housing. In the year ended July 1, 1975, industrial production declined about 12 per cent. Bankruptcies increased in the first half of 1975, industrial jobs dropped, and unemployment rose. See FRANCE.

Italy, considered "the sick man of Europe" in 1974, recovered slightly in 1975. Imports declined by 23 per cent and the country reduced its 20 per cent inflation rate slightly. Unemployment was still high and capital investment was weak. See ITALY.

Great Britain suffered a continuing economic crisis with its high inflation rate, and several companies hovered on the brink of bankruptcy at year-end. Canada was forced to install income and price controls in October in an attempt to bring inflation under control. Australia, in generally better health than most other countries, nonetheless considered its economic situation one of the predominant issues in its December election. See AUSTRALIA; CANADA; GREAT BRITAIN.

A report on Russia's annual economic plan in December underscored how vulnerable its economy is to the uncertainties of agriculture. The poor 1975 grain crop – about one-third below the target – forced the Soviet government to scale down economic goals. The industrial growth rate in 1975 was 7.5 per cent, and national income rose by only 4 per cent. Economic goals were lowered for 1976, largely at the expense of the Russian consumer. See AGRICULTURE; RUSSIA.　　　Warren W. Shearer

Ecuador's President Guillermo A. Rodriguez Lara returns triumphantly to Quito after defeating an attempted coup d'état by army officers.

ECUADOR. President Guillermo A. Rodriguez Lara survived a violent right wing attempt at a coup d'état on Sept. 1, 1975, in which 22 persons were killed and about 100 wounded. The attempt was due partly to the example set by the ouster of neighboring Peru's President Juan Velasco Alvarado in August and unpopular new taxes on consumer imports. The coup was led by General Raul González Alvear, head of the joint chiefs of staff.

González, who succeeded in taking over the presidential palace in Quito, received the support of centrist and conservative politicians, grouped in a newly formed Civic Junta for Institutional Restoration. He also was endorsed by former President José María Velasco Ibarra, who issued a radio statement from exile in Argentina backing the coup. But the navy, the air force, and the Guayaquil army command remained loyal to Rodriguez, who fought his way back into the capital at the head of an armored column. González fled to the residence of the Chilean ambassador and later flew to exile in Chile. On September 4, the government announced the court-martial of 14 senior military officers who had participated in the coup attempt. Mass arrests of political leaders were ordered; the Civic Junta was disbanded.

The coup attempt confirmed Rodriguez in his reluctance to contemplate any return to civilian rule. But it did not produce the violent lurch to the left that was widely expected. The new Cabinet, which replaced the one that resigned on September 3, was dominated by personal supporters of the president as well as pragmatists, such as Colonel Jaime Dueñas, the oil minister, and Jaime Morillo, the civilian finance minister.

The Economy. Ecuador became the only member of the Organization of Petroleum Exporting Countries to report a trade deficit in 1975. By midyear, this had risen to $170 million. Ecuador's oil exports dropped 49 per cent between January and June. This was partly due to a landslide in March that closed down for a month the trans-Andean pipeline, an essential means of moving the crude oil from the jungles of Oriente province. But the Texaco-Gulf consortium, whose local subsidiary, Venture, was marketing 75 per cent of Ecuador's production abroad, also claimed that high export taxes were pricing Ecuador's crude oil out of the market and making production only marginally profitable. Production had fallen to 165,000 barrels a day from a potential of 210,000 barrels per day.

A belated step was taken to rectify the situation on July 9, when the government lowered the price by 43 cents a barrel from the old price of $10.84 per barrel, retroactive to July 1. The tax rate was cut from 58.5 per cent to 53.1 per cent, and the royalty rate was maintained at 16.67 per cent.   Robert Moss

See also LATIN AMERICA (Facts in Brief Table).

EDUCATION. Two-thirds of the world's 800 million adult illiterates are women, a United Nations Educational, Scientific, and Cultural Organization (UNESCO) study revealed in September, 1975. The report, given at the International Symposium for Literacy, held at Persepolis, Iran, showed that the number of female illiterates is growing more rapidly than the number of male illiterates.

"What holds women back is not so much male attitudes of dominance [although these are widely prevalent] as...social inhibitions and traditional restrictions...usually transmitted by women themselves, from mother to daughter to granddaughter," said Helen Callaway, an American anthropologist doing research on illiteracy at Oxford University in England. "Nearly everywhere, males are given preference for general education and for technical training; they are the ones who are encouraged to venture into the wider world."

Functional Illiterates. As if to underscore the UNESCO study on world literacy, the U.S. Office of Education released in October results of a four-year study that showed that 23 million adult Americans are *functionally illiterate*—unable, for example, to read newspaper help-wanted ads.

The College Entrance Examination Board released figures in September showing that the verbal and mathematical aptitude scores of college-bound high school students had dropped 10 points

Striking teachers picket Chicago's Board of Education in September. The 11-day walkout shut down classes for 530,000 students.

and 8 points, respectively, in 1975, the steepest decline in 20 years. Some observers blamed increased television viewing, and others criticized teaching methods. "We don't know the reasons for it...." said Sam A. McCandless, director of the board's admissions testing program. "I suspect that it may be a combination of various factors."

Perhaps in response to growing public concern, U.S. elementary schools increased their emphasis on the three R's. Alternative schools, dedicated to traditional instruction, were introduced in a number of communities (see Section Five, ALTERNATIVE SCHOOL). In higher education, more students turned to such traditional subjects as economics, mathematics, and the sciences, often in preparation for admission to business, law, and medical schools.

Teachers' Strikes. The largest number of teachers' strikes in recent history kept a total of 2 million schoolchildren out of school for varying periods at the start of the academic year in September. The most notable stoppages were in New York City, with an enrollment of 1.1 million pupils, and Chicago, with 530,000. Also affected by strikes were cities in California, Delaware, Massachusetts, New Jersey, Ohio, Pennsylvania, Rhode Island, and Washington.

The two largest U.S. teacher organizations – the National Education Association (NEA) with 1.7-million members and the American Federation of Teachers (AFT) with 456,000 members – continued to compete with each other for power. Moreover, both organizations escalated their efforts to gain collective-bargaining rights for college and university faculties, and they were joined in that fight by the American Association of University Professors, an old-line academic organization that previously condemned industrial-type bargaining and strikes. About 12 per cent of the faculty members in U.S. colleges and universities are now covered by collective-bargaining agreements.

Busing. In Detroit, a federal court in August declined to order the busing of children to achieve desegregation. The court pointed out that, since only about one-fourth of the enrollment was white, effective citywide integration could not be achieved simply by massive busing, which might prompt more whites to leave the public school system. On August 16, District Court Judge Robert E. De-Mascio instead ordered the school board to devise a plan that would improve integration, with less busing.

Major busing was ordered in Boston and Louisville, Ky. Opponents tried to block the programs through protests, and there was sporadic violence. But extensive work by local and state police, aided by federal law-enforcement agents, permitted the schools to return quickly to relative peace. After initial protests that resulted in scores of injuries

Paul Tran, right, is one of thousands of young refugees who entered Canadian and U.S. schools after fleeing South Vietnam.

and more than 400 arrests on September 8 and 9, the two school districts of Louisville and Jefferson County, Kentucky, which had been joined by the desegregation order, appeared ready to accept the busing of 11,300 white students and an equal number of black students out of a total enrollment of 118,000. Resistance declined in Boston, too, but there were indications that many white pupils were leaving the public school system. Informal estimates showed that Boston public schools lost nearly 10,000 pupils in 1974 and probably 7,000 more in 1975. Since 1972, enrollment has declined from 96,000 to 84,000. See BOSTON.

Total Enrollment in U.S. schools and colleges declined for the third successive year, after almost three decades of constant growth. High school and college enrollments continued to increase, but elementary enrollments have dropped about 600,000 in each of the past three years.

Total enrollments in public and private institutions at all levels declined from slightly more than 59 million to 58.9 million. The elementary grades (kindergarten through grade 8) enrolled 34 million, a decline of 619,000, with 30.4 million in public schools. High schools (grades 9 through 12) enrolled 15.6 million. The 14.3 million in public high schools represented an increase of only about 160,000, indicating that the high school population is also moving toward a no-growth era.

The 1975 high school graduating class totaled 3.1 million, and the class of 1976 is expected to be slightly larger, establishing another record in American secondary education. About 975,000 bachelor's degrees, 54,000 first professional degrees, 280,000 master's degrees, and 35,000 doctorates were earned during the academic year.

Higher education had an enrollment of 11.1 million, 8.8 per cent above the previous year for the largest year-to-year increase since 1965. Only 3-million students attended private colleges and universities. Two-year public community colleges showed the greatest growth – 16.6 per cent.

Teachers. There were 3.1 million teachers working at all levels of U.S. education, including some 650,000 in colleges and universities. In addition, some 300,000 persons were employed as superintendents, principals, and other supervisors. The NEA estimated the supply of new teachers at 300,000 annually. This compares with a demand for only 160,000 per year.

The average teacher's salary for the 1974-1975 school year was $11,513, and $11,234 for elementary-school teachers, compared with $11,199 and $10,337, respectively, in the previous year. Averages ranged from Mississippi's $8,057 to Alaska's $16,387. The range was $7,457 to $15,547 in the 1973-1974 fiscal year. Other states above the $13,000 level were California, Hawaii, Illinois, and New York.

Education Expenditures at all levels in 1975-1976 were estimated by the U.S. Office of Education at $119 billion from local, state, federal, and private sources, compared with $108 billion the previous year. However, the increase was generally attributed to inflation rather than to growing support. The total national education expenditure remained fixed at just below 8 per cent of the gross national product. The average per-pupil outlay was $1,163, an 8.7 per cent increase.

Legislation. President Gerald R. Ford vetoed a $7.9-billion appropriation for education on July 25, charging it would have an inflationary impact on the economy. However, Congress decisively overrode the veto on September 10. While Ford had complained that the appropriation exceeded his budget request by $1.5 billion, the congressional majority replied that the bill constituted only a 3.6 per cent increase over the previous year's appropriations, though the inflation rate was 8 per cent.

Fiscal Crunch. School districts throughout the country felt severe budget pressures. The problem was dramatically underscored in New York City, the nation's largest school district with more than 900 schools, when the board of education was forced to cut its $2.8-billion 1976 budget by $285-million, which led to 9,000 teacher layoffs.

College Tuitions and fees rose by almost 12 per cent at public four-year colleges and by more than 8 per cent at private ones. According to a survey by the College Scholarship Service of the College Entrance Examination Board, total costs now average $3,594 annually for students living on campus and $3,186 for commuters.

Bureau of the Census statistics show that about 47 per cent of all high school students go directly to college after graduation. However, the percentages vary dramatically by family income. In families with incomes of less than $3,000 a year, only 12.7 per cent go to college. For families with incomes between $5,000 and $8,000, the figure rises to 23.7 per cent. More than 53 per cent of students in families above the $15,000 bracket go on to college.

Compared with the turbulent mood of the 1960s, campuses were quiet, with students once again absorbed in academic matters. But, while little attention was paid to it, a new militancy shattered the peace in some places. There were more demonstrations and protests in the spring of 1975 than at any time since 1971, the last year of the earlier era of rebellion. On a number of campuses – including Brown University in Providence, R.I.; Brandeis University in Waltham, Mass.; and the University of California, Santa Barbara – students occupied academic buildings, largely in protest against rising tuition and reduced scholarship opportunities for minority students. William J. McGill, president of Columbia University in New York City, warned that the relative calm on the campuses could be "deceptive."

Jobs. Despite gloomy forecasts, the final tally for 1975 graduates appeared slightly more encouraging than had been predicted. University placement directors estimated that 90 per cent of the graduates found jobs. Many of them, however, had to wait longer and take lesser jobs at lower pay than they had hoped. The decline in job offers was sharpest for engineers and Ph.D.'s.

The National Science Foundation predicted that between 375,000 and 400,000 Ph.D.'s in science and engineering will be competing for approximately 295,000 job openings by 1985. This suggests that many Ph.D.'s will have to accept jobs that currently call for lesser degrees.

Following a 10-year decline in enrollments, engineering schools reported a 22 per cent increase. This included a first-year 1974-1975 enrollment of 4,140 women – a 69 per cent increase – and 2,740 blacks, a gain of 30 per cent.

Law school applications showed the first slight decline, but even that drop left about five applicants for each law school opening.

F. David Mathews, former president of the University of Alabama, was confirmed as secretary of health, education, and welfare on July 22 (see MATHEWS, F. DAVID). John E. Ryor became president of the NEA.   Fred M. Hechinger

See also Section One, FOCUS ON EDUCATION.

EGYPT. President Anwar al-Sadat's official visit to the United States in November, 1975, capped a year of accomplishments that earned him high rank among the world's leaders. His major achievement was the signing of an interim peace agreement with Israel on September 4 that called for withdrawal of their forces in the Sinai Peninsula. The agreement, forged after months of "shuttle diplomacy" by U.S. Secretary of State Henry A. Kissinger, also provided for the stationing of American radar technicians in the Sinai to monitor the disengagement. Israel handed the Ras Sudar oil field back to Egypt on October 5, with the larger Abu Rudeis oil fields returned on December 1. Israel had held both fields since the six-day war in 1967. Sadat was criticized by Libya, Syria, and the Palestine Liberation Organization, but most of the Arab states supported the agreement.

Another significant Sadat success was the reopening of the Suez Canal, closed for eight years, on June 5. By October 17, some 3,000 vessels had passed through the waterway.

Domestic Affairs. Some unrest was caused by economic strains. There were riots and strikes early in the year as workers in Cairo's industrial suburbs and at the Helwan iron and steel complex voiced their grievances. On April 13, Sadat dismissed Prime Minister Abdul Aziz Hegazi and formed a new Cabinet, headed by Interior Minister Mamduh Muhammad Salim, to correct domestic ills.

The trial of Moslem extremists for the April, 1974, attack on the Cairo Military Academy in a plot to overthrow Sadat ended with death sentences for the three leaders and prison terms for 29 others. But Sadat continued to break with the policies of the late President Gamal Abdel Nasser. On April 5, a Cairo court awarded $75,000 to a political prisoner tortured by Nasser's secret police, and the last political prisoners from that period were released in March.

Economic Affairs. Egypt received some large amounts of foreign aid and marked some economic gains of its own. The Ramadan field in the Gulf of Suez began pumping oil on February 18 with an output of 100,000 barrels per day. Egypt's first natural gas field, Abu Maadi off Alexandria, also began producing. Suez Canal tolls were $24.7 million for the first three months of operation. Loans from the United States, Iran, and oil-producing Arab countries were expected to cover most of the annual deficit of $2.3 billion.

Um Kalthoum, the most popular singer in the Arab world, died in Cairo on February 3 at the age of 76. Her distinctive Arabic singing captivated millions during her 50-year career.   William Spencer

See also MIDDLE EAST (Facts in Brief Table).

The Egyptian destroyer *October Six*, with President Sadat aboard, steams south from Port Said on June 5 to reopen the Suez Canal after eight years.

John A. Durkin, front, and Louis C. Wyman, right, testify in January before a Senate subcommittee about their disputed New Hampshire election.

ELECTIONS. Democrats won most of the major 1975 elections, but Republicans clearly gained strength in some areas. Boston Mayor Kevin H. White and Kentucky Governor Julian Carroll survived an antibusing backlash to win election. However, a major setback for feminists occurred in November, when New York and New Jersey voters rejected state equal rights amendments.

Special Congressional Elections. Perhaps the most closely watched contest in 1975 was the special election held on September 16 between Democrat John A. Durkin and Republican Louis C. Wyman for the vacant U.S. Senate seat in New Hampshire. Neither state election officials nor the U.S. Senate had been able to determine which man won the contested November, 1974, election.

After six months of partisan wrangling, the Senate washed its hands of the dispute and sent the matter back to New Hampshire for a new election. Durkin captured 53.5 per cent of the vote.

In January, W. Henson Moore became the second Republican in more than 100 years to win a congressional seat in Louisiana, defeating Democrat Jeff LaCaze in a rerun. Their 1974 race had been voided because of voting irregularities.

In California, Shirley N. Pettis was elected on April 30 to fill the congressional seat left vacant when her husband, Republican Jerry L. Pettis, was killed in a plane crash on February 14. In Illinois,

Democrat John G. Fary won a special election on July 8 to fill the vacancy created by the death on January 27 of Congressman John C. Kluczynski. On November 25, Democrat Clifford R. Allen won an election to replace Congressman Richard H. Fulton (D., Tenn.), who had been elected mayor of Nashville.

Gubernatorial Contests. Strong emotions about court-ordered busing plans were a factor in Kentucky's gubernatorial election. But Acting Governor Carroll won a four-year term on November 4, even though his Republican opponent, Robert Gable, campaigned on antibusing sentiment.

In Mississippi, Republican Gilbert E. Carmichael narrowly lost the governor's chair to Democrat Charles C. (Cliff) Finch. The closeness of the race seemed to indicate that the Republicans were gaining strength in Mississippi.

Two women were elected lieutenant governor — Thelma Stovall in Kentucky and Evelyn Gandy in Mississippi. Edwin W. Edwards, a Democrat, was re-elected governor of Louisiana on November 1.

Mayoral Races. In the November elections, voters retained the incumbent mayors of Baltimore; Boston; Cleveland; Hartford, Conn.; Gary, Ind.; Madison, Wis.; Miami and Miami Beach, Fla.; and Philadelphia. On April 1, Chicago's Mayor Richard J. Daley was overwhelmingly re-elected to a sixth term, and Dallas Mayor Wes Wise won a third term. Patience S. Latting was re-elected mayor of Oklahoma City, Okla., in March. However, Salt Lake City, Utah, voters unseated incumbent Mayor Conrad Harrison in November, electing Democrat Ted Wilson. See BALTIMORE; BOSTON; CHICAGO; CLEVELAND; DALEY, RICHARD J.; DALLAS-FORT WORTH; PHILADELPHIA.

In Phoenix, Ariz., Vice-Mayor Margaret Hance defeated seven other candidates in November to become the city's first woman mayor. In Minneapolis, Minn., independent Charles S. Stenvig upset incumbent Democratic Mayor Albert J. Hofstede. See MINNEAPOLIS-ST. PAUL.

In Indianapolis, former Congressman William H. Hudnut III won the mayor's seat on November 4, preserving Republican control of Indiana's largest city. Seattle Mayor Wesley G. Uhlman defeated an effort by city workers to recall him from office. See SEATTLE.

Houston Mayor Fred Hofheinz was re-elected in a December run-off election (see HOUSTON). George R. Moscone was elected mayor of San Francisco in a run-off election on December 11. See SAN FRANCISCO-OAKLAND.

Voting Rights. On August 6, President Ford signed into law a seven-year extension of the Voting Rights Act of 1965 and broadened its coverage to include Spanish-speaking Americans and other minority-language groups. The act originally applied to seven Deep South states and some counties in the North. The extension covers the same Southern states plus Alaska, Texas, and parts of 12 other states. The extension also permanently banned literacy tests as a voting qualification.

Campaign Spending Law. The six-member Federal Election Commission, chaired by former Congressman Thomas B. Curtis (R., Mo.), was sworn in on April 4 to enforce the 1974 Federal Election Campaign Act. This law, which took effect on Jan. 1, 1975, limits individual campaign contributions and spending by candidates in national elections.

A strong challenge to the law by Senator James L. Buckley (Cons., N.Y.), Independent presidential candidate Eugene J. McCarthy, and civil liberties groups was brought before the Supreme Court of the United States on November 10. They argued that the limits on donations and spending in the new law unconstitutionally restrict the political expression of contributors and candidates. A similar challenge was rejected on August 15 by a U.S. Court of Appeals.

The Federal Communications Commission on September 25 exempted candidates' news conferences and political debates from its rule requiring radio and television stations to provide equal time for all qualified candidates. William J. Eaton

See DEMOCRATIC PARTY; REPUBLICAN PARTY.

ELECTRIC POWER. See ENERGY.

ELECTRONICS. Scientists in the United States and Europe announced in 1975 that they have perfected electronic systems that are the visual equivalent of the phonograph. To be marketed in late 1976, the systems play *videodisks*—metal-coated plastic disks 12 inches (30.5 centimeters) in diameter that hold 30 minutes of a motion picture or other feature on each side. The systems hook up to the antenna leads of an ordinary television set.

Videodisk Players. Two systems led the competition to be first in what experts believe may become a $700-million annual market for videodisk players and videodisks by 1980. In the United States, RCA Corporation's Selecta-Vision uses a sapphire stylus to sense changes in electrical properties as it glides in the videodisk groove. Philips Gloeilampfabriken of the Netherlands, and MCA, Incorporated, of California have jointly developed Disco-Vision, a player that uses a laser to pick up sound and picture information without touching the spinning disk. Although both players attach to television sets to produce pictures, they require different types of videodisks. They are expected to sell for about $500, and an album containing a feature-length movie will cost about $15.

The electronics industry picked up momentum during 1975 by making known technologies and concepts more widely and practicably available. These technologies include the semiconductor logic devices called integrated injection logic, computerized systems for handling financial transactions without handling money, and such low-cost digital-processing power as microprocessors.

Microprocessors. A complete computing device on one fingernail-sized semiconductor chip, the microprocessor continued to develop in 1975. Some microprocessors were available with about twice as many computing functions as in 1974. Others had more storage space.

RCA Corporation Chairman Robert W. Sarnoff announced in March that microprocessors could boost automobile mileage 40 per cent in standard-size vehicles according to preliminary tests. Automobile makers and other semiconductor manufacturers were skeptical of so dramatic a gain. But most agreed that inexpensive, mass-produced devices that contain microprocessors to adjust ignition timing and other factors will produce more efficient fuel consumption in cars of the future.

Although the microprocessor itself did not invade the home in 1975, sophisticated processorlike devices called read only memory (ROM) semiconductor chips were in many new appliances. For example, the Singer Company of New York City began selling a sewing machine that uses an ROM to control stitch width, length, and density. This tiny device replaces 350 mechanical parts on the $800 machine. ROM's also made it possible for manufacturers to put electronic temperature con-

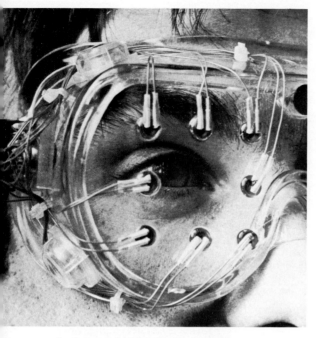

An electronic device that turns sound into lights and vibrations is being developed at Ohio State University as an aid to the deaf.

trols on stoves, electronic timing controls on microwave ovens, and all-electronic (varactor) tuners on television sets to replace the electromechanical tuners that click from channel to channel.

Integrated Injection Logic (IIL) promised to put more information on a single chip that could be retrieved faster than with other types of logic. It appeared in several commercial applications, most notably in electronic-watch circuits and in telephone terminal equipment circuits. The first IIL 4,000-bit capacity random access memory (RAM) was developed by Fairchild Camera and Instrument Corporation of California. A bit is the basic information unit in a computer. The development should further open up the IIL market.

Electronic Funds Transfer Systems were also being tested in 1975 after many years of speculation. Tests were set up in California, Illinois, Massachusetts, and New York. Merchants with computer terminals in their shops relay a customer's purchases directly to the bank. The terminals eliminate the use of money, checks, and bank-issued credit cards. See BANKS and BANKING.

Computerized checkout units were also being tested in a number of United States supermarkets. See RETAILING (Close-Up).   Marilyn J. Offenheiser

EL SALVADOR. See LATIN AMERICA.

EMPLOYMENT. See ECONOMICS; EDUCATION; LABOR; SOCIAL SECURITY; SOCIAL WELFARE.

ENERGY. With known fossil energy resources dwindling, and their availability uncertain, many nations investigated renewable sources of energy in 1975. For instance, Australian engineers took a fresh look at feasibility studies of tidal power. With prices of fossil fuels such as coal and oil increasing, proposals to tap the 40-foot (12-meter) tides on the northwestern coast of Western Australia to generate electricity became more attractive.

Japanese researchers studied ocean waves as a power source. At the Third International Ocean Development Conference in Tokyo in August, they reported that a disk-shaped buoy containing turbines could generate 3 megawatts (Mw) of electricity as cheaply as conventional generators.

In Canada, British Columbia reversed this trend toward using renewable resources. The province has historically relied almost completely on water power to generate its electricity. But officials announced in July that more than half of the province's projected new power capacity will be coal-fired. The move to develop the province's large coal deposits will save an estimated $1 billion.

U.S. Plans. The Energy Research and Development Administration (ERDA) outlined its goals to Congress on June 30. The ERDA plan covers immediate, medium-range, and long-range energy needs in research and development, designed to make the country less "vulnerable to undesirable external influence on U.S. foreign and domestic policy."

ERDA urged programs to increase the recovery of oil from U.S. fields, most of which are now abandoned after only one-third of the oil has been recovered. This increased domestic production would allow time to develop other medium-range energy measures, such as increasing coal production, removing oil from shale, and producing synthetic oil and gas from coal.

For the long-range, turn-of-the-century goals, ERDA proposed an integrated plan that includes the development of nuclear breeder reactors — reactors that will produce more fuel than they consume. It also calls for the development of nuclear fusion reactors and solar energy.

President Gerald R. Ford's plan to spend $100-billion on new energy projects was announced on September 22. Ford proposed creating a new government body called the Energy Independence Authority that would help provide massive financing for energy development.

U.S. Electric Utilities had another disappointing year in the face of rising costs and lagging rates. The hoped-for resurgence of kilowatt-hour (kwh) sales of electricity in 1975, after almost no growth in 1974, did not materialize. Utilities saw their sales nudge up 2 per cent from 1974's sales. But in spite of efforts to conserve energy by government utilities and private groups, residential sales of electricity sprang back to a near-normal 6.2 per cent increase, while commercial sales topped out at over 7 per cent. In sharp contrast, industrial sales were down about 5 per cent, primarily because of the recession and industry's strong efforts at conservation and improved management of its energy supplies. Some 18 per cent of all residential electric heating installations during 1975 used the efficient heat pump.

In the face of climbing fuel costs and a critical shortage of needed capital, the U.S. electric utility industry reported the following:

	1974	1975	% gain
	(in millions)		
Total capability (kw)	475	505	6.3
Utilities generation (kwh)	1,830,000	1,863,600	2.0
Utilities sales (kwh)	1,700,000	1,735,000	2.0
Utilities revenue*	$35,000	$42,700	22.0

*For investor-owned companies

Nuclear Energy in the electric utilities staggered under attacks by environmental and safety forces, burgeoning costs, construction delays, and a reassessment of projected load growth. After a decade of reasonably steady advances, manufacturers of nuclear reactors that generate electric power face the most uncertain period in their history. Only five new nuclear units were ordered through October, and only four units previously postponed were reinstated. During the same period, four previously ordered units totaling 4,500 Mw were canceled, and 16 units totaling 17,500 Mw were delayed.

The inherent low cost of nuclear fuel was being questioned in some circles, especially in regions where coal is readily available. American Electric Power (AEP), which started operating its first nuclear unit in March and was completing a second, was leaning to coal to meet its estimated annual growth rate of about 8 per cent. But, with vast coal reserves bought before prices rose, AEP is far from typical of the utilities.

In contrast, John W. Simpson, chairman of the Atomic Industrial Forum and past president of Westinghouse Power Systems Company, told the International Energy Engineering Congress on November 5 that 56 nuclear plants in the United States generated nearly 10 per cent of the nation's electricity in 1975 and, on average, produced that electricity for 40 per cent less cost than coal-fired plants and 65 per cent less than oil-fired plants.

U.S. Nuclear Attitudes. A major public-opinion survey by Louis Harris and Associates, Incorporated, showed U.S. leaders have underestimated public acceptance of nuclear power. The survey, termed by pollster Harris the most comprehensive in-depth study of U.S. public attitudes on this subject ever done, was conducted for Ebasco Services, a prominent firm of consulting engineers and man-

Energy Secretary Anthony Wedgwood Benn, center, opens a valve to pump ashore Great Britain's first North Sea oil on June 18.

Crude-oil storage tanks that hold 500,000
barrels each are being built at Valdez,
the southern end of the Alaska pipeline.

plants. Each park could generate up to 10 billion watts of electricity. Energy parks would also produce steam for nearby industries, thus improving energy efficiency, reducing costs, and easing thermal effects on the environment.

At Year's End, the worldwide energy picture reflected a truly paradoxical situation. Some energy sources are abundant — with the United States leaning heavily on its rich coal reserves. However, their recovery may be too costly or socially undesirable in many cases. In spite of this, increased energy use by an ever-expanding population, especially in the developing countries, requires the use of energy resources once classified as uneconomic.

In 1975, more than 18 per cent of all U.S. raw-energy supplies was imported, and dependence on foreign sources of energy increased rapidly. At the 1975 rate, raw-energy imports will make up from 40 to 50 per cent of the total within 10 years. Production of domestic oil and natural gas, two principal U.S. fossil fuels, has peaked and is declining at an annual rate of 8 per cent. Even coal, the most abundant fuel resource in the United States, is not being produced in sufficient quantity; annual production has leveled at about 600 million short tons (540 million metric tons). Energy experts estimate that this output must double within 10 years for the U.S. to meet demand.   James J. O'Connor

ENGINEERING. See BUILDING & CONSTRUCTION.

agers. Probably the most important question asked of the 1,537 adults polled was: Do you favor or oppose the building of more nuclear power plants? The answers were 63 per cent in favor, 19 per cent opposed, and 18 per cent not sure.

Energy Management. Squeezing the most work from every British thermal unit (B.T.U.) and every kwh took on added meaning during 1975. American industry put high priority on energy conservation, reducing waste while maintaining or increasing industrial output. Consulting engineers and industrial managers applied present-day equipment and available technology to reduce energy consumption 15 to 50 per cent in both new and existing buildings. Thermal insulation proved a basic element in energy-saving programs in industrial plants, commercial buildings, and homes.

Electric motors designed for industry or home use are now being manufactured to higher efficiency standards, trimming back consumption. Electric motors account for a major portion of industrial electricity use; so, the typical industrial motor user, with 300 to 500 motors per plant, could save up to $10,000 annually by switching to the more efficient motors.

The Energy Parks concept got attention in planning sessions by Washington officials and electric utilities. Energy parks, if developed, would consist of groups of coal-fired or nuclear generating

ENVIRONMENT. Major inroads are being made on "our irreplaceable environmental capital in pursuit of short-term economic benefits," Maurice F. Strong, executive director of the United Nations (UN) Environment Program, warned on April 17, 1975. Speaking at a meeting in Nairobi, Kenya, Strong cited the "proliferating commitment" to nuclear energy and lack of progress in protecting endangered wildlife species as prime problems. An international coalition of environmental groups charged in a petition to the UN on October 24 that "too little has been done" to adopt the earth-care policy endorsed by the UN Conference on Human Environment in June, 1972.

The UN Law of the Sea Conference concluded an eight-week session in Geneva, Switzerland, on May 9 without reaching agreement (see OCEAN). Delegates to the conference were hopeful, however, that a consensus was developing for the session scheduled to open in New York City on March 24, 1976. The U.S. Congress, critical of the slow progress in reaching international agreement, moved to establish a 200-nautical-mile protective fishing zone around U.S. shores. The House of Representatives approved a 200-mile limit on October 9 that would lapse with U.S. ratification of an international treaty. On October 15, Iceland became the first European nation to establish such a 200-mile fishing zone. See FISHING INDUSTRY.

ENVIRONMENT

In the United States, President Gerald R. Ford's Administration subordinated environmental goals to fight the economic recession. He said in July that, while he advocated a "détente with nature," some environmental goals must be tempered to allow economic progress. The environmental movement remained a powerful political force. An October poll by the Opinion Research Corporation found that 60 per cent of Americans favor paying the costs of environmental protection as opposed to 21 per cent who want to keep prices and taxes down at the risk of increased pollution. The polling firm said that the environmental movement shows "little sign of abating even during a period of economic stress."

Energy Conflicts. While President Ford and Congress wrestled indecisively on the politics of meeting the nation's energy problems, environmentalists urged more emphasis on energy conservation and developing new forms of energy. A national plan for energy research, unveiled by the Ford Administration on June 30, was faulted by conservationists at hearings on September 3 as being biased in favor of atomic energy and not placing enough stress on cutting energy use. The National Wildlife Federation said the blueprint played down the potential for solar and geothermal energy.

The weakness of the largely voluntary energy conservation measures was underlined when the International Energy Agency reported in October that the United States ranked 15th among 18 oil-importing nations in conservation efforts. The Ford Administration's proposal for a $100-billion government corporation to help finance energy projects was greeted skeptically by many conservationists. They feared the massive development of synthetic fuels envisioned by the proposal would inflict a disastrous ecological toll through strip-mining of coal and oil shale.

Government experts predicted a long-range role for solar power, which many ecologists regard as the most environmentally sound form of energy use. The Energy Research and Development Administration said on August 13 that the sun may provide about 7 per cent of U.S. energy needs by the end of this century.

The Supreme Court of the United States ruled unanimously on March 17 that the federal government owns the oil and gas resources on the Atlantic outer continental shelf beyond the 3-nautical-mile limit. Following the decision, the U.S. Department of the Interior pushed aggressively to open new "frontier" areas off the Atlantic and Pacific coasts for oil drilling.

The Alaska oil pipeline, a prime target of environmentalists in the late 1960s, moved ahead of schedule in October and was expected to begin providing 600,000 barrels of oil daily by April, 1977. The optimistic outlook developed after the last of 47 barges carrying vital equipment reached Prudhoe Bay in the Arctic Coastal Plain on September 30. The barge fleet had been blocked for three months by weather that prevented the normal summer breakup of the Arctic ice pack.

Air Pollution. The Environmental Protection Agency (EPA) on March 5 extended until 1978 the deadline for automakers to meet stricter anti-pollution standards on exhaust emissions. This third extension of the curbs, which were originally scheduled to take effect in 1975, was strongly criticized by the National Clean Air Coalition.

Warnings were voiced throughout the year that the earth's ozone layer was threatened with depletion by freon gases released from aerosol cans. Some scientists said a perilous weakening of the ozone shield that surrounds the earth's atmosphere could take place, permitting damaging ultraviolet radiation from the sun to reach the earth. This could cause an increase in the incidence of skin cancer and ultimately threaten all life on earth. Spokesmen for the aerosol industry dismissed the warnings as theoretical. See Close-Up; Section One, FOCUS ON SCIENCE.

Land Programs. The House of Representatives failed on June 11 to override President Ford's veto of legislation to control strip-mining of coal. The bill would have imposed stiff federal standards on surface mining and provided for reclamation of land already damaged. A similar bill was vetoed by President Ford on Dec. 30, 1974. Environmentalists fought hard for the bill and won substantial backing in Congress. The Senate approved it 84 to 13 on March 13, 1975, and the House passed it 333 to 86 on March 18. The President's argument that the bill threatened plans to meet energy needs was instrumental in sustaining his vetoes.

A drive by environmentalists to revive land-use legislation collapsed on March 17 when the Ford Administration opposed the bill because of "overriding economic and budget problems." The legislation would have provided $800 million in funds to encourage the states to develop their own land-use controls.

Water Cleanup. The National Commission on Water Quality reported on September 6 that the effort to clean up the nation's waterways is running far behind schedule. EPA Administrator Russell E. Train said the preliminary report "completely lacks balance." The final report was to be made to Congress in March, 1976.

One cause of EPA's slow disbursement of funds for sewage-treatment plants was eliminated on February 18, when the Supreme Court ruled that President Richard M. Nixon exceeded his authority in 1972 when he impounded $9 billion in funds for fighting water pollution.　Andrew L. Newman

See also CONSERVATION.

Is That Spray Can Dangerous?

"It is difficult to perceive that when you are spraying an antiperspirant in your bathroom, you are endangering the health of everyone in the world." Russell W. Peterson, chairman of the U.S. Council on Environmental Quality, voiced feelings shared by many Americans in 1975's biggest environmental flap, which focused on the convenient — and perhaps harmful — aerosol can.

The first shot was fired in June, 1974, by chemists F. Sherwood Rowland and Mario J. Molina of the University of California, Irvine. They suggested that molecules of the fluorocarbons used in more than half the 3 billion aerosol cans sold annually are rising slowly into the stratosphere. There, these supposedly harmless "inert" gas molecules are breaking down the earth's ozone shield, a layer of gas that prevents the sun's most harmful ultraviolet (UV) radiation from reaching the earth and greatly reduces less damaging UV radiation. If more of the most dangerous UV radiation reaches the earth's surface, some scientists fear it could cause an increase in cataracts and human skin cancer. If present gas production trends continue, 30 per cent of the stratospheric ozone could be destroyed by 1994, according to some estimates. This could produce an additional 100,000 to 300,000 cases of skin cancer a year in the United States alone. Scientists also warned that increased UV radiation could cause genetic damage to plant and animal life.

Environmentalists quickly called for a ban on fluorocarbon gases. But estimates of the danger varied widely. Industry spokesmen pointed out that much more testing was needed before scientists could be sure of the gases' effects on the ozone layer. They noted that ozone levels fluctuate naturally.

They also said a complete ban on the gases would seriously affect the refrigeration and foamed-plastics industries, which use fluorocarbons. The DuPont Company, the biggest manufacturer of the gases, describes the production, packaging, and marketing of fluorocarbons as an $8-billion U.S. industry involving near-

ly a million workers. So the lines were drawn in a classic confrontation between economic need and environmental peril.

A special government task force reported on June 12, after five months of study, that "there seems to be legitimate cause for concern" about the effects of fluorocarbons on ozone. They said that the ozone concentration may already have been reduced 1 per cent and may eventually be reduced 3 per cent by gas molecules drifting up to the stratosphere. They called for a ban on the use of fluorocarbons as aerosol propellants by January, 1978, unless new evidence shows the gases are harmless.

But the new evidence reported later in the summer supported the ozone-depletion theory. Research teams from the National Center for Atmospheric Research (NCAR) and the National Oceanic and Atmospheric Administration reported that their field tests produced data so close to laboratory predictions it was "absolutely astounding." John Gille, head of NCAR's Upper Atmosphere Project said, "I think our results have drastically narrowed room for doubt" that fluorocarbons are affecting the ozone shield. A key study by the National Academy of Sciences is now underway.

The ozone controversy emphasizes the difficulties an industrial society has in choosing between a short-term economic good and a possible environmental hazard. If the gases are banned, it will cause economic dislocation. Substitutes must then be found for the Freon gas used in refrigerators and air conditioners. If the gases are not banned, the scientific data points more and more to the possibility of great environmental hazard.

Although industry opposed a ban, the Johnson Wax Company has switched from fluorocarbons to another propellant, and makers of the gases reported sales declines of up to 25 per cent. Industry spokesmen acknowledged that many consumers were avoiding fluorocarbon aerosols. Perhaps people were making their own decisions about aerosols and ozone. Edward G. Nash

Aerosol can

ETHIOPIA. The military government that ousted Emperor Haile Selassie I abolished Ethiopia's monarchy on March 21, 1975. After deposing Selassie in September, 1974, the government invited his eldest son, Crown Prince Asfa Wossen, to return from Europe to be crowned as a figurehead king. However, the crown prince remained in exile. On August 27, the 83-year-old Selassie died.

The provisional military government announced on March 9 that it would not relinquish power until the people were judged ready to rule themselves. However, the new government faced increasing opposition throughout the year.

Eritrean Rebels. The most serious challenge came from Eritrean nationalists who sought to transform their province of about 2 million persons into a separate nation. On January 31, heavily armed guerrillas attacked Ethiopian Army positions in Asmara, Eritrea's capital. The fighting lasted three days. The army and the rebels fought another large battle in late February near Keren.

The rebels reportedly received weapons from Arab nations, while the Ethiopian Army received arms from the United States. The rebels demanded that the United States stop supplying the Ethiopian Army. They kidnaped five Americans from a U.S. communications base near Asmara, two on July 14, two on September 12, and one on December 21. One condition for the release of the hostages was a halt to U.S. arms shipments.

As of November, there seemed to be a stalemate in the fighting. Government forces held the major towns, and the secessionists controlled almost all the countryside, except the southern part of the province. In southern Eritrea, a separate antigovernment movement emerged. In late May and early June, Afar tribesmen attacked government troops along the vital road linking Addis Ababa, Ethiopia's capital, with the port of Assab. The dispute was reportedly over radical land reforms.

The government had nationalized all agricultural land without compensation on March 4. It encouraged peasants to join large communal farms. The reforms appeared to be popular in Ethiopian provinces where absentee landlords had rented parts of their large tracts to peasants for farming. However, in several areas, landlords with strong local roots organized armed resistance.

Labor Opposition. On September 24, the Confederation of Ethiopian Trade Unions threatened a general strike if the government did not permit political parties, freedom of speech, and other democratic liberties. On September 25, security forces in Addis Ababa killed seven airline employees who were demonstrating and distributing antigovernment literature.   John D. Esseks

See also AFRICA (Facts in Brief Table).

Ethiopian veterans march in February in downtown Addis Ababa to show their support of government policy toward Eritrean rebels.

EUROPE reeled from the force of worldwide recession in 1975 and struggled to lower inflation and unemployment while revitalizing the economy. In the fall, all of the nine European Community (Common Market) countries except Great Britain and Ireland implemented recovery programs that were timed to coincide with similar efforts in the United States and Japan. But average annual inflation remained above 10 per cent.

Portugal remained Europe's real trouble spot in 1975, as a power struggle between Communists and Socialists nearly brought about civil war (see PORTUGAL). The future of Cyprus remained unresolved despite United Nations (UN) efforts, and the island was still partitioned between Greeks and Turks (see CYPRUS). Greece applied for full market membership in June and received British, French, and Italian pledges of support in the fall (see GREECE). Italian regional elections in June sounded an ominous note, making the Communist Party the strongest in seven of 15 regions, including major cities (see ITALY).

Angry demonstrations throughout Europe followed the execution of five political activists in Spain on September 27. Involved in the Basque separatist struggle, they had been sentenced under new antiterrorism laws despite repeated appeals for clemency from Pope Paul VI, UN Secretary-General Kurt Waldheim, and European leaders.

Israeli and European Community representatives sign a pact in Brussels in May cutting tariffs on Common Market exports to Israel 60 per cent.

Spanish consulates and embassies were sacked, and Britain, Germany, the Netherlands, and Norway were among the first to recall their ambassadors. The government of General Francisco Franco isolated itself from practically every important section of Spanish society. Franco died on November 20, and Prince Juan Carlos was proclaimed king two days later. See JUAN CARLOS I; SPAIN.

Security Summit. Delegations from 35 governments, including the leaders of Eastern and Western Europe, Canada, the United States, and Russia, filed into Finlandia Congress Hall in Helsinki, Finland, on July 30 to open the third stage of the Conference on Security and Cooperation in Europe (CSCE).

The conference, culminating 22 months of talks, ended three days later with the signing of a document that set goals of "peace, security, justice, and cooperation." The English-language version was 106 pages long and dealt with issues of human contacts, including family reunification, travel and tourism, and the flow of information; economic cooperation; cooperation in education and culture; principles governing relations between countries; and measures to increase mutual trust, including advance notification of military maneuvers. While the measures have no binding force, all participating countries were committed to publish them and to abide by them. The participating nations

pledged to "broaden, deepen, and make continuing and lasting the process of détente."

But the spirit of détente received an early setback when the Turkish delegation walked out as Cyprus President Archbishop Makarios III took the floor. Turkish Prime Minister Suleyman Demirel told the meeting that Turkey could not consider any conference decision about Cyprus binding. In a peacekeeping effort on July 31, U.S. President Gerald R. Ford offered Turkey $50 million in arms aid and stepped-up efforts to solve the Cyprus dispute. In exchange, Turkey was to keep open U.S. bases that monitor Russian military communications. Demirel rejected the offer.

President Ford and other heads of state also held private talks on issues outside the CSCE program. On his way to Helsinki, President Ford met West German Chancellor Helmut Schmidt in Bonn. They agreed to integrate the economic policies of West Germany and the Common Market with those of the United States. In a 24-hour visit to Warsaw, Poland, Ford reviewed with Polish Communist Party First Secretary Edward Gierek the implementation of 1974 bilateral agreements.

The stagnant international economic situation concerned all the Common Market leaders at the CSCE. Rampaging inflation – running at an average annual rate of over 10 per cent for the Common Market countries – and rising unemployment

305

Facts in Brief on the European Countries

Country	Population	Government	Monetary Unit*	Foreign Trade (million U.S. $) Exports	Imports
Albania	2,563,000	Communist Party First Secretary Enver Hoxha; Premier Mehmet Shehu; People's Assembly Presidium Chairman Hashi Lleshi	lek (10.25 = $1)	74	116
Andorra	19,000	The bishop of Urgel, Spain, and the president of France	French franc and Spanish peseta	no statistics available	
Austria	7,639,000	President Rudolf Kirchschlaeger; Chancellor Bruno Kreisky	schilling (18.2 = $1)	7,161	9,023
Belgium	9,907,000	King Baudouin I; Prime Minister Leo Tindemans	franc (40.6 = $1)	28,260 (includes Luxembourg)	29,703
Bulgaria	8,822,000	Communist Party First Secretary & State Council Chairman Todor Zhivkov; Premier Stanko Todorov	lev (1 = $1.10)	3,836	4,326
Czechoslovakia	14,830,000	Communist Party First Secretary & President Gustav Husak; Premier Lubomir Strougal	koruna (11.5 = $1)	7,053	7,532
Denmark	5,134,000	Queen Margrethe II; Prime Minister Anker Henrik Jorgensen	krone (6.1 = $1)	7,718	9,902
Finland	4,663,000	President Urho Kekkonen; Prime Minister Martti Miettunen	markka (3.9 = $1)	5,538	6,870
France	53,607,000	President Valéry Giscard d'Estaing; Prime Minister Jacques Chirac	franc (4.5 = $1)	46,473	52,914
Germany, East	16,975,000	Communist Party First Secretary Erich Honecker; State Council Chairman Willi Stoph; Prime Minister Horst Sindermann	mark (2.4 = $1)	8,748	9,646
Germany, West	63,670,000	President Walter Scheel; Chancellor Helmut Schmidt	Deutsche mark (2.6 = $1)	89,055	68,897
Great Britain	56,858,000	Queen Elizabeth II; Prime Minister Harold Wilson	pound (1 = $2.02)	38,640	54,144
Greece	9,030,000	President Constantine Tsatsos; Prime Minister Constantine Caramanlis	drachma (33.3 = $1)	2,030	4,385
Hungary	10,565,000	Communist Party First Secretary Janos Kadar; President Pal Losonczi; Prime Minister Gyorgy Lazar	forint (20.4 = $1)	5,130	5,576
Iceland	220,000	President Kristjan Eldjarn; Prime Minister Geir Hallgrimsson	króna (166 = $1)	331	518
Ireland	3,087,000	President Cearbhall O'Dalaigh; Prime Minister Liam Cosgrave	pound (1 = $2.02)	2,628	3,799
Italy	55,883,000	President Giovanni Leone; Prime Minister Aldo Moro	lira (684.8 = $1)	30,240	40,927
Liechtenstein	22,000	Prince Francis Joseph II	Swiss franc	no statistics available	
Luxembourg	359,000	Grand Duke Jean; Prime Minister Gaston Thorn	franc (40.6 = $1)	28,260 (includes Belgium)	29,703
Malta	316,000	President Sir Anthony J. Mamo; Prime Minister Dom Mintoff	pound (1 = $2.52)	134	361
Monaco	25,000	Prince Rainier III	French franc	no statistics available	
Netherlands	13,981,000	Queen Juliana; Prime Minister Johannes Martin den Uyl	guilder (2.7 = $1)	33,016	34,204
Norway	4,060,000	King Olav V; Prime Minister Trygve Bratteli	krone (5.5 = $1)	6,242	8,423
Poland	34,140,000	Communist Party First Secretary Edward Gierek; President Henryk Jablonski; Premier Piotr Jaroszewicz	zloty (33.2 = $1)	8,315	10,482
Portugal	8,720,000	President Francisco da Costa Gomes; Prime Minister José Pinheiro de Azevedo	escudo (27 = $1)	2,277	4,496
Romania	21,698,000	Communist Party General Secretary & President Nicolae Ceausescu; Prime Minister Manea Manescu	leu (4.9 = $1)	3,751	3,704
Russia	258,542,000	Communist Party General Secretary Leonid I. Brezhnev; Premier Aleksey N. Kosygin; Supreme Soviet Presidium Chairman Nikolay V. Podgorny	ruble (1 = $1.43)	27,405	24,890
San Marino	19,000	2 regents appointed by Grand Council every 6 months	Italian lira	no statistics available	
Spain	36,119,000	King Juan Carlos I; Prime Minister Carlos Arias Navarro	peseta (58.8 = $1)	7,098	15,382
Sweden	8,352,000	King Carl XVI Gustaf; Prime Minister Olof Palme	krona (4.4 = $1)	15,912	15,813
Switzerland	6,736,000	President Rudolf Gnaegi	franc (2.7 = $1)	11,865	14,431
Turkey	40,909,000	President Fahri S. Koruturk; Prime Minister Suleyman Demirel	lira (14.9 = $1)	1,574	3,775
Yugoslavia	21,615,000	President Josip Broz Tito; Prime Minister Dzemal Bijedic	dinar (17.9 = $1)	4,071	8,071

*Exchange rates as of Dec. 1, 1975

bedeviled all of Europe. The Common Market finance ministers told all member countries except Britain and Ireland on August 24 that they should produce economic activity by reflation. Belgium, France, Luxembourg, the Netherlands, West Germany, and, to a lesser degree, Denmark and Italy soon announced deficit-spending programs to stimulate their economies.

Unemployment skyrocketed in all Common Market countries except Ireland during the year that ended July 31. A Common Market plan to guarantee certain workers 80 per cent of normal salaries if they lose their jobs was dropped over West German opposition.

Economic Summit. At the invitation of French President Valéry Giscard d'Estaing, the leaders of Britain, France, Italy, Japan, West Germany, and the United States met from November 14 to 17 at the Château de Rambouillet, a turreted castle about 35 miles (55 kilometers) southwest of Paris. They pledged to work closely together to "assure the recovery" of their economies and "to reduce the waste of human resources involved in unemployment." Although they formulated no detailed plans, the heads of state hoped to avoid renewed inflation and protectionist trade policies that might help one nation's recovery but hurt others.

The summit caused some bitterness among those Western industrialized nations that were not invited, especially the Netherlands. Nor was the call for growth particularly well received at the 27-seat Conference on International Economic Cooperation that convened in Paris on December 16. Oil exporters sided with representatives from developing nations in calling for more production equipment and capital. See INTERNATIONAL TRADE AND FINANCE.

Agricultural Policy Disputes. Britain demanded radical changes in the Common Market's Common Agricultural Policy (CAP), which aims to provide security of farm supplies at stable prices. The demand was part of the renegotiation terms before a June 5 referendum in which Britons voted 2 to 1 to stay in the Common Market. Britain wanted a new marketing system for beef, with subsidies paid to producers, rather than Common Market price supports. Britain claimed that this would prevent a beef surplus. The market accepted the British plan on February 13 in return for higher prices for dairy products.

British and French poultry farmers carried on an "egg war" with the European Commission, a Common Market executive group. Backed by the West Germans and Italians, the British and French walked out of a meeting in Brussels, Belgium, on May 13 because they said the Common Market had failed to deal with an extreme crisis in their industry. British farmers complained that supply was outstripping demand by 4 per cent and asked

for a subsidy on early slaughter of hens. On July 2, the commission agreed to suspend import subsidies until November 1, but it refused Britain's request for a complete export ban because it would interfere with free trade flow in the Common Market.

Europe had huge dairy produce surpluses and, by August 29, a dried skimmed-milk "mountain" had risen to 1,065,000 short tons (966,000 metric tons) and the surplus of butter to 312,000 short tons (283,000 metric tons), most of it stored in France. Farm experts hoped the continued drought would help to reduce the glut. The Common Market adopted a $32-million plan to increase milk drinking in schools, sell more cheap powdered milk to developing countries, and provide cheaper butter for Europe's needy.

The Wine War between France and Italy was a more serious threat to CAP. A drop in consumption led to a Common Market wine "lake" of 500-million gallons (1.9 billion liters). French growers complained that 80 per cent of the 1974 harvest was unsold and that their income had fallen 30 per cent in two years. They asked for an import ban on cheap Italian wine. However, Italy blocked a French attempt to slap a 17 per cent tax on wine imports at a meeting of agricultural ministers on September 9. The ministers failed to find a solution after 20 hours of continuous discussion. On Sep-

Leaders of 35 nations meet in Helsinki, Finland, on July 30 to cap the Conference on Security and Cooperation in Europe.

tember 12, France imposed a 12 per cent import tax on inexpensive Italian wines.

On September 18, the German delegation stormed out of a wine-market management committee meeting in Venice, Italy, to protest the commission's decision to abolish a 12 per cent tax on wine exports to West Germany. The Germans charged the commission with shifting the consequences of the wine dispute "into the West German wine market." On October 29, the commission ordered France to lift its tax on Italian wine.

Fishing Limits continued to vex the Common Market. Iceland decided to extend its fisheries limit from 50 to 200 nautical miles after October 15, precipitating a renewal of the 1972 "cod war." Icelandic gunboats cut the fishing-net towlines of British trawlers, and British Royal Navy frigates and tugboats were sent to run interference. Shots were fired on December 12. West Germany and Belgium agreed to limit their fishing there.

Market Unity. Despite the agricultural and fishing conflicts, unity came from a meeting on December 3. Leaders of the nine market nations avoided a split when Britain dropped its demand for a separate voting seat at the Conference on International Economic Cooperation. Seven of the leaders agreed to hold direct elections for the European Parliament in 1978, and all agreed on a uniform passport for community citizens, to be issued in 1978. France ended its maverick energy policy by agreeing to share oil in times of emergency.

Regional Fund. The Common Market's long-promised regional development fund of $1.4 billion was distributed for the first time in 1975. Chief beneficiaries were Italy (40 per cent), Britain (28 per cent), and Ireland (6 per cent). The funds are to be used over three years either to help maintain present jobs or to create new ones. On August 10, Britain was told firmly that the fund must not be used for projects already in progress.

Monetary Reform Urged. Commission President François-Xavier Ortoli stressed on July 14 the importance of a return to monetary stability and fixed exchange rates. His remarks came shortly after France rejoined the *snake,* the system by which currencies float jointly within narrowly defined limits. Ortoli said it was important that the three remaining "defectors" — Britain, Italy, and Ireland — should rejoin the snake as soon as possible. After eight months of negotiations, Switzerland decided on November 20 not to join the snake.

Third World Help. The 32 developing countries hardest hit by high energy costs received a $100-million grant from the Common Market on January 22 following their $150-million 1974 allocation. The market signed a five-year agreement with 46 developing African, Caribbean, and Pacific countries in Lomé, Togo, on February 28. The pact guarantees duty-free access for their agricultural and industrial exports and provides about $4 billion in development funds for the 46 countries, most of which are former colonies of Common Market nations. The deal ensured for Common Market countries 1.4 million short tons (1.2 million metric tons) of sugar a year for seven years.

In Brussels on May 11, the market signed a preferential agreement with Israel under which Israeli exports may enter European markets free of duty after July 1, 1977. The pact was regarded as a break from Europe's pro-Arab Middle East policy. Although protesting the Israeli pact, Arab League nations met with the Common Market in Cairo, Egypt, on June 10 to discuss economic, technical, and cultural cooperation. On July 28, the Common Market agreed to supply Egypt with $250 million worth of wheat, sugar, meat, and dairy produce.

Equal Rights. The Common Market stepped up pressure on member states to reduce discrimination against working women. Commission Vice-President Patrick J. Hillery promoted a directive on eliminating legal and administrative measures that discriminate against working women on the basis of sex, marital, or family status. He said that laws to protect women should be in force in member countries by June, 1976.

Defense. Britain on April 20 eased a plan to cut its armed forces by 10 per cent over 10 years, following an urgent plea from the North Atlantic Treaty Organization (NATO). When President Ford addressed a NATO summit meeting in Brussels on May 29, he warned France and Greece, which have withdrawn from the military alliance, and Portugal that the integrity of NATO could be preserved only through unqualified participation. He promised the United States would make no unilateral cuts in its NATO forces. The NATO heads of government affirmed their resolve "to preserve the solidarity of the alliance and restore it where impaired."

Communist Relations. The Common Market established formal relations with China on September 15. It also held its first official talks in Moscow from February 4 to 7 with its Eastern Europe counterpart, the Council for Mutual Economic Assistance (COMECON). The talks failed to produce agreement for a more substantive meeting.

The COMECON countries maintained growth rates of between 5 and 7 per cent at the expense of more consumer goods. Premiers and chief planners approved "a concerted plan of multilateral integration measures" for the planning period 1976 to 1980 at a meeting in Budapest, Hungary, in June. Russia had more than doubled crude oil prices in January, but the only mention of the burden that this placed on other COMECON members was a note to give "special attention to problems of fuel-energy supplies." Kenneth Brown

EXPLOSION. See DISASTERS.

The annual international industrial fair, held in Hannover, West Germany, in May, was one of the world's largest trade fairs.

drew crowds. The 49th annual Feast of San Gennaro was held from September 14 to 21 and drew nearly 1 million visitors to its array of clams, calzone, gelati, zeppole, and sausages and pepper. San Francisco's 75,000 Chinese residents held their 124th New Year celebration from February 15 to 23, honoring the Year of the Hare. Half a world away, millions of Chinese celebrated the 26th anniversary of the People's Republic of China on October 1 with festivals throughout the nation.

Ocean Expo '75, the first international exhibition devoted to marine life, opened on July 19 on Okinawa under the sponsorship of the Japanese government. The 50 pavilions, scheduled to be open until Jan. 18, 1976, were expected to draw 2.3 million tourists. The opening festivities were marred by two young radicals who tossed a fire bomb at Japanese Crown Prince Akihito and Princess Michiko. They were unhurt.

Amsterdam, the Netherlands, founded about 1275, celebrated its 700th anniversary with a series of theater, music, and art exhibits, the opening of a children's museum, and an international congress on education. The observance began on October 27. More than 6 million visitors poured into Munich, West Germany, for the annual Oktoberfest, which opened on September 20.　　Lynn Beaumont

See also BICENTENNIAL, U.S.

FARM MACHINERY. See MANUFACTURING.

FAIRS AND EXHIBITIONS. More than 600 major international trade fairs were held in 1975, ranging from general product sales shows to highly specialized fairs designed to attract buyers of specific products. The Frankfurt Book Fair from October 9 to 14 in West Germany was a gathering of the world's largest and most important international publishers. It included the People's Republic of China as a first-time exhibitor.

The 31st International Air and Space Show, held in Paris every other year since 1909, attracted more than half a million visitors between May 30 and June 8. The first worldwide machine-tool exhibition, held in Paris from June 17 to 26, attracted 1,370 exhibitors from 25 countries. The Argentine Rural Society Annual Fair, the most impressive livestock show in South America, celebrated its 100th anniversary in August, in Buenos Aires.

U.S. Exhibits. There were 1,800 state, district, and county fairs and more than 300 individual fairs held throughout the United States. The annual Eastern States Exhibition, one of the country's largest and most colorful agricultural and industrial exhibits, drew 933,184 visitors to West Springfield, Mass., from September 10 to 21.

Two of the oldest and best-known ethnic and cultural fairs in the United States—the Feast of San Gennaro in New York City's Little Italy and San Francisco's Chinese New Year celebration—

FASHION in 1975 touched on everything from loose peasant garments to tailored blazer suits, jumped from "uniform thinking" to "fantasy expressions," and maintained an overriding concern with quality. The message from designers was refinement and sophistication—a belief that timeless clothes make sound investments. Quality meant expensive fabrics—Harris tweed, wool flannel, cashmere, camel's hair, pure cotton, and pure silk—all those splendid materials that stand up to the test of time.

The Main Trends. It was not a year for major upheavals. The Big Look of 1974 was cleaned up and toned down. The new shapes leaned toward the body, and even when they moved away, their fullness was tamed. There was a tendency to pare the silhouette, as in Calvin Klein's reefer coats and Yves Saint Laurent's tube dresses. Designers such as Geoffrey Beene also softened the bulk by wrapping the waist, and balancing smocklike overshirts with slim skirts and straight-leg trousers. Savile Row tailoring and Anglo-Saxon conceits such as blazers, vests, hacking jackets, haberdasher's suits, and polo coats reappeared. Skirts sported dressmaker details: yokes, tucks, pleats, smocking, dirndl gathers, wraps, cargo pockets, or ropes.

Layering, the art of piling garment upon garment, also aided a rich look. Layering savvy consisted of double blouses, multiple sweaters of vary-

Denim, the familiar blue-jeans material, moved into fashion respectability as young and old flocked to wear it in a wide variety of costumes.

ing lengths, pants under tunic dresses, jumpers over dresses, double coats (a paper-thin rain shell over a warm wool, knit, or fur version), hoods under hats, and shawls over everything. The triangular scarf was the ultimate layer.

Neutral colors from nature – beige, sage, and blush – in one-color combinations played up the luxurious textures. The most vital color was charcoal gray or pale gray, with overtones of violet and blue. Also prominent were charcoal navy, loden green, wine red, winter red, and clear scarlet. Squishy cloche hats, crushed boots, pouch bags, ombré-shaded sunglasses, and polished wood, silver, and gold jewelry completed the picture.

Back to the Past. Lingerie evening dresses in peach, pink, ivory, or café au lait struck a note of pampered, indolent femininity of bygone days. Melon-pink silk robes and floating pajamas in shades of the Jazz Age slinked out of the boudoir to attend parties.

Old clothes – meticulously made castoff finery – once the special domain of eccentrics, became the rage. Young people flocked to the spate of antique-vestments boutiques that sprang up everywhere, swooping up hand-me-down evening bags, Art Deco jewelry, smudgy-pink georgette dresses, and the wispy undergarments of the 1930s.

Laborers' Looks. Along with the quest for quality ran a total rejection of it. A craze for khaki, olive-drab, and workmen's clothes threatened to knock out jeans and T-shirts as America's favorite uniform.

The jumpsuit was the runaway success of the year. It came in hard-working fabrics – twill, drill, duck, baby-wale corduroy, and seersucker. Uniform components included parachuter's or painter's pants, clam-diggers, culottes, butcher-apron wraps, military fatigues pushed into combat boots, naval-inspired dresses, and a whole battalion of epaulets, zip-up pockets, and webbing belts.

Eastern Orientation. A handful of designers turned to the mysterious East to fuel their fantasies. Fashion's Orient Express picked up steam with Kenzo Takada's spring showing in Paris. It contained a treasure trove of sensuous, silken chinoiserie.

In America, Cuban-born Adolfo interpreted dynastic styles with mandarin-collared, frog-fastened knit pants suits. Korean-born Cathy Hardwick flung huge porcelain-type flowers on quilted cotton coats of red and plum. German-born Britta of Cinnamon Wear cut drop-shouldered coolie jackets in proletarian-posh dark muslins. Exploring further into the exotica of the East was American designer Mary McFadden with opulent coats batiked in Java, hand-painted tunics, and pajamas and jackets that sang of Persia, India, or Tibet.

By year's end, the fantasy mood of designers shifted from the hills of China to other, wilder shores of fashion influence. Paris packed a playful batch of resort-bound looks into the October ready-to-wear collections. Saint Laurent echoed the languid cotton shirts of Marrakech. Kenzo Takada longed for Africa with hip-sashed skirts, slit-happy dresses, and bare-shoulder tops.

Menswear came closer to translating the high European tailoring tradition into comfortable contemporary clothes for American men. The so-called American suit, characterized by the soft-shoulder jacket and straight pants, was further modified to resemble the closer-fitting European model. The new look, called the quasi-European suit, had slightly padded shoulders, higher armholes, a more prominent waist suppression, open-patch pockets, and a light flare to both jacket and pants. Part of this trend was the reappearance of the vest with almost every suit. Also emerging was a fashion for sham-suede apparel.

The Coty Awards. Geoffrey Beene received another citation on the Coty Hall of Fame Award that he won in 1974. Elected to the Hall of Fame were Calvin Klein and Piero Dimitri, the first menswear designer to be so honored. The Return Award went to Bill Kaiserman of Rafael for innovative men's separates, and the Winnie for women's design went to Carol Horn's Habitat. Special award recipients were Nancy Knox of Intercuerros and Monika Tilley of Elon..   Kathryn Zahony Livingston

FINLAND. Disagreement over how to solve inflation and other economic problems forced the government of Prime Minister Kalevi Sorsa to resign on June 4, 1975. But an election on September 21 and 22 brought little change in the balance between left and nonleft parties in parliament. Sorsa's four-party coalition fell because it could not agree on how to deal with Finland's 17 per cent rate of inflation and a $1.5-billion trade deficit.

Following a radio and television appeal by President Urho Kekkonen, five parties formed a "national emergency" coalition government on November 30. Led by Prime Minister Martti Miettunen, the Social Democrats took five of the 18 Cabinet posts. The Center and Communist parties each took four seats.

To help correct its economic woes, Sorsa's government had clamped a 15 per cent surcharge on imports on March 24. It affected about 60 per cent of commodity imports, but not Russian oil.

Industrial output dropped in the first three months of 1975. The cost of living rose 5.9 per cent in the first four months. Unemployment rose, too, and the government revised the two-year wage agreement negotiated in March, 1974. Wages generally increased by 5 per cent in April, but low-income groups gained more.   Kenneth Brown

See also EUROPE (Facts in Brief Table).

FIRE. See DISASTERS.

FISHING. Delegates to the National Wildlife Federation Convention, meeting in Pittsburgh on March 16, 1975, called for a new national policy that would strip American Indians of their special fishing rights. The delegates said Indians are entitled to the same rights as other citizens – but no more. A 1973 decision by U.S. District Court Judge George Boldt gave Indians virtually unlimited control over salmon and steelhead trout fishing in the state of Washington, and Indians in many Western states are not required to buy fishing licenses or abide by creel and bag limits. Lynn A. Greenwalt, director of the U.S. Fish and Wildlife Service, said in July, "The Indians have a right to fish, but not to exhaust the resource."

Limits on the catch of Atlantic bluefin tuna, a prime target of sports fishermen, were established by the National Oceanic and Atmospheric Administration to help save the threatened species.

Clashes between sports and commercial fishermen on North Carolina's Outer Banks led to closing of the Cape Hatteras area to commercial fishing on weekends. Sports anglers protested that commercial seine hauling disrupted surfcasting.

A record 27 million U.S. fishermen spent $128-million on state fishing licenses in 1974. The most heavily fished states were California, Michigan, and Texas. Wisconsin attracted the most out-of-state fishermen.   Andrew L. Newman

FISHING INDUSTRY. United States tuna-boat skippers protested vigorously in August, 1975, over fishing out of season for yellowfin tuna by other nations in a conservation zone in the eastern Pacific Ocean. The skippers charged that other countries failed to enforce restrictions that U.S. boats must observe in a zone extending from southern California to Chile.

Tuna fleet spokesmen said the U.S. share of the world yellowfin tuna catch had declined from 90 per cent in 1966 to 60 per cent in 1975. In an effort to force other nations to abide by the restrictions imposed in a 1966 treaty, the United States on November 1 imposed an embargo on imports from Spain of yellowfin tuna, the principal species used in the United States.

Fish Catch. United States commercial fishermen increased their catch 4 per cent in 1974 to 4.9 billion pounds (2.2 billion kilograms). As the result of larger landings of less expensive fish for industrial use and a sharp decline in the price fishermen received for shellfish, the total catch was valued at $898.5 million, 1 per cent less than the 1973 catch. Per capita consumption of fish dropped to 12 pounds (5 kilograms) in 1974 from the record 1973 level of 12.7 pounds (6 kilograms). Total imports reached a record high of $1.69 billion, up 7 per cent from 1973. The Port of Los Angeles led U.S. ports in both size and value of landings.

New England, with its fish catch down a drastic 51 per cent from 1965, tried to popularize "underutilized species," such as the red crab, to provide new markets. New England fishermen blame the invasion of the George's Bank area, off Cape Cod, by huge Russian and Japanese stern trawlers for the depletion of traditional New England catches such as cod, haddock, and halibut.

Fishing Limits. The House of Representatives on October 9 approved a limit of 200 nautical miles to protect historic U.S. fishing grounds. Foreign fleets would have access to the grounds only when stocks are considered ample. The measure would extend the U.S. fishing zone from its present limit of 12 nautical miles, beginning July 1, 1976. The Ford Administration has opposed extending the limit unilaterally on the grounds that other countries might retaliate unless the limits were set by international agreement. See ENVIRONMENT.

The United States and Canada in September won the approval of 15 other nations for a 10 per cent cut in the proposed 1976 quota for taking finfish off the New England and mid-Atlantic coasts. The United States had protested that the quota of 800,000 short tons (724,000 metric tons), including squid, posed a serious threat to future productivity.   Andrew L. Newman

FLOOD. See DISASTERS.

FLORIDA. See STATE GOVERNMENT.

FLOWER. See GARDENING.

FOOD

Two average families, U.S., *top,* and English, *above,* are surrounded by the staggering quantities of food they consume each year.

Representatives of 69 nations, meeting in Rome, agreed on Nov. 1, 1975, to set up a fund to help produce food in the world's least-developed countries. An initial aid target of $1.2 billion was set, with contributions split evenly between the developed industrial nations and the oil-exporting nations. The fund was first suggested at the United Nations (UN) World Food Conference held in Rome in November, 1974, which was attended by delegates from 130 countries.

Bleak Red Harvest. The disastrous 1975 grain harvest in Russia may have serious effects on international food markets and supplies as well as in the Soviet Union. The annual Soviet economic report, released on December 2, did not give figures on the harvest. However, analysis of such figures as industrial growth rate and national income clearly showed a serious agricultural shortfall. The U.S. Department of Agriculture (USDA) earlier had estimated the Russian grain harvest at 176 million short tons (160 million metric tons), more than 25 per cent below the planned 237.6 million short tons (215.6 million metric tons). Later estimates, however, indicated a much worse harvest of 152 million short tons (138 million metric tons).

By December 1, Russia had bought 22 million short tons (20 million metric tons) of grain from the West, including 14.3 million short tons (13-million metric tons) from the U.S. See RUSSIA.

New Look for Labels. More nutritional information began to appear on food labels in the United States during the year as the result of Food and Drug Administration (FDA) food-labeling regulations that went into effect on July 1. These regulations prescribe when and how food labels must provide information on the nutritional content of foods. Nutrition labeling is voluntary for most foods, but if the food is *fortified* (has nutrients added) or a nutritional claim is made for it, the label must show how much of 10 nutrients it contains.

Another new label is the Universal Product Code (UPC) symbol, a series of black parallel bars of varying widths. These bars identify the product to a computer. The UPC symbol appeared on more than 60 per cent of all supermarket products by the end of 1975. See RETAILING (Close-Up).

In a controversial development, a federal appeals court ruled that the USDA had the right to put new beef-grading standards into effect. Under the new standards, some beef previously graded "good" would qualify for "choice" grade. The USDA contended that the new standards would lead to lower meat prices by allowing leaner, grass-fed beef to qualify for higher grades.

The Russian purchase of U.S. wheat and corn, the high cost of fuel and fertilizer, and increasing food-marketing costs contributed to the food-price spiral in the United States in 1975. According to the USDA and the Bureau of Labor Statistics, retail food prices rose 8.7 per cent overall for the year ending September 30, while the retail price of meats, poultry, and fish rose more than 20 per cent.

New Products continued their record-breaking pace. For the first 10 months, the U.S. new-product introduction rate was 13.6 per cent ahead of 1974. Three types of food – categorized as imitation, convenience, and natural – accounted for a majority of the new products. Meat substitutes, light beer, imitation cheese, and low-calorie margarine were some of the new imitation products. New convenience foods included canned cooky doughs, frozen pancake batter, individual desserts, and frozen individual hamburgers. Yogurt set the pace in natural foods by becoming a basic ingredient in ready-to-eat salads, frozen desserts, and salad dressing. The new brands of natural foods included breakfast cereals, breads, and beverages with a greater proportion of fruit juices.

Food Consumption Patterns in the United States showed few significant changes in 1975. Consumption of sugar declined 10 per cent; eggs, 5 per cent; meat, 4 per cent; coffee, 4 per cent; and margarine, 3 per cent. On the other hand, consumption of canned fruits increased 11 per cent; frozen fruits and fruit juices, 8 per cent; ice cream, 5 per cent; and frozen vegetables, 5 per cent.

Per Capita U.S. Food Consumption, 1974-1975

	Pounds (Kilograms)	
	1974	1975
Milk and cream	284.0 (128.8)	290.0 (131.5)
Beef	116.8 (53)	120.3 (54.6)
Potatoes	115.9 (52.6)	117.0 (53.1)
Fresh vegetables	101.2 (45.9)	100.2 (45.45)
Sugar	97.0 (44.0)	87.3 (39.6)
Fresh fruits	78.1 (35.4)	79.7 (36.1)
Pork	66.6 (30.2)	54.6 (24.8)
Canned vegetables	52.7 (23.9)	54.3 (24.6)
Chicken	41.1 (18.6)	40.2 (18.2)
Canned fruits	19.7 (8.9)	21.9 (9.9)
Ice cream	17.5 (7.9)	18.4 (8.3)
Cheese	14.6 (6.62)	14.7 (6.68)
Coffee	12.8 (5.8)	12.3 (5.6)
Frozen fruits and fruit juices	11.3 (5.1)	12.2 (5.5)
Fish	12.0 (5.44)	12.1 (5.48)
Margarine	11.3 (5.0)	11.0 (5.1)
Frozen vegetables	10.2 (4.62)	10.7 (4.85)
Turkey	8.8 (4.0)	8.2 (3.7)
Butter	4.6 (2.1)	4.6 (2.1)
Veal	2.3 (1.0)	3.4 (1.5)
Lamb and mutton	2.3 (1.0)	2.0 (0.9)
Tea	0.80 (0.362)	0.81 (0.367)
Eggs	287 eggs	273 eggs

Food Additives were attacked as dangerous to health during the year. For example, the meat-curing agents sodium nitrate and sodium nitrite were linked to cancer, while the color additive Food, Drug, and Cosmetics Dye Red Number 2 was attacked as a possible cause of miscarriages and genetic damage, as well as cancer. On the regulatory side, the USDA proposed on November 11 to prohibit the use of nitrate and reduce the levels of nitrite used in most cured meat and poultry products. However, an FDA hearing on November 20 and 21 again left the food additive status of the Red Number 2 dye unchanged.

The FDA also proposed banning certain kinds of polyvinyl chloride food-packaging materials, specifically the rigid and semirigid polyvinyl used to package luncheon meat and to make bottles for salad dressings and vegetable oils. Polyvinyl film wraps were not included in the FDA proposal. FDA Commissioner Alexander M. Schmidt said on August 28 that the "FDA and the scientific community agree that vinyl chloride poses certain risks to human health." Vinyl chloride, from which polyvinyl is made, has been implicated in at least 19 cases of a rare, fatal form of liver cancer in people who worked in the industry. See CHEMICAL INDUSTRY.   John B. Klis and Howard W. Mattson

UCLA flanker Wally Henry begins the startling Rose Bowl upset of Ohio State with this soaring touchdown catch. Bruins beat Buckeyes. 23-10.

FOOTBALL. Labor and economic problems shook both professional and college football in 1975. Among the professionals, the National Football League (NFL) completed its second season without a labor contract, and the rival World Football League (WFL) went out of business midway through its second season. Meanwhile, college coaches had to dress fewer players for games because of cost-cutting measures instituted by the National Collegiate Athletic Association (NCAA) (see SPORTS).

The most successful teams in a highly exciting season were the Pittsburgh Steelers and Dallas Cowboys in the NFL and Oklahoma and Ohio State among the colleges. The most successful players were quarterback Fran Tarkenton of the Minnesota Vikings and running back Archie Griffin of the Ohio State Buckeyes.

In the NFL, 26 teams played 14 regular-season games each from September to December. Eight teams qualified for the play-offs, with the Steelers and Cowboys, the two survivors, advancing to the Super Bowl on Jan. 18, 1976, in Miami, Fla.

The Steelers won their second straight Super Bowl game, 21-17, with a fourth-quarter comeback that netted them 14 points. The defense sparked the rally with a blocked punt that rolled out of the Dallas end zone for a safety and a pass interception that led to a Roy Gerela field goal.

For a time, there was a fear that there would be no season at all. The NFL's contract with the NFL Players Association had expired in January, 1974, and no agreement was reached despite a 42-day players' strike as the 1974 training season started. A short-lived strike in September by five teams forced cancellation of one 1975 preseason game.

The walkout was initiated by the New England Patriots, who voted on September 13 to stop practicing because no player-management agreement had been reached. Their action forced cancellation of the team's final exhibition game the following day against the New York Jets. By September 17, the Jets, Washington Redskins, New York Giants, and Detroit Lions had also voted to strike. However, a truce ended the strike, and the season went on. Once again, the players returned to work without a contract.

The dispute between management and players revolved around the so-called Rozelle rule. The rule permitted a player to play out the option year of his contract and then move to another team, but the new team had to compensate his former team with players and/or draft choices. If the teams could not agree on compensation, the NFL commissioner, Alvin (Pete) Rozelle, decided.

The players said the Rozelle rule discouraged such movement of players because the compensation might be too costly. They called the rule a violation of antitrust laws, and on December 30, after a 55-day trial in Minneapolis, U.S. District Court Judge Earl Larson ruled in favor of the players. However, the judge stayed the ruling to allow appeal, and no changes in NFL policies were expected for at least two or three years.

The negotiations, or non-negotiations, left a bad taste. John Hollis wrote in *Pro Football Weekly:* "If the people in pro football don't think the world can get along without them, they're not very realistic. . . . Children's games, while interesting and entertaining, are not a vital part of the world's survival kit."

The WFL started the 1974 season with 12 teams and proclaimed itself a second major league. It played entertaining football, but it was underfinanced and received little money for television rights, and it lost at least $10 million.

It tried again in 1975, buoyed by such NFL players as Larry Csonka, Jim Kiick, Paul Warfield, Calvin Hill, and Ted Kwalick. But new financing was inadequate, television was not interested, and crowds dwindled to an average of 13,000 per game. Even with most players earning only $500 a game, losses mounted, and the league collapsed in October. Memphis and Birmingham, its two most solvent franchises, applied for 1976 NFL franchises, but the NFL turned it back. Rozelle also ordered NFL clubs not to sign any players from the defunct league until the season ended. He rescinded that order after a court ruled that WFL players not under contract should be allowed to sign.

The NFL Season. Another sore point was attendance, which dropped about 10 per cent from near-capacity levels. The NFL blamed the federal law that forbids local television blackouts when a game is sold out 72 hours in advance. There were empty seats in good weather, many empty seats in bad. The NFL feared that ticket buyers today would stay at home tomorrow, but Congress decided to keep the law. Despite the problems, the season produced stirring football. There were more sudden-death games, especially involving the Washington Redskins. There were more touchdowns and more touchdown passes.

The best records were produced by the Steelers, Vikings, and Los Angeles Rams, each with 12 victories and 2 defeats during the regular season. Also in the play-offs were the Oakland Raiders, Cincinnati Bengals, and St. Louis Cardinals, each 11-3, and the Cowboys and Baltimore Colts, each 10-4. The Miami Dolphins and Houston Oilers became the first teams with 10-4 records to fail to qualify for the play-offs.

Defense made the difference in the American Football Conference (AFC) play-offs, as Pittsburgh defeated Baltimore, 28-10, and Oakland held off Cincinnati, 31-28. Pittsburgh beat Oakland, 16-10, in the AFC final, though the Raiders recovered an onside kickoff with 12 seconds remaining and almost scored again.

In the National Football Conference (NFC) play-offs, Los Angeles defeated St. Louis, 35-23, and Dallas upset Minnesota, 17-14, on a 50-yard touchdown pass from Roger Staubach to Drew Pearson with 24 seconds remaining. Minnesota argued that Pearson had pushed his defender, and a game official close to the play was struck on the head by a whiskey bottle thrown from the stands. Dallas then upset Los Angeles, 37-7, in the NFC final, as Staubach passed for three touchdowns and the Rams's running game collapsed.

The Steelers, defending Super Bowl winners, relied on a defense led by linebackers Jack Lambert

1975 College Conference Champions

Conference	School
Atlantic Coast	Maryland
Big Eight	Oklahoma-Nebraska (tie)
Big Sky	Boise State
Big Ten	Ohio State
Ivy League	Harvard
Mid-American	Miami (Ohio)
Missouri Valley	Tulsa
Ohio Valley	Tenn. Tech-W. Kentucky (tie)
Pacific Eight	UCLA-California (tie)
Southeastern	Alabama
Southern	Richmond
Southwest	Arkansas-Texas-Texas A. & M. (tie)
Western Athletic	Arizona State
Yankee	New Hampshire

The Bowl Games

Bowl	Winner	Loser
Astro-Bluebonnet	Texas 38	Colorado 21
Cotton	Arkansas 31	Georgia 10
Fiesta	Arizona State 17	Nebraska 14
Gator	Maryland 13	Florida 0
Liberty	USC 20	Texas A. & M. 0
Orange	Oklahoma 14	Michigan 6
Peach	W. Virginia 13	N.C. State 10
Rose	UCLA 23	Ohio State 10
Sugar	Alabama 13	Penn State 6
Sun	Pittsburgh 33	Kansas 19

All-America Team (as picked by UPI)

Offense
Wide receiver—Steve Rivera, California.
Tight end—Ken MacAfee, Notre Dame.
Tackles—Bob Simmons, Texas; Dennis Lick, Wisconsin.
Guards—Terry Webb, Oklahoma; Randy Johnson, Georgia.
Center—Rick Bonness, Nebraska.
Quarterback—Gene Swick, Toledo.
Running backs—Archie Griffin, Ohio State; Ricky Bell, Southern California; Chuck Muncie, California.
Place-kicker—Chris Bahr, Penn State.

Defense
Ends—Leroy Cook, Alabama; Jimbo Elrod, Oklahoma.
Tackles—Leroy Selmon, Oklahoma; Steve Niehaus, Notre Dame.
Middle guard—Dewey Selmon, Oklahoma.
Linebackers—Ed Simonini, Texas A. & M.; Greg Buttle, Penn State; Woodrow Lowe, Alabama.
Defensive backs—Chet Moeller, Navy; Tim Fox, Ohio State; Pat Thomas, Texas A. & M.

and Jack Ham, cornerback Mel Blount, and tackle Joe Greene. On offense, Franco Harris became the second runner in NFL history (the first was Jim Brown) to gain 4,000 yards in his first four seasons.

The Cowboys, in the play-offs for the ninth time in 10 years, became the first *wild-card* play-off team to reach the Super Bowl. A wild-card team is the divisional second-place team with the best record in its conference. The Cowboys' success was unexpected because they were rebuilding a team that had grown old, and 12 of the 43 players were rookies.

The Baltimore Colts were the surprise of the season. They became the first NFL team to rise from last place in their division to first in one season. The man most responsible was Joe Thomas, the

general manager who had achieved similar success with expansion teams in Minnesota and Miami.

When Thomas took over in 1972, he benched 39-year-old John Unitas, who held every important NFL career passing record, and traded many older players. He drafted Bert Jones in 1973, and Jones became one of the NFL's best quarterbacks. The young defensive line he drafted in 1973 and 1974 led the NFL in 1975 quarterback *sacks* (tackles behind the line of scrimmage) with 59.

The 1975 Colts also had a new head coach in Ted Marchibroda, a former quarterback who had spent the nine previous years as George Allen's offensive coordinator in Los Angeles and Washington. Under Marchibroda, the Colts won their last nine

Standings in National Football Conference

Eastern Division

	W.	L.	T.	Pct.
St. Louis	11	3	0	.786
Dallas	10	4	0	.714
Washington	8	6	0	.571
New York Giants	5	9	0	.357
Philadelphia	4	10	0	.286

Central Division

	W.	L.	T.	Pct.
Minnesota	12	2	0	.857
Detroit	7	7	0	.500
Chicago	4	10	0	.286
Green Bay	4	10	0	.286

Western Division

	W.	L.	T.	Pct.
Los Angeles	12	2	0	.857
San Francisco	5	9	0	.357
Atlanta	4	10	0	.286
New Orleans	2	12	0	.143

Standings in American Football Conference

Eastern Division

	W.	L.	T.	Pct.
Baltimore	10	4	0	.714
Miami	10	4	0	.714
Buffalo	8	6	0	.571
New England	3	11	0	.214
New York Jets	3	11	0	.214

Central Division

	W.	L.	T.	Pct.
Pittsburgh	12	2	0	.857
Cincinnati	11	3	0	.786
Houston	10	4	0	.714
Cleveland	3	11	0	.214

Western Division

	W.	L.	T.	Pct.
Oakland	11	3	0	.786
Denver	6	8	0	.429
Kansas City	5	9	0	.357
San Diego	2	12	0	.143

National Conference Individual Statistics

Scoring

	TDs.	E.P.	F.G.	Pts.
Foreman, Minn.	22	0	0	132
Fritsch, Dall.	0	38	22	104
Bakken, St. L.	0	40	19	97
Dempsey, L. A.	0	31	21	94

Passing

	Att.	Comp.	Pct.	Yds.	TDs.
Tarkenton, Minn.	425	273	64.2	2,994	25
Staubach, Dall.	348	198	56.9	2,666	17
Kilmer, Wash.	346	178	51.4	2,440	23
Harris, L. A.	285	157	55.1	2,148	14

Receiving

	No. Caught	Total Yds.	Avg. Gain	TDs.
Foreman, Minn.	73	691	9.5	9
Payne, G. B.	58	766	13.2	0
Marinaro, Minn.	54	462	8.6	3
Taylor, Wash.	53	744	14.0	6

Rushing

	Att.	Yds.	Avg. Gain	TDs.
Otis, St. L.	269	1,076	4.0	5
Foreman, Minn.	280	1,070	3.8	13
Hampton, Atl.	250	1,002	4.0	5
Newhouse, Dall.	209	930	4.4	2

Punting

	No.	Yds.	Avg.	Longest
H. Weaver, Det.	80	3,361	42.0	61
Wittum, S.F.	67	2,804	41.9	64
James, Atl.	89	3,696	41.5	75
Clabo, Minn.	73	2,997	41.1	62

Punt Returns

	No.	Yds.	Avg.	TDs.
Metcalf, St. L.	23	285	12.4	1
Chapman, N. O.	17	207	12.2	0
Livers, Chi.	42	456	10.9	0
Taylor, S.F.	16	166	10.4	0

American Conference Individual Statistics

Scoring

	TDs.	E.P.	F.G.	Pts.
Simpson, Buff.	23	0	0	138
Stenerud, K.C.	0	30	22	96
Banaszak, Oak.	16	0	0	96
Gerela, Pitt.	0	44	17	95

Passing

	Att.	Comp.	Pct.	Yds.	TDs.
Anderson, Cin.	377	228	60.5	3,169	21
Dawson, K.C.	140	93	66.4	1,095	5
Jones, Balt.	344	203	59.0	2,483	18
Bradshaw, Pitt.	286	165	57.7	2,055	18

Receiving

	No. Caught	Total Yds.	Avg. Gain	TDs.
Rucker, Cleve.	60	770	12.8	3
Mitchell, Balt.	60	544	9.1	4
Chandler, Buff.	55	746	13.6	6
Burroughs, Hou.	53	1,063	20.1	8

Rushing

	Att.	Yds.	Avg. Gain	TDs.
Simpson, Buff.	329	1,817	5.5	16
Harris, Pitt.	262	1,246	4.8	10
Mitchell, Balt.	289	1,193	4.1	11
Pruitt, Cleve.	217	1,067	4.9	8

Punting

	No.	Yds.	Avg.	Longest
Guy, Oak.	68	2,979	43.8	64
Bateman, Buff.	61	2,536	41.6	74
J. Wilson, K.C.	54	2,233	41.4	64
Cockroft, Cleve.	82	3,317	40.5	67

Punt Returns

	No.	Yds.	Avg.	TDs.
Johnson, Hous.	40	610	15.3	3
Colzie, Oak.	48	655	13.6	0
Solomon, Mia.	26	320	12.3	1
Upchurch, Den.	27	312	11.6	0

regular-season games, and he was chosen NFL coach of the year.

Another team that did better than expected was the Dolphins, who had won four straight AFC Eastern Division titles. Although they lost three offensive stars (Csonka, Kiick, and Warfield) to the WFL and three defensive stars (Dick Anderson, Nick Buoniconti, and Manny Fernandez) to injuries, they tied the Colts for 1975 division honors. They lost a play-off berth to the Colts because Baltimore beat them in two regular-season meetings.

Individual Honors. Tarkenton, in his 15th NFL season, broke three lifetime records that had taken Unitas 18 seasons to set. Tarkenton's records were 5,225 passes, 2,931 completions, and 291 touchdown passes. He also drew close to Unitas' record of 40,239 yards gained by passing.

Chuck Foreman, Tarkenton's Minnesota teammate, led the league with 73 pass receptions, the most by a running back in NFL history. He also led his conference in scoring with 132 points, and the 1,070 yards he gained rushing left him only six yards behind the conference leader, Jim Otis of St. Louis.

Foreman scored 22 touchdowns, tying Gale Sayers' one-season record. O. J. Simpson of the Buffalo Bills surpassed both with 23 touchdowns, and his 1,817 yards rushing led all players.

Charlie Taylor of Washington broke Don Maynard's lifetime record of 633 pass receptions. Terry Metcalf of St. Louis broke Mack Herron's year-old record of 2,444 by amassing 2,462 all-purpose yards (rushing, pass receiving, and kick returning). Place-kicker George Blanda of Oakland, 48 years old and in his 26th pro season, passed 2,000 points in scoring.

Canadian Football. The Canadian Football League (CFL) opened up its game with 12 rules changes in 1975. For the first time, it allowed blocking above the waist on punt returns, making long returns possible. The crowds responded by turning out in record numbers. Attendance for 72 regular-season and 18 preseason games totaled 2,180,993.

In the Grey Cup game for the CFL championship, the Edmonton Eskimos defeated the Montreal Alouettes, 9-8, on Dave Cutler's three field goals on November 23 in Calgary, Alberta.

Willie Burden, a rookie running back for the Calgary Stampeders, was voted the season's Most Valuable Player. He set a CFL record of 1,896 yards rushing, an astounding figure in a game that relies essentially on passing.

The College Season. Ohio State was headed for the national championship until its shocking defeat by the University of California, Los Angeles (UCLA), in the Rose Bowl game. That gave the unofficial national title to Oklahoma.

Ohio State was one of only three major teams that completed the regular season undefeated and untied; the others were Arizona State and Arkansas State. Ohio's Buckeyes led the final regular-season polls of the Associated Press board of writers and broadcasters and the United Press International board of coaches. Griffin, the Ohio tailback, was everyone's choice as player of the year, and the Football Writers' Association of America voted Woody Hayes of Ohio State the coach of the year.

But Ohio State lost to UCLA, a 15-point underdog, 23-10, on Jan. 1, 1976, in Pasadena, Calif. In Miami that night, Oklahoma defeated Michigan in the Orange Bowl, 14-6.

Oklahoma, ranked second in the nation until then, was first in the final wire-service polls. The Sooners had gone 37 games without a defeat until a 23-3 upset by Kansas on November 8.

Ohio State gained solace from Griffin's achievements. He completed his four-year college career by becoming the first player in major-college history to run for more than 5,000 yards. He set another record by running for 100 or more yards per game for 31 consecutive games. He also became the first two-time winner of the Heisman Trophy as the outstanding college player.

Attendance rose almost half a million in 1975. The NCAA's 634 football-playing colleges reported total attendance of 31,687,847. The Big Ten Conference averaged 59,000 a game; the Big Eight, 53,000.
Frank Litsky

FORD, GERALD RUDOLPH (1913-   ), 38th President of the United States, concentrated in 1975 on being elected President in his own right. Unlike every other U.S. President in the 20th century, Ford had never taken part in a national campaign for either President or Vice-President. Former President Richard M. Nixon appointed Ford Vice-President in 1973, and Ford assumed the presidency after Nixon resigned in 1974. Critics said few Americans knew anything about him.

However, the American people learned more about Ford during 1975. Compared to Nixon, Ford was an open, frank, and unassuming man. But he reminded Americans – and the rest of the world – of his enormous power in May, when he ordered a swift attack on Khmer (Cambodia) after Khmer forces captured a U.S. merchant ship, the *Mayaguez*. See KHMER.

Then, in November, he abruptly dismissed Secretary of Defense James R. Schlesinger and Central Intelligence Agency (CIA) Director William E. Colby, indicating the extent of his personal power. However, the firings provoked a great deal of criticism. Some observers believed that Ford was consistently overreacting to prove his strength. But according to the President, the changes in his Cabinet and the CIA only signaled an effort to establish his "own team." See CABINET, U.S.; PRESIDENT OF THE UNITED STATES.

Newsmen on July 5 record President Ford's
first dip in the new White House pool, which
was paid for by private, tax-free donations.

ousine was accidentally struck by another car at an
unguarded street intersection in Hartford, Conn.,
on October 14. Despite the very real danger to his
life. Ford refused to cut out most of his public appearances.

White House Life. As President, Ford worked
long hours, rising at about 5:15 A.M. to begin his
18-hour working day. In April, presidential press
secretary Ronald H. Nessen revealed that Ford
reads about a dozen newspapers a day, plus books,
magazines, and news summaries prepared for him.

In spite of his heavy workload and the enormous
responsibility of his office, Ford made it a policy to
read about 50 letters a week from the average of
about 5,000 received daily at the White House.

Ford's permanent White House staff numbered
about 530. But there were 1,194 employees under
the direct control of the President in 1975, 14 more
than during his first year in office.

The First Lady. Betty Ford presented her personal views frankly and forthrightly. She was an
outspoken supporter of the Equal Rights Amendment. In a television interview on August 10, the
first lady commented that she would not be surprised if her teen-age daughter, Susan, had an
affair. The comment shocked some Americans, but
others praised her honesty.   Carol L. Thompson

See also Section One, FOCUS ON THE NATION.

Presidential Bid. The nomination of an incumbent President by his own party is traditionally
assured. But Ford did not become President in a
traditional manner, and his right to the 1976 Republican nomination was not guaranteed.

Ford formally announced his candidacy for the
Republican nomination on July 8. He said that he
would enter every primary to meet a strong challenge from the conservative former governor of
California, Ronald Reagan (see REAGAN, RON-
ALD). Ford politicked across the country, trying to
woo conservatives. See REPUBLICAN PARTY.

The President's travel expenses – approximately
$500,000 for the year – were charged to the White
House until December 31. In 1976, travel expenses
for all presidential primary campaigns, including
Ford's, must be deducted from the $10 million
allowed by the Federal Election Commission.

Narrow Escapes. The President twice escaped
death at the hands of would-be assassins. On September 5, Lynette Alice Fromme pointed a loaded
pistol at the President as he stood shaking hands
with a crowd in Sacramento, Calif. The gun, however, did not go off. Fromme was convicted of attempted assassination on November 26. On September 22, Sara Jane Moore fired at, but missed,
the President in San Francisco. Fromme and Moore
both received life prison sentences.

The President also escaped injury when his lim-

In the playful clutches of daughter Susan,
the first lady places a call to son Michael
from President Ford's desk in the Oval Office.

FOREST AND FOREST PRODUCTS. An extremely low pace in housing starts held down lumber and plywood output and prices in the United States in 1975. The industry also received a heavy blow on August 22 when a federal appeals court upheld a ban on clear-cutting timber in national forests in four Southern states. Conservation groups called it a landmark victory. But the U.S. Forest Service said that the ruling, if applied to all its operations, could force a 75 per cent reduction in the agency's plans to sell 12 billion board feet (28 million cubic meters) of timber in 1976.

Government researchers announced in March that a new method of converting trees into lumber products produces twice as much usable wood as conventional methods. The method, called COMPLY, bonds waste materials such as chips, shavings, and sawdust with glue and sheathes them with solid wood facings.

A new attack was launched in June on the gypsy moth, which is moving south after defoliating trees on more than 750,000 acres (300,000 hectares) in the Northeastern States in 1974. Workmen sprayed an artificial *pheromone* (sex scent) over Maryland forests to confuse the male moths and lure them away from females, preventing breeding. If not halted, the gypsy moth could wreak havoc on major Southern hardwood forests.   Andrew L. Newman

FOUR-H CLUBS. See YOUTH ORGANIZATIONS.

French President Giscard d'Estaing, right center, and his wife watch a dancer in Ringeldorf in May. Later, they dined with all 69 of the villagers.

FRANCE struggled in 1975 to keep unemployment below 1 million while reviving the economy and safeguarding the franc. President Valéry Giscard d'Estaing agreed with West German Chancellor Helmut Schmidt in Bonn, West Germany, on July 27 that parallel recovery programs in the two countries would help Europe.

Economic Recovery Programs. President Giscard d'Estaing announced stimulation measures on April 23, a $3.7-billion program that involved cheap loans to industry. The plan also gave $2.6-million in development aid to the underindustrialized west and central regions of France. But industrial production fell 12 per cent from July, 1974, to July, 1975, and unemployment rose from 500,000 to 900,000 over the same period. Although exports remained at the 1974 dollar level, they were down in volume, negating the value of the first eight months' trade surplus, which totaled more than $2-billion.

The government approved a second program on September 13 and coordinated it with its European partners. The plan provided for new expenditures and credits totaling $7 billion, more than 2 per cent of France's gross national product. In another stimulating move on September 5, the Bank of France cut its bank rate to 8 per cent, the fifth and largest drop since the rate stood at 13 per cent at the start of 1975.

Presidential Image. In a New Year broadcast, Giscard d'Estaing expressed hope that 1975 would be "a year of fraternity." He announced that he and his wife would dine in the homes of French families of every background and profession "to have a personal and direct contact, and so that each can speak in his own way about his own problems." In the first year of his presidency, Giscard d'Estaing's informal style apparently pleased most of the people.

His first "meet-the-people" luncheon was in the three-room Paris apartment of a picture framer, his wife, and their son, a law student. All the chefs in France advised the hostess on television, radio, and in print on what to serve and how to cook it. She settled for cress soup, sea bass, fillet of beef, and strawberry charlotte.

Labor Unrest. France encountered protest on the part of servicemen, fishermen, prostitutes, and winegrowers during the year. About 150 soldiers marched in Karlsruhe, West Germany, on January 13 demanding improved army benefits. Lieutenant General Marcel Bigeard became defense secretary on January 31, and he tripled draftees' pay to about $50 per month on March 4, but it was still the second lowest in Europe after Italy. Fishermen protested low fish prices and high fuel costs by blockading ports from Dunkerque to Bayonne from February 17 to February 21, when the government offered subsidies of $11 million and temporarily banned seafood imports from non-Common Market countries.

Sixty Lyon prostitutes occupied the church of St. Nizier on June 2 to protest alleged police harassment. Prostitutes also protested in Nice and Marseille. Judge Guy Pinot was appointed on July 23 to draw up a report for the Cabinet on prostitution.

More difficult to quell were protests by winegrowers in southern France, who wanted the government to stop cheap wine imports. The French franc rejoined the Common Market's joint floating currency system on July 10. See EUROPE.

Island Problems. Two French policemen were killed on the French island of Corsica on August 22 in an outbreak of violence by separatists who want more autonomy for Corsica. Giscard d'Estaing appointed a Corsican, Jean Riolacci, as prefect with wide powers to deal with the revolt. Unrest continued, however, and militant Corsicans led a general strike on September 1. The Comoro Islands, four perfume-exporting islands in the Indian Ocean, declared their independence on July 6. But on August 3, a pro-France group seized power.

In October, France said that it planned to change the status of St. Pierre and Miquelon islands, located off Newfoundland, Canada, from a territory to a department.   Kenneth Brown

See also EUROPE (Facts in Brief Table).

FRASER, MALCOLM (1930-   ), became prime minister of Australia after an election on Dec. 13, 1975, gave his Liberal-National Country Party coalition a stunning victory over the Labor Party led by Gough Whitlam. See AUSTRALIA.

John Malcolm Fraser was born on the sprawling family ranch near Melbourne, Victoria. He attended Melbourne Grammar School and Magdalen College at Oxford University in England. He returned home as a *grazier* (gentleman rancher), and immediately entered politics. He won election to Parliament on his second try in 1956.

After the Liberal sweep in 1966, Fraser became minister for the army, though he never served in the armed forces because he was too young for World War II service. In 1968, he became minister for education and science, and minister for defense 18 months later. He became Liberal Party leader on March 21, 1975. Seven months later, he led the fight to block Whitlam's budget, thus leading to Whitlam's ouster and his becoming prime minister.

Fraser is a political conservative, noted for a single-minded concentration on work. In 1956, he married Tamara Beggs, daughter of a Russian aristocrat. They have four children. Kathryn Sederberg.

FUTURE FARMERS OF AMERICA (FFA). See YOUTH ORGANIZATIONS.

GABON. See AFRICA.

GAMBIA. See AFRICA.

GAMES, MODELS, AND TOYS. Indoor games, particularly those known as "conflict simulation" games, gained popularity in 1975. An industry spokesman attributed the widespread interest in such board games in the United States to parental fears that the family is drifting apart. He said games enabled parents to create a more attractive home life for all members of the family. Nearly 100 conflict games were on the market with names such as Tank Battle, Skirmish, War in the East, and Panzerblitz.

Monopoly Variations. Games deriving from the all-time favorite Monopoly were also popular. One of the most elaborate variations was Petropolis, which involved oil, politics, and economics and sold for $790. The game board was made of leather, and its oil rigs were silver- and gold-plated.

The backgammon rage continued undiminished. Games in which electric calculators can be used were explained in *The Calculating Book,* by James T. Rogers. Many of the games were based on the fact that the calculator's stylized numbers form certain letters when turned upside down.

Old and New Toys. An old stand-by toy, the inexpensive yoyo, surged in popularity, as it usually does in times of recession. Flambeau Products Corporation, which controls about 85 per cent of the American yoyo market, turned out 100,000 yoyos a day in 1975. Skateboard sales also boomed. Bahne Skateboards, a California company that makes the boards out of fiberglass and polyurethane, began the year selling about 100 a week. By July, Bahne was selling thousands of the skateboards a week.

In May, Mattel, Incorporated, which brought out Barbie dolls in 1958, introduced a new female member of the Barbie doll family called Growing Up Skipper. When the doll's left arm was rotated, its body grew three-fourths of an inch (19 millimeters) taller and small plastic breasts appeared on its chest. This trend toward realism in toys was also exemplified in two other new dolls, one of which crawled and another that sneezed.

The year marked the 200th anniversary of the invention of the jigsaw puzzle. In January, one puzzle manufacturer said sales had increased by 30 per cent since the beginning of the energy crisis in late 1973. Worldwide sales more than doubled since 1965.

Model Champs. At the National Miniature Aircraft Championships in Lake Charles, La., in August, Mike Ransom of Pryor, Okla., won both the grand national and open national championships. Brian Pardue of Greensboro, N.C., won the senior national championship, and the junior national championship went to Barry Pailet of Glen Head, N.Y. The Chicago Aeronuts and the Dixie Whiz Kids retained their titles as club team and national team champions.   Theodore M. O'Leary

GANDHI, INDIRA PRIYADARSHINI (1917-
), prime minister of India, was found guilty on
June 12, 1975, of illegal campaigning during her
1971 election victory in Uttar Pradesh state. Gandhi denied the charge and appealed the ruling to
India's supreme court. She also rejected demands
that she resign, and on June 26 declared a national
emergency, banning major opposition groups and
arresting thousands of political foes. In August,
the government passed a new voting law that
nullified the charges against her, and the supreme
court later reversed the lower court's decision. She
clamped a strict censorship on India's press, and
assumed extraordinary emergency powers. Gandhi
maintained that emergency measures were necessary because of opposition leader Jayaprakash Narayan's call for a nationwide campaign of civil dis-
obedience. See INDIA.

Gandhi is the only child of the late Jawaharlal
Nehru, India's first prime minister. She was born
in Allahabad and attended Santiniketan University in India and Oxford University in England. In
1942, she married Feroze Gandhi (no relation to
Mohandas K. Gandhi), who died in 1960. They
had two sons. She served as president of the Indian
National Congress, India's leading political party,
in 1959 and 1960 and as minister of information
and broadcasting from 1964 until she became
prime minister in 1966.   Foster Stockwell

Alice Vonk of Sully, Iowa, and David
Burpee examine a new white marigold she
developed. It brought her a $10,000 award.

GARDENING. An international agreement to protect endangered wild plant and animal species
went into force on July 1, 1975. Sponsored by the
United Nations Environment Program, the Convention on International Trade in Endangered
Species of Wild Fauna and Flora restricts trade in
plants and animals that are near extinction. Plant
dealers and collectors, for example, have put increasing pressure on many rare cactuses and or-
chids. But, as the convention went into effect, only
12 nations had ratified it.

Interest in Plants and gardening in the United
States continued to expand. Rising food prices
prompted people to grow their own vegetables, and
many house and apartment dwellers turned to pot-
ted plants to add a touch of life to their surroundings. There were shortages of some larger, slower-
growing, indoor trees, but a greater variety was
available. Uncommon species such as the triangle-
leaf fig (*Ficus triangularis*) became popular.

Warning Note. John Davis, Gallup Poll vice-
president, warned the Mail-Order Nurserymen's
Association that "all research shows that, although
more persons than ever are gardening today, there
could very well be a decline in gardening starting
two years from now." Studies showed a large number of dropout gardeners, most of them persons
whose hopes of large savings on food were frus-
trated by their lack of gardening know-how.

An aid for beginning gardeners that showed
growing popularity was the slow-release fertilizer.
Acting on the same principle as timed-release cold
capsules, these fertilizers gradually release their nutrients over an entire growing season.

New Plants included three All-America Award-
winning flowers and three vegetables. The flowers,
all bronze-medal winners, were the early blooming
dahlia "Redskin"; the new pansy "Imperial Blue,"
praised for its long flowering season; and the fra-
grant, scarlet carnation "Juliet." The three vegetables were a large-headed broccoli, "Premium
Crop," which won a silver medal; the cauliflower
"Snow Crown," a silver-medal winner notable for
heads weighing up to 2 pounds (0.91 kilogram);
and the sweet, yellow-fleshed watermelon "Yellow
Baby," given a bronze medal.

The 1976 All-America Award-winning roses
were golden-apricot floribunda "Cathedral," orange hybrid tea "Yankee Doodle," salmon-pink
climber "America," and the pink-gold hybrid
tea "Seashell." The W. Atlee Burpee Company announced in August that it had finally found a long-
sought white marigold. A $10,000 prize went to its
developer, amateur gardener Alice Vonk of Sully,
Iowa. Seed of the new flower will be increased for
future commercial release.   Phil Clark

GAS AND GASOLINE. See ENERGY; PETROLEUM
AND GAS.

GEOLOGY. Remains of the largest winged reptile known to have flown were unearthed in Big Bend National Park in southwest Texas in rocks of the late Cretaceous Period, some 65 to 70 million years ago. Vertebrate paleontologist Douglas A. Lawson of the University of California at Berkeley announced the discovery on March 14, 1975. The reptile, which had a wingspread of about 51 feet (15.5 meters) has been named *Quetzalocoatlus northropi*. It was a member of the order Pterosauria (winged lizard).

The reptile's wingspread was more than five times that of the condor, largest bird living today, and 13 feet (4 meters) greater than that of the U.S. F-4 fighter plane. Its estimated size was based on the partial remains – wing, neck, jaw, and back bones – of three of the creatures found at Big Bend between 1972 and 1975.

The Big Bend fossils were discovered in rock formations that were once continental sediments. Other pterosaurs had previously been found in rocks from marine sediments. This suggests that the reptiles did not feed on ocean fish, as scientists assume the related species did. Lawson has theorized that this species may have eaten *carrion* (dead and rotting flesh). If this is true, it implies greater variation in this group of reptiles than scientists had previously suspected.

Lawson based his theory on the fact that the huge reptile had an unusually long neck, and each neck vertebra was attached to the next by a complex interlocking process that must have provided great flexibility and sturdy support. The creature's long neck would have allowed it to reach deep into the carcasses of dinosaurs.

Oldest Fossils. Geologists from Virginia Polytechnic Institute, Duke University, and the Smithsonian Institution excavated the oldest known worm fossils in North America in May, 1975, from deposits of volcanic ash rock in North Carolina. The fossils were imprints of large marine worms in rock-hardened mud more than 620 million years old. The worms lived during pre-Cambrian times, long before any vertebrates evolved on earth. Since that time, the North American and the African continents separated and moved apart to create an ocean, then came back together again and moved apart once more to form today's Atlantic Ocean.

The fossils are similar to others found in England, Australia, and Newfoundland. The worms, some more than 1 foot (30 centimeters) long, had segmented bodies.

Predicting an Earthquake. Chinese geologists accurately predicted a major earthquake on Feb. 4, 1975, in Liaoning Province. As a result of the warning, precautionary measures reduced the loss of life and property in the area. The epicenter of the earthquake, which registered 7.3 on the Richter scale, was about 35 miles (56 kilometers) from the

Hawaii's Mauna Loa volcano erupts in July for the first time in 25 years. Lava and smoke pour from a crack near the summit.

leading Chinese iron and steel complex at Anshan, a highly industrialized and heavily populated area in northeastern China. Geologists throughout the world generally agreed that this was the most significant earthquake prediction yet made.

Earlier, U.S. geologists predicted a minor earthquake, measuring 5.2 on the Richter scale. Scientists at the U.S. Geological Survey's National Center for Earthquake Research in Menlo Park, Calif., forecast the quake that occurred on Nov. 28, 1974, near Hollister, Calif., though the prediction was not reported to the public until early in 1975.

California is especially prone to earthquakes because the San Andreas Fault, a boundary between two large rigid plates, runs through the state for about 600 miles (965 kilometers). The Pacific Plate, to the west, is moving slowly northwest and pushes against the American plate to the east. This movement causes many slight tremors and occasional earthquakes around the fault as pressures in the rocks caused by their pushing against one another are relieved.

Earth Shift. Geologists at the Massachusetts Institute of Technology reported in August that satellite pictures taken by the Earth Resources Technology Satellite have confirmed the theory that the land mass of India, which rides on one of the giant plates that form the earth's surface, is pushing against another plate that includes China. The collision of the two land masses is pushing China eastward at a rate of more than 1 inch (2.5 centimeters) a year. It also accounts for China's unusual pattern of earthquakes.

The results of the satellite study were confirmed by visiting Chinese geologists in a meeting at Columbia University in New York City in October. The Chinese said that their studies, completed after scaling Mount Everest to collect samples of rocks from various heights and exploring remote regions in Central Asia, showed that Asia is the product of several such continental collisions, one of which is still crumpling and twisting the landscape. The successive collisions have produced the largest continent, the highest mountains, and the loftiest plateaus on earth.

This research shows that Asia's complex and perplexing pattern of earthquake activity results from crustal movements on a grand scale. Sections of the earth's crust are being pushed in various directions by the northward drive of India, much as ice floes are scattered by an icebreaker. The Chinese scientists, using radioactive-dating techniques to date limestones taken from Mount Everest, found that the rock was laid down between 410-million and 575 million years ago, presumably on the floor of a sea that lay between India and what was then the continent of Asia.   Thomas X. Grasso

GEORGIA. See ATLANTA; STATE GOVERNMENT.

GERMANY, EAST. West German Chancellor Helmut Schmidt criticized the "uncompromising attitude" of East German leaders on Jan. 30, 1975, for slowing the development of relations between the two Germanys and the progress of détente in Europe. However, the two governments were in constant contact throughout the year. There also were signs of a more accommodating attitude on reuniting families divided by the border. Schmidt and East Germany's Communist Party First Secretary Erich Honecker met in Helsinki, Finland, on July 31, in the first such meeting in five years.

Diplomatic Ties. East Germany signed a consular pact with Austria on March 26 in Berlin. The agreement was the first with a Western nation that recognized East Germany as a separate nation. In Helsinki, in August, Honecker and Canadian Prime Minister Pierre Elliott Trudeau agreed to exchange diplomatic missions. On September 9, Australia named Malcolm Morris as its first resident ambassador to East Germany.

Monsignor Agostino Casaroli, the Vatican's special envoy for foreign affairs, visited East Berlin from June 9 to 15 at the invitation of Foreign Minister Oskar Fischer. It was the first visit by an envoy of the Holy See to East Germany, which has about 1.5 million Roman Catholics. East Germany asked that its ecclesiastical districts be made independent of West German dioceses. Casaroli said

that any departure from the 1933 Reich Concordat, which groups the East and West German churches together, must be discussed with West Germany.

Economic Growth. A report by the Central Statistical Board (CSB) on the first six months of 1975 said that the National Economic Plan was being fulfilled with an upswing in the economy. The CSB reported that national income rose 5.5 per cent and manufacturing output gained 6.8 per cent. Foreign trade with countries of the Council for Mutual Economic Assistance (COMECON) rose 11 per cent. About 45,000 dwellings were built and nearly 20,000 were converted, expanded, or modernized. Labor productivity increased 6 per cent, largely because of "acceleration of the intensification effort and the resulting rise in efficiency." The report claimed full employment but noted that 58,000 jobs had been "reorganized or rearranged, using scientific methods of labor organization."

Russia raised the prices of its oil, natural gas, and other raw materials to world market levels, but East Germany adjusted to this inflationary trend better than most other COMECON countries by a policy of fuel economy, greater use of lignite, and improved labor productivity. A revised treaty with Russia, signed on October 7, made no mention of reunifying the two German states.   Kenneth Brown

See also EUROPE (Facts in Brief Table).

GERMANY, WEST. The deepest and longest recession since World War II struck West Germany in 1975. Unemployment rose to about 1.1 million in September, the highest jobless level in 16 years. About 800,000 people worked short hours. Despite an economic recovery package of $680 million and a $5.6-billion tax cut at the end of 1974, exports fell 13 per cent during the first six months of 1975, the gross national product dropped 5 per cent, and the trade surplus dropped to $9.4 billion from $11.9-billion. Foreign orders were down 15 per cent, and industry worked at only 74 per cent capacity.

Construction Recovery Program. As one of a series of international measures that Chancellor Helmut Schmidt hoped would lift the world from recession, he introduced a $2.2-billion recovery program on August 27. Belgium, Denmark, France, Italy, Luxembourg, and the Netherlands announced parallel plans. Schmidt's recovery package included nearly $2 billion in unemployment funds, urban modernization funds, and subsidies for repairing older houses and building some new housing. The federal government placed orders worth $240 million with the ailing building industry to develop its own investment projects and help to preserve jobs.

Budget Deficit. The program pushed the expected federal deficit over $15 billion. On August 29, the Bonn government proposed a "painful"

draft budget to pull the state finances out of deficit by 1980. Federal spending increases in 1976 will be limited to 4.1 per cent to give a budget total of $65 billion. But Finance Minister Hans Apel and Economics Minister Hans Friderichs said it would be 1977 before the federal finances began to shift from their serious deficit position. The government plan calls for budget cuts and tax increases for 1976 and 1977. Unemployment insurance for workers would go up from 2 to 3 per cent of income beginning Jan. 3, 1976. Value-added taxes on every purchase would go up in 1977.

State Elections. Schmidt's ruling coalition of Social Democrats and Free Democrats, looking ahead to a November, 1976, general election, were heartened by state election results in March, April, and May. Although the opposition Christian Democrats made small gains, the coalition claimed to have reversed the tide of opinion that had been running against it.

However, voters in the state of Bremen expressed uneasiness over Schmidt's economic program in elections on September 28. The Social Democrats retained control but fell 6 per cent, while the Free Democrats gained strength.

Foreign Workers. High unemployment led to a February government investigation into immigration. About 6.3 per cent of West Germany's 2.5-million foreign workers were unemployed. Complaints by trade unions led to a second, more searching, inquiry in June. The Baden-Württemberg state government offered foreign workers 75 per cent of a year's unemployment benefit as a premium for going home. About 1,750 accepted the offer. Most were from the Volkswagen automobile plants.

Warsaw Pact. Schmidt and Polish Communist Party First Secretary Edward Gierek agreed on August 2 in Helsinki, Finland, to allow an estimated 125,000 ethnic Germans to leave Poland over the next four years. In return, West Germany agreed to grant $400 million in trade credits to Poland at an interest rate of 2.5 per cent plus a lump sum of $504 million.

United States Visits. West German President Walter Scheel conferred with President Gerald R. Ford in Washington, D.C., on June 10, and addressed a joint session of Congress the next day. Scheel was the first West German head of state to visit the United States in 17 years. Schmidt met President Ford on October 3. He emphasized his concern over high U.S. interest rates that he believed were attracting investment money out of West Germany.   Kenneth Brown

See also EUROPE (Facts in Brief Table).

GIRL SCOUTS. See YOUTH ORGANIZATIONS.

GIRLS' CLUBS. See YOUTH ORGANIZATIONS.

Tight security, including car checks by West German border guards, was maintained during trial of alleged terrorists in Stuttgart in May.

GOLF. Jack Nicklaus of Columbus, Ohio, was the 1975 golfer of the year. He won five tournaments, more than anyone else, on the Professional Golfers' Association (PGA) tour. Of the four grand-slam tournaments, he won two – the Masters and the PGA – and was beaten by two strokes in the United States Open and one stroke in the British Open. He won $298,149 in official prize money and led the tour for the seventh time in earnings and the sixth in victories.

Major Tournaments. Nicklaus won the Masters in April at Augusta, Ga., for the fifth time, his 276 beating Tom Weiskopf and Johnny Miller by a stroke. The key shot came on the 16th hole of the final round when his 40-foot (12-meter) putt broke two ways before dropping into the cup for a birdie.

The next grand-slam tournament was the United States Open in June in Medinah, Ill. Lou Graham of Nashville, Tenn., and John Mahaffey of Houston, Tex., tied at 287 after 72 holes, and Graham won an 18-hole play-off by two strokes with a 71.

Tom Watson of Kansas City, Mo., and Jack Newton of Australia tied at 279 in the British Open in July at Carnoustie, Scotland, and Watson's 71 beat Newton by a stroke in the play-off. Nicklaus failed to tie when his chip on the 72nd hole missed.

In the PGA championship in August in Akron, Ohio, Nicklaus' 276 beat Bruce Crampton by two

Lee Elder, the first black golfer to play in the Masters tournament at Augusta, Ga., failed to qualify for the last two rounds in April.

strokes. This was Nicklaus' fourth PGA title and 16th in a so-called major tournament. He had also won five Masters, three United States Opens, two British Opens, and two United States Amateurs.

Miller, who set an all-time earnings record of $353,030 in 1974, started quickly in 1975. He won the first two tournaments – the Phoenix Open by 14 strokes and the Tucson Open by nine – and he shot a 61 in each. He finished with four tournament victories. In addition to the British Open, Watson won the Byron Nelson Classic in Dallas and the World Series of Golf in Akron.

Gene Littler won three major tournaments – the Bing Crosby National Pro-Amateur in Pebble Beach, Calif.; the Memphis Classic; and the Westchester Classic in Harrison, N.Y. Hale Irwin scored three major victories – in the Atlanta Golf Classic; the Western Open in Oak Brook, Ill.; and the Piccadilly world match-play tournament in England.

The 45-year-old Littler finished fifth in tour earnings with $182,883, and he was the eighth golfer to pass $1 million in career earnings. Only three years before, he had undergone surgery to remove cancerous growths in the lymph glands under his left arm.

En route to the $50,000 first prize in the Westchester Classic, he earned $8,000 for a hole in one. He donated the $8,000 to the American Cancer

Society in memory of Gary Sanders, a 25-year-old touring professional who had died of a cerebral hemorrhage a week earlier. Sanders was to have undergone cancer surgery.

Lee Trevino, Jerry Heard, and Bobby Nichols, all leading tournament players, had a brush with death during the Western Open when they were stunned by lightning bolts during a heavy rain. They were hospitalized briefly.

The PGA's 41 tournaments were worth $7.41-million, compared with 1974's 43 tournaments worth $7.71 million. The Ladies Professional Golf Association (LPGA) tour embraced 27 official tournaments.

Women's Tour. Sandra Palmer of Fort Worth, Tex., 5 feet 1½ inches (156 centimeters) tall, and Carol Mann of Towson, Md., 6 feet 3 inches (191 centimeters), had a successful year on the LPGA tour. Palmer won the $180,000 Colgate-Dinah Shore Winners Circle in Palm Springs, Calif., and the $55,000 United States Open at Atlantic City, N.J. She led the tour in earnings with $76,374, finished in the top ten 18 times in 25 tournaments, and averaged 71.95 strokes per round. Mann, the LPGA president, won four tournaments in three months. Kathy Whitworth, Donna Caponi Young, and JoAnne Gunderson Carner won three each. Carner earned $64,842; Mann, $64,727.   Frank Litsky

GOVERNORS, U.S. See STATE GOVERNMENT.

GREAT BRITAIN pulled back from the brink of economic chaos in 1975. Whether it turns out to have been simply a short respite on the way to national bankruptcy or a watershed heralding the beginning of national salvation remains to be seen.

Two critical developments helped to stave off the worst. On June 5, two-thirds of the people going to the polls in the country's first referendum voted to keep Britain in the European Community (Common Market). A month later, the Labour government announced a new plan for wage restraint, the first serious attempt to control the country's rocketing wage inflation since Labour came to power in February, 1974.

The Referendum settled an issue that had divided the nation for more than 15 years. Labour Prime Minister Harold Wilson emerged triumphant in his two major objectives – Britain stayed in the European Community and the Labour Party was not split permanently in the process.

The government successfully renegotiated the membership terms in March. About $250 million was lopped off Britain's contribution to the Common Market budget, special arrangements were made for continuing New Zealand butter imports, and changes were promised in the common agricultural policy. Wilson then announced that he would advise British voters to vote "yes for Europe" in a national referendum.

Margaret Thatcher celebrates her election as the first woman leader
of the Conservative Party with her son Mark and husband, Denis.

Anti-Market Forces. A formidable array of political strength was lined up against Wilson. One-third of his Cabinet, a substantial number of junior ministers, half the Labour Party Parliament members, most of the Labour Party executive, and nearly all the important unions in the Trades Union Congress (TUC) campaigned for withdrawal.

The country was treated to the unusual spectacle of major Cabinet figures taking diametrically opposite positions in public. The Conservatives had a field day as the Labour Party publicly ripped itself apart. Only a handful of right wing Conservatives opposed the official Conservative policy supporting membership. When the House of Commons voted on April 9, the renegotiated terms were approved by 396 votes to 170.

The Campaign. The issue then went to the voters. The question proposed by the referendum was simple and neutral: "Do you think the United Kingdom should stay in the European Community? Yes/No."

By early May, both sides had grouped into broad umbrella organizations. The "Britain in Europe" campaign contained all the Liberals, most of the Conservatives, and most of Labour's leading moderates, such as Home Secretary Roy Jenkins. It was lavishly financed by big business and private contributions. The "Get Britain Out" group worked on a shoestring budget and consisted of an uneasy alliance of right wing Conservatives, such as Enoch Powell (now an Ulster Loyalist), and leading Labour left wingers, such as Anthony Wedgwood Benn, secretary for industry, and Michael Foot, the employment minister.

About 65 per cent of the electorate turned out to vote on June 5. Only the Shetland Islands and the Hebrides voted against the referendum. Scotland, Wales, and Northern Ireland all voted yes, though by smaller majorities than England. It was a unanimous pro-Europe chorus, with even a majority of Labour voters approving membership. It was a great victory for Wilson. But it had its price.

Back to Basics. For four critical months, the referendum battle took the nation's eye off the rapidly worsening economic situation. It was a dangerous distraction for a country on the brink of hyperinflation and mass unemployment.

By February, it was clear that the economy was suffering from excessive wage and price inflation, rising unemployment, a large trade deficit, weak monetary-exchange rates, and a dismal investment outlook. The government's social contract with the unions, whereby the unions agreed to moderate their wage demands in return for certain socialistic measures, was in tatters. By March, prices were rising at the annual rate of 25 per cent, but basic wage rates were increasing by an incredible 33 per cent annually, well ahead of any of Britain's European competitors. At the same time, production was declining. Labour moderates watched with growing despair as union leaders disregarded the social contract in the scramble for massive wage increases.

However, Chancellor of the Exchequer Denis Healey did not try to tackle excessive wage increases or rising prices in his April budget. He went out of his way to stress the need for quickly reducing the size of pay settlements, but he made only vague threats about what he would do if that did not happen. Instead, he imposed a 25 per cent value-added tax on luxury goods; increased the duty on wine, spirits, and tobacco; raised the vehicle license fee $30 a year; and boosted income tax rates 4 per cent. He was trying to siphon off some of the purchasing power that had resulted from the social contract's failure and also boost revenue in order to reduce the enormous budget deficit. But the program's most immediate effect was to add yet another twist to the inflationary spiral.

Wage Restraints. By July, external pressure forced Healey to act again. A run on the pound gathered momentum, partly because international bankers had lost confidence in the pound, and partly because Arab oil producers threatened to move their funds from London. Healey tried to restore confidence by fixing a ceiling of $12 a week on wage raises for the next 12 months. He wanted to reduce the rate of inflation to less than 10 per cent by the end of 1976. Employers who granted raises topping $12 would be subject to sanctions.

The government's greatest success was in winning union support for this plan. Its stanchest ally in this battle turned out to be Jack Jones, leader of the 1.8-million member transport union and a former left wing militant, who sold the $12 ceiling to the rest of the trade-union movement.

Labour Goes Moderate. The income policy was a symbol of the Wilson government's swing back to the center. Labour had been elected in 1974 on its most socialistic program since 1945, but throughout 1975 the Labour left grumbled of a sellout as the party moderates regained the upper hand. The ground was cut from under the left when the TUC decided to support wage restraints.

The government kept its side of the social contract by extending nationalization. A national enterprise board was formed to share in the manufacturing industry and make planning agreements with major companies. Development land for new housing was nationalized. And the unions received a host of new rights and privileges in a series of legislative measures written largely by the TUC.

Early in November, the government announced a new industrial strategy. It promised that, in the future, the private sector would be allowed to make profits and that public money would go to back industrial winners rather than bolster lame ducks.

Yet, in April, the government had bailed out the bankrupt British Leyland Motor Company with $3.5 billion over the next seven years, and had nationalized the company on August 11. Five weeks after announcing its new industrial strategy, the government gave $330 million in loans and guarantees to Chrysler Corporation, which had threatened to pull out of Britain after incurring record losses. The need to save jobs as unemployment mounted was the primary reason for the decisions.

North Sea Oil remained the one flicker of light in the economic gloom. Amid great ceremony, Queen Elizabeth II went to Aberdeen, Scotland, in November to press a button symbolically starting the flow of oil from the Forties field. When it reaches peak production of 200,000 barrels of oil per day by 1980, the Forties oil field will meet 20 per cent of Britain's oil needs. By the early 1980s, Britain should be bringing ashore enough to make the country self-sufficient in oil, with some for export.

The government introduced a petroleum-revenue tax that gives the state up to 70 per cent on profits from the biggest fields. A newly formed British national oil corporation will control the 51 per cent government participation being negotiated with the oil companies.

The Conservatives elected Margaret Thatcher their new leader on February 11. Former Conserv-

Queen Elizabeth II inspects the Gurkha Honour Guards in Hong Kong in May. Her visit was the first by a reigning British monarch.

Conservative Reginald Maudling, left, and Labourite Roy Jenkins urge
voters to support Britain's continued membership in the Common Market.

ative Prime Minister Edward Heath's failures in
the two 1974 elections provoked mounting criticism among Conservative Parliament members,
and he agreed to put the leadership up for vote.
Thatcher was a surprise nominee, and, even more
surprising, she emerged a clear victor. Her victory
was interpreted as a swing to the right. See
THATCHER, MARGARET HILDA ROBERTS.

Home-Rule Moves. On November 19, the government proposed the most far-reaching constitutional changes in more than 200 years. It plans to
introduce legislation in Parliament in October,
1976, to establish elected assemblies in Scotland
and Wales with wide powers over domestic affairs.

The government hopes that home rule will reduce the appeal of nationalist parties that want
outright independence for Scotland and Wales. But
three weeks after the plan was announced, an opinion poll showed that the Scottish Nationalists had
become Scotland's largest party with 37 per cent of
the votes, 7 per cent ahead of Labour. For the first
time, London commentators started to talk seriously about the breakup of Britain.

Parliament also passed a law against sex discrimination, aimed at giving women equal opportunity in jobs, pay, and other conditions. It went
into effect December 29. Employers have five years
to overhaul their employment practices. Andrew F. Neil

See also EUROPE (Facts in Brief Table).

GREECE sought full membership in the European
Community (Common Market) on June 12, 1975.
Greece had been an associate member from 1962 to
1967, when a military dictatorship took over the
government. Membership was restored in 1974
with the return of democratic rule to Greece. Ste-
phan Stathatos, Greece's Common Market representative, said the application for full membership
was "based on our earnest desire to consolidate
democracy in Greece within the broader democratic institutions of the European community to
which Greece belongs."

Relations with Turkey. Although Greece urged
Turkey to apply for Common Market membership
to improve relations, the two countries remained
split over a Cyprus settlement and ownership of the
potentially oil-rich Aegean Sea continental shelf.
On January 27, Prime Minister Constantine Caramanlis proposed to Turkey that the Aegean oil dispute be settled by the International Court of Justice in The Hague, the Netherlands. The first
Greek-Turkish summit since the Cyprus war ended
in Brussels, Belgium, on May 31 with Caramanlis
and Turkish Prime Minister Suleyman Demirel
shaking hands. The two agreed to have the International Court decide the oil issue.

Frontier Pledge. On July 2, Caramanlis met
Bulgarian Communist Party First Secretary Todor
Zhivkov in Sofia to receive assurances about the

inviolability of the Greek-Bulgarian frontier in the event of a Greek-Turkish war. They decided to invite their Balkan neighbors to a conference to define areas of Balkan cooperation.

Defense Plans. On April 29, the United States and Greece announced the end of homeporting of U.S. warships at Elevsis, near Athens, and the closing of an American air base at Athens airport. The announcement came after three weeks of talks on limiting American military forces in Greece.

On August 23, former dictator George Papadopoulos and two aides were sentenced to death for high treason, but were later reprieved. Papadopoulos was sentenced to 25 years imprisonment in December for bloody suppression of a 1973 student revolt. Parliament elected Constantine Tsatsos, 76, as president on June 19 under a new Constitution. He replaced Michael Stassinopoulos.   Kenneth Brown

See also CYPRUS; EUROPE (Facts in Brief Table); TURKEY.

GRENADA. See LATIN AMERICA; Section Five, GRENADA.

GUATEMALA. See LATIN AMERICA.

GUINEA. See AFRICA.

GUINEA-BISSAU. See AFRICA; Section Five, GUINEA-BISSAU.

GUYANA. See LATIN AMERICA.

HAITI. See LATIN AMERICA.

Members of the military junta that ruled Greece from 1967 to 1974 are sentenced to death for treason in August. They were later reprieved.

HANDICAPPED. Representatives from 30 nations, members of the World Federation of the Deaf, met in August in Washington, D.C., to discuss the problems of the deaf. The group meets every four years, but this was its first meeting in the United States. The delegates agreed to launch a worldwide program to provide better immunization against diseases that cause deafness, such as German measles, mumps, and Rh factor disease. Their panel on vocational rehabilitation recommended that all training programs include instruction on how to use leisure time. And the panel studying communication recommended that each country develop ways to communicate televised emergency announcements to deaf citizens.

In the United States, the growth in special education for the handicapped was greeted in 1975 as an important part of the civil rights movement. Organizations such as Disabled in Action and special groups of handicapped students demanded not just an education but an equal education, side by side with nondisabled pupils, where possible.

Until now, there has been a tendency for schools to treat handicapped students in a second-class manner. Often, classes for the handicapped are located in school basements or in out-of-the-way parts of the building where there can be little contact between the disabled and normal children.

The efforts of the handicapped groups and many rehabilitation workers are now focused on bringing handicapped and nonhandicapped students together as much as possible. The program, called *mainstreaming,* is designed to benefit all students. The handicapped are treated as normal students, and the other pupils discover that their disabled colleagues are real people, too.

At the same time, there is an increasing awareness on the part of the public that the handicapped are a growing social and political force in the United States. There are an estimated 20 million physically handicapped persons in the United States and they are applying pressure to obtain what able-bodied Americans take for granted: a drink of water within reach; buildings they can enter from the front; and intersections they can cross safely.

In December, President Gerald R. Ford signed a bill that extends federal grants to states and localities for the education of the handicapped. The legislation sets up a formula in which each state receives grants for handicapped pupils based on percentages of what is spent nationally for the average nonhandicapped pupil.

The proponents of mainstreaming could look with interest to developments in Mexico. There the American Foundation for Overseas Blind (AFOB) is administering a program in the public schools that will integrate blind youngsters with sighted pupils. The educational plan, financed by the Mexican government and the AFOB, will train teachers in special education and develop an orientation and mobility program for blind students.

Aids for the Handicapped. Howard M. Jenkins of Huntington, N.Y., was granted a patent for a wheel chair that will climb stairs. He assigned the rights to Ramby, Incorporated, which has set up offices in Stamford, Conn. The Ramby, as the chair is called, has been produced in manually and electrically operated models, but the manufactured product will be battery powered. The chair does not have the usual wheels; it runs on two pairs of tracks that consist of sprockets mounted on endless belts. The seat is electrically self-leveling.

An optical instrument used by the U.S. Army to see enemy soldiers at night during the Vietnam War is being field-tested by the Northeastern Rehabilitation Center for the Blind in Albany, N.Y., for possible use by people with night blindness or other vision problems. The device, called a passive night vision scope, looks like a miniature movie camera. It is less than 5 inches (13 centimeters) long, and is powered by a 1.4-volt battery. The instrument amplifies tiny amounts of light from 300 to 10,000 times. For example, a person sitting in a darkened room can look through the device and see other persons in the room almost as clearly as in daylight.   Joseph P. Anderson

HARNESS RACING. See HORSE RACING.

HARRIS, FRED ROY (1930-   ), a former U.S. senator from Oklahoma, announced his candidacy for the 1976 Democratic presidential nomination on Jan. 11, 1975. The announcement came as no surprise, because Harris has spent most of his time since he left the Senate in 1972 trying to build popular support for the 1976 campaign.

Fred Harris was born into a poor sharecropping family in Walters, Okla., on Nov. 13, 1930. He grew up in the Oklahoma Dust Bowl during the Great Depression. He married LaDonna Crawford, a Comanche Indian, in 1949. They both worked to finance his studies at the University of Oklahoma, where he earned a B.A. degree in 1952 and a law degree in 1954. Harris practiced law in Lawton, Okla., until he was elected to the U.S. Senate in 1964, to complete the term of the late Senator Robert S. Kerr. He was re-elected in 1966.

Harris began his Senate career as a conservative Democrat with the support of the powerful Kerr family. However, as the Vietnam War continued, and domestic problems mounted, Harris moved toward the liberal Democratic bloc. He was chairman of the Democratic National Committee in 1969 and 1970. He left the Senate in 1972 after making a brief bid for the presidential nomination.

Harris and his wife have three children. They live in Lawton and McLean, Va.   Edward G. Nash

HAWAII. See STATE GOVERNMENT.

HEALTH AND DISEASE. Officials of the World Health Organization (WHO) predicted in September, 1975, that the worldwide battle against smallpox would end soon. They also said that they expect two years of searching after the last smallpox case is cured before an international commission can declare officially that the dread disease has been wiped out. They said WHO knew of only 16 persons in the world still infected with the most devastating kind of smallpox, and all of these were quarantined in Bangladesh.

Other diseases took their toll in 1975, however. A severe cholera epidemic struck Bangladesh in October. That country had also suffered an earlier outbreak of the disease, one of the worst in Asia's history, in 1974. The worst outbreak of malaria in 20 years surged through India in May, though there were relatively few fatalities, according to WHO officials. And influenza swept across Europe in January, reaching epidemic proportions in such countries as Czechoslovakia, France, and Italy.

In the United States, the decade's most severe outbreak of encephalitis, an inflammation of the brain, occurred in July and August. A dozen states reported hundreds of cases, and the disease reached epidemic proportions in Illinois and Mississippi. Although about 10 per cent of encephalitis cases prove fatal, officials at the Center for Disease Control in Atlanta, Ga., noted that fewer than 1 in 100 persons bitten by an infected mosquito actually become ill. For still unexplained reasons, most of the year's encephalitis victims were elderly persons. The Center for Disease Control reported in August that the nationwide measles immunization campaign had prevented 24 million cases of measles, and 2,400 deaths in 10 years.

Cancer struck an estimated 665,000 Americans and killed some 365,000 in 1975, an all-time high. While there were no major breakthroughs in cancer therapy, a report on 22 years of cancer statistics published by the American Cancer Society produced some encouraging news. The report showed that the incidence of several major forms of cancer, including stomach cancer, cancer of the esophagus, and ovarian cancer, dropped dramatically and that survival rates for cancer victims were improving. Twenty-five years ago, only 1 of every 4 cancer patients survived for at least five years after diagnosis of their illness. Today 1 of every 3 survives.

The National Cancer Institute published a study that surveyed the cases of 219,493 white and 21,088 black patients over a nine-year period. The study showed that whites had significantly higher survival rates than did blacks. The researchers theorized that the immune systems of blacks may react differently to cancer.

The National Cancer Institute also published charts in August that verified the fact that a significant proportion of all cancers are caused by

Brazil's Health Minister Paulo de Almeida Machado receives an inoculation against meningitis as part of a nationwide battle against the disease.

HILLS, CARLA ANDERSON (1934-   ), was confirmed as U.S. secretary of housing and urban development on March 5, 1975. She is only the third woman Cabinet member in U.S. history and the first since 1955. Sworn in on March 11, she promised to make "substantial strides toward that goal of achieving for every American family decent shelter and a proper living environment."

Carla Anderson was born in Los Angeles on Jan. 3, 1934, the daughter of a wealthy building materials distributor. She attended private schools and graduated with honors from Stanford University in 1955. After receiving her law degree from Yale University Law School in 1958, she married Roderick M. Hills, also a lawyer. She was admitted to the bar in 1959.

From 1959 to 1961, she was assistant United States attorney in Los Angeles. In 1962, she became a partner with her husband and three other lawyers in a Los Angeles law firm specializing in antitrust and securities law. In 1974, she was named assistant attorney general in charge of the Justice Department's Civil Division, where she supervised more than 200 lawyers.

Hills is coauthor of *Federal Civil Practice* (1961) and coauthor and editor of *Antitrust Adviser* (1971). In her moments away from official duties, she enjoys tennis and cooking. She and her husband have four children.   Kathryn Sederberg

chemical agents in the environment. The charts showed that areas of the country that have many chemical plants and large amounts of chemical pollution have the highest death rates from lung, liver, and bladder cancers.

Heart Disease. There was encouraging news about the coronary death rate in 1975. Statistics showed that public health efforts to change people's smoking and eating habits have begun to show results, and the coronary death rate has been dropping since the late 1960s. From 1968 to 1972, the coronary death rate for white men between the ages of 35 and 64 dropped 8.7 per cent, with similar drops among black men and among black and white women. The reduction in the number of people who smoke cigarettes, changes in eating habits, and better management of high blood pressure were all credited for the decrease in deaths.

On August 26, the U.S. Food and Drug Administration (FDA) issued a new warning on oral contraceptives, particularly for women over 30 years old. The FDA said the risk of a fatal heart attack was nearly three times higher among women using oral contraceptives who are from 30 to 39 than among those not using them. For women over 40 who use the pill, the threat of a fatal heart attack was nearly five times greater.   Dianne Rafalik

HIGHWAY. See BUILDING AND CONSTRUCTION; TRANSPORTATION.

HOBBIES. Dealers in craft materials and supplies reported in 1975 that their business was increasing despite the U.S. economic recession. Figures from the Hobby Industry Association of America, published in April, showed that annual sales of hobby materials rose from $652 million to $1 billion between 1965 and 1974. The growth continued in 1975. Hobbies provided a relatively inexpensive way for people to spend their leisure time.

Bicentennial Hobbies. The approaching U.S. Bicentennial stimulated interest in the hobby field. "Collectors of military figures are now avid for miniatures of the American Revolution," said Arthur Etchells, a spokesman for the Miniature Figure Collectors of America. Interest in such early American crafts as weaving, spinning, and candle making also increased.

A vase containing a lock of George Washington's hair sold for $41,400 at a London auction on May 27. The so-called Poole Vase was made by Josiah Wedgwood II in 1791. The lock of hair apparently had little effect on the price.

Collectors' Items. President Gerald R. Ford's letters brought higher prices than expected at auction in New York City. For example, a letter estimated to be worth $100 brought $525 on February 27, the highest price paid for a Ford letter until then. The letter, discussing the Vietnam War, was dated Jan. 22, 1968, when Ford was in the House of

Friedrich Karl Baas displays a 500-year-old
Gutenberg Bible he found in a church attic
in West Germany. It might be worth $3 million.

Representatives. On January 23, a book inscribed
by Ford when he was a congressman sold for $300.
In the inscription, he misspelled the word *personal*
as *personel*. Ford had written the book, *Portrait of
the Assassin,* about Lee Harvey Oswald in collaboration with John R. Stiles in 1965.

A chair in which John F. Kennedy sat when he
was a student at Choate Academy in Wallingford,
Conn., brought $300. It was sold at an auction of
furnishings from the Peapack, N.J., home of Jacqueline Kennedy Onassis on January 8.

Seventy antique and classic automobiles belonging to Oklahoma collectors sold for almost $1.2-
million at a Dallas auction on June 1. J. Lou Gep-
hart of Inglebrook, Ohio, paid the highest price,
$150,000, for a 1932 Duesenberg Model J.

A 99-piece silver service that purportedly belonged to Adolf Hitler sold at auction on April 24
in Indianapolis for $32,000. The anonymous seller,
a former U.S. Army officer, said he found the silver
at Hitler's Munich headquarters. The pieces were
engraved with the initials A.H., swastikas, and ea-
gles. Hitler's black 1940-1941 Mercedes-Benz parade car sold for $141,000 at a Dunedin, Fla., auc-
tion on February 11. The seller, Bob Pass of St.
Louis, said he paid $176,000 for the car. A double-
barreled flintlock gun believed to have been owned
by Napoleon Bonaparte sold for $57,960 in London
on May 14. Theodore M. O'Leary

HOCKEY. The Philadelphia Flyers retained the
National Hockey League (NHL) championship in
the 1974-1975 season, a result of their rough style
and the coaching of Fred Shero. They won the
Stanley Cup play-offs for the second consecutive
year and produced the Most Valuable Players in
the regular season (center Bobby Clarke) and play-
offs (goalie Bernie Parent).

With the addition of teams in Washington and
Kansas City, the NHL expanded to 18 teams. It
abandoned its traditional alignment of East and
West Divisions and established two new conferences (Clarence Campbell and Prince of Wales)
and four new divisions (Lester Patrick, Conn
Smythe, Charles F. Adams, and James Norris).

The four division champions were the Flyers,
Vancouver Canucks, Buffalo Sabres, and Montreal
Canadiens. The Flyers defeated the Sabres, 4
games to 2, in the Stanley Cup finals and proved,
said Parent, "that we were no fluke champion."

Roughness a Problem. The Flyers often intimi-
dated their opponents, but they were not the only
team involved in rough hockey. The Flyers and the
California Golden Seals accumulated 232 minutes
in penalties, an all-time record, in one game. Seven
weeks later, the St. Louis Blues and New York
Rangers broke the record with 246 minutes in penalties, 180 in one period alone.

The most publicized incident happened on January 4 in Bloomington, Minn., when Dave Forbes of
the Boston Bruins struck Henry Boucha of the
Minnesota North Stars over the right eye with his
hockey stick. Boucha required 25 stitches, later underwent surgery, and still was reported suffering
from double vision.

Forbes was arrested and tried for aggravated
assault, but a mistrial was declared when the jury
could not agree on a verdict. This was the first
prosecution in the United States of a professional
athlete for an alleged criminal act committed during a sports event.

Bobby Orr of Boston won the Art Ross Trophy
as scoring champion and his eighth James Norris
Trophy as the outstanding defenseman. He was
named to the All-Star team with Denis Potvin of
the New York Islanders on defense, Parent in goal,
Clarke at center, and Rick Martin of Buffalo and
Guy Lafleur of Montreal at wing.

The 27-year-old Orr had one year remaining on
his five-year, $200,000-a-year contract. The Min-
nesota Fighting Saints of the rival World Hockey
Association (WHA) offered him $4 million over
five years. Orr asked the Bruins for $1 million a
year for seven years or $250,000 a year for life. He
made a compromise deal with the Bruins, then underwent knee surgery two weeks before the start of
the 1975-1976 season. By the time he returned to
action in November, his high-scoring teammate,
Phil Esposito, had been traded to the Rangers. Orr

had a second operation on the same knee on November 29.

The WHA started its third season with 14 teams realigned into three divisions – Eastern, Western, and Canadian. Two teams, Indianapolis and Phoenix, were new, and the New England Whalers moved from Boston to Hartford, Conn.

The Whalers, Houston Aeros, and Quebec Nordiques won the division titles. Houston won the World Cup play-offs for the second straight year, sweeping the finals from Quebec in four games.

Houston's star was Gordie Howe, an NHL stand-out for 25 years before joining the WHA. The 47-year-old Howe was named club president and decided to play another season.

Andre Lacroix of San Diego barely beat Bobby Hull of the Winnipeg Jets for the scoring title. Hull edged Lacroix for the Most Valuable Player award, mainly because of his 77 goals. Lacroix, Hull, and Howe were named to the All-Star team with defensemen Kevin Morrison of San Diego and J. C. Tremblay of Quebec, and goalie Ron Grahame of Houston.

Although the Michigan franchise failed to survive and every team again lost money, the WHA moved toward stability. Regular-season attendance increased 47.8 per cent to 4.1 million. NHL attendance was 9.5 million. Frank Litsky

HOME FURNISHINGS. See INTERIOR DESIGN.
HONDURAS. See LATIN AMERICA.

Standings in National Hockey League
Clarence Campbell Conference

Lester Patrick Division	W.	L.	T.	Points
Philadelphia	51	18	11	113
N.Y. Rangers	37	29	14	88
N.Y. Islanders	33	25	22	88
Atlanta	34	31	15	83
Conn Smythe Division				
Vancouver	38	32	10	86
St. Louis	35	31	14	84
Chicago	37	35	8	82
Minnesota	23	50	7	53
Kansas City	15	54	11	41

Prince of Wales Conference

Charles F. Adams Division	W.	L.	T.	Points
Buffalo	49	16	15	113
Boston	40	26	14	94
Toronto	31	33	16	78
California	19	48	13	51
James Norris Division				
Montreal	47	14	19	113
Los Angeles	42	17	21	105
Pittsburgh	37	28	15	89
Detroit	23	45	12	58
Washington	8	67	5	21

Scoring Leaders	Games	Goals	Assists	Points
Bobby Orr, Boston	80	46	89	135
Phil Esposito, Boston	79	61	66	127
Marcel Dionne, Detroit	80	47	74	121
Guy Lafleur, Montreal	70	53	66	119
Pete Mahovlich, Montreal	80	35	82	117
Bobby Clarke, Philadelphia	80	27	89	116
Rene Robert, Buffalo	74	40	60	100

Leading Goalies	Games	Goals against	Avg.
Bernie Parent, Philadelphia	68	137	2.03
Wayne Stephenson, Philadelphia	12	29	2.72
Bobby Taylor, Philadelphia	3	13	6.50
Philadelphia Totals	80	181	2.26
Rogie Vachon, Los Angeles	54	121	2.24
Gary Edwards, Los Angeles	27	61	2.34
Los Angeles Totals	80	185	2.31
Glenn Resch, N.Y. Islanders	25	59	2.47
Billy Smith, N.Y. Islanders	53	156	2.78
N.Y. Islanders Totals	80	221	2.76

Awards
Calder Trophy (best rookie)—Eric Vail, Atlanta
Hart Trophy (most valuable player)—Bobby Clarke, Philadelphia
Lady Byng Trophy (sportsmanship)—Marcel Dionne, Detroit
Norris Trophy (best defenseman)—Bobby Orr, Boston
Art Ross Trophy (leading scorer)—Bobby Orr, Boston
Conn Smythe Trophy (most valuable player in Stanley Cup play)—
  Bernie Parent, Philadelphia
Vezina Trophy (leading goalie)—Bernie Parent, Philadelphia
Bill Masterton Trophy (perseverance, dedication to hockey)—
  Don Luce, Buffalo

Standings in World Hockey Association

East Division	W.	L.	T.	Points
New England	43	30	5	91
Cleveland	35	40	3	73
Chicago	30	47	1	61
Indianapolis	18	57	3	39
West Division				
Houston	53	25	0	106
San Diego	43	31	4	90
Minnesota	42	33	3	87
Phoenix	39	31	8	86
Baltimore	21	53	4	46
Canadian Division				
Quebec	46	32	0	92
Toronto	43	33	2	88
Winnipeg	38	35	5	81
Vancouver	37	39	2	76
Edmonton	36	38	4	76

Scoring Leaders	Games	Goals	Assists	Points
Andre Lacroix, San Diego	78	41	106	147
Bobby Hull, Winnipeg	78	77	65	142
Serge Bernier, Quebec	76	54	68	122
Ulf Nilsson, Winnipeg	78	26	94	120
Larry Lund, Houston	78	33	75	108
Wayne Rivers, San Diego	78	54	53	107
Anders Hedberg, Winnipeg	65	53	47	100
Gordie Howe, Houston	75	34	65	99
Wayne Dillon, Toronto	77	29	66	95
Mike Walton, Minnesota	75	48	45	93

Leading Goalies	Games	Goals against	Avg.
Ron Grahame, Houston	43	131	3.03
Wayne Rutledge, Houston	35	113	3.24
Houston Totals	78	244	3.12
Bob Whidden, Cleveland	29	89	3.23
Gerry Cheevers, Cleveland	52	167	3.26
Cleveland Totals	78	256	3.25
Jack Norris, Phoenix	33	107	3.27
Gary Kurt, Phoenix	47	156	3.29
Phoenix Totals	78	263	3.29

Awards
Gary L. Davidson Trophy (most valuable player)—
  Bobby Hull, Winnipeg
W.D. (Bill) Hunter Trophy (leading scorer)—
  Andre Lacroix, San Diego
Lou Kaplan Award (best rookie)—Anders Hedberg, Winnipeg
Ben Hatskin Trophy (leading goalie)—Ron Grahame, Houston
Dennis A. Murphy Award (best defenseman)—
  J.C. Tremblay, Quebec
Howard Baldwin Award (coach of the year)—
  Sandy Hucul, Phoenix

HORSE RACING

HORSE RACING. Forego successfully defended his title in 1975, proving again to be the best handicap horse in the United States. He won major stakes throughout the year and beat late-season challenger Wajima in the Woodward Stakes at Belmont Park on September 27.

Wajima, a 3-year-old, missed the Triple Crown races, but defeated Kentucky Derby winner Foolish Pleasure and Belmont Stakes victor Avatar while winning the Marlboro Cup Handicap on September 13 at Belmont. Winner of five stakes and $497,451 in 1975, Wajima was retired to stud at a record syndication price of $7.2 million.

Foolish Pleasure met Ruffian, winner of the Triple Crown for Fillies and considered the best female race horse in decades, in a $350,000 match race at Belmont Park on July 6. Ruffian broke down during the race and was humanely destroyed when she responded poorly to surgery on broken bones in her right foreleg. Ruffian was undefeated in her 10 races as a 2-year-old and 3-year-old.

Susan's Girl, champion handicap filly of 1973, returned to her best form to win six stakes, including the Delaware Handicap, Beldame, and Spinster, bringing her career earnings to more than $1.2 million.

Two-year-old fillies Dearly Precious and Optimistic Gal were the best of their division, with

Major Horse Races of 1975

Race	Winner	Value to Winner
Belmont Stakes	Avatar	$116,160
Canadian International Championship Stakes	Snow Knight	113,220
Epsom Derby (England)	Grundy	215,060
Irish Sweeps Derby	Grundy	129,280
Irish St. Leger	Caucasus	27,658
Kentucky Derby	Foolish Pleasure	209,600
King George VI & Queen Elizabeth Stakes	Grundy	165,458
Marlboro Cup Handicap	Wajima	150,000
National Thoroughbred Championship	Dulcia	240,000
Preakness Stakes	Master Derby	158,100
Prix de L'Arc de Triomphe	Star Appeal	350,000
Queen's Plate Stakes (Canada)	L'Enjoleur	95,351
Santa Anita Derby	Avatar	82,900
Washington, D.C., Int'l	Nobiliary	100,000

Major U.S. Harness Races of 1975

Race	Winner	Value to Winner
American Pacing Classic	Young Quinn	$ 45,000
Cane Pace	Nero	70,000
Hambletonian	Bonefish	116,096
Kentucky Futurity	Noble Rogue	41,500
Little Brown Jug	Seatrain	54,690
Messenger Pace	Brets Champ	77,111
Roosevelt International	Savoir	100,000

A plastic cast on her broken foreleg, Ruffian is led away after injury halted $350,000 match race in July. The filly was later destroyed.

Dearly Precious winning eight of nine starts, including seven stakes races. Optimistic Gal was victorious in five stakes but lost to Dearly Precious in their two encounters.

Honest Pleasure clearly was the best among the year's 2-year-old colts, winning four consecutive major stakes and earning $370,227 in taking six of eight starts.

A Record Price for a thoroughbred sold at public auction was established at Belmont Park on October 15 when Brereton C. Jones paid $730,000 for Key to the Kingdom, a 5-year-old stakes winner whose bloodlines make him an outstanding prospect for the stud.

Another world record auction price was the $715,000 for a yearling full brother to 1969 Kentucky Derby winner Majestic Prince at the Keeneland sales in July. The son of Raise a Native and Gay Hostess was sold by Spendthrift Farm to Mr. and Mrs. Franklin Groves of Minneapolis, Minn.

Harness Racing. Savoir, winner of the Roosevelt International, in November became harness racing's seventh $1-million winner. Bonefish won the Hambletonian, and Seatrain captured the Little Brown Jug.

Quarter Horse Racing. Bugs Alive in 75 earned first money of $330,000 in the All-American Quarter Horse Futurity for 2-year-olds at Ruidoso Downs, N. Mex.   Jane Goldstein

HOSPITAL administrations tried to reconcile economic pressures with better care for patients in 1975. When the U.S. Department of Health, Education, and Welfare eliminated an 8.5 per cent Medicare nursing differential in July that was designed to pay part of the extra nursing care required by aged patients, hospital spokesmen expressed concern that the change would lower the level of care available. They took the matter to court, and, on August 1, the American Hospital Association (AHA), the American Protestant Hospital Association, the Catholic Hospital Association, and the Federation of American Hospitals won an injunction barring termination of the differential.

The cost of malpractice insurance affected every hospital's ability to provide care and the costs of that care. Between January and March, premiums increased as much as 700 per cent for some hospitals. The costs were passed on to patients in higher charges. See INSURANCE (Close-Up).

The AHA registered 7,250 hospitals with a total of 1.5 million beds in 1974. Outpatient visits continued to increase at a faster rate (7.2 per cent) than inpatient admissions (3.4 per cent), totaling 250.5 million and 35.5 million, respectively, for all hospitals. There were 3.2 million full- and part-time hospital employees.   Madison B. Brown

In the nation's first major walkout by doctors, interns and residents picketed 21 New York City hospitals in March for better work conditions.

HOUSING. Severe depression struck the U.S. home-building industry in 1975. High prices of homes, a tight money market, lowered federal subsidies, a high inventory of unsold homes, and the generally depressed state of the economy all contributed to the decline in housing construction.

Housing starts in February fell to an annually adjusted rate of only 977,000 units, 48 per cent fewer than in February, 1974. The U.S. Department of Commerce reported new housing starts in July were up to an annual adjusted rate of 1.2 million units, but still down 6 per cent from July, 1974. Furthermore, the Commerce Department had reported on January 17 that housing starts in 1974 had fallen to an eight-year low of 1.4 million units, 35 per cent fewer than in 1973.

The poor 1974 and 1975 records promised a crisis of increasing proportions as the number of new homes being produced fell further behind the 2-million units that must be built each year to meet U.S. housing needs.

Bail-Out Legislation. President Gerald R. Ford signed into law two bills designed to help stimulate the housing industry. On March 29, he signed a bill allowing home buyers in 1975 to deduct 5 per cent of the sale price from their 1975 income tax, up to $2,000. However, the Federal Home Loan Bank Board (FHLBB) reported on July 9 that the tax credit had not been enough to bring about a major reduction in the inventory of unsold homes.

On July 2, the President signed the Emergency Housing Act of 1975, giving the government authority to purchase an additional $10 billion in low-interest mortgages. Under this program, the lender charges an interest rate as low as 7.5 per cent, and the government absorbs the difference between that and the current interest rates of more than 9 per cent. The new law also authorized government-guaranteed loans to unemployed persons who would otherwise lose their homes because of mortgage foreclosures. But on June 24, President Ford vetoed a $1.2-billion housing bill that would have provided relief from high mortgage-interest rates and down-payment requirements for middle-income families.

Administration Policies. The FHLBB, on June 16, made it easier for persons with small down payments to purchase new homes. It increased from 10 per cent to 15 per cent the amount of assets that savings and loan associations could lend for mortgages exceeding 90 per cent of a home's value.

On January 20, the Administration released $900 million for low-income and senior-citizen rent subsidies. At the same time, the Department of Housing and Urban Development (HUD) permitted government loans for construction of rental housing for elderly and handicapped persons.

In January, HUD began ending its aid to developers of planned new communities. Fifteen new

Apartment hunters in Moscow scan lists of offers
to trade apartments. Bulletin boards are part
of plan to ease Russia's housing shortage.

towns were promised continued, but limited, federal aid to stave off financial failure.

Closing Costs. The federal Real Estate Settlement Procedures Act became effective on June 20. It requires lenders to give home buyers 12 days advance notice of all fees and charges to be levied when the formal purchase takes place. It also prohibits kickbacks and referral fees. Lending institutions claimed that the new procedures increased paperwork and delayed completion of transactions.

Suburban Zoning. The Supreme Court of the United States, on June 25, rejected a challenge to suburban zoning laws. The challengers argued that, by keeping housing costs high, such laws excluded low-income and racial-minority groups from the community. In a 5 to 4 vote, the court dismissed the suit brought against Penfield, N.Y., a suburb of Rochester. The court ruled that the plaintiffs – a group of inner-city residents, a city taxpayer's group, and a fair-housing organization – lacked legal standing to pursue the suit, because none of them had been injured by the laws.

Housing Trends. On August 21, HUD reported that about 4 million Americans were living in either condominium or cooperative housing and that condominium ownership was likely to become more popular. The report noted that the number of condominiums has increased 15 times to about 1.25-million units since 1970.   James M. Banovetz

HOUSTON. Mayor Fred Hofheinz failed to win a clear majority of votes against three other candidates in the Nov. 4, 1975, election and was forced into a run-off with his closest opponent, Frank Briscoe. The outcome was finally decided on December 2, with Hofheinz as the winner.

Police Problems. Police Chief Carroll M. Lynn accused the Houston Police Department of illegal wiretapping. Testifying before a congressional committee on May 22, Lynn also charged that the Federal Bureau of Investigation failed to respond adequately to his request for an investigation and that his own phone had been tapped. Lynn, who became chief when Mayor Hofheinz took office in 1974, reported that police wiretapping had been going on since 1967 or 1968.

Mayor Hofheinz reported on January 6 that the police department had compiled dossiers on a substantial number of Houston residents, including Congresswoman Barbara C. Jordan (D., Tex.). He said he ordered the files cleared of such dossiers and added that the persons responsible would be punished. The police department also withdrew from the national Law Enforcement Intelligence Unit (LEIU), claiming that the organization encouraged a national network of police spying. However, LEIU officials claimed that Houston had been expelled for illegal wiretapping.

Magnet Schools. The board of trustees of the Houston public schools recommended on May 6 that magnet-school programs be developed as an alternative to court-ordered pairing of elementary schools to achieve greater integration. Magnet schools offer specialized programs, such as music, with enrollment open to anyone in the school district. The program went into effect in September, with more than 30 magnet-school programs designed to attract students with special interests.

Economic Conditions in Houston remained relatively strong. From mid-1974 to mid-1975, department store sales increased 18 per cent, and construction activity was up 4.7 per cent. Food costs rose 11.3 per cent during the same period. The unemployment rate was only 4.9 per cent, but this was an increase of 3.9 per cent over mid-1974. However, the cost of living rose 12 per cent between July, 1974, and July, 1975. The average annual income of factory workers increased only 8.1 per cent as of mid-1975, to $11,766. The average pump price of regular gasoline rose 3.6 per cent to 51.6 cents per gallon (3.8 liters) by June.

Census. A midyear report by the U.S. Census Bureau revealed that Houston's population had increased by 7 per cent between 1970 and 1973. Houston's population was estimated to be 1,320,018 as of July 1, 1973. Only Houston and Washington, D.C., among large cities, were expected by the National Planning Association to sustain a significant rate of growth.   James M. Banovetz

HUMPHREY, HUBERT HORATIO (1911-   ), former Vice-President and unsuccessful presidential candidate in 1968, showed surprising strength in 1975 public-opinion polls on Democratic Party presidential possibilities. In a November Gallup Poll, Humphrey was picked over 10 active Democratic candidates by 30 per cent of those questioned, far surpassing all the others. In an October test, Humphrey polled 23 per cent.

Throughout the year, Humphrey insisted that he had no intention of seeking the nomination. But he said he would accept if the Democratic National Convention offered it to him.

Humphrey was born in Wallace, S. Dak. He received a B.A. degree from the University of Minnesota in 1939 and an M.A. degree from Louisiana State University in 1940.

Prior to serving as Vice-President under Lyndon B. Johnson from 1965 to 1969, Humphrey was mayor of Minneapolis from 1945 to 1948 and U.S. senator from Minnesota from 1949 to 1964. After his defeat in the 1968 presidential election by Richard M. Nixon, he taught political science at Macalester College in St. Paul and the University of Minnesota in Minneapolis. He was elected to the U.S. Senate again in 1970, taking the seat vacated by Eugene J. McCarthy.

Humphrey married Muriel Fay Buck in 1936. They have four children.   Foster Stockwell

HUNGARY continued its policy of economic and political retrenchment at home in 1975 and strengthened its economic ties with Russia and other Communist countries. Janos Kadar was reelected first secretary for another five years at the Communist Party Congress in Budapest in March. But Rezsö Nyers and Lajos Feher were dropped from the Politburo. The two leaders were closely associated with the 1968 economic reform move that decentralized economic planning and increased availability of consumer goods.

Prime Minister Jenö Fock, another prominent member of the original reform team, resigned on May 15 "for health reasons" after eight years in office. He was replaced by economic planner Gyorgy Lazar (see LAZAR, GYORGY).

In March, Hungary signed an agreement with the United States to set up a joint economic council and, on June 28, agreed to compensate United States holders of pre-World War II Hungarian bonds. But Hungary rejected the emigration clauses attached to the U.S. Trade Reform Act of December, 1974.

Vatican Relations. Joseph Cardinal Mindszenty, exiled anti-Communist Roman Catholic primate of Hungary, died in Vienna on May 6. Pope Paul VI had named nine new Hungarian bishops on January 10.   Chris Cviic

See also EUROPE (Facts in Brief Table).

HUNTING. *Guns of Autumn,* a Columbia Broadcasting System (CBS) television documentary on hunting broadcast Sept. 5, 1975, caused such a storm of controversy in the United States that CBS broadcast a follow-up, *Echoes of Guns of Autumn,* on September 28. The second show included views of those who thought the first program was unfair. A Federal Communications Commission spokesman said most of those complaining said *Guns of Autumn* showed only the worst examples of the sport. The documentary showed hunting at a city dump, running bears with dogs, and hunting at game preserves where kills are guaranteed.

The complaints reflected the increasing resentment of some sports groups over what they charge is an organized campaign to misrepresent hunting. The fifth International Big Game Hunters' and Fishermen's Conference in San Antonio in May called for a "declaration of war" on organized antihunting groups. Speakers at the Western Association of State Fish and Game Commissioners July meeting in Seattle assailed what they saw as federal interference with effective state fish and wildlife management.

Increases in most waterfowl populations brought good fall flights for hunters in most flyways. Snow-goose hunting was opened for the first time in 44 years and Atlantic brant hunting for the first time since 1972.   Andrew L. Newman

ICE SKATING. Sheila Young of Detroit won most of the world-championship races for women speed skaters on successive February weekends in 1975. The first meet, the world sprint championships on February 15 and 16 at Göteborg, Sweden, featured two 500-meter and two 1,000-meter races. The 24-year-old Young won three of the four races and became overall champion for the second time in three years.

The world all-around championships for women, held at Assen, the Netherlands, on February 22 and 23, consisted of races at 500, 1,000, 1,500, and 3,000 meters. Young won two of the first three races and was the overall leader going into the final race. However, she fell to third place in the final standing because she finished ninth in that 3,000-meter race, and Karin Kessow of East Germany became the overall world champion.

In men's speed skating, Harm Kuipers of the Netherlands, a 24-year-old medical student, won the world all-around championship. Alexander Safranov of Russia won the world sprint championship, and Rich Wurster of Grafton, Wis., won the U.S. and North American outdoor titles.

Figure Skating. Russians won three of the four titles in the world championships held from March 4 to 8 in Colorado Springs, Colo. The only non-Russian winner was Diane De Leeuw, who finished far ahead in women's singles. Although she repre-

Diane De Leeuw, who skated for the Netherlands but lived and trained in California, won the women's world figure-skating title in March.

sented the Netherlands and had won five Dutch championships, the 19-year-old De Leeuw lived and trained in Paramount, Calif.

The Russians who won world titles were Sergei Volkov in men's singles, Irina Rodnina and Alexander Zaitsev in pairs, and Irina Moiseyeva and Andrei Minenkov in dance. Volkov became the first Russian world champion in singles.

Rodnina's world title was her seventh straight — three with Zaitsev and the preceding four with Alexei Ulanov. The Russian husband-wife team of Alexander Gorshkov and Ludmilla Pakhomova, winners of five consecutive world and six consecutive European dance titles, withdrew from the world championships when Gorshkov contracted pneumonia.

Americans did as well as expected in the world championships. Eighteen-year-old Dorothy Hamill of Riverside, Conn., finished second in women's singles. Colleen O'Connor and Jim Millns of Colorado Springs placed second in dance. Gordon McKellen, Jr., 23, of Lake Placid, N.Y., was fifth in men's singles. All had retained their titles in the United States championships held January 29 to February 1 in Oakland, Calif.   Frank Litsky

ICELAND. See Europe.

IDAHO. See State Government.

ILLINOIS. See Chicago; State Government.

INCOME TAX. See Taxation.

INDIA would long remember June 12, 1975. That morning, the high court in Prime Minister Indira Gandhi's hometown of Allahabad, in the state of Uttar Pradesh, ruled that she had won her seat in parliament by corrupt means and must give it up. The court also barred her from elective office for six years.

By sundown that same day, she was dealt another blow. Her Congress Party was beaten by a five-party coalition in an election in Gujarat state, where she had campaigned tirelessly for a month. The coalition was led by her enemy, former Deputy Prime Minister Morarji Desai.

On June 26, the prime minister and her advisers took a step that sharply changed India's course. President Fakhruddin Ali Ahmed declared that "a grave emergency exists whereby the security of India is threatened by internal disturbances." Among the government's first actions was a roundup of opponents, including Desai and 72-year-old Jayaprakash Narayan, who had emerged as leader of a movement to clean up government corruption. The government said 10,000 persons were arrested in the next 90 days; foreign observers put the total as high as 60,000.

Emergency Laws. In explaining her actions, Gandhi referred to a "deep and widespread conspiracy" throughout the land. Her law minister told parliament on July 23 that, "in the public interest," the government could not tell the courts the details of the "plot."

Both houses of parliament approved the emergency laws on July 23 and 24. It was easy, because Gandhi's Congress Party held a heavy majority. About 30 of the opposition members of parliament were under arrest, and other members of the opposition boycotted the proceedings. One of the new laws permitted the prime minister to rule by proclamation. Another barred the courts from reviewing her actions. A third, signed by the president on August 10 — just one day before Gandhi was to begin her appeal to the supreme court — changed the election law retroactively to absolve her of any past criminal offenses.

On legal grounds, the supreme court on November 7 reversed Gandhi's June 12 conviction. Since the court did not challenge the emergency laws, it had no choice but to clear her. But only five days later, the court refused to reconsider its two-year-old decision restricting parliament's power to amend the Constitution so as to alter it radically.

Civil Liberties fared badly under the emergency. An ordinance ruled that a detained person did not have to be told the grounds for his arrest, and he could be held without trial. The press was forbidden to print "unauthorized, irresponsible, or demoralizing news items." Later, Gandhi credited the censorship for the general calm. "When there are no papers, there's no agitation," she said. Some

Prime Minister Indira Gandhi sternly silenced her critics in India after a court convicted her in June for illegal campaigning in 1971.

foreign newsmen were expelled, and many opposition leaders remained under arrest, their names never mentioned in the Indian press. Narayan was freed on a 30-day parole in early November.

At year's end, Gandhi's Congress Party decided to delay general elections, due in March, 1976, for at least a year. It also decided to extend the state of emergency, and all its powers, for at least another six months.

The government insisted the state of emergency brought economic success, and it was partly right. The 30 per cent inflation rate of 1974 was sharply cut. Arrests checked hoarding and smuggling. Strikes were banned. A few rural reforms, long on the books, were put into effect, but peasant distress persisted. After two drought years and heavy floods, India expected a record harvest. But not all signs were cheery. Economic stagnation continued, and exports could not pay for essential imports.

Kashmir. Sheik Mohammad Abdullah was reinstated on February 25 as head of the Kashmir state government. Dismissed from the post 22 years earlier because he was suspected of wanting to separate Kashmir, a predominantly Moslem state, from the rest of India, he had been detained by India for a total of 14 years since 1953. Sheik Abdullah announced that he would abandon his long struggle for a plebiscite. Mark Gayn

See also ASIA (Facts in Brief Table).

INDIAN, AMERICAN. The wave of Indian militancy continued in 1975. Two agents of the U.S. Federal Bureau of Investigation and one Indian were killed on June 26 in a gun battle on the Pine Ridge Indian reservation in South Dakota, when the agents attempted to arrest four men on charges of kidnaping.

The incident occurred against a background of continued warfare on the reservation between backers of the militant American Indian Movement (AIM) and supporters of the Oglala Sioux tribal president, Richard Wilson. AIM and its supporters, who are among the most poverty-stricken residents of the reservation, have charged Wilson with corrupt practices, such as giving patronage jobs to his supporters. The conflict resulted in a breakdown in order, and at least eight Indians were killed in disputes between the two groups.

Indian Militants seized an unused Roman Catholic seminary near Gresham, Wis., on January 1. They demanded that the Alexian Brothers religious order turn over the 225-acre (91-hectare) facility to the Menominee tribe. The Indians ended their occupation of the novitiate on February 4, when the Alexians agreed to deed the facility to the Menominees for use as a health-care center. On July 10, however, the Alexians said they were forced to back down on the agreement, because they feared the tribe could not adequately meet costs.

Armed Indians occupy a Roman Catholic seminary near Gresham, Wis., in January, demanding that it be turned over to the Menominee tribe.

tending the provision of the Voting Rights Act of 1965 to cover Indians.

Rights and Resources. The 26 Indian tribes of the Northern Great Plains published a "Declaration of Indian Rights to the Natural Resources in the Northern Great Plains States" in August. The Plains area is targeted for massive development of coal resources, which requires much water. Consequently, the tribes strongly asserted their rights to water, and asked that a moratorium be placed on water allocations until Indian rights are protected. As coal prices escalated, both the Cheyenne and the Crow tribes of Montana pressed legal actions to renegotiate coal-development contracts they had signed in the 1960s.

The Crow lost a battle over fishing rights on a 50-mile (80-kilometer) stretch of the Big Horn River, which flows through their Montana reservation. On April 9, a U.S. District Court judge reversed two previous rulings and said that the riverbed belonged to the state, not to the Crow. The ruling could provide a basis for challenges to Indian water-rights claims based on sovereignty granted by treaties.

The largest Indian-owned year-round resort, a $15-million recreation complex on the Mescalero Apache reservation in New Mexico, opened to the public on July 11.   Andrew L. Newman

INDIANA. See STATE GOVERNMENT.

On February 21, AIM militants occupied an electronics plant operated by the Fairchild Camera and Instrument Corporation on the Navajo reservation at Shiprock, N. Mex., to protest the layoff of 140 Navajo workers. The group left about a week later, but Fairchild closed the plant permanently in March, throwing more than 500 out of work.

The Navajo Tribal Council voted 48 to 0 on June 5 against allowing the AIM group to hold its annual convention on the Navajo reservation. The decision reflected the conviction of many Indian leaders that Indians should turn from violence and push their causes in Congress, the courts, and the U.S. Bureau of Indian Affairs (BIA).

New Law. A key instrument for such Indian advancement was approved on January 4, when President Gerald R. Ford signed the Indian Self-Determination and Education Assistance Act. The legislation gives Indian tribes increased opportunities to govern their own affairs and provides for grants to strengthen tribal governments. It directs the BIA to contract with tribes – upon their request – to operate reservation programs. The legislation also gives the Indian community a stronger role in deciding how special funds will be used for Indian children in public schools. The government issued proposed regulations for implementing the act on September 4, after more than 30 meetings with Indian groups. In August, Ford signed a bill ex-

INDONESIA may well remember 1975 as the year of the "Pertamina Scandal." Pertamina is a government-controlled conglomerate based on Indonesia's vast oil wealth. But it is more than just the state oil company. Under its flamboyant president, H. Ibnu Sutowo, a former physician and soldier turned businessman, it had invested in steel, fertilizer, an airline, and rice plantations to make it the greatest industrial complex in the underdeveloped world, with assets worth $3.1 billion. As the Pertamina empire grew, so did its foreign debt – to a total exceeding $1.5 billion. When the time came in February and March to repay two loans totaling $100 million, mostly to U.S. banks, Pertamina could not.

Rather than face the collapse of Pertamina's – and its own – credit standing abroad, the Indonesian government took over the debts. But the rescue operation required new foreign loans that may have reached $1 billion, as well as a change in the country's development plans.

Two reasons for Pertamina's woes may have been Japan's declining purchases of oil and China's readiness to sell oil to Japan and the Philippines at prices that undercut Indonesia's. The country's oil exports in 1974 were worth $2.6 billion. But another reason was the rivalry between Sutowo and the "Berkeley Mafia," a group of government planners trained at the University of California.

Communist Tide. If Pertamina was one of President Suharto's worries, so was the Communist triumph in Indochina. Although Indonesia's Communists were bloodily purged after a group of leftist army officers tried to seize power in September, 1965, the soil remained fertile for unrest. The annual income of most of the 130 million Indonesians remained around $40; some 4 million persons were without jobs, and perhaps 30 million were only partly employed; and the inflation rate, down from 50 per cent in 1974, still ran as high as 18 per cent.

Suharto's argument has been that, to combat Communism, Indonesia needed "national resilience" – a viable economy and a public feeling that life was becoming better. But, on a visit to Washington, D.C., on July 5, he also sought arms to fight home-grown insurgency and urged the United States to maintain its naval presence in Southeast Asia.

Student Unrest, which broke into violence in January, 1974, was muted in 1975. The courts were still trying Communists arrested in 1965. Amnesty International, a London-based organization, put the total of political prisoners still held at 55,000.

Terrorists from South Molucca hijacked a train and took over the Indonesian Embassy in the Netherlands in December. They were demanding independence from Indonesia.   Mark Gayn

See also Asia (Facts in Brief Table).

Dr. Louis Lewis stages an impromptu concert in San Francisco during anesthesiologists' strike protesting high malpractice insurance rates.

INSURANCE. Underwriting losses for property and liability insurance companies in the United States were expected to exceed $3.5 billion by the end of 1975, making the year one of the most costly on record. Losses for the first six months of the year exceeded $1.8 billion, nearly reaching the $1.91-billion underwriting losses for all of 1974.

Automobile insurance was the principal problem, but by no means the only one. The cost of repairing vehicles climbed as inflation drove up the price of replacement parts and labor. However, insurance premiums paid by car owners did not increase at a comparable rate. Inflation also hiked medical and hospital costs, but damage to cars was responsible for more of the insurance losses than bodily injuries.

As the energy crisis eased in 1975, automobile mileage surged. This caused a 5.7 per cent increase in accident frequency and a 13.8 per cent increase in the average cost of an accident involving private passenger cars in the first half of 1975.

The cost of claims under homeowners' insurance also showed a serious upward trend in 1975. Insurers attributed this to a greater frequency of losses, higher construction costs, and inadequate premium charges. Product liability claims, with nearly 1 million pending lawsuits, also contributed to the bleak underwriting picture, as did malpractice claims (see Close-Up).

Financial Status. Insurance companies and their rating bureaus sought approval throughout the year from state insurance commissioners for higher premium rates. They had varying degrees of success, but generally, in their words, what they got was too little and too late to compensate for increased claims. The easy availability of insurance coverage that characterized 1973 and 1974 eroded in 1975 as companies became more selective and far less eager for business.

Fears for the financial health of some insurers at the start of 1975 eased at midyear because of a fortunate upturn in the stock market. Major insurance companies invest a large portion of their assets in stocks. When the stock market slumps, the insurers suffer. Because of increases in the value of their investments, the industry's surplus – the amount available to pay claims – increased by $3.9-billion in 1975 after a severe shrinkage of $6 billion in 1974. Nevertheless, by the end of September, 26 smaller insurance companies that wrote about $120 million in annual premiums voluntarily ceased business. In addition, about a dozen others became insolvent.

No-Fault Insurance. Efforts to enact federal guidelines for no-fault automobile insurance continued. The Senate Commerce Committee in June approved a new version of a bill that would set federal minimum standards for state no-fault laws,

Malpractice Headaches

Medical malpractice insurance problems, which had been building up for nearly a decade, reached crisis levels in the United States in 1975. Malpractice insurance is designed to protect doctors and hospitals against claims of negligence or error. It provides funds for investigating claims, preparing legal defenses, or ultimately, paying damages to the patient-victims as directed in court judgments or settlements.

Authoritative estimates indicate that the number of claims has risen about 180 per cent since 1969. By 1975, there was an average of 1 suit for every 10 doctors. The average jury award for damages had also gone up.

The rise in lawsuits has been partly attributed to changing public attitudes toward the medical profession because of sharp advances in fees and not as much personal attention by doctors. Greater sophistication in surgical procedures has also led to an increasing belief that all medical failures are caused by negligence. The medical infallibility popularized in such television shows as "Marcus Welby, M.D.," has created unrealistic expectations on the part of the public. Finally, high awards, some exceeding $1 million, have encouraged a growing number of suits.

Insurance industry sources indicate that doctors win 8 out of 10 cases that are brought to trial. Yet the ultimate cost of paying claims is estimated at about $250 for every $100 collected in premiums.

Malpractice insurance is ordinarily written on an "occurrence" basis, to cover all future claims of malpractice incidents in any given year as long as the claim is made within the time period covered by the statutes of limitations. This is the "long tail." It means that claims are covered even if filed five or six years after an alleged incident occurred. In the case of minors, this time period is extended to 20 years. The insurance industry and the medical field have criticized this unknown factor as a Damoclean scalpel that makes proper measurement of risks and rates virtually impossible.

As a result of the growing number of lawsuits and the increase in awards, insurance rates have risen sharply. For example, New York City neurosurgeons, one of the highest-risk specialties, paid annual malpractice premiums of $659 in 1964 for standard coverage limits of $100,000 per claim and $300,000 per year. Orthopedic surgeons paid $601 for the same coverage. By 1974, the premium for neurosurgeons was $11,045 and for orthopedic surgeons, $7,272. Rates vary from city to city, but they have skyrocketed in similar proportions across the country.

In late 1974, the Argonaut Insurance Company announced its intention to triple the premiums in the state of New York. Argonaut had taken over coverage for the 23,000-member New York State Medical Society six months earlier. The bid for a premium hike failed, and the company announced that all coverage would expire on June 30, 1975. It then withdrew from other malpractice risks throughout the country.

Other insurers threatened to cancel malpractice insurance in at least 20 states, and many of them did so. In protest, anesthesiologists and surgeons in New York, California, and Ohio prepared to stage "job actions," refusing to perform anything but emergency surgery. Such walkouts were actually staged briefly in northern California and some Ohio cities.

Temporary corrective action came quickly. Legislatures in 26 states authorized the creation of joint underwriting pools to spread the insurance risk among all licensed liability companies. In addition, legislation in New York and Maryland and two other states permitted doctors to form their own mutual insurance companies.

Some of the 1975 laws included such reforms as curtailing the statutes of limitations, requiring binding arbitration, placing ceilings on "pain and suffering" awards, establishing stricter review and disciplinary systems to monitor doctor performance, and limiting the fee system for plaintiffs' lawyers. There is no universal approval for any of these legislative solutions, but they ended the crisis, at least temporarily.　　Emanuel Levy

"Dr. Frankenstein . . . your monster is suing you for malpractice."

under which accident victims are reimbursed by their own insurance companies. The bill was rewritten to meet objections from U.S. Attorney General Edward H. Levi, who said that a provision requiring state officials to administer federal law might be unconstitutional. Under the rewritten bill, the U.S. Department of Transportation would administer the system in states that do not adopt the federal guidelines.

The House Consumer Protection Subcommittee began hearings in August on three separate no-fault bills. A final version was expected to reach the floor of the House sometime in 1976. However, President Gerald R. Ford remained opposed to a federal law, arguing that the states should adopt the concept individually.

On the state level, only North Dakota adopted a no-fault law in 1975. It was to become effective on Jan. 1, 1976. Although many other state legislatures considered no-fault bills, none were passed. Laws enacted in 1974 became effective in 1975 in four states—Georgia, Kentucky, Minnesota, and Pennsylvania.

Constitutional challenges against no-fault laws in Connecticut, Kentucky, Michigan, New York, and Pennsylvania failed, and the laws were upheld. A challenge against the no-fault property damage law in Michigan was successful in a lower court and was appealed.   Emanuel Levy

INTERIOR DESIGN. A mood of nostalgic memories of times gone by and reflections of Early American life styles highlighted interior design in the United States in 1975. Manufacturers made all-out efforts to feature Early American designs as the country approached the 1976 American Revolution Bicentennial celebration. A category known as country casual appeared in seating selections for living rooms, dens, and family rooms. Wall coverings and paints used colonial and Americana themes with names relating to such historic places as Valley Forge, Jamestown, and Bunker Hill.

Contemporary Styles. Despite a strong movement toward colonial styles, contemporary stylings were most prominent in the new furniture selections shown at the home furnishings markets. *Home Furnishings Daily,* the trade newspaper, reported that contemporary and modern designs were the most popular. They were followed by Early American and colonial styles. Traditional styles, including Italian, French, and 18th-century Georgian, were in third place. The once-popular Mediterranean style trailed in last place.

A major trend in contemporary seating was the flexible arrangement known as the "pit group." These modular seating units, ideal for use in limited spaces, were an updated version of the sectional sofas that were so fashionable during the 1930s. The units included sofas, love seats, and chairs, with one arm or none. The user could put them together to form U-shaped, L-shaped, square, or other seating arrangements. They were completely upholstered and deeply padded.

Leisure-Living Furniture of wrought iron, reed, rattan, aluminum, wicker, or metal and glass was extremely popular with young homemakers. This furniture was often available in knockdown versions to be assembled by the buyer. It was easy to move and store, simple to care for, and less costly than upholstered furniture. Buyers could use it in family rooms, dens, and dining rooms, as well as outdoors, in porches, patios, and gardens. As the acceptance and sales potential of leisure furniture soared, manufacturers began turning away from canvas and vinyl materials and showed leisure furnishings in smart tweeds and print coverings of nylon, olefin, and blends of cotton and rayon.

The natural look was popular in colors, textures, and designs. Fabrics and wall and floor coverings were shown in colors such as terra cotta, sand, and rock. Also popular was the traditional red, white, and blue combination, especially in Early American offerings. Nylon, olefin, and synthetic fiber fabrics appeared often because of their durability.

The Consumer Product Safety Commission challenged the fabric and upholstery industry to work harder to make their products less susceptible to fire and to label fiber content clearly. California enacted a law listing inflammability standards to reduce injuries from fires in upholstered furniture.

New, soft floor coverings and rugs followed the mood of the year's furniture. Earth-tone carpets with nubby textures and tweed surfaces were most popular. Sculptured shags and plushes were also good sellers. The Berber wool area rug appeared in contemporary, Early American, and country-casual interiors.

Industry Awards. Ada Louise Huxtable, architecture critic for *The New York Times,* received the National Home Fashions League Trailblazer Award for her writing on design, architecture, and environment. Elmer Klein, vice-president of Futorian Manufacturing Company of Chicago, was named Polymer Man of the Year by the Furniture Division of the Society of Plastics Industry for his leadership in promoting the use of plastics in furniture and building public confidence in the plastics furniture industries.

The year opened on a dark economic note for the industry. There were 193 bankruptcies in the first quarter of 1975, compared to 130 for the same period in 1974. Financial analysts attending the Southern Furniture Market at High Point, N.C., in April agreed that an upturn would come gradually as consumer spending increased during the year. By October, the industry appeared to be on the threshold of recovery from its worst sales slump since World War II.   Helen C. Schubert

INTERNATIONAL TRADE AND FINANCE

World trade declined sharply in 1975 for the first time in 25 years because of the global economic recession. Trade volume in the first half of the year, after adjusting for higher prices, was down 10 per cent. This contrasted with average annual growth of 8.5 per cent in the 1960s, 11 per cent in 1973, and 6 per cent in 1974. In effect, nations with sluggish economies – and that included all the major industrial countries – imported less from each other and also from the less-developed countries.

Fortunately, the trade decline was not caused by protectionist measures against imports in order to preserve jobs at home. Such measures could have led to widespread retaliation. All the major countries, except Great Britain, continued to abide by the trade pledge they negotiated in the Organization for Economic Cooperation and Development that committed them to avoid import restraints such as higher tariffs. Britain enacted selective import quotas in December. This was in marked contrast to the experience during the Great Depression of the 1930s, when widespread trade restraints only made the depression worse.

The Oil Deficit. The year's most striking feature was a major change in world trade patterns. In 1974, nearly all oil-importing countries had deficits in the "current account" part of their balance of payments, which covers trade and other payments except capital investment. In 1975, the rest of the world continued to run a large deficit – estimated at $40 to $45 billion – with the oil-producing countries, but the industrial countries as a group were back in balance and probably showed a small surplus. This meant that the entire oil deficit shifted to those less-developed countries that produce no oil.

The less-developed countries encountered increasing difficulty in borrowing enough money to cover their deficits. Some had to cut back their imports and economic development programs. For the second year, the International Monetary Fund (IMF) operated a special "oil facility," a fund that made loans to many countries based on the extra cost of their oil imports. This helped, but it covered only about one-tenth of the total gap.

Apart from this problem, the massive flow of funds to the oil-producing countries was handled remarkably well. At no time was there danger of a financial crisis. The oil producers spent part of

International Monetary Fund representatives decide to continue a special fund to help members cope with the high cost of oil imports.

their money on a rapidly rising volume of imports. Another part was given in a slowly rising volume of aid to the less-developed countries. However, it was unevenly distributed, with much of it going to Arab and other Moslem countries. The rest was loaned or invested in the industrial countries.

Coping with the Problem. Early in 1975, the industrial countries agreed to set up a $25-billion financial support fund, or "safety net," to help those who could not cope with the balance-of-pay-

ments problem caused by the higher cost of imported oil. Although the plan had been proposed by the United States, congressional ratification moved slowly. At the end of the year, it still was not clear whether the fund would be approved. Without the United States, the plan could not go into effect.

Luckily, there was no need for it in 1975, though a few countries, such as Great Britain and Italy, continued to have balance-of-payments difficulties. Most of the major countries, however, showed a surplus. The United States was on the way to a record trade surplus. Both agricultural and industrial exports held up well, and imports dropped sharply because of the recession.

Exchange Rates. The world continued to operate successfully on a system of floating currency exchange rates. Rates were determined mainly by supply and demand in daily trading in foreign exchange markets, though central banks intervened from time to time to check large shifts up or down. The currencies of eight European countries floated together in what is known as the "snake." This kept exchange rates stable for trade among themselves, while the entire snake moved up or down against the dollar. Early in the year, the dollar declined substantially, but in June it began a strong rise against the European snake and, to a lesser extent, against the Japanese yen.

France and the United States were the main an-

Orders

ARAB ARMS PURCHASE LIST

ARAB ANTI-JEWISH BLACKLIST

U.S.

©1975 HERBLOCK

tagonists on the issue of fixed versus floating exchange rates. In mid-November, they reached a compromise during an economic "summit" meeting of the six leading industrial nations in France. The dollar will continue to float, but central national banks will probably intervene more often in daily trading to moderate its swings. In effect, the United States accepted the French desire for more stability in exchange rates, while France accepted the U.S. view that floating rates had been an essential element in cushioning the world against monetary shocks and heading off periodic crises. The rest of the world seemed likely to accept the compromise, which would be a key element in modernizing the international monetary system.

The Role of Gold. The negotiators agreed in August on future rules for gold, with the aim of gradually phasing out its use in the monetary system. Critics feared, however, that the agreement would not accomplish that purpose. If the IMF gold agreement is eventually ratified by world governments, there will no longer be an official price for gold and it will become more like an ordinary commodity, though it will remain in official monetary reserves for years to come.

As part of the plan, the IMF will sell one-sixth, or 25 million troy ounces (775 million grams), of its gold holdings. The proceeds will go to help the world's poorer countries. The threat of such a sale

was an important factor in driving down the gold price, which fell from a high of nearly $200 per troy ounce (31 grams) at the beginning of the year to below $130 in early September, then recovered somewhat.

Americans, on Dec. 31, 1974, were permitted to own gold for the first time in 41 years, but no gold rush developed.

Trade Negotiations. The U.S. Congress at the end of 1974 passed sweeping new trade legislation that authorized further reductions in U.S. tariffs and other trade barriers. As a result, negotiations began in Geneva, Switzerland, in February for a new round of mutual trade concessions, aimed at further expanding world trade. The negotiations had a more ambitious scope than those in the past. They dealt with such difficult problems as nontariff trade barriers, limits on the use of export controls (known as assuring access to supply), and new ground rules for export subsidies. The negotiations moved slowly and were not expected to be completed before 1977. But their very existence – with the objective of expanding trade rather than restricting it – probably helped nations with record postwar unemployment to resist the temptation to erect new import barriers.   Edwin L. Dale, Jr.

See also ECONOMICS; Section One, FOCUS ON THE ECONOMY.

IOWA. See STATE GOVERNMENT.

IRAN. Shah Mohammad Reza Pahlavi declared Iran a one-party state on March 2, 1975, and urged all Iranians to join the new party, the Iran Resurgence Party. He appointed Prime Minister Amir Abbas Hoveyda secretary-general of the party. The shah also proclaimed increased public and worker ownership of state and private industries.

Designation of Iran as a single-party state did not completely silence opposition to the shah. Terrorists from a group called the Iranian Peoples Warriors assassinated two U.S. Air Force officers in Teheran on May 21, allegedly to avenge the April execution of nine revolutionaries for plotting against the shah.

Foreign Affairs. The year saw considerable success for Iranian foreign policy. The shah's military aid to Sultan Sayyid Qaboos of Oman in the sultan's war against rebels in Dhofar province was a major factor in controlling the rebellion. Iran reached a March agreement with Iraq that settled long-standing border disputes and solidified Iran's dominant position in the Persian Gulf and northern Indian Ocean. The agreement also added to Iran's financial burden because of the influx of 250,000 Kurdish refugees from Iraq; the Kurdish rebel movement collapsed after the agreement. As part of his effort to build a regional security structure in the Persian Gulf, the shah purchased six missile-equipped destroyers from the United States in February for $660 million. Iran also made plans to buy three U.S. diesel-powered submarines.

The Economy. In September, the shah estimated income from oil and natural gas at $21.9 billion for the year. With such enormous funds available, Iran could afford to buy heavily abroad. In addition to $2 billion in arms purchases, 35.9 per cent of all U.S. arms sales abroad, Iran signed a billion-dollar agreement with Canada on July 9 for nuclear power plants. Additional power plants costing $7-billion were ordered from the United States in March. Agreements to obtain uranium for the nuclear plants were signed with Australia and France. Iran also signed a $15-billion, five-year trade agreement with the United States to buy arms and development projects.

The main domestic problems were inflation and shortages of skilled labor and adequate port facilities for exports. In July, the shah began a campaign against the profiteering and price fixing that had driven prices up 25 per cent. Prison terms and heavy fines were imposed on thousands of businessmen for violations. Iran signed an agreement with the United States and West Germany on September 10 for 220 mobile vocational training centers to provide on-the-job training.   William Spencer

See also IRAQ; MIDDLE EAST (Facts in Brief Table); OMAN.

IRAQ. The border treaty with Iran, mediated by Algeria in March, 1975, ended a long-standing boundary dispute in the Shatt al Arab estuary, which links the Tigris and Euphrates rivers to the Persian Gulf. The new boundary follows the mid-point of the main navigable channel. The two countries also agreed to exercise joint control over their borders and to halt infiltration. See IRAN.

Kurds End Fight. This part of the agreement abruptly ended the Kurdish insurrection. The Kurds, who had held a mountain enclave along the border for a year despite massive Iraqi Army assaults, gave up the fight when Iranian equipment and supplies were cut off. Mustafa Barzani, leader of the Kurds' struggle for autonomy for 25 years, took refuge in Iran along with 250,000 compatriots.

With the Iraqi Army in full control of Kurdistan, the government issued an amnesty offer; returning Kurds were required to surrender their weapons but otherwise would be treated as erring brothers to encourage reintegration. About 50,000 Kurds returned from refuge in Iran. But others, following the leadership of former Barzani associate Jalal Talabani, swore to continue the struggle.

Relations with Russia deteriorated even as those with Iran improved. In August, the Iraqi government demanded the withdrawal of 6,700 Soviet military advisers. Iraq and Saudi Arabia signed a

Hundreds of Kurdish rebels turn in weapons and accept amnesty from the Iraqi government as their long struggle for independence ends.

border agreement dividing the neutral zone between the two countries on April 8. But Iraq's relations with Syria were soured by a dispute over the distribution of Euphrates River water, impounded by Syria's Tabqa Dam. Severe drought in southern Iraq made the problem worse. On June 3, Syria agreed to release 3.9 million cubic yards (3 million cubic meters) of water to Iraq. But relations remained strained between the two countries as the Iraqi and Syrian branches of the Baathist Party squabbled. In a protest to the Arab League, Iraq accused Syria of violating its airspace and ambushing armored patrol vehicles and civilian automobiles on the Iraqi side of the border. Syria, in turn, charged Iraq with arresting several hundred "progressives" and executing 50 of them.

As oil royalties continued to pour in, a budget of $13.5 billion was approved on May 23. Iraq's second five-year plan, introduced on July 17, earmarked $30 billion for development, most of it in agriculture and petrochemicals. New projects included a $12-million cement plant with a 220,000-short-ton (200,000-metric-ton) annual capacity at Al Fallujah and a 407-mile (655-kilometer) pipeline from the northwestern Al Hadithah oil field to the Persian Gulf port of Al Faw. The pipeline will provide an alternative to Syrian refineries for Iraqi oil. William Spencer

See also MIDDLE EAST (Facts in Brief Table).

IRELAND spent 1975 grappling unsuccessfully with its most serious economic crisis since the 1930s. By summer, inflation reached an annual rate of 25 per cent, and more than 100,000 persons – 12 per cent of the labor force – were unemployed. The outlook for 1976 seemed just as bleak. Prime Minister Liam Cosgrave's coalition of *Fine Gael* (Gaelic People) and Labour parties came under mounting attack from the opposition *Fianna Fáil* (Soldiers of Destiny), but Fine Gael won a surprise victory in an autumn by-election.

Economic Strain. The depth of the recession surprised everyone, most of all the government, which expected the economy to pick up after midyear. Finance Minister Ritchie Ryan's January budget was modestly expansionary, designed to keep the economy moving until world trade picked up. Ryan announced large increases in social-welfare benefits and income tax allowances, while granting $25 million in relief to industry.

In April, the unions signed a national agreement that linked pay increases to the cost of living. By June, however, it was clear that earlier optimistic forecasts would not come true.

Faced with drops in output, consumption, and investment, a foreign-trade gap, and wages rising faster than elsewhere in Europe, Ryan introduced another budget in June. Despite widespread demands for a wage freeze, the government struck a voluntary bargain with the unions. In return for a $45-million package of food, transportation, and fuel subsidies, the unions agreed to accept lower wage increases.

The budget pleased no one, and criticism grew on all sides as price increases and unemployment began to bite deeper. But government ministers stuck grimly to a policy of weathering the economic storm by massive external borrowing and an internal budget deficit of more than $500 million. The business community wanted public-spending cuts and a wage freeze, while the unions sought more expansion.

Northern Ireland. The economic depression deflected the Irish from their abiding concern with Ulster. Relations with Great Britain remained cool as political progress in the north halted. The fragile bipartisan policy between the coalition Irish government and Fine Gael ended in the fall when Fine Gael called for British withdrawal from the north.

Tiede Herrema, the Dutch managing director of Ferenka Steel Cord Factory, a Dutch company in Limerick, was kidnaped early in October by Irish Republican Army terrorists. After an 18-day siege of a council house in Monasterevan, near Dublin, Herrema was released on November 7 when his captors surrendered. Andrew F. Neil

See also EUROPE (Facts in Brief Table); GREAT BRITAIN; NORTHERN IRELAND.

ISRAEL agreed to a long-sought interim agreement with Egypt on Sept. 4, 1975, in Geneva, Switzerland, calling on both sides to pull back Sinai forces. But the agreement was a mixed blessing for Israel.

The presence of American technicians in the Sinai to monitor the cease-fire compensated in part for the Israeli commitment – which was more of a calculated risk than Egypt's – not to resort to force in future disputes. As a result of the agreement, a Greek freighter with a cargo of Romanian cement bound for Elat passed through the Suez Canal on October 23, the first ship carrying an Israeli cargo to do so in 23 years. But the return of the Ras Sudar and Abu Rudeis oil fields in the Sinai to Egypt represented a significant economic loss. The two oil fields, held since the 1967 war, had been supplying 55 per cent of Israel's petroleum needs. See EGYPT.

Prime Minister Yitzhak Rabin emerged almost unchallenged as Israel's top political leader. Although he was off to a shaky start in 1974, the near-unanimous support for the interim agreement in the Knesset (parliament) demonstrated solid parliamentary support for Rabin. Even the opposition Likud Party, led by militant Menachem Begin, supported the agreement. Only former Defense Minister Moshe Dayan held out.

A new political alignment, Moked, was formed in July by former left wing Zionists and advocates of a peace settlement with the Arabs. Its platform, adopted on July 20, called for negotiations with Egypt, Syria, Jordan, and the Palestine Liberation Organization for a settlement.

Israel's Borders with her Arab neighbors remained quiet except for the Lebanese. In January and February, Israel mounted a number of raids into southern Lebanon against Palestinian guerrillas allegedly operating from refugee camps and Lebanese villages. The escalation of civil war in Lebanon reduced the border tension drastically, though as late as December 2, Israeli planes attacked suspected guerrilla sites around Tripoli in northern Lebanon and along the Lebanese border, killing at least 70 persons. Twice – in May and December – Israel and Syria agreed to an extension of the United Nations (UN) peacekeeping role on the Golan Heights. See SYRIA.

Although not on the scale of previous years, there was intermittent terrorism within Israel. Frogmen landed on a Tel Aviv beach and invaded the seaside Savoy Hotel on March 5; 18 persons were killed, including seven guerrillas. A bomb exploded in Jerusalem on July 4, killing 14. Twenty Israelis were injured by a grenade on May 15, Israel's Independence Day, at a Dead Sea picnic.

At the UN, Israel suffered some setbacks, the most serious being a General Assembly resolution on November 10 that classified Zionism as a "form of racism." See UNITED NATIONS (UN).

Economic Affairs. The continued defense burden, along with sky-high inflation and the worldwide recession, put an almost intolerable strain on the economy. In addition to loss of the Sinai oil fields, world prices of potash, one of Israel's few money-earning exports, declined 40 per cent because of an oversupply of fertilizers. Tourism was down 17 per cent. A long-term favorable step was a preferential trade pact signed with the European Community (Common Market) on May 11. The agreement cuts tariffs on Common Market exports to Israel 60 per cent. But inflation and a shortfall in revenues indicated a $6-billion budget deficit.

Faced with near-ruin, the Rabin government devalued the Israeli pound four times. The last devaluation, on Jan. 2, 1976, made it 7.2 Israeli pounds to the U.S. dollar. To hold the economy in line, the government froze basic wages and public construction, eliminated 500 civil service jobs, cut 5,000 workers in defense industries, reduced cost-of-living allowances, and increased indirect taxes 5 to 10 per cent, making the Israelis the most heavily taxed people anywhere. Meanwhile, the government awaited either massive U.S. aid or the miracle of permanent peace. William Spencer

See also MIDDLE EAST (Facts in Brief Table).

More than 20,000 Israeli demonstrators march near Nabulus, on the west bank of Jordan, in March, demanding the right to settle there.

ITALY. President Giovanni Leone, who is rarely heard from in political affairs, warned Parliament on Oct. 15, 1975, that Italy was in serious trouble. In the first State of the Nation message in 12 years, he said Italy suffered from too many strikes and too much absenteeism, bureaucracy, corruption, and other ills. He proposed laws to regulate unions. Despite his critical tone, Leone said he hoped the message would be seen as an "act of faith in our future as a free and democratic nation."

Regional Elections. Italy's Communist Party emerged as the strongest single party in seven of the 15 regions in which elections were held on June 15. The gains were mainly in the cities, including Rome, Bologna, Genoa, Turin, Milan, Florence, and Naples. The ruling Christian Democrats' share of the 34.8 million votes dropped from 38 per cent in the 1972 regional elections to 35 per cent, while the Communists' share went up from 28 to 33 per cent.

The elections were the first since the voting age was lowered from 21 to 18. It was also the first time that the Roman Catholic Church did not urge support of the Christian Democrats, who fought the campaign largely on the law-and-order issue. On May 21, the government passed a strong law to curb crime and political violence. The Communists opposed the law, which strengthened the powers of police and of magistrates in pretrial proceedings. A rash of bombings, political kidnapings, and street fighting had prompted the legislation and continued through the month-long campaign.

Fanfani Goes. Christian Democrats blamed party secretary Amintore Fanfani for the Communist advance and pressured him to resign. On June 26, he stood firm when the Socialists, who won 12 per cent of the vote, refused to join any center-left coalition. But he resigned on July 22 after losing a vote of confidence in his party's national council by 103 to 69. Four days later, Benigno Zaccagnini, 63, took over as a compromise leader.

Economic Recovery. Italy's economy improved dramatically during the first six months of 1975. Inflation averaged 10 per cent, down from 25 per cent in 1974. In July, Italy posted its first monthly trade surplus in three years, with a seven-month trade deficit only about 25 per cent that of the same period in 1974. However, industrial production fell 12.2 per cent, and more than a million persons were unemployed. Wildcat strikes disrupted production and transportation throughout the year.

Prime Minister Aldo Moro's government on August 8 approved a recovery package designed to inject $5.25 billion into the faltering economy. Deputy Prime Minister Ugo la Malfa appealed for everyone's help "to avoid the threat of a collapse which hangs over our economy."   Kenneth Brown

See also EUROPE (Facts in Brief Table).

IVORY COAST. See AFRICA.

JACKSON, HENRY M. (1912-   ), United States senator from Washington since 1952, announced on Feb. 6, 1975, that he would seek the Democratic nomination for President in 1976. Jackson has been a leading conservationist throughout his legislative career. He criticized the 1974 nuclear arms limitation agreement with Russia, saying the U.S. should seek balanced disarmament instead. He also led a U.S. Senate move in 1974 that tied trade concessions to relaxed Russian emigration rules for Soviet Jews.

Jackson was born in Everett, Wash., on May 31, 1912, the youngest of four children. His parents had emigrated from Norway in the 1880s. He acquired his nickname "Scoop" while delivering papers for the Everett *Herald* as a teen-ager. He worked his way through college and received his LL.B. degree from the University of Washington Law School in 1935.

Jackson practiced law in Everett until 1938, when he was elected Snohomish County prosecuting attorney. In 1940, he was elected to the U.S. House of Representatives, where he served six terms.

Jackson married Helen Eugenia Hardin in 1961. They have a son and a daughter. Since 1952, Jackson has donated all his earnings from speaking and writing to scholarship funds.   Robert K. Johnson

JAMAICA. See WEST INDIES.

JAPAN. The first state visit to the United States by a reigning Japanese ruler occurred in 1975, when Emperor Hirohito toured the nation. The visit began on September 30 at Williamsburg, Va., and then the imperial party visited President Gerald R. Ford in Washington, D.C. While in Washington, the emperor expressed his regret over World War II, his gratitude for U.S. assistance in Japan's postwar reconstruction, and his hope for everlasting friendship.

The emperor, a noted marine biologist, visited the Woods Hole Oceanographic Institution in Massachusetts and the Scripps Institution of Oceanography in La Jolla, Calif. Empress Nagako, a gifted artist, visited several art museums. The principal cities on their itinerary were New York City, Chicago, Los Angeles, San Francisco, and Honolulu. Security measures were strict.

Other Visits. Prime Minister Takeo Miki visited President Ford in August. They agreed that the U.S. secretary of state and the Japanese foreign minister would meet twice a year to review bilateral and world matters of common concern, discussed the post-Vietnam situation in Asia, and agreed to work closely on a number of world economic problems. For the prime minister, it was a return to the United States, where he had studied in the 1930s.

Meanwhile, U.S. Secretary of Defense James R. Schlesinger visited Japan in August and urged the

Japanese to improve their military capacity. However, he emphasized that the United States was urging Japan to stress the defensive ability of its forces – which, he said, were not now sufficient to fulfill their defensive mission – not to assume a military role outside of Japan.

Queen Elizabeth II and the Duke of Edinburgh paid a ceremonial state visit to Japan in May. It was the first visit by a British monarch and repaid a visit to England by the emperor and empress in October, 1971.

Prime Minister Miki's first year in office was politically uneventful. One of his predecessors, Eisaku Sato, who served the longest continuous term as a Japanese prime minister, died in Tokyo on June 3 after a stroke.

Economic Recession posed the most difficult problem for Japan and its prime minister. During the first nine months of the year, the government announced four plans to stimulate the economy. The first three involved advancing spending from the second half of the fiscal year to the first. The fourth called for more than $6.7 billion of additional government spending, especially on public works. It was designed to achieve a 2.2 per cent rate of real growth in the gross national product during the current fiscal year. In 1974, the gross national product had dropped 1.8 per cent, the first "minus growth" since 1951. The nominal increase was 18.6 per cent, but inflation caused the minus.

Unemployment was 870,000, or 1.6 per cent of the work force, in September. Deputy Prime Minister Takeo Fukuda announced that inflation had been brought under control, with the most recent wholesale price index being only 1 per cent above that of 1974. The annual spring "labor offensive" resulted in a 13.1 per cent pay increase for workers in major enterprises, as compared with 32.9 per cent in 1974.

Japan's External Trade showed a striking gain for the fiscal year that ended on March 31. Exports increased 47 per cent to $57.3 billion and imports 40 per cent to $53.2 billion. However, the global price spiral accounted for the increases in large part. Japan's balance-of-payments deficit dropped to $3.4 billion as compared with $13.4 billion a year earlier. However, a 10 per cent September increase in crude oil prices was expected to cost Japan $2-billion a year.

On March 10, Japan's famed Shinkansen high-speed express-train line was extended from Okayama to Fukuoka in northern Kyushu island, 668 miles (1,075 kilometers) from Tokyo. The train can cover this distance in about seven hours. However, Japan National Railways, which operates the Shinkansen, appeared on the verge of bankruptcy with a cumulative deficit of more than $7 billion.

Relations with China, Russia. In February, Russia proposed a treaty of good neighborliness

Ryokichi Minobe, re-elected to third term as mayor of Tokyo, puts the final touches on the blank eye of a Dharma doll in celebration rite.

and cooperation with Japan. But Prime Minister Miki held that a treaty of peace should take precedence. However, a peace treaty has been stalled for years over the ownership of several small islands north of Japan.

A peace treaty with the People's Republic of China has been delayed by China's insistence on a clause opposing political domination in the Asia-Pacific area by any other country. Japan does not favor the demand, which is clearly directed against Russian influence in the area. Trade between Japan and China increased 63.4 per cent to $3.3 billion in 1974, making China Japan's eighth-largest trading partner.

Miscellany. On May 16, Junko Tabei, a 35-year-old, 98-pound (44-kilogram) housewife, became the first woman to reach the summit of Mount Everest. A member of a 15-woman Japanese climbing expedition, she was accompanied by Ang Tsering, a Sherpa guide.

The modestly scaled International Ocean Exposition opened on Okinawa on July 20. Political extremists tossed a fire bomb at Crown Prince Akihito and Crown Princess Michiko at the opening ceremony, but neither was injured. The exposition was scheduled to run for six months. One of its features was Aquapolis, the world's first experimental floating city.   John M. Maki

See also ASIA (Facts in Brief Table).

JEWS throughout the world were alarmed in 1975 by the demands of Arab and other nonaligned, or third world, countries that the United Nations (UN) oust or suspend Israel. But the UN's credentials committee accredited the Israeli delegation on September 29.

In November, the UN General Assembly passed a resolution defining Zionism as "a form of racism," which many Jewish leaders denounced as a new example of anti-Semitism in the world. On November 12, the government of Israel and the World Zionist Organization announced that they would meet in Jerusalem before the end of the year to consider means of countering the UN resolution.

In Syria, the 4,000-member Jewish community continued to live under severe government restrictions and suffered frequent harassment. According to the Committee of Concern and the Committee for the Rescue of Syrian Jews, the community experienced civil, religious, and political persecution at the hands of the government during the year.

Jewish activists in Russia continued to stage militant protests, demanding permission to emigrate to Israel. The Soviet government likewise continued its campaign against the militants, with trials and other repressive measures.

In the United States, Rabbi Arnold Sobel of Congregation Emanu-El (Reform) and Monsignor

Toronto Reform Rabbi W. Gunther Plaut examines the initial volume of his commentary on the *Torah,* the first officially authorized American commentary.

Joseph Regny of Saint Patrick's Cathedral exchanged pulpits in New York City for one Sunday service in January. It was the first time such an exchange had ever taken place. Congregation Emanu-El is the nation's largest synagogue, and St. Patrick's is the seat of the Roman Catholic Archdiocese of New York. On January 12, Pope Paul VI reaffirmed the Catholic Church's rejection of "every form of anti-Semitism."

Women. On April 20, the U.S. Rabbinical Assembly (Conservative) took one more step toward the ordination of women. Incoming president Mordecai Waxman predicted that women would be admitted to the Rabbinical Assembly in the future.

In June, Barbara Herman, an alto, became the first woman in the history of Reform Judaism to be designated officially as a *cantor* (solo singer in a synagogue). She received her investiture at the annual commencement exercises of the Hebrew Union College – Jewish Institute of Religion in Temple Emanu-El. Reform Judaism ordained the first woman rabbi, Sally J. Preisand, in 1972.

***Torah* Commentary.** The first volume of a new commentary on the *Torah,* the five books of Moses, was published on January 15 by the Union of American Hebrew Congregations, which represents Reform Judaism. The 585-page volume, a commentary on Genesis, reflects a liberal interpretation. It treats the first book of the *Torah* as sacred writing, but also interprets it as literature with a message for modern man. The book was written by Rabbi W. Gunther Plaut of Holy Blossom Temple in Toronto, Canada, a leading Reform theologian.

The Jewish Publication Society of America announced in June that it had formulated plans for a new English-language commentary on the Hebrew Scriptures. The society said the commentary will be the first to be prepared in more than 30 years.

World Population. The 1973 Jewish population – the most recent year for which figures are available – was 14,150,000, down from 14,370,000 in 1972. The *American Jewish Year Book,* which listed the figures in its 1975 edition, said the decrease reflected a lower estimate of 5,732,000 for the Jewish population in the United States. In the U.S. Jewish population, 40.5 per cent of the household heads identified themselves as Conservative, 30 per cent as Reform, 11.4 per cent as Orthodox, 12.4 per cent as unaffiliated, and 5.7 per cent as atheist or agnostic.

A number of prominent Jews died in 1975. Jacob Adler, the Yiddish humorist who contributed to the *Jewish Daily Forward,* under the pseudonym B. Kovner, died at 101 on January 1 in St. Petersburg, Fla. Mordecai Namir, 77, former secretary-general of the Israeli labor organization Histadrut, and former mayor of Tel Aviv-Yafo, Israel, died on February 22 in Tel Aviv.   Judah Graubart

See also ISRAEL; MIDDLE EAST.

JORDAN improved its relations with neighboring Syria and Iraq in 1975. This, along with continued financial support from Kuwait and Saudi Arabia, strengthened Jordan's position and compensated for the 1974 Arab snub of King Hussein I. In 1974, at an Arab summit conference in Rabat, Morocco, the Arab states chose the Palestine Liberation Organization (PLO), rather than Hussein, to represent all Palestinians.

On June 10, Syria's President Hafiz al-Asad became the first Syrian head of state to visit Jordan since 1957. In a surprise move, the two neighbors, who nearly went to war in 1970 over Hussein's crackdown on Palestinians, agreed to form a joint military high command. They agreed also on economic cooperation and a waiver of passports for citizens of each country traveling in the other.

Aid to Oman. Jordan sent a 650-man battalion to aid Sultan Sayyid Qaboos of Oman against rebels in the Oman province of Dhofar. The unit was withdrawn in September after suffering 5 per cent casualties. See OMAN.

On March 17, Hussein postponed elections for a new National Assembly indefinitely. The legislature was suspended in November, 1974. The king wanted to exclude from the legislature all deputies from the Israeli-occupied west bank of the Jordan River.

A number of protesting military officers were arrested and a student strike closed the University of Jordan on April 23. However, both groups were protesting Jordanian involvement in the Oman war, rather than demonstrating against the continued lack of constitutional liberties.

Economic Aid contributed to Jordan by the Arab oil producers as one of the "confrontation states" against Israel continued to pump money into the Jordanian economy. In February, Qatar gave $9 million and Kuwait sent $50 million. Saudi Arabia pledged $47 million.

On July 28, President Nicolae Ceausescu of Romania became the first Communist head of state to visit Jordan. Romania agreed to increase its annual Jordanian phosphate purchases from 110,000 short tons (100,000 metric tons) to 550,000 short tons (500,000 metric tons) by 1980, and Romanian technicians began building a 27-mile (43-kilometer) oil pipeline at Az Zarqa. Loans totaling $49.5 million from the World Bank, the United States, and Kuwait financed roadbuilding to relieve traffic congestion in Amman, the capital.

On October 8, the 72-mile (116-kilometer) rail line from Hittiya to Aqaba went into operation. It will provide an all-weather link from Jordan's southern phosphate mines to its only seaport.

On October 20, the United States loaned an additional $6.1 million to Jordan for the country to purchase 40,000 short tons (36,300 metric tons) of wheat.   William Spencer

See also MIDDLE EAST (Facts in Brief Table).

JUAN CARLOS I (1938-   ) was installed as king of Spain in a brief ceremony on Nov. 22, 1975, following the death of Francisco Franco, dictator of Spain, two days earlier. Juan Carlos had assumed temporary power on October 31 as Franco lay near death. He is Spain's first king in 44 years. He promised to stimulate "profound improvements," and many observers felt he would try to gradually lead Spain toward greater democracy. See SPAIN.

Juan Carlos Alfonso Victor Maria de Borbón y Borbón was born in Rome on Jan. 5, 1938. His parents were living there in exile with his grandfather, King Alfonso XIII, who abdicated the throne in 1931. At the age of 10, Juan Carlos went to Spain to be groomed as future king under Franco's personal supervision. Juan Carlos studied at the military academies of all three branches of the armed services.

He was officially designated as Franco's successor in 1969. After that, he appeared more frequently in public and made official visits abroad. When Franco fell ill in July, 1974, he delegated his powers to Juan Carlos. But the shift was only temporary, as a recovered Franco resumed power in September.

Juan Carlos married the Greek Princess Sophia in 1962. They have three children.   Kathryn Sederberg

JUNIOR ACHIEVEMENT (JA). See YOUTH ORGANIZATIONS.

KANSAS. See STATE GOVERNMENT.

KARAME, RASHID (1921-   ), became premier of Lebanon for the ninth time since 1955 on May 28, 1975. Karame is a Moslem of the Sunni sect as all premiers are by custom in Lebanon, which has a Moslem majority. See LEBANON.

Karame's return to government after a five-year absence came during a period of tension and extensive street fighting between the Christians and Moslems that later in the year developed into full-scale civil war.

Karame was born in 1921 in Tarabulus (Tripoli), the second-largest city in Lebanon, where his family has been politically prominent for many years. He received his law degree from Fuad al-Awal University in Cairo, Egypt, in 1947. He practiced law in Beirut, Lebanon, and traveled during the next three years. In 1950, his father died, and Karame became the political leader of Tarabulus. He was elected to parliament in 1951, and in 1955, at the age of 34, he became the youngest premier in Lebanese history.

In addition to the premiership, Karame has held several other Cabinet posts. He is known for his flexibility in the complicated politics of Lebanon. His five-year absence from government is generally attributed to the intense dislike that President Sleiman Frangie has for him.

Karame is a bachelor. His hobby is collecting birds.   Edward G. Nash

KENNEDY, EDWARD MOORE (TED)

KENNEDY, EDWARD MOORE (TED) (1932-), was the favorite presidential choice in 1975 of both Democratic politicians and voters for that party's nomination in 1976, according to many public opinion polls. But the Massachusetts senator repeatedly refused to run. He announced that if his name were entered in a state primary, he would withdraw, and that he would not accept a convention draft. Nevertheless, polls showed him to be the favorite among Democrats, and many party officials nourished hopes he would reconsider.

Kennedy's reluctance apparently stemmed from personal and family considerations. His wife, the former Virginia Joan Bennett, was recovering from emotional stress that required hospitalization in 1974. His 13-year-old son, Ted, Jr., lost his leg to cancer in 1973 and was still undergoing treatment. The 1969 Chappaquiddick Island incident still concerned many voters. And Kennedy undoubtedly bore in mind that two of his brothers – President John F. Kennedy and Senator Robert F. Kennedy – were assassinated while in office.

Kennedy was born in Boston in 1932. He graduated from Harvard University and received his law degree in 1959 from the University of Virginia. He was elected to the Senate in 1962. He and his wife have three children, Kara Ann, Edward Moore, and Patrick Joseph. Edward G. Nash

KENTUCKY. See STATE GOVERNMENT.

KENYA. The murder of Josiah M. Kariuki, one of Kenya's most popular politicians, in March, 1975, touched off a wave of political unrest. Kariuki, a member of the National Assembly and a former Cabinet minister, had developed a large following by championing Kenya's poor majority. Kariuki spoke openly of himself as a successor to aging President Jomo Kenyatta. Many Kenyans suspected that his murder was instigated by political enemies.

A parliamentary committee set up to investigate the murder reported on June 3 that senior police officials had covered up evidence and had either taken part in the crime or had been accomplices.

Kenyatta's administration tried to prevent the National Assembly from accepting the report, but it was adopted on June 11 by a majority vote. Although all Assembly members belonged to Kenya's only party, the Kenya African National Union (KANU), dissident party members in effect formed an opposition to the government. To regain its authority, the KANU leadership decreed on September 20 that any Assembly member who deviated from the party position would be expelled. On October 15, two members of parliament, both outspoken dissidents, were arrested.

Several terrorist incidents occurred during the year. The worst was a bombing in a Nairobi bus station on March 1 that killed 27. John D. Esseks

See also AFRICA (Facts in Brief Table).

KHALID IBN ABD AL-AZIZ AL-SAUD (1913-), became king of Saudi Arabia immediately after the March 25, 1975, assassination of his half brother, King Faisal. A decision on his succession had been made only weeks before by the house of Al-Saud, the ruling family of the oil-rich kingdom. The family, several thousand strong, picked the quiet Khalid as a compromise to avoid dissension. Khalid named a brother, Prince Fahd, crown prince and deputy prime minister.

A son of Ibn Saud, the founder of Saudi Arabia, Khalid was born in 1913. He received a traditional Moslem education from tutors and in religious schools. He became an assistant to Prince Faisal and was named deputy prime minister and crown prince in 1965, after Faisal became king.

Khalid has represented the Saudi government at many international conferences, but he has never been prominent in public affairs and has shown little taste for government. He retains a deep liking for the Bedouin desert life.

He has a passion for falconry and maintains one of the finest collections of falcons in the world. A heart ailment has curtailed his activities in recent years.

The new king is popular in Saudi Arabia. He is a devoted family man with seven daughters and five sons. Edward G. Nash

See also SAUDI ARABIA.

KHMER. The Khmer Republic (formerly Cambodia) fell under Communist control in 1975 with the military defeat of a regime supported by the United States. The regime was established in March, 1970, by a group led by Lon Nol, who overthrew the government of Prince Norodom Sihanouk.

While Sihanouk lived in exile in Peking, China, a Communist-led movement, the Khmer Rouge, fought the Lon Nol regime with North Vietnamese backing. By January, 1975, the movement had reduced government control to a few cities plus southwestern Khmer. As the Khmer Rouge tightened their siege around the capital, Phnom Penh, President Gerald R. Ford asked Congress for added military aid. But Congress never approved the President's request.

Lon Nol left the country on April 1, and Senate President Saukham Khoy became interim president, hoping to negotiate with the enemy. But the Khmer Rouge spurned talks. With Khmer Rouge forces pressing closer around Phnom Penh, U.S. Marines evacuated the U.S. Embassy's staff, journalists, and some Cambodians by helicopter on April 12. Later that day, an emergency "summit committee," headed by the army chief of staff, Lieutenant General Saksut Sakhan, and including Prime Minister Long Boret, was formed to try to continue the war. However, Phnom Penh was captured by the Khmer Rouge on April 16.

Foreign refugees ride trucks to the Khmer border and then walk to freedom in Thailand after fall of the Lon Nol government in April.

Leaders Executed. Long Boret, former acting Prime Minister Sisowath Sirik Matak, Lon Nol's brother Lon Non, and others were later reported to have been executed. Almost all of Phnom Penh's 2-million people were turned out of the city, apparently because the Khmer Rouge could not feed them there. Several other cities were also evacuated. Refugee reports said many died during the trip into the countryside. The U.S. Department of State reported that "orders were issued by the Khmer Rouge to their outlying commanders to kill top political and military leaders."

Mayaguez Incident. Khmer gunboats captured the U.S. ship *Mayaguez* and its 39-man crew on May 12. United States Marines landed on Tang Island on May 14 to try to rescue the ship and its crew, while American planes bombed the mainland. Khmer authorities in Phnom Penh released the 39 men, and they left with the Marines. During the rescue attempt, 15 marines were killed, 3 were reported missing, and 50 were wounded.

First Deputy Prime Minister Khieu Samphan appeared to head the new Khmer regime. Sihanouk returned home on September 9, but he remained only 19 days, then went abroad. Forty-two of his associates decided not to stay in Phnom Penh. They accused the Khmer Rouge of failing to respect the political program agreed on.　　Henry S. Bradsher

See also ASIA (Facts in Brief Table).

KIWANIS INTERNATIONAL. Delegates to the 60th annual convention in Atlanta, Ga., in June, 1975, confirmed Ted R. Osborn of Lexington, Ky., as president. The Kiwanis International Board of Trustees was restructured to include a representative of the European federation, an administrative unit. The board moved to establish a life-member designation that would be available to a limited number of members for a $150 fee.

The annual Kiwanis Decency Award for decency in communication went to the producer and cast of the popular television series "The Waltons."

In other 1975 actions, the board established an International Goodwill Week for fall, 1976, that will extend the principles exemplified by the Canada-United States Goodwill Week worldwide. It also approved Kiwanis sponsorship of local Builders' Clubs — junior high school youth-service organizations. The clubs will have only a local structure and membership in them will be open to both sexes.

The 5,800 United States Kiwanis Clubs received official Bicentennial kits that outline the part Kiwanians can play in observing the American Revolution Bicentennial in 1976. The kit explains the Kiwanis program that has as its theme the "Volunteer and the Nation." Official celebration by Kiwanis International began Oct. 1, 1975, and runs through September, 1976.　　Joseph P. Anderson

KLEPPE, THOMAS S. (1919-   ), was sworn in as the new U.S. secretary of the interior on Oct. 17, 1975. He replaced Stanley K. Hathaway, who served as interior secretary from June 13 to July 25. Hathaway resigned after being hospitalized for "moderate depression" brought on by overwork.

When President Gerald R. Ford nominated him for the Cabinet post, Kleppe was serving as head of the Small Business Administration (SBA). Critics had attacked the SBA while it was under Kleppe's direction for alleged political favoritism and poor management. However, Kleppe was not accused of any wrongdoing, and the Senate confirmed his nomination on October 9.

Thomas Savig Kleppe was born on July 1, 1919, in Kintyre, N. Dak. After attending Valley City State Teachers College for a year, he worked first as a bank bookkeeper, then as an assistant cashier. During World War II, he was in the Army.

In 1946, Kleppe became a bookkeeper for a glass-wax marketing firm, the Gold Seal Company, rising to president in 1958. From 1964 to 1966, he was vice-president of an investment banking firm in Minneapolis, Minn.

Meanwhile, Kleppe became involved in politics. He was mayor of Bismarck, N. Dak., from 1950 to 1954 and a Republican congressman from 1967 to 1970. In 1971, he became head of the SBA. Kleppe and his wife have four children.   Darlene R. Stille

KOREA, NORTH. President Kim Il-song traveled widely in 1975. He went to the People's Republic of China in April, a visit believed related to the collapse of regimes backed by the United States in South Vietnam, Laos, and Khmer. Kim possibly saw that as a sign of U.S. weakness and sought Chinese support for military pressure on South Korea, which has U.S. protection. But if he did ask such backing, China voiced support only for peaceful reunification of Korea. There were reports that Kim sought but failed to receive an invitation to Moscow because Russia was also reluctant to get involved in a Korean war.

A South Korean proposal on July 4 to resume talks on peaceful reunification was rejected by North Korea.

Kim's younger brother, who had long been in ill health, faded from the political scene, and his son, Kim Chong-il, 36, began to gain prominence. This suggested to many observers that Kim intends to have his son succeed him.

North Korea's drive for rapid industrialization ran into some trouble. The worldwide decline in metals prices severely cut export earnings after the regime had contracted to buy large amounts of foreign industrial equipment. North Korea thus became the first Communist country to fail to meet payment on its Western debts.   Henry S. Bradsher

See also ASIA (Facts in Brief Table).

KOREA, SOUTH. Internal tension over the powers of President Chung Hee Park's government and external tensions over the possibilities of war beset South Korea in 1975. Domestic opponents conducted a running battle with Park, but he used his authoritative powers to deny them the support of an independent press and restrict their protests. On December 19, Park carried out a major Cabinet reshuffle, replacing long-time Prime Minister Kim Jong Pil and nine other top officials. Park named Choi Kyn Ha prime minister.

A referendum held on February 12 reportedly gave Park's regime a 73 per cent vote of approval for the constitutional changes he made in 1972 to strengthen his powers. The regime began to release political prisoners on February 15. On February 28, 13 of them charged that they had been tortured while in prison.

Criticism Banned. The government majority in the National Assembly on March 19 passed a bill prohibiting Koreans from criticizing their government to foreigners. The opposition New Democratic Party found itself locked out of the session that voted on the bill. The opposition leader, Kim Young-sam, defied the law, but officials did not move against him. On May 13, Park issued a decree prohibiting all criticism of the government or spreading rumors harmful to national security.

Argument between U.S. Army major and North Korean newsman erupts into a fist fight on June 30 at meeting of the Armistice Commission at Panmunjom.

University students, Christian religious groups, and intellectuals challenged the tight official control most actively. Demonstrations were banned on university campuses on April 8, and troops occupied the Korea University campus in Seoul to ensure order. The next day eight men were hanged for plotting to overthrow the government.

War Fears. The fall of American-backed regimes in South Vietnam, Khmer, and Laos caused grave concern in South Korea, which has depended upon U.S. defense guarantees since the Korean War truce in 1953. Park feared the Communist victories would make North Korea more aggressive. An estimated 1 million persons, including opposition leaders, attended a May 10 rally to show public support for Park's call for increased vigilance.

The United States offered on June 27 to abolish the United Nations (UN) Command that had fought the war if North Korea and China would agree to substitute permanent agreement for the truce. The two countries rejected this, but demanded the withdrawal of U.S. troops. United States Secretary of Defense James R. Schlesinger visited South Korea in August to reaffirm American intentions to protect the country with American soldiers, who are stationed there separate from the UN Command. The UN Security Council refused South Korea's membership request.   Henry S. Bradsher

See also ASIA (Facts in Brief Table).

KUWAIT voters elected 25 new National Assembly deputies on Jan. 27, 1975, when 65 per cent of the electorate turned out to vote. Prime Minister Jabir al-Ahmad al-Sabah formed a new 17-member Cabinet on February 9. The election was another step toward more representative government.

The government announced in August that military equipment worth $250 million had been delivered to Kuwait from Russia, including MIG-23 jets, tanks, torpedo boats, and surface-to-air missiles. The move brought sharp criticism from Iran and Saudi Arabia. Kuwait also purchased $366-million in arms from the United States.

A census taken on May 12 showed the population had increased 36 per cent since 1971 to 1,180,000. But national wealth increased even more. The budget approved on July 14 anticipated revenues of $5.6 billion, up 81 per cent over 1974, and a surplus of $2.7 billion. The national income came to $11,000 per capita, highest in the world. In August, the Kuwaiti civil service was streamlined, with stricter educational requirements.

The government took complete control of the Kuwait Oil Company from the British Petroleum Company and Gulf Oil Corporation in December. Kuwait made a variety of loans during the year; the largest was $415 million to the Arab states opposing Israel.   William Spencer

See also MIDDLE EAST (Facts in Brief Table).

LABOR. American workers began to see the light at the end of the tunnel in 1975, despite severe rates of unemployment and inflation. In November, 7.7-million Americans were unemployed, an increase of 1.7 million over November, 1974. The unemployment rate lessened considerably, however, after reaching a 34-year high of 9.2 per cent in May. It stood at 8.3 per cent as of December.

Total employment began to rise, but unemployment remained high because the economy, while growing, was barely keeping pace with an expanding labor force. About 85.3 million Americans were employed as of November.

The Cost of Living. The Bureau of Labor Statistics (BLS) Consumer Price Index rose 9.1 per cent from Dec. 31, 1974, to Dec. 31, 1975. The rise, while steep, was a definite improvement over the 12.2 per cent price index rise in 1974.

Workers' purchasing power dropped again in 1975, but the reduction was less severe than in 1974. Real spendable weekly earnings declined 2.9 per cent in the one-year period ending in September. The 9.1 per cent rise in the price index and a drop of 1.4 per cent in average hours worked per week more than offset a 6.2 per cent rise in average hourly earnings.

Rising labor costs, a major factor in the recent inflation, tend to be offset by gains in productivity. Productivity, measured as worker output per hour in the private economy, increased at an annual rate of 9.5 per cent as of the third quarter of 1975.

Preliminary BLS estimates given in the following table show major employment changes in 1975:

	1974	1975*
	(in thousands)	
Total labor force	**93,240**	**94,657**
Armed forces	2,229	2,188
Civilian labor force	91,011	92,469
Unemployment	5,076	7,890
Unemployment rate	5.6%	8.5%
Change in real weekly earnings (Workers with 3 dependents— private nonfarm sector)	−5.2%	−2.9%†
Change in output per man-hour (Private nonfarm sector)	−3.7%	1.9%‡

*January to September average, seasonally adjusted, except for armed forces data.
†For 12-month period ending Sept. 30, 1975.
‡Third quarter of 1975, compared to third quarter of 1974.

Collective Bargaining. Major settlements reached in the first nine months of 1975 provided average increases of 10.3 per cent for the first year of the contracts and 7.8 per cent over the life of the agreements. This compares to 9.0 per cent for the first year and 7.3 per cent for the life of contracts negotiated in 1974. Only 2.5 million workers were covered by major contracts scheduled to expire or be reopened in 1975, down sharply from 1974.

Rail Contracts. The United Transportation Union and six other unions reached settlements between January and March affecting 275,000 rail-

A wave of layoffs left 8 million Americans idle, and the lines of those seeking benefits to cushion the financial blow grew longer.

road workers. The three-year contracts with the nation's railroads provided 10 per cent wage hikes retroactive to January 1, with additional 5 per cent increases as of October 1; 3 per cent as of April 1, 1976; and 4 per cent as of July 1, 1977. The pacts also re-established cost-of-living clauses and instituted a 10th holiday and a dental insurance plan.

In July, the Brotherhood of Railway, Airline, and Steamship Clerks reached a settlement for an additional 117,000 railroad workers. In addition to the provisions of the earlier rail pact, the clerks' settlement provided for another cost-of-living adjustment on Jan. 1, 1978.

On September 2, President Gerald R. Ford invoked the Railway Labor Act to postpone a strike by four shopcraft unions, representing 70,000 workers, for 60 days. A tentative agreement reached on December 4 averted a walkout. The three-year pact, retroactive to January 1, was similar to the earlier rail settlements, but it also limited the railroads' ability to subcontract, a major issue.

Postal Employees, represented by four unions, won a three-year settlement with the United States Postal Service on July 21. The pact provided a $400 annual pay raise effective immediately, with additional $250 increases in March, 1976, and November, 1976, plus $600 in July, 1977. The contract also provided for semiannual cost-of-living adjustments, and the Postal Service agreed to assume 75 per cent of the cost of employees' health insurance, instead of 65 per cent.

Farmworkers. The Agricultural Labor Relations Act was signed into law by California Governor Edmund G. Brown, Jr., on June 5. It was designed to ease the jurisdictional turmoil between the Teamsters and the United Farm Workers of America (UFW) unions over the state's 250,000 farmworkers. The law, which became effective on August 28, provided for secret-ballot representation elections within seven days after at least 50 per cent of a farm's employees file a petition endorsing a particular union. A second union can compete if at least 20 per cent of the workers petition for it. The ballot also contains a no-union choice.

Other Settlements covered 70,000 workers in the Western lumber industry, 95,000 Amalgamated Clothing Workers of America members who produce cotton garments and outerwear, 70,000 members of the Retail Clerks International Association employed by southern California food- and drugstore chains, and 25,000 seamen.

Longshoremen on the Pacific Coast won a three-year contract in July with the Pacific Maritime As-

A month-long strike by 2,300 United Mine Workers of America (UMW) members in eastern Pennsylvania's hard-coal fields ended on April 29, after miners ratified a three-year settlement. The contract included an hourly wage increase of $2.10 over the three-year term. Union officials claimed the pact was the best ever negotiated in the hard-coal industry.

From August 11 to September 10, a wildcat miners' strike over a local grievance in Logan County, West Virginia, spread throughout the state and then to nearby states. It eventually affected 80,000 soft-coal miners. The miners were dissatisfied over such issues as giving up their right to local strikes and delays in the implementation of a grievance procedure. The UMW was fined $700,000 by a federal judge because of the illegal walkouts.

Union Affairs. George Meany, 81, was re-elected to his 11th term as president of the American Federation of Labor and Congress of Industrial Organizations (AFL-CIO) at the organization's annual convention in October in San Francisco. UFW leader Cesar Chavez addressed the delegates, and Meany castigated the International Brotherhood of Teamsters for its tactics in organizing farmworkers in California. He accused the Teamsters of marching "shoulder-to-shoulder with the organized financial-agricultural structure of this state." The Teamsters' executive board canceled its mutual aid and no-raiding pacts with 22 AFL-CIO unions.

Former Teamsters chief James R. Hoffa disappeared near Detroit on July 30, and his family feared that he had been murdered. The Federal Bureau of Investigation entered the case on August 3. A grand jury was also convened to look into his disappearance. See CRIME.

On September 11, former UMW President W. A. (Tony) Boyle was sentenced to three consecutive life terms by a judge in Pennsylvania for ordering the 1969 murders of union rival Joseph A. Yablonski and his wife and daughter.

On May 28, Louis Stulberg, 74, announced his retirement as president of the International Ladies' Garment Workers' Union, effective September 1. The union's executive board elected Sol C. Chaikin to succeed him.

Jobless Issues. In January, President Ford signed a trade reform act providing benefits for workers who lose their jobs because of competition from imported products. The workers were entitled to up to 70 per cent of their pay for one year. The act also provides job-search money, 80 per cent of moving expenses up to $500, and up to three years' job training.

The United Automobile Workers (UAW) union petitioned for benefits for 41,000 laid-off Chrysler Corporation workers, claiming that the firm's automobile imports from Canada "contributed importantly" to the layoffs. On August 1, the Department

sociation. The pact, affecting 12,000 workers, raised wages $2.15 an hour over the three years.

Public Employee strikes affected many cities and states. Tight government budgets clashed with efforts by workers to keep pace with inflation. In September, teachers in more than 100 school districts went on strike, postponing the opening of schools. Other strikes included one by San Francisco's police and firemen in August and one by Pennsylvania's state employees in July. See CITY; EDUCATION.

Some 3.5 million federal classified and military personnel received a 5 per cent pay raise on October 1. Earlier, President Ford had rejected an advisory committee's call for an 8.6 per cent hike.

Strike Activity declined in 1975 after a sharp rise in 1974. The BLS reported 31.3 million days of idleness in the first nine months of 1975, as opposed to 38.6 million in the same 1974 period.

There were doctors' strikes in New York City, San Francisco, and Chicago during the year. In New York City, interns and residents struck the 21-member League of Voluntary Hospitals from March 17 to 20 over excessive working hours. See CHICAGO; HOSPITAL; INSURANCE (Close-Up); SAN FRANCISCO-OAKLAND.

On December 6, some 16,700 United Airlines machinists went on strike, grounding all flights. A settlement approved on December 21 provided a $2.36 an hour pay increase over three years.

LABOR

A Decade of U.S. Inflation

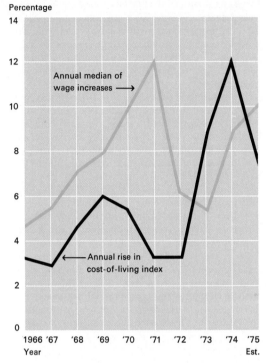

Percentage

Annual median of
wage increases →

← Annual rise in
cost-of-living index

1966 '67 '68 '69 '70 '71 '72 '73 '74 '75
Year   Est.

LAOS. The Communists completed their take-over of Laos in 1975. The 600-year-old monarchy was formally dissolved on December 3, and the People's Democratic Republic of Laos came into being. King Savang Vatthana was replaced by a president, Prince Souphanouvong, who for many years headed the pro-Communist Popular Front of Laos. Prince Souvanna Phouma, who had tried for 10 years to reconcile the rightists and the Communist-led Pathet Lao, was pushed aside. Strong man of the new regime was Kayson Phomvihan, head of the Marxist-Leninist Laos People's Party.

Game Plan. The formal take-over provided a climax to a game plan that began in March with a push against the royal army troops. The only effective resistance was offered by the Meo guerrillas of General Vang Pao, who were armed and financed by the U.S. Central Intelligence Agency (CIA).

Communist-led groups in the capital city, Vientiane, began antigovernment demonstrations late in April. With this background, Pathet Lao deputy ministers seized control of the government and the army, sending the rightist ministers fleeing to Thailand. Throughout the country, Communist-led revolutionary committees displaced members of the old administration.

Political Seminars. By August, some 3,000 senior officers had been ordered to Xam Nua, the

of Labor certified some 18,000 Chrysler Corporation workers as eligible for an estimated $45 million in benefits. By November 1, another 20,000 workers in other industries had been certified as eligible.

Union members held two rallies in Washington, D.C., during the year, calling on the Administration to adopt policies that would create more jobs.

On May 8, General Motors Corporation (GM) and the UAW jointly announced that their Supplemental Unemployment Benefits (SUB) fund for laid-off workers had been depleted. The benefit cutoff affected 55,000 GM workers. Chrysler's SUB fund was depleted on April 1, affecting 33,000 employees. At the peak of the layoffs in early 1975, 250,000 UAW members employed by Detroit automakers were out of work.

Grain Shipments. In mid-August, AFL-CIO maritime unions refused to load grain on ships bound for Russia, claiming the sale of grain to Russia would raise U.S. food prices. The unions also demanded that most of the grain be delivered by U.S. ships. The shipments resumed in September, after President Ford prohibited further sales until mid-October and worked out new guidelines for negotiating such sales. See AGRICULTURE.

John T. Dunlop became secretary of labor in March. See DUNLOP, JOHN T.   Leon Bornstein

See also ECONOMICS; Section One, FOCUS ON THE ECONOMY.

Public ceremonies in which village officials
confess their wrongdoings became common
when Communist Pathet Lao took control in Laos.

Pathet Lao capital, for "re-education." Souvanna Phouma's staff was also required to attend political seminars. On September 4, the properly briefed Supreme Court found 31 top officials guilty of "brutal, barbarous crimes," and General Vang Pao and five others were sentenced to death. The defense and finance ministers of the old regime were sentenced to life in prison. However, most of the sentenced officials had already fled the country. Newspapers were placed under strict control and banks were nationalized.

A new national flag was adopted in September. It has two narrow red stripes above and below a large blue stripe, with a large white circle at the center. It replaced the old flag that had a three-headed elephant on a red background.

"Down with U.S." The United States found itself under fire in June. A student blockade forced the U.S. Information Service offices to close. The number of American personnel in Laos, which included many CIA agents, was cut from 1,200 in 1973 to 28 by October, 1975. But the U.S. Embassy remained open.

With rice and gasoline in short supply, the new regime asked that the United States continue some of its economic aid. Meanwhile, Russia assumed many aid functions, including planning a new capital in the Plain of Jars.   Mark Gayn

See also ASIA (Facts in Brief Table).

LATIN AMERICA. Spiraling inflation, growing trade deficits, and political unrest created turbulent undercurrents in Latin America in 1975. Simultaneously, they helped to stimulate an ever-widening surge toward self-reliance and economic stability.

Instability in some governments was apparent during the year. The regime of Peru's President Juan Velasco Alvarado was ousted in a bloodless coup d'état on August 29, while President Guillermo A. Rodriguez Lara of Ecuador barely survived a violent right wing attempt to overthrow him on September 1. No less threatened was Argentina's President María Estela (Isabel) Martínez de Perón. The threats she faced were not as violent, but they were persistent. Nevertheless, she managed to survive the year in office. The Honduran Armed Forces Superior Council dismissed General Oswaldo López Arellano as president on April 22. See ARGENTINA; ECUADOR; PERU.

Paraguay remained under the rule of President Alfredo Stroessner's Colorado Party, which maintained a paper-thin façade of democracy at best. No such illusions existed in Bolivia, where the military regime of President Hugo Banzer Suarez unhesitatingly announced there would be no return to civilian government before 1980. Brazil also remained in the firm grip of a military regime, and the prospect of return to full democracy in the immediate future was unlikely.

The governments of Chile, Colombia, Cuba, Guyana, Haiti, Mexico, Uruguay, and Venezuela remained stable. In several other instances—notably in Grenada and Surinam, which achieved full independence in 1975, and Antigua and St. Vincent, which have been promised nationhood in the near future—forebodings of inner conflicts proved largely unjustified.

In the Central American republics, notably Nicaragua and Guatemala, dissident workers and students frequently disagreed with their government's policies and demonstrated against dire economic conditions. However, there were no serious threats of overthrow.

Central America. Costa Rica's government was under internal and external pressures to expel U.S. financier Robert L. Vesco, who had fled the United States to escape prosecution for allegedly "looting" mutual funds managed by the International Controls Corporation's Investors Overseas Services, Limited. In addition, many Costa Ricans were dissatisfied because retired U.S. citizens living in Costa Rica were granted special privileges, such as tax breaks.

Subversive activities flourished in the Dominican Republic, notably in March and April, when hundreds of university students clashed with police. A wave of arrests followed reports in June that a guerrilla landing had been made near San José de Oca, west of Santo Domingo, the capital.

Student demonstrators were also active in El Salvador. About 3,000 university students clashed with police in the streets of San Salvador in July. The spark that set off the rioting was the staging of a Miss Universe contest in San Salvador, for which the government had paid $1 million in promotional fees. Student leaders maintained the money would have been better spent on education. Two urban guerrilla movements also contributed to the unrest in El Salvador — the left wing People's Revolutionary Army and a right wing terrorist group that took upon itself the task of countering leftist underground movements.

Guatemala was embroiled with Great Britain over the status of Belize (formerly British Honduras), a British colony over which Guatemala has claimed sovereignty for more than 100 years. Great Britain said it supported Belizean aspirations for independence, despite Guatemala's demand for sovereignty over the colony. Belize insisted on exercising its own prerogatives in 1975 and disavowed any ties with Guatemala. On November 30, Britain and Guatemala agreed to resume negotiations, which had been broken off under threats of open hostilities. Wide-ranging talks on the colony's status were to begin in February, 1976.

Regional Groups. As part of a trend toward self-help, several regional groups were active during the year. The Inter-American Development

Bank (IADB) held its 16th annual assembly in Santo Domingo, Dominican Republic, from May 19 to May 21. In its annual report, the IADB told the 1,000 delegates and guests from nearly 40 European, Asian, African, and North and South American nations that it had provided $1.11 billion in social- and economic-development loans to its members in 1974. In order to sustain projected levels of development through 1976, the organization said it needed an additional $4 billion in capital. The United States announced on May 20 that it would contribute $1.8 billion to the IADB to promote economic programs. A previous commitment from 10 European nations, as well as Israel and Japan, guaranteed an additional $745 million.

The United Nations Economic Commission for Latin America (ECLA) adopted a plan for regional economic development at a meeting held in Port-of-Spain, Trinidad, from May 6 to May 14. Of the 18 nations attending, 17 Latin American and Caribbean nations voted for the plan; the United States voted against it. Proposals adopted included the establishment of multinational enterprises in Latin America and the creation of a regional authority to encourage interactivity in investment, production, and trade among countries and groups of countries. The plan also proposed that new organizations be formed for raw-material exporters. Their prime function would be to protect the prices of Latin American exports in international markets.

Facts in Brief on Latin American Political Units

Country	Population	Government	Monetary Unit*	Foreign Trade (million U.S. $) Exports	Imports
Argentina	25,391,000	President María Estela Martínez de Perón	peso (52.8=$1)	4,005	3,570
Bahamas	217,000	Governor General Sir Milo B. Butler; Prime Minister Lynden O. Pindling	dollar (1=$1)	1,444	1,906
Barbados	241,000	Governor General Sir Arleigh Winston Scott; Prime Minister Errol W. Barrow	dollar (2=$1)	84	203
Belize	144,000	Governor General Richard Neil Posnett; Premier George Price	dollar (1.7=$1)	22	39
Bolivia	5,756,000	President Hugo Banzer Suarez	peso (20=$1)	280	196
Brazil	110,829,000	President Ernesto Geisel	cruzeiro (8.6=$1)	7,968	14,039
Chile	9,639,000	President Augusto Pinochet Ugarte	peso (7.8=$1)	2,481	1,911
Colombia	25,511,000	President Alfonso Lopez Michelsen	peso (29.4=$1)	1,353	1,337
Costa Rica	2,089,000	President Daniel Oduber Quirós	colón (8.6=$1)	433	716
Cuba	9,470,000	President Osvaldo Dorticos Torrado; Prime Minister Fidel Castro	peso (1=$1.22)	887	1,427
Dominican Republic	4,825,000	President Joaquín Balaguer	peso (1=$1)	637	774
Ecuador	7,439,000	President Guillermo A. Rodriguez Lara	sucre (23.8=$1)	1,062	948
El Salvador	4,315,000	President Arturo Armando Molina Barraza	colón (2.5=$1)	463	562
Grenada	98,000	Governor General Sir Leo V. DeGale; Prime Minister Eric M. Gairy	dollar (2.2=$1)	5	21
Guatemala	6,288,000	President Kjell Eugenio Laugerud Garcia	quetzal (1=$1)	586	700
Guyana	826,000	President Raymond Arthur Chung; Prime Minister Forbes Burnham	dollar (2.5=$1)	178	186
Haiti	5,513,000	President Jean-Claude Duvalier	gourde (5=$1)	52	74
Honduras	3,036,000	Chief of State Juan Alberto Melgar Castro	lempira (2=$1)	258	382
Jamaica	2,033,000	Governor General Florizel A. Glasspole; Prime Minister Michael Norman Manley	dollar (1=$1.10)	649	936
Mexico	60,176,000	President Luis Echeverría Alvarez	peso (12.5=$1)	3,540	6,504
Nicaragua	2,450,000	President Anastasio Somoza Debayle	cordoba (7.1=$1)	381	562
Panama	1,715,000	President Demetrio B. Lakas; Chief of the Government Omar Torrijos Herrera	balboa (1=$1)	205	800
Paraguay	2,950,000	President Alfredo Stroessner	guarani (126=$1)	170	174
Peru	16,334,000	President Francisco Morales Bermudez Cerruti; Prime Minister Oscar Vargas Prieto	sol (41.4=$1)	1,511	1,531
Puerto Rico	2,958,000	Governor Rafael Hernández Colón	dollar (U.S.)	3,093	3,580
Surinam	473,000	President Johan H.E. Ferrier; Prime Minister Henck A.E. Arron	guilder (1.8=$1)	179	157
Trinidad & Tobago	1,103,000	Governor General Sir Ellis Emmanuel Innocent Clarke; Prime Minister Eric E. Williams	dollar (2.3=$1)	2,038	1,848
Uruguay	3,100,000	President Juan M. Bordaberry Arocena	peso (2.7=$1)	382	487
Venezuela	12,539,000	President Carlos Andres Pérez	bolívar (4.3=$1)	10,769	4,200

*Exchange rates as of Dec. 1, 1975

Delegates from 78 nonaligned nations discuss economic and political problems at a five-day conference held in Lima, Peru, in August.

The proposal also urged the creation of a regional authority to regulate the activities of foreign multinational corporations.

In addition, the provisos would place more emphasis on existing regional integration programs, especially the Latin American Free Trade Association and the Central American Common Market; they also call for the creation of a fund to aid Latin American countries with serious balance-of-payments deficits. Over the objections of the United States, Great Britain, France, and Canada, the ECLA delegates voted to exclude all developed countries outside the region from participating in work groups set up to study various aspects of regional economic development and integration.

The formation of a Latin American Economic System (SELA) was proposed jointly by President Luis Echeverría Alvarez of Mexico and President Carlos Andres Pérez of Venezuela in Mexico City on March 20. The two leaders urged that the heads of state of 24 Latin American and Caribbean nations appoint representatives to organize meetings that would plan formation of the agency. They proposed SELA "to encourage Latin American nations to rely on their own, permanent systems of consultation and economic cooperation . . . which should be capable of truly and effectively responding to their common needs and aspirations." The proposal also emphasized that SELA would not duplicate or replace existing regional organizations, notably the Organization of American States (OAS).

In the weeks preceding the proposal by Echeverría and Andres Pérez, Venezuelan and Mexican representatives had traveled throughout the region seeking support for SELA. Cuba, Ecuador, Peru, and several other nations publicly endorsed the plan; Brazil, though sympathetic, said it would not join an organization whose objectives would lead to a confrontation with the United States.

However, representatives of 25 regional governments, including Brazil, signed the SELA charter on October 17, at the conclusion of a three-day SELA meeting in Panama City, Panama. The organization's new headquarters will be in Caracas, Venezuela. Its first secretary-general is Jaime Moncayo, a former finance minister of Ecuador. The United States was excluded from participation.

Threat to Free Press. About 400 editors and publishers from Latin American and Caribbean countries, the United States, and Canada attended the 31st general assembly of the Inter-American Press Association (IAPA) from October 22 to 24 in São Paulo, Brazil. Delegates approved a report prepared by the IAPA's Freedom of the Press Committee which found that press freedom in the Western Hemisphere was under severe threat.

The report charged that press freedom did not exist in 10 countries (Brazil, Chile, Cuba, Guyana,

Haiti, Nicaragua, Panama, Paraguay, Peru, and Uruguay) and that problems existed between the news media and the government in seven others (Antigua, Argentina, the Bahamas, Grenada, St. Kitts, St. Vincent, and Trinidad and Tobago).

Communist party leaders representing 24 Latin American and Caribbean countries met in Havana, Cuba, in June. In a statement issued on June 16, the group sharply denounced the United States as Latin America's "principal and common enemy." It also attacked the People's Republic of China for supporting unidentified "groups of pseudorevolutionaries who . . . divide the left, attack the Communist parties, block the progressive process, and often behave as agents of the enemy at the core of the revolutionary movement."

The OAS held its General Assembly from May 8 to May 19 in Washington, D.C. Throughout the sessions, U.S. Secretary of State Henry A. Kissinger urged foreign ministers of the member nations to work toward closer ties between Latin America and the United States. Most of the participants, however, were adamantly opposed to a new U.S. trade law that denies preferential benefits to members of the Organization of Petroleum Exporting Countries (OPEC). Venezuela and Ecuador, OPEC's two Latin American members, led the protests, characterizing the law as "offensive." In a January meeting of the OAS's permanent council, 20 of the members denounced the trade act as "discriminatory and coercive."

Among its actions, the OAS approved a Mexican proposal to review the organization's diplomatic and commercial sanctions against Cuba. But the vote fell short of the two-thirds vote required; 14 members approved, 4 disapproved, and 5 abstained. The members agreed to postpone further action. That action came at a meeting of OAS foreign ministers in Costa Rica on July 29, when 15 Latin American countries and the United States voted to lift the sanctions. At the same meeting, Alejandro Orfila, former Argentine ambassador to the United States, succeeded Galo Plaza of Ecuador as secretary-general. Newly independent Grenada became the 24th active member of the OAS.

CIA in Latin America. The U.S. Central Intelligence Agency's (CIA) activities in Latin America came under the scrutiny of the U.S. Congress during the year. The Senate Select Committee on Intelligence reported on November 20 that, on the basis of its findings, the United States had actively supported and sought to instigate a coup against the government of the late President Salvador Allende Gossens of Chile in 1970. It also reported that the CIA instigated at least eight separate plots against Prime Minister Fidel Castro of Cuba between 1960 and 1965.   Paul C. Tullier

LAW. See Civil Rights; Courts and Laws; Crime; Supreme Court of the United States.

LAZAR, GYORGY (1924-   ), an economic planner, was appointed prime minister (president of the Council of Ministers) of Hungary on May 15, 1975. Lazar succeeded Jenö Fock, who resigned "for health reasons." He had previously served as deputy prime minister and chairman of the National Planning Office. Although Lazar is Hungary's official chief of state, real political power rests in the hands of Communist Party head Janos Kadar.

Lazar was born in 1924 at Isaszeg. He went to a trade school and went to work in 1948 as a technical draftsman. Within a year, he joined the newly created National Planning Office. He became chief department head in 1953 and vice-president of the office in 1958. Concerned with matters of economy, investment, finance, and labor, Lazar wrote many articles on questions pertaining to the national economy and local planning.

He was appointed minister of labor and co-president of the National Council of Youth Policy in February, 1970. In June, 1973, he became vice-president of the Council of Ministers and president of the new State Planning Committee.

Lazar joined the Hungarian Socialist Workers' (Communist) Party in 1945. In November, 1970, he was elected to the party's Central Committee, and in March, 1975, the 11th Party Congress elected him to the Politburo.   Robert K. Johnson

See also Hungary.

LEBANON. Wracked by bloody urban civil war, Lebanon sank near complete political and economic collapse in 1975. The capital, Beirut, lay in ruins. More than 6,000 persons had been killed and thousands wounded by late December.

The fighting began in January with the familiar tale of clashes between Palestinian guerrillas and Israeli forces in south Lebanon. The government's inability – or unwillingness – to control the Palestinians prompted public criticism by Pierre Gemayel, leader of the Christian Phalangist Party, whose well-armed 5,000-man militia and 20,000 irregulars were a potent military force. On April 13, fighting broke out between the Phalangists and various Palestinian factions.

A cease-fire on April 18, the first of many, quickly broke down. Fighting began to resemble a religious civil war between Lebanon's politically dominant Christians and the more numerous Moslems, who had long been restive under a Constitution politically weighted in favor of the Christians. Camille Chamoun's Maronite Christian National Liberal Party joined the Phalangists, and Prime Minister Rashid Solh, a Moslem, quit on May 15.

After a brief experiment with an all-military Cabinet, President Sleiman Frangie called on Rashid Karame to form a new government that included Chamoun as interior minister but excluded both Moslem and Christian extremists. But the

Masked Christian Phalangist militiamen, armed with a recoilless rifle, patrol a Beirut street during bitter fighting with Lebanese Moslems.

LÉGER, JULES (1913-   ), Canada's 21st governor general, carried out a full round of functions in 1975, after his convalescence from a stroke suffered in 1974.

With his wife, Gabrielle, he traveled widely in Canada, from Nova Scotia to Alberta and Saskatchewan. The pair spent a month at the Citadel in Quebec, Que., the traditional summer home of the governor general. They also visited Léger's birthplace, St.-Anicet, Que., southwest of Montreal, where a street had been named in honor of the governor general and his brother, Paul-Émile Cardinal Léger.

As head of state in Canada, Léger entertained British Prime Minister Harold Wilson; Prince Charles of Great Britain; President Suharto of Indonesia and his wife; President Kristjan Eldjarn of Iceland; and other official visitors. He also presided over investitures for the Order of Canada, the Order of Military Merit, and bravery decorations.

A new governor general's medal was designed by the Canadian painter Alexander Colville. It featured profiles of Léger and his wife, as well as representations of the crown, the maple leaf, and the owl, symbolizing learning. The medal has been awarded since 1874 for academic achievement in Canada. The reverse side is used as the governor general's personal seal.   David M. L. Farr

LESOTHO. See Africa (Facts in Brief Table).

LEVI, EDWARD HIRSCH (1911-   ), was sworn in as U.S. attorney general on Feb. 7, 1975. Almost all of his previous career had been spent at the University of Chicago.

Levi was born in Chicago and received his law degree from the University of Chicago in 1935. He was admitted to the bar in 1936, and became an assistant professor at the University of Chicago Law School the same year. From 1940 to 1945, he was on a leave of absence as a special assistant to the U.S. attorney general. He worked most of this period in the Department of Justice antitrust division. He returned to the University of Chicago in 1945 as a professor of law, and in 1950, he became dean of the law school. In 1962, he was named provost, and, on Nov. 14, 1968, he was appointed president of the university.

In 1950, he was chief counsel to the House Judiciary Committee's Subcommittee on Monopoly Power. He served on the White House Central Group on Domestic Affairs in 1964 and the White House Task Force on Education in 1966 and 1967. He was also a member of the President's Task Force on Priorities in Higher Education in 1969 and 1970.

Balding and bespectacled, Levi is noted as a legal scholar with no definite political label. He and his wife, the former Kate Sulzberger Hecht, have three sons.   Kathryn Sederberg

LIBERIA. See Africa (Facts in Brief Table).

new government was reluctant to use the army to control the fighting, because many of its officers are Christians and the ranks are divided between Christians and Moslems.

By October, all-out war had developed in Beirut, punctuated by brief cease-fires. On November 29, Frangie and Karame agreed to meet with other Lebanese leaders to negotiate changes in the Lebanese political structure to reduce the discord.

On December 8, Moslem gunmen in Beirut began an all-out drive to cut off the Christian forces holed up in the once-swank sea-front hotel district. Interior Minister Chamoun called out the armed forces for the first time, and tried to place army units between the battling guerrillas. But fighting continued into the new year.

The Economy. With street fighting, murders, and kidnapings almost daily fare, dozens of international banks and multinational industrial corporations hastily moved their headquarters from Beirut to more tranquil Middle East cities, such as Cairo, Egypt, and Amman, Jordan. The economic life of Beirut, once known as the "Zurich of the Middle East," came to a complete standstill. The cost to the Lebanese economy was estimated at nearly $2 billion; the cost to Lebanese society was incalculable.   William Spencer

See also Karame, Rashid; Middle East (Facts in Brief Table).

LIBRARY. Money was at the root of most library problems in the United States and Canada in 1975. New York City, teetering on the edge of bankruptcy, ordered libraries in the boroughs of Brooklyn, Manhattan, and Queens to cut $6.2 million from their budgets. Library officials said the cut would force branch closings, reduced hours, and staff layoffs. John Corey, director of libraries in Manhattan, the Bronx, and Staten Island, forecast a 20 per cent reduction in staff and a 50 per cent drop in services if the cuts were carried out. Deficits and cutbacks faced many other library systems, such as those in Chicago; Cleveland; Hartford, Conn.; and San Francisco. In Canada, the North York (Ont.) Public Library was forced to turn back to the city $1.8-million that had been set aside for a $9.4-million central library.

On the brighter financial side, Texas and Minnesota increased their allocations for libraries. The Texas budget was up a whopping 195 per cent to $8.36 million. Funding for service to the blind and handicapped was also up. Minnesota increased its aid by 25 per cent for each of the next two years.

Balanced Funding. A study of library funding alternatives prepared for the U.S. National Commission on Libraries and Information Science called for a new funding approach. It said that local governments have been assuming an unfair share – 81 per cent – of library costs, while the federal government and most state governments have not been supplying adequate funds. The study recommends a balanced system that would provide up to $2.1 billion in library revenues.

Stir Over Boorstin. President Gerald R. Ford's appointment of historian Daniel J. Boorstin as Librarian of Congress dismayed many librarians. Since the retirement of L. Quincy Mumford in 1974, John Lorenz, deputy Librarian of Congress, had served as acting librarian. Library groups had hoped that Ford would appoint a professional librarian experienced in library administration and problems. Boorstin, a noted writer and senior historian at the National Museum of History and Technology, was neither, they said. Boorstin supporters said that the Librarian of Congress should be, in the words of Senator Charles H. Percy (R., Ill.), "primarily a scholar." After committee hearings in July and August, Boorstin was approved by the Senate on September 26.

Library Meetings. "Information Power" was the theme of National Library Week, from April 13 through 19. The International Federation of Library Associations 41st General Council met in Oslo, Norway, in August to discuss "The Future of International Library Cooperation."   Robert J. Shaw

See also AMERICAN LIBRARY ASSOCIATION; CANADIAN LIBRARY ASSOCIATION.

The Library of Congress celebrated its 175th anniversary in 1975. The library's ornate main reading room, *above*, was completed in 1897.

LIBYA. Discontent in the ruling Revolutionary Command Council with the policies and leadership of President Muammar Muhammad al-Qadhaafi led to an attempted coup in August, 1975. The attempt was led by Major Omar Meheishi, minister of planning and scientific research, and Major Bashir Hawadi, secretary-general of the Libyan Arab Socialist Union (LASU), Libya's only legal political organization. Dissatisfaction stemmed from Qadhaafi's foreign policy. His financial support of Palestinian extremist groups, Moslem factions in Lebanon, and a variety of revolutionary organizations around the world had increasingly isolated Libya from other Arab states.

Egyptian authorities reportedly alerted Qadhaafi to the plot when they became convinced it would fail. Hawadi and some 30 officers were arrested, but Meheishi escaped to Tunisia.

The Egyptian tipoff improved the strained relations between the two North African neighbors. Egyptian newspapers had been banned in Libya in February for criticizing Qadhaafi. About 160 Egyptian advisers were deported on April 16 for protesting public criticism of Egyptian President Anwar al-Sadat.

After the Coup Attempt, the government issued a series of drastic edicts. Libyans were not allowed to leave the country for several weeks. Death was decreed for anyone convicted of supporting or belonging to any political organization other than LASU or for contacts with foreign agents. Qadhaafi also cracked down on profiteering. The housing and automobile-import industries were nationalized in September, and Libyans owning businesses worth more than $100,000 were required to sell 85 per cent of their stock on the open market.

The "Popular Revolution" continued. An April 7 law divided the country into municipalities, subdivided into quarters, with elected "popular committees" responsible for local administration.

On May 10, a Tripoli court reduced the death sentence passed in absentia on exiled King Idris to seven years in prison.

Libya agreed in January to finance a $739-million petrochemical complex in Turkey in return for medical and engineering help. The government also signed an agreement with Russia on June 2 for construction of a nuclear reactor.

On October 2, Libya halted all oil production by Occidental Petroleum Corporation in apparent retaliation for Occidental's $1-billion damage suit. The suit was filed with the World Court in The Hague, the Netherlands, in September, after Libya ordered Occidental to reduce its production by 325,000 barrels a day. The case was settled out of court in early December.   William Spencer

See also AFRICA (Facts in Brief Table).

LIECHTENSTEIN. See EUROPE.

LIONS INTERNATIONAL held its annual convention in Dallas, Texas, in June, 1975. An estimated 40,000 members attended. In his inaugural speech as president for 1975-1976, Harry J. Aslan of Kingsburg, Calif., proclaimed "Lionism Is Opportunity" as the theme during his presidency. He also encouraged all clubs to study their communities and begin at least one new service program during the year.

During the convention there was a memorial service to Helen Keller, who challenged delegates at the 1925 convention in Cedar Point, Ohio, to become "Knights of the Blind." Since then, the service organization's program for sight conservation and aid to the blind has originated and sponsored glaucoma screening clinics and eye banks, examination clinics, and research centers.

As of June 30, the Lions International Foundation had received contributions totaling $719,417. The foundation first began distributing funds in 1972, largely for humanitarian and disaster relief programs. A number of clubs and individual members assisted South Vietnamese refugees.

Lions membership was reported at 1,100,854 after the convention. These members belonged to some 28,707 clubs located in about 150 countries and territories. October 8 was World Lions Service Day, during which all members of each club focused on a single project.   Joseph P. Anderson

LITERATURE. Despite gloomy early forecasts, book-publishing profits and authors' royalties were eminently satisfactory in 1975. This was the consensus of the world's major publishers who were represented — some by their best-selling authors — at the international Frankfurt Book Fair held from October 9 to 14 in Frankfurt, West Germany. Individual European publishers predicted that overall sales would be up 20 per cent by year's end, an optimism shared by most publishers in the United States, Canada, and Great Britain. Even publishers from Panama and the People's Republic of China, both of whom participated in the fair for the first time, reported their best sales in years. See PUBLISHING.

Part of the increase was due to booming sales of the publishers' less expensive paperbacks. That was not the whole story, however. Higher book prices were an important factor.

Although spiraling U.S. publishing costs had forced hard-cover book prices up, the average increase was less than that of the overall cost of living. Actually, at various times, more than half the books on the bestseller list sold for $10 or more, indicating little consumer resistance to these higher prices.

Another reason for the industry's ability to weather the economic storm was prudence — sometimes an excessive prudence. Many American publishers cut back the number of their titles, and the first to suffer the ax were first novels, whose number dropped to half that of 1974. A final reason for the book industry's good fortune seemed to be that it is comparatively "recession proof," for books appear to be among the last items a consumer will cut back on.

As far as literary quality was concerned, the book harvest of 1975 was bountiful in two major areas — novels and biographies. It was more than adequate in two others — history and current affairs.

Fiction. Only in first novels and short stories — both genres that usually lose money — was there a drought in both quality and quantity. Of the few first novels of note, James McCourt's *Mawrdew Czgowchwz* (pronounced "Mardu Gorgeous"), a rich, comic novel about an operatic diva, was the most satisfying.

In short-story collections, the incomparable Russian-American Vladimir Nabokov dusted off 13 pieces written in his youth and published them as *Tyrants Destroyed*. They turned out to be as cultivated and elegant as his mature work.

A younger writer, Leonard Michaels, earned considerable praise for *I Would Have Saved Them If I Could*. A collection of stories about coming of age in the 1950s, they were written with considerable sensitivity and verve.

Well-established talents produced almost all the year's many noteworthy novels. Three of the best were unconventional, yet each won much praise. The first of these was Peter Matthiessen's *Far*

Booksellers and publishers' representatives discuss business during the 75th American Booksellers Association Convention in New York City.

Tortuga, a long, lyrical, and finely etched prose poem about turtle fishermen in the West Indies, told in the musical dialect of the area. Another was William Gaddis' *J R,* which explored the American lust for wealth in a long novel composed only of dialogue, in which characters are rarely if ever identified. The novel's passionate, hypnotizing drive overcame the complexities that made it a struggle for most readers.

Then there was E. L. Doctorow's *Ragtime,* the year's most-talked-about novel. Unconventional but easy to read, it was a wide-ranging yet tightly controlled satire of America in the early 1900s. Many historical figures appear in cameo roles in the novel, an engaging blend of comedy and social commentary—and a considerable best seller.

Also popular with readers was *Humboldt's Gift,* by Saul Bellow. The tale of a failed poet and a rising playwright, it was as packed with ideas as his previous works, yet had an openness and warmth that recalled the youthful vitality of Bellow's earliest novels.

Two younger novelists contributed splendid work in 1975. Both their books, coincidentally, were old-fashioned regional family chronicles. One was *The Surface of Earth,* by Reynolds Price, a Southerner; the other was *Beyond the Bedroom Wall,* by Larry Woiwode, a Midwesterner.

Other solid American novels of the year were *A Month of Sundays,* by John Updike; *Sneaky People,* by Thomas Berger; *The Great Victorian Collection,* by Brian Moore; *The Dead Father,* by Donald Barthelme; and *Cockpit,* by Jerzy Kosinski.

Foreign Novels. There was a heavy infusion of good novels from abroad, especially from Germany, which contributed three noteworthy works: Uwe Johnson's *Anniversaries,* 1972 Nobel prize-winner Heinrich Böll's *The Lost Honor of Katharina Blum,* and Lothar-Gunther Buchheim's *The Boat.*

Four excellent novels also arrived from English-speaking nations: Doris Lessing's *The Memoirs of a Survivor* and Margaret Drabble's *The Realms of Gold,* both from Britain; Nadine Gordimer's *The Conservationist,* from South Africa; and *The Cockatoo,* by Australian Patrick White, winner of the 1973 Nobel Prize for Literature.

Rounding out the imports were Yasunari Kawabata's *Beauty and Sadness,* from Japan; Mario Vargas Llosa's *Conversation in the Cathedral,* Peru; and V. S. Naipaul's *Guerrillas,* Trinidad.

Biography and Autobiography. Always a reliable field for quality in both scholarship and style, biography was handsomely served in 1975.

Six biographies of historical figures stood out. One of the most fascinating was Vincent Cronin's *Louis and Antoinette,* a mildly flawed but nevertheless sparkling apologia for the monarchs who were victims of the French Revolution. Another was

Frances Donaldson's *Edward VIII,* also a sympathetic treatment of its subject, the late Duke of Windsor.

The others were Amos Elon's *Herzl,* an absorbing study of Theodor Herzl, the founder of modern Zionism; Daniel Thomas' *Cardigan,* a fine examination of the leader of the Charge of the Light Brigade; Richard Hall's *Stanley,* a scholarly yet exciting life of African explorer Henry Morton Stanley; and Robert Skidelsky's *Oswald Mosley,* about the pre-World War II British Fascist leader.

Literary biographies were also well represented. The year's most sumptuous book of any kind was Samuel Schoenbaum's *William Shakespeare: A Documentary Life.* Other biographies of English men of letters were *Samuel Johnson,* by John Wain; *Shelley: The Pursuit,* by Richard Holmes; *Wilfred Owen,* by John Stallworthy; and *Kipling,* by Philip Mason.

Important American literary biographies were *Edith Wharton,* by R. W. B. Lewis; *Romantic Revolutionary,* a biography of radical journalist John Reed, by Robert Rosenstone; and *Thurber,* an overlong, overdetailed, yet hypnotizing life of the humorist by Burton Bernstein.

Three on a Tower: The Lives and Works of Ezra Pound, T. S. Eliot and William Carlos Williams, by Louis Simpson, was an adroit synthesis of the lives and works of three vastly different but equally important 20th century poets.

Among 1975's few good autobiographies were three stand-outs: *The Twenties,* Edmund Wilson's chronicle of his life and loves in predepression America's literary world; the late Hungarian prelate Joseph Cardinal Mindszenty's challenging *Memoirs;* and British art critic Kenneth Clark's *Another Part of the Wood: A Self-Portrait.*

History. Slavery in America continued to preoccupy many historians. Two major books in this category were *The Problem of Slavery in the Age of Revolution 1770-1823,* by David Brion Davis, and *The Rise and Fall of Black Slavery,* by C. Duncan Rice. Ira Berlin's *Slaves Without Masters* explored the history of the free Negro in the pre-Civil War South. And one of 1974's major books on slavery, Robert W. Fogel and Stanley L. Engerman's *Time on the Cross,* a computer-analyzed study of the statistics of slavery, came under heavy attack in 1975, especially from Herbert Gutman in *Slavery and the Numbers Game.*

Another subject of continuing interest was the archipelago of slave-labor camps in Russia. Several books explored various aspects of these camps, but none was as authoritative as 1970 Nobelist Alexander I. Solzhenitsyn's *The Gulag Archipelago,* the second volume of which appeared in 1975.

In other areas, Walter Laqueur contributed *Weimar: A Cultural History 1918-1933,* a thoroughgoing examination of German life in the years just before Adolf Hitler rose to power. Lucy S. Dawidowicz explored the other side of that coin in her definitive history of Hitler's genocidal policy, *The War Against the Jews 1933-1945.* Charles H. Mee, one of a growing number of unconventional "revisionist" historians, upset accepted theories in *Meeting at Potsdam,* which painted Franklin D. Roosevelt and Winston Churchill as bumbling villains whose misjudgments led to the Cold War.

From abroad came the year's most shining example of the historian's art — Volume II of Frenchman Fernand Braudel's *The Mediterranean and the Mediterranean World in the Age of Philip II.* To many, it was perhaps the finest historical work of our day.

Letters and Journals. Collections of the correspondence of literary figures dominated the year's offerings. In one, another stone was added to the monument of the great American novelist Henry James with Volume II of the projected four-volume *Letters of Henry James,* edited by his biographer Leon Edel.

The first books of two multivolume collections also appeared in 1975. One was Volume I of *The Letters of Sean O'Casey,* covering the correspondence of the Irish playwright from 1910 to 1941, edited by David Krause. Another was *The Letters of Virginia Woolf, Volume I: 1888-1912,* edited by Nigel Nicolson and Jeanne Trautman.

Agatha Christie, whose detective Hercule Poirot met his end in her 1975 best seller, *Curtain,* relaxes with her husband, Sir Max Mallowan.

The Letters of Bernard De Voto, the American novelist-historian-editor, were edited by his friend and fellow novelist Wallace Stegner. The result was splendid. So was Elaine Steinbeck's memorial to her husband John – *Steinbeck: A Life in Letters.*

Among collections of the letters of political figures was *Roosevelt and Churchill: Their Secret Wartime Correspondence,* edited by Francis Loewenheim, Harold D. Langley, and Manfred Jonas. It was an engrossing insight into war strategy.

Current Affairs. As expected, the "Watergate industry" continued to pour out volumes on the scandal that toppled President Richard M. Nixon. Among them were *Before the Fall,* former White House aide William Safire's personal story of the months before the 1972 presidential campaign; *How the Good Guys Finally Won,* Jimmy Breslin's immensely entertaining chronicle of the impeachment process in the House of Representatives; and Theodore H. White's best-selling but disappointing *Breach of Faith.* The best of these was the calm, reasoned, and very perceptive *Washington Journal: The Events of 1973-1974,* by Elizabeth Drew.

The controversy surrounding huge increases in oil-company earnings spawned *The Seven Sisters: The Great Oil Companies and the World They Made,* a classic example of corporate muckraking by Anthony Sampson. And the increasing power of multinational corporations – those with plants and offices in several countries – resulted in an equally outstanding book, *Global Reach,* by Richard Barnet and Ronald Müller.

The year's most talked-about book in the current affairs category was Susan Brownmiller's *Against Our Will,* a wide-ranging and sometimes shocking study of rape throughout history, which won enthusiastic initial notices.

Miscellaneous. *Sylvia Porter's Money Book,* which offered expert advice on a wide variety of financial matters, was one of the year's outstanding best sellers. Two important books in the field of language were Walker Percy's *The Message in the Bottle,* which studied the relationships between human consciousness and the structure of language, and Paul Fussell's *The Great War and Modern Memory,* which explored how the horrors of World War I forever changed ways of describing war.

Among the significant works of poetry to be published during the year were two posthumous volumes: *Thank You, Fog,* by W. H. Auden, who died in 1973; and *The Awful Rowing Toward God,* by Anne Sexton, who died a suicide in 1974. Another collection of superior poetry was *Poems: Selected and New,* by Adrienne Rich.   Henry Kisor

See also AWARDS AND PRIZES (Literature Awards); LITERATURE FOR CHILDREN; NOBEL PRIZES; POETRY; PULITZER PRIZES.

LITERATURE, CANADIAN. See CANADIAN LIBRARY ASSOCIATION; CANADIAN LITERATURE.

LITERATURE FOR CHILDREN. Because of rising printing costs, several publishers indicated in 1975 that the full-color illustrations so characteristic of children's books may become a rarity in the future. Feeling the pinch of inflation, publishers began turning to black-and-white illustrations or using less color.

A recurring topic in the year's books is the theme of death, which found its way into books for all ages from the very youngest up. The *didactic* (instructional) approach so obvious in books for young people in recent years seems to be less in vogue now. Many of the new books deal with fantasy from a variety of angles, perhaps an indication of the increasing popularity of fantasy with young adults.

Among the outstanding books of 1975 were:

Picture Books

I Am a Giant, by Ivan Sherman (Harcourt). "Little children eat broccoli. I eat apple trees" – so begins this imaginative description of what a giant does. Small children will enjoy the tall-tale humor. Ages 4 to 8.

Creepy Castle, by John S. Goodall (McElderry/Atheneum). A brave medieval mouse and his lady explore a deserted castle in this story without words; the charming illustrations are in full color. All ages.

Marie Louise's Heyday, by Natalie Savage Carlson, pictures by Jose Aruego and Ariane Dewey (Scribners). Delightful pictures of five little possums engaged in various activities form the chief attraction in this account of mongoose Marie Louise's busy baby-sitting session. Ages 4 to 8.

A Beastly Collection, by Jonathan Coudrille (Warne). A highly original set of drawings and their alliterative descriptions make this alphabet book fun not only for the young child listener, but also for the adult reader. All ages.

Pickles and Jake, by Janet Chenery, illustrated by Lilian Obligado (Viking). Sam thinks his dog is the best pet, and Emily likes her cat. But despite the competition they feel, they find that their best effort at the pet show comes from their unpremeditated cooperation. Ages 6 to 9.

Tim Mouse Goes Down the Stream, by Judy Brook (Lothrop). Tim Mouse and Mr. Brown the hedgehog boldly set out to rescue Willy Frog, who has been captured by rats. Attractive, detailed illustrations add much to the adventure. Ages 5 to 9.

Little Toot Through the Golden Gate, by Hardie Gramatky (Putnam). With his usual verve, Little Toot tackles a new experience; lively pictures show him exploring San Francisco Bay and becoming acquainted with the boats there. Ages 5 to 9.

Big Bear to the Rescue, by Richard Margolis, pictures by Robert Lopshire (Greenwillow Read-Alone). Big Bear sees Mole sleeping in the well and organizes a rescue. Entertaining pictures make this

Arrow Maker fitted the Boy to his bow and drew it. The Boy flew into the heavens. In this way, the Boy traveled to the sun.

Gerald McDermott makes bold and brilliant use of Pueblo Indian art motifs to illustrate the award-winning *Arrow to the Sun,* a Pueblo Indian tale.

fast paced and amusing enough to lure beginning readers.

The Story of Christmas, by Felix Hoffmann (McElderry/Atheneum). Told in simple language that stays close to the Biblical account, this appealing book has full-color pictures of simplicity and dignity. Ages 4 and up.

Things to Do

Op Art Coloring Book, by Jean Larcher (Dover). These intriguing designs may take on the appearance of movement as they are colored, making this book fun for the Op Art fan from age 12 through college years.

Sandwichery: Riddles, Recipes and Funny Facts about Food, by Patricia Stubis, pictures by Talivaldis Stubis (Parents' Magazine Press). This attractive collection of sandwich recipes, some quite unusual, has riddles and bits of food history tucked here and there, and offers its information in an attractive, unusual way. Ages 4 to 9.

The International Cookie Jar, by Anita Borghese, drawings by Yaroslava Mills (Scribners). Interesting and mouth-watering cookie recipes from 65 countries should make this book fascinating to the older, experienced cook as well as the young and aspiring one. Ages 10 and up.

Mobiles You Can Make, by Loretta Holz (Lothrop). This well-illustrated introduction to the making of various kinds of mobiles combines nu-merous craft techniques with interesting projects for individuals or groups. Ages 8 and up.

Plays from African Folktales, with ideas for acting, dance, costumes, and music, by Carol Korty (Scribners). These four simple plays should be interesting and enjoyable for elementary school students, requiring very little in the way of costumes or props. Ages 7 to 12.

How to Sharpen Your Study Skills, by Sigmund Kalina and illustrated by Richard Rosenblum (Lothrop). An experienced teacher-tutor gives concrete suggestions to young students on ways to organize their time, how to study for and take various kinds of tests, and how to gain confidence in their ability to cope. Ages 10 to 14.

Mary Poppins in the Kitchen; a Cookery Book with a Story, by P. L. Travers and Maurice Moore-Betty, illustrated by Mary Shepard (Harcourt). One of the charms of the book – aside from its Mary Poppins atmosphere – is the unusual nature of some of the daily menus and recipes. They should tempt adult as well as younger appetites, especially with Mary Poppins to recommend them. All ages.

Animals, Science, and Information

Pets in a Jar, Collecting and Caring for Wild Animals, by Seymour Simon, illustrated by Betty Fraser (Viking). Filled with excellent information about collecting and observing insects, snails, and other small creatures, this book should be inspiring

A month-long exposition, Children's Books
International, displayed children's literature
from many nations at the Boston Public Library.

and fascinating to the 8- to 12-year-old amateur
naturalist.

A Zoo in Your Room, by Roger Caras, illustrated
by Pamela Johnson (Harcourt). This is a sensible
book containing the information that one needs to
keep small mammals, birds, amphibians, and other
animals happy and healthy indoors. It also considers which animals make appropriate pets, and gives
their food and housing requirements. Ages 10 to 14.

Woodchuck, A Science I Can Read Book, by
Faith McNulty, pictures by Joan Sandin (Harper).
A female woodchuck is followed through a year's
activities, which include the birth and raising of her
family. For the beginning reader.

The Harlequin Moth, by Millicent Selsam, illustrated by Jerome Wexler (Morrow). Excellent photographs, some in color, follow the moth through its
life cycle, showing how a caterpillar sheds its skin,
and what goes on in a cocoon. Ages 7 to 10.

Sportsmath: How It Works, by Lee Arthur, Elizabeth James, and Judith Taylor (Lothrop). Using
real games in five major sports as examples, the
authors introduce the concepts necessary for keeping statistics for each sport. This should be one way
to appeal to the nonmathematical sports lover. Ages
11 and up.

The Code and Cipher Book, by Jane Sarnoff and
Reynold Ruffins (Scribners). This is an easy and
fun introduction to basic types of codes and ciphers,

presented with examples for decoding and encod-
ing. Illustrations and bits of history add to the interest. Ages 8 to 14.

How to Count Like a Martian, by Glory St. John
(Walck). This is a fascinating exploration of various
historical numbering systems, during which the
reader quite painlessly learns something about various numerical bases and a little about how a computer works. Ages 10 and up.

The Story of the Dictionary, by Robert Kraske
(Harcourt). Anyone who enjoys words should enjoy
this account of the origin of some famous diction-
aries, the changes words have undergone through
the years, and some of the peculiarities of the English language. Ages 10 and up.

Fiction

The Grey King, by Susan Cooper, illustrated by
Michael Heslop (McElderry/Atheneum). The
fourth volume in *The Dark Is Rising* series features
Will on his first mission by himself. It is told with
the same imagination and high excitement that distinguished the best of the earlier books. Ages 12 and
up.

Touchmark, by Mildred Lawrence, illustrated by
Deanne Hollinger (Harcourt). Orphan Nabby
longed to be an apprentice pewterer, but for a girl
in pre-Revolutionary Boston, this seemed an impos-
sibility. Her curiosity, determination, and lively
personality win her friends, a family, and eventually enable her to fulfill her desire. Full of action, the
book catches the atmosphere and excitement of a
tumultuous time. Ages 9 to 12.

The Great Ghost Rescue, by Eva Ibbotson, illustrated by Giulio Maestro (Walck). This book often
has the reader laughing aloud at this highly original and very humorous story of a family of ghosts
who are the inspiration for the establishment of a
ghost sanctuary for English ghosts displaced by
progress. Ages 9 to 12.

Below the Root, by Zilpha Keatley Snyder, illustrated by Alton Raible (Atheneum). The reader
follows the suspenseful adventures of Raamo from
the moment he learns with shocked wonder that he
is to be one of the Chosen until he unravels the
mystery of the terror that lives below the root of the
Green Sky world. Ages 12 and up.

The Towers of February, by Tonke Dragt, translated from the Dutch by Maryka Rudnik
(Morrow). Establishing a strong sense of mood almost immediately, this unusual science fantasy has
an air of mystery and suspense. Ages 12 and up.

The Spell of the Northern Lights, by Lucy Johnston Sypher, illustrated by Ray Abel (Atheneum).
This story of the author's childhood in Wales, N.
Dak., begins with her 11th birthday, when she discovers she might have had a "spell" put on her
when she was born. Ages 10 to 14.

The Watchers, by Jane Louise Curry (Mc-
Elderry/Atheneum). Ray, sent by his remar-

ried father back to his dead mother's clannish kin in the West Virginia hills, finds himself able to see people from another time who inhabit the area and wishes to defend his new home from the evil that threatens it – an unusual and fascinating fantasy. Ages 12 and up.

The Nunga Punga and the Booch, by Jean Kennedy, drawings by Anne Burgess (Scribners). The Nunga Punga, a tall, thin friend, and the Booch, a short, round friend, have to use their heads in this amusing story of their adventures in getting rid of a hungry tiger. Ages 8 to 10.

To Live a Lie, by Anne Alexander, illustrated by Velma Ilsley (Atheneum). Jennifer has decided not to make friends at her new school and to deny she has a mother, because the agony of her parents' divorce has made her feel angry and unwanted. How the events at the new school lead her to face her new circumstances makes a well-told and believable story. Ages 12 to 14.

The Haunting of Ellen, by Catherine Sefton (Harper). When an overflow of guests forces two young sisters to move into an old cottage, strange things begin to happen to Ellen, who finally solves the mystery of the uneasy ghost. Ages 10 to 14.

Romansgrove, by Mabel Esther Allan, illustrated by Gail Owens (Atheneum). A contemporary brother and sister make friends with a 14-year-old girl living in 1902 and, as the friendship progresses, realize that they are influencing events that took place before they were born. Ages 12 and up.

The Magic Meadow, by Alexander Key (Westminster). One of five children in a hospital ward for incurables finds his way to another world and comes back to get the others to join him in the new adventures. Ages 9 to 12.

Awards in 1975 included:
American Library Association Children's Service Division Awards: The *Newbery Medal* for "the most distinguished contribution to American literature for children" was awarded to *M. C. Higgins, the Great,* by Virginia Hamilton (Macmillan). This book also won the National Book Award for children's literature. The *Caldecott Medal* for "the most distinguished American picture book for children" went to *Arrow to the Sun,* by author-illustrator Gerald McDermott (Viking). The *Laura Ingalls Wilder Award,* presented every five years to an author "whose books, published in the United States, have over a period of years made a substantial and lasting contribution to literature for children," was given to Beverly Cleary.

British Book Awards: The *Carnegie Medal* went to Mollie Hunter for *The Stronghold.* The *Kate Greenaway Medal* was awarded to Pat Hutchins for illustrating *The Wind Blew.* Lynn de Grummond Delaune

LIVESTOCK. See AGRICULTURE.

LONG BEACH, CALIF. See LOS ANGELES-LONG BEACH.

LOS ANGELES-LONG BEACH. A California court of appeals on March 10, 1975, reversed a lower court decision requiring the Los Angeles public school system to desegregate. The contested integration decision, handed down in 1970, found the city board of education guilty of deliberate segregation and ordered large-scale busing of public school students to remedy the situation. However, the three-member appellate court panel ruled that the Los Angeles Board of Education had not "intentionally discriminated against minority students by practicing a deliberate policy of racial segregation." Therefore, the busing plan was held to be unnecessary.

Police and Crime. Under tentative guidelines published by the city in April, political beliefs, sexual habits, drinking habits, and ecological beliefs were eliminated as reasons for opening or maintaining police files on individuals or groups. As a result, more than 2 million data cards on 55,000 groups and individuals were destroyed.

Los Angeles police concluded their biggest manhunt since the 1969 Charles Manson "family" murder case on February 3, when they arrested Vaughn Greenwood on suspicion of murdering nine persons in December, 1974, and January, 1975. The murders were called the skid row slasher case because the victims, most of them derelicts, were killed with a knife.

There were also 26 gang-related slayings in the Los Angeles area during the first five months of the year. Assistant School Superintendent William L. Lucas testified before Congress on June 18 that there were 143 youth gangs in the city's schools and that 630 assaults against students and school staff members occurred during the first four months of the year.

Living Costs rose 9.6 per cent in the Los Angeles-Long Beach area between August, 1974, and August, 1975. Much of the increase could be traced to housing costs. Meanwhile, food prices increased 9.3 per cent and gasoline 3.3 per cent to a pump price of 56.7 cents per gallon (3.8 liters) for regular gasoline. The average annual earnings of factory workers in the area reached $10,272 by mid-1975, up 9.1 per cent.

According to figures reported in mid-1975 by the U.S. Census Bureau, the metropolitan area suffered a population decline of 1.2 per cent between 1970 and 1973. Los Angeles lost 2.3 per cent of its population, and Long Beach lost 3.4 per cent. The July 1, 1973, population was estimated at 2,746,854 for Los Angeles and 346,793 for Long Beach, including areas annexed since 1970.

In late November, brush fires raged out of control in the hills around Los Angeles, forcing hundreds of persons to flee their homes. James M. Banovetz

LOUISIANA. See NEW ORLEANS; STATE GOV'T.

LUMBER. See FOREST AND FOREST PRODUCTS.

LUXEMBOURG

LUXEMBOURG enjoyed one of the lowest inflation rates of any European Community (Common Market) country during 1975. Largely because of healthy exports, the rate was 10.8 per cent for the 12-month period that ended in September, 1975. But the worldwide steel market collapsed early in 1975, and output and prices fell about 35 per cent during this period. As a result, the gross national product (GNP) was down 3.5 per cent. Steel production accounts for about 25 per cent of Luxembourg's GNP and 40 per cent of the employment.

In June, the European Commission asked the steel industry to voluntarily curb production 17 per cent. Steel mills were closed during much of August and September, and the government began a $3-million-per-month program to employ idled steelworkers in public works projects. In September, the Organization for Economic Cooperation and Development forecast a continued decline in industrial production.

The economic news was not all bad, however. The government raised the guaranteed minimum wage an average of 14.9 per cent at the beginning of 1975. Steelworkers got 17 per cent; bank employees, 13 per cent; and civil servants, 9 per cent. Along with raising the minimum taxable income, the pay raise increased personal income and helped keep up consumer demand.   Kenneth Brown

See also EUROPE (Facts in Brief Table).

MACHEL, SAMORA MOISES (1933-   ), became the first president of Mozambique on June 25, 1975, the day the country officially won independence from Portugal. Machel was a leader of the Mozambique Liberation Front (FRELIMO), which fought a 10-year guerrilla war for independence. See MOZAMBIQUE.

Machel was born in the Limpopo Valley of southern Mozambique. He received only six years of schooling at a Roman Catholic mission school before going to work. He then attended evening classes and trained as a medical assistant at a hospital in Lourenço Marques. During this time, Machel became interested in ways of correcting the inequities practiced against black Africans by Portuguese colonists in Mozambique.

In the early 1960s, he met Eduardo Chivambo Mondlane, a founder and president of FRELIMO, who inspired him to go to Tanzania and then Algeria for military training. After Machel returned, he fought with FRELIMO forces throughout the guerrilla war that began in September, 1964.

He became FRELIMO's secretary of defense in 1967, and was elected to the party's central committee in 1968. Mondlane was assassinated in 1969, and Machel succeeded him as leader. Machel continued to visit the combat zones and areas held by FRELIMO forces, preparing for his take-over of the government.   Darlene R. Stille

MAGAZINE. The Audit Bureau of Circulations in Chicago reported a 1.2 per cent drop in total circulation for its 309 consumer- and farm-magazine members for the first six months of 1975 compared with the same period in 1974. Newsstand sales declined 4.9 per cent, while subscriptions rose slightly. *Money, People,* and *Smithsonian* posted large circulation gains.

The industry continued to worry about increasing postal costs. After 22 months of hearings before the U.S. Postal Rate Commission, the administrative law judge recommended on May 28 that magazine postage rates be more than doubled. On August 28, however, the commission rejected the judge's recommendation and approved only moderate increases. To offset increased costs of postage, paper, and printing, a number of publishers raised advertising rates and both newsstand and subscription prices. Several magazines also reduced their circulation, particularly subscriptions, in an effort to cut costs.

New Magazines made their debuts while a small number ceased publication. *Sprint,* a biweekly published by Scholastic Magazines, Incorporated, is aimed at fourth-, fifth-, and sixth-grade students reading at second-grade level. The National Geographic Society started a children's magazine in September. A monthly aimed at children ages 8

National Geographic World, a monthly magazine for children, made its debut in September. It features cutouts, posters, and puzzle mazes.

through 12, *National Geographic World* covers topics similar to those in *National Geographic,* but attempts to make learning fun through the use of mazes, cutouts, and posters.

Today's Viewpoint, another monthly launched in September, is edited by women for single women. It focuses on the practical needs of unmarried women. *Backpacking Journal,* edited for backpackers, hikers, and campers, was introduced in April by Davis Publications, Incorporated, on a semiannual basis.

The Girl Scouts of the United States of America started a new magazine, *Daisy,* in January. An educational magazine for girls of Brownie and Junior Girl Scout age — from 7 to 11 years old — *Daisy* will be published nine times a year.

Discovery was introduced by Black Sports, Incorporated, in 1975 as a quarterly and will be published monthly in 1976 during the school year. It offers black college students career and travel information; humor; audio, record, and book reviews; and such cultural coverage as fashion news.

Celebrity, published by the Magazine Management Company, Incorporated, premièred in June and concentrates on celebrities who are currently in the news. Challenge Publications' *In the Know,* which began publication in May, is similar in format. The Braille Sports Foundation in Minneapolis, Minn., began publication of *Feeling Sports* in February. This monthly is available in braille or on cassettes and is the only sports publication that is written and edited exclusively for those who are visually handicapped.

Among magazines that ceased publication were the 44-year-old *Science & Mechanics,* a Davis Publications, Incorporated, magazine; the monthly recreational-vehicle magazine *Wheels Afield,* a Petersen Publishing Company magazine; and *Lithopinion,* a showcase magazine for the New York Amalgamated Lithographers of America Local 1.

Changing ownership or merging were *1,001 Decorating Ideas,* sold to Family Health Magazine, Incorporated, by Consolidated Foods Corporation; *True,* sold by Petersen Publishing Company to Lopez Publications Incorporated; and *Camera 35,* sold to Popular Publications by American Express.

Awards. Winners of the National Magazine Awards in 1975 were *Consumer Reports* for public service, *Medical Economics* for specialized journalism, *National Lampoon* and *Country Journal* for visual excellence, *Redbook* for fiction, *The New Yorker* for reporting excellence, and *Esquire* for service to the individual. The awards are sponsored by the American Association of Magazine Editors and administered by the Columbia University Graduate School of Journalism.　　　Gloria Ricks Dixon

See also ADVERTISING.

MAINE. See STATE GOVERNMENT.

MALAGASY REPUBLIC. See AFRICA.

MALAWI. See AFRICA.

MALAYSIA. The "Voice of Malayan Revolution," a radio station in southern China, filled the airwaves of Malaysia in 1975 with reports of victories in the jungle and with appeals to the "toiling masses" to join in a "people's war." Prime Minister Abdul Razak bin Dato Hussein responded with reports of guerrilla losses, appeals to the guerrillas to surrender, and threats of harsh punishment.

Razak termed the insurrection "a serious and growing threat." Despite the fact that the old pro-Chinese faction of Chin Peng was being challenged by two rival factions, the rebellion grew and spread into the cities. Notable were the August bombing of a national monument marking the victory over the Communists and a September attack on the police field force headquarters in Kuala Lumpur.

The government reacted in early October with a set of emergency laws. The new laws required families to report the movements of their members and guests; suspects had to prove their innocence; and compulsory vigilante groups were created in towns and villages.

Ailing Economy. One reason for the growing guerrilla activity was mounting resentment among the Chinese Malaysians, who were finding their way into the civil service and many other occupations blocked by the national policy of preference for Malays. But another reason was the crisis pro-

Demanding release of comrades in Japanese jails, terrorist takes hostages to airport in Kuala Lumpur, Malaysia, for flight to Libya.

duced by dropping world prices for lumber, palm oil, rubber, and tin. The boom of the early 1970s had ended. There was privation in the countryside, where nearly 70 per cent of the peasants own less than the 6 acres (2 hectares) said to be necessary for a modest livelihood, and in the cities, where the unemployment rate exceeded 10 per cent.

To allay public discontent, the newly elected Paramount Ruler Yahya Petra ibni Al-Marhum Sultan Ibrahim ordered his own salary cut 5 per cent. Razak and the 13 state chief ministers did the same. The impact of their action may have been lessened by disclosure that Tun Dato Haji Mustapha, chief minister of the oil-rich state of Sabah, owned a great deal of property in England.

Neutrality. While fighting the Communists at home, Razak sought better relations with Communist nations, notably China. As he had in the past, he urged a neutralization of Southeast Asia, guaranteed by the major powers.

One of the lesser government preoccupations was with pollution in the Strait of Malacca, the busy corridor linking the Indian Ocean and the South China Sea. Collisions involving tankers were fouling the coastline, compelling Malaysia, Singapore, and Indonesia to seek controls.   Mark Gayn

See also ASIA (Facts in Brief Table).

MALDIVES. See ASIA.

MALI. See AFRICA.

MALLOUM, F. NGAKOUTOU BEY-NDI (1932-

), became head of the nine-member Supreme Military Council ruling Chad on April 15, 1975. Military forces overthrew the civilian government of President N'Garta Tombalbaye in a coup on April 13. See CHAD.

Brigadier General Malloum was arrested in 1973 on charges of plotting to overthrow the Tombalbaye government. Malloum denied the charges, but was still under house arrest when the government was toppled.

After taking office, Malloum stated that the army was "engaged in a battle for national reconstruction" to wipe out the "political incoherence and injustice" that had existed under the former regime. However, his government took a moderate stand on national issues and called mainly for increased agricultural production.

Malloum was born on Sept. 10, 1932, at Fort-Archambault in southern Chad. He received his military training in France and with French forces in Africa.

In 1968, he was promoted to the rank of colonel and became chief of Chad's military cabinet. In 1971, he became chief of the general staff, and in 1972, he was made commander in chief of the armed forces.   Darlene R. Stille

MALTA. See EUROPE.

MANITOBA. See CANADA.

MANUFACTURING. Industry in the United States spent 1975 trying to recover from the worst recession since the Great Depression of the 1930s. Recovery began slowly in April and May, accelerated during the summer, and began to moderate in October. The Federal Reserve Board saw this as evidence that manufacturers were not rushing to build up inventories following the massive liquidations of the summer.

Industrial Production spurted during the summer, and showed solid gains of 1.6 per cent in August and 1.8 per cent in September – an 11-year high. In October, however, production rose only 0.4 per cent. Although this was the sixth monthly gain in a row, it was the slimmest since May. The Federal Reserve's Industrial Production Index rose to 116.5 in October – with the 1967 level representing a base of 100. But it was still 6.7 per cent below October, 1974.

Business inventories rose in August and September following six months of steady, and at times rapid, liquidation of stocks. The U.S. Department of Commerce reported that inventories in September rose 0.2 per cent to $265.1 billion. As the year drew to a close, economists generally agreed that the rate of change in inventories would be the key factor in determining the strength of the economic recovery. An inventory reduction means manufacturers are filling at least some orders from existing supplies. An increase in inventories generally points to a boost in orders, productivity, and jobs.

Durable Goods orders, which increased for six straight months through August, declined 1.1 per cent in September, then rebounded 1.3 per cent in October. The Commerce Department saw this as a sign that the recovery was not faltering as suggested by the September figures, but was still registering real growth, even if at a slower pace. Durable goods orders climbed $552 million in October to $42.8-billion, compared to $42.3 billion in September, when orders declined $461 million. The major surge in October came from primary metals and machinery, which overcame weaknesses in transportation orders. Shipments in October continued to outpace orders, rising $785 million, or 1.8 per cent, to $44.1 billion.

Unfilled orders of durables declined for two successive months, dropping 0.9 per cent in September and 1.1 per cent in October. The October backlog dropped to $115.1 billion, a decline of $25 billion from the high in September, 1974.

Plant Utilization. The summer recovery was reflected in greater plant utilization during the three-month period ending in September. Industry operated at 69 per cent of capacity during that period, compared to only 67 per cent during the previous quarter. While the pickup was encouraging, it must be measured against 27 years of such statistics compiled by the Federal Reserve Board.

U.S. Productivity Lags

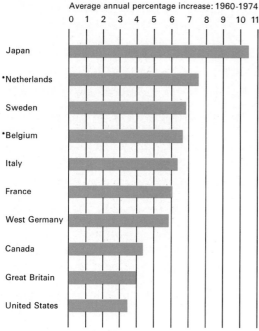

Average annual percentage increase: 1960-1974

*Average increase, 1960-1973
Source: U.S. Department of Labor

Until the 1974 recession, plant utilization had never dropped below 72.5 per cent.

A glance at operations of two of the nation's bellwether industries showed some of the reasons for the unused capacity. While reporting an increase in orders since August, the chairman of National Steel Corporation said that industry shipments for the year would total only 95 million short tons (86 million metric tons), compared with shipments of 109.5-million short tons (99 million metric tons) in 1974 and a record 111.4 million short tons (101 million metric tons) in 1973. The Aluminum Association reported shipments of about 4.8 million short tons (4.4 million metric tons), down 2 million short tons (1.8 million metric tons).

The reduced level of plant utilization caused manufacturers to trim capital spending throughout the year. The Commerce Department estimated capital spending at $113.5 billion, up 1 per cent from 1974's record of $112.4 billion. However, McGraw-Hill's Economic Department estimated that real spending was down 9 per cent, after discounting the effects of price increases.

Productivity surged and labor costs dropped as the tempo of the recovery increased. The U.S. Department of Labor reported that overall productivity rose at an annual rate of 11 per cent in the third quarter. This was almost triple the 4.2 per cent rate in the second quarter, and the largest gain since the first quarter of 1971. Manufacturing productivity in the third quarter rose at an annual rate of 9.5 per cent, well ahead of the second quarter's 2.8 per cent. As a result, unit labor costs fell 4.1 per cent. This was the largest quarterly drop since the third quarter of 1965.

Unemployment, which became a national issue in 1974, continued to plague the United States. Unemployment jumped to 8.6 per cent of the work force in October, reversing a trend set by four consecutive months of declining unemployment. Unemployment reached a post-depression high in May when it soared to 9.2 per cent. The Labor Department attributed the October upsurge to persons re-entering the labor market as factory production rose. McGraw-Hill estimated that 1.1 million workers had re-entered the labor force since June.

New Technology. The need to conserve fuel continued to spark new technological developments. Parker-Hannifin Corporation set up a production line at its Waverly, Ohio, plant to turn out a new hydraulic system that it claims reduces the energy required to accomplish many jobs by 25 to 50 per cent. The system, several years in development, consumes only the energy needed to perform a given task. It would replace more conventional systems that consume an equal amount of energy for each task, regardless of size.

The first large plant to convert coal into oil came closer to reality in January when the U.S. government awarded a $237.2-million contract to a joint venture of Union Carbide Corporation and General Tire & Rubber Company to build a demonstration plant near Belleville, Ill. Scheduled to begin operation in 1980, the plant will turn 2,600 short tons (2,360 metric tons) of coal a day into 3,900 barrels of synthetic crude oil and 22 million cubic feet (623,000 cubic meters) of "natural" gas.

Government safety standards that take effect in July, 1976, were also responsible for new products and production methods to reduce worker hazards. Raybestos-Manhattan Incorporated claimed to have a new process to make asbestos textile products safely. Asbestos is a fibrous silicate mineral that is used in more than 3,000 products from gaskets to paint and wallboard. The new patented and trademarked system, Novatex, was placed in commercial production at the company's North Charleston, S.C., plant. The system involves bathing the asbestos in chemicals and detergents. The company claims the Novatex "wet process" will reduce the hazards to workers, but will not eliminate the asbestos properties of flexibility, strength, and resistance to high temperatures.

As a direct result of the recession, many companies encouraged cost-cutting measures. One pronounced move was a trend toward fewer and standardized parts. Chrysler Corporation reported it reduced the number of parts needed for automobile

A textile engineer holds a candle to children's night clothes in a safety test to measure how well various products can resist flames.

assembly 20 per cent or more between its 1970 and 1976 models. Ford reduced the number of engine parts an average of 56 per cent between initial production of 1975 cars and 1976 models.

Machine Tool Orders declined in November to $103.7 million, after registering their best month in a year in October with $119.8 million. However, the November total was still 30 per cent better than in November, 1974. Through November, orders tapped only 60 per cent of the industry's shipment capability. Shipments fell 13 per cent from $208.2-million in October to $180.9 million in November, about the same as in November, 1974. At the end of November, the order backlog was $1.37 billion, down from $1.45 billion in October and only about half the $2.69-billion backlog in November, 1974.

Electrical Products. Sharp decreases in residential and commercial building, and various energy-conservation measures imposed during the year were the main reasons that shipments of electrical products dropped 1 per cent to $65 billion. The only increases were in electronics-communications products, which rose 6 per cent to $22.4 billion, and industrial equipment, which increased 5 per cent to $10.5 billion. Consumer products remained even at $13.7 billion. Insulated wire and cable dropped 20 per cent to $1.4 billion; insulating materials were down 17 per cent to $1 billion; building equipment was down 11 per cent to $2.5 billion; power equip-

ment was down 9 per cent to $6.5 billion; and lighting equipment was down 4 per cent to $4.3 billion.

Rubber Products. The slumping auto industry used less rubber and helped account for the sharp decrease in rubber consumption. Total rubber consumption was 2.8 million short tons (2.6 million metric tons), compared to 3.4 million short tons (3.1-million metric tons) the previous year. Production of synthetic rubber dropped from 2.6 million short tons (2.4 million metric tons) to 2.1 million short tons (1.9 million metric tons), and accounted for only 74 per cent of the total, down from 77 per cent in 1974. Tire production fell from 208,633,000 to 196,779,000.

The Paper Industry, which entered the year in a steep downtrend, ended it on an equally steep uptrend. The American Paper Institute estimated that paper and paperboard production totaled 52.8 million short tons (47.9 million metric tons), 13 per cent below the 61 million short tons (55.3 million metric tons) produced in 1974. Yet by year-end, the annual rate was 59 million short tons (53.5 million metric tons), up from a rate of 48 million short tons (43.6 million metric tons) at the beginning of the year and a low of 46 million short tons (41.7 million metric tons) in March.   George J. Berkwitt

MARINE CORPS, U.S. See ARMED FORCES.
MARYLAND. See BALTIMORE; STATE GOV'T.
MASSACHUSETTS. See BOSTON; STATE GOV'T.

MATHEWS, F. DAVID (1935-   ), president of the University of Alabama, was confirmed by the Senate on July 22, 1975, as United States secretary of health, education, and welfare. The youngest member of President Gerald R. Ford's Cabinet, he replaced Caspar W. Weinberger, who resigned for personal reasons. See CABINET, U.S.

During his Senate confirmation hearings, Mathews expressed doubt about the value of busing schoolchildren to achieve racial balance. However, he swore to uphold the law in this regard.

Forrest David Mathews was born in Grove Hill, Ala., on Dec. 6, 1935. He attended the University of Alabama and earned his Ph.D. from Columbia University in New York City in 1965. In 1960, he went to work for the University of Alabama and became president of the institution in 1969.

Since the late 1960s, he has served on several governmental and educational advisory panels, including the National Programming Council for Public Television. In addition, he has written several works on Southern history and on U.S. higher education. In 1969, the Junior Chamber of Commerce named him one of the 10 outstanding young men in America.

Mathews married Mary Chapman in 1960. They have two daughters.   Darlene R. Stille

MAURITANIA. See AFRICA.

MAURITIUS. See AFRICA.

MEDICINE. The European Community (Common Market) decided on Feb. 11, 1975, to allow the 400,000 doctors in member countries to practice medicine anywhere in the nine nations. The decision, made by the group's health ministers at a meeting in Brussels, Belgium, creates for the first time a European status for a profession in the Common Market. The new system is based on mutual recognition of national diplomas and certificates.

On the Picket Line. In the United States, the sight of doctors picketing hospitals – unimaginable only a few years ago – became a common one in 1975. In several states, including California and New York, doctors withheld their services to protest their difficulties in getting malpractice insurance coverage. In New York City, a unionlike group of interns and residents successfully struck the city's voluntary hospitals – private, not-for-profit institutions – in March to win shorter workweeks and better working conditions. Other young physicians went on strike over working conditions in Los Angeles in May and in Chicago in October.

The most discussed issue in medicine was the soaring number of malpractice suits brought against doctors and the high premiums doctors had to pay for malpractice insurance. As private insurers dropped out of the malpractice market, it became increasingly difficult for doctors, particularly in such high-risk specialties as orthopedics, to get

malpractice insurance. See INSURANCE (Close-Up).

Organized Medicine. For the American Medical Association (AMA), it was a bad year. Because of a $3-million deficit, the organization had to trim its staff from approximately 1,000 to 800 persons, slash its budgets, and reorganize its structure. In the midst of these adjustments, it was discovered that a staff member who dubbed himself "Sore Throat" was leaking confidential information to consumer groups, congressmen, and reporters. In the furor that resulted, the AMA was accused of possible income tax evasion, misuse of postal privileges, and illegal political contributions.

Other groups within organized medicine had their share of headaches, too. The Department of Justice charged the American Society of Anesthesiologists with price fixing in September, alleging that the society's "relative value" fee guide restrains price competition and denies patients the right to obtain anesthesia services at lower fees.

The American College of Surgeons, the American Surgical Association, and other private and governmental agencies released a report in 1975 that showed a surplus of as many as 30,000 surgeons in the United States. The study, which was expected to lead to drastic changes in how and how many new surgeons are trained, recommended stricter hospital regulations in granting surgical privileges,

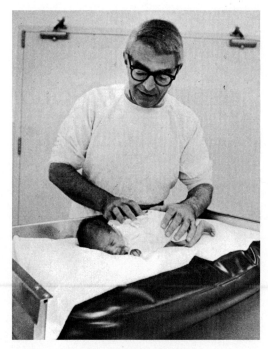

Doctors at University Hospital in San Diego place premature babies on water beds in an experiment to guard against crib death.

fewer training positions in surgery, and periodic reassessment of the competence and performance of surgeons.

Medical Ethics. Law courts were called upon to rule on two issues that have been debated by doctors for several years – a doctor's liability in aborting a possibly *viable fetus* (one potentially able to survive outside the mother's womb) and the right to withdraw treatment for a patient being kept alive by mechanical means.

On February 15, Kenneth C. Edelin, a Boston obstetrician, was convicted of manslaughter in an abortion operation and sentenced to a year's probation. Right-to-life groups hailed the decision as a victory in their anti-abortion campaign.

New Jersey Superior Court Judge Robert Muir, Jr., ruled on November 10 that the parents of 21-year-old Karen Ann Quinlan did not have the right to withdraw treatment so she could die with "grace and dignity." The young woman had been in a coma for months and had suffered permanent brain damage. Her parents asked court permission to disconnect the respirator keeping her alive. The case raised theological, legal, and ethical questions about the rights of patients kept alive by mechanical means.

Health Manpower. Legislation linking federal support to medical schools with a requirement that some graduating doctors serve for a time in areas that do not have enough doctors seemed most favored in the U.S. Congress. Emphasis in manpower discussions has shifted from the number of physicians available to concern over their specialties and where they will practice. There now are too many doctors in too few places (primarily parts of large cities) and too few in too many places (mainly rural areas). There also are more than enough specialists and too few general practitioners.

Enrollments in U.S. medical schools rose to record highs in 1975. In September, 14,874 students enrolled in 114 medical schools. In the past 10 years, first-year medical school enrollments have increased 70 per cent. The number of women in medical schools set a record in 1975, comprising 22 per cent (3,275 students) of the total freshman class.

Heart Surgery. Christiaan N. Barnard of Cape Town, South Africa, repeated his spectacular parallel heart transplant, in which he implanted a donor's heart without removing the recipient's, twice in 1975. The first patient to undergo the operation in November, 1974, died in April of complications unrelated to the operation. Other developments in heart surgery in 1975 included the perfection of a balloon pump to relieve the stress on the heart of patients who have had open-heart surgery and the use of patches – dacron umbrellalike devices inserted by catheter – to repair defects in the heart without open-heart surgery.   Dianne Rafalik

See also HEALTH AND DISEASE.

MENTAL HEALTH. The Supreme Court of the United States upheld the rights of mental patients on June 26, 1975. In a unanimous, precedent-setting decision, the court ruled that a mentally ill person cannot be institutionalized if the hospital is not offering treatment, the patient is not dangerous to himself or others, and the patient is capable of living in the community with the help of friends and family.

The plaintiff in the case, Kenneth Donaldson, was confined to a Florida state hospital for 15 years without treatment after being diagnosed as a "paranoid schizophrenic" in 1957. Donaldson, a Christian Scientist, refused treatment, and tried again and again to win release. In 1971, he sued the hospital superintendent, James B. O'Connor, for depriving him of the right to be either treated or released. In response, hospital authorities released Donaldson 10 days before the trial began. The trial jury awarded Donaldson $38,500 in damages. The ruling was upheld by an appellate court before O'Connor petitioned the Supreme Court for a review of the decision.

Legal authorities speculated that there were many other persons deprived of treatment in state institutions. But, because the Supreme Court failed to define precisely such terms as "dangerous" and "capable of living in the community," the decision did not lead to a wholesale release of mental patients from institutions. The court ducked such tough legal questions as the rights of dangerous persons confined without treatment and of nondangerous persons receiving treatment but confined against their will. A number of cases were filed in lower courts in 1975 to expand the ruling.

The Donaldson decision may lead to a wider range of treatment choices for mental patients. One effect of the ruling may be the development of more community-based facilities for the mentally ill. Such services would help patients confined for years in state hospitals to adjust to an outside life.

Drug Misuse. In the wake of the controversy over the right-to-treatment ruling, a Senate subcommittee investigating juvenile delinquency uncovered evidence of widespread misuse of tranquilizers in government mental institutions. Several physicians and former mental patients told of institutions where inmates regularly received high doses of such tranquilizers as chlorpromazine. James Clements, former president of the American Association of Mental Deficiency, estimated that as many as 80 per cent of the inmates in retardation centers in Georgia were kept on tranquilizers.

Theories of Mental Illness. The controversy over what mental illness is and what can and should be done about it continued. In the past 25 years, the main emphasis in psychiatric treatment has shifted from Freudian psychoanalytical approaches to chemical and biological methods.

Clinical research in 1975 provided more evidence that heredity and brain disturbances can be important factors in certain mental diseases. Genetic studies at Harvard University and the National Institute of Mental Health, for example, showed a significant hereditary component in schizophrenia and manic depression.

The studies at the National Institute of Mental Health identified a genetic factor in schizophrenia, a crippling emotional state that isolates victims from reality. Nongenetic factors, such as environment and nutrition, also were found to contribute to the disorder. Schizophrenia, which afflicts about 1 per cent of the population, has been shown to be a "class" disease. Found most often among the lower social and economic classes in urbanized and industrialized areas, it is much rarer among the poor in rural regions and small towns and among people of higher social standing.

Manic Depression also has biochemical origins, according to researchers at Harvard who are formulating a biochemical theory of depression based on their finding that a family of key body chemicals, the catecholamines, are imbalanced in certain types of depressed patients. As a result of drug treatment, the success rate for alleviating depression has risen from 30 to 90 per cent in the past 25 years.   Dianne Rafalik

METRIC SYSTEM. After almost 200 years of sporadic debate, the United States Congress in 1975 passed legislation setting up a federal mechanism to help the country shift over to the metric system of measurement. The United States is the last major country to commit itself to the metric system. Although the Metric Conversion Act of 1975 does not require anybody to change and does not specify any target date for conversion, it authorizes the establishment of a U.S. Metric Board to help coordinate the inevitable changeover.

Many U.S. companies and government agencies are already moving briskly ahead with plans for the changeover. One of every three automobiles on U.S. roads now requires metric nuts, bolts, and tools. Boards of education and legislatures in 29 states have begun to encourage the use of metric measurements. Metric road signs are beginning to appear in a dozen states, and North Dakota now requires metric signs in its state parks. A Pennsylvania test found people did not mind buying gasoline by the liter (0.26 gallon).

On the federal level, the Civil Service Commission began metric courses in 1975, the Department of Defense said metric measurements will be considered in buying all new equipment, and the Treasury Department required that all wine be bottled in metric containers by 1979.   Daniel V. De Simone

"The next thing you know they'll be calling us two point five four centimeter worms."

MEXICO. The ruling Institutional Revolutionary Party (PRI) gave its presidential nomination to Finance Minister José Lopez Portillo on Sept. 22, 1975. Traditionally, the nomination virtually assures Lopez victory in the July, 1976, election. Party leaders indicated Lopez would follow incumbent President Luis Echeverría Alvarez' "revolutionary policies," which include efforts to achieve greater economic independence from the United States and further nationalization of private businesses.

The Mexican Communist Party, the Mexican Workers Party, the Socialist Action and Unity Movement, and the Socialist Organization Movement announced on April 22 they would cooperate in efforts to reform the nation's electoral law. Among other things, the law withholds legal recognition from any party with fewer than 60,000 members. None of the groups had legal recognition.

The Socialist Workers Party, a fifth group, was formed on May 1. It also promised to actively promote "revolutionary development" in Mexico and strenuously oppose the PRI candidate in 1976.

Extreme leftist groups continued active throughout the year. Five persons were killed and about 19 were seriously injured on January 27 by terrorist bombs set off in San Luis Potosí. Other bombs exploded that same day in Mexico City and Oaxaca. The People's Union was blamed for the bombings.

Mexico's President Luis Echeverría Alvarez addresses delegates to World Conference on International Women's Year in Mexico City.

It was also implicated in a November terrorist bomb explosion in Mexico City. However, there were no casualties in the November bombing.

Economic Conditions. During the first half of 1975, wholesale prices in Mexico rose 8.9 per cent over those for the same period in 1974. Inflation continued to rise at an average rate of 15 per cent annually. Unemployment was a growing problem, notably in the 10-year-old border industries program. Because of rising wages and a growing recession in the United States, about 25,000 Mexicans—25 per cent of the work force in factories along the Mexican-U.S. border—had been fired. Since 1971, unemployment in Mexico had quadrupled. Tourism was down 30 per cent.

Oil Boom. The discovery of new offshore oil deposits in the Gulf of Campeche was reported on August 13. New oilfields were also found in the Cotaxtla region of Veracruz state in March. The Chiapas and Tabasco states fields discovered in 1974 produced a total of 100 million barrels of crude oil over the year ending Aug. 1, 1975.

Crude-oil exports were averaging 89,000 barrels per day. Pemex, the government oil monopoly, estimated that, with the new finds, Mexico had some 20 billion barrels of proven petroleum reserves.

International Relations. Between July 8 and August 22, President Echeverría toured 14 nations in the Caribbean, Africa, Asia, and the Middle East and signed numerous agreements with his host countries. Among the agreements was one calling for commercial cooperation between Mexico and the European Community (Common Market). Another calls for economic and technological cooperation with the Council for Mutual Economic Assistance (COMECON), the Communist economic alliance in Eastern Europe.

Domestic criticism of the president's trip was widespread. Many critics felt that the $20-million tour had been primarily used to further Echeverría's chances of being elected United Nations (UN) secretary-general in December, 1976.

Mexico City was host from June 19 to July 2 to a world conference sponsored by the UN as part of its observance of International Women's Year. On October 17, Mexico was one of 70 nations that voted to adopt a UN General Assembly resolution declaring Zionism "a form of racism and racial discrimination." After that vote, members of the U.S. Jewish community began canceling vacation trips to Mexico. By year's end, the Mexican Bureau of Tourism reported that between 60,000 and 80,000 hotel reservations had been canceled, costing Mexico from $4 million to $5 million in foreign revenue. In December, Mexico's Foreign Minister Emilio O. Rabasa went to Israel to explain the vote, then resigned from office.

Paul C. Tullier

See also LATIN AMERICA (Facts in Brief Table).

MICHIGAN. See DETROIT; STATE GOV'T.

Israeli tanks pull back from the Sinai front as a symbolic peace
gesture preceding the June 5 reopening of Egypt's Suez Canal.

MIDDLE EAST. With the September, 1975, signing of a disengagement agreement in the Sinai Peninsula, Egypt and Israel took a giant step toward
the elusive permanent settlement of the Arab-
Israeli conflict. Nudged along by the "shuttle diplomacy" of U.S. Secretary of State Henry A. Kissinger, Egyptian and Israeli representatives signed
a historic agreement on September 4 in Geneva,
Switzerland. The new pact had more far-reaching
concessions on both sides than its January, 1974,
predecessor, which established a United Nations
(UN) buffer zone to separate the two nations.

The nine articles in the 1975 agreement showed
how far both sides moved from earlier positions and
also demonstrated the extent of their reliance on
U.S. impartiality. Both agreed specifically to continue to observe the cease-fire and to renounce the
use of force to resolve their differences. Israel was to
withdraw its forces 12 to 26 miles (19 to 42 kilometers) east of its former positions. A greater expanded buffer zone manned by UN troops replaced the
former Israeli occupation area. Israeli forces were
to be redeployed east of the high ground surrounding the strategic Giddi and Mitla passes, and the
passes demilitarized. However, Israel retained its
electronic early-warning station at the eastern end
of Giddi Pass and its air base at Bir Gifgafa. Maximum troop strength on each border of the UN
buffer zone would be 8,000 men. No troops other

than the soldiers of the UN emergency force were to
be permitted in the buffer zone.

American Monitors. A key feature in the agreement – particularly for Israel – is the stationing of
200 American civilian technicians at surveillance
posts in the passes for electronic monitoring of the
cease-fire. This represents the first organized American "presence" in the Middle East since the
landing of Marines in Lebanon in 1958. Congressional approval was required, and some congressmen voiced fears of another Vietnam-type involvement. However, Congress approved the action and
cleared the way for Israel's acceptance of the pact.

Another bastion of Arab resistance to Israel's
right to function as a state crumbled when Egypt
agreed to allow the passage through the reopened
Suez Canal of nonmilitary cargoes destined for Israeli ports. On October 23, the Greek freighter
Olympus, with a cargo of cement destined for the
Israeli port of Elat, passed through the canal.

On its part, Israel agreed to return the Sinai oil
fields captured in 1967 to Egyptian control. It was a
costly economic concession, because the fields were
supplying 55 per cent of Israel's domestic requirements. The smaller Ras Sudar field was returned to
Egypt on October 5 and Abu Rudeis on December
1. The disengagement operations were planned to
take place in stages over a 4^{1}/$_{2}$-month period, ending on Feb. 22, 1976.

Egyptian President Anwar al-Sadat's international stature and his image as a moderate Arab leader were greatly enhanced by the agreement. Despite some ill-timed criticism of Zionism and Jews in general during his U.S. visit in November, he came away with pledges of $750 million in military and economic aid, a 300 per cent increase over the previous year. It now seemed vitally important to American policymakers to shore up Egypt's struggling economy.

Israel Isolated. In contrast, Israel was faced with increasing international isolation and pressure for a settlement that would recognize the Palestinians' territorial "rights." Over Israeli objections, two more UN specialized agencies, the Food and Agriculture Organization and the International Labor Organization, granted observer status to representatives of the Palestine Liberation Organization (PLO) in June. The United Nations Educational, Scientific, and Cultural Organization (UNESCO), which in 1974 barred financial aid to Israel, voted to ban Israeli experts at conferences on education in the Mediterranean area.

In addition, a solid bloc of Arab and other third world countries passed a UN General Assembly resolution in November denouncing Zionism as "a form of racism and racial discrimination" (see UNITED NATIONS). The resolution aroused a storm of protest in the United States and other Western countries. Christian clergymen and lay leaders joined Jewish leaders in affirming the historical meaning and mission of the movement. However, Russia and China voted in favor of the resolution. An Israeli air strike against PLO bases in Lebanon on December 2 served further to isolate Israel. The attack, involving 30 planes, hit PLO centers along the border and in north Lebanon, near Tripoli, killing at least 70 persons.

Arab Criticism. Despite these developments, the Arab world was anything but united over the question of a settlement with Israel. Syria denounced the Sinai agreement. The Syrian Baath Party's official newspaper called it a blow to Arab solidarity and a unilateral action by Egypt to abandon the Arabs' "Three No" policy — no peace, no negotiations, no recognition — toward Israel. Nevertheless, Syria twice — in May and November — approved continuing the UN buffer zone on the Golan Heights. The PLO, equally angered by the Egyptian government's shutdown on September 11 of its Voice of Palestine Cairo broadcasts, accused Sadat of selling out Palestinian interests. See EGYPT; ISRAEL; SYRIA.

Iran, Iraq Agree. The Israeli-Egyptian agreement overshadowed a number of earlier significant events with implications for the area's future. In

Facts in Brief on the Middle East Countries

Country	Population	Government	Monetary Unit*	Foreign Trade (million U.S. $) Exports	Imports
Bahrain	256,000	Amir Isa bin Salman Al Khalifa; Prime Minister Khalifa bin Salman Al Khalifa	dinar (1=$2.53)	1,164	446
Cyprus	671,000	President Archbishop Makarios III	pound (1=$2.54)	158	407
Egypt	38,456,000	President Anwar al-Sadat; Prime Minister Mamduh Muhammad Salim	pound (1=$2.56)	1,516	2,349
Iran	34,384,000	Shah Mohammad Reza Pahlavi; Prime Minister Amir Abbas Hoveyda	rial (65.3=$1)	24,000	5,672
Iraq	11,471,000	President Ahmad Hasan al-Bakr	dinar (1=$3.41)	7,413	1,175
Israel	3,453,000	President Ephraim Katzir; Prime Minister Yitzhak Rabin	pound (7.1=$1)	1,825	5,389
Jordan	2,820,000	King Hussein I; Prime Minister Zayd Rifai	dinar (1=$3.06)	155	488
Kuwait	1,180,000	Emir Sabah al-Salim al-Sabah; Prime Minister Jabir al-Ahmad al-Sabah	dinar (1=$3.42)	11,246	1,529
Lebanon	3,517,000	President Sleiman Frangie; Prime Minister Rashid Karame	pound (2.4=$1)	500	1,218
Oman	787,000	Sultan Sayyid Qaboos bin Said Al Bu Said	rial (1=$2.60)	1,294	199
Qatar	101,000	Amir & Prime Minister Khalifa bin Hamad Al-Thani	riyal (4.1=$1)	2,304	271
Saudi Arabia	9,157,000	King & Prime Minister Khalid ibn Abd al-Aziz Al-Saud	riyal (3.5=$1)	35,657	3,473
Sudan	18,343,000	President Sayed Gaafar Mohamed Nimeiri	pound (1=$2.87)	350	642
Syria	7,604,000	President Hafiz al-Asad; Prime Minister Mahmud al-Ayyubi	pound (3.7=$1)	784	1,230
Turkey	40,909,000	President Fahri S. Koruturk; Prime Minister Suleyman Demirel	lira (14.9=$1)	1,574	3,775
United Arab Emirates	228,000	President Zayid bin Sultan al-Nuhayan; Prime Minister Maktum ibn Rashid al-Maktum al-Falasa	dirham (3.9=$1)	7,371	1,145
Yemen (Aden)	1,705,000	Presidential Council Chairman Salim Ali Rubayya; Prime Minister Ali Nasir Muhammad	dinar (1=$2.90)	113	172
Yemen (Sana)	6,660,000	Command Council Chairman Ibrahim Mohamed al-Hamdi; Prime Minister Abdulaziz Abdul Ghani	rial (4.6=$1)	13	190

*Exchange rates as of Dec. 1, 1975

March, Iran and Iraq defined their common border along the Shatt al Arab estuary linking the Tigris and Euphrates rivers to the Persian Gulf. The new border, defined as the midpoint of the channel, removed a source of friction dating back decades.

The main result of the agreement, however, was to pull the rug from under the Kurdish rebellion against the Iraqi government, because Iran withdrew its support of the Kurds. Deprived of their only source of weapons and equipment and cut off in their mountain enclave from sanctuary in Iran, the Kurds gave up their 13-year struggle for internal autonomy on their own terms. Mustafa Barzani, the Kurdish leader, took refuge in Iran, with thousands of his countrymen.

The agreement with Iraq underlined Shah Mohammad Reza Pahlavi's intentions of making Iran the leader of a united group of Persian Gulf states. Iranian forces assisting Sultan Sayyid Qaboos bin Said Al Bu Said of Oman were credited with the success of Omani forces against another rebellion, this one in Dhofar Province by rebels who were supported intermittently by Yemen (Aden). See IRAN; IRAQ; OMAN; YEMEN (ADEN).

Moroccan March. Elsewhere, the Middle East was relatively free of major upheavals and disturbances. Spain's announcement on May 23 that it would grant independence to its Spanish Sahara colony did arouse Morocco. After an opinion by the International Court of Justice earlier had denied the validity of Moroccan and Mauritanian claims to the territory, King Hassan II organized an October march by 350,000 unarmed Moroccans to stake their claim to Spanish Sahara. By early November, thousands of marchers were 6 miles (10 kilometers) inside the Spanish Sahara border. They halted there while Hassan negotiated with Spanish emissaries. On November 19, the king sent the marchers home after Spain agreed to divide the mineral-rich colony between Morocco and Mauritania. Another neighbor, Algeria, called for independence for Spanish Sahara. See ALGERIA; MOROCCO.

The Glaring Exception to relative regional stability was Lebanon. Beginning with clashes in January and February between Israeli raiders and Palestinian commandos based in Lebanon, fighting spread to Lebanese cities. Communal battles finally engulfed the capital, Beirut, in civil war. Battles between several sects and groups of Moslems and the Phalangists, a well-trained Christian militia, severely damaged the city.

More than a dozen truces were arranged by Prime Minister Rashid Karame and other leaders. Each broke down. The political basis for the fighting was Lebanon's traditional governmental structure, which gives slightly more power to Lebanese Christians, even though they are no longer a majority in the country. An added factor was Moslem support for the Palestinian guerrillas against Israel.

Pullback in the Sinai

In late November, former French Prime Minister Pierre Couve de Murville helped to arrange negotiations on constitutional reforms in discussions with Karame, a Moslem; President Sleiman Frangie, a Christian; and other leaders.

The Lebanese economy was paralyzed. Its banking system, which had negotiated investments of $1.25 billion before the fighting, closed down in October as Lebanon's reputation for free exchange and financial stability was destroyed. Between April and November, the conflict left an estimated 6,500 dead and 15,000 injured, and caused $500 million in property damage. In addition to the banks, some 60 foreign firms moved their headquarters to other Middle Eastern cities such as Cairo, Egypt; Manama, Bahrain; and Amman, Jordan. Perhaps the one saving grace of the Lebanese crisis was a tacit agreement by outside powers not to intervene. See KARAME, RASHID; LEBANON.

Economy. Despite giving nearly $25 million in revenues to Egypt through tolls in its six months of operation, the reopened Suez Canal was more a political than an economic success. Otherwise, the year saw large amounts of money, mainly petrodollars, changing hands from the major oil-producing states to less fortunate neighbors with few concrete results, other than enlarging the already enormous stockpiles of weapons in the Middle East.

William Spencer

MINES AND MINING. The world faces a future plagued by mineral shortages, according to a National Academy of Sciences report issued in February, 1975. The 348-page report asserts that the U.S. government should pursue a national policy of conservation of materials, energy, and environmental resources. It suggests that the first real shortages may be only a few years away.

According to the academy, substitutes must be found as soon as possible for chromium, gold, mercury, palladium, and tin. In addition, substitutes for antimony, silver, tungsten, vanadium, and zinc should also be assessed. On the bright side, world coal resources appear to be adequate for hundreds of years. See COAL.

The Copper Supply is seriously short in the United States, according to the report, and significant discoveries must be made if the current U.S. production rate is to be maintained until the end of the century. The prime cause of dwindling supplies is the price cutting that has persisted for months in the major copper-producing nations, according to Herbert Barchoff, president of the American Copper Council, a trade group. After a six-week tour of major copper-exporting nations – Chile, Peru, Zaire, and Zambia – Barchoff said that, with prices hovering at 60 cents a pound (0.45 kilogram), production was being cut.

Silhouetted against the sky, the headframe of a South African gold mine stands over the entrance to the mine near Johannesburg.

United States producers attended a United Nations special session on raw materials and development in September and opposed U.S. Secretary of State Henry A. Kissinger's plan for establishing international agreements for key resources. Thirteen domestic copper producers, representing over 90 per cent of U.S. copper production, argued that such an international agreement would not ensure adequate U.S. copper supplies. They said ample foreign copper supplies are restricting the ability of U.S. companies to exploit domestic reserves.

Search for Uranium. The energy crisis of 1974 spurred new uranium hunts. By early 1975, stockpiled uranium fuel at U.S. nuclear power plants totaled about 20,000 short tons (18,000 metric tons). An additional 4,300 short tons (3,900 metric tons) was still in the hands of miners who also refine the ore. By the year 2000, the United States will need an additional 1.5 to 2.2 million short tons (1.4 to 2.0 million metric tons) of the fuel for its nuclear power plants if current plans do not succumb to growing opposition. See SCIENCE AND RESEARCH.

Gold Bust. The U.S. gold boom collapsed in January almost before it got underway. With the government making private possession of gold legal for the first time since 1933, the expected rush to buy bullion at nearly $200 per troy ounce (31 grams) did not materialize. By the end of September, bullion had fallen to less than $130.

Strip Mining. In early October, Congress acted to halt strip mining in the Death Valley National Monument in California. Large-scale strip mining has been going on in the national monument for four years as several large corporations hunted for minerals. Mining in Death Valley was made possible by Congress in 1933 shortly after the national monument was created. Mining on public lands was approved at the time on behalf of the pick-and-shovel miner, who had been trying to scratch ore out of Death Valley since the mid-1800s.

But Congress failed to enact tough environmental controls on strip mining, especially for coal in the Western states. On May 7, Congress cleared a bill similar to the one President Gerald R. Ford pocket-vetoed in December, 1974. But coal and utility interests mounted a successful lobbying campaign, charging that coal production would drop if the bill became law. President Ford vetoed it and Congress could not override his veto.

Discharges into Lake Superior by the Reserve Mining Company constitute a potential threat to the public health, the U.S. Circuit Court of Appeals in St. Louis ruled on March 14. Nevertheless, the court refused to sustain an earlier court order closing the company's plant in Silver Bay, Minn. The plant, which discharges 67,000 short tons (61,000 metric tons) of ground taconite into the lake every day, was given "reasonable time" to clean up the water pollution.   Mary E. Jessup

MINNEAPOLIS-ST. PAUL. Charles S. Stenvig defeated incumbent Mayor Albert J. Hofstede in the Nov. 4, 1975, election for mayor of Minneapolis. Stenvig, a former policeman, had been the mayor of Minneapolis when Hofstede defeated him in November, 1973. Stenvig's campaign centered around the issues of crime and pornography.

Plans and Studies. A master plan to control urban growth in the 10-county Twin Cities metropolitan area won a unanimous vote of approval by the Metropolitan Council in late March. The plan limited most new development to areas with existing water and sewer facilities.

According to a U.S. Census Bureau report issued in June, Minneapolis lost 12 per cent of its population and St. Paul 7.3 per cent between 1970 and 1973. As of July 1, 1973, Minneapolis' population was 382,423; St. Paul's, 287,305.

The Minneapolis Downtown Council reported in January that state aid to suburban Hennepin County averaged $951 per household as opposed to only $520 for every household in Minneapolis. The council also noted that the tax rate in Minneapolis could be cut by 33 per cent if state aid to the city was raised to the same level as aid to the suburbs.

According to a report issued in July by the Minnesota Planning and Development Department, racial segregation in Minneapolis housing changed little between 1960 and 1970. The study called for home rehabilitation and rent subsidies as part of a strategy to increase the supply of middle-income housing available to minorities.

In April, the federal Environmental Protection Agency found that St. Paul's drinking water contained small amounts of organic chemicals suspected of causing cancer in laboratory animals.

Sports and Recreation. Special task forces of the Minneapolis and St. Paul chambers of commerce recommended in March that a domed sports arena be built in the Twin Cities area.

Restored and reconstructed Fort Snelling officially reopened as a historic attraction on May 1. Guides, who provided daily tours of the facility during the summer, spent a weekend in April living in the fort under the same conditions as the soldiers who first occupied it in the early 1820s.

Living costs in the Twin Cities area rose 8.9 per cent between July, 1974, and July, 1975. Food prices rose 1.6 per cent in the year ending in June, while gasoline prices remained fairly stable. The average price of 1 gallon (3.8 liters) of regular gasoline in June was 55.7 cents.   James M. Banovetz

MINNESOTA. See MINNEAPOLIS-ST. PAUL; STATE GOVERNMENT.

MISSISSIPPI. See STATE GOVERNMENT.

MISSOURI. See SAINT LOUIS; STATE GOV'T.

MONACO. See EUROPE.

MONGOLIA. See ASIA.

MONTANA. See STATE GOVERNMENT.

MOROCCO. With a single bold stroke, King Hassan II ended a long dispute with Spain in 1975 and gained control of the northern half of phosphate-rich Spanish Sahara. The chain of events began in May, when Spain announced it would grant independence to Spanish Sahara, long a center of dispute with Morocco. On October 16, Hassan announced that he would lead 350,000 civilians on a march into the sparsely populated colony. Thousands of unarmed Moroccans began moving toward the border about a week later. The smooth efficiency of the government's arrangements for the march had clearly taken months of planning. More than 3,000 trucks and hundreds of support personnel, including doctors and nurses, were part of the enthusiastic march.

The Moroccans crossed the border at two points in early November. Spanish troops retired to positions well inside the border, behind mine fields. The prospect of firing on unarmed civilians, with its inevitable effect on world opinion, pushed Spain to a diplomatic solution. After negotiations, Spain agreed on November 14 to partition Spanish Sahara, the northern half going to Morocco and the southern to Mauritania. Algeria opposed the partition (see ALGERIA).

Hassan ordered the marchers home on November 19. On November 22, he named the director of the

Spanish Sahara: A Mineral-Rich Prize

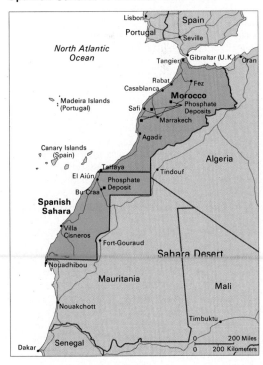

royal Cabinet, Ahmed Bensouda, governor of Morocco's new possession, which Spain was to leave on Feb. 28, 1976. Representatives of the Saharan tribes pledged support to Hassan on November 30.

Domestic Affairs. The Spanish Sahara issue increased Hassan's domestic support. As a result, he eased some political restrictions in Morocco. The Party for Progress and Socialism, organized in 1974 as successor to the banned Moroccan Communist Party and Party for Liberation and Socialism, held its first open party congress on February 21.

In March, Hassan once again delayed the often-postponed Chamber of Representatives elections to await "the return of plundered territories"—the Spanish Sahara and the northern coastal enclaves of Ceuta and Melilla. Some 250 persons jailed for antigovernment activities were released in April.

The Economy. Exploitation of rock-salt deposits near Mohammadia represents a major economic breakthrough for Morocco. The deposits contain reserves of 3.3 billion short tons (3 billion metric tons) of pure sodium chloride. When full production begins, they will earn the country $40 million annually in exports of chlorine, caustic soda, soda ash, and polyvinyl chloride. In March, Morocco increased prices for its phosphates, the major export, with 22 million short tons (20 million metric tons) produced annually. William Spencer

See also AFRICA (Facts in Brief Table).

MOTION PICTURES.

Although movies themselves were not better than ever in 1975, the movie business certainly was. American motion pictures sold well in other countries, while foreign films did unusually well in the United States.

By late fall, 1975, box-office receipts seemed certain to go beyond the $2-billion mark in the United States alone to surpass the previous year's record-breaking $1.9-billion gross. Inflated ticket prices accounted for a good part of the year's increased revenues, of course. Theaters in large cities, such as New York City, asked as much as $4 to $5 for admission to first-run films. But an estimated increase of some 2 million admissions per week over 1974's 21 million weekly average suggested that the gains were in numbers of customers as well as in ticket prices. It was clear that after some 25 years of falling revenues and floundering experiments to entice customers, such as 3-D and Cinerama, the U.S. film industry was thriving once again. For while Americans had not regained the same movie-going habit—before television 80 million people went to the movies each week—the public was attending much-publicized movies in large numbers.

Jaws, an extraordinary blockbuster, was the major movie event in 1975. In a mere four months, the film earned an estimated $150 million at the box office in the United States and Canada alone. It was still doing an impressive business at the end of the year. With the receipts from foreign trade not yet counted in its earnings, *Jaws* had evidently become the top-grossing movie of all time.

Technically intricate and expertly crafted by 27-year-old director Steven Spielberg, *Jaws* concerns a mammoth, man-eating, white shark that has made the shore of a small resort community its feeding grounds. The film touches briefly on the theme of social responsibility, when officials at the resort community attempt to cover up this threat to the town's prosperity. But most of the movie is given over to the thrills and chills of the pursuit of the great white fish by a monomaniacal seaman, who is ultimately killed by it.

Obviously indebted to both Henrik Ibsen's *An Enemy of the People* and Herman Melville's *Moby Dick* for its subject matter, and to Alfred Hitchcock's movies for its surprise and shock techniques, *Jaws* had little to offer viewers in the way of originality. Nor had it much new to tell the motion-picture industry about the formula for success. But *Jaws* did underscore the potency that violence and terror have in attracting audiences to movies.

The greater portion of the top-grossing films of the 1970s held out similar promises to viewers—that they would be treated to blood and gore and to spine-tingling horrors. In 1972, *The Godfather's* explicit imagery of "Mafia"-inspired garrotings and shootings drew record-breaking crowds into movie theaters. In 1974, *The Exorcist's* vision of supernatural possession proved even more tantalizing than did violent death to viewers throughout the world. And through 1974 and 1975, a series of disaster films, such as *Earthquake* and *The Towering Inferno*, made it clear that large-scale disaster had immense appeal to mass audiences.

Star Power? *Jaws* also seemed to confirm the declining power of the star. As had been true of *The Exorcist*, not one of *Jaws'* leading players—neither Richard Dreyfuss, nor Robert Shaw, nor Roy Scheider—was particularly well known. The fact that top-name players in 1975 releases, such as Robert Redford in *The Great Waldo Pepper* and Paul Newman in *The Drowning Pool*, did poorly at the box office made the relative insignificance of the movie star to a film's grosses even more emphatic.

If stars were not significant to *Jaws'* success, its source in a best-selling novel apparently was. At the time of *Jaws'* release, 5.5 million copies of Peter Benchley's thriller were in print. Significantly, *The Godfather* and *The Exorcist* had also been adapted from highly popular works of fiction.

But while adaptation from a successful prior source proved the rule for money-making films during 1975, books were certainly not the only "proven properties" on which successful movies were based. Among the year's top-grossing films were also a number of sequels to popular films of the past. *Funny Lady* continued the life story of comedi-

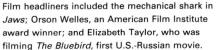

Film headliners included the mechanical shark in *Jaws*; Orson Welles, an American Film Institute award winner; and Elizabeth Taylor, who was filming *The Bluebird*, first U.S.-Russian movie.

enne Fanny Brice, begun with 1969's hugely successful *Funny Girl*. It again starred Barbra Streisand in the leading role. *The Godfather, Part II* added to the saga of the Corleone family first presented in *The Godfather*. Robert de Niro played Don Vito as a young man, and Al Pacino continued in the role of Michael. And *The Return of the Pink Panther* offered a new set of adventures for Peter Sellers as the bumbling Inspector Clouseau.

In addition to these films, other top-grossing movies in 1975 were *Lenny*, adapted from Julian Barry's play and starring Dustin Hoffman as the late Lenny Bruce; Woody Allen's comedy, *Love and Death*; *Murder on the Orient Express*, adapted from Agatha Christie's thriller; and *Shampoo*, starring and coauthored by Warren Beatty. Surprising to many in the industry was the failure of Robert Altman's *Nashville* to be among these top-grossing films. But though it was considered by the overwhelming majority of critics to be the finest American film released in 1975, it had only middling box-office success. More promising financially was another of the year's critical successes, *One Flew Over the Cuckoo's Nest*, adapted from Ken Kesey's novel of the same name and starring Jack Nicholson.

Big Productions. Significantly, as in 1974, the 10 top-grossing 1975 films accounted for somewhere between 40 and 50 per cent of the industry's total box-office gross for the year. This fact, together

with the impressive profits gleaned in both 1974 and 1975, confirmed the financial effectiveness of the pattern of production and distribution that had been asserting itself recently. Instead of diffusing energy, talent, and money among many small productions, the various movie companies tended more and more to concentrate their efforts behind a small number of large productions, spending as much as $4 million on publicity for a potential blockbuster. But while this pattern obviously led to increased profits for producers and distributors, it also created a problem for the thousands of theater owners.

The great cry from exhibitors throughout 1975 was "product shortage." Movie companies simply weren't providing enough films to supply all the theaters. In the first 10 months of 1975, only 128 new films were released, compared with 155 in 1974. And in the 1960s, when movie attendance was considerably lower than it was in 1975, as many as 207 new films were released annually. However, there was some indication that this trend might be reversed; there were 20 per cent more films in production in 1975 than in 1974.

Foreign Films. The year 1975 was the best in recent memory for the foreign-language film market in the United States. Ingmar Bergman's *Scenes from a Marriage* and Federico Fellini's *Amarcord*, each originally released in 1974 and each an award-winning film, did extremely well at the box office. So did the late Vittorio De Sica's *A Brief Vacation*, which grossed well over $1 million.

But *Scenes from a Marriage* and *Amarcord* notwithstanding, the 1975 profits from imports came less from films of aesthetic value than from French pornography such as *Emmanuelle, Exhibition*, and *The Story of O*. Less explicit than American pornography, these imports seemed to owe their success largely to the fact that they were booked into first-run art houses where they gained an aura of respectability and attracted mixed audiences.

It was, perhaps, ironic that the New York Film Festival chose 1975 as the year to include its first hard-core pornographic movie in its program. For 1975 was also the centennial of the birth of D. W. Griffith, the great movie pioneer whose emphatically Victorian sensibility permeated his hundreds of films. But, if the many Griffith retrospectives offered during the year by the American Film Institute and the Museum of Modern Art in New York City made clear the degree to which the movies had changed in their handling of sex and violence, they also showed how unchanged was the art of screen narrative. All the basic principles of this art were discovered and demonstrated by Griffith in the early years of this century.   Joy Gould Boyum

See also AWARDS AND PRIZES (Theater and Motion Picture Awards); BURSTYN, ELLEN; CARNEY, ART; COPPOLA, FRANCIS FORD; ULLMANN, LIV.

MOYNIHAN, DANIEL PATRICK (1927-   ), was confirmed by the Senate on June 9, 1975, as the chief United States representative to the United Nations (UN). An educator and an outspoken authority on the problems of urban minorities, Moynihan has held several federal posts. He served as ambassador to India from 1973 to 1975.

At the UN, Moynihan became an outspoken critic of the majority of underdeveloped nations that regularly vote against the United States. He became so embroiled in controversy that his resignation was rumored in November. But President Gerald R. Ford expressed full confidence in him. See UNITED NATIONS.

Moynihan was born on March 16, 1927, in Tulsa, Okla., but grew up in slum neighborhoods in New York City. A graduate of the Tufts University Fletcher School of Law and Diplomacy, he served on the staff of New York Governor W. Averell Harriman in the late 1950s and under Presidents John F. Kennedy, Lyndon B. Johnson, and Richard M. Nixon. From 1966 to 1969, he directed the Joint Center for Urban Studies at Massachusetts Institute of Technology and Harvard University where he was professor of education and urban politics.

Moynihan married Elizabeth Therese Brennan of Boston in 1955. They have three children. For relaxation, Moynihan enjoys fishing, hiking, and eating gourmet food.   Robert K. Johnson

MOZAMBIQUE. Portuguese colonial rule formally ended and Mozambique became independent on June 25, 1975. Samora Moises Machel, leader of the Mozambique Liberation Front (FRELIMO), the nation's only legal political party, became Mozambique's first president (see MACHEL, SAMORA M.). FRELIMO had waged a guerrilla war against Portugal for 10 years until a new Lisbon government decided in 1974 to liquidate Portugal's African colonial empire.

Marxist State. The new nation's Constitution provides for a 210-member People's Assembly as the supreme policy-making body. However, most observers believed that real power is likely to reside with the Marxist-Socialist FRELIMO leadership.

On July 27, Machel's government closed all private schools, nationalized private health-care facilities, and announced that priority in agriculture would be given to collective farms.

Economic Problems. At the time of independence, agricultural products—sugar, cotton, cashew nuts, and sisal—were Mozambique's main exports. There are coal, bauxite, iron, and other mineral deposits in the north, but they are undeveloped because of a lack of capital and skilled manpower.

The skilled-labor problem grew worse just before independence as whites fled the country. Mozambique's white population, about 200,000 in 1973, accounted for most of the professional and other highly skilled workers. The prospect of black African rule caused most of them to leave the country. By June, 1975, only an estimated 75,000 whites remained. To encourage trained white persons to stay, FRELIMO professed to be nonracial and permitted whites to join the party. Three ministers of the new government were white.

A Difficult Choice faced the government. Should it maintain economic ties with white-ruled Rhodesia and South Africa or break relations? The Rhodesian and South African consulates were closed, but both governments continued to operate trade offices in Lourenço Marques.

Despite FRELIMO's sympathy for black African nationalist movements, there were strong practical reasons for Mozambique not to join in trade embargoes or other economic sanctions against the two neighbors. For example, about 100,000 Mozambicans work in South African mines, and South Africa remits part of their pay to Mozambique in the form of gold. When sold on the free market, the gold earns valuable hard currency for Mozambique. The heavy flow of South African goods through the port of Lourenço Marques and Rhodesian goods through the port of Beira provides jobs for thousands of Mozambicans.

In addition, the vast Cabora Bassa hydroelectric project in northern Mozambique will export most of its power to South Africa.   John D. Esseks

See AFRICA (Facts in Brief Table).

President Samora M. Machel, right, and
Vice-President Marcelino Dos Santos salute
Mozambique's birth as an independent nation.

MULDOON, ROBERT DAVID (1921-   ), became prime minister of New Zealand on Nov. 29,
1975, when his National Party scored a surprising
upset victory over Wallace E. Rowling's Labour
Party. Muldoon announced that he would also
serve as finance minister. See NEW ZEALAND.

Muldoon was born in Auckland on Sept. 25,
1921. He studied accounting while serving as an
infantryman during World War II and took his
final examinations in an army tent in Italy. After
the war, he worked as an accountant and taught
auditing. He was elected to Parliament in 1960
after two earlier unsuccessful campaigns, and
quickly made his mark as one of a group of young
back-benchers who argued as strongly with their
own leadership as with the Labour Party. He became undersecretary of finance in 1964 and minister of tourism and publicity briefly in 1967 before
becoming minister of finance that same year. When
the Labour Party came to power in 1972, he was
deputy leader of the Opposition and took over as
leader in July, 1974.

Muldoon is regarded as an able administrator
and one of New Zealand's most forceful political
leaders. He is noted for his aggressive, abrasive personality and traded punches with hecklers during
his election campaign. In quieter moments, he cul-
tivates lilies. He married Thea Dale Flyger in 1951.
They have three children.   Kathryn Sederberg

MUHAMMED, MURTALA RAMAT (1937-   ),
a 38-year-old brigadier in the Nigerian Army,
became head of the government on July 29, 1975.
Muhammed, who is a member of the Hausa tribe,
succeeded Yakubu Gowon, an Anga tribesman who
was deposed in a bloodless military coup d'état after
a nine-year rule. See NIGERIA.

Muhammed was born in northern Nigeria in
June, 1937. He received his primary and secondary
school education in government schools. He also
attended Ahmadu Bello University in Zaria; Sand-
hurst, Great Britain's Royal Military College; and
Britain's Royal School of Signals.

After completing his studies, Muhammed was
appointed to a Nigerian Army staff position. In
August, 1967, when secessionist Biafran forces had
pushed to within 70 miles (110 kilometers) of
Lagos, Muhammed was given command of a new
army division assigned to reinforce the front. He
received considerable recognition for his leadership
during the war. In April, 1968, he returned to a
staff officer's post as inspector of communications,
with the rank of brigadier. Early in 1975, he was
appointed to a new federal executive council, a position that made him second in command to the
head of state.

Muhammed is a modest man who neither drinks
nor smokes. He is married and lives with his wife
and children on Ikoyi Island.   Paul C. Tullier

MURPHY, BETTY SOUTHARD (1928-   ), a
lawyer, was confirmed by the U.S. Senate as chairman of the National Labor Relations Board
(NLRB) on Feb. 5, 1975. She is the first woman
member of the NLRB. As a lawyer specializing in
labor issues, she served clients from both labor
and management.

Betty Southard Murphy was born on March 1,
1928, in East Orange, N.J., and she grew up in
Atlantic City, N.J. Murphy began her career as a
journalist, not as a lawyer. After studying at Ohio
State University and at the Sorbonne and Alliance
Française in Paris, she worked as a free-lance reporter in Asia, Europe, and the Middle East before
becoming a Washington, D.C., correspondent for
United Press International.

She then decided she would like to cover the Supreme Court of the United States and took law
courses to prepare herself for such an assignment.
However, the law became her primary interest, and
she obtained her degree in 1958.

Murphy then became a staff attorney for the
NLRB, but left in 1959 to join a private firm, where
she established her reputation as a labor law expert.
In July, 1974, President Richard M. Nixon ap-
pointed her head of the U.S. Department of Labor
Wage and Hour Division.

She and her husband, Cornelius, a radiologist,
have two children.   Darlene R. Stille

MUSEUMS

MUSEUMS. The combined effects of inflation and recession forced many museums to curtail services and increase their money-raising efforts in 1975. Operating deficits for museums in New York state totaled $3 million, and endowment values for these museums dropped 30 per cent, according to a report issued in January. To cut costs, the Boston Museum of Fine Arts closed one day each week and raised admission prices. The Metropolitan Museum of Art in New York City temporarily cut its schedule to five days a week in July.

Museum Growth. Expansion in Canadian museums included an astronomical observatory for the National Museum of Science and Technology in Ottawa, Ont., and a $4-million fund drive for additions to the Montreal Museum of Fine Arts. The British government opened its National Railway Museum in York in September to mark the 150th anniversary of British railways.

The American Museum of Atomic Energy in Oak Ridge, Tenn., opened its new $3.6-million building in February. Scottish Rite Masons launched a $6-million Museum of Our National Heritage at Lexington, Mass., on April 20. In New York City, the American Museum of Natural History moved its research collection of vertebrate fossils, 250,000 specimens, into the new 10-story, $4.5-million Charles Frick Wing.

The U.S. Bicentennial. To celebrate 200 years of American independence, city and county taxpayers voted $6 million in bonds to provide a new home for the Charleston (S.C.) Museum, which was established in 1773. The National Portrait Gallery in Washington, D.C., presented a special exhibition brilliantly tracing the steps toward independence from September, 1774, to July, 1776. Another Bicentennial exhibition showed "Paul Revere's Boston: 1735–1818" in that city's Museum of Fine Arts. The Museum of Science and Industry in Chicago began a three-year exhibit and activity program concerning 200 years of "America's Inventive Genius." "The World of Franklin and Jefferson," a major exhibit by American designers Charles and Ray Eames, opened in Paris, then traveled to Warsaw, Poland, and London before its 1976 U.S. tour.

Cultural Exchanges between the United States and Russia brought masterpieces from Leningrad museums for temporary display at the National Gallery of Art, Washington, D.C., and later at galleries in Detroit, Houston, Los Angeles, and New York City. Russia also loaned the Metropolitan Museum of Art in New York City an exhibition of ancient Scythian artifacts from Russian museums. New York City's Museum of Modern Art prepared a loan exhibit for Australian museums. From Paris, the Musée Guimet sent a traveling exhibition of rare Asian art.   Ralph H. Lewis

MUSIC, CLASSICAL. Composers and musical groups all over the United States were preparing in 1975 for the American Revolution Bicentennial. Gian Carlo Menotti was writing an opera for the Philadelphia Lyric Opera and a choral work for the Washington, D.C., Cathedral. Carlisle Floyd was busy with an opera for the Houston Opera. Eleven composers were producing music for the National Symphony Orchestra, Washington, D.C.

The Seattle Symphony programmed 11 compositions by Americans into its 1975-1976 schedule, calling the gesture "Salute to Bicentennial." The Los Angeles Philharmonic was in the midst of "Orchestra America," an opportunity for patrons to hear the music of such U.S. composers as Samuel Barber, Leonard Bernstein, Aaron Copland, George Gershwin, Roy Harris, and Walter Piston. The San Francisco Symphony included the works of a U.S. composer in almost every program.

Probably the most ambitious Bicentennial salute came at the Newport, R.I., Music Festival from July 24 to August 3. In three concerts a day, musicians paid tribute to American composers except for occasional foreign-produced works that have an American theme, such as *Die Amerikanerin*, a cantata by Johann Christoph Friedrich Bach, son of Johann Sebastian Bach. Music performed included Dudley Buck's cantata *The Midnight Ride of Paul Revere* and Julian Edwards' opera *The Patriot*,

The new wing on the Metropolitan Museum of Art in New York City, which opened in May, houses the Lehman Collection.

which deals with an assassination plot against George Washington and how it was foiled by the daughter of a tavernkeeper who substitutes herself for Washington. Ballads and folk songs from the Revolutionary period were programmed, along with music by Cecil Burleigh, John Alden Carpenter, George Chadwick, and others.

Money Woes. All this attention to native-born talent had a heartening tone. But when all the celebrating was done, there remained the danger that many U.S. musical organizations might not be around to see much of the nation's third century.

The National Endowment for the Arts provided $2 million in grants to 27 opera companies, and $4.2 million to 69 orchestras. More than 100 com-

posers received stipends, too. But a depressed stock market limited private and foundation giving, and the increased cost of living held down the public's ability to buy tickets, while inflation ballooned music budgets dangerously.

The nation's "big four" opera companies — the Metropolitan Opera, the New York City Opera, Chicago's Lyric Opera, and the San Francisco Opera — sought at least $15 million in 1975 to pay their bills. The five leading orchestras — Boston, Chicago,

With films behind the performers and transparent images on a screen in front, the New York City Opera's 1975 *Die tote Stadt* is a stunning show.

Cleveland, New York City, and Philadelphia—were searching for another $10 million. As an example, Chicago's Lyric Opera needed $3.2 million in gifts to meet expenses in 1975, despite a 100 per cent ticket sellout.

To trim costs, production schedules and season lengths were cut. The New Jersey Symphony and the Kansas City Philharmonic cut back their schedules. General purpose, unrestricted endowments, raised over the course of nearly a century, were wiped out at the Metropolitan and the Chicago Symphony. The St. Paul Opera canceled its summer season.

Even in Europe, where government subsidies have historically been more generous, the picture was bleak. For instance, London's Royal Opera dipped into 1976 funds to pay for the 1975 season. Italy's opera houses were in a panic.

All this was occurring as the pressure for more music was building. Public-opinion analyst Louis Harris, who was elected chairman of the Associated Councils of the Arts in 1975, urged Congress to increase the arts endowment to about $180 million in fiscal 1977, $210 million in 1978, and $250 million in 1979. Harris said that the arts can no longer "be looked on as a commodity only for a few, as something for highbrows; they are becoming a major part of the mainstream of life, and as the demands for services rise, we must be prepared to meet a flood of demands for the arts. . . . The American people are looking for a quality of experience to fit the quality of life."

Revivals and Premières. A nearly forgotten American opera was revived on Broadway in October. Ragtime-great Scott Joplin's *Treemonisha,* produced by the Houston Opera, brought nightly cheers and frequent standing ovations from New York City audiences. Among the new operas were *Gulliver* by Easley Blackwood, Elliot Kaplan, and Frank Lewin; and Conrad Susa's *Black River,* done by the Minnesota Opera. *Captain Jinks of the Horse Marines* by Jack Beeson was commissioned by the National Endowment for the Arts for the Kansas City Opera. A morality play set to music, *The Last Lover* by Robert Starer, turned up at the Caramoor Festival in New York. Allan Davis' *The Departure,* offered at the University of Montevallo in Alabama, turned out to be a Reconstruction drama involving voodoo and death.

Yvan Semenoff's *Sire Halewyn,* about a Flemish Bluebeard who is finally undone by a young virgin who brings the evil man's head to her father à la *Salome,* was introduced in Brussels, Belgium. The Schwetzingen Festival in West Germany performed Günther Bialas' *Puss in Boots,* an attempt at 12-tone humor that includes a feline concert of falsetto meows. *Gränskibbutzen (The Border Kibbutz)* by Maurice Karkoff premièred in Stockholm, Sweden, while police stood by in case of disturbances; the opera is set in an Israeli air-raid shelter and deals heavily with Middle East politics. Giselher Klebe's *A True Hero,* based on Irish dramatist John Synge's *The Playboy of the Western World,* was heard first in Zurich, Switzerland.

Marxist composer Luigi Nono had La Scala's stage in Milan, Italy, for his *To the Great Sun Charged with Love,* a revolutionary item about the 1871 Commune in Paris done to words by Bertolt Brecht, Maxim Gorki, Karl Marx, Fidel Castro, and Ché Guevara. In one scene, chorus members are strapped to huge rotating planks to express a sort of crucifixion of mankind in the continuing "class struggle."

In the United States, more opera was being done in English. Wagner particularly had an English-language year. The Seattle Opera did two *Ring* cycles, one in German and the other in English. The San Diego Opera performed *The Valkyrie (Die Walküre)* in English. The Kansas City Opera did *The Flying Dutchman.*

Orchestra premières included Cecil Effinger's *Capriccio for Orchestra* and Louis Weingarden's *Piano Concerto* in Denver; *Goerdeler Triptych* by Heuwell Tircuit and Michael Colgrass' *Concertmasters* for three violins and orchestra in Detroit; Paul Chihara's *Symphony in Celebration* in Houston; and *Mississippi Heritage of Folk Songs* by Wil-

Sarah Caldwell makes her conducting debut at the New York Philharmonic on November 10, with a program of works by five women composers.

Beverly Sills, one of America's foremost sopranos, makes her debut at the Met in April, in Rossini's *Siege of Corinth*.

Soprano Beverly Sills made her long-awaited debut at the Metropolitan in April. The Boston Opera's Sarah Caldwell conducted a program of music by women composers in her debut with the New York Philharmonic in November. Lyric soprano Elisabeth Schwarzkopf said farewell to the United States in a cross-country series of packed recitals.

Birgit Nilsson, the famed Wagnerian soprano, cut down her traveling. She canceled U.S. performances after losing an income tax case. The U.S. government reported that she owed nearly $500,000 in back taxes and penalties. Her decision sent such opera houses as the Met and Chicago scurrying for substitutes.

Reinterpretations of opera were numerous. Donizetti's *Elixir of Love*, done in Jackson, Miss., by Opera/South, had its scene switched to a delta town, and the characters turned into a schoolteacher, a local cotton planter, and a patent-medicine man. The locale of Verdi's *A Masked Ball* in a Madison, Wis., production was changed to a pre-World War I Balkan nation, and, in Berlin, the same opera was transplanted to a New Orleans ruled by a dictator. Ulrica, the sorceress, sang voodoo on the old plantation. La Scala's *Siegfried* delved into contemporary politics. The hero was a brown-shirted, leather-clad Hitler youth, Mime's cave was a modern foundry, and the dragon was personified by a Mafia gang.   Peter P. Jacobi

liam Presser in Jackson, Miss. Dominick Argento's *From the Diary of Virginia Woolf*, which won the 1975 Pulitzer Prize for music, and Eric Stokes' *The Continental Harp and Band Report* were performed by the Minnesota Symphony; Roger Dickerson's *Orpheus* in New Orleans; and Barbara Kolb's *Soundings* and Carman Moore's *Wild Fires and Field Songs* in New York City.

First heard in Pittsburgh were George Rochberg's *Concerto* for violin and orchestra, Ezra Laderman's *Celestial Bodies*, and *Air Music* by Ned Rorem. Gyorgy Ligeti's *San Francisco Polyphony* and Carman Moore's *Gospel Fuse* were performed in San Francisco; Elie Siegmeister's *Shadows and Light* in Shreveport, La.; *Choreographie* by André Prevost in Toronto, Canada; and Henri Lazarof's *Spectrum for Trumpet and Orchestra* by the Utah Symphony. Antal Dorati's *Piano Concerto* was performed by the National Symphony in Washington, D.C., and Alan Hovhaness' *Cello Concerto* by the Western Symphony in Washington state.

Changes and Debuts. Schuyler Chapin was replaced as general manager of the Metropolitan Opera by attorney Anthony A. Bliss, who became executive director, and conductor James Levine, who became music director. Seiji Ozawa resigned as head of the San Francisco Symphony. Toronto got Andrew Davis as its music director, and St. Louis welcomed George Semkow.

MUSIC, POPULAR. The discothèque returned as an important medium of exposure for popular music in many United States cities in 1975. The "discos" played mainly black soul music, designed for dancing. The music is strongly dominated by bass and drum rhythms, and the records usually last five minutes, almost twice as long as regular jukebox records. This was the second time around for the discothèque in the United States, but this time it was on a much more influential scale than during its previous wave of popularity in the 1960s. Discothèques became showcases for Gloria Gaynor, billed as the "Queen of Disco," Barry White, Van McCoy, and many other performers. The success of the music in discothèques forced radio stations to program records in this style.

The Superstars. The most popular new artist was singer-composer-guitarist Bruce Springsteen. For most of his 26 years, Springsteen lived in obscurity and poverty in the New Jersey towns of Freehold and Asbury Park. Then he was discovered by John Hammond of Columbia Records, who also launched the recording career of Bob Dylan. Springsteen already had two albums out, which had attracted only moderate attention, when his third album, "Born to Run," became a million-dollar gold album six weeks after its release.

Accompanied by his E Street Band, Springsteen let go wildly in his songs and monologues. His

Olivia Newton-John, *left,* and Stevie Wonder
shared plaudits in 1975 as two of the most
successful stars in American popular music.

moods varied from raucous and brazen to simple and poignant. Critics compared him to Dylan, Elvis Presley, and Buddy Holly, and admired his songs about alienation, hot-rodders, mysterious women, and lonely men. They claimed he brought back to rock some of the power it had in the 1960s.

The superstar stature of Elton John, established in 1974, was reaffirmed when he became the first pop star to fill Dodger Stadium in Los Angeles since the Beatles' one-night stand in 1966. John played there for two nights at the end of October.

Stevie Wonder, the most widely honored recording star of the 1970s, became the most successful in the history of commercial recording in 1975. Motown Records offered the 26-year-old singer-songwriter-producer a record-breaking guarantee of $13 million over seven years.

Music on Film. A significant movement was the large number of musical subjects filmed or prepared for filming as major motion-picture features. *Nashville* received critical acclaim. *Lisztomania* appealed to the youth-rock market. *Tommy* was a movie version of the rock opera, which had originally been produced as a record album.

In production or planning late in 1975 were movies about singer Buddy Holly, ragtime composer Scott Joplin, folksingers Huddie (Leadbelly) Ledbetter and Woody Guthrie, pop hero Nat (King) Cole, and blues queen Bessie Smith. Robbie

Benson was set to play the title role in *Ode to Billie Joe,* based on Bobbie Gentry's hit song, and Barbra Streisand was to star with Kris Kristofferson in a new version of *A Star Is Born.*

New Directions. While modern musicians and their songs dominated the scene, several old song hits—most of them from the 1930s and 1940s—enjoyed new fame in contemporary versions. Art Garfunkel rode high with "I Only Have Eyes For You." The Ritchie Family had similar success with "The Peanut Vendor" and "Brazil," Deodato with "Caravan," and Freddy Fender with "Secret Love." Fender, along with Johnny Rodriguez and several others, illustrated a new trend—Chicano country music—featuring country-style vocals in both English and Spanish.

Natalie Cole, 25-year-old daughter of the late Nat, gained national recognition as a strong rhythm-and-blues-oriented singer with her first album, "Inseparable." "This Will Be," a tune from her album, rose to the number-one spot on the soul-record charts.

For the first time, black American singers enjoyed great popularity in South Africa. Playing for white, black, and occasionally integrated audiences, they were welcomed with minimal racial problems. Among them were singer Lovelace Watkins, with a band led by Monk Montgomery; Della Reese; the Supremes; and the Drifters.

Another new direction was the "progressive-country" trend, represented by such rebel artists as Waylon Jennings, Willie Nelson, and Jessi Colter.

The Jazz Scene. Musicians and others interested in jazz founded the World Jazz Association in Los Angeles. Its objectives were to persuade the media to give more coverage to jazz, and to offer its members reduced prices for records and concert tickets. The association soon affiliated with other organizations such as the new Las Vegas Jazz Society.

Lonnie Liston Smith, a pianist and composer, rose to prominence with a cool, undulating style of abstract music that he described as "cosmic funk." Composer Quincy Jones, back in action after serious brain surgery, toured successfully in Japan and the United States. His "Body Heat" and "Mellow Madness," both skillfully mixing soul, rock, and jazz elements, were among the year's biggest-selling albums by a jazz-associated star. Also prominent were flutist Hubert Laws, with a classically influenced jazz style, and his brother, saxophonist Ronnie Laws, with a semirock style. Following the soul-jazz trend, saxophonists Grover Washington, Jr., Stanley Turrentine, and Eddie Harris reached new crests of acceptance, as did pianists Keith Jarrett and Chick Corea.   Leonard Feather

See also AWARDS AND PRIZES (Arts Awards); RECORDINGS.

NAMIBIA. See AFRICA.

NASH, JOYCE (1935-   ), was chosen the first woman president of the New Democratic Party (NDP), Canada's third largest party, in July, 1975. She succeeded Donald MacDonald, who held the post for four years. At the same meeting, Edward Broadbent, who had been the NDP's parliamentary leader, was elected national head of the party.

Nash was born in North Battlefield, Sask., and moved to British Columbia when she was 2. She has been an active party organizer for 20 years, and is known as a quiet, capable, energetic campaign organizer. As a member of the governing council since 1969 and an NDP vice-president since 1971, she has been involved in financial and organizational matters rather than policy issues.

She has been campaign manager for the federal and provincial constituencies in the Nanaimo area since 1962. She also has been serving as temporary secretary of the British Columbia NDP while on leave from her job as constituency representative for Parliament member Thomas C. Douglas.

Nash lives in Nanaimo with her husband, George, a real estate salesman. They have two grown children. She is an avid reader and swimmer and likes to knit, crochet, and cook. Kathryn Sederberg

NATIONAL DEFENSE. See ARMED FORCES.

NATIONALIST CHINA. See TAIWAN.

NAVY. See ARMED FORCES.

NEBRASKA. See STATE GOVERNMENT.

NEPAL. Birendra Bir Bikram Shah Dev was at last crowned king on Feb. 24, 1975, some 37 months after he ascended the throne. The date had been picked in 1974 by royal astrologers. But the coronation pageantry also served to bolster the monarchy at a difficult time, after the government's relations with India had reached a breaking point. Anti-Indian riots occurred in Nepal in September, 1974, following India's annexation of Sikkim.

In April, 1975, Nepal's Prime Minister Nagendra Prasad Rijal, a major landowner, formed a pro-Indian government. Nepal needs friendly relations with India because 90 per cent of its 1974 trade was with this neighbor to the south. When an accord was reached in August, India insisted that Nepal pay for coal, iron, oil, and steel not in rupees – the usual medium – but in silver and gold, of which Nepal's reserves had dropped to just $60 million by October. In December, Rijal was replaced by the king's aide, Tulsi Giri.

Nepal's survival between India and China remained the overriding problem. The government removed one irritant early in 1975, when its troops drove the Khampas, anti-China Tibetan guerrillas, out of the Himalayan passes. China responded on February 2 by granting $80 million for a 244-mile (393-kilometer) highway, and promising aid for Nepal's new five-year plan.   Mark Gayn

See also ASIA (Facts in Brief Table).

NETHERLANDS. Queen Juliana announced plans to cut defense spending in her speech from the throne on Sept. 16, 1975. She said the Netherlands would withdraw a guided missile cruiser from the North Atlantic Treaty Organization (NATO) force in October, two years earlier than planned. In January, 1976, 15 Neptune long-distance patrol aircraft assigned to NATO were to be grounded. But the government canceled the plans in October in response to strong NATO protests. On May 27, with Belgium, Denmark, and Norway, the government agreed to buy U.S.-built F-16 jet fighter aircraft. See ARMED FORCES.

Economic Recovery Plan. On September 16, the government proposed a 1976 budget that would continue economic stimulation and curb unemployment. The proposals called for subsidies for employers' social security payments and financing of projects to stimulate the construction industry, where unemployment was highest. A rise in the value-added tax from 16 to 18 per cent was postponed until July 1, 1976, in a bid to stimulate consumer demand. The measures will cost the Netherlands about $1.16 billion and raise the expected 1976 deficit to nearly $5.5 billion.

More than 5 per cent of the work force was unemployed because the Netherlands' six most important trading partners cut back Dutch imports almost 10 per cent in the first six months of 1975. The government approved a plan on August 28 to raise its share of ownership in the Royal Dutch Airlines (KLM) from 70 to 78 per cent. The airline was in financial difficulty.

War on Automobiles. The government intensified its war on the use of private automobiles in towns and cities on September 16. It raised the yearly tax on large private vehicles to almost $700. "A multiyear plan for passenger transportation will be presented soon," Queen Juliana told parliament.

Barges' Blockade. About 1,000 freight barges blockaded the Rhine River and entrances to major ports, including Rotterdam, the world's largest port, on August 25. The barge owners were protesting proposed legislation that would put many of the barges out of business. The blockade ended on August 28 when the government threatened to bring in the navy and parliament killed the legislation.

The government granted independence on November 25 to Surinam, a South American territory ruled by the Netherlands for more than 300 years. See SURINAM. Kenneth Brown

See also EUROPE (Facts in Brief Table).

NEVADA. See STATE GOVERNMENT.

NEW BRUNSWICK. See CANADA.

NEW GUINEA. See PACIFIC ISLANDS.

NEW HAMPSHIRE. See STATE GOVERNMENT.

NEW JERSEY. See NEWARK; STATE GOVERNMENT.

NEW MEXICO. See STATE GOVERNMENT.

NEW ORLEANS. A nationwide investigation of crime in the grain-export business centered on New Orleans, the world's largest grain port, in 1975. It resulted in 57 indictments against grain companies and their employees on charges of conspiracy, bribery, theft, and income tax evasion. Twenty-two indictments, handed down on August 7, involved a case in which more than $1 million in grain was stolen, sometimes by the barge load, in New Orleans between 1971 and 1975. By October, 47 corporations and individuals had either been convicted or had pleaded guilty.

New Orleans longshoremen tried in 1975 to stop loading grain on ships bound for Russia to protest the sale of U.S. grain. The work stoppage was halted by a federal court order on September 5.

Financial Affairs. New Orleans faced an $11.5-million budget deficit during 1975. Mayor Moon Landrieu blamed the fund shortage on an inadequate tax base rather than on excessive pay demands by municipal employees. Mayor Landrieu, who served as president of the U.S. Conference of Mayors during the year, led the nation's mayors in their effort to win greater federal aid for cities, specifically for beleaguered New York City. See CITY; NEW YORK CITY.

New Orleans received $14.8 million in federal aid under the 1974 Housing and Community Development Act. The city developed a two-part program for distributing the funds to needy neighborhoods. The first step was the development of an urban blight index for ranking neighborhoods on the basis of need. The second step involved extensive city-wide and neighborhood hearings at which programs were explained. Money was ultimately allocated for projects involving recreation, housing rehabilitation, neighborhood health clinics, garbage removal, and street improvement.

An 80-day strike of the city's bus and streetcar drivers ended on March 7. The settlement called for most disputes to be submitted to arbitration.

Superdome Opens. After extensive delays, New Orleans' new Superdome, built on 52 acres (21 hectares) near the central business district, opened to the public on August 3. Its first exhibition football game was played on August 9.

The Economy. Unemployment in the New Orleans area stood at 8.1 per cent by mid-1975, up 1 per cent from mid-1974. The average annual earnings of a factory worker in the area reached $10,034 by midyear, an increase of only 5.3 per cent over 1974. Department store sales rose 12.4 per cent, and construction activity fell 4.7 per cent between mid-1974 and mid-1975. The pump price of regular gasoline reached 56.9 cents per gallon (3.8 liters) in June, up 4.2 cents since January 1. James M. Banovetz

NEW YORK. See NEW YORK CITY; STATE GOV'T.

The massive $163-million Superdome covers 52 acres (21 hectares) in New Orleans. The big arena opened in August with a football game.

NEW YORK CITY, weighted down by billions of dollars in debts, narrowly missed bankruptcy on four occasions in 1975. Banks refused to help the city refinance its debts. The city finally avoided insolvency on November 26, when President Gerald R. Ford agreed to allow federal aid. Ford's action came a day after the New York state assembly had approved $200 million in tax increases for New York City as part of a complex $6.6-billion financing plan for the city. Congress approved, and on December 9 President Ford signed, the New York City Seasonal Financing Act of 1975. Funds were appropriated on December 18.

The federal act authorized $2.3 billion a year in short-term federal loans to the city through June, 1978. Each loan, which would have to be paid back within a year, would have an interest rate 1 percentage point higher than the U.S. Treasury borrowing rate. The secretary of the treasury may refuse to make the loans if prospects for repayment are inadequate. He may also withhold federal-aid payments if the city does not repay on time.

The Fiscal Crisis had been building for years as New York City's spending increasingly exceeded its income from taxes and other revenue. Economists and government officials blamed the general economic recession, heavy welfare costs, a shrinking city tax base, financial mismanagement, and the demands of municipal employee unions.

The city's first bankruptcy threat was forestalled on June 10, when the state assembly set up the Municipal Assistance Corporation (MAC) to market bonds that would refinance $3 billion worth of short-term city debts. New York City pledged almost $1 billion a year from its sales and stock-transfer taxes as security for the bonds. The city also had to turn over partial control of its budget to MAC, which placed a ceiling on city borrowing.

However, in August, investors refused to purchase any more MAC bonds, and in September, New York was again on the verge of bankruptcy. Leaders of four municipal unions used $100 million from their pension funds to buy MAC bonds, thus helping the city meet its September 6 bills. On September 9, the state assembly approved a $2.3-billion financial-aid plan. The measure also set up an Emergency Financial Control Board, which assumed complete control over all city revenue. In October, the board called for drastic cuts in the city budget, which meant cutbacks in city services.

Default again threatened the city on October 17, but was avoided when the teachers' union agreed to use $150 million from its pension fund to buy MAC bonds. Finally, a December default was avoided when President Ford agreed to federal assistance.

City Employee Cutbacks. There was a confusing series of layoffs and rehirings of city employees. In an effort to forestall the crisis, Mayor Abraham D. Beame announced on January 15 that 4,050 city

Mayor Abraham Beame, right, greets City Council members before a speech calling for budget cuts that would cost 40,000 their city jobs.

employees would be laid off. However, most of the layoffs were averted on February 1, when unions agreed to forego some benefits. Another 19,000 jobs were eliminated on July 1, when the mayor's $12.08-billion "crisis budget" went into effect. The mayor's austerity plan called for the eventual elimination of 40,000 city jobs.

From July 1 to 3, city garbage collectors staged a wildcat strike to protest layoffs in the Sanitation Department. Police and firemen also protested. On July 3, the city agreed to rehire more than 5,000 employees. On July 31, labor leaders representing more than half of the city's employees agreed to wage freezes. But, despite the crisis, New York City's public-school teachers defied a court order and went on strike on September 9. Although they claimed wages were not an issue, the settlement reached on September 16 called for pay increases of up to $1,500 a year.

Terms for Federal Aid. President Ford was at first strongly opposed to federal aid for the city. The President agreed to grant federal aid only after the state assembly enacted city tax increases on November 25, including an average 25 per cent increase in the city's personal income tax.

Eleven persons were killed and more than 70 injured on December 29, when a bomb exploded in the luggage-claim area of New York City's La Guardia Airport.   James M. Banovetz

NEW ZEALAND. In a surprising upset, the National Party under Robert D. Muldoon defeated Prime Minister Wallace E. Rowling's Labour government in elections on Nov. 29, 1975. The upset climaxed a year of economic uncertainty and acrimonious political debate. The political controversy revolved around the performances of Muldoon and Rowling, the role of the Security Intelligence Service, the availability of abortions, and questions of Maori land rights. See MULDOON, ROBERT D.

The economy was under constant discussion throughout the year. Although the inflation rate was relatively low – 12.6 per cent in May and 14.9 per cent in July – and unemployment was less than 1 per cent of the labor force, the country faced balance-of-payments difficulties, which it avoided only by overseas borrowing. The Reserve Bank reported in July that annual export revenues were down 5 per cent, while the cost of imports rose 28 per cent.

The Drop in Exports was caused largely by a decline in demand for meat and wool. Butter, forest products, and manufactured exports all increased. New Zealand showed great energy in finding new markets for its exports. The chairman of the Dairy Board announced in May that 67 per cent of dairy earnings were coming from markets other than Great Britain, compared with 37 per cent in 1970. Trade missions and other means were used to diversify export sales. New Zealand signed contracts with Russia, Japan, China, West Germany, and several nations in the Middle East.

Yet New Zealand was still concerned about the British market, especially when Britain renegotiated the terms of its membership in the European Community (Common Market). Government and opposition parties united in demanding long-term access to the British market. A Common Market summit meeting decided in March that New Zealand would not be deprived of essential markets for butter, and that under certain circumstances, cheese would be allowed into Britain after 1977.

There was some disagreement with Australia about terms of the New Zealand-Australia Free Trade Agreement, especially regarding free entry into Australia for New Zealand carpets, cheese, and clothes driers, but a compromise was worked out. New Zealand's balance of payments proved so shaky, however, that the government devalued the New Zealand dollar 15 per cent on August 10. This increased farm income from exports.

Foreign Affairs. The Rowling government pursued a course of sympathy with developing countries, especially the Pacific Islands. It persisted in trying to establish a nuclear-free zone in the Pacific Ocean. In August, New Zealand announced that it would withdraw its troops from Singapore in the next two years. J. D. B. Miller

See also ASIA (Facts in Brief Table).

NEWARK. Budget crises plagued city officials during 1975. On January 16, Mayor Kenneth A. Gibson announced that 370 employees would be laid off to reduce an anticipated 1975 budget deficit of $35.7 million. An additional 348 employees were dismissed on March 17. The city council adopted a $252-million city budget for 1975 on March 31. The city increased the property tax and called for the elimination of an additional 600 city workers.

The school board announced on April 30 that an anticipated $14-million school deficit would force the firing of 900 teachers and 700 other school-system employees. The board also planned to eliminate most athletic, music, business education, and industrial arts programs. This sparked a seven-day student boycott, which ended on May 19, when the board promised to find another solution.

In August, 44,200 persons were receiving unemployment insurance payments in Newark, an increase of 29.6 per cent over the previous year. The unemployment rate was 10.8 per cent. The cost of living in the northeastern New Jersey area rose 6.7 per cent between August, 1974, and August, 1975, but the average income of factory workers increased 7.6 per cent during the same period. A U.S. Census Bureau report issued in June estimated Newark's population as of July 1, 1973, at 367,683, a drop of 3.7 per cent since 1970. James M. Banovetz

NEWFOUNDLAND. See CANADA.

NEWSPAPER. Labor problems, tied in with economic problems, were an important factor in the newspaper industry throughout the world in 1975. In the United States, the *Washington Post* was temporarily forced to shut down in October when pressmen went out on strike. Vandalism in the pressroom caused electrical and mechanical damage that put all of the *Post*'s 72 printing units out of operation. The *Post* was published temporarily on other presses until its own were repaired. Publisher Katharine Graham hinted in November that the newspaper may never settle with the striking pressmen. Strikes also occurred in several other cities.

International Troubles. The French press faced a crisis in May when all Paris papers were struck for 24 hours in support of a walkout at the tabloid *Le Parisien Libere.* The strike was merely a symptom of deeper turmoil in an industry faced with rising labor, paper, and printing costs. The provinces responded with increasing newspaper mergers. And in Paris, publication of *Le Figaro* was suspended for 24 hours in July as journalists protested the sale of the paper.

Drastic economy efforts swept newspapers in Great Britain. *The Observer, The Financial Times, The Daily Mirror, The Evening News,* and *Sunday People* made plans to cut labor costs and introduce computer technology. *The Daily Telegraph,* one of Britain's most successful newspapers, announced plans in September to cut its production staff by more than one-third to fight rising costs.

A national postal workers' strike in Canada cut off the printing of newspaper mail editions in October. Newspaper syndicates distributing comics, features, and columns called upon emergency air, railroad, and truck services to deliver their materials.

Total Daily Circulation of U.S. newspapers dipped close to the 60 million mark, after a record high of 63 million in the late 1960s and early 1970s. Circulation price increases produced some losses. Many newspapers eliminated costly distribution by truck to distant points. Increases in second-class mail rates also caused some newspapers to drop subscribers. There were 1,789 dailies in the United States – 340 morning papers and 1,449 evening.

New Technology. A prototype ink-jet plateless printing press was shown at a newspaper production conference in Houston in June. Although not yet ready for commercial use, the new system would allow production of custom-tailored area editions without stopping the press.

The Wall Street Journal in November became the first newspaper to use satellite transmission in its printing process when it began sending full pages from its printing plant in Chicopee Falls, Mass., to a new facility in Orlando, Fla.   Gerald B. Healey

NICARAGUA. See LATIN AMERICA.

NIGER. See AFRICA.

NIGERIA. President Yakubu Gowon was forced from office by junior military officers in a bloodless coup on July 29, 1975. At the time, he was in Uganda, representing Nigeria at a summit meeting of the Organization of African Unity.

The deposed leaders were not arrested, but "retired." In addition to Gowon, they included all officers of major-general rank or higher. Almost 8,000 civil servants were also dismissed.

Brigadier Murtala Ramat Muhammed became the new chief of state. Muhammed, a Moslem, belongs to the Hausa, a northern tribe. Some observers believed that he might arouse strong opposition in Nigeria's southern states, which have traditionally feared domination by the Moslem north. See MUHAMMED, MURTALA RAMAT.

Redressing Grievances. The new government redressed an important southern grievance by nullifying the 1973 census and retaining the 1963 count as the basis for such official purposes as distributing development funds. Many Nigerians believed that the tabulations in both censuses had been manipulated to the north's political advantage, but the 1973 count gave the north a much larger edge.

In October, Muhammed announced plans to transfer power to an elected government by October, 1979, and appointed a constitutional drafting committee. The delay in returning Nigeria to civilian rule was an important grievance that made the Gowon administration vulnerable to a coup. Muhammed announced that a constituent assembly, partly elected and partly appointed, would convene in 1978, and that the ban on party politics would be lifted in October, 1978, in preparation for the election of federal and state legislatures.

Soaring Inflation, fed in 1975 by large wage increases, was another cause of discontent with the Gowon government. After a two-year wage freeze, public employees received raises in January of up to 130 per cent.

Gowon's government had moved to dampen inflationary pressures by buying more foreign goods. Nigeria's large earnings from oil exports could support higher levels of imports, but its port facilities were unable to cope with the increased flow of goods. By October, more than 300 ships – most of them carrying cement – were awaiting berths at Apapa, the port of Lagos. The congestion threatened to obstruct fulfillment of the country's Third Five-Year National Development Plan.

The main source of development funds is Nigeria's oil industry, which became the world's seventh most important supplier in 1974. In early 1975, Nigeria's known oil reserves were estimated to be capable of sustaining the 1974 production level for more than 40 years.   John D. Esseks

See also AFRICA (Facts in Brief Table).

Murtala Ramat Muhammed, left, Nigeria's new head of state, listens while the armed forces chief of staff speaks to reporters in Lagos.

NIXON, RICHARD MILHOUS (1913-   ), the first President of the United States to resign from office, re-emerged into public view in 1975. But the Watergate scandal that drove him from office in August, 1974, still shadowed his life. Throughout 1975, Nixon tried unsuccessfully to gain possession of the controversial tapes and documents that recorded his years in the White House and, allegedly, his involvement in the Watergate affair.

Tape Custody Fight. United States District Court Judge Charles R. Richey ruled on January 31 that the documents and tapes were government property. But in a deposition given in July, Nixon declared that only he had the right to decide what sections of his papers and tapes should be made public. The deposition was for a suit he had brought in 1974, claiming that a law giving the federal government custody of his papers was unconstitutional. The Department of Justice released a brief on September 8 contending that he might tamper with the material. The suit was still pending at the end of the year. See WATERGATE.

Presidential Memories. Nixon claimed he wanted the files of his years in the White House to help in writing his memoirs. Warner Paperback Library bought the rights to the memoirs in late 1974 for a rumored advance of $175,000.

On August 9, Nixon agreed to a series of televised interviews with television personality David Frost for an undisclosed amount. The series will be presented as four 90-minute programs sometime after the November, 1976, elections.

Continuing Investigations. Nixon testified in San Clemente, Calif., before two grand jury members on June 23 and 24 about the Watergate affair. The contents of the statement were not made public, but on September 20, Nixon's attorney revealed that the former President had denied under oath any responsibility for the 18½-minute gap in conversation on one of the White House tapes.

In August, the Senate Select Committee on Intelligence asked for some Nixon documents. The committee was investigating the Administration's role in Central Intelligence Agency activities in Chile. On September 4, presidential counsel Philip W. Buchen announced that the subpoenaed papers would be released to the committee.

Out of Seclusion. As Nixon's health improved, he began to appear in public more frequently. On October 9, he took part in a Teamsters Union golf tournament in California.

In August, Nixon invited former White House photographer Oliver (Ollie) Atkins to San Clemente to take pictures. The photographs showed a smiling Nixon busy composing his memoirs, relaxing at the piano, and walking with his wife, Pat, outside their San Clemente villa.   Carol L. Thompson

David Frost and Richard M. Nixon discuss their agreement to tape the former President's memoirs for worldwide showing on television.

NOBEL PRIZES in peace, literature, economics, and science were presented in 1975. However, the Russian government refused to allow Andrei D. Sakharov, the first Russian to win the prize for peace, to attend the formal presentation ceremony in Oslo, Norway. Sakharov's troubles with his government recalled similar difficulties faced by Alexander I. Solzhenitsyn, who won the Nobel Prize for Literature in 1970, and Boris L. Pasternak, who received the literature award in 1958.

Peace Prize was given to Russian physicist Andrei D. Sakharov, 54, one of the developers of the Russian hydrogen bomb and a long-time campaigner against nuclear tests and the Cold War arms race. He is one of Russia's most outspoken supporters of civil liberties. His views have incurred the hostility of authorities in the Soviet Union. "Andrei Dmitriyevich Sakharov has addressed his message of peace and justice to all peoples of the world," the Nobel committee said. "For him it is a fundamental principle that world peace can have no lasting value unless it is founded on respect for the individual human being in society."

Literature Prize was awarded to Eugenio Montale, 79, an Italian poet, for his interpretation of human values under "an outlook on life with no illusions." Literary and music critic for the Milan newspaper *Corriere della Sera*, Montale published his first volume of poems *Bones of the Cuttlefish* in

Because her husband was not allowed to leave Russia, Mrs. Andrei Sakharov, left, accepts his peace prize at Nobel ceremonies in Oslo.

1925. His other books include *The Occasions* (1939), *The Storms and Other Things* (1956), *Satura* (1962), and *Diario del '71 e del '72* (1973). The award committee said each volume strengthened his position as a major poet, and his books have "continued to capture the interest of young people in Italy and abroad."

Economic Science Prize was shared by two specialists in *econometrics* (the branch of economics that uses statistical methods to treat economic relationships), one a Russian and the other a Dutch-born American. Leonid V. Kantorovich, 63, of Moscow, and Tjalling C. Koopmans, 65, of Yale University, were cited "for their contributions to the theory of optimum allocation of resources." Kantorovich, whose work was downgraded during the rule of Joseph Stalin, proposed a novel mathematical technique to improve central planning in Russia shortly before World War II.

Chemistry Prize was jointly awarded to John W. Cornforth, 58, of the University of Sussex in England, and Vladimer Prelog, 69, of the Federal Technical University in Zurich, Switzerland, for their work in stereochemistry. Both have spent a lifetime studying the build-up, breakdown, and architecture of complex biological molecules, such as cholesterol and the antibiotics. Cornforth was born in Australia and studied at Oxford University in England. Prelog was born in Yugoslavia and is now a citizen of Switzerland. He developed the system for determining D- and L-isomerism in molecules (the right- or left-handedness of certain compounds with the same chemical formulas).

Physics Prize went to one American and two Danish physicists "for the discovery of the connection between collective motion and particle motion in atomic nuclei and the development of the theory of the structure of the atomic nucleus based on this connection." The winners are James Rainwater, 58, of Columbia University; Aage N. Bohr, 53, of the Institute for Theoretical Physics in Copenhagen, Denmark; and Ben Mottelson, 49, of the Nordic Institute of Technology, also in Copenhagen. Bohr's father, Neils Bohr, won the Nobel physics prize in 1922 for studying the structure of atoms and their radiations.

Physiology and Medicine Prize went to three Americans who discovered how viruses can cause malignant tumors in humans. They are David Baltimore, 37, professor of microbiology at the Center for Cancer Research of the Massachusetts Institute of Technology; Renato Dulbecco, 61, Italian-born biologist now with the Imperial Cancer Research Fund Laboratory in London; and Howard M. Temin, 41, professor of *oncology* (tumor research) at the University of Wisconsin's McArdle Memorial Laboratory. They were honored for discoveries concerning the interaction between tumor viruses and the genetic material of the cell. Foster Stockwell

403

NORDLI, ODVAR (1927-   ), an accountant and parliamentary leader of Norway's Labor Party, was unanimously appointed by the party's National Executive Committee on Sept. 25, 1975, to succeed Trygve Bratteli as prime minister. Bratteli had announced his intention to resign in January, 1976. Nordli said he would continue Bratteli's policies, especially in pursuing measures to stimulate the economy and boost employment. See NORWAY.

Nordli was born on Nov. 3, 1927, in Stange in Hedmark County. He completed his education after World War II and served in municipal and county auditing offices until he became district auditor for Hedmark County in 1957.

He was vice-mayor of the Stange Municipal Council from 1951 to 1963 and an alternate member of the *Storting* (parliament) from 1954 to 1961, when he became a full member. In parliament, he served on or chaired committees dealing with municipal and social affairs. He has also held numerous party posts.

In March, 1971, he became minister of labor and municipal affairs in Bratteli's first government, which resigned in October, 1972.   Robert K. Johnson

NORTH ATLANTIC TREATY ORGANIZATION (NATO). See EUROPE.

NORTH CAROLINA. See STATE GOVERNMENT.

NORTH DAKOTA. See STATE GOVERNMENT.

NORTHERN IRELAND continued a vain search for some degree of reconciliation between its warring Roman Catholic and Protestant communities in 1975. The British government spent the year clinging to a cease-fire with the Irish Republican Army (IRA), while keeping Ulster's politicians at arm's length in the hope that the two sides would agree to a power-sharing formula if left to their own devices.

The year finished with both strategies in shambles. The cease-fire had been exposed as a sham, with a summer of sectarian murders and revenge killings in Belfast followed by an autumn of terror in London. Meanwhile, hopes of any political progress were crushed when a Protestant loyalist-dominated constitutional convention rejected sharing power with Catholics.

Constitutional Convention. The three Protestant parties of the United Ulster Unionist Council took 46 of the 78 seats in a May 1 election for a constitutional convention to decide the future government of the province. The loyalists offered the Catholic Social Democratic and Labour Party (SDLP) a two-tier system of government, in which the SDLP would have a major role in the second tier of all-party committees. But the SDLP would settle for nothing less than full power sharing at the executive level.

Wary British soldiers patrol Belfast streets in August as rallies are held on the fourth anniversary of imprisonment without trial.

In November, the loyalists pushed through a report recommending what amounted to a return to old-style Protestant supremacy, with the resurrection of a Stormont parliament resembling the one that was dissolved in 1972. The report obviously did not meet Britain's criterion of finding a solution acceptable to both Protestants and Catholics. But Merlyn Rees, Britain's secretary of state for Ulster, was left with a dilemma. His latest initiative, the convention, had failed, and there was a complete policy vacuum in London about what to do next.

Cease-Fire Fails. Rees's hopes of a truce with the IRA were also squashed. After hectic negotiations between government officials and Sinn Féin, the IRA political wing, the 1974 Christmas cease-fire was extended indefinitely on Feb. 10, 1975. Loyalist politicians accused Rees of making a deal with terrorists and argued that the IRA would use the cease-fire as an opportunity to regroup and rearm.

Unfortunately, the cease-fire proved to be a sham and, by summer, shootings and bombings escalated again. The violence worsened when an internal feud broke out within the IRA in the autumn. Nevertheless, by early December, Rees had kept his promise to release all IRA terrorists detained without trial, thus removing a major propaganda weapon from the IRA. On the other hand, a number of known gunmen were once again free.   Andrew F. Neil

See also EUROPE (Facts in Brief Table).

King Olav V of Norway holds a bouquet as he reaches to shake hands with a boy outside a Norwegian Lutheran Church in Chicago in October.

NORWAY. Prime Minister Trygve Bratteli announced on Sept. 25, 1975, that he would resign in January, 1976. His successor was to be the ruling Labor Party's parliamentary leader, Odvar Nordli. The move followed a weakening of support for the party. In municipal elections held on September 14 and 15, the Conservative Party gained from 3.5 per cent to 21.4 per cent of the votes compared with 1971 results, and Labor lost 3.4 per cent to 38.2 per cent, its worst showing in 30 years. The Socialist Left Party, an association of several left wing parties, was the big loser, getting only half the votes it had in the 1971 parliamentary elections. The Socialists lost mayoral offices in Oslo, Bergen, and other cities.

Oil Boom. The *Storting* (parliament) approved a new tax law on oil production from the North Sea fields on May 29. Oil companies will pay a 25 per cent surcharge on top of the 50.8 per cent corporate income tax. The tax was expected to bring in more than $1 billion annually for the next 20 years. The industries ministry lowered its 1975 production estimate in June for the Ekofisk field from 76.3 to 56.5-million barrels of gas and oil, meaning Norway will become a net exporter of gas and oil in 1976, a year later than originally planned. Total production should surpass 500 million barrels in 1980, according to the new survey. Bratteli resisted pressure from energy-hungry Western European nations in

September and restated his government's position that oil money would not be allowed to fuel inflation and disrupt the country's social fabric.

Fishing Limits. Negotiations continued through the year on plans to extend fishing limits to 50 and ultimately to 200 nautical miles. Norway charted three no-trawling zones off its northern coast on January 31, after negotiating with other nations. The ban is effective for five winter months. None of the zones extend beyond 35 nautical miles.

Price Freeze. Only 1 per cent of the work force was jobless, but the rate of inflation continued above 11 per cent. The government, unions, and employers agreed to an economic plan on September 10 to lower the inflation rate by 2 percentage points in 1976. Large groups of workers, whose raises are tied to a cost-of-living index, agreed to accept only 80 per cent of their cost-of-living raises. Only 30 per cent will be in direct pay increases, while the other 50 per cent will take the form of increased family allowances, tax concessions, and food subsidies. Prices were frozen from September 1 to December 31.

The world shipping slump and the disastrous slump in tanker loadings idled about 16 per cent of Norway's merchant fleet by August.   Kenneth Brown

See also EUROPE (Facts in Brief Table); NORDLI, ODVAR.

NOVA SCOTIA. See CANADA.

NUTRITION. The crisis atmosphere that marked nutritional science a year earlier dissipated during 1975. The dire predictions of mass starvation were not fulfilled, and there was time to plan against worldwide famine. Food experts hoped that the record United States grain harvest would permit a build-up of reserves and some measure of security against poor harvests in the future. But the failure of the Russian grain harvest and attempts by the Soviet Union to buy large amounts of grain from Australia, Canada, and the United States may slow any plans for grain stockpiling.

While mass starvation has been averted for the near future, malnutrition continues to plague much of the world. Protein shortages are particularly critical in developing nations.

Protein Fortification. Because proteins vary in quality according to the types of their amino acid subunits, nutritionists have proposed to improve the poorer classes of proteins by adding missing amino acids to food, much as vitamins are now added to wheat and corn flours. Some nutritionists question this fortification scheme because not enough is known about the body's ability to metabolize the added amino acids. Nancy L. Canolty of the University of California at Davis studied the absorption of a particularly important amino acid, methionine. Soybeans, a protein source proposed for meat-short areas, are low in methionine. Canolty reported in July that the body absorbed free methionine more rapidly than methionine contained in a protein. This finding was not unexpected because proteins have to be broken before their amino acid subunits can be absorbed. But Canolty also found that amino acid levels in blood serum changed after a meal containing added methionine and that the serum amino acid pattern changed during long periods of eating the supplemented diets. This change affects many areas of protein metabolism and may cause nutritional difficulties if large-scale amino-acid fortification programs are undertaken.

Another problem with protein supplements is the fact that amino acids come in two forms—D and L—related to the molecular arrangement of their atoms. Constance Kies and her colleagues at the University of Nebraska have investigated the use of both forms of methionine in humans. Experimental work indicates that rats metabolize both the L, the natural form, and artificially produced D. Fortification in human food would be most economically feasible if a mixture of the D and L forms could be used because the chemical process used in manufacturing methionine produces a mixture of the two. But Kies found in 1975 that humans use the L form of methionine most readily. The experimenters concluded that allowance will have to be made for this when fortification programs are planned for protein-short diets. Such fortification is unnecessary in most developed nations but may become impor-

tant if vegetable protein replaces meat. The effect on growing children, in particular, must be more carefully evaluated.

Quality, Not Quantity. In the United States, food quality has been of more concern than quantity. While false advertising has long been prohibited, nutritional claims in advertising have begun to receive close scrutiny because many claims are ambiguous. The Federal Trade Commission has proposed to define such terms as "better than," "equal to," and "organically grown" when they are applied to food products. Critics of the legislation regard it as vague and too restrictive.

The need for some regulation was emphasized by the findings of Mary A. Anderson and Bluebell R. Standal at the University of Hawaii. After studying the beliefs of individuals who use "natural foods," they reported in August that these people were quite concerned with the nature of their diet and tried to follow the most healthful practices. Most of those questioned, however, sought advice first from the owners of health food stores and only rarely consulted a nutritionist or dietician. The study showed that, in choosing or avoiding foods, they followed a mixture of valid reasoning, exaggerated claims, and false information. Advertising may confuse, and there seems to be no effective method to bring information to the public.   Paul E. Araujo

OAKLAND. See SAN FRANCISCO-OAKLAND.

OCEAN. The Fourth United Nations Law of the Sea Conference in Geneva, Switzerland, which ended on May 9, 1975, produced a treaty draft that could bring order to ocean law. Drafted by delegates from 140 nations, the treaty would allow coastal states to establish a 200-nautical-mile economic zone of jurisdiction over marine resources. The zone of full territorial sovereignty would be extended from 3 to 12 nautical miles.

Russian Sub Salvaged. After holding the story for months at the request of United States Central Intelligence Agency (CIA) Director William E. Colby, the news media reported on March 18 that the CIA had recovered large pieces of a sunken Russian submarine during the summer of 1974. The ballistic-missile, diesel-powered submarine sank in 1968, about 750 miles (1,200 kilometers) northwest of Hawaii in water 16,000 feet (4,900 meters) deep. The secret salvage operation was disguised as an ocean-mining expedition by the *Glomar Explorer,* a vessel supposedly built to mine manganese nodules on the ocean floor.

Troubled Waters. United States Deep Sea Drilling Project (DSDP) scientists who concluded a two-month expedition on February 15 found evidence that the ancient Atlantic Ocean was subjected to tremendous environmental stress, especially during its early formative period. Prior to their work, oceanographers believed the ancient ocean

Congressman Bill Alexander (D., Ark.), left,
and Senator Lowell Weicker, Jr. (R., Conn.),
center, make a test dive in an underwater lab.

had a stable environment throughout its history.

Operating off the southwest coast of Africa, the DSDP drilling ship *Glomar Challenger* obtained fossil remains of plants and animals. These remains suggest that the rift that developed when the continents of Africa and South America began drifting apart originally contained fresh water from deep lakes similar to today's East African rift-valley lakes. As the rift broadened, ocean waters entered, changing the lakes from fresh to salt water. The deep basins apparently became stagnant because of sluggish circulation and, over a period of 20 million years, filled with massive alternating layers of organic-rich shales and sand washed from the adjacent continents.

Scientists theorize that waters from the stagnant seaway seeped across the already forming Walvis Ridge toward the equator as the split between the continents extended northward. The rate of evaporation there soon exceeded the rate of water input. Within a few million years — a brief instant in geologic time — a massive layer of evaporite minerals and rock salt was deposited along the axis of the splitting crust. The mass of salt deposited — 8,000 feet (2,440 meters) thick — is equivalent to about 10 per cent of all the dissolved salt in the rest of the world's oceans. Salt deposition ended abruptly, but stagnation continued until South America had drifted so far west that the north coastline of what is

now Brazil had moved totally clear of the bulge of West Africa.

Record Drill. During the expedition, the *Glomar Challenger* achieved a major technological feat by drilling a hole 4,311 feet (1,314 meters) beneath 14,954 feet (4,558 meters) of water, the deepest penetration of the sea floor ever attained. The drilling ship made two unexpected discoveries in a subsequent summer cruise that ended on August 12. It found the most deeply subsided former island — more than 2½ miles (4 kilometers) below sea level — on the crest of a submarine ridge southwest of the Grand Banks, off Newfoundland. This ridge apparently began gradually sinking more than 105-million years ago. Volcanic rock recovered at the bottom of the drill hole indicates that the sunken island was once an unusual portion of the Mid-Atlantic Ridge that extended above sea level.

The ocean floor core also contains a continuous record of microscopic fossils from the late Cretaceous to Tertiary periods. A continuous fossil record between these two time periods is rare in either continental or marine records. Study of the recovered sedimentary record may shed new light on the mysterious time about 65 million years ago when many species of marine animals, as well as land animals, became extinct.   Arthur G. Alexiou

OHIO. See CLEVELAND; STATE GOVERNMENT.

OKLAHOMA. See STATE GOVERNMENT.

OLD AGE. The National Council on the Aging (NCOA), in September, 1975, called for government action to prevent discrimination in employment on account of age for people over 65. But the Supreme Court of the United States on November 3 let stand without comment a lower court ruling against an elderly civil service employee. An accountant in a state hospital in New Orleans, she lost her job when she became 65. In refusing to reinstate her, the lower court said there was a "rational basis" for the law. Legal experts saw the case as an unclear test of the constitutionality of forced-retirement laws.

The NCOA convention, held in Washington, D.C., was typical of the increased political activism among the elderly. Although the U.S. Congress and most state legislatures are under pressure to hold down taxes and spending, the elderly have pressed them to provide more money for pensions and a variety of social services. The National Council of Senior Citizens, the American Association of Retired Persons, the National Retired Teachers Association, and the Gray Panthers all called in 1975 for greater attention to the financial, health, and social needs of the elderly. For example, hundreds of elderly Americans picketed on June 10 outside the Department of Housing and Urban Development (HUD) in Washington, D.C. They objected to a proposed change in the way HUD grants loans to nonprofit organizations to build housing for elderly and handicapped people.

Despite such pressure, the Ford Administration stood firm in its resolve to limit increases in Social Security benefits to 5 per cent, but Congress forced an 8 per cent increase. See SOCIAL SECURITY.

Volunteer activity by elderly people increased during the year. According to a Harris poll, 22 per cent of those Americans who are 65 or older do volunteer work, apart from paid work. Another 10 per cent would like to do volunteer work. Among older people who are college graduates, 42 per cent do volunteer work.

The Public's Image. During the year, the NCOA released results of a Harris poll on the nature and needs of elderly people. Eighty-six per cent of those polled who were 18 and over agreed with the statement, "Nobody should be forced to retire because of age, if he wants to continue working and is still able to do a good job." Four out of five persons believe government should help support older people with the taxes collected from all Americans.

Nevertheless, the NCOA launched a public-relations drive to "counter the notion that old people are frail, sickly, and vulnerable." The organization began a Senior Citizen of the Month award. Its first winner was Hoyt Catlin, an 85-year-old Connecticut nursery owner whose employees average 65 years of age.   Robert J. Havighurst

OLYMPIC GAMES. Preparations continued in 1975 without major problems for the 1976 Olympic Winter Games in Innsbruck, Austria. Preparations continued with all kinds of problems for the 1976 Olympic Summer Games in Montreal, Canada.

Montreal's major concern resulted from frequent strikes by workmen building Olympic facilities, especially the 70,000-seat main stadium. Many Canadians feared the stadium would not be ready for the opening ceremonies on July 17, 1976. Mayor Jean Drapeau of Montreal insisted everything would be ready.

There were financial concerns, too. In 1972, officials estimated the cost of the 1976 games at $310-million. By 1975, the estimate was $1 billion, and in November the Quebec provincial government took over construction and financing of the facilities from Montreal. Provincial officials said they expected the deficit to be about $600 million.

President Gerald R. Ford appointed an 18-member President's Commission on Olympic Sports to determine why U.S. Olympic teams had had so many problems in the past and how the problems could be eliminated. Commission members include such sports figures as Bill Toomey, Donna de Varona, Rafer Johnson, Jack Kemp, Micki King, Ernie Vandeweghe, Willye White, and Charles (Bud) Wilkinson.   Frank Litsky

See also PAN AMERICAN GAMES.

OMAN. The Popular Front for the Liberation of Oman (PFLO) rebellion against Sultan Sayyid Qaboos bin Said Al Bu Said in Dhofar Province affected the interests of other Arab and Persian Gulf states in 1975. In February, Iran promised to protect Omani airspace against foreign aircraft. The move was directed against Yemen (Aden), which supports the rebels. Yemeni airmen reportedly have made occasional flights over western Oman.

The sultan's army, bolstered by Iranian and Jordanian battalions, struck hard against the PFLO. The main rebel strongholds in the mountainous Jabal Akhdar area were sealed off in August, and Iranian forces captured the key town of Rakhyut. Two PFLO commanders surrendered on August 20 in Salalah, the Dhofari capital. The Jordanians withdrew in September.

Heavy military expenditures estimated at $375-million, 40 per cent of total Omani revenues, produced a financial crisis in spite of $900 million in oil revenue. Saudi Arabia loaned Oman $100 million on May 28 to meet current cash obligations on condition that expenditures be cut 30 per cent. But Qaboos refused to cut military costs. The World Bank loaned Oman $150 million.   William Spencer

See also MIDDLE EAST (Facts in Brief Table).

ONTARIO. See CANADA.

OPERA. See MUSIC, CLASSICAL.

OREGON. See STATE GOVERNMENT.

PACIFIC ISLANDS. All island groups experienced inflation and a downturn in their economies in 1975. They had to pay more for goods imported from the industrial countries and for transport. At the same time, the tourist boom subsided in such places as Fiji.

Independence Moves. The most important political event was Papua New Guinea's achievement of total independence from Australia on September 16. Papua New Guinea, somewhat smaller in size and population than New Zealand, is the largest and most populous of all the island territories. Its independence was celebrated in the face of a secession attempt by the outlying island of Bougainville, site of the vast Bougainville copper mine. The Papua New Guinea Cabinet proposed to give all mine royalties to the Bougainville provincial government after June, but the proposal failed to deter the Bougainville separatists, who unilaterally declared their independence on September 1. Nonetheless, the secession attempt did not lead to violence, though fighting had occurred at the mine on May 12 for other reasons, and a compromise seemed possible. An attempt to establish an independent Papua failed. See PAPUA NEW GUINEA.

The Solomon Islands became self-governing in December, with the promise of independence in 1977. The Ellice Islands separated from their former partners, the Gilbert Islands, in October to

Joining the U.S. Family

The Mariana Islands voted on June 17, 1975, to join the United States as a commonwealth, the first step in a process that will make the Marianas the first new U.S. territory since the Virgin Islands were added in 1917.

Nearly 80 per cent of the voters approved the union, a move the islanders have been seeking for 20 years. But the change will not take place overnight. The U.S. Congress must first ratify the agreement. Then the islanders must get the President to approve a constitution. Finally, the United Nations (UN) Security Council must approve dissolution of the UN Trust Territory of the Pacific Islands, also known as Micronesia, of which the Marianas have been a part since 1947. This cannot be done until some provision has been made for self-government in the other districts. The Marianas probably will not achieve complete commonwealth status until 1980 or 1981.

The Marianas are a group of 15 islands in the western Pacific Ocean. Some of World War II's fiercest fighting occurred on these islands.

Today, the Marianas show little evidence of their bloody past. Golden beaches sweep down to azure seas and lush, verdant foliage covers craggy mountaintops. The 14 northern islands, which will form the new commonwealth, have been administered by the United States as one of six districts in the UN trust territory. Guam, the 15th Mariana, has been a U.S. territory since 1898.

Under an agreement signed in February, the islanders will become U.S. citizens and will govern their own internal affairs. However, they will not be able to vote for President or for members of Congress, and the United States will control defense and foreign affairs.

The Marianas will receive $14 million in U.S. aid, adjusted to 1975 dollars, each year for at least seven years. All federal taxes paid by the islanders will be kept on the islands. United States immigration laws will not apply, so that foreign labor can be obtained more easily; and the minimum wage will apply only to employees of the U.S. government and its contractors.

One of the most significant aspects of the agreement is its military importance. The acquisition gives the United States a strategic western Pacific base. Although the Marianas are about 5,600 miles (9,000 kilometers) from the U.S. mainland, the group is only about 2,000 miles (3,200 kilometers) from China and 1,400 miles (2,250 kilometers) from Japan. The United States government will lease about two-thirds of the island of Tinian, which will be converted into an air and naval base. In addition, the United States gets a harbor area on Saipan and the uninhabited island of Medinilla, which it will use for a bombing range. The United States will pay $19.5 million in return for a 50-year lease, renewable for another 50 years.

The Marianas are the most economically advanced of the Micronesian districts. A growing tourist economy is making them more prosperous than many other islands in Micronesia. Most residents have attended high school and speak English as well as the native language.

The rest of Micronesia is going ahead with plans for a unified government, though the islanders are divided among themselves as well as with the United States on many key issues. Most of them appear to want either self-government or looser ties with the United States than those accepted by the Marianas. Until the negotiations are completed, the trusteeship continues.   Kathryn Sederberg

become a separate British territory named Tuvalu. The New Hebrides began a slow and hesitant move toward greater self-management with municipal elections in August and national elections in November. Olivier Stirn, the French secretary of state for overseas departments and territories, visited France's Pacific territories early in the year. He did not promise independence, but indicated that more local autonomy would be given to French Polynesia. Australia set up a royal commission to consider Norfolk Island's future.

The people of the Marianas, part of the United Nations (UN) Trust Territory of the Pacific Islands, voted on June 17 by a 76 per cent majority to accept commonwealth status with the United States (see Close-Up). The other members of the trust territory signed a constitution in November for a proposed Federated States of Micronesia. Under the proposal, the Micronesians would handle internal affairs, while the United States would take care of defense and foreign relations.

Fijian Leader. Ratu Sir Kamisese Mara, prime minister of Fiji, was the most prominent island leader. Along with representatives of other former European dependencies, he obtained good terms from the European Community (Common Market) for Fiji's sugar exports. He also tried to edge Australia out of the sugar market in other island groups and offered to help Papua New Guinea develop a local sugar industry.

Fiji gained a majority interest in the Air Pacific airline. It also was prominent at the South Pacific Commission meetings in Nauru in October. The South Pacific Forum in July agreed to set up a regional shipping line, but Sir Kamisese warned that its success would depend largely on the attitudes of the Australian and New Zealand maritime unions.

Other Developments. An unusual dispute arose about Ocean Island, a barren phosphate island administered by Great Britain as part of the Gilbert group. The Gilberts receive much of their revenue from Ocean Island's phosphate royalties. The Banabans, former inhabitants of the island, were resettled after World War II on Rabi Island near Fiji, 1,600 miles (2,600 kilometers) from Ocean Island. But they want to go home, and they are trying by court action in Great Britain and pressure at the United Nations to have Ocean Island detached from the Gilberts and made independent, perhaps in association with Fiji.

Migration, especially to New Zealand and the United States, continued from islands with expanding populations, such as Samoa, Niue, and the Cook Islands, and from Fiji and the UN Trust Territory. New Zealand encountered some agitation for migrants to be placed on probation before final acceptance as residents.   J. D. B. Miller

PAINTING. See VISUAL ARTS.

PAKISTAN. Hayat Mohammad Khan Sherpao, home minister of the North-West Frontier province and a close friend of Prime Minister Zulfikar Ali Bhutto, was killed by a bomb on Feb. 8, 1975, in Peshawar, the provincial capital. Within 48 hours, the main opposition group, the National Awami Party (NAP) was banned. Its leader, Abdul Wali Khan, and some 400 other persons were arrested.

Bhutto, who hurriedly returned from a visit to the United States, charged that the NAP was getting money, guns, and sympathy from neighboring Afghanistan. The arrests did not end widespread unrest in the North-West Frontier, and the province was placed under federal rule on February 17.

After Wali Khan's arrest, other opposition members walked out of the lower house of Parliament and announced they would boycott its sessions. In their absence, the government amended the Pakistan Constitution to make parliamentary approval unnecessary in proclaiming a state of emergency.

New Leader. Meanwhile, another formidable rival emerged to challenge Bhutto. He was Ghulan Mustafa Khar, once regarded as Bhutto's heir apparent. Dismissed as governor of Punjab Province in July, the 39-year-old Khar resigned from Bhutto's dominant Pakistan People's Party in September and joined the Muslim League. Khar is a native of Punjab, which, with 60 per cent of the nation's 70 million people, is the most important of the four provinces. He played up the fact that Bhutto came from Sind Province, hoping to reduce the massive Punjab vote that Bhutto won in 1970.

Recession. Violence, separatism in the North-West Frontier and Baluchistan provinces, and the decline of his People's Party were not Bhutto's only woes. Caught in a budgetary squeeze, the government, on February 1, raised the prices of 223 commodities, including gasoline. On April 7, wheat, sugar, and vegetable oil prices were also raised sharply by cutting off part of the state subsidy for these items. The price rises led to more riots.

Foes and Friends. In this crisis, the government of Iran and various oil sheiks helped Pakistan. They provided loans and grants worth more than $500-million. Of course, they had helped to create some of Pakistan's financial problems. Thanks to the Arab oil squeeze, Pakistan's oil bill had risen from $60 million in 1970 to $450 million in 1975. Pakistan continued to see India and Afghanistan as its principal enemies. The Afghans apparently hoped to detach the North-West Frontier and Baluchistan provinces in order to create a new pro-Afghan state of Pakhtoonistan.

On February 24, the United States announced it was lifting its 10-year-old ban on the sale of U.S. arms to Pakistan. One reason for this was presumably to bolster Pakistan against India, which had been getting Russian weapons.   Mark Gayn

See also ASIA (Facts in Brief Table).

PAN AMERICAN GAMES. Athletes from the United States won most of the honors in the 1975 Pan American Games held from October 13 to 26 in Mexico City, Mexico. That was expected. What was not entirely expected was the often-fierce anti-American outbursts by the Mexican crowds.

Larry Young of Columbia, Mo., was closing in on the two Mexican leaders in the 20-kilometer road walk when Mexican spectators pushed him, shoved him, and spat upon him. Dianne Dunbar, a 15-year-old gymnast from Pleasanton, Calif., was booed during her routine because the Mexican who preceded her had received low scores. Jenny Chandler, a 16-year-old diver from Lincoln, Ala., was so unnerved by hooting and derogatory yelling that she ruined one dive. The jury allowed her to repeat the dive without penalty, and she did it well enough to win the gold medal.

Why the anti-American feeling? It stemmed partly from the traditional overwhelming U.S. success in these quadrennial Olympic-type games encompassing 22 sports. The hostility was attributed partly to long-time economic domination of Mexico by the United States and partly to the temperament of the Mexican people.

The United States won a total of 247 medals — 117 gold, 85 silver, and 45 bronze. Cuba was second with 56-46-30 — 132. Next were Canada with 18-35-39 — 92, Mexico with 8-13-37 — 58, and Brazil with 7-12-22 — 41.

Although many of the best American track athletes and swimmers did not compete, the United States scored heavily in these showcase sports. It won 12 of the 23 gold medals in men's track, 7 of 14 in women's track, 14 of 15 in men's swimming, and 13 of 14 in women's swimming.

The United States also won 14 of 18 gold medals in shooting, 7 of 10 in Greco-Roman wrestling, 5 of 10 in free-style wrestling, 5 of 6 in equestrian events, and 3 of 4 in yachting. It won all 6 gold medals in women's gymnastics, all 5 in tennis, and all 3 in synchronized swimming. It also won men's and women's basketball.

The outstanding performance came in men's track and field, where João Oliveira, a 21-year-old Brazilian soldier, triple-jumped 58 feet 8¼ inches (18 meters). That broke the world record by almost 18 inches (46 centimeters).

Ann Carr, a 17-year-old gymnast from Philadelphia, won five gold medals. Seventeen-year-old Kathy Heddy of Summit, N.J., and 18-year-old Kim Peyton of Portland, Ore., won four gold medals each in swimming. Hershel Anderson, a 38-year-old Army sergeant from Tracy City, Tenn., won four gold medals and two silver medals in pistol shooting.   Frank Litsky

Joni Huntley of Sheridan, Ore., clears the bar at 6 feet 2½ inches (189 centimeters), a Pan American Games women's high jump record.

PANAMA. Negotiations on a new Panama Canal treaty with the United States remained a central concern in 1975. Many issues, including the treaty's duration, economic benefits to be accorded Panama, and the right of the United States to expand canal facilities, contributed to the intensely hostile atmosphere in which the negotiators worked.

Students demonstrating against U.S. control of the Canal Zone attacked the U.S. Embassy in Panama City in September, breaking many windows before police stopped them. However, U.S. Ambassador Ellsworth Bunker announced in Washington, D.C., on December 2 that a preliminary agreement had been reached. Under its terms, the United States would retain "primary responsibility" for operating the canal. The duration of the treaty had not been agreed upon.

On October 17, at a meeting in Panama City, 25 Latin American and Caribbean countries initialed an agreement creating the Latin American Economic System. The new alliance was pledged to defend regional economic interests. Panama military representatives also attended a conference with the United States and several Latin American countries that was held in Montevideo, Uruguay, from October 20 to October 25. The representatives approved a policy designed to end Communist subversion in the Western Hemisphere.   Paul C. Tullier

See also LATIN AMERICA (Facts in Brief Table).

Statehood for Papua New Guinea, an Australian-administered territory, becomes official in September with the symbolic lowering of Australia's flag.

PAPUA NEW GUINEA, a Pacific island nation that includes Bougainville island in its boundaries, gained independence on Sept. 16, 1975. Michael Somore, head of the Papua and New Guinea Union Party, was sworn in as prime minister at Independence Day ceremonies in Port Moresby, the new nation's capital. Australia, which had administered the country since the end of World War I, promised continued financial aid.

Independence came only after long arguments over provisions of the new Constitution. One of the most controversial was whether Papua New Guinea should have a head of state. The arguments were resolved on July 29, when the Papua New Guinea Constituent Assembly adopted a 150-page Constitution accepting Queen Elizabeth II of Great Britain as head of state.

Separatist groups were active throughout the year. One group, led by Josephine Abaijah, the country's leading feminist, favored independence for a southern region of the country. There was also a strong separatist movement on copper-rich Bougainville, where 37 members of the provincial assembly voted on August 27 to secede. On September 1, another group known as the Republican Government of North Solomons declared Bougainville independent. The Papua New Guinea government ignored the action.   Paul C. Tullier

See also ASIA (Facts in Brief Table).

PARAGUAY. President Alfredo Stroessner's Colorado Party won an expected landslide victory in the municipal elections held on Oct. 27, 1975. The party polled 87 per cent of the votes, compared with only 10 per cent for the main opposition group, Domingo Laino's Liberal Radical Party. Fraud and coercion had been standard features in Paraguayan elections, and Laino provided a fresh example. He claimed that, when he went to the booth to cast his own vote, he found that there were no ballot papers there.

The democratic façade was paper-thin, but Stroessner, in power since 1954, remained one of the most solidly entrenched rulers in Latin America. The only significant stirring of dissent during the year came from a conference of Roman Catholic bishops held in March, during which the prelates were highly critical of the methods used by the secret police.

Foreign Policy. Stroessner continued to find his friends among right wing authoritarian regimes. South African Prime Minister Balthazar Johannes Vorster visited Asunción from August 13 to 16; after conferring with Stroessner, he agreed to lend $9 million for housing and agricultural projects. Brazil's President Ernesto Geisel paid a state visit in December. Stroessner himself visited Taiwan.

Because Paraguay was well off the mainstream of world politics, the country continued to escape the attention of the radical lobby at the United Nations (UN), though the alleged mistreatment of the Ache Indians was raised before the UN Commission on Human Rights in September.

The Itaipu Scheme. Economic hopes centered on the $4-billion Itaipu hydroelectric power scheme, a joint Brazilian-Paraguayan project for which Paraguay will supply vast quantities of timber, sand, and cement. The Paraguayans also expected to resell to Brazil most of their half-share in the power produced by the scheme. Some doubts were expressed about the steady drift of Brazilian farmer-settlers into the country's four northern departments—Alto Paraná, Caaguazú, Amambay, and Kanendiyu—which was accelerating as work on the scheme got underway. But a relatively low birth rate and the emigration of about 1 million Paraguayans since Stroessner came to power had left the country sparsely populated and in need of immigrants.

Paraguay signed an agreement with Brazil in July under which the two countries jointly agreed to build a $46-million steel-rolling mill outside Asunción. Three U.S. oil companies—Exxon Corporation; Texaco, Incorporated; and Pennzoil Company—began exploring for oil in the bleak Chaco plain in northwestern Paraguay in January. Controversy arose over their contracts.   Robert Moss

See also LATIN AMERICA (Facts in Brief Table).

PARENTS AND TEACHERS, NATIONAL CONGRESS OF (PTA), voted to support laws on handgun control at its 1975 convention in Atlantic City, N.J., in June. The delegates also passed resolutions promoting the health and welfare of Vietnamese refugee children and demanding a reduction of violence in television programs. Other resolutions supported adequate labeling of additives in food products, adoption of the metric system in schools, and the upgrading of courses in family life.

Mrs. Walter G. Kimmel of Rock Island, Ill., was elected president; Mrs. William C. Baisinger, Washington, D.C., first vice-president; and Wilson C. Riles, Sacramento, Calif., second vice-president.

The PTA sponsored conferences in several regions to encourage making family-life education part of public school curriculums. With a $20,000 grant from Sears, Roebuck and Company, the PTA began a one-year project to study the causes of school absenteeism in five states.

A joint program with the National Institute on Alcohol Abuse and Alcoholism (NIAAA) to combat the misuse and abuse of alcohol by the nation's youth continued. The program is funded by nearly $100,000 provided by NIAAA. The PTA annually awards mini-grants to state parent-teacher groups to conduct community alcohol education programs.

A 10-cent annual increase in national dues took effect on April 1.   Joseph P. Anderson

PELÉ (1941-   ), Brazilian soccer star, signed a three-year contract for about $4.7 million in June, 1975, with the New York Cosmos in the North American Soccer League. Pelé had retired from international competition in 1971.

Pelé is acclaimed as the world's greatest soccer player. He led Brazil's national team to three World Cup championships, the first when he was 17. The World Cup is an international tournament held every four years. An inside-left forward, Pelé has scored more than 1,200 goals in his professional career. He was the first player to score more than 1,000 goals. Prior to his retirement, the government declared him a national treasure to prevent foreign teams from luring him out of Brazil. He became a millionaire.

Edson Arantes do Nascimento was born into a poor family in Três Corações (Three Hearts), Brazil. He quit school after the fourth grade and worked briefly as a cobbler's apprentice. When he was 14, a family adviser took him to Santos, where he started his soccer career. Soccer fans nicknamed him Pelé. He is also called *Perola Negra* (Black Pearl) in Brazil, *La Tulipe Noire* (The Black Tulip) in France, *El Peligro* (The Dangerous One) in Chile, and *Il Re* (The King) in Italy. Joseph P. Spohn

See also SOCCER.

PENNSYLVANIA. See PHILADELPHIA; STATE GOVERNMENT.

PERSONALITIES OF 1975 included the following newsmakers:

Blair, Frank, 59, television newscaster, read his last news on NBC-TV's "Today" show on March 14. He retired from the network after 22 years of broadcasting.

Boorstin, Daniel J., prizewinning historian, was confirmed as the United States 12th Librarian of Congress on September 26. Boorstin had served as senior historian of the Smithsonian Institution's National Museum of History and Technology since 1973. He was director of the museum from 1969 to 1973, after serving as professor of history at the University of Chicago for 25 years. He received the 1974 Pulitzer Prize in History for *The Americans: The Democratic Experience,* the final volume in a massive historical trilogy.

Chaplin, Charlie, 86, famed as the baggy-trousered tramp of silent movies, was knighted March 4 by Queen Elizabeth II of Great Britain. He almost turned the moment into another "silent." "I was too dumbfounded to talk to the queen," he said later. He also said he preferred to be known as Sir Charles, not Sir Charlie.

Cotton, Norris, who retired as senator from New Hampshire in January after 20 years service, was down to zero seniority when he was sworn in for a two-week term on September 3. Norris was reappointed by New Hampshire Governor Meldrim

Prince Charles of Great Britain dons an
inflatable diving suit for an icy dip in
the Arctic Ocean during a tour of Canada.

tion's "Man on the Trail" list in August because he
is "an outdoor type with executive demeanor."

Fulbright, J. William, 70, was awarded an honorary knighthood in the Order of the British Empire
on June 30 in London. The former Democratic senator from Arkansas, who attended Oxford University in the 1920s, was honored for sponsoring the
Fulbright scholarship program, which began in
1946. More than 37,000 American Fulbright scholars have participated in the program, and more
than 96,000 foreign students and teachers have
studied in the United States.

Hagins, Clarence, 33, a Richmond, Va., artist
suffered from an overdose of wining and dining in
September. His problem started when he encountered a stranger, a Saudi Arabian businessman, in a
London pub. The stranger insisted on buying
drinks for Hagins' group and later invited them to a
luxury hotel. "He took me for Prince Qaboos of
Oman," Hagins said. "He thinks I'm traveling in-
cognito. Nothing will persuade him that I'm just
plain Clarence Hagins. I just get this nod of secret
understanding."

Harvey, Dodie, 37, of New Hope, Minn., waited
19 years after passing her written driver's test before she took the road test and got her license in
1975. During all those years, she had an instruction
permit that allowed her to drive when accompanied

Thompson, Jr., after the Senate failed to settle a
contested election between Democrat John A. Durkin and Republican Louis C. Wyman. Durkin won
a new election on September 16, thus ending Cotton's brief post-retirement legislative stint.

Droyer, Claude, 29, and Patrice Pelayo, 24,
French mountain climbers, scaled the wall of
Europe's tallest office building, the Maine-
Montparnasse Tower in Paris, in June. The building is 700 feet (213 meters) high. They made the
5½-hour climb to draw attention to the lack of
government aid for mountain climbing. Police and
firemen waited at the top to take the climbers into
custody, but they released them when it was discovered that they had broken no French law.

Ellis, Rob, 25-year-old outfielder for the Sacramento Solons, was disappointed in his 1975 season
and his .250 batting average. So he paid $40 to run
an ad apologizing to the team's fans in the September 2 issue of the Sacramento *Union.* "I felt terrible and played the same way," he wrote. "I'm sorry
I couldn't have done better." Solons' manager
Harry Bright said he had never heard of a ballplay-
er apologizing in that way.

Ford, Steven, 19-year-old son of President
Gerald R. Ford, was named by the Girls Rodeo
Association of Spring Creek, Nev., as the man they
would most like to ride with "on the trail to happy
destiny." Ford was picked to head the organiza-

Richard Washington of New Milford, Conn., tries
on the costume he wears to portray his famous
ancestor, George, in Bicentennial celebrations.

by a licensed driver. She renewed the permit each year, but used it to drive only once—when she and her husband drove to California in 1967. "I just thought I wouldn't add to all the nuts already on the road," she explained.

Hiss, Alger, 70, was reinstated as a member of the Massachusetts bar in August, the first time that state has reversed a disbarment. Hiss was disbarred in 1952 after being convicted of perjury for denying that he had ever turned over State Department documents to Communists. The Massachusetts Supreme Judicial Court ruled unanimously on August 5 that Hiss had demonstrated "moral and intellectual fitness" and ordered him readmitted to legal practice.

Hoak, Sandra, of Akron, Ohio, entered her second year as the only female football official in Ohio. She officiates at games in the semipro Northern Ohio Football League. "I'm not the women's libber type," she said, "but I do believe that people should do what they want to do." She went to school to learn the trade after puzzling about the strange gestures officials made at football games.

Humphrey, Hubert H., Democratic senator from Minnesota, was allowed to sit in on a press conference of coach Bud Grant of the Minnesota Vikings football team held on August 28. But there was a condition. "Nice to see you," Grant greeted him. "If you keep your mouth shut, you can sit in." Humphrey replied, "Don't worry, I'm just here to watch."

Johnson, Stancil E. D., a psychiatrist in Pacific Grove, Calif., has written what may be the definitive treatise on the Frisbee. Titled *Frisbee,* it compiles records, traces the disk's history, and tells how to play various games with it. Johnson is so enamored of it that he asked to be cremated when he dies and have his ashes mixed with the finest grade of polyethylene to make 25 Frisbees.

Masoud Sharif Al Hamdan, Sheik, of Saudi Arabia discovered in January that some things cannot be bought, even with Arab oil money. It all started when the sheik's son fell in love with the Alamo while attending a program for foreign military officers at a Texas air base. "Contact the proper people," the sheik wrote to a Texas lawyer. "I want to present it as a gift to my son." The state of Texas, which owns the shrine, said it would not sell the fort where 187 men died fighting for Texas independence in 1836. But it offered a replica that had been built for a movie set.

Mathews, F. David, U.S. secretary of health, education, and welfare, informed department employees in September that he prefers letters to be signed "Cordially," rather than "Sincerely." However, "Sincerely" is still preferable for reports to Congress and for letters of condolence. For the President, the signature should be "Faithfully yours," his memo added.

Junko Tabei, the first woman to climb Mount Everest, waves the flags of Japan and Nepal as she stands on the summit of the mountain.

Mira, George, quarterback for the Jacksonville (Fla.) Express football team, was injured by a giant zipper on September 14 during a World Football League game at the Aloha Stadium in Honolulu. Mira's left index finger caught in a zipper on the field's artificial surface. "It looked like someone had bitten it off," said trainer Brady Greathouse. "When it heals, it'll be a quarter-inch shorter."

Nadjari, Maurice H., special prosecutor for the state of New York, received a taste of his own medicine in January. Nadjari, who lives in Huntington, N.Y., was ticketed for going 73 miles (118 kilometers) per hour in a 55-mph (88-kph) zone on the Seaford-Oyster Bay Expressway. Nadjari accepted his ticket "very graciously, like a gentleman," according to the county patrolman who stopped him.

Nelson, Ed, of London, won the great London commuter race in January by traveling from Marble Arch to Waterloo Station in seven minutes on his motor scooter. Most other contestants went by bus or subway, but one rode horseback, one ran the distance, and one dodged among passing cars on a pair of roller skates.

Onassis, Christina, 24, daughter of the late Aristotle Onassis, married Greek shipping heir Alexandros Andreadis, 32, in July after a month-long courtship. The wedding, in a tiny seaside chapel, united two of Greece's great fortunes. Christina inherited the bulk of the Onassis fortune after her father's death in March. Her husband, a private in the Greek army, is the second son of Stratis Andreadis, a prominent banker, industrialist, and shipping magnate.

Onassis, Jacqueline Kennedy, widow of President John F. Kennedy and Aristotle Onassis, joined Viking Press Inc., New York City, as a $200-a-week consulting editor in September. She does not work set hours, but her duties are related to all divisions of the book-publishing company. Before marrying Kennedy, she worked briefly as an inquiring photographer for the *Washington Times-Herald.*

Patton, George S., III, 51, a major general, took over his father's old division in August. Patton was a West Point cadet when his father, General George S. Patton, Jr., led the Second Armored Division in North Africa in World War II. The son commanded a tank company in Korea and the 11th Armored Cavalry Regiment in South Vietnam. "My father favored my joining the Army," he said, "but never influenced me one moment in my entire life. I just always wanted to be in the Army."

Slayton, Donald K., 51, had an excuse that was out of this world when he failed to appear in a St. Louis court on July 15 to testify for a 51-year-old colleague who had been removed from flight duties for the McDonnell Douglas Corporation because of age. Slayton was orbiting the earth in the joint U.S.-Russian Apollo-Soyuz mission.

Smokey Bear, the widely recognized symbol of fire prevention, lost both his job and his name in 1975. Smokey promoted fire safety for 25 years after being rescued as a cub from a New Mexico forest fire in 1950. But the Forest Service retired him when he reached the human equivalent of 70, mandatory retirement age for federal employees. A younger, more active bear will take over.

Tabei, Junko, a 35-year-old Japanese housewife, became the first woman to scale Mount Everest, the world's highest mountain at 29,141 feet (8,845 meters), on May 16. Afterward, she confessed that she was more afraid of flying than she was of climbing mountains.

Waller, Sir John, 58, of London, admitted in September that his newborn daughter was "not exactly the boy we had hoped for." Under the terms of his aunt's will, Sir John will receive $1 million as soon as he and his 31-year-old wife produce a male heir. "Of course, I'm disappointed," he said, "but we will have another go."

Yeager, Charles E., 52, the first man to fly faster than the speed of sound, retired from the U.S. Air Force on February 28 after 34 years of military service. A brigadier general, he was director of aerospace safety for the Air Force. As one of the country's leading test pilots, he first cracked the sound barrier in 1947 in a Bell X-1 rocket plane. In 1953, he set another record when he flew 2½ times the speed of sound in a Bell X-1A.   Kathryn Sederberg

PERU. President Juan Velasco Alvarado was ousted, after nearly seven years in office, in a bloodless coup d'état on Aug. 29, 1975. He was replaced by General Francisco Morales Bermudez Cerruti, who was sworn in on August 30. Peru's military-led revolution was thus channeled into a more conservative course, with emphasis being placed on careful economic management.

The influence of General Morales, senior officer in the Peruvian army and a former minister of economy, had grown rapidly since Velasco became ill on February 28, the latest in a series of serious health problems that followed the amputation of his right leg in 1973. While Velasco spent a month convalescing in the south, Morales ran the country.

Morales' hand was evident in the new economic plan announced on June 30, which stressed monetary restraint, cut food subsidies, brought realistic price increases for many basic commodities, and provoked a general strike in the southern town of Arequipa. Morales also approved of the clampdown on the extreme left in August. After strong pressure from right wing ministers, the radical paper *Marka* was closed, and 28 journalists, trade unionists, and politicians were expelled.

After the Coup, which occurred during a meeting of nonaligned nations in Lima, Morales assured the delegates that "the revolution that bids you

Throngs of banner-carrying workers representing Peru's powerful labor unions stage an orderly celebration in downtown Lima on May Day.

farewell is the same one that welcomed you a few days ago." However, it later became clear that things had changed.

A civilian, Luís Barua Castañeda, was named minister of economy and finance – the first since the coup in 1968. A general amnesty was decreed for the political victims of that coup, and ex-president Fernando Belaúnde Terry, forced into exile by that coup, returned to Peru on Jan. 4, 1976.

Labor Troubles. The year began with a police strike, which was suppressed by the army. Nearly 100 persons were killed in the disturbances. Price inflation added to labor unrest throughout the year, spearheaded by the Communist-run General Confederation of Peruvian Workers and a confederation of peasants, which organized widespread land seizures.

The Economy. The new government instituted the first official devaluation of the sol since 1967. It also edged away from the strident economic nationalism of the Velasco regime. The possibility emerged of negotiated compensation for the American-owned Marcona Mining Company, the country's main iron-ore concern, which was seized in July. The new government also backpedaled on the land-redistribution program; its disruptive effects had cut the agricultural production growth rate to just over 1 per cent in 1974.   Robert Moss

See also LATIN AMERICA (Facts in Brief Table).

Owner Barbara Vanword with Ch. Sir Lancelot of Barvan after the old English sheep dog won Westminster Kennel Club best-of-show honors.

PET. The implications of a U.S. pet-population explosion became clearly evident in 1975. The *Congressional Quarterly* estimated that between 2,000 and 3,500 puppies and kittens were born in the United States every hour. The Humane Society of the United States estimated that there were 34 million dogs and 46 million cats in the United States, along with 23 million pet birds, 340 million fish, and 125 million other kinds of pets. The sale of one popular pet, small turtles, was banned by the U.S. Food and Drug Administration in June, because turtles carry an organism that causes intestinal distress in humans.

Animal shelters were forced to destroy about 90 per cent of the 15 million animals turned over to them during the year. The National League of Cities reported that dog- and other pet-control problems were the number-one source of citizen complaints to mayors. The development of a birth-control pill for dogs, Ovaban, was announced by the Schering Corporation in April.

Pet Food Drain. Figures published by the *Congressional Quarterly* in 1975 showed that pet food was the largest-selling dry- or canned-food item in grocery stores. Americans spend more than $2 billion annually on pet foods – four times as much as they spend on baby foods.

Canine News. For the first time since 1914, an old English sheep dog was judged best-in-show at the Westminster Kennel Club dog show in New York City in February. Ch. Sir Lancelot of Barvan, owned by Mr. and Mrs. Ronald Vanword of Newmarket, Canada, was chosen from among 3,035 dogs. Best-in-show honors at the International Kennel Club show, which attracted 3,018 dogs to Chicago in March, went to Ch. Cummings Gold-Rush Charlie, a golden retriever owned by Liz Clark of Middleburg, Va., and L. C. Johnson of Princeton, N.J.

Registration figures released by the American Kennel Club in March showed that poodles were the most popular breed of dog in the United States for the 15th consecutive year. Following in order were German shepherds, Irish setters, beagles, dachshunds, Doberman pinschers, miniature schnauzers, Labrador retrievers, cocker spaniels, and Saint Bernards.

Cat Winners. The Cat Fanciers' Association named Gr. Ch. Hawthorne Nite Liter of Lee, a black Persian male owned by Mr. and Mrs. William Lee of Grand Rapids, Mich., as *Best Cat of the Year*. *Best Alter* was a sable Burmese spay, Gr. Pr. Crestvue's Hether of Colchester, owned by Sandy and Rita Krebs of Gaithersburg, Md. The *Best Kitten* award went to a blue-cream Persian female, Gr. Ch. Bryn Mawr Georgie Girl. The young Persian is owned by Werner, Irene, and Mike Kachel of Dayton, Ohio.   Theodore M. O'Leary

PETROLEUM AND GAS. Canada, once a prime supplier of oil to the United States, reduced its exports sharply in 1975. Donald S. Macdonald, minister of energy, mines, and resources, set maximum exports to the United States at 750,000 barrels a day for the last half of 1975. In 1974, Canadian oil exports to the United States averaged 791,000 barrels a day. "The United States can make arrangements for alternative supplies of oil if required to do so," Macdonald said on May 5. Canada, traditionally the second-largest oil supplier to the United States market after Venezuela, cut its exports because of threatened shortages at home.

Meanwhile, the first oil from Great Britain's North Sea project was brought in from the offshore fields in mid-June, starting a flow potentially worth $414 billion. A consortium, partly owned by the Rio Tinto-Zinc Corporation of Britain and Texaco, Incorporated, of the United States, anchored the first tanker carrying North Sea oil in the Thames River estuary near London on June 18.

U.S. Fuel Supply. The *Oil & Gas Journal* predicted on May 20 that the United States would have adequate supplies of gasoline and other refined petroleum for the rest of 1975 if imports were not restricted.

However, the U.S. Geological Survey (USGS) expressed a different and more alarming view in

New gasoline additive!

© 1975 by the Chicago Tribune

June, after a second study of the nation's petroleum resources. The USGS had estimated in March, 1974, that the nation's undiscovered recoverable reserves, onshore and offshore, ranged from 200 to 400 billion barrels. After another year of study, however, the USGS lowered the estimate to from 50 to 130 billion barrels of recoverable reserves, figures more in line with estimates made by the petroleum industry and the National Academy of Sciences.

This drastically lowered estimate of the nation's oil resources prompted Senator Ernest F. Hollings (D., S.C.), chairman of the National Ocean Policy Study, to issue the group's sharply critical analysis of the Administration's accelerated program for offshore leasing, a key part of the effort to make the United States self-sufficient in energy. The report said that the ultimate effect of increased domestic production would be just the opposite, because by the end of the century, the United States will have completely depleted its domestic supplies before substitutes can be provided.

The United States currently produces about 65 per cent of the 6.3 billion barrels of oil and natural gas liquids it uses each year. About 12 per cent of its production comes from the outer continental shelf, which has an estimated 32 to 61 per cent of the undiscovered recoverable oil.

The Supreme Court of the United States unanimously ruled on March 17 that the federal government has exclusive rights to any oil and gas resources on the Atlantic outer continental shelf beyond the 3-nautical-mile (5.6-kilometer) limit. The ruling cleared the way for the U.S. Department of the Interior to call for bids from major oil companies for leasing these offshore reserves. In August, however, a number of states, including New York, New Jersey, and Massachusetts, announced that they were preparing lawsuits against the Department of the Interior to halt its proposed auction of 10 million acres (4 million hectares) of offshore oil-extraction rights.

Alaska Pipeline. One of the largest construction forces in U.S. history raced to build the 798-mile (1,284-kilometer) trans-Alaska pipeline. Despite bad weather, labor problems, and rising costs, work on the project neared the halfway mark in October, with about 16,000 workers operating out of 29 camps. The cost of the project, initially estimated at $6 billion, may run as high as $10 billion.

Oil Pricing. In his State of the Union message in January, President Gerald R. Ford announced plans to impose a new tariff on petroleum imports that would start at $1 a barrel and rise to $3. In July, the President announced a plan for the gradual removal of all price controls on domestic oil over a 30-month period. His proposal, which would have raised the price of gasoline and fuel oil by about 7 cents per gallon (3.8 liters) by the end of 1977, was rejected by Congress. But Congress eventually

Leaders of the Organization of Petroleum Exporting Countries hold their first summit meeting in Algiers, Algeria, in early March.

passed, and the President signed on December 22, an energy bill that ended the import tariff and initially reduced domestic crude oil prices.

Discussions with the Organization of Petroleum Exporting Countries (OPEC) concerning proposed price hikes of from 10 to 25 per cent per barrel of exported oil continued. Finally, at an OPEC conference in Vienna, Austria, in September, the price of OPEC oil was raised 10 per cent to $11.51 per barrel and was frozen there until June 30, 1976. The increase followed a fourfold increase over the previous two years.

Natural Gas shortages have plagued the United States every winter since 1969. The scarcity threatened for the winter of 1975-1976 was expected to be the worst, according to Senator Hollings. In October, he predicted that supplies would fall 1.3 trillion cubic feet (36.8 billion cubic meters), or about 19 per cent below potential demand, producing a shortage 30 per cent worse than in 1974-1975.

With natural gas accounting for about one-third of all the energy consumed in the United States, especially in the cold Northeastern and Midwestern states, the results would be serious. In earlier winters, gas companies unable to meet demands generally cut off service to industry. However, some observers said that some of the 55 per cent of American homes heated by natural gas might be unable to get gas.

The price of gas piped across state lines is set by the Federal Trade Commission at 52 cents per thousand cubic feet (28.3 cubic meters). The Ford Administration favors removing all price controls and letting a free market set the price in order to encourage further drilling. The Senate Interior Committee, on the other hand, favors a bill that would gradually raise the price of interstate gas over four years to $1.25 per thousand cubic feet (28.3 cubic meters), the price now charged for intrastate gas. On December 31, the Federal Power Commission ordered a two-stage price rise for interstate natural gas that would give gas producers a 21 per cent increase by July 1, 1976.

Concern over the natural gas shortages prompted Congress and federal agencies to consider legislation that would speed construction of a $10-billion pipeline to transport gas from Alaska's North Slope. The Federal Power Commission was studying two plans. One calls for a 2,600-mile (4,200-kilometer) pipeline system from the North Slope and Canada's Mackenzie Delta to Calgary, Alta. From there, other lines would carry the gas to the Western and Midwestern states. The other plan would build an 809-mile (1,301-kilometer) pipeline from Prudhoe Bay, Alaska, to the southern coast of Alaska. The gas would be liquefied there and shipped by tanker to southern California.   Mary E. Jessup

See also CANADA; ENERGY.

PHILADELPHIA. Mayor Frank L. Rizzo was re-elected in November, 1975, despite losing the support of the city's regular Democratic Party organization. The organization supported state Senator Louis G. Hill in the primary, because Rizzo had supported President Richard M. Nixon and other Republicans. But Rizzo defeated Hill and four other candidates in the May 20 primary. Then he easily beat Republican city councilman Thomas M. Foglietta in November.

A Transit Strike halted bus and subway commuter service on March 15, leaving 400,000 commuters searching for other means of transportation. Cars jammed the streets, and special parking areas had to be set up around the city. The strike was settled on March 25.

A strike of 270 mailers halted publication of the *Inquirer* and the *Daily News* on June 20. Pressmen on the rival *Evening Bulletin* temporarily stopped publication of that newspaper on June 24, after it added the *mastheads* (names) of the struck papers to its editions. The work stoppage ended on June 26.

Desegregation Plan. The Philadelphia Board of Education on January 10 ordered its staff to develop a plan that would put the city's 270,000 pupils in desegregated classrooms one day each week. They would spend the remaining four days in their neighborhood schools. A state court had ordered both the board and the state human relations commission to develop a plan by January 31.

A study of the city's public schools released on February 1 by the Federal Reserve Bank of Philadelphia reported that elementary pupils seemed to learn better in integrated schools. However, black junior high school students apparently benefited when surrounded by a black majority. The report also noted that the teacher's race and amount of advanced education and the school's facilities did not appear related to student achievement.

The Economy. Living costs rose 7.9 per cent in the Philadelphia area between August, 1974, and August, 1975. But the average income of factory workers kept pace, showing an 8.2 per cent annual rate of increase by mid-1975. However, food prices rose 9.7 per cent; housing costs, 9.2 per cent; and health and recreation prices, 8.7 per cent. The unemployment rate stood at 11 per cent in mid-1975, down 3.6 per cent. Department store sales registered a 5.4 per cent increase, while construction activity fell by 15.5 per cent. Gasoline prices remained nearly stable, increasing only 0.8 cent to 55.7 cents for a gallon (3.8 liters) of regular.

The Port of Philadelphia handled the largest volume of international commerce in the nation in 1974, according to a report released on May 17 by the Delaware River Port Authority. International shipping through Philadelphia reached a record high of 80.8 million short tons (73.3 million metric tons). James M. Banovetz

PHILIPPINES moved in 1975 to adjust to what President Ferdinand E. Marcos on May 23 called "the emerging realities in Asia." Marcos visited China from June 7 to June 11. On June 9, he signed a pact with Chinese Premier Chou En-lai to establish diplomatic relations. Taiwan immediately broke off its relations with the Philippines.

As American-backed regimes were falling in South Vietnam and Khmer (Cambodia), the Philippine government announced on April 12 that it was reassessing its defense agreements with the United States. Marcos expressed fear that American presidential agreements and other commitments were no longer binding. The status of Clark Air Force Base and the Subic Bay Naval Base, the largest U.S. Air Force and Navy bases in the western Pacific, was under review during the year.

Support for Marcos. The Philippine Supreme Court ruled 10 to 1 on February 1 that the martial law Marcos had proclaimed in 1972 was legal. This cleared the way for a February 27 referendum on Marcos' continued exercise of martial-law powers. The vote was conducted by an open show of hands at village meetings—a system that critics charged was rigged to produce the results Marcos wanted. Announced results gave 90 per cent approval for continuing the emergency powers that Marcos had assumed in 1972, and 80 per cent approval for presidential appointment of local officials instead of election. On November 6, Marcos appointed his wife to head a new government for the metropolitan Manila area.

Former Senator Benigno S. Aquino, Jr., the most prominent prisoner of the martial-law regime, ended a 40-day hunger strike on May 14. He had been protesting what he termed an illegal attempt to put him on trial. He remained in prison.

Purge Ordered. Marcos announced a wide-ranging purge of senior officials at September 19 celebrations of the third anniversary of martial law. Focusing on corruption, the president said a "sweeping, complete, and exhaustive reorganization of the government" would be made. He admitted that cleanup drives in 1972 and early 1973 had not been effective, and that authoritative controls had created new opportunities for corruption.

There was controversy whether land reform brought significant results, but rural areas prospered with one of the best rice crops in years. Foreign trade suffered from low prices for raw material exports.

Efforts to settle the Moslem rebellion in the southern islands had limited success. Secessionist groups denied repeated government claims of settlements, and guerrilla attacks continued. The New People's Army also battled the Philippine Army with a Maoist-style Communist challenge to the nation's social and economic order. Henry S. Bradsher

See also ASIA (Facts in Brief Table).

PHOTOGRAPHY. The international recession slashed profits and caused production cutbacks in many camera factories in 1975. It also held down the number of job opportunities. But despite a slowdown in world markets, the photography industry was alive and expanding. Ironically, popularity of the simple 110-format camera developed in the United States mushroomed in Japan and West Germany, the principal sources of complex cameras. Japanese importers of the German Leica cameras had their most prosperous year in a long time.

Photography's popularity continued to grow. A museum show in the United States featured *holograms* as art. These are three-dimensional images, normally used in industrial, medical, and space research, that can be viewed without special glasses or screens.

A new museum devoted to photography opened at the University of Arizona in Tucson in May. It exhibits the professional work of prominent photographers, along with papers and memorabilia that give an insight into their work and ideas.

New Cameras. Prototype cameras introduced in 1974, such as the Zeiss/Yashica Contax RTS and the full-frame Minox, actually arrived on the market during 1975. Two roll-film SLR cameras with offbeat picture formats were announced—the Mamiya 645 and the Bronica ETR. Both had for-

mats of 4.5 × 6 centimeters (1.8 × 2.4 inches), hardly a new size, but one not used before in modern, automated cameras.

Pentax, whose screw-thread lens mount was long almost a standard for many other cameras, introduced three new camera models featuring a bayonet lens mount, together with a new series of lenses. The switch from screw-thread to bayonet mount makes it possible to change lenses much faster.

Olympus introduced the OM-2, an automatic version of its little 35-millimeter (mm) SLR OM-1. It has an unusually interesting light meter. The built-in meter uses photocells that face the shutter and film surfaces and read the light reflected from them to determine exposure, instead of reading the light directly through the lens. This system permits the use of a special automatic flash unit whose light output is controlled by the same photocells.

Lens Technology continued to advance, with previously announced types such as the solid *catadioptrics* (combined lens and mirror) going on sale. Another noteworthy trend was the arrival of various zoom lenses with close-focusing capability in the *photomacrographic* (near actual size) range.

A new 50-mm lens from Leitz has a remarkable f/1 aperture—almost half again as fast as the highest-speed (f/1.2) still-camera lenses commonly available previously. Another Leitz introduction

Chicago Tribune photographer Ovie Carter won top prize in the World Press Photo Contest for a picture from his series on "The Faces of Hunger."

was a 180-mm f/3.4 apochromatic telephoto lens that virtually eliminates chromatic aberration — that is, it focuses light of all colors in the same plane to eliminate the colored halos that sometimes form around bright images.

Other Developments. The startling promise of cameras with automatic or near-automatic focusing was held out by an electronic-circuit chip announced by Honeywell, Incorporated. The company offered the chip for sale to camera makers.

In the movie field, the Eastman Kodak Company marketed a Super-8 sound camera that accepts a 200-foot (60-meter) cartridge of sound-striped film — four times the capacity of its previous film cartridges. This capacity makes the camera useful in such areas as television news coverage.

Photography suffered inevitable losses with the death of a number of leading figures. Among them were photographers Wynn Bullock, Walker Evans, and John Vachon; writers Arvel Ahlers, Joseph Cooper, Norris Harkness, and H. M. Kinzer; and W. Nelson Goodwin, Jr., 98, inventor of the Weston exposure meter and system of film-speed ratings.

The year closed with preparations underway in Cologne, West Germany, for the biennial *photokina* (World's Fair of Photography) in September, 1976. Many new products and processes will be revealed at the fair to continue photography's advance as an art, science, and craft.   Kenneth Poli

PHYSICS. One of the most remarkable developments in 25 years, discovery of psi particles, dominated news in the physics world in 1975. This discovery may be as important to understanding elementary particle physics as the hydrogen atom has been to atomic physics.

The Psi Particles. In November, 1974, two independent experimental groups simultaneously announced discovery of the first in a series of important new particles. One group was from the Massachusetts Institute of Technology (M.I.T.). The other was a collaboration of California research groups from the Stanford Linear Accelerator Center (SLAC), the Lawrence Berkeley Laboratory, and the University of California at Berkeley (UCB). Existence of the new particle — called the "J" by the M.I.T. group — was quickly confirmed in European laboratories. As 1974 ended, the California researchers found a second, heavier, but related new particle they called the "psi-prime."

These discoveries stimulated a huge research effort during 1975. At SLAC, the new particles are produced when beams of electrons and their antiparticles, positrons, collide head-on and annihilate each other in a race-tracklike device called the Stanford Positron-Electron Accelerating Ring (SPEAR). By midyear, the researchers at SPEAR had measured important physical properties of the new particles and found evidence of a third short-lived particle heavier than the psi-prime. They discovered that the psi-prime usually changes into the psi — thus establishing that the two particles are intimately related.

In July, a collaboration of West German and Japanese physicists using DORIS, the electron-positron accelerating ring in Hamburg, West Germany, reported that the psi-prime can also change into at least one new particle whose mass is intermediate between the psi and the psi-prime. By September, the SPEAR researchers had confirmed this result and discovered that the psi-prime changes into at least two new intermediate particles. Physicists at Cornell University in Ithaca, N.Y.; the Fermi National Accelerator Laboratory in Batavia, Ill.; SLAC; and the European Center for Nuclear Research's intersecting storage rings at Geneva, Switzerland, also studied the psi particles.

Theoretical Interpretation. Meanwhile, theorists tried to square the family of new particles with their understanding of the *strong force* — the one that holds protons and neutrons together in atomic nuclei. The most successful modern theory of the strong force holds that three tiny fundamental particles called *quarks* combine in various ways to form the 100 or so particles that interact via the strong force. In 1964, theorists Sheldon L. Glashow of Harvard University and James D. Bjorken of SLAC suggested that a fourth type of quark may exist. They believed it would be endowed with an abstract property curiously called *charm*. Charm would be conserved in strong interactions in very much the same way that the total amount of ordinary electric charge does not change. The fact that the psi lives at least 100 times longer than expected suggests that it may be a charmed quark and its antiparticle bound together. The discoveries of the psi-prime and the intermediate-mass particles support this hypothesis. All of them can be interpreted as excited states of the basic pair of charmed quarks. The next step in confirming this theory would be to observe a single charmed quark bound to one or more ordinary quarks.

Monopole!? A team of physicists from UCB and the University of Houston reported in August that they have discovered what they believe to be a magnetic monopole — a single pole of a magnet comparable to a single unit of electric charge. They based their announcement on an unusual track left by a particle that passed through 33 plastic sheets and a layer of photographic emulsion and film dangling from a balloon some 130,000 feet (40,000 meters) over Sioux City, Iowa, in 1973. Other physicists suggested that an ordinary platinum nucleus in the cosmic rays near the top of the atmosphere left the track. But the announcement generated immense excitement because the hypothetical monopole has been the subject of speculation and search since it was predicted in 1931.   Thomas O. White

PITTSBURGH. A celebration of overjoyous Pittsburgh football fans turned into a violent confrontation with police on Jan. 12, 1975, when the Pittsburgh Steelers won their first Super Bowl championship in New Orleans by defeating the Minnesota Vikings. About 11,000 fans swarmed into the downtown area following the game, and violence broke out. Sixty persons, including 2 policemen, were injured, and 250 persons were arrested.

Newspaper Strike. Pittsburgh's two newspapers were closed for a month by 700 striking members of the Teamsters Union who worked on the trucks and loading docks. The walkout started on June 27 at the *Press* in a dispute over reassignment of a dockworker. The strike also closed the *Post-Gazette,* which was printed by the *Press.* A total of 2,300 persons were idled by the strike. The papers resumed publication on July 28, after a settlement was reached that gave the company the right to change work assignments and gave the union a new method of calculating cost-of-living pay increases.

Pittsburgh teachers went on strike on December 1 over a pay dispute. Union officials speculated that the strike might last two months.

Mass Transit Success. Passenger use of public transit facilities in Pittsburgh increased during the first quarter of 1975 by 4.4 per cent over the 1974 level. More than 36 million passengers used the transit facilities of the Allegheny County Port Authority Transit (PAT) during the first three months of 1975. This record stands in contrast to the declining use of mass transit in other major cities.

The increased patronage resulted from an aggressive PAT marketing system that held down fares and increased services. The campaign to promote ridership used such devices as "wild card buses," on which service is free; attractively decorated vehicles; and reduced fares during nonrush hours.

Typical incentives were the "Early Bird Special" and the "Tuesday Special," which offered a 15-cent reduction in the 40-cent fare to persons riding before 7 A.M. or during off-peak hours on Tuesdays.

Living Costs in the Pittsburgh area rose 9 per cent between July, 1974, and July, 1975, but the average income of a factory worker rose only 3.5 per cent to an annual $12,151. Food costs rose 9.2 per cent between June, 1974, and June, 1975, while the average pump price of 1 gallon (3.8 liters) of regular gasoline increased 4.1 per cent to 56.8 cents.

The number of persons receiving unemployment benefits in August, 1975, reached 41,700, an increase of 105 per cent over the previous year. Department store sales in the area were up 5.5 per cent, but construction activity was down 13 per cent from the August, 1974, level.

A U.S. Census Bureau report released in mid-1975 showed that the city's population fell 7.8 per cent, to an estimated 479,276 persons from 1970 to July 1, 1973.   James M. Banovetz

POETRY. A poet – Eugenio Montale of Italy – won the 1975 Nobel Prize for Literature. His work is distinguished for its terse, deeply profound statements on the human condition. See NOBEL PRIZES.

Another Nobelist, Saint-John Perse (Alexis Léger) of France, the Homer of our racial unconscious, died on September 20. His books, such as *Anabase* (*Anabasis*), *Exil* (*Exile*), and *Vents* (*Winds*), won the Nobel Prize for him in 1960.

Other Prizewinners. Gary Snyder of California received the Pulitzer Prize for Poetry. His book, *Turtle Island,* takes its title from "the old/new name for the continent, based on many creation myths of the people who have been here for millennia."

Marilyn Hacker won the National Book Award for her volume, *Presentation Piece.* The Lamont Award for the most outstanding second book of poetry went to Lisel Mueller. Other important poetry prizes included the Edgar Allan Poe Award to Charles Simic for *Return to a Place Lit by a Glass of Milk;* the Walt Whitman Award to Reginald (Reg) Saner; and the Copernicus Award to Kenneth Rexroth, recognizing his lifetime achievement and his latest book, *New Poems.*

New Works. Among the established poets who gained critical attention were Michael Anania, Hayden Carruth, Josephine Jacobsen, Donald Finkel, Marvin Bell, John Ashbery, Ted Berrigan,

Reginald Saner of the University of Colorado won the Copernicus Society of America's first Walt Whitman Award for an unpublished poet.

Richard Howard, Robert Watson, Daryl Hine, David Ignatow, John Hollander, Donald Davie, Miller Brand, Arthur Gregor, James Schulyer, David Slavitt, and Kenneth Koch. An outstanding book, *Poem in Progress* by John Logan, explored the complexities of fathers and sons, and men who love young men.

Younger poets who brought out notable volumes included Charles Plymell, Richard Friedman, Anne Waldman, and Charles Wright. Ira Sadoff won the Yale Younger Poets Prize with *Settling Down.* Albert Goldbarth's *Jan. 31* was a National Book Award nominee.

Outstanding Translations. Patrick K. Ford translated *The Poetry of Llywarch Henn,* the sixth-century Welsh poet and warrior whose poems "poignantly describe the degradation and spiritual impoverishment of old age." Another outstanding translation was *Sir Gawain and the Green Knight: A Comedy for Christmas,* translated by Theodore Silverstein. David M. Vieth edited *The Complete Poems of John Wilmot, Earl of Rochester,* the first uncensored text of the Restoration poet.

Important criticism came from Karl Shapiro, whose irreverent, often brilliant, collection of essays was called *The Poetry Wreck;* Helen Vendler, *The Poetry of George Herbert;* Renato Poggioli, *The Oaten Flute: Essays on Pastoral Poetry;* and Robert Penn Warren, *Democracy and Poetry.*   Paul Carroll

POLAND expanded its political and business relations with both the West and the East in 1975. However, growing economic troubles at home soured the political climate prior to the Communist Party Congress in December. Edward Gierek was again named first secretary, while Franciszek Szlachcic was dropped from the Politburo. He had been considered a potential threat to Gierek.

The government's undoubted success was its deal with West Germany, originally made between Chancellor Helmut Schmidt and Gierek at the Helsinki, Finland, summit on August 2 (see WEST GERMANY). Gierek also reached an economic agreement with Sweden during his visit there in June. That same month, Poland signed documents strengthening cultural, economic, and political ties with France and obtained a $1.75-billion credit during President Valéry Giscard d'Estaing's visit.

U.S. Settlement. Poland settled its outstanding debts with the United States in May. American holders of $40 million in defaulted pre-World War II Polish bonds will receive 36 per cent of their nominal value and Poland will defer repurchase of the $20 million in Polish zlotys still in the United States from shipments of surplus agricultural goods to Poland in the late 1950s. President Gerald R. Ford visited Poland in July on his way to Helsinki. On October 20, U.S. Secretary of Commerce Rogers C. B. Morton concluded an agreement with Po-

land to increase mutual trade to $2 billion by 1980. In November, Poland agreed to buy annually an average of 2.75 million short tons (2.5 million metric tons) of U.S. grain through 1980.

Food Shortages, especially meat, led to widespread dissatisfaction in March and again later in the year. Poland's Planning Commission Chairman Mieczyslav Jagielski was replaced on October 23 by Tadeusz Wrzaszczyk, former minister for industry. A Politburo meeting on November 12 noted deteriorating labor discipline. The number of days not worked – excluding holidays – in key industries was 9.1 per cent higher in the first six months of 1975 than during the same period in 1974.

Far-reaching administrative reform, effective on June 1, changed Poland's three-level system of local government into a two-level system by abolishing 390 districts, or counties. The counties were absorbed by the larger *voivodships* (provinces), whose number increased from 22 to 49. Only 11 of the previous party secretaries in the voivodships were reappointed; 38 new appointments were made. The bureaucratic reorganization eliminated an estimated 13 per cent, or about 200,000, of Poland's civil service jobs, and increased Gierek's power by reducing the size and increasing the number of voivodships.   Chris Cviic

See also EUROPE (Facts in Brief Table).

POLLUTION. See ENVIRONMENT.

POPULATION, WORLD. The already vast number of people in the world increased at an extraordinary rate in 1975. The estimated population, as of December 31, stood at an all-time high of 4.2-billion persons. It represented an increase of some 90 million over the preceding year and, if it continued to increase at the current 2.2 per cent annual growth rate, population would double to some 8.4 billion in about 30 years.

Latin America, where the population was increasing at the rate of 2.9 per cent annually, had the highest growth rate in the world. Africa stood second, with a growth rate of 2.8 per cent, while Asia's total population was increasing at the annual rate of 2.5 per cent. Europe, with an 0.8 per cent growth rate, had the lowest per annum increase. The population of the North American continent was increasing 1.0 per cent annually.

The overall world birth rate, according to a report prepared by the Environmental Fund of Washington, D.C., was 35 per 1,000 population. The death rate was 13 per thousand. It was this gross imbalance – more people being born, fewer dying – that preoccupied demographic experts, governments, governmental agencies, and privately funded organizations. Their major cause of concern was the world's continuing depletion of its food resources in the face of the very high rate of population increase.

Dwindling Food Supply. Most demographers and agricultural experts agreed that food resources were inadequate to meet the needs of the burgeoning population. A World Fertility Survey, being conducted under the supervision of British statistician Sir Maurice G. Kendall, was one of a number of major long-range international investigations of the anticipated population crisis and its ultimate effect on food supply.

Concern was also reflected in a report issued by the National Research Council of Washington, D.C., on September 22. The council's introductory report, "Population and Food—Crucial Issues," was part of a major effort launched by the National Academy of Sciences and the National Science Foundation to bring the food problem into focus.

Birth Control. Many nations in Africa, Asia, and Latin America had difficulty in getting their people to use birth-control devices as a means of controlling runaway population growth. In India, efforts to curb population growth were floundering despite the fact that the government ordered stepped-up production of birth-control pills and even considered compulsory family-planning methods. In Africa, where the total population could reach 525 million by the year 2000, birth-control programs had proved to be "dismal failures," according to United Nations officials.　　　　　Robert C. Cook

PORTUGAL. The military regime survived revolts in 1975 by both left wing and right wing forces. By year's end, moderate elements appeared to be in control. Abroad, Portugal granted independence to Angola on November 11, but serious fighting among rival factions continued through the year (see ANGOLA). Other former colonies gained independence—Mozambique on June 25, Cape Verde Islands on July 5, and São Tomé and Príncipe on July 12 (see CAPE VERDE ISLANDS; MOZAMBIQUE; SÃO TOMÉ AND PRÍNCIPE).

Leftists Quashed. Extreme leftist paratroopers seized three major air bases and the air-force headquarters in Lisbon on November 25. President Francisco da Costa Gomes declared a state of emergency and sent loyal commandos to retake the installations. Three persons died in the fighting that ended the uprising the following day. Gomes discharged the army and navy chiefs and ousted the military-security police chief, General Otelo Saraiva de Carvalho, a leader of the ultraleftists. About 50 rebel officers were imprisoned in Porto.

The aborted November coup capped a year during which Portugal stood on the brink of civil war as ultraleftists, Communists, and Socialists vied for power. Yet, despite the intense political turmoil, fewer than 20 persons had been killed since the Armed Forces Movement (MFA)—the ruling or-

Portuguese workers, sailors, and soldiers took to the streets in 1975 as political power swung to the far left, then shifted to the middle.

ganization of young officers – seized power on April 25, 1974.

Spínola Flees. General António de Spínola – the former provisional president who was ousted in September, 1974 – fled to Spain on March 11 after an unsuccessful coup attempt by his rightist supporters. On March 12, the 200-member MFA set up a Supreme Revolutionary Council with full legislative powers. The leftist forces consolidated their power by nationalizing banks and insurance companies. Prime Minister Vasco dos Santos Gonçalves formed a fourth provisional government on March 25. But the moderate Socialist Party, led by Mario Soares, won 115 seats in elections on April 25, giving a clear lead in the 247-seat General Assembly to the three main non-Communist parties (see SOARES, MARIO). The Communist Party got only 12.5 per cent of the vote, or 30 seats.

Tensions Mount. Communist printers closed the Lisbon Socialist newspaper *Republica* on May 20 and sealed its offices. Socialists refused to participate in the government unless the Communists were restrained. They suspended their boycott on May 28 after the MFA intervened, and on May 30 *Republica* reappeared, printed on secret presses. Clashes continued, and Soares rallied the Socialists to oppose the left wing military rulers, accusing them of wanting to set up a Communist dictatorship. He led his party out of the government on July 11, and the coalition collapsed six days later, leaving the military in control.

Generals Lead. In a victory for the extreme left on July 25, the MFA concentrated all political and military power in the hands of three generals, Gonçalves, Gomes, and Otelo Saraiva. Following riots in northern towns, a new government was sworn in on August 7. Moderate military leaders began a campaign to oust the pro-Communist Gonçalves. In the face of sustained opposition, he quit, abandoning attempts to become commander in chief of the armed forces on September 5. A sixth provisional government, more moderately based, then took office on September 19 under Prime Minister José Pinheiro de Azevedo, who pledged to pursue broad Socialist policies (see AZEVEDO, JOSÉ PINHEIRO DE).

Weak Economy. Wage and price freezes and other austerity measures continued throughout 1975. With inflation running above 30 per cent annually, the United States and the European Community (Common Market) granted Portugal $272-million in emergency aid in October following the ouster of Gonçalves.

Island Trouble. Indonesian troops invaded Portuguese Timor on December 7 after months of civil war. Lisbon broke diplomatic ties with Indonesia and called for United Nations Security Council action. See ASIA.   Kenneth Brown

See also AFRICA; EUROPE (Facts in Brief Table).

POSTAL SERVICE, UNITED STATES. An off-again, on-again postal rate hike finally went into effect on Dec. 31, 1975, boosting the cost of a first-class letter from 10 cents to 13 cents. The price of post cards went up to 9 cents, and parcel-post rates were increased an average of 10 per cent. Other rates also were increased.

The rate hike, which was originally scheduled to take effect on December 28, was blocked on December 16 by U.S. District Judge John Sirica, who said the scheduled rate increases were illegal because the Postal Service failed to take all the steps required in raising rates. Sirica's decision was overturned by a federal appeals court on December 29, allowing the new rates to go into effect.

Postal officials had estimated that the new rates would provide $2.4 billion a year in additional revenue. But even with the increase, and a postal subsidy of $1.6 billion for the year ending June 30, 1976, they had predicted a $1.4-billion deficit for fiscal 1976.

Benjamin F. Bailar succeeded Elmer T. Klassen as postmaster general on February 15. Bailar, 40, joined the Postal Service in 1972 after serving as vice-president of American Can Company, which Klassen headed before taking the postal job.

Bailar proposed that Congress boost its subsidy by $1 billion a year for the next two or three years to avoid the need for additional rate increases and help the Postal Service eliminate its deficit. The new postmaster general promised to reduce labor costs by reassigning postal workers and going ahead with a controversial system for readjusting letter carriers' workloads.

Bailar also promised to take a "hard look" at the possibility of closing post offices in small towns. The General Accounting Office (GAO) recommended on June 5 that 12,000 rural post offices be closed. The GAO said it cost $270 million to operate these small post offices in 1973, though they only brought in revenues of $160 million.

Labor Agreement. Fears of a postal strike were eased in July when the Postal Service agreed on a new three-year contract with four unions covering 600,000 workers. Pay increases over the three-year period would total $1,500 a year, bringing the average, top-scale postal worker's pay to about $15,000. In addition, cost-of-living adjustments would be due in May and November, raising pay 1 cent an hour for each four-tenths of a point rise in the Consumer Price Index.

A provision barring layoffs was retained in the agreement, despite Postal Service efforts to change it. However, the Postal Service was allowed to hire temporary employees for up to 180 days, instead of the previous 89 days. These temporary employees are not covered by the no-layoff provision, and can constitute no more than 10 per cent of the work force at any location.   William J. Eaton

POVERTY. The International Bank for Reconstruction and Development (World Bank) announced on March 8, 1975, that it would increase its investment funds to $1 billion a year by 1979 to aid the poorest people in rural areas of developing countries. The bank defined the poorest people as those with an annual per capita income of $50 or less. The World Bank estimates that about 640 million persons fall into this category. About 80 per cent of these, or 512 million, live in rural areas.

The World Bank hopes to improve the productivity of the small farmer by consolidating land holdings, making better seeds available, improving health facilities, and developing farm-credit systems and new markets for agricultural products.

In its work to improve the health of the world's poor, the World Bank is shifting its emphasis from large building projects, such as hospitals, to preventive medicine and health education training programs for poor rural people.

UN Special Session. The United Nations (UN) General Assembly held a special session from September 1 to 16 to discuss ways to aid developing countries and narrow the economic gap between them and the industrial and oil-producing nations. The Assembly adopted a resolution on September 16 that called for stabilizing international commodities trade, which fluctuates wildly, often to the detriment of the farmer. It also urged greater financial aid, more scientific and technological aid, and agricultural assistance to developing countries.

It was also clear at the meeting that developing countries want to exert greater influence themselves over international economic decisions that will affect their futures.

In the United States, President Gerald R. Ford signed into law the Head Start, Economic Opportunity, and Community Partnership Act on Jan. 4, 1975. The bill extends economic opportunity programs for three years and replaces the Office of Economic Opportunity with the Community Service Administration. The new law provided for $330-million for fiscal year 1975 and open-ended authorizations for 1976 and 1977 for Community Action Program grants and contracts. It provided for $50-million for 1975 and set no maximum limit for 1976 and 1977 for community partnership projects. The bill did not set a fund limit for the Head Start program, but added a requirement that handicapped children make up at least 10 per cent of the Head Start enrollment. The Follow Through program was allocated $60 million. The bill also included authorization for grants and contracts to conduct research, demonstrations, and pilot programs on new ways to help American Indians become economically and socially self-sufficient.

The President had reservations about some features of the bill but decided it was the best compromise to break the deadlock between Congress and the executive branch on the future of the Community Action Program and an independent Office of Economic Opportunity. The President favors placing the agency under the Department of Health, Education, and Welfare, but there was strong congressional sentiment against such a move.

The President said that he believes strongly that federal social and economic assistance programs should be developed and operated with great sensitivity to the needs of the poor, but that those needs would be better served when programs that benefit the disadvantaged are managed together. Therefore, he ordered the development of a reorganization plan.

Food Stamps. By voting (374 to 38) on February 4 to freeze the price of government food stamps for the rest of the year, the U.S. House of Representatives rejected a Ford Administration plan to ease the rising federal cost of the food-stamp program. The Senate agreed the next day by a vote of 76 to 8, and the President, though he refused to sign the bill, allowed it to become law without his signature.

On Jan. 1, 1975, 17.1 million Americans were participating in the program, an increase of 1.2-million in a single month. As a result, the program was expected to cost at least $4 billion in 1975. The Administration had hoped to save $650 million by raising the price of the stamps from an average 23 per cent of the recipient's net income, figured on a sliding income scale, to a flat 30 per cent of each recipient's income. United States Department of Agriculture experts estimated this would have cut the number of stamp buyers by 10 to 20 per cent.

By June, the food-stamp program had 19.1 million persons enrolled; this total dropped slightly in July. On July 25, Ford asked Congress for an additional $3.8 billion to pay for the fiscal 1976 program, and the controversy between the Administration and Congress over the program continued to rage. Ford called it "another massive . . . program, almost uncontrolled. . . ." "We begin with the best of intentions," Treasury Secretary William E. Simon said on August 12, "but wind up with social programs that are spinning out of control." He termed the food-stamp program "a well-known haven for chiselers and ripoff artists." On the other hand, Senator George S. McGovern (D., S.Dak.) called it "the best social program we've got on the books, with the exception of Social Security. . . ."

Variations on a Theme. The food-stamp program produced a number of similar proposals in 1975. For instance, clothing stamps that would be issued to the poor were proposed by a New York City apparel industry official and were being studied by congressional staff analysts. And energy stamps, proposed by the Utility Rates Division of the Wisconsin Public Service Commission, would provide lower rates and lower utility taxes on electric bills.   Joseph P. Anderson

PRESIDENT OF THE UNITED STATES

Gerald R. Ford faced unusual problems during 1975. He was not the nation's elected leader; he became President under the terms of the 25th Amendment to the U.S. Constitution. He had been elected only as a Republican representative to Congress from Grand Rapids, Mich. He had been appointed Vice-President by Richard M. Nixon in 1973 and became President after Nixon resigned in 1974. Ford's Administration depended on many Nixon appointees, but Ford needed a new, untainted image. As President, he also faced enormous problems of inflation and unemployment at home, and he had to contend with the aftermath overseas of the U.S. defeat in Indochina.

On Nov. 3, 1975, President Ford announced far-reaching Cabinet shifts. He dismissed James R. Schlesinger as secretary of defense and named White House Chief of Staff Donald H. Rumsfeld to succeed Schlesinger. Richard B. Cheney, Rumsfeld's deputy, became the new White House chief of staff. The President also fired Central Intelligence Agency (CIA) Director William E. Colby and named George H. W. Bush, the U.S. representative in China, to replace him. The powerful Henry A. Kissinger remained secretary of state, but relinquished his post as the President's national security adviser. Air Force Lieutenant General Brent Scowcroft, a Kissinger supporter, became the national security adviser. That same day, the President named U.S. Ambassador to Great Britain Elliot L. Richardson as secretary of commerce to succeed Rogers C. B. Morton, who had asked to be replaced. Almost simultaneously, Vice-President Nelson A. Rockefeller announced that he would not be a candidate for the Republican vice-presidential nomination in 1976. See CABINET, UNITED STATES; ROCKEFELLER, NELSON ALDRICH.

Relations with Congress. In his State of the Union message to Congress on January 15, President Ford sounded a somber note, saying, "The state of the Union is not good." He urged Congress to support his programs for energy self-sufficiency and to avoid inflationary appropriations. He also asked for a free hand in making foreign-policy decisions. But throughout 1975, the President and Congress were in conflict over a national energy policy and over the broader questions of foreign policy and executive power.

A startled President Ford ducks during two assassination attempts—one in Sacramento, Calif., *above,* the other in San Francisco.

As part of his proposed energy independence plan, the President suggested a $2-per-barrel tax on all imported crude oil. He also proposed an amendment to the Clean Air Act that would delay rigorous emission-control standards for cars built from 1977 through 1981. In addition, President Ford called for removal of price controls from domestic oil and natural gas. However, Congress extended controls on oil prices twice. Then, on December 17, it finally passed an energy bill calling for oil-price

controls and price rollbacks. The President signed the bill on December 22.

The President also clashed with Congress over social-welfare legislation and tax legislation. Since assuming office in 1974, he had vetoed more than 40 bills passed by Congress, usually because he regarded them as inflationary. Only three laws were passed over his veto in 1975 – a $7.9-billion education bill; a $2-billion health care act; and the National School Lunch and Child Nutrition Act.

The President proposed a $16-billion tax reduction on January 13, including $12 billion in rebates of up to $1,000 on individual 1974 income tax payments. The tax bill finally passed by Congress and signed by the President on March 29 called for a $22.8-billion tax cut, with a maximum rebate of $200.

On October 6, President Ford suggested to Congress that the 1975 income tax cuts be made permanent and asked Congress for a corresponding cut in federal expenditures. Congress voted the tax cuts on December 17, but the measure did not limit federal spending. Ford vetoed it. Congress failed to override the veto, on December 18, but worked out a compromise extending the 1975 tax cuts for six months; the President signed it on December 23.

The President also clashed with Congress in 1975 on the subject of aid to Indochina. In the final days of the war in Khmer (Cambodia) and Vietnam, he asked Congress for military aid to stave off the

Communist victory, but Congress refused to appropriate the funds. Congress also established an arms embargo against Turkey in February despite the President's opposition, and lifted the embargo only partially in October. See ASIA; CONGRESS OF THE UNITED STATES; TURKEY.

National Energy Moves. On January 23, President Ford signed a proclamation raising the excise tax on imported crude oil by $1 per barrel, effective February 1. He imposed a second $1-per-barrel rise on June 1 and imposed a 60-cents-per-barrel duty on refined petroleum products. However, a U.S. court of appeals in Washington, D.C., ruled on August 11 that the President had no authority to impose taxes on imported oil. The court ruled invalid both Ford's $2-per-barrel fee and Nixon's 1973 graduated tax on crude oil. The Administration appealed the ruling, but on September 22, announced the elimination of the 60-cents-per-barrel fee on imported refined petroleum products, retroactive to September 1.

Foreign Policy. The United States finally abandoned its commitment in Southeast Asia in 1975 and accepted Communist victories in Vietnam and Khmer. On April 16, President Ford said the United States was responsible in a large measure for the "tragic situation" in South Vietnam as Communist troops overwhelmed government forces. Ford said

that Congress had not granted South Vietnam enough military aid in recent years. But in a speech at Tulane University in New Orleans on April 23, President Ford declared that "as far as America is concerned," the war in Indochina was over. He pleaded for a "great national reconciliation" in the aftermath of the long and costly conflict that had been opposed by so many Americans. The President ordered U.S. forces to help evacuate those Vietnamese who were afraid to remain in Vietnam under the Communists.

On May 12, shortly after the war ended, the U.S. merchant ship *Mayaguez* and its crew were captured by the Khmer Navy. When the *Mayaguez* was not immediately released, the President reacted swiftly. He dispatched U.S. Marines to attack Khmer's Tang Island and ordered a bombing attack on Ream Harbor. The ship and its crew were released even before the attacks.

Most Americans applauded the President's strong action. But some observers thought he had overreacted in order to show that the United States was still a mighty power. See KHMER.

Détente. The Administration continued to pursue a policy of détente with Russia. President Ford vigorously defended the Administration's agreements to sell wheat to the Soviet Union despite protests from labor unions. On October 20, the White

Emperor Hirohito of Japan, on his state visit, responds to President Gerald R. Ford's greeting outside the White House.

President Ford and Romanian President Nicolae Ceausescu, right, join in a Romanian folk dance during Ford's visit to Bucharest in August.

House announced a five-year agreement with Russia, providing for the shipment of up to 8.8 million tons (8 million metric tons) of U.S. grain a year. The White House also released a copy of a letter of intent that declared that the United States would be able to buy up to 200,000 barrels a day of Russian oil and petroleum products. See AGRICULTURE; LABOR; RUSSIA.

One of the year's greatest diplomatic triumphs for President Ford and Secretary of State Kissinger was the September Sinai agreement, ending the long conflict between Egypt and Israel. Congress agreed on October 9 to the stationing of U.S. civilians in the Sinai to monitor the terms of the agreement. See MIDDLE EAST.

Presidential Travel. President Ford traveled extensively throughout the United States in 1975. In addition, he made three trips to Europe and a trip to China. He made his first European visit in May and June. On May 28, he arrived in Brussels, Belgium, to reassure the North Atlantic Treaty Organization allies that the United States commitment to the alliance "will not falter." He flew to Madrid, Spain, on May 31 to discuss the presence of U.S. naval units in Spain with Generalissimo Francisco Franco. He then conferred with Egypt's President Anwar al-Sadat in Salzburg, Austria, and called on Pope Paul VI and Italian President Giovanni Leone in Rome.

He again flew to Europe in late July for the Helsinki, Finland, Conference on Security and Cooperation in Europe. He visited the concentration camp site in Auschwitz, West Germany, and conferred with West German Chancellor Helmut Schmidt. He also visited government leaders in Poland, Romania, and Yugoslavia. On November 16, the President flew to France for an economic conference at Rambouillet, near Paris. See EUROPE; INTERNATIONAL TRADE AND FINANCE.

On November 30, the President left for a five-day visit to China, where he met with various Chinese leaders, including Communist Party Chairman Mao Tse-tung. On the way back, he visited Indonesia and the Philippines. Ford conferred with Philippines President Ferdinand E. Marcos on the future of U.S. bases in the Philippines. He also stopped in Honolulu, Hawaii, for December 7 ceremonies marking the 34th anniversary of the Japanese attack on Pearl Harbor.

Presidential Politics. President Ford also campaigned hard for the 1976 Republican presidential nomination, trying to head off a challenge by the conservative former governor of California, Ronald Reagan. Ford formally announced his candidacy on July 8, and for the rest of the year continually voiced his own conservative viewpoints. In a speech in Chicago on August 25, he promised to "get the federal government out of your business, out of your lives, out of your pockets, and out of your hair." He stated his opposition to forced school busing, and he pushed for deregulation of the nation's railroads, air transport, and trucking systems. He pledged a strong effort to balance the federal budget and criticized beleaguered New York City for its liberal welfare and spending policies. See NEW YORK CITY; REPUBLICAN PARTY.

Perils of the Presidency. President Ford's life was in danger three times in 1975. On September 5, Lynette Alice Fromme pointed a loaded pistol at the President while he stood on a sidewalk in Sacramento, Calif., shaking hands with well-wishers. Fromme was convicted of attempting to assassinate the President and, on December 17, was sentenced to life in prison.

On September 22, Sara Jane Moore fired at the President outside the St. Francis Hotel in San Francisco, but missed. In December, she pleaded guilty to a charge of trying to kill the President. On Jan. 15, 1976, she was sentenced to life in prison.

Despite the danger, President Ford maintained that public appearances were an important part of his job. At times, he appeared to be wearing a bulletproof vest, but Secret Service agents refused to divulge what precautions were being taken. The President escaped injury in an automobile accident on October 14 in Hartford, Conn. See FORD, GERALD RUDOLPH.

White House Visitors. Many foreign heads of state and high officials visited the White House. Emperor Hirohito of Japan paid a state visit to the United States in October. Japanese Prime Minister Takeo Miki also visited the President in August.

British Prime Minister Harold Wilson went to the White House for talks with the President in January and again in May. The President also met with the leaders of Australia and New Zealand in May.

Ford discussed Middle East developments with Israeli Prime Minister Yitzhak Rabin at the White House on June 11 and 12 and with Egyptian President Anwar al-Sadat on October 27.

Jordan's King Hussein I visited the White House in April, and the Shah of Iran visited in May. In June, President Nicolae Ceausescu of Romania met with the President to discuss U.S. trade agreements.

Watergate Ghosts. *Washington Post* investigative reporters charged on December 18 that they had uncovered information showing that President Ford had been pressured into granting Nixon a pardon in August, 1974, and that Ford had told a Nixon aide there would be a pardon 10 days before it was granted. The newspaper claimed that a Nixon speechwriter had drafted Ford's statement about the pardon. However, Ford denied the charges and continued to maintain that he had acted on his own in granting the pardon in September, 1974. See WATERGATE.   Carol L. Thompson

PRINCE EDWARD ISLAND. See CANADA.

PRISON. A distinct upsurge in prison population led to serious overcrowding in many United States penal institutions in 1975, and correctional authorities warned that the trend could lead to severe problems in coming years. After relatively little prison construction in recent years, due in part to a leveling of inmate numbers, the new trend took many prison officials by surprise.

Prison Population. A Law Enforcement Assistance Administration study showed that nine prison systems in the South were filled far beyond listed capacity. Federal judges in Alabama, Florida, Georgia, and the District of Columbia ordered officials to relieve congestion or face contempt citations. Florida had been housing inmates in tent cities, and Louisiana was considering taking a World War II ship out of moth balls to serve as a floating prison. Georgia released up to 1,000 prisoners prematurely in October to make room for new ones.

Slightly more than 360,000 inmates were incarcerated in federal, state, and local centers on a typical day during the year. That number included about 24,000 in 35 federal institutions (a 10-year high), some 200,000 in 550 major adult and juvenile facilities operated by the states and the District of Columbia, and about 140,000 in county and municipal jails.

John J. Flanagan, a researcher at the University

Chicago's new triangular-shaped federal detention center may represent the prison of the future, with its barless windows and individual rooms.

of Wisconsin, released a study in November predicting a continued upsurge in prison population and overtaxed facilities until 1985. He attributed the increase to rising crime rates; an increase in the number of men in the 20- to 30-year-old "prison age bracket"; the increased popularity of mandatory jail sentences to deter crime; and fewer offenders being diverted into nonprison sentences.

Jail Disturbances. Overcrowding was blamed for the year's biggest prison outbreak, a 17-hour disturbance by 1,800 inmates at New York City's Rikers Island Detention Center in the Bronx on November 23 and 24 that caused an estimated $2-million damage. Over objections of guards and others, prison officials granted total amnesty to the rioters in return for the safe release of five guards seized as hostages. City officials promised action on prisoner complaints about overcrowding, poor medical treatment, and lack of visiting privileges.

The debate over the value of prison rehabilitation programs continued. A survey taken by the American Bar Association's *Corrections* magazine indicated that 77 per cent of the nation's ranking prison administrators opposed ending rehabilitation programs, but only 25 per cent cited rehabilitation as their primary goal. David C. Beckwith

PRIZES. See AWARDS AND PRIZES; CANADIAN LIBRARY ASSOCIATION; CANADIAN LITERATURE; FASHION; NOBEL PRIZES; PULITZER PRIZES.

PROTESTANT. Internationally, Protestant turmoil in 1975 was reflected in a number of issues, most of them having to do with religious repression by military regimes. In South Korea, many Protestant ministers were exiled or imprisoned by President Chung Hee Park. Protestants in Zaire were inhibited by the new policies of President Mobutu Sese Seko, who moved the celebration of Christmas to June 24, restored pre- or anti-Christian rites, and banned religious instruction in Zaire schools. The ultraconservative Lutheran churches in Chile opposed their 42-year-old bishop, Helmut Frenz, for his criticism of the new right wing government. In Norway, the conservative Lutheran bishop Per Lønning resigned his office in protest against the government's support of legalized abortion.

The international religious scene was not given over only to dispute and conflict. The World Council of Churches met in November in Nairobi, Kenya, to discuss "Christ Frees – Christ Unites." The conclave brought Protestant and Eastern Orthodox leaders together, while the Roman Catholic Church sent observers. The gathering revealed that, despite deep cleavages over theology and social policy both within the World Council and between it and other Christians, not everyone had given up on the quest for Christian unity.

Women. Whether or not International Women's Year lived up to its expectations, 1975 was unques-tionably "the year of the woman" in U.S. Protestantism. Church after church struggled with "sexist language" in their liturgies and constitutions. The Church of the Brethren, having set out to minimize exclusively masculine references in its literature, found itself obliged to confront the denomination's very name.

Symbolic of the new breakthroughs for women was the naming of Sallie TeSelle as dean of the Vanderbilt University Divinity School in Nashville, Tenn. She is the first woman to lead a prestigious theological institution.

The biggest church news concerning women, however, was the yearlong preoccupation with the question of women's ordination in the Episcopal Church. The conflict generated by this issue forebodes deeper Episcopal conflicts in the future.

While more than 70 Protestant denominations now ordain women, the Episcopal Church officially does not. Episcopalianism, part of the Anglican Communion, adheres to what many describe as a "catholic-sacramental" view of the ministry. This means, among other things, that ordination is taken especially seriously in the theology and canons of the church. To include women in the priesthood is a particularly difficult issue in such a context.

Despite official opposition to their envisioned new role, scores of women were registering at Episcopal seminaries, and scores more were already serving as deacons, the order of ministry next in line to priesthood. They found support from what some regarded to be a surprising source, the new archbishop of Canterbury, the Most Reverend F. Donald Coggan. Archbishop Coggan, regarded as a relatively conservative evangelical churchman and one not eager to stimulate controversy, publicly supported women's ordination in 1975. Meanwhile, Canadian Anglicans authorized women to become priests, though they permitted considerable variety of interpretation and practice, depending upon diocese.

Four U.S. Episcopalian women were ordained on September 7 by the Right Reverend George W. Barrett, retired bishop of Rochester, in Washington, D.C. Eleven women were ordained in 1974. Barrett and other bishops who have taken part in such rites were censured by their colleagues, and male priests who permitted or authorized these women to administer the sacraments were also subjects of "godly admonition." Throughout the year, there were repeated instances of trials, censures, and controversy.

Debate raged over whether the women who were not waiting for full church approval were creating a backlash that would delay a vote of support for women's ordination by the church's House of Deputies and General Convention, or were hastening that day. Episcopalian conservatives were also expressing discontent over a new trial version of their *Book of Common Prayer.*

Lutheran Conflicts. Even more troubled were the debates in the 2.8-million-member Lutheran Church — Missouri Synod. The largely Midwestern church has been torn by controversy since conservative members began to dominate its leadership in 1969. At the 1975 biennial convention in Anaheim, Calif., in July, the conservative majority passed a number of measures designed to suppress the dissent of moderates. They reaffirmed past restrictive measures against the moderates and condemned the new 400-student Concordia Seminary in Exile (Seminex) in St. Louis, an institution, established in 1974, that resulted from conscientious objection to what its professors and students saw to be repressive policies. They denounced Evangelical Lutherans in Mission, an organization that rallied many of those opposed to administration policies, and served notice against at least eight district presidents — the equivalent of bishops — who ordained Seminex graduates and whose other activities did not always conform to majority policies.

The district presidents firmly defended their activities. Evangelical Lutherans in Mission declared in August that they intended to stay together and continue their form of witness, even if it meant being evicted from the Missouri Synod.

Other denominations also saw conflict. An intransigent Wesleyan group called The Good News

Movement at its summer convention denounced the moderation or liberalism of the United Methodist Church, asked for control of at least one seminary and a separate ecclesiastical jurisdiction, and in other ways made sounds that many Methodists interpreted as schismatic.

Hartford Statement. The year was generally quiet theologically. Few new books or statements of major importance awakened response. An exception was the statement issued in January by 18 theologians — Protestant, Roman Catholic, and Eastern Orthodox — who met at Hartford, Conn. The highly publicized gathering denounced several trends among Protestant theologians that came to be known as the "Hartford Heresies."

At the heart of their concern was what they believe to be a neglect of the sense of "transcendence" in Christian leaders' thought today. They charged that these leaders were not sufficiently accenting the distinctiveness of the church's doctrines, its exclusiveness, or its regard for God's "otherness."

Responses to the statement varied. Because the signers named no names, some churchmen claimed that such generalized criticism spread false impressions as to the extent and character of the "heresies." It was hard to find a prominent thinker who recognized himself or herself in the Hartford statement. Others averred that almost no one held

Moderates of the Evangelical Lutherans in Mission decide in Chicago in August to split with the conservative Lutheran Church — Missouri Synod.

to these "heresies," though these views had been more visible 10 years earlier. The conservative religious press, both Roman Catholic and Protestant, devoted the most space to the event. It gave their editors an opportunity to tell readers that even liberals – and most Hartford participants had been typed as liberals – were disgusted with theological extremism. The response also indicated that thousands of Protestants welcomed the manifesto as a sign of new theological seriousness and steadiness. Those who had called the conference reconvened the group in September and announced a series of publications and future organizational activities on the subject.

Church Membership. Statistically, it was not an especially good year for Protestant churches in the United States. The fundamentalist, Pentecostal, and conservative evangelical denominations continued to hold their own, but their growth was not sufficient to compensate for the decline in other groups. Those supporters who remained active in all the churches were faithful in their financial offerings. In most cases, giving reached new highs.

In 1974, some 40 percent of the American people told polltakers they had been in church the week before – down from a high of 49 per cent in 1958. Among Protestants, 30 per cent said that they attended church weekly.　　　　Martin E. Marty

See also RELIGION.

PSYCHOLOGY. Researchers at Tulane University in New Orleans reported in June, 1975, that they had identified the action of two *neurotransmitters* (chemicals that transmit impulses in the brain). The psychologists – Jack D. Maser, Gordon G. Gallup, Jr., and Lou E. Hicks – used the neurotransmitters noradrenalin (NA) and serotonin (5-HT), which are apparently reciprocally related, on chickens. They used the chemicals to study tonic immobility, a relatively prolonged paralysis that occurs when most animals, including chickens, are suddenly released from manual restraints. For a time after release, the animals exhibit a waxy flexibility in their limbs – much like catalepsy in humans – and muscular tremors.

The psychologists first induced tonic immobility in the chickens and then injected them with NA, and found that this chemical prolonged the time that the chickens remained immobilized. When the researchers injected 5-HT, the time of immobility was much shorter. They also injected the hallucinating drug LSD, which is known to deplete the brain's natural supply of 5-HT, and found that LSD also prolongs the time of tonic immobility.

Although there are more differences than similarities between tonic immobility in animals and cataleptic disorders in human beings, it is possible that chemicals can control catalepsy just as they control tonic immobility.

Learning to be Helpless. Psychologists Martin E. Seligman and Robert A. Rosellini of the University of Pennsylvania conducted experiments in 1975 on learned helplessness, a phenomenon discovered by Seligman more than a decade ago. Learned helplessness involves limits on an animal's ability to learn when it is restrained during punishment. For example, dogs that are given electric shocks from which they cannot escape have great difficulty learning to escape from such shocks when they are later free to do so. In contrast, dogs that have not been previously shocked, or dogs that are given shocks from which they can escape, learn quickly to run away from the shocking mechanism. Although the studies of Seligman and his associates relate only to animals, the work may have important implications for human educational theories and for problems of social learning. Seligman and Rosellini suggest that exposure to unavoidable punishment conditions any living organism to accept frustration passively.

In their latest experiments, Seligman and Rosellini showed that learned helplessness also limits learning in other situations. They found that hungry animals that had first learned to be helpless through exposure to inescapable shocks could look for food only where they had been previously taught to find it. When the food was not there, they passively accepted the frustration.　　　Robert W. Goy

PUBLISHING. Major mergers and general belt-tightening characterized the book-publishing industry in 1975. One of the largest take-overs was the November sale of Viking Press, New York City, to Penguin Books, the giant British paperback publisher, for a reported $12 million. The sale was seen as part of a trend away from independent publishing companies, and toward more concentration in the industry. Other important mergers were the sale of E. P. Dutton & Company to a Dutch company during the summer, and MCA Incorporated's acquisition of G. P. Putnam's Sons in September.

Economic Woes. Major hard-cover book publishers in the United States approached the year with caution, saying that new book titles might be cut as much as 30 per cent. They announced plans to cut back authors' advances and royalties, and indicated that they would tend to look for sure-fire sellers in buying manuscripts. Despite the economic slump, however, new titles in the first half of the year totaled 14,998, some 200 more than in the first six months of 1974. Including new editions of old titles, the total number of books published during the year was expected to increase 5 to 7 per cent.

One bright spot on the scene was found at the university presses, which are switching from academic subjects to more general-interest books.

Copyright Controversy. National controversy over the reproduction and distribution of written

Publishers' representatives from five continents gather for a gala opening night dinner at the first Montreal International Book Fair in May.

PUERTO RICO. A five-year dispute over the use of Culebra Island and its surrounding keys as U.S. Navy gunnery targets ended amicably in 1975. Under an executive order signed by President Gerald R. Ford on September 10, the Navy agreed to cease testing ship-to-shore weapons in the area and relinquished all control over the leased property it held on Culebra. Puerto Rico announced it would establish a recreational area on the property.

A new civil service law provoked a one-day walkout and a march through the streets of San Juan by thousands of public employees on October 8. The government maintained the law would offer job security and protection from political reprisals. The workers insisted the law put them at the mercy of their employers. A simultaneous strike by the National Maritime Union against the Puerto Rican Merchant Marine severely cut Puerto Rico's food supply for a time.

The island's economy was in serious straits, with revenues from manufacturing, construction, and tourism dwindling steadily. Unemployment was reported at 19.9 per cent as of August 1, but it was closer to 40 per cent if those who had given up looking for work were included. An estimated 71 per cent of Puerto Rico's 2.9 million residents depended on food stamps for survival.   Paul C. Tullier

See also LATIN AMERICA (Facts in Brief Table).

materials supposedly covered by copyright continued to simmer. A deadlocked Supreme Court of the United States left the issue undecided in February when it upheld a lower court ruling that a medical publisher could not collect fees from libraries that copy its articles without charge. The issue has set libraries and others against composers, authors, and publishers who argue that the growing use of duplicating machines causes them to lose buyers. Librarians and educators argue that duplication is crucial in providing access to knowledge.

A broad-based coalition of literary, musical, news, and educational publishers and audiovisual groups joined forces in March to fight for a revised federal copyright law that would cover "fair use" of copyrighted works and library photocopying. The group said it does not oppose making single copies for personal use, but it opposes massive copying in which one copy of a book or magazine is used as a master to produce repeated duplicates.

Subcommittees of the United Nations Educational, Scientific, and Cultural Organization and the World Intellectual Property Organization at a joint session in June declined to recommend photocopying standards for their members. The group recommended that national solutions be found for the problem.   Gerald B. Healey

See CANADIAN LITERATURE; LITERATURE; MAGAZINE; NEWSPAPER; POETRY.

Puerto Rico's Governor Rafael Hernández Colón, speaking from the governor's mansion in San Juan, announces his antirecession budget.

PULITZER PRIZES in journalism, letters, and music were announced in New York City on May 5, 1975. In the 59th year of awards, the prizes were:

Journalism

Public Service. A gold medal to *The Boston Globe*, for "massive and balanced coverage of the Boston school desegregation crisis." The award cited more than 400 articles published by the newspaper, beginning on April 1, 1974.

General Local Reporting. $1,000 to *The Xenia* (Ohio) *Daily Gazette*, for its coverage of the tornado that devastated Xenia on April 3, 1974, killing 30 persons, injuring 1,600, and causing an estimated $100-million damage. Although its plant was damaged and many employees had lost homes, the paper did not miss a day of publication.

Special Local Reporting. $1,000 to the *Indianapolis Star*, for a six-month investigation of police corruption that led to the resignation of three Indianapolis, Ind., officials and the subsequent election defeat of the Marion County prosecutor.

National Reporting. $1,000 to Donald L. Barlett, 39, and James B. Steele, 32, of the *Philadelphia Inquirer*, for a seven-part investigative series on the Internal Revenue Service that exposed "the unequal application of federal tax laws."

International Reporting. $1,000 to William Mullen, a 30-year-old reporter, and Ovie Carter, a 29-year-old photographer, of the *Chicago Tribune*, for a five-part series on famine in Africa and India. The two newsmen traveled over 10,000 miles (16,000 kilometers) in their investigation.

Editorial Writing. $1,000 to John Daniell Maurice, 61, editor of the *Charleston* (W. Va.) *Daily Mail*. Maurice wrote nearly 50 editorials that helped to shape responsible public opinion during the bitter textbook controversy in Kanawha County, West Virginia. He has worked at the *Daily Mail* since 1937.

Spot News Photography. $1,000 to Gerald H. Gay, 29, of the *Seattle Times* for a photo of four weary Seattle firemen resting after fighting a fire that destroyed a waterfront home on Oct. 11, 1974.

Feature Photography. $1,000 to Matthew Lewis, 45, staff photographer for the *Washington Post* for his color photography in the newspaper's Sunday supplement, *Potomac Sunday*.

Distinguished Commentary. Mary McGrory, columnist of the *Washington Star*, for her discussions of public affairs. McGrory joined the *Star* in 1947. Her column appears in some 50 newspapers.

Distinguished Criticism. $1,000 to Roger Ebert, 33, film critic for the *Chicago Sun-Times*. Ebert has been with the *Sun-Times* since 1966, when he abandoned graduate studies at the University of Chicago. His reviews, syndicated to nearly 100 newspapers, prompted the Chicago Newspaper Guild to praise him for "ushering in a new era of criticism in Chicago."

Editorial Cartooning. $1,000 to Gary Trudeau, 26-year-old creator of "Doonesbury," which is syndicated in almost 300 newspapers. "Doonesbury" developed in 1969 out of a comic strip Trudeau drew for the *Yale Daily News* when he was a student there. He has since used the strip to comment vigorously and humorously on the Vietnam War, the Nixon Administration, and the Watergate scandals. "Doonesbury" is the first comic strip to win a Pulitzer Prize.

Letters

Biography. $1,000 to Robert A. Caro, 39, for his controversial biography *The Power Broker: Robert Moses and the Fall of New York*. Caro spent seven years writing the massive, often highly critical, study of city planner Robert Moses, who built many of New York City's bridges, tunnels, and expressways.

Drama. $1,000 to Edward Albee, 47, for his philosophical comedy *Seascape*. Albee won a Pulitzer in 1967 for *A Delicate Balance*. His best-known and most important play, *Who's Afraid of Virginia Woolf?*, was rejected by the Pulitzer Prize advisory board in 1962.

Fiction. $1,000 to Michael Shaara, 46, for his second novel, *The Killer Angels*. The book tells the story of the Battle of Gettysburg from the point of view of historic participants, such as Confederate

Gary Trudeau's hard-hitting commentaries on the Watergate affair helped him win the Pulitzer Prize for his "Doonesbury" strip.

generals Robert E. Lee and James Longstreet. An associate professor at Florida State University in Tallahassee, Shaara has been on a medical leave of absence since a 1974 motorcycle accident.

General Nonfiction. $1,000 to Annie Dillard, 30, for *Pilgrim at Tinker Creek*, a lyrically philosophical celebration of nature around Tinker Creek in the Roanoke River Valley of Virginia.

History. $1,000 to Dumas Malone, 83, for the first five volumes of a projected six-volume *Jefferson and His Time*, a biography of Thomas Jefferson. Malone began his work in 1943 and is working on the final volume. A professor of history at Columbia University from 1945 to 1959, he is now a professor of history and biographer in residence at the University of Virginia.

Poetry. $1,000 to Gary S. Snyder, 45, for *Turtle Island*, a work that "harks back to these roots" of the peoples of North America. He is a serious student of American Indian cultures and Zen Buddhism and is generally considered to have been the model for the character Japhy Ryder in *The Dharma Bums* by Jack Kerouac.

Music. $1,000 to Dominick Argento, 48, for his song cycle *From The Diary of Virginia Woolf*, which was first performed by Janet Baker in Minneapolis, Minn., in January, 1975. Argento has been a professor of music at the University of Minnesota since 1958.   Edward G. Nash

QATAR completed its take-over of the assets of the Shell Oil Company of Qatar and the Qatar Petroleum Company in May, 1975. The two companies received compensation of $35 million.

Prime Minister Khalifa bin Hamad Al-Thani announced an ambitious three-year, $250-million industrial plan on September 5 that is designed to lessen Qatar's dependence on oil. The industrialization plan will use the country's extensive natural gas holdings, which are expected to last long after Qatar's oil runs out. The plans include new steel and aluminum industries and the expansion of existing cement and fertilizer factories, and harbor facilities at Qatar's main ports, Doha and Musayid.

The national budget approved on January 20 totaled $460 million, a 60 per cent increase over 1974. The major allocations were $150 million for housing and $120 million for agriculture.

Qatar joined with other Persian Gulf states and Iran in forming a $7-million Regional Fisheries Project under the technical direction of the United Nations Food and Agriculture Organization. The group will coordinate fishing activities and survey fishery resources in the gulf. In September, Qatar loaned Egypt $100 million.   William Spencer

See also MIDDLE EAST (Facts in Brief Table).

QUEBEC. See CANADA.

RACING. See AUTOMOBILE RACING; BOATING; HORSE RACING; SWIMMING; TRACK AND FIELD.

RADIO made a serious attempt in 1975 to separate its legislative interests from those of television in the United States. In a move to become a "total radio" organization, the National Association of FM Broadcasters changed its name in September to the National Radio Broadcasters Association. Its first move was to seek a new license-renewal regulation that would cover radio only.

The National Association of Broadcasters protested, contending that radio and television were "inextricably entwined." But the Federal Communications Commission (FCC) and the White House Office of Telecommunications Policy (OTP) indicated their support of the idea.

Regulations Eased. The FCC in September proposed a test suspension of the fairness doctrine for radio stations in major cities when broadcasting political news. Under the fairness doctrine, broadcasters are compelled to provide equal time for opposing views on controversial issues. The following month, the OTP drafted a more ambitious legislative plan that would exempt radio outlets in the top 10 markets from almost all government regulations for five years. Both proposals were based on the theory that there were enough radio stations in those markets to ensure an overall balance. Both plans met with strong opposition from congressional committees and public interest groups.

The power of protest organizations was illustrated in August when Starr Broadcasting made a precedent-setting agreement with two citizens' groups—Classical Radio for Connecticut and the WNCN Listeners' Guild. Starr agreed to drop its all-rock music format on New York City's WQIV-FM, to restore the outlet's all-classical music format and former call letters (WNCN-FM), and to sell the station to the GAF Corporation.

Program Trends. Rock and middle-of-the-road (soft pop) music formats continued as favorites in 1975. By fall, the new disco music fad—the revival of hard rock with a danceable beat—was a growing programming influence. Other program staples included all-news formats and consumer-help shows. In line with the first trend, NBC Radio introduced its National News and Information Service, a syndicated, round-the-clock, all-news service.

Collective sales revenues for network radio in 1975 were expected to be the best in two decades. The sales gain was partially attributed to the recession, which made radio seem a better media value to advertisers.

An Arbitron radio survey found that 36.4 per cent of all radio listeners in the top 10 markets were tuned to FM stations in 1975. The study said that FM listenership had increased 81 per cent since 1970. FM station sales in the million-dollar-plus price range continued to boom. Two FM outlets—KOST-FM in Los Angeles and KRBE-FM in Houston—sold for $2.5 million each. June Bundy Csida

RAILROAD operations in the United States suffered in 1975 from the business recession. The U.S. Congress passed a $6.5-billion aid bill on December 19, but President Gerald R. Ford said he would veto it as being too costly. A wage-contract agreement in December averted a nationwide strike.

United States railroads showed their first overall net operating income deficit in history – $94 million – in the first three months of 1975, the Association of American Railroads said. Through September, losses totaled about $128 million, against profits of $553 million a year earlier. Freight traffic fell 11.7 per cent through mid-December, but the downward trend seemed reversed late in the year. Increased grain shipments led the turnaround.

Operating revenues were about $12 billion in the first nine months, 5 per cent below the same period in 1974. The Interstate Commerce Commission (ICC) stalled a 7 per cent freight-rate boost early in 1975, but finally allowed that rise and two others for a total 14.5 per cent increase by October.

A Midwest line, the Chicago, Rock Island & Pacific Railroad, joined eight Northeastern railroads in bankruptcy proceedings on March 17. Delayed for 12 years by the ICC, its plan to merge with the Union Pacific Railroad fell apart, and the U.S. Railway Association (USRA), a government corporation, refused to grant an emergency loan.

On July 28, USRA issued its "Final System Plan" for restructuring seven of the bankrupt Northeastern lines into Consolidated Rail Corporation (Conrail), a federally backed private railroad. The plan was tacitly adopted on November 9, when Congress did not act to reject it before then. The Conrail plan involves $2.1 billion in federal financing; abandonment or federal-state subsidy of 5,700 miles (9,200 kilometers) of money-losing branch lines; and purchase by the solvent Chessie System, Incorporated, holding company for the Chesapeake & Ohio Railway and the Baltimore & Ohio Railroad, of 2,000 miles (3,200 kilometers) of Northeastern track, to give Conrail competition.

Conrail funding was part of the package of railroad legislation Congress enacted in December. The bill also gave railroads considerable freedom from ICC regulation in setting freight rates, in line with Administration proposals on rail aid and "deregulation."

Travel on trains run by the National Railroad Passenger Corporation (Amtrak) declined 9 per cent through September, to 12 million passengers, as people who rode trains during the 1974 gasoline crunch went back to their cars. The fiscal 1976 operating deficit was estimated at $460 million, up from $278 million in fiscal 1975, with costs climbing and several new routes added. Congress, on May 26, enacted $1.1 billion in legislation to cover Amtrak losses and buy new equipment.   Albert R. Karr

See also TRANSPORTATION.

Transrapid 4, a magnetic suspension train built in West Germany, reaches a top speed of 120 miles (200 kilometers) per hour in tests in May.

REAGAN, RONALD (1911-   ), the former motion-picture star and two-term governor of California, became a candidate for the Republican nomination for President on Nov. 20, 1975 (see RE- PUBLICAN PARTY). Reagan, considered a spokesman for the party's conservative wing, called on Republicans to raise an ideological banner "of bold colors and no pale pastels."

Ronald Wilson Reagan was born in Tampico, Ill., and graduated from Eureka College in Illinois. He became a radio sports announcer in Des Moines, Iowa, in the 1930s. He acted in his first movie in 1937. His best-known films included *Kings Row* (1941), *This Is the Army* (1943), and *Storm Warning* (1950). During the 1940s and 1950s, he also served as president of the Screen Actors Guild and as head of the Motion Picture Industry Council.

Reagan entered national politics in 1964 when he campaigned on television for the Republican presidential candidate, Senator Barry Goldwater of Arizona. He was elected governor of California in 1966, campaigning on a promise to reduce government spending and the role of government in society. He was re-elected in 1970, and ran unsuccessfully for the Republican nomination for President in 1968. He married Jane Wyman in 1940, and they were divorced in 1948. They have two children. He married Nancy Davis in 1952, and they have two children.   Foster Stockwell

RECORDINGS. Federal grand juries in Los Angeles; Newark, N.J.; and Philadelphia indicted 16 persons and six record companies on June 24, 1975, on charges of bribing radio-station employees to plug their records. The U.S. Department of Justice said the payola investigation grew out of a separate probe into alleged income tax evasion by two former officials of CBS Records. The two were indicted in New York City.

Figures released in 1975 showed that dollar sales of records and tapes in the United States reached an all-time high of $2.2 billion in 1974. Album sales were up 8.8 per cent over 1973, while the dollar volume for single records rose only 2.1 per cent. These figures were somewhat misleading in that they reflected the higher prices charged for records. The actual number of albums sold dropped from 280 million to 276 million, while the number of single disks slipped from 228 million to 204 million. Prerecorded tapes rose in unit sales from 108 million to 114 million, however.

Pop and Rock continued to dominate the market, accounting for two-thirds of all sales. Classical record sales dropped slightly while jazz recordings increased from 1.3 per cent to 4.5 per cent of the total. The growth was due to the so-called "crossover" trend that saw many jazz artists performing pop-oriented material to boost sales.

So-called middle-of-the-road records, by singers who are over 30, became more popular. However, many artists in this field started their own record companies because they felt they were being swamped by the companies' concentration on pop and rock. Among the artists were Robert Goulet and Tony Bennett. Several radio stations banded together to form an organization known as Group 12 to create a middle-of-the-road music library.

Milestones. Ray Conniff set a precedent, becoming the first U.S. pop star to record in Russia. His "Ray Conniff in Moscow" album, with a Russian vocal chorus and orchestra, featured songs by contemporary Soviet writers. Elton John won a gold record for $1 million in sales and led the pop charts within a week of release with two albums during 1975.

Classical and Semiclassical. Scott Joplin's ragtime works continued to dominate both in record sales and air play. A definitive five-volume album, "Scott Joplin: The Complete Works for Piano," played by Dick Hyman, earned widespread critical acclaim. Other noteworthy classical music albums were Modest Mussorgsky's *Pictures at an Exhibition* in an electronic version performed in Japan by Isao Tomita; Gioacchino Antonio Rossini's *The Siege of Corinth* by the London Symphony Orchestra; and Igor Stravinsky's *The Rite of Spring* by the Chicago Symphony Orchestra.   Leonard Feather

RED CROSS. According to a study released in October, 1975, the Red Cross is plagued by such internal problems as a shortage of funds, poor planning, and a growing inability to act as a movement. The study was commissioned by the International Committee of the Red Cross and the League of Red Cross Societies, both of Geneva, Switzerland, to provide constructive criticism. While saying that the Red Cross still enjoyed international respect, the study warned the organization against living off its reputation.

In the United States, hundreds of American Red Cross volunteers and staff members worked with the U.S. military services and various volunteer agencies in 1975 to assist more than 100,000 Southeast Asian refugees. The refugees fled to U.S. refugee centers from South Vietnam in boats, ships, and planes after that country fell to the Viet Cong.

The Red Cross played a vital role in providing communications, counseling, social workers, mail service, first aid, and supplementary nursing care. Red Cross workers also helped the refugees move from the camps to permanent homes in communities throughout the United States.

The American Red Cross's 50th national convention was held in Boston in April. Chairman Frank Stanton called for a continuing analysis of the needs and resources of communities so the Red Cross could serve better in time of need. Joseph P. Anderson

Composer Marvin Hamlisch signs his autograph and holds one of four National Academy of Recording Arts and Sciences Grammy awards he won March 1.

RELIGION. South Vietnam's surrender in April, 1975, focused the attention of religious analysts on the state of religion in that Southeast Asian nation. Thousands of Roman Catholics had fled there from North Vietnam in the early 1950s, and some Western observers feared that the North Vietnamese victory would lead to a blood bath against the Catholics. As the North Vietnamese and Viet Cong troops approached Saigon, Roman Catholic priests and Buddhist monks gathered in the Catholic cathedral for the first such joint service in Vietnamese history.

But the Communists announced after the city fell that they were including freedom of religion in their program, and there was no news of an extensive purge in the months that followed. Increased communication with North Vietnam also permitted the Western world to see that much Roman Catholicism had survived in that country.

In the Middle East, there was an eruption of military action across religious lines. In Lebanon, Arab Moslems fought Arab Christians in a struggle that resembled, in some respects, the tensions in Northern Ireland. That is, differences between the two sides were political and social, but they were intensified by deep religious commitments and allegiances. The Christian Phalange Party, a neo-fascist group with its own 5,000-man army, was engaged in war with the 10,000 Palestinian guerrillas of the Palestine Liberation Organization.

In Japan. While religion offers meaning, ritual, and solace for most people most of the time, its public side often finds it centered in conflict. This was the case in Japan where there were reports of the continued political and statistical growth of *Soka Gakkai* (Value Creation Academy). This Buddhist sect's aggressive leader, Daisaku Ikeda, visited the United States early in the year. Soka Gakkai has deep roots in Japanese history, and stresses puritan living standards and aggressive power.

In Africa, religion was an element in most trouble spots. Ethiopia, one year after the coup that displaced Emperor Haile Selassie, was torn by a kind of civil war. Coptic Christianity is the religion of most of the people in Ethiopia. But in Eritrea, the northernmost province, dissidents were almost entirely Moslem. Jehovah's Witnesses, who had two years earlier moved from Malawi to neighboring Mozambique to escape religious persecution, were now forced back into Malawi by the newly independent government in Mozambique. They reported a renewal of the Malawi persecutions.

In North America, Eastern religions continued to make their presence felt, though there was some lessening of interest in them. Several years earlier, versions of Hinduism or Buddhism were regarded as exotic or eccentric intrusions, and received much press coverage. The shock had worn off by 1975, and the Eastern religions were an accepted reality. Embarrassing conflicts between mother and son

U.S. Church Membership Reported for Bodies with 150,000 or More Members*

African Methodist Episcopal Church	1,166,301
African Methodist Episcopal Zion Church	1,024,974
American Baptist Association	1,071,000
American Baptist Churches in the U.S.A.	1,579,029
The American Lutheran Church	2,437,862
Armenian Church of America, Diocese of the (Including Diocese of California)	372,000
Assemblies of God	1,239,197
Baptist Missionary Association of America	211,000
Christian Church (Disciples of Christ)	1,312,326
Christian Churches and Churches of Christ	1,034,047
Christian Methodist Episcopal Church	466,718
Christian Reformed Church	206,000
Church of God (Anderson, Ind.)	161,401
Church of God (Cleveland, Tenn.)	328,892
The Church of God in Christ	425,000
The Church of God in Christ, International	501,000
The Church of Jesus Christ of Latter-day Saints	2,683,573
Church of the Brethren	179,387
Church of the Nazarene	430,128
Churches of Christ	2,400,000
Conservative Baptist Association of America	300,000
The Episcopal Church	2,907,293
Free Will Baptists	215,000
General Association of Regular Baptist Churches	250,000
Greek Orthodox Archdiocese of North and South America	1,950,000
International General Assembly of Spiritualists	164,072
Jehovah's Witnesses	539,262
Jewish Congregations	6,115,000
Lutheran Church in America	2,986,970
The Lutheran Church—Missouri Synod	2,769,594
National Baptist Convention of America	2,668,799
National Baptist Convention, U.S.A., Inc.	5,500,000
National Primitive Baptist Convention, Inc.	1,645,000
Orthodox Church in America	1,000,000
Polish National Catholic Church of America	282,411
Presbyterian Church in the U.S.	896,203
Progressive National Baptist Convention, Inc.	521,692
Reformed Church in America	354,004
Reorganized Church of Jesus Christ of Latter Day Saints	156,687
The Roman Catholic Church	48,701,835
The Salvation Army	366,471
Seventh-day Adventists	479,799
Southern Baptist Convention	12,513,378
Unitarian-Universalist Association	192,510
United Church of Christ	1,841,312
The United Methodist Church	10,063,046
United Pentecostal Church, International	270,000
The United Presbyterian Church in the U.S.A.	2,723,565
Wisconsin Evangelical Lutheran Synod	388,865

*Majority of figures are for the years 1974 and 1975.
Source: National Council of Churches, *Yearbook of American and Canadian Churches* for 1976.

Roman Catholic, Eastern Orthodox, and Anglican clergymen attend the January investiture of F. Donald Coggan as archbishop of Canterbury.

came to light when the 17-year-old Maharaj Ji, regarded as a divine figure by followers of the Divine Light Mission, was removed from his post and accused of being "a spiritually imperfect playboy" by his mother, Shri Mataji.

Sun Myung Moon, whose Unification Church was popular in Korea, increased his real estate holdings in the United States. He claimed that income from the street sale of candles and literature by his followers, popularly called "Moonies," financed his investments of more than $10 million.

Black Muslims. On February 25, death took Elijah Muhammad, leader of the Black Muslims, the most successful black religious group outside the Christian orbit in America. He had fused some Moslem terms and ideas with his own vision in a movement preaching black power and pride. He preached that blacks were of a superior and good race that had long been held back by a devilish white race. The day of the reversal of fortunes, he taught, was at hand. Shortly before his death, Muhammad began to revise the sect's ideology and spoke in increasingly friendly tones about the role of whites in the world's future. Muhammad's son Wallace Muhammad was named leader of the sect. However, many observers predicted ongoing power struggles in the group.   Martin E. Marty

See also EASTERN ORTHODOX CHURCHES; JEWS; PROTESTANT; ROMAN CATHOLIC CHURCH.

REPUBLICAN PARTY. Severe infighting among Republicans in 1975 jeopardized President Gerald R. Ford's chances of winning nomination as the 1976 Republican presidential candidate. Ford formally declared his candidacy on July 8. Former California Governor Ronald Reagan announced on November 20 that he would challenge Ford for the Republican nomination. Vice-President Nelson A. Rockefeller withdrew from consideration as Ford's 1976 running mate, but refused to rule himself out of the presidential contest. Former Texas Governor John B. Connally, Jr., stated that he was keeping his options open in terms of a presidential bid, and Senator Charles McC. Mathias, Jr., of Maryland said that he or another moderate Republican might enter the contest.

Basis for Battle. Normally, an incumbent President has little difficulty in getting his party's nomination to seek another term. However, Ford's situation was anything but normal.

To begin with, Ford had not been elected either Vice-President or President. President Richard M. Nixon selected Ford, then Republican leader in the U.S. House of Representatives, to be his Vice-President after Spiro T. Agnew, surrounded by scandal, resigned the office in 1973. When Nixon himself resigned on Aug. 9, 1974, Ford was sworn in as President. Ford's subsequent pardon of Nixon for crimes he committed or may have committed in connection with the Watergate affair, a recession coupled with high unemployment, and certain aspects of U.S. foreign policy soon gave Ford serious political problems.

Conservative Challenge. Reagan, a spokesman for the right wing of the Republican Party, took a strong anti-Communist line and criticized Ford's policy of détente with Russia. Reagan was an appealing alternative to conservative party members.

A Reagan campaign committee was formed on July 15, headed by Senator Paul Laxalt of Nevada. Two months later, the Conservative Party of New York state endorsed Reagan for President.

The Rockefeller Affair. Ford's attitude toward Rockefeller seemed to cool as the Reagan challenge became more serious. Early in the year, Ford strongly backed the former New York governor. By late summer, however, Ford's campaign chairman, Howard H. (Bo) Callaway, said Rockefeller would be a liability to Ford in a contest with Reagan.

On November 3, Rockefeller dropped out as a possible 1976 vice-presidential nominee, and Ford did not try to talk him out of the move. While Rockefeller gave no reason for his decision, aides said he felt he was attacked unfairly by right wing Republicans and was ignored on major policy matters. Rockefeller later attributed his decision to "party squabbles." He also differed with Ford's opposition to any federal aid for near-bankrupt New York City. See NEW YORK CITY.

REPUBLICAN
...ERSHIP CONFEREN...
...ve're out to win!...

Ford's Campaign. On October 3, Lee Nunn, a key aide, left Ford's campaign committee. Nunn reportedly quit because he was unhappy with the way Callaway was managing the campaign. David Packard quit as Ford's finance chairman on November 14. Ford himself admitted that his campaign "could be better." Proof of that came early in December when a Gallup Poll showed that Reagan outpolled Ford 40 per cent to 32 per cent.

Ford said his name would be entered in every presidential primary election in 1976. He stated that he would not withdraw from the race before the Republican National Convention.

Ford called for more openness in the party. A poll conducted for the Republican National Committee

President Ford, a contender for the Republican presidential nomination, gives a pep talk to party leaders in Washington, D.C., on March 7.

and released in March showed that only 18 per cent of the voters considered themselves Republicans.

"The standing of our party has hit its lowest point," Ford said on March 7. "We must discard the attitude of exclusiveness that has kept the Republican Party's door closed too often. . . ." The party, Ford said, should appeal to everyone who wants to work within it for common goals. Reagan, in contrast, said Republicans should not sacrifice basic beliefs just to attract more followers.

RETAILING

While not a declared candidate, Connally regarded himself as a third force in the presidential race. He resumed speaking at Republican events after being acquitted on April 17 of federal charges that he took a $10,000 payoff for his help in raising milk subsidies in 1971 when he was secretary of the treasury. Although claiming to support Ford, Connally said that Ford has "yet to prove himself" and could not be rated an "automatic winner" of the presidential nomination.

Convention Decisions. The Republicans on September 8 chose Kansas City, Mo., as the site of their 1976 convention. The convention was set to begin on Aug. 16, 1976.

In March, conservatives narrowly won a fight to restrict the "positive action" rule designed to attract more blacks, women, and young people into Republican affairs. Under the revised rule, state organizations were told to seek a broader base, but they would not be penalized for not doing so.

On September 30, a U.S. Circuit Court of Appeals upheld a "victory bonus" rule that awards additional delegates to states that went Republican in the last two presidential elections. The rule had been challenged by Republican liberals and moderates who claimed the bonus would give control of the 1976 convention to conservatives. William J. Eaton

See also FORD, GERALD R.; REAGAN, RONALD; ROCKEFELLER, NELSON A.

A W. T. Grant store announces its closing in Atlanta. The giant retail chain shut down 576 stores in 1975 as it struggled to survive.

RETAILING. Retail sales in the United States for early 1975 reflected declining consumer confidence and rising unemployment. Surprisingly, there was a major upturn in the second quarter. Consumer confidence improved, and alert retailers became increasingly sensitive to consumer psychology. They also tightened inventory controls, cut overhead, and increased productivity.

The nation's sixth largest general merchandise chain nearly collapsed in 1975. The W. T. Grant Company suffered staggering losses because of a now-deposed management that was not marketing oriented and that expanded nationally beyond its resources, while granting customer credit too liberally. In December, the firm, which once operated more than 1,200 stores with annual sales approaching $2 billion, was being reorganized under Chapter 11 of the bankruptcy laws. A new management planned to retrench to a company of about 500 stores concentrated in the Northeast.

Most chains curtailed their expansion programs. But, because of previous commitments, the industry continued to add new stores. Seeking greater sales per unit of space, many chains trimmed the size of the average new store and sought better ways to use vertical as well as horizontal space.

The catalog-showroom industry had a year of retrenchment, but its sales volume was computed at over $2.8 billion, as against $800 million in 1970.

Demand Changes. Americans' fast-changing life styles were reflected in the demand for casual attire and shrinking interest in formality. Denim apparel rose to new heights of popularity for all ages, often being given designer treatment and pricing. The "natural look" was a winner in home furnishings. The trend to apartment dwelling increased the demand for compact furnishings and appliances. Sales of do-it-yourself items showed noteworthy gains.

The Fair Credit Billing Act, which became effective in 1975, set strict standards for settling billing disputes (see CONSUMER AFFAIRS). The well-intentioned legislation, however, added to retailers' expenses. Sears, Roebuck and Company estimated that it would cost some $100,000 a year simply to notify its customers of the new law.

Slow deliveries during the holiday season were a major concern in many merchandise categories as stores sought to replenish stocks. Cautious manufacturers were reluctant to take great risks in anticipating demand, while most retailers tried to buy goods on shorter projections so that they could swing quickly with changing consumer preferences.

Sales increases for the 1975 Christmas season averaged close to 14 per cent for major retailing groups—winding up a relatively good year. Smaller stores gained only 3 to 4 per cent. Joseph R. Rowen

RHODE ISLAND. See STATE GOVERNMENT.

Markets Check Out Computers

A coded message appeared on many boxes, cans, and packages on supermarket shelves in 1975 – a series of black lines of varying width underscored by two 5-digit numbers. The pattern is the item's universal product code (UPC). The UPC means nothing to the shopper, but it is a unique fingerprint to the laser-beam scanner, or eye, of a computer checkout system.

By the end of 1975, more than 25 supermarkets throughout the United States were testing automated checkout systems based on UPC. A typical system consists of a computer and its memory, which contains all the price information, linked to a number of checkstands in place of the conventional store checkout counters. Each checkstand has an electronic terminal, a scanner, and a televisionlike display screen.

A checker passes each package being purchased over the window of the scanner, and its laser light "reads" the UPC symbol and relays the coded information to the store's computer. In less than a second, the computer flashes the product's name and price on the checkstand display screen and adds the same information to a printed, itemized receipt. Because meat and produce items are coded by a special machine in the store, the checker only touches the electronic terminal keys to ring up sales of those items lacking a UPC.

Many computer and grocery industry executives see the new computer checkout systems as a way to increase profits and stem rising prices. They claim that the system not only increases the checker's speed and accuracy, but also provides more detailed information to the customer. For example, where a cash register receipt would show an entry "GROC .59" for a box of rice, the computer system can print "QUICK-B RICE .59." As the computer records each purchase, it also adjusts various store records. So it also helps the store manager control inventory.

Because the computer reads only the UPC, the price does not have to be stamped on each item. Prices could appear only on grocery shelves and on the customer's itemized receipt. Eliminating the stamped prices would represent savings in labor.

Some labor and consumer organizations oppose computer checkout systems. Labor groups believe the increased automation will mean fewer jobs. Consumer advocates fear that shoppers will find it more difficult to compare prices if the price is not stamped on each item. Because of these concerns, lawmakers are studying legislation that would require a price on every item.

Such resistance presents a dilemma to store owners. A system that has 10 checkstands costs about $125,000. Unless a store can realize some savings through the use of fewer employees, its system could be uneconomical. Consequently, the decision to install the new system may depend on how much the computer can help the store managers' record keeping.

Because the computer systems provide better inventory control and collect complete and accurate information on each sale, other retailers are installing them. In variety stores, a machine encodes the necessary fingerprint on each sales tag – either as a magnetic strip or a special code of green, black, and white bars similar to a UPC. The tag machine also prints readable information for the consumer, such as size, color, and price. A salesperson passes a wandlike sensor over the code on the tag to ring up a sale, and the computer does the rest.

The entry of computers into the checkout lane may be only a temporary solution to an increasingly outmoded form of retailing. Investigators at the Massachusetts Institute of Technology in Cambridge have studied the use of computers, communications systems, and automatic food-handling equipment. They proposed in early 1975 four automated systems that might eliminate self-service and checkout lanes. On the basis of consumer response to computer checkout systems, however, such schemes as ordering groceries by telephone after seeing items displayed on a color television set are futuristic, indeed. Such systems could be built, but the consumer may not be ready for them.   Robert K. Johnson

Universal product code

RHODESIA. Throughout 1975, there were on-again, off-again constitutional talks between the white-minority government and black nationalists. Competing black nationalist groups had united tenuously in the African National Council (ANC) in December, 1974, for the negotiations. The most important nationalists included Joshua Nkomo, president of the Zimbabwe African People's Union (ZAPU); Ndabaningi Sithole, head of the rival Zimbabwe African National Union (ZANU); and Methodist Bishop Abel Muzorewa, compromise president of the ANC.

South African Prime Minister Balthazar Johannes Vorster reportedly pressured Rhodesian Prime Minister Ian D. Smith to negotiate with the blacks and to accept greater black participation in Rhodesia's government. The alternative would most likely be a civil war, which Rhodesia's small white population – about 5 per cent of the total – could not win. The situation became especially urgent after Mozambique gained independence in June, 1975. Mozambique's long border with Rhodesia was potentially open to guerrilla operations. See MOZAMBIQUE.

The talks were delayed by arguments over preconditions, the location for the conference, and disagreements between black nationalists. Fighting broke out between ZANU and ZAPU members in Salisbury on June 1. Riot police killed 13 blacks and wounded 28 others during the melee.

The Meetings. Talks finally began on August 25 in a railway car parked in neutral territory on the Victoria Falls bridge between Zambia and Rhodesia. Both Vorster and President Kenneth D. Kaunda of Zambia attended. However, Smith insisted that all future sessions be held inside Rhodesia rather than on the neutral ground of the railway car. This demand was unacceptable to Sithole and other ANC leaders, who feared that they would be arrested if they returned to Rhodesia. So negotiations broke down.

The ANC then split into two divisions. An external wing, the Zimbabwe Liberation Council (ZLC), was based in Zambia and headed by Sithole. An internal faction under Nkomo was based in Rhodesia. On September 11, Bishop Muzorewa, based in Zambia, expelled Nkomo from the ANC for allegedly collaborating with Smith. Nkomo's supporters in Rhodesia held a special ANC conference on September 28 and elected him president in place of Muzorewa. The ZLC reportedly began readying a new guerrilla offensive against the Smith government in September. Nkomo was open to further negotiations, and he and Smith met in Rhodesia on November 1.   John D. Esseks

See also AFRICA (Facts in Brief Table).

ROADS AND HIGHWAYS. See TRANSPORTATION.

ROCKEFELLER, NELSON ALDRICH (1908-), Vice-President of the United States, announced in a letter to President Gerald R. Ford on Nov. 3, 1975, that he was withdrawing as Ford's 1976 running mate. Rockefeller at first gave no reason for his decision. The letter simply stated, "I wish you to know this for your own planning."

Party Squabbles. At a press conference on November 6, Rockefeller admitted that "party squabbles" were responsible for his decision. Republican Party conservatives had been unhappy with Ford's choice of the moderate Rockefeller as Vice-President. When Ronald Reagan, a leading conservative, launched a strong challenge for the Republican presidential nomination, some of Ford's aides began to view Rockefeller as a political liability. This apparently was the main reason for Rockefeller's withdrawal. "I eliminated the issue, which was the basis of a lot of the squabble," the Vice-President said. Rockefeller did not, however, rule out the possibility that he might make his own bid for the presidential nomination. See REAGAN, RONALD; REPUBLICAN PARTY.

During an interview in October, Rockefeller said that he believed he could have been elected President if he had switched from the Republican to the Democratic Party.

The Rockefeller Commission. On January 5, President Ford appointed Rockefeller head of an

Rhodesian police try to stop fight at black nationalist meeting, then fire into crowd; 13 blacks are killed and 28 others are hurt.

Mrs. Nelson Rockefeller arrives at the Washington mansion that became the official residence of U.S. Vice-Presidents in September.

eight-member commission to look into charges of illegal domestic spying by the Central Intelligence Agency (CIA). Rockefeller had been involved in intelligence matters since 1969, when he became a member of the President's Foreign Intelligence Advisory Board.

On June 10, the Rockefeller Commission released its report, detailing unlawful domestic spying by the CIA. The commission found that the CIA had tapped phones, bugged rooms, opened the mail of U.S. citizens, and compiled records containing the names of 300,000 individuals and organizations. The Rockefeller Commission urged tighter controls on the CIA, including a congressional joint committee on intelligence to oversee the agency. Meanwhile, a Senate committee found more illegal CIA activity. See UNITED STATES, GOVERNMENT OF.

Official Residence. The Vice-President and his wife, Margarette (Happy), welcomed the first guests to the new official vice-presidential residence on September 7. The Rockefellers gave nine housewarming parties for members of Congress and other dignitaries in September and October.

The 33-room mansion, known as Admiral's House, stands on the Naval Observatory grounds in Washington, D.C., and formerly housed chiefs of naval operations. Following extensive renovations, the house opened in 1975 as the first official residence for U.S. Vice-Presidents.   Darlene R. Stille

ROMAN CATHOLIC CHURCH. The issue of whether women should be ordained to the priesthood attracted considerable attention in 1975. Pope Paul VI asserted on April 18 that the church cannot ordain women because Christ's call to women to be "disciples and collaborators" but not ordained ministers cannot be changed by the church. But Johannes Cardinal Willebrands of the Netherlands said that the issue needs deeper study. He contended that a decision by the Episcopal Church to ordain women "would create a serious new element in the dialogue on the nature of ministry." But he also said, "I claim there is no theological argument at the level of faith against the ordination of women."

Numerous meetings were held to discuss the issue. One of the largest, titled "Women in the Future Priesthood Now: A Call for Action," was sponsored by the University of Detroit from November 28 to 30. Significantly, there are more than 300 nuns engaged in campus ministry in the United States.

Abortion continued to be a central concern among U.S. Roman Catholics. About 50,000 Catholics demonstrated in Washington, D.C., on January 22 in favor of a constitutional amendment to "undo" the 1973 decision by the Supreme Court of the United States permitting abortion. Bishop Leo T. Maher of San Diego, in a controversial pastoral letter read at all Masses in San Diego parishes on

Tapestry of Mother Seton hangs from a balcony of St. Peter's Basilica during the canonization of the first U.S.-born saint.

May 12 and 13, announced that persons advocating abortion or members of societies endorsing it would be barred from receiving any of the sacraments.

The Charismatic Movement among Catholics maintained its momentum. Leon-Joseph Cardinal Suenens of Belgium told 10,000 charismatics on May 13, during a convention at St. Peter's Church in Rome, "This is the day the church said to you, 'Welcome!'" Pope Paul gave permission for use of the main altar for the concluding Mass of the convention, and said extemporaneously, "Your joy and your love will renew the church." The U.S. Bishops Committee for Pastoral Research and Practice neither endorsed nor condemned the movement but asked charismatics to continue contacts with their pastors and bishops. William Storey, a Notre Dame theologian, alleged that there were grave abuses at a charismatic center called True House, in Notre Dame, Ind., but Cardinal Suenens challenged Storey's charges. The Catholic bishops of Canada on May 8 praised the Christian joy of the charismatic movement but noted some of its negative aspects such as élitism, emotionalism, and fundamentalism.

The Ecumenical Movement in the United States seemed to drift. The dominant concern at the National Catholic Workshop on Christian Unity, held in San Diego in February, was that though some official Catholic-Protestant dialogue groups have reached agreement on the Eucharist, priesthood, and the papacy, Rome has been reluctant to approve these developments.

The Vatican Congregation for the Doctrine of the Faith warned Swiss theologian Hans Küng on February 20 that his opinions on infallibility were "erroneous," reducing infallibility to indefectibility. Küng also endorsed consecration of the Eucharist by the laity in times of emergency. The Swiss Bishops Conference supported the warning, but Küng retorted that the Vatican was "inquisitorial" and that he intended to teach in "an ecumenical spirit." Ordinary parishioners were reported to be apathetic about ecumenism.

Jewish Dialogue. The newly created Vatican Commission for Religious Relations with the Jews released a new set of guidelines on January 3 for the continuing Catholic-Jewish dialogue. *Guidelines and Suggestions for Implementing the Conciliar Declaration Nostra Aetate, No. 4* represents the fruits of 10 years of experience in this dialogue since Vatican II published *Nostra Aetate, No. 4,* its statement on the Jews. Favorably received by most Jewish leaders, the document has stimulated dialogue. However, Jewish leaders have protested the absence of any reference to the state of Israel and have deplored the text's lack of an expression of contrition for long centuries of Catholic persecution of Jews.

Bicentennial. The U.S. Bishops Bicentennial Committee held six meetings in various cities, beginning in February, in preparation for the celebration of the 1976 American Bicentennial. The meetings dealt with the topic of global justice for humankind. Theodore M. Hesburgh, president of Notre Dame University in Indiana, announced plans for "a global lobby," patterned after Common Cause, to tackle development, poverty, and hunger issues.

Poverty and Farmworkers. The 24 Catholic bishops of Appalachia issued a stirring pastoral letter – in free verse – in February, promising to work with the poor against "a powerlessness common to the rest of society." The National Catholic Educational Association chose "Seeking a Just Society" as the theme for its annual meeting in Atlantic City, N.J., in April. Dolores Huerta, organizer for the United Farm Workers of America (UFW) and one of the main speakers, urged the delegates to support a national boycott of grapes, lettuce, and Gallo wine. A new sensitivity to the human rights of Chicanos and American Indians was expressed in many Catholic circles in 1975.

The main support for the UFW in its struggle for free elections of union representatives came from U.S. Catholic bishops. The union, led by Cesar Chavez, won a victory with the California Agricultural Labor Relations Act, which became effective on August 29. The law permits collective bargaining, strikes, and secondary boycotts, and establishes a board to oversee elections and handle disputes involving farmworkers, unions, and growers.

Other Issues. Monsignor George Higgins, secretary of research for the United States Catholic Conference, told the Subcommittee on Immigration of the U.S. House of Representatives on April 3, "It is unconscionable that our government should even consider separating families by forcing a mass exodus or deportation of literally millions of men, women, and children." He was referring to congressional proposals designed to stop the flow of illegal aliens into the country. Some legislators estimate there are 10 million such persons in the U.S., many of them Mexican. The conference on August 20 assailed an "illegal aliens bill," one of several introduced but not passed by Congress, as a "scapegoat solution" to the current unemployment problem.

Many of the Vietnamese refugees brought to the United States after the war ended are Catholics, and Catholic relief organizations were hard pressed to take care of them. In the face of widespread protests against bringing these refugees to the United States, Archbishop Joseph L. Bernardin insisted on May 15 that high unemployment should not impede Catholic generosity. In April, Catholic Relief Services was reportedly feeding 800,000 refugees daily in the United States and in Vietnam.

The church in various Latin American countries continued to protest against oppressive political regimes in 1975. The mood of progressive Latin American Catholics was mirrored in Gustavo Gutiérrez' *Theology of Revolution,* a book that warned public officials that bloody revolution might be a lesser evil than the institutionalized ·violence of the establishment. Liberation theology was propounded by Latin American theologians in a six-day June conference in Detroit. They advocated a modified Marxism along with the theme that American economic imperialism is the primary cause of poverty and oppression in Latin America.

Mother Seton Canonized. Probably the brightest day of the year for many U.S. Catholics was September 14, when Mother Elizabeth Ann Bayley Seton was canonized in St. Peter's Square. She was venerated as founder of the Catholic school system in America. Also canonized, on October 12, was Oliver Plunkett, an Irish archbishop executed by the British in 1681 on a charge of treason.

Catholic Membership. The Official Catholic Directory for 1975 reported that the number of converts increased from 74,741 in 1974 to 75,123 in 1975. The total Catholic population increased by more than 236,000 to 48,701,835 in 1975. There were 58,909 priests as against 56,712 in 1974. The total number of nuns dropped from 139,963 to 135,225. High school enrollment increased from 911,730 in 1974 to 920,516 in 1975. Elementary school enrollment decreased from 2,717,898 to 2,599,227.   John B. Sheerin

ROMANIA distanced itself still further from other Warsaw Pact nations in 1975, but its policy at home showed little change. Forced economic development, strict political discipline, and intense nationalism remained the order of the day.

Prime Minister Manea Manescu declared at the Council for Mutual Economic Assistance (COMECON) summit meeting in Budapest, Hungary, in June that individual COMECON countries must have bilateral relations with the European Commission, administrative body of the European Community (Common Market). These ties should be separate from any relations between the two organizations, he said. Romania announced in July that it would appoint an ambassador to the Common Market. Manescu was unenthusiastic about Russian plans to integrate the economies of COMECON nations for the five-year-plan period from 1976 to 1980.

Romania and Russia also clashed at the Conference on Security and Cooperation in Europe in Geneva, Switzerland, in July over such matters as notification of military maneuvers. Romanian officials also met with Italian and Spanish Communist leaders and two Yugoslav party leaders in June to discuss their opposition to Russian domination of the proposed European Communist Conference.

Romania announced in April that it and Yugoslavia were jointly producing a new jet fighter and a new multibarrel missile launcher. President Gerald R. Ford visited Romania in August to sign a document conferring most-favored-nation status on Romania's exports to the United States. The U.S. Congress had approved the concession on July 28 after having satisfied itself that Romania has a liberal emigration policy.

Third World Ties. Romania continued to pursue vigorously its links with the developing nations. It sent an observer to the nonaligned nations' preparatory meeting in Lima, Peru, in August and announced that it would attend the group's conference in 1976. President Nicolae Ceausescu visited the Philippines, Pakistan, Tunisia, and Jordan in April, and Brazil, Venezuela, Mexico, and Senegal in June. In November, he visited Portugal, where Romania backed the Socialist Party rather than the pro-Russian Communist Party.

Floods in July covered one-third of the country and caused heavy losses. About 200 industrial plants and 100,000 houses were heavily damaged. About 10,000 cattle, 80,000 pigs, 100,000 sheep, and 3 million fowl were lost. More than 25 per cent of the grain and wheat crops were in the most severely flooded areas. In September, following strong criticism of the quality of industrial consumer goods, Lina Ciobanu replaced Gheorghe Couzan as minister of light industry.   Chris Cviic

See also EUROPE (Facts in Brief Table).

ROTARY INTERNATIONAL. A new recreational fellowship, the International Art Fellowship of Rotarians, was established in 1975 for all Rotary International members interested in artistic activities. The new fellowship is expected to promote art holidays, organize exhibits of works of art, and promote the use of art for better understanding. The group was approved at the annual convention of Rotary International, held in Montreal, Canada, in June.

It was announced at the convention that nearly 800 students are studying abroad under Rotary Foundation awards and that 900 young business and professional men are participating in group-study exchange programs sponsored by the foundation. Earlier in the year, the Rotary International board of directors clarified the role of the Rotary Institute, which has been established for past, present, and incoming officers.

Ernesto Imbassahy DeMello of Rio de Janeiro, Brazil, was elected president of Rotary International on July 1. There were 16,543 clubs with an estimated 774,500 Rotarians in 151 countries and geographical regions. There were also 2,195 Rotaract Clubs (for 18- to 28-year-olds) with an estimated membership of 43,940 in 65 countries, and 3,316 Interact Clubs (for preuniversity students) with 72,918 members in 69 countries.   Joseph P. Anderson

ROWING. See SPORTS.

RUBBER. See MANUFACTURING.

RUSSIA continued to expand its business relations with the West in 1975. However, its disagreements with the United States and other Western countries over the interpretation of détente sharpened during the second half of the year. Russia stayed on the sidelines in the Middle East, but it intervened openly in Africa. Its relations with China continued to deteriorate. At home, the crackdown on political dissidents continued. Bad weather caused the worst grain harvest since 1965.

Communist Party General Secretary Leonid I. Brezhnev attended the 35-nation summit meeting in Helsinki, Finland, from July 30 to August 1 that marked the end of the 2¹/₂-year-long Conference on European Security and Cooperation. Russia welcomed the adoption of the final document, especially the references to the permanence of the territorial status quo in Europe. But Russia and its Eastern European partners gave a restrictive interpretation to parts of the document dealing with the freer flow of people and ideas between East and West. See EUROPE.

At the same time, Russia's increasingly open backing of the Portuguese Communist Party caused concern in the West. United States Secretary of State Henry A. Kissinger said on August 14 that the United States would "stand by to help a democratic Portugal." In October, Brezhnev rejected out of hand a call by French President Valéry Giscard d'Estaing for an ideological détente between East and West. Russia and West Germany failed to make progress on a cultural, legal, and scientific agreement during a visit to Moscow by West German President Walter Scheel in November.

Foreign Minister Andrei A. Gromyko and Kissinger discussed ways of breaking the deadlock at the Strategic Arms Limitation Talks in Geneva, Switzerland, when they met in September in New York City and Washington, D.C. On November 10, Kissinger announced that Russia had rejected an American compromise proposal for breaking the deadlock. Russia replied four days later that the United States had violated the 1974 Vladivostok agreement on the ceiling of 2,400 strategic vehicles by proposing to exempt two new weapons systems—the new American cruise missile and the Soviet Backfire-B bomber. See ARMED FORCES.

In the Middle East, Russia shelved its demand for another Geneva peace conference after Kissinger-Gromyko talks in Vienna, Austria, in May. Relations with Egypt deteriorated after Egypt and Israel reached their second Sinai disengagement agreement in August with the help of the United States. Brezhnev's scheduled June visit to Egypt was called off.

Instead, Russia concentrated on wooing other Arab states. Soviet Premier Aleksey N. Kosygin visited Tunisia and Libya in May. President Hafiz al-Asad of Syria obtained promises of new arms

The geometric pattern of an arched roof engulfs two men as they stand on a platform in a new Russian subway link between Kharkov and a suburb.

supplies when he visited Moscow in October. Relations with the Palestine Liberation Organization remained close. In November, Russia renewed its demand for another Geneva conference.

Moscow extended military aid to the Communist-led Popular Movement for the Liberation of Angola (MPLA) before and after Angola gained independence from Portugal on November 11 (see ANGOLA). Soviet support of the MPLA, at the expense of two other nationalist movements, brought Russia into conflict with the Organization of African Unity, whose chairman, Uganda President Idi Amin Dada, ordered the Russians on November 12 to close their embassy in Kampala. However, normal relations were resumed within a week.

In Asia, Russia fully supported India's Prime Minister Indira Gandhi in June after she proclaimed a state of emergency and arrested her political opponents. India and Russia agreed in October to double their trade by 1980. Russia and its allies stepped up their supplies to the victorious Communist forces in Indochina in May after the non-Communist regimes in South Vietnam, Khmer (Cambodia), and Laos collapsed. North Vietnam's Communist Party Secretary Le Duan visited Moscow in October.

Border talks with China – which had resumed in February – were broken off indefinitely in May. In August, the Soviet party monthly, *Kommunist,* pub-

lished an article that launched a big anti-Maoist campaign throughout Eastern Europe.

In Europe, Russia's attempt to organize a World Communist Conference to condemn China ran into severe trouble. Several Communist parties in Western Europe and Romania and Yugoslavia in Eastern Europe opposed the project for a preliminary European Communist Conference. The conference was to have been held in East Berlin following the Helsinki meeting, but was postponed indefinitely.

But Russia used its new power as almost the sole supplier of raw materials and fuels to accelerate its drive for closer economic integration. Romania openly opposed these plans in June at the Council for Mutual Economic Assistance (COMECON) meeting in Budapest, Hungary. Nevertheless, Moscow concluded bilateral agreements with all COMECON members in Europe, tying their economic programs closer than ever before to Russia's.

Russia had a successful year in space. On July 17, U.S. and Russian spaceships docked in orbit. In October, two unmanned Russian craft landed on Venus. See SPACE EXPLORATION.

Trade with the West. Russia boosted its trade with the West in 1975 by purchasing more than $2-billion worth of Western grain. Because of bad weather, the Soviet harvest was about 152 million short tons (138 million metric tons), according to Western estimates, about one-third less than

451

planned. By the end of October, Russia had purchased at least 22 million short tons (20 million metric tons) of Western grain, over half of it from the United States. On October 20, Russia and the United States signed a deal under which Russia promised to buy 6.6 million to 8.8 million short tons (6 to 8 million metric tons) of U.S. grain a year for five years, beginning Oct. 1, 1976. The United States can block sales if it believes that its supplies are too low. A reciprocal agreement on sales of 200,000 barrels a day of Russian oil to the United States went unsigned.

The poor harvest caused overall economic growth of only 4 per cent instead of the revised target of 6.5 per cent, the Soviet government said in December. It sharply lowered 1976 targets, especially in consumer goods production, which was to grow only 2.7 per cent.

Cancels U.S. Trade Pact. On January 10, Russia canceled its 1972 trade agreement with the United States whereby trade restrictions were to be eliminated. The move came in response to the Trade Reform Act passed in December, 1974. The act linked most-favored-nation status to freer emigration policies. Moscow charged the act violated "the principle of noninterference in domestic affairs." Soviet officials were also disappointed at the size of the trade credit available to Russia.

A new railroad bridge over the River Ob near Surgut, Russia, is part of a line that will transport Siberian oil to industrial centers.

Domestic Affairs. The act's free-emigration clause was primarily intended to prod Moscow into a softer stance on the emigration of Jews. But only about 7,000 Russian Jews were allowed to emigrate by November 3, a fraction of the figure for 1974. On July 1, Moscow announced that a 30 per cent tax would be levied on moneys received from abroad, starting Jan. 1, 1976. The tax is in addition to a 30 per cent bank handling fee and was seen as a move to prevent outside support of Jews who lose jobs after trying to emigrate.

Andrei D. Sakharov, a famous physicist and campaigner for civil rights in Russia, was awarded the Nobel Prize for Peace on October 10, but Russian officials turned down his visa application to travel to Oslo, Norway, to receive the prize, on the grounds that he knew too many state secrets.

Alexandr N. Shelepin, former head of the secret police, was dropped from the Politburo on April 16 and from his post as head of the Soviet trade unions on May 22. Speculation about Brezhnev's ill health was fueled throughout the year by several long absences. But a Central Committee meeting on December 1 slated him to deliver the keynote report at the 25th Party Congress in 1976.   Chris Cviic

See also EUROPE (Facts in Brief Table); Section Two, RUSSIA TODAY: REALITY AND THE FADING DREAM.

RWANDA. See AFRICA.

SAFETY. Experts on highway safety throughout the world continued to urge the use of safety belts in automobiles and trucks in 1975 as a means of cutting down the number of motor-vehicle fatalities. Switzerland enacted a law making the use of safety belts mandatory for adults. The new law also requires children under 12 years of age to sit in the rear seat of a car unless that seat is already filled by other children. The law is the first requiring that safety belts be installed and used in delivery vans and minibuses, as well as in automobiles.

The new Swiss law also sets requirements for belts themselves, calling for "three-point belts that are simple to use, comfortable, and do not impede, and so endanger, the driver." Failure to observe the new law is punishable by a fine.

Safety-belt laws also went into effect on June 1 in Belgium and the Netherlands. Similar laws were under consideration in Finland, Luxembourg, and West Germany. Australia, New Zealand, and Sweden already had laws requiring safety-belt use. Czechoslovakia and France require only that belts be used outside cities. Puerto Rico is the only major jurisdiction in the United States that requires safety belts to be used.

For the second straight year, motor-vehicle fatalities in the United States were relatively low in comparison to the number of fatalities prior to the enactment of the national speed limit of 55 miles (89 kilometers) per hour. Safety officials again attributed the reduction to the speed limit, to less traffic because of higher gasoline prices, and to smoother traffic flow on the nation's highways. During the first seven months of 1975, the National Safety Council (NSC) reported there were 6,000 fewer traffic accident deaths – a drop of 19 per cent – than in the same period in the pre-energy crisis year of 1973. However, the toll was 4 per cent higher than in the first seven months of 1974.

Accidental Deaths and Death Rates

| | 1974 | | 1975† | |
	Number	Rate††	Number	Rate††
Motor Vehicle	47,880	22.7	46,960	22.1
Work	13,700	6.5	13,200	6.2
Home	26,000	12.3	25,500	12.0
Public	24,500	11.6	23,000	10.8
Total*	107,500	51.0	104,500	49.2

†For 12-month period up to Aug. 30, 1975.
††Deaths per 100,000 population.
*The total does not equal the sum of the four classes because *Motor Vehicle* includes some deaths also included in *Work* and *Home*.

Source: National Safety Council estimates.

Safety Factors. During 1975, NSC researchers made a careful study of the 20,630 traffic fatalities recorded in 1974, which was 17 per cent lower than the 1973 toll. The researchers determined that lower speeds accounted for nearly 10 percentage points of this reduction. Less travel, particularly at night, and fewer riders in vehicles accounted for another 2 per cent, as did increased use of safety belts. Unknown factors contributed an additional 2 per cent, while the increased use of motorcycles and small cars combined to produce 1 per cent.

Work Accidents. Accident-prevention measures were stressed as a tool against inflation during the year by safety leaders. Statisticians at the NSC estimated that about 1 million productive man-years had been lost in 1974 because of work accidents. These cost $15 billion, including medical expenses, lost wages, administrative costs, property losses caused by hazards such as fire, and related costs.

Safety officials pointed out that when the $10-billion cost of wages lost due to home, public, and motor-vehicle accident injuries is added to the cost of work accidents, the total for productivity loss in the United States increases to $25 billion. This represents about 2 per cent of the gross national product. Eliminating this loss, the officials said, would cut the overall inflation rate about 16 per cent.

Accidents of all kinds in 1974 cost an estimated $43.3 billion. This included deaths and injuries, as well as motor-vehicle accidents in which no one was injured. The costs exceeded the total that all U.S. manufacturing and mining industries spent for new plants and equipment. Vincent L. Tofany

SAINT LOUIS. The population of St. Louis fell to its lowest level since 1890, according to figures released in mid-1975 by the U.S. Census Bureau. The bureau estimated that the city's population was 558,006 as of July 1, 1973, a decline of 10.3 per cent since the 1970 census. Enrollment in St. Louis public schools for the fall, 1975, term dropped 2.5 per cent to 191,017 pupils.

The city also faced a financial crisis. Its new fiscal year budget, beginning on May 1, projected a deficit of $20 million. Since such deficits are prohibited by state law, the city enacted a 10.34 per cent property-tax increase and eliminated 481 municipal jobs to equalize revenues and expenditures.

Official Corruption. For the first time in more than 50 years, a top-level St. Louis city official was convicted of a felony involving his public office. Building Commissioner Kenneth O. Brown was found guilty of extortion and six counts of mail fraud on August 29.

The president of the East St. Louis Board of Education and five other school officials were convicted in May on charges of conspiracy, extortion, and racketeering. The six were stripped of their public offices, sentenced to prison, and enjoined from any future participation in school district affairs.

Also, an alderman filed charges in late September accusing the mayor, the city comptroller, and the license collector of not requiring a written contract with a company doing business with the city and of not properly licensing businesses in the city.

Zoning Case. The Supreme Court of the United States on June 23 upheld a lower court ruling that a zoning ordinance in a St. Louis suburb had the effect of excluding blacks from the community. The federal government initially brought the court action against Blackjack, Mo., in 1971. The government argued that a zoning ordinance that barred construction of multiple-family dwellings prevented inner-city black residents from finding housing they could afford in the suburb. About 79 per cent of St. Louis' blacks earn less than $10,000 a year.

Living Costs in the St. Louis area rose 11 per cent between June, 1974, and June, 1975. Food costs were up 10.8 per cent, housing prices rose 15.3 per cent, clothing costs increased 4.6 per cent, and health and recreation expenditures were up 10.3 per cent. The price of gasoline remained steady, however. Regular gasoline averaged 55.9 cents per gallon (3.8 liters). At the same time, department store sales rose 4.1 per cent, and construction activity was up 5.1 per cent. The average annual income of a factory worker in the St. Louis area increased 8.6 per cent to $11,083. Persons receiving unemployment insurance benefits in the area increased 108.3 per cent to a total of 45,400 between August, 1974, and August, 1975. A strike at the McDonnell Douglas Corporation plant idled 11,500 workers between February 10 and May 11. James M. Banovetz

SALVATION ARMY started a new program in 1975 to help prisoners who have not completed their sentences. Working with state and local authorities in several states, the army now houses in its men's social service centers prisoners who have been approved for work-release programs. The men live at the army centers in or near their home communities and work nearby. They may have contact with their families, and weekend passes are available. After work, the men share in the centers' therapy, recreation, and counseling programs. The program is an extension of the army's traditional activities in the rehabilitation of former convicts.

Unmarried mothers, who no longer need the long-term shelter traditionally provided by the Salvation Army, now can use army community centers that provide prenatal and postnatal care, including dental treatment. Continuing high school and vocational education and counseling for the unmarried parents and their families are also available.

The army's worldwide network of missing persons bureaus continues to reunite lost people. The army's Southern territorial office reports success in about half of the cases it handles.

Salvation Army members in the United States contributed $3 million in 1975 through "self-denial giving" to support army activities in developing countries. Seventy-four American officers served in Africa, Asia, and South America.   Joseph P. Anderson

SAN FRANCISCO-OAKLAND. Police demanding a 13 per cent pay raise went on strike in San Francisco on Aug. 18, 1975, leaving the city unprotected except for emergency calls. Two days later, the city's firemen joined the walkout. After first threatening to fire the strikers, Mayor Joseph L. Alioto capitulated on August 21 and negotiated a settlement giving the strikers their demanded raises. The city's Board of Supervisors immediately rejected the settlement. But Alioto used emergency powers because public safety was threatened, and granted increases raising base pay of the police and firemen to $18,816.

Anesthesiologists in the San Francisco area went on strike May 1 to protest massive increases in their malpractice insurance premiums. The strike lasted until May 28, when Governor Edmund G. Brown, Jr., signed emergency legislation setting up pools of insurance companies to underwrite short-term malpractice insurance. See INSURANCE (Close-Up).

Bay Area Crimes. San Francisco was the scene of an attempted presidential assassination. Sara Jane Moore, a former informant for federal law enforcement agencies, fired a handgun at President Gerald R. Ford on September 22. On September 5, Charles Manson "family" cultist Lynette Alice (Squeaky) Fromme also made an attempt on the President's life in Sacramento, Calif. See CRIME; PRESIDENT OF THE UNITED STATES.

Patricia C. Hearst, missing since her abduction by members of the Symbionese Liberation Army (SLA) on Feb. 4, 1974, was captured in San Francisco on September 18 (see CRIME). Two other SLA members, Russell J. Little and Joseph M. Remiro, were convicted on June 9 of slaying Oakland Schools Superintendent Marcus Foster in 1973 and of trying to murder his assistant, Robert Blackburn.

Living Costs rose 10.3 per cent in San Francisco between June, 1974, and June, 1975. During the same period, food costs rose 10.8 per cent; housing, 10.9 per cent; and health and recreation costs, 11.6 per cent. By mid-1975, however, the average annual earnings of factory workers had reached $12,922, an increase of 11.7 per cent since mid-1974. The unemployment rate stood at 9.8 per cent, down 0.5 per cent from mid-1974. During the same period, department store sales rose 13.5 per cent, while construction activity fell 11 per cent. The price of regular gasoline reached 58.3 cents a gallon (3.8 liters) in June, up from 57.6 cents in June, 1974.

In the November 4 mayoral election, state Senator George Moscone and John Barbagelata, a city supervisor, emerged as the two top contenders to replace Alioto, who did not run. In the December 11 run-off, Moscone was elected.   James M. Banovetz

See also CITY; STATE GOVERNMENT.

SAN MARINO. See EUROPE.

San Francisco police struck in August, demanding a 13 per cent pay hike; Mayor Joseph Alioto agreed after three days.

SANFORD, TERRY (1917-   ), president of Duke University and former governor of North Carolina, announced in May, 1975, that he would seek the Democratic nomination for President in 1976. A political supporter of John F. Kennedy in 1960, Sanford sees himself as a moderate Southern alternative to Governor George C. Wallace of Alabama, also an announced candidate.

James Terry Sanford was born on Aug. 20, 1917, in Laurinburg, N.C. He earned a B.A. degree from the University of North Carolina in 1939. A special agent for the Federal Bureau of Investigation in 1941 and 1942, he resigned to become a paratrooper in World War II. He continued his law studies after the war and received his law degree in 1946.

Sanford practiced law in Fayetteville, N.C., from 1948 to 1960 and became active in state politics. He served as a state senator in 1953 and 1954. Then, in 1960, he was elected governor, defeating a strong segregationist candidate. As governor he led a far-reaching educational reform program and helped broaden North Carolina's industrial base beyond tobacco, textiles, and furniture. In 1969, he became president of Duke University. Although he started a sabbatical leave in January, 1976, he retained his university post while campaigning.

Sanford married Margaret Rose Knight of Hopkinsville, Ky., on July 4, 1942. They have a son and a daughter.   Robert K. Johnson

SÃO TOMÉ AND PRÍNCIPE, two small islands off the coast of West Africa, became an independent republic on July 12, 1975. The new nation, which had been under Portuguese rule for nearly 500 years, is the fourth and smallest of Portugal's African territories to emerge from colonial status since 1974. See PORTUGAL.

On July 10, Manuel Pinto da Costa was unanimously named head of state by the political bureau of the Gabon-based Movement for the Liberation of São Tomé and Príncipe. A constituent assembly elected the week before immediately proclaimed Da Costa the first president. The last Portuguese troops left the islands on July 11.

The new nation faced a bleak and financially troubled future. The economy was close to collapse because of a steep drop in the world price of cacao, the principal crop. In addition, most of the 1,000 white settlers who ran the cacao plantations and the Cape Verdeans who were foremen left the islands.

There is practically no industrial production. It was hoped, however, that the Organization of African Unity, which admitted the new nation to membership on July 18, would assist in economic development. Talks were also being held with a British firm to persuade it to resume oil explorations interrupted in 1972.   Paul C. Tullier

See also AFRICA (Facts in Brief Table).

SASKATCHEWAN. See CANADA.

SAUDI ARABIA. King Faisal's assassination on March 25, 1975, while he was holding court in Riyadh, silenced an important voice in Middle Eastern politics and world economics. The assassin, Prince Faisal ibn Musad Abdel Aziz, was a nephew of King Faisal and a former student at the University of Colorado. He allegedly acted to revenge the death of a brother during a 1964 riot. Musad was publicly beheaded in Riyadh on June 18.

The royal family closed ranks smoothly behind Faisal's half-brother, 62-year-old Crown Prince Khalid ibn Abd al-Aziz Al-Saud. Another half-brother, Prince Fahd, became heir apparent and deputy prime minister. On May 8, King Khalid, who underwent open-heart surgery in 1974, turned over decision-making powers in both domestic and foreign affairs to Fahd, subject to the king's final approval. See KHALID IBN ABD AL-AZIZ AL-SAUD.

Saudi Arabia's vast wealth was still its principal leverage in Arab and international affairs. Cash reserves of $22 billion and growing oil profits permitted massive foreign spending without slowing domestic development. The budget, approved on July 9, called for $30 billion in expenditures. The second five-year plan, which began in July, authorized $145 billion to develop industry.   William Spencer

See also MIDDLE EAST (Facts in Brief Table).

SCHOOL. See CIVIL RIGHTS; EDUCATION; Section One, FOCUS ON EDUCATION.

SCIENCE AND RESEARCH. About 140 molecular biologists from 16 countries made an unprecedented attempt at self-regulation of scientific research in 1975. They met at the Asilomar Conference Center in Pacific Grove, Calif., in February to establish tighter standards for research in genetic engineering – the manipulation of genes, which carry the heredity of all living things. The new guidelines were designed to prevent medical risks to man, while allowing beneficial experiments.

The events leading to the gathering began about 1972, when molecular biologists discovered a special class of enzymes called restriction enzymes, which can cut specific subunits of the double-stranded genetic material deoxyribonucleic acid (DNA) in such a way that strips of DNA from a different organism can be joined to them, and then the restructured DNA molecules can *replicate*, or reproduce. Molecular biologists can learn many things about the properties of the genetic code by studying such man-made organisms.

Most of the DNA for such experiments comes from a bacteria called K12, a special laboratory strain of *Escherichia coli*, a bacterium that lives in the intestines of human beings and many animals. Because the bacterium is common in human beings, scientists fear that such laboratory experiments in genetic engineering might lead to the transfer of new infections or even cancer viruses to man.

SCIENCE AND RESEARCH

The safeguards established at the Asilomar conference were designed to prevent the escape of potentially harmful organisms from the laboratory, and they replace a voluntary postponement of some kinds of genetic-engineering research that was originally proposed by a group of U.S. biologists led by Paul Berg of Stanford University.

Abortion Conviction. The year also saw a marked increase in both scientific and public debate over the proper limits of human biomedical research and treatment. "Right to life" forces scored a major victory on February 15, when a Boston jury found Dr. Kenneth C. Edelin guilty of manslaughter because he performed a therapeutic abortion on a woman in the second trimester of pregnancy. Also in Boston, Drs. Stanley Walzer and Park Gerald of Harvard Medical School were forced to terminate a seven-year, XYY-chromosome genetic-screening program because of pressure. Other scientists insisted the program was unethical and harmful because of its possible stigmatizing effects on male children. The XYY chromosome has been erroneously called the "criminal chromosome" because it has been found in the cells of some convicted felons. However, it appears to be associated with learning disabilities and certain other problems.

After a moratorium of more than a year, the U.S. Department of Health, Education, and Welfare in July ended a ban on federally funded research with human fetuses, subject to extensive safeguards recommended by a national review board. The moratorium was ordered by Congress in 1974.

Many scientists believe that fetal research is proper and vital to improved health. Opponents of abortion have objected strenuously to such research on the grounds that it violates the rights of unborn human beings. The law enacted in June, 1974, called for the moratorium until a national advisory council, set up by the law, delivered recommendations on the controversial issue.

The advisory council is also considering ethical problems connected with research on penitentiary inmates and the use of drugs and radical brain surgery to deal with behavioral problems.

Science Adviser. Although largely symbolic, President Gerald R. Ford's decision to re-establish the post of science adviser in the White House was important to scientists. President Dwight D. Eisenhower created the post in 1957, largely because of concern over the launching of Russia's *Sputnik I*. President Richard M. Nixon abolished it in 1973.

President Ford advised a group of congressmen in May that he wanted the science advisory apparatus restored, this time by statute instead of executive order, with the adviser subject to Senate confirmation. He submitted a bill to Congress in July for-

". . . and now, Dr. Preston, reporting on some interesting side effects of moose hormone experimentation."

mally requesting creation of an Office of Science and Technology Policy, and Vice-President Nelson A. Rockefeller testified as an Administration witness in support of the measure at a congressional hearing.

Federal Spending for U.S. research and development continued its upward trend, though the increase was largely nullified by inflation. Spending was expected to total $21.7 billion in fiscal 1976 (July 1, 1975, to June 30, 1976), an increase of 11 per cent. Areas showing the sharpest increases were energy, 37 per cent; national defense, 20 per cent; and the space programs, 13 per cent.

Nuclear Power. Scientific debate in the United States quickened on the large-scale use of nuclear power. More than 30 prominent scientists, including Hans A. Bethe, Cornell University physicist, and 10 other winners of the Nobel Prize, issued a declaration in January that the only reasonable way to satisfy U.S. energy needs is by increasing the use of nuclear power. But on the 30th anniversary of the nuclear bomb detonation over Hiroshima, Japan, in August, the Union of Concerned Scientists produced a petition signed by 2,300 U.S. scientists warning of "grave potential hazards" in nuclear energy and calling for a "drastic" curtailment in the U.S. nuclear program.   Henry T. Simmons

See also the various science articles.

SCULPTURE. See VISUAL ARTS.

SEATTLE residents gave Mayor Wesley G. Uhlman, a Democrat in the middle of his second four-year term, a strong vote of confidence in a special recall election on July 1, 1975. The situation leading to the recall began on Dec. 23, 1974, when Uhlman dismissed Fire Chief Jack N. Richards after receiving a highly critical report on the fire department's operations. Uhlman gave the job to City Budget Officer Walter Hundley, a black who had authored the report.

Within a month, the fire fighters' union demanded an election to recall Uhlman from office, charging that the mayor was guilty of appointing as fire chief an "unqualified and incompetent" person. It secured 83,000 signatures on recall petitions.

Employees of the city's utility company and other municipal workers who opposed the mayor's attempts to increase employee efficiency and productivity joined with the fire fighters. The municipal employees were unhappy because Mayor Uhlman had laid off nearly 500 persons since taking office in 1969 and had tried to curb what he regarded as wasteful work practices. Some observers believed there were also racial undertones. Black fire fighters, many of whom had been hired under Uhlman's minority jobs program, refused to campaign against him. Uhlman won the election.

Local Economy. The unemployment rate at midyear was 9.7 per cent in the metropolitan area,

To move a floating dry dock 1 foot (0.305 meter) wider than Seattle's Ballard Locks, engineers tilted the dry dock with ballast.

but close to 20 per cent within the city. United States Department of Labor statistics showed that 33,600 persons in the Seattle area were receiving unemployment benefits in August, 1975, an increase of 44 per cent from August, 1974.

Other economic indicators, however, were more encouraging. Department store sales registered an annual increase of 8.6 per cent by mid-1975, and construction activity increased 7.6 per cent. The average earnings of a factory worker rose 14.8 per cent to $12,503. Living costs, on the other hand, rose 10 per cent between August, 1974, and August, 1975, while food costs showed an annual increase of 9.2 per cent as of June. The pump price of regular gasoline rose 3 per cent during the same period to an average of 56.2 cents a gallon (3.8 liters).

The U.S. Census Bureau reported in mid-1975 that Seattle's estimated population as of July 1, 1973, was 503,073, down 5.2 per cent from 1970.

Free Bus Service in downtown Seattle was continued for two more years under an agreement announced in late January by city officials and the Metro Transit System. The experimental program began in September, 1973. The free-ride zone was also enlarged from 105 to 111 square blocks, covering the downtown business district.   James M. Banovetz

SENEGAL. See AFRICA.

SERVICE CLUBS. See KIWANIS INTERNATIONAL; LIONS INTERNATIONAL; ROTARY INTERNATIONAL.

SHAPP, MILTON J. (1912-   ), governor of
Pennsylvania, announced on Sept. 25, 1975, that he
was a candidate for the Democratic presidential
nomination. He said he was campaigning on a platform of "common sense" government.

Shapp was born in Cleveland, the son of Republican Aaron Shapiro, a hardware wholesaler. His
mother, a Democrat, was a social activist and a
leader in Cleveland's women's rights movement.
Shapp received a degree in electrical engineering
from Case Institute of Technology in Cleveland in
1933. After serving with the U.S. Army Signal
Corps in North Africa, Italy, and Austria during
World War II, Shapp founded Jerrold Electronics
Corporation, a pioneer in the development of the
cable-television industry in 1947. Shapp made a
fortune in this business. He sold it in 1966.

He was elected governor of Pennsylvania in 1970
and re-elected in 1974, both times with the largest
margins ever accorded a Democratic candidate for
that office. He achieved national prominence as a
tough but fair negotiator when he successfully mediated a national strike by independent truckers in
February, 1974. A month later, he helped prevent a
shut-down of the nation's gas stations, and he de-
fused a second truckers' strike in May, 1974.

Shapp is married to the former Muriel Matzkin.
They have three children.   **Foster Stockwell**

SHIP AND SHIPPING. Commercial ship demand
slipped throughout the world in 1975, pulled down
by a severe slump in orders for crude-oil tankers.
Despite this, U.S. Navy business boomed. The Suez
Canal, closed for eight years, reopened on June 5.

Lloyd's Register of Shipping said there were
2,276 merchant vessels under construction on June
30, off 1.3 per cent from the same date in 1974.
Shipbuilding orders, including ships under construction, fell to 4,798 from 5,179.

U.S. Shipbuilders enjoyed a record and expanding peacetime order book of more than $15 billion.
The Maritime Administration reported dollar value
of commercial-vessel orders on October 1 at about
$4.4 billion, up from $4.2 billion in 1974. Some 81
ocean and lake vessels were scheduled for completion by 1980, down from 92 a year earlier.

The Ford Administration announced approval in
June of $170.4 million in contracts—partly subsi-
dized by the government—for Avondale Shipyards
Incorporated in New Orleans to build three oil
tankers and enlarge two container ships. Each tanker will cost an estimated $43.4 million.

Supertanker Glut. But the tanker segment of the
maritime business was badly depressed, as worldwide oil consumption dropped. Shippers had more
tankers than were needed, and shipping rates
dropped sharply. Some oil-carrying charter rates

Krim, the first Russian-built supertanker, undergoes sea trials. The ship
displaces 182,000 gross tons. Many such supertankers were idle in 1975.

fell more than 90 per cent below those of late 1973. Seatrain Shipbuilding Corporation obtained a $40-million federally guaranteed loan in May and negotiated new bank loans to resume work on two tankers, after closing in January. On October 1, there were 49 tankers on order at U.S. shipyards, down 6 from 1974, according to the Shipbuilders Council of America.

United States Navy contracts, on the other hand, surged. The order book for Navy work on December 15 was about $11.4 billion, climbing from about $9.8 billion in 1974. New orders included seven destroyers, two Trident nuclear-powered submarines, a nuclear-fueled missile-firing cruiser, and three attack submarines.

Russia agreed in September to pay $16 per metric ton, up from a previous $9.50 rate, for U.S. grain shipped to Russian Black Sea ports. Maritime unions had called for a boycott of U.S. grain shipments to Russia on August 18, but a court ordered longshoremen back to work on August 26. The merchant-marine industry was also helped by legislation that increased from $5 billion to $7 billion the authorized federal mortgage insurance for vessels built in U.S. yards.

President Gerald R. Ford on September 19 named Karl E. Bakke as chairman of the Federal Maritime Commission. Albert R. Karr

SHOOTING. See Hunting; Sports.

SHRIVER, SARGENT (1915-   ), officially entered the race for the Democratic presidential nomination on Sept. 20, 1975. In his announcement speech, he laid claim to the political legacy of the Kennedy family, which he joined in 1953 with his marriage to Eunice Mary Kennedy, sister of President John F. Kennedy.

Robert Sargent Shriver, Jr., was born in Westminster, Md. He received a bachelor's degree from Yale University in 1938, and his law degree in 1941. He served in the U.S. Navy during World War II.

After a brief stint as assistant editor for *Newsweek* magazine, he joined the staff of Joseph P. Kennedy, his future father-in-law. He managed Kennedy's Merchandise Mart in Chicago from 1948 to 1960. While in Chicago, he served as president of the Chicago Board of Education from 1955 to 1960. He was named director of the Peace Corps in 1961, and head of the Office of Economic Opportunity in 1964. He served as U.S. ambassador to France from 1968 to 1970. He ran for Vice-President with Senator George S. McGovern of South Dakota in the 1972 campaign.

He lives in Rockville, Md., with his wife and their five children. Kathryn Sederberg

SIERRA LEONE. See Africa.

SIKKIM. See Asia.

SINGAPORE. See Asia.

SKATING. See Hockey; Ice Skating.

SKIING. The World Cup circuit, skiing's showcase event, changed its rules for 1975 to provide greater rewards for all-around competitors at the expense of specialists. Yet, at season's end, the champions were familiar. Annemarie Proell Moser of Austria won the women's title for the fifth consecutive year, and Gustavo Thoeni of Italy captured men's honors for the fourth time in five years.

The World Cup series embraced 14 meets for men and 13 for women from December, 1974, to March, 1975, in six European nations and Japan, Canada, and Sun Valley, Ida. In addition to the usual points for high finishes in special slalom, giant slalom, and downhill races, bonus points were awarded for all-around excellence at three men's and three women's meets.

Going into the final men's race on March 23 at Val Gardena, Italy, there was a three-way tie for first place among the 24-year-old Thoeni, Ingemar Stenmark of Sweden, and Franz Klammer of Austria. The final race was the first dual slalom in World Cup history. In a format borrowed from the professional tour, the skiers raced side by side down parallel courses in direct eliminations.

Dramatically, Thoeni and Stenmark reached the final. When Stenmark hit the next-to-last gate of the first run and was disqualified, Thoeni became champion. He finished with 250 points for the sea-

Annemarie Proell Moser, 22, of Austria, won the women's title in World Cup skiing for the fifth consecutive year.

son to 245 for Stenmark and 240 for Klammer. Moser finished the women's series with 305 points to 199 for Hanni Wenzel of Liechtenstein.

The most successful American was 20-year-old Cindy Nelson of Lutsen, Minn., who won a women's giant slalom at Whistler Mountain, British Columbia, Canada, and a downhill at Saalbach, Austria. She finished eighth in the final standing. No American man won a race, and the highest final ranking by an American was 19th by Greg Jones of Tahoe City, Calif.

Professional Skiing. The professional circuit consisted of 14 meets in the United States, Canada, and Europe. Each meet had special slalom and giant slalom races over parallel courses, with total prize money of $410,000. Hank Kashiwa of Old Forge, N.Y., won the series title with 360 points to 346 for Henri Duvillard, a new pro from France.

Nordic Skiing. America's best Nordic skiers were Tim Caldwell of Putney, Vt.; Martha Rockwell of West Lebanon, N.H.; and Jerry Martin of Minneapolis, Minn. Caldwell won one North American and two United States cross-country titles. Rockwell won all three individual cross-country titles for women in the United States championships, raising her career total to 15. Martin, who is blind in one eye, captured his third United States jumping title. He also won the national title in ski flying (jumping for distance).   Frank Litsky

SOARES, MARIO (1924-   ), the leader of Portugal's Socialist Party, worked with other moderates in 1975 to force Prime Minister Vasco dos Santos Gonçalves from power and to quash a revolt by far left wing troops. Soares had served as foreign minister in the first two provisional coalition governments that ruled following the April, 1974, overthrow of dictator Marcello Caetano. Soares' party received the most votes in April, 1975, elections. See PORTUGAL.

Soares was born on Dec. 7, 1924, in Lisbon, the son of a minister in Portugal's first republic. He studied at the University of Lisbon from 1942 to 1951 and earned a law degree from the Sorbonne in Paris in 1957. Politically active, Soares helped found the youth branch of the United Democratic Movement in 1946 and was a member of its first central committee until the movement was outlawed in 1948.

Soares was imprisoned more than a dozen times for his political activities and exiled twice. He was teaching in exile at the University of Paris when he was called back to Portugal in 1974 to become foreign minister. He traveled widely, pleading for continued economic support from Western nations and overseeing the negotiations that led to independence for Portugal's former African colonies.

He married actress Maria Barroso in 1949, while in prison. They have two children.   Robert K. Johnson

SOCCER has thrived in the rest of the world, yet has struggled for years for recognition in the United States. But American soccer reached its zenith in 1975, when the New York Cosmos of the North American Soccer League (NASL) signed Pelé of Brazil, generally recognized as the world's greatest player until he retired in 1974.

Pelé, 34 years old and a wealthy man with many business interests, was lured out of retirement by a contract worth about $4.7 million over three years, making him the highest-salaried athlete in any sport. He agreed to play about 100 games, including exhibitions, and assist the Cosmos and their parent company, Warner Communications, Incorporated, in public relations. See PELÉ.

Warner and the Cosmos expected to make money on the deal. The Cosmos, who averaged 4,700 in attendance in 1974 and 6,500 in the five 1975 home games before Pelé's arrival, started selling out their stadium, which seats 22,500. Almost all their road games sold out, and they collected large guarantees for exhibition games.

The NASL hoped that the arrival of Pelé would help it get a national television contract. His first game with the Cosmos, an exhibition against the Dallas Tornado on June 15, was televised in 13 nations, including the United States. CBS estimated that 5 million people in the United States watched the game, and the Neilsen ratings showed that 35 per cent of all sets turned on in the New York City area were tuned to the game.

Despite the presence of Pelé, the Cosmos finished third in the NASL's five-team Eastern Division. The league's 20 teams played 22 games each from April to August. The Tampa Bay Rowdies of Florida, a first-year team, won the championship by defeating the Portland (Ore.) Timbers, 2-0, in the play-off final on August 24 in San Jose, Calif.

Steve David of the Miami Toros, the scoring champion, was chosen Most Valuable Player in a poll of players. Pelé was second in the voting.

Other Champions. The American Soccer League, older but less prestigious than the NASL, had two champions. When the New York Apollos and Boston Astros played 67 scoreless minutes of overtime in the title game, Commissioner Bob Cousy declared them co-champions.

The Los Angeles Maccabi won the United States Open championship by defeating Inter-Giuliana of New York, 1-0, in the title game on June 15 in Torrance, Calif. The Chicago Kickers gained the national amateur championship.

Overseas, Bayern Munich of West Germany won the European Cup; Borussia MG of West Germany, the European Union Cup; and Dynamo Kiev, the European Cup Winners Cup, the first major European title for a Russian team. Derby captured the English League's first-division title, and Aston Villa won the English League Cup.   Frank Litsky

Brazilian star Pelé, right, joined the New York Cosmos, and North American Soccer League attendance immediately increased.

SOCIAL SECURITY. About 32 million persons in the United States received regular monthly social security benefit checks in 1975 under old-age, survivors, and disability insurance. Others received benefits under such programs as Medicare and Medicaid. The government paid out over $100 billion and concern spread in President Gerald R. Ford's Administration over the continuing escalation of such payments.

President Ford urged Congress on January 21 to set a 5 per cent ceiling on automatic cost-of-living increases. However, July payments contained an 8 per cent cost-of-living increase, since no action had been taken by Congress on Ford's request.

An advisory council of prominent private citizens, established to review the social security system, announced on January 24 that benefits would exceed tax receipts in 1976 by several billion dollars. They recommended changes that would convert slightly more than half of the financing of Medicare to general U.S. Treasury revenues.

The fact that benefits will exceed tax receipts in 1976 posed no threat to the benefits, the advisory group pointed out, because of the cushion of the $50-billion social security trust fund. But if their recommendations are implemented, the advisers said, the government would not have to take money from the trust fund, and could keep that fund growing. The advisory council was under the chairmanship of W. Allen Wallis, chancellor of the University of Rochester in New York.

Direct Deposit. The direct depositing of social security checks in financial institutions – long in the planning stage and tested in Georgia and Florida in 1974 – went into effect in 1975. The voluntary program for recipients of retired, disabled, and survivors social security payments went into effect in 23 states west of the Mississippi River on August 1. Beneficiaries in the Central and Southeastern states became eligible on September 1; the rest of the nation, on October 1.

Under the new method, checks are less likely to be lost, stolen, destroyed, or forged. This system also eliminates waiting in line to cash checks and the difficulty of cashing them in unfamiliar places. Some banks announced that they would guarantee their customers that payments would be credited to their accounts each month whether or not the social security check arrived on time.

The new arrangement lays the groundwork for the anticipated electronic fund-transfer system, which may eventually replace the issuance and delivery of individual checks. The change grew out of the need for a fast, simple method of getting the enormous volume of social security payments from the government to individuals.

Discrimination. The Supreme Court of the United States in March unanimously struck down a section of the Social Security Act that denied widowers with children the same social security survivors' benefits as widows receive. The justices said that the law unconstitutionally discriminated against female wage earners by providing less protection for their survivors than it provided for the survivors of male employees.

Under the Social Security Act, benefits based on the earnings of a deceased husband and father covered by the act are payable, with some limitations, both to the widow and to the couple's minor children in her care. But if a wife and mother dies, the widower gets none of the benefits based on her earnings. They go only to the minor children.

The decision led to a re-examination of the entire social security law by Social Security Commissioner James B. Cardwell. He told the Senate Special Committee on Aging in October that other provisions of the act discriminated between men and women and should be corrected. He said that the agency should be able to correct all but one provision "without incurring significant additional cost, without adding to the administrative complexity of the program or, for that matter, without affecting large numbers of people."

That one provision, however, presumes that a wife is dependent on her husband, while a man has to prove dependency, Cardwell said. This provision would be difficult to resolve.   Joseph P. Anderson

SOCIAL WELFARE officials looked for new ways to guarantee that every needy American had adequate food, housing, and other necessities in 1975 as unemployment reached 9.2 per cent and statistics indicated that 23.8 million persons were living below the poverty level in the United States. Many believed that the best way to ensure equitable distribution of aid was to shift all of the welfare responsibility to the federal government.

During 1975, the federal government paid slightly more than half of all welfare bills. Many state officials said their agencies could no longer handle the huge welfare burden. In addition, the 50 states had widely varying standards of how much welfare recipients should get, how county and state governments should share the burden, and how to detect and remove ineligible recipients from welfare rolls.

Inflation added to the amount of money needed for survival, and allotments for food stamps rose $8 more per month on July 1 to meet rising costs resulting from inflation. All in all, welfare rolls have increased nearly 38 per cent and payments were up 11.3 per cent since 1968.

Flat Grants. More than half the states have turned to flat grants as a simple way of distributing welfare payments issued in Aid to Families with Dependent Children (AFDC). Under this system, many of the basic and special-needs cash payments

Social workers throughout the United States found it increasingly difficult to keep up with the mounting welfare caseload in 1975.

are consolidated and paid in a lump sum. Payments are based on the size of each AFDC family. In one state, this has reduced payments for 55 special-needs items to a single payment. In another state, 12 allowances were consolidated into one.

In 1975, 27 states used this kind of AFDC payment program. Most of them instituted it after the U.S. Department of Health, Education, and Welfare (HEW) opened a drive in 1973 to eliminate payment errors in the $8-billion AFDC program.

"The movement to flat grants and away from complicated individualized payments to AFDC families will go a long way toward correcting overpayment and underpayment errors." HEW Secretary Caspar W. Weinberger said in mid-1975. "Flat grants already have helped a number of states to reduce errors related to the previously complex methods of determining payment amounts for welfare families."

HEW had reported in December, 1973, that 10.2 per cent of all AFDC cases were ineligible, 22.8 per cent were overpaid, and 8.1 per cent were underpaid. The agency insisted that states must reduce such errors by July 1, 1975, to no more than 3 per cent for ineligibility and no more than 5 per cent each for overpayment and underpayment, or they would face the loss of the federal share of costs.

Food Stamps. President Gerald R. Ford's Administration sent a food-stamp reform bill to Congress on October 20. The Administration said it would save taxpayers $1.2 billion annually by either eliminating from the relief rolls or reducing benefits for almost half of the 18.8 million persons now receiving food coupons.

The plan would limit eligibility to those whose net income falls below the poverty level — $2,590 for a single person, $5,050 for a family of four — eliminating 1 million households, or 3.4 million people, from the rolls. It would also change the method of determining who is eligible for food stamps, reducing benefits for an additional 5.3 million persons who would still qualify under the new standards.

In transmitting the plan to Congress, President Ford said, "My recommendations for dealing with the food-stamp assistance program follow a fundamental principle on which I stand: The federal government should help, within the limits of natural resources, those who are in need; but we should not give one dollar . . . to those not in need."

The plan would limit participation by workers who lose their jobs through layoffs or strikes. For such workers, food-stamp eligibility would be determined by their average income for three months, rather than just for one month as is done under the present food-stamp program. The Administration program was severely criticized by liberal members of Congress.　　　　　　　　Joseph P. Anderson

SOMALIA. See AFRICA.

SOUTH AFRICA. The white-minority government relaxed its *apartheid* system of racial segregation somewhat in 1975. The government said on April 25 that nonwhites would be recruited for the diplomatic service. In May, the first soldiers of mixed racial backgrounds (Coloreds) were appointed as officers in the army.

A significant improvement for blacks who work in urban areas came in May when they were allowed to hold leases up to 30 years. Blacks may only rent in segregated residential areas. Since 1968, they had been compelled to rent on a month-to-month basis, because the government wanted to discourage settlement in urban areas by blacks.

Homeland Independence. On April 23, it was announced that the Transkei *Bantustan* (black homeland) would become an independent nation in October, 1976. All Bantustans are eventually to be politically independent. However, except for the Transkei, all the homelands consist of scattered parcels of land. In March, the government introduced a plan to reduce the number of parcels from more than 100 to 36. Nevertheless, all of the homelands would comprise only 13 per cent of South Africa's land, while the blacks comprise 70 per cent of the population.

Internal Politics. Elections for the Colored Persons Representative Council were held on March 19. South Africa's 2 million Colored citizens live in white areas and elect representatives to the council, a body with limited powers in local government. The Colored Labor Party defeated the progovernment Federal Party by winning 31 of the 40 elected seats.

Two of the three white opposition parties announced their merger in May to form the Progressive-Reform Party. The new party advocates a federal system of government and strict constitutional safeguards to prevent one race from dominating another.

Prime Minister Balthazar Johannes Vorster continued trying to normalize relations with black-ruled African countries. In February, he secretly visited Liberia for talks with President William R. Tolbert, Jr. During the year, he cooperated with Zambia, Botswana, and Tanzania in pushing Rhodesian blacks and whites toward a negotiated settlement (see RHODESIA).

Namibia (South West Africa) made some progress toward independence from South Africa. A conference of representatives of the territory's tribes resolved in September that an independence constitution be drafted by the end of 1978.　John D. Esseks

See also AFRICA (Facts in Brief Table); TELEVISION (Close-Up).

SOUTH AMERICA. See LATIN AMERICA and articles on Latin American countries.

SOUTH CAROLINA. See STATE GOVERNMENT.

SOUTH DAKOTA. See STATE GOVERNMENT.

SPACE
EXPLORATION

United States astronauts eased an *Apollo* spacecraft into contact with a manned Russian *Soyuz* craft on July 17, 1975, and locked the two vehicles together as they orbited 138 miles (229 kilometers) above Earth (see Close-Up). The mission, called the Apollo-Soyuz Test Project (ASTP), symbolized détente in space between the two superpowers. ASTP was the last manned space flight planned by the National Aeronautics and Space Administration (NASA) until 1979, when the space shuttle, a combination spacecraft and aircraft, is scheduled to begin space flights.

Salyut and Soyuz. In contrast, the Soviets are flying longer manned missions. In December, 1974, they placed the *Salyut 4* space station in orbit. On Jan. 11, 1975, cosmonauts Alexei A. Gubarev and Georgi M. Grechko docked *Soyuz 17* with the station. The two spent 30 days aboard *Salyut 4* – a record for Russian cosmonauts – and landed on February 9.

On April 5, a second crew bound for *Salyut 4* was forced to make an emergency landing in western Siberia when the upper stage of the launch rocket failed to separate from a lower stage. The aborted mission, coming only three months before the joint ASTP flight, generated concern about the Russian's technical competence and the safety of American astronauts. However, the Russians successfully launched cosmonauts Petr I. Klimuk and Vitaly I. Sevastyanov on May 24, and they spent 63 days aboard *Salyut 4.* They conducted experiments similar to those performed on the 28-, 59-, and 84-day American *Skylab* missions in 1973 and 1974. The Russian results agree with a NASA conclusion that daily exercise is necessary to keep an astronaut's cardiovascular system and body muscles from deteriorating during long periods of weightless flight.

Venus Probes. The Soviet Union also continued its program of unmanned planetary flights in 1975. In October, *Venera 9* and *Venera 10* made the first twin landings on another planet – Venus – and transmitted the first pictures from the surface of another planet. The surface of the landing sites, 1,320 miles (2,200 kilometers) apart, appeared rocky, which is evidence against the theory scientists have held that the surface has been extensively eroded.

Venera 9 operated for 53 minutes on the surface and *Venera 10* for a record 65 minutes. Atmospheric pressure 90 times that on Earth and temperatures of about 900°F. (482°C) presumably prevented a

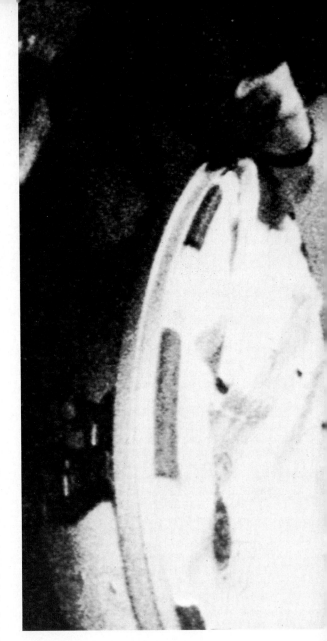

Historic handshake in space on July 17, 1975, is shown in photograph made from a frame of 16mm motion-picture film.

longer life for instruments. The Soviet landers were released from orbiting craft and descended by parachutes, transmitting data on the thick cloud cover of Venus as they fell.

Mariner 10 took the first close-up pictures of these clouds as it flew by Venus in February, 1974. The photographs revealed circulation patterns that resemble those in the tropical regions of Earth. Some bands of clouds travel around Venus at speeds of 200 miles (320 kilometers) per hour.

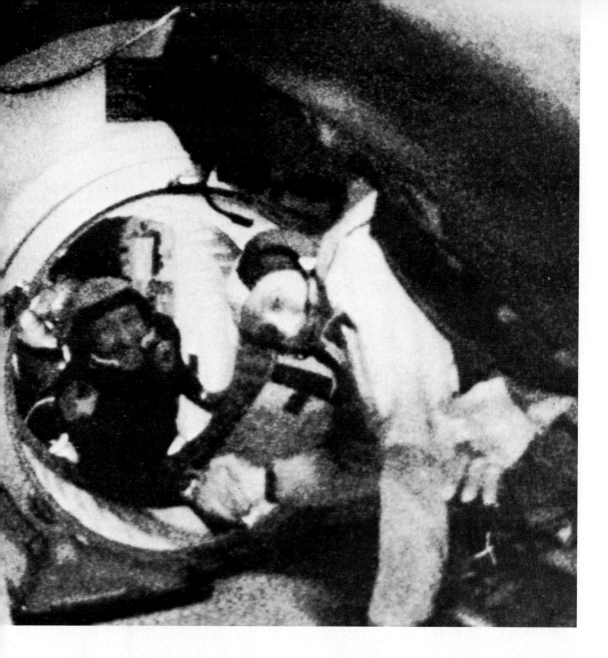

Mercury and Jupiter. *Mariner 10* also passed Mercury for the third time on March 16, 1975. At that time, it came as close as 200 miles and verified that Mercury has its own magnetic field. The field was detected on a pass in March, 1974, but scientists did not know then if it was Mercury's own field or the result of solar winds blowing across the planet. The 1975 pass showed that the field is generated in the interior of Mercury.

United States scientists were also busy in 1975 examining data from *Pioneer 11,* which flew by Jupiter in December, 1974, and sped on to a 1979 rendezvous with Saturn. The probe found that the magnetic field of Jupiter sometimes is stretched to distances of 9 million miles (14.5 million kilometers)

by pressure from the solar wind. When the wind changes direction, the magnetic boundary moves back toward the planet at speeds as fast as 200,000 miles (320,000 kilometers) per hour, and the field may lose 75 per cent or more of its volume.

Belts of intense radiation inside this pulsating field temporarily interfered with the operation of some instruments and caused a loss of data. However, *Pioneer 11* flew as close as 26,000 miles (42,000 kilometers) and sent back new details about the radiation belts, the polar regions, and the large moons of Jupiter. Some scientists have speculated that the Jovian polar regions may be warm and stable enough for living organisms to originate and survive there.

Détente In Space

United States astronaut Thomas P. Stafford shook the hand of Russian cosmonaut Alexei A. Leonov on the afternoon of July 17, 1975, after their spacecraft joined together in orbit 138 miles (229 kilometers) over the Earth. It was both a technical and a political milestone. The mission, called the Apollo-Soyuz Test Project (ASTP), marked the first time that spacemen from two nations joined their ships in orbit and carried out joint experiments. The handshake symbolized cooperation in space between two superpowers that have been unceasing rivals since 1945.

The ASTP mission grew out of an agreement to cooperate in space that was signed on May 24, 1972, during a visit by President Richard M. Nixon to Russia. The two nations agreed to develop systems that would permit their spacecraft to dock in space so they could rescue stranded spacefarers and conduct joint scientific experiments.

After three years of preparation, the Soviet Union launched a *Soyuz* spacecraft from the Baikonur Cosmodrome in southwest Soviet Asia on July 15. Cosmonauts Leonov — an air force colonel and the first man to walk in space — and Valery N. Kubasov, a civilian flight engineer, were on board. For the first time, the Soviet government permitted live television coverage of a space launch.

The United States launched an *Apollo* spacecraft from the Kennedy Space Center at Cape Canaveral, Fla., 7½ hours later. In addition to Stafford, an Air Force major general and veteran of three space flights, the crew included civilians Vance D. Brand and Donald K. (Deke) Slayton. The two crews maneuvered their spacecraft together, with *Apollo* making the final approach to *Soyuz*. A color TV camera on *Apollo* allowed the world to watch as the two vehicles were *docked* (joined) and locked together. Two orbits later, Stafford crawled through a tunnel connecting the vehicles and shook Leonov's hand.

During the next two days, the spacemen visited each other's ships, exchanging national flags and signing international certificates. Each

American and Russian spacemen initial official certificates.

astronaut visited the foreign craft at least once. Soviet Communist Party General Secretary Leonid I. Brezhnev complimented the crews in a message read by mission control in Moscow. U.S. President Gerald R. Ford talked with them via a telephone link-up. The crews later conducted scientific experiments, television "tours" of each spacecraft, and a press conference.

After almost 44 hours together, and on the fourth day of the mission, the vehicles undocked on July 19. Then they docked briefly and undocked a second time before going their separate ways. The cosmonauts touched down in a cloud of smoke in Kazakhstan, northeast of the Baikonur Cosmodrome on July 21. On emerging from the heat-scorched capsule, Leonov said, "We worked strictly on schedule, and it was hard."

The *Apollo* astronauts continued to perform experiments in orbit. These included the discovery of at least one source of extreme ultraviolet radiation in the universe. The crew conducted nearly 30 experiments, five with the Russians, before splashing down in the Pacific Ocean about 300 miles (500 kilometers) west of Honolulu, Hawaii, on July 24.

The mission's only serious problem arose during re-entry when the astronauts failed to shut off a small rocket-thruster system. Gaseous nitrogen tetraoxide fumes entered the *Apollo* cabin, and Brand momentarily blacked out. The men were hospitalized in semi-isolation in Honolulu until July 30.

Senator John H. Glenn (D., Ohio), the first American to orbit the Earth, called the flight a "symbolic gesture, more political than substantive." Critics complained that the mission's $250-million cost was too high a price for a symbolic gesture that may yield no definite and lasting benefit. They also charged that the United States gave away valuable technical knowledge to the Soviet Union. Officials of the National Aeronautics and Space Administration denied these charges but conceded that ASTP would not have been flown solely for technical and scientific reasons.   William J. Cromie

Search for Life. The United States launched two *Viking* spacecraft in 1975 to search for signs of life on Mars. The first left Cape Canaveral, Fla., on August 20. It is scheduled to go into orbit around Mars in June, 1976, and release an instrument package that may land on July 4. A second *Viking*, launched on September 20, is slated to land no earlier than Sept. 4, 1976. The landing sites will be low, humid areas where the probability of encountering liquid water is highest. A scoop 10 feet (3 meters) long will pick up samples of soil from Mars's surface, which will be examined in an automatic biological laboratory for traces of organisms — living or dead.

Other Missions. India joined the space explorers when Russia launched its *Aryabhata* satellite on April 20, 1975. The Netherlands joined the list of space-exploring countries in August, 1974, with the launch of its first satellite. West Germany launched the *Helios* spacecraft in December, 1974, and it came closer to the Sun than any previous man-made object — to within 28 million miles (45 million kilometers).

The European Space Agency was born in Paris on May 30, when 10 European nations banded together for $380 million worth of nonmilitary space research. William J. Cromie

See also Section Two, UPDATING OUR PERSPECTIVE ON THE PLANETS.

SPAIN. General Francisco Franco, who ruled Spain as a dictator for 39 years, died on Nov. 20, 1975, after lying near death for a month. Franco's designated successor, Prince Juan Carlos, became king on November 22. He swore allegiance to the Franco regime's principles but promised to make "profound improvements" (see JUAN CARLOS I).

As his first major political act, the 37-year-old king granted limited pardons to some political prisoners and common criminals. The act did not apply to those held under Spain's antiterrorism decree, which went into effect on August 27. The decree forces judges to impose death sentences on those found guilty of killing policemen, soldiers, or government officials. It was used in the military trial of 11 political terrorists, five of whom were executed on September 27 despite appeals for clemency from many of the world's political and religious leaders. Two of the five were members of the outlawed Basque separatist movement.

Europe Protests. After the executions, at least 15 countries recalled their ambassadors. Protestors rioted in France, Great Britain, the Netherlands, and Portugal. President Luis Echeverría Alvarez of Mexico called on the United Nations Security Council to expel Spain, and the European Community (Common Market) broke off trade talks with Spain because Franco had "violated the very principle of human rights."

In response, Prime Minister Carlos Arias Navarro said on September 30 that "Spain is not prepared to pay the price of its dignity to win approval abroad." About 150,000 persons turned out for a Madrid rally on October 1 in support of Franco.

But political killings continued. Gunmen shot three policemen, which stiffened the government's determination to "carry out the law," according to a communiqué issued on October 3. Three more policemen were killed in the Basque country on October 5, and five people were shot dead in a gun battle in Barcelona on October 8.

Strikes and Riots. The September executions followed months of riots and strikes by workers and students backed by Roman Catholic priests. On February 4, the government imposed without trial $60,000 in fines on 19 priests for delivering sermons in Pamplona sympathizing with striking miners.

With thousands of students and workers on strike for freedoms, Arias Navarro changed his Cabinet on December 11. He gave key posts to reformers.

U.S. Bases. The United States retained use of air and naval bases in Spain under an agreement announced on October 4. Spain averted a crisis with Morocco by agreeing on November 14 to partition its Spanish Sahara colony between Morocco and Mauritania (see MOROCCO). Kenneth Brown

See also EUROPE (Facts in Brief Table).

His hand on a Bible, King Juan Carlos I is sworn in on Nov. 22, 1975, two days after the death of dictator General Francisco Franco.

SPORTS. Economic problems struck the sports world hard in 1975. The major casualty was the World Football League (WFL), which lost $10 million in 1974, its first season. Attendance in 1975 averaged only 13,000, and in midseason, with losses in the millions, the league folded. See FOOTBALL.

Just before the WFL expired, the World Hockey Association started its fourth season, and it had fewer high-paid players. Ben Hatskin, its chief executive officer, said, "We started three years ago and signed a lot of our players to three-year contracts. After the three years, the fringe players and bench-sitters found themselves without a new contract." See HOCKEY.

The nine-year-old American Basketball Association (ABA) was down to 10 teams, and all 10 applied in vain for franchises in the older National Basketball Association (NBA). "There's no way professional basketball can survive if 25 of the 28 teams in both leagues lose substantial amounts of money every year," ABA President John Y. Brown said. NBA salaries averaged more than $100,000 a year, ABA salaries slightly less. Brown said the two leagues lost a total of $16 million during the 1974–1975 season. By December, three ABA teams had folded and the league was down to seven teams. The Baltimore club franchise was revoked in October, San Diego folded in November, and the Utah team went out of business in December. See BASKETBALL.

NCAA Economies. The National Collegiate Athletic Association (NCAA) said 80 per cent of its more than 700 member colleges lost money on their 1974 athletic programs. It held a special convention to cut costs, and it expected its changes to save $15 million.

For the 234 large colleges grouped in NCAA Division One, the total number of players on football scholarships at one time was cut from 105 to 95. Coaching staffs, previously unlimited in size, were limited to 11 for football and four for basketball. The total number of scholarships for so-called non-revenue sports—all except football and basketball—was set at 80 for the larger colleges and 60 for the smaller. The $15-a-month payment that most athletes on athletic scholarships received for incidental expenses was eliminated.

Among the reforms was a limit on the number of players a college football team could dress for a game—60 players at home, 48 on the road. Previously, there was no limit. The University of Alabama, calling the new rule unfair to players who practiced all week but could not play in a game, got a court injunction against the limit, but that was overruled by a higher court on appeal.

Equality in Sports. A new law, Title IX, gave women's rights in sports a boost. It provides that separate teams in any contact sport may be provided if a significant number of female students want

More than 4,000 runners create a different kind of traffic jam on a road outside Tokyo during a marathon race in February.

the teams. The same percentage of athletic scholarships, based on the number of participants, must also be offered to women. The law does not require that women be allowed to play on men's teams unless a school cannot provide a women's team and has discriminated against women in noncontact sports.

Among the Winners in 1975 were:

Curling. Switzerland won the world championship by defeating the United States, 7–3, in March in Perth, Scotland. The Seattle rink that represented the United States had won the U.S. title earlier in March, eliminating the Superior, Wis., rink that won the 1974 world title.

Fencing. Russia repeated as team champion and won three of the eight titles in the world championships in July in Budapest, Hungary. The United States finished sixth in team saber.

Handball. Jay Bilbeu of Fresno, Calif., won the U.S. Handball Association (USHA) four-wall championship in a field of 291. Fred Lewis of Cleveland, the 1974 USHA champion, played on an eight-city professional tour and won the title.

Rowing. East Germany, which had won six of the eight titles in the 1974 world championships, won five of eight in the 1975 competition in August in Nottingham, England. The United States finished fifth in eights and fifth in pairs with coxswain. Harvard was the best college eight.

Shooting. Gary Anderson, a state senator from Axtell, Nebr., won the United States high-powered rifle title in the national championships at Camp Perry, Ohio, in August. The six-day championships drew 725 competitors.

Weight Lifting. Vassili Alexeev of Russia won the world super heavyweight title in Moscow in September for the sixth consecutive year and set world records of 542$\frac{1}{2}$ pounds (246 kilograms) for the clean and jerk and 948 pounds (430 kilograms) for the snatch and the clean and jerk combined in one meet. Russia won the world title.

Wrestling. Russia won its ninth straight team title in the world championships in Moscow in August. The United States was fifth but won no medals, though five Americans placed fourth in their divisions. Mike McCready of Dubuque, Iowa, won the unlimited-weight class in both Amateur Athletic Union (AAU) national championships — free-style and Greco-Roman.

Other Champions. *Archery,* world champions: men, Darrell Pace, Reading, Ohio; women, Zebiniso Rustamova, Russia. U.S. champions: men, Pace; women, Irene Lorensen, Phoenix, Ariz. *Badminton,* U.S. champions: men, Mike Adams, Flint, Mich.; women, Judianne Kelly, Norwalk, Calif. *Biathlon,* world champion: Heikki Ikola, Finland. *Billiards,* U.S. pocket champion: Dallas West, Rockford, Ill. *Bobsledding,* world champions: four-man, Switzerland (Erich Scharer, driver); two-man, Italy (Giorgio Alvera, driver). *Canoeing,* world 500-meter champions: men's canoe, S. Pterenko, Russia; men's kayak, G. Csapo, Hungary; men's kayak slalom, Siegbert Horn, East Germany. *Casting,* U.S. all-around champion: Steve Rajeff, San Francisco. *Court tennis,* U.S. open champion: Gene Scott, New York City. *Cross-country,* U.S. champions: AAU, Greg Fredericks, Philadelphia; NCAA, Craig Virgin, Illinois. *Cycling,* world champions: men's amateur sprint, Daniel Morelon, France; women's amateur sprint, Sue Novarra, Flint, Mich.; world pro road, Hennie Kuiper, the Netherlands. *Field hockey,* world champion: India. *Gymnastics,* women's all-around champions: European, Nadia Comeneci, Romania; World Cup, Ludmilla Turisheva, Russia. *Horseshoe pitching,* U.S. champion: Elmer Hohl, Wellesley, Canada. *Judo,* AAU grand champion: Tommy Martin, Stockton, Calif. *Karate,* world sparring champion: Masahiko Tanaka, Japan. *Lacrosse,* college: Maryland. National Lacrosse League: Quebec Caribous. *Luge* (tobogganing), world champions: men, Wolfram Fiedler, East Germany; women, Margit Schumann, East Germany. *Modern pentathlon,* World Cup: Pavel Lednev, Russia. *Motorcycling,* U.S. grand national champion: Gary Scott, Springfield, Ohio. *Parachuting,* U.S. overall champions: men, Jimmy Davis, Charlotte, N.C.; women, Debbie Schmidt, Joliet, Ill. *Polo,* U.S. open champion: Milwaukee. *Racquetball,* U.S. champion: Charlie Brumfield, San Diego. *Racquets,* world champion: William Surtees, Chicago. *Rodeo,* national all-around champion: Leo Camarillo, Oakdale, Calif. *Roller skating,* U.S. champions: men, Michael Glatz, San Diego; women, Moana Brigham, San Diego. *Rugby,* Great Britain, Rugby Union: club champion, Bedford; county champion, Gloucestershire; International champion, Wales. Rugby League: Challenge Cup, Widnes. *Sled-dog racing,* world champion: Dick Moulton, Center Harbor, N.H. *Softball,* U.S. fast-pitch champions: men, Rising Sun Hotel, Reading, Pa.; women, Raybestos Brakettes, Stratford, Conn. *Squash racquets,* U.S. champion: Victor Neiderhoffer, New York City. *Squash tennis,* U.S. champion: Pedro Bacallao, New York City. *Surfing,* U.S. champions: men, Aaron Wright, Pedro Point, Calif.; women, Sally Prange, Honolulu, Hawaii. *Synchronized swimming,* world champion: Gail Johnson Buzonas, Santa Clara, Calif. *Table tennis,* world champions: men, Istvan Jonyer, Hungary; women, Yung Sun Kim, North Korea. *Trampoline,* AAU champions: men, Stuart Ransom, Memphis, Tenn.; women, Shelly Grant, Springfield, Ill. *Volleyball,* AAU champions: men, Honolulu Outriggers; women, British Columbia Chimo. International Volleyball Association: Los Angeles Stars. *Water polo,* world: Russia. *Water skiing,* world overall champions: men, Carlos Suarez, Venezuela; women, Liz Allan Shetter, Groveland, Fla. **Frank Litsky**

SRI LANKA. The capital, Colombo, buzzed with rumors of an imminent split in Prime Minister Sirimavo Bandaranaike's three-party leftist United Front throughout August, 1975. Finally, on the night of September 1, President William Gopallawa sent blunt letters to three ministers of the Trotskyite Equality Party — including those of finance and plantations — telling them they had been fired. The finance portfolio was given to Prime Minister Bandaranaike's nephew, Felix Bandaranaike. He was in Washington, D.C., at the time, but this did not matter. He was sworn in at the precise moment picked for the event by the prime minister's astrologers.

Tea Plantations were at the root of the discord. Tea is the nation's main money-maker, earning $150 million a year in foreign sales. Bandaranaike's Sri Lanka Freedom Party and the Trotskyites agreed on the need to nationalize the 396 tea estates still in private hands. But Bandaranaike was apparently willing to break relations with her far-left partners rather than let them control the plantations. To allow the Trotskyites, who already dominated key unions as well as the university campuses, to dominate the tea industry as well was something she clearly did not want.

With more than 90 seats in the 157-seat National State Assembly, and with 6 more held by the allied pro-Moscow Communists, Bandaranaike did not have to fear a parliamentary upset.

Far more worrisome, however, was the deep and growing public discontent. After two years of drought, rains at last promised a good harvest. But the nation was still spending half of its export earnings to buy food from other countries. A black market flourished in bicycle tires, chili peppers, cotton textiles, flashlight batteries, and other essentials that were in desperately short supply. And, in this land with a soaring birth rate, the year 1975 saw an additional 300,000 persons added to the army of jobseekers.

Crowded Jails. The wheels of justice have moved slowly since April, 1971, when thousands of youths, led by leftist extremists, tried to seize power in Sri Lanka. By September, 1975, some 229 of the arrested youths had been given prison terms ranging from one year to life imprisonment, and 2,376 received suspended sentences.

Meanwhile, thousands remained in jail awaiting trial. In that 1971 "children's uprising," Russia, China, and India all provided arms and cash to Bandaranaike. The United States continued its aid, even as Sri Lanka politicians denounced American villainy. Now, with the Trotskyites out, some expected Bandaranaike to move closer to the middle of the road. But in a near-bankrupt nation, with discontented people and feuding political parties, moderation may be only a dream. **Mark Gayn**

See also ASIA (Facts in Brief Table).

STAMP COLLECTING. Striking increases in the value of rare stamps were registered in 1975. Scott's *1975 Specialized Catalogue of U.S. Stamps* showed 22,782 price changes, virtually all of them representing price increases from 1974. For example, the *Graf Zeppelin* airmail stamps of 1930 rose in one year from a catalog value of $784 for a block of three to $1,060. Also indicative of the trend was the $1,014,185 gross realized at the Rarities of the World auction in New York City on March 25, an American record for a one-day auction. One block of six 1867 U.S. stamps embossed with a waffle design brought $159,500. The same issue, offered individually and listed at $25,000, sold for $42,500, the highest auction price ever paid for a used U.S. stamp.

An 1850 cover with a pair of black-on-rose, two-penny British Guiana stamps sold for $190,000 to an unnamed American buyer at an auction in Geneva, Switzerland, on May 5. An 1859 letter with three 40-centesima Parma stamps brought $140,000. The Stanley Gibbons Group of London reported in July that Great Britain's rarest and most valuable stamp, the Edward VII sixpenny purple IR official of 1904, had increased in value from 13,500 to 15,000 British pounds in six months. (In July, the British pound was worth $2.15.) The British Guiana one-penny black-on-magenta of 1856 —

the world's most valuable stamp — jumped in value from 130,000 to 150,000 British pounds in the space of one year.

Commemoratives. Besides issuing several stamps commemorating prominent persons and events pertaining to the American Revolution Bicentennial, the U.S. Postal Service issued four stamps on March 25 honoring the memory of "Contributors to the Cause" who are little known today. The honored patriots were Haym Salomon (10 cents), who helped finance the Revolutionary War; Salem Poor (10 cents), a free black who fought bravely at the Battle of Bunker Hill against the British; Sybil Ludington (8 cents), who rode through the night to arouse militiamen; and Peter Francisco (18 cents), who enlisted in the colonial army at the age of 15. The Postal Service said in August that it would issue a sheet of 32 stamps reproducing the Declaration of Independence with each stamp showing part of the document. The American Philatelic Society "black blotted" the proposed sheet, and collectors resented having to buy all 32 stamps to have a complete collection. The Postal Service canceled the issue in November.

The United States and Russia jointly commemorated the July link-up of the *Apollo* and *Soyuz* spaceships. They issued two stamps, one of American and one of Russian design.   Theodore M. O'Leary

"Spain '75," an exhibition of stamps from 125 countries, is held in the Crystal Palace of the Madrilian Casa del Campo in Madrid in April.

STATE GOVERNMENT. Many states took severe, bullet-biting action in 1975 to stave off financial deficits. They acted after a federal report predicting financial problems for the states proved painfully accurate. The report, made after a May survey, showed that the 48 contiguous states had a net surplus of $3.9 billion on June 30, 1975, down from $6.5 billion a year earlier. Most of this was concentrated in 21 states. Eighteen states with unemployment at or above the national average had a combined surplus of only $400 million, down 83 per cent from June 30, 1974.

Faced with impending revenue shortfalls, the states began to act. They cut spending across the board, increased taxes, left vacant state jobs unfilled, restricted pay raises, and laid off employees.

The most dramatic example of belt-tightening came in New York state, where the legislature on November 25 passed a measure that increased New York City taxes $200 million. State officials said it was necessary to get federal aid for the debt-ridden city. The tax package was only part of a $6.6-billion financing program that Governor Hugh L. Carey devised to meet the city's immediate cash needs and refinance its debt over a three-year period. See NEW YORK CITY.

Other states also began trimming their budgets. For example, Connecticut Governor Ella T. Grasso announced a three-phase layoff of 6,000 state workers on December 4 in an effort to erase a projected $80-million deficit. Faced with a $460-million budget deficit, the Massachusetts legislature passed $364 million in new taxes and voted to cut the state budget 10 per cent. Alaska, Arkansas, Florida, Illinois, Michigan, Nebraska, and Ohio also acted.

Taxes Go Up. Faltering gasoline-tax revenues and the possibility that the federal government would tax gasoline heavily to conserve energy forced many states to re-examine their gasoline taxes. At least seven states increased their gas tax. Hawaii raised the tax 3½ cents per gallon (3.8 liters) for 14 months. Arkansas made a 1-cent increase permanent. Other increases included Minnesota, 2 cents; Wyoming, 1 cent; Rhode Island, 2 cents; South Dakota, 1 cent; and Oregon, 1 cent.

At least two states raised cigarette taxes — Maryland to 10 cents per package and Rhode Island from 5 to 18 cents per pack. Massachusetts and Connecticut increased general sales taxes. Despite severe fiscal problems, most states continued to provide property-tax relief.

Medical Malpractice Insurance. Skyrocketing malpractice-insurance rates for physicians and hospitals virtually dominated many state legislative discussions. Nearly half of the states enacted legislation. Some simply created special commissions to monitor the rising rates, but California, Florida, Idaho, Illinois, Louisiana, New York, and Pennsylvania set limits on malpractice claims that ranged

from $100,000 to $500,000. A district court voided Idaho's limit on damages in September, but a state court upheld Illinois' limit in the same month. Hawaii, Maryland, New York, North Carolina, South Carolina, Wisconsin, and others created pools to fund malpractice claims. Other states created medical excess-damage-award funds, provided self-insurance for doctors, or authorized the state insurance commissioner to create malpractice-insurance programs. See INSURANCE (Close-Up).

Bond Issues Suffer. Voters showed a disdain for bond programs in elections on November 4, possibly because of the controversy over New York City's financing situation. Of $6.33 billion worth nationwide, $5.87 billion were defeated. Ohio voters rejected $4.5 billion in bond proposals, while New Jersey voters turned down $922 million in bonds for transportation, housing, and water and sewer systems. New York state voters disapproved a $250-million bond proposal for housing for the elderly. Maine, Oregon, and Pennsylvania voters approved bond programs, however.

Election procedures should become easier in several states. The legislatures in California, Iowa, New York, Oregon, Tennessee, Utah, and Wisconsin enacted such measures as voter registration by mail and authorized mobile-unit voter registration.

Government Ethics. The shape of the political election process changed, too, in the continuing trend toward higher ethical standards. Wyoming barred associations or organizations from contributing directly to candidates; contributions must be made through political parties. Kansas passed a law permitting its classified public employees to run only for nonpartisan offices. A new California law requires that political announcements in newspapers be explicitly labeled. In Nevada, voters may mark a block on the ballot indicating they support none of the candidates on the ballot. The Texas legislature created new campaign spending limits and expanded coverage of the 1973 law on campaign finance reporting. A new Virginia law requires fuller public disclosure of election finances. Hawaii, Nevada, and South Dakota now limit campaign spending and require that expenditures be reported. Arkansas, Louisiana, South Carolina, and Tennessee required additional reporting.

At least 17 states enacted codes of ethics in 1975 with such provisions as financial disclosure by public officials, stronger conflict-of-interest regulations, expanded powers for public ethics commissions, and more "openness" in government activity. For example, the state of Washington, with one of the toughest governmental-ethics laws in the nation, modified its law governing financial disclosure by public officials, reducing some requirements and tightening others.

Energy Legislation. Soaring electrical utility costs sparked much of the 1975 energy action.

Selected Statistics on State Governments

State	Resident Population(a)	Governor	Senate (D.)	(R.)	House (D.)	(R.)	State tax rev. (c)	Tax rev. per cap. (d)	Public school enrollment 1974-75 (e)	Pub. school expenditures per pupil in aver. daily attendance 1974-75(f)
Alabama	3,614	George C. Wallace (D.)	35	0	105	0	$1,111	$308	764	$ 871
Alaska	352	Jay S. Hammond (R.)	13	7	30	9(g)	203	578	81	1,624
Arizona	2,224	Raul H. Castro (D.)	18	12	27	33	938	422	517	1,176
Arkansas	2,116	David Pryor (D.)	34	1	98	2	653	308	446	896
California	21,185	Edmund G. Brown, Jr. (D.)	25	15(k)	55	25	9,565	451	4,419	1,210
Colorado	2,534	Richard D. Lamm (D.)	16	19	39	26	866	342	568	1,188
Connecticut	3,095	Ella T. Grasso (D.)	29	7	118	33	1,059	342	662	1,507
Delaware	579	Sherman W. Tribbitt (D.)	13	8	25	16	336	581	132	1,485
Florida	8,357	Reubin O'D. Askew (D.)	27	12(g)	86	34	2,791	334	1,524	1,147
Georgia	4,926	George D. Busbee (D.)	51	5	155	24(h)	1,548	314	1,075	1,000
Hawaii	865	George R. Ariyoshi (D.)	18	7	35	16	576	665	177	1,384
Idaho	820	Cecil D. Andrus (D.)	13	22	27	43	298	364	187	910
Illinois	11,145	Dan Walker (D.)	34	25	101	76	4,410	396	2,300	1,376
Indiana	5,311	Otis R. Bowen (R.)	23	27	56	44	1,854	349	1,196	1,074
Iowa	2,870	Robert D. Ray (R.)	26	24	61	39	1,062	370	626	1,240
Kansas	2,267	Robert F. Bennett (R.)	14	26	53	72	769	339	457	1,444
Kentucky	3,396	Julian M. Carroll (D.)	30	8	78	22	1,284	378	703	864
Louisiana	3,791	Edwin W. Edwards (D.)	38	1	100	4	1,529	403	834	1,034
Maine	1,059	James B. Longley (Ind.)	14	19	91	59(g)	369	348	243	1,007
Maryland	4,098	Marvin Mandel (D.)	39	8	126	15	1,731	422	902	1,369
Massachusetts	5,828	Michael S. Dukakis (D.)	33	7	190	45(i,k)	2,219	381	1,193	1,356
Michigan	9,157	William G. Milliken (R.)	24	14	66	44	3,486	381	2,106	1,547
Minnesota	3,926	Wendell R. Anderson (D.)	38	28(g)	103	31	2,022	515	893	1,423
Mississippi	2,346	Charles D. Finch (D.)	50	2	119	3	797	340	515	834
Missouri	4,763	Christopher S. Bond (R.)	23	11	114	49	1,303	274	1,011	1,078
Montana	748	Thomas L. Judge (D.)	30	20	67	33	233	311	171	1,269
Nebraska	1,546	J. James Exon (D.)	49(j)		(Unicameral)		425	275	321	1,211
Nevada	592	Mike O'Callaghan (D.)	17	3	31	9	267	451	134	1,101
New Hampshire	818	Meldrim Thomson, Jr. (R.)	12	12	167	233	172	211	170	1,095
New Jersey	7,316	Brendan T. Byrne (D.)	29	10(g)	49	31	2,101	287	1,468	1,380
New Mexico	1,147	Jerry Apodaca (D.)	29	13	51	19	520	453	281	1,052
New York	18,120	Hugh L. Carey (D.)	26	34	88	62	8,939	493	3,419	2,005
North Carolina	5,451	James E. Holshouser, Jr. (R.)	49	1	111	9	1,900	349	1,163	1,052
North Dakota	635	Arthur A. Link (D.)	17	34	40	62	264	415	138	1,032
Ohio	10,759	James A. Rhodes (R.)	21	12	59	40	3,039	282	2,358	1,144
Oklahoma	2,712	David L. Boren (D.)	39	9	76	25	884	326	595	1,009
Oregon	2,288	Robert Straub (D.)	22	7(g)	38	22	793	347	472	1,425
Pennsylvania	11,827	Milton J. Shapp (D.)	29	20	114	89	4,733	387	2,302	1,446
Rhode Island	927	Philip W. Noel (D.)	46	4	83	17	350	377	183	1,493
South Carolina	2,818	James B. Edwards (R.)	44	2	107	17	957	339	621	984
South Dakota	683	Richard F. Kneip (D.)	19	16	33	37	171	251	156	973
Tennessee	4,188	Ray Blanton (D.)	20	12(g)	63	35(g)	1,141	272	894	903
Texas	12,237	Dolph Briscoe (D.)	28	3	134	16	3,637	297	2,754	894
Utah	1,206	Calvin L. Rampton (D.)	15	14	40	35	399	331	303	942
Vermont	471	Thomas P. Salmon (D.)	12	18	65	75(l)	187	397	105	1,095
Virginia	4,967	Mills E. Godwin, Jr. (R.)	35	5	78	17(m)	1,663	335	1,076	1,054
Washington	3,544	Daniel J. Evans (R.)	30	19	62	36	1,554	439	781	1,199
West Virginia	1,803	Arch A. Moore, Jr. (R.)	26	8	86	14	741	411	405	910
Wisconsin	4,607	Patrick J. Lucey (D.)	19	14	63	36	2,141	465	979	1,323
Wyoming	374	Ed Herschler (D.)	15	15	29	32(g)	154	412	85	1,322
District of Columbia	716								135	1,814

(a) Numbers in thousands, provisional estimates as of July 1, 1975 (Bureau of the Census)
(b) As of Dec. 31, 1975
(c) 1975 preliminary figures in millions (Bureau of the Census)
(d) 1975 preliminary figures in dollars (*State Taxes 1975*)
(e) Numbers in thousands, fall, 1974 (U.S. Office of Education, *Digest of Educational Statistics, 1974*)
(f) Number in dollars, 1974-75 (U.S. Office of Education, *Statistics of Public Elementary and Secondary Day Schools, Fall 1974*)
(g) 1 Independent
(h) 1 vacancy
(i) 3 Independents
(j) Nonpartisan
(k) 2 vacancies
(l) 10 Independents
(m) 5 Independents

States stepped in to check charges by the Federal Energy Administration that electrical utility customers may have been overcharged from $250 million to $500 million during the Arab oil embargo of 1973 and 1974. They also looked into charges of price-gouging for such other energy resources as coal used for electric generation. A 1975 Indiana law requires hearings for electricity-rate increases that are due to fuel charges, and a new Maryland law requires utilities to justify all fuel rate increases.

To ease the burden of increased electric power costs on senior citizens and others, some states, including California, enacted "life-line" legislation, holding utility costs at a minimum for those who use small amounts of power.

Rhode Island gave its public utility commission authority to force utilities to pay refunds and authorized the state attorney general to investigate complaints against utilities. In Connecticut, utility companies were prohibited from passing on to customers the cost of political or image-making ads.

In other energy areas, 10 more states acted to regulate surface strip mining of coal and other resources, and four granted the governor additional powers during energy emergencies or the authority to require information on energy supply and demand from suppliers. New Mexico, North Carolina, and Oregon created new energy agencies or councils. Kentucky and Colorado created energy offices.

Geothermal, solar, or nuclear energy were subjects of legislation in at least seven states. Iowa became the first state to use solar energy to heat a capitol building complex. Utah and Wisconsin enacted power-plant-siting legislation.

Environment. Oregon became the first state to ban the sale of aerosol spray cans containing fluorocarbons because of potential danger to the atmosphere's ozone layer. The Oregon ban becomes effective on March 1, 1977 (see ENVIRONMENT [Close-Up]). California and Minnesota banned flip-top cans, effective 1979 and 1977, respectively.

A steadily increasing tide of land-planning and land-use legislation flowed through the legislative halls of at least 17 states. Six states — Florida, Idaho, Montana, Nebraska, Virginia, and Wyoming — enacted laws requiring local or regional land-use planning. Florida and Virginia required political subdivisions to establish land-use commissions and to produce master plans for land use. California, Hawaii, Maryland, and New York enacted environmental or land-planning legislation concerned with coastal and wetlands protection.

Criminal Justice. A decided trend emerged in the revision of state rape laws. Thirteen states enacted laws containing such provisions as prohibiting introduction of testimony about a rape victim's past sexual behavior; eliminating the necessity for corroborating evidence in rape cases; and establishing degrees of rape.

Ray Rayner conducts a televised lottery drawing on May 8. Illinois was the first state to provide live lottery coverage under a new federal law.

Alabama, Maryland, Missouri, and Virginia reinstated the death penalty, bringing to well over 30 the number of states with capital-punishment laws. Nine states enacted new laws concerning firearms. New Jersey and Hawaii banned the cheap handguns commonly known as "Saturday night specials." California, Connecticut, and Florida mandated sentences or stiffened penalties for crimes committed with firearms. California enacted a 15-day waiting period for persons who buy handguns from dealers.

Alaska, Arkansas, California, Colorado, Maine, and Ohio eased penalties for persons who use marijuana. White-collar crime, such as embezzlement, fraud, and forgery, was the subject of new legislation in five states.

Health and Welfare. Legislative activity largely involved elderly citizens in 1975. Eleven states passed laws governing and regulating nursing homes. In Oregon, the legislature provided an extra $1 million to provide health and housekeeping services for the elderly as alternatives to nursing homes. An omnibus bill to aid the elderly in Iowa provided $1.7 million for meals, dental clinics, nursing-home inspections, job transportation, and winterizing homes. Three states provided free college tuition for senior citizens, and Utah enacted legislation prohibiting job discrimination because of age.   Ralph Wayne Derickson

STEEL INDUSTRY. Steel production in the non-Communist countries declined throughout much of 1975, mainly because of the worldwide economic recession. The International Iron and Steel Institute reported in July that Free World production in June was down 14.5 per cent. Some individual nations fared worse: U.S. production dropped 28 per cent for that month; Great Britain was down 28.5 per cent; and the total European Community (Common Market) production was down 30 per cent in July, with Belgium and Luxembourg down 45.7 per cent and 37.2 per cent, respectively. The U.S. picture improved later, but European recovery was slow in coming.

United States Production lagged until mid-August, when there was a six-week spurt in demand for cold-rolled sheets – a product used extensively by the automotive and appliance industries. This increase was caused by announced steel price rises of from 5 to 6 per cent that became effective on October 1. Even so, the output of 107.9 million short tons (97.9 million metric tons) poured by the week ending November 29 was 19.4 per cent below the 133.9 million short tons (121.5 million metric tons) produced during the same period in 1974, said the American Iron and Steel Institute (AISI).

Layoffs and Imports. With production and sales down and widespread layoffs common – some U.S. steel companies had laid off as much as 10 per cent of their work force by mid-May – steel companies worried about imports of foreign steel. Although imports had been falling steadily since November, 1974, AISI figures showed that foreign steel accounted for almost 13 per cent of the nation's "total apparent supply" in July, 1975. Citing what it termed the adverse effects of foreign imports, the United States Steel Corporation filed complaints with the U.S. Treasury Department, asking for increases in import duties on Common Market steel.

Pollution Curbs Scored. An all-out drive by the industry to have pollution-control regulations modified was urged at the annual AISI meeting in New York City in May. The AISI chairman, Frederick G. Jaicks, urged industry spokesmen to use findings of a cost-impact study made by Arthur D. Little, Incorporated, to convince members of Congress and the Administration that easing the restrictions would be in the nation's best economic interest and could be done without significant environmental damage. The Little study showed that the steel industry would have to spend some $1.4 billion a year through 1983 for pollution control, more than 25 per cent of its projected annual capital spending.

The Environmental Protection Agency announced on June 14 that it was requiring steelmakers to reduce their water pollution by mid-1977 and make further improvements by mid-1983. The agency said it was setting a series of detailed guidelines for 12 segments of the industry.   Mary E. Jessup

STEVENS, JOHN PAUL (1920-   ), a judge of the U.S. Circuit Court of Appeals since 1970, was sworn in as a justice on the Supreme Court of the United States on Dec. 19, 1975, by Chief Justice Warren E. Burger. He succeeded retired Justice William O. Douglas. See SUPREME COURT OF THE UNITED STATES.

Stevens was born in Chicago, the son of the man who built the Stevens Hotel (now the Conrad Hilton), one of the world's largest hotels. He graduated from the University of Chicago in 1941 and from Northwestern University School of Law in 1947, ranking first in his law-school class. From 1942 to 1945, he served as a U.S. Navy pilot and won a Bronze Star.

Stevens was a law clerk to U.S. Supreme Court Justice Wiley B. Rutledge in 1947 and 1948, then entered private practice in Chicago, specializing in antitrust and commercial law.

From 1953 to 1955, he was a member of the Attorney General's National Committee to Study Antitrust Laws. He also taught law part time from 1952 to 1956, first at Northwestern University and then at the University of Chicago.

In 1969, he was chief counsel for the special commission that investigated charges of impropriety against two Illinois Supreme Court justices. The investigation led to the resignation of both men. He is married and has four children.   Foster Stockwell

STOCKS AND BONDS. Stock market prices in the world's financial centers regained lost ground in 1975 from the lows of 1974. In the United States, the Dow Jones average of 30 blue-chip industrial stocks closed the year at 852.41, up 38.3 per cent, but still under the all-time peak of 1051.70 recorded on Jan. 11, 1973. Standard and Poor's broad-based index of 500 common stocks closed at 90.19, up 31.5 per cent. Trading volume on the New York Stock Exchange topped 4.69 billion shares. Other stock exchanges in the United States and around the world experienced a volume pickup as share prices advanced with economic recovery.

Interest rates on new U.S. bond issues remained below the cyclical highs of the previous year during early 1975. However, interest rates generally moved up as the economy expanded from the recession's low point in the first quarter. Interest rates for long-term government issues surpassed previous records in the United States and Canada.

U.S. Public Debt. Considerable slowing in the rising rate of U.S. inflation served to moderate further inflationary expectations. This was reflected in easier credit markets. An offsetting factor was the federal government deficit, which amounted to $43.6 billion in fiscal 1975.

The gross U.S. public debt totaled $533.2 billion on June 30, 1975. Private investors held $303.2 billion, of which $221.6 billion was marketable, or

Stocks Seek Recovery in 1975

New York Stock Exchange composite averages

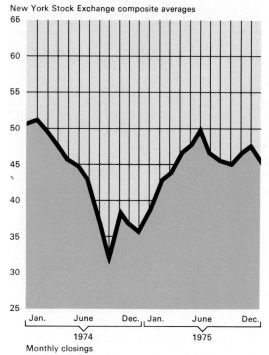

1974   1975

Monthly closings

contrast to net sales of $1.4 billion in 1974. Sales were particularly brisk early in the year when stock prices were advancing significantly and interest rates were falling. The market value of mutual funds was $42.9 billion at the end of July, up 14 per cent from a year earlier.

The Securities Industry. Ray Garrett, Jr., resigned as chairman of the Securities and Exchange Commission (SEC) on October 28. He was succeeded by White House aide Roderick M. Hills, husband of Carla A. Hills, secretary of the Department of Housing and Urban Development. During Garrett's two years in office, a number of changes in securities market regulation occurred, including setting commission rates competitively on both large and small transactions. The latter became effective on May 1. Prodded by the SEC, the industry took a significant step toward a nationwide stock market in June when composite stock tickers went into operation, giving price and volume data for securities traded on all major exchanges.

President Ford signed a new securities law on June 4 that widens the SEC's power over exchanges by limiting their self-regulating authority. However, the securities industry opposed any radical change in its operations until it makes final its plans for a single nationwide stock market, as ordered by Congress.   William G. Dewald

See also ECONOMICS.

able to be traded. More than half of the marketable debt was due to mature within a year. The average maturity of federal marketable debt was about three years, well below the nine-year average at the end of World War II. Nonmarketable federal debt, including savings bonds and notes held by individuals and special issues held by official foreign holders, totaled $90.9 billion at the end of June.

The Bond Market. Higher stock prices and profit prospects and lower interest rates attracted heavier new issues by U.S. corporations in 1975. Bonds, the interest costs of which are tax deductible, made up over 80 per cent of gross proceeds of new corporate issues. Gross proceeds in the first half of 1975 were 40 per cent above the pace a year earlier.

New issues of state and local government bonds reflected the increased risk of default by carrying higher interest rates. Nevertheless, state and local governments issued 30 per cent more debt than a year earlier. New York City nearly defaulted on its debts. President Gerald R. Ford opposed congressional proposals for federal aid to the city until a program had been worked out to cut spending, raise taxes, and restructure the debt. Congress then passed a bill providing federal loans to the city of up to $2.3 billion, which the President signed on December 9. See NEW YORK CITY.

Net sales of mutual fund shares during the first seven months of 1975 reached nearly $1 billion, in

SUDAN. President Sayed Gaafar Mohamed Nimeiri thwarted an attempt to overthrow him on Sept. 5, 1975. Rebel officers and leftists seized the radio station in Omdurman, across the Nile River from Khartoum, the capital. The bulk of the army remained loyal, however, and the revolt was crushed that day.

Although the country's lack of oil resources has kept it from playing a major role in Arab and African affairs, Sudan's agricultural potential began to attract the interest of many nations. In March, a United Nations project began to use U.S. satellite photographs to survey Sudan's undeveloped land, estimated at from 100 million to 200 million acres (40 to 80 million hectares) of arable land. Cultivating this land could make Sudan a major exporter of food, capable of meeting from 35 to 40 per cent of the food needs of the Middle East by 1985. Kuwait, Libya, Qatar, Saudi Arabia, and the United Arab Emirates agreed on a development program to aid the Sudan when the survey is completed.

The Arab Fund for Economic and Social Development, the World Bank, and Kuwait loaned the Sudan $121 million in March for the 300,000-acre (121,000-hectare) Ar-Rahad agricultural scheme in Gezira Province south of Khartoum. Iraq loaned $300 million on May 21 for a sugar refinery and textile plant.   William Spencer

See also AFRICA (Facts in Brief Table).

SUPREME COURT OF THE UNITED STATES.
Justice William O. Douglas, who served on the court longer than any other justice in history, retired on Nov. 12, 1975, because of his health. The 76-year-old Douglas, who first took his seat on the court on April 17, 1939, suffered a disabling stroke on Dec. 31, 1974. John Paul Stevens of Chicago was sworn in as his successor on December 19 (see STEVENS, JOHN PAUL).

Douglas' health handicapped operations of the Supreme Court throughout the year. He was unable to participate fully in court deliberations, and the court postponed consideration of a dozen cases expected to be decided by close margins. These cases included reconsideration of imposing the death penalty for certain crimes.

Despite this, the court issued significant opinions in 1975 that extended the rights of women, students, and mental patients. A number of other decisions emphasized that the court was retreating only slowly and reluctantly from principles established during the "Warren Court" era, particularly those regarding protections for accused criminals and persons seeking to exercise rights granted by the First Amendment to the U.S. Constitution.

Individual Rights. In a landmark opinion that strengthened the right to personal freedom, a unanimous court ruled on June 26 that mental patients who are not dangerous to others can no longer be placed in institutions against their will. In *O'Connor v. Donaldson*, Justice Potter Stewart declared, "Mere public intolerance or animosity cannot constitutionally justify the deprivation of a person's physical liberty."

The court struck a blow for women's rights on January 21 when it ruled unconstitutional a Louisiana law that discriminated against women in the selection of jury members. In another equal rights ruling, the court unanimously struck down part of the Social Security law that provided survivor's benefits to widows with children, but not to widowers. The Supreme Court ruled that the plan "unjustifiably discriminated against women wage earners by affording them less protection for their survivors than is provided to male employees."

In two close decisions on student rights, the justices ruled that public school students have the right to a hearing before being seriously disciplined, and that students can sue school officials for damages sustained during illegal disciplinary action. See CIVIL RIGHTS (Close-Up).

Although the court refused to consider many cases that would advance criminal rights, important decisions supported the rights of suspects against law enforcement efforts. The court limited the right of border-patrol officers to stop and search cars in attempting to block illegal entry. It also held that a person arrested without a warrant cannot be jailed without a hearing to determine if there was

Supreme Court Justice William O. Douglas, partially paralyzed by a stroke, retired in November after more than 36 years on the court.

sufficient cause to arrest him. And it ruled that a defendant who remained silent when he was arrested could not be questioned at his trial about his failure to produce an alibi.

First Amendment. The court continued to modify a 1973 ruling that appeared to leave obscenity standards up to local authorities. It decisively overturned a Jacksonville, Fla., ordinance banning nudity in films shown at outdoor movie theaters. It also ruled that Chattanooga, Tenn., could not arbitrarily deny use of the municipal auditorium for production of the rock musical *Hair* before opening night. The ruling extended to live theater the same constitutional guarantees against prior censorship enjoyed by newspapers, books, and motion pictures.

In an 8 to 1 vote, the justices ruled unconstitutional a Georgia law that prohibited the publication of a rape victim's name. The press cannot be punished for accurately publishing what appears in court records, the majority stated.

Legal Profession. The court unanimously ruled on June 16 that antitrust laws apply to lawyers. The decision outlawed as illegal price fixing the traditional minimum fee schedules.

By a 6 to 3 margin on June 30, the court ruled that a criminal defendant has the right to reject a court-appointed lawyer and insist on acting as his own attorney. One dissenter, Justice Harry A. Blackmun, complained that the majority was bestowing "a constitutional right on one to make a fool of himself."

The court continued its discouragement of class-action lawsuits in a divided decision on May 12. By denying plaintiffs in certain public-interest suits the right to collect attorney's fees from defendants, the justices rejected efforts of environmentalists to recover court costs by calling themselves "private attorneys general."

Other Decisions. On February 18, the court ruled unanimously that President Richard M. Nixon acted illegally in 1972 when he impounded water-pollution-control funds authorized by Congress. In a close 5-to-4 decision on June 25, the court refused to consider a suit challenging municipal zoning laws that effectively keep out the poor and minority groups.

Businessmen were hit by two High Court rulings. In an important labor case, *Albemarle Paper Co. v. Moody*, the court ruled that victims of discrimination in hiring or promotion were entitled to back pay even when the employer had acted in good faith. In a crackdown on white-collar crime, the court ruled 5 to 3 in *United States v. Park* that a corporate officer is criminally liable for illegal actions committed by persons under him, even if he did not know or participate in the unlawful conduct. David C. Beckwith

SURGERY. See MEDICINE.

SURINAM, an overseas territory of the Netherlands for more than 300 years, became independent on Nov. 25, 1975. Prime Minister Henck A. E. Arron, who had headed the autonomous pre-independence government, remained in his post. Johan H. E. Ferrier was elected to serve as the new nation's president.

A new Constitution, including a proviso for a general election in 1976, was unanimously approved by the Surinamese Parliament on December 2. Its adoption, however, was marred by racial discord between the two major ethnic groups: the East Indians, or Hindustani, and the Creoles. The Hindustani bitterly opposed any provisions they thought might favor the Creoles. The Creoles, a minority group of blacks and mulattoes, feared the Hindustani would incorporate provisos in the Constitution that would perpetuate Hindustani control over the nation's commerce. Only after both groups had secured constitutional guarantees that allayed their fears was the Constitution adopted.

Prior to independence, many residents left for the Netherlands, particularly Hindustani who feared reprisals from Prime Minister Arron's predominantly black, five-party coalition government. By year's end, about 140,000 Surinamese had fled to the Netherlands. Paul C. Tullier

See also LATIN AMERICA (Facts in Brief Table).

SWAZILAND. See AFRICA.

SWEDEN. The *Riksdag* (parliament) approved plans on May 28, 1975, that would make Sweden the world's largest per capita consumer of nuclear power. Four nuclear power reactors were operating in 1975, and the plan calls for 11 by 1985. By the year 2000, some 24 reactors will supply about two-thirds of Sweden's energy needs.

Scientists, politicians, and environmental organizations waged a vigorous campaign against the scheme, and the ruling Social Democrats split over the issue. Prime Minister Olof Palme said the Swedes use more energy per capita than any other European nation, and he wanted to restrain annual energy consumption growth to 2 per cent.

Economic Slump. The recession sharply halted export orders and idled 1.4 per cent of the work force by August. The Central Bureau of Statistics reported on July 14 that prices rose an average 9 per cent for the year ending in May. Industrial deliveries dropped 2 per cent, and new orders were 10 per cent lower than in 1974. Shipbuilding, paper, pulp, steel, and textile industries were hard hit.

The government announced plans on July 22 to inject about $2 billion into the economy to combat winter unemployment. Labor Minister Ingemund Bengtsson said the measures, including state grants to industry to provide education instead of layoffs, would save 200,000 jobs.

Flames engulf the West German Embassy in Stockholm, Sweden, after political terrorists set off explosives on April 24.

SWIMMING

Tax Dodgers. More than 100 members of parliament of all five parties demanded tax reforms on August 27 after tax authorities confirmed newspaper reports that rich people had used the generous tax-deduction laws to whittle down taxable incomes. Finance Minister Gunnar Sträng and Tord Magnusson, the king's brother-in-law, were among those named. Sweden's biggest industrial enterprise, Volvo of Sweden, paid no state taxes in 1974 on gross profits of more than $90 million.

The strong reaction to the disclosures stemmed from the fact that Swedes pay very high taxes to support an extensive welfare state. Palme promised more social legislation by the end of 1975 to give workers a minimum of five weeks annual vacation. And on October 20, the government announced plans for a flexible pension plan that will allow workers to taper off from a full workweek at age 60 to a minimum of 17 hours a week at age 70. Physicians and psychologists recommended the program.

Tradition Dies. The 1975 session of parliament opened on January 10 in its own chambers for the first time. King Carl XVI Gustaf, reduced to a figurehead under the 1974 Constitution, wore a dark suit when the speaker invited him to open the session. For 400 years, parliament had gathered with much ceremony at the royal palace in Stockholm at the king's bidding.   Kenneth Brown

See also EUROPE (Facts in Brief Table).

Jenny Turrall, 15, of Australia rejoices after breaking the world 800-meter free-style record at a March swimming meet in London.

SWIMMING. The world's best swimmers in 1974 were Tim Shaw of Long Beach, Calif., and Kornelia Ender of East Germany. The world's best swimmers in 1975 were the same two – Shaw, a 17-year-old high school senior, and Ender, a 16-year-old schoolgirl.

They were also the stars of the world championships held from July 19 to 27 in Cali, Colombia. Ender won four gold medals (two in relays) and set world records for the 100-meter free-style (56.22 seconds) and the 100-meter butterfly (1 minute 1.24 seconds). Shaw won the three longest free style races for men – 200, 400, and 1,500 meters. The world championships demonstrated what everyone in swimming knew – that the American men were far ahead of the others and that the East German women were still the best.

The American men won eight of their 15 swimming events, and they did it even though two of their stars – breast-stroker John Hencken of Santa Clara, Calif., and backstroker John Naber of Menlo Park, Calif. – passed up the meet. East Germans won 10 of 14 women's events; Americans won 3.

New Records. The world-record toll during the year was comparatively mild for this volatile sport. Male swimmers broke eight of their 16 records and women nine of their 15. Shaw set three records, and 18-year-old Bruce Furniss of Santa Ana, Calif., broke two in individual events and two in relays.

Shaw and Furniss were teammates on the Long Beach Swim Club, and they endured long, hard workouts together. "It doesn't feel like work to me," said Shaw.

Jim Montgomery of Madison, Wis., made a comeback of sorts. Montgomery, a 20-year-old junior at Indiana University, had enjoyed mixed success since winning five gold medals in the 1973 world championships. In the Amateur Athletic Union national outdoor championships at Kansas City, Kans., he set a world record of 50.59 seconds for the 100-meter free style in the afternoon trials on August 23. After a cheeseburger, a nap, and a quick look at television, he won the evening final in 51.04, beating Jonty Skinner of South Africa by a hundredth of a second.

The most successful American woman was 18-year-old Shirley Babashoff of Fountain Valley, Calif., a sophomore at Golden West College. She won two gold medals (200-meter and 400-meter free style), three silver, and one bronze in the world championships. She did it with hard work, saying, "I don't think there's such a thing as a natural swimmer. You've got to work at everything if you want to be good."

Diving. Two of the four world champions were Americans – Air Force Lieutenant Phil Boggs of Colorado Springs, Colo., in men's springboard and Janet Ely of Dallas in women's platform. Frank Litsky

SWITZERLAND. Police fought rioters on April 25, 1975, and again on September 7 and 8 in the industrial town of Moutier. The demonstrators were part of a separatist movement that wants the town to join the new French-speaking *canton* (province) of Jura rather than stay with the predominantly German-speaking canton of Bern. Moutier's citizens voted on September 7 to stay in Bern. Three other towns also voted to stay, while six voted to join Jura.

The Swiss people approved a referendum on June 8 to increase income, gasoline, and sales taxes. They rejected a tax increase on heating fuel. The government began an antirecession program on July 1 that pumped money into the building industry, raised export guarantees, and increased unemployment-insurance coverage. More than 6,500 Swiss citizens were out of work in May, 1975, compared to only 64 a year earlier.

European Community (Common Market) finance ministers agreed on September 22 that Switzerland should join the "snake" – the joint currency float that keeps most Common Market currencies closely tied to one another and to the currencies of Norway and Sweden. But on November 20, the Swiss government announced that it was unwilling to accept the conditions France had put on its entry.   Kenneth Brown

See also EUROPE (Facts in Brief Table).

SYRIA. President Hafiz al-Asad was re-elected to a four-year term as secretary-general of the ruling Syrian Baath Party on Aug. 8, 1975. Asad's personal popularity enabled him to steer a middle course in Arab affairs and to take initiatives abroad that would have been impossible for any previous Syrian head of state.

For example, the government approved two 6-month extensions of the United Nations observer force on the Golan Heights, while insisting on no compromise with Israel. Syria bitterly criticized Egypt for the Sinai disengagement agreement with Israel that was signed on September 4, but Asad did not rule out a similar agreement for Syria. Relations with neighboring Jordan also improved.

Political Difficulties that have always plagued Syria surfaced within the Baath Party during its sixth regional congress in April. The opposition challenged the official Asad-backed candidates for party offices. Some 120 party members were arrested on April 11 for allegedly spying for Iraq. The rival Iraqi Baathist government was also accused of supporting sabotage by members of the underground Arab Communist Organization (ACO). Five ACO members received death sentences after a mass trial in July. The strained relations with Iraq were complicated further by a dispute over water distribution rights on the Euphrates River, which flows through Syria into Iraq. See IRAQ.

Members of the right wing, fundamentalist Muslim Brotherhood were arrested for plotting against the regime in July. Three Brotherhood members were hanged after riots in Aleppo on July 21.

Economic Policies. Asad's relatively moderate policies enabled the government to devote more attention to economic development. On May 2, the new Jbessa oil field near the Iraqi border went into production. Its output of 440,000 short tons (400,000 metric tons) annually will account for 4 per cent of Syria's total production. Contracts for offshore oil exploration were awarded to a U.S. company on March 19 and to a Hungarian company on May 27 for drilling in a desert area near Palmyra. Syrian oil production for 1975 was expected to be 11 million short tons (10 million metric tons). Cotton sales also rose, with production of 148,000 short tons (134,000 metric tons) exported at a price 17.5 per cent above that received in 1974. About 90 per cent of Syria's cotton was sold to Greece. As a result, the gross national product rose to $4.8 billion for a per capita income of $400.

The government inaugurated development projects costing $1 billion on September 5 for the fourth five-year plan. The largest project is a $265-million refinery at Baniyas, being built by Romanian engineers and technicians.   William Spencer

See also MIDDLE EAST (Facts in Brief Table).

Syria's President Asad, right, and President Sadat of Egypt arrive at the guest palace in Riyadh, Saudi Arabia, to meet with King Khalid.

An elaborately decorated hearse with the coffin of Chiang Kai-shek leads
his funeral procession through the streets of Taipei, Taiwan, in April.

TAIWAN. President Chiang Kai-shek, the leader of Nationalist China for half a century, died on April 5, 1975, at the age of 87. He had been so ill for three years that he took no active part in running Taiwan. Vice-President C. K. Yen succeeded him as president. See DEATHS OF NOTABLE PERSONS (Close-Up).

Chiang's son, Chiang Ching-kuo, had been effectively running Taiwan as premier since 1972, so the death did not significantly affect official policies. The premier promised to carry on his father's programs (see CHIANG CHING-KUO). In a last political will, Chiang Kai-shek asked the people to continue struggling "to recover the Chinese mainland, rehabilitating the national culture, and staying in the camp of democracy."

The first military parade in many years was held on October 10, National Day, to symbolize Taiwan's continued defiance of Peking. Locally made weapons, including jet fighters and helicopters, were shown to emphasize Taiwan's self-reliance.

American Reduction. The last squadron of U.S. Air Force F-4 Phantom fighter-bombers, capable of carrying nuclear weapons, left Taiwan in May. This was part of a reduction to 2,800 military men, most of them planning staff and monitors of mainland communications. The American withdrawal from Indochina worried Taiwan, but the U.S. commitment to the Nationalist regime was reaffirmed.

President Gerald R. Ford's trip to China in December, 1975, stirred apprehension in Taiwan. The Nationalists feared that Ford might make a deal with the Communist Chinese that would be detrimental to the Taiwan government. Two factors made any weakening of U.S. support untimely, however. One was an official American desire to show reliability to its allies. The other was domestic political pressure on Ford not to abandon Taiwan.

But the changing Asian situation left Taiwan more isolated. The Philippines and Thailand, long staunch supporters of Taiwan, established diplomatic relations with China. But Japan resumed airline ties with Taiwan on August 10.

Prisoner Problem. While showing patience about its goal of gaining control of Taiwan, China kept up its political pressure against the island. Peking released 10 Nationalist generals who had spent 26 years in Chinese prisons, and 144 other persons identified as Nationalist agents who landed in amphibious raids from 1962 to 1965. Taiwan was wary about taking them back, but accepted 60.

Premier Chiang announced on September 23 that new economic conditions were forcing the government to draft a new development plan for the period from 1976 to 1981. Economic growth dropped in 1975 to 2.5 per cent, low by Taiwan's boom standards.   Henry S. Bradsher

See also ASIA (Facts in Brief Table).

TANZANIA. Julius K. Nyerere was elected to a fourth term as president on Oct. 26, 1975. National Assembly elections were also held on October 26. Under Tanzania's concept of one-party democracy, two candidates can compete from each parliamentary district, but both must be members of the Tanganyika African National Union (TANU). Voters rejected incumbent cabinet ministers in two districts, and in a third, a junior minister lost his seat.

While TANU is the sole party on Tanzania's mainland, the Afro-Shirazi Party (ASP) dominates politics on the off-shore island of Zanzibar. The two parties have ruled jointly at the national level. However, in September, Nyerere called for their merger.

Tanzania's economy was caught in a price squeeze. While the prices of imports remained high, those for key exports fell. Sisal prices reportedly dropped 20 per cent between 1974 and mid-1975. Furthermore, drought forced the government to import large quantities of grain. On June 12, the finance minister estimated that grain and petroleum imports would consume half of Tanzania's 1975 export earnings.

Despite these difficulties, the government continued its program to regroup all rural residents into compact villages by the end of 1976.   John D. Esseks

See also AFRICA (Facts in Brief Table); ZAIRE.

TAXATION. The total costs of federal, state, and local government in the United States rose to more than $555 billion in 1975, according to the Tax Foundation, a private research association established to educate the public regarding fiscal-management aspects of government. The foundation predicted that the American taxpayer would face an even heavier tax burden during the rest of this century.

The U.S. Department of Labor reported that 23 per cent of the 1975 income of high-income families was paid in withholding taxes and social security taxes, while 16 per cent of the income of low-income families went for these taxes. The comparable figures in 1968 were 17 per cent and 12 per cent, respectively.

Federal Taxes. Both houses of Congress approved a $22.8-billion net federal income tax cut for 1975 on March 26. Personal income taxes were cut $24.8 billion, a reduction that was offset by a rise of $2 billion in business taxes. In order to stimulate the economy, taxpayers received rebates on their 1974 taxes of between $100 and $200 per family, and low-income families that paid no taxes received a small *negative tax* (cash) payment.

In October, President Gerald R. Ford urged Congress to pass legislation extending the tax reduction and simultaneously setting a $395-billion

Former captive Carrie Hunter, left, waits to greet Stephen Smith in July in Tanzania after his release by Zaire guerrillas who kidnaped them in May.

U.S. merchants tried to use the federal
income tax rebate to push special sales in
an effort to shake the 1975 business slump.

in 1976. The taxable wage base on 1975 income was
$14,100. The taxable wage base on 1976 income
will be $15,300. Thus the maximum social security
tax for a wage earner in 1976 will be $895.05 (the
1975 maximum was $824.85). Workers earning less
than $14,100 a year will not have to pay any addi-
tional tax. Wage base increases go into effect automatically whenever cost-of-living benefits are instituted.

Although the social security trust funds will receive about $2.1 billion more because of these in-
creases, the deficit in the trust funds was estimated
at $3 billion in 1975, and it is expected to be $6-
billion in 1976. Social security beneficiaries received
an 8 per cent increase in benefits in 1975.

It was estimated that the social security tax base
will rise to $16,800 in 1977, yielding a maximum
social security tax payment of almost $1,000 a year.
The tax rate is scheduled to rise to 6.05 per cent in
1978. The first social security taxes imposed in 1937
were levied at 1 per cent of the first $3,000 of a
worker's income, a maximum tax of $30 a year. The
wage base has been increased 20 times since then.

Campaign Financing. Thomas B. Curtis, chairman of the Federal Election Commission, reported
in July that the checkoff of $1 out of an individual's
personal income tax as a contribution to
presidential-primary campaigns, instituted in 1973
is expected to provide more than $100 million in tax
funds to help finance the 1976 presidential campaign. The optional checkoff produced $30 million
from 1973 and 1974 tax returns. In order to qualify
for these preconvention funds, a candidate must
raise $5,000 privately in contributions of no more
than $250 apiece in each of at least 20 states.

State and Local Taxes. State tax collections rose
8 per cent in fiscal 1975 to $80.1 billion. During the
same period, local taxing units collected about
$61.3 billion, 23.5 per cent less than the state total.

Sales and gross-receipts taxes again represented
the largest single source of state tax revenue, a total
of $43.3 billion. About $24.8 billion of this was in
general sales and gross receipts taxes. Selective sales
and gross receipts totaled $18.6 billion.

Altogether, 44 states collected $18.8 billion in in-
dividual income taxes, a 10.2 per cent increase. All
50 states levied some form of sales and gross-
receipts tax.

Eight states collected more than half of all the
state tax revenues in fiscal 1975. California led with
a total of $9.6 billion. New York was the second
largest tax collector, with $8.9 billion. In order, the
next six were Pennsylvania, Illinois, Texas, Michigan, Ohio, and Florida.

Tax revenues increased by at least 15 per cent in
11 states in fiscal 1975. Eleven others showed an
increase of less than 5 per cent, and two —
Connecticut and Michigan — showed a net decline
in tax collections.   Carol L. Thompson

ceiling on federal spending in fiscal 1977 – a $28-
billion cut in federal spending. Congress approved
legislation extending the 1975 tax cut temporarily
on December 17, but without the ceiling on federal
spending. The President vetoed the measure that
same day, saying that a tax cut without a limit on
federal spending would "risk a new round of
double-digit inflation." The House of Representatives failed to override the President's veto, voting
only 265 to 167 to override on December 18.

Congress then passed another tax-cut bill on December 19, which contained a nonbinding commitment to control government spending. This was acceptable to the President, and he signed it on December 23. The action was the last major one taken
by the first session of the 94th Congress. By barring
a tax rise, it will save individuals $7.4 billion and
corporations about $1 billion between January 1
and June 30, 1976.

Federal Tax Collections in fiscal 1975 (from July
1, 1974, through June 30, 1975) totaled $293.4 bil-
lion. Of this, $226 billion came from individual in-
come and employment taxes; $46 billion from taxes
on corporations; $4.6 billion from estate and gift
taxes; and $16.8 billion from excise and other taxes.

Social Security. The social security tax rate was
raised in 1975. In October, the Ford Administration announced that some 18 million workers would
pay up to $70.20 in additional social security taxes

TELEVISION. A large segment of the U.S. public was up in arms against excessive violence and sex on television in 1975. Complaints to the Federal Communications Commission (FCC) about video crime shows rose almost 1,000 per cent. Pressured by Congress to "do something" about the situation, the FCC in turn pressured broadcasters to develop the so-called family-viewing-time policy. The plan, endorsed by the National Association of Broadcasters (NAB) in April, stipulated that "programming inappropriate for viewing by a general family audience" should not be aired from 7 P.M. to 9 P.M. (6 P.M. to 8 P.M. in the Central Time Zone).

Family Time Flops. The controversial compromise was introduced in September and, it quickly became evident, was a fiasco. Only two of the fall season's 16 new family-hour shows made the Nielsen Survey's list of the 30 most-watched programs.

On October 30, the Writers Guild of America, the Directors Guild of America, and the Screen Actors Guild filed suit against the three networks—American Broadcasting Companies (ABC), Columbia Broadcasting System (CBS), and National Broadcasting Company (NBC)—the FCC, and the NAB. The suit questioned the constitutionality of family viewing time, charging that the government was imposing censorship by inducing the networks to adopt the self-regulatory plan. The action contended that lack of family viewing standards and increased blue-penciling of scripts by the networks

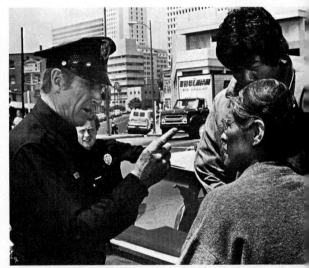

Television programs ranged from classics to police series. Colleen Dewhurst starred with Jason Robards in *Moon for the Misbegotten, above*; Lloyd Bridges was "Joe Forrester," *top right*; and Lee Remick played "Jennie," *right*.

Television Goes International

Prime Minister Indira
Gandhi inaugurates
India's new satellite
TV system to villages.

Television truly became worldwide on May 5, 1975, when South Africa—the last major nation without TV—beamed the first test transmissions of its new video system.

During the year, at least 146 countries provided television for an estimated 364 million TV sets with a potential viewing audience of more than 1 billion persons. About one-third of those nations had color TV facilities, and about half carried commercials on at least some of their channels. The United States had by far the most television sets with 112.1 million. Next came Russia with 45 million sets; Japan, 25 million; Great Britain, 20 million; and West Germany, 17.4 million. Fewer than 40 countries lacked TV.

Law-and-order shows were staple television fare throughout the world. Two American detective series, "Columbo" and "Kojak," were particularly popular on foreign TV in 1975. West Germany's favorite home-grown TV law-and-order series were "Tatort," featuring Klaus Schwarzkopf, and "Der Comisar." Schwarzkopf also dubs Peter Falk's lines in "Columbo" for German TV. West Germany dubs all TV imports, though many other countries use subtitles.

"Columbo" was Japan's number-one television program in 1975 for the third year in a row. The Japanese are the world's most avid TV fans, with the United States and Canada tied for second. Japanese viewers watch television an average of 7 hours and 17 minutes daily. They watch it almost as much during the early morning and noon hours as they do at night. Both daytime and late-night TV in Japan feature nudity and explicit sexuality. One of the most popular late-night programs is titled "Member of Upper House of Parliament with His Nude Show."

Television in Great Britain is noted for its superb dramatic presentations and documentaries. Some of the most impressive programs on U.S. public television have been British imports, such as "Masterpiece Theatre," "Civilisation," and "The Ascent of Man." The British Broadcasting Corporation's "Newsround" is one of the few news shows in the world that is prepared especially for children. More than 5 million British youngsters watch it.

However, British TV, like that in the United States, draws many of its highest ratings with situation comedies such as "Till Death Us Do Part"—the inspiration for "All in the Family"—and "It Ain't Half Hot," about army life in India.

Italian TV viewers like musicals and quiz shows. One of Italy's most popular programs in 1975 was a Roman version of the old U.S. "$64,000 Question."

Television's impact—for better or worse—on the lives of viewers in all parts of the world has long been commented upon. Noting this impact, some countries exercise rigid controls over programming. For example, Spain's top-rated show, "35 Million Spaniards," a consumer-action series, was canceled in January, 1975, allegedly because it probed too deeply into some questionable business practices.

South Africa delayed introducing television on the grounds that it could be morally corrupting. However, another reason might have been the government's fear that television would transcend illiteracy. South Africa is an *apartheid* (racially segregated) country of more than 25-million persons, with four blacks for every white.

When the Canadian Broadcasting Corporation introduced television to the Eskimos living in the Northwest Territories in the early 1970s, the Eskimos quickly became dissatisfied with their primitive life style, as contrasted with what they saw on TV.

India hopes for more positive results from its controversial, but innovative, Satellite Instructional Television Experiment. India has television in four cities, but most of its more than 600 million people live in villages without it. In August, 1975, a U.S. satellite started sending a signal to nearly 2,400 of these villages, allowing India's peasants to see educational shows as well as entertainment programs. Each village has one set, and a local resident is trained to operate it.   June Bundy Csida "chilled the creative activity of artists" and threatened "to set back TV's move . . . toward realism."

At the same time, public protest groups accused the networks of following an "anything goes" policy after 9 P.M. Television resembled a crime ghetto from 9 P.M. to 11 P.M., with 24 of the fall season's 29 law-and-order shows crammed into that "adult" time period. A final irony was that the NAB family rule did not apply to programs that independent stations had purchased. Thus, some outlets were free to program such syndicated crime series as "The Untouchables" and "Mod Squad."

New Programs. Melting-pot casting dominated TV programming in 1975. More than 20 fall shows featured ethnic characters – black, Greek, Irish, Italian, Jewish, Mexican, Polish, Puerto Rican, and others. Ethnic titles were also in vogue. The new fall programs included "The Montefuscos," "The Family Holvak," "Kate McShane," "Bronk," and "Starsky and Hutch."

However, the only new fall show to score in the early top 10 ratings was "Phyllis," a fresh, funny spin-off from "The Mary Tyler Moore Show" with Emmy-winner Cloris Leachman as a dizzy, newly widowed WASP trying to cope with a new life style.

Among the older ethnic and irreverent situation comedies, "All in the Family" was still a big favorite, as were "Rhoda," "Chico and the Man," "Sanford and Son," "M*A*S*H," "Maude," and "Good Times." Also high-rated were "The Waltons," and "The Six Million Dollar Man."

The biggest disappointment of the fall season was "Beacon Hill," a lavish American version of the hit British import "Upstairs, Downstairs." The highly touted but low-rated series was canceled in October. Also axed were more than half of the new fall series, along with such long-running favorites as "Mannix," "The Odd Couple," "Kung Fu," and – after 20 years – "Gunsmoke."

Impressive Specials were *Love Among the Ruins*, a multi-Emmy winner starring Katharine Hepburn and Sir Laurence Olivier; Eugene O'Neill's *Moon for the Misbegotten; A Girl Named Sooner*, with versatile Cloris Leachman as an aged sharecropper; *Fear On Trial*, a fine dramatization of the John Henry Faulk blacklisting case, with George C. Scott and William Devane; *The Guns of Autumn*, a painful-to-watch documentary about hunters and their prey; *Judgment: The Court Martial of Lt. William Calley*; Elizabeth Montgomery in *The Legend of Lizzie Borden; Queen of the Stardust Ballroom*, starring Maureen Stapleton; and Diana Rigg in *In This House of Brede*.

Outstanding Bicentennial programs – the first of many ambitious American history specials scheduled through July 4, 1976 – were David Brinkley's *Life*, the first of three specials focusing on Thomas Jefferson; a six-part series starring Hal Holbrook as Carl Sandburg's "Abe Lincoln"; and a "Ben

Franklin" series with four different actors portraying the statesman at different times in life.

Baseball was the most popular game on television in October when an estimated cumulative audience of 367 million persons watched the World Series. It was the largest video audience in World Series history. The seventh game, viewed by 71 million, was number one in its prime-time period.

The Public Broadcasting Service (PBS) provided more quality programs than usual in 1975. Particularly outstanding were the National Geographic Society's *The Incredible Machine*, featuring a fascinating X-ray tour of the human body, and Frederick Wiseman's *Welfare*, a grim dissection of New York City's welfare system.

Other choice PBS offerings were "The Ascent of Man," the late British scientist Jacob Bronowski's personal view of man's intellectual evolution; "Classic Theater: The Humanities in Drama"; *The Plutonium Connection*, on "Nova," a demonstration of how easy it would be to build a nuclear bomb; "The Tribal Eye"; *World Hunger: Who Will Survive?*; and three British mini-series – "Shoulder to Shoulder," the story of England's suffragette movement; "Notorious Woman," the saga of George Sand; and "Jennie," with Lee Remick as Winston Churchill's mother.

News Programs. The most exciting TV news coverage in 1975 took place on July 17 with a historic handshake between American and Russian astronauts in space. On July 21, some 30 million viewers for the first time watched a Russian spacecraft touch down on land. The networks also provided unforgettable footage of the evacuation of Vietnam and Khmer (Cambodia) in April and May, and the resettlement of refugees in the United States.

A controversial television news practice was "checkbook journalism." CBS paid sizable sums to Watergate figures H. R. Haldeman and G. Gordon Liddy for exclusive interviews in the spring. They drew negative reactions from the public and other news media, and NBC broke off negotiations to purchase former President Richard M. Nixon's televised memoirs for a reported $600,000. Nixon subsequently made a deal in August to film four 90-minute interviews with British producer David Frost, to be aired after the 1976 election.

FCC Rulings. Politicians – at least Republicans – were pleased in late September when the FCC decreed that all press conferences and political debates could be treated by broadcasters as on-the-spot coverage of bona-fide news events and, therefore, exempt from equal-time requirements.

Citizen protest groups received a setback in September when the FCC declared improper an agreement signed on Oct. 1, 1973, between KTTV, Los Angeles, and the National Association for Better Broadcasting. As part of the pact, KTTV had agreed to blacklist 40 children's shows. The FCC said KTTV relinquished too much control.

Seventeen state attorneys general formally asked the FCC in July to ban over-the-counter drug commercials on TV between 6 A.M. and 9 P.M. because, they alleged, such advertising sparked drug abuse by children. A June, 1975, RAND Corporation study of television and human behavior said that "exposure to drug advertisements is positively correlated in young boys with use of over-the-counter drugs." As of November, the FCC had not ruled.

Other Developments. Citizen groups throughout the United States claimed commercial interests were beginning to exert too much influence on public TV. Private companies spent $17.5 million for public television network shows in 1975, compared with less than $12 million in 1974. Mobil Oil Corporation, for example, budgeted $2 million for public television in 1975. However, underwriting advocates note that the amount is an insignificant part of the total $220 million that was spent on public television in 1974.

The first pay-cable satellite feed to systems in Florida and Mississippi was inaugurated at the end of September by Home Box Office, Incorporated. This marked the first regularly scheduled use of domestic satellites for television communication within the United States.   June Bundy Csida

TENNESSEE. See STATE GOVERNMENT.

TENNIS. Chris Evert of Fort Lauderdale, Fla., and Arthur Ashe of Richmond, Va., two American favorites, won major tennis honors in 1975. Jimmy Connors of Belleville, Ill., the world's most successful male player in 1974, lost the important tournaments but he managed to win when huge purses were at stake.

The 32-year-old Ashe, an international star for 10 years, enjoyed his best year. He won the Wimbledon title on July 5 in England, and he also won the World Championship Tennis (WCT) play-off final. His earnings for the year exceeded $315,000, the most by any tennis player in a year from tournament purses; he ranked number one nationally.

The 20-year-old Evert earned more than $300,000, the most by any woman athlete. With her patient, mechanical backcourt game, she won the United States, French, Italian, and Virginia Slims play-off titles, among others. She won 58 straight tournament matches from April to July.

Connors' Year. Connors lost in three major finals – to Ashe at Wimbledon, to Manuel Orantes of Spain in the United States Open at Forest Hills, N.Y., and to John Newcombe of Australia in the Australian Open. However, Connors was the hero of a new form of entertainment, the big-money televised tennis match.

He defeated 36-year-old Rod Laver of Australia in four sets in Las Vegas, Nev., on February 2 for a winner's purse of $100,000. On April 26, again in Las Vegas, he beat Newcombe in four sets for the winner's prize of $150,000 (when fringe benefits were counted, his purse neared $500,000).

Orantes, a toothy, cheerful, 26-year-old left-hander, won the U.S. Open by upsetting Connors in straight sets. Bjorn Borg of Sweden won the French Open, beating Guillermo Vilas of Argentina. Vilas was leading scorer in the 43 tournaments on the Commercial Union Grand Prix circuit.

Grand Prix Tournaments carried prize money of more than $4 million. In addition, there was a $750,000 bonus pool at the end of the season and a Masters tournament for the eight leading finishers in December in Stockholm, Sweden, which Ilie Nastase of Romania won.

Traditionally, most tournaments have been played on clay. The only major tournaments still played on grass were the championships of England (Wimbledon), the United States, and Australia, and a few other tournaments in those nations.

In 1975, however, the U.S. Open abandoned grass because the grass courts at the West Side Tennis Club had become too expensive to maintain. Instead, the Open was played there on an artificial surface made of ground rock. It was similar to clay, a slower surface than grass, and it favored players who relied on touch and patience, not power.

Jimmy Connors shakes hands with John Newcombe after beating him in a challenge match that netted Connors nearly $500,000.

Evert's only major defeat came at Wimbledon, where 31-year-old Billie Jean King of San Mateo, Calif., eliminated her on July 2 in the semifinals. Two days later, King won her sixth Wimbledon singles title and said she would never play a major singles competition again.

Evonne Goolagong of Australia won her national title but lost in the U.S. Open and Wimbledon finals. She led the Pittsburgh Triangles to the World Team Tennis (WTT) championship and was voted the most valuable player in the 10-team league.

Evert Joins WTT. One player who had declined to join WTT was Evert, but she signed with the Phoenix Racquets to play in 1976 for $160,000 a year. Another recruit was Martina Navratilova, an 18-year-old Czechoslovak left-hander who defected to the United States in September. A finalist in the Australian, French, and Italian opens and the Virginia Slims finals, she joined the Cleveland Nets.

Sweden beat Czechoslovakia to win the Davis Cup in December. The United States team, eliminated by Mexico in February, made major changes for 1976. Tony Trabert replaced Dennis Ralston as captain, and Connors, who boycotted cup play for three years because he and his manager, Bill Riordan, disliked Ralston, rejoined the team. But the U.S. lost to Mexico in December.   Frank Litsky

TEXAS. See DALLAS-FORT WORTH; HOUSTON; STATE GOVERNMENT.

THAILAND elected 269 new National Assembly members on Jan. 26, 1975, under its new Constitution. M. R. Seni Pramot formed a two-party coalition government, but it lost a confidence vote and fell on March 6. His younger brother, Khukrit Pramot, then formed a seven-party coalition and became prime minister on March 17.

The Communist victories in Indochina caused problems for Thailand. Planes and ships brought refugees from South Vietnam and Khmer (Cambodia). New regimes in Saigon, South Vietnam; Phnom Penh, Khmer; and Vientiane, Laos, asked that the planes and ships be returned, but the United States asserted title to those it had provided as aid and flew some planes away.

Guerrilla Worries. A guerrilla war had been smoldering in Thailand for years, and Thais feared that, with the end of the Indochina war, North Vietnam would give more weapons and support to the guerrillas. Thai intelligence reports said that the weapons the guerrillas received came across Laos from North Vietnam. At the same time, the Communist Pathet Lao take-over in Laos led to increased tensions with that Thai neighbor and a renewal of old territorial disputes.

In these unsettled circumstances, Thailand wanted to keep a military tie with the United States. Members of the Southeast Asia Treaty Organization decided on September 24 to phase out within two years the structure based in Bangkok, but their 1954 regional defense treaty was left intact as the only treaty link between Bangkok and Washington, D.C.

U.S. Withdrawal. The new Thai government asked the United States to withdraw the U.S. forces that had used Thailand as a base during the Indochina war. United States B-52 bombers were taken out in June. Khukrit agreed on June 4 with the United States that the last 23,000 men would be gone by March 20, 1976. The talks were complicated when the United States used Thai bases in rescuing the U.S. merchant ship *Mayaguez* and its crew in May without formal Thai permission.

Khukrit and Chinese Premier Chou En-lai established diplomatic relations in Peking on July 1. Khukrit said later that Chinese leaders told him they did not support Thai guerrillas.

Efforts by left wing students and farmers' organizations to achieve rural land reform and establish village self-help programs contributed to tensions between Thai conservatives and liberals in August. Bangkok student activists accused the government of plotting against reform. Some of the student leaders were murdered in villages, and nine were arrested. Their release after student protests angered Bangkok police, who wrecked Khukrit's home on August 19.   Henry S. Bradsher

See also ASIA (Facts in Brief Table).

THATCHER, MARGARET HILDA ROBERTS

(1925-   ), became the first woman to head a British political party when she was elected leader of the Conservatives on Feb. 11, 1975. More significant, in defeating former Prime Minister Edward Heath for the party leadership, she led a rebellion from the ranks in a party that traditionally has little room for outsiders. She could become Britain's first woman prime minister if the Conservative Party comes to power.

Margaret Roberts, the daughter of a grocer, was born on Oct. 13, 1925, in Grantham, England. She went through school on scholarships and received a degree in chemistry from Oxford University. From 1947 to 1951, she worked as a research chemist and studied law at night. In 1951, she married oil executive Denis Thatcher. After the birth of twins in 1953, she became a barrister, working in tax law.

She has served in Parliament since 1959. From 1970 to 1974, she was secretary for education and science in the Conservative Cabinet. In this post, she aroused severe criticism when she raised the price of school lunches and cut off free milk for schoolchildren to help finance education reform. After the Labour Party came to power in 1974, she was the principal parliamentary spokesman for the Opposition on economic and tax policy. She is known as an effective and energetic debater. Her major recreational interest is music. Kathryn Sederberg

THEATER

Some of America's finest plays took the 1975 spotlight in celebration of the Bicentennial. An outstanding success was the Circle in the Square Broadway revival of Arthur Miller's *Death of a Salesman*. George C. Scott's bald, grimacing salesman was a shambling, defeated corpse of a man, an unsympathetic Willy Loman who fails by his own standards of success. During the play's initial run in the 1950s, Miller commented that the audience's personal interpretation of the play might obscure its larger intent. The new production clarifies his theme that failure is a tragedy in a society that puts a high value on personal and material success.

Materialism also concerned Eugene O'Neill, who was working on a trilogy on that subject when he died in 1953. The destructive force of greed is seen in both *Desire Under the Elms*, offered by the American Conservatory Theatre in San Francisco, and *Long Day's Journey into Night*. The latter was produced by the American Bicentennial Theatre at the John F. Kennedy Center for the Performing Arts in Washington, D.C., with Jason Robards portraying the miserly father in the autobiographical work. A more idealistic treatment of the same family is seen in *Ah, Wilderness!* revived by the Circle in the Square repertory group. The same company also presented the first major revival since 1924 of O'Neill's *All God's Chillun Got Wings*.

One of T. S. Eliot's plays contributed to the Bicentennial season. A major revival of *The Cocktail Party* was staged by Nina Vance at the Alley Arena Stage in Houston. Robert Lowell is another American poet whose plays enriched the season. The Goodman Theatre in Chicago staged *Benito Cereno*, and the American Place Theatre, in New York City, original producers of *The Old Glory* in 1964, revived it for the Bicentennial celebration.

Other Favorites. Since their debuts, Tennessee Williams' plays have been in constant production. The Guthrie Theater in Minneapolis, Minn., presented *A Streetcar Named Desire*, and the Academy Festival Theater in Lake Forest, Ill., offered *Sweet Bird of Youth*, which subsequently toured Eastern theaters. *Summer and Smoke* was seen off-Broadway at the Roundabout Theater, and an early, poignant one-act play, *27 Wagons Full of Cotton*, opened the 1975-1976 season of the Phoenix Theatre in New York City.

The first play of the Bicentennial season on Broadway was a revival of Thornton Wilder's *The Skin of Our Teeth*, but even the sprightliness of Elizabeth Ashley as the maid could not conceal the fact that the play seemed quaint and outdated. *The Matchmaker*, a more durable candidate for revival,

was staged in a zany and fast-paced production by San Francisco's American Conservatory Theatre. Wilder's farce is also the book of *Hello, Dolly!*, itself a veritable musical classic. It toured the United States in 1975 with Pearl Bailey as the indomitable Mrs. Levi. In Providence, R.I., audiences applauded an outstanding revival of Lillian Hellman's duet of plays about a grasping Southern family in the late 1800s. *Another Part of the Forest* was followed by *The Little Foxes*, so that the rise and fall of the

Dancers holding their publicity photos compete for jobs in *A Chorus Line,* an innovative musical that opened off-Broadway in May.

Hubbard family could be viewed as an American counterpart to Greek tragedy.

Revivals of 19th-century plays re-created the stage of the past for modern audiences. Dion Boucicault's 1865 melodrama, *Rip Van Winkle*, was produced by the Clarence Brown Company at the University of Tennessee in Knoxville. Anthony Quayle played the title role, which was written originally for the great American actor Joseph Jefferson. William Gillette was represented by two plays on Broadway, the long-running *Sherlock Holmes* and another thriller, *Secret Service*, revived by the Phoenix Theatre.

The emergence of realism in the theater in the early 1900s was seen in two revivals scheduled for the spring of 1976. Langdon Mitchell's *The New York Idea*, a 1906 social comedy about divorce, was planned by the McCarter Theatre in Princeton, N.J., and Edward Sheldon's *The Boss*, a 1911 depiction of industrial corruption, by the Chelsea Theatre Center in Brooklyn, N.Y.

Shakespeare, the first playwright produced in the colonies, remained a force in the American theater in 1975. The Royal Shakespeare Company of England's sunny and delightful production of *Love's Labour's Lost*, offered at the Brooklyn Academy of Music and on tour, was a major event.

The Musical. Four outstanding musicals lit up the Broadway scene during the year, despite a 25-day musicians' strike in the fall. The most innova-

Striking musicians blacked out the marquees of Broadway's music theaters for 25 days, closing nine musicals and delaying several opening nights.

tive was *A Chorus Line*, directed by Michael Bennett, which moved to Broadway from the New York Shakespeare Festival Public Theatre. A tribute to the chorus dancer, it depicts the lives of eight dancers who survive tryouts and land jobs in the chorus line. Six months of rehearsal allowed Bennett to achieve a perfect ensemble effect, and the entire chorus line is the star. *Shenandoah* is a dramatic, moving musical about the upheavals caused by the Civil War. A Virginia farmer, played by John Cullum, wishes to remain uninvolved, but is forced to take action when his son is kidnaped by Union soldiers. An artistic re-creation of music of the period, the score incorporates ballads, lullabies, hymns, and other musical forms.

A fast-moving Afro-American musical, *The Wiz*, is based on *The Wizard of Oz*. Fifteen-year-old Stephanie Miles gave a spirited performance as Dorothy, and the production received an Antoinette Perry (Tony) Award for best musical. *Chicago* is a stylized, satiric musical in which director Bob Fosse caricatures, through show-business idiom, the corrupt criminal and legal world of Chicago in the 1920s. Gwen Verdon was superb as Roxie Hart, acquitted of murder because of her lawyer's "razzle-dazzle" skill at evading the truth.

Although Broadway's dramatic hits, such as *Equus* and *Sherlock Holmes*, and off-Broadway productions were not affected by the musicians' strike,

the nine musicals that were affected lost some \$3.5-million in box-office receipts. Restaurants, parking lots, and New York's taxi industry also suffered financially from the strike. Several opening nights were delayed. Among them was *Treemonisha*, the only opera written by Scott Joplin, whose ragtime music is enjoying a popular revival. A number of long-running musicals simply went back into rehearsal during the musicians' strike to sharpen performances that might have become dulled after months of repetition.

New Plays of merit included *The Taking of Miss Janie*, Ed Bullins' penetrating analysis of racial and class attitudes in the 1960s. Tom Stoppard's verbally dazzling *Travesties* envisions the imaginary meeting in Zurich, Switzerland, in 1917 of James Joyce, Tristan Tzara, and V. I. Lenin, leading revolutionaries in literature, art, and politics. A narrator argues against their proposed innovations. Edward Albee's *Seascape* won a Pulitzer Prize over objections from many drama critics, who found the dialogue between a middle-aged couple and two lizardlike creatures banal and humdrum. Alice Griffin

See also AWARDS AND PRIZES (Arts Awards); ULLMANN, LIV.

TIMOR. See PORTUGAL.

TOGO. See AFRICA.

TORNADOES. See DISASTERS; WEATHER.

TOYS. See GAMES, MODELS, AND TOYS.

TRACK AND FIELD. Filbert Bayi, a 21-year-old Tanzanian, and John Walker, a 23-year-old New Zealander, wiped Jim Ryun's name from the world-record book in 1975. Bayi ran the mile in 3 minutes 51.0 seconds in May, trimming a tenth of a second from Ryun's 1967 record, and Walker reduced it to 3 minutes 49.4 seconds in August.

Bayi, slim and graceful, was the attraction for the so-called Dream Mile on May 17 in Kingston, Jamaica. The mile record seemed ready to fall to his effortless, front-running style. It did. Bayi led from the start. See BAYI, FILBERT.

Walker's Record race came on August 12 at Göteborg, Sweden. He won by 40 yards (37 meters), but there was no strong opposition because the meet promoters did not want anyone to interfere with his record attempt. See WALKER, JOHN G.

Marty Liquori, Ryun's successor as America's premier miler, ran fast races all summer — one in 3 minutes 52.2 seconds. He thought a mile in 3 minutes 45 seconds was "definitely possible." But a meeting between Walker and Bayi seemed unlikely until the 1976 Olympic Games in Montreal, Canada, and the event there would be 1,500 meters rather than the slightly longer distance of 1 mile.

Brian Oldfield. Despite the attention they created, the record miles did not compare in excellence to the world-record triple jump of 58 feet 8¼ inches (18 meters) by João Oliveira of Brazil, or the record shot-put performance by Brian Oldfield of Cupertino, Calif. Oldfield put the 16-pound (7.3-kilogram) shot exactly 75 feet (22 meters) in an International Track Association (ITA) professional outdoor meet on May 10 in El Paso, Tex. Three of Oldfield's six puts that day bettered the recognized world record of 71 feet 7 inches (23 meters) set by Al Feuerbach of San Jose, Calif., in 1973.

Oldfield's performance, like those of other pros, was not recognized by the International Amateur Athletic Federation (IAAF), which rules amateur track and field around the world, or the Amateur Athletic Union (A.A.U.), America's ruling body. That prevented official recognition of such professional achievements as Steve Smith's three record pole vaults indoors — 18 feet 2½ inches (5.55 meters) in Montreal; 18 feet 4 inches (5.59 meters) in Portland, Ore.; and 18 feet 5 inches (5.62 meters) in New York City.

Death took distance runner Steve Prefontaine, of Coos Bay, Ore., who held seven American records. Prefontaine, 24, was killed in an auto accident on May 30, while driving home from a party.

The ITA survived its third year despite financial problems. It staged nine meets indoors and six outdoors (two in Great Britain), with attendance averaging 8,910.

World Track and Field Records Established in 1975

Event	Holder	Country	Where made	Date	Record
Men					
100 yards	Houston McTear	U.S.A.	Winter Park, Fla.	May 9	:09.0*
100 meters	Silvio Leonard	Cuba	Ostrava, Czech.	June 5	:09.9*
	Steve Williams	U.S.A.	Siena, Italy	July 16	:09.9*
	Steve Williams	U.S.A.	West Berlin	August 22	:09.9*
200 meters	Don Quarrie	Jamaica	Eugene, Ore.	June 7	:19.8*
	Steve Williams	U.S.A.	Eugene, Ore.	June 7	:19.8*
220 yards	Don Quarrie	Jamaica	Eugene, Ore.	June 7	:19.9
	Steve Williams	U.S.A.	Eugene, Ore.	June 7	:19.9*
1 mile	John Walker	New Zealand	Göteborg, Sweden	August 12	3:49.4
110-meter hurdles	Guy Drut	France	West Berlin	August 22	:13.0*
3,000-meter steeplechase	Anders Garderud	Sweden	Stockholm, Sweden	July 1	8:09.7
1-mile relay	Ray, Taylor, Peoples, Vinson	U.S.A.	Durham, N.C.	July 19	3:02.4
Pole vault	Dave Roberts	U.S.A.	Gainesville, Fla.	March 28	18 ft. 6½ in. (5.65 meters)
Triple jump	João Oliveira	Brazil	Mexico City	October 15	58 ft. 8¼ in. (18 meters)
Discus throw	John Powell	U.S.A.	Long Beach, Calif.	May 4	226 ft. 8 in. (69 meters)
Hammer throw	Walter Schmidt	W. Germany	Frankfurt, W. Germany	August 14	260 ft. 2 in. (80 meters)
Decathlon	Bruce Jenner	U.S.A.	Eugene, Ore.	August 9-10	8,524 pts.
Women					
440 yards	Irina Szewinska	Poland	London	August 31	:51.3
3,000 meters	Grete Anderson	Norway	Oslo, Norway	June 24	8:46.6
440-yard relay	Helten, Wilkes, Kroniger, Gang	W. Germany	Durham, N.C.	July 18	:44.07
1-mile relay	Krause, Fost, Weinstein, Barth	W. Germany	Durham, N.C.	July 19	3:30.3
3,200-meter relay	Shtereva, Tomova, Peklivanova, Zlateva	Bulgaria	Sofia, Bulgaria	August 30	8:05.2
Shot-put	Marianne Adam	E. Germany	East Berlin	August 6	70 ft. 10½ in. (22 meters)
Discus throw	Faina Melnik	U.S.S.R.	Zurich, Switzerland	August 20	230 ft. 4 in. (70 meters)

*Equals record

491

Filbert Bayi sets record, *left,* in Jamaica's
Dream Mile race on May 17. But John Walker
breaks it, *right,* on August 12 in Sweden.

Among the successful Americans were Dave
Roberts of Gainesville, Fla., in the pole vault; John
Powell of San Jose, Calif., discus throw; Bruce Jenner of San Jose, decathlon; Steve Williams of New
York City, sprints; Jim Bolding of Los Angeles,
400-meter hurdles; Dwight Stones of Glendale,
Calif., high jump; and Will Rodgers of Boston,
marathon. Roberts, Powell, and Jenner broke
world records.

East German Women won the Europa Cup and
ranked as the best in the world. But several Ameri-
cans were close to the top, including Madeline
Manning Jackson of Cleveland at 800 meters;
Francie Larrieu of Los Angeles, 1,500 meters; Jane
Frederick of Los Angeles, pentathlon; Kathy
Schmidt of Long Beach, Calif., javelin throw; Joni
Huntley of Sheridan, Ore., high jump; and Kathy
McMillan, 17, of Raeford, N.C., long jump.

Jackson retired after winning the 800-meter gold
medal in the 1968 Olympics. She married, had a
child, and worked for the Salvation Army. Running again in 1975, she lowered her U.S. record to 2
minutes 0.5 second and then 2 minutes 0.3 second.
Larrieu set American records indoors and outdoors
at 1,500 meters and 1 mile. After a 23-hour flight
from China, she slept for 15 hours and then set an
American mile outdoor record of 4 minutes 31.6
seconds on May 31 in Wichita, Kans.   Frank Litsky

See also PAN AMERICAN GAMES.

TRANSIT systems serving U.S. urban communities
in 1975 barely held the ridership gains they picked
up during the 1974 energy crisis. The American
Public Transit Association reported that city mass-
transit operations carried 4.96 billion passengers
from January through October, only 0.92 per cent
above the same 1974 period.

An increase for 1975 would mark the third
straight year of ridership rises, reversing a trend of
patronage decline since 1945. After a tiny rise in
1973, ridership spurted in 1974 as commuters abandoned their cars to avoid long gas station lines and
climbing gasoline prices.

More transit operators used special-fare induce-
ments and other sales pitches to win new customers
and keep recent converts in 1975. Free-fare plans
mushroomed. For example, Dallas began a "Free-
bus" downtown service, and Nashville, Tenn., moved
a "Fareless Flyer" over different routes on an irregular schedule. There were new reduced-fare plans
for the elderly, the handicapped, students, and
other groups, particularly at nonrush-hour times.

Federal Funding policies were formulated to
keep financing for city systems in check, as hopes
for costly new rapid-transit systems mounted.
Funding for fiscal year 1976 reached $1.7 billion
under a six-year, $11.8-billion program launched
in 1974. But Transportation Secretary William T.
Coleman, Jr., said that "when stacked against the
staggering costs of elaborate transit projects . . . it
does not require great mathematical skill to realize
that $11.8 billion is not going to provide money for
everyone."

The demand for federal transit dollars expanded
as rail-system costs escalated. In Washington, D.C.,
for example, an original $2.5-billion cost estimate
for the new 98-mile (158-kilometer) Metro system
rose to $4.7 billion. Government analysts suggested
the cost could eventually reach $6 billion.

The Urban Mass Transportation Administration
(UMTA) issued new guidelines aimed at forcing
cities to examine possible less-costly alternatives to
big rail systems—mainly improved bus service. It
started guaranteeing a set level of new long-term
funding for some urban rapid-transit projects—
$600 million for Atlanta, Ga., and $500 million for
Baltimore. But it insisted that remaining and rising
costs be covered locally. And the federal government issued a set of rules on September 22 to require urban-planning authorities seeking federal
funds to develop in-depth plans to integrate mass
transit with other transportation schemes, revitalize
existing facilities, and keep down costs.

Meanwhile, the Department of Transportation
said it will begin demonstration programs of
"auto-free" or "auto-restricted" zones in cities,
which were encouraged to use highway funds for
transit. Washington, D.C.'s response, a proposal to
switch $286.6 million earmarked for two interstate

roads to build its Metro system, was approved by Coleman on October 3.

Landmark Aid. The first federal operating subsidies for transit systems began in 1975. The nation's commuter-system deficit rose to more than $1 billion, increasing the need for federal or other nonfare-box subsidies. New York City was allowed to borrow $87.5 million in May from capital improvement grant funds to help pay operating costs. In June, UMTA gave New York City the first direct federal operating subsidy, $30.9 million. Grants to other cities followed.

Technology. UMTA finally decided to pay for completion of the controversial driverless Personal Rapid Transit (PRT) system on West Virginia University's campus in Morgantown. Despite climbing costs, UMTA on May 21 committed up to $112 million for the automatically controlled PRT, which began service in October. Congress's Office of Technology Assessment issued a report on June 10 accusing the UMTA of emphasizing big systems like the PRT without regard for translating the research dividends into small workable mass transit systems for urban areas. Meanwhile, such cities as Dayton, Ohio; Denver, Colo.; Detroit; and Chicago showed interest in using cheaper *light-rail,* or trolley-type, systems.   Albert R. Karr

See also TRANSPORTATION.

TRANSPORTATION. The force of the worldwide recession, inflated fuel and other costs, and an Administration push to "deregulate" transportation unsettled the United States transportation industries in 1975. Airlines and railroads plunged into deficits, and truckers sustained a sharp earnings drop as transport traffic fell. Losses deepened because regulatory bodies – under fire for alleged favoritism to the industries they oversee – stalled on granting rate and fare increases, though they began allowing hikes later in the year.

Traffic Decline. Transportation in the United States was hit hard by the economic slowdown early in 1975 but seemed to recover during the last six months. The total U.S. transportation tab for the year was about $290 billion. This was a 1.4 per cent increase over 1974, according to a preliminary estimate by the Transportation Association of America (TAA). The trade group estimated that overall U.S. mainland intercity freight volume declined 6 per cent, led by drops of from 10 to 11 per cent in rail and truck traffic. Pipeline freight was up about 1 per cent, Great Lakes traffic rose about 3.5 per cent, rivers and canals were about the same, and air cargo fell about 5 per cent.

The TAA estimated that intercity passenger traffic increased about 3 per cent because of a 4.5 per cent climb in automobile travel. As the 1974 gaso-

Metro Center Station will be the major transfer point in Washington, D.C.'s new rail rapid-transit system, part of which was scheduled to open in 1976.

line pinch eased, drivers and passengers returned to their cars, and public transportation suffered as a result. The TAA estimated that rail and bus traffic both fell about 8 per cent.

Auto travel did not return to the higher speeds prevalent before the energy crisis, however. Many drivers continued to adhere fairly closely to the federally mandated 55-mile (89-kilometer) per hour speed limit, and several states stepped up enforcement of the limit.

Department of Transportation (DOT). A new secretary of transportation, William T. Coleman, Jr., took office on March 7 (see COLEMAN, WILLIAM T., JR.). On September 17, he issued the department's first statement of national transportation policy. President Ford signed a $4.86-billion appropriations bill on November 24 funding DOT and related agencies for fiscal 1976. The bill earmarked $90 million for the recall of unemployed maintenance men to rehabilitate deteriorated railroad track.

The new secretary spearheaded major new legislation to partially deregulate service, rates, and fares for railroad, airline, truck, and intercity bus operations. The measures were to give carriers more freedom from regulation, stimulating competition, and thus provide consumers with better and cheaper transportation. Airline and truck groups, comfortable with regulation, opposed the plans (see AVIATION; TRUCK AND TRUCKING). The Ford Administration backed a plan by the U.S. Railway Association to restructure bankrupt Northeast railroads under a 1973 law. At year's end, the President had not taken action on a measure passed by Congress (see RAILROAD).

President Ford also proposed legislation on July 7 to extend the 19-year-old highway trust fund beyond 1977. But the bill would cut back the fund's size, permitting completion of only the 42,500-mile (68,400-kilometer) interstate highway system. The Federal Highway Administration estimated that the last 5,500 miles (8,900 kilometers) would cost $39 billion. Other highways would be funded by general revenues. Both the House of Representatives and the Senate passed bills in December to extend federal funding for all road programs to Sept. 30, 1978. On February 11, President Ford said he would release $2 billion in impounded highway funds to produce jobs. Another $9 billion was pried loose by court and congressional action.

Canada's Minister of Transport Jean Marchand issued his own policy statement in June, shortly before resigning from office for health reasons. He said that Canadian subsidy and regulation policies should be re-examined. On October 4, the new Mirabel International Airport opened north of Montreal.   Albert R. Karr

See also AUTOMOBILE; COAL; SHIP AND SHIPPING; TRANSIT.

TRAVEL. Recession and inflation forced many American travelers to stay closer to home in 1975. Nevertheless, worldwide tourism increased more than 5 per cent, and it remained one of the largest single factors in world trade. About 15.4 million travelers from other countries visited the United States during the year, 9 per cent more than in 1974. But the number of Americans visiting other countries dropped sharply.

Most American travelers took shorter trips and stayed in one place longer. They carefully mapped their itineraries to avoid delays and random side trips that wasted time and money. The cost of restaurant meals rose 10 per cent; hotel and motel rooms, 8.5 per cent; and recreation, 8.8 per cent.

Automobile travel accounted for an estimated 70 per cent of American tourism. By the end of June, the American Automobile Association of New York had prepared routes for 139,113 trips, 26 per cent more than in 1974. About 37 million American adults visited American Bicentennial sites.

Americans vanished in the prime European markets in 1975. Those who went pinched pennies, a severe blow to luxury hotels used to Yankees spending 50 per cent more than other tourists. Prices for food, lodging, and travel in Europe increased up to 20 per cent, with the $3 dry martini and the $50 hotel room not at all unusual. American tourism in West Germany dropped nearly 9 per cent, and American business in Spain, Great Britain, Scandinavia, and Italy was off by at least 20 per cent. Mexico's tourist industry suffered severely after it voted favorably on a United Nations motion equating Zionism with racism (see MEXICO).

Visitors to the U.S. About 9.4 million Canadians visited the United States, an increase of 8 per cent, and they spent $1.5 billion. Mexico showed the largest increase in travel to the United States, 14 per cent. More than 2 million Mexican visitors spent over $1 billion in the United States.

Japanese tourists formed the largest group of overseas visitors to the United States. In 1975, some 850,000 Japanese, 11 per cent more than in 1974, came and spent $497 million in the U.S. Among other countries, British visitors increased 2 per cent to 460,000; West Germany, 5 per cent to 310,000; and France, 5 per cent to 175,000.

An estimated 23.3 million U.S. citizens visited other countries, down 6.6 per cent. However, 14.8-million went to Canada, an increase of 3.4 per cent.

Cruises Gain. A notable exception to the general decrease in American travel abroad was cruising, mainly in Caribbean waters. Some 850,000 passengers sailed from Miami, Fla., an increase of 15 per cent. Cruise itineraries were shorter and many were packaged with air fares.

While cruise capacity rose to nearly a million berths, transatlantic sailing virtually died. The Italian Line discontinued transatlantic service, leaving

More than 2,000 original employees gather to mark the fourth anniversary of Walt Disney World in Florida. The park has had 45 million visitors.

only the Cunard Line on that route. The Swedish American Line went out of the passenger business, selling its two luxury liners to cruise operators.

Air Fares rose a total of 20 per cent. However, new low charter fares that became available under less restrictive conditions in September promised to make air travel cheaper for Americans. The system covers conventional domestic and overseas pleasure travel and trips to special events. For example, a 7-day Washington, D.C.-Paris round-trip ticket bought 30 days in advance could cost only $360.27 for flight and hotel. The lowest previous discount fare for the plane ticket alone was $353, if purchased 60 days in advance.

One of the most successful travel offerings of the year was the "no frills" fare, a $61 one-way fare between New York City and Florida during certain months. National Airlines introduced the "no frills" fare and was quickly followed by American, Continental, Delta, and Eastern airlines. Food and drink service was originally eliminated on "no frills" flights, but the frills were soon restored as competition increased.

Rail fares generally increased by 9 per cent, but the U.S. National Railroad Passenger Corporation (Amtrak) introduced a special Bicentennial Colonial Corridor coach fare of $40 between Washington, D.C., and Boston on September 8, a saving of about 33 per cent.

Travel Agency Defaults, in which the agencies issued airline tickets but failed to pay the carriers, increased from 44 in 1973 to nearly 100 in 1975, with losses of more than $4 million.

The World Tourism Organization held its first general assembly in Madrid, Spain, in May. An affiliated agency of the United Nations, with 98 nations as members, it will administer approved projects to promote world tourism and help protect the cultural, social, architectural, and physical environment of tourist sites from the occasionally disruptive impact of millions of tourists.

In an effort to speed the tracing of lost luggage and cut down on the number of passengers who pick up the wrong suitcases, the airlines, on September 21, began refusing baggage unless the owner's name was firmly affixed to the outside.

New Travel Chief. The U.S. Senate on October 3 confirmed the appointment of Creighton D. Holden, a former hotel executive, as assistant secretary of commerce for tourism. He will direct the U.S. Travel Service program, which has a budget of $90 million from July 1, 1975, to Sept. 30, 1978, for the promotion of foreign tourism to the United States. The service will also spend $8.1 million for a three-year domestic program to encourage Americans to travel in the United States.   Lynn Beaumont

See also BICENTENNIAL, U.S.

TRINIDAD AND TOBAGO. See WEST INDIES.

Titan, called the world's biggest truck, can haul about 350 short tons (317 metric tons). The huge vehicle is intended for off-highway uses.

TRUCK AND TRUCKING. The economy's decline severely hampered the U.S. trucking industry in 1975, though not as much as it did other forms of transportation. Because of a 12.5 per cent decrease in tonnage hauled, total motor-carrier revenues dropped 4 per cent to $21.4 billion, the American Trucking Associations, Incorporated (ATA) estimated. Net earnings were about $350 million, a 30 per cent decline from 1974 earnings.

Truckers experienced their worst first quarter in 14 years, showing a net loss of $7.4 million, against a profit of $93.8 million during the same part of 1974. However, results through the first nine months of the year showed some improvement. Motor carriers earned $254 million through September, 35 per cent below 1974. Operating revenues fell 5.5 per cent.

A sharp drop in freight traffic explained much of the financial problem. The ATA's general truck-freight tonnage measurement began the year more than 20 per cent below 1974 and fell 25.1 per cent behind in March. By October the fall-off had narrowed to 10.2 per cent, however.

Trucking firms gained compensation to cover increased labor and other costs from a series of freight-rate hikes that were approved by the Interstate Commerce Commission (ICC). They included boosts of from 2 to 8 per cent on July 1 to cover a wage rise under a contract agreement with the Teamsters Union. The union outlined demands for new wage boosts and benefits in December. If accepted, the package could boost labor costs as much as 50 per cent between 1976 and 1979.

Following the January 4 enactment of a federal law boosting the weight limit on the nation's interstate highway system to 80,000 pounds (36,000 kilograms), the ATA counted 28 states that had raised or were raising their limits to the new level.

President Gerald R. Ford sent Congress a proposal to reduce motor-carrier regulations on November 13, and it provoked an angry reaction from the ATA. His legislation would limit rate setting by industry rate bureaus and reduce rate supervision by the ICC. Ford said the plan "will reduce or eliminate many of the inefficiencies which have crept into the motor-carrier industry during 40 years of regulatory control." The legislation followed similar railroad and airline bills designed to encourage greater competition. It would permit truck-freight rates and intercity bus fares to go up or down eventually by up to 15 per cent a year without prior ICC approval, and make it easier for small independent truckers to get into the business. The ATA said the plan would destroy the "essential stability" of transport, "completely disrupt the nation's entire marketing and distribution system," harm small shippers, and mean loss of truck service for small towns.   Albert R. Karr

TRUDEAU, PIERRE ELLIOTT (1919-   ), completed his seventh year as prime minister of Canada on April 20, 1975, but the pressing issues he faced were different from those for which he entered politics. He entered federal politics to establish genuine bilingualism in Canada and to bring about constitutional changes that would secure Quebec's membership in Confederation. He made significant progress on the first objective, but little on the second.

These issues no longer commanded the attention in 1975 that they had in the mid-1960s. The concerns of Canada were now economic – inflation, depression, energy supplies, food shortages, and access to foreign markets. Trudeau appeared less interested in these questions. For much of the year, he seemed to stand aside from involvement in Canada's pressing economic difficulties.

Sensing the need for action in October, Trudeau dramatically abandoned the position on which he won a national election 15 months earlier and committed his government to stiff income and price controls. His attempt to rally the country against continuing inflation proved a severe test to his leadership. Nevertheless, his political standing remained high. His leadership was confirmed in November at a national convention of the Liberal Party. Trudeau and his wife, Margaret, became the parents of a third son, Michel Charles-Emile, on October 2.   David M. L. Farr

TUNISIA. The National Assembly passed a constitutional amendment on March 18, 1975, making Habib Bourguiba president of Tunisia for life. The Constitution had limited an elected president to three consecutive five-year terms.

Despite Bourguiba's mandate, opposition to the single-party system increased. Tunisia's first teachers' strike took place on January 14, as teachers demanded the release of those jailed since August, 1974, during student unrest. On July 11, a state court sentenced 30 persons to prison terms of up to two years on various charges, such as insulting the head of state and falsely criticizing ministers. At the same time, a manifesto of the opposition Movement for Popular Unity Party, allegedly founded by former Minister of Economy Ahmed Ben Salah, began circulating in Tunis.

Although the gross national product increased 10.9 per cent, unemployment hit 15 per cent, with the greatest impact falling on university graduates and other young people.

In January, a phosphoric acid plant with an annual capacity of 275,600 short tons (250,000 metric tons) went into production at Sfax. Three offshore natural gas fields with reserves of 52 billion cubic feet (1.47 billion cubic meters), enough to meet domestic needs for 20 years, were discovered on April 23.   William Spencer

See also AFRICA (Facts in Brief Table).

TURKEY ended six months of political crisis on March 31, 1975, when former Prime Minister Suleyman Demirel, head of the conservative Justice Party, formed a coalition government. Demirel's new Cabinet, an alignment of three small parties with the Justice Party majority, won a narrow vote of confidence in the National Assembly on April 6.

Demirel's program called for a two-zone federation on Cyprus, extension of Turkey's territorial waters to 12 nautical miles to permit offshore oil exploration, and development of eastern provinces.

His first test of strength came in the October 12 off-year elections to fill 54 of the 153 Senate seats. The campaign was marked by violence, underlining the extreme polarization of Turkish politics. There were 19 politically motivated murders during the summer, and Demirel was attacked with brass knuckles in May by a young unemployed Turk. Demirel suffered a broken nose. About 60 per cent of the nation's 8.7 million registered voters cast ballots. The Justice Party lost 5 seats and the opposition Republican People's Party gained 17, but the coalition kept its Senate majority with 89 seats.

U.S. Relations. Turkey's touchiness about its continued occupation of one-third of Cyprus was largely responsible for a distinct cooling in relations with the United States (see CYPRUS). After a July 24 vote in the U.S. House of Representatives to

Soldiers help U.S. Secretary of State Henry A. Kissinger lay a wreath on the grave of modern Turkey's founder, Kemal Atatürk, in Ankara.

continue the six-month-old arms embargo against Turkey, Demirel's government closed down all 27 U.S. military installations, and abrogated the 1969 joint defense agreement. On October 2, Congress eased the arms ban by allowing Turkey to buy equipment contracted for before the ban.

The political uncertainty made economic prospects seem even gloomier. Turkey's foreign trade deficit rose to $1 billion for the first half of 1975, prompting three devaluations of the lira. Equally critical was the decline in money sent home by Turks working in Western Europe due to the recession. Some 30,000 workers were repatriated from West Germany alone, and remittances dropped 39 per cent to $524 million. Turkey's inflation rate was estimated at 30 per cent in 1975.

Bright Spots. Iron ore deposits of 772 million short tons (700 million metric tons) were discovered in the Black Sea region on August 15, and a new natural gas field was found near Nusaybin on September 12. An aluminum-tube plant with an annual export capacity of 100 million tubes went into production in Konya in July. Equally promising were labor agreements with Libya and Saudi Arabia signed in August.

A severe earthquake struck eastern Turkey on September 7. The tremor killed more than 2,000 persons and destroyed several towns.   William Spencer

See also MIDDLE EAST (Facts in Brief Table).

UDALL, MORRIS KING (1922-   ), an Arizona congressman, campaigned in 1975 for the 1976 Democratic presidential nomination. He was the first Democrat to enter the race officially, announcing on Nov. 23, 1974. A liberal closely allied with conservationist causes, Udall focused his campaign on what he called the "three E's," economy, energy, and environment.

Udall was born in St. Johns, Ariz., on June 15, 1922. He entered the University of Arizona in 1940, but his studies were interrupted by service in the U.S. Army Air Corps from 1942 to 1946. He returned to the university after World War II and received a law degree in 1949. Despite the loss of an eye in a childhood accident, the 6-foot 6-inch (198-centimeter) Udall played basketball for the University of Arizona and later for the Denver Nuggets, a professional team.

In 1949, he joined his brother Stewart in law practice in Tucson, Ariz. He practiced law until 1961, when his brother, by then a congressman, was appointed secretary of the interior by President John F. Kennedy. Udall was elected to fill the congressional seat vacated by his brother, and has held it ever since. In 1969, he created a congressional furor by unsuccessfully attempting to oust John W. McCormack as speaker of the House.

Udall married Ella Royston in 1968. He has six children by a previous marriage.   Edward G. Nash

UGANDA. Actions by President Idi Amin Dada damaged relations with several other countries during 1975. On June 11, an Ugandan military tribunal sentenced Denis Cecil Hills, a British citizen, to death for calling Amin a "village tyrant" in a book Hills wrote. Amin offered to pardon Hills if British Foreign Secretary James Callaghan would come to Uganda. Instead, Queen Elizabeth II sent two army officers carrying her personal plea. Zaire also reportedly interceded, and Amin announced on July 1 he would pardon Hills. Callaghan then went to Uganda for talks, and Hills was released on July 10.

In March, Uganda began receiving shipments of Russian arms, including a squadron of MIG-21 aircraft. However, Amin demanded in November that Russia explain its recognition of a political faction fighting for control of Angola (see ANGOLA).

United States relations were also severely strained. In a speech to the United Nations (UN) on October 1, Amin called for the "extinction of Israel as a state." The U.S. ambassador to the UN, Daniel P. Moynihan, responded by calling Amin a "racist murderer," in reference to the alleged murders of thousands of Amin's opponents in Uganda.

Uganda hosted the summit meeting of the Organization of African Unity in July, and as leader of the host country, Amin was chairman. John D. Esseks

See also AFRICA (Facts in Brief Table).

ULLMANN, LIV JOHANNE (1939-   ), one of the most brilliant motion-picture stars acting under Swedish director Ingmar Bergman, made her American stage debut in New York City in 1975. She appeared in Henrik Ibsen's *A Doll's House.*

Ullmann was born on Dec. 16, 1939, in Tokyo, Japan, where her father, a Norwegian aircraft engineer, was working. The family did not return to Norway until after World War II ended. After studying drama in London, she joined a repertory company in Stavanger, Norway. In 1959, she joined the National Theatre and the Norwegian Theatre in Oslo.

She met Bergman in 1964, and appeared in his film *Persona* (1967). This was the beginning of an intense personal and professional relationship. She had leading roles in several Bergman films.

Ullmann also appeared in non-Bergman films. The most acclaimed was a two-part epic based on the immigration of Swedish peasants to America. The first part, *The Emigrants,* was shot in Sweden in 1970 and released in the United States in 1972. The second part, *The New Land,* was released a year later.

She lives in Stommen, Norway, with her daughter, whose father is Bergman.   Kathryn Sederberg

UNEMPLOYMENT. See ECONOMICS; LABOR.
UNION OF SOVIET SOCIALIST REPUBLICS (U.S.S.R.). See RUSSIA.

UNITED ARAB EMIRATES (UAE). Dubayy nationalized its oil resources and installations of the five oil companies operating there on July 10, 1975. The five foreign oil companies, including Continental Oil Company of the United States, were guaranteed $110 million in compensation. They will continue their own marketing operations at their own cost, but a state agency was set up to manage the oil industry, which produces about 300,000 barrels a day.

Its wealth enabled the UAE to take an active role in world oil affairs. In January, the UAE joined the Organization of Petroleum Exporting Countries (OPEC) as its third largest contributor.

The UAE approved a budget of $700 million on May 27. But revenues for Abu Zaby, the richest member, were $3.3 billion, and its contribution to the federal budget was $500 million. Abu Zaby's Fund for Arab Economic Development approved loans totaling $180 million to eight Arab states and Bangladesh.

The first UAE paint factory opened in Dubayy in July. The plant will supply 3,300 short tons (3,000 metric tons) of paint annually to the Persian Gulf states. Agreement was reached in principle for a UAE federal army and diplomatic service on May 12. William Spencer

See also MIDDLE EAST (Facts in Brief Table).

UNITED NATIONS (UN). The 30th General Assembly provoked protest throughout the Western world in 1975 by acting against Zionism, the Jewish return movement on which the nation of Israel is based. On November 10, the Assembly adopted a resolution by a vote of 72 to 35, with 32 abstentions, saying Zionism is "a form of racism and racial discrimination."

All Western countries, together for once, voted against the resolution. The Arab-African coalition, solid since the 1973 Arab oil embargo, fell apart as 17 African countries voted against the resolution or abstained. They feared the loss of Western support for their campaign against South African racial discrimination. Israeli Ambassador Chaim Herzog tore the resolution up, saying, "The Jewish people will treat it as no more than a piece of paper."

PLO Power. The resolution was among new gains of the Palestine Liberation Organization (PLO), the anti-Israeli guerrilla group backed by Arab, nonaligned, and Communist delegations. Granted observer status in the Assembly and UN conferences in 1974, the PLO won admittance to Security Council debates in 1975. On November 30, Syria consented to a six-month renewal of the UN Disengagement Observer Force (UNDOF) mandate on the Syria-Israel sector but gained the Council's agreement to let the PLO into a full Mid-

Construction of United Nations City buildings, due to be finished in 1978, continues along the Danube River in Vienna, Austria.

International Women's Year

The generally poor and oppressed condition of women throughout the world prompted the United Nations (UN) to designate 1975 as International Women's Year, symbolized by a specially designed dove. A world conference, held in Mexico City, Mexico, from June 19 to July 2, highlighted the observance.

International Women's Year called attention to the fact that, in most countries, women do not have the same chance as men to gain an education, work in the job they want, or participate fully in politics. According to 1970 UN statistics, about 40 per cent of the world's women cannot read or write, as opposed to 28 per cent of the men. The situation is much worse in developing nations. In Africa, more than 83 per cent of the women are illiterate; in the Arab states, over 85 per cent. In the industrialized nations, where great strides have been made toward equalizing educational opportunity, the UN reported, the subjects studied by boys nevertheless differ significantly from those studied by girls.

The UN found it more difficult to assess the situation of women in the world labor market. Uncounted millions of women in developing nations work as domestics or subsistence farmers to support their families while their husbands work in distant cities or mining areas. However, the UN estimated that there are 562 million working women, about 34 per cent of the world's labor force. But even in industrialized nations, they earn only from 50 to 80 per cent of what their male counterparts earn.

The legal and political rights of women vary widely from country to country. In most of the UN's more than 140 member nations, women are allowed to vote in all elections and run for political office on an equal basis with men. But nine nations do not allow women to vote at all.

In many countries, the popular culture regards women as inferior, and these countries still have laws that discriminate against women in marital and family matters. For example, a wife needs her husband's permission to apply for employment, and she does not have the legal right

to own property or file for divorce.

The delegates from 133 nations who attended the Mexico City conference discussed these problems and sought ways to improve the lives of women and "raise the consciousness of the world." While the official conference was being held at the Mexican Foreign Ministry, an unofficial UN-sponsored conference, or Tribune, attracted about 5,000 women to the Mexico City Medical Center. The conference passed 34 resolutions and a World Plan of Action for the advancement of women that called for increased literacy, job training, and more employment opportunities. The conference also adopted the Declaration of Mexico, which linked women's equality to a redistribution of the world's wealth.

However, the event did not occur without differences among delegates and criticism by feminists from industrialized nations and representatives from the developing world. The feminists from the industrialized nations objected to the conference being held in Mexico, which they regarded as a bastion of male supremacy. They also criticized the fact that a man—Mexico's attorney general—was named president of the conference and that 20 per cent of the delegates were male.

Representatives from developing nations complained that their concerns did not have much in common with those of the industrialized nations. Delegates from the developing nations were more interested in social and economic reforms that would aid both men and women living at subsistence levels—suffering from hunger and extreme poverty.

Other critics pointed out that conference discussions often veered from women's issues to political concerns, such as the Arab-Israeli issue and the rift between China and Russia.

Nevertheless, International Women's Year and its culminating conference were the first events of this kind. And, though there were differences in viewpoint and doubts about the ultimate effectiveness of the documents produced, the event marked a milestone in the history of womankind.   Darlene R. Stille

Women's Year stamp

dle East debate in January, 1976. The vote was 13 to 0, with China and Iraq not participating. On December 4, Egypt induced the Council to seat the PLO immediately as a participant in a debate on Egyptian and Lebanese complaints of Israeli air raids on Palestinian camps in Lebanon. The vote was 9 to 3 with 3 abstentions. The United States and Great Britain, with Costa Rica, voted against the move, but they could not veto it because it was procedural.

On December 8, the United States stood alone in its veto of a resolution by nonaligned nations to condemn Israel. The Council had rejected U.S. amendments to condemn all acts of violence — including PLO attacks on Israel.

Middle East Peacekeeping. Israel readily agreed to the Council's every extension of the mandate of a UN buffer force, but the Arabs pressed for an end to Israeli occupation of their territory. Secretary-General Kurt Waldheim had to go to the Middle East to gain Arab consent. Egypt agreed on April 17 to the renewal of the UN Emergency Force (UNEF) in the Sinai for only three months instead of the usual six months. Again, on July 24, Egypt agreed, but only after a special appeal from the Council president, Eugenio Plaja of Italy. But the new Egyptian-Israeli disengagement agreement signed on September 4 required a year's extension each time, and the Council voted one on October 23. The agreement necessitated UNEF's expansion from about 4,000 men to almost 5,000, to handle heavier duties. Syria gave last-minute consent to the Council's renewal of UNDOF on the Golan Heights on May 28.

The Assembly held special debates on Palestine and the Middle East. On November 10, it adopted an Egyptian-promoted resolution calling for the PLO's participation in the Geneva Conference and all UN-sponsored peace efforts. It also adopted a PLO-promoted resolution establishing a committee to give the next Assembly a program for enabling the Palestinians to exercise "inalienable rights" to national independence and a return home to what is now Israel. The United States and Israel voted against both resolutions. The Assembly voted on December 6 to ask the Security Council to draft a timetable for a settlement among all parties, including the PLO. The resolution was to ensure Israeli withdrawal from all occupied territories and attainment of Palestinian "national rights."

The Assembly passed a new Russian disarmament proposal on December 11. The resolution asked for an international agreement to ban "new types of weapons of mass destruction." A draft was attached for the Geneva Disarmament Conference to work from.

Chile Scored. The Assembly approved on December 9 a declaration against police torture and a resolution charging that torture of prisoners was "institutionalized" in Chile — a charge Chile denied. The torture declaration was drafted at a September UN crime-prevention congress that was switched to Geneva, Switzerland, from Toronto because of Canadian protests against admitting PLO observers. The resolution against Chile was based on a report prepared from interviews outside Chile by an investigating team of the UN Commission on Human Rights. Chile had agreed to admit the team but reneged at the last minute, claiming that pronouncements of other UN bodies had prejudged the outcome.

Action on Africa. The Assembly on December 10 strongly condemned collaboration with "the racist regime of South Africa" and urged the United States, Britain, France, West Germany, Japan, and Italy to limit trade with that country. The South African delegation, ousted from the 1974 Assembly, stayed away from the 1975 session.

In the Security Council on June 6, the United States, Britain, and France vetoed a mandatory arms embargo on South Africa proposed as pressure to force South Africa to turn over control of Namibia (South West Africa) to the UN (see AFRICA). Spain's November agreement to turn over Spanish Sahara to Morocco and Mauritania, despite Algeria's insistence that the colony become independent, led the General Assembly on December 10 to adopt two "self-determination" resolutions. The pro-Algerian resolution won by a vote of 80 to 0, and the pro-Moroccan by a vote of 56 to 42. The Spanish agreement followed Moroccan King Hassan II's recall of thousands of civilian marchers he had sent into Spanish Sahara in spite of three appeals from the Council that he call off the march. See MIDDLE EAST; MOROCCO.

Southeast Asia. After years of passing only pro-South Korean resolutions, the Assembly finally passed a pro-North Korean one on November 18. First it passed a pro-South Korean measure calling for talks among the United States, South Korea, China, and North Korea to keep the 1953 armistice agreement but dissolve the UN military command. Then it passed a measure calling for talks between the United States and North Korea to replace the armistice with a peace agreement.

The Korean question figured in Security Council consideration of UN membership applications by North Vietnam and South Vietnam, which were filed in mid-July after the April Communist victory. The United States vetoed both applications on August 11 and again on September 30, after a General Assembly appeal for reconsideration. It gave as its reason the Council's refusal to take up South Korea's renewed membership application.

North and South Korea both have only observer status. But the new Communist governments of Khmer (Cambodia) and Laos inherited UN memberships. Their UN delegations joined China in

Daniel P. Moynihan, top right, found that his
hard-hitting style in defense of the United
States was coolly received by some UN delegates.

aligning with the third world. Prince Norodom Sihanouk, speaking as president of Khmer on October 6, thanked Assembly members who had asserted his right to Khmer's seat since his 1970 ouster.

In Cyprus, the UN conducted talks between Greek and Turkish Cypriots in search of a political settlement. However, they broke down on February 13, when the Turkish Cypriots proclaimed a separate state in the northern part of the island. The Turks wanted eventual federation with a Greek Cypriot state instead of the old single Cyprus under Greek Cypriot domination. The Security Council, meeting at Cyprus' request, unanimously asked Waldheim on March 12 to reconvene the talks. He did so in Vienna, Austria, from April 28 to May 3, from June 5 to 9, from July 31 to August 2, and again at UN headquarters on September 10. But a UN spokesman finally reported there were "no concrete proposals." The Assembly called on November 20 for immediate resumption of negotiations, but Turkey opposed the resolution. The Security Council on December 13 extended the term of the UN peacekeeping force stationed in Cyprus for six months. See CYPRUS.

The UN Children's Fund (UNICEF) and the UN high commissioner for refugees, Prince Sadruddin Aga Khan, gave emergency relief to Laos and both North and South Vietnam. UNICEF also provided aid in Khmer. An appeal from the secretary-general for $100 million brought $27 million from various governments. Meanwhile Sadruddin arranged resettlement abroad for more than 60,000 Khmer, Laotian, and Vietnamese refugees who did not want to go home. He registered some 1,700 persons who wished to return to their homes, but authorities were slow in taking them.

The Trusteeship Council lost its next-to-last trust territory on September 16 when Papua New Guinea became independent from Australia (see PAPUA NEW GUINEA). This left only the U.S.-administered Pacific Islands under UN trusteeship, and in a plebiscite on June 17 the northern Mariana Islands voted to seek U.S. commonwealth status (see PACIFIC ISLANDS [Close-Up]).

The UN University Council, meeting in January in Tokyo, agreed that the evolving world network of higher learning institutes should focus its research on world hunger, resource management, and human development.

World Conferences. The International Women's Year Conference in Mexico City, Mexico, from June 19 to July 2, was attended by 891 women delegates from 133 countries and over 6,500 others from organizations and news media. The delegates adopted a World Plan of Action for Women's Rights and a Declaration of Mexico calling for a just society and the elimination of Zionism.

The Food and Agriculture Organization (FAO) conference in Rome elected Edouard Somma of Lebanon on November 10 to succeed Addeke H. Boerma of the Netherlands as FAO director-general.

The Third Conference on the Law of the Sea met in Geneva from March 17 to May 9 and planned a fourth session to be held in New York City in 1976. See OCEAN.

The UN General Assembly, at a seventh special session in September devoted to development and international economic cooperation, passed a resolution spelling out measures to get developing countries more trade and aid.

Gaston Thorn, prime minister of Luxembourg, was elected president of the three-month regular session. Daniel P. Moynihan, who succeeded John Scali as chief U.S. representative to the UN on June 30, caused controversy with hard-hitting speeches.

Moynihan's Style. For example, Moynihan used the phrase "racist murderer" in a speech on October 3 to describe Uganda's President Idi Amin Dada. Before the Assembly on October 1, Amin had called for the "extinction" of Israel as a nation. President Gerald R. Ford supported Moynihan on October 8, and as the session wore on, Moynihan continued to voice a new, tough U.S. position against the third world UN majority that berates and votes against the United States on many issues. "There are some things you cannot do to us and some things you cannot say about us," Moynihan told representatives of the third world. "And we will just not take that, and we will find ways to discourage it."

Moynihan was about to resign in late November because of lack of support from the U.S. Department of State. He decided to stay following a talk at the White House with President Ford on November 24. An official statement released after their meeting urged him "to continue to speak out candidly and forcefully on major issues before the United Nations." But some moderate third world delegates and even European delegates argued that his remarks were needlessly divisive. See MOYNIHAN, DANIEL PATRICK.

Miscellaneous. The Cape Verde Islands, São Tomé and Príncipe, Mozambique, Papua New Guinea, the Comoro Islands, and Surinam were admitted to the United Nations during the year, boosting its membership to 144. The Assembly elected five countries – Dahomey (now Benin), Libya, Pakistan, Panama, and Romania – to two-year terms on the 15-member Security Council. It named 18 countries to three-year terms on the 54-member Economic and Social Council, all beginning in 1976. They are Afghanistan, Algeria, Austria, Bangladesh, Bolivia, Brazil, Cuba, France, West Germany, Greece, Malaysia, Nigeria, Portugal, Togo, Tunisia, Uganda, Venezuela, and Yugoslavia.   William N. Oatis

UNITED STATES, GOVERNMENT OF. The United States in 1975 moved into the last quarter of the 20th century with a new balance of power in its federal government. The crisis atmosphere of the Watergate years had subsided, and the power of the U.S. presidency was in check. The long and ambivalent U.S. involvement in Indochina had ended, and in its place politics, the state of the economy, and alleged illegal activities by the Central Intelligence Agency (CIA) and the Federal Bureau of Investigation (FBI) held the nation's attention.

The United States went through its most serious economic recession since the 1930s in 1975 (see ECONOMICS; LABOR). The Democrat-controlled Congress and the conservative Republican President could not agree on how to fight inflation and reduce unemployment. And with the 1976 elections drawing closer, both the President and Congress had their eyes on politics.

CIA and FBI Probes. A presidential commission chaired by Vice-President Nelson A. Rockefeller scrutinized the activities of the CIA in 1975. Both the CIA and the FBI were investigated by select committees in the Senate and the House of Representatives. The Rockefeller Commission completed its investigation in June. The Rockefeller Commission declared that the CIA had indulged in an illegal domestic spying operation. See ROCKEFELLER, NELSON ALDRICH.

The Senate Select Committee on Intelligence was chaired by Frank Church (D., Ida.); and the House Select Committee on Intelligence, by Otis G. Pike (D., N.Y.) (see CHURCH, FRANK). The Senate released the results of its investigation on November 20, despite President Ford's efforts to block part of the report. The Senate investigators found that the CIA was involved in plots to kill leaders in five foreign countries – Chile, the Congo (now Zaire), Cuba, the Dominican Republic, and South Vietnam. The report also revealed that CIA officials had not always informed their White House superiors of their plans, but that U.S. Presidents may have been aware of the assassination plots. The CIA also reportedly opened the foreign mail of prominent Americans between 1953 and 1973. The CIA did not obey the orders of President Richard M. Nixon to destroy stockpiled poisons that had been produced during a supersecret 18-year, $3-million project. The CIA also tested mind-altering drugs on unsuspecting persons, and this resulted in the 1953 death of one government employee, who was given a dose of LSD.

The Senate committee reported that the FBI had secretly sent a harassing letter to civil rights leader and Nobel Prizewinner Martin Luther King, Jr. King reportedly interpreted the letter as an attempt to force him to commit suicide. The letter was sent

A new vice-presidential seal, designed by Vice-President Nelson Rockefeller, was officially adopted in October.

Major Agencies and Bureaus of the U.S. Government*

Executive Office of the President

President, Gerald R. Ford

Vice-President, Nelson A. Rockefeller
White House Staff Coordinator, Richard B. Cheney
Presidential Press Secretary, Ronald H. Nessen
Central Intelligence Agency—George H. W. Bush, Director
Council of Economic Advisers—Alan Greenspan, Chairman
Council on Environmental Quality—Russell W. Peterson, Chairman
Council on Wage and Price Stability—Michael H. Moskow, Director
Domestic Council—James M. Cannon, Executive Director
Economic Policy Board—L. William Seidman, Executive Director
Office of Management and Budget—James T. Lynn, Director

State Department

Secretary of State, Henry A. Kissinger

Agency for International Development—Daniel Parker, Administrator
U.S. Representative to the United Nations—Daniel P. Moynihan

Department of the Treasury

Secretary of the Treasury, William E. Simon

Bureau of Alcohol, Tobacco, and Firearms—Rex D. Davis, Director
Bureau of Engraving and Printing—James A. Conlon, Director
Bureau of the Mint—Mary Brooks, Director
Comptroller of the Currency—James E. Smith
Internal Revenue Service—Donald C. Alexander, Commissioner
Treasurer of the United States—Francine Neff
U.S. Customs Service—Vernon D. Acree, Commissioner
U.S. Secret Service—H. Stuart Knight, Director

Department of Defense

Secretary of Defense, Donald H. Rumsfeld

Joint Chiefs of Staff—General George S. Brown, Chairman
Secretary of the Air Force—Thomas C. Reed†
Secretary of the Army—Martin R. Hoffmann
Secretary of the Navy—J. William Middendorf II

Department of Justice

Attorney General, Edward H. Levi

Bureau of Prisons—Norman A. Carlson, Director
Drug Enforcement Administration—Peter Bensinger,† Administrator
Federal Bureau of Investigation—Clarence M. Kelley, Director
Immigration and Naturalization Service—Leonard F. Chapman, Jr., Commissioner
Law Enforcement Assistance Administration—Richard W. Velde, Administrator
Solicitor General—Robert H. Bork

Department of the Interior

Secretary of the Interior, Thomas S. Kleppe

Bureau of Indian Affairs—Morris Thompson, Commissioner
Bureau of Land Management—Curt Berklund, Director
Bureau of Mines—Thomas V. Falkie, Director
Bureau of Outdoor Recreation—(vacant)
Bureau of Reclamation—Gilbert G. Stamm, Commissioner
Geological Survey—Vincent E. McKelvey, Director
National Park Service—Gary E. Everhardt, Director
Office of Territorial Affairs—Fred Zeder, Director
U.S. Fish and Wildlife Service—Lynn A. Greenwalt, Director

Department of Agriculture

Secretary of Agriculture, Earl L. Butz

*As of Jan. 1, 1976;   † nominated but not yet confirmed

Agricultural Economics—Don A. Paarlberg, Director
Agricultural Marketing Service—Erwin L. Peterson, Administrator
Agricultural Stabilization and Conservation Service—Kenneth E. Frick, Administrator
Farmers Home Administration—Frank B. Elliott, Administrator
Federal Crop Insurance Corporation—Melvin R. Peterson, Manager
Forest Service—John R. McGuire, Chief
Rural Electrification Administration—David A. Hamil, Administrator
Soil Conservation Service—Kenneth E. Grant, Administrator

Department of Commerce

Secretary of Commerce, Elliot L. Richardson

Bureau of the Census—Vincent P. Barabba, Director
National Bureau of Standards—(vacant)
National Oceanic and Atmospheric Administration—Robert M. White, Administrator
Office of Minority Business Enterprise—Alex M. Armendaris, Director
Patent and Trademark Office—C. Marshall Dann, Commissioner

Department of Labor

Secretary of Labor, John T. Dunlop

Bureau of Labor Statistics—Julius Shiskin, Commissioner
Labor-Management Services Administration—Paul J. Fasser, Jr., Administrator
Occupational Safety and Health Administration—Morton Corn, Administrator

Department of Health, Education, and Welfare

Secretary of Health, Education, and Welfare, F. David Mathews

Administration on Aging—Arthur S. Flemming, Commissioner
Alcohol, Drug Abuse, and Mental Health Administration—James D. Isbister, Administrator
Food and Drug Administration—Alexander M. Schmidt, Commissioner
Health Resources Administration—Kenneth M. Endicott, Administrator
Health Services Administration—(vacant)
National Institute of Education—Harold L. Hodgkinson, Director
National Institutes of Health—Donald S. Fredrickson, Director
Office of Consumer Affairs—Virginia H. Knauer, Director
Office of Education—Terrell H. Bell, Commissioner
Public Health Service—Theodore Cooper, Administrator
Social and Rehabilitation Service—James S. Dwight, Jr., Administrator
Social Security Administration—James B. Cardwell, Commissioner

Department of Housing and Urban Development

Secretary of Housing and Urban Development, Carla A. Hills

Community Planning and Development—(vacant)
Federal Disaster Assistance Administration—Thomas P. Dunne, Administrator
Federal Housing Commissioner—David S. Cook
Federal Insurance Administration—John Robert Hunter, Acting Administrator
New Communities Administration—(vacant)

Department of Transportation

Secretary of Transportation, William T. Coleman, Jr.

Federal Aviation Administration—John L. McLucas, Administrator
Federal Highway Administration—Norbert T. Tiemann, Administrator
Federal Railroad Administration—Asaph H. Hall, Administrator
National Highway Traffic Safety Administration—James B. Gregory, Administrator
U.S. Coast Guard—Admiral Owen W. Siler, Commandant
Urban Mass Transportation Administration—Robert E. Patricelli, Administrator

Congressional Officials

President of the Senate pro tempore—James O. Eastland
Speaker of the House—Carl B. Albert
Architect of the Capitol—George M. White
Comptroller General of the U.S.—Elmer B. Staats
Congressional Budget Office—Alice M. Rivlin, Director
Librarian of Congress—Daniel J. Boorstin
Office of Technology Assessment—Emilio Q. Daddario, Director
Public Printer of the U.S.—Thomas F. McCormick

Independent Agencies

ACTION—Michael P. Balzano, Jr., Director
American Revolution Bicentennial Administration—
   John W. Warner, Administrator
Civil Aeronautics Board—John E. Robson, Chairman
Civil Service Commission—Robert E. Hampton, Chairman
Community Services Administration—Bert Gallegos, Director
Consumer Product Safety Commission—S. John Byington,†
   Chairman
Energy Research and Development Administration—
   Robert C. Seamans, Jr., Administrator
Environmental Protection Agency—Russell E. Train,
   Administrator
Equal Employment Opportunity Commission—Lowell W. Perry,
   Chairman
Export-Import Bank—Stephen McKenzie Dubrue, Jr.,†
   President
Farm Credit Administration—W. Malcolm Harding, Governor
Federal Communications Commission—Richard E. Wiley, Chairman
Federal Deposit Insurance Corporation—Frank Wille, Chairman
Federal Election Commission—Thomas B. Curtis, Chairman
Federal Energy Administration—Frank G. Zarb, Administrator
Federal Home Loan Bank Board—(vacant)
Federal Maritime Commission—Karl E. Bakke, Chairman
Federal Power Commission—Richard L. Dunham, Chairman
Federal Reserve System—Arthur F. Burns, Board of Governors
   Chairman
Federal Trade Commission—(vacant)
General Services Administration—Jack M. Eckerd, Administrator
Indian Claims Commission—Jerome K. Kuykendall, Chairman
Interstate Commerce Commission—George M. Stafford, Chairman
National Aeronautics and Space Administration—
   James C. Fletcher, Administrator
National Credit Union Administration—Herman Nickerson, Jr.,
   Administrator
National Foundation on the Arts and Humanities—Paul Berman,
   Director
National Labor Relations Board—Betty Southard Murphy,
   Chairman
National Mediation Board—George S. Ives, Chairman
National Science Foundation—H. Guyford Stever, Director
National Transportation Safety Board—John H. Reed,
   Chairman
Nuclear Regulatory Commission—William A. Anders, Chairman
Occupational Safety and Health Review Commission—Frank R.
   Barnako, Chairman
Overseas Private Investment Corporation—Marshall T. Mays,
   President
Securities and Exchange Commission—Roderick M. Hills,
   Chairman
Selective Service System—Byron V. Pepitone, Director
Small Business Administration—Mitchell P. Kobelinski,†
   Administrator
Smithsonian Institution—S. Dillon Ripley, Secretary
Tennessee Valley Authority—Aubrey J. Wagner, Chairman
U.S. Arms Control and Disarmament Agency—Fred C. Ikle,
   Director
U.S. Commission on Civil Rights—Arthur S. Flemming, Chairman
U.S. Information Agency—James Keogh, Director
U.S. International Trade Commission—Will E. Leonard, Jr.,
   Chairman
U.S. Postal Service—Benjamin F. Bailar, Postmaster General
Veterans Administration—Richard L. Roudebush, Administrator

allegedly because FBI Director J. Edgar Hoover believed that King might have been under Communist influence. The FBI also placed informers and provocateurs in civil rights and antiwar groups and committed 238 illegal burglaries against dissidents between 1952 and 1966.

The House Select Committee on Intelligence focused on the effectiveness of CIA activities with regard to anticipating international crises. The House committee reported on September 11 that the CIA had failed to predict the 1973 Middle East war, even though it had all the intelligence data. The committee also investigated intelligence gathering before the 1968 Tet offensive in Vietnam and the role of the CIA in the dispute between Turkey and Greece over Cyprus. However, the committee had difficulty obtaining secret documents.

The Executive Branch. In November, President Ford executed a surprising Cabinet shuffle, which he said was a move to bring in his "own team." White House Chief of Staff Donald H. Rumsfeld replaced James R. Schlesinger as secretary of defense and Elliot L. Richardson replaced Rogers C. B. Morton as secretary of commerce. In addition, William E. Colby was dismissed as director of the CIA, and George H. W. Bush, U.S. liaison officer with China, succeeded him. See CABINET, U.S.; PRESIDENT OF THE UNITED STATES.

President Ford traveled abroad four times in 1975 – to Europe in May, July, and November, and to China, Indonesia, and the Philippines on a December trip.

There were two assassination attempts against him. Nevertheless, he maintained that meeting the voters was an important part of his job. But many Americans wondered whether the President should avoid dangerous public exposure.

The Legislative Branch. The Democrat-controlled 94th Congress disagreed with President Ford's positions on tax cuts, budget cuts, a national energy policy, welfare measures, and military and foreign aid. But despite the large Democratic congressional majority, only three measures passed over the President's veto – a $2-billion health-care bill; a $7.9-billion education bill; and the National School Lunch and Child Nutrition Act of 1975.

Other major legislation passed by Congress in 1975 included: a law reducing federal personal income taxes in 1975 and providing a small tax rebate for 1974; an extension of the 1975 tax reduction to cover 1976 taxes; an oil price-control bill; a freeze on food-stamp prices; a modified bill to aid the ailing housing industry; and an extension of emergency unemployment compensation. See CONGRESS OF THE UNITED STATES; ENERGY; HOUSING; SOCIAL WELFARE; TAXATION.

Judicial Branch. Justice William O. Douglas, suffering from a continuing illness, retired from the Supreme Court of the United States on November

Federal Spending and Revenue Receipts

Estimated U.S. Budget for Fiscal 1976*

	Billions of dollars
National defense	94.0
International affairs†	6.3
Science and space research	4.6
Natural resources, environment, energy	10.0
Agriculture	1.8
Commerce and transportation	13.7
Community and regional development	5.9
Education, manpower, social services	14.6
Health	28.0
Income security	118.7
Veterans benefits and services	15.6
Law enforcement and justice	3.3
General government	3.2
General revenue sharing	7.2
Interest	34.4
Allowances	8.0
Undistributed funds	—20.2
Total	349.4

*July 1, 1975, to June 30, 1976

†Includes foreign aid

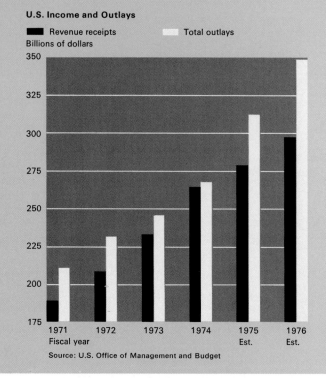

U.S. Income and Outlays

■ Revenue receipts   ▢ Total outlays

Billions of dollars

Source: U.S. Office of Management and Budget

12. He had served a record 36 years as a justice. On November 28, President Ford appointed John Paul Stevens, a federal appeals court judge from Chicago, to succeed Douglas. The Senate confirmed Stevens on December 17, and he was sworn in on December 19. See STEVENS, JOHN PAUL.

The Supreme Court handed down several rulings on the rights of citizens. On June 26, it ruled unanimously that a mental patient cannot be confined in a mental institution against his will if he is not being treated and if he is not dangerous to others and can survive in society.

Three decisions dealt with the rights of schoolchildren. See CIVIL RIGHTS (Close-Up).

Other important Supreme Court decisions:

■ A state of Utah law setting different ages for adulthood for men and women is unconstitutional.

■ A Pennsylvania law providing state aid for auxiliary services in private and parochial schools is unconstitutional.

■ The city of Richmond, Va., may annex a white suburb to alter the city's racial composition if the move serves a valid government end. See CITY.

■ States cannot refuse to pay unemployment compensation to a woman simply because she is in the last three months of pregnancy or has recently borne a child.   Carol L. Thompson

See also SUPREME COURT OF THE UNITED STATES; Section One, FOCUS ON THE NATION.

UNITED STATES CONSTITUTION. Proponents of the Equal Rights Amendment (ERA) to the Constitution, guaranteeing equal rights for women, were dealt a serious blow on Nov. 4, 1975. New Jersey and New York state voters turned down equal rights amendments for their state constitutions. Some observers speculated that the anti-ERA sentiment in those traditionally liberal states might set back efforts to win final ratification of the ERA for the U.S. Constitution.

North Dakota became the 34th state to ratify the ERA on February 3. However, ratification by 38 states is needed to make the amendment part of the Constitution. The ERA failed to win any other state ratifications, but 13 states voted it down.

Two amendments affecting the election of U.S. Presidents were under consideration by Congress. An amendment proposed on February 25 by Senator John O. Pastore (D., R.I.) would require a special presidential election if an appointed Vice-President becomes President more than a year before regular elections. Under the 25th Amendment, Gerald R. Ford became President without having been elected either President or Vice-President.

An amendment to abolish the Electoral College and allow the President to be elected by direct popular vote was cleared by the Senate Judiciary Subcommittee in May.   Darlene R. Stille

UPPER VOLTA. See AFRICA.

URUGUAY. Criticism of the military regime of President Juan M. Bordaberry Arocena was widespread throughout 1975. In part, it was due to the government's efforts to restrict such criticism. But much of it resulted from a spiraling inflation rate, an annual trade deficit of $100 million, a public debt of about $780 million, and the loss in buying power of the average worker's paycheck.

The government acted frequently to control adverse criticism. Late in April, about 2,000 workers and students were arrested to prevent demonstrations planned by the General Labor Confederation (CNT) on May 1. The CNT had been outlawed on April 15 and its funds and property confiscated. A crackdown on the leftist March 26th Movement was carried out on May 7, when 53 alleged members were arrested.

Arrests and Censorship. Other government moves against critics included the arrest on March 4 of Horacio Bazzano, secretary-general of the Uruguayan Student Federation, and several key officials of the Uruguayan Railroad Workers Union. All of them had been highly critical of the government's repressive measures.

The government also staged new attacks on the local and foreign press. A clash over agrarian policy in May involving Bordaberry and his military commanders brought strict press censorship, with newspapers forbidden to report details of the conflict. Argentine and Brazilian newspapers circulating in Uruguay that referred to the controversy were confiscated. On April 8, the weekly magazine *9 de Febrero* was banned; *Visperas*, a Roman Catholic magazine, was also closed.

Economy Measures. In March, the Bordaberry regime announced measures designed to bolster the sagging economy. They included tax exemptions for imports and wage increases of about $12 a month for all workers. To balance the wage raises, fuel prices were increased 17 per cent, and public utility rates went up 10 per cent. Uruguay also received a $17.25-million Special Drawing Rights loan from the International Monetary Fund to help hold down the country's balance-of-payments deficit and control inflation.

On May 1, the Inter-American Development Bank (IADB) approved a $14.4-million loan to help expand Uruguay's cement production. A February IADB loan was used to bolster the Uruguayan telecommunications system. Uruguay also signed an agreement to sell Brazil 55,000 short tons (50,000 metric tons) of wheat for $3 million. In other moves, severe restrictions were placed on power consumption in an effort to cut oil and petroleum imports. Paul C. Tullier

See also LATIN AMERICA (Facts in Brief Table).

UTAH. See STATE GOVERNMENT.

UTILITIES. See COMMUNICATIONS; ENERGY; PETROLEUM AND GAS; TELEPHONE.

VENEZUELA ended nearly half a century of foreign domination of its petroleum industry in 1975. On August 29, President Carlos Andres Pérez signed into law a bill nationalizing the industry and empowering the government to take complete control on Jan. 1, 1976. The 21 producing firms, the largest of them U.S.-owned, had fixed assets in Venezuela of about $5 billion. On October 28, they agreed to accept a government offer of $1.1 billion in compensation. The nation's iron-mining industry had already been nationalized on January 1, with the government agreeing to pay $101.3 million in compensation to the U.S. companies that owned the industry.

The government continued to strengthen its domestic reform programs. On January 23, Andres Pérez announced a massive Cabinet reshuffle in which 10 of the 19 posts changed hands. Two of the most significant involved an exchange of portfolios between Foreign Minister Efrain Schacht and Ramon Escovar Salom, secretary-general of the presidency. Schacht had been widely criticized for failing to maneuver the lifting of sanctions imposed against Cuba during an Organization of American States meeting considering the move in 1974. Salom, who took over as foreign minister, was an ardent supporter of a high-price policy for Venezuelan oil products in world markets.

Prisoners Escape. A third Cabinet change, the resignation of Interior Minister Luis Pinerua Ordaz, had political implications involving the escape on January 18 of 23 political prisoners from the San Carlos military prison in Caracas. The escapees included such left wing guerrilla leaders as Carlos Betancourt and Gabriel Puerta of the Red Flag movement and Francisco Prada of the National Liberation Armed Forces.

Pinerua Ordaz, as interior minister, had been criticized for laxity in guarding the prisoners. In its efforts to recapture the guerrillas, the government declared a state of emergency for all security forces. It launched a sweeping series of arrests that resulted in the detention of hundreds of Venezuelans. Leftist political leaders denounced the measures.

Foreign Affairs. Meeting in Mexico City, Mexico, on March 20, Andres Pérez and Mexico's President Luis Echeverría Alvarez formally proposed the creation of a Latin American Economic System (SELA). In a joint communiqué, the two heads of state urged the governments of 24 regional nations to help organize SELA constituent meetings.

Andres Pérez signed a joint declaration with the presidents of Colombia, Costa Rica, and Panama in March, supporting Panama's claim to full sovereignty over the Panama Canal. On April 3, Venezuela and 11 other nations formed the Association of Iron Ore Producing Countries. Paul C. Tullier

See also LATIN AMERICA (Facts in Brief Table).

VERMONT. See STATE GOVERNMENT.

VETERANS. President Gerald R. Ford formally declared an end to the "Vietnam era" on May 7, 1975, when he ended wartime veterans' benefits for new military recruits. The proclamation ended such benefits as burial allowances and death pensions. The President also sent legislation to Congress that would terminate GI Bill educational benefits for future recruits. The measure was passed by the House on October 6 and sent to the Senate. The education benefits were enacted after World War II, and continued for Korean War and Vietnam War veterans.

Unemployment Problems. Meanwhile, nearly 2-million Americans who served in the armed forces during the Vietnam era were either jobless, untrained, or uncounseled. Unemployment among Vietnam-era veterans from 20 to 24 years of age was 10.8 per cent among whites and 22.7 per cent among minorities, compared to a first-quarter unemployment rate of 8.2 per cent for all Americans.

Although the Department of Labor found that twice as many counseled applicants find jobs as do veterans who are not counseled, only about 5 per cent of the veterans applying for jobs at state employment offices receive counseling. By federal law, veterans must be given priority in job placement by federally funded state employment offices. Unqualified veterans must be enrolled promptly in training programs or given job counseling.

Federal law requires major government contractors to list openings with state employment offices. Instead of waiting for companies to list jobs, observers suggest that employment officials should go to employers to find new job openings.

Veterans Pension Study. A Veterans Administration (VA) study of pensions for veterans and their widows aged 72 and older was completed in 1975. Although the report concluded that the pension system is effective, 30.1 per cent of the veterans and 36.8 per cent of the widows said that they cannot afford to buy all the food they need.

Another 29.9 per cent said they do not have enough money for other needs. About 25 per cent have trouble paying for housing, and 28 per cent said they cannot afford needed medical care. The VA said many pensioners do not take advantage of other programs – only 3 per cent get food stamps, for example. However, if a veteran receives more than $1,500, or $3,000 for a family of two, he is not eligible for food stamps.

Disability Compensation. President Ford signed legislation on August 5 to provide cost-of-living increases in compensation payments to service-disabled veterans and to widows and children receiving dependency and indemnity compensation. The first checks bearing the increases began arriving on September 1.

The new laws increased monthly compensation rates by about 10 per cent for veterans rated as being from 10 to 50 per cent disabled. The monthly compensation for veterans who are more than 60 per cent disabled increased by 12 per cent. The allowance for dependents of veterans who are more than 50 per cent disabled was raised about 10 per cent. The law also liberalized the effective date for award hikes based on increased severity of the service-connected disability. The annual special clothing allowance was raised and dependency and indemnity rates for widows and children were increased 12 per cent.

Veterans Organizations. The American Legion held its 57th national convention in Minneapolis, Minn., from August 15 to 21. Delegates voted to increase the national organization's share of total local dues from $250 to $350, effective July 1, 1976. They also voted to join the American Cancer Society in an intensive effort to fight cancer. Harry G. Wiles of Topeka, Kans., was elected national commander.

The Veterans of Foreign Wars held its 76th national convention in Los Angeles from August 15 to 22. Delegates elected Thomas C. Walker of New London, Conn., commander in chief.

The American Veterans Committee held its 32nd convention from June 27 to 29 in South Fallsburg, N.Y. F. J. Pepper of Washington, D.C., was chosen national chairman.   Joseph P. Anderson

VICE-PRESIDENT. See Rockefeller, Nelson.

VIETNAM, NORTH. The goal of the late President Ho Chi Minh was finally achieved in 1975 with the defeat of South Vietnam. Ho had never accepted the division of Vietnam after his force defeated French forces in 1954. He sent army divisions and political workers into South Vietnam – many of the men came from there originally – and their victory on April 30 cleared the way for eventual reunification of the country under Communist rule from Hanoi. In December, officials announced reunification was set for April 30, 1976.

Le Duan, secretary-general of North Vietnam's Communist Party and the government's most important leader, traveled extensively. He went to Khmer (formerly Cambodia) in August, to China in September, and to Eastern Europe in October.

The China visit ended in apparent disagreement between the two governments. The Chinese were disturbed over Russian influence in Vietnam. North Vietnam increasingly took Russia's side in international affairs on which Moscow and Peking disagreed. In addition, China and Vietnam have long had territorial disputes in the South China Sea.

North Vietnam applied for United Nations membership in July. But the United States vetoed the application because Communist and other nations refused to consider a similar application from South Korea.   Henry S. Bradsher

See also Asia (Facts in Brief Table).

Hanoi billboard showing Ho Chi Minh proclaiming the reunification of
Vietnam celebrates the capture of Saigon and victory in the south.

VIETNAM, SOUTH. The long war in Vietnam
ended on April 30, 1975, with a complete Communist victory. North Vietnam immediately began reorganizing South Vietnam in preparation for reunification of the two countries on April 30, 1976.

Phuoc Binh, capital of Phuoc Long province, fell
to North Vietnamese Army troops on Jan. 7, 1975.
Encouraged by this victory, North Vietnam sent
more troops into South Vietnam. The fall of Ban
Me Thuot on March 10 caused South Vietnam's
President Nguyen Van Thieu to order the Central
Highlands evacuated. This turned into a rout. Hue
and Da Nang, the main cities in northern South
Vietnam, fell on March 26 and 29.

The South Vietnamese Senate on April 2 overwhelmingly approved a resolution that a "government of national union" be formed to end the
war. Politicians who normally strongly supported
Thieu in all his actions joined in approving the call
for a new government. Only one member of the
Senate voted against the resolution. The senators
criticized both Thieu and the United States for the
position in which South Vietnam found itself. They
blamed Thieu for mistakes and the United States
for not supporting the Saigon regime fully enough.

Meanwhile, Communist demolition units and
division-sized infantry units supported by tanks
were drawing closer to the South Vietnamese capital. Refugees poured into the city.

Aid Asked. President Gerald R. Ford asked the
U.S. Congress for an extra $300 million in military
aid for Saigon on January 28, but it had not been
approved by March. Ford then asked for $972 mil-
lion in emergency help on April 10, but this request
was also never approved.

As Communist forces gathered to attack Saigon,
Thieu resigned on April 21. In an impassioned address to the nation, he defended his character and
the accomplishments of his regime, while chroni-
cling its collapse. He called for peace, but also said
the successor government would fight on. He devoted most of his speech to scathing criticism of the
United States, saying that former President Richard M. Nixon had promised Saigon not only military and economic aid, but also "direct and strong
United States military intervention" in the event
the Communists broke the Paris agreement of 1973.
It was the breaking of this agreement, according to
Thieu, that resulted in South Vietnam's defeat.

Thieu was succeeded by Vice-President Tran
Van Huong, but the Communists refused to negotiate with Huong. On April 28, Duong Van Minh
became president, hoping to negotiate peace. But
the final attack was already underway. On orders
from President Ford, U.S. troops were evacuated
from Saigon on April 29 and 30. A fleet of 81 helicopters flew 1,373 Americans and 5,695 Vietnamese
to U.S. Navy ships in the South China Sea. More

509

Tent city erected on Guam housed Vietnamese refugees until they could move to quarters at reopened army camps in the United States.

than 140,000 refugees left on helicopters, planes, ships, and fishing boats. About 132,000 settled in the United States and some in other countries, but 1,546 sailed back to Vietnam in October.

Communist troops entered Saigon on April 30. They forced Minh to surrender unconditionally.

The New Regime posted military management committees in South Vietnamese cities. The Provisional Revolutionary Government (PRG) formally took over control on June 6, the sixth anniversary of its founding by the Viet Cong's National Liberation Front. But the PRG remained curiously invisible and seemingly powerless. A member of the North Vietnamese Communist Party's Politburo, Pham Hung, who had directed the war in the south, was given the senior position in public appearances, ahead of PRG officials.

Indoctrination programs were run for government and military personnel of the Thieu regime. Some former officials were resettled in rural areas, and the new official newspaper in Saigon said on October 4 that some 1.5 million of the city's 4 million inhabitants would be moved to farms.

The PRG applied for membership in the United Nations in July, but the United States vetoed the application. Henry S. Bradsher

See also ARMED FORCES; ASIA (Facts in Brief Table).

VIRGINIA. See STATE GOVERNMENT.

VISUAL ARTS. Financial problems affected many United States museums in 1975. An immediate solution – used at Detroit; Cincinnati, Ohio; and the Museum of Modern Art and the Metropolitan Museum of Art in New York City – was to shorten the museum week and raise admission prices.

Compared to the financial problem, security caused little concern in the United States. Although U.S. museums were plagued by ongoing minor thefts, they experienced nothing like the enormous thefts prevalent in the European museum world. Italy had special problems. Three Renaissance paintings – one by Raphael and two by Piero della Francesca – were stolen from the Ducal Palace in Urbino in February in one of the country's most sensational art thefts. Official statistics showed that nearly 11,000 works of art were stolen in Italy in 1974.

Other major European thefts in 1975 included two multimillion-dollar burglaries in Milan and the theft of art worth more than $4.6 million in Hannover, West Germany. In the Netherlands, a vandal slashed Rembrandt's *The Night Watch* with a bread knife, but experts said they could restore the famous painting.

International Exchanges. The year's exotic exhibitions depended upon continuing international museum cooperation. An exhibition of 30 works from the Hermitage and the Russian Museum in

Leningrad, the first old master loan exhibition from the Soviet Union to the United States, opened at the National Gallery of Art in Washington, D.C., and traveled across the country. Another Russian exhibition – "From the Land of the Scythians: Ancient Treasures 3000 B.C.-100 B.C." – was brought to the United States from museums in Ukraine through a special exchange agreement between the Metropolitan Museum and Russia. "Archaeological Finds of the People's Republic of China," already seen in Europe, was displayed at the National Gallery of Art.

International cooperation was also involved in "From David to Delacroix: French Painting 1774-1830." This vast collection of 200 works, many borrowed from French museums, was seen at the Detroit Institute of Arts and the Metropolitan Museum of Art. Among other French exhibitions was "The Age of Louis XV: French Painting 1710-1774," presented by the Art Institute of Chicago, the Toledo Museum of Art, and the National Gallery of Canada in Ottawa, Ont. "The Impressionist Epoch" at the Metropolitan Museum was small, but highly successful, partly because of an elaborate educational device accompanying the paintings. The Art Institute of Chicago presented a large survey of Claude Monet's works to record crowds.

The world of Oriental art, both Near and Far Eastern, was well represented. To coincide with the United States visit of Japanese Emperor Hirohito, 35 works from the Japanese imperial collections were displayed at the Smithsonian Institution in Washington, D.C. The influence of Japanese art in 19th-century Europe was seen in the Cleveland Museum of Art's "Japonisme" exhibition with more than 300 works. The Metropolitan Museum not only presented "Momoyama: Japanese Art in the Age of Grandeur," but also opened its new Islamic Galleries devoted to that culture's lavish decorative arts.

The American View. Several U.S. museums began to present Bicentennial celebration exhibitions. "Paul Revere's Boston 1735-1818" at the Boston Museum of Fine Arts offered colonial visual culture. Boston also displayed "Frontier America: The Far West," scheduled to travel in Europe after its American tour. "The European Vision of America" at the Cleveland Museum of Art showed how the New World appeared to artists of the Old World from the time of Columbus to the 1800s. The Brooklyn Museum displayed "Vision and Fantasy in American Painting."

The clear emphasis in several exhibitions on the academic tradition of the 1800s was part of a move to correct the imbalance imposed by the decades-long prevalence of the modern tradition. The National Collection of Fine Arts in Washington, D.C., presented "Academy: The Academic Tradition in American Art." New York City's Cultural Center,

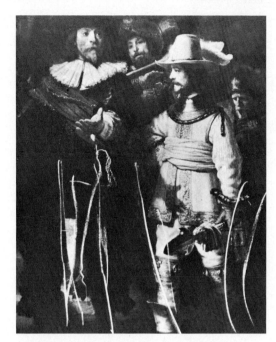

Rembrandt's famous painting *The Night Watch*, slashed in September by a man wielding a bread knife, was expected to be successfully restored.

which closed permanently later in the year, showed "Three Centuries of the American Nude," from Benjamin West to the present.

The modern tradition of the 1900s was seen in "Avant-Garde Painting and Sculpture in America 1910-1925" at the Delaware Art Center in Wilmington, where the works of 56 artists, some of them little known, illustrated the sources of American modernism. The fine abstract artist Bradley Walker Tomlin had an exhibition at the Albright-Knox Art Gallery in Buffalo, N.Y. The paintings and collages of the pioneer American modernist Arthur Dove were assembled in a traveling exhibition by the San Francisco Museum of Art.

Sculpture. Two important sculpture exhibitions were devoted to pioneer modernists. The Whitney Museum of American Art in New York City exhibited the sculpture and drawings of Elie Nadelman, the Polish-born artist whose elegant, often humorous work now seems quite contemporary. Work of the French-American Gaston Lachaise was presented by Cornell University's Johnson Art Museum in Ithaca, N.Y. The traveling exhibition was an example of the many and often little-known exhibitions offered by university galleries across the United States. Other sculpture exhibitions included the Whitney Museum's unusual gesture in placing the large abstract works of Mark di Suvero throughout New York City, while showing his smaller works in

Titan of The Arts

The world in 1975 celebrated the 500th anniversary of the birth of Michelangelo, one of the titans of art. Michelangelo Buonarroti was born in Italy in 1475. While still in his 20s, he became one of the most famous artists in Europe, and by the time he was in his late 30s, he was recognized as the greatest of living artists. Five centuries later, he is still a serious candidate to be the greatest visual artist who ever lived, a man to rank with Beethoven in music or Shakespeare in literature.

Michelangelo, more than any other, established the notion of the primary importance of the artist and of himself, in particular, as a man with a distinct and unique personality. To him, the artist was a superior being whose least action was worthy of remark and record. In his own case, he was quite right. Even more than his versatile contemporary Leonardo da Vinci, Michelangelo changed the artist's position from that of craftsman to that of a creative figure who could speak to princes, religious and secular, as their equal.

No artist other than Picasso has been so completely recorded. Yet, while more is known about Michelangelo than about almost any other great figure in the visual arts, he remains as mysterious and unapproachable as Mozart or Beethoven.

There is a consistency and pride throughout Michelangelo's life that make him at once the most transparent of artists and the most completely remote and unreachable. The intensity of his feelings is expressed in the most amazing technique in the history of Western art. But his work also embodies profound thought processes. The emotional quality of his work may be indistinctly felt, but only with a clear knowledge of his intellectual world is it possible to gauge the subtlety of his references.

Michelangelo's *Pietà*

Michelangelo is considered the greatest of tragic artists. This perhaps is an unfortunate use of the word, yet the more precise *pathetic* seems hopelessly out of place. The Italian word *terribilità* seems to capture most completely the man and his art. Sadly, it cannot be put into English, which lacks a word with the same connotation of awesome, even frightening, majesty. It also implies being far larger than life – in scale, in form, and in feeling.

Michelangelo invented the sense of the grandly heroic for Western art, and his vision has thoroughly influenced all artists who have seen his work. El Greco, who intensely disliked Michelangelo's *The Last Judgment* and proposed to do a new version, still reflects in his complicated structures a direct, if unintentional, legacy from Michelangelo. Bernini in the 1600s, Rodin in the 1800s, and even Maillol in the 1900s, all owe a debt to Michelangelo's way of seeing. It is not that Michelangelo's vision emerged without roots, but that the intensity of his vision is so powerful that the beholder innocently supposes it to be *completely* Michelangelo's invention.

The quality of Michelangelo's feeling, its intensity, and the magnificent way in which it is communicated set him apart as the first modern man, the most intensely personal of all artists, and, ultimately, the most remote. He demanded empathy from the viewer to re-create feelings of an equal intensity and quality.

His work contains the elements of classic tragedy – pity and fear to purge the emotions. This pity and fear suffuses the prophets and sibyls of the Sistine Chapel ceiling, the figures from the tomb of Pope Julius II, and the *Madonna and Child* of the Medici tombs. The joining of the most glamorous and touching physical beauty with the most intense sadness and terror produces images that haunt all subsequent representations of the human form.

Michelangelo's perfection of the heroic and elegiac style make him the most intense of all artists, full of grandeur and infinite sadness – the sadness of being aware of human imperfectibility in spite of incomparable physical beauty. The implications of transient beauty and final corruption are truly terrifying and totally sad. The result is an expression beyond tears and beyond the ordinary limits of human feeling. The beholder is genuinely in an Olympian presence.

John Maxon

Empty frames litter the Gallery of Modern Art in Milan, Italy, mute evidence of the museum's second multimillion-dollar art theft in May.

Atlanta, Ga., explored a more elegant aspect of current tendencies.

Modern European work was seen in the exhibition of the pioneer Czechoslovak abstract artist Vrantisek Kupka at the Guggenheim Museum in New York City. The Los Angeles County Museum of Art celebrated its 10th anniversary with the oft-neglected "European Painting of the 1970s."

The Art Market Place. Quality work continued to bring high prices at auctions. For instance, an important Tahitian portrait by Paul Gauguin sold for $950,000, the highest price ever paid for his work. *La Fille a l'accroche-coeur (The Girl with the Kiss-Curl)* by Henri de Toulouse-Lautrec brought a record $460,000. There was continuing speculation that the Near East would become a major world art center, and results of an old master painting auction held in Teheran, Iran, justified this expectation.

The year's major museum acquisitions were highlighted by the Metropolitan Museum's purchase of the Packard collection for $5.1 million. The 412 rare Japanese art objects, originally collected by art collector Harry Packard, were said to have exhausted the museum's purchase funds for the next five years, and this started an immediate controversy.   Joshua B. Kind

VITAL STATISTICS. See CENSUS, UNITED STATES; POPULATION, WORLD.

the museum galleries. Many hold Di Suvero to be one of the finest U.S. sculptors. The Museum of Modern Art showed the works of the English sculptor Anthony Caro. An exhibition at the Walker Art Center in Minneapolis, Minn., emphasized Claes Oldenburg's use of inanimate objects in his sculpture. Oldenburg was also commissioned to construct a large work beside a newly completed federal building in Chicago. Suburban Rolling Meadows added to the Chicago area's large group of major outdoor works with the completion of Pablo Picasso's *The Bather* in concrete. The work was constructed by a Norwegian artist, Carl Nesjar.

New Techniques. The increasing use of video as an art form was seen in both exhibition and planning. The Rockefeller Foundation awarded a small,. but significant grant to the Long Beach Museum in California for a video-editing facility; area artists will have free access to it. The new facility includes a TV station. The Long Beach Museum also was one of several to offer large anthologies of video activity. Others were the Wadsworth Atheneum in Hartford, Conn.; the Museum of Contemporary Art in Chicago; and the Whitney Museum.

The "radical new" was also seen in "Bodyworks" at Chicago's Museum of Contemporary Art. In this art form, the artist's body is used as the work of art. An exhibition of drawings by Sol LeWitt – often done on the wall – at the High Museum of Art in

WALKER, JOHN GEORGE (1952-   ), New Zealand distance runner, set a world record of 3 minutes 49.4 seconds for the mile run on Aug. 12, 1975, in Göteborg, Sweden. Walker clipped 1.6 seconds off the mark set by Filbert Bayi of Tanzania, his greatest rival, in May. See BAYI, FILBERT.

Walker's record performance came after he talked Göteborg meet officials into changing the race from a 1,500-meter run to the full mile so he could try for the record. It climaxed an impressive European tour in which he won the mile run at a June meet in Stockholm, Sweden, and the 1,500-meter run in Oslo, Norway, in August while competing in 15 international meets.

Walker first gained world prominence as a runner in 1973, and he was named the top miler of 1974 by *Track and Field News*. However, he lost to Bayi in the mile run twice during 1975, both indoor races.

Walker is one of the biggest world-class milers, standing 6 feet ¼ inch (184 centimeters) tall and weighing about 165 pounds (75 kilograms). The son of an Auckland cement contractor, Walker now works as an advertising salesman for an Auckland radio station.

Walker lives at home with his parents, and he runs more than 85 miles (137 kilometers) a week in training.   Joseph P. Spohn

See also TRACK AND FIELD.

WALLACE, GEORGE CORLEY (1919-   ), governor of Alabama, declared himself a candidate for the Democratic presidential nomination on Nov. 12, 1975. He had delayed the announcement for months to weigh the choice between running for the Democratic nomination or on a third-party ticket. Before making his announcement, he visited Europe to meet with foreign leaders. He vowed to conduct an active primary campaign.

Even before his formal announcement, Wallace ran well in the public opinion polls, and his aides initiated a massive fund-raising effort and began setting up campaign organizations in several states. Wallace continued to criticize the federal bureaucracy, and advocated that more attention be given to middle-class Americans.

Wallace carried five states running as the American Independent Party candidate for President in 1968. He was shot in May, 1972, while campaigning for the Democratic presidential nomination and was left paralyzed from the waist down. But he brushed off doubts about his physical condition in 1975, and two of his doctors said he was fit to run.

Wallace was elected to his third term as governor of Alabama in November, 1974. His first wife, Lurleen, died in 1968. He married Cornelia Ellis Snively on Jan. 4, 1971.   Kathryn Sederberg

WASHINGTON. See STATE GOVERNMENT.

WASHINGTON, D.C. Walter E. Washington became Washington, D.C.'s first elected mayor when he was sworn into office on Jan. 2, 1975. Mayor Washington, a black, had served as the appointed mayor of the city since 1967.

School superintendent Barbara A. Sizemore was dismissed from her post on October 9 after a five-month dispute over her job performance. The District of Columbia Board of Education charged her with insubordination and poor administration. Reportedly, Sizemore, a black, believed the move against her was inspired by the board's desire to retain control of the schools and to resist any decentralization moves that would give blacks more control of local schools.

Bombings and Protests. A bomb exploded in the U.S. Department of State headquarters on January 29, causing $350,000 damage to the building and leading to a rash of bomb scares and evacuations in other federal buildings. The radical Weather Underground group claimed responsibility for the blast. Two small bombs went off in offices of Aeroflot, the Russian airline, and in the Mexican Embassy on May 10, during meetings of the Organization of American States. Then, on October 27, a bomb again damaged the State Department building. A Puerto Rican nationalist group claimed responsibility.

The massive J. Edgar Hoover FBI Building in Washington, D.C., dedicated in September, is the law enforcement agency's new home.

A jobs rally sponsored by labor unions drew an estimated 60,000 persons to the national capital on April 26. A similar rally on February 5 drew an estimated 10,000 unemployed auto workers. On April 8, 2,000 strip-mine workers staged a protest against pending legislation that would apply stricter controls to such mining operations. About 6,000 demonstrators marched on the Capitol on October 25 to protest forced school busing.

Union pressmen struck the *Washington Post* on October 1 in a dispute over cuts in the number of union members employed on each shift. The pressmen damaged all presses used by the *Post* to print its daily newspaper editions. After losing a day of publication, the *Post* resumed publication on October 3 by printing at out-of-town locations. It resumed full publication in its own pressroom on October 13, with the strike still in progress.

Living Costs rose 7 per cent in the Washington, D.C., area between August, 1974, and August, 1975. By mid-1975, food costs had registered a 9.9 per cent increase over the preceding year and the unemployment rate had risen 1.1 per cent to 6.1 per cent, while the average earnings of factory workers went up 9.8 per cent to $11,607 per year.

The U.S. Census Bureau reported in 1975 that Washington lost 3 per cent of its population between 1970 and 1973. The city had an estimated 733,801 persons as of July 1, 1973.   James M. Banovetz

WATERGATE. The Watergate special prosecutor's office wound up its work on Oct. 15, 1975, reporting the conviction of 51 persons and 19 corporations in a final summary of its investigation of the greatest political scandal in American history. Yet it never solved some major Watergate mysteries.

Charles F. Ruff became the fourth special prosecutor on October 17, replacing Henry S. Ruth, Jr. The unit was maintained mainly to prepare arguments against appeals of Watergate convictions.

The Final Report did not summarize the evidence against former President Richard M. Nixon, who escaped prosecution because President Gerald R. Ford pardoned him. Although Nixon never admitted any guilt in the Watergate affair, the report stated: "These transcripts showed his early involvement in the cover-up and belied contrary claims that he had repeatedly made. . . ."

The report recommended a constitutional amendment to make clear whether an incumbent President can be indicted, and if so, for what types of crimes. The Watergate prosecutors also recommended a series of steps to prevent more Watergates that included establishing a division of government crimes in the Department of Justice to make a concentrated effort against corrupt officials.

The report advised against the appointment of an attorney general who had served in any high political position. The report added that heads of the Federal Bureau of Investigation (FBI), the Secret Service, and the Internal Revenue Service (IRS) should be chosen from highly qualified individuals outside of politics.

To prevent the political use of the Central Intelligence Agency, the FBI, or the IRS, the report called for adoption of written policies on intelligence gathering that would be made public after review by a presidential board.

The Trials. On January 1, a federal jury returned guilty verdicts against four of Nixon's men – former advisers H. R. Haldeman and John D. Ehrlichman, former Attorney General John N. Mitchell, and former campaign official Robert C. Mardian. Kenneth W. Parkinson, a lawyer for the re-election campaign, was acquitted of obstruction of justice charges.

Federal Judge John J. Sirica in February sentenced Haldeman, Mitchell, and Ehrlichman to prison terms of at least $2^1/2$ years and not more than 8 years for conspiracy, obstruction of justice, and lying under oath. Mardian, convicted only of conspiracy, was sentenced to at least 10 months and not more than 3 years in prison. They appealed their convictions. Conspiracy charges against Gordon C. Strachan, a Haldeman aide, were dropped on March 10. Strachan claimed he had been promised limited immunity in return for his testimony at the cover-up trial.

Nixon Testifies. Two members of the Watergate grand jury and members of the special prosecutor's staff questioned Nixon under oath for 11 hours on June 23 and 24 in San Clemente, Calif. The extraordinary arrangement was made because of Nixon's health and "other legal considerations," the prosecutors said. Nixon apparently did not provide any more incriminating information, because the third and last Watergate grand jury was dismissed on July 3 without returning additional indictments.

Nixon submitted to questioning again in August for a civil suit he brought to challenge a 1974 law providing for federal custody of the White House tapes and other documents that Nixon claimed belonged to him. See NIXON, RICHARD M.

Remaining Mysteries. The report conceded that the prosecutors were unable to determine who was responsible for the $18^1/2$-minute gap in a taped conversation between Haldeman and Nixon that took place three days after the break-in at Democratic National Headquarters in the Watergate complex.

No prosecution was possible in the cases of wiretapping of 17 persons for alleged national security reasons or the harassment of White House "enemies" by the IRS. The Watergate investigators did not prosecute anyone in connection with a secret $100,000 cash contribution made by recluse industrialist Howard Hughes in 1970 to Nixon's friend, Charles G. (Bebe) Rebozo.

John B. Connally, Jr., *wearing hat, left,* was acquitted of bribery charges. Maurice H. Stans, *above,* was fined for violating campaign laws.

Related Cases. Former Secretary of Commerce Maurice H. Stans pleaded guilty in March to five misdemeanor charges of violating campaign-finance laws and was fined $5,000 on May 14.

On April 17, former Treasury Secretary John B. Connally, Jr., was acquitted of charges that he accepted $10,000 as a payoff for his 1971 support of increased milk subsidies. After the acquittal, the Watergate prosecutor's office dropped charges of perjury and conspiracy to obstruct justice against Connally.

On November 12, literary appraiser Ralph G. Newman was convicted of making false statements regarding Nixon's vice-presidential papers. Nixon had donated the papers to the government and claimed a huge tax deduction.

Although most of the charges were leveled against Republicans, the Democratic Party did not escape without blemish. Jack L. Chestnut, campaign manager in 1970 for Senator Hubert H. Humphrey (D., Minn.), was convicted on May 8 of accepting an illegal $12,000 contribution from Associated Milk Producers, Incorporated. But the prosecutor's office announced that it would not prosecute Democratic National Committee Chairman Robert S. Strauss on charges of accepting an illegal $50,000 campaign contribution from Ashland Oil Company in 1971, because the statute of limitations had expired.   William J. Eaton

WEATHER. The United States and Russia submitted a joint proposal to the world disarmament conference in Geneva, Switzerland, on Aug. 21, 1975, that would outlaw attempts to manipulate the weather or change the environment for military or other hostile purposes.

The U.S.-Russian accord resulted from a decision reached at the July, 1974, meeting in Moscow between President Richard M. Nixon and Communist Party General Secretary Leonid I. Brezhnev. Discussions were continuing, and the final text was expected to be submitted to the 1976 session of the United Nations General Assembly.

Weather Satellites. The second Synchronous Meteorological Satellite (SMS-2) was launched on February 6, first photographing West Africa. It was permanently positioned in a stationary orbit and, like SMS-1, will continuously monitor weather conditions in and near the United States. The two satellites can also obtain extremely accurate pictures. The SMS-2 was launched by the National Aeronautics and Space Administration (NASA).

The Ozone Problem. The dilemma over what caused the decline in upper atmospheric ozone continued in 1975. There was a strong possibility that chlorofluorocarbon gases released into the air from aerosol spray cans and nitric oxides from industrial pollutants were reducing the ozone layer in the atmosphere through a series of chemical reactions.

NASA plans to use the Copernicus Orbiting Astronomical Laboratory now in orbit to investigate this.

Meanwhile, the National Oceanic and Atmospheric Administration issued a report in August indicating that scientists do not understand why the amount of ozone in the atmosphere fluctuates. They pointed out that the recent decline in ozone may not be caused by particles or gases released by man. The rate of ozone decrease was 0.7 per cent in 1971 and 1972, but only 0.2 per cent in 1973 and 1974. See ENVIRONMENT (Close-Up).

Project Dustorm, a unique experiment to investigate the role that dust plays in changing severe storms, was conducted from April 8 to May 8. The study focused particularly on storms that produce hail and tornadoes. Researchers used instrumented aircraft, weather balloons, and radar to gather data. They collected hailstones over a 12-state area and analyzed them for their dust content. They also looked for a possible correlation between the size and distribution of hailstones and the amount of clay and organic aerosol particles they contained.

The first results from the study showed that storms that collected the largest amounts of dust were less likely to produce large tornadoes. Dust sucked into these storms could be observed from surface stations as well as through high-resolution satellite pictures. The assumption that dust particles may play a role in the hailstorm appears to be supported by the data gathered thus far.

U.S. Weather. There was seasonable weather over much of the United States in 1975, with several short periods of abnormalities. The most noteworthy weather problem was damage to the wheat crop in the Red River Valley of North Dakota and Minnesota in June. An early freeze throughout the North-Central states in September caused only minor damage. Dry weather in the Western plains delayed the planting of the winter wheat crop.

Russia had a very poor growing season. A drought combined with very high temperatures resulted in a poor grain crop. See AGRICULTURE; RUSSIA.

Tornadoes and Hurricanes. Several hundred tornadoes occurred in the United States, but only a few caused severe damage. Most states had fewer than the average number of tornadoes, but Florida and Nebraska were notable exceptions. A tornado roared through Omaha, Nebr., on May 6, killing three persons and causing $150 million in damage.

On September 23, Hurricane Eloise struck the west Florida Panhandle. Damage was most severe near the coast, where high winds, heavy rains, and a large storm surge occurred.   Edward W. Pearl

See also DISASTERS.

WEIGHT LIFTING. See SPORTS.

Some fully clothed Parisians and tourists take a cooling dip near the Eiffel Tower to get relief from a hotter-than-normal European summer.

WEST INDIES

WEST INDIES. A labor crisis, an international dispute, and a rising sense of nationalism played dominant roles in the English-speaking islands of the Caribbean in 1975. In March and April, the island state of Trinidad and Tobago endured a series of crippling crises in its oil and sugar industries. Workers in the two major industries went on strike, demanding wage increases, more fringe benefits, and nationalization of the oil industry. After eight weeks of turmoil, with frequent clashes between strikers and police, the government offered compromises, and the sugar workers eventually returned to work on April 19. The oil workers remained intransigent, however, and the government, to ensure distribution of oil and petroleum products, called out the army and took over all gasoline stations.

Fishing Dispute. Negotiations broke down in August between the United States and the Bahamas in a dispute involving lobster-fishing rights. The dispute had arisen when the Bahamian government enacted a law prohibiting lobster fishing in an area covering about 100,000 square miles (260,000 square kilometers) of the continental shelf. The United States regards half of the area as international waters in which about 2,000 U.S. fishermen have been active. Following Bahamian rejection of a $6-million settlement proposed by the United States, the U.S. government announced it would submit the case to the International Court of Justice in The Hague, the Netherlands, for arbitration.

Jamaica continued to consolidate its control over its bauxite industry, a major source of national income. It announced in January that it had acquired a 51 per cent share in various privately owned bauxite companies operating on the island and had also canceled land concessions. The companies involved were given seven-year management contracts, and compensation was being worked out.

Anguilla was granted a larger measure of self-government on May 30, under a compromise agreement arranged by the West Indies Associated States of St. Christopher (St. Kitts)-Nevis-Anguilla. Under the new arrangement, Anguilla – which helped to found the association in 1967 – gains control of additional ministries.

Independence Plans. Two islands, St. Vincent and Antigua, began negotiating to gain independence from Great Britain. On January 3, St. Vincent's Governor Sir Rupert John announced that a formal request had been made to the British government. A similar announcement was made by Antigua on May 9. Both islands hoped to become independent in 1976.   Paul C. Tullier

See also LATIN AMERICA (Facts in Brief Table).

WEST VIRGINIA. See STATE GOVERNMENT.

WILDLIFE. See CONSERVATION.

Archbishop Makarios, president of Cyprus, discusses his country's plight at a Commonwealth conference held from April 29 to May 6 in Jamaica.

WILSON, MARGARET BUSH (1920-   ), a St. Louis civil rights attorney, became chairman of the National Association for the Advancement of Colored People (NAACP) on Jan. 13, 1975. She succeeded Bishop Stephen G. Spottswood, who died in December, 1974.

Wilson is the daughter of the late James Bush, Sr., a real estate broker who was the primary organizer of black real estate brokers in bringing a suit against restrictive covenants in housing. Their successful case, *Shelley v. Kramer* (1948), was to housing discrimination what the historic *Brown v. Board of Education of Topeka* decision in 1954 was to segregated education. Margaret Wilson's first case after graduation from Lincoln University Law School in Jefferson City, Mo., in 1943 involved incorporating the brokers who brought that suit.

She majored in economics and mathematics at Talladega (Ala.) College before studying law, then practiced real estate law in St. Louis and served as an assistant attorney general in Missouri. She first became active in the NAACP in St. Louis.

Wilson was elected the first woman president of the 6,000-member NAACP branch in St. Louis in 1958. Later, she served as president of the Missouri State Conference of NAACP Branches for four years. In 1963, she was elected to the NAACP National Board of Directors.   Foster Stockwell

WISCONSIN. See STATE GOVERNMENT.

WOHLHUTER, *WOOL hutter,* **RICK** (1948-   ), track star, won the Sullivan Award in February, 1975, as the United States outstanding amateur athlete in 1974. Wohlhuter won 26 straight races and set world records in the 880-yard run and the 1,000-meter run and a United States record in the 800-meter run.

The 135-pound (61-kilogram) Wohlhuter is a tenacious competitor noted for his ability to sustain a punishing pace. He fell during his semifinal heat in the 800-meter run at the 1972 Olympic Games. He raced to catch up, but was eliminated by a stride.

Wohlhuter began running in junior high school in St. Charles, Ill., and won the half-mile in the Illinois state high school meets in 1966 and 1967. Leg injuries hampered him during his college career at Notre Dame University. However, Wohlhuter continued to run after his graduation in 1971. Now an insurance claim adjuster in Chicago, he runs for the University of Chicago Track Club.

Because of leg problems, Wohlhuter runs only from 40 to 50 miles (64 to 80 kilometers) a week in training. Most top runners run much more in practice. He passed up a chance to become a professional runner in 1975 and began competing in the mile run. Wohlhuter hoped to compete in the 1976 Olympics in Montreal, Canada.   Joseph P. Spohn

WRESTLING. See SPORTS.

WYOMING. See STATE GOVERNMENT.

YEMEN (ADEN). The People's Democratic Republic of Yemen, maverick of the Arab world with its extreme socialism and militant support of revolutionary groups in the Arabian Peninsula, moderated its position in 1975 to reduce its political and economic isolation. Aden limited its support of the Popular Front for the Liberation of Oman (PFLO) rebels against Omani Sultan Sayyid Qaboos bin Said Al Bu Said largely to propaganda attacks on Qaboos for his use of Iranian troops.

On October 17, however, Omani airplanes and artillery struck PFLO headquarters and other rebel targets near Hauf in Yemen. The air strike also hit a Yemeni security barracks in the area. During the same operation, Iranian troops tried to cut rebel supply lines into Oman. See IRAN; OMAN.

At the sixth general congress of the ruling National Front (NF) in March, NF Secretary-General Abd al-Fattah Ismail said Aden would establish relations with Bahrain, Qatar, and the United Arab Emirates on a basis of mutual respect. In September, discussions began with the Yemen Arab Republic (Yemen [Sana]) to revive plans for unity.

In May, the government leased Perim Island, at the southern entrance to the Red Sea, to Egypt, acting as the Arab League agent, in return for financial aid from Arab oil-producing states.

A major factor in Yemen's policy shift was the emergence of a moderate government faction, led by Presidential Council chairman Salim Ali Rubayya, that is more concerned with economic progress than political ideology. Pay increases and a pension plan fully financed by the government and public corporations went into effect on March 25. The working day was set at eight hours, with Thursday afternoons and Fridays days of rest.

Foreign Economic Aid. In February, Yemen and Iraq set up a joint fishing company, with $30-million in capital, to exploit Yemen's rich Red Sea and Indian Ocean fisheries. The World Bank also loaned $1.6 million in January for fisheries development and $15.5 million on May 22 for a highway running 222 miles (358 kilometers) from the port of Al Mukalla through the fertile Hadhramaut Valley. Kuwait's Fund for Arab Economic Development loaned $15 million for the same project. In June, Libya funded a fish-processing plant.

The June reopening of the Suez Canal spurred efforts to revive the port of Aden. A ministry of trade and supply was established in April, and the government completed an emergency plan on June 3 to permit ships of up to 120,000 tons, with a maximum draft of 43 feet (13.2 meters), to enter the harbor. A new crane was installed to handle heavy cargo. To encourage trade, Aden retained the anchorage and docking fees charged before the canal was closed in 1967, and a special free-trade zone was established for transit goods.   William Spencer

See also MIDDLE EAST (Facts in Brief Table).

YEMEN (SANA). Friction between the civilian Cabinet of Prime Minister Muhsin bin Ahmad al-Ayni and Command Council Chairman Ibrahim Mohamed al-Hamdi came to a head on Jan. 16, 1975. Colonel Hamdi, who holds supreme power in the Yemen Arab Republic, dismissed Ayni, charging that he had lost the confidence of the Consultative Assembly formed to write a constitution for the country. Sources said that Ayni had tried to reduce or cut off government subsidies paid to the tribal sheiks, who are strongly represented in the Assembly. Abdulaziz Abdul Ghani, founder of the Central Bank of Yemen, succeeded Ayni.

But factional rivalries continued to delay the constitution. In April, Hamdi dismissed a number of senior army officers and ministers who had supported Ayni. More ministers were sacked in July, and a new central organization for state security, responsible only to Hamdi, was set up. A tribal plot to restore the monarchy under Prince Mohammed ben Hussein, who lives in exile in Saudi Arabia, was uncovered on August 16. Sheik Bazel al-Wajih was arrested and police found evidence that Hussein and some army officers and tribal sheiks were plotting. Hussein is the cousin of the former ruler, Iman Mohammed al-Badr. Concern over this loss of tribal support led Hamdi to order all Russian military advisers to leave the country.   William Spencer

See also MIDDLE EAST (Facts in Brief Table).

YOUNG MEN'S CHRISTIAN ASSOCIATION (YMCA). Canada's YMCA in 1975 became the first in the world to elect a woman as national president. Raynell Andreychuk, a 30-year-old lawyer from Moose Jaw, Sask., became leader of the organization, whose membership is about 42 per cent women, in May.

Through the World Alliance of YMCA's, the International Division of the United States YMCA helped care for 132,000 Vietnamese in refugee camps. It also tried to "internationalize" every YMCA in the United States to gain additional financial support for the work of the World Alliance, involving 100 million people in 86 countries.

The YMCA also launched a development program called repositioning "to provide greater service for a greater number and wider spectrum of people; [achieve] a more favorable and penetrating impact on the nation; and [develop] more and new financial resources." As part of this project, more than 600 of the 1,842 YMCA's, in cooperation with educational and medical organizations, began a six-year cardiovascular health program, and 132 YMCA's in minority communities are scheduled to develop ethnic cultural centers.

The American YMCA's registered membership reached 8.5 million in 1975. Of these, 34.6 per cent were women. Operating revenues went over the $300-million mark.   Joseph P. Anderson

YOUNG WOMEN'S CHRISTIAN ASSOCIATION (YWCA). With the theme "Women — Empowered and Acting," four national YWCA meetings took a serious look at the impact of the economic crisis on women in the United States and around the world in 1975. They emphasized the status of women in developing countries.

YWCA's in more than 400 communities across the United States worked on a variety of programs in 1975. These included consciousness-raising sessions, intervention projects designed to help young women who might otherwise face imprisonment, and resource centers designed to help women and girls who are rape victims.

A new pamphlet, *A Job at the End — Guidelines for Teen Counseling, Training, and Career Development*, offers exercises and advice designed to prepare young women for employment. It is designed to be used with two other YWCA publications, *Attention Is Needed, Action Is Called For*, and *Let's Try a Workshop with Teen Women*, both based on 1,100 questionnaires answered by teen-agers who indicated that job counseling was one of their greatest needs.

Also published in 1975 were *From Deep Roots — the Story of the YWCA's Religious Dimensions* and *Women — A Power for Change*, the report of an international consultation of YWCA leaders from 16 countries, held in 1974.   Joseph P. Anderson

YOUTH ORGANIZATIONS in the United States emphasized Bicentennial programs and further cooperation with the President's Council on Physical Fitness and Sports in promoting fitness in 1975.

Boy Scouts of America (BSA). The 14th World Jamboree opened on July 30 at the Norwegian resort town of Lillehammer. Some 2,500 American scouts were among the 15,000 participants.

The newly elected president of the BSA, Arch Monson, of San Francisco, announced that physical fitness will play an even larger role in future plans of the organization. "Be Prepared for Life, Be Safe, Be Fit" was adopted as the national theme for 1975. Programs emphasizing fitness and safety included an effort to teach every Scout and Cub Scout to swim, and the Cub Scout Bicycle Safety Program, which emphasizes knowledge of traffic rules and bicycle maintenance.

Boys' Clubs of America adopted "Gift of Service to the Nation" as the 1975 Bicentennial theme. Individual clubs were helped by a how-to-do-it Bicentennial kit. The 69th annual conference of Boys' Clubs was held in Chicago from May 25 to 29 with delegates representing 1,100 Boys' Clubs attending. The National Boy of the Year for 1975, Kenneth Ivory, 17, of the Milwaukee Boys' Club was honored by President Gerald R. Ford at the White House in March. The Epstein Memorial Foundation, which assists Boys' Club members who have

Boy Scouts from all over the world exchange names and addresses
with new-found friends at the 1975 World Scout Jamboree in Norway.

special talents in the arts, celebrated its 25th anniversary in 1975.

Camp Fire Girls. The National Council of Camp Fire Girls approved a design for the future of the organization at the quadrennial meeting in Houston in November, 1975. A planning committee, given the task of analyzing the future needs of youth and the organization's ability to meet them, presented its recommendations in 1974.

Camp Fire experimented with new approaches to leadership. Traditionally, Camp Fire groups have been led by one or two adults and assisted by a local sponsor. To encourage groups in difficult-to-serve areas and provide leadership stability and variety, pilot-project councils were tested. In this test, expanded teams of from two to five adults – both women and men – share responsibility for each group of girls.

4-H Clubs concentrated on Bicentennial programs in 1975. In one county, 4-H'ers planted more than 200 trees. Many clubs in northern Rhode Island restored historical cemeteries in their communities. Early colonists maintained a family burial plot on nearly every farm, and many of these have been forgotten. But 4-H'ers looked up the records and restored the cemeteries.

Michigan's 4-H has introduced heritage programs for Americans of African and Spanish descent. The programs are designed to help 4-H'ers learn more about the cultures of Africa and Spanish America, and include studies of music, dance, drama, food, crafts, and history.

Future Farmers of America (FFA). With the 1975 theme of "A Chance for Growth," the national FFA organization did just that last year. Membership increased by more than 20,000 to 485,000 in more than 7,700 chapters.

The FFA Foundation announced sponsorship of the first world conference in agricultural education. The conference, to be held in Kansas City, Mo., during the National FFA Convention in 1976, will feature seminars on worldwide vocational agriculture education.

A record 20,200 FFA members, vocational agriculture instructors, and guests attended the 48th National FFA Convention in Kansas City in November. FFA's highest awards, Star Farmer and Star Agribusinessman of America, were presented to Daniel Worcester, a 21-year-old livestock and crop farmer from Hill City, Kans., and Bryce Westlake, a 20-year-old custom meat processor from Kinnear, Wyo. The Bowman FFA chapter of Bowman, S.C., was judged the best in the FFA community-improvement program, Building Our American Communities.

Girl Scouts of the United States of America reached the midpoint in their three-year Bicentennial project in 1975. "Find America's Hidden Heroines" is a major part of the program, and millions of Girl Scouts have set out to discover the unknown women and girls who contributed to the building of the nation.

By searching through historical documents and interviewing individuals, Girl Scouts have discovered women and girls who accomplished daring or unusual feats. For example, Tiny Broadwick of North Carolina made history in Los Angeles in 1913 by making the first parachute jump from an airplane. And JoAnn Winkler of Madison, Wis., successfully protested against discrimination on the basis of sex and in 1974 became the first newspaper-delivery girl in Madison. Julia Joe, a Navajo Indian from Arizona, set an unusual record by weaving the largest Navajo rug ever made. It was 36 by 26 feet (11 by 8 meters), and weighed 250 pounds (110 kilograms).

Community groups in Wenatchee, Wash., rallied around a Girl Scout plan to turn Dry Gulch, an old 6-acre (2.4-hectare) gravel quarry and dump, into an arboretum. The city commissioners approved the plan, and the mayor asked the National Guard to help clean up the dump. Local landscape architects, nursery owners, and the Audubon Society helped the girls plant trees and develop trails. When the arboretum is completed in 1976, the Girl Scouts' Bicentennial gift to their city will serve as a recreational area and outdoor classroom.

Gloria D. Scott was elected president of the Girl Scouts at the 1975 National Convention, held in October in Washington, D. C. The 37-year-old educator is the first black woman to hold the post in the 63-year history of the group. The convention also voted overwhelmingly not to admit boys.

Girls Clubs of America (GCA) held its 30th annual conference in New York City in April, 1975, with almost 500 representatives attending. "Expectations Unlimited" was the theme, and the keynote session was a salute to International Women's Year, in which Congresswoman Shirley Chisholm (D., N.Y.) and Lieutenant Governor Mary Anne Krupsak of New York participated.

GCA now has 230 centers serving more than 180,000 girls from 6 years of age to high school age. The centers usually function in areas unserved by other youth agencies. Approximately 68 per cent of the clubs are located in low-income areas and 30 per cent of the members are black, Indian, Oriental, or Spanish-speaking.

Junior Achievement (JA). The 32nd National Achievers Conference was held in August in Bloomington, Ind. The 2,500 teen-agers surveyed at the conference called for a reduced federal budget and revitalization of the private economic sector.

The young conference delegates represented almost 200,000 students who operated businesses on their own in the national Junior Achievement business education program. Joseph P. Anderson

YUGOSLAVIA intensified its crackdown on dissenters in 1975 and searched for greater economic stability. Relations with Russia deteriorated late in the year, while those with the West became closer.

Eight liberal Marxist professors were suspended from the Philosophy Department of Belgrade University on January 28, and their scholarly journal, *Praxis*, was suppressed in Zagreb on February 18. It had been the only legal publication that criticized the government. Writer and university lecturer Mihajlo Mihajlov was sentenced in Novi Sad on February 28 to seven years at hard labor for "hostile propaganda."

The Yugoslav state presidency set up a special top-level Committee for the Defense of the Constitutional Order on February 20, under the chairmanship of Vladimir Bakaric. The powerful eight-man unit was to exert stricter controls within the country and serve as a kind of "superpresidency." On May 12, Bakaric became vice-president.

Seven pro-Russian activists were sentenced to prison terms ranging from 18 months to nine years in Tuzla, Bosnia, on July 2, for their "dogmatic, Cominformist, Stalinist" attitudes. Other alleged Soviet sympathizers were arrested between August and October in various parts of Yugoslavia. On October 15, the presidium launched a formal campaign against pro-Russian Stalinists and, in No-

Yugoslav President Josip Broz Tito cuts his 83rd birthday cake during celebrations in Belgrade on May 25 as his wife Jovanka looks on happily.

vember, accused Russia of backing the Stalinists.

Yugoslav Prime Minister Dzemal Bijedic visited China in October. Yugoslavia continued to improve relations with China's ally, Albania, and with Greece, whose proposal for a Balkan Economic Conference was accepted by Yugoslavia.

Western Ties. Yugoslavia signed a treaty with Italy on November 10, formally confirming the 1953 division of the disputed Trieste territory. Relations with Austria, which grew tense in May over the rights of the Slovene minority in Austria, calmed down in October when the two countries signed a cultural agreement. Yugoslavia and the United States signed an agreement to step up mutual economic cooperation on May 13, and President Gerald R. Ford visited Yugoslavia in August.

Trade Deficit. Yugoslavia's trade deficit was $2.8 billion at the end of August, $1.5 billion of it with European Community (Common Market) countries. Exports to the West went down 25 per cent in the first seven months of the year, while imports rose 12 per cent. Exports to other Communist countries were 23 per cent higher and imports from them 8 per cent higher. Yugoslavia's annual inflation rate topped 30 per cent and nearly 600,000 persons were unemployed in July. Labor productivity increased only 0.3 per cent, and the 1975 harvest was the worst in 10 years.   Chris Cviic

See also EUROPE (Facts in Brief Table).

ZAIRE. President Mobutu Sese Seko said on June 17, 1975, that his government had uncovered a plot to assassinate him. Several generals were among those arrested. On September 1, a military tribunal sentenced seven army officers to death and 26 others to prison terms.

Mobutu's government charged that the United States Central Intelligence Agency (CIA) had sponsored the plot, and Mobutu expelled the U.S. ambassador on June 18. However, some observers believed that this charge was designed to rebut criticism that Mobutu was too pro-American and to divert attention from Zaire's internal problems.

Falling world prices for copper, Zaire's main export, along with rising import costs for oil and other items plunged Zaire into serious economic difficulty. In April, copper prices fell to about half their 1974 level, and by June, Zaire was unable to make payments on its foreign debts. Mobutu was forced to seek additional U.S. aid.

Marxist rebels in eastern Zaire crossed Lake Tanganyika on May 19, kidnaped three American students and one Dutch student from an animal research center in Tanzania, and held them for ransom. They released the hostages one by one over the next two months, freeing the last on July 25, after receiving a ransom of $40,000.   John D. Esseks

See also AFRICA (Facts in Brief Table).

ZAMBIA. See AFRICA.

ZOOLOGY. Robert B. Lockard and Donald Owings of the University of Washington in Seattle reported in 1975 that bannertail kangaroo rats, which normally forage for food at night, stop or greatly reduce their foraging when the moon is bright. After conducting a series of experiments, the researchers concluded the rats reduce their activity when the moon is bright because such predators as coyotes, kit foxes, and owls can easily see them in bright moonlight.

Lockard and Owings used automatic recorders to determine when the rats ate at specific bait stations. For one hour each night over a period of six weeks, they placed an artificial moon – a bright disk – above each station that appeared only when the real moon was not visible. Rat activity was greatly reduced when either the artificial moon or the real moon was shining. During the next month, the artificial moons were not used, and the rats were less active while the moon was shining. Then, during the next six weeks the scientists placed a dim, artificial moon at each station that produced some light for one hour each night. However, rat foraging did not subside under the dim, artificial moonlight.

The scientists concluded that only a certain amount of light above a given threshold level caused the rats to stop foraging. It was not some biological clock within the rats, running on lunar time, they decided. Nor was it the appearance of a luminous disk, because the dim, artificial moon had no effect. In other words, the rats' protective action was triggered by the amount of light by which predators might discover their presence at night.

Fish Antifreeze. Such fish as winter flounders and Atlantic tomcod, which live in subzero waters in winter, are known to have large-molecule compounds in their blood that serve as an antifreeze. John G. Duman and Arthur L. DeVries of the Scripps Institution of Oceanography in La Jolla, Calif., reported in 1975 that these fish synthesize the antifreeze compounds only when they need them. They stop producing the antifreeze when the days grow longer and temperatures rise. Both changes are necessary to stop the production of antifreeze.

The scientists reported that southern varieties of one species of arctic fish cannot produce the antifreeze substance, but their northern cousins can. They said that the ability to stop or start producing the antifreeze is presumably an adaptation developed because production requires so much energy that it is worthwhile to stop production when it is not needed.

It was announced in May that the first specimen of an as yet unnamed fish was found in the Pacific Ocean off the Northwest coast of the United States. According to Robert Lavenberg of the Los Angeles County Museum of Natural History, it is a member of the *Psychrolutidae* (cold-swimming) family, genus *Psychroluten*.   Barbara N. Benson

Smokey Bear, symbol of fire prevention, bowed to age in May. An arthritic 25, he retired to the National Zoo in Washington, D.C.

ZOOS AND AQUARIUMS. With conservation their predominant concern, officials of zoological parks and aquariums throughout the world continued to emphasize breeding captive species. Notable achievements in 1975 included the hatching of mountain toucans (tropical American birds) at the Los Angeles Zoo; a Bataleur eagle at the St. Louis Zoo, and a cock of the rock (South American bird) and a kiwi (New Zealand bird) at the National Zoological Park in Washington, D.C.

Other rarities included a Fiji Island iguana born in the William Land Park Zoo at Sacramento, Calif.; the births of spot-necked otters at the North Carolina Zoological Park, Raleigh; and a manatee at the Miami Seaquarium in Florida. Significant, too, were second-generation births of an Asiatic elephant at the Los Angeles Zoo and of a clouded leopard at Cheyenne Mountain Zoo in Colorado Springs, Colo.

Protecting Threatened Species. However, even as zoos continued to record breeding successes, more species were added to the list of those threatened with extinction. Particular attention was focused on the plight of six different species of marmoset whose natural ranges in South America are rapidly disappearing as their tropical forest homelands are destroyed for agricultural and industrial development. One of the six, the golden lion marmoset, is becoming well established in breeding col-

onies in several U.S. zoos, while the wild population in Brazil has dwindled to probably less than 600 animals. Another species, the cotton-top marmoset, has been commonly sold in pet stores but is now recognized as an endangered species.

The New York Zoological Society set up a survival center on St. Catherine's Island in Georgia for breeding and maintaining endangered species. Among the animals there are the addax, gemsbok, and sable antelope.

New Exhibits. The American Association of Zoological Parks and Aquariums exhibits award went to Brookfield Zoo, near Chicago, for its realistic Saharan Predator exhibit. In addition to simulating the desert habitat closely, the exhibit promotes the natural behavior of desert lions and panthers.

The National Zoological Park in Washington completely renovated its Monkey House and remodeled its yards for pachyderms. Lions and cheetahs also have new facilities at the Cincinnati Zoo, and the Indianapolis Zoological Park has new units for lions and leopards. The zoo in Denver opened its Bird World, with more than 100 species of birds in 12 major exhibits, and the Philadelphia Zoological Gardens added to its African Plains exhibit.

A large aquarium and a dolphinarium were planned as part of a 700-acre (283-hectare) park at Teheran, Iran. Zoos were also under construction in Saudi Arabia and Kuwait.   George B. Rabb

Section Five

World Book Supplement

In its function of keeping WORLD BOOK owners up to date, THE WORLD BOOK YEAR BOOK herewith presents significant new articles from the 1976 edition of THE WORLD BOOK ENCYCLOPEDIA. These articles should be indexed in THE WORLD BOOK ENCYCLOPEDIA by means of THE YEAR BOOK cross-reference tabs.

INDIAN RESERVATION

INDIAN RESERVATION, in the United States, is an area set aside for the use of Indians. The nation's approximately 285 federal and state Indian reservations cover more than 50 million acres (20 million hectares) in about 30 states. About 800,000 Indians live in the United States, and almost half of them make their home on a reservation.

Indian reservations are owned by the Indians and are held in trust for them by the federal or state governments. The Bureau of Indian Affairs, an agency of the Department of the Interior, manages most of the federal programs on reservations.

Canada has more than 2,200 areas set aside for Indians. These areas are called *reserves*.

Description. Indian reservations differ greatly in size and population. Some California reservations known as *rancherias* cover less than 10 acres (4 hectares) each and have fewer than 10 Indians. The Navajo reservation, the largest U.S. Indian reservation, is about the size of West Virginia. It covers about 14 million acres (6 million hectares) in Arizona, New Mexico, and Utah. About 100,000 Navajos live there.

Indian reservations consist of a wide variety of land. Some spread across desert and mountain areas of the Southwest, and others occupy forest and lake regions of the Midwest and Northwest. Still others cover the great plains between Oklahoma and Montana.

Farming ranks as the chief economic activity on most Indian reservations. Manufacturing provides a small but growing source of employment and income. Leading industries on Indian lands include jewelry making and wood processing. A number of tribes lease mineral rights, operate businesses, and offer tourist attractions on their reservations. But most reservations lack well-developed economies. About 40 per cent of the reservation Indians have no job. Indians who live on reservations have the highest unemployment rate and the lowest average income of any U.S. group.

Living conditions on the reservations are generally substandard. Some Indian lands have modern homes, but inadequate housing is a widespread problem. Reservation Indians also have the least education and the poorest health among all U.S. groups.

History. In 1758, the New Jersey Colony established the first Indian reservation in North America. The colony set aside land for the Delaware Indians at Indian Mills in what is now Burlington County.

During the early and mid-1800's, advancing white settlers claimed more and more Indian lands. The federal government moved the eastern Indians to newly established reservations west of the Mississippi River. By the late 1800's, most of the Indians in the United States had been moved to reservations in the West.

The Bureau of Indian Affairs was established in 1824. Its activities included the lease or sale of forest, mineral, and other natural resources on Indian reservations to non-Indians. The bureau used the income from these activities to help provide welfare and other federal services to the Indians.

The bureau maintained strong control over federal reservation programs during the first half of the 1900's. Then, in the 1960's, many tribal leaders and younger Indians began a movement to give control of these programs to the Indians themselves. President Richard M. Nixon sent a special message to Congress in 1970, calling for a new era of Indian self-determination. Since then, the government has given the tribes increased authority over reservation facilities.   Leon F. Cook

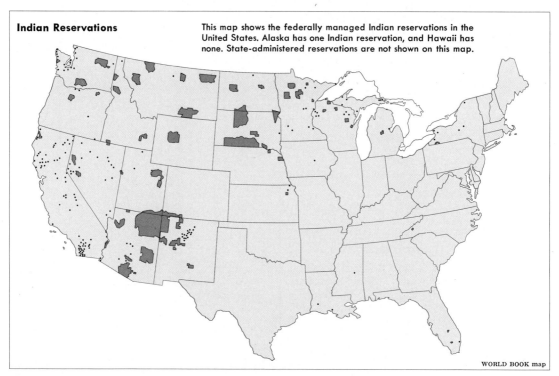

Indian Reservations

This map shows the federally managed Indian reservations in the United States. Alaska has one Indian reservation, and Hawaii has none. State-administered reservations are not shown on this map.

WORLD BOOK map

GYMNASTICS is a sport in which each contestant performs acrobatic exercises on various gymnasium equipment. Two or more teams compete in a gymnastics meet, which takes place in a gymnasium. Men's and women's teams have separate meets. Judges watch each gymnast's performance, called a *routine*, and decide what score he or she has earned.

Gymnastics helps develop balance, endurance, flexibility, and strength. A good gymnast must devote many hours to practice. Most women gymnasts reach their peak in their teens. The top performers in men's gymnastics average 21 years old.

Friedrich Jahn, a German schoolteacher, built the first modern gymnastics equipment in the early 1800's. Gymnastics has been a part of the Olympic Games since the modern Olympics began in 1896. During the 1970's, worldwide television coverage of the Olympics helped gymnastics grow remarkably as a spectator sport.

Men's Events

A men's gymnastics meet consists of six events that are held in a set order. These events, in order of performance, are the (1) floor exercise, (2) pommel horse, (3) rings, (4) long horse vault, (5) parallel bars, and (6) horizontal bar. Men who compete in all six events are called *all-around gymnasts*. Those who enter only one or two events are called *specialists*.

The Floor Exercise is performed on a mat that measures about 40 feet (12 meters) square. The gymnast performs a continuous series of movements that require balance, flexibility, and strength. These movements include handsprings, leaps, somersaults in the air, and tumbling. The floor exercise must be completed in not less than 50 seconds and not more than 70 seconds.

The Pommel Horse, also called the *side horse*, is named for the padded piece of equipment on which this event is held. The horse measures about 64 inches (163 centimeters) long and about 14 inches (36 centimeters) wide. It has two wooden handles on top called *pommels*. The pommels are about 50 inches (127 centimeters) from the floor. The gymnast uses the pommels to support his weight entirely with his hands. He swings his legs in complete circles around the sides and top of the horse without stopping. He also performs a movement called the *scissors*, beginning with one leg on each side of the horse. He switches the positions of his legs as he swings them from side to side. The contestant must frequently support himself with only one hand while raising the other hand to swing his legs past.

The Rings. This event is performed on two wooden rings suspended from cables about 105 inches (267 centimeters) above the floor. The gymnast leaps up and grasps the rings and then tries to keep them motionless while performing various movements. These include handstands and complete circular swings. The athlete supports his body in various *strength positions*, which require exceptional power. In a movement called the *cross*, for example, he supports himself in an upright position with his arms extended sideways. The event also includes *holding positions*, which require him to remain motionless for three seconds.

The Long Horse Vault is performed on a stand that resembles the pommel horse but has no handles. In this event, the gymnast vaults across the length of the horse. He approaches the horse at a run and jumps up and

John Messineo, Tom Stack & Associates

The Pommel Horse event is performed on a piece of equipment called a *horse*. The gymnast uses his hands to support his weight and performs a variety of leg movements without stopping.

John Messineo, Tom Stack & Associates

The Rings is an event held on two wooden rings that are suspended from cables. The competitor tries to keep the rings motionless while he executes a number of maneuvers with his body.

forward from a low springboard. He places one or both hands on the horse for support as he goes over. He may twist around in the air, do a somersault, or perform any one of several movements. The gymnast vaults twice, but only his higher score counts.

The Parallel Bars. In this event, the gymnast performs on two long wooden bars about 65 inches (165 centimeters) high and slightly more than shoulder width apart. He supports himself on the bars with his hands

GYMNASTICS

The Parallel Bars event takes place on two long wooden bars. While supporting himself with his hands, the gymnast carries out acrobatic exercises and movements that require great strength.

Sundby Sports Publications

The Balance Beam is held on a long wooden beam. The gymnast tries to use the full length of the beam while she performs acrobatic movements, jumps, leaps, running steps, and turns.

Bruce Curtis

while performing handstands, swings, twists, and other acrobatic movements. The gymnast also performs several *holding positions* on the parallel bars. In each one, he must remain motionless for two seconds. In addition, he performs various *strength movements* that require great arm power and must be done slowly.

The Horizontal Bar event takes place on a somewhat flexible steel bar fastened about 100 inches (250 centimeters) above the floor between two supports. The gymnast holds the bar with both hands and swings around it repeatedly. He performs several acrobatic movements without coming to a full stop. During this routine, he must reverse his position, which involves a change of grip on the bar. He also must perform maneuvers that require him to release his grip and regain it again while in the air. Many gymnasts finish this event with a spectacular *dismount* from the bar. They

swing rapidly around the bar, let go, and twist or somersault in the air before landing on their feet.

All-Around Competition for men consists of all six events. In college and international meets, an all-around competitor must perform a *compulsory routine* in each event. This routine involves a set sequence of movements. The gymnast then performs an *optional* routine in each of the six events, doing whatever movements he chooses. Only all-around gymnasts compete in international meets.

Women's Events

A women's gymnastics meet has four events. In order of performance, they are the (1) balance beam, (2) side horse vault, (3) uneven parallel bars, and (4) floor exercise. Most women gymnasts are all-around competitors who enter all these events.

The Balance Beam. This event involves a long wooden beam about 4 inches (10 centimeters) wide. Competitors perform jumps, leaps, running steps, and turns on it and try to use the full length of the beam. The best performers in this event also do cartwheels, back handsprings, and somersaults. The routine must be performed in not less than 1 minute 20 seconds and not more than 1 minute 45 seconds.

The Side Horse Vault is performed on the same equipment used in men's long horse vaulting. But women gymnasts vault across the width of the horse rather than its length. As in the men's event, the gymnast vaults twice, but only the higher of the two scores counts.

The Uneven Parallel Bars. In this event, gymnasts compete on two parallel wooden bars, one about 90 inches (228 centimeters) above the floor and the other about 60 inches (152 centimeters) high. The athlete swings around one bar at a time, performing maneuvers that require great flexibility and agility. She switches rapidly back and forth from one bar to the other, trying to keep in constant motion.

The Floor Exercise is performed on a mat that resembles the one used in the men's floor exercise. Women gymnasts perform this event with a musical accompaniment. Each contestant designs her routine to match the tempo and mood of the music she has selected. She must take at least 1 minute and not more than 1 minute 30 seconds to demonstrate her skill in acrobatics, dancing, and tumbling.

All-Around Competition for women includes all four events. In national and international meets, every competitor performs a compulsory routine in each event and then an optional routine in each. International meets are open only to all-around gymnasts.

Gymnastics Competition

Judging. Judges of gymnastics meets carefully watch each compulsory routine for such flaws as falls, improper body position, omissions, slowness, and stops. In the optional routines, the judges base their decision on difficulty, form, and the appropriate combination of movements.

A perfect score for any event is 10.00. The judges subtract points or tenths of a point for each flaw. In optional routines, the judges may award bonus points for especially difficult or original movements.

Five judges, including one called a superior judge, score the performance of each contestant. In most cases, the score of the superior judge is not used. Instead, the superior judge takes the scores of the other four judges and eliminates the highest and lowest ones. The superior judge computes an athlete's final score by averaging the two middle scores. If the difference between the two middle scores exceeds a certain range, the superior judge uses his score as a guide in adjusting the final score. At an international meet, each team's top five individual all-around scores are added together for the team score.

Organization. The United States Gymnastics Federation (USGF) governs amateur gymnastics in the United States. This organization is a member of the International Gymnastics Federation, which governs international amateur gymnastics.

In the United States, many states hold a championship gymnastics competition for high school athletes.

Guus De Jong, Photo Trends

The Side Horse Vault consists of leaping across the width of the horse. After a running start, the gymnast jumps forward from a springboard, bracing her hands on the stand as she goes over.

Jerry Cooke

The Uneven Parallel Bars event is performed on two wooden bars. The competitor swings back and forth from bar to bar and executes difficult maneuvers while remaining in constant motion.

At the college level, the National Association of Intercollegiate Athletics (NAIA), the National Collegiate Athletic Association (NCAA), and the National Junior College Athletic Association (NJCAA) have men's regional or national championships.

The USGF conducts programs for men and women that determine the United States teams for international competition. Such competition includes the Olympic Games, the Pan-American Games, the World Games, and the World University Games. FRANK L. BARE

Kennedy Galleries, Inc.

Walters Art Gallery

West Point Museum

Independence

The Westward Movement

The Civil War

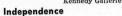

The History of the United States spans 200 years. It is an exciting tale of the birth and growth of one of the world's freest, richest, and most powerful nations.

UNITED STATES HISTORY

UNITED STATES, HISTORY OF THE. The history of the United States is the story of a great nation that was carved out of a wilderness by a brave and freedom-loving people. The men and women who built the United States came from almost every part of the world. They represented many different nationalities, races, and religions. Through the years, the people and their descendants learned to live and work together, and to take pride in being Americans. This spirit of cooperation and pride helped make the United States the huge, powerful, and wealthy nation it is today. It also helped the country and its people survive many challenges and hardships—including dangers in the wilderness, wars, social turmoil, and economic depressions.

Background

As late as the 1400's, Indians and Eskimos were the only inhabitants of the Western Hemisphere. During the next 200 years, people from several European countries sailed across the Atlantic Ocean to North and South America. Among them were colonists—chiefly British—who settled along the eastern coast of North America between what are now Maine and Georgia. These hard-working colonists built up a series of thriving permanent settlements in the wilderness. They lived under British rule for many years. But their dedication to liberty led them to declare their independence and form the United States of America in 1776.

Growth and Expansion

The American people dedicated their new nation to the principles of democracy, freedom, equality, and

opportunity for all. From the start, the United States welcomed immigrants to its shores. Attracted by the opportunity for freedom and a chance for a better life, newcomers from many lands poured into the United States by the millions. Immigration and natural growth caused the country's population to mount steadily—from fewer than 3 million in 1776 to more than 200 million today.

As the population grew, the American people spread out across North America. Wherever they went, these pioneers worked hard to turn the wilderness into a place where they could earn a living. They formed thriving farms in places where the soil was good. They searched for minerals and other valuable resources, and established towns where they found resources. Cities grew up along the main transportation routes and business and industry prospered there.

America's rapid growth made it one of the world's largest nations in both size and population. The country's bustling economic activity turned it into a land of enormous wealth.

Today, the United States ranks as the world's leading producer of farm products and manufactured goods, and its people have the highest standard of living in the world. The United States also became a world leader in many other fields, including science, medicine, technology, and military strength.

Challenges and Hardships

The United States grew and prospered in spite of many challenges and hardships. At the start, the very survival of the new nation was in doubt. The colonists

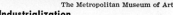
The Metropolitan Museum of Art
Industrialization

Brown Bros.
The Great Depression

NASA
The Space Age

who founded the United States had to defeat the mighty British Empire in the Revolutionary War to make their claim to independence stick. They succeeded despite great odds against them.

Both the colonists and the pioneers who moved westward across the country faced many dangers, including disease, starvation, and attacks by Indians. In the 1860's—less than 100 years after the Revolution—the survival of the United States was threatened again. Eleven Southern states withdrew from the Union and tried to establish an independent nation. The tragic, bloody Civil War between the North and the South followed. The North won the Civil War and the country remained united.

The American ideals of equality and opportunity for all did much to help the United States grow and prosper. Yet the ideals have not always been followed in practice. From colonial times until the end of the Civil War, many black Americans were slaves. In addition, some Americans have suffered from discrimination in jobs and other areas because they were immigrants, or because of their race or religion.

America's economic growth, though amazingly rapid, has not always been smooth. Periodically, severe depressions have brought the economy to a near standstill. At such times, large numbers of Americans lost their jobs and lived in poverty.

During the 1900's, the United States became one of the world's strongest military powers. As such, it took on the role of defending democracy throughout the world. This role led the United States into two World Wars and other conflicts. In the mid-1900's, many Americans began protesting against their country's military role, while others defended it. This issue led to bitter disputes among the people.

Today, like always, the United States faces a wide range of problems. They include the existence of poverty amid tremendous wealth, recurring slumps in the overall economy, disputes over foreign policy, and pollution of the environment. But the American people retain a deep pride in their country and the belief and hope that they can overcome their difficulties as their forefathers did in the past.

About This Article

The contributor of this article is Oscar Handlin, Carl H. Pforzheimer University Professor at Harvard University. He is the author of many books on American history, including The Uprooted—*a winner of the Pulitzer prize—and* The Americans: A New History of the People of the United States.

The article traces the history of the United States from its beginnings to the present day. The outline below shows the major sections of the article. WORLD BOOK *also has many individual articles on important events and people in United States history. Cross-references that appear within this article refer the reader to other* WORLD BOOK *articles for additional details on key topics. The Study Aids section at the end of the article includes a listing of related articles.*

Article Outline:

531

The French Arrive in Florida (1591), an engraving by Theodore de Bry based on a painting by Jacques le Moyne; Library of Congress

European Explorers from several countries made voyages to America during the 1500's. The scene above shows French explorer Jean Ribaut and his crew approaching the Florida coast in 1562. Friendly Indians gathered along the shore to greet the newcomers.

UNITED STATES HISTORY / *America Before Colonial Times*

For thousands of years, Indians were the only inhabitants of the Western Hemisphere. They had wandered into North America from Asia more than 20,000 years ago. They spread across the hemisphere to the tip of South America. About 10,000 years ago, Eskimos—another Asian people—moved to the Western Hemisphere. But they settled only in the far north, near the Arctic Circle (see Eskimo).

The Vikings were probably the first white men to reach America. A band of these venturesome seamen is believed to have explored part of the east coast of North America about 1,000 years ago. But European exploration and settlement of America did not begin for another 500 years. Then, in 1492, Christopher Columbus sailed westward from Spain, seeking a short sea route to the Far East, or Orient. He found, instead, a vast New World. Following Columbus' voyage, explorers, soldiers, and settlers from several European countries flocked to America. The process through which white men took control of the Indian homeland was underway.

The First Americans

About 20 million Indians were living in the Americas when Columbus reached the New World. About 15 to 20 million Indians lived between what is now Mexico and the tip of South America. About 1 million Indians lived in what are now the United States and Canada.

The American Indians formed hundreds of tribes, with many different languages and ways of life. Some tribes in the south—including the Aztec, Inca, and Maya—established advanced civilizations. They founded cities that had huge, magnificent buildings. They also accumulated gold, jewels, and other riches. Most American Indians north of Mexico lived in small villages. They hunted game and raised such crops as *maize* (corn), beans, and squash. Some tribes traveled continuously in search of food and never established permanent settlements.

Some Indian tribes of North America helped early European settlers survive in the wilderness of the New World. But as settlers moved westward, they became a threat to the Indian way of life, and Indians and whites became enemies. For a detailed story of the first Americans, see Indian, American.

European Discovery

The Vikings. About A.D. 1000, Vikings from Greenland explored part of the North American mainland—probably what is now Newfoundland, Canada. Led by Leif Ericson, they were probably the first white men to reach the mainland of the continent. But the Vikings did not establish permanent settlements, and their voyages were soon forgotten.

Columbus. Before Columbus' voyage, Europeans did not know the Western Hemisphere existed. During the 1400's, Europeans became interested in finding a short sea route to the Far East—a region of spices and other valuable goods.

Columbus, an Italian navigator, believed he could find a short route to the East by sailing west. Financed by the Spanish king and queen, he set sail westward from Spain on Aug. 3, 1492. Columbus reached land on October 12, and assumed he had arrived in the Far East. Actually, he landed on San Salvador, one of the islands just east of the North American mainland.

Columbus died in 1506, still believing he had sailed to the Far East. But other Europeans realized he had come upon an unexplored land. They called it the *New World*, and honored Columbus as its discoverer. Europeans also called the Western Hemisphere *America*, after Amerigo Vespucci. An Italian, Vespucci claimed he made voyages to the New World for Spain and Portugal beginning in 1497.

Exploration and Early Settlement

The discovery of the existence of America caused a wave of excitement in Europe. To many Europeans, the New World offered opportunities for wealth, power, and adventure. European rulers and merchants wanted to gain control of the hemisphere's resources in order to add to their wealth. Rulers also sought to gain New World territory, and thus increase their power and importance. Christian clergymen were eager to spread their religion to the Indians. Explorers and others viewed the New World as a place to seek adventure, as well as gain personal fame and fortune. Before long, Europeans from several countries sailed across the Atlantic to explore America and set up trading posts and colonies.

For details on the early exploration, see EXPLORATION AND DISCOVERY.

The Spanish and Portuguese. During the 1500's, the Spanish and Portuguese spread out over the southern part of the Western Hemisphere in search of gold and other riches. The Spaniards quickly conquered the Inca of Peru, the Maya of Central America, and the Aztec of Mexico. The Portuguese took control of what is now Brazil. By 1600, Spain and Portugal controlled most of the hemisphere from Mexico southward.

Also during the 1500's, Spaniards moved into what is now the Southeastern and Western United States. They did not discover riches there, as they did farther south. But they took control of Florida and of the land west of the Mississippi River. In 1565, the Spanish founded St. Augustine, Fla., the oldest city in what is now the United States. They also established missions and other settlements in the West and South. See MISSION LIFE IN AMERICA; SPAIN (The Spanish Empire).

The British and French began exploring eastern North America about 1500. At first, both nations sent only explorers and fur traders to the New World. But after 1600, they began establishing permanent settlements there. The French settlements were chiefly in what is now Canada. The British settlements included the 13 colonies that later became the United States.

For many years, Great Britain and France struggled for control of the land between the Atlantic Ocean and the Mississippi River, and for Canada. Britain finally won out in 1763 when it defeated France in the French and Indian War.

The Land That Became the United States

The explorers who came to the northern part of the hemisphere did not find gold and other riches, as did the Spanish in the south. Nor did these explorers find large Indian civilizations to help supply their needs. Instead, they found a wilderness sparsely inhabited by Indians.

The first settlers encountered many hardships as they attempted to establish colonies along the eastern coast. They had no way of knowing that beyond their settlements lay a vast and unbelievably rich and varied land. But later, the resources of this new land—its fertile soils, abundant water supplies, and plentiful minerals—would help the United States grow into one of the world's largest and most prosperous nations.

Period Facts in Brief

Important Dates

1492 Christopher Columbus sailed from Spain to the Western Hemisphere. Europeans honored him as the discoverer of America.

1497 John Cabot made the first voyage to North America for England.

1500 Portuguese explorer Pedro Álvares Cabral reached what is now Brazil.

1513 Ponce de León of Spain began exploring Florida, seeking the Fountain of Youth.

1521 Spanish conquistador Hernando Cortes defeated the Aztec of Mexico.

1534 Jacques Cartier of France became the first European to reach the Gulf of St. Lawrence in Canada.

1540-1542 Francisco Coronado of Spain explored the American Southwest.

1565 Spaniards founded St. Augustine, Fla., the oldest city in what is now the United States.

1585 Sir Walter Raleigh tried unsuccessfully to establish a permanent British settlement in America.

Andreas Feininger, Time-Life Picture Agency © Time, Inc.

An Acoma Indian Village, *above,* is one of the oldest continuously inhabited settlements in the United States. Located on a *mesa* (flat-topped hill) in New Mexico, it probably dates from the 1300's.

Penn's Treaty with the Indians (1771), an oil painting on canvas by Benjamin West; Pennsylvania Academy of the Fine Arts, Philadelphia

Early Colonists worked to maintain good relations with the Indians. William Penn, *arms extended,* made his first treaty with the Indians in 1682. His fair dealings with the Indians helped the colony of Pennsylvania grow and prosper.

UNITED STATES HISTORY: 1607-1753 / *The Colonial Heritage*

The first British attempt to establish a colony in what is now the United States took place in 1585. Sir Walter Raleigh sent settlers to Roanoke Island, off the coast of North Carolina. But this attempt at colonization failed (see LOST COLONY).

In 1607, a small band of about 100 British colonists reached the coast near Chesapeake Bay. They founded Jamestown, the first permanent British settlement in North America (see JAMESTOWN). During the next 150 years, a steady stream of colonists came to America and settled near the coast. Most of them were British, but they also included people from France, Germany, Holland, Ireland, and other countries.

The earliest colonists faced great hardship and danger in the wilderness. They suffered from lack of food and from disease, and were sometimes attacked by Indians. But the colonists soon established productive farms and plantations; built towns, roads, churches, and schools; and began many small industries. They prospered economically and, for the most part, maintained peaceful relations with the Indians.

The American colonists also developed political practices and social beliefs that have had a major influence on the history of the United States. They made strides toward democratic government, and they placed a high value on individual freedom and on hard work as a means of getting ahead.

The Thirteen Colonies

In the early 1600's, the British king began granting charters for the purpose of establishing colonies in America. The charters went to companies of merchants and to individuals called *proprietors.* The merchants and proprietors were responsible for recruiting people to settle in America and, at first, for governing them. By the mid-1700's, most of the settlements had been formed into 13 British colonies. Each colony had a governor and legislature, but each was under the ultimate control of the British government.

The 13 colonies stretched from what is now Maine in the north to Georgia in the south. They included the New England Colonies of Massachusetts, Connecticut, Rhode Island, and New Hampshire in the far north; the Middle Colonies of New York, New Jersey, Pennsylvania, and Delaware; Virginia and Maryland along Chesapeake Bay; and the Southern Colonies of North Carolina, South Carolina, and Georgia in the far south.

Virginia and Maryland were among the earliest British colonies. They were founded for different reasons, but they developed in much the same way.

Virginia began with the Jamestown settlement of 1607. The London Company, an organization of English merchants, sent the settlers to America, hoping that they would find gold and other treasures. But the settlers found no treasures, and faced great hardships. Captain John Smith played a leading role in helping the colony survive in its early days. In about 1612, some Jamestown colonists began growing tobacco, which the London Company sold in Europe. The crop soon became popular, and—as tobacco production mounted—Virginia prospered. New farms and settlements sprang up in the colony.

Maryland was founded by the Calverts, a family of wealthy English Roman Catholics. Catholics were persecuted in England, and the Calverts wanted to provide a place where Catholics could enjoy freedom. In 1632, Cecilius Calvert became proprietor of the Maryland area. Colonists, led by Leonard Calvert, established the first Maryland settlement in 1634. The Maryland settlers also raised tobacco. As tobacco production increased, their colony grew and prospered.

The people of Virginia and Maryland made important strides toward democracy and individual liberty. The Virginians appealed to the London Company for a voice in their local government. The company wanted to attract newcomers to its colony, and so it agreed. In 1619, it established the House of Burgesses, the first representative legislature in America (see HOUSE OF BURGESSES). Maryland attracted both Catholic and Protestant settlers. In 1649, the Calverts granted religious freedom to people of both faiths. This was the first religious toleration act in North America.

New England. Puritans, originally financed by English merchants, founded the New England Colonies. Puritans were English Protestants who faced persecution because of their opposition to the Church of England, Britain's official church. See PURITAN.

In 1620, a group of *Separatists* (Puritans who had separated from the Church of England) and other colonists settled in New England. Called *Pilgrims*, they founded Plymouth Colony—the second permanent British settlement in North America. Between 1628 and 1630, Puritans founded the Massachusetts Bay Colony at what are now Salem and Boston. Plymouth became part of Massachusetts Colony in 1691. See PLYMOUTH COLONY; MASSACHUSETTS BAY COLONY.

Settlers spreading out from Massachusetts founded the three other colonies in New England. Connecticut was first settled in 1633 and became a colony in 1636. Colonists settled in Rhode Island in 1636. Rhode Island became a colony in 1647. New Hampshire, first settled in 1623, became a colony in 1680.

Important Puritan leaders of the New England Colonies included governors William Bradford of Plymouth and John Winthrop of Massachusetts, and Roger Williams, the founder of Rhode Island.

Life in New England centered around towns. Each family farmed its own plot of land, but they all lived close together in a town. The early New England colonists relied on farming to earn a living. But before long, the New Englanders started many small industries, including fishing, lumber, and crafts.

The Puritans also contributed to democracy in

Period Facts in Brief

First Permanent Settlement, Each Colony

Virginia (1607), Massachusetts (1620), New Hampshire (1623), New York (1624), Connecticut (1633), Maryland (1634), Rhode Island (1636), Delaware (1638), Pennsylvania (1643), North Carolina (about 1653), New Jersey (1660), South Carolina (1670), Georgia (1733).

Important Dates

1607 About 100 colonists founded Jamestown, the first permanent British settlement in North America.

1619 Virginia established the House of Burgesses, the first representative legislature in America.

1620 The Pilgrims founded Plymouth Colony, the second permanent British settlement in North America.

1624 The Dutch established the settlement of New Netherland.

1636 Harvard—the first college in the colonies—was founded.

1638 People from Sweden established the settlement of New Sweden.

1647 Massachusetts established the first colonial public school system.

1649 Maryland passed the first religious toleration act in North America.

1664 England took control of New Netherland and New Sweden.

1672 The Boston Post Road was completed, linking Boston and New York City.

1704 *The Boston News-Letter,* the first successful colonial newspaper, began publication.

1752 Benjamin Franklin flew a homemade kite during a storm to prove that lightning is a form of electricity.

Population Growth and Change

Total population, about 100

1607
Rural, 100%

Total population, 1,328,000

1753
Rural, 98%   Urban, 2%

WORLD BOOK map

The Thirteen Colonies stretched along the eastern coast of North America. French territory lay to the north and west of the colonies, and Spanish territory lay to the south.

America. The Pilgrims created the *Mayflower Compact*, an agreement among the adult males to provide "just and equal laws" for all (see MAYFLOWER COMPACT). The New England Puritans also held town meetings, where the adult males worked together to frame laws.

The Middle Colonies. Soon after British settlement started, the Dutch founded New Netherland, a trading post and colony that included what are now New York and northern New Jersey. They began a permanent settlement in New York in 1624, and in New Jersey in 1660. In 1638, the Swedes established a trading post and settlement called New Sweden in present-day Delaware and southern New Jersey. The Dutch claimed New Sweden in 1655. But in 1664, the British—far better established in America than the Dutch—took over New Netherland and New Sweden.

King Charles II of England gave the New York and New Jersey territory to his brother, James, Duke of York. Friends of the duke founded huge farming estates in northern New York. New York City developed from the Dutch city of New Amsterdam in southern New York. It became a shipping and trading center. The Duke of York gave New Jersey to two of his friends who allowed much political and religious freedom. As a result, New Jersey attracted many settlers.

Swedes established a small settlement in what is now Pennsylvania in 1643. In 1681, William Penn of England received a charter that made him proprietor of Pennsylvania. Penn was a *Quaker*—a religious group that was persecuted in many countries (see QUAKERS). At Penn's urging, Quakers and other settlers who sought freedom flocked to Pennsylvania. Penn carefully planned settlements in his colony, and Pennsylvania thrived. Philadelphia, one of the settlements, became the largest city in colonial America. Penn also became proprietor of the Delaware area.

The Southern Colonies. In 1663, King Charles II gave the land between Virginia and Florida, called Carolina, to eight proprietors. Virginians had set up a settlement in the northern part of Carolina about 10 years earlier. After 1663, Carolina attracted British settlers, French Protestants called Huguenots, and Americans from other colonies. In 1712, the northern two-thirds of the region was divided into two colonies, North Carolina and South Carolina. North Carolina developed as a colony of small farms and fur trading activity. In South Carolina, wealthy landowners established rice and indigo plantations. The plantations required many laborers, and landowners filled this need by bringing many blacks to the colony as slaves. The coastal settlement of Charleston, S.C., became a rich seaport and lively social center.

The southern one-third of Carolina remained largely unsettled until 1733. Then, James Oglethorpe of England founded Georgia there. Oglethorpe hoped Georgia would become a colony of small farms. The colony's charter prohibited the importation of blacks so that neither slavery nor plantations would develop. But by 1750, Georgia law had been changed to allow settlers to bring in slaves, and plantations soon developed.

Life in Colonial America

Reports of the economic success and religious and political freedom of the early colonists attracted a steady flow of new settlers. Through immigration and natural growth, the colonial population rose to $1\frac{1}{3}$ million by 1753. Most of the settlers came from Britain, but the colonies also drew newcomers from almost every other country of Western Europe. In addition, the slave trade brought in so many Africans that, by the 1750's, blacks made up about 20 per cent of the population. Yet despite the varied backgrounds of the early settlers, Americans of the mid-1700's had—as one writer said—"melted into a new race of men."

The Colonists. Europeans knew that a person who went to America faced great hardship and danger. But

Detail of *Baltimore in 1752* (about 1807), an aquatint by Daniel Bowley based on a drawing by John Moale; Maryland Historical Society, Baltimore

Many of the Early Settlers grouped together in small villages. Baltimore, Md., *above*, began as a cluster of houses and other buildings along the banks of the Patapsco River. Colonists fished in the river, *left foreground*, and grew tobacco in a large field, *far right*.

Library of Congress

New York Public Library, Arents Collection

The Industrious Colonists worked hard to establish communities in the wilderness. A Northern colonist, *left*, shaves a board to size for a house he is building. Slaves on a Southern plantation, *right*, pack tobacco for shipment to Europe as plantation owners look on.

the New World also offered people the opportunity for a new start in life. As a result, many people were eager to become colonists.

Some Europeans came to America seeking religious freedom. In addition to the Puritans, Roman Catholics, Quakers, and Huguenots, they included Jews and members of German Protestant sects.

Other Europeans became colonists for economic reasons. Some of them were well enough off, but saw America as a place where they could become rich. Many poor Europeans also became colonists. Most of them came to America as *indentured servants*. An indentured servant agreed to work for another person, called a *master*, in America. In return, the master paid for the servant's transportation and provided him with food, clothing, and shelter. Agreements between servants and masters lasted up to seven years, after which the servant was free to work for himself.

Still other people who came to America had no choice in the matter. They included prisoners from overcrowded English jails, Irishmen captured by the English in battle, and black Africans captured in intertribal warfare and sold to European traders. The prisoners and captives were sold into service in America.

At first, the blacks had the same legal status as white indentured servants. But by about 1660, black equality had faded. Many masters began extending the period of service of their black servants indefinitely. This marked the beginning of slavery in North America. Some people in all the American colonies owned slaves, but slavery became more common in the South than in the North. The South had plantations that required large numbers of laborers, and the plantation owners found it profitable to buy slaves to do the work.

The Economy. The earliest colonists had to struggle to produce enough food to stay alive. But before long, colonial America had a thriving economy. Planters grew large crops of rice, indigo, and tobacco. Small farmers raised livestock and such crops as corn and wheat. When not busy in their fields, many farmers fished or hunted. Some cut lumber from forests to provide the materials for such products as barrels and ships. The colonists used part of what they produced, but they exported large quantities of goods. They traded chiefly with Britain, whose manufacturing firms depended on raw materials from its colonies. In return, they received manufactured goods. The colonies also traded with the French, Dutch, and Spanish.

Economic and Social Opportunity. Colonial America, like Europe, had both wealthy upper-class people and poor lower-class people. But in Europe, old traditions made economic and social advancement rare. America had no such traditions. Advancement was possible for everyone willing to work hard except slaves. In the New World, land was plentiful and easy to obtain, and there were many opportunities to start new businesses. Indentured servants often obtained land or worked in a trade after their period of service ended. Often, they or their sons became well-to-do merchants or landowners. The colonies had a great need for professional people, such as clergymen, lawyers, physicians, and schoolteachers. Because little training was required for these jobs, they were open to almost everyone.

The Colonists and Government. The colonists rejected the old idea that government was an institution inherited from the past. Instead, they regarded it as something they themselves had created for their own use. The colonists lived under British rule. But to them, laws made in Britain meant little until they were enforced on the spot. They often ignored British laws. This independent attitude would soon lead to a clash between the Americans and the British.

For more information on life in the American Colonies, see COLONIAL LIFE IN AMERICA.

Detail of *Raising the Liberty Pole*, an engraving by John McRae; Kennedy Galleries, Inc., New York City

Joyful Celebrations followed the signing of the Declaration of Independence on July 4, 1776. The scene above shows colonists raising a liberty pole to mark the occasion. At the right, colonial army officers sign up a volunteer for service in the war for independence against Great Britain.

UNITED STATES HISTORY: 1754-1783 / The Movement for Independence

Relations between the American Colonies and Great Britain began to break down during the mid-1700's. Little by little, Britain tightened its control over the colonies. Its leaders passed laws that taxed the colonists and restricted their freedom. The colonists had become accustomed to governing themselves, and had developed a sense of unity and independence. As a result, they deeply resented what they considered British interference in their affairs. Friction between the Americans and British mounted, and, on April 19, 1775, the Revolutionary War broke out between the two sides. During the war—on July 4, 1776—the colonists boldly declared their independence from their mighty British rulers. In 1783, they defeated the British and made their claim to independence stick.

Background to the Revolution

The French and Indian War. Great Britain and France had struggled for control of eastern North America throughout the colonial period. As their settlements moved inland, both nations claimed the vast territory between the Appalachian Mountains and the Mississippi River. The struggle led to the outbreak of the French and Indian War in 1754.

The British won the war, and, under the Treaty of Paris of 1763, Britain gained control of: (1) all of what is now Canada, and (2) all French territory east of the Mississippi River except New Orleans. Britain also received Florida from Spain in 1763. As a result, the British controlled all of North America from the Atlantic Ocean to the Mississippi River.

The French and Indian War was a turning point in American history. It triggered a series of British policy changes that eventually led to the colonial independence movement. See FRENCH AND INDIAN WARS (The French and Indian War).

British Policy Changes. The French and Indian War created problems for the British. After the war, Britain had to find ways to strengthen its control over its enlarged American territory. Also, Britain had spent so much money fighting the French and Indian War that its national debt had nearly doubled. George III, who had become king of Great Britain in 1760, instructed the British Parliament to establish policies to solve these problems. Parliament soon began passing laws that restricted the freedom of the American colonists, taxed them, or both.

In 1763, Parliament voted to station a standing army in North America to strengthen British control. Two years later, in the Quartering Act, it ruled that colonists must provide British troops with living quarters and supplies. Britain also sought to keep peace in North America by establishing good relations with the Indians. The Indians had already lost a good deal of territory to the white settlers. A British proclamation of October, 1763, prohibited American colonists from settling west of the Appalachian Mountains until treaties with the Indians might open up areas there.

King George and Parliament believed the time had come for the colonists to start obeying trade regulations and paying their share of the cost of maintaining the British Empire. In 1764, Parliament passed the Sugar Act. This law provided for the efficient collection of taxes on molasses brought into the colonies. It also gave British officials the right to search the premises of persons suspected of violating the law. The Stamp Act of 1765 extended to the colonies the traditional English tax on newspapers, legal documents, and other printed matter (see STAMP ACT).

Colonial Reaction. The colonists bitterly opposed the new British policies. They claimed that Britain had no right to restrict their settlement or deny their freedom in any other way. They also strongly opposed British taxes. The colonists were not represented in Parliament. Therefore, they argued, Britain had no right to tax them. The colonists expressed this belief in the slogan, "Taxation Without Representation is Tyranny."

To protest the new laws, colonists organized a widespread boycott of British goods. Many colonists joined secret clubs called *Sons of Liberty*. These groups threatened to use violence to prevent enforcement of the laws (see SONS OF LIBERTY). In 1765, representatives of nine colonies met in the Stamp Act Congress to consider joint action against Britain.

A Brief Easing of Tensions. The colonial boycott and resistance alarmed Britain's leaders. In 1766,

Parliament repealed the offensive Stamp Act. But at the same time, it declared that Britain still had the right to make laws for the colonies.

The Road to Independence

Renewed Conflict. The relaxation of tensions between the Americans and the British proved to be short-lived. In 1767, Parliament passed the Townshend Acts, which taxed lead, paint, paper, and tea imported into the colonies. These and other laws renewed discontent among the colonists. As tensions between the Americans and British grew, Britain reacted by sending troops into Boston and New York City.

The sight of British troops in the city streets aroused colonial anger. On March 5, 1770, Boston civilians taunted a group of troops. The troops fired on the civilians, killing three persons and wounding eight others, two of whom died later. This incident, called the Boston Massacre, shocked Americans and unnerved the British. See BOSTON MASSACRE.

In 1770, Parliament repealed all provisions of the Townshend Acts with one exception—the tax on tea. Three years later, Parliament reduced the tax on tea sold by the East India Company, a British firm. The British actions offended the colonists in two ways. They reaffirmed Britain's right to tax the colonists and gave

Period Facts in Brief

Important Dates

1756 A stagecoach line linked New York City and Philadelphia.

c. 1757 The first street lights in the colonies were installed in Philadelphia.

c. 1760 The first Conestoga wagons were built.

1763 Britain defeated France in the French and Indian War and gained control of eastern North America.

1763 Britain stationed a standing army in North America and prohibited colonists from settling west of the Appalachian Mountains.

1765 The British Parliament passed the Stamp Act, taxing newspapers, legal documents, and other printed matter in the colonies.

1766 The first permanent colonial commercial theater opened in Philadelphia.

1770 British troops killed American civilians in the Boston Massacre.

1773 Colonists staged the Boston Tea Party, dumping British tea into Boston Harbor.

1774 The Intolerable Acts closed Boston Harbor and included other steps to punish the colonists.

1774 The First Continental Congress met to consider action against the British.

1775 The Revolutionary War between the colonists and the British began.

1776 The colonists adopted the Declaration of Independence and formed the United States of America.

1781 The Americans defeated the British at Yorktown, Va., in the last major battle of the Revolutionary War.

1783 The Treaty of Paris officially ended the Revolutionary War.

Population Growth and Change

Total population, 1,360,000

1754

Rural, 98%   Urban, 2%

Total population, 3,125,000

1783

Rural, 96%   Urban, 4%

Manuscript Division, New York Public Library

Rare Book Division, New York Public Library; Astor, Lenox, and Tilden Foundation

The Stamp Act, passed by Parliament in 1765, required colonists to buy stamps as a tax on printed matter. A tax stamp appears at the left, *above*. A colonial illustrator drew a skull and crossbones—a symbol of death—*right*, to protest the law.

the East India Company an unfair advantage in the tea trade. Furious Americans vowed not to use tea and colonial merchants refused to sell it. On Dec. 16, 1773, a group of American colonists staged the Boston Tea Party to dramatize their opposition. Dressed as Indians, the colonists boarded East India Company ships and threw tea the ships contained into Boston Harbor. See BOSTON TEA PARTY.

In 1774—in the Quebec Act—Britain extended the boundary of its colony of Quebec to include territory north of the Ohio River. Quebec had a large French population, and the Americans resented the expansion of the colony. See QUEBEC ACT.

The Intolerable Acts. Angered by the Boston Tea Party, Parliament passed laws to punish the colonists early in 1774. Called the Intolerable Acts by the Americans, the laws included provisions that closed the port of Boston, gave increased power to the British royal governor of the colony of Massachusetts, and required the colonists to house and feed British soldiers. See INTOLERABLE ACTS.

The First Continental Congress. The Intolerable Acts stirred colonial anger more than ever before. On Sept. 5, 1774, delegates from 12 colonies met in the First Continental Congress in Philadelphia. The delegates were responsible men who disliked lawlessness, and they still hoped for a settlement with the British. They reaffirmed American loyalty to Britain and agreed that Parliament had the power to direct colonial foreign affairs. But at the same time, the delegates called for an end to all trade with Great Britain until Parliament repealed the Intolerable Acts. King George shattered hope for reconciliation by insisting that the colonies either submit to British rule or be crushed. See CONTINENTAL CONGRESS.

The Revolutionary War Begins. On April 19, 1775, British troops tried to seize the military supplies of the Massachusetts militia. This action led to the start of the Revolutionary War. Colonists—first at Lexington, and then at Concord, Mass.—took up arms to turn back the British. At Concord, the determined Americans stopped the British advance. Word of their success spread, and hope for victory over Britain grew. Colonial leaders met in the Second Continental Congress on May 10, 1775. The Congress faced the task of preparing the colonies for war. It organized the Continental Army, which colonists from all walks of life joined. On June 15, the Congress named George Washington of Virginia commander in chief of the army.

King George officially declared the colonies in rebellion on Aug. 23, 1775. He warned the Americans to end their rebellion or face certain defeat by Britain. But the threat had no effect on the colonists' determination to fight on. Some of the people—called *Loyalists*—favored submission to British rule, but a growing number of Americans now supported the fight for independence. Many people who had been unsure were convinced by reading Thomas Paine's pamphlet *Common Sense*. Paine—in this brilliant plea for the cause of freedom—stated the simple alternatives open to the Americans: They must either accept the tyranny of the British Crown or throw off their shackles by proclaiming a republic.

The Declaration of Independence. On July 4, 1776, the Second Continental Congress officially declared independence and formed the United States of America by adopting the Declaration of Independence. Written by Thomas Jefferson of Virginia, the declaration was a sweeping indictment of the king, Parliament, and the British people. It also set forth certain self-evident truths that were basic to the revolutionary cause. It said that all men are created equal, and are endowed by their Creator with rights to life, liberty, and the pursuit of happiness. To protect those rights, men organized governments, and the governments derived their powers from the consent of the governed. But

Detail of *The Battle of Lexington, April 19th, 1775* (1775), an engraving by Amos Doolittle; Connecticut Historical Society, Hartford

The Revolutionary War began on April 19, 1775, on the village green in Lexington, Mass., *left*. British troops, *in red coats*, routed the Americans. But later in the day, colonists at nearby Concord stopped a British advance.

when a government ceased to preserve the rights, it was the duty of the people to change the government, or abolish it and form a new one.

Thus the colonists were fighting for philosophical principles as well as specific objectives. The spirit aroused by the Declaration of Independence was an important factor in the ultimate American victory. See DECLARATION OF INDEPENDENCE.

Victory Over a Great Empire. The Americans were challenging the world's most powerful empire in the Revolutionary War. They lacked a well-trained army, officers who were accustomed to commanding troops, and munitions and money. But they had the advantage of fighting on their home territory. The British, on the other hand, had well-trained and well-equipped troops and officers, but they were fighting in an unfamiliar land thousands of miles from home. The American cause was also helped by aid from France and other European nations that opposed Britain.

The Revolutionary War raged on through the 1770's. Then, on Oct. 19, 1781, the Americans won a decisive victory at the Battle of Yorktown in Virginia. The main part of the British Army surrendered there, and the Americans had—in effect—won the war. Two years of peace negotiations and occasional fighting followed. Finally, on Sept. 3, 1783, the Americans and the British signed the Treaty of Paris of 1783, officially ending the Revolutionary War.

For a detailed account of the war for independence, see REVOLUTIONARY WAR IN AMERICA.

American Attitudes and Independence

Through the years, the American people had developed attitudes that help explain their strong desire to gain freedom from the British. These attitudes included a deep belief in government by the people, a sense of unity, an optimistic view of the future, and strong nationalistic feelings.

Government by the People. When the American colonies were first settled, merchants and large land-owners held most of the political power. But little by little, other colonists began to use the political process to express their views on important issues. Such issues included the ownership of land, representation in government, taxation, and the role of the church in society. The colonists learned to back candidates for public office who would represent their views and challenge the power of the ruling class.

The ruling merchants and landowners presented only half-hearted resistance to this widening of political power. They needed the aid of the lower classes to back their opposition to British policy. Furthermore, the very argument for self-government that the colonial leaders used against the British justified those seeking to share political power within the colonies. By 1774, America no longer was a society in which the few ruled with the passive consent of the many. Instead, large numbers of people had an active voice in government.

Unity, Optimism, and Nationalism. Through the years, the colonists had developed feelings of unity. Their opposition to the British led them to rely on one another more and more. Groups called *Committees of Correspondence* were set up throughout the colonies to provide organized opposition to Britain. Supported voluntarily by the people, the committees decided what action should be taken against the British in times of crisis. See COMMITTEES OF CORRESPONDENCE.

The colonial Americans also shared an optimistic view of their future. They were impressed by the rapid growth of their colonies, and they loved to calculate how much more their population and wealth would yet increase.

Unity and progress led to an increasing sense of nationalism among the people. By 1774, the colonists no longer thought of themselves as transplanted Europeans, but rather as Americans.

Congress Voting Independence (1785), an oil painting on canvas by Robert Edge Pine and Edward Savage; Historical Society of Pennsylvania, Philadelphia

The Vote for Independence from Great Britain took place on July 2, 1776. On July 4, the Second Continental Congress officially adopted the Declaration of Independence, and the United States of America was born.

Election Day at the State House (1816), India ink and water color on paper by John Lewis Krimmel; Historical Society of Pennsylvania, Philadelphia

Democratic Elections were among the important features written into the new nation's Constitution by the Founding Fathers. Large numbers of voters, *above*, turned out in Philadelphia for an election in 1816. American flags waving in the breeze added to the patriotic spirit of the event.

UNITED STATES HISTORY: 1784-1819 / *Forming a New Nation*

As a result of the Treaty of Paris of 1783, the new nation controlled all of North America from the Atlantic Ocean to the Mississippi River between Canada and Florida. Canada, to the north, remained British territory. Great Britain returned Florida to Spain, and Spain continued to control the area west of the Mississippi River.

The original 13 colonies made up the first 13 states of the United States. Eventually, the American land west of the Appalachian Mountains was divided into territories.

At the end of the Revolutionary War, the new nation was still a loose confederation of states. But in 1787, American leaders got together and wrote the Constitution of the United States. The Constitution became the country's basic law and welded it together into a solid political unit. The men who wrote it included some of the most famous and important figures in American history. Among them were George Washington and James Madison of Virginia, Alexander Hamilton of New York, and Benjamin Franklin of Pennsylvania. The authors of the Constitution, along with other early leaders such as Thomas Jefferson of Virginia, won lasting fame as the Founding Fathers of the United States.

At the start of its history, the United States faced severe financial problems. But before long, the skill of its leaders and the spirit and hard work of its people put the country on a sound economic footing. Early America also faced threats from powerful European nations. But masterful diplomacy by Washington and other leaders guided the country through its early years in peace. The peace ended with the War of 1812, in which the United States and Great Britain fought to a standstill. After the war, America focused its attention on its own development, and entered a period of bustling economic growth.

Establishing a Government

The American people began setting up a new system of government as soon as they declared their independence. Each of the new states had its own constitution before the Revolutionary War ended. The state constitutions gave the people certain liberties, usually including freedom of speech, religion, and the press. In 1781, the states set up a federal government under laws called the Articles of Confederation. But the Articles proved to be inadequate for running the government. The shortcomings of the Articles led to the formation of a new government under the Constitution.

Background to the Constitution. The Articles of Confederation gave the federal government the power to declare war and manage foreign affairs. But the Articles did not allow the government to collect taxes, regulate trade, or otherwise direct the activities of the states.

542

Under the Articles, each state worked independently for its own ends. Yet the new nation faced problems that demanded a strong federal government. The United States had piled up a huge national debt during the Revolutionary War. But since the federal government could not collect taxes, it was unable to pay the debt and put the country on a sound economic footing. The government even lacked the means for raising money to provide for national defense. The federal government had no power to regulate the nation's trade. In addition, some states issued their own paper money, causing sharp changes in the value of currency and economic chaos. See ARTICLES OF CONFEDERATION.

Creating the Constitution. In 1786, Virginia persuaded five states to send delegates to a convention at Annapolis, Md., to discuss interstate commerce. The delegates decided that the Articles of Confederation would have to be revised and wrote a report calling for all states to join in a new convention. In 1787, delegates from every state except Rhode Island met in Philadelphia's Independence Hall to consider revisions to the Articles. Rhode Island did not take part because it resented "outside interference" in its affairs. The delegates decided against simply revising the Articles of Confederation. Instead, they agreed to write an entirely new Constitution. The convention chose George Washington as presiding officer.

The delegates debated long and hard over the contents of the Constitution. Some of them wanted a document that gave much power to the federal government. Others wanted to protect the rights of the states and called for a weak central government. Delegates from large states claimed their states should have greater representation in Congress than the small states. But small-state delegates demanded equal representation.

The delegates finally reached agreement on a new Constitution on Sept. 17, 1787. The document they produced has often been called a work of political genius. The authors skillfully worked out a system of government that satisfied the opposing views of the people of the 1780's. At the same time, they created a system of government flexible enough to continue in its basic form to the present day.

The Constitution provided for a two-house legislature—a House of Representatives and a Senate. Representation in the House was based on population in order to satisfy the large states. All states received equal representation in the Senate, which pleased the small states. The Constitution gave many powers to the federal government, including the rights to collect taxes and regulate trade. But it also reserved powers for the states. The Constitution provided for three branches of government: the executive, headed by a President; the legislature, made up of the two houses of Congress; and the judiciary, or federal court system. In a master stroke of government organization, the creators of the Constitution provided for a system of checks and balances among the three branches. Each branch received powers and duties that ensured that the other branches would not have too much power.

Adopting the Constitution. Before the Constitution became law, it needed *ratification* (approval) by nine states. Some Americans still opposed the Constitution,

Period Facts in Brief

Presidents (with political parties and dates of service)
George Washington, no political party, 1789-1797
John Adams, Federalist, 1797-1801
Thomas Jefferson, Democratic-Republican, 1801-1809
James Madison, Democratic-Republican, 1809-1817
James Monroe, Democratic-Republican, 1817-1825

States in the Union

The 13 states that ratified the Constitution:
Delaware (1787), Pennsylvania (1787), New Jersey (1787), Georgia (1788), Connecticut (1788), Massachusetts (1788), Maryland (1788), South Carolina (1788), New Hampshire (1788), Virginia (1788), New York (1788), North Carolina (1789), Rhode Island (1790).

New states added through 1819:
Vermont (1791), Kentucky (1792), Tennessee (1796), Ohio (1803), Louisiana (1812), Indiana (1816), Mississippi (1817), Illinois (1818), Alabama (1819).

Important Dates

1787 The Founding Fathers wrote the Constitution.
1790's The first U.S. political parties developed.
1790 Samuel Slater built the country's first successful water-powered machines for spinning cotton.
1793 Eli Whitney invented the cotton gin.
1800 Washington, D.C., became the national capital.
1803 The Louisiana Purchase doubled the size of the United States.
1811 Work began on the National Road, which—when completed—linked the East and the Midwest.
1812-1814 The United States and Great Britain fought the War of 1812.
1814 Francis Scott Key wrote "The Star-Spangled Banner."

Population Growth and Change

Total population, 3,240,000
1784
Rural, 96%   Urban, 4%

Total population, 9,358,000
1819
Rural, 93%   Urban, 7%

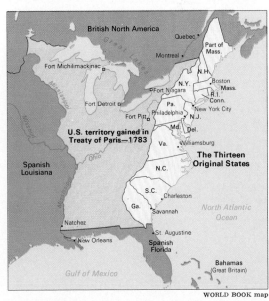

WORLD BOOK map

The United States After the Revolution extended from the Atlantic Ocean to the Mississippi River. British territory lay to the north, and Spanish territory lay to the west and south.

543

and fierce debate over ratification broke out. Hamilton, Madison, and John Jay responded to criticism of the document in a series of letters to newspapers. Called *The Federalist*, the letters gained much support for the Constitution (see FEDERALIST, THE). On June 21, 1788, New Hampshire became the ninth state to ratify.

The Bill of Rights. Much opposition to the new Constitution stemmed from the fact that it did not specifically guarantee enough individual rights. In response, 10 amendments known as the Bill of Rights were added to the document. The Bill of Rights became law on Dec. 15, 1791. Among other things, it guaranteed freedom of speech, religion, the press, and the rights to trial by jury and peaceful assembly.

For more details, see CONSTITUTION OF THE UNITED STATES; BILL OF RIGHTS.

Setting Up the Government. The Constitution provided that the President be elected by an Electoral College, a group of men chosen by the states (see ELECTORAL COLLEGE). In 1789, the Electoral College unanimously chose Washington to serve as the first President. It re-elected him unanimously in 1792. The people elected the members of the first House of Representatives, as they do today. But the senators were chosen by the state legislatures, a practice that continued until the early 1900's. The government went into operation in 1789, with its temporary capital in New York City. The capital was moved to Philadelphia in 1790, and to Washington, D.C., in 1800.

Early Problems and Politics

Solving Financial Problems. Financial problems plagued the new government. The national debt piled up during the Revolutionary War threatened the financial structure of the United States. The nation also needed internal improvements such as roads and bridges, but the federal government could not afford to pay for them.

Americans split over how to deal with the financial problems. One group, led by Secretary of the Treasury Alexander Hamilton, wanted the federal government to take vigorous action. Another group, headed by Secretary of State Thomas Jefferson, opposed government participation in economic affairs.

Hamilton proposed that the government increase tariffs and tax certain products made in the United States, such as liquor. The government would use the tax money to pay both its debts and those of the states. It would also have money for ongoing expenses and internal improvements. Hamilton also proposed a government-supported national bank to control government finances.

Jefferson and his followers, who included many Southerners, denounced all of Hamilton's plans. But Jefferson later agreed to support some of Hamilton's financial proposals. In return, Hamilton agreed to support a shift of the national capital to the South. Congress approved Hamilton's financial plan and agreed to locate the capital in the South. Jefferson continued to oppose the national bank proposal. But in 1791, Congress chartered a national bank for 20 years (see BANK OF THE UNITED STATES).

Enforcing Federal Law. The new tax program led to the Whiskey Rebellion. In 1794, farmers in Pennsylvania who made whiskey refused to pay the tax on liquor. President Washington sent in troops who ended the rebellion. Washington's action did much to establish the federal government's authority to enforce its laws within the states. See WHISKEY REBELLION.

Foreign Affairs. The new government also faced problems in foreign affairs. In 1793, France went to war against Britain and Spain. France had helped the Americans in the Revolutionary War, and it now expected U.S. assistance in its war. Americans disagreed over which side to support. Jefferson and his followers wanted the United States to back France, while Hamilton and his group favored the British.

President Washington insisted that the United States

Signing the Constitution (1860's), an oil painting on canvas by Thomas Rossiter; Independence National Historical Park Collection, Philadelphia

The Signing of the Constitution, above, ranks among the most historic events in American history. The delegates to the Constitutional Convention signed the document in 1787. Ratified in 1788, the Constitution has served as the basic law of the United States ever since.

remain neutral in the European war. He rejected French demands for support, and also sent diplomats to Britain and Spain to clear up problems with those countries. Chief Justice John Jay, acting for Washington, negotiated the Jay Treaty with Britain in 1794. The treaty's many provisions included a trade agreement with Britain which—in effect—ended American trade with France. It also included a British promise to remove troops still stationed on U.S. territory. In 1795, Thomas Pinckney negotiated the Pinckney Treaty, or Treaty of San Lorenzo, with Spain. This treaty settled a dispute over the Florida border between the United States and Spain and also gave the United States free use of the Mississippi River. See JAY TREATY; PINCKNEY TREATY.

In 1796, Washington—annoyed by the disputes within his Administration—refused to seek a third term as President. John Adams succeeded him in 1797. At about that time, French warships began attacking American merchant vessels. Adams, like Washington, hoped to use diplomacy to solve foreign problems. He sent diplomats to France to try to end the attacks. But three agents of the French government insulted the diplomats with dishonorable proposals, including a demand for a bribe. The identity of the agents was not revealed. They were simply called X, Y, and Z, and the incident became known as the XYZ Affair.

The XYZ Affair created a furor in the United States. Hamilton and his followers demanded war against France. But Adams was determined to keep the peace. In 1799, he again sent diplomats to France. This time, the United States and France reached a peaceful settlement. See XYZ AFFAIR.

Establishing Political Parties. Washington and many other early American leaders opposed political parties. But in the 1790's, the disputes over government policies led to the establishment of two parties. Hamilton and his followers, chiefly Northerners, formed the Federalist Party. The party favored a strong federal government and generally backed Britain in international disputes. Jefferson and his followers, chiefly Southerners, established the Democratic-Republican Party. The party wanted a weak central government and generally sided with France in foreign disputes. See FEDERALIST PARTY; DEMOCRATIC-REPUBLICAN PARTY.

The Alien and Sedition Acts. The XYZ Affair had a major impact on American internal policies and politics. After the affair, the Federalists denounced the Democratic-Republicans for their support of France. The Federalists had a majority in Congress. They set out to silence their critics, who included Democratic-Republicans and foreigners living in the United States. In 1798, the Federalist Congress and President Adams —also a Federalist—approved the Alien and Sedition Acts. These laws made it a crime for anyone to criticize the President or Congress, and subjected foreigners to unequal treatment.

A nationwide outcry against these attacks on freedom followed. The protests included the Kentucky and Virginia Resolutions. The resolutions were statements by the Kentucky and Virginia state legislatures that challenged the constitutionality of the Alien and Sedition Acts. The most offensive parts of the Acts soon expired

George Washington, *far right,* became the first American President in 1789. The other men in the picture are the members of his first Cabinet. They are, *left to right,* Henry Knox, Thomas Jefferson, Edmund Randolph, and Alexander Hamilton.

or were repealed. However, the laws gave the Federalists the reputation as a party of oppression. See ALIEN AND SEDITION ACTS; KENTUCKY AND VIRGINIA RESOLUTIONS.

Jeffersonian Democracy

Public reaction to the Alien and Sedition Acts helped Jefferson win election as President in 1800 and again in 1804. Jefferson's political philosophy became known as *Jeffersonian Democracy.* It called for as little government as possible. Jefferson envisioned the United States as a nation of small farmers. In Jefferson's ideal society, the people would lead simple, but productive, lives and be able to direct their own affairs. Therefore, the need for government would decline. Jefferson took steps to reduce government expenses and the national debt. But in spite of his beliefs and practices, Jefferson found that as President he could not avoid actions that expanded the role of government.

The Louisiana Purchase, the first major action of Jefferson's presidency, doubled the size of the United States. In 1801, Jefferson learned that France had taken over from Spain a large area between the Mississippi River and the Rocky Mountains called Louisiana. Spain was a weak nation, and did not pose a threat to the United States. But France—then ruled by Napoleon Bonaparte—was powerful and aggressive. Jefferson viewed French control of Louisiana as a danger to the United States.

In 1803, Jefferson arranged the purchase of the area from France for about $15 million. The Constitution did not authorize the government to buy foreign territory. Jefferson, a defender of strict interpretation of the Constitution, had to admit that he had "stretched the Constitution until it cracked."

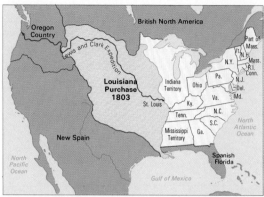

The Louisiana Purchase of 1803 added to the United States the territory between the Mississippi River and the Rocky Mountains. The purchase doubled the size of the country.

WORLD BOOK map

The Louisiana Purchase added 827,987 square miles (2,144,476 square kilometers) of territory to the United States. In 1804, Jefferson sent Meriwether Lewis and William Clark to explore the land. Lewis and Clark traveled all the way to the Pacific Ocean. Their reports provided valuable information about the Indians and the natural wealth of the West. See LOUISIANA PURCHASE; LEWIS AND CLARK EXPEDITION.

The Supreme Court. John Marshall became chief justice of the United States in 1801. Under Marshall, the Supreme Court became a leading force in American society. In 1803, in the case of *Marbury v. Madison*, the court asserted its right to rule on the constitutionality of federal legislation (see MARBURY V. MADISON). From then until Marshall's death in 1835, the court reviewed about 50 cases involving constitutional issues. This role of Marshall's court strengthened the nation by providing a way to ensure that government remained within constitutional bounds. But the Supreme Court also did much to increase the power of the federal gov-

ernment, a development Jefferson had opposed. For example, in *McCulloch v. Maryland* (1819), the court ruled that the federal government has implied powers in addition to those specified in the Constitution. It also said federal authority prevails over state authority when the two conflict (see McCULLOCH V. MARYLAND).

Jefferson and Foreign Policy. In 1803, Great Britain and France went to war again, and both nations began seizing American merchant ships. The British also *impressed* American seamen, seizing them and forcing them into British service.

Jefferson again found it necessary to use government powers, this time to protect American shipping. At his request, Congress passed trade laws designed to end British and French interference. The Embargo Act of 1807 made it illegal for Americans to export goods to foreign countries. But the embargo threatened to ruin the nation's economy, and was repealed in 1809. The Non-Intercourse Act of 1809 prohibited Americans from trading with Britain and France. But the warring nations still interfered with American trade.

The War of 1812

James Madison succeeded Jefferson as President in 1809. France soon promised to end its interference with American shipping, but Britain did not. Also, people believed the British were encouraging Indians to attack American pioneers moving westward. For these reasons, many Americans demanded war against Britain. They were led by members of Congress from the West and South called *War Hawks*, including Henry Clay of Kentucky and John C. Calhoun of South Carolina. Other Americans, especially New Englanders, opposed the War Hawks' demand. But on June 18, 1812, at Madison's request, Congress declared war on Britain and the War of 1812 had begun.

Neither side gained much advantage early in the war. But on Aug. 24, 1814, British troops captured Washington, D.C., and burned the Capitol and other government buildings. This British action made Americans

Capture of the City of Washington (1815), an anonymous engraving;
Anne S. K. Brown Military Collection, Brown University Library, Providence, R.I.

British Troops captured Washington, D.C., in 1814— during the War of 1812. The British set fire to the United States Capitol, the White House, and other government buildings in the city.

realize their nation's survival was at stake. Large numbers of volunteers rushed into service, and helped stop the British offensive. The Treaty of Ghent of Dec. 24, 1814, officially ended the War of 1812. Neither side won the war and little was gained from the struggle. See WAR OF 1812.

Growing Nationalism

A strong spirit of nationalism swept through the United States following the War of 1812. The war itself gave rise to increased feelings of self-confidence and unity. The peace that followed enabled the nation to concentrate on its own affairs. The bitterness that had marked political disputes eased with the break-up of the Federalist Party. Meanwhile, the nation expanded westward, new states entered the union, and the economy prospered. Historians sometimes call the period from about 1815 to the early 1820's *The Era of Good Feeling* because of its relative peace, unity, and optimism about the future.

Nationalism and the Economy. After the War of 1812, Henry Clay and other nationalists proposed economic measures that came to be called the *American System*. They said the government should raise tariffs to protect American manufacturers and farmers from foreign competition. Industry would then grow and employ more people. More employment would lead to greater consumption of farm products, and so farmers would prosper and buy more manufactured goods. In addition, tariff revenues would enable the government to make needed internal improvements.

The government soon put ideas of the American System into practice. In 1816, Congress enacted a high tariff, and it rechartered the national bank to give the government more control over the economy. The government also increased its funding of internal projects. The most important funding increase was for the National Road, the building of which had begun in 1811. The road—when completed—stretched from Cumberland, Md., to Vandalia, Ill. It became an important route for the shipment of goods and the movement of settlers westward (see NATIONAL ROAD).

A National Culture. Many early Americans had tried to pattern their culture after European civilization. Architects, painters, and writers tended to imitate European models. But in the late 1700's and early 1800's, art and culture more and more reflected American experiences. Architects designed simple, but beautiful, houses that blended into their surroundings. Craftsmen built sturdy furniture that was suited to frontier life, yet so simply elegant as to be considered works of art. The furniture of the Shakers, a religious group, is an example. The nation's literature flourished when it began reflecting American experiences. Political writings such as the works of Thomas Paine and the authors of *The Federalist* had high literary merit. The works of Washington Irving, one of the leading early authors, included tales based on American folklore.

Decline of the Federalists. In 1814 and 1815, New England Federalists held a secret political meeting in Hartford, Conn. Their opponents charged that they had discussed the *secession* (withdrawal) of the New England States from the Union (see HARTFORD CONVENTION). The Federalists never recovered from the charge, and the party broke up about 1816. James Monroe, the Democratic-Republican presidential candidate in the election of 1820, was unopposed.

New Territory. The United States gained two new pieces of territory between 1815 and 1820. In 1818, a treaty with Britain gave the country the Red River Basin, north of the Louisiana Territory. Spain ceded Florida to the United States in 1819.

"A Fire Bell in the Night." The Era of Good Feeling did not mean an end to all the country's disputes. The issue of slavery was causing deep divisions among the people. Many Northerners were demanding an end to slavery, while Southerners were defending it more and more. Jefferson, then retired, accurately viewed the growing dispute as a warning of approaching disaster, "like a fire bell in the night."

Detail of *Fairview Inn* (1889), a water color on paper by Thomas C. Ruckle;
Maryland Historical Society, Baltimore

The National Road was one of the major transportation routes in early America. When completed, it stretched from Maryland to Illinois. A steady stream of pioneers moved westward along the road. Inns, like the one above, provided resting and eating stops for travelers.

Prairie Scene: Mirage (1837), a water color by Alfred Jacob Miller; Walters Art Gallery, Baltimore

Americans Moved Westward by the thousands during the early 1800's. Hardy pioneers, *above*, piled all their belongings into covered wagons and set out to find new homes in the West. The push westward continued until the nation stretched from coast to coast.

UNITED STATES HISTORY: 1820-1849/*Expansion*

During the early 1800's, settlers by the thousands moved westward over the Appalachian Mountains into the new states and territories. Many of these pioneers even settled beyond the country's western boundary. They flocked into Texas, California, and other western lands belonging to Mexico. Americans also settled in the Oregon Country, a large territory between California and Alaska claimed by both Britain and the United States. In the mid-1800's, the United States gained control of the Mexican lands and the southern part of the Oregon Country, and the nation extended from coast to coast.

The pioneers were brave, hardy people who went west in search of a better life. They were attracted by the West's open land, good farmland, and rich mineral and forest resources. Through hard work, they settled the Western wilderness—as earlier Americans had done in the East.

The build-up of the West gave rise to changes in American politics. As areas in the West gained large populations, they were admitted to the Union as states. But wealthy Easterners continued to control governmental and economic policy. Western farmers and frontiersmen, as well as city laborers and craftsmen, soon banded together politically to promote their interests. They found a strong leader in Andrew Jackson, and helped elect him President in 1828. Jackson took steps to reduce the power of wealthy Easterners and aid the "common man." At the same time, other Americans were working for such reforms as women's rights, im-

provements in education, and the abolition of slavery.

The United States and Europe maintained peaceful relations during the Expansion Era. But in 1823, President James Monroe issued the Monroe Doctrine, a statement that warned European countries not to interfere with any of the free nations of the Western Hemisphere (see MONROE DOCTRINE).

America Moves West

By 1820, American pioneers had established many frontier settlements as far west as the Mississippi River. By the 1830's, the Westward Movement had pushed the frontier across the Mississippi, into Iowa, Missouri, Arkansas, and eastern Texas. The land beyond, called the *Great Plains*, was dry and treeless, and seemed to be poor farmland. But explorers, traders, and others who had journeyed farther west told of rich farmland and forests beyond the Rocky Mountains. In the 1840's, large numbers of pioneers made the long journey across the Great Plains to the Far West.

The Pioneers included Easterners from both the North and South. Many other pioneers came from Europe seeking a better life. Some people went west in search of religious freedom. The best known of these were the Mormons, who settled in Utah in 1847.

Most of the pioneers became farmers who owned their own plots. But urban life also moved westward with the frontier. Bustling towns and cities grew up in the West. There, traders in farm goods and other products of the West carried on brisk businesses. The urban centers also attracted churches, banks, stores, and hotels; and clergymen, craftsmen, doctors, lawyers, lawmen, and schoolteachers.

For more details on the pioneers, see PIONEER LIFE IN AMERICA; WESTWARD MOVEMENT.

Manifest Destiny. By the mid-1840's, thousands of Americans lived in the Oregon Country and on the western land claimed by Mexico. By then, large numbers of Americans had come to believe in the doctrine of *manifest destiny*. That is, they thought the United States should control all of North America. Stirred by this belief, Americans demanded control of Oregon and the Mexican territory.

The conflicting claim with Britain over Oregon was settled with relative ease. Britain decided that the effort needed to hold all of Oregon was not worth while. In 1846, the British turned over to the United States the part of the territory south of the 49th parallel, except Vancouver Island. See OREGON TERRITORY.

The struggle over the Mexican territory was more complicated. It began in Texas in 1835, when the American settlers there staged a successful revolt against Mexican rule. In 1836, the settlers proclaimed Texas an independent republic, but also requested U.S. statehood. Nine years later, the United States annexed Texas and made it a state.

The United States gained more Mexican territory as a result of the Mexican War. In 1846, President James K. Polk sent General Zachary Taylor to occupy land near the Rio Grande that both the United States and Mexico claimed. Fighting broke out between Taylor's troops and Mexican soldiers. On May 13, 1846, at Polk's request, Congress declared war on Mexico. The United States quickly defeated its weak neighbor. The Treaty of Guadalupe Hidalgo, signed on Feb. 2, 1848, officially ended the war. The treaty gave the United States a vast stretch of land from Texas west to the Pacific and north to Oregon.

In 1853, in the Gadsden Purchase, America bought

Period Facts in Brief

Presidents (with political parties and dates of service)

James Monroe, Democratic-Republican, 1817-1825
John Quincy Adams, Democratic-Republican, 1825-1829
Andrew Jackson, Democrat, 1829-1837
Martin Van Buren, Democrat, 1837-1841
William H. Harrison, Whig, 1841
John Tyler, Whig, 1841-1845
James K. Polk, Democrat, 1845-1849
Zachary Taylor, Whig, 1849-1850

States in the Union

Number at start of period: 22
Number at end of period: 30
States added during the period:
Maine (1820), Missouri (1821), Arkansas (1836), Michigan (1837), Florida (1845), Texas (1845), Iowa (1846), Wisconsin (1848).

Important Dates

1820 The Missouri Compromise ended a slavery dispute.
1823 The Monroe Doctrine warned Europeans against interference in Western Hemisphere affairs.
1825 The Erie Canal opened, providing a water route from the Atlantic Ocean to the Great Lakes.
1830 The *Tom Thumb*, the nation's first commercial steam locomotive, operated in Baltimore.
1832 South Carolina threatened secession over a tariff.
1834 Cyrus McCormick patented the reaper.
1837 Samuel F. B. Morse demonstrated the first successful telegraph in the United States.
1846 Britain ceded the southern part of the Oregon Country to the United States.
1848 Victory in the Mexican War gave the United States vast new territory in the West.
1848 The discovery of gold in California triggered the Gold Rush.

Population Growth and Change

Total population, 9,638,453
1820
Rural, 93%   Urban, 7%

Total population, 22,488,000
1849
Rural, 85%   Urban, 15%

Settlement of Immigrants in Missouri (about 1850), a lithograph by E. Sachse; Missouri Historical Society, St. Louis

A Pioneer Homestead in Missouri, *above*, consisted of a log cabin and a small piece of farmland. The farmer cleared timber from the surrounding forest to build his house and to burn as fuel.

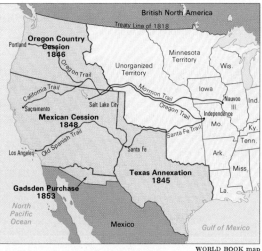

WORLD BOOK map

Expansion in the Mid-1800's extended the nation westward to the Pacific Ocean. The Oregon Country was ceded to the U.S. by Britain. The rest of the new territory came from Mexico.

549

Detail of *The Trail of Tears* (1942), an oil painting on canvas by Robert Lindneux; Woolaroc Museum, Bartlesville, Okla.

Eastern Indians were forced to move west of the Mississippi River during the Expansion Era as whites took over their land. The difficult journey, *above*, became known as the *Trail of Tears* among the Cherokee and Choctaw Indians.

from Mexico the strip of land that makes up the southern edge of Arizona and New Mexico. The United States then owned all the territory of its present states except Alaska (purchased from Russia in 1867) and Hawaii (annexed in 1898). See MEXICAN WAR; GADSDEN PURCHASE.

The western territory gained by the United States added to the American spirit of national pride and was a key factor in the nation's economic growth. But it also helped widen the split between the North and South, and helped bring on the Civil War. See *The Irrepressible Conflict* section of this article.

Expansion and the Indians. As the pioneers moved westward, they took over much of the land that Indians had occupied for thousands of years. Fighting often broke out between the pioneers and Indians. The United States government sent soldiers to battle the Indians and the soldiers won most of these so-called Indian Wars. By the 1840's, the soldiers had driven most eastern Indians west of the Mississippi River. See INDIAN WARS (Along the Frontier).

Expansion and the Economy. Expansion into the rich interior of the continent enabled the United States to become the world's leading agricultural nation. Many of the pioneer farmers found they could produce more than they needed for their families. They then concentrated on products with high sales value. Cotton was in great demand by textile mills in Europe and the Eastern United States. Farmers in the South as far west as Texas raised cotton to supply the mills. Many settlers in Kentucky and Tennessee prospered by growing tobacco. Midwesterners produced large crops of corn and wheat, and also raised much livestock. Farmers in the Far West raised wheat, fruit, and other valuable products.

New techniques and machines boosted the output of America's farms. The cotton gin, invented by Eli Whitney in 1793, came into widespread use in the 1800's. It enabled cotton growers to separate cotton fiber from the seeds as fast as 50 people could by hand. The reaper, patented by Cyrus McCormick in 1834, allowed farmers to harvest grain much more quickly than before. See COTTON GIN; REAPING MACHINE.

The discovery of minerals in the West also aided America's economy. The most famous mineral strike took place in 1848, when gold was discovered at Sutter's Mill in California. See FORTY-NINER; GOLD RUSH.

The period also marked the beginning of large-scale manufacturing in the United States. Previously, most manufacturing was done by craftsmen at home or in small shops. But beginning in the early 1800's, businessmen erected factories equipped with modern machinery that enabled them to produce goods more rapidly. Manufacturing remained centered in the East, but some Western towns developed industries.

Developments in transportation also contributed immensely to America's economic growth. New or improved roads—such as the National Road in the East and the Oregon and Santa Fe trails in the West—eased the difficulty of traveling and shipping goods by land (see TRAILS OF EARLY DAYS with its *Related Articles*).

In 1807, Robert Fulton demonstrated the first commercially successful steamboat, the *Clermont*. The steamboat soon became the fastest and most important means

Detail of *A Cotton Plantation on the Mississippi* (1884), a Currier and Ives lithograph based on a painting by W. A. Walker; Museum of the City of New York

Cotton Plantations sprang up throughout the South in the 1800's. Cotton became so important to the Southern economy that people called the crop "King Cotton." Many whites used black slaves to work in their fields. They claimed that slave labor was vital to the South's economy.

The Camden and Amboy Railroad with the Engine "Planet" in 1834 (1904), an oil painting on canvas by Edward Lamson Henry; Graham Gallery, New York City

Railroads and Steamboats became important means of transportation during the Expansion Era. In the scene above, New Jersey travelers transfer from a steamboat, *background,* to a train. A stagecoach and a carriage—two other means of transportation—appear at the right.

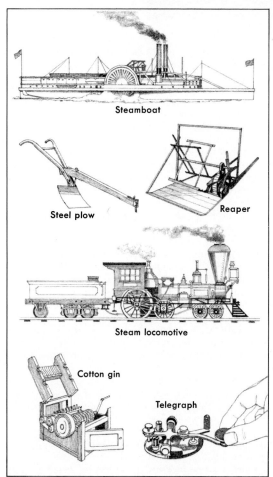

Steamboat

Steel plow

Reaper

Steam locomotive

Cotton gin

Telegraph

WORLD BOOK illustrations by David Cunningham

Technological Advances in transportation, farming, and communication greatly aided America's economic growth during the early 1800's. Some of the developments are shown above.

of shipping goods. Americans of the early 1800's built many canals to connect their natural waterways. The Erie Canal, the most important one, was completed in 1825. It opened a water passage from the Hudson River in New York to the Great Lakes in the Midwest. Boats used the canal to carry manufactured products from the East to the West and farm products and raw materials from the West to the East (see ERIE CANAL).

The steam-powered railroad soon rivaled the steamboat in importance as a means of shipping. In the 1820's, American railroads were still in the experimental stage. But by 1850, about 9,000 miles (14,500 kilometers) of railroad lines were in operation.

In 1837, Samuel F. B. Morse demonstrated the first successful telegraph in the United States. The telegraph soon gave businessmen the fastest means of communication yet known. An expanded postal system also helped speed communications.

Cultural Change. After 1820, the wilderness seemed less and less hostile to the American people. Increasingly, society glorified the frontier and nature. The public eagerly read the novels of James Fenimore Cooper, which described Indians and frontiersmen as pure of heart and noble in deeds. Ralph Waldo Emerson and other American philosophers praised nature as a source of truth and beauty available to all people, rich and poor alike.

Developments in printing spread art and information to more people than ever before. A new printing process called *lithography* enabled artists to produce many copies of their works cheaply. Large numbers of Americans bought and decorated their homes with lithographs. The lithographs of Nathaniel Currier and James Merritt Ives were especially popular. They depicted everyday American scenes, customs, and events—often in a sentimental style. Faster printing presses reduced the cost of printing newspapers. After 1835, many newspaper publishers lowered the cost of their papers to a penny, a price even poor people could afford. But the spoken word remained an important means of mass communication. Large numbers of people attended gatherings

551

Political Candidates and other orators traveled far and wide to bring their messages to frontier audiences. Public speeches from platforms like the one at the left became known as *stump speeches*.

Detail of *Stump Speaking* (1854), an oil painting on canvas by George Caleb Bingham; Boatmen's National Bank of St. Louis

where political candidates, pleaders of special causes, and famous clergymen and lawyers made speeches.

City people of the Expansion Era flocked to theaters to enjoy plays, minstrel shows, and other forms of entertainment. Groups of entertainers also toured the country, performing before small-town audiences. P. T. Barnum, the most famous showman of the time, fascinated the public with exhibitions of midgets, "fat ladies," and other unusual attractions.

Politics and the "Common Man"

The Election of 1824 led to renewed political friction in the United States. Four Democratic-Republicans, including John Quincy Adams and Andrew Jackson, sought to succeed Monroe as President. Jackson received the most electoral votes. But he did not win a majority, so it fell upon the House of Representatives to select the new President. The House chose Adams. Embittered, Jackson and his followers formed a separate wing of the Democratic-Republican Party, which soon developed into the Democratic Party.

Jacksonian Democracy. Adams and all the earlier Presidents came from well-to-do Eastern families. Jackson, by contrast, was born in a log cabin into a poor family. He won national fame as an Indian fighter and as a hero of the War of 1812.

Jackson ran for President again in 1828. He appealed for support from Western farmers and frontiersmen, and city laborers and craftsmen. He promised to end what he called a "monopoly" of government by the rich and to protect the interests of the "common man." His policy of equal political power for all became known as *Jacksonian Democracy*. Jackson's background and policies gained him much support in the West and in the nation's growing cities. The voters elected him President by wide margins in 1828 and again in 1832.

Jackson as President. When Jackson became President, many wealthy Easterners held what were, in

effect, lifelong appointments to federal government jobs. Jackson dismissed many of these people from office, replacing them with his supporters. Some historians consider this action the start of the spoils system in the federal government. See SPOILS SYSTEM.

Jackson's main crusade against the wealthy involved the second Bank of the United States. The bank's duties included regulating the nation's money supply. Jackson believed the bank operated as a monopoly that favored the wealthy. In 1832, Congress voted to re-charter the bank, but Jackson vetoed the bill. He soon withdrew the government's money from the bank, and the bank later collapsed.

The other great issue of Jackson's Administration involved the tariff and nullification. In 1828, Congress passed a bill that placed high tariffs on goods imported into the United States. The South believed the bill favored New England manufacturing interests, and denounced it as a "Tariff of Abominations." Speaking for South Carolina, Calhoun (then the Vice-President) claimed any state could nullify a federal law it deemed unconstitutional. In 1832, Congress lowered tariffs somewhat, but not enough to please South Carolina. South Carolina declared the tariff acts "null and void," and threatened to secede from the Union if the federal government tried to collect tariffs in the state. This action created a constitutional crisis. Jackson believed in states' rights, but maintained the Union must be preserved. In 1833, he persuaded Congress to pass the *Force Bill*, which allowed him to use the armed forces to collect tariffs. But Congress lowered tariffs to a point acceptable to South Carolina, and the nullification crisis ended. See NULLIFICATION.

Politics After Jackson. Jackson's influence on politics continued after he left office. As undisputed leader of the Democrats, Jackson designated Martin Van Buren to be the party's candidate in the 1836 presidential election. Jackson's opponents had formed the

Whig Party four years earlier. In an attempt to attract followers of Jackson, most Whigs supported William Henry Harrison to oppose Van Buren. Harrison, like Jackson, had won fame as a war hero. But the voters, still loyal to Jackson, elected Van Buren.

A depression called the Panic of 1837 crippled the American economy shortly after Van Buren took office, but prosperity later returned. The presidential election of 1840 again matched Van Buren and Harrison. In their campaign, the Whigs made some attempt to criticize Van Buren's economic policies, but for the most part they ignored issues. Instead, they promoted Harrison as a war hero and associated him with hard cider, the log cabin, and other symbols of the frontier. In this way, they appealed to many of Jackson's frontier supporters, and Harrison won the election.

Social Reform

During the Expansion Era, many Americans came to believe that social reforms were needed to improve their society. Churches and social groups set up charities to aid the poor and teach them how to help themselves. Reformers worked to reduce the working day of laborers from the usual 12 or 14 hours to 10 hours. Prohibitionists—convinced that drunkenness was the chief cause of poverty and other problems—persuaded 13 states to outlaw the sale of alcohol between 1846 and the Civil War. Dorothea Dix and others worked to improve the dismal conditions in the nation's prisons and insane asylums. Other important targets of reformers were women's rights, improvements in education, and the abolition of slavery.

The Drive for Women's Rights. Early American women had few rights. There were almost no colleges for women, and most professional careers were closed to them. A married woman could not own property. Instead, any property she had legally belonged to her husband. In addition, American women were barred from voting in all elections.

A women's rights movement developed after 1820, and brought about some changes. In 1835, Oberlin College became the first men's school to admit women. Other men's colleges soon began admitting women, and new colleges for women were built. In 1848, New York became the first state to allow married women to own real estate. That same year, Lucretia Mott and Elizabeth Cady Stanton organized a Woman's Rights Convention in Seneca Falls, N.Y. The convention issued the first formal appeal for *woman suffrage* (the right to vote). But nationwide suffrage did not come about until 1920.

Education Reform. In the early 1800's, most good schools in the United States were expensive private schools. Poor children went to second-rate "pauper," or "charity," schools, or did not go at all. During the 1830's, Horace Mann of Massachusetts and other reformers began demanding education and better schools for all American children. States soon began establishing public school systems, and more and more children received an education. Colleges started training teachers for a system of public education based on standardized courses of study. As a result, schoolchildren throughout the country were taught much the same

lessons. For example, almost all children of the mid-1800's studied the *McGuffey*, or *Eclectic*, *Readers* to learn to read. These books taught patriotism and morality as well as reading (see McGuffey, William H.).

The Abolition Movement became the most intense and controversial reform activity of the period. Beginning in colonial times, many Americans—called *abolitionists*—had demanded an end to slavery. By the early 1800's, every Northern state had outlawed slavery. But through the years, the plantation system of farming had spread throughout the South, and the economy of the Southern States depended more and more on slaves as a source of cheap labor.

The question of whether to outlaw or allow slavery became an important political and social issue in the early 1800's. Through the years, a balance between the number of *free states* (states where slavery was prohibited) and *slave states* (those where it was allowed) had been sought. This meant that both sides would have an equal number of representatives in the United States Senate. As of 1819, the federal government had achieved a balance between free states and slave states. There were 11 of each.

When the Territory of Missouri applied for admission to the Union in 1818, bitter controversy broke out over whether to admit it as a free or slave state. In either case, the balance between free and slave states would be upset. But in 1820, the nation's leaders worked out the Missouri Compromise, which temporarily maintained the balance. Massachusetts agreed to give up the northern part of its territory. This area became the state of Maine, and entered the Union as a free state in 1820. In 1821, Missouri entered as a slave state, and so there were 12 free and 12 slave states.

The Missouri Compromise had another important provision. It provided that slavery would be "forever prohibited" in all the territory gained from the Louisiana Purchase north of Missouri's southern border, except for Missouri itself. See Missouri Compromise.

The Missouri Compromise satisfied many Americans as an answer to the slavery question. But large numbers of people still called for complete abolition. In 1821, Benjamin Lundy, a Quaker, pleaded for gradual abolition in a journal called *The Genius of Universal Emancipation*. William Lloyd Garrison, a fiery New England journalist, opposed even gradual abolition. Garrison demanded an immediate end to slavery. He founded *The Liberator*, an important abolitionist journal, in 1831. Many blacks who had gained their freedom became important spokesmen for the abolition movement. They included Frederick Douglass and Sojourner Truth. See Abolitionist.

The growing strength of the abolition movement raised fears among Southerners that the federal government would outlaw slavery. Increasingly, the South hardened its defense of slavery. Southerners had always argued that slavery was necessary to the plantation economy. But after 1830, some Southern leaders began arguing that blacks were inferior to whites, and therefore fit for their role as slaves. Even many Southern whites who owned no slaves took comfort in the belief that they were superior to blacks. As a result, Southern support of slavery increased.

The First Day at Gettysburg (1863), an oil painting on canvas by James Walker; West Point Museum, U.S. Military Academy

The Civil War ranks among the most tragic events of United States history. Fought between 1861 and 1865, it pitted Northerners against Southerners in bloody battle. In the Battle of Gettysburg, above, about 40,000 Americans were killed or wounded in just three days.

UNITED STATES HISTORY: 1850-1869/*The Irrepressible Conflict*

The long dispute between the North and South over the issue of slavery came to a head after the Mexican War ended in 1848. The vast new area the United States had acquired in the West during the 1840's created a problem Americans could not evade. It was obvious that the new land would sooner or later be split up into territories, and then into states. Proslavery Americans—chiefly Southerners—argued against any restraints on slavery in the new territories and states. Antislavery Americans—mainly Northerners—wanted the federal government to outlaw slavery in the newly acquired lands. Still others proposed the doctrine of *popular sovereignty*. That is, they said the people of the territories and states should decide whether or not to allow slavery.

At first, the sides tried to settle their differences through debate and compromise. But the dispute over slavery proved to be an "irrepressible conflict," as Senator William H. Seward of New York termed it. During the 1850's, the North and South drew further and further apart over the issue. In the early 1860's, 11 Southern states seceded from the Union. The North insisted that the South had no right to secede and that the Union must be preserved at all costs. On April 12, 1861, the Civil War broke out between the North and South. In this tragic chapter of United States history, Americans faced Americans in bloody battle. The Civil War took more American lives than any other war. It left large parts of the South in ruins, and created long-lasting feelings of bitterness and division between the people of the North and South.

The North won the Civil War in 1865. The North's victory preserved the Union. And, soon after the war, slavery was outlawed throughout the United States.

Debate and Compromise

California applied for statehood in 1849. The application triggered debate over whether California should be admitted as a free state or a slave state. It also heightened the long-standing argument over how to deal with the slavery question.

Congressional Views. Members of Congress became spokesmen for the various views about slavery. Calhoun, then a senator from South Carolina, expressed the views of Americans who believed in the right to own slaves. Senator Seward was one of many spokesmen for people with strong antislavery beliefs. He said moral law—a higher law than the Constitution—required that the government abolish slavery nationwide. Senator Clay of Kentucky represented Americans who held views between those of Calhoun and Seward. Clay urged both the North and South to compromise because—he said—the alternative was the end of the Union.

The Compromise of 1850. Clay and others succeeded in bringing about agreement on the California slavery question. They won approval of the Compromise of 1850, a series of laws that made concessions to both the North and South. Measures designed to satisfy the North included the admission of California to the Union as a free state and the abolition of the slave trade in Washington, D.C. As part of the Compromise, Congress created the territories of New Mexico and Utah. To try to satisfy Southerners, Congress ruled that when these territories became states, the residents would decide whether or not to allow slavery. Also for the South, Congress agreed to strict measures designed to aid the capture of runaway slaves.

Many Americans thought the Compromise of 1850 provided a final solution to the slavery problem. The Compromise did cool the heated argument over the issue—but only for a while. See COMPROMISE OF 1850.

The Kansas-Nebraska Act. In the early 1850's, Congress began considering the creation of new territories in the area roughly between Missouri and present-day Idaho. Bitter debate flared up over whether the territories should ban or allow slavery. Those who called for a ban cited the Missouri Compromise to back their position. The land under consideration was part of the area in which the Compromise had "forever prohibited" slavery. But on May 25, 1854, Congress passed the Kansas-Nebraska Act, a law that changed this provision. The law created two territories west of Missouri—Kansas and Nebraska. It provided that the people of Kansas and Nebraska would decide whether or not to allow slavery. See KANSAS-NEBRASKA ACT.

Nationwide Turmoil

Few, if any, American laws have had more far-reaching effects than the Kansas-Nebraska Act. Furious antislavery Americans denounced both Northerners and Southerners who had supported the act. Others staunchly defended the act. Everywhere, attitudes toward the slavery question hardened, and capacity for further compromise diminished. Political and social turmoil swept through the country, and the United States was on the road to war.

Political and Institutional Splits. Angered by the Kansas-Nebraska Act, a group of antislavery Americans formed the Republican Party in 1854. Many Democrats and Whigs who opposed slavery left their parties and became Republicans. Other Americans, puzzled by the national turmoil, sought simple answers to the country's problems. They joined the Know-Nothing (or Ameri-

Period Facts in Brief

Presidents (with political parties and dates of service)

Zachary Taylor, Whig, 1849-1850
Millard Fillmore, Whig, 1850-1853
Franklin Pierce, Democrat, 1853-1857
James Buchanan, Democrat, 1857-1861
Abraham Lincoln, Republican, 1861-1865
Andrew Johnson, National Union, 1865-1869
Ulysses S. Grant, Republican, 1869-1877

States in the Union

Number at start of period: 30
Number at end of period: 37
States added during the period:
California (1850), Minnesota (1858), Oregon (1859), Kansas (1861), West Virginia (1863), Nevada (1864), Nebraska (1867).

Important Dates

1850 The Compromise of 1850 temporarily ended a national crisis over the slavery question.

1854 Passage of the Kansas-Nebraska Act led to nationwide turmoil over the slavery issue.

1856 The first American kindergarten opened in Watertown, Wis.

1860 Pony express riders began carrying mail from St. Joseph, Mo., to the Far West.

1861-1865 The North and the South fought each other in the Civil War.

1863 The Emancipation Proclamation declared freedom for all slaves in Confederate-held territory.

1865 The 13th Amendment outlawed slavery throughout the United States.

1867 The United States bought Alaska from Russia.

1868 The House of Representatives impeached President Andrew Johnson, but the Senate did not remove him from office.

Population Growth and Change

Total population, 23,191,876

1850

Rural, 85%   Urban, 15%

Total population, 37,816,000

1869

Rural, 75%   Urban, 25%

The Old Print Shop, Inc., New York City

The Compromise of 1850 temporarily cooled the heated dispute over slavery between the North and South. Henry Clay, *center above*, led the effort in Congress to pass the Compromise.

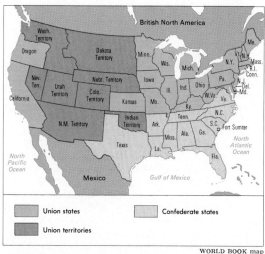

WORLD BOOK map

The Civil War (1861-1865) split the nation into two parts—the Confederacy and the Union. The Confederacy was made up of 11 Southern States that withdrew from the Union in 1860 and 1861.

Detail of *The Slave Auction* (1862), an oil painting on canvas by Eyre Crowe; Kennedy Galleries, Inc., New York City

Slaves Were Sold at public auctions in the South. Pictures of blacks being sold like merchandise stirred much resentment against slavery in the North.

can) Party, which blamed the problems on immigrants and Roman Catholics.

The stability of the two main political parties before 1854 had helped keep the nation together. Thus, the political splits deprived the country of an important unifying force. Religious denominations had also been a unifying force. But beginning in the 1840's, large church groups split along sectional lines and another unifying institution was lost. By the mid-1850's, the Supreme Court seemed to be the only institution to command nationwide respect. But in 1857, the court ruled—in the Dred Scott Decision—that Negroes were not citizens and that laws limiting the spread of slavery were unconstitutional. The court then lost much of its influence in the North. See DRED SCOTT DECISION.

Social Disorder. After 1854, Southerners increasingly referred to themselves as a separate national group. In the North, abolitionists stepped up their campaign against slavery. Harriet Beecher Stowe's novel *Uncle Tom's Cabin* (1851-1852) became one of the most widely read books in America. This powerful work about the horrors of slavery helped stir antislavery feelings to a fever pitch. In Kansas, fierce fighting broke out in 1856 between proslavery and antislavery settlers. See UNCLE TOM'S CABIN; KANSAS ("Bleeding Kansas").

On Oct. 16, 1859, abolitionist John Brown and a small band of followers seized the federal arsenal at Harpers Ferry, Va. (now W. Va.). Brown intended the action as the first step in a general slave uprising. But federal troops easily captured him, and—after a trial— he was hanged. Brown's plan had almost no chance of success. The odds against him were so great that many people believe he was insane at the time of the Harpers Ferry incident. Even so, many Northerners thought of him as a martyr, while many Southerners genuinely believed his attack was part of an organized movement to end slavery. These attitudes perhaps best show how divided the United States had become in the 1850's.

The Election of 1860 also reflected the nation's division. The Democratic Party split into Northern and Southern wings, with each wing slating its own candidate for President. The Whig Party, weakened by desertions, disbanded before the election. Conservative Whigs and Know-Nothings formed the Constitutional Union Party, which ran its own candidate for President. Only the Republicans remained united. They nominated Abraham Lincoln, an Illinois lawyer, for President. The Republican unity helped Lincoln win the election on Nov. 6, 1860.

Secession. Lincoln had earned a reputation as an opponent of slavery, and his election was unacceptable to the South. Southerners feared the new President would restrict or end slavery. Alarmed by this prospect, South Carolina seceded from the Union on Dec. 20, 1860, well before Lincoln took office. Alabama, Florida, Georgia, Louisiana, and Mississippi seceded in January, 1861. The six seceded states formed the Confederate States of America in February. Later in 1861, Arkansas, North Carolina, Tennessee, Texas, and Virginia seceded and joined the Confederacy.

Lincoln took office on March 4, 1861. The new President insisted above all else on the preservation of the Union. To him, the seceded states were still part of the United States, and there was yet hope for reconciliation. But a little more than a month later, the North and South were at war.

The Civil War and Reconstruction

The Civil War began on April 12, 1861, when Southern troops fired on Fort Sumter, a military post in Charleston Harbor. Both sides quickly prepared for battle after the Fort Sumter clash. The North had superior financial and industrial strength, and more manpower than the South. But the South fought valiantly to defend its cause. The South gained the upper hand at first, but the North gradually turned the tide. Finally, Confederate resistance wore down, and Union armies swept through the South. On April 9, 1865, General

Library of Congress

The South Lay in Ruins at the end of the Civil War. A scene showing shells of burned-out buildings in Richmond, Va., above, provides an example of the destruction brought on by the war.

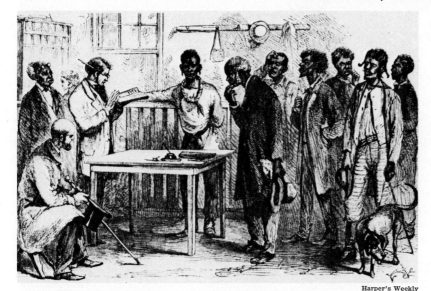

Reconstruction Measures passed by Congress after the Civil War included the establishment of election boards to register black voters. The scene at the left shows blacks lined up to register in Macon, Ga.

Harper's Weekly

Robert E. Lee—commander of the Confederate Army—surrendered to the Union commander General Ulysses S. Grant at Appomattox Court House in Virginia. The last Confederate troops surrendered on May 26.

The four years of bloody fighting between the North and South had staggering effects on the nation. About 360,000 Union troops and perhaps 260,000 Confederate troops—all Americans—died in the conflict. No other war in history has taken so many American lives. Property damage was enormous, especially in the South. Many Southern cities, towns, plantations, factories, and railroads lay in ruin. The war also took an emotional toll on the nation. It caused deep and long-lasting feelings of bitterness and division between the people of the North and the South.

For a detailed account of the war, see CIVIL WAR.

The Emancipation Proclamation. At the start of the Civil War, Lincoln's main goal was the preservation of the Union. But as battlefield casualties mounted, he decided that another goal—the emancipation of the slaves—was necessary to justify the cost of the war. On Jan. 1, 1863, Lincoln issued the Emancipation Proclamation. The proclamation declared freedom for all slaves in the areas under Confederate control at the time. See EMANCIPATION PROCLAMATION.

Reconstruction. Toward the end of the Civil War, the North set out to establish terms under which Confederate states would be readmitted to the Union. The process through which the South returned, as well as the period following the war, is called *Reconstruction*.

Northerners divided into two groups over Reconstruction policy. One group, called the *moderates*, wanted to end the bitterness between the North and South and favored avoiding harsh treatment of the rebels. Members of the other group, the *radicals*, believed the South should be punished for its rebellion. They also wanted a policy that would ensure that blacks received better treatment in the South than they had before the war.

President Lincoln led the moderates. But assassin John Wilkes Booth shot him on April 14, 1865. Lincoln died the next day, less than a week after Lee's surrender. Vice-President Andrew Johnson became President. He tried to carry out Lincoln's moderate policy, but he was unable to overcome radical opposition. The radicals included many of the most powerful Republican members of Congress. They controlled enough votes in Congress to push through their own Reconstruction policy and override Johnson's vetoes. Johnson's opposition to the radicals almost led to his removal from office. In 1868, the House of Representatives impeached the President. But the Senate voted against removing him from office by the margin of a single vote. For details, see JOHNSON, ANDREW.

The Reconstruction program drafted by Congress included laws to further the rights of blacks. The 13th Amendment to the Constitution (1865) outlawed slavery throughout the United States. The 14th Amendment (1868) confirmed the citizenship of Negroes, and the 15th Amendment (1870) made it illegal to deny the right to vote on the basis of race.

Congress also stationed troops in the South. Republicans, protected by the troops, took control of local Southern governments. White Southerners loyal to their old traditions bitterly resented the new political system. Many of them joined the Ku Klux Klan, a secret society that used violence to keep blacks from voting and trying to achieve equality (see KU KLUX KLAN).

Congress insisted that the Confederate states agree to follow all federal laws before being readmitted to the Union. Between 1866 and 1870, all the Confederate states returned to the Union. By the early 1870's, interest in Reconstruction in the North had faded. However, Reconstruction did not end officially until 1877, when the last federal troops left the South.

Reconstruction had limited success. It expanded the legal rights of Negroes, and some blacks advanced politically. But the old social order, based on white supremacy, soon returned to the South. The fundamental problem of the black's place in society remained to haunt future generations. See RECONSTRUCTION.

Forging the Shaft: A Welding Heat (1877), an oil painting on canvas by John Ferguson Weir;
The Metropolitan Museum of Art, New York City, Gift of Lyman G. Bloomingdale, 1901

America Became an Industrial Giant during the late 1800's. The nation's factories, such as the
iron foundry above, began turning out products on a much larger scale than before. Millions of rural
Americans and immigrants flocked to the country's cities to work in the booming industries.

UNITED STATES HISTORY: 1870-1916 / *Industrialization and Reform*

The industrial growth that began in the United States in the early 1800's continued steadily up to and through the Civil War. Still, by the end of the war, the typical American industry was small. Hand labor remained widespread, limiting the production capacity of industry. Most businesses served a small market and lacked the capital needed for business expansion.

After the Civil War, however, American industry changed dramatically. Machines replaced hand labor as the main means of manufacturing, increasing the production capacity of industry tremendously. A new nationwide network of railroads enabled businessmen to distribute goods far and wide. Inventors developed new products the public wanted, and businessmen made the products in large quantities. Investors and bankers supplied the huge amounts of money that businessmen needed to expand their operations. Many big businesses grew up as a result of these and other developments. They included coal mining, petroleum, and railroad companies; and manufacturers and sellers of such products as steel, industrial machinery, automobiles, and clothing.

The industrial growth had major effects on American life. The new business activity centered in cities. As a result, people moved to cities in record numbers, and the cities grew by leaps and bounds. Many Americans amassed huge fortunes from the business boom, but others lived in extreme poverty. The sharp contrast between the rich and the poor and other features of American life stirred widespread discontent. The discontent triggered new reform movements, which—among other things—led to measures to aid the poor and control the size and power of big business.

The industrial growth centered chiefly in the North. The war-torn South lagged behind the rest of the country economically. In the West, frontier life was coming to a close.

America's role in foreign affairs also changed during the late 1800's and early 1900's. The country built up its military strength and became a world power.

The Rise of Big Business

The value of goods produced by American industry increased almost tenfold between 1870 and 1916. Many interrelated developments contributed to this growth.

Improved Production Methods. The use of machines in manufacturing spread throughout American industry after the Civil War. With machines, workers could produce goods many times faster than they could by hand. The new large manufacturing firms hired hundreds, or even thousands, of workers. Each worker was assigned a specific job in the production process. This system of organizing laborers, called the *division of labor*, also sped up production. The increased production speed had a tremendous impact on the economy. It enabled businessmen to charge lower prices for products. Lower prices, in turn, meant more people could afford the products, and so sales soared.

Development of New Products. Inventors created, and businessmen produced and sold, a variety of new products. The products included the typewriter (1867), barbed wire (1873), the telephone (1876), the phonograph (1877), the electric light (1879), and the gasoline automobile (1885). Of these, the automobile had the greatest impact on the nation's economy. In the early 1900's, Ransom Eli Olds and Henry Ford began turning out cars by mass production. Automobile prices dropped, and sales soared. The number of automobiles owned by Americans jumped from 8,000 in 1900 to almost 3,500,000 in 1916.

Natural Resources. America's rich and varied natural resources played a key role in the rise of big business. The nation's abundant water supply helped power the industrial machines. Forests provided lumber for construction and wooden products. Miners took large quantities of coal and iron ore from the ground. Andrew Carnegie and other businessmen made steel from these minerals. Steel played a vital role in the industrialization process. It was used to build machines, railroad tracks, bridges, automobiles, and skyscrapers. Other industrially valuable minerals included copper, silver, and petroleum. Petroleum—the source of gasoline—became especially important after the automobile came into widespread use in the early 1900's.

A Growing Population. More than 25 million immigrants entered the United States between 1870 and

Period Facts in Brief

Presidents (with political parties and dates of service)
Ulysses S. Grant, Republican, 1869-1877
Rutherford B. Hayes, Republican, 1877-1881
James A. Garfield, Republican, 1881
Chester A. Arthur, Republican, 1881-1885
Grover Cleveland, Democrat, 1885-1889
Benjamin Harrison, Republican, 1889-1893
Grover Cleveland, Democrat, 1893-1897
William McKinley, Republican, 1897-1901
Theodore Roosevelt, Republican, 1901-1909
William H. Taft, Republican, 1909-1913
Woodrow Wilson, Democrat, 1913-1921

States in the Union

Number at start of period: 37
Number at end of period: 48
States added during the period:
Colorado (1876), North Dakota (1889), South Dakota (1889), Montana (1889), Washington (1889), Idaho (1890), Wyoming (1890), Utah (1896), Oklahoma (1907), New Mexico (1912), Arizona (1912).

Important Dates

1876 Alexander Graham Bell invented the telephone.
1877 Thomas Edison invented the phonograph.
1879 Edison invented the electric light.
1884 The world's first skyscraper was begun in Chicago.
1886 The American Federation of Labor was founded.
1898 The United States defeated Spain in the Spanish-American War.
1903 The Wright Brothers made the first successful airplane flight at Kitty Hawk, N.C.
1913 The 16th Amendment gave the federal government the power to levy an income tax.
1914 World War I began in Europe.

Population Growth and Change

Total population, 38,558,371
1870
Rural, 74%   Urban, 26%

Total population, 99,871,604
1916
Rural, 51%   Urban, 49%

Automobile

Gas range

Skyscraper

Telephone

Electric light

Gas-powered tractor

Trolley streetcar

Phonograph

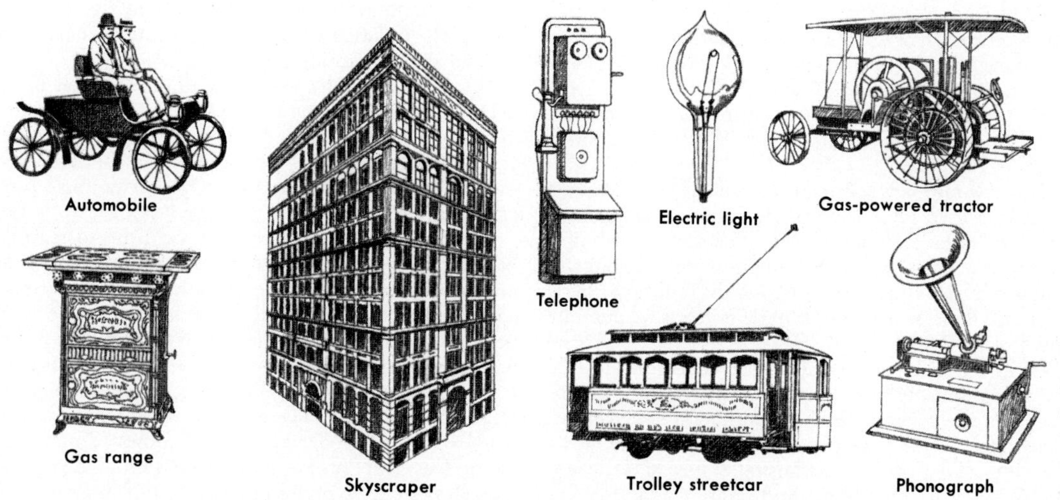

WORLD BOOK illustrations by David Cunningham

Many New Products came into use during the period of industrialization. Their manufacture and sale contributed greatly to the economic boom. Some of the new products are shown above.

Alfred Stieglitz photo; The Museum of Modern Art

Immigrants flocked into the United States by the millions during the late 1800's and early 1900's. A shipload of newcomers from Europe is shown above.

Immigration to the United States Between 1870 and 1916

The largest number of immigrants between 1870 and 1916 came from southern and eastern Europe. Earlier, the number of immigrants from northern and western Europe had far surpassed the total from any other part of the world.

Source: U.S. Bureau of the Census

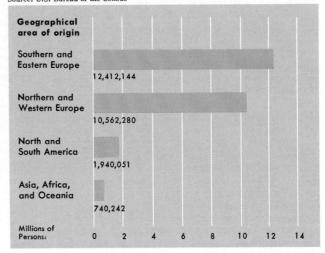

Geographical area of origin	
Southern and Eastern Europe	12,412,144
Northern and Western Europe	10,562,280
North and South America	1,940,051
Asia, Africa, and Oceania	740,242

Millions of Persons: 0 2 4 6 8 10 12 14

1916. Immigration plus natural growth caused the U.S. population to more than double during the same period, rising from about 40 million to about 100 million. Population growth helped the economic boom in two ways. It increased the number of consumers, and thus enlarged the market for products. It also provided the additional workers needed for the jobs created by the new business activity.

Distribution, Sales, and Communication. In the late 1800's, the American railroad system became a nationwide transportation network. The distance of all railroad lines in operation soared from about 9,000 miles (14,500 kilometers) in 1850 to almost 200,000 miles (320,000 kilometers) in 1900. A high point in railroad development came in 1869, when workers laid tracks that joined the Central Pacific and Union Pacific railroads near Ogden, Utah. This event marked the completion of the world's first transcontinental railroad system. The system linked the United States by rail from coast to coast.

The new railroads spurred economic growth. Mining companies used them to ship raw materials to factories over long distances quickly. Manufacturers distributed their finished products by rail to points throughout the country. The railroads became highly profitable businesses for their owners, including Cornelius Vanderbilt and Jay Gould.

Improved sales methods also aided economic growth. Owners of big businesses sent salesmen to all parts of the country to promote their products. Enterprising merchants opened huge department stores in the growing cities. They included Marshall Field of Chicago, R. H. Macy of New York, and John Wanamaker of Philadelphia. The stores offered a wide variety of products at reasonable prices. Other merchants—including Montgomery Ward and Richard Sears—began mail-

order companies, chiefly to serve people who lived far from stores. The companies published catalogs that showed their products. Buyers used the catalogs to order goods by mail.

Advances in communication provided a boost for the economy. Railroads replaced such mail-delivery systems as the stagecoach. In 1876, Alexander Graham Bell invented the telephone. These developments, along with the telegraph, provided the quick communication that is vital to the smooth operation of big business.

Investment and Banking. The business boom triggered a sharp increase in investments in the stocks and bonds of corporations. As businesses prospered, persons eager to share in the profits invested heavily. Their investments provided capital that companies needed to expand their operations.

New banks sprang up throughout the country. Banks helped finance the nation's economic growth by making loans to businesses. Some bankers of the era, especially J. P. Morgan, assumed key positions in the American economy because of their ability to provide huge sums of capital.

Monopolies. The government did little to regulate business during the 1800's. Unrestricted, American businessmen struggled to wipe out competition and gain complete control of their industries. They formed monopolies, which—for the most part—are illegal today. Some businessmen in the same industry *merged* (united to form a single company) in order to reduce or eliminate competition. Other businessmen formed *trusts*. A trust was a monopoly in which a group of managers controlled rival businesses without formal ownership (see MONOPOLY AND COMPETITION; TRUST).

The monopolies had some favorable effects on the economy. They helped make possible the giant, efficient corporations that contributed so much to economic growth. The monopolies also enabled businessmen to avoid sharp fluctuations in price and output, and thus keep sales steady. On the other hand, monopolies gave some businessmen so much power that they could take unfair advantage of others. A businessman with little or no competition could demand goods from suppliers at low cost, while charging high prices for his products. The businessman could also save money by reducing the quality of his products.

The South and the West

The War-Torn South. After the Civil War, Americans in the South faced the task of rebuilding their war-torn society. The South lagged behind the rest of the nation economically. Some industry developed in the region, but the South remained an agricultural area throughout the period of industrialization.

Many Southern farmers—both black and white—owned the land they worked. But in general, the land of these small, independent farmers was poor. The best land was given over to tenant farming—a system in which laborers farm the land and pay rent in money or crops to the owner. The tenant farming system had neither the virtues of the plantation system of pre-Civil War days nor of the independent owner system. The tenant farmers lacked the incentive to improve land that was not their own, and the owners did not have full control over production. For these and other reasons, agriculture remained more backward in the South than elsewhere.

The End of the Western Frontier. The long process of settling the United States from coast to coast drew to a close after the Civil War. In 1862, Congress passed the Homestead Act, which offered public land to people free or at very low cost. Thousands of Americans and immigrants started farms in the West under the provisions of the act. They settled chiefly on the Great Plains, which—contrary to earlier beliefs—included much excellent farmland. Miners flocked to the West as the demand for minerals soared. Towns sprang up near the mines. Cattle ranching spread throughout the Southwest after the Civil War.

After 1870, settlement became so widespread in the West that it was no longer possible to draw a continuous frontier line. The United States Census of 1890 officially recognized the fact that America's frontier had ended. See WESTWARD MOVEMENT (The Last Frontiers); WESTERN FRONTIER LIFE.

The settlement of the West brought an end to the American Indian way of life. Farmers occupied and fenced in much of the land. White men moving westward slaughtered buffalo herds on which Indians depended for survival. Some Indians retaliated against the whites by attacking wagon trains and homes. But as in earlier days, the federal government sent soldiers to crush the Indian uprisings. In the end, the Indians were no match for the soldiers and their superior weapons. Through the years, the federal government pushed more and more Indians onto reservations. Reservation Indians suffered from poverty and illness, and could not adjust to the new way of life forced upon them. By 1900, the separate Indian way of life had become a thing of the past. For more details, see INDIAN, AMERICAN (The

Farmers Flocked to the Great Plains during the late 1800's. The Kansas farm family above built their house from sod. The Plains had few trees, and so lumber for building was scarce.

Fall of Indian America); INDIAN RESERVATION; INDIAN TERRITORY; INDIAN WARS.

Life During the Industrial Era

The industrial boom had major effects on the lives of the American people. The availability of jobs in industries drew people from farms to cities in record numbers. In 1870, only about 25 per cent of the American people lived in urban areas. By 1916, the figure had reached almost 50 per cent.

The lives of people in the cities contrasted sharply. A small percentage of them had enormous wealth and enjoyed lives of luxury. Below them economically, the larger middle class lived comfortably. But at the bottom of the economic ladder, a huge mass of city people lived in extreme poverty.

The Wealthy. The business boom opened up many opportunities for financial gain. The economic activity it generated enabled many people to establish successful businesses, expand existing ones, and profit from investments. Some businessmen and investors were able to amass huge fortunes. The number of millionaires in the United States grew from perhaps about 20 in 1850 to more than 3,000 in 1900. Among the millionaires was a small group who accumulated fortunes of more than $100 million each. They included Andrew Carnegie, Marshall Field, J. P. Morgan, John D. Rockefeller, and Cornelius Vanderbilt. The wealthy Americans built enormous mansions, wore the finest clothing, ate in the best restaurants, and could afford to buy almost anything they desired.

The Middle Class. Other city people prospered enough to live lives of comfort, if not wealth. They included owners of small businesses, and such workers as factory and office managers. They became part of America's growing middle class.

The Underprivileged. The laborers who toiled in factories, mills, and mines did not share in the benefits of

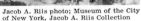

The Lives of the Poor and the Rich contrasted sharply during the industrial period. Poor city people, *left,* lived in a crowded tenement and could barely afford the necessities of life. But the wealthy, such as the well-dressed antique shoppers at the right, enjoyed lives of luxury.

the economic growth. They usually worked at least 60 hours a week for an average pay of about 20 cents an hour, and had no fringe benefits.

As the nation's population grew, so did the competition for jobs. The supply of workers outstripped the demand. Businessmen felt little pressure to improve the lot of workers. They knew that job competition meant poor people would work under almost any conditions. The oversupply of workers led to high unemployment. In addition, depressions slowed the economy to a near standstill in 1873, 1884, 1893, and 1907. Unemployment soared during the depressions. Workers suffered through the periods of idleness without the unemployment benefits that are available today. Such economic hardship meant that, in many cases, every family member except very young children had to seek a job.

The everyday life of the city poor was dismal and drab. The poor lived crowded together in slums. Much of their housing consisted of cheap apartment buildings called *tenements.* The crowded slum neighborhoods bred crime. Overwork, poor sanitation, and inadequate diet left slum dwellers vulnerable to disease. Many poor children received little or no education, because they had to work to contribute to their families' welfare. In addition, schools in the slums were poorly equipped for educating those who attended them.

In spite of harsh living conditions, hope made the lives of many of the poor tolerable. The poor knew that economic advancement was possible in the United States. Some families, through hard work and saving, were able to start small businesses. And—even if a worker himself could not advance economically—he believed that in America his children would.

The Farmers. American farmers also suffered hardships after the Civil War. Advances in agricultural equipment and techniques had enabled most of the

farmers to increase their production. However, *middlemen* between the farmers and the consumers took a large share of the money earned from farm products. The middlemen included owners of railroads, grain elevators, mills, and gins.

The Gilded Age. American author Mark Twain called the era of industrialization "The Gilded Age." Twain used this term to describe the culture of the newly rich of the period. Lacking tradition, the wealthy developed a showy culture supposedly based on the culture of upper-class Europeans. The enormous mansions of the newly rich Americans imitated European palaces. The wealthy filled the mansions with European art works, antiques, rare books, and gaudy decorations. They spent their leisure time attending operas, relaxing at luxurious resorts, or engaging in other functions they believed were signs of refinement.

Most Americans, however, had a far different idea of culture. They enjoyed fairs that exhibited industrial machines, the latest inventions, and other items related to America's material progress. The fairs included the Philadelphia Centennial Exposition of 1876 and the Chicago World's Columbian Exposition of 1893. The American people were eager spectators at circuses, vaudeville shows, and sporting events. Baseball became so popular after 1900 that it was called the *national pastime.* Also after 1900, a new kind of entertainment, the motion picture, began attracting public interest. Many Americans of the industrial era enjoyed playing popular songs from sheet music on parlor pianos, or, after 1877, from records on crude phonographs. The people liked magazines filled with pictures, and *dime novels*—inexpensive books that emphasized adventure and the value of hard work and courage.

Government and the People. After the Civil War, the Democratic and Republican parties developed strong *political machines.* Members of these organizations kept in contact with the people, and did them favors in return for votes. But in general, political and government leaders strongly favored business interests. They did little to interfere with business or to close the gap between the rich and poor.

Government of the era was also marked by widespread corruption. Ulysses S. Grant became President in 1869. Members of Grant's Administration used their government positions for their own financial gain (see GRANT, ULYSSES S. [Political Corruption; Government Frauds]). Corruption also flourished in state and local government. The people seemed little concerned, however. For example, in 1872, Grant won a second term and received more votes than he did the first time.

Reform

A strong spirit of reform swept through the United States during the late 1800's and early 1900's. Large numbers of Americans called for changes in the country's economic, political, and social systems. The reformers wanted to reduce poverty, improve the living conditions of the poor, and regulate big business. They worked to end corruption in government, make government more responsive to the people, and accomplish other goals.

During the 1870's and 1880's, the reformers made relatively little progress. But after 1890, they gained much public support and influence in government. By 1917, the reformers had brought about many changes. Some reformers called themselves *progressives*. As a result, the period of American history from about 1890 to about 1917 is often called the *Progressive Era*.

Early Reform Efforts included movements to organize laborers and farmers. In 1886, skilled laborers formed the American Federation of Labor (AFL)—now the American Federation of Labor-Congress of Industrial Organizations (AFL-CIO). Led by Samuel Gompers, this union bargained with employers and gained better wages and working conditions for its members. Farmers founded the National Grange in 1867 and Farmers' Alliances during the 1870's and 1880's. These groups helped force railroads to lower their charges for hauling farm products and assisted the farmers in other ways.

Unskilled laborers had less success in organizing than did skilled laborers and farmers. The Knights of Labor, a union open to both the unskilled and skilled workers, gained a large membership during the 1880's. But its membership declined sharply after the Haymarket Riot of 1886. In this incident, someone threw a bomb in Haymarket Square in Chicago during a labor dispute. The bomb killed eight policemen and two other persons. Many Americans blamed the disaster on the labor movement. The Haymarket Riot aroused antilabor feelings and weakened the cause of unskilled workers.

The drive for woman suffrage became strong after the Civil War. In 1869, Susan B. Anthony and Elizabeth Cady Stanton founded the National Woman Suffrage Association. The Territory of Wyoming gave women the right to vote the same year. Soon, a few states allowed women to vote, but only in local elections.

Early reformers brought about some changes in government. In 1883, their efforts led to passage of the Pendleton, or Civil Service, Act. This federal law set up the Civil Service Commission, an agency charged with granting federal government jobs on the basis of merit, rather than as political favors. The commission was the first federal government regulatory agency in the nation's history. In 1884, Democrats and liberal Republicans joined together to elect Grover Cleveland President. A reform-minded Democrat, Cleveland did much to enforce the Pendleton Act.

The Progressive Era. The outcry for reform increased sharply after 1890. Clergymen, social workers, and others studied life in the slums and reported on the awful living conditions there. Educators criticized the nation's school system. A group of writers—called *muckrakers* by their critics—published exposés about such evils as corruption in government and how some businessmen cheated the public. The writers included Upton Sinclair, Lincoln Steffens, and Ida M. Tarbell. Increasingly, unskilled workers resorted to strikes in an attempt to gain concessions from their employers. Often, violence broke out between the strikers and strikebreakers hired by the employers. Socialists and others who opposed the U.S. economic system of capitalism supported the strikers and gained a large following.

Corning-Painted Post Historical Soc., Corning, N.Y.　　Sy Seidman (WORLD BOOK photo)　　　　　　　　　　Culver

Popular Entertainment of the period included circuses, dime novels, and—after 1900—motion pictures. A circus parade through a small-town street, *left*, was a highly exciting event. A dime novel, *center*, taught the value of courage. Many movies featured slapstick comedy, *right*.

These and other developments caused many middle-class and some upper-class Americans to back reforms. The people wondered about the justice of a society that tolerated such extremes of poverty and wealth. More and more, the power of big business, corruption in government, violent strikes, and the inroads of socialism seemed to threaten American democracy.

As public support for reform grew, so did the political influence of the reformers. In 1891, farmers and some laborers formed the People's, or Populist, Party. The Populists called for government action to help farmers and laborers. They gained a large following, and convinced many Democrats and Republicans to support reforms. See POPULIST PARTY.

Reformers won control of many city and some state governments. They also elected many congressmen who favored their views. In addition, the first three Presidents elected after 1900—Theodore Roosevelt, William Howard Taft, and Woodrow Wilson—supported certain reform laws. These political developments resulted in a flood of reform legislation on the local, state, and federal levels.

Local and State Legislation. Reformers in local and state government passed many laws to help the poor. Such laws provided for tenement house inspection, playgrounds, and other improvements of life in the slums. Some reform governments expanded public education and forced employers to protect workers against fires and dangerous machinery in factories. The many reformers in local and state government included mayors Samuel M. "Golden Rule" Jones of Toledo, Ohio, and Tom L. Johnson of Cleveland; and governors Woodrow Wilson of New Jersey and Robert M. "Battling Bob" La Follette of Wisconsin. Wisconsin went so far as to pass an income tax, a measure bitterly opposed by the wealthy Americans.

Federal Legislation. In 1890, the federal government passed the Sherman Antitrust Act. This act outlawed trusts and other monopolies that hindered free trade. But the government did little to control monopolies until after Theodore Roosevelt became President in 1901. Roosevelt was a liberal Republican who called for a "square deal" for all Americans. He won lasting fame as a "trust buster." Roosevelt did not oppose monopolies altogether, but he believed they should be regulated whenever they operated against the public interest. In 1903, Roosevelt established the Bureau of Corporations, an agency that collected information on businesses. When the bureau found that a business was violating the Sherman Antitrust Act, the government sued. During Roosevelt's presidency, the government brought suits against more than 40 companies. The most famous suit broke up John D. Rockefeller's Standard Oil Company in 1911.

Roosevelt became the first President to aid laborers in a strike against employers. In 1902, the United Mine Workers struck for better wages and working conditions. Roosevelt asked the miners and the mine owners to settle their differences through arbitration, but the mine owners refused. Angered, the President threatened to have the Army take over the mines. The owners gave in, and reached a compromise with the miners.

In 1906, Upton Sinclair published *The Jungle*, a novel about unsanitary conditions in the meat-packing industry. Roosevelt ordered an investigation of Sinclair's charges, and found they were true. At Roosevelt's urging, Congress passed the Meat Inspection Act and the Federal Food and Drugs Act to regulate food and drug processing.

Republican William Howard Taft succeeded Roosevelt in 1909. Although a conservative, Taft helped further the cause of reform. He brought twice as many suits against businesses as Roosevelt did. He also extended civil service and called for a federal income tax.

In 1912, conservative Republicans backed Taft for their party's presidential nomination, and liberal Republicans supported Roosevelt. Taft won the nomination. The liberals then formed the Progressive, or "Bull Moose," Party and nominated Roosevelt for President. The Republican split enabled reform Democrat Woodrow Wilson to win the presidency. The Democrats also gained control of Congress.

The reform movement flourished under Wilson. Two amendments to the Constitution proposed during Taft's Administration were ratified in 1913. The 16th Amendment gave the federal government the power to levy an

The Progressive Era was marked by widespread demands for reform. Young socialist women, *left,* marched in a parade to demand better treatment of laborers. Such public demonstrations became common tactics among the reformers of the era.

Detail of *Battle of Manila Bay, May 1, 1898*, a lithograph by an unknown Japanese artist; Chicago Historical Society

Victory in the Spanish-American War set the United States on the road toward becoming a world power. The war lasted less than a year. In the Battle of Manila Bay, *above,* American ships commanded by Commodore George Dewey destroyed a Spanish fleet in the Philippines.

income tax. The 17th Amendment provided for the election of U.S. senators by the people, rather than by state legislatures. The Clayton Antitrust Act of 1914 struck a blow against monopolies. It prohibited corporations from grouping together under interlocking boards of directors. It also helped labor by making it impossible to prosecute unions under antitrust laws. In 1914, the government set up the Federal Trade Commission (FTC) to handle complaints about unfair business practices. The many other reform measures passed during Wilson's presidency included the Underwood Tariff Act of 1913, which lowered a high tariff that protected American business from foreign competition.

For more details on this era of reform in the United States, see PROGRESSIVE MOVEMENT.

Foreign Affairs

During the 1870's and 1880's, the United States paid relatively little attention to foreign affairs. In comparison to such European nations as France, Germany, and Great Britain, America was weak militarily and had little influence in international politics. Among Europeans, American diplomats had the reputation of being bumbling amateurs. German leader Otto von Bismarck summed up the European attitude toward America. He said, "A special Providence takes care of fools, drunkards, and the United States." During the 1890's and early 1900's, however, the United States developed into a world power and took a leading role in international affairs.

The Spanish-American War of 1898 marked a turning point in U.S. foreign policy. Spain ruled Cuba, Puerto Rico, the Philippines, and other overseas possessions during the 1890's. In the mid-1890's, Cubans revolted against their Spanish rulers. Many Americans demanded that the United States aid the rebels. On Feb. 15, 1898, the U.S. battleship *Maine* was blown up off the coast of Havana, Cuba. No one is certain who

caused the explosion, but many Americans blamed the Spaniards. Demands for action against Spain grew, and "Remember the *Maine*" became a nationwide war cry. On April 25, 1898, at the request of President William McKinley, Congress declared war on Spain. The United States quickly defeated Spain, and the Treaty of Paris of Dec. 10, 1898, officially ended the war. Under it, the United States received Guam, Puerto Rico, and the Philippines from Spain. Also in 1898, the United States annexed Hawaii. See SPANISH-AMERICAN WAR; HAWAII (History).

A World Power. Roosevelt succeeded McKinley as President in 1901. He expressed his foreign policy strategy with the slogan, "Speak Softly and Carry a Big Stick." Roosevelt meant that the country must back up its diplomatic efforts with military strength.

The United States built up its armed forces under Roosevelt. In 1902, Germany, Great Britain, and Italy blockaded Venezuela in an attempt to collect debts from that South American nation. Citing the Monroe Doctrine, Roosevelt forced the Europeans to withdraw. In 1903, the President used a threat of force to gain the right to dig the Panama Canal (see PANAMA CANAL [History]). America took over the finances of the Dominican Republic in 1905 to keep that country stable and free from European intervention. In 1916, during Wilson's Administration, American troops occupied the Dominican Republic to keep order there. These and other actions showed that the United States had emerged as a world power.

War Clouds in Europe. In 1914, long-standing problems among European nations led to the outbreak of World War I. In this fierce, destructive struggle, the *Central Powers* (Germany and a few other nations) lined up against the *Allies* (France, Great Britain, Italy, Russia, and many smaller countries). Before long, events would drag the United States into the war and test its new role as a world power.

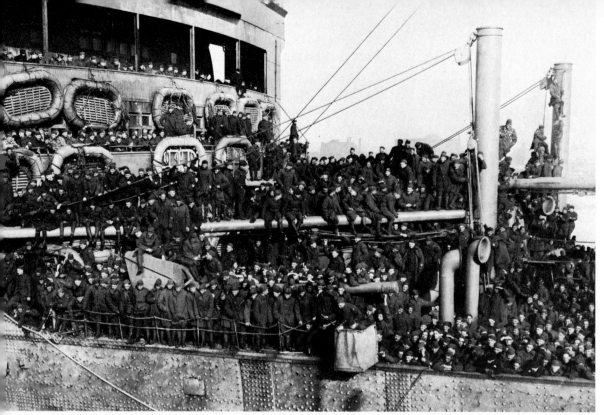

World War I marked the first time the United States had fought a full-scale war on foreign territory. In 1917 and 1918, troopships carried about 2 million American fighting men across the Atlantic to Europe. Called *doughboys*, the Americans helped the Allies defeat Germany.

UNITED STATES HISTORY: 1917-1929 / A New Place in the World

The United States stayed out of World War I until 1917. But then, German acts of aggression convinced President Wilson and most other Americans of the need to join the war against Germany in order to make the world "safe for democracy." For the first time in its history, the United States mobilized for a full-scale war on foreign territory. About 2 million American fighting men soon crossed the Atlantic in troopships. The *doughboys*, as the troops were called, played an important role in the Allied victory in 1918.

The decade following World War I brought sweeping changes to American life. The economy entered a period of spectacular—though uneven—growth. Spurred on by the good times and a desire to be "modern," large numbers of Americans adopted new attitudes and life styles. The booming economy and fast-paced life of the decade gave it the nickname of the *Roaring Twenties*. But the good times ended abruptly. In 1929, a stock-market crash triggered the worst and longest depression in America's history.

World War I and the Peace

The United States in the War. After World War I began in 1914, the United States repeatedly stated its position of neutrality. But increasingly, German acts of aggression brought America closer to joining the Allies. On May 7, 1915, a German submarine sank the British passenger ship *Lusitania*. The attack killed 1,198

people, including 128 American passengers. Wilson and other Americans bitterly protested this killing of defenseless civilians, and Germany agreed to stop such attacks.

Wilson won re-election in November, 1916, using the slogan, "He Kept Us Out of War." But four months later, German submarines began sinking American merchant ships. This and other acts of aggression led the U.S. to declare war on Germany on April 6, 1917.

The American people rallied around their government's decision to go to war. Almost 2 million men volunteered for service, and about 3 million were drafted. The doughboys fought valiantly in the trenches, forests, and fields of France and helped the battered Allies turn back a major German offensive. On the home front, the spirit of patriotism grew to a fever pitch. Americans willingly let the government take near full control of the economy for the good of the war effort. The people bought billions of dollars worth of Liberty Bonds to help pay the cost of the war. Movie stars, including Charlie Chaplin and Mary Pickford, toured the country to promote bond sales. Fiery patriotic songs such as George M. Cohan's "Over There" and "You're a Grand Old Flag" gave a lift to the spirits of the doughboys and the public alike.

World War I ended in an Allied victory with the signing of an armistice on Nov. 11, 1918. For a detailed account of the conflict, see WORLD WAR I.

The Peace Conference and Treaty. In 1919, the Allies held the Paris Peace Conference to draw up the terms of the peace with Germany. Wilson viewed the conference as an opportunity to establish lasting peace among nations. He proposed a list of terms called the *Fourteen Points* to be used as a guide for the peace settlement. The terms included arms reductions and settlement of disputed territorial claims (see FOURTEEN POINTS). But the other leading Allies were chiefly interested in gaining territory and war payments from Germany. They adopted the Treaty of Versailles, which ignored almost all of Wilson's proposals. The treaty stripped Germany of its armed forces and much territory, and forced it to pay high war damages.

The Treaty of Versailles did make provision for one of Wilson's proposals—an association of nations (later called the League of Nations) that would work to maintain peace. But Wilson suffered a final blow to his peace plans when the United States Senate failed to ratify the Treaty of Versailles. Thus, the Senate rejected U.S. participation in the League of Nations. See VERSAILLES, TREATY OF; LEAGUE OF NATIONS; WILSON, WOODROW (Wilson's Second Administration).

Life During the Roaring Twenties

In many ways, the 1920's marked the point at which the United States began developing into the modern society it is today. During and after World War I, people continued to move from farms to cities in record numbers. The 1920 United States Census reported that, for the first time, a majority of Americans lived in urban areas. By the end of the Roaring Twenties, such features of modern life as the automobile, telephone, radio, and electric washing machine had become part of millions of American households. In 1927, aviation pioneer Charles A. Lindbergh helped launch the modern air age when he made the first solo flight across the Atlantic Ocean.

The role of American women changed dramatically during the 1920's. The 19th Amendment to the Constitution, which became law on Aug. 26, 1920, gave women the right to vote in all elections. In addition, many new opportunities for education and careers opened up to women during the decade.

Modern Life and Social Change. Developments of the 1920's broadened the experiences of millions of Americans. The mass movement to cities meant more people could enjoy such activities as movies, plays, and sporting events. Radio broadcasting began on a large scale during the 1920's. It brought news of the world and entertainment into millions of urban and rural homes. The automobile gave people a new way to get around—whether for business, or to see far-off places, or just for fun. Motion-picture theaters became part of almost every city and town during the 1920's. They became known as *dream palaces* because of their fancy design and the excitement and romance that movies provided for the public. The new role of women also changed society. Many women who found careers outside the home began thinking of themselves more as the equal of men, and less as housewives and mothers.

Change and Problems. The modern trends of the 1920's brought about problems as well as benefits.

Many Americans had trouble adjusting to the impersonal, fast-paced life of cities. This disorientation led to a rise in juvenile delinquency, crime, and other antisocial behavior. The complex life in cities also tended to weaken the strong family ties that had always been part of American society. See CITY (City Problems [Social Problems]).

The 18th Amendment to the Constitution, called the prohibition amendment, caused unforeseen problems. It outlawed the sale of alcoholic beverages throughout the United States as of Jan. 16, 1920. Large numbers of otherwise law-abiding citizens considered prohibition a violation of their rights. They ignored the law and bought liquor provided by underworld gangs. The supplying of illegal liquor, called *bootlegging*, helped many gangs prosper. In addition, competition for control of the lucrative bootlegging business led to many gang wars. See PROHIBITION.

The Flaming Youth. In an effort to be modern, many young men and women of the Roaring Twenties adopted a life style that earned them the nickname of the *Flaming Youth*. Women began wearing radically new clothing styles. Short skirts, rolled-down stockings, and short "bobbed" hair replaced the full-length dresses and long hair of earlier days. Women who wore such clothes became known as *flappers*. The flappers and their *beaus* (boyfriends) enjoyed such new thrills as speeding around in automobiles. They—along with many of their elders—often visited supposedly secret

Period Facts in Brief

Presidents (with political parties and dates of service)
Woodrow Wilson, Democrat, 1913-1921
Warren G. Harding, Republican, 1921-1923
Calvin Coolidge, Republican, 1923-1929
Herbert C. Hoover, Republican, 1929-1933

States in the Union
Number at start of period: 48
States added during the period: none.

Important Dates
1917-1918 The United States fought in World War I.
1920 The Senate rejected American participation in the League of Nations.
1920 The U.S. Census showed that, for the first time, the majority of Americans lived in urban areas.
1920 The 18th Amendment, prohibiting the sale of alcoholic beverages nationwide, became effective; the 19th Amendment gave women complete suffrage.
1922 The government raised tariffs to the highest level ever.
1925 The Scopes Trial in Dayton, Tenn., upheld the right of a state to ban the teaching of evolution in public schools.
c. 1925 The Golden Age of radio broadcasting began.
1927 Charles A. Lindbergh made the first solo flight across the Atlantic Ocean.
1927 *The Jazz Singer*, the first motion-picture "talkie," appeared.
1929 The stock-market crash brought financial ruin to thousands of investors.

Population Growth and Change
Total population, 101,297,851
1917
Rural, 50%   Urban, 50%
Total population, 121,670,000
1929
Rural, 44%   Urban, 56%

Ford Archives, Henry Ford Museum, Dearborn, Mich.

Automobile Ownership soared in the 1920's. During the decade, the number of automobiles in the United States nearly tripled. Cars soon crowded the streets of every American city and town.

Jazzmen Photo from Ramsey Archive

A Jazz Band and dancers dressed in flapper costumes entertain a nightclub audience, *above*. Jazz became so popular in the 1920's that the decade is sometimes called the *Jazz Age*.

Brown Bros.

Revival Meetings attracted large numbers of people during the 1920's. At these meetings, evangelists such as Billy Sunday, *on platform above*, delivered emotional sermons.

nightclubs called *speakeasies*. At the speakeasies, people drank bootleg liquor; listened to jazz, the latest craze in popular music; and danced the Charleston and other modern steps.

An Age of Heroes. Americans of the Roaring Twenties developed strong admiration for individual accomplishment. Lindbergh's transatlantic flight made him a national hero. Sports superstars of the 1920's won the public's admiration for their ability to excel within the rules of the game. The stars included Red Grange of football, Jack Dempsey of boxing, Bobby Jones of golf, Bill Tilden and Helen Wills of tennis, and—most of all—baseball's Babe Ruth. Even attitudes toward big businessmen changed during the 1920's. Despised by many in earlier days, businessmen gained widespread admiration for their accomplishments.

The movies provided the public with daring fictional heroes, including good, strong cowboys who always defeated bad Indians or outlaws. In literature, F. Scott Fitzgerald created fictional characters whose pleasure-seeking lives won public admiration. But other authors saw little glamour in American life. For example, Sinclair Lewis won fame for novels that portrayed the "average American" as narrow-minded and dull. Ernest Hemingway scorned society's values and made heroes of the "lost generation"—people who did not fit into modern life.

Looking Backward. Not all Americans saw the changes brought about during the Roaring Twenties as being desirable. Many people yearned for a return to old American traditions, a trend that was reflected in many areas of life. In politics, it led to the return of a conservative federal government. In his successful presidential campaign of 1920, Warren G. Harding used the slogan "A Return to Normalcy." To many people, returning to "normalcy" meant ending the strong role of the federal government that marked the early 1900's. It also meant *isolation*, a turning away from the affairs of the outside world. Isolation—a reaction to World

Wide World   Culver

Heroes of the 1920's included Babe Ruth and Charles A. Lindbergh. Ruth became the most famous sports star of the decade. Lindbergh made the first solo flight across the Atlantic Ocean.

War I—became a feature of American foreign policy during the 1920's.

In religion, the trend toward tradition led to an upsurge of *revivalism* (emotional religious preaching). Revival meetings were most common in rural areas, but also spread to cities. Billy Sunday, once a major-league baseball player, drew wildly enthusiastic crowds to his revivals in big cities.

The conservative Americans of the Roaring Twenties also called for a return to law and order. They denounced violations of prohibition and other crimes. However, few people seemed too bothered when, in 1923, investigators revealed widespread corruption in the Harding Administration (see HARDING, WARREN G. [Government Scandals]; TEAPOT DOME).

The Ku Klux Klan had died out in the 1870's, but a new Klan gained a large following during the 1920's. The new Klan had easy answers for Americans troubled by modern problems. It blamed the problems on "outsiders," including blacks, Jews, Roman Catholics, foreigners, and political radicals. Both Northerners and Southerners joined the Ku Klux Klan. At its height, the Klan had perhaps 5 million members. See KU KLUX KLAN (In the 1900's).

The Economy—Boom and Bust

During the 1920's, the American economy soared to spectacular heights. Wartime government restrictions on business ended. Conservatives gained control of the federal government and adopted policies that aided big business. New technological developments also contributed to business growth.

But in spite of its growth and apparent strength, the economy was on shaky grounds. Only one segment of the economy—manufacturing—prospered. The distribution of wealth grew lopsided. Businessmen grew rich, but farmers and laborers became worse off than before the war. Finally, in 1929, wild speculation led to a stock-market crash that toppled the economy like a house of cards.

Government and Business. The American people grew tired of the federal government's involvement in society that marked the Progressive Era and the war years. They elected to Congress conservatives who promised to reduce the role of government. Also, all three Presidents elected during the 1920's—Harding, Calvin Coolidge, and Herbert Hoover—were Republicans who agreed with the policy.

The federal government, however, did what it could to promote American business. In 1922, the government passed the Fordney-McCumber Act, which raised tariff duties to the highest level ever in order to keep foreign goods from competing with American products. This and other measures did much to help American business flourish.

Technology enabled American manufacturers to develop new products, improve existing ones, and turn out goods much faster and more cheaply than ever before. Sales of such items as electric washing machines, refrigerators, and radios soared. But the manufacturing boom depended most heavily on the growth of the automobile industry. Before and during the 1920's, Henry Ford and others refined car manufacturing to a science.

The cost of automobiles continued to drop and sales soared. In just 10 years between 1920 and 1930, the number of cars registered in the United States almost tripled, growing from about 8 million to 23 million. The thriving automobile industry triggered growth in such related industries as steel, road construction, gasoline sales, and tourism.

Agriculture and Labor did not share in the prosperity. A reduced market for farm goods in war-torn Europe and a slowdown in the U.S. population growth led to a decline in the demand for American farm products. Organized labor suffered major setbacks during the 1920's. A lack of government support reduced the power of unions in their dealing with employers, and workers in many new industries remained unorganized. Widespread poverty among farmers and laborers cut into the demand for manufactured goods, a contributing factor to the upcoming depression.

Investments, Speculation, and the Crash. The economic growth of the 1920's led more Americans than ever to invest in the stocks of corporations. The investments, in turn, provided companies with a flood of new capital for business expansion. As investors poured money into the stock market, the value of stocks soared. The upsweep led to widespread speculation, which pushed the value of stocks far beyond the level justified by earnings and dividends. Much of the speculation involved buying stocks *on margin;* that is, paying a fraction of the cost and borrowing the rest.

Such unsound investment practices led to the stock-market crash of 1929. In late October, a decline in stock prices set in. Panic selling followed, lowering stock prices drastically and dragging investors to financial ruin. When the year ended, the government estimated that the crash had cost investors $40 billion. The crash combined with the other weaknesses in the economy to bring on the Great Depression of the 1930's.

For more details on the decade of the 1920's, see ROARING TWENTIES.

Wide World

The Stock-Market Crash of 1929 brought an abrupt end to the prosperity of the Roaring Twenties. Crowds of panic-stricken investors gathered aimlessly on Wall Street after the crash, *above.*

The Great Depression of the 1930's spread poverty throughout the United States. Hungry, unemployed Americans stood in long "bread lines" to receive food paid for by charitable donations. The hard times dragged on until 1942, after the United States entered World War II.

UNITED STATES HISTORY: 1930-1959/Depression and a World in Conflict

The United States suffered through the Great Depression that followed the stock-market crash of 1929 for more than 10 years. During the depression, millions of workers lost their jobs and large numbers of farmers were forced to abandon their farms. Poverty swept through the nation on a scale never before experienced.

The Great Depression was not limited to the United States. It struck almost every other country in the world. In some countries, the hard times helped bring to power dictators who promised action to restore the economy. The dictators included Adolf Hitler in Germany and a group of military leaders in Japan. Once in power, both Hitler and the Japanese rulers began conquering neighboring lands. Their actions led to World War II, the most destructive conflict in the history of man. The United States fought in the war from 1941 to 1945, and played a key role in defeating Germany and Japan.

Victory in World War II brought a spirit of great relief and joy to the United States. The postwar economy boomed. More people shared in the prosperity than ever before, creating a huge, well-to-do middle class. Even so, Americans still faced problems. Chief among them were the new threat of nuclear war, the growing strength of Communism, and discontent among Americans who did not share in the prosperity.

The Great Depression

The Road to Ruin. The stock-market crash sent shock waves through the American financial community.

Banks greatly curtailed their loans to businesses, and businessmen then cut back on production. Millions of people lost their jobs because of the cutbacks. Spending then dwindled, and businesses suffered even more. Factories and stores shut down, causing even higher unemployment. Consumption of farm products declined, and farmers became worse off than ever. Thousands of banks failed during the depression and foreign trade decreased sharply. By the early 1930's, the nation's economy was paralyzed.

The Depression and the People. At the height of the depression in 1933, about 13 million Americans were out of work, and many others had only part-time jobs. Farm income declined so sharply that more than 750,000 farmers lost their land. The Dust Bowl, the result of a terrible drought on the western Great Plains, also wiped out many farmers (see DUST BOWL). Hundreds of thousands of people lost their life savings as a result of the bank failures.

Throughout the depression, many Americans went hungry. People stood in "bread lines" and went to "soup kitchens" to get food provided by charities. Often, two or more families lived crowded together in a small apartment. Some homeless people built shacks of tin and scraps of wood in vacant areas. They called these clumps of shacks *Hoovervilles*—a scornful reference to Herbert Hoover, President when the depression struck. In 1932, about 15,000 World War I veterans marched on Washington, D.C., to demand an early payment of a government bonus owed them. Hoover ordered troops to drive them out of the city.

Roosevelt, Recovery, and Reform. Early in the Great Depression, Hoover promised that prosperity was "just around the corner." But the depression deepened as the election of 1932 approached. The Republicans slated Hoover for re-election. The Democrats chose Franklin Delano Roosevelt. In his campaign, Roosevelt promised government action to end the Great Depression and reforms to avoid future depressions. The people responded, and Roosevelt won a landslide victory.

Roosevelt's program for recovery and reform was called the *New Deal*. Its many provisions included public works projects to provide jobs, relief for farmers, aid to manufacturing firms, and the regulation of banks. A solidly Democratic Congress approved almost every measure Roosevelt proposed. Many new government agencies were set up to help fight the depression. The agencies included the Civilian Conservation Corps (CCC) and the Works Progress Administration (WPA), both of which provided jobs; the Farm Credit Administration (FCA), which extended credit to farmers; and the Social Security Board, which developed the social security system.

The New Deal helped relieve the hardship of many Americans. But hard times dragged on until World War II military spending stimulated the economy.

Roosevelt's efforts to end the depression made him one of the most popular U.S. Presidents. The voters elected him to four terms. No other President won election more than twice. Roosevelt's New Deal was a turning point in American history. It marked the start of a strong government role in the nation's economic affairs that has continued and grown to the present day. See GREAT DEPRESSION; NEW DEAL.

The United States in World War II

World War II began on Sept. 1, 1939, when German troops overran Poland. France, Great Britain, and other nations (called the Allies) went to war against Germany.

Period Facts in Brief

Presidents (with political parties and dates of service)
Herbert C. Hoover, Republican, 1929-1933
Franklin D. Roosevelt, Democrat, 1933-1945
Harry S. Truman, Democrat, 1945-1953
Dwight D. Eisenhower, Republican, 1953-1961

States in the Union

Number at start of period: 48
Number at end of period: 50
States added during the period:
Alaska (1959), Hawaii (1959).

Important Dates

1930's The United States suffered through the Great Depression.
1933 President Franklin D. Roosevelt began the New Deal program to try to end the depression.
1941-1945 The United States fought in World War II.
1945 An American airplane dropped the first atomic bomb used in warfare on Hiroshima, Japan.
1945 The United States became a charter member of the United Nations (UN).
1947 President Truman announced the Truman Doctrine, which pledged American aid to nations threatened by Communism.
1950's Television became part of most American homes.
1950 Senator Joseph R. McCarthy gained national fame by charging that Communists had infiltrated the federal government.
1950-1953 The United States fought in the Korean War.
1954 The Supreme Court ruled compulsory segregation in public schools unconstitutional.
1955 Martin Luther King, Jr., began organizing a movement to protest discrimination against blacks.
1957 Russia launched *Sputnik I*—the first space satellite—causing the United States to place more emphasis on space research.

Population Growth and Change

Total population, 122,775,046
1930
Rural, 44%   Urban, 56%

Total population, 175,608,490
1959
Rural, 31%   Urban, 69%

Library of Congress

The Dust Bowl spread across the Great Plains and the Southwest during the Depression, destroying much farmland. It was caused by a drought accompanied by severe dust storms.

Wide World

World War II Defense Workers included many women. The women filled jobs vacated by men who entered the armed forces. They helped supply the men with planes, ships, and weapons.

American Planes Dropped Atomic Bombs on the Japanese cities of Hiroshima and Nagasaki in 1945. The destruction from these blasts caused Japan to surrender, ending World War II.

At first, America stayed out of the war. But on Dec. 7, 1941, Japanese planes bombed the U.S. military base at Pearl Harbor, Hawaii. The United States declared war on Japan on December 8, and on Germany and Italy—Germany's chief ally—three days later.

The War Effort. The American people backed the war effort with fierce dedication. About 15 million American men served in the armed forces. They ranged from teenagers to men well over 40. More than 200,000 women volunteered for service. At home, automobile plants and other factories were converted into defense plants where airplanes, ships, weapons, and other war supplies were made. The country had a shortage of civilian men, and so thousands of women worked in the defense plants. With a combination of humor and admiration, people called the women defense workers "Rosie the Riveter." Even children took part in the war effort. Boys and girls collected used tin cans, old tires, and other "junk" that could be recycled and used for war supplies.

Allied Victory. On May 7, 1945, after a long, bitter struggle, the Americans and other Allies forced the mighty German war machine to surrender. Vice-President Harry S. Truman had become President upon Roosevelt's death about a month earlier. Truman demanded Japan's surrender, but the Japanese continued to fight on. Truman then made one of the major decisions in history. He ordered the use of the atomic bomb, a weapon many times more destructive than any previous weapon. An American airplane dropped the first atomic bomb used in warfare on Hiroshima, Japan, on Aug. 6, 1945. A second atomic bomb was dropped on Nagasaki on August 9 (see ATOMIC BOMB). Japan formally surrendered on September 2, and the war was over. For more details, see WORLD WAR II.

The Threat of Communism

The United States and Russia both fought on the side of the Allies during World War II. But after the war, the two countries became bitter enemies. Russia, as a Communist country, opposed democracy. It helped Communists take control of most of the countries of Eastern Europe and also aided Communists who seized control of China.

Russia and China then set out to spread Communism to other lands. The United States, as the world's most powerful democratic country, took on the role of defending non-Communist nations threatened by Communist take-over. The containment of Communism became the major goal of U.S. postwar foreign policy.

The Cold War and Foreign Policy. The postwar struggle between the American-led non-Communist nations and Russia and its Communist allies became known as the *Cold War.* It was so named because it did not lead to fighting, or a "hot" war, on a major scale.

Both the United States and Russia built up arsenals of atomic bombs, more powerful hydrogen bombs, and other nuclear weapons. The nuclear weapons made each nation capable of destroying the other. The threat of nuclear war made both sides cautious. As a result, Cold War strategy emphasized threats of force, propaganda, and aid to weak nations. The United Nations (UN), founded in 1945, provided a forum where the nations could try to settle their Cold War disputes.

Truman and Dwight D. Eisenhower, the first two Presidents of the Cold War era, pledged American military support to any nation threatened by Communism. Also, the United States provided billions of dollars to non-Communist nations. See COLD WAR.

The Korean War resulted from the Cold War friction. On June 25, 1950, troops from Communist North Korea, equipped by Russia, invaded South Korea. The UN called on member nations to help restore peace. Truman sent American troops to aid South Korea, and the UN sent a fighting force made up of troops from many nations. The war lasted for three years, ending in a truce on July 27, 1953. See KOREAN WAR.

Communism and Internal Friction. The spread of Communism caused deep divisions within the United States. Conservatives blamed the Roosevelt and Truman Administrations for allowing the Communist postwar gains. They also claimed that Communists were infiltrating the American government. The charges led to widespread investigations of—and debate over—the extent of Communist influence in American government and society. Conservatives believed the investigations were needed to save the country from Communist control. Liberals charged the conservatives with conducting "witch hunts"; that is, trying to fix guilt on people without evidence. See UN-AMERICAN ACTIVITIES COMMITTEE; HISS, ALGER; McCARTHY, JOSEPH R.

Postwar Society

After World War II, the United States entered the greatest period of economic growth in its history. Periods of *inflation* (rapidly rising prices) and *recession* (mild business slumps) occurred. But overall, businesses and people prospered. Prosperity spread to more Americans than ever before, resulting in major changes in American life. However, not all people shared in the prosperity. Millions of Americans—including a high percentage of the nation's blacks—continued to live in poverty. The existence of poverty amid prosperity

Suburban Housing Developments sprang up around American cities after World War II. The postwar prosperity enabled millions of people to afford new houses in the suburbs.

A Civil Rights Law banning compulsory school segregation led to a dramatic incident in 1957. President Eisenhower sent federal troops to escort black students into an all-white Arkansas school.

brought on a period of active social protest that has continued to the present day.

Prosperity Returns. Military spending during World War II drew the United States out of the Great Depression. Major industries, such as automobile manufacturing and housing construction, had all but stopped during the war. After the war, these industries resumed production on a much larger scale than ever. Relatively new industries such as electronics, plastics, frozen foods, and jet aircraft became booming businesses.

The shortage of goods during the war and other factors combined to create a vast market for American products. A soaring birth rate boosted the number of consumers. Between 1950 and 1960 alone, the population of the United States grew by about 28 million. Labor unions became stronger than ever, and gained high wages and other benefits for their members. Wage laws and other government regulations also helped give workers a greater share of the profits of business. These developments also meant that more Americans had more money to spend on goods.

A New Life Style resulted from the prosperity. After the war, millions of people needed, and were able to afford, new housing. Construction companies quickly built up huge clusters of houses in suburbs around the nation's cities. Vast numbers of Americans moved from cities to suburbs. The suburbs attracted people for many reasons. They offered newer housing, more open space, and—usually—better schools than the central cities. See SUBURB; CITY (Metropolitan Cities).

A rise in automobile ownership accompanied the suburban growth. The majority of suburbanites worked in the central cities and depended on cars to get to and from work. Most suburbs lacked good local transportation systems, and so families relied on cars to go shopping or almost anywhere else. Between 1940 and 1960, the number of automobiles registered in the United States jumped from about $27\frac{1}{2}$ million to $61\frac{1}{2}$ million. By 1960, over three-fourths of all American families

owned a car, and almost a fifth owned more than one.

Increased automobile traffic led to the building of a nationwide network of superhighways. The car and prosperity enabled more people than ever to take vacation trips. New motels, fast-service restaurants, and gas stations sprang up to serve the tourists.

Prosperity and technological advances changed American life in other ways. Television—an experimental device before the war—became a feature of most American homes during the 1950's. This wonder of modern science brought scenes of the world into the American living room at the flick of a switch. Fascinated, large numbers of people made TV watching one of their main leisure-time activities (see TELEVISION [History]). New appliances made household work easier for American families. They included automatic washers, driers, dishwashers, and garbage disposers.

Poverty and Discrimination. In spite of the general prosperity, millions of Americans still lived in poverty. The poor included members of all races, but the plight of the nation's poor blacks seemed especially bleak. Ever since emancipation, blacks in both the North and South had faced discrimination in jobs, housing, education, and other areas. A lack of education and jobs made poverty among blacks widespread.

During the early 1900's, blacks, joined by many whites, had begun a movement to extend civil rights to blacks. The movement gained momentum after World War II. Efforts of civil rights leaders resulted in several Supreme Court decisions that attacked discrimination. In the best-known case, *Brown v. Board of Education of Topeka* (1954), the court ruled compulsory segregation in public schools illegal.

In spite of the gains, many civil rights leaders became dissatisfied with the slow progress of their movement. In 1955, Martin Luther King, Jr., a Baptist minister, began organizing demonstrations protesting discrimination. Before long, the public protest would become a major tool of Americans seeking change.

A Photograph of the Earth taken by astronauts orbiting the moon, *above*, is an example of America's leading role in science and technology. But despite its many accomplishments, the United States today faces a variety of problems and challenges—just as it has throughout its history.

UNITED STATES HISTORY / *America Since 1960*

The period of American history since 1960 has been marked by a continuation of many postwar trends. For much of the period, the country's foreign policy remained focused on the containment of Communism. The economy continued to expand, despite recurring periods of inflation and recession. The movement of people from cities to suburbs continued steadily. The 1970 U.S. Census showed that, for the first time, more Americans lived in suburbs than in cities.

The country continued to be a leader in scientific and technological advancements. It made great strides in medicine that helped reduce human suffering, and its technological skill provided the means for a new and exciting field of exploration—outer space.

At the same time, events and new public attitudes brought dramatic social changes to the United States. The black civil rights movement grew in intensity during the 1960's. Many other groups—including American Indians, Mexican Americans, and women—also began demanding fuller rights. In the mid-1960's, many Americans began challenging their government's foreign-policy decisions. Protesters of all kinds staged demonstrations to try to bring about change. Most demonstrations were conducted peacefully. But in some cases, they led to violence.

Crime and violence soared in the United States after 1960, and pollution threatened the environment. Concern over political corruption grew in the 1970's, and helped bring about the first resignation of an American President, Richard M. Nixon.

As in every other period of history, the list of the nation's problems was long. But at the same time, most Americans maintained a deep pride in their country. The many accomplishments of the American people throughout the nation's 200-year history gave hope for the future.

The 1960's

The Civil Rights Movement. The black civil rights movement became the main domestic issue in the United States during the early 1960's. Increasingly, blacks—joined by whites—staged demonstrations in order to dramatize their demands for rights and equality. One of the highlights of the movement came on Aug. 28, 1963, when more than 200,000 people staged a *freedom march* called the March on Washington in Washington, D.C.

John F. Kennedy, who became President in 1961, urged Congress to pass legislation outlawing discrimination on the basis of race. Kennedy was killed by an assassin on Nov. 22, 1963, and Vice-President Lyndon B. Johnson became President. Johnson, a former U.S. senator skilled in dealing with legislators, persuaded Congress to pass many major civil rights laws.

The Civil Rights Act of 1964 outlawed discrimination in employment, voter registration, and public accommodations. The Civil Rights Act of 1968 was designed to end discrimination in the sale and renting of housing. Congress, at Johnson's urging, also provided financial aid for the needy as part of a program that Johnson called the War on Poverty. For a detailed account of the civil rights movement, see the NEGRO article.

Urban Unrest. In spite of government aid and a generally booming economy, poverty remained a major problem in America's central cities. Discontent among blacks in poor, decaying neighborhoods grew. In the mid-1960's, blacks staged riots in the ghettos of Chicago, Cleveland, Detroit, Los Angeles, New York City, Newark, and other cities. They also rioted in 1968, following the assassination of Martin Luther King, Jr.

The number of such crimes as murder, robbery, and rape soared during the 1960's. The crime rate was especially high in the central cities, but also increased rapidly in suburbs and elsewhere. Sociologists attributed the rising crime rate to many factors, including the weakening of the family, poverty, mental illness, drug addiction, and a feeling of hopelessness and alienation.

The Vietnam War brought further turmoil to the United States in the 1960's. The war had begun in 1957 as a battle for control of South Vietnam between the non-Communist government and Communists. In the late 1950's and early 1960's, Presidents Eisenhower and Kennedy sent military aid and advisers to support the South Vietnam government. Soon after Johnson became President, the Communists threatened to topple the government. Johnson responded to the threat by sending hundreds of thousands of American combat troops to help South Vietnam fight the Communists. By the mid-1960's, the United States was deeply involved in the Vietnam War.

Public response to the Vietnam War differed sharply from the near unanimous public support in World Wars I and II. A majority of Americans supported the war effort at first, but others bitterly opposed it. In the late 1960's, opposition to the war grew. The war critics argued that the United States had no right to interfere in Vietnamese affairs. Throughout the nation, college students and others staged demonstrations to protest America's involvement in Vietnam.

Johnson, discouraged by the criticism of his Vietnam policy, refused to run for re-election in 1968. The people elected Richard M. Nixon, partly because he pledged to end U.S. involvement in the war. But as the 1960's drew to a close, American troops were still fighting in Vietnam.

Space Exploration by American astronauts provided a high note during the troubled 1960's. On May 5, 1961, astronaut Alan B. Shepard soared into space from a launching pad at Cape Canaveral, Fla. Shepard earned the distinction of becoming the first American in space. Throughout the 1960's, the United States and Russia matched their technological skills in a race to land the first person on the moon. Then, on July 20, 1969, millions of people watched on television as U.S. astronaut Neil A. Armstrong climbed down from his spacecraft and became the first person to set foot on the moon. For the story of America's accomplishments in space, see SPACE TRAVEL.

Recent Developments

The Spreading Drive for Equality. The drive for equality that began with blacks spread to other minority groups. American Indians, Mexican Americans, and others organized active movements aimed at gaining equality (see INDIAN, AMERICAN [Indians Today]; MEXI-

Period Facts in Brief

Presidents (with political parties and dates of service)

Dwight D. Eisenhower, Republican, 1953-1961
John F. Kennedy, Democrat, 1961-1963
Lyndon B. Johnson, Democrat, 1963-1969
Richard M. Nixon, Republican, 1969-1974
Gerald R. Ford, Republican, 1974-

States in the Union

Number at start of period: 50
States added during the period: none.

Important Dates

1961 Astronaut Alan B. Shepard became the first American in space.

1962 Russia removed missiles from Cuba, ending a threat of war with the United States.

1963 More than 200,000 civil rights demonstrators staged the March on Washington in Washington, D.C.

1964 Congress passed a flood of important civil rights legislation.

1965 American combat troops began fighting in the Vietnam War.

1965 The first of a series of urban riots by blacks broke out in the Watts section of Los Angeles.

1969 Astronaut Neil A. Armstrong became the first person to set foot on the moon.

1973 The United States removed its last combat troops from Vietnam.

1974 Richard M. Nixon became the first American President to resign from office.

1976 The United States celebrated its bicentennial—the 200th anniversary of its founding.

Population Growth and Change

Total population, 179,323,175

1960

Rural, 30%   Urban, 70%

Total population, 217,544,000

1976

Rural, 24%   Urban, 76%

Wide World

Civil Rights for Blacks became a major national issue during the 1960's. About 200,000 persons, including both blacks and whites, took part in the March on Washington in 1963.

David Burnett

Protest Demonstrations became a common tool among Americans seeking change in the 1960's. The young people above called for an end to U.S. participation in the Vietnam War.

Alex Webb, Magnum

The Watergate Scandal forced President Richard M. Nixon, *left on carpet,* to resign from office in 1974. Vice-President Gerald R. Ford, *right,* succeeded Nixon as President.

CAN AMERICANS). In addition, large numbers of women began calling for an end to discrimination based on sex. Their activities became known as the Women's Liberation Movement. The movement helped bring about greater equality for women in employment and other areas (see WOMAN [Woman's Roles Today]).

Pollution and Conservation. As the country's industry and population grew, so did the pollution of its environment. Smoke from factories and fumes from automobiles filled the air with dangerous gases. Wastes from factories and other sources polluted many rivers and lakes. In the late 1960's, large numbers of Americans began demanding government action to control environmental pollution. In response to these demands, the government passed many antipollution laws. But the pollution problem remains severe. See ENVIRONMENTAL POLLUTION.

The need to conserve energy has become another pressing problem for the country. America's many industries, households, cars, and other energy users place a drain on the nation's limited energy supply. The energy crisis was highlighted in 1973, when a fuel shortage reduced the supply of oil available for heating homes and the gasoline supply for automobiles and other vehicles. See ENERGY SUPPLY.

Foreign Policy. Nixon removed America's last combat troops from Vietnam in 1973—after he had won a second term as President. Two years later, in 1975, South Vietnam and neighboring Cambodia and Laos fell to the Communists. For fuller details on the conflict, see VIETNAM WAR.

As President, Nixon took steps to reduce the Cold War tensions between the United States and China and Russia, the two leading Communist powers. In 1972, he visited the two countries. Nixon reached agreements with the Chinese and Russian leaders that seemed to improve relations between the United States and the

Communist powers, at least temporarily. The relaxing of tensions between the United States and the Communists came to be called *détente.*

Political Scandals rocked the United States in the 1970's. Investigators revealed many cases of graft and other corruption in local and state government, but the nation's attention focused chiefly on charges of corruption on the federal level.

In 1973, Spiro T. Agnew, Nixon's Vice-President, came under criminal investigation. A federal grand jury began hearing charges that he participated in widespread graft in Maryland. The investigation covered the period Agnew had served as an officeholder in Maryland and as Vice-President. Agnew resigned from the vice-presidency on Oct. 10, 1973. See AGNEW, SPIRO T.

In 1972, campaign workers for President Nixon's reelection committed a burglary at the Democratic political headquarters in the Watergate building complex in Washington, D.C. Nixon was later charged with covering up the burglary and with other illegal activities. In July, 1974, the Judiciary Committee of the House of Representatives voted articles of impeachment against the President. Evidence against Nixon mounted until it became apparent that the full House of Representatives would impeach him and that the Senate would remove him from office. On Aug. 9, 1974, Nixon resigned from the presidency. He was the only American President ever to resign.

Gerald R. Ford, who had been appointed Vice-President following Agnew's resignation, succeeded Nixon. He pardoned Nixon for all federal crimes the former President might have committed while in office. See WATERGATE and NIXON, RICHARD M., for more details on the Watergate scandal and resignation.

The Economy. In spite of its overall strength, the American economy ran into deep trouble during the late 1960's and early 1970's. The worst period of inflation in the nation's history began in the late 1960's. During the early 1970's, a severe recession led to the country's highest unemployment rate since the Great Depression.

Historically, recessions have brought an end to inflation. In the 1970's, however, inflation continued in spite of the recession. This development left the nation's economic planners unsure as to how to deal with the problem. They knew that measures such as large tax cuts and increased government spending might help end the recession. But at the same time, they were aware that such measures could raise the rate of inflation.

America at the Bicentennial. In 1976, the American people celebrated the *bicentennial* (200th anniversary) of their nation's founding. They marked the occasion with parades, re-enactments of historical events, and other patriotic celebrations.

The bicentennial also provided a chance for a pause in the fast-paced life of the 1970's. As Americans looked back on their country's history, they saw that their forefathers had overcome great hardships and difficult problems. The examples of the past gave the people pride, and the hope that they and future Americans could do as well.   OSCAR HANDLIN

UNITED STATES HISTORY/*Study Aids*

Related Articles. WORLD BOOK has hundreds of separate articles that provide information on aspects of American history. See the articles on each President and the *History* section of the articles on each state. The many other related articles in WORLD BOOK include:

HISTORICAL PERIODS AND WARS

Civil War	Pioneer Life in America
Cold War	Progressive Movement
Colonial Life in America	Reconstruction
Exploration and Discovery	Revolutionary War in
French and Indian Wars	America
Gay Nineties	Roaring Twenties
Gold Rush	Spanish-American War
Great Depression	Vietnam War
Immigration and Emigration	War of 1812
Indian Wars	Western Frontier Life
Industrial Revolution	Westward Movement
Korean War	World War I
Mexican War	World War II

IMPORTANT DOCUMENTS

Articles of Confederation	Four Freedoms
Atlantic Charter	Fourteen Points
Compromise of 1850	Gettysburg Address
Constitution of the	Homestead Act
United States	Kansas-Nebraska Act
Declaration of	Mayflower Compact
Independence	Missouri Compromise
Emancipation Proclamation	Monroe Doctrine
Federalist, The	Northwest Ordinance

OTHER RELATED ARTICLES

American Literature	Panama Canal
Bicentennial Celebration,	Political Party
American	Slavery
Continental Congress	Space Travel
Flag	States' Rights
Indian, American	Trails of Early Days
Lewis and Clark	United States
Expedition	United States,
Louisiana Purchase	Government of the
Money	United States Capitals

Outline

I. America Before Colonial Times
  A. The First Americans
  B. European Discovery
  C. Exploration and Early Settlement
  D. The Land That Became the United States
II. The Colonial Heritage (1607-1753)
  A. The Thirteen Colonies
  B. Life in Colonial America

III. The Movement for Independence (1754-1783)
  A. Background to the Revolution
  B. The Road to Independence
  C. American Attitudes and Independence
IV. Forming a New Nation (1784-1819)
  A. Establishing a Government
  B. Early Problems and Politics
  C. Jeffersonian Democracy
  D. The War of 1812
  E. Growing Nationalism
V. Expansion (1820-1849)
  A. America Moves West
  B. Politics and the "Common Man"
  C. Social Reform
VI. The Irrepressible Conflict (1850-1869)
  A. Debate and Compromise
  B. Nationwide Turmoil
  C. The Civil War and Reconstruction
VII. Industrialization and Reform (1870-1916)
  A. The Rise of Big Business
  B. The South and the West
  C. Life During the Industrial Era
  D. Reform
  E. Foreign Affairs
VIII. A New Place in the World (1917-1929)
  A. World War I and the Peace
  B. Life During the Roaring Twenties
  C. The Economy—Boom and Bust
IX. Depression and a World in Conflict (1930-1959)
  A. The Great Depression
  B. The United States in World War II
  C. The Threat of Communism
  D. Postwar Society
X. America Since 1960
  A. The 1960's
  B. Recent Developments

Questions

What were the 13 original colonies? When was the first permanent settlement in each colony made?

What was the Stamp Act? The Sugar Act?

Why did the early American leaders decide to write the Constitution?

What was the Louisiana Purchase?

When did the British capture Washington, D.C.?

What was the doctrine of manifest destiny?

How did westward expansion contribute to America's economic growth?

Who were some of the leading abolitionists?

What were some effects of the Civil War?

How did the lives of the rich and the poor contrast during the era of industrialization?

What was prohibition?

Whom did the nickname "Rosie the Riveter" describe?

What was the March on Washington?

Grenada Tourist Board

Saint George's, the scenic capital of Grenada, lies among thickly forested hills on the island's southwest coast. Grenada's lovely scenery helps make tourism a leading economic activity.

GRENADA, *greh NAY duh,* is an island nation in the West Indies. It lies in the Caribbean Sea, about 90 miles (140 kilometers) north of Trinidad. The nation of Grenada also consists of Carriacou and several other small islands of the Grenadine chain. But the island of Grenada makes up most of the country. A pleasant climate and beautiful scenery and beaches attract many tourists to Grenada. The nation ranks as one of the world's leading producers of nutmeg and other spices.

Grenada was a dependency of Great Britain from the late 1700's until 1974, when it gained independence. St. George's is the capital and only sizeable city. About 9,000 persons, or about 10 per cent of Grenada's population, live there.

Government. Grenada is a constitutional monarchy and a member of the Commonwealth of Nations. The national legislature consists of a 13-member Senate and a 15-member House of Representatives. The people elect the members of the House. The prime minister, who is the nation's chief executive, heads the majority party of the House and is appointed by the governor general. The British monarch appoints the governor general on the advice of the prime minister. The governor general appoints the senators, chiefly on the advice of the prime minister and other political leaders.

People. About 95 per cent of Grenada's people have African or mixed African and European ancestry. Descendants of East Indians or of Europeans make up the

Gustavo A. Antonini, the contributor of this article, is Associate Professor of Geography and Latin American Studies and Director of Research at the Center for Latin American Studies at the University of Florida.

rest of the population. Most Grenadians speak English or a *dialect* (local form) of English. The people of some regions speak a French dialect. More than half the population are Roman Catholics. Other religious groups include Anglicans, Methodists, and Presbyterians.

Grenada has about 60 elementary schools, about 10 high schools, and several vocational schools. The government provides all or some of the funds to support most of these schools. More than 30,000 students are enrolled in elementary or high school in Grenada, but attendance is not required by law.

Land and Climate. The mountainous, thickly forested countryside of the island has many gorges and waterfalls. Grand Etang, a lake in the crater of a volcano, lies near the center of Grenada.

FACTS IN BRIEF

Capital: St. George's.

Official Language: English.

Official Name: State of Grenada.

Form of Government: Constitutional Monarchy.

Area: 133 sq. mi. (344 km²). *Greatest Distances*—north-south, 21 mi. (34 km); east-west, 12 mi. (19 km). *Coastline*—75 mi. (121 km).

Elevation: Highest—Mount Saint Catherine, 2,757 ft. (840 m). *Lowest*—sea level.

Population: *Estimated 1976 Population*—98,000; density, 738 persons per sq. mi. (285 per km²). *1970 Census*—94,500; *Estimated 1981 Population,* 100,000.

Chief Products: *Agriculture*—bananas, cocoa, mace, nutmeg. *Manufacturing*—food products, beer, rum.

National Anthem: "The Grenada National Anthem."

Flag: The red-bordered flag has a yellow triangle at the top and bottom and a green triangle on each side. A yellow and brown nutmeg represents Grenada's chief product, and seven gold stars symbolize its seven *parishes* (districts). Adopted 1974. See FLAG (picture: Flags of the Americas).

Money: *Basic Unit*—East Caribbean Dollar.

Temperatures in Grenada seldom fall below 69° F. (21° C) in winter or rise above 90° F. (32° C) in summer. The annual rainfall averages 60 inches (150 centimeters) on the coast and up to 200 inches (510 centimeters) in the mountains.

Economy of Grenada is based chiefly on agriculture and tourism. The nation has few factories. The standard of living remains low because most Grenadians either cannot find work or must work for low wages. The island's chief exports include bananas, cocoa, nutmeg, and a spice called *mace.* Other products include coconut, cotton, limes, and sugar cane. Grenada needs many products made in other countries, and so it imports more than it exports. St. George's is the chief port, but the country also has several smaller ports.

Great Britain, Canada, and the United States rank as Grenada's leading trade partners. In 1974, Grenada sought to increase trade with its neighbors by joining the Caribbean Community and Common Market, an economic union of 13 nations.

Grenada has about 600 miles (970 kilometers) of roads, most of which are surfaced. The nation has an

Grenada

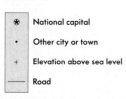

⊛ National capital

• Other city or town

+ Elevation above sea level

▬ Road

WORLD BOOK map

ORGANIZATION OF PETROLEUM EXPORTING COUNTRIES (OPEC) is an association of 13 nations that depend largely on oil exports for their income and foreign trade. The members of OPEC are Algeria, Ecuador, Gabon, Indonesia, Iran, Iraq, Kuwait, Libya, Nigeria, Qatar, Saudi Arabia, the United Arab Emirates, and Venezuela.

OPEC provides a common oil policy for its member nations. For example, it establishes taxes, royalties, and various trade rules on the oil exported by those countries. The members of OPEC produce more than half the oil used in the world. They also supply about 85 per cent of the oil imported by nonmember nations. As a result, OPEC has a major influence on the petroleum industry throughout the world (see PETROLEUM [In Other Countries; The Rising Cost of Oil]).

The Organization of Petroleum Exporting Countries was established in 1960 and has four main governing bodies. The OPEC Conference, the highest authority of the organization, meets twice a year to formulate general policies. The Economic Commission advises the conference on oil price matters. The Board of Governors, which consists of one representative from each member nation, meets at least twice annually. It supervises the affairs of the Secretariat, the administrative branch of OPEC. The Secretariat has permanent headquarters in Vienna, Austria.   ZUHAYR MIKDASHI

PALESTINE LIBERATION ORGANIZATION (PLO) is the political body that represents the Arab people of Palestine. Its chief goal is to establish a Palestinian state for these Arabs.

There are more than 3 million Palestinian Arabs. More than 700,000 of them became refugees as a result of the Arab-Israeli war of 1948, when Israel was founded. By the mid-1970's, about 2 million Palestinian Arabs lived outside what was once Palestine. The area that had formed Palestine now consists of Israel, the Gaza Strip, and the west bank of Jordan.

The PLO includes guerrilla groups and associations of doctors, laborers, lawyers, students, teachers, and women. Some Palestinian Arabs are independent members of the PLO. The guerrilla groups, such as *Al Fatah* and *As Saiqa*, dominate the organization.

The main organs of the PLO are the Executive Committee, the Central Committee, and the Palestine National Council. The Executive Committee, the main PLO decision-making body, consists of representatives of the major guerrilla groups and some independent members. The Central Committee, which includes representatives of all the guerrilla groups, acts as an advisory group to the Executive Committee. The Palestine National Council, which has about 180 members, serves as the assembly of the Palestinian people.

The Palestine Liberation Organization was founded in 1964. The Arab governments recognized it in 1974 as the "sole, legitimate representative of the Palestinian people." Later that year, the United Nations (UN) recognized the PLO as the representative of the Palestinian Arabs.   MICHAEL C. HUDSON

See also ARAFAT, YASIR; PALESTINE.

airport and bus service but no railroads. Two newspapers and a radio station serve the island.

History. Arawak Indians were the first people to live in what is now Grenada. During the 1400's, Carib Indians from South America took over the island. In 1498, Christopher Columbus became the first European explorer to land there. He named the island *Concepcion*, but other Europeans later called it Grenada. The Caribs defeated early European attempts to colonize Grenada. In 1650, the Caribs sold the island to the French, who later slaughtered many of the Indians.

Control of Grenada shifted between France and Great Britain several times before the island became a British colony in 1783. Through the years, European planters brought many African slaves to work on plantations there. After the British ended slavery in 1834, many East Indians came to work in Grenada.

In the mid-1900's, the British gave Grenada some control over its own affairs. In the early 1970's, Prime Minister Eric M. Gairy led a movement for independence. Political unrest developed because some groups opposed independence and accused Gairy of becoming a dictator. In 1974, Grenada gained independence and joined the United Nations.   GUSTAVO A. ANTONINI

See also GRENADINES; SAINT GEORGE'S; WEST INDIES.

GUINEA-BISSAU, *GIHN ih bih SOW*, is a small, independent country on the bulge of Africa's west coast. The nation also includes the offshore Bijagós (or Bissagos) Islands. Guinea-Bissau is slightly larger than Delaware and Maryland combined, but it has fewer people than Baltimore. Bissau is the capital, chief port, and largest city (see BISSAU).

Most of the people of Guinea-Bissau are farmers. The leading crops include peanuts and rice, which thrive in the country's tropical climate. Guinea-Bissau was Portuguese Guinea, an overseas province of Portugal, until 1974. That year, the province won its independence after an 11-year war against Portuguese rule.

Government. Guinea-Bissau is a republic. The National Popular Assembly, composed of 120 members, acts as the lawmaking body. The Assembly chooses 15 of its members to form the State Council, which performs duties assigned to it by the Assembly. The president of the council serves as the nation's president. The Council of State Commissioners, made up of the heads of the government departments, manages government programs.

The members of the National Popular Assembly, who are called deputies, represent individual regions of Guinea-Bissau. The people in each region elect a regional council, which chooses the deputies from the region. Deputies serve a three-year term.

Guinea-Bissau has only one political party, the African Party for the Independence of Guinea and Cape Verde. It is usually known by the initials PAIGC, the abbreviation of its name in Portuguese. The head of the party, the general secretary, ranks as Guinea-Bissau's most powerful leader. The PAIGC is also the main party in the Cape Verde Islands, an independent country about 475 miles (764 kilometers) northwest of

---

John A. Marcum, the contributor of this article, is Provost of Merrill College at the University of California in Santa Cruz and former President of the African Studies Association.

Guinea-Bissau. Until 1975, the islands were an overseas province of Portugal.

People. Guinea-Bissau has about 533,000 persons. Black Africans make up about 85 per cent of the people. Most of the rest consist of *mestizos* (persons of mixed

─────────── **FACTS IN BRIEF** ───────────

Capital: Bissau.

Official Language: Portuguese.

Official Name: Republic of Guinea-Bissau.

Form of Government: Republic. *Head of State*—President.

Area: 13,948 sq. mi. (36,125 km²). *Greatest Distances*—north-south, 120 mi. (193 km); east-west, 200 mi. (322 km). *Coastline*—247 mi. (398 km).

Elevation: *Highest*—near the northeastern border, about 1,000 ft. (300 m) above sea level. *Lowest*—sea level.

Population: *Estimated 1976 Population*—533,000; distribution, 80 per cent rural, 20 per cent urban; density, 47 persons per sq. mi. (18 per km²). *1970 Census*—487,448. *Estimated 1981 Population*—574,000.

Chief Products: Palm kernels, peanuts, rice.

Flag: A black star is centered on a red vertical stripe to the left of two horizontal stripes. The top horizontal stripe is yellow, and the bottom one is green. See FLAG (picture: Flags of Africa).

Money: *Basic Unit*—escudo. One hundred centavos equal one escudo.

---

black African and Portuguese ancestry). The black Africans belong to about 20 tribal groups. The largest groups, in order of size, consist of the Balante; the Fulani; the Manjako; and the Malinke, or Mandingo (see FULANI; MALINKE).

Most people in Guinea-Bissau live in rural areas and make a bare living farming. Many of them live in straw huts with thatched roofs. Most of the people practice *animism*, the belief that everything in nature has a spirit (see ANIMISM). Many other people are Moslems. The official language of Guinea-Bissau is Portuguese. But instead of Portuguese, most people more often use *crioulo*, a local language that combines other local African languages and Portuguese.

While under Portuguese rule, the people of Guinea-Bissau received little education. When the country won its freedom, only about 5 per cent of the people could read and write. During the war for independence, rebel leaders began many schools and adult education programs in areas under their control. After the war, the new government turned several former Portuguese military buildings into schools.

Land and Climate. Guinea-Bissau covers 13,948 square miles (36,125 square kilometers). The coastal area consists of rain forests and thick swamps. Mangrove trees grow in the water along the shore. The land slopes upward from the coast, and grasslands called *savannas* cover most of the inland regions. Many rivers flow through the country. The chief rivers include the Cacheu, the Corubal, and the Geba.

Guinea-Bissau has a tropical climate with a dry and a wet season. During the dry season, which lasts from December to May, temperatures average 74° F. (23° C). During the wet season, which lasts from June to November, temperatures average 83° F. (28° C). The heaviest

Robert F. Van Lierop

Shoppers in a Rural Village of Guinea-Bissau buy food and other items at small open-air shops. About 80 per cent of the country's people live in rural areas.

Victory Celebrations took place in Bissau, the capital of Guinea-Bissau, after Portugal granted the country independence in September, 1974. Rebel forces in the former colony had fought for freedom from Portuguese rule for more than 10 years.

Alain DeJean, Sygma

rains fall in July and August. The yearly rainfall averages 95 inches (241 centimeters) along the coast and 55 inches (140 centimeters) inland.

Economy. Guinea-Bissau's agriculture, industry, and mineral resources are underdeveloped. More than half of all workers are farmers. The chief crops include beans, coconuts, corn, palm kernels, peanuts, and rice. During the war for independence, farming was disrupted, and rice and many other crops were destroyed. The province, which had been a rice exporter, had to import rice.

Guinea-Bissau's few industries employ only a small percentage of the nation's workers. Building construction and food processing are the chief industries.

Peanuts rank as the country's main export. Other exports include coconuts and palm kernels, both of which

grow on the Bijagós Islands and along the coast. Leading imports include fuels and textiles. Guinea-Bissau trades chiefly with Portugal.

After the war ended, one of the new government's chief goals was to increase farm production to meet the country's food needs. The government planned projects to cultivate unused land and to modernize farming methods. These projects were also aimed at providing jobs for war veterans. The government also planned to develop the nation's mineral resources with the mining of bauxite, copper, phosphates, zinc, and other minerals.

Guinea-Bissau has few paved roads. Rivers serve as a chief means of transportation. The Cacheu, Corubal, and Geba rivers are deep enough for some oceangoing ships to travel about 80 miles (130 kilometers) upstream. The nation has several small airfields.

History. Many tribes of black Africans lived in what is now Guinea-Bissau before Portuguese explorers arrived in 1446. From the 1600's to the 1800's, the Portuguese used the region as a base for the slave trade. The region became a Portuguese colony called Portuguese Guinea in 1879. It became an overseas province of Portugal in 1951.

During the 1950's and 1960's, an independence movement swept across Africa. In 1956, African nationalist leaders in Portuguese Guinea founded the African Party for the Independence of Guinea and Cape Verde (PAIGC). Amilcar Cabral headed the party from 1956 to 1973, when he was assassinated. During the early 1960's, the PAIGC trained many Portuguese Guinean farmers in the hit-and-run tactics of *guerrilla* warfare.

The war for independence began in 1963. By 1968, the PAIGC controlled about two-thirds of the province. The people in these areas elected the first National Popular Assembly in 1972. The next year, the Assembly declared the province to be an independent nation called Guinea-Bissau. Luis Cabral, a PAIGC leader and a brother of Amilcar Cabral, became the new nation's first president. The war ended in 1974, when Portugal recognized Guinea-Bissau's independence. The PAIGC, under General Secretary Aristides Pereira, began work to rebuild and develop the country. The party also worked to unite Guinea-Bissau and the Cape Verde Islands under one government.   JOHN A. MARCUM

Guinea-Bissau

⭐ Capital
• Other City or Town
—— Road

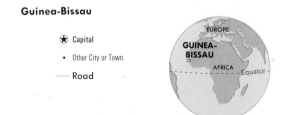

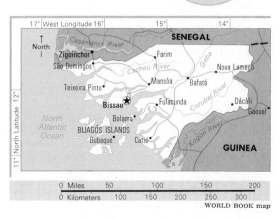

WORLD BOOK map

581

ALTERNATIVE SCHOOL

ALTERNATIVE SCHOOL is any school that differs from traditional schools in curriculum, purpose, or teaching methods. Most alternative schools attempt to establish a less formal relationship between pupils and teachers. They also try to make greater use of community facilities outside the school and to involve parents in the educational process. Alternative schools developed because of dissatisfaction with the quality and aims of public and private schools.

Alternative schools have voluntary enrollments. A typical alternative school has from 30 to 40 students. A school of this size can easily adjust its program to fit individual needs and desires. Some work only with elementary-school children, and others accept only teenagers. Many alternative schools put students of several ages into one class.

In the United States in the mid-1970's, at least 500 alternative schools operated independently of the public school system. These schools, which are privately run, are usually called *free schools*. The word *free* refers to the independence of such schools. It also describes the emphasis of the schools in allowing students to make their own decisions in various matters.

About 500 other alternative schools operated as part of the public school system in the United States. Such schools may be located in one area of a public school building or in a separate building provided by the school system.

Features of Alternative Schools

The basic principle followed by alternative schools is that not all children have the same goals and the same ways of learning. Many of the people involved in operating these schools do not want to convert the whole school system to their methods. They want to provide the opportunity for a different kind of education for children who would benefit from it.

The major feature of many alternative schools is the *open classroom*. The teacher of an open classroom, instead of lecturing most of the time, helps students find interesting ways to learn on their own. Many kinds of educational materials are kept in the classroom. The students work with these materials alone or in groups, and the teacher gives the students individual help and instruction.

Most alternative schools lack adequate funds and such facilities as gymnasiums, laboratories, and shops. Parents and volunteers provide most of the schools' finances, help run the classes, and aid in maintaining the buildings.

Many forms of alternative schools have developed in response to various needs. *Street academies* and *dropout centers*, which function in the poor sections of big cities, help high school dropouts continue their education. *Storefront schools* have developed from child-care and kindergarten facilities. *Work schools* hold classes part of the day, and the students work at regular jobs the rest of the day.

The *school without walls* plan, used in some large cities, takes advantage of the educational opportunities provided by businesses and institutions of the community. Students may spend part of the day at an artist's studio, a factory, a museum, a newspaper office, a repair shop, a theater, or a government or private agency. The purpose of the school without walls method is to make learning more realistic and enjoyable. The program also broadens the experiences offered high school students.

Some alternative schools emphasize the study of the culture and history of a certain minority group. Some accept only students from one such group. Other alternative schools seek students from several cultures and races.

A number of alternative schools have been designed for children from middle- or upper-class families. Such schools are in suburban or rural areas. Most of them stress the independence of each student and have no required subjects.

A trend in the development of alternative schools has been the establishment of such schools within the public school system. One plan offers a variety of learning environments from which students, parents, and teachers may choose. At the elementary school level, parents can choose to place their children in a traditional classroom or in one of several kinds of open classrooms. High school students decide whether to enter a free school with few course requirements, or one of several programs within the regular high school program.

History

Experimental schools similar to alternative schools have been set up throughout the history of public education. But the term *alternative school* first came into widespread use during the 1960's. It referred to a wide variety of programs and institutions that differed greatly from private schools and special programs within public schools. Most private schools had been established for the children of wealthy families. Most special programs worked only with students who had special problems or exceptional ability. But most alternative schools welcomed any student.

Blacks in the Southern States set up some of the first alternative schools. During the 1960's, these people established *freedom schools* in communities where public schools refused to admit their children. In many Northern cities, blacks established alternative schools because of dissatisfaction with the treatment of their children in public schools.

Many people began to realize that a public school system could hurt, rather than help, some children. These people declared that parents and educators should have the freedom to set up alternative methods of education.

During the late 1960's, several groups began a movement that created open classrooms modeled on Great Britain's *infant schools*. Such schools are attended by children from age 5 to 7. In the United States, similar classrooms were set up in a number of public schools. Their success contributed to the growth of the alternative school movement.   BEATRICE GROSS and RONALD GROSS

ALTERNATOR. See ELECTRIC GENERATOR.

ALTGELD, JOHN PETER. See ILLINOIS (Industrial Development).

ALTHING. See ICELAND (Government).

Section Six

Dictionary Supplement

This section lists important words from the 1976 edition of
THE WORLD BOOK DICTIONARY. This dictionary, first published
by Field Enterprises Educational Corporation in 1963, keeps abreast
of our living language with a program of continuous editorial revision.
The following supplement has been prepared under the direction of
the editors of THE WORLD BOOK ENCYCLOPEDIA and
Clarence L. Barnhart, editor in chief of THE WORLD BOOK DICTIONARY.
It is presented as a service to owners of the dictionary and as an
informative feature to subscribers of THE WORLD BOOK YEAR BOOK.

A

ab|he|sive (ab hē′siv, -ziv), *adj., n.* —*adj.* not sticking to other material; slippery: *an abhesive plastic.*
—*n.* an abhesive substance.
[< *ab-¹* off, away from + (ad)*hesive*]

acoustic perfume, an overlay of nondescript sound to cover up distracting or annoying noises; white noise: *The most popular form of acoustic perfume, of course, is music—piped, canned, or live* (Eugene Raskin).

a|cous|to|e|lec|tron|ics (ə küs′tō i lek′tron′iks, -kous′-; -ē′lek-), *n.* a branch of electronics dealing with the conversion of electrical signals into a flow of acoustic waves traveling along a solid surface.

af|ror|mo|si|a (af′rôr mō′zē ə), *n.* a strong West African hardwood resembling teak. [< New Latin *afrormosia* the species name]

am|ni|o|cen|te|sis (am′nē ō sen tē′sis), *n.* the insertion of a special hypodermic needle into the amnion to remove a sampling of fetal cells from the amniotic fluid for diagnostic purposes: *Amniocentesis can tell expectant parents that their child will be genetically defective* (Science News). [< New Latin *amniocentesis* < Greek *amnion* amnion + *kéntēsis* act of puncturing]

ar|chae|o|mag|net|ism (är′kē ə mag′nə tiz əm), *n.* the measurement of residual magnetism, used especially as a method to determine the age of an archaeological specimen by relating the permanent magnetism it acquired at its creation to the amount of magnetism retained at the time of measurement.

asphalt cloud, particles of combustible asphalt discharged in great masses by an antiballistic missile in the path of an enemy missile or missiles.

B

ba|ro|co|co (bə rō′kə kō′), *adj.* grotesquely elaborate. [blend of *baroque* and *rococo*]

Barr body (bär), a piece of chromosomal material in the nuclear membrane of female cells which stains darkly and is the remnant of one of the two female chromosomes (X chromosomes); sex chromatin. [< Murray *Barr,* born 1908, a Canadian anatomist, who discovered these bodies in 1949]

BASIC or **Basic²,** *n.* a computer language made up of a blend of simple English and elementary algebra, used to introduce students to programming. [< *B*(eginners) *A*(ll-purpose) *S*(ymbolic) *I*(nstruction) *C*(ode)]

best|er (bes′tər), *n.* a hybrid sturgeon developed in the Soviet Union for its ability to spawn in its home grounds instead of migrating upstream. [< *bel*uga + *ster*let]

beta cloth, a fabric made from a very fine, nonflammable glass fiber, used especially for making space suits. [< *Beta,* a trademark for the glass fiber]

bi|o|cy|ber|net|ics (bī′ō sī′bər net′iks), *n.* the study of automatic control and communication in living systems.

bi|o|eth|ics (bī′ō eth′iks), *n.* the study of the ethical problems involved in biological research, such as the ethics of organ transplantation and genetic engineering.

bi|stat|ic radar (bī stat′ik), a radar system based on two widely separated locations, one for transmitting signals to a body in outer space, another for receiving them as they reflect back to earth.

black lung, a form of pneumoconiosis which affects coal miners: *"Black lung" is caused by the inhalation of fine particles of coal dust* (Atlantic).

blood-brain barrier (blud′brān′), *Medicine.* a barrier in the central nervous system that prevents chemicals injected into blood vessels from entering the brain.

Boston arm, an artificial arm that is battery-powered and activated by electric signals from the amputee's remaining arm or shoulder muscles. [< *Boston,* Massachusetts, where it was developed]

C

car|be|cue (kär′bə kyü), *n.* a device for melting down and compacting scrap automobiles. [< *car* + (bar)*becue*]

car|di|o|ver|ter (kär′dē ō vér′tər), *n.* a device for restoring normal heartbeat by means of electric shock: *Electric current from the cardioverter being applied directly to a patient's heart by doctors at the National Heart Hospital London* (London Times). [< *cardio-* + Latin *vertere* to turn]

ca|se|id|in (kā sē′ə dən), *n.* one of a group of substances in the milk of mammals that provide infant immunity against certain infectious diseases. [< Latin *cāseus* cheese + English *-id* + *-in*]

Chan|dler wobble (chan′dlər), a slight eccentric oscillation of the earth on its axis recurring in cycles which last approximately 14 months: *The Earth's pole undergoes a mutation, the Chandler wobble, ... whose motion is somehow kept going despite the substantial effects of viscous damping forces* (New Scientist and Science Journal). [< Seth Carlo *Chandler,* 1846-1913, an American astronomer, who made a study of it]

chem|o|tax|on|o|my (kem′ō tak son′ə mē), *n.* the classification of living plant and animal species on the basis of their chemical constituents.

D

da|ta|phone (dā′tə fōn′, dat′ə-, dä′tə-), *n.* an apparatus for sending information from one machine to another over telephone lines. Electronic computers send vast quantities of information by dataphone.

dead drop, a telephone booth, public lavatory, or similar site used in espionage to deposit and pick up messages and other material according to a prearranged schedule: *In a dead drop ... the sender and receiver avoid the risk entailed in making a transfer during a personal encounter* (New Yorker).

de|boost (dē büst′), *v., n.* —*v.i.* to reduce the thrust of a spacecraft or missile in flight, especially in order to lower the orbiting altitude of a spacecraft or to slow down a warhead before impact: *This combination would prevent anti-ballistic missile radar ... from ascertaining the point of impact until the rocket "deboosts"—about three minutes and 500 miles from target* (Time).
—*n.* the act of reducing the thrust of an orbiting spacecraft or missile: *The second "deboost" maneuver dropped Or-biter 2 from its taxiing orbit of 1,150 miles high and 130 miles low to a new orbit of 1,149 miles high and 31.3 miles low* (New York Times).

decision tree, a diagram in the form of a branching tree representing alternate strategies or methods and the respective values assigned to them, used to help make decisions or plans in any system.

deke (dēk), *n., v.,* **deked, dek|ing.** *Canadian Slang.* —*n.* a sham maneuver in hockey; feint.
—*v.t.* to maneuver (a shot, movement, or player) in hockey by feinting.
[< *decoy*]

des|mo|sine (des′mə sīn), *n.* an amino acid that serves as a cross-link for molecules of elastin: *Desmosine* [*is*] *probably largely responsible for the elasticity and stability of elastin, the main protein of the aortic wall* (Scientific American). [< Greek *desmós* chain, bond + English *-ine²*]

di|a|grid (dī′ə grid′), *n.* a framework of diagonally intersecting bars of metal or concrete, used as a supporting structure in a building, reactor, or the like. [< *dia*(gonal) *grid*]

E

eb|ul|lism (eb′yə liz əm), *n.* the bubbling of body fluids resulting from a sudden reduction of air pressure: *The absence of an atmosphere on the Moon brings hazards of suffocation with a time of useful consciousness limited to a few seconds due to lack of oxygen and the ebullism—boiling of body fluids—due to lack of atmospheric pressure* (Science Journal). [< Latin *ēbullīre* boil up + English *-ism*]

e|lec|tro|sleep (i lek′trō slēp′), *n.* sleep induced by passing an electric current through the brain between electrodes placed on the temples: *Soviet physicians have indicated "good results" in using electrically induced relaxation and sleep—electrosleep—to treat various ailments* (New York Times).

el|lip|som|e|ter (i lip som′ə tər), *n.* an instrument for measuring ellipticity, used especially to determine the thicknesses of extremely thin films.

en|dis|tance (en dis′təns), *v.t.,* **-tanced, -tanc|ing.** to make (an audience) feel distant from the action or characters of a play or motion picture, as by having the actors wear masks or continually shift roles: *... a deliberate attempt to "endistance" the audience from the subject matter of the film, in a manner to which we may apply ... the now overused term "Brechtian"* (London Times).

e|qui|axed (ē′kwə akst′), *adj. Crystallography.* **1** having about the same dimensions on all sides; regular in shape: *equiaxed crystal grains.* **2** consisting of equiaxed grains formed in the center of an alloy casting: *an equiaxed zone.* [< *equi-* + *ax*(is) + *-ed²*]

e|quipe or **é|quipe** (ā kēp′), *n.* a sports or racing crew and its equipment; team: *a motorcycle equipe, a Grand Prix equipe.* [< French *équipe* gang, crew]

es|bat (es′bat), *n.* a meeting of witches: *Apart from the festivals, the covens meet once a month as near as possible to the time of the full moon to celebrate a less important ceremony known as the esbat* (Atlantic). [probably < Old French *esbat* a frolic, gambol (French *ébats*) < *esbatre* to frolic, ultimately < Latin *ex-* out + *battere* to beat]

e|vap|o|tran|spire (i vap′ō tran spīr′), *v.t.*, **-spired, -spir|ing.** to cause the return of (water) to the atmosphere by evaporation and transpiration: *Water-use efficiency can be expressed in a variety of ways, such as tons of hay or bushels of potatoes per acre-inch of water evapotranspired, crates of marketable lettuce per acre-foot of water, or as a weight ratio, kilogram per kilogram* (E. G. Viets, Jr.). [back formation < *evapotranspiration*]

F

fake book, *U.S.* a book reproducing the melodies or similar shorthand versions of copyrighted popular songs without permission of the copyright owners.

fat city, *U.S. Slang.* a very good, comfortable, or successful state or condition: *Johnny ... announced that he was in "fat city" and everything was "swave"* (New York Times).

fine-tune (fīn′tün′, -tyün′), *v.t.*, **-tuned, -tun|ing.** to make fine adjustments in the operation or performance of; regulate.

Flo|ry temperature (flôr′ē, flōr′-), a specific temperature at which any one polymer exists in an ideal state for study of its properties in comparison with those of other polymers: *The Flory temperature ... became the basis for the development of hundreds of different plastics and synthetics* (Time). [< Paul J. *Flory,* born 1910, an American chemist, who discovered it]

foil|borne (foil′bōrn′, -bôrn′), *adj., adv.* — *adj.* **1** supported by hydrofoils: *a foil-borne craft.* **2** involving the use of hydrofoils: *foilborne operations, foilborne speeds.* — *adv.* on hydrofoils: *It is designed to be operated foilborne in waves up to 15 feet* (London Times).

Fourth World or **fourth world**, the poor countries of the world, as distinguished from the oil-rich countries of the Third World: *Called the "Fourth World" ... they comprise nearly one billion people in some 40 undeveloped nations in Africa, Asia, and Latin America* (Time).

G

ga|len|ics (gə len′iks, -lē′niks), *n.* **1** the art or science of preparing galenicals. **2** the art or science dealing with the optimum form of drugs and medicines.

gar|bo (gär′bō), *n., pl.* **-bos.** (in Australia) a garbage or trash collector. [alteration of *garbage*]

genetic counseling, the counseling of prospective parents on possible birth defects in their children on the basis of chromosomal tests and such medical procedures as amniocentesis: *A couple may seek genetic counseling if they believe they might pass on certain inherited defects to their children* (Saburo Hara).

geodetic satellite, an earth satellite designed to make simultaneous observations of the earth's surface from two or more points in order to obtain data on the exact shape and size of the earth and the exact position of areas on the earth's surface.

Geor|gian|ism (jôr′jē niz əm), *n.* a movement in British poetry character-

ized by attention to nature and pastoral life, as in the poems of Rupert Brooke, John Drinkwater, W. W. Gibson, and Harold Monro. [< *Georgian* (George V, in whose reign the anthologist Edward Marsh, 1872-1953, initiated it) + *-ism*]

ghe|rao (ge rou′), *n., v.* — *n.* (in India and Pakistan) a coercive tactic used by striking workers, in which employers or managers are barricaded in their offices until they meet the workers' demands. — *v.t.* to subject to a gherao: *The directors of one steel concern were "gheraoed" next to the blast furnace* (New York Times). [< Hindustani *gherao* encirclement, siege]

glas|phalt (glas′fôlt, -falt; gläs′-), *n.* a material made from glass for paving roads: *An experimental product called "glasphalt" ... uses finely ground glass granules to replace the rock aggregates now used as a construction material for highways* (Time). [blend of *glass* + *asphalt*]

gyp|lure (jip′lùr′), *n.* a synthetic form of the sex attractant of the female gypsy moth. [< *gyp*(sy moth) + *lure*]

H

hedge fund, *U.S.* an investment fund set up as a limited partnership for investing private capital speculatively: *The hedge funds, so-called, have been operating on borrowed money in order to concentrate the capital gains of their customers* (Harper's).

hem|bar (hem′bär), *n.* a hybrid variety of barley developed in 1969 by the U.S. Department of Agriculture. [coined by Dr. Robert T. Ramage, research scientist of the U.S. Department of Agriculture in Arizona < arbitrary prefix *hem-* + *bar*(ley)]

high profile, an attitude or position that is direct, open, and emphatic; a conspicuously clear-cut stance.

hol|o|thu|rin (hol′ə thùr′in, hō′lə-), *n.* a poisonous substance that is a complex mixture of steroid glycosides, extracted from a species of sea cucumber and used experimentally in medicine to destroy bacteria and suppress the growth of tumors: *In addition to their hemolytic activities, holothurins cause irreversible inhibition of nerve conduction* (J. W. Daly). [< *holothur*(ian) + *-in*]

I

im|mu|no|dif|fu|sion (i myü′nō di fyü′zhən), *n.* a process for separating the components of an antigen-antibody complex by the diffusion of antigen and antibody solutions through a gel.

in|cap (in′kap), *n. Slang.* an incapacitant.

in|di|ca (in′də kə), *n.* a fine-grained variety of Asian rice that is not sticky and is rich in amylose, used in developing new hybrid types of rice. [< New Latin *indica* < Latin *Indica,* feminine of *Indicus* Indian, Indic]

in|fus|er (in fyü′zər), *n.* **1** a person or thing that infuses. **2** a device for automatically injecting at preset intervals a dose of a drug into a person's vein. It is strapped to the arm and consists of a hypodermic syringe and a tiny battery-operated motor. *Patients with osteoporosis ... could also be helped by using infusers to inject low doses of parathyroid hormones* (New York Post).

ir|tron (ėr′tron), *n.* a galactic source of strong infrared radiation: *Irtrons radiate fantastic amounts of energy, in some cases many times more than the total power emitted by all the stars in the largest galaxies* (Science News). [< *i*(nfra)*r*(ed) (spec)*tr*(um) + *-on*]

J

ja|gad|gu|ru (jə gəd gü′rü, -gü rü′), *n.* the title of a widely revered Hindu guru or religious leader. [< Hindustani *jagadgurū* < Sanskrit *jagat* world + *guru* revered]

ju|gate (jü′gāt, -git), *adj., n.* — *adj.* **1** *Biology.* occurring in pairs; connected; yoked, as a pinnate leaf in which the leaflets are in pairs. **2** (of impressions stamped on coins) placed side by side. — *n.* **1** a jugate impression on a coin. **2** *U.S.* a button pairing the pictures of a presidential candidate and his running mate. [< Latin *jugātus,* past participle of *jugāre* join < *jugum* yoke]

L

lap|a|ro|scope (lap′ə rə skōp), *n.* a tubelike optical instrument for illuminating and examining internal organs from the outside. [< Greek *lapárā* flank + English *-scope*]

Law|son criterion (lô′sən), *Nuclear Physics.* a criterion that establishes the point at which a fusion reaction becomes self-sustaining, formulated by the British physicist J. D. Lawson in the 1960's.

leap second, an extra second added to clock time each year by international agreement in order to keep the time signals used by navigators synchronized with the actual motion of the earth: *The latest leap second was celebrated New Year's Eve at the stroke of midnight Greenwich Mean Time, when around the world ... radio stations added an extra "beep" to their hourly time signals* (Science News). [patterned on *leap year*]

lev|a|pad (lev′ə pad′), *n.* a device for supporting an air cushion vehicle, consisting of a perforated flat plate through which air up to 100 pounds per square inch is forced under pressure. [< Latin *levāre* to lift, raise + English *pad*[1]]

lex|i|gram (lek′sə gram), *n.* a geometric form or other symbol that stands for a word. Lexigrams are used to teach animals, such as chimpanzees, to communicate with humans.

M

mag|lev or **mag-lev** (mag′lev), *n.* a high-speed train supported above the ground and guided by a system of superconducting electromagnets. [< *mag*(netic) *lev*(itation)]

Pronunciation Key: hat, āge, cāre, fär; let, ēqual, tėrm; it, īce; hot, ōpen, ôrder; oil, out; cup, pùt, rüle; child; long; thin; ᵺen; zh, measure; ə represents a in about, e in taken, i in pencil, o in lemon, u in circus.

magnetic bubble, a tiny, circular, movable, magnetic domain formed in an orthoferrite, used experimentally as a miniature computer processing unit or telephone switching unit.

me|di|a|gen|ic (mē'dē ə jen'ik), *adj.* suitable for the communications media; having an attractive or appealing public image: [*He*] *hopes to find someone young and mediagenic, politically moderate to balance his own brand of midwest conservatism* (Newsweek). [patterned on *photogenic*]

mi|cro|proc|es|sor (mī'krō pros'əs ər; *especially British* -prō'səs-), *n.* an electronic computer or processor contained in a chip as small as a quarter of an inch square and able to perform the sensing, communication, and control functions of a standard-sized computer or processor: *The microprocessor is basically a grouping of thousands of tiny transistors and other electronic components ... Together, they form a miniature computer that can govern the use of fuels to their maximum efficiency* (New York Times).

N

negative feedback, feedback in which the output and input remain in a state of equilibrium; normal or stable feedback.

new penny, *pl.* **new pence**. the British penny in the decimal system established in 1971, equal to $1/100$ of a pound and corresponding to 2.4 pence in the old system: *The minimum cost of a call would go down from 6d.—the equivalent of 2½ new pence—to 2 new pence with a compensating adjustment in the length of the call* (London Times). *Abbr:* np (no periods).

notch|back (noch'bak'), *n.* an automobile with a sloping or slanting roof and a pronounced rear bumper.

O

object art, a form of abstract sculpture that emphasizes the sculptured object by deliberately understating its shape, texture, and color: *The "object art" and "thingish" novel of the sixties are resurrections of the Cubist spirit* (Harold Rosenberg).

O|kun's law (ō'kənz), *U.S. Economics.* a formula that shows the correlation between the rate of unemployment and the gross national product. Okūn's law indicates how much unemployment will rise for every $1-billion decline in the gross national product. [< Arthur M. Okun, born 1928, an American economist]

o|lim (ō lēm'), *n.pl. Hebrew.* 1 Jewish immigrants to Israel: *Positively, the nation* [*Israel*] *feels refreshed by olim, the homecoming immigrants, justified in its deepest purpose, and strengthened to build a new life on its corner of the earth* (London Times). 2 (literally) those who ascend. See also **aliyah**.

P

pa|le|o|chro|nol|o|gy (pā'lē ō krə nol'ə jē, pal'ē-), *n.* the dating of fossil animals and plants, as by counting the ridges on fossil shells and corals.

par|a|le|gal (par'ə lē'gəl), *adj.* of or having to do with law in an auxiliary capacity: *Greater use can be made of paralegal aides—nonlawyers who are specially trained to do minutiae that require an inefficiently large amount of an attorney's time* (Time). [< *para-*[1] + *legal*]

pet|ro|dol|lars (pet'rō dol'ərz), *n.pl.* surplus U.S. dollars obtained by oil-rich countries from increased oil revenues and usually spent by investing heavily in foreign, especially large industrial, countries: *The Arabs, using excess dollars (the so-called petrodollars) from the quadrupling of crude oil prices, ... invested close to $11 billion in the U.S. in 1974* (New York Sunday News).

Pho|to-Re|al|ism (fō'tō rē'ə liz əm), *n.* a form of painting based on and often imitating still photographs: *Photo-Realism is photographic (many of the Photo-Realist painters simply copy blown-up photographs they have projected onto their enormous canvases) and cruelly noticing of things as they are* (New Yorker). **— Pho'to-Re'al|ist**, *adj.*

pres|er|va|tor (prez'ər vā'tər), *n. U.S.* a person in charge of preserving a historic site or other landmark restoring it to its original form: *A Columbia University professor of architectural history will be named the first Preservator of Central Park* (New York Times).

pull date, the date stamped on packaged food to show the limit of its shelf life. See also **open dating**.

R

rurp (rėrp), *n.* a type of piton shaped somewhat like a picture hook: *Scott uses a number of American rurps ... whose blades are only 9¾ inches long* (Sunday Times). [< *r*(ealized) *u*(ltimate) *r*(eality) *p*(iton)]

S

Sa|hel|i|an (sə hel'yən, -hē'lē ən), *adj.* 1 of or having to do with the group of countries below the Sahara including Chad, Gambia, Mali, Mauritania, Senegal, Upper Volta, and Niger: *the Sahelian region, zone, or strip.* 2 (originally) of the Sahel, or coastal plain of Tunisia. [< Arabic *sāhel* coastal strip]

sand sink, a method of removing oil spilled at sea by spraying the oil with a mixture of chemically treated sand and water which sticks to the oil causing it to sink.

sea grant college or **university**, *U.S.* an institution that receives a grant of money from the government to engage in oceanographic study and research. [patterned after *land grant college* or *university*]

simian line or **crease**, a single deep line or crease running across part of the palm of the hand nearest the fingers instead of the two separate lines found normally: *The so-called simian crease ... is normally rare but occurs frequently in Down's syndrome, or mongolism* (Scientific American). [so called from its being typical of the palms of simians]

T

tan|noy (tan'oi), *n. British.* a public-address system: *It was just one of the hundreds of routine messages broadcast daily over the tannoy of any international airport* (Manchester Guardian Weekly). [< *Tannoy*, a trademark for such a system]

throw weight, the delivery power of a ballistic missile or rocket, expressed in megatons, size of a missile payload: *The SS-9 and the new SS-18 have throw weights capable of launching warheads packing 25 megatons* (Time).

tri|age (trē äzh'; *especially for 1 and 2 also* trī'ij), *n.* 1 the act of sorting, as according to kind or quality. 2 something sorted out, as the broken coffee beans separated from the whole coffee in sorting. 3 the act or fact of assigning priorities according to urgency or expediency, especially in military and political planning and in the choice of giving medical treatment to casualties most likely to survive when only limited help is available. *In the West, there is increasing talk of triage, a common-sense if callous concept that teaches that when resources are scarce they must be used where they will do the most good* (Time). [< Old French *triage* < *trier* to pick, cull]

V

va|rac|tor (və rak'tər), *n.* a type of semiconducting diode whose capacitance varies with the applied voltage. [probably < *var*(iable cap)*ac*(i)*tor*]

vex|il|lol|o|gy (vek'sə lol'ə jē), *n.* the study of flags: *Vexillology is not normally a very vexed subject. It concerns the design, making and history of flags* (Daily Telegraph). [< Latin *vexillum* a flag or banner + English *-logy*]

W

water cannon, a large nozzle usually mounted on a truck to shoot water at high pressure, used especially in riot control: *Water cannon were brought in to break up the crowds* (Sunday Times).

X

X-rat|ed (eks'rā'tid), *adj. U.S.* 1 produced for exhibition or viewing by adult audiences; having an X rating: *an X-rated motion picture.* 2 *Informal.* **a** sexually explicit; pornographic: *X-rated books, an X-rated show.* **b** obscene: *X-rated language.*

Y

YIG (yig), *n.* a synthetic garnet of yttrium and iron oxide having versatile magnetic properties, used especially in laser modulation. [< *Y*(ttrium) *I*(ron) *G*(arnet)]

Z

zo|o|se|mi|ot|ics (zō'ə sē'mē ot'iks), *n.* the study of communication among animals.

Section Seven

Index

How to Use the Index

This index covers the contents of the 1974, 1975, and 1976 editions of THE WORLD BOOK YEAR BOOK.

Each index entry is followed by the edition year (in *italics*) and the page numbers, as:

ADVERTISING, *76*-166, *75*-184, *74*-178

This means that information about Advertising begins on the pages indicated for each of the editions.

An index entry that is the title of an article appearing in THE YEAR BOOK is printed in capital letters, as: **AUTOMOBILE.** An entry that is not an article title, but a subject discussed in an article of some other title, is printed: **Pollution.**

The various "See" and "See also" cross references in the index list are to other entries within the index. Clue words or phrases are used when two or more references to the same subject appear in the same edition of THE YEAR BOOK. These make it easy to locate the material on the page, since they refer to an article title or article subsection in which the reference appears, as:

Emission standards: automobile, *76*-198, *75*-214; environment, *74*-309

The indication *"il."* means that the reference is to an illustration only. An index entry in capital letters followed by *"WBE"* refers to a new or revised WORLD BOOK ENCYCLOPEDIA article that is printed in the supplement section, as:

UNITED STATES, HISTORY OF THE, *WBE, 76*-530

A

U

V

Acknowledgments

The publishers acknowledge the following sources for illustrations. Credits read from left to right, top to bottom, on their respective pages. An asterisk (*) denotes illustrations created exclusively for THE YEAR BOOK. All maps, charts, and diagrams were prepared by THE YEAR BOOK staff unless otherwise noted.

3	Joseph Erhardt*
8	Pictorial Parade
9	Wide World
10	Bob Fila, *Chicago Sun-Times;* Wide World; Photoreporters
11	Wide World
12	C. Salhani, Sygma; Wide World; Wide World; Wide World; J. P. Laffont, Sygma
13	NASA; Wide World; Wide World
14	Wide World; Wide World; Paul Quirico; Wide World
15	Diego Goldberg, Sygma; Wide World; Bob Clay, Pledge
16	Wide World; Wide World; United Press Int.
18	Richard Sparks*
19	Boris Spremo*
20	Wide World
21	Diego Goldberg, Sygma
22	Allis-Chalmers Corp.
23	Wide World
24	Richard Sparks*
25	Robert Isear*
26	Bettmann Archive
27	Wide World
28	Harvard University
30	Richard Sparks*
31	Robert Isear*
32-35	Wide World
36	Richard Sparks*
37	Joseph Erhardt*
38	University of California at Irvine
39	Joseph Erhardt*
40	Wide World
41	International Minerals & Chemical Corp.
42	Richard Sparks*
43	Dan Budnik*
44	Bettmann Archive
45	WORLD BOOK photo*
46	Perry Riddle, *Chicago Daily News*
48	Richard Sparks*
49	Dan Budnik*
50	Wide World
51	Robert Walker, *The New York Times*
52	RKO Radio Pictures
53	Edmund Jarecki, *Chicago Daily News*
54	Richard Sparks*
55	J. R. Eyerman*
56-58	Wide World
60-61	Joseph DeVelasco*
63	Mark Godfrey, Magnum
64	LeRoy Woodson; Donald McCullin, Magnum
66-71	Joseph DeVelasco*
72-73	Fred Ward, Black Star; Nathan Benn; Fred Mayer, Woodfin Camp, Inc.
74	Marilyn Silverstone, Magnum
76-79	Joseph Erhardt*
81	John Downs*
83-85	Joseph Erhardt*
87	John Downs*
90	Joseph Erhardt*
93	John Downs*
95-98	Joseph Erhardt*
101	John Downs*
102-103	Joseph Erhardt*
105-106	John Downs*
108	NASA
110-111	U.S. Geological Survey
113	NASA
114-121	Jet Propulsion Lab.
122	NASA
124-135	Gilbert Stone*
138-139	Mario de Biasi, *Epoca* from Pictorial Parade; Emil Schulthess, Black Star; Alex Borodulin, De Wys, Inc.
141	Ken Regan, Camera 5; Howard Sochurek, Woodfin Camp, Inc.
142	Mario de Biasi, *Epoca* from Pictorial Parade
143	Howard Sochurek, Woodfin Camp, Inc.; Emil Schulthess, Black Star
145	Howard Sochurek, Woodfin Camp, Inc.
146-147	Elliott Erwitt, Magnum; Leon V. Kofod
149	Mario de Biasi, *Epoca* from Pictorial Parade
150	Jason Laure, Woodfin Camp, Inc.; Mario de Biasi, *Epoca* from Pictorial Parade
151	Mario de Biasi, *Epoca* from Pictorial Parade
154	*Harper's Weekly,* 1875; Bettmann Archive; *Harper's Weekly,* 1875; Bettmann Archive; Brown Brothers
157	*Harper's Weekly,* 1875; Culver Pictures; *Harper's Weekly,* 1875; *Leslie's Illustrated Weekly,* 1875 (The Newberry Library, Chicago)
159	Brown Brothers; Bettmann Archive; Bettmann Archive; *Illustrated London News,* 1875; Bettmann Archive
162	Culver Pictures; Bettmann Archive; Ames, a McDonough Company; *Leslie's Illustrated Weekly,* 1875, (The Newberry Library, Chicago)
166	Ralston Purina Co. & The Project Group Inc.
167	CARE
169	J. P. Laffont, Sygma
170	United Press Int.
172	Gamma from Liaison
174	United Press Int.
176	Wide World
177	Photo Trends
178	Sygma
179	Robin A. Barraco, Wayne State University
181	Wide World
182	Nathaniel Lieberman, American Institute of Architects
183	Keystone
184	General Dynamics
186-187	United Press Int.
190	Wide World
191	Sovfoto
193	Western International Hotels
194	*Mercury,* Hobart
197	Chrysler Corporation
199-200	United Press Int.
207	*Saturday Review* & Joseph Farris
209-213	Wide World
215	Teresa Zabala, *The New York Times*
216	General Electric Research & Development Center
218	National Academy of Sciences
219	United Press Int.
221	Wide World
223	*The New York Times*
224	Mobil Oil Corporation
225-227	Wide World
228	© CN Tower Limited
229	Edward Hausner, *The New York Times*
231	Wide World
232	International Harvester
235	Canada Post Office
237	Robin Laurance, *The New York Times*
238	Pictorial Parade
241	Sovfoto
242	Bob Fila, *Chicago Sun-Times*
243	Charles Gerretsen, Gamma from Liaison
244	Keystone
245	Wide World
247	Buescher, © King Features Syndicate 1975
248-249	Wide World
250	WORLD BOOK photo*
252	*The New York Times*
253	Wide World
255	Wide World

605

260	Wide World
261	John Fischetti, © 1975 *Chicago Daily News*
262	Camerapix
264	The First National Bank of Boston
266	Bob Clay, Pledge
267	Wide World
271	Myra Armstrong
272	Jorge Fatauros
273	Wide World
274	Wide World; Jean Guyaux; Wide World; Wide World
275-276	Wide World
277	*Chicago Sun-Times;* Wide World; Wide World; Wide World
278	Wide World; United Press Int.; United Press Int.; Harper & Row
279	Roy Doty, *Newsweek*
280	Photoreporters
282	Pontiac Stadium
283	Wide World
284-285	Pictorial Parade
287	Wijesoma, *Ceylon Observer*, Columbo from *Atlas World Press Review;* John Fischetti, © 1974 *Chicago Daily News;* Vadillo, *Siempre*, Mexico City from *Atlas World Press Review*
290	Pictorial Parade
292-293	Wide World
294	David Strick, *The New York Times*
296	Wide World
297	United Press Int.
299	Wide World
300	Keystone
301	Wide World
303	Joseph Erhardt*
304	Wide World
305	United Press Int.
307	Alain Nogues, Sygma
309	*The New York Times*
310	Joseph Erhardt*
312	DuPont; Photo Trends
314	Wide World
318	The White House
319	Wide World
320	Keystone
321-325	Wide World
326	Pictorial Parade
327-328	United Press Int.
329	Keystone
331-336	Wide World
337	United Press Int.
339-340	Wide World
341	United Press Int.
342	Tom Darcy, *Newsday*
344	Wally McNamee, *Newsweek*
346	© 1975 by Herblock, *The Washington Post*
347	Photo Trends
349-352	Wide World
355	Pictorial Parade
356	United Press Int.
358-359	Bill Ray
360	Wide World
363	Diego Goldberg, Sygma
365	Wide World
366	George Tames, *The New York Times*
368	Tom Hollyman
369	*Boston Herald-American* from Dodd, Mead
371	Reprinted by permission of Viking Press from *Arrow to the Sun* by Gerald McDermott, Copyright © 1974 by Gerald McDermott
372	Carol Schene, Boston Public Library
375	Wide World
378	*The New York Times*
379	Wide World
381	© 1975 Bill Hoest, reprinted by permission of *Saturday Review*
382	United Press Int.
383	Keystone
386	South Africa Chamber of Mines
389	Georgia Harbison, *Time;* American Film Institute; 20th Century-Fox
391	J. P. Laffont, Sygma
392	William E. Sauro, *The New York Times*
393	Beth Bergman
394	Elliott Erwitt, Magnum
395	Wide World
396	Wide World; Motown
398	Louisiana Superdome
399-401	Wide World
402-403	United Press Int.
404	Photo Trends
405-411	Wide World
412	Australian Information Service
414-415	Wide World
416	Pictorial Parade
417	Wide World
418	© 1975 by the *Chicago Tribune*
419	Henri Bureau, Sygma
421	Guy Bona, *Chicago Tribune*
423	Robert Jackson, Folger Shakespeare Library
425	United Press Int.
428-429	© 1975 Elizabeth Sunflower, Pledge; United Press Int.
430-431	Wide World
432	Jack Lenahan, *Chicago Sun-Times*
434	Evangelical Lutherans in Mission
436	Nancy Crampton; *The New York Times*
437	© 1975 G. B. Trudeau, distributed by Universal Press Syndicate
439	United Press Int.
440	Wide World
442	Pictorial Parade
443	Wally McNamee, *Newsweek*
444	Ron Sherman
445	International Business Machines
446-451	Wide World
452	Sovfoto
454	Wide World
456	Joseph Dawes, *The Wall Street Journal*
457	Wide World
458	Pictorial Parade
459	Wide World
461	*New York Daily News*
462	Michael Evans
464-466	NASA
467-468	Wide World
470	Photo Trends
473	Illinois State Lottery
476	Penelope Breese, *Newsweek*
477	Photoreporters
478-481	Wide World
482	James De Pree
483	ABC Television; NBC; Public Broadcasting Service
484-486	Wide World
488-489	Martha Swope
490	Robert Walker, *The New York Times*
492	Wide World; Photoreporters
493	Washington Metropolitan Area Transit Authority
495	© Walt Disney Productions
496	Photo Trends
497	Wide World
499	*The New York Times*
500	United Nations
502	Bernard Gotfryd, *Newsweek*
503	United Press Int.
509	Fotolib
510	Lester Sloan, *Newsweek*
511	Keystone
512-513	Wide World
514	Federal Bureau of Investigation
516	Wide World
517	F. Proust, Sygma
518	United Press Int.
521	Boy Scouts of America
522	United Press Int.
524	Wide World

A Preview of 1976

January

S	M	T	W	T	F	S
				1	2	3
4	5	6	7	8	9	10
11	12	13	14	15	16	17
18	19	20	21	22	23	24
25	26	27	28	29	30	31

1 New Year's Day.
6 Epiphany, 12th day of Christmas, celebrates visit of the Three Wise Men.
18 Jaycee Week, through January 24, marks founding of Jaycees.
World Religion Day, emphasizes need for world religious unity.
19 94th Congress convenes for second session.
31 Chinese New Year, begins year 4674 of the ancient Chinese calendar, the Year of the Dragon.

February

S	M	T	W	T	F	S
1	2	3	4	5	6	7
8	9	10	11	12	13	14
15	16	17	18	19	20	21
22	23	24	25	26	27	28
29						

1 National Freedom Day.
American Heart Month through February 29.
Boy Scouts of America Anniversary Celebration through February 29.
2 Ground-Hog Day. Legend says six weeks of winter weather will follow if ground hog sees its shadow.
4 Olympic Winter Games, through February 15, in Innsbruck, Austria.
12 Abraham Lincoln's Birthday, observed in 26 states.
Holiday of the Three Hierarchs. Eastern Orthodox holy day, commemorating Saints Basil, Gregory, and John Chrysostom.
14 Saint Valentine's Day, festival of romance and affection.
15 Brotherhood Week to February 22.
Susan B. Anthony Day, commemorates the birth of the suffragist leader.
16 George Washington's Birthday, according to law, is now legally celebrated by federal employees, the District of Columbia, and 42 states on the third Monday in February, not on the actual anniversary, the 22nd.
21 National FFA Week, through February 28, publicizing the role of Future Farmers of America in U.S. agriculture.
29 Leap Year Day.

March

S	M	T	W	T	F	S
	1	2	3	4	5	6
7	8	9	10	11	12	13
14	15	16	17	18	19	20
21	22	23	24	25	26	27
28	29	30	31			

1 Easter Seal Campaign through April 18.
Red Cross Month through March 31.
2 Mardi Gras, last celebration before Lent, observed in New Orleans, La., and many Roman Catholic countries.
3 Ash Wednesday, first day of Lent, the penitential period that precedes Easter.
5 World Day of Prayer.
7 Girl Scout Week, through March 13, marks the organization's 64th birthday.
Save Your Vision Week through March 13.
14 Camp Fire Girls Birthday Week, to March 20, marks 66th birthday of the organization.
16 Purim, commemorates the saving of Jews through the death of the ancient Persian despot Haman.
17 St. Patrick's Day, honoring the patron saint of Ireland.
20 First Day of Spring, 6:50 A.M., E.S.T.
21 Earth Day, opens yearlong program to replenish the earth.

April

S	M	T	W	T	F	S
				1	2	3
4	5	6	7	8	9	10
11	12	13	14	15	16	17
18	19	20	21	22	23	24
25	26	27	28	29	30	

1 April Fools' Day.
Cancer Control Month through April 30.
4 National Boys' Club Week through April 10.
National Library Week through April 10.
11 Palm Sunday, marks Jesus' final entry into Jerusalem along streets festively covered with palm branches.
Holy Week, through April 17, commemorates the Crucifixion and Resurrection of Jesus Christ.
14 Pan American Week through April 20.
15 Maundy Thursday, celebrates Christ's injunction to love each other.
Passover, or Pesah, first day, starting the 15th day of the Hebrew month of Nisan. The eight-day festival celebrates the deliverance of the ancient Jews from bondage in Egypt.
16 Good Friday, marks the death of Jesus on the cross. It is observed as a public holiday in 17 states.
18 Easter Sunday, commemorating the Resurrection of Jesus Christ.
25 Eastern Orthodox Easter Sunday.

30 Walpurgis Night, according to legend, the night of the witches' Sabbath gathering in Germany's Harz Mountains.

May

S	M	T	W	T	F	S
						1
2	3	4	5	6	7	8
9	10	11	12	13	14	15
16	17	18	19	20	21	22
23	24	25	26	27	28	29
30	31					

1 May Day, observed as a festival of spring in many countries.
Law Day, U.S.A.
Kentucky Derby at Churchill Downs, Louisville, Ky.
Mental Health Month through May 31.
2 National Music Week through May 9.
9 Mother's Day.
10 Salvation Army Week through May 16.
15 Armed Forces Day.
22 National Maritime Day.
27 Ascension Day, 40 days after Easter Sunday, commemorating the ascent of Jesus into heaven.
30 Indianapolis 500-Mile Race in Indianapolis, Ind.
31 Memorial Day, according to law, is the last Monday in May.

June

S	M	T	W	T	F	S
		1	2	3	4	5
6	7	8	9	10	11	12
13	14	15	16	17	18	19
20	21	22	23	24	25	26
27	28	29	30			

1 Stratford Festival, drama and music, Ontario, Canada, through October 31.
4 Shabuot, Jewish Feast of Weeks, marks the revealing of the Ten Commandments to Moses on Mount Sinai.
6 D-Day, commemorates the day the Allies landed to assault the German-held continent of Europe in 1944.
Whitsunday, or Pentecost, the seventh Sunday after Easter, commemorating the descent of the Holy Spirit upon Jesus' 12 apostles.
12 Queen's Official Birthday, marked by trooping of the colors in London.
13 National Flag Week through June 19.
14 Flag Day, commemorates the adoption of the Stars and Stripes in 1777 as the official U.S. flag.
20 Father's Day.
21 First Day of Summer, 1:24 A.M., E.S.T.
27 Freedom Week through July 4.

607

A Preview of 1976

July

S	M	T	W	T	F	S
				1	2	3
4	5	6	7	8	9	10
11	12	13	14	15	16	17
18	19	20	21	22	23	24
25	26	27	28	29	30	31

1 **Dominion Day** (Canada), celebrates the confederation of the provinces in 1867.

4 **Independence Day,** marks Continental Congress's adoption of Declaration of Independence in 1776.

14 **Bastille Day** (France), commemorates popular uprising against Louis XVI in 1789 and seizure of the Bastille, the infamous French prison.

15 **Saint Swithin's Day.** According to legend, if it rains on this day, it will rain for 40 days.

17 **Summer Olympic Games,** Montreal, Canada, through August 1.

18 **Captive Nations Week** through July 24.

20 **Moon Day,** the anniversary of man's first landing on the moon in 1969.

28 **Salzburg International Music and Drama Festival,** Salzburg, Austria, through August 27.

August

S	M	T	W	T	F	S
1	2	3	4	5	6	7
8	9	10	11	12	13	14
15	16	17	18	19	20	21
22	23	24	25	26	27	28
29	30	31				

5 **Tishah B'ab,** Jewish fast day, on ninth day of Hebrew month of Ab, marking Babylonians' destruction of the First Temple in Jerusalem in 587 B.C.; Roman destruction of the Second Temple in A.D. 70; and Roman suppression of Jewish revolt in A.D. 135.

14 **V-J Day** (original) marks Allied victory over Japan in 1945.

15 **Feast of the Assumption,** Roman Catholic and Eastern Orthodox holy day, celebrates the ascent of the Virgin Mary into heaven.

19 **National Aviation Day.**

22 **Edinburgh International Festival,** music, drama, and film, through September 11.

24 **Ramadan,** the ninth month of the Moslem calendar begins, observed by fasting.

26 **Women's Equality Day,** commemorating the ratification of the 19th Amendment, giving women the vote.

September

S	M	T	W	T	F	S
			1	2	3	4
5	6	7	8	9	10	11
12	13	14	15	16	17	18
19	20	21	22	23	24	25
26	27	28	29	30		

6 **Labor Day** in the United States and Canada.

8 **Harvest Moon,** the full moon nearest the autumnal equinox of the sun, shines with special brilliance for several days and helps farmers in the Northern Hemisphere to get more field work done after sunset.

22 **First Day of Autumn,** 4:48 P.M., E.S.T.

24 **American Indian Day,** honoring native Americans.

25 **Rosh Hashanah,** or Jewish New Year, the year 5737 beginning at sunset. It falls on the first day of the Hebrew month of Tishri and lasts for two days.

October

S	M	T	W	T	F	S
					1	2
3	4	5	6	7	8	9
10	11	12	13	14	15	16
17	18	19	20	21	22	23
24	25	26	27	28	29	30
31						

1 **Anniversary of the 1949 Chinese Communist Revolution,** China's national holiday.

3 **National Employ the Physically Handicapped Week** through October 9.
National 4-H Week through October 9.
Fire Prevention Week through October 9.

4 **Yom Kippur,** or Day of Atonement, most solemn day in the Jewish calendar, marking the end of the period of penitence.

9 **Sukkot,** or Feast of Tabernacles, begins the nine-day Jewish observance, which originally celebrated the end of harvest season.
Leif Ericson Day, honoring early Norse explorer of North America.

10 **National Y-Teen Week** through October 16.

11 **Thanksgiving Day,** Canada.
Columbus Day, commemorates Columbus' discovery of America in 1492. Previously celebrated on October 12.

24 **National Cleaner Air Week** through October 30.

25 **Veterans Day,** observed on the fourth Monday in October.

31 **Halloween,** or All Hallows' Eve.
Reformation Day, celebrated by Protestants, marks the day in 1517 when Martin Luther nailed his Ninety-Five Theses of protest to the door of a church in Wittenberg, Germany.
United Nations Children's Fund (UNICEF) Day.

November

S	M	T	W	T	F	S
	1	2	3	4	5	6
7	8	9	10	11	12	13
14	15	16	17	18	19	20
21	22	23	24	25	26	27
28	29	30				

1 **All Saints' Day,** observed by the Roman Catholic Church.
Christmas Seal Campaign through December 31.

2 **Election Day,** United States.

5 **Guy Fawkes Day** (Great Britain), marks the failure of a plot to blow up King James I and Parliament in 1605 with ceremonial burning of Guy Fawkes in effigy.

7 **Anniversary of 1917 Bolshevik Revolution,** Russia's national holiday, through November 8.

8 **National Children's Book Week** through November 14.

14 **American Education Week** through November 20.

25 **Thanksgiving Day,** United States.

28 **Advent,** first of the four Sundays in the season preceding Christmas.

December

S	M	T	W	T	F	S
			1	2	3	4
5	6	7	8	9	10	11
12	13	14	15	16	17	18
19	20	21	22	23	24	25
26	27	28	29	30	31	

2 **Pan American Health Day.**

6 **Saint Nicholas Day,** when children in parts of Europe receive gifts.

10 **Human Rights Week** through December 17.
Nobel Prize Ceremony, in Stockholm, Sweden, and Oslo, Norway.

15 **Bill of Rights Day,** marks the ratification of that document in 1791.

17 **Hanukkah,** or Feast of Lights, eight-day Jewish holiday beginning on the 25th day of the Hebrew month of Kislev that celebrates the Jewish defeat of the Syrian tyrant Antiochus IV in 165 B.C. and the rededication of The Temple in Jerusalem.

21 **First Day of Winter,** 12:36 P.M., E.S.T.

25 **Christmas.**

31 **New Year's Eve.**